Español
Santillana

Santillana USA is proud to announce the University of Salamanca's endorsement

VNiVERSiDAD
Ð SALAMANCA
CAMPUS DE EXCELENCIA INTERNACIONAL

CURSOS
Internacionales

A Message to Educators and Parents:

Since its inception in 1218, *Universidad de Salamanca* has been linked to the teaching, learning, and dissemination of the Spanish language. It was in Salamanca where the first grammar of the language was published in 1492, and where, at the beginning of the XX Century, Spanish as a foreign language studies were first and fully integrated into the academic programs of a university.

Throughout its historical dedication to the teaching of the Spanish language and culture, *Universidad de Salamanca* has nurtured a tradition of sharing its knowledge and efforts with select educational institutions and organizations. This pedagogical philosophy has led *Cursos Internacionales de la Universidad de Salamanca* to reach an agreement with Editorial Santillana — leader in the publication of instructional materials throughout the world — to carry out a study of Santillana's Spanish as a world language program in order to accredit the program's suitability for educational use in the United States.

Cursos Internacionales de la Universidad de Salamanca, after carefully evaluating **Español Santillana**, has endorsed the linguistic and cultural excellence of this program based on the following findings:

- Reflects the latest pedagogical and methodological research-based approaches that current investigations deem appropriate to the teaching and learning of Spanish as a second language
- Is linguistically and grammatically accurate, and reflects the current use of Spanish around the world
- Presents authentic culture in meaningful contexts to support language instruction
- Aligns to the U.S. National Language Standards, preparing students to become college and career ready
- Fosters progressive Spanish language acquisition to achieve the highest possible level of communicative proficiency

In order to continue to support the further spread and study of the Spanish language, *Cursos Internacionales de la Universidad de Salamanca* is pleased to collaborate with Santillana in its efforts to promote the Spanish language in the United States with quality materials, and appreciates the confidence that Santillana has placed in our institution to evaluate **Español Santillana**.

José Miguel Sánchez Llorente
Consejero Delegado
Cursos Internacionales de la Universidad de Salamanca

High School **3**

Español
Santillana

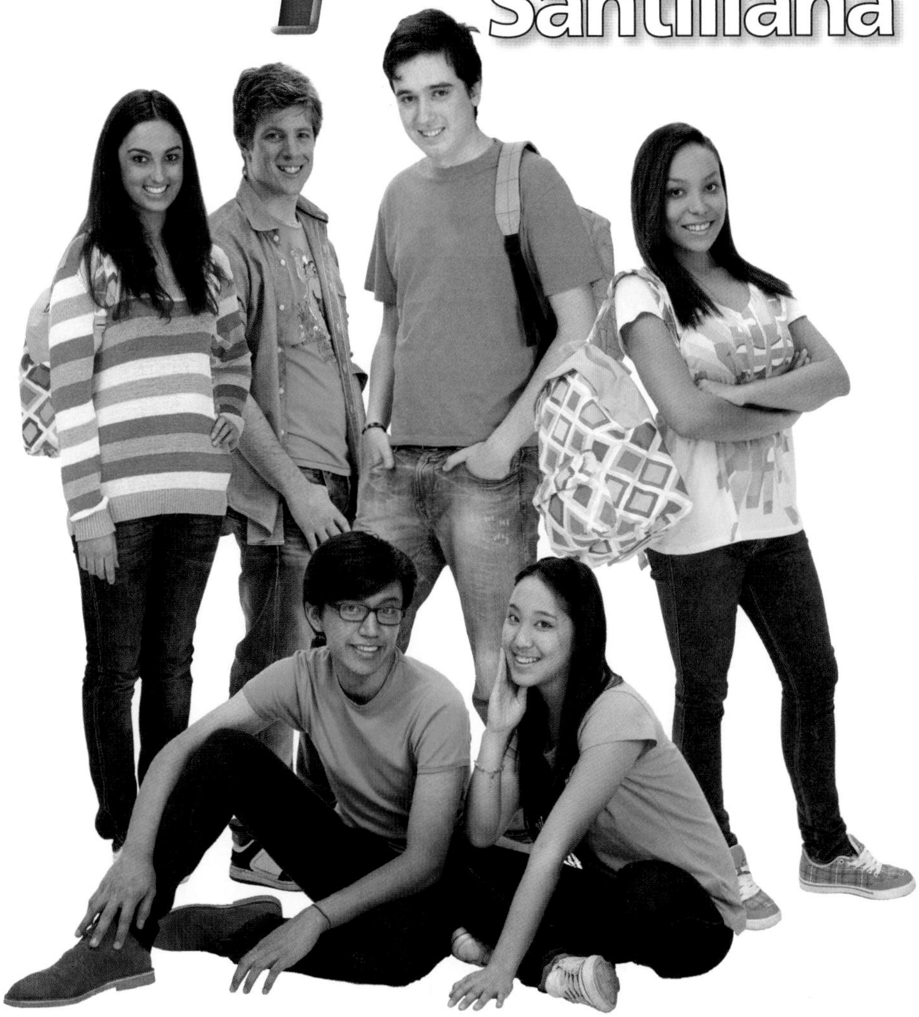

SANTILLANA USA
Language Education Experts

Español Santillana is a collaborative effort by two teams specializing in the design of Spanish-language educational materials. One team is located in the United States and the other in Spain.

Published in the United States of America.

Español Santillana
Teacher's Edition Level 3
ISBN-13: 978-1-61605-913-2
ISBN-10: 1-61605-913-3

Illustrator: **Bartolomé Seguí**
Picture Coordinator: **Carlos Aguilera**

Cartographers: **José Luis Gil, Tania López**
Cartographic Coordinator: **Ana Isabel Calvo**

Production Manager: **Jacqueline Rivera**

Production Coordinator: **Julio Hernández**

Design and Layout: **Jorge Borrego**

Proofreaders: **Nuria del Peso, Elizabeth A. Pease, Marta López**

Photo Researchers: **Mercedes Barcenilla, Amparo Rodríguez**

Santillana USA Publishing Company, Inc.
2023 NW 84th Avenue, Doral, FL 33122

Printed by Worzalla Publishing Co.

4 5 6 7 8 9   18 17 16

Editorial Staff in the United States
Anne Smieszny
Ana Isabel Antón

Editorial Staff in Spain
Susana Gómez
Belén Saiz
Clara Alarcón

Mercedes Fontecha
M.ª Antonia Oliva

Linguistic and Cultural Advisers in Latin America and in the United States

Antonio Moreno
Content Director, Santillana México

Mayra Méndez
Editorial Director, Santillana Puerto Rico

Claudia Noriega
Editorial Director, Santillana Guatemala

Cecilia Mejía
Editorial Director, Santillana Perú

Graciela Pérez de Lois
Editorial Director, Santillana Argentina

Rodolfo Hidalgo
Editorial Director, Santillana Chile

Mario Núñez
Director of Professional Development, Santillana USA

Reviewers

Francesc Borrull
Chicago, IL

Anna Budiwsky
Villanova, PA

Lorrie Ann Button-Edelson
Katy, TX

Donna Clementi
Oshkosh, WI

Frances S. Hoch
Raleigh, NC

Gudrun Martyny
Orlando, FL

Nieves Pérez-Knapp
Provo, UT

Carol Radchik
La Jolla, CA

Mónica Ruiz-Meléndez
West Chester, PA

Eugenia Sarmiento
Centennial, CO

Carlos Soler Montes
Albuquerque, NM

Alicia Vinson
Lexington, KY

James Zavodjancik
Milford, CT

Clare Ziff
Villanova, PA

Writers (Teacher's Edition)

Paloma Lapuerta
New Britain, CT

María Á. Pérez
Tenerife, Spain

María Lourdes Casas
New Haven, CT

Lisa Berliner
Farmington, CT

Elizabeth Millán
Highland Park, IL

Jan Ferrier Sands
North Granby, CT

Writers (Student Book)

Paloma Lapuerta
teaches Spanish Language, Literature and Culture at Central Connecticut State University. She graduated from the University of Salamanca, Spain, and received her PhD from the University of Geneva, Switzerland. She has taught in different countries and is co-author of several Spanish textbooks.

María Lourdes Casas
received her Masters of Arts and PhD in Spanish at the University of Wisconsin-Madison. Dr. Casas has taught Spanish Language and Literature at the University of Wisconsin-Madison, Connecticut College, and Southern Connecticut State University. Currently she is an Assistant Professor at Central Connecticut State University.

Lisa Berliner
received her MA in Educational Leadership from Central Connecticut State University. She is currently pursuing a Masters degree in Spanish. She teaches Spanish at the secondary level in Simsbury, CT.

Jan Ferrier Sands
received her BS in Spanish and MS in Curriculum and Supervision from Central Connecticut State University. She is a career teacher of Spanish at Simsbury High School, Simsbury, CT. From 2005 to 2008, she served as the World Languages Teacher-in-Residence at the Connecticut State Department of Education.

María Á. Pérez
received her MA in Spanish from Portland State University. She was the assistant director for the Spanish Basic Language Program at the University of Illinois in Chicago. She has taught college-level Spanish at several institutions, and has worked as an editor and writer for various publishers.

Contributing Writers

Ana Isabel Antón
Miami, FL

Clara Alarcón
Madrid, Spain

Susana Gómez
Madrid, Spain

Mercedes Fontecha
Madrid, Spain

Contributors

Janet L. Glass
Dwight-Englewood School
Englewood, NJ

Jan Kucerik
Pinellas County Schools
Largo, FL

Carol McKenna Semonsky
Georgia State University
Atlanta, GA

Gerardo Piña-Rosales
North American Academy of the Spanish Language
The City University of New York, New York, NY

Dr. Emily Spinelli
AATSP
University of Michigan-Dearborn, Dearborn, MI

Brandon Zaslow
Occidental College
Los Angeles, CA

Advisers

Paula Hirsch
Windward School, Los Angeles, CA

María Orta
Kennedy High School, Chicago, IL

Developmental Editor
Belén Saiz and María Á. Pérez

Editorial Coordinator
Anne Smieszny

Editorial Director
Enrique Ferro

Índice

Español Santillana. **Presentation**

Scope and Sequence

Key Ideas for Today's Language Classroom

Unidad preliminar. Un paso más

Unidad 1. ¿Cómo eres?

Unidad 2. Entre amigos

Unidad 3. Tus cosas

Unidad 4. Vida sana

Unidad 5. ¿Trabajas?

Unidad 6. Tus aficiones

Unidad 7. Por el planeta

Unidad 8. En sociedad

Appendices

Español Santillana

Key Ideas

1. A motivating story

1. *Español Santillana* tells a story of travels and challenges.

Four pairs of enthusiasts of the Spanish language and Hispanic culture want to explore the Spanish-speaking world: its people, its cities, its regions, and its cultures. Because of this, they have decided to create the *Fans del español* website and to travel to different countries in order to discover and show unique aspects of each place. In each country, the four teams compete, taking on different *desafíos*, or challenges, that they must complete.

The community of *Fans* has grown, and in Level 3, new fans will take on all-new challenges with the same objective: to get to know the places, the cultures, and the lifestyles of Spanish-speaking countries.

2. The challenges present exceptionally motivating situations and fascinating places.

Each unit presents several challenges (four in Levels 1 and 2; three in Level 3) related to the people, the regions, or the cultures of a country or geographic area. For example, the teams participate in the ritual of the *voladores de Papantla* in Mexico (Level 1), act in a *telenovela* in Buenos Aires (Level 2), and prepare a typical dish of *ropa vieja* with a recipe from the Canary Islands (Level 3).

3. The students decide which team wins the challenge in each unit.

In Levels 1 and 2, students discuss the challenges at the beginning of each unit, and make predictions about which pair will win. At the end of the unit, students take a vote to decide the winners of the challenge according to a previously established criterion: the most original, the most fun, the most relevant, and so on.

In Level 3, students get to choose one of the pairs' challenges in order to perform a task related to it.

Active participation in the storyline promotes student involvement and motivation.

TU DESAFÍO

The *Tu desafío* section that appears on certain pages of Levels 1 and 2 is intended to motivate students and promote independent work. Upon accessing the *Fans del español* website to do the proposed activity, students earn points, which they can accumulate throughout the year.

In Level 3, the students' challenges are linked to the challenges that the three pairs take on in each unit.

¿Quién ganará?

ciento cuarenta y nueve 149

¿Quién ganará?

Estudiantes	México						Puerto Rico						Guatemala						Perú					
1																									
2																									
3																									
4																									
5																									
6																									
7																									
8																									
9																									
10																									

Español
Santillana

Key Ideas

2. The integration of culture into the units

1. Culture is the framework for learning Spanish.

Culture is present throughout the unit: in the challenges, in the boxes that feature the five Cs of language learning, in the section titled *Mapa cultural*, in the readings, and in the final project.

Culture is also present in the practice activities: students analyze the cultural perspectives, practices, and products of a country or cultural area, compare it with their own country, and transfer what they have learned to their own reality.

DESAFÍO 1

La máscara de jade

Diana y Rita

Find a jade mask in Antigua.

2. Culture is presented in an original way.

Each challenge features a **cultural element** related to the theme of the unit. For example, *Desafío 1* in Guatemala (Level 1) showcases an element of traditional Guatemalan culture: jade masks.

Elements of the culture related to the theme of the unit are also presented in an organized way in the *Mapa cultural* section.

3. Culture is recognized in all its richness.

Culture is explored as a perspective, a practice, and a product. For example, students reflect about the festivals, customs, traditions, family dynamics, table manners, courtesy expressions, dances, foods, etc.

Culture is exhibited from a variety of angles:

▶ Major cities such as Mexico City, San Juan in Puerto Rico, Antigua Guatemala, Santo Domingo, Cartagena de Indias, Buenos Aires, Seville, etc.

▶ Archeology, architecture, and the fine arts: Teotihuacan, Tikal, Machu Picchu, the Zócalo, the El Morro fortress in San Juan, the Alhambra, Frida Kahlo, Diego Rivera, Pablo Picasso, Fernando Botero, etc.

▶ Customs such as festivals, traditional clothing, foods, and sports.

▶ Youth culture, such as music and fashion.

Guatemala

T8

An example of the integration of culture

Level: 1 **Country:** Guatemala **Theme:** Shopping and clothing

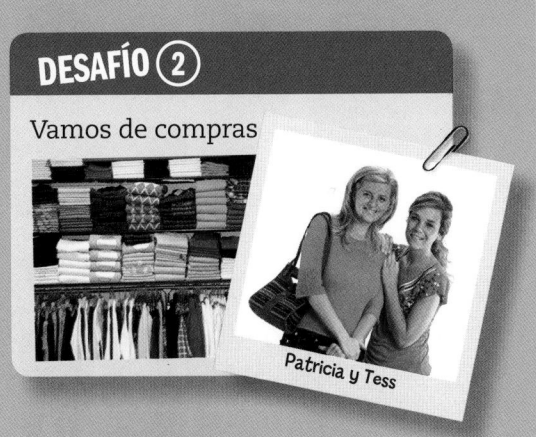

DESAFÍO 2
Vamos de compras
Patricia y Tess

Buy articles of clothing in a mall in Guatemala.

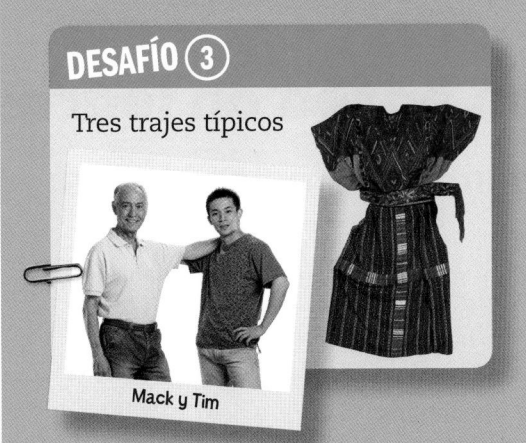

DESAFÍO 3
Tres trajes típicos
Mack y Tim

Acquire three traditional garments in Tikal.

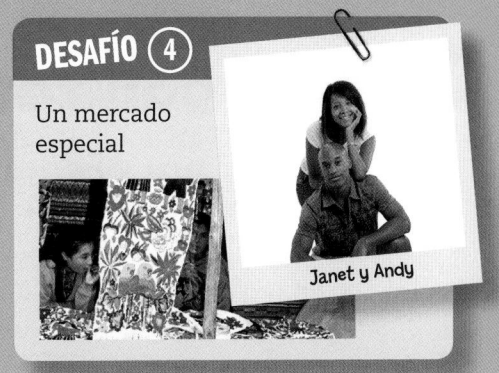

DESAFÍO 4
Un mercado especial
Janet y Andy

Locate a bag of worry dolls in the Chichicastenango market.

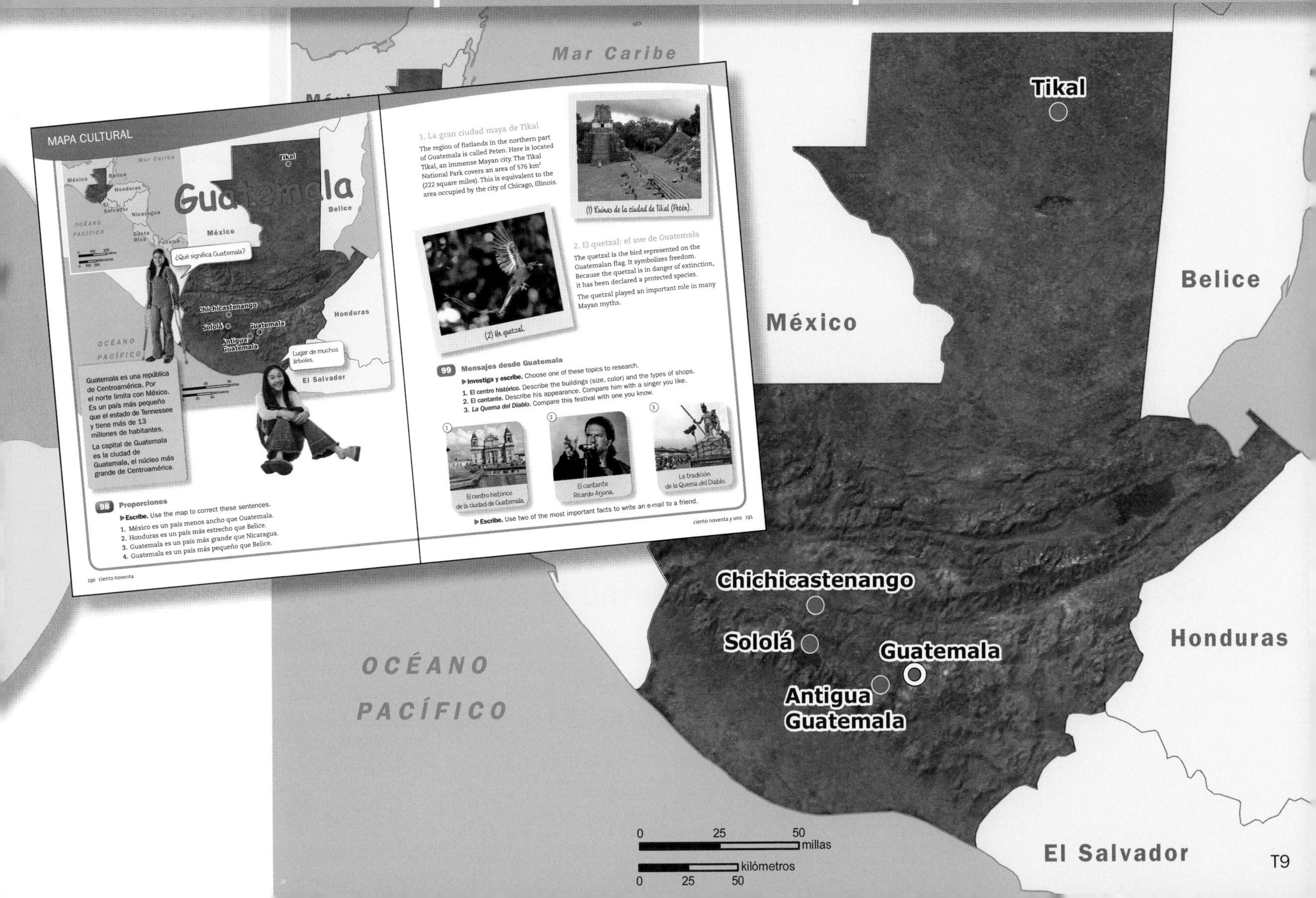

Mar Caribe
Tikal
Belice
México
Honduras
Chichicastenango
Sololá
Guatemala
Antigua Guatemala
OCÉANO PACÍFICO
El Salvador
0 25 50 millas
kilómetros 0 25 50

MAPA CULTURAL

Guatemala

¿Qué significa Guatemala?

Lugar de muchos árboles.

Guatemala es una república de Centroamérica. Por el norte limita con México. Es un país más pequeño que el estado de Tennessee y tiene más de 13 millones de habitantes.

La capital de Guatemala es la ciudad de Guatemala, el núcleo más grande de Centroamérica.

98 Proporciones

▶**Escribe.** Use the map to correct these sentences.

1. México es un país menos ancho que Guatemala.
2. Honduras es un país más estrecho que Belice.
3. Guatemala es un país más grande que Nicaragua.
4. Guatemala es un país más pequeño que Belice.

190 ciento noventa

1. La gran ciudad maya de Tikal

The region of flatlands in the northern part of Guatemala is called Peten. Here is located Tikal, an immense Mayan city. The Tikal National Park covers an area of 576 km^2 (222 square miles). This is equivalent to the area occupied by the city of Chicago, Illinois.

(1) Ruinas de la ciudad de Tikal (Petén).

2. El quetzal: el ave de Guatemala

The quetzal is the bird represented on the Guatemalan flag. It symbolizes freedom. Because the quetzal is in danger of extinction, it has been declared a protected species.

The quetzal played an important role in many Mayan myths.

(2) Un quetzal.

99 Mensajes desde Guatemala

▶**Investiga y escribe.** Choose one of these topics to research.

1. **El centro histórico.** Describe the buildings (size, color) and the types of shops.
2. **El cantante.** Describe his appearance. Compare him with a singer you like.
3. ***La Quema del Diablo.*** Compare this festival with one you know.

① El centro histórico de la ciudad de Guatemala.

② El cantante Ricardo Arjona.

③ La tradición de la Quema del Diablo.

▶**Escribe.** Use two of the most important facts to write an e-mail to a friend.

ciento noventa y uno 191

Español Santillana

Key Ideas

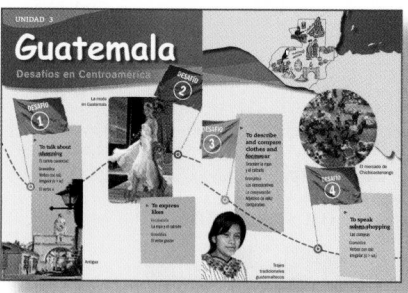

3. An organization based on learning

1. The units are organized in three major blocks.

1. **The linguistic nucleus:** this is the fundamental and most extensive part of the unit. It is centered around the vocabulary, the grammar, and the practice of communication in the context of the travels and the challenges.

   In Level 3, this part includes a ***Lectura*** section in which three types of texts are used: dialogues, informative texts, and literary texts.

   La llegada

2. **An in-depth look into culture:** this has as its core the ***Mapa cultural***. This section presents some of the characteristic cultural aspects of a country (Level 1), a region (Level 2), or a theme (Level 3).

   The *Mapa cultural* is complemented by a ***Lectura*** section (Levels 1 and 2), in which students learn about a cultural aspect while practicing reading comprehension skills and strategies, or by an ***Escritura*** section (Level 3).

   Los desafíos

3. **Putting knowledge into action:** the ***Repaso*** pages and the ***Proyecto.*** Students review the vocabulary and grammar of the unit, then do a project in which they integrate the unit's key linguistic and cultural concepts in a communicative way.

   Todo junto

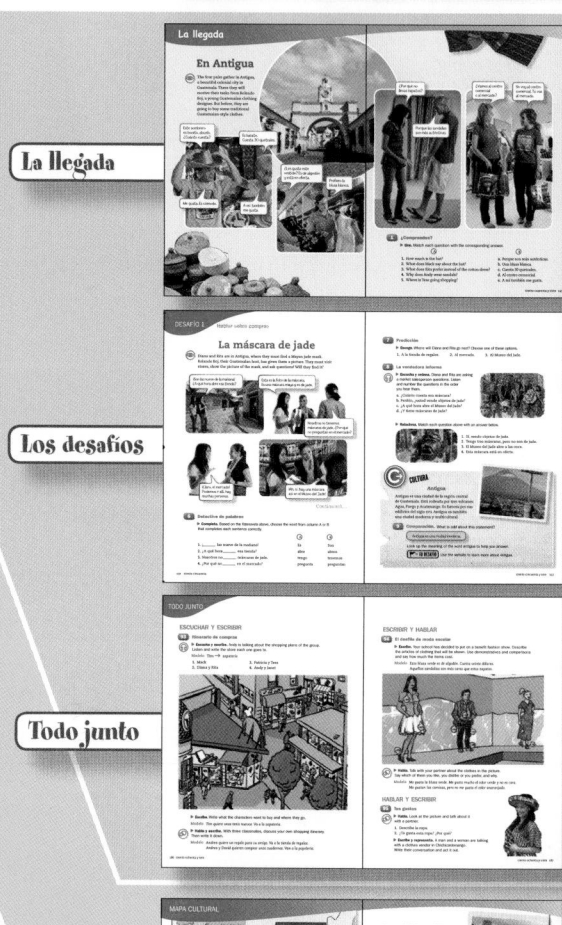

El mapa

2. Vocabulary and Grammar are presented in short, well-defined sections.

Vocabulary and Grammar have been organized in short, unified, two-page sections. This system facilitates focus on the topic being studied.

Los repasos

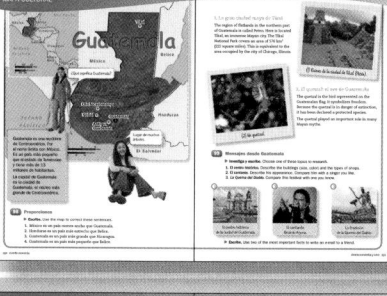

In Levels 1 and 2, there are four *desafíos* per unit. In Level 3, there are three.

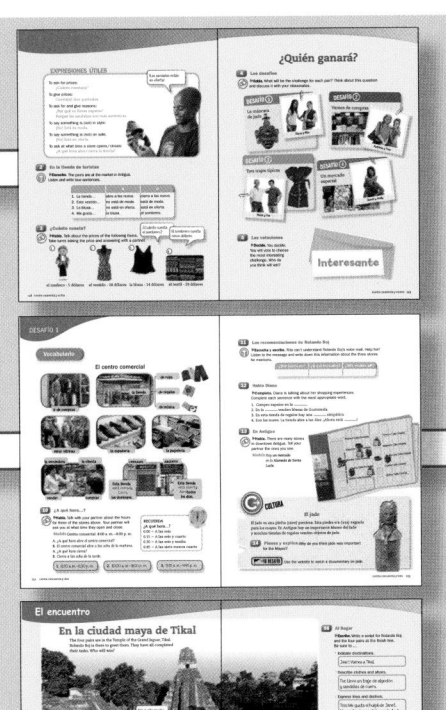

El encuentro

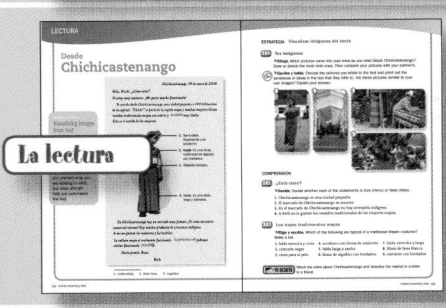

La lectura

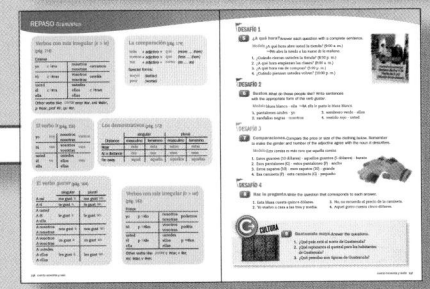

El proyecto

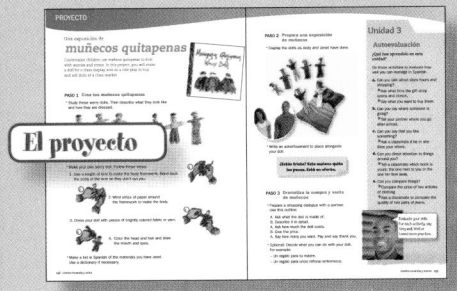

Organization of the Unit: The Challenges

The first part of the unit tells the story of the teams and the challenges they undertake.

1. *Las tareas*

In Level 3, each unit starts with two sections:

▶ A text that presents the cultural challenges that the pairs have to resolve. This text offers some contextualized examples of the vocabulary and the grammar of the unit.

▶ The **Antes de empezar** section, in which students learn some useful expressions related to the topic, and review the basic vocabulary that they have learned in previous levels.

2. The *Desafíos*

In this part, the plot of the unit is developed and students practice the language concepts (vocabulary and grammar) in detail.

Each **Desafío** features one of the teams, who has to resolve a cultural challenge. In Levels 1 and 2 there are four *Desafíos* per unit; in Level 3 there are three.

3. *Para terminar*

The **Para terminar** section ends the *Desafío* part of the unit. In Level 3, this section is divided into two parts:

▶ **Todo junto** contains communicative activities that integrate vocabulary and the key grammatical structures from the unit.

▶ **Tu desafío** proposes that the students choose and develop one task related to the cultural challenges that the teams have completed in the unit.

Level 3

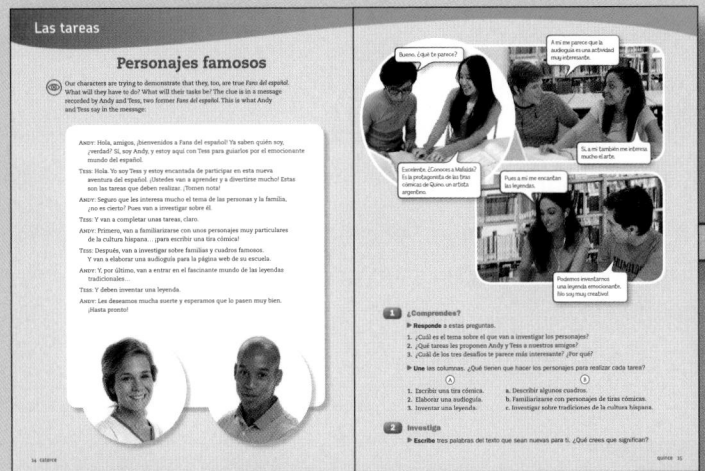

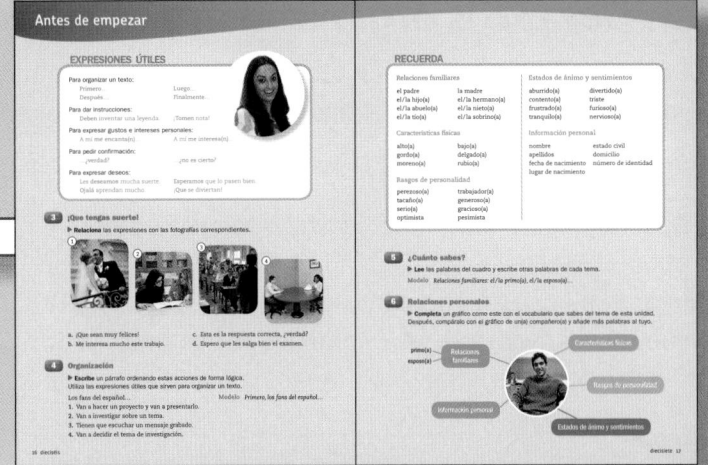

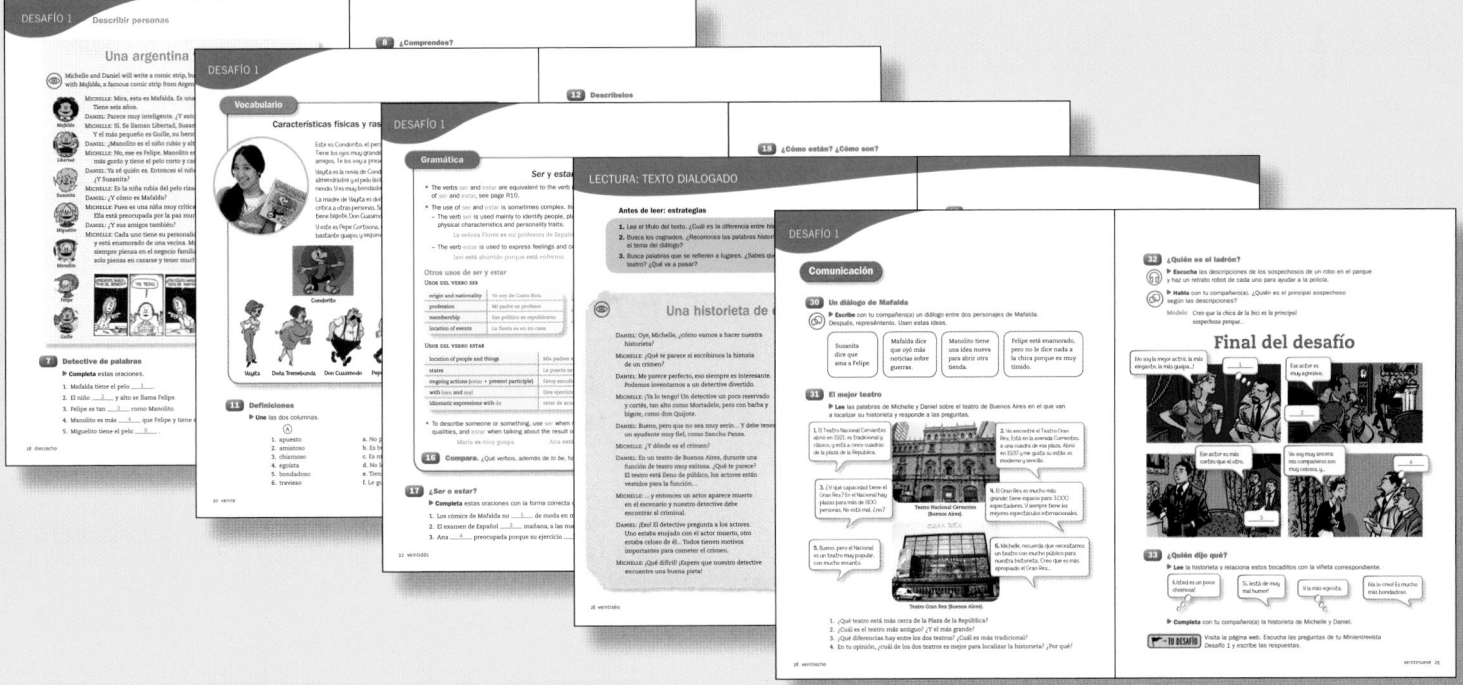

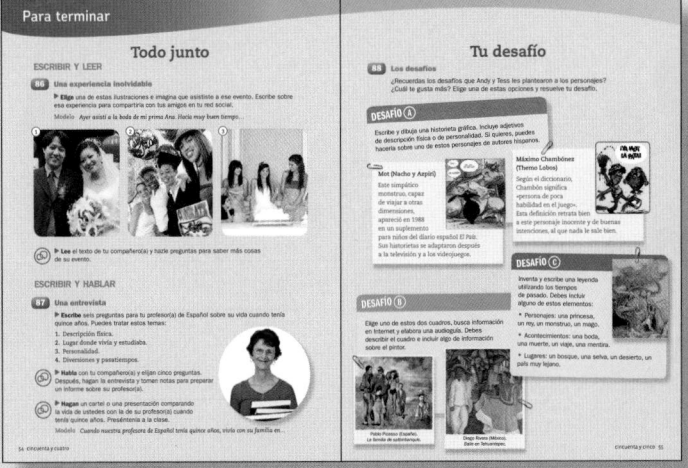

Organization of the Unit: The Structure of a *Desafío*

Each *Desafío* is organized into five sections.

The *Desafío* is the story of each team's challenge, and is therefore the basis of the storyline. It also develops key vocabulary and grammar around a communicative function.

1. *El desafío* (presentation)

The **Desafío** begins with a text in which the characters talk about their challenge using the target vocabulary and grammar in a context. The context allows the students to become familiar with the new words and structures, and to make hypotheses about their meaning and their usage.

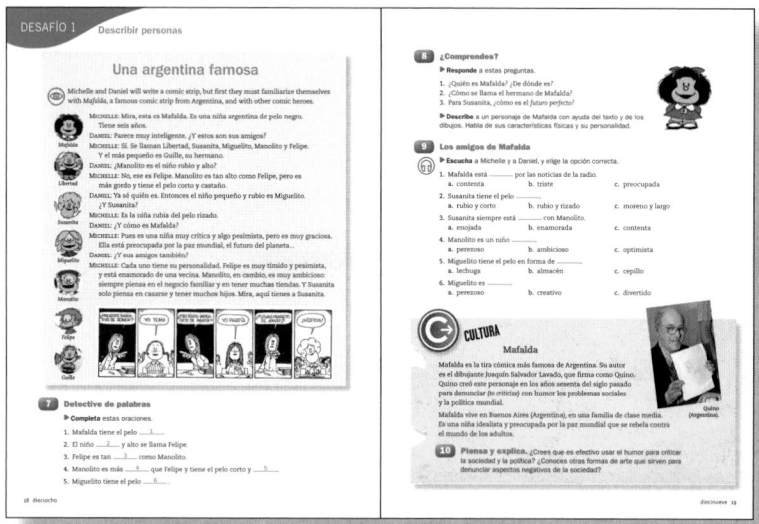

3. *La gramática*

On the **grammar** pages, students are given explanations of key structures, which are practiced along with the key vocabulary.

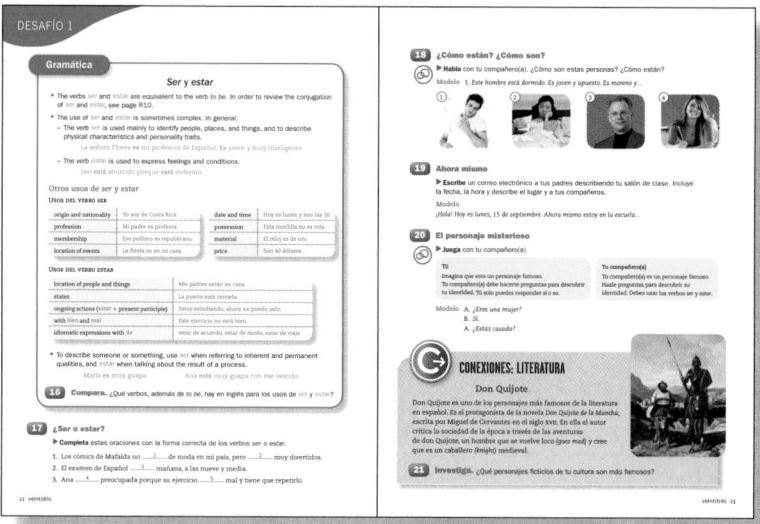

2. *El vocabulario*

On the **vocabulary** pages, the new words and phrases are presented with the support of images and language context. Students use the vocabulary in follow-up activities.

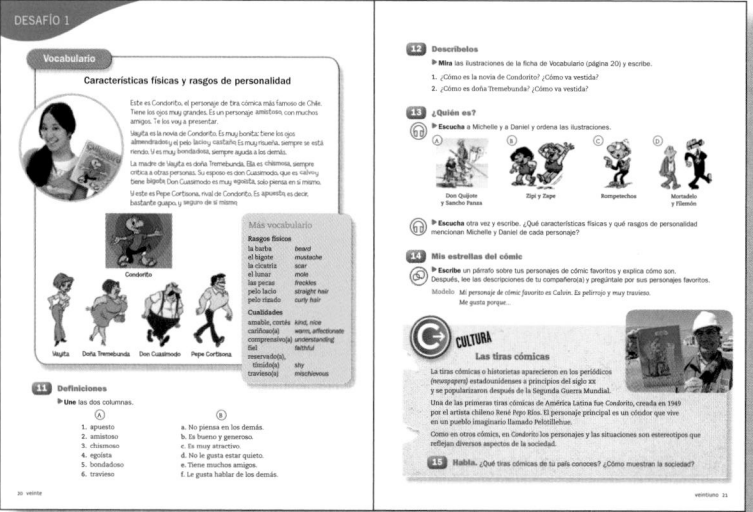

4. *La lectura*

In each *Desafío* in Level 3, **reading** is practiced via a written dialogue, an informative text, or a literary text.

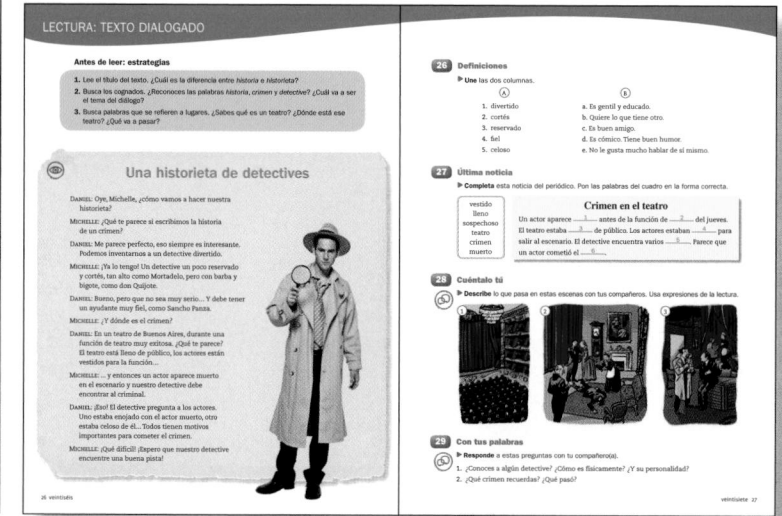

5. *La comunicación*

On the **communication** pages, there are progressively more open-ended activities that allow students to apply the key vocabulary and grammar in communicative situations.

The *Desafío* ends with a *fotonovela*, which is a continuation of and a conclusion to the initial text.

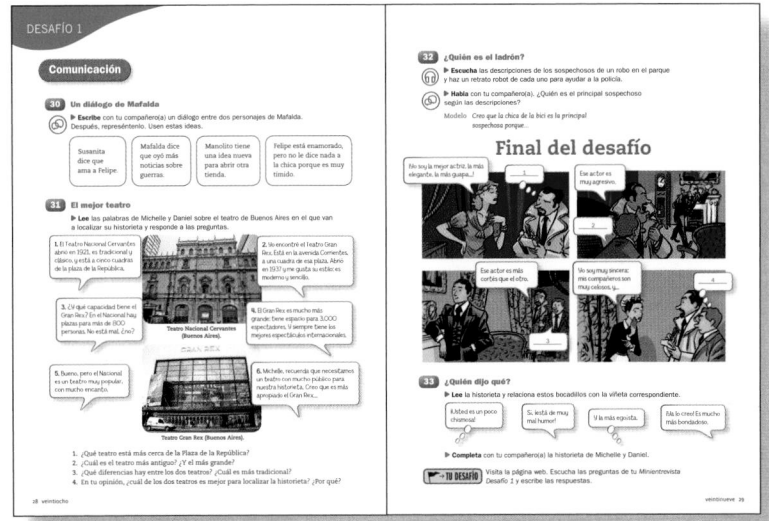

The "C-Boxes"

The linguistic material presented in each *Desafío* is complemented with boxes in which four of the five C's from the standards are developed: **Culture**, **Comparisons**, **Communities**, and **Connections**.

Communication is developed throughout the book in the vocabulary and grammar activities. A section at the end of each *Desafío* is also dedicated to Communication.

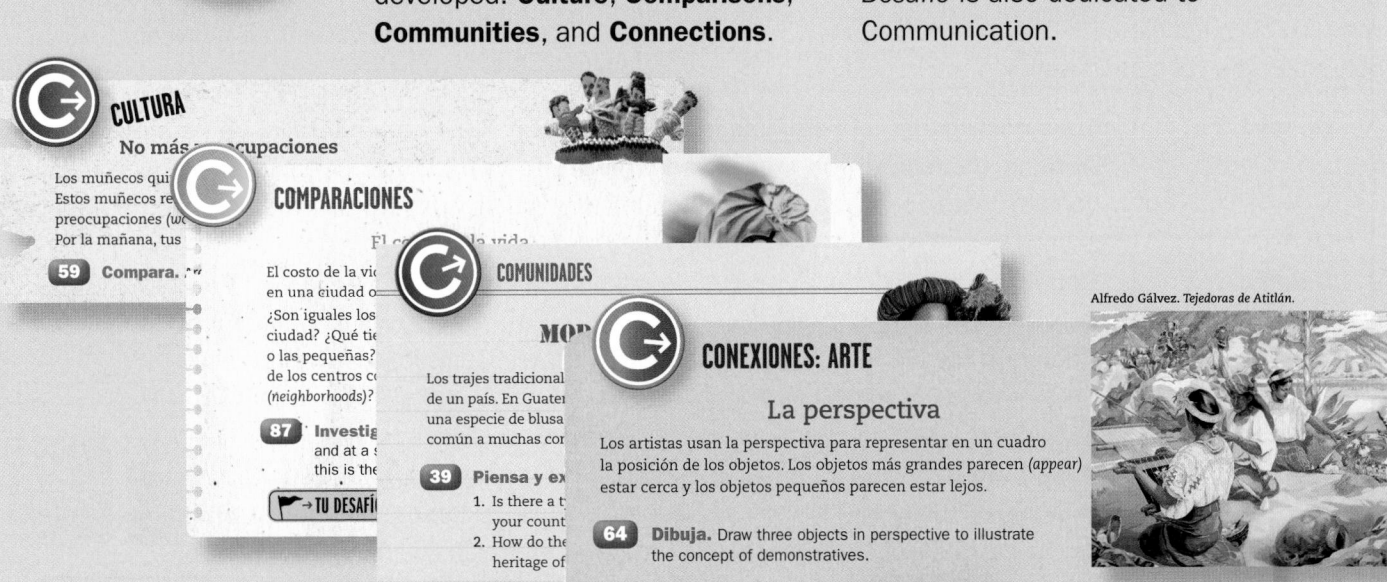

Alfredo Gálvez. *Tejedoras de Atitlán.*

CONEXIONES: ARTE

La perspectiva

Los artistas usan la perspectiva para representar en un cuadro la posición de los objetos. Los objetos más grandes parecen (*appear*) estar cerca y los objetos pequeños parecen estar lejos.

64 Dibuja. Draw three objects in perspective to illustrate the concept of demonstratives.

The Vocabulary

A careful selection.

Key vocabulary has been selected, considering the specifications of organizations dedicated to the instruction and evaluation of Spanish, including the *Instituto Cervantes* and the American Association of Teachers of Spanish and Portuguese (AATSP).

In general, the most commonly used and standard Spanish terms have been chosen, rather than regional variants. Whenever possible, words close to their English counterparts (cognates) have been included.

The basic criteria for the selection of vocabulary were frequency of use and relevance to students' everyday life, interests, and needs.

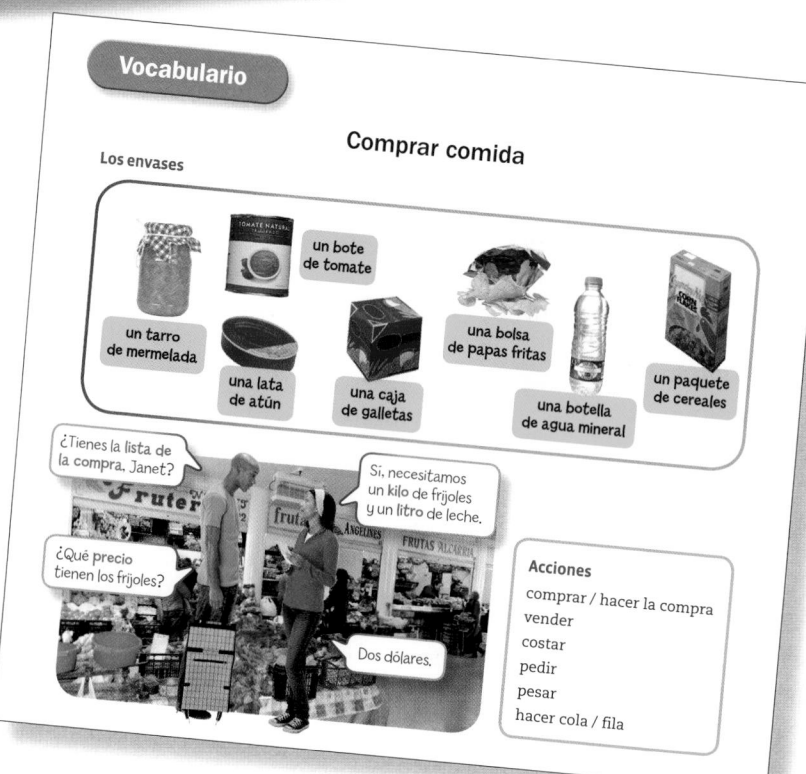

Organization by topic or situations.

The vocabulary is organized by topic or by situations related to the theme of the unit. For example, a unit dedicated to the theme of food includes words relating to foods and beverages, meals, and food stores.

Level 2, Unit 4. Theme: Food

Desafío 1	**Foods**: los pescados, los mariscos, el salmón, los camarones, el atún, los cereales, el pan, la pasta, el arroz, la carne, los frijoles, las lentejas, los guisantes, los lácteos, el queso, la leche, el yogur, la mantequilla, las frutas, las fresas, las uvas, la sandía, el melón, la piña, la pera, las verduras, las hortalizas…
Desafío 2	**Food containers**: un bote, una lata, una caja, una bolsa, una botella, un paquete. **Actions, measures, and other words related to buying food**: comprar, hacer la compra, vender, costar, pedir, pensar, hacer cola / fila; un kilo, un litro; la lista de la compra, el precio.
Desafío 3	**Condiments**: el aceite, el vinagre, la sal, la pimienta, el azúcar, la salsa de tomate, la mayonesa, la mostaza. **Actions in the kitchen**: pelar, cortar, echar, mezclar, batir, cocer, hervir, freír, asar.
Desafío 4	**In the restaurant**: el menú del día, de primero, de segundo. **At the table**: el mantel, la servilleta, el cuchillo, el tenedor, el vaso, la cuchara. **Describing foods and beverages**: agrio(a), dulce, picante, salado(a), soso(a), amargo(a), bueno(a), malo(a), delicioso(a), caliente, frío(a), fresco(a). **Preparing food**: frito(a), asado(a), a la plancha, cocido(a), hervido(a), empanado(a).

The instructional focus: work on many levels.

1. *Fotonovelas* and *Desafío* presentation texts

These include new vocabulary words and expressions that students can understand through their visual or verbal context. The activities help students focus on the lexical items and formulate hypotheses about their meaning.

2. *Vocabulario*

The new words and expressions are presented on the vocabulary pages in each *Desafío* with the support of images and / or language contexts.

Students practice the vocabulary first in closed-ended activities (less difficult) and then in open-ended activities (more difficult), where they can apply the vocabulary in real-life situations.

3. *Gramática, Comunicación,* and *Todo junto*

Key vocabulary is reinforced and used in different contexts, along with recycled vocabulary from previous units.

4. *Repaso*

At the end of the unit, vocabulary is reviewed and pre-assessment activities are included.

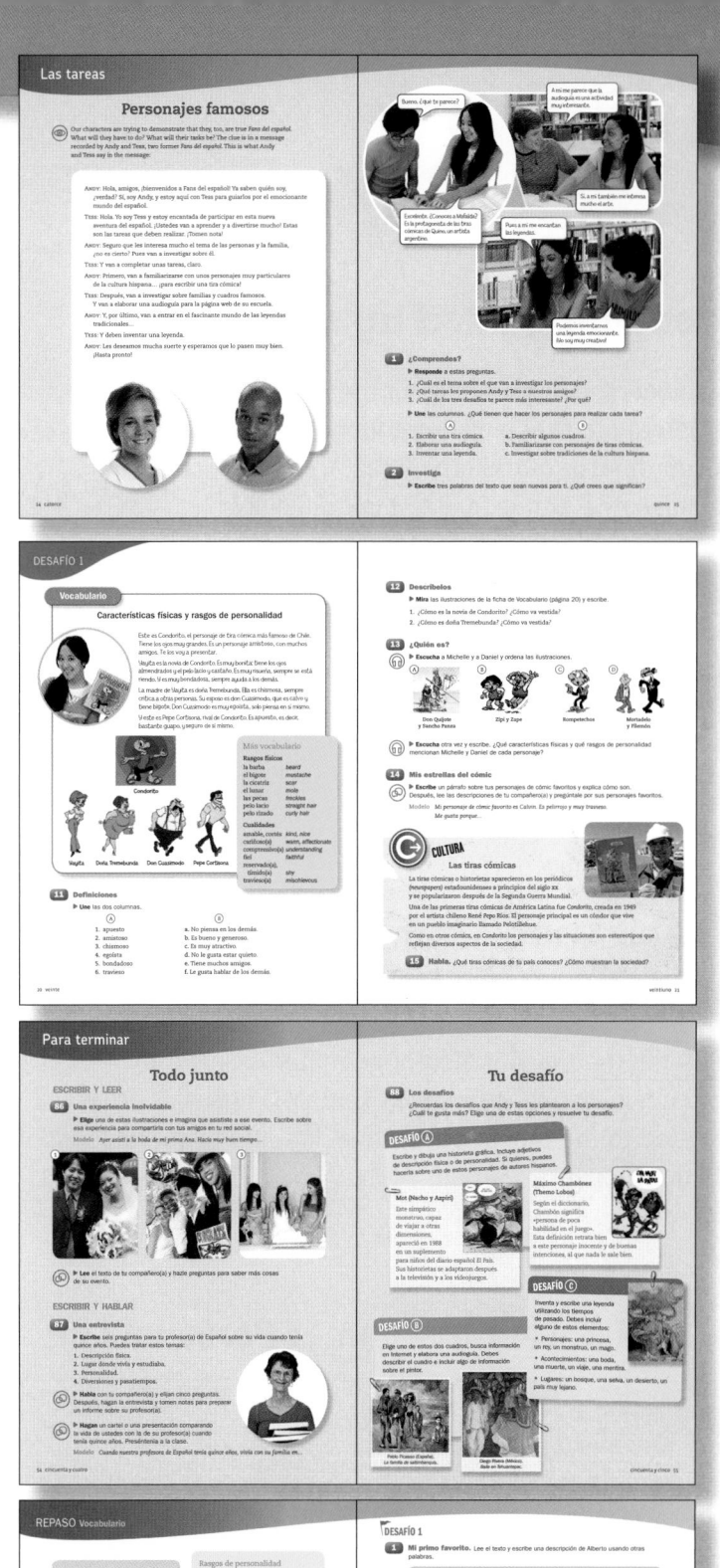

The Grammar

A decision guided by experience.

The selection and sequence of the grammatical elements was determined keeping three fundamental criteria in mind: the use of the structures, their productivity in communicative contexts, and their difficulty.

For example, the verbs *ser*, *estar*, and *tener* are presented before the verb *gustar* because they are more frequently used, they are more productive, and they present fewer difficulties for English speakers than the verb *gustar*.

Organization: Grammar linked to communicative functions.

In general, the presentation of grammar is linked to a communicative function. For example, in Level 2, Unit 1, dedicated to the theme of personal life, the following functions and structures are learned:

Gramática

Verbos con raíz irregular (e > ie)

Verbos irregulares

- Irregular verbs do not follow typical conjugation patterns. Ser and tener, for example, are irregular verbs.

  ser → yo soy, tú eres...   tener → yo tengo, tú tienes...

- Irregular verbs may change the stem or the endings.
  Remember: To identify the stem of a verb, delete the -ar, -er, -ir endings from the infinitive form.

  lav -a̶r̶   prend -e̶r̶   abr -i̶r̶

Verbos con raíz irregular (e > ie)

- Some verbs, like cerrar *(to close)*, require a stem change from e to ie.

VERBO CERRAR *(TO CLOSE)*. PRESENTE

Singular		Plural	
yo	cierro	nosotros nosotras	cerramos
tú	cierras	vosotros vosotras	cerráis
usted él ella	cierra	ustedes ellos ellas	cierran

Note: The e > ie stem change affects all the present tense forms except nosotros, nosotras and vosotros, vosotras. This is why these verbs are called "boot or shoe verbs."

- Other verbs like cerrar are:

  empezar *(to begin)* → yo empiezo
  entender *(to understand)* → yo entiendo
  pensar *(to think)* → yo pienso

  preferir *(to prefer)* → yo prefiero
  querer *(to want)* → yo quiero

15 **Comparación.** What irregular English verbs do you know? Give three examples and explain why they are irregular.

Level 2, Unit 1. Theme: Personal Life

Desafío 1 Identifying yourself and others	Possessive adjectives and pronouns
Desafío 2 Describing people	Adjectives and nouns
Desafío 3 Expressing states and feelings	Comparison and superlative
Desafío 4 Asking questions	Interrogatives

Didactic Focus: the use of concise and organized information.

1. *Fotonovelas* and *Desafío* presentation texts

The beginning texts of each *Desafío* include new structures that students can comprehend by their visual or linguistic context. The activities help students to focus on these structures and to formulate hypotheses about their meaning and usage.

2. *Gramática*

The grammar boxes contain explicit information about the structures presented in the initial text. They present the information supported by concise, visually organized graphics, tables, and diagrams. Each grammar box concludes with a comparison between Spanish and English.

The grammar activities are sequenced according to difficulty, from closed-ended activities to open-ended and personalized activities.

3. *Comunicación* and *Todo junto*

Key grammatical structures are reinforced by their application in open-ended, communicative activities.

4. *Repaso*

Key grammar is reviewed at the end of the unit by means of pre-assessment activities.

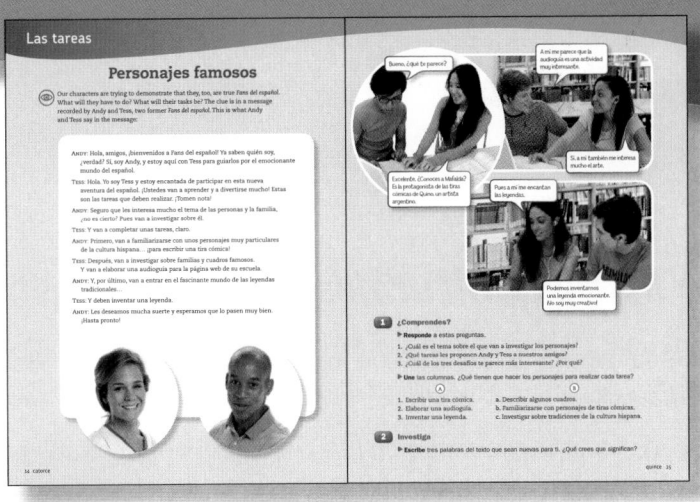

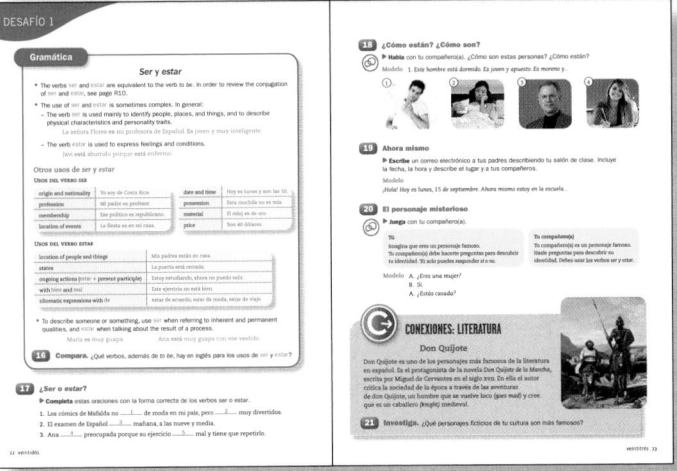

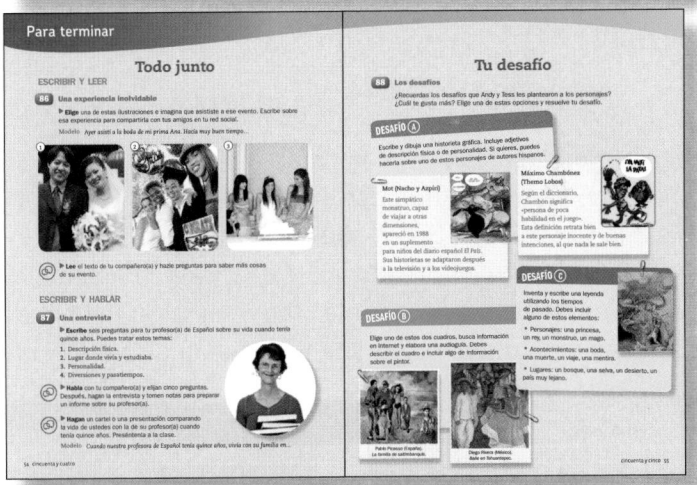

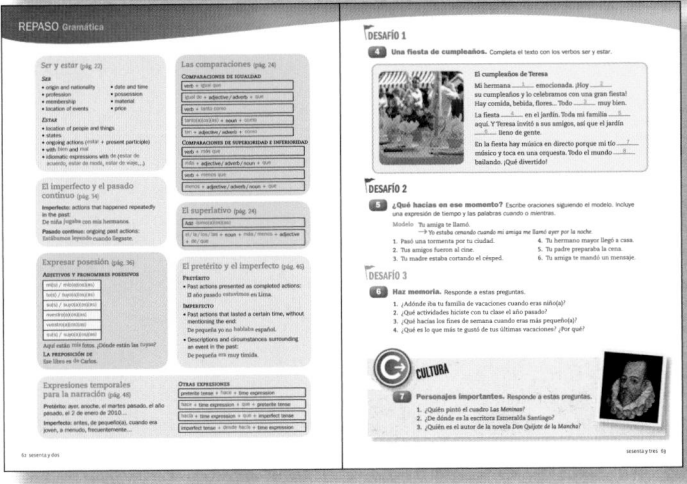

The *Mapas Culturales*

The *Mapas Culturales* propose a systematic study.

The *Mapa cultural* is the section in which students study Hispanic cultures in an organized and systematic way.

In Levels 1 and 2, the *Mapa cultural* is based on the study of a country or a geographical region with cultural similarities: Central America, the Antilles, the Río de la Plata region, etc.

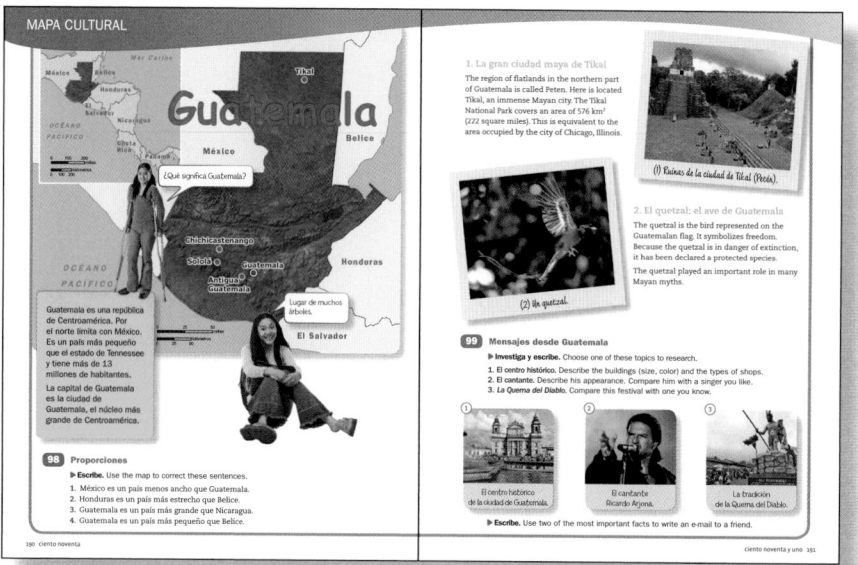

The first page contains **general information** about the country or cultural area which is being studied: its location, size, the countries in this region, main cities, etc.

The *Mapa cultural* offers a selection of representative cultural aspects: places, people, traditions, customs, and folklore.

In Level 3, the *Mapa cultural* compares a cultural practice or product in different Spanish-speaking countries: the festivals (the *Desfile de Llamadas* in Uruguay, the *Grito de Dolores* in México, the *castells* and the *fallas* in Spain, the Flower Bearers Parade in Colombia), the traditional sports (*tejo* in Colombia, the *charreada* in Mexico, *pato* in Argentina, stone lifting in Spain), urbanism in colonial cities, the universities, etc. The integrated thematic structure allows students to make comparisons and to appreciate the richness and diversity of the Spanish-speaking world.

Culture in the *Mapas Culturales*

Level 1

México	La antigua Tenochtitlán El sur: la población indígena
Puerto Rico	El Viejo San Juan La salsa, la esencia de Puerto Rico
Guatemala	La gran ciudad maya de Tikal El quetzal: el ave de Guatemala
Perú	Los incas, reyes de las montañas Las líneas de Nazca
España	Madrid: paraíso de pintores El sur: la herencia árabe
Estados Unidos	Huellas hispanas en los Estados Unidos Estados con historia hispana Concentración hispana en las ciudades
Argentina	El tango Buenos Aires
Chile	La Isla de Pascua Pablo Neruda Los chinchineros

Level 2

Centroamérica	Mestizaje y cultura Riqueza natural
Las Antillas	Barrios coloniales Música caribeña
Andes centrales	Quechuas y aymaras Los equecos Las islas Galápagos
Norteamérica	El Camino Real de Tierra Adentro Los chicanos
España	Paisaje mediterráneo La Noche de San Juan Las lenguas romances
Caribe continental	Símbolos nacionales El mestizaje y los bailes Cocina del Caribe: color y sabor
Río de la Plata	Influencia italiana Cultura rioplatense El chipá
La Panamericana	Variedad geográfica El mundo hispano

Level 3

La población latinoamericana	Tres culturas (indígenas, europeos, africanos) Fisonomía latinoamericana (mestizaje)
La fiesta: expresión comunitaria	El Desfile de Llamadas (Uruguay) El Grito de Dolores (México) Los castells (España)
La ciudad colonial	El modelo urbanístico de las ciudades coloniales (Santo Domingo, La Habana, Ciudad de México, Cartagena de Indias, Lima...)
Alimentos básicos en el mundo hispano	El maíz (México y Centroamérica) El trigo (España) La papa (Perú) La yuca (Paraguay)
Universidades hispanas	Universidad de Chile Universidad de Alcalá (España) Universidad Nacional Autónoma de México
Deportes con tradición	El tejo (Colombia) La charreada (México) El pato (Argentina) El levantamiento de piedras (España)
Espacios naturales singulares	Cabo de Hornos (Chile) Lanzarote (España) Las Yungas (Argentina) Arrecife Alacranes (México)
Una ciudad con historia: Barcelona	La antigua Barcino La Barcelona medieval La Barcelona moderna La Barcelona actual

Reading

Reading materials, linked to a comprehension strategy, build competency for reading in Spanish.

The reading materials present an opportunity to practice the given vocabulary and grammatical structures, while improving students' ability to interpret new vocabulary and grammatical structures in contexts. The use of numerous cognates makes the context more understandable and helps students to increase their vocabulary.

In Levels 1 and 2, each unit focuses on a specific reading strategy: identifying cognates; identifying key concepts; making inferences; and so on. Applying these strategies, students develop their ability to understand Spanish texts.

The readings work with different types of texts.

In Levels 1 and 2, the readings are linked to the culture of a country or cultural area, or with the theme of the unit, and represent different writing genres.

In each unit of Level 3, reading is practiced systematically with three types of texts: a written dialogue, an informative text, and a literary text.

Level 1

Theme	Type of Text
• Teotihuacán	An informative text.
• El Morro	A travel blog.
• Desde Chichicastenango	A letter.
• Festividad inca del Inti Raymi	A travel brochure.
• El *Guernica*, de Pablo Picasso	An art catalog.
• Celebramos la Herencia Hispana	An invitation.
• *La vuelta al mundo de Cinthia Scoch*	A short story.
• *Oda a la manzana,* de Pablo Neruda	A poem.

Level 2

Theme	Type of Text
• El blog de Ichxel	A personal blog.
• Estilo de vida caribeño	A travel magazine.
• Textiles andinos bolivianos	A museum brochure.
• La receta del guacamole	An instructional text.
• *Figura en una ventana,* de Salvador Dalí	A descriptive text.
• El Dorado, ecos de una leyenda	An informative text.
• Un cuento de Benedetti	A narrative text.
• El Tapón de Darién	An argumentative text.

Level 3

Textos informativos	Textos literarios
• Una breve biografía de Frida Kahlo	• *Los hermanos Ayar* (leyenda inca)
• Juegos precolombinos	• *El mensaje*
• Guía de viajeros: un hotel inolvidable	• *La casa de muñecas*
• El blog personal de Sara	• *La leyenda del maíz* (leyenda azteca)
• Manuel Jalón, un inventor humanista (reportaje)	• *Música*, de Ana María Matute
• Historia de los Juegos Panamericanos	• *Galletitas*, de Jorge Bucay
• Las tradiciones del Sol	• *El eclipse*, de Augusto Monterroso
• Entrevista a Debra McKeon	• *La muralla*, de Nicolás Guillén

Writing

Writing moves toward the production of more complex texts.

In Levels 1 and 2, writing is practiced within the framework of the *Desafíos* by way of short, simple texts: lists, notes, e-mails, schedules, recipes, etc. In Level 3, there is an additional composition included and the students are required to create somewhat more complex compositions: a character sketch, an essay, a report, or an opinion article.

Through these activities, students have the opportunity to express their ideas and become accustomed to formal and creative writing in Spanish.

Compositions are developed within the framework of the writing process.

Writing is developed in a four-step process:

1 *Piensa* (Plan) **2** *Escribe* (Write) **3** *Revisa* (Revise and correct) **4** *Comparte* (Share and publish)

In this process, students frequently exchange their writing with their peers in the tasks of planning and revision, thus taking full advantage of collaborative work.

Level 3. Composition Tasks

- Un personaje interesante (bosquejo biográfico)
- ¿Un poema o un dibujo? ¡Un caligrama!
- Un ensayo de moda
- Una receta típica

- Una carta formal
- Un cuento
- Un reportaje medioambiental
- Y tú, ¿qué opinas? (un texto de opinión)

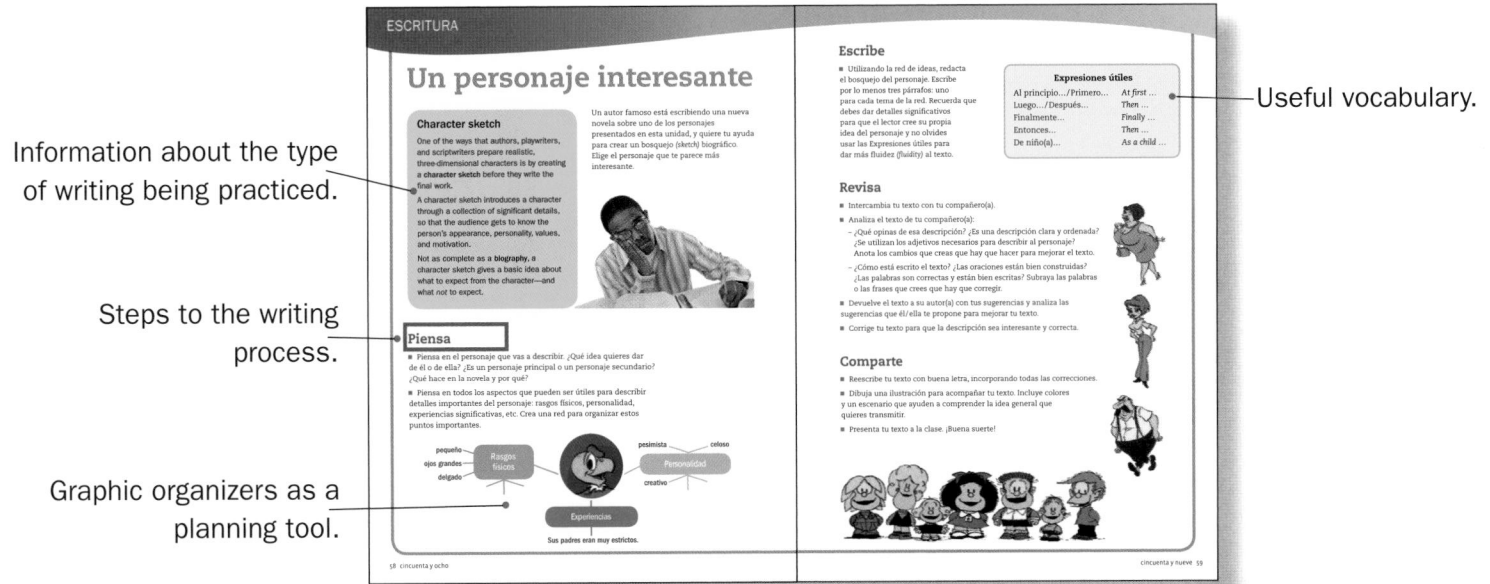

Information about the type of writing being practiced.

Steps to the writing process.

Graphic organizers as a planning tool.

Useful vocabulary.

The Project

The project provides an opportunity for integrating and applying knowledge.

Each unit closes with a project that encourages students' creativity and communicative capacity, while activating vocabulary and grammatical structures that students have learned. Each project develops a communicative activity that integrates cultural and linguistic information.

The activities are separated into steps.

Each project develops from a set of activities presented sequentially in separate steps. Each step is clearly defined and includes guidelines to help students complete the activities.

Una exposición de muñecos quitapenas

PASO 1	**Crea tus muñecos quitapenas**
PASO 2	**Prepara una exposición de muñecos**
PASO 3	**Dramatiza la compra y venta de muñecos**

Project Tasks
Level 1

México	Una presentación sobre Diego Rivera
Puerto Rico	Una visita guiada por la Casa Blanca
Guatemala	Una exposición de muñecos quitapenas
Perú	Nuestros restaurantes
España	Un póster sobre hábitos de higiene
Estados Unidos	Un cartel sobre un hispano famoso
Argentina	Crónica de un viaje
Chile	Un póster sobre animales en peligro

Project: *Una exposición de muñecos quitapenas*

Vocabulary	• Clothing. Characteristics, materials, and colors of clothing • Shopping
Grammar	• The verb *gustar* • Demonstrative adjectives • Comparisons • Present tense of irregular verbs
Culture	• Indigenous traditions • Traditional handicrafts from Guatemala

Level 2

Centroamérica	Una historia sobre personajes de Guatemala
Las Antillas	Un juego en las calles de Santo Domingo
Andes centrales	Una revista sobre moda andina
Norteamérica	Un menú con ingredientes americanos
España	Una presentación sobre hábitos de alimentación
Caribe continental	Un folleto sobre la laguna de Guatavita
Río de la Plata	Un guión para una telenovela
La Panamericana	Un boletín sobre la predicción meteorológica

Level 3

Las personas y la familia	Un álbum de fotos de tu vida
Vida social	Un plan de actividades con tus amigos
La ropa y la vivienda	Una feria sobre ciudades coloniales hispanas
La alimentación y la salud	Una guía para una vida saludable
El trabajo y las profesiones	Un proyecto de una organización solidaria
El tiempo libre y los viajes	Un plan para un viaje de estudios
La naturaleza y el medio ambiente	Una campaña publicitaria en favor del medio ambiente
Historia, política y sociedad	Una presentación sobre un país de Latinoamérica

The unit closes with a self-evaluation.

At the end of each unit is a self-evaluation section with questions that correspond to the unit objectives, so that students can reflect upon their progress.

Presentation of the task.

Steps.

Project instructions.

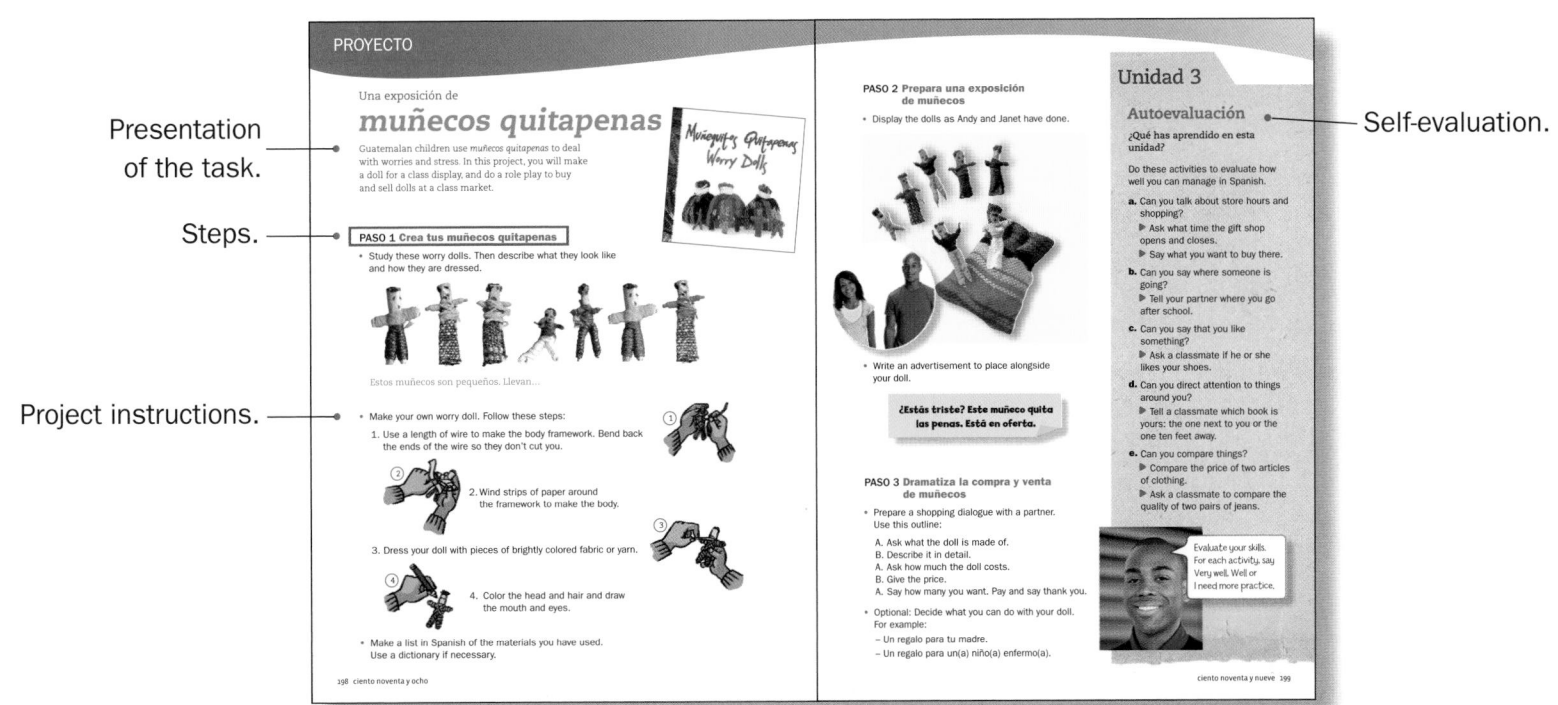

Self-evaluation.

The *Teacher's Edition*

Keys for teaching and learning.

The pages at the beginning of each unit offer a broad overview as well as tools for the organization and planning of school activities.

Objectives, contents, and evaluation criteria.

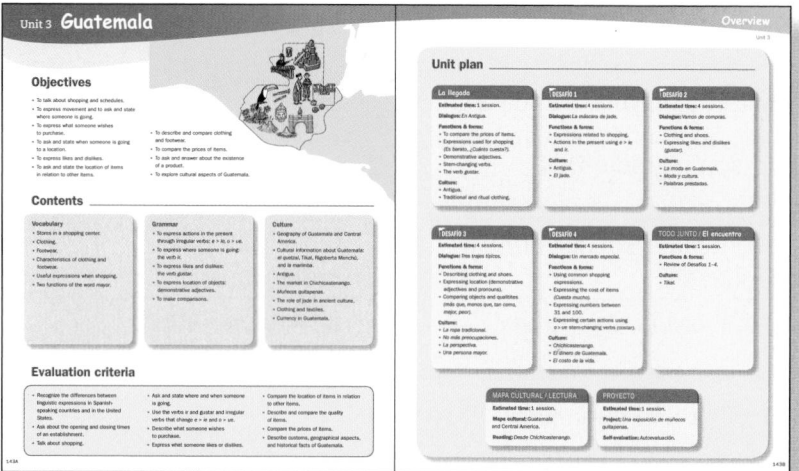

Outline of the unit and estimated time for completing each section.

Detailed description of the standards for learning Spanish in the unit.

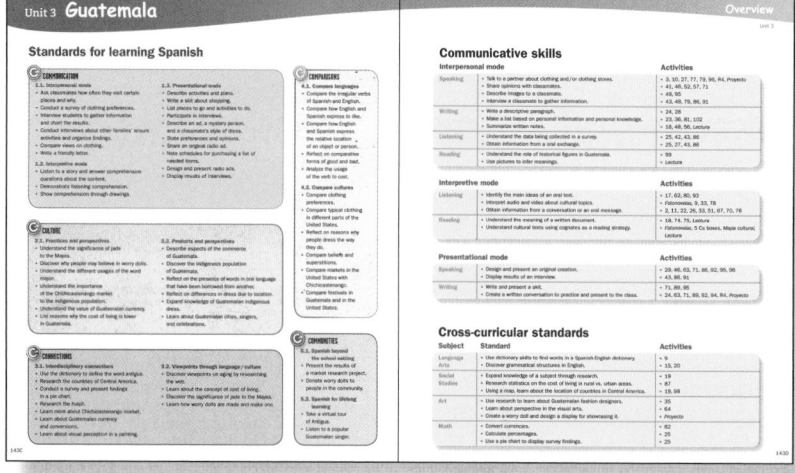

Communicative abilities practiced in the unit classified by skill (speaking, writing, listening, and reading) and by use (interpersonal, interpretative, and presentational).

Standards for other areas also discussed.

Detailed lesson plans for 50- and 90-minute classes.

Audio scripts.

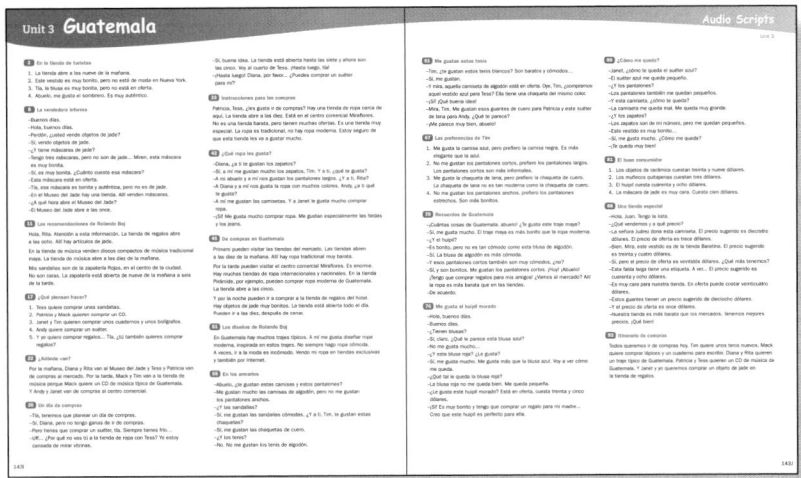

The instructional guides offer numerous resources for making the teacher's job easier.

General overview of the section.

Explanation of key educational and methodological solutions for interpreting the material.

Additional information about the cultural topics discussed.

Methodological proposals and suggestions: how to present the material, what to do with the class, how to prevent common errors, etc.

Differentiated instruction: developing learners, expanding learners, heritage language learners, special-needs learners, cooperative learning, multiple intelligences, critical thinking, etc.

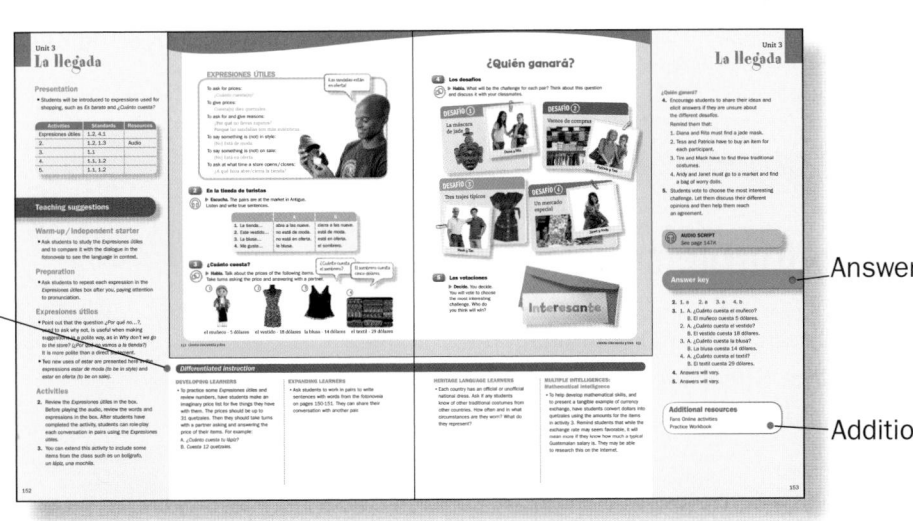

Answer key.

Additional resources.

Technology

A wide variety of technological resources.

Español Santillana relies on broad technological support, including digital versions of print materials (books, workbooks, and teacher's guides), plus an extensive offering of specific resources: visual presentations, videos, audio materials, a webpage, and more.

Visual presentations in the *fotonovelas* and the challenges.

The *fotonovelas* that present the characters' arrival in the country and their challenges are supported by visual presentations that replicate the dialogues and the story. The visual presentations offer an excellent method for improving students' listening comprehension ability.

Videos for enjoying the Spanish-speaking world's cultures.

The unit begins with a video that gives students an overview of the country or cultural area and the challenges that the characters will undertake. Each *Mapa cultural* is also accompanied by a video that offers a detailed view of the country or cultural area, its landscapes, and its most outstanding characteristics. In addition, each unit includes two other videos on significant cultural topics: the house of Frida Kahlo (Mexico), Old San Juan (Puerto Rico), the market of Chichicastenango (Guatemala), and so on. The videos are highly evocative, serving to motivate students and reinforce their listening skills while promoting learning.

The audios, an invaluable tool.

The books are accompanied by an Audio CD containing recordings of all the listening activities. The Speaking and Listening Workbook (see page T31) is also accompanied by an Audio CD.

The webpages are a fundamental element of *Español Santillana.*

The webpage **Fans del español** (www.fansdelespañol.com) features the basic plot of the story. The characters decide to create the website *Fans del español* in order to share what they know about the Spanish-speaking world. Characters post information about themselves and about challenges that students can access on this webpage. In this manner, fiction becomes reality.

Additionally, the **Español Santillana** series is supported by the **Fans Online** website (campus.fansdelespañol.com), which offers countless activities, photogalleries, games, and other resources for the student, as well as an extensive bank of Assessment activities for the teacher to use (Online Assessments).

The digital versions of the Student Book and Teacher's Edition provide a complete multimedia experience.

Both the Student Book and Teacher's Edition are available in an interactive digital format:

▶ The **Interactive Student Book** contains numerous multimedia resources that enhance and complement learning Spanish: videos, visual presentations, audios, photogalleries, flashcards, etc. Students can listen to the pronunciation of the dialogues and vocabulary words, and can also use interactive tools such as highlighters and sticky notes.

▶ The **All-in-One Digital Teacher's Edition** brings together all of the elements that the teacher needs to plan and teach a class:

- The *Interactive Student Book* and its multimedia resources. This version of the *Student Book* is designed so that the teacher can project the pages onto a screen and can also activate the videos, the visual presentations, the audios, and other features.
- The *Teacher's Edition* pages.
- The *Teacher's Annotated Edition* of the *Practice Workbook* and the *Speaking and Listening Workbook*, with its corresponding audio tracks.
- The Assessment Program, with answer keys for the teacher.
- An editable version of the Lesson Plans, so that the teacher can personalize the lesson plans to his or her needs.

The Workbooks

Three workbooks to practice with.

Español Santillana features three student workbooks: the *Practice Workbook*, the *Speaking and Listening Workbook*, and the workbook for heritage Spanish speakers (the *Cuaderno para hispanohablantes*).

The *Practice Workbook* deepens the study of the language independently.

This is the perfect complement to the Student Book. Here students will find many opportunities to work with the linguistic and cultural contents of the series. It contains all the information (word glossaries and grammar summaries) that students need, and the activities have been designed so that students can work them out without having to consult other sources.

The *Speaking and Listening Workbook* consolidates two fundamental skills.

This workbook deals specifically with comprehension and verbal expression.

The listening activities can be used in the classroom or at home. The Audio CD that accompanies the workbook allows the students to work independently. In contrast, the speaking activities are designed to be used in the classroom.

The speaking and listening activities allow students to practice the key vocabulary and grammatical structures presented in the books.

The workbook for heritage Spanish speakers improves their reading comprehension and writing ability.

This workbook complements the *Español Santillana* textbook and is for heritage Spanish speakers capable of completing an activity in Spanish by themselves.
The workbook maintains the themes and structures of the Student Book, allowing heritage Spanish speakers to work with the textbook in class while completing tasks appropriate to their language level in the workbook.

The objectives of the workbook are the following:

- To develop reading comprehension (Reading).
- To expand students' vocabulary (Vocabulary).
- To improve students' handling of written expression for various purposes (Spelling, Writing).
- To encourage understanding of and appreciation for differences in cultural origins (Connections, Communities).

Scope and Sequence High School 1

Contents

Unidad	Vocabulario
Unit 1 **México** 30–85	• People • Physical characteristics • Personality traits • Family • States and conditions
Unit 2 **Puerto Rico** 86–143	• The house • Furniture and objects in a house • Household chores • Leisure activities
Unit 3 **Guatemala** 144–199	• The shopping center • Clothing and footwear • Describing clothing and footwear • Shopping
Unit 4 **Perú** 200–255	• Foods and beverages • Food stores • At the table • Describing food
Unit 5 **España** 256–309	• Parts of the body • Personal hygiene • Symptoms and illnesses • Basic remedies • Healthy habits
Unit 6 **Estados Unidos** 310–363	• The world of work • Hobbies • Free time • Sports
Unit 7 **Argentina** 364–417	• Transportation • Travel • Destinations and lodging • The city. Location and directions
Unit 8 **Chile** 418–471	• The universe • Geography • Political divisions • Numbers from 101 to 1,000 • Nature and the environment

Gramática		Cultura	

• Subject pronouns
• The verb *ser*
• Adjectives
• The verb *tener*
	• Expressing possession:
	  – Possessive adjectives
	  – The preposition *de*
	• The verb *estar*
		• *Mapa cultural:* Mexico
		  • Mexico City: Tenochtitlan
		  • The south: the indigenous
		    population
			• *Lectura: Teotihuacán, ciudad
			  de los dioses*

• Nouns
• Articles. Agreement with nouns
• Expressing existence.
  The verb *haber*
• Expressing location
• Regular *-ar* verbs, present tense
	• Regular *-er* and *-ir* verbs,
	  present tense
	• Expressing obligation:
	  – *Tener que* + infinitive
	  – *Hay que* + infinitive
	• Adverbs of frequency
		• *Mapa cultural:* Puerto Rico
		  • Old San Juan
		  • Salsa, the essence of
		    Puerto Rico
			• *Lectura: El Morro: Blog
			  de viajes*

• Stem-changing verbs (*e > ie*)
• The verb *ir*
• The verb *gustar*
• Demonstratives
	• Comparison. Comparative
	  adjectives
	• Stem-changing verbs (*o > ue*)
		• *Mapa cultural:* Guatemala
		  • The great Mayan city of Tikal
		  • The quetzal, national bird
		    of Guatemala
			• *Lectura: Desde
			  Chichicastenango*

• Adverbs of quantity
• Expressing want, preference,
  and rejection. The verbs
  querer and *preferir*
	• Irregular verbs in the *yo* form
	• Direct object pronouns
	• Indirect object pronouns
	• Stem-changing verbs (*e > i*)
		• *Mapa cultural:* Peru
		  • The Incas, kings of the
		    mountains
		  • The Nazca lines
			• *Lectura: Festividad inca
			  del Inti Raymi*

• The verbs *ver, oír, oler,
  and decir*
• Reflexive verbs
• The verb *doler*
	• The verb *sentirse*
	• Affirmative *tú* commands.
	  Regular verbs
		• *Mapa cultural:* Spain
		  • Madrid: a painter's paradise
		  • The south: an Arabic
		    heritage
			• *Lectura: El Guernica,
			  de Pablo Picasso*

• Affirmative commands.
  Irregular verbs
• *Ir a* + infinitive. Time
  markers in the future
• The present progressive
	• The present participle
	• Stem-changing verbs (*u > ue*)
		• *Mapa cultural:* United States
		  • Hispanic influence
		    in the United States
		  • States with Hispanic history
			• Concentration of Hispanic
			  people in cities
			• *Lectura: Celebramos
			  la Herencia Hispana*

• The preterite tense of regular
  -ar verbs
• The preterite tense of regular
  -er and *-ir* verbs
	• Time markers in the past
	• The preterite tense of the
	  verbs *ser* and *ir*
	• Negative commands
		• *Mapa cultural:* Argentina
		  • The tango
		  • Buenos Aires
			• *Lectura: La vuelta al mundo
			  de Cinthia Scoch*

• Expressing cause: *porque*
  and *por*
• Expressing quantity. Indefinites
• Irregular verbs in the
  preterite. *Decir* and *hacer*
	• Irregular verbs in the
	  preterite. *Estar* and *tener*
	• Expressing permission and
	  prohibition
		• *Mapa cultural:* Chile
		  • Easter Island
		  • Pablo Neruda
		  • The chinchineros
			• *Lectura: Oda a la manzana*

Scope and Sequence High School 2

Contents

Unidad	Vocabulario
Unit 1 **Centroamérica** 28–79	• Personal and family relationships • Physical characteristics and personality traits • Emotional states and feelings • Personal information
Unit 2 **Las Antillas** 80–131	• The house. Household chores • Furniture and objects in a house • Electrical appliances • The neighborhood. Places and services
Unit 3 **Andes centrales** 132–183	• Clothing and accessories • Describing clothes • Stores and establishments • Shoppping
Unit 4 **Norteamérica** 184–235	• Foods • Buying food • In the kitchen • In the restaurant
Unit 5 **España** 236–287	• Parts of the body • Personal hygiene • Health: symptoms and illnesses • Healthy habits
Unit 6 **Caribe continental** 288–339	• Trips and excursions • On the train and on the plane • The car • The hotel. The bank
Unit 7 **Río de la Plata** 340–391	• The school • Professions • Hobbies, free time activities, and entertainment • Sports
Unit 8 **La Panamericana** 392–443	• Geography • Countries • The weather • Nature and environment

Gramática		Cultura	

• Possessives
• Adjectives and nouns
	• Comparisons and superlatives
	• Interrogatives
		• *Mapa cultural:* Centroamérica
		  • Mestizaje y cultura
		  • Riqueza natural
			• *Lectura: El blog de Ichxel*

• The present progressive
• Direct object pronouns
	• Indirect object pronouns
	• Demonstratives
		• *Mapa cultural:* Las Antillas
		  • Barrios coloniales
		  • Música caribeña
			• *Lectura: Estilo de vida caribeño*

• The preterite tense of regular
  -ar verbs
• The preterite tense of regular
  -er and *-ir* verbs
	• The preterite tense of the verbs *ser, ir,*
	  decir, tener, estar, and *hacer.*
	• The preterite tense of
	  stem-changing *-ir* verbs
		• *Mapa cultural:* Andes centrales
		  • Quechuas y aymaras
		  • Los equecos
		  • Las islas Galápagos
			• *Lectura: Textiles andinos bolivianos*

• Expressing amount. Indefinites
• Singular affirmative commands
	• Plural affirmative commands
	• Negative commands
		• *Mapa cultural:* Norteamérica
		  • El Camino Real de Tierra Adentro
		  • Los chicanos
			• *Lectura: La receta
			  del guacamole*

• The past participle
• Adverbs ending in *-mente*
	• *Por* and *para*
	• Making recommendations
		• *Mapa cultural:* España
		  y el Mediterráneo
		  • Paisaje mediterráneo
		  • La Noche de San Juan
		  • Las lenguas romances
			• *Lectura: Figura en una ventana,
			  de Salvador Dalí*

• The imperfect tense
• The preterite tense of the verbs
  dar, poder, poner, querer, saber,
  and *venir*
	• Talking about past actions. The preterite
	  and the imperfect tenses
	• Talking about past actions and describing
	  in the past. The preterite and imperfect
	  tenses
		• *Mapa cultural:* Caribe continental
		  • Símbolos nacionales
		  • El mestizaje y los bailes
		  • Cocina del Caribe: color
		  y sabor
			• *Lectura: El Dorado, ecos
			  de una leyenda*

• Expressing existence. Indefinites
• The present subjunctive
  of regular verbs
	• The present subjunctive of
	  stem-changing verbs
	• The present subjunctive of
	  irregular verbs
		• *Mapa cultural:* El río de la Plata
		  • Influencia italiana
		  • Cultura rioplatense
		  • El chipá
			• *Lectura: Un cuento de Benedetti*

• The relative superlative
• Expressing plans
  and intentions
	• The future tense
	• Hiding the agent. The pronoun *se*
		• *Mapa cultural:* La ruta Panamericana
		  • Variedad geográfica
		  • El mundo hispano: unidad
		  y diversidad
			• *Lectura: El Tapón de Darién:
			  un corte en la ruta Panamericana*

Scope and Sequence High School 3

Contents

Unidad	Vocabulario
Unit 1 **¿Cómo eres?** 12–65	• Physical characteristics and personality traits • Family relationships • Biographies
Unit 2 **Entre amigos** 66–119	• Personal relationships • Introductions. Expressions to invite, accept, and reject an invitation • Phone calls
Unit 3 **Tus cosas** 120–173	• Clothing • Describing objects • Household chores and professions
Unit 4 **Vida sana** 174–227	• Foods • Healthy habits • The doctor's office. The human body
Unit 5 **¿Trabajas?** 228–281	• Jobs and professions • Work and technology • Volunteering and community service
Unit 6 **Tus aficiones** 282–335	• Free time and events • Sports • Travel and lodging
Unit 7 **Nuestro planeta** 336–389	• Nature and the environment • The weather. The universe • Natural disasters. Natural resources
Unit 8 **En sociedad** 390–443	• Historical figures, events, civilizations • Politicas and government • Society

Gramática		Cultura		Escritura
• *Ser* and *estar* • Comparatives and superlatives • The imperfect and the past progressive	• Expressing possession • The preterite and the imperfect tenses • Time expressions for narration	• Lectura informativa: *Una breve biografía* • Lectura literaria: *Los hermanos Ayar* (leyenda inca)	• Mapa cultural: La población latinoamericana	Un bosquejo biográfico
• Direct object and indirect object pronouns • Reflexive and reciprocal verbs • Expressing wishes, likes, and preferences	• Non-reflexive verbs used with pronouns • Expressing need and obligation • Speaking about the future	• Lectura informativa: *Juegos precolombinos* • Lectura literaria: *El mensaje*	• Mapa cultural: La fiesta: expresión comunitaria	Un caligrama
• The past participle • Talking about recent actions. The present perfect tense • Indefinites	• Impersonal constructions. The pronoun *se* • The past perfect tense • Demonstratives	• Lectura informativa: *Guía de viajeros: un hotel inolvidable* • Lectura literaria: *La casa de muñecas*	• Mapa cultural: La ciudad colonial	Un ensayo
• Commands • Verbs that express change • *Para* and *por*	• Making value statements • The conditional tense • Giving advice and recommendations	• Lectura informativa: *El blog personal de Sara* • Lectura literaria: *La leyenda del maíz* (leyenda azteca)	• Mapa cultural: Alimentos básicos en el mundo hispano	Una receta
• Expressing certainty and doubt • The imperfect subjunctive • Giving details. The relative pronoun *que*	• The gender of nouns • Expressing feelings • Expressing difficulty	• Lectura informativa: *Manuel Jalón, un inventor humanista* • Lectura literaria: *Música* (Ana María Matute)	• Mapa cultural: Universidades hispanas	Una carta formal
• Expressing opinion • Grammatical forms of courtesy • Expressing probability	• Expressing purpose • Indirect speech • Expressing place	• Lectura informativa: *Historia de los Juegos Panamericanos* • Lectura literaria: *Galletitas* (Jorge Bucay)	• Mapa cultural: Deportes con tradición	Un cuento
• Expressing condition (I) • Expressing condition (II) • Expressing time	• The present perfect subjunctive • Expressing cause and consequence • The personal *a*	• Lectura informativa: *Las tradiciones del Sol* • Lectura literaria: *El eclipse* (Augusto Monterroso)	• Mapa cultural: Espacios naturales singulares	Un reportaje
• The passive voice • The past tenses (review) • Referring to the stages of an action	• Uses of the indicative (review) • Articles • Uses of the subjunctive (review)	• Lectura informativa: *Entrevista a Debra McKeon* • Lectura literaria: *La muralla* (Nicolás Guillén)	• Mapa cultural: Una ciudad con historia: Barcelona	Un texto de opinión

The Spanish Language of the United States

Gerardo Piña-Rosales The North American Academy of the Spanish Language

First of all, dear reader, let us focus on the title of this essay: "The Spanish Language *of* the United States" instead of "The Spanish Language *in* the United States." The difference between these two prepositions is an essential one: it implies that we have begun to speak of a United States Spanish with its own characteristics, as one more of the multiple variants of the Spanish language spoken around the world.

Spanish Speakers in the United States

It is estimated that there are some 45 million Spanish-speaking people in the United States, which translates into 15 percent of the nation's population, and it is expected that this figure will rise to more than 150 million Spanish speakers by 2050. In other words, it is highly probable that the United States will become the country with the largest number of Spanish-speaking inhabitants on our planet. More than half of the 45 million Spanish speakers were born in this country, and they make up a younger-than-average portion of the overall population: 48 percent of Hispanics are younger than 25 years of age. Whether or not a minority language replaces the language spoken by the majority depends, above all, on the new generations; thus, the relative youth of the Hispanic population will undoubtedly influence the future of the Spanish language in the United States.

Spanish Variants

When we speak of the Spanish language of the United States, it is important to point out that we are not referring to a monolithic, uniform language, but to one that encompasses a number of variants. In this regard, we can divide the country into several linguistic areas, each with its own distinct characteristics. In the West and Southwest, where 60 percent of Hispanics reside, a *chicano* variant of Spanish is spoken; in Florida, and especially in Miami, a Cuban variant of Spanish is heard. In the Northeast, including New York, New Jersey, and Connecticut, a Caribbean form of Spanish is spoken. Furthermore, one can hear *isleño* Spanish in Louisiana and a distinctive form of Spanish spoken in the region of the Sabine River (Louisiana and Texas).

English Influences

The massive influence of English has imparted a unique imprint on the Spanish language of the United States, which contrasts with that of other Spanish-speaking countries.

This particular influence is manifested in new vocabulary, much of it based on "borrowed" words, which have contributed to the incorporation of *anglicisms* into the Spanish spoken in those countries.

English Influence at Work

Hispanic immigrants try to learn and speak English at their workplace and in their associations with Americans. This effort to communicate tends to facilitate the use of *Spanglish*. In time, if they have a certain level of education, they learn both languages well and become bilingual. There is a desire to acquire a better knowledge not only of English but also of the Spanish of their heritage.

Spanglish

A distinctive characteristic of the Spanish language of the United States is the so-called "code-switching," which consists of a speaker's use of both languages during a conversation. Since this means of communication has not been methodically studied until recently, a certain notion exists—both among the general public and among certain educators—that it is a random mixture of languages, i.e., *Spanglish*. In fact it is a process with its own structural conventions, one that also plays a unique role among bilingual Spanish speakers, precisely as an alternative to communicating in a single language. The economic importance of the Spanish language of the United States is greater than that of any other Spanish-speaking country. The Spanish language would survive if only for the United States.

Bibliography

Amastae, Jon and Lucía Elías-Olivares. *Spanish in the United States: Sociolinguistic Aspects.* Cambridge: Cambridge University Press, 1982.

Elías-Olivares, Lucía, ed. *Spanish in the U.S. Setting: Beyond the Southwest*. Rosslyn, VA: National Clearinghouse for Bilingual Education, 1983.

Lipski, John M. *Varieties of Spanish in the United States*. Washington DC: Georgetown University Press, 2008.

López-Morales, Humberto, ed. *Enciclopedia del español en los Estados Unidos.* Madrid: Instituto Cervantes/Santillana, 2008.

Teaching and Learning: Language and Culture

Janet Glass Dwight Englewood School, Englewood, New Jersey, Rutgers University

Alfred Nobel's Peace Prize wished to reward "the person who shall have done the most or the best work for fraternity between nations." What could be more critical today? As teachers of world languages, our medium is language, but our message is one of cultural ambassador. Besides, what is more intriguing to a student than to learn how to make a new friend from another culture, to enter another world? This motivation is what stimulates our students' curiosity and helps them master the language. But once hooked, how can we make the most of their interest?

Five-Senses Culture

We can start by integrating culture into the whole language instruction process, making sure that culture underscores every language activity and is at the core of the unit. We can go beyond cultural "awareness" and try to experience the target culture in the classroom with smells, touches, simulations, tastes, rhythms, and video clips. Learning is enhanced when exchanges with people from the target culture happen early and often. As Byram et al. say in "Developing Intercultural Competence in Practice," "the task is rather to facilitate learners' interactions with some small part of another society and its cultures … and encouraging them to investigate for themselves the otherness around them." Let's lift it off the page!

Measuring Culture

When it comes to culture, students are always asking, "Does it *count*?" Although we have currently come a long way in measuring the language proficiency of our students, we are challenged to do as well with testing cultural appropriateness. Culture has to be taught systematically and then, assessed. How powerful it is to show students evidence of their own cultural competence, yet more exploration of how to best assess cultural competence is needed.

Seeing Our Own Culture with New Eyes

As language teachers, we also make the most of students' interest when we show how language shapes our thoughts, and leads to how we behave. Most of us don't become aware of our own cultural assumptions until confronted by another world view. When I was in Japan, for example, people frequently apologized as part of their daily conversation. They said, "Sorry I disturbed you" when calling someone on the phone. How does this habit of polite language reflect its culture? Accepting responsibility is a very high priority in Japan. As a result, we find it is a culture that discourages blame and is relatively free of lawsuits. Cultural instincts become internal, hidden, and subconscious. Through the target language, we strive to have our students uncover these influences, empathize with the people, and be able to interact in culturally appropriate ways.

Research Says

Meanwhile, research has confirmed what we have sensed. In a survey of young students studying language and culture, their responses to "People from other countries are scary" and "Hearing a language that's not English makes me nervous" was a resounding "No!" Students not in the program answered "Maybe" and "Yes."

So, as we make the foreign become familiar, the familiar will become a bit more foreign. By bringing cultural experiences into the classroom, measuring the outcomes, aiming for deep understanding and exchanges, we put linguistic and cultural abilities together and at the forefront of our shrinking world. *¡Sí, se puede!*

Bibliography

Byram, Michael, A. Nichols, and D. Stevens. "Developing Intercultural Competence in Practice." *Multilingual Matters Ltd*. 3 (2001).

Kennedy, Teresa, et al. "The FLES Attitudinal Inventory." *Foreign Language Annals*, ACTFL 33(3), May/June 2000: 278–289.

Wright, David A. "Culture as Information and Culture as Affective Process: A Comparative Study." *Foreign Language Annals*, ACTFL 33(3), May/June 2000: 330–341.

The Integration of Language, Culture, and Content in the Three Modes of Communication

Brandon Zaslow Site Director, California Foreign Language Project, Department of Education, Occidental College, Los Angeles, California

Work with teachers who are implementing a standards-based instructional approach shows that the integration of language, culture, and content is the area of greatest challenge and the aspect of standards-based practice that has the most transformative effect on student learning.

Preparing students to use language for real-world purposes in culturally appropriate ways requires that teachers specify the tasks students will need to carry out in order to function in target-language communities. The most efficient way to gain access to language, culture, and content is through the use of authentic materials, those that are designed for individuals who speak the language and share the culture and its perspectives on content. Semi-authentic video, audio, or print media are often used to ensure that all of the language, culture, and content necessary for successful real-world language use are available for learning.

Interpretive Mode

Teachers use a variety of strategies for making language, culture, and content comprehensible. They prepare students for interpretation by interesting them in the theme of the lesson, building on previous knowledge, and previewing key language, culture, and content. They ask students to make predictions, provide non-linguistic supports to meaning, and work with texts multiple times using different interpretive tasks that focus student attention on language, culture, or content. Often teachers break up texts into smaller segments in order to help students skim for main ideas and then scan for supporting details. Texts with storylines or content that can be divided into logical parts are easier to understand and recall.

Interpersonal Mode

When learners understand the materials used during interpretive communication, they need a great deal of practice to use the language, content, and cultural knowledge and skills to participate in real-world tasks. In order to gain proficiency in interpersonal communication, learners need to practice carrying out real-world tasks in multiple settings combining various elements of language, culture, and content. Recycling communicative elements that will occur in culminating tasks ensures that students will be successful in spontaneous, unrehearsed interpersonal communication.

As students gain proficiency using their language in a variety of culturally-authentic settings, teachers integrate language, culture, and content in more demanding simulations or real-world interpersonal tasks.

Presentational Mode

When students have had an opportunity to practice with others and carry out a number of interpersonal tasks using language, culture, and content, they will have developed the skills necessary to carry out real-world presentational tasks with sufficient clarity and accuracy to be successfully understood by a target-culture audience. Presentational tasks can be oral or written or combine both speech and writing. It is important when constructing presentational tasks to focus learner attention on culturally appropriate behavior and target-culture audiences. In written presentational tasks, rubrics are useful to guide the many drafts that may be necessary to produce a clear and accurate text that communicates effectively with the target audience.

Conclusion

Although challenging, the integration of language, culture, and content in interpretive, interpersonal, and presentational communication will transform world language classrooms and prepare students to function effectively in target-language communities.

Bibliography

National Standards in Foreign Language Education Project. *Standards for Foreign Language Learning in the 21st Century*. Lawrence, KS: Allen Press, Inc., 1999.

Anderson, Nancy, ed. *Spanish for Native Speakers*. AATSP, 2000.

Ballman, Terry L., Judith E. Liskin Gasparro, and Paul B. Mandell, eds. *The Communicative Classroom*. AATSP, 2001.

Birckbichler, Diane W. and Robert M. Terry, eds. *Reflecting on the Past to Shape the Future*. ACTFL, 2000.

Galloway, Vicky, ed. *Teaching Cultures of the Hispanic World: Products and Practices in Perspective*. AATSP, 2001.

Gunterman, Gail, ed. *Teaching Spanish with the Five C's: A Blueprint for Success*. ACTFL, 2000.

Heining-Boynton, Audrey L., ed. *2005-2015: Realizing Our Vision of Languages for All*. ACTFL, 2006.

Lafayette, Robert C., ed. *National Standards: A Catalyst for Reform*. ACTFL, 1996.

Omaggio-Hadley, Alice. *Teaching Language in Context*, 3rd ed. Boston: Heinle and Heinle, 2001.

Shrum, Judith L. and Eileen W. Glisan, *Teacher's Handbook: Contextualized Language Instruction*, 4th ed. Boston: Heinle and Heinle, 2010.

Teaching Vocabulary and Grammar Using Authentic Literary Texts and Other Reading Selections

Emily Spinelli Executive Director, American Association of Teachers of Spanish and Portuguese.
Professor Emerita of Spanish, University of Michigan-Dearborn

For many years the foreign language profession viewed the teaching of language and the teaching of literature as two very separate and distinct activities. At all educational levels the reading of literary texts was often seen as a task that only very advanced students could undertake. As a result, the early years of instruction were generally devoted to learning the language so that students could study literature in upper-level courses.

Authentic Texts Defined

In the 1970s this separation of language and literature teaching was challenged as researchers in language acquisition advocated for the use of authentic texts and materials in the language classroom. Widdowson pointed out that the language presented to students does not need to be simplified for easy access. He further stated that, "Nowadays there are recommendations that the language presented should be authentic." Wallace later defined authentic language as that found in "…real-life texts, not written for pedagogic purposes." Soon thereafter, authentic materials gradually made their way into textbooks in the form of advertisements, brochures, menus, schedules, and other items utilized in daily life. However, literature was still not viewed as suitable material for language learning.

Contemporary View of Literary Texts

Recently, a report from the Modern Language Association called for an end to the separation of language courses and literature courses and recommended a curriculum "in which language, culture, and literature are taught as a continuous whole." This contemporary view of the role of literature reinforces the notion that literary texts can be used to teach language beginning at the earliest levels. In addition to providing language models for students, literary selections also provide authentic cultural information, help critical thinking skills, and emphasize historical and literary traditions.

Reading Strategies and Activities to Promote Comprehension

It is now generally accepted that literary and other authentic texts should not be simplified or modified in order to help students comprehend them. Rather, students should be provided with reading strategies and activities prior to reading the selection. In turn, these strategies and activities will help students comprehend the authentic material.

Pre-reading, During-reading, and Post-reading Activities

Generally the strategies, explanations, and activities related to a reading selection fall into three categories called pre-reading, during-reading, and post-reading activities, depending on when they are used in relation to reading the selection. Pre-reading strategies provide students with reading techniques such as reading for gist, understanding the genre of the text, or forming hypotheses about the theme or topic of the text. Pre-reading activities can involve a presentation or review of vocabulary or grammar structures used within the literary selection. Vocabulary activities typically focus on cognate recognition, word families, prefixes and suffixes and other information designed to assist students with comprehending individual words. Grammar activities generally focus on recognition of parts of speech, verb forms and tenses, and word order. Other pre-reading activities focus on cultural information that have students compare or contrast cultural products, practices or perspectives found in the text with those found in their own cultures. During-reading activities generally help students focus on the pre-reading strategies and other information taught or reviewed in the pre-reading phase. Finally, the post-reading activities focus on comprehension and ask students to demonstrate what they learned while reading.

By helping students comprehend authentic texts through the use of pre-reading strategies and activities, we expand their language capabilities while strengthening their cross-cultural and literacy skills.

Bibliography

Bernardo, Sacha Anthony. "The Use of Authentic Materials in the Teaching of Reading." *The Reading Matrix* 6 (2006): 60–69.

Foreign Languages and Higher Education: New Structures for a Changed World. New York: Modern Language Association, 2006.

Wallace, Catherine. *Reading.* Oxford: Oxford University Press, 1992.

Widdowson, Henry G. *Aspects of Language Teaching.* Oxford: Oxford University Press, 1990.

Motivation

Jan Kucerik Pinellas County Public Schools, Pinellas County, Florida

A seventh grade student known to his Spanish teacher as "Juanito" ambles reluctantly into his beginning Spanish classroom. He greets the teacher, not with an enthusiastic "Buenos días, señora," but instead with the question on the mind of many of his classmates, "What are we doing in here today?" Although we would like to believe that the question has been posed out of genuine interest in the classroom activities, we realize that Juanito's question is motivated by self-preservation. He worries that he might be unprepared for, or embarrassed by, the activities Señora has planned for the day.

What Motivates Our Students

Motivation is crucial to teaching and learning. Whenever we feel a desire or need for something, we are in a state of motivation. Juanito is motivated to survive the class period, and his teacher wants him to thrive and share her passion for the Spanish language and Hispanic culture. He has a need to feel safe, yet his teacher understands that he must take risks in order to acquire language. He wants to avoid struggle, and she knows that great effort is involved in negotiating meaning and learning from mistakes. Although human beings are motivated to learn from birth, students are often not motivated to learn what we want them to learn in the way that we want them to learn it. They do, however, select information and learning experiences that are important to them every day. Teachers continue to work tirelessly to motivate their students, but most focus on extrinsic motivators, which may not be enough to truly engage students in the long term. How do we make students feel connected to learning? How do we make them feel as if the learning could not happen without them? How do we create excitement for learning, resulting in students eagerly entering our classrooms each day?

Relationships Are Key

We rely on the standards and performance guidelines to articulate authentic tasks and clear goals. We persevere in our commitment to adjust the learning environment and the content to attract students. Most importantly, we recognize that our relationships with our students and their relationship with the learning process are crucial. Students must believe that they can be successful and experience incremental growth through learning experiences carefully designed around small chunks of meaningful language, leading to purposeful communication. Learning must be fun. Students are more likely to retain the language they acquire in a learning context that they enjoy.

They must feel that they are part of the learning environment, that they belong to the target culture, while they are acquiring their new language. They must understand the purpose of the lesson and have the freedom to select language that is important to them along the way.

Motivation and Learning

Students are motivated to take part in Spanish class when the context through which the language is presented and practiced is meaningful, serves a purpose, and relies on the students to bring it to life. Effective teachers understand the link between motivation and learning, and select language and cultural contexts that rely on the students to tell the story. "What are we doing in here today, Señora?" "We need you, Juanito, to help guide us on our learning journey."

Bibliography

Blaz, Deborah. *Foreign Language Teacher's Guide to Active Learning.* Larchmont, NY: Eye on Education, Inc., 1999.

———. *Bringing the Standards for Foreign Language Learning to Life.* NY: Eye on Education, Inc., 2002.

Curtain, Helena, and Carol A. Dahlberg. *Languages and Children—Making the Match.* Boston: Allyn and Bacon, 2004.

High, Julie. *Second Language Learning through Cooperative Learning.* San Clemente, CA: Kagan Publishing, 1993.

Marzano, Robert J., Debra J. Pickering, and Jane E. Pollock. *Classroom Instruction that Works.* Baltimore: ASCD, 2001.

Omaggio, Alice H. *Teaching Language in Context.* Florence, KY: Cengage and Heinle, 2000.

Patrick, Paula. *The Keys to the Classroom.* Alexandria, VA: The American Council on the Teaching of Foreign Languages, 2007.

Rogers, Spence. *21 Building Blocks Critical to Leaving No Child Left Behind.* Evergreen, CO: PEAK Learning Systems, Inc., 2003.

Rogers, Spence, Jim Ludington, and Becky Graf. *Teaching and Training Techniques: Lighting the Way to Performance Excellence.* Evergreen, CO: PEAK Learning Systems, Inc., 2003.

Rogers, Spence, Jim Ludington, and Shari Graham. *Motivation and Learning: A Teacher's Guide to Building Excitement for Learning and Igniting the Drive for Quality.* Evergreen, CO: PEAK Learning Systems, Inc., 1999.

Shrum, Judith L., and Eileen W. Glisan. *Teacher's Handbook: Contextualized Language Instruction.* Florence, KY: Cengage and Heinle, 2005.

Features of Backwards Design Found in *Español Santillana*

Carol McKenna Semonsky Associate Professor Emerita, Georgia State University

Principles of Backwards Design

Backwards Design, developed by Grant Wiggins and Jay McTighe, is an approach to unit development that puts the emphasis on big ideas and enduring understandings rather than on discrete skills and coverage. It has three main steps: 1) identify desired results; 2) determine acceptable evidence; and 3) plan learning experiences and instruction. Assessments are performance-based, reflect the big ideas, and are designed before the instructional activities.

Step One: Identify Desired Results

In step one, teachers define the unit's goals, its essential questions and enduring understandings, as well as the key language skills students will acquire as a result of the unit. Enduring understandings are those that have value in real life beyond the classroom, that have a potential for engaging students, and that include core tasks that are essential and integral to the subject matter. For world language teachers, national, state, and local standards as well as thematic planning provide essential guidelines and contexts when defining desired results.

Español Santillana's overall format, that of thematic units centered around young people traveling in various Spanish-speaking countries, addresses enduring understandings, such as, "Who are the Spanish-speaking peoples of the world and how do they live?" and "How are our lives similar and different?" The themes are broad and reflect cultural perspectives. For instance, in Level 1, *Unidad 3*, the stated theme is "shopping in the context of Mayan cultures and Guatemala's historic cities."

Step Two: Determine Acceptable Evidence

In step two, teachers decide which evidence will show that students have a grasp of the big ideas and enduring understandings. Wiggins and McTighe suggest that performance tasks provide the best evidence. For world language teachers, performance-based assessments, focused on student use of extended, communicative language in authentic situations, are recommended. However, the use of extended language requires initial skill building where core vocabulary and structures are mastered first.

Español Santillana offers a wide selection of contextualized formative assessments centered on these core skills as well as summative assessments that prompt extended and authentic language. Students are given an opportunity to reflect on their accomplishment of the goals by using the *Autoevaluación* at the end of each unit.

Step Three: Plan Learning Experiences and Instructions

It is in step three, in the planning for learning experiences, where *Español Santillana* excels. Both the textbook and ancillaries offer plentiful and contextualized practice of essential skills that form the building blocks necessary for meaningful communication. Practice exercises represent real-life situations. Daily plans found in the Teacher's Edition facilitate planning for both regular and block scheduling. The Teacher's Edition directly links unit content to standards and offers many ideas to address individual differences, including suggestions for reaching all learners via multiple intelligences and differentiated instruction. *Español Santillana* has a selection of ancillary materials, including websites, DVDs, and other multimedia from which teachers may choose in order to design the most effective instruction, matching both their initial desired results and their students' individual needs.

Bibliography

Center for Advanced Research on Language Acquisition. *Creating an Assessment Unit Process: Backwards Design.* University of Minnesota. July, 2010. <http://www.carla.umn.edu/assessment/vac/CreateUnit/p_1.html>.

National Standards in Foreign Language Education Project. *Standards for Foreign Language Learning in the 21st Century.* Lawrence, KS: Allen Press, Inc., 1999.

Wiggins, Grant and Jay McTighe. *Understanding by Design.* Power Point presentation. Winter 2004. <http://www.grantwiggins.org/documents/mtuniontalk.pdf>.

———. *Understanding by Design, Expanded 2nd Edition.* Alexandria, VA: Association for Supervision and Curriculum Development, 2005.

Español
Santillana

fans del Español

Español Santillana is a collaborative effort by two teams specializing in the design of Spanish-language educational materials. One team is located in the United States and the other in Spain.

Editorial Staff in the United States
Anne Silva
Ana Isabel Antón

Editorial Staff in Spain
Susana Gómez
Clara Alarcón
Belén Saiz
Mercedes Fontecha
M.ª Antonia Oliva

Linguistic and Cultural Advisers in Latin America and in the United States

Antonio Moreno
Content Director, Santillana México

Mayra Méndez
Editorial Director, Santillana Puerto Rico

Claudia Noriega
Editorial Director, Santillana Guatemala

Cecilia Mejía
Editorial Director, Santillana Perú

Graciela Pérez de Lois
Editorial Director, Santillana Argentina

Rodolfo Hidalgo
Editorial Director, Santillana Chile

Mario Núñez
Director of Professional Development, Santillana USA

Reviewers

Francesc Borrull
Chicago, IL

Anna Budiwsky
Villanova, PA

Lorrie Ann Button-Edelson
Katy, TX

Donna Clementi
Oshkosh, WI

Frances S. Hoch
Raleigh, NC

Gudrun Martyny
Orlando, FL

Nieves Pérez-Knapp
Provo, UT

Carol Radchik
La Jolla, CA

Mónica Ruiz-Meléndez
West Chester, PA

Eugenia Sarmiento
Centennial, CO

Carlos Soler Montes
Albuquerque, NM

Alicia Vinson
Lexington, KY

James Zavodjancik
Milford, CT

Clare Ziff
Villanova, PA

Published in the United States of America.

Español Santillana
Student Book Level 3
ISBN-13: 978-1-61605-910-1
ISBN-10: 1-61605-910-9

Illustrator: **Bartolomé Seguí**
Picture Coordinator: **Carlos Aguilera**

Cartographer: **José Luis Gil, Tania López**
Cartographic Coordinator: **Ana Isabel Calvo**

Production Manager: **Ángel García Encinar**

Production Coordinator: **Julio Hernández**

Design and Layout: **Hilario Simón, Antonio Díaz**

Proofreaders: **Elizabeth A. Pease, Marta López**

Photo Researchers: **Mercedes Barcenilla, Amparo Rodríguez**

Santillana USA Publishing Company, Inc.
2023 NW 84th Avenue, Doral, FL 33122

1 2 3 4 5 6 7 8 9 10   16 15 14 13 12

Writers

Paloma Lapuerta
teaches Spanish Language, Literature and Culture at Central Connecticut State University. She graduated from the University of Salamanca, Spain, and received her PhD from the University of Geneva, Switzerland. She has taught in different countries and is co-author of several Spanish textbooks.

María Lourdes Casas
received her Masters of Arts and PhD in Spanish at the University of Wisconsin-Madison. Dr. Casas has taught Spanish Language and Literature at the University of Wisconsin-Madison, Connecticut College, and Southern Connecticut State University. Currently she is an Assistant Professor at Central Connecticut State University.

Lisa Berliner
received her MA in Educational Leadership from Central Connecticut State University. She is currently pursuing a Masters degree in Spanish. She teaches Spanish at the secondary level in Simsbury, CT.

Jan Ferrier Sands
received her BS in Spanish and MS in Curriculum and Supervision from Central Connecticut State University. She is a career teacher of Spanish at Simsbury High School, Simsbury, CT. From 2005 to 2008, she served as the World Languages Teacher-in-Residence at the Connecticut State Department of Education.

María Á. Pérez
received her MA in Spanish from Portland State University. She was the assistant director for the Spanish Basic Language Program at the University of Illinois in Chicago. She has taught college-level Spanish at several institutions, and has worked as an editor and writer for various publishers.

Contributing Writers

Ana Isabel Antón
Miami, FL

Clara Alarcón
Madrid, Spain

Susana Gómez
Madrid, Spain

Mercedes Fontecha
Madrid, Spain

Anne Silva
Miami, FL

Contributors

Janet L. Glass
Dwight-Englewood School
Englewood, NJ

Jan Kucerik
Pinellas County Schools
Largo, FL

Carol McKenna Semonsky
Georgia State University
Atlanta, GA

Gerardo Piña-Rosales
North American Academy of the Spanish Language
The City University of New York, New York, NY

Emily Spinelli
AATSP
University of Michigan-Dearborn, Dearborn, MI

Brandon Zaslow
Occidental College
Los Angeles, CA

Advisers

Paula Hirsch
Windward School, Los Angeles, CA

María Orta
Kennedy High School, Chicago, IL

Developmental Editor
Susana Gómez

Editorial Coordinator
Anne Silva

Editorial Director
Enrique Ferro

Bienvenidos a

Las parejas

Eva Bishop y Ethan Thomas

Nosotros somos fans del español por el arte y la música. Nos encantan.

Daniel García y Michelle Liu

A nosotros nos interesan las costumbres y las tradiciones del mundo hispano.

Español Santillana

Quiénes somos

Somos una comunidad de fans del español y de la cultura hispana. Nuestro objetivo es dar a conocer el mundo que habla español: sus gentes, sus ciudades, sus fiestas y tradiciones, sus alimentos… Y para eso hemos creado la página web Fans del Español (www.fansdelespañol.com).

Nuestra historia

Nuestra página web nació hace unos años con los primeros fans del español: Andy y su hermana Janet; Tess y su madre Patricia; Diana y su tía Rita; y Tim y su abuelo Mack. Las cuatro parejas decidieron viajar por los países hispanohablantes para resolver unos desafíos: encontrar los lugares más sorprendentes, los vestidos más exóticos, las costumbres y tradiciones más divertidas…

Los desafíos continúan

Hoy formamos una gran comunidad con muchas personas que quieren participar y saber más sobre Latinoamérica y sobre España.

Este año nuestros protagonistas son tres parejas: Eva y Ethan; Daniel y Michelle; y Asha y Lucas. Los seis están estudiando High School y son grandes fans del español. Por eso están dispuestos a enfrentarse a nuevos desafíos. Su objetivo: mejorar su español y conocer mejor la cultura y las formas de vida de los países hispanos.

¿Quieres pertenecer a nuestra comunidad? Puedes seguir nuestras aventuras a través de este libro y de nuestra página web. Tú también tienes Tu Desafío.

Asha Patel y Lucas Cardoso

Los veteranos

Andy, Tess, Diana y Tim

Queremos viajar por el mundo hispano. Hay lugares increíbles.

¡Adelante!

(1) Mercado de Chichicastenango
(Guatemala)

(2) Día de Puerto Rico
(Nueva York)

(3) Ruinas mayas de Monte Albán
(México)

Los temas de los desafíos

Las tres parejas y los veteranos han hecho un listado de temas de su interés. Seguro que tú ya sabes algo sobre esos temas.

Las personas y la familia

¿Qué personajes y leyendas del mundo hispano conoces?

Vida social

¿Qué fiestas del mundo hispano conoces? ¿En qué países se celebran?

La ropa y la vivienda

¿Qué ciudades coloniales hay en las Américas? ¿Cómo es su estilo arquitectónico?

La alimentación y la salud

¿Qué comida latina prefieres? ¿De dónde es esa comida?

El trabajo y las profesiones

¿Qué hispanos célebres conoces? ¿A qué se dedican?

El tiempo libre y los viajes

¿Qué países atraviesa la ruta Panamericana?

La naturaleza y el medio ambiente

¿Dónde está la Patagonia? ¿Qué clima tiene esa región?

Historia, política y sociedad

¿Qué países conservan restos de la cultura maya? ¿Y de la cultura inca?

Los escenarios de los desafíos

¡El mundo hispano es tan grande! ¡Y es tan diverso! México, Guatemala, El Salvador, Honduras… Con la ayuda del mapa, responde a estas preguntas:

1. ¿En qué países de América se habla español?

2. ¿A qué países corresponden estas capitales?

   - Bogotá
   - Santo Domingo
   - Madrid
   - San Juan
   - Buenos Aires
   - Lima
   - Managua
   - La Paz

Tu desafío

Tú también tienes unos desafíos que resolver. En cada unidad vas a elegir el desafío de una pareja para hacer una tarea relacionada con él. Ese será TU DESAFÍO.

→ TU DESAFÍO

CANADÁ

ESTADOS UNIDOS

OCÉANO ATLÁNTICO

OCÉANO ATLÁNTICO

España

Mar Mediterráneo

0   375   750
millas

kilómetros
0   375   750

BAHAMAS

CUBA

REPÚBLICA DOMINICANA

HAITÍ

PUERTO RICO

JAMAICA

MÉXICO

BELICE

HONDURAS

GUATEMALA

Mar Caribe

EL SALVADOR

NICARAGUA

COSTA RICA

PANAMÁ

VENEZUELA

GUYANA

Guayana Francesa

COLOMBIA

SURINAM

ECUADOR

PERÚ

BRASIL

OCÉANO

PACÍFICO

BOLIVIA

PARAGUAY

CHILE

URUGUAY

ARGENTINA   Río de la Plata

0   500   1.000
millas

kilómetros
0   500   1.000

Contents

¿Cómo eres?

Las personas y la familia

Video Program

Videos

- ¿Cómo eres?
- Fiestas familiares
- El mundo según los mayas
- Mapa cultural. La población latinoamericana

Audiovisuales

 Personajes famosos

 Una argentina famosa

 Una historieta de detectives

 Retratos de familia

 Flor de leyendas

www.fansdelespañol.com

UNIDAD 2

Entre amigos

Vida social

Video Program

Videos

- Entre amigos
- El juego de pelota
- El baile en el mundo latino
- Mapa cultural. La fiesta: expresión comunitaria

Audiovisuales

 ¡Vamos a divertirnos!

 El Día de san Jordi

 Del amor… y del olvido

 Un juego milenario

 Un concurso de baile

www.fansdelespañol.com

UNIDAD 3

Tus cosas

La ropa y la vivienda

Video Program

Videos

- Tus cosas
- El vestido en América Latina
- Los patios cordobeses
- Mapa cultural. La ciudad colonial

Audiovisuales

Tradiciones con mucho estilo

Un traje muy especial

Un traje tradicional

En busca del símbolo perdido

Un festival de flamenco

www.fansdelespañol.com

XV

UNIDAD 4

Vida sana

La alimentación y la salud

Video Program

Videos

- Vida sana
- Platos latinos
- Punta del Este
- Mapa cultural. Alimentos básicos en el mundo hispano

Audiovisuales

 *Nos cuidamos*

 *La ropa vieja*

 *La mejor receta*

 *Un balneario uruguayo*

 *El hospital más antiguo de las Américas*

www.fansdelespañol.com

UNIDAD 5

¿Trabajas?

El trabajo y las profesiones

Video Program

Videos

- ¿Trabajas?
- Medios de comunicación hispanos en los Estados Unidos
- El turismo en América Latina
- Mapa cultural. Universidades hispanas

Audiovisuales

 *Ciudadanos responsables*

 *El Día de César Chávez*

 *Una vida interesante*

 *El trabajo perfecto*

 *Por el bien común*

www.fansdelespañol.com

Tus aficiones

El tiempo libre y los viajes

DESAFÍO ①

DESAFÍO ②

Video Program

Videos

- Tus aficiones
- Pasión por el surf
- La Ruta Quetzal
- Mapa cultural. Deportes con tradición

DESAFÍO ③

Audiovisuales

 Viajes por el mundo hispano

 Un cartel de cine

 De cine

 Un deporte extremo

 Colaboradores en la Ruta Quetzal

www.fansdelespañol.com

UNIDAD 7

Por el planeta

La naturaleza y el medio ambiente

Video Program

Videos

- Por el planeta
- Mariposas viajeras
- La Noche de san Juan
- Mapa cultural. Espacios naturales singulares

Audiovisuales

 *¡Salvemos el planeta!*

 *Una maravilla de la naturaleza*

 *¡Ayudemos a las mariposas monarca!*

 *La fiesta del Sol*

 *Un desafío muy justo*

www.fansdelespañol.com

UNIDAD 8

En sociedad

Historia, política y sociedad

Las tareas

Video Program

Videos

- En sociedad
- Patrimonio de la Humanidad
- La misión de la OEA
- Mapa cultural. Una ciudad con historia: Barcelona

DESAFÍO ③

▶ **Expresar deseos, opinar y valorar**

Audiovisuales

 *Pasado y presente del mundo hispano*

 *Un mapa muy valioso*

 *La Escalinata de los Jeroglíficos*

 *Una organización multinacional*

 *Un calendario multicultural*

www.fansdelespañol.com

Objectives

- To talk about current actions and situations.
- To describe routines.
- To talk about past actions.
- To tell someone to do something.
- To ask and answer questions appropriately.
- To use regular and irregular verbs properly.
- To compare and contrast information.
- To initiate and engage in meaningful conversations.
- To distinguish between true and false statements.
- To describe a class schedule.
- To talk about travel and vacation destinations.
- To talk about past experiences.
- To give suggestions or advice.

Contents

Vocabulary

- The school.
- Everyday actions.
- Free-time activities.
- Travel vocabulary.
- Healthy habits.

Grammar

- The present tense.
- The present progressive.
- Regular verbs in the past tense.
- Irregular verbs in the past tense.
- Informal and formal commands.
- Interrogatives.

Evaluation Criteria

- Recognize and use verbs in the present tense.
- Recognize and use verbs in the present progressive tense.
- Recognize and use regular and irregular verbs in the past tense.
- Form sentences using appropriate verb tenses.
- Write sentences to describe an image.

- Create an original story.
- Compare information in written form.
- Give commands using affirmative imperative verb tenses.
- Give suggestions or advice.
- Engage in conversations to elicit or provide information.
- Recognize and use interrogatives to write questions.

- Answer questions appropriately.
- Write sentences or a short summary about personal experiences.
- Organize images to show the proper sequence of events.
- Detail a classroom schedule.
- Describe past vacations or travel experiences.

Unit Plan _____

Presentación del nivel/ Páginas preliminares

Estimated time: 1 session.

Level 3 presentation: Pages IV–VII.

Unit presentation: Unit opener.

1. CONTAR HECHOS ACTUALES

Estimated time: 1 session.

Functions & forms:
- To talk about current actions.
- The present tense.
- The present progressive tense.
- Regular and irregular verbs.

2. CONTAR HECHOS PASADOS

Estimated time: 1 session.

Functions & forms:
- To talk about actions completed in the past.
- Regular verbs in the preterite tense.

3. CONTAR HECHOS PASADOS

Estimated time: 1 session.

Functions & forms:
- To talk about actions completed in the past.
- Irregular verbs in the preterite tense.

4. DAR ÓRDENES E INSTRUCCIONES

Estimated time: 1 session.

Functions & forms:
- To tell someone to do something.
- Formal and informal commands.
- Regular and irregular verbs in command form.

5. HACER PREGUNTAS / EVALUACIÓN

Estimated time: 1 session.

Functions & forms:
- To ask simple and complex questions.
- Interrogatives.

Assessment: Test.

Standards for Learning Spanish

 **COMMUNICATION**

1.1. Interpersonal mode

- Exchange personal opinions and experiences.
- Engage in oral conversations using personal knowledge and experience.
- Compare and contrast information with a partner.
- Ask and answer questions on different topics.
- Ask a partner questions and take notes.

1.2. Interpretive mode

- Demonstrate understanding of oral and written expressions.
- Demonstrate understanding of questions relating to familiar and less familiar topics.
- Understand written exchanges.

- Understand and obtain information from audio or video recordings.
- Extract information from an informative text.
- Understand new vocabulary presented in Spanish.

1.3. Presentational mode

- Write sentences or paragraphs comparing information.
- Complete sentences with relevant information or correct verb tenses.
- Write answers to given questions.
- Write questions for an interview and present the results.
- Create a list of information and present it to the class.
- Write sentences or a paragraph summarizing information.

 CULTURE

2.1. Practices and perspectives

- Learn about activities people in Hispanic countries do in their leisure time.
- Learn about places people visit in Hispanic countries.

2.2. Products and perspectives

- Learn about ancient structures in Hispanic countries.

 CONNECTIONS

3.1. Interdisciplinary connections

- Understand the similarities and differences between some aspects of grammar in English and in Spanish.
- Reinforce grammatical concepts.

- Conjugate verbs in different verb tenses.
- Use reading strategies and previous knowledge to help comprehend texts and new vocabulary in Spanish.

 COMPARISONS

4.1. Compare languages

- Compare the formation and use of various verb tenses in English and in Spanish.
- Compare how sentences and questions are formed in English and in Spanish.

4.2. Compare cultures

- Compare leisure activities in Hispanic cultures and in the United States.

 COMMUNITIES

5.1. Spanish within and beyond the school setting

- Discuss class schedules and school activities.
- Imagine situations in which Spanish could be used.
- Discuss leisure activities done in one's community.
- Discuss vacations and past actions experienced outside the classroom.

5.2. Spanish for lifelong learners

- Discuss ways in which Spanish can be used in future life experiences.
- Discuss suggested life practices to use now and in the future.

Communicative Skills

Interpersonal Mode   Activities

Speaking	• Engage in conversation with a classmate. • Ask and answer guided questions. • Interview a classmate. • Invent a story with a classmate.	• 2, 15 • 8, 11 • 3, 17, 19 • 7
Writing	• Write descriptive or narrative sentences. • Make questions for an interview and take notes from an interview. • Write sentences giving advice. • Write a paragraph comparing or summarizing information.	• 4, 5, 7, 9 • 17, 19 • 14 • 3, 11, 19
Listening	• Understand sentences or questions and respond appropriately. • Understand simple oral exchanges and react appropriately or apply information to a task.	• 3, 8, 11, 17, 19 • 11, 15, 17
Reading	• Understand a list of items or simple texts that provide information.	• 12

Interpretive Mode   Activities

Listening	• Obtain information from a conversation. • Understand simple oral descriptions or oral orders. • Understand oral answers to choose the correct questions.	• 2, 5 • 2, 13 • 17
Reading	• Understand and take part in brief written exchanges. • Understand descriptive or narrative texts. • Understand an informative text.	• 14, 18 • 6, 10 • 12, 19
Viewing	• Connect information to images. • Obtain information from an image.	• 5, 13 • 4, 7

Presentational Mode   Activities

Speaking	• Present information to the class.	• 19
Writing	• Summarize information. • Write descriptive sentences or a narrative text based on pictures. • Compare information in written form.	• 11, 19 • 5, 7 • 3, 11
Visually Representing	• Present information in a chart or table.	• 3, 11

Cross-Curricular Standards

Subject	Standard	Activities
Language Arts	• Write a paragraph about past experiences. • Write a profile.	• 11 • 19

Lesson Plans (50-Minute Classes)

Day	Objectives	Sessions	Activities	Time	Standards	Resources / Homework
1	To introduce Level 3 and the *Unidad preliminar*	**Introduction** • *Bienvenidos a Español Santillana* Level 3 (IV–VII) • Unit presentation: Unit opener (1)		30 m. 20 m.	1.2, 1.3, 2.1, 2.2, 3.1, 5.1, 5.2	
2	To talk about current actions and situations	**1. Contar hechos actuales** (2–3) • Warm-Up: Independent Starter • Grammar: *El presente de indicativo* • Grammar: *El presente continuo*	1–3 4	5 m. 25 m. 20 m.	1.1, 1.2, 1.3, 3.1, 4.1, 5.1	Audio Practice Workbook
3	To talk about actions completed in the past	**2. Contar hechos pasados** (4–5) • Warm-Up: Independent Starter • Grammar: *El pretérito. Verbos regulares*	5–8	5 m. 45 m.	1.1, 1.2, 1.3, 3.1, 5.1	Audio Practice Workbook
4	To talk about actions completed in the past	**3. Contar hechos pasados** (6–7) • Warm-Up: Independent Starter • Grammar: *El pretérito. Verbos irregulares*	9–11	5 m. 45 m.	1.1, 1.2, 1.3, 2.1, 3.1, 5.1	Audio Practice Workbook
5	To tell someone to do something	**4. Dar órdenes e instrucciones** (8–9) • Warm-Up: Independent Starter • Grammar: *El imperativo afirmativo*	12–15	5 m. 45 m.	1.1, 1.2, 1.3, 3.1, 5.2	Audio Practice Workbook
6	To ask simple and complex questions	**5. Hacer preguntas / Assessment** (10–11) • Warm-Up: Independent Starter • Grammar: *Los interrogativos* • Test	16–19	5 m. 35 m. 10 m.	1.1, 1.2, 1.3, 3.1, 5.1	Audio Practice Workbook

Lesson Plans (90-Minute Classes)

Day	Objectives	Sessions	Activities	Time	Standards	Resources / Homework
1	To introduce Level 3 and the *Unidad preliminar*, and to talk about current actions and situations	**Introduction / 1. Contar hechos actuales** (1–3) • Warm-Up: Book orientation • *Bienvenidos a Español Santillana* Level 3 (IV–VII) • Unit presentation: Unit opener (1) • Grammar: *El presente de indicativo* • Grammar: *El presente continuo*	1–3 4	5 m. 15 m. 10 m. 30 m. 30 m.	1.1, 1.2, 1.3, 2.1, 2.2, 3.1, 4.1, 5.1, 5.2	Audio Practice Workbook
2	To talk about actions completed in the past	**2. Contar hechos pasados / 3. Contar hechos pasados** (4–7) • Warm-Up: Independent Starter • Grammar: *El pretérito. Verbos regulares* • Grammar: *El pretérito. Verbos irregulares*	5–8 9–11	5 m. 40 m. 45 m.	1.1, 1.2, 1.3, 2.1, 3.1, 5.1	Audio Practice Workbook
3	To tell someone to do something and to ask simple and complex questions	**4. Dar órdenes e instrucciones / 5. Hacer preguntas** (8–11) • Warm-Up: Independent Starter • Grammar: *El imperativo afirmativo* • Grammar: *Los interrogativos*	12–15 16–19	5 m. 45 m. 40 m.	1.1, 1.2, 1.3, 3.1, 5.1, 5.2	Audio Practice Workbook
4	To assess student proficiency	**Assessment** • Test (See Day 1 Unit 1)		20 m. (70 m.)	1.1, 1.2, 1.3	

Audio Scripts

Icons

The (🎧) symbol is used to refer to audio activities. The audio scripts for these activities are found in each unit at the end of the Overview section.

The (👁) symbol is used to refer to activities that are accompanied by a visual presentation. The scripts for these presentations are identical to the dialogues found in the texts that present the cultural challenges in the Student Book.

The (🗣) symbol is used to refer to speaking activities. These activities require spoken expression by the student and do not follow any particular script.

2 Tu horario, mi horario

–Hola, Ethan. ¿Qué tal tu primer día de clase?

–Pues no muy bien. No me gusta el horario.

–¿Qué clases tienes?

–Tengo Biología, Álgebra, Español, Historia y Literatura. Pero el problema no son las clases; las clases me gustan. El problema es el horario.

–Bueno, ya sabes que a veces las cosas no son como queremos. Yo quiero tomar clases de Arte, pero este año no ofrecen Arte.

–Es cierto. Y tampoco hay clases de Fotografía.

–Pero tenemos buenos maestros y unos compañeros muy simpáticos.

–Sí, ¡y eso es lo más importante!

5 ¡Me perdí!

–Hola, Sonia. Te llamé por teléfono el fin de semana, pero no respondiste.

–Es que mis padres alquilaron una cabaña en el bosque y pasamos el fin de semana allí.

–¡Qué bien!

–No tan bien. En realidad me pasó algo horrible. El sábado mi padre salió a pescar al lago y mi madre recibió una llamada y se quedó en la cabaña hablando por teléfono.

–¿Y tú?

–Yo salí a pasear por el bosque, ¡y me perdí!

–¿Te perdiste? ¿Cómo?

–No sé. Caminé y caminé, pero no logré encontrar la cabaña.

–¿Llamaste a tus padres?

–No. ¡No llevé el celular!

–¿Y qué pasó?

–Pues esperé hasta que me encontraron mis padres. Llegaron rápidamente.

–¡Qué susto!

9 ¿Quién hizo qué?

1. Hola, soy Lucas. Yo hice un viaje por México.
2. Yo soy Ethan y fui a la costa.
3. Yo soy Michelle. Este verano dormí mucho. ¡Me encanta dormir!
4. Hola, soy Eva. Este verano saqué la licencia de conducir.
5. Yo soy Daniel y estuve en las montañas.
6. Yo me llamo Asha y tuve un verano muy aburrido.

13 Todos damos órdenes

1. Vaya al médico.
2. Hable más alto, por favor. No le oigo.
3. Presten atención y tomen apuntes.
4. Dime la verdad, Sonia.
5. ¡Ánimo, chicos! Jueguen bien y ganen.
6. Ponte el cinturón de seguridad.

17 ¿Cuál fue la pregunta?

1. De Colombia.
2. El baloncesto.
3. Hace un año, creo.
4. A mi país, a Colombia.

Un paso más

The Unit

- This unit is a review of the main objectives of Spanish Levels 1 and 2. Students will review the following topics:
  - The present tense to talk about current actions and describe routines.
  - The present progressive tense to talk about actions that are happening at the moment of speaking.
  - The regular and irregular preterite tense conjugations to talk about actions completed in the past.
  - The regular and irregular affirmative command forms to tell someone to do something.
  - The interrogatives in order to ask and answer questions.

Activities	Standards	Resources
Un paso más	1.2	

Teaching Suggestions

Preparation

- Invite students to introduce themselves to the class. Then direct their attention to the pictures on this page and on pages IV and V, and explain that in Spanish Level 3 they will meet three new pairs of Spanish-language enthusiasts who will take on *desafíos* assigned to them by the four veteran *Fans del español* (Andy, Diana, Tess, and Tim). You may want to introduce the new participants by giving students some information on each one (e.g., name, age, hometown, interests).

- Direct students to page VI and introduce them to the topics or themes of Spanish Level 3. Explain that they will learn new and exciting information about each of these topics, but that there are also many things they already know about the Spanish-speaking world and these topics. Divide the class into eight groups, assign each group one of the topics, and have them answer the questions posed for their topic. Encourage students to go beyond the questions and brainstorm more information about their assigned topic, since they will surely know more.

UNIDAD

preliminar

Un paso más

¡Descubre con nosotros el mundo del español!

Hola, fan del español. Y felicidades: ¡¡ya estás en tercero!! Eso quiere decir que puedes usar el español para comunicarte con personas de Latinoamérica y de España. Y también que conoces muchas cosas sobre los países hispanos y su cultura. Sí, no hay duda, eres un(a) auténtico(a) fan del español.

Este año vas a conocer a nuevos fans del español: Eva, Ethan, Daniel, Michelle, Lucas y Asha. Ellos te van a ayudar a descubrir muchos aspectos del mundo hispano que todavía desconoces. Y con ellos vas a vivir nuevos y emocionantes desafíos.

¿Te gusta dibujar? Pues vas a conocer algunos personajes de cómic famosos.

¿Te gusta bailar? Pues vas a saber algo más sobre el flamenco y la salsa.

¿Te gusta leer? Pues vas a poder leer leyendas muy interesantes y otros relatos en español.

¿Te gusta viajar? Pues vas a conocer las expediciones de la ruta Quetzal.

¿Te gusta ayudar a los demás? Pues vas a poder hacer tu propio proyecto de voluntariado.

The Veterans

ANDY DOUGLAS
Andy used to travel with his sister, Janet. He is from Atlanta, GA.

DIANA ROBLES
Diana used to travel with her aunt, Rita. She is from Lawrenceville, NJ.

TESS WILLIAMS
Tess used to travel with her mother, Patricia. She is from San Antonio, TX.

TIM TAYLOR
Tim used to travel with his grandfather, Mack. He is from San Francisco, CA.

The New Participants

EVA BISHOP
Age: 17 years old
Hometown: Chula Vista, CA
Interests: science and technology
Spanish-language experience: Started studying Spanish in middle school.

ETHAN THOMAS
Age: 18 years old
Hometown: Chula Vista, CA
Interests: writing and playing guitar
Spanish-language experience: Started studying Spanish in 10th grade.

¡Suerte!

Y, por supuesto, vas a aprender a hacer nuevas cosas en español: expresar tus sentimientos y opiniones, hacer recomendaciones, expresar tus deseos, gustos y preferencias, hablar de tus experiencias, hacer peticiones de manera cortés...

Adelante. Te espera una tarea apasionante. Pero antes de empezar, vamos a repasar algunas cosas que ya conoces.

1. Contar hechos actuales
El presente de indicativo
El presente continuo

2. Contar hechos pasados
El pretérito. Verbos regulares

3. Contar hechos pasados
El pretérito. Verbos irregulares

4. Dar órdenes e instrucciones
El imperativo afirmativo

5. Hacer preguntas
Los interrogativos

MICHELLE LIU

Age: 17 years old
Hometown: Tallahassee, FL
Interests: traveling and art
Spanish-language experience: Started studying Spanish in 9th grade.

DANIEL GARCÍA

Age: 17 years old
Hometown: Tallahassee, FL
Interests: cooking and art
Spanish-language experience: Started studying Spanish two years ago, but his family speaks Spanish at home.

ASHA PATEL

Age: 16 years old
Hometown: New York, NY
Interests: music and soccer
Spanish-language experience: Started studying Spanish in kindergarten.

LUCAS CARDOSO

Age: 17 years old
Hometown: New York, NY
Interests: nature and basketball
Spanish-language experience: Started studying Spanish in 8th grade, but he already knew some Spanish.

Preliminary Unit
Un paso más

- After students have answered the questions in their groups and recorded any additional information, call on each group to share their information with the class. If some students in the class have personal knowledge of any of the topics, invite them to share their experiences with the class.

- Ask students to read silently the objectives for this unit listed on page 1. Then, in order to assess your students' proficiencies, give them this performance pretest. If students are not able to perform certain tasks, this will be a good indication that you might need to spend some extra class time reviewing the corresponding structures.

1. Contar hechos actuales

- Have students
  – Describe their daily school routines and schedules.
  – Describe what they do in their leisure time and talk about their likes and dislikes regarding free-time activities.
  – Describe what two of their classmates are doing at this very moment.

2. Contar hechos pasados

- Have students
  – Talk about the last time they did something and tell what happened.

3. Contar hechos pasados

- Have students
  – Tell what they and their family did on their last vacation, where they went, where they stayed, and whether they had a good time.

4. Dar órdenes e instrucciones

- Have students
  – Tell a classmate what to do to foster the learning of Spanish.
  – Offer their advice for healthy living to their Spanish teacher.

5. Hacer preguntas

- Have students
  – Interview a classmate to get to know him or her better.

Objectives

- In this unit, students will
  – Express habitual actions in the present tense.
  – Express likes and dislikes.
  – Express the progress of an action.
  – Talk about actions completed in the past.
  – Give recommendations and advice.
  – Ask questions.

1. CONTAR HECHOS ACTUALES

Gramática – El presente de indicativo. El presente continuo

Presentation

- In this section, students will review the present tense to talk about current actions and describe routines. They will also review the present progressive tense to talk about actions that are happening at the moment of speaking.

Activities	Standards	Resources
Gramática	1.2, 3.1, 4.1	
1.	1.2, 1.3	
2.	1.1, 1.2, 1.3, 5.1	Audio
3.	1.1, 1.2, 1.3, 5.1	
4.	1.3	

Teaching Suggestions

Warm-Up / Independent Starter

- Have students think about their typical school day this semester and ask them to come up with five sentences describing their day. For example: *Llego a las 7:45. Tengo clase de Álgebra a las 8:00.*

Preparation

- Have students work in groups of three to share their Independent Starters. For example:
  A. *Yo llego a las 7:45 a la escuela. ¿A qué hora llegan ustedes?*
  B. *Yo llego a las 7:30. ¿Y tú, Jack, a qué hora llegas?*
  C. *Yo llego a las 7:40.*

- Have groups elect one member to compile the information and another to report it to the class. The third group member may write some of their sentences on the board. Ask the class to identify the verb in each of the sentences. If necessary, review some of the present tense conjugations.

- To illustrate the difference between the present tense and the present progressive, ask students to describe what they are doing right now. Point out that they used the present tense to describe what they do on a typical school day, whereas they used the present progressive to describe what they were doing at the moment of speaking.

Gramática

El presente de indicativo

- In Spanish we use the present tense to talk about current actions and situations, and to describe routines.

  Yo **estudio** Español en la escuela.
  Nosotros **vamos** a clase todos los días.

  See the following pages for a review of the present indicative conjugations.
    – Regular verbs: page R9.
    – Irregular verbs: page R9.
    – Verbs like *gustar*: page R11.

El presente continuo

- We use the present progressive to talk about actions that are happening at the moment of speaking.

  En este momento **estoy hablando**.

- The present progressive is formed with the verb estar and the present participle (normally ending with -ando or -iendo).

  See page R12 for a review of the present progressive conjugations.

¿Qué haces durante la semana?

¡Muchas cosas! Los lunes por la mañana **voy** a clase, después...

1 En la escuela de Eva

▶ **Une** las tres columnas y escribe oraciones lógicas. Usa el presente.

	(A)	(B)	(C)
1.	Mi amiga Laura y yo	comenzar	sus puertas a las 7:30 a. m.
2.	La escuela	ser	a las 12:00 p. m. en la cafetería.
3.	La primera clase	terminar	compañeras en la clase de Arte.
4.	Los estudiantes de Español	leer	terminar las tareas en clase.
5.	Algunos estudiantes	abrir	a las 8:00 a. m.
6.	A veces yo no	volver	textos en español.
7.	Los maestros	almorzar	a explicar si no entendemos algo.
8.	El día escolar	poder	a las 3:30 p. m.

Modelo   1. *Mi amiga Laura y yo somos compañeras en la clase de Arte.*

Differentiated Instruction

DEVELOPING LEARNERS

- For additional practice with irregular verbs, have students complete these sentences with the present tense form of the verb in parentheses.

  1. *Bill y Diana (querer) ir al cine. (quieren)*
  2. *Sam (jugar) muy bien al tenis. (juega)*
  3. *Yo (saber) escribir mi nombre en chino. (sé)*
  4. *Mi padre (perder) el celular. (pierde)*
  5. *Carla (contar) el dinero antes de pagar. (cuenta)*
  6. *¿Qué (pedir) tú de postre? (pides)*
  7. *Yo no (conocer) bien a mis compañeros. (conozco)*

EXPANDING LEARNERS

- Have students create a two-paragraph narrative with the information in their Independent Starters. Remind them to use sequence connectors (e.g., *primero, después, también, por último*) to give their paragraphs coherence, and encourage them to use a variety of verbs.

- Once students have finished their narratives, ask them to white out the verbs. Then have them exchange papers with a partner and ask partners to write in the verbs they think best complete the text.

2 Tu horario, mi horario

 ▶ **Escucha** a Ethan y a Eva hablando sobre su horario. Decide si estas oraciones son ciertas o falsas. Si son falsas, corrígelas.

1. A Ethan no le gustan sus clases.
2. Eva quiere tomar clases de Arte.
3. Ethan tiene una clase de Fotografía.
4. Los compañeros de Ethan y Eva son simpáticos.

▶ **Habla** con tu compañero(a) sobre las clases y el horario que tienen este año.

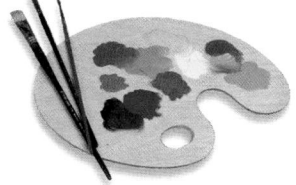

Modelo A. ¿Cuál es tu horario este año?
B. A las 8 a. m. tengo Geometría. Después…

 3 Mi fin de semana

▶ **Completa** una tabla como esta sobre tu fin de semana típico.

▶ **Entrevista** a un(a) compañero(a) sobre su fin de semana y escribe sus respuestas en la tabla.

Modelo A. ¿Vas de compras los fines de semana?
B. Sí, me gusta mucho comprar.

▶ **Escribe** un párrafo para comparar lo que hacen tu compañero(a) y tú.

Actividad	Yo	Él/Ella
ir de compras	✔	
dormir mucho		
limpiar el dormitorio		
ver la televisión		
hacer deporte		
salir con amigos		

 4 Ahora mismo en la escuela

▶ **Escribe** oraciones sobre qué están haciendo estas personas ahora mismo. Usa los verbos del cuadro.

escribir   comer   tocar   correr

ellas

mis amigos y yo

ella

yo

tres 3

HERITAGE LANGUAGE LEARNERS

• Discuss with students that some verbs have spelling or phonological irregularities that may pose problems. You may wish to give them some examples: *satisfacer →
satisfago, satisfaces*; *dirigir → dirijo, diriges*; *caber → quepo, cabes*; *oler → huelo, hueles*; *huir → huyo, huyes*; *cocer → cuezo, cueces*; *convencer → convenzo, convences*.

• Have students work with a partner to compile a list of irregular verbs in the present tense that pose them spelling problems. Then ask them to write a story, a poem, or a song using as many of those verbs as possible.

TOTAL PHYSICAL RESPONSE (TPR)

• Ask for a volunteer to pantomime an activity such as talking on the phone or cooking. Then have the rest of the class guess what he or she is doing in the present progressive tense. For example, a male student is cooking. Students will respond: *Él está cocinando*.

---

1. CONTAR HECHOS ACTUALES

Gramática – El presente de indicativo. El presente continuo

Activities

2. Have students read the four statements before playing the audio. Then play the audio two times. Tell students to simply listen the first time and complete the activity the second time.

3. Once students have finished, have them rate the activities in terms of how much they like them. Students may add two more things they do on weekends. Have them write their names on sticky notes. Then create a bar graph on the board using the students' sticky notes. Which activities are the most popular?

 AUDIO SCRIPT
See page XXVF.

Answer Key

1. Answers will vary. Sample answers:
2. La escuela abre sus puertas a las…
3. La primera clase comienza a las 8:00 a. m.
4. Los estudiantes de Español leen textos…
5. Algunos estudiantes almuerzan a las…
6. A veces yo no puedo terminar las…
7. Los maestros vuelven a explicar si no…
8. El día escolar termina a las 3:30 p. m.

2. 1. F. A Ethan no le gusta su horario.
2. C.
3. F. Ethan quiere tomar una clase de Fotografía.
4. C.
▶ Answers will vary.

3. Answers will vary.
▶ Answers will vary.
▶ Answers will vary.

4. 1. Ellas están corriendo.
2. Mis amigos y yo estamos comiendo.
3. Ella está escribiendo.
4. Yo estoy tocando el violín.

Additional Resources

Fans Online activities
Practice Workbook

3

2. CONTAR HECHOS PASADOS

Gramática – El pretérito. Verbos regulares

Presentation

■ In this section, students will review the regular preterite tense conjugations to talk about actions completed in the past.

Activities	Standards	Resources
Gramática	1.2, 3.1	
5.	1.2, 1.3	Audio
6.	1.2, 1.3	
7.	1.1, 1.2, 1.3	
8.	1.1, 5.1	

Teaching Suggestions

Warm-Up / Independent Starter

■ Have students think about this past weekend and list two things they did on Saturday and two they did on Sunday. To get them started you may give them these verbs: *hablar, cenar, comprar, lavar, celebrar, bailar, visitar, comer, salir, escribir.*

Preparation

■ Have students interview two classmates to find out what they did on the weekend. Ask students to complete a table like the one below.

	Sábado	*Domingo*
Yo	*compré una camiseta, lavé la ropa*	*preparé el desayuno, salí al cine*
Janice	*lavó la ropa, visitó a su abuela*	*se levantó tarde, cenó con su novio*
Mark	*compró unos pantalones*	*celebró su cumpleaños, bailó con sus invitadas*

■ Then invite volunteers to report to the class the activities that both their interviewees and they themselves did during the weekend. For example: *Janice y yo lavamos la ropa el sábado. Mark y yo compramos ropa el sábado. Él compró unos pantalones y yo, una camiseta.*

■ Remind students that the present and preterite *nosotros* form of regular *-ar* and *-ir* verbs have the same endings. Context will tell them whether the action is in the past or present.

4

Gramática

El pretérito. Verbos regulares

● In Spanish we use the preterite tense to talk about actions completed in the past.

Anoche **salí** con mis amigos y **cenamos** juntos.

● See page R12 for a review of the regular preterite tense conjugations.

¿Qué te pasó?

¡No lo vas a creer! Doblé rápidamente con la bici en una esquina y perdí el equilibrio.

¿Y terminaste en el suelo?

Sí, y me rompí el brazo.

Regular preterite -*ar* verb endings:

-é	-amos
-aste	-asteis
-ó	-aron

Regular preterite -*er* and -*ir* verb endings:

-í	-imos
-iste	-isteis
-ió	-ieron

5 ¡Me perdí!

▶ **Escucha** lo que le pasó a Sonia el fin de semana y ordena las ilustraciones.

▶ **Escribe** pies para las ilustraciones anteriores. Usa estas expresiones en el pretérito.

recibir una llamada   pescar en un lago   perderse en el bosque
alquilar una cabaña   encontrar a Sonia

Differentiated Instruction

DEVELOPING LEARNERS

● Ask students to rewrite these sentences in the past tense, using the preterite form of each underlined verb.

1. *Estudio para el examen de Historia.* (Estudié)
2. *¡Qué rápido subes las escaleras!* (subiste)
3. *Llegamos a tiempo al cine.* (Llegamos)
4. *Ellos hablan por teléfono.* (hablaron)
5. *Carl bebe un vaso de leche.* (bebió)
6. *Corremos en una competición.* (Corrimos)
7. *Usted no come ensalada.* (comió)
8. *Escribimos un ensayo sobre las últimas elecciones.* (Escribimos)

EXPANDING LEARNERS

● Have pairs of students play an association game. One partner calls out a part of the school and the other partner creates a complete sentence saying something that happened there. Then partners switch roles. For example:

A. *La cafetería.*
B. *Mis amigos y yo almorzamos ayer en la cafetería.*
B. *El gimnasio.*
A. *Entrené para el partido de baloncesto en el gimnasio.*

6 Un pequeño accidente

 ► **Completa** el mensaje de correo de Daniel.

| chocar | recoger | mirar | ocurrir | romper | subir |

De: Daniel
Para: Michelle
Asunto:
Cuerpo del texto | Anchura variable | A+ A+ | B I U | ≡ ≡ ≡ | ≣ ≣ |

¡Hola, Michelle!
Ayer no te llamé porque __1__ un pequeño accidente. Mi padre me __2__ en la escuela por la tarde. Yo __3__ al coche y, al salir del estacionamiento, mi padre no __4__ y... ¡ __5__ con otro coche! Estamos bien, pero el coche se __6__ .

7 ¿Qué pasó?

► **Observa** estas fotos que tomó Michelle y escribe tres oraciones para contar qué pasó.

Modelo 1. *La mujer llegó tarde y perdió el autobús.*

llegar

comprar

celebrar

 ► **Habla** con tu compañero(a) e inventen una pequeña historia.

Modelo *El despertador no sonó, por eso la mujer perdió el autobús…*

8 La última vez que...

 ► **Habla** con tu compañero(a). Pregúntale cuándo hizo estas actividades por última vez y qué pasó.

1. comprar algo
2. visitar a un(a) amigo(a)
3. asistir a una fiesta
4. comer demasiado
5. viajar a otra ciudad

¿Cuándo compraste algo por última vez?

La semana pasada. Compré unos pantalones muy modernos.

cinco 5

Gramática – El pretérito. Verbos regulares

Activities

5. Have students use their captions to write a narrative summarizing Sonia's mishap. Remind them to use sequence words (e.g., *primero, después, luego, por último*). Then play the audio again and have students check their narrative. Did they get the sequence and the events right?

6. To extend this activity, have students add two more sentences to the story. They may, for instance, focus on what happened right after the crash: *Después del choque llamamos a la policía. Yo me asusté un poco, pero no pasó nada serio.*

8. Invite volunteer pairs to act out some of their dialogues for the class. After each presentation, ask the class comprehension questions.

 AUDIO SCRIPT
See page XXVF.

Answer Key

5. E, D, C, A, B.
   ► Answers will vary. Sample answers:
   A. Sonia se perdió en el bosque.
   B. Los padres encontraron a Sonia.
   C. La madre de Sonia recibió una llamada.
   D. El padre de Sonia pescó en un lago.
   E. Los padres de Sonia alquilaron una cabaña.

6. 1. ocurrió   3. subí   5. chocamos
   2. recogió   4. miró   6. rompió

7. Answers will vary. Sample answers:
   2. La chica compró muchas cosas.
   3. La chica celebró el cumpleaños con sus amigos.
   ► Answers will vary.

8. Answers will vary.

HERITAGE LANGUAGE LEARNERS

• Have students visit a news website from their country of origin and take notes on the most important news. Based on what they read, have students write their own news report, including at least six events. For example: *Dos vehículos chocaron en la avenida Simón Bolívar. Tres personas resultaron heridas, pero ninguna de gravedad.* Ask students to read their reports to the class. Encourage the class to ask for repetition or clarification of words and phrases they didn't understand.

MULTIPLE INTELLIGENCES: Visual-Spatial Intelligence

• Have pairs draw a series of scenes on construction paper to illustrate one of the stories they came up with for activity 7. Alternatively, they may use pictures from old magazines or the Internet.

• Display students' scenes around the classroom. Ask for volunteers to narrate the story based on the scenes.

Additional Resources

Fans Online activities
Practice Workbook

3. CONTAR HECHOS PASADOS

Gramática – El pretérito. Verbos irregulares

Presentation

- In this section, students will review the irregular preterite tense conjugations to talk about actions completed in the past.

Activities	Standards	Resources
Gramática	1.2, 3.1	
9.	1.2, 1.3, 2.1, 5.1	Audio
10.	1.2, 1.3, 2.1	
11.	1.1, 1.2, 1.3, 5.1	

Teaching Suggestions

Warm-Up / Independent Starter

- Have students select six verbs from the grammar presentation on page 6 and write down one thing they associate with each verb they selected. For example: *dar → un consejo; hacer → la tarea*.

Preparation

- Have students come up with a sentence in the preterite about themselves or someone else in which they use the verbs and associations from their Independent Starters.

- Ask students to get together with a partner and share their sentences. Then have them choose five sentences to write a brief story. It can be a funny or silly story, but it should be coherent. For example: *Ayer le di un consejo a mi amiga Clara, pero no quiso escucharme. Hizo una mueca y se fue corriendo.* Invite pairs to read their stories to the class and hold a class vote to select the funniest or most entertaining story.

- As students read their stories aloud, write some of the verbs on the board and discuss these verbs' preterite conjugations. Remind students that *ir* and *ser* have the same forms in the preterite. Context will tell them which verb is being used.

Activities

9. Before you play the audio, ask students to conjugate the verbs in column B in the *yo* form of the preterite tense.

6

Gramática

El pretérito. Verbos irregulares

- Remember: we use the preterite tense to talk about actions completed in the past.

  Yo **fui** de vacaciones a México y mi amigo Carlos **estuvo** en Colombia.

- See page R13 for a review of the irregular preterite tense conjugations.

¡Qué moreno estás! ¿Adónde **fuiste** de vacaciones?

Fui a Puerto Rico y **estuve** un mes en la playa. ¿Y tú qué **hiciste**?

Yo **tuve** que estudiar, pero también **pude** descansar.

¡Qué bien!

Some common irregular verbs in the preterite:

dar	→	di
decir	→	dije
dormir	→	dormí
estar	→	estuve
hacer	→	hice
ir	→	fui
pedir	→	pedí
poder	→	pude
poner	→	puse
querer	→	quise
saber	→	supe
ser	→	fui
tener	→	tuve
traer	→	traje
venir	→	vine

9 ¿Quién hizo qué?

▶ **Escucha** y une las dos columnas para escribir oraciones lógicas. ¿Qué hicieron los chicos en sus vacaciones?

Ⓐ
1. Lucas
2. Ethan
3. Michelle
4. Eva
5. Daniel
6. Asha

Ⓑ
a. estar en las montañas
b. tener un verano aburrido
c. sacar la licencia de conducir
d. ir a la costa
e. dormir mucho
f. hacer un viaje por México

Modelo 1. *Lucas hizo un viaje por México.*

Pirámide de Kukulkán (México).

▶ **Escribe** oraciones sobre tus vacaciones. Utiliza los verbos de la ficha de Gramática.

Modelo *Yo estuve de vacaciones con mi familia. Fuimos a...*

6 seis

Differentiated Instruction

DEVELOPING LEARNERS

- Ask students to go through Asha's blog entry and classify all the verbs by their tense, conjugation, infinitive form, and use. For example, the first sentence says, *Estoy a más de 3.000 metros de altitud, en una ciudad de los Andes peruanos.* The verb *estoy* is the present tense *yo* form of the verb *estar*. Asha uses it to talk about the place where she is currently located.

- Once students have finished, have them get together with a partner to compare their verb classifications. Do they need to make any corrections to their classifications?

EXPANDING LEARNERS

- In groups of four, have students create a story about an event in the past. Ask them to elect one person to write. Taking turns within the group, each person has to add a line to the story. You may wish to give them the first line to get them started. For example: *Un ruido despertó anoche a Tania.* Ask students to keep adding lines until everyone in the group has added three lines. Then invite volunteers to read the stories aloud to the class.

10 Un viaje de altura

▶ **Lee** la entrada en el blog de viajes de Asha y escribe la respuesta a estas preguntas.

Huancayo (Perú), 22 de julio

Estoy a más de 3.000 metros de altitud, en una ciudad de los Andes peruanos. Llegué ayer en el tren turístico Lima-Huancayo. Por la noche fui a un restaurante típico peruano. Cené muy bien y los meseros me dijeron qué lugares debo visitar hoy en la ciudad.

El viaje en tren desde Lima fue impresionante. Pasamos por más de 60 túneles en las montañas. Hicimos dos paradas en el camino y también tuvimos un problema mecánico. Por eso el viaje fue más largo de lo normal. ¡Pero valió la pena!

1. ¿Adónde fue Asha anoche?
2. ¿Qué le dijeron los meseros a Asha?
3. ¿Cómo fue el viaje en tren desde Lima?
4. ¿Qué ocurrió en ese viaje?
5. ¿Qué opina Asha de su viaje en tren?

11 Vacaciones

▶ **Habla** con dos compañeros(as) sobre sus vacaciones y completa una tabla como esta con sus respuestas.

Información	Compañero(a) 1	Compañero(a) 2
¿Adónde fue?	a la playa	
¿Qué hizo?	nadar y leer	
¿Cuánto tiempo estuvo?	un mes	
¿Cómo fueron las vacaciones?	divertidas y largas	

▶ **Escribe** un párrafo comparando lo que hicieron tus dos compañeros y tú en las vacaciones.

Modelo

Estas vacaciones Sally fue a la playa con su familia, pero Peter y yo fuimos a las montañas. Los tres…

Gramática – El pretérito. Verbos irregulares

10. Have students read the blog entry in small groups. Ask them to stop after each sentence to summarize what they just read in Spanish. Then have them answer the questions and use their answers to write a paragraph to summarize the reading.

11. Invite volunteer groups to act out their paragraphs. Each student in the group pantomimes what he or she did while on vacation and the rest of the class guesses. For example:
Student A: [Student pantomimes getting a suntan and reading.]
Class: *Tomó el sol y leyó.*

 AUDIO SCRIPT
See page XXVF.

Answer Key

9. 2. d   3. e   4. c   5. a   6. b
▶ Answers will vary.

10. Answers will vary. Sample answers:
1. Asha fue a un restaurante típico peruano.
2. Los meseros le dijeron qué lugares visitar en la ciudad.
3. El viaje en tren fue impresionante.
4. Pasaron por más de 60 túneles, hicieron dos paradas y tuvieron un problema mecánico.
5. Ella piensa que el viaje valió la pena.

11. Answers will vary.
▶ Answers will vary.

Additional Resources

Fans Online activities
Practice Workbook

HERITAGE LANGUAGE LEARNERS

• Remind students of some irregularities in the preterite that may pose spelling problems. Verbs ending in -car, -gar, and -zar: *tocar* → *toqué*; *llegar* → *llegué*; *empezar* → *empecé*. Verbs that change *i* to *y*: *concluir* → *concluyó*. Very irregular verbs: *ir* → *fui, fuiste*; *tener* → *tuve, tuviste*; *estar* → *estuve, estuviste*; *poder* → *pude, pudiste*; *querer* → *quise, quisiste*; *saber* → *supe, supiste*.

• Have pairs of students compile a list of irregular verbs in the preterite that pose problems for them. Post the list for all in the class to use as reference.

MULTIPLE INTELLIGENCES: Verbal-Linguistic Intelligence

• Have students hypothesize about the preterite tense conjugations of the following verbs: *predecir* (to predict), *imponer* (to impose), *contener* (to contain), *impedir* (to prevent, to block), *rehacer* (to redo, to rebuild), and *prevenir* (to warn, to prevent). Ask students to think of reasons for the conjugation patterns they noticed for these verbs. Are they able to extrapolate a rule from these patterns? Students should associate these verbs with the core verb (e.g., *predecir* → *decir*).

4. DAR ÓRDENES E INSTRUCCIONES

Gramática – El imperativo afirmativo

Presentation

- In this section, students will review regular and irregular affirmative command forms.

Activities	Standards	Resources
Gramática	1.2, 3.1	
12.	1.1, 1.2, 1.3, 5.2	
13.	1.2	Audio
14.	1.2, 1.3	
15.	1.1, 5.2	

Teaching Suggestions

Warm-Up / Independent Starter

- Have students complete a table like the one below with the affirmative command forms of the following verbs: *hablar, correr, escribir, cerrar, pedir, probar, tener, hacer, poner, venir, salir, ser, decir, ir,* and *dar.*

Infinitivo	tú	usted	ustedes
hablar	habla	hable	hablen

Preparation

- Ask students to get together with a partner and compare their tables. Have them make the necessary corrections and keep the table as a reference for this lesson's activities.

- Then have pairs play a game to practice these command forms. One student will give a command and his or her partner models the action. Be sure students switch roles.

Activities

12. Invite volunteers to share with the class other health or lifestyle recommendations that are common in other cultures they know.

13. Before playing the audio, give students a couple of minutes to look at the pictures and write down one possible command or instruction for each picture. Then play the audio and have students complete the activity. Did they guess some of the commands correctly?

Gramática

El imperativo afirmativo

- To tell one person or more than one person to do something, you can use an informal or a formal command.

  Haz más ejercicio para estar en forma.
  Salid a pasear todos los días.
  Coma más verduras y **beba** mucha agua.
  Vayan al médico una vez al año.

- See page R18 for a review of both the formal and informal affirmative command forms.

¡Come las verduras, Javi!

Es que no me gustan.

12 **Diez consejos para vivir mejor**

▶ **Lee** estos consejos para vivir mejor. Luego escríbelos en tu cuaderno usando la forma *tú* del imperativo.

Modelo
Sonríe con frecuencia.

▶ **Ordena** los consejos del 1 al 10 según la importancia que tienen para ti.

▶ **Compara** tu lista con la de tu compañero(a). ¿Son similares?

CONSEJOS PARA VIVIR MEJOR

- Sonreír con frecuencia.
- Hacer ejercicio diariamente.
- Dormir de 7 a 8 horas al día.
- Seguir una dieta equilibrada.
- Ayudar a otras personas.
- Salir al aire libre y pasear.
- Ser honesto.
- Tener pensamientos positivos.
- Practicar meditación o relajación.
- Tener buenas relaciones personales.

8 ocho

Differentiated Instruction

DEVELOPING LEARNERS

- Have students play "Concentration." Write affirmative commands on a set of index cards and write the corresponding personal pronouns (*tú, usted, vosotros, ustedes*) on another set of cards. Place the cards facedown on a table and have students take turns trying to match each command with the corresponding pronoun. If they make a match, they get to keep their cards, but only if they say a sentence using the command. If no match is made, or if the sentence is not correct, players must return the cards. The winner is the player with the most cards when you call time.

EXPANDING LEARNERS

- Ask students to think about their favorite dish and the steps involved in preparing it. Then have students work with a partner to give each other step-by-step instructions on how to prepare the dish. They should not tell their partner the name of the dish; just give him or her detailed instructions. For example: *Primero corta en cuadritos una cebolla, un tomate y un chile. Después fríelos en aceite. Añade…* Have partners take notes. Once they have all the steps, ask them to try to guess the dish.

13 Todos damos órdenes

▶ **Escucha** estas órdenes e indicaciones y decide a qué fotografía corresponden.

14 Los consejos de Asha

▶ **Escribe.** ¿Qué consejos les da Asha a estas personas? Usa estos verbos.

| hablar | ponerse | practicar | hacer | ir | viajar |

1. Su maestra: «Tengo gripe y me siento mal».
2. Dos compañeros de clase: «Queremos estar en buena forma física».
3. Una amiga: «No sé qué ponerme para el baile de graduación».
4. Unos amigos de sus padres: «No sabemos qué hacer estas vacaciones».
5. Lucas: «Estoy muy triste. Mi novia y yo discutimos».
6. El padre de su mejor amigo: «Estoy muy estresado».

15 ¿Qué me recomiendan?

▶ **Habla** con dos compañeros(as). Piensen en dos problemas cada uno. Por turnos, dense consejos.

Últimamente estoy muy cansada.

Haz ejercicio. Eso da mucha energía.

O duerme más. Por lo menos, 7 horas al día.

nueve 9

HERITAGE LANGUAGE LEARNERS

• In parts of South and Central America, *vos* is used instead of *tú* for informal situations. This is called *voseo*, and the verb endings employed with *vos* are different from those used with *tú*. Some students in your class may be familiar with *voseo*. Give those who are not some examples of *vos* commands: *hablar → hablá; comer → comé; salir → salí; levantarse → levantate; ir → andá; dormir → dormí*. Ask students to rewrite the list of recommendations in activity 12 using the *vos* command forms. Invite volunteers to read their lists to the class.

COOPERATIVE LEARNING

• Have students work in small groups to come up with a list of seven rules for fostering the learning of Spanish in their Spanish classroom. They should first write the rules using informal command forms and then rewrite them using formal commands. Have groups read their lists to the class and afterward, engage them in a discussion about the effectiveness of each rule. Then hold a class vote to select the six most effective rules. You may want to post these rules in the classroom.

Gramática – El imperativo afirmativo

15. To expand this activity, ask students to think of reasons for not following their partners' recommendations and encourage the partners to offer alternative recommendations. For example:

A. *Me duele la cabeza.*
B. *Toma una aspirina.*
A. *Soy alérgica a las aspirinas.*
B. *Descansa en un sitio oscuro.*

 AUDIO SCRIPT
See page XXVF.

Answer Key

12. Haz ejercicio diariamente.
Duerme de 7 a 8 horas al día.
Sigue una dieta equilibrada.
Ayuda a otras personas.
Sal al aire libre y pasea.
Sé honesto.
Ten pensamientos positivos.
Practica meditación o relajación.
Ten buenas relaciones personales.
▶ Answers will vary.
▶ Answers will vary.

13.
1. C	3. A	5. B
2. F	4. E	6. D

14. Answers will vary. Sample answers:
1. Vaya al médico.
2. Hagan/Haced ejercicio.
3. Ponte un vestido de fiesta.
4. Viajen por América del Sur.
5. Habla con ella.
6. Practique yoga.

15. Answers will vary.

Additional Resources

Fans Online activities
Practice Workbook

9

Preliminary Unit

5. HACER PREGUNTAS

Gramática – Los interrogativos

Presentation

- In this section, students will review the interrogatives in order to ask and answer questions.

Activities	Standards	Resources
Gramática	1.2, 3.1	
16.	1.1, 1.2	
17.	1.1, 1.2, 1.3	Audio
18.	1.1, 1.2	
19.	1.1, 1.2, 1.3, 5.1	

Warm-Up / Independent Starter

- Have students read the grammar presentation silently. Then ask them to think of the questions they would need to ask to get the following information from someone:

  – Nombre   – Lugar de nacimiento
  – Domicilio   – Fecha de nacimiento
  – Edad   – Número de identidad

Preparation

- For privacy reasons, ask students to make up an address and identification number for today's activities. Then have them create a questionnaire with the questions from their Independent Starter. Remind students that questions in Spanish have two question marks, one at the beginning and another at the end. Question words have an accent mark and some of these words agree in number and/or gender with the noun.

- Once students have created their questionnaires, ask them to pair up with a classmate and answer each other's questions in writing. Invite volunteer pairs to act out their interview.

Activities

16. Have small groups come up with a list of questions one might find in the other three forms mentioned in the second part of this activity. Ask groups to share one of their lists of questions without specifying which type of form it is. Have the class guess the form.

10

Gramática

Los interrogativos

- When we ask questions that can be answered with *sí* or *no*, we put the verb at the beginning of the sentence.

  —¿Estudias Español?   —¿Tienes un bolígrafo?
  —Sí.   —No, lo siento.

- When we ask questions that need to be answered with more information, we use interrogatives. Normally, interrogatives go at the beginning of a sentence, before the verb.

  ¿Cómo te llamas?   ¿De dónde eres?   ¿Cuántos hermanos tienes?

- See page R7 for a review of the most common interrogatives in Spanish.

¿Cómo estás? ¿Por qué no me llamaste anoche? ¿Dónde estás?

¡Uf! ¿Qué es esto? ¡Cuántas preguntas!

16 **Lucas completa un formulario**

▶ **Completa** las preguntas del formulario con el interrogativo que corresponde.

Cuántas	Dónde	Cómo	Qué	Cuál	Cuándo

1. ¿_____ te llamas?
2. ¿_____ naciste?
3. ¿_____ es tu número de identidad?
4. ¿_____ vives?
5. ¿_____ personas viven en tu domicilio?
6. ¿_____ promedio *(average)* de notas tienes?

▶ **Elige.** ¿Qué tipo de formulario está completando Lucas?

a. Entrevista de trabajo.   c. Cuestionario médico.

b. Inscripción en un gimnasio.   d. Solicitud de beca *(scholarship application)*.

10 diez

DEVELOPING LEARNERS

- If students have difficulties using *qué* and *cuál(es)*, remind them that *cuál(es)* is used to ask about one or more elements in a group, and that it is generally followed by a verb. Have students choose the correct word to complete these questions.

  1. ¿Qué / Cuál es tu clase favorita? (Cuál)
  2. ¿Qué / Cuál de estos es tu libro? (Cuál)
  3. ¿Qué / Cuál hora es? (Qué)
  4. ¿Qué / Cuáles idiomas hablas? (Qué)
  5. ¿Qué / Cuál es el mejor coche? (Cuál)
  6. ¿Qué / Cuáles clases tienes hoy? (Qué)

EXPANDING LEARNERS

- Ask students to think of a famous person they would like to interview. The person could be an artist, sports personality, politician, writer, etc. They need to identify the person, and then write ten questions using a variety of interrogatives, as well as some yes/no questions. If time permits, have other students play the role of the interviewee and, working in pairs, deliver the interview before the class.

17 **¿Cuál fue la pregunta?**

▶ **Escucha** las respuestas que Marco da a Lucas y elige la pregunta correcta en cada caso.

1. a. ¿Dónde naciste?
   b. ¿De dónde eres?
   c. ¿Adónde vas?

2. a. ¿Cuál es tu deporte favorito?
   b. ¿Cómo juegas?
   c. ¿A qué juegas con tus amigos?

3. a. ¿De dónde viniste?
   b. ¿Por qué viniste a esta ciudad?
   c. ¿Cuándo llegaste a esta ciudad?

4. a. ¿Cómo vas de vacaciones?
   b. ¿Adónde vas de vacaciones?
   c. ¿Qué haces en las vacaciones?

▶ **Habla** con tu compañero(a). Hazle las preguntas que Lucas le hizo a Marco.

▶ **Escribe** las respuestas de tu compañero(a) y compáralas con las respuestas de Marco.

18 **Conversaciones incompletas**

▶ **Completa** los siguientes diálogos con una pregunta o una respuesta lógica.

1. —¿Por qué estás tan contenta hoy, Asha?

   —_____.

2. —¿_____, Asha?

   —Hablo español, inglés y francés.

3. —Lucas, ¿_____?

   —Historia y Español.

4. —¿Te gustan las películas de acción?

   —_____.

5. —¿_____?

   —Vivo en la calle Wilburn.

¿Adónde vas?

Voy a la biblioteca.

19 **¡Soy periodista!**

▶ **Escribe** seis preguntas que necesitas hacerle a un(a) compañero(a) para escribir una reseña *(profile)* de esa persona en el periódico de la escuela.

▶ **Entrevista** a tu compañero(a) y toma nota de sus respuestas.

▶ **Escribe** la reseña. Después, preséntala a la clase.

Camila Jiménez
Camila es una estudiante nueva en nuestra escuela. Es de Orlando, Florida. Tiene...

---

5. HACER PREGUNTAS

Gramática – Los interrogativos

18. There are several possible answers for each blank in 1, 3, and 4. To extend this activity, have students think of at least two answer options for each of those blanks.

19. Call on volunteers to read the profiles they created without mentioning the name of the student they are describing. Have the class guess the student's identity. How did they know?

> **AUDIO SCRIPT**
> See page XXVF.

Answer Key

16. 1. Cómo   3. Cuál   5. Cuántas
   2. Cuándo   4. Dónde   6. Qué
   ▶ (d) Solicitud de beca.

17. 1. b   2. a   3. c   4. b
   ▶ Answers will vary.
   ▶ Answers will vary.

18. Answers will vary. Sample answers:
   1. Porque salí bien en el examen de Ciencias.
   2. ¿Qué idiomas hablas, Asha?
   3. Lucas, ¿cuáles son tus clases favoritas?
   4. Sí, me gustan mucho.
   5. ¿Dónde vives?

19. Answers will vary.
   ▶ Answers will vary.
   ▶ Answers will vary.

Additional Resources

Fans Online activities
Practice Workbook

HERITAGE LANGUAGE LEARNERS

• Have students create clues for a crossword puzzle to practice the different interrogatives. For instance, the clues may consist of questions that are missing the question word, like in activity 16. If access to computers is available, ask students to use software to create the crossword grid. When they complete their task, ask volunteers from among the other students to try to solve the puzzle.

CRITICAL THINKING

• Discuss with students the advantages to having two interrogative marks in Spanish. You may remind them that Spanish doesn't use an auxiliary verb such as *do* to form questions. For instance, "Do you know the answer?" becomes *¿Sabes la respuesta?* in Spanish. Without the question marks, it is a statement: *Sabes la respuesta.* (You know the answer.) Ask students what would happen if there was only one question mark in cases like these (e.g., **Sabes la respuesta?*). Elicit that the reader would not know until reaching the end whether he or she is reading a question or a statement.

Unit 1 ¿Cómo eres?

Objectives

- To describe people's physical characteristics and personality traits.
- To express states of being and feelings.
- To provide personal information.
- To make comparisons and use superlatives.
- To talk about past actions.
- To describe family relationships.

- To express ownership with possessive adjectives and pronouns.
- To narrate and describe in the past.
- To talk about life stages and events in a biography.
- To identify main ideas and significant details in a variety of texts.

- To write descriptive, narrative, or informative texts.
- To know and apply the different stages of the writing process: planning, writing, revising, and sharing.
- To explore cultural aspects of the Latin American population.

Contents

Vocabulary

- Useful expressions to organize a text, to give instructions, to express personal likes and interests, to ask for confirmation, and to express wishes.
- Review: Words for personal information and family relationships, and words to describe people.
- Physical characteristics and personality traits.
- Family relationships.
- Marital status.
- Life stages and events, rites and celebrations, and religions.

Grammar

- The verbs *ser* and *estar*.
- Comparisons and superlatives.
- The imperfect and the past progressive tenses.
- To express ownership with possessive adjectives and pronouns.
- The preterite and the imperfect tenses.
- Time expressions to narrate in the past.

Culture

- *Mafalda* by the strip cartoonist Quino.
- Comic strips in Hispanic culture.
- *Don Quijote.*
- Spanish court painters: Diego Velázquez and Francisco de Goya.
- *Estereotipos familiares.*
- *Fiestas familiares.*
- Traditional Hispanic legends.
- Esmeralda Santiago: *Cuando era puertorriqueña.*
- *Leyendas de Guatemala.*
- A legend of the origin of the Inca Empire.
- Latin American population.

Evaluation Criteria

- Describe people's physical characteristics and personality traits.
- Express states of being and feelings.
- Use and differentiate the uses of the verbs *ser* and *estar*.
- Recognize and use possessive adjectives and pronouns.
- Compare people to express equality, inequality, and extreme degree of an adjective.

- Identify family members and describe family relationships.
- Use the forms of the imperfect tense.
- Recognize and use the past progressive tense.
- Recognize and use possessive adjectives and pronouns.
- Narrate events in the past using the preterite and the imperfect and differentiate the uses of both tenses.

- Recognize and use time expressions to narrate in the past.
- Express understanding of the origin, history, and diversity of the Latin American population.
- Write a character sketch.
- Read different types of texts and identify main ideas and significant details in them.
- Write guided texts giving information, describing, or narrating events.

Unit Plan _____

Las tareas/Antes de empezar

Estimated time: 1 session.

Text: *Personajes famosos.*

Functions & forms:

- Useful expressions to organize a text, to give instructions, to express personal likes and interests, to ask for confirmation, and to express wishes.
- Review of known vocabulary for personal information and family relationships, and for describing people.

DESAFÍO 1

Estimated time: 5 sessions.

Text: *Una argentina famosa.*

Functions & forms:

- To describe people.
- Physical characteristics and personality traits.
- The verbs *ser* and *estar*.
- Comparisons and superlatives.

Culture:

- *Mafalda.*
- *Las tiras cómicas.*
- *Don Quijote.*

Reading: *Una historieta de detectives.*

DESAFÍO 2

Estimated time: 5 sessions.

Text: *Retratos de familia.*

Functions & forms:

- To talk about past actions.
- Family relationships and marital status.
- The imperfect and the past progressive tenses.
- To express ownership.

Culture:

- *Los pintores de la corte.*
- *Estereotipos familiares.*
- *Fiestas familiares.*

Reading: *Una breve biografía.* Frida Kahlo.

DESAFÍO 3

Estimated time: 6 sessions.

Text: *Flor de leyendas.*

Functions & forms:

- To narrate and describe in the past.
- Biographies. Life stages and events, rites and celebrations, and religions.
- The preterite and the imperfect tenses.
- Time expressions to narrate in the past.

Culture:

- *Las leyendas tradicionales.*
- *Cuando era puertorriqueña.*
- *Leyendas de Guatemala.*

Reading: *Los hermanos Ayar: una leyenda sobre el origen del imperio inca.*

Para terminar

Estimated time: 1 session.

Todo junto: Review of *Desafíos 1–3.*

Tu desafío:

- *Desafío A:* Write and draw a comic strip.
- *Desafío B:* Describe a painting and give information about the artist.
- *Desafío C:* Invent and write a legend.

MAPA CULTURAL

Estimated time: 1 session.

Mapa cultural: La población latinoamericana.

ESCRITURA

Estimated time: 1 session.

Writing: *Un personaje interesante.*

PROYECTO

Estimated time: 1 session.

Project: *Un álbum de fotos de tu vida.*

Standards for Learning Spanish

COMMUNICATION

1.1 Interpersonal mode
- Exchange personal opinions and experiences.
- Engage in oral conversations using personal knowledge and experience.
- Talk about past and present habits.
- Compare information with a partner.
- Prepare and conduct an interview.
- Role-play an interview.
- Ask and answer questions on different topics orally.
- Write a message for a social-networking website with personal knowledge.
- Write a dialogue with a partner.

1.2. Interpretive mode
- Demonstrate understanding of oral and written idiomatic expressions.
- Demonstrate understanding of questions relating to familiar and less familiar topics.
- Understand and obtain information from audio or video recordings.
- Understand written exchanges.
- Extract information from a biography.
- Identify main ideas and significant details from a traditional legend orally and in writing.
- Draw conclusions and make judgments from oral and written texts.
- Interpret texts on topics of other cultures and relate them to personal knowledge and experience.

1.3. Presentational mode
- Dramatize a situation.
- Produce and present an original creation orally.
- Describe people with detail.
- Write a descriptive and informative paragraph about a painting.
- Narrate past events.
- Write a summary of a narrative text.
- Write a descriptive paragraph comparing or summarizing information.
- Compose a comic strip.
- Compose an original legend.
- Write a character sketch.

CULTURE

2.1. Practices and perspectives
- Discover some cultural stereotypes about the family in Hispanic culture and compare them with stereotypes in students' own culture.
- Read about some family celebrations in Hispanic countries and compare them with family celebrations in the United States.

2.2. Products and perspectives
- Read about some Hispanic comic strips and cartoonists.
- Reflect on the influence of comic strips in society and explore their connection to the "real world."

- Read about some fictitious characters in Hispanic culture in order to understand cultural stereotypes.
- Compare fictitious characters in Hispanic culture and in students' own culture.
- Learn about important Hispanic paintings and artists.
- Read about traditional Hispanic legends and understand their cultural importance.
- Read about and research relevant Hispanic writers.

CONNECTIONS

3.1. Interdisciplinary connections
- Understand the similarities and differences between some aspects of grammar in English and in Spanish.
- Learn about renowned Hispanic paintings and painters.
- Explore traditional Hispanic legends.

- Learn about relevant Hispanic writers.
- Create a comic strip.
- Write a character sketch.

3.2. Viewpoints through language / culture
- Read comic strips in Spanish.
- Read a traditional legend in Spanish.

COMPARISONS

4.1. Compare languages
- Compare the uses of the Spanish verbs ser and estar with the English verb to be.
- Compare the formation and the uses of past progressive in English and in Spanish.
- Compare possessives in English and in Spanish.
- Compare the uses of past tenses in English and in Spanish.
- Compare expressions to talk about the past in English and in Spanish.

4.2. Compare cultures
- Compare stereotypes about the family in Hispanic culture and in the culture of the United States.
- Compare family celebrations in Hispanic countries and in the United States.

COMMUNITIES

5.1. Spanish within and beyond the school setting
- Describe a work of art.
- Promote a positive attitude toward other cultures.

5.2. Spanish for lifelong learners
- Learn the writing process.
- Encourage the love of art.
- Contribute to the positive valuation of traditional stories.

Communicative Skills

Interpersonal Mode

		Activities
Speaking	• Exchange opinions, experiences, or information. • Describe a character to a partner. • Engage in conversation with a classmate. • Compare pictures or information with a classmate. • Ask and answer questions with a partner. • Prepare and perform an interview.	• 9, 25, 32, 78, 89 • 14, 18, 51, *Proyecto* • 29, 52, 58 • 45, 58, 87 • 14, 20, 86, *Proyecto* • 83, 87
Writing	• Write a message for a social-networking website. • Write a dialogue with a classmate. • Write a descriptive paragraph comparing or summarizing information. • Write questions for an interview and write a report with the results.	• 19, 86 • 30, 33 • 52, 58 • 83, 87
Listening	• Understand simple descriptions.	• 86, *Proyecto*
Reading	• Understand descriptive sentences or paragraphs.	• 14, 25

Interpretive Mode

		Activities
Listening	• Obtain information from a conversation. • Understand oral descriptions or narrations.	• 9, 24, 62, 63, 72 • 13, 32, 36, 40, 49, 63
Reading	• Demonstrate comprehension of written exchanges and longer written dialogues. • Infer meanings based on a text. • Reflect on cultural topics in relation to personal knowledge and experience. • Understand and obtain information from a descriptive or narrative text. • Obtain information and draw conclusions from an informative text.	• 1, 8, 27, 31, 33, 50, 60, 85 • 2, 11, 26, 38, 65, 66 • 10, 15, 21, 37, 41, 46, 64, 69 • 25, 44, 62, 73, 77, 79, 80, 81 • 34, 35, 53, 54, 55, 56, 83
Viewing	• Connect information or descriptions to images. • Obtain information from an image or visual.	• 13, 36, 49, 84 • 18, 28, 33

Presentational Mode

		Activities
Speaking	• Present information, a description, or a story to the class. • Present an original creation to the class.	• 57, 58 • *Proyecto*
Writing	• Write sentences or a paragraph to describe people. • Write a comic strip. • Write a summary of a traditional legend or an original legend.	• 8, 14, 25, 60, 88, R1, *Escritura* • 33, 88 • 63, 82, 85, 88
Visually Representing	• Draw a comic strip, or illustrate a legend or a character sketch. • Create a poster.	• 33, 73, 88, *Escritura* • 87

Cross-Curricular Standards

Subject	Standard	Activities
Language Arts	• Compare elements of Spanish grammar with English equivalents. • Use the writing process to write a character sketch.	• 16, 22, 42, 47, 70, 74 • *Escritura*
Literature	• Read about and research relevant Hispanic writers.	• *Vocabulario D3*, 69, 78
Art	• Study different renowned works by Hispanic painters. • Design a comic strip or create a personal photo album.	• *Lectura D2*, 35, 36, 37, 60, 88 • 73, 82, 88, *Proyecto*
Social Studies	• Read about the origin and history of the Latin American population. • Read about traditional Hispanic legends.	• *Mapa cultural* • 73, *Lectura D3*

Lesson Plans (50-Minute Classes)

Day	Objectives	Sessions	Activities	Time	Standards	Resources/Homework
1	To introduce personal relationships and the characters' challenges, and to review learned vocabulary	**¿Cómo eres?/Las tareas/Antes de empezar** (12–17) • Warm-Up: Topic orientation • Presentation: *Personajes famosos* • *Expresiones útiles* and *Recuerda*	 1–2 3–6	 10 m. 20 m. 20 m.	1.1, 1.2, 1.3, 2.1, 2.2, 3.1, 5.1, 5.2	Visual Presentation Video Practice Workbook
2	To describe people	**Desafío 1 – Una argentina famosa** (18–19) • Warm-Up: Independent Starter • *Texto: Una argentina famosa* • *Cultura: Mafalda*	 7–9 10	 5 m. 35 m. 10 m.	1.1, 1.2, 1.3, 2.1, 2.2, 3.1, 4.2, 5.1	Visual Presentation Audio
3	To talk about physical characteristics and personality traits	**Desafío 1 – Vocabulario** (20–21) • Warm-Up: Independent Starter • Vocabulary: *Características físicas y rasgos de personalidad* • *Cultura: Las tiras cómicas*	 11–14 15	 5 m. 35 m. 10 m.	1.1, 1.2, 1.3, 2.1, 2.2, 4.2, 5.1	Audio Visual Presentation
4	To learn the uses of the verbs ser and estar	**Desafío 1 – Gramática** (22–23) • Warm-Up: Independent Starter • Grammar: 'Ser' y 'estar' • *Conexiones: Don Quijote*	 16–20 21	 5 m. 35 m. 10 m.	1.1, 1.2, 1.3, 2.1, 2.2, 3.1, 4.1, 4.2, 5.1, 5.2	Practice Workbook
5	To make comparisons and use superlatives	**Desafío 1 – Gramática** (24–25) • Warm-Up: Independent Starter • Grammar: *Las comparaciones y el superlativo*	 22–25	 5 m. 45 m.	1.1, 1.2, 1.3, 2.2, 3.1, 4.1, 5.1	Audio Practice Workbook
6	To understand a dialogue and to integrate vocabulary and grammar	**Desafío 1 – Lectura/Comunicación** (26–29) • Warm-Up: Independent Starter • *Lectura: Una historieta de detectives* • *Comunicación:* Review • *Final del desafío*	 26–29 30–32 33	 5 m. 20 m. 15 m. 10 m.	1.1, 1.2, 1.3, 2.2, 3.1, 3.2, 5.1	Visual Presentation Audio Practice Workbook *Tu desafío* Quiz on *Desafío 1*
7	To talk about past actions	**Desafío 2 – Retratos de familia** (30–31) • Warm-Up: Correct quiz on *Desafío 1* • *Texto: Retratos de familia* • *Conexiones: Los pintores de la corte*	 34–36 37	 5 m. 35 m. 10 m.	1.1, 1.2, 1.3, 2.1, 2.2, 3.1, 3.2, 4.2	Visual Presentation Audio
8	To talk about family relationships and about marital status	**Desafío 2 – Vocabulario** (32–33) • Warm-Up: Independent Starter • Vocabulary: *Relaciones familiares* • *Cultura: Estereotipos familiares*	 38–40 41	 5 m. 35 m. 10 m.	1.1, 1.2, 1.3, 2.1, 2.2, 3.1, 3.2, 4.2	Audio Practice Workbook
9	To learn the imperfect and the past progressive tenses	**Desafío 2 – Gramática** (34–35) • Warm-Up: Independent Starter • Grammar: *El imperfecto y el pasado continuo* • *Cultura: Fiestas familiares*	 42–45 46	 5 m. 35 m. 10 m.	1.1, 1.2, 1.3, 2.1, 3.1, 3.2, 4.1, 4.2, 5.1	Video Practice Workbook
10	To express ownership	**Desafío 2 – Gramática** (36–37) • Warm-Up: Independent Starter • Grammar: *Expresar posesión*	 47–52	 5 m. 45 m.	1.1, 1.2, 1.3, 3.1, 4.1, 5.1	Audio Practice Workbook

Day	Objectives	Sessions	Activities	Time	Standards	Resources / Homework
11	To understand a biography and to integrate vocabulary and grammar	**Desafío 2 – Lectura / Comunicación** (38–41) • Warm-Up: Independent Starter • *Lectura: Una breve biografía* • *Comunicación:* Review • *Final del desafío*	 53–56 57–59 60	5 m. 20 m. 15 m. 10 m.	1.1, 1.2, 1.3, 2.1, 2.2, 3.1, 3.2, 4.2, 5.1	Audio Practice Workbook *Tu desafío* Quiz on *Desafío 2*
12	To narrate and describe in the past	**Desafío 3 – Flor de leyendas** (42–43) • Warm-Up: Correct quiz on *Desafío 2* • *Texto: Flor de leyendas* • *Conexiones: Las leyendas tradicionales*	 61–63 64	5 m. 35 m. 10 m.	1.1, 1.2, 1.3, 2.1, 2.2, 3.1, 3.2, 4.2	Visual Presentation Audio
13	To talk about life stages, rites and celebrations, and religions	**Desafío 3 – Vocabulario** (44–45) • Warm-Up: Independent Starter • Vocabulary: *Biografías* • *Conexiones: Cuando era puertorriqueña*	 65–68 69	5 m. 35 m. 10 m.	1.1, 1.2, 1.3, 2.1, 2.2, 3.2, 5.1	Audio Practice Workbook
14	To learn the preterite and the imperfect tenses	**Desafío 3 – Gramática** (46–47) • Warm-Up: Independent Starter • Grammar: *El pretérito y el imperfecto*	 70–73	5 m. 45 m.	1.1, 1.2, 1.3, 2.2, 3.1, 4.1	Audio Practice Workbook
15	To learn time expressions to narrate in the past	**Desafío 3 – Gramática** (48–49) • Warm-Up: Independent Starter • Grammar: *Expresiones temporales para la narración* • *Cultura: Leyendas de Guatemala*	 74–77 78	5 m. 35 m. 10 m.	1.1, 1.2, 1.3, 2.2, 3.1, 4.1, 5.1	Video Practice Workbook
16	To understand a legend	**Desafío 3 – Lectura** (50–51) • Warm-Up: Independent Starter • *Lectura: Los hermanos Ayar: una leyenda sobre el origen del imperio inca*	 79–82	5 m. 45 m.	1.1, 1.2, 1.3, 2.2, 3.1, 3.2	
17	To integrate vocabulary and grammar	**Desafío 3 – Comunicación** (52–53) • Warm-Up: Independent Starter • *Comunicación:* Review • *Final del desafío*	 83–84 85	5 m. 30 m. 15 m.	1.1, 1.2, 1.3, 2.1, 5.1	Audio Practice Workbook Quiz on *Desafío 3* **Para terminar – Tu desafío** (55)
18	To integrate language in context	**Para terminar** (54–55) • Warm-Up: Correct quiz on *Desafío 3* • *Todo junto* • *Tu desafío* presentations	 86–87 88	5 m. 20 m. 25 m.	1.1, 1.2, 1.3, 2.1, 2.2, 3.1, 5.1, 5.2	Practice Workbook
19	To assess student proficiency and to learn about the Latin American population	**Evaluación / Mapa cultural** (56–57) • Warm-Up: Independent Starter • Quiz on *Desafíos 1–3* • *Mapa cultural: La población latinoamericana*	 89	5 m. 15 m. 30 m.	1.1, 1.2, 1.3, 2.1, 2.2, 3.1, 3.2	Video Practice Workbook
20	To create a character sketch	**Escritura** (58–59) • Warm-Up: Independent Starter • *Escritura: Un personaje interesante*		5 m. 45 m.	1.1, 1.2, 1.3, 2.2, 3.1	Project work
21	To create a photo album	**Proyecto** (64–65) • Warm-Up: Prepare project presentations • Project presentations		10 m. 40 m.	1.1, 1.2, 1.3, 2.1, 2.2, 3.1, 5.1, 5.2	**Repaso – Vocabulario** (60–61) **Repaso – Gramática** (62–63) **Autoevaluación** (65)

Lesson Plans (90-Minute Classes)

Day	Objectives	Sessions	Activities	Time	Standards	Resources / Homework
1	To introduce personal relationships and the characters' challenges, and to review learned vocabulary	(See Day 4 Preliminary Unit) ***¿Cómo eres?/Las tareas/Antes de empezar*** (12–17) • Warm-Up: Topic orientation • Presentation: *Personajes famosos* • *Expresiones útiles* and *Recuerda*	 1–2 3–6	(20 m.) 10 m. 30 m. 30 m.	1.1, 1.2, 1.3, 2.1, 2.2, 3.1, 5.1, 5.2	Visual Presentation Video Practice Workbook
2	To describe people and to talk about physical characteristics and personality traits	***Desafío 1 – Una argentina famosa/Vocabulario*** (18–21) • Warm-Up: Independent Starter • *Texto: Una argentina famosa* • *Cultura: Mafalda* • Vocabulary: *Características físicas y rasgos de personalidad* • *Cultura: Las tiras cómicas*	 7–9 10 11–14 15	 5 m. 30 m. 10 m. 35 m. 10 m.	1.1, 1.2, 1.3, 2.1, 2.2, 3.1, 4.2, 5.1	Visual Presentation Audio Practice Workbook
3	To learn the uses of the verbs *ser* and *estar,* and to make comparisons and use superlatives	***Desafío 1 – Gramática*** (22–25) • Warm-Up: Independent Starter • Grammar: 'Ser' y 'estar' • *Conexiones: Don Quijote* • Grammar: *Las comparaciones y el superlativo*	 16–20 21 22–25	 5 m. 35 m. 10 m. 40 m.	1.1, 1.2, 1.3, 2.1, 2.2, 3.1, 4.1, 4.2, 5.1, 5.2	Audio Practice Workbook
4	To understand a dialogue, to integrate vocabulary and grammar, and to assess student proficiency	***Desafío 1 – Lectura/Comunicación/Evaluación*** (26–29) • Warm-Up: Independent Starter • *Lectura: Una historieta de detectives* • *Comunicación:* Review • *Final del desafío* • Quiz on *Desafío 1*	 26–29 30–32 33	 5 m. 35 m. 25 m. 10 m. 15 m.	1.1, 1.2, 1.3, 2.2, 3.1, 3,2, 5.1	Visual Presentation Audio Practice Workbook *Tu desafío*
5	To talk about past actions and to talk about family relationships and about marital status	***Desafío 2 – Retratos de familia/Vocabulario*** (30–33) • Warm-Up: Independent Starter • *Texto: Retratos de familia* • *Conexiones: Los pintores de la corte* • Vocabulary: *Relaciones familiares* • *Cultura: Estereotipos familiares*	 34–36 37 38–40 41	 5 m. 30 m. 10 m. 35 m. 10 m.	1.1, 1.2, 1.3, 2.1, 2.2, 3.1, 3.2, 4.2	Visual Presentation Audio Practice Workbook
6	To learn the imperfect and the past progressive tenses and to express ownership	***Desafío 2 – Gramática*** (34–37) • Warm-Up: Independent Starter • Grammar: *El imperfecto y el pasado continuo* • *Cultura: Fiestas familiares* • Grammar: *Expresar posesión*	 42–45 46 47–52	 5 m. 35 m. 10 m. 40 m.	1.1, 1.2, 1.3, 2.1, 3.1, 3.2, 4.1, 4.2, 5.1	Audio Video Practice Workbook

Day	Objectives	Sessions	Activities	Time	Standards	Resources / Homework
7	To understand a biography, to integrate vocabulary and grammar, and to assess student proficiency	**Desafío 2 – Lectura/Comunicación/Evaluación** (38–41) • Warm-Up: Independent Starter • *Lectura: Una breve biografía* • *Comunicación:* Review • *Final del desafío* • Quiz on *Desafío 2*	 53–56 57–59 60	 5 m. 35 m. 25 m. 10 m. 15 m.	1.1, 1.2, 1.3, 2.1, 2.2, 3.1, 3.2, 4.2, 5.1	Audio Practice Workbook *Tu desafío*
8	To narrate and describe in the past and to talk about life stages, rites and celebrations, and religions	**Desafío 3 – Flor de leyendas/Vocabulario** (42–45) • Warm-Up: Independent Starter • *Texto: Flor de leyendas* • *Conexiones: Las leyendas tradicionales* • Vocabulary: *Biografías* • *Conexiones: Cuando era puertorriqueña*	 61–63 64 65–68 69	 5 m. 30 m. 10 m. 35 m. 10 m.	1.1, 1.2, 1.3, 2.1, 2.2, 3.1, 3.2, 4.2, 5.1	Visual Presentation Audio Practice Workbook
9	To learn the preterite and the imperfect tenses and to learn time expressions to narrate in the past	**Desafío 3 – Gramática** (46–49) • Warm-Up: Independent Starter • Grammar: *El pretérito y el imperfecto* • Grammar: *Expresiones temporales para la narración* • *Cultura: Leyendas de Guatemala*	 70–73 74–77 78	 5 m. 40 m. 35 m. 10 m.	1.1, 1.2, 1.3, 2.2, 3.1, 4.1, 5.1	Audio Video Practice Workbook
10	To understand a legend, to integrate vocabulary and grammar, to integrate language in context, and to assess student proficiency	**Desafío 3 – Lectura/Comunicación/Evaluación/Todo junto** (50–54) • Warm-Up: Independent Starter • *Lectura: Los hermanos Ayar: una leyenda sobre el origen del imperio inca* • *Comunicación:* Review • *Final del desafío* • *Todo junto* • Quiz on *Desafío 3*	 79–82 83–84 85 86–87	 5 m. 25 m. 20 m. 10 m. 15 m. 15 m.	1.1, 1.2, 1.3, 2.1, 2.2, 3.1, 3.2, 5.1	Audio Practice Workbook **Para terminar – Tu desafío** (55)
11	To learn about the Latin American population and to create a character sketch	**Tu desafío/Mapa cultural/Escritura** (55–59) • Warm-Up: Independent Starter • *Tu desafío* presentations • *Mapa cultural: La población latinoamericana* • *Escritura: Un personaje interesante*	 88 89	 5 m. 15 m. 30 m. 40 m.	1.1, 1.2, 1.3, 2.1, 2.2, 3.1, 3.2, 5.1, 5.2	Video Practice Workbook **Repaso – Vocabulario** (60–61) **Repaso – Gramática** (62–63) Quiz on *Desafíos 1–3* Project work
12	To create a photo album	**Proyecto/Assessment** (64–65) • Warm-Up: Correct quiz on *Desafíos 1–3* • Project presentations • *Autoevaluación* • Test (See Day 1 Unit 2)		 5 m. 15 m. 10 m. 15 m. (45 m.)	1.1, 1.2, 1.3, 2.1, 2.2, 3.1, 5.1, 5.2	

9 Los amigos de Mafalda

–Antes de hacer nuestra propia tira cómica, tenemos que entender bien las personalidades de los personajes de *Mafalda*.

–De acuerdo.

–¿Qué sabes sobre Mafalda?

–Pues que es una niña baja, con el pelo negro. Y también sé que no le gusta nada la sopa. Frecuentemente está preocupada por las noticias que escucha en la radio.

–¿Y cómo se llama la mejor amiga de Mafalda?

–Susanita.

–Es la niña con el pelo rubio y rizado, ¿verdad?

–Sí. Ella tiene ideas muy tradicionales.

–Creo que siempre está enojada con Manolito, ¿no?

–Así es, no se llevan bien. Manolito es ambicioso. Él sueña con tener muchas tiendas cuando sea mayor y por eso siempre piensa en ideas para mejorar el negocio familiar.

–¡Qué gracioso! Tiene el pelo en forma de cepillo.

–¡Tienes razón! Y Miguelito, otro amigo de Mafalda, tiene el pelo como una lechuga.

–¿Qué más sabemos sobre Miguelito?

–Yo sé que es el más pequeño de todos y que tiene mucha imaginación.

–Bueno, todavía tenemos que hablar sobre sus amigos Felipe y Libertad, su hermanito Guille y sus padres.

–¡A leer más tiras! ¡Qué investigación tan divertida!

13 ¿Quién es?

–¿Conoces a este personaje?

–Sí, claro, es la figura más conocida de la literatura española, don Quijote de la Mancha. Esta es una versión en dibujos animados. Él es alto y muy delgado, y su compañero, Sancho Panza, es bajo y gordo. Don Quijote es idealista y Sancho es su fiel ayudante.

–¿Y quién es este personaje calvo y con gafas?

–Es Rompetechos. Es muy optimista y siempre está de buen humor, pero tiene muy mala suerte.

–¿Sabes quiénes son estos niños?

–Sí, son Zipi y Zape. Son gemelos, uno es rubio y el otro es moreno. ¡Son muy traviesos!

–A estos sí los conozco. Son los famosos Mortadelo y Filemón. Son detectives y viven muchas aventuras. Filemón es el jefe, y el que está vestido de negro es Mortadelo.

–Así es. Filemón es muy serio, al contrario que Mortadelo, que es divertido y creativo: ¡siempre va disfrazado!

23 Los vecinos

–Nuestros vecinos son muy interesantes.

–¿Por qué lo dices?

–Porque son hermanos, pero no son parecidos.

–Tienes razón. Xavi es muy alto y David es muy bajo.

–¡Y David es mayor!

–Sí. Además, Xavi es optimista. Siempre es muy positivo mientras que David siempre es negativo.

–Pues, aunque David no es el chico más optimista del mundo, es muy amistoso. Me ayuda siempre que lo necesito.

–Y Xavi también. Los dos son bondadosos.

–Y corteses; siempre me saludan.

–Sí, los dos son corteses, pero por lo general Xavi no habla mucho. Es muy tímido. En cambio, David no para de hablar.

–Es cierto, pero son buenos vecinos y me caen muy bien.

32 ¿Quién es el ladrón?

1. Yo vi a una mujer bajo un árbol. Era alta y creo que tenía el pelo castaño y corto y los ojos verdes. Llevaba un vestido muy bonito con flores rosadas. Estaba jugando con su perrito y parecía muy cariñosa.

2. Yo observé a dos hombres sentados en un banco. Estaban almorzando. Uno era bajo y tenía los ojos azules y grandes y el pelo negro, muy corto. Tenía bigote. El otro no era ni alto ni bajo, era de estatura media. Tenía el pelo rubio y una cicatriz en la cara. Los dos llevaban traje. Creo que eran hombres de negocios.

3. Yo vi a una chica joven montando en bici por el parque. Tenía el pelo negro y largo. Llevaba unos jeans y una camiseta negra. Creo que tenía los ojos negros, pero no la vi muy bien porque parecía tener mucha prisa.

36 Descripciones

En este cuadro de Botero vemos a cinco figuras en una escena típicamente familiar. Todos los personajes están bastante gordos, que es una de las características más representativas de los cuadros y las esculturas de este artista. En la parte central del cuadro está la familia: el padre, sentado en una silla, con su hijo en brazos; la madre, de pie a su lado. Entre los dos, la hija mayor. Y el hijo más pequeño al lado de su madre. Al fondo vemos un paisaje con árboles.

40 ¡Adivina!

Hola, yo soy Eva y voy a presentarles a mi familia. Mis padres son Thomas y Samantha. Y tengo una hermana menor; se llama Sabrina. Mis abuelos paternos están divorciados, pero se llevan muy bien. Son Jeff y Mary. Además de mi padre, tienen otro hijo, mi tío Larry. Él es muy simpático. Tiene novia, pero no está casado. Mis abuelos maternos, los padres de mi madre, se llaman Anthony y June. Mi madre tiene una hermana, Lucy. Ella está casada con Jack. Lucy y Jack tienen dos hijos: mi primo Jason, de catorce años, y Rachael, que tiene diez años.

49 ¿De quién es?

¡Qué desorden! ¡Cuántas cosas hay por la sala! Aquí hay un libro. A ver... No es mío, es de mi ahijado. También hay unas revistas que no son mías... Ah, son las de mi abuelo. ¡Vaya! Mis padres se fueron de vacaciones y se olvidaron de la cámara de fotos. ¿Y qué es esto que hay debajo del sofá? Es el monopatín de mi hermana. ¡Qué desastre!

59 Recuerdos de infancia

De pequeño vivía en Boston con mi familia. Mis padres, mis hermanos y yo vivíamos en un apartamento bastante grande en el centro de la ciudad. Me gustaba mucho, pero veíamos poco a mis abuelos porque entonces no vivían con nosotros. Ellos estaban en Nueva York, donde vivo yo ahora. Mis hermanos y yo íbamos a la escuela en autobús. Nos llevábamos bien, pero a veces discutíamos. Lo normal entre hermanos, ¿no? Lo mejor eran las vacaciones de verano. Mis tíos venían a visitarnos y hacíamos muchas excursiones con ellos y con mis dos primos.

63 La leyenda de las cataratas del Iguazú

–¿Conoces alguna leyenda hispana, Asha?

–Sí, conozco una leyenda argentina muy bonita. ¿Te la cuento?

–Claro. ¿Cómo se llama?

–Es la leyenda de las cataratas del Iguazú. Cuenta que hace muchos años, en el río Iguazú, vivía una enorme serpiente que se llamaba Boi. Los indígenas guaraníes tenían que sacrificar a una joven todos los años y entregársela a Boi, lanzándola al río.

–¡Qué horrible!

–Sí. Un año los indígenas eligieron a una joven llamada Naipí para el sacrificio. Pero llegó allí un joven muy valiente llamado Tarobá, que se enamoró de Naipí y quiso salvarla de la muerte. Por la noche, la metió en su canoa y los dos escaparon por el río. Pero Boi, la serpiente, se enojó mucho y partió el río en dos, formando las cataratas.

–¿Y Tarobá y Naipí se salvaron?

–No. La serpiente transformó a Tarobá en los árboles que hay en la parte superior de las cataratas, y a Naipí en la caída de agua. Así los separó para siempre.

–¡Qué historia tan triste!

–No, qué va. La leyenda también dice que los días de sol, cuando se forma el arco iris, Tarobá y Naipí vuelven a unirse.

68 Conversaciones

1. Carlos y Ana se casaron ayer.
2. Luisa anunció su embarazo el mes pasado.
3. María Luisa fue al almacén y eligió un vestido precioso.
4. Claudia dio a luz el 14 de febrero.
5. Después de trabajar toda su vida como profesores, decidieron jubilarse en junio.
6. Este año me gradúo de la universidad.

72 La investigación

–Lucas, ¿qué tal tu investigación? ¿Encontraste información sobre leyendas tradicionales hispanas?

–Sí, claro. Primero fui a la biblioteca. Había muchos libros de leyendas, pero eran muy largas y muy difíciles.

–¿No leíste ninguna?

–Sí, tranquila. Leí una leyenda corta muy interesante. Y también encontré otras en Internet. ¿Y tú?

–Yo fui a la universidad. Conozco a un profesor de Español y lo entrevisté. Y también fui a un restaurante mexicano que hay en mi barrio y hablé con algunas personas.

–¡Qué buena idea!

–Me contaron una leyenda muy bonita. ¿Quieres oírla?

–Claro. Cuéntamela.

84 Los momentos de la vida

1. Diego y Cristina se casaron el 22 de junio en la catedral.
2. Era el veinte de mayo cuando me gradué de la universidad.
3. Elena y Carlos hicieron un viaje a Hawái para celebrar su aniversario.
4. Carolina estaba embarazada cuando vino a vivir a Nueva York.
5. El jueves pasado Antonio le regaló un anillo a Anita. Creo que se van a casar el próximo año.

Unit 1
¿Cómo eres?

The Unit

- The theme for Unit 1 is personal relationships. The participants will learn how these relationships are expressed as they describe people's physical characteristics and personality traits, family relationships, and the cycle of life.

- Andy and Tess, two veterans of *Fans del español*, will give the participants their tasks.
  - *Desafío 1.* Michelle and Daniel have to find out more about a famous comic strip from Argentina and then write and illustrate their own original comic strip.
  - *Desafío 2.* Eva and Ethan will learn about some famous works of art by Hispanic painters and then create an audio guide for their school's art department webpage.
  - *Desafío 3.* Asha and Lucas will explore some well-known Hispanic legends and then try their hand at writing one of their own.

Activities	Standards	Resources
¿Cómo eres?	1.2, 2.2, 3.1	Video

Teaching Suggestions

Warm-Up / Independent Starter

- Have students look at the photos, and ask them to come up with a "story" for one of the images. Students who are familiar with the cartoon strip, Botero's art, or *la Llorona* may include some of this information; others must rely on their imagination. Have students write their stories.

Preparation

- Ask students to read the captions and predict the topic for each challenge. For example, they may answer that the first image is a cartoon; the second is about paintings, portraits, or politics; and the last image deals with legends.

- Have students read each *Desafío's* objective, as well as the vocabulary and grammar goals, then discuss how each illustration might relate to these objectives and goals.

12

UNIDAD 1

¿Cómo eres?
Las personas y la familia

Fernando Botero (Colombia).
La familia presidencial

DESAFÍO 1

▶ **Describir personas**

Vocabulario
Características físicas y rasgos de personalidad

Gramática
Ser y *estar*

Las comparaciones y el superlativo

Personajes de *Mafalda* (Argentina)

DESAFÍO 2

▶ **Hablar de acciones pasadas**

Vocabulario
Relaciones familiares

Gramática
El imperfecto y el pasado continuo

Expresar posesión

12 doce

The Challenge

DESAFÍO 1

Personajes de *Mafalda*

Mafalda is the main character of an Argentinean comic strip that ran from 1964 to 1973. It became popular in many countries, generating two animated cartoons and a movie. Mafalda is an unusually perceptive 6-year-old girl who is concerned about humanity and world peace. Her reflections often echoed existing political and social issues. The comic strip also introduces readers to Mafalda's parents, siblings, and friends, including one very little friend called Libertad (Freedom), suggesting the cartoonist's interpretation of the little freedom there is in society.

DESAFÍO 2

Fernando Botero. *La familia presidencial*

Works by Colombian artist Fernando Botero (b. 1932) are easily identifiable; the people and objects depicted are disproportionately large. These exaggerated figures, which some call *boterismo*, show people in daily life, as well as historical characters and events. Botero often paints figures of power and authority, but the irony and criticism in his work are most often shown with good humor. Botero's style eliminates brushwork and texture to obtain a smooth look as in *La familia presidencial*, where characters all seem to have an inflated sense of importance.

¿Cómo eres?

DESAFÍO 3

▶ **Narrar y describir en pasado**

Vocabulario
Biografías

Gramática
El pretérito y el imperfecto

Expresiones temporales para la narración

La leyenda de la Llorona (México)

trece 13

Picture Discussion

- Have students look at the images again and review their predictions about each topic. Then ask them to read the stories from their Independent Starters and share their predictions and any information they may have on these topics in a class discussion.

Personajes de *Mafalda* (Argentina)

- Ask students to describe the physical characteristics of the characters pictured and then predict what they think these characters' personalities might be like. Students should use both *ser* and *estar* in their descriptions. For example: *El primer personaje es un señor moreno, que tiene una nariz muy grande. Parece que está cansado.* Encourage students to be creative.

Fernando Botero (Colombia). *La familia presidencial*

- Focus students' attention on the shapes of the people in the foreground and the mountains in the background of the painting. What do they have in common? (They are all rotund figures.) Explain that the artist also painted himself in the background. Ask students why they think Botero might have done this. Do they know any other works of art in which the artist included himself or herself?

La leyenda de la Llorona (México)

- Have students focus on the figure of the woman in the image and ask them what they think she is doing. (crying) Do they think she is a comical or tragic figure? What natural feature can they identify in the image? (a river) How do they think this body of water will play into the legend? Can they name other tragic characters from legends they may know?

Objectives

- By the end of Unit 1, students will be able to
  - Describe and compare people.
  - Talk about customary and ongoing actions in the past.
  - Express possession.
  - Talk about the cycle of life.
  - Tell a story in the past.
  - Talk about famous Hispanic cartoon characters, describe some famous portraits by Hispanic painters, and familiarize themselves with some legends from around the Hispanic world.

DESAFÍO 3

La leyenda de la Llorona

While many legends explain the origins of things or natural phenomena, others are cautionary tales that parents might use to foster proper behavior in their children. La Llorona is of this latter category. The legend, which has several versions, tells the story of a beautiful woman who kills her own children. Although she is deeply remorseful, her repentance does not grant her peace and she is condemned to walk the Earth sobbing. Parents often use this legend to warn their children that they may be taken by the Llorona if they behave badly or stay out late at night.

13

Unit 1
Las tareas

Presentation

- In this section, the three pairs listen to a message recorded by Andy and Tess, former participants in *Fans del español*, who describe the challenges that lie ahead. Students will preview useful expressions for organizing a text, giving instructions, expressing likes and personal interests, asking for confirmation, and expressing hopes and wishes.

Activities	Standards	Resources
Texto	1.2, 2.1, 2.2, 3.1, 5.1	Vis. Pres.
1.	1.1, 1.2, 2.1, 2.2, 3.1	
2.	1.1, 1.2, 1.3	

Teaching Suggestions

Warm-Up / Independent Starter

- Have students list, in a three-column chart, all of the expressions they know in Spanish for organizing a text (i.e., sequence words), giving instructions, and expressing likes and personal interests. For example:

Organizar	Instrucciones	Gustos
primero	tener que + infinitive	gustar

Preparation

- Acquaint or reacquaint students with Andy and Tess. Explain that Andy is from Atlanta, GA, and that he used to travel with his older sister, Janet. Tess is from San Antonio, TX, and she used to travel with her mother, Patricia.

- Invite volunteers to share their Independent Starters. Discuss the uses of the expressions students mention. Then ask students to read through the text on this page and classify, in the same chart, the expressions they find for organizing a text, giving instructions, and expressing likes and personal interests.

- You may want to review the construction *ir a +* infinitive as another way to indicate the future. Ask students to point out this use in the text.

14

Las tareas

Personajes famosos

 Our characters are trying to demonstrate that they, too, are true *Fans del español*. What will they have to do? What will their tasks be? The clue is in a message recorded by Andy and Tess, two former *Fans del español*. This is what Andy and Tess say in the message:

ANDY: Hola, amigos, ¡bienvenidos a Fans del español! Ya saben quién soy, ¿verdad? Sí, soy Andy, y estoy aquí con Tess para guiarlos por el emocionante mundo del español.

TESS: Hola. Yo soy Tess y estoy encantada de participar en esta nueva aventura del español. ¡Ustedes van a aprender y a divertirse mucho! Estas son las tareas que deben realizar. ¡Tomen nota!

ANDY: Seguro que les interesa mucho el tema de las personas y la familia, ¿no es cierto? Pues van a investigar sobre él.

TESS: Y van a completar unas tareas, claro.

ANDY: Primero, van a familiarizarse con unos personajes muy particulares de la cultura hispana… ¡para escribir una tira cómica!

TESS: Después, van a investigar sobre familias y cuadros famosos. Y van a elaborar una audioguía para la página web de su escuela.

ANDY: Y, por último, van a entrar en el fascinante mundo de las leyendas tradicionales…

TESS: Y deben inventar una leyenda.

ANDY: Les deseamos mucha suerte y esperamos que lo pasen muy bien. ¡Hasta pronto!

Differentiated Instruction

DEVELOPING LEARNERS

- Have students answer the following questions about Andy and Tess's message. Then have them use the answers to summarize what was written. Finally, have students read their summaries to a partner.
  1. ¿Quiénes asignan las tareas?
  2. ¿Cuáles son las tres tareas que les asignan a las tres parejas?
  3. ¿Cómo van a prepararse para las tareas?
  4. ¿Qué les desean Andy y Tess a los participantes?

EXPANDING LEARNERS

- Have students write a response to Andy and Tess. They must:
  - Introduce themselves to Andy and Tess, including a physical description of themselves.
  - Tell how they feel about the challenges in this unit and how they think each participant pair will fare.
  - Conclude their response with a bit of personal knowledge on each of the challenges.
- Once students have finished with their responses, ask volunteers to read their responses to the class.

Bueno, ¿qué te parece?

A mí me parece que la audioguía es una actividad muy interesante.

Sí, a mí también me interesa mucho el arte.

Excelente. ¿Conoces a Mafalda? Es la protagonista de las tiras cómicas de Quino, un artista argentino.

Pues a mí me encantan las leyendas.

Podemos inventarnos una leyenda emocionante. ¡Yo soy muy creativo!

1 **¿Comprendes?**

▶ **Responde** a estas preguntas.

1. ¿Cuál es el tema sobre el que van a investigar los personajes?
2. ¿Qué tareas les proponen Andy y Tess a nuestros amigos?
3. ¿Cuál de los tres desafíos te parece más interesante? ¿Por qué?

▶ **Une** las columnas. ¿Qué tienen que hacer los personajes para realizar cada tarea?

Ⓐ

1. Escribir una tira cómica.
2. Elaborar una audioguía.
3. Inventar una leyenda.

Ⓑ

a. Describir algunos cuadros.
b. Familiarizarse con personajes de tiras cómicas.
c. Investigar sobre tradiciones de la cultura hispana.

2 **Investiga**

▶ **Escribe** tres palabras del texto que sean nuevas para ti. ¿Qué crees que significan?

quince 15

Unit 1

Las tareas

👁 Texto: Personajes famosos

- Read the introduction to the text. Then ask students why they believe it is significant for two former *Fans del español* to introduce the challenges to the new participants. Ask for two volunteers to read the text aloud. What do students think about the challenges?

- Ask students to get into pairs and read the dialogues on page 15 to find out what the participants think about the challenges. Discuss with students the participants' reactions.

Activities

2. After completing this activity, ask students to identify any false cognate in the text, say what it means, and explain how it might be confused. (*realizar*: to accomplish; it could be confused with "to realize," which is *darse cuenta*) Point out the word *particulares* in Andy's dialogue and brainstorm with the class other words that he might have used to convey the same meaning: *especiales, singulares, propios*. You may want to point out the other meaning of *particulares*: private, as in *un asunto particular* (a private matter). *Particular* also means "peculiar." Finally, *particular* is often used in expressions such as *este trabajo no tiene nada de particular* (there's nothing special about this job). Have students compare and contrast these meanings with the word *particular* in English.

Answer Key

1. 1. Van a investigar sobre el tema de las personas y la familia.

2. Escribir una tira cómica, elaborar una audioguía para la página web de su escuela e inventar una leyenda.

3. Answers will vary.

▶ 1. b 2. a 3. c

2. Answers will vary.

Additional Resources

Fans Online activities
Practice Workbook

HERITAGE LANGUAGE LEARNERS

- Have students write about the challenge that is the most appealing to them and explain why. They should also include a list of the kind of personality traits or skills that are necessary to successfully complete the task, and explain how they would complete the challenge.

CRITICAL THINKING

- Ask students to think about the challenges for this unit. Have them explain why the challenges begin with *una tira cómica*, continue with *una audioguía*, and end with *una leyenda*. Remind them to think about what kind of preparation is involved for each challenge and the skills necessary to accomplish the task. Have students first write their ideas on a sheet of paper. Then ask volunteers to share their ideas with the class.

15

Unit 1
Antes de empezar

Presentation

- In this section, students will learn a variety of useful expressions, some for organizing a text, others for giving instructions, expressing likes and personal interests, asking for confirmation, and expressing hopes and wishes.
- Students will also review nouns that name family relationships and adjectives that describe physical characteristics, personality traits, feelings and states of mind, as well as vocabulary used for obtaining personal information.

Activities	Standards	Resources
Expresiones útiles	1.2, 2.1	
3.	1.1, 1.2, 2.1, 5.1, 5.2	
4.	1.2, 1.3	
Recuerda	1.2	
5.	1.2, 1.3	
6.	1.1, 1.2, 1.3	

Teaching Suggestions

Warm-Up / Independent Starter

- Have students list words they know that describe people's physical characteristics and personality traits. To get them started you may suggest: *alto, bajo, rubio, guapo, simpático, antipático, tímido.*

Preparation

- Go over the *expresiones útiles* by using them in personalized contexts. For example, you might give students instructions by telling them the following: *Primero abran el libro. Después lean las palabras de la página 17. Luego busquen las palabras que no recuerden en el diccionario. Finalmente, describan a un(a) compañero(a), sin decir su nombre, usando por lo menos cinco de estas palabras.*
- Have students read their descriptions aloud and ask volunteers to guess who is being described. As students read their descriptions, write any words on the board that listeners appear to have trouble identifying and clarify their meaning. Remind students that adjectives must agree with the noun they are modifying.

16

EXPRESIONES ÚTILES

Para organizar un texto:
- Primero…
- Después…
- Luego…
- Finalmente…

Para dar instrucciones:
- Deben inventar una leyenda.
- ¡Tomen nota!

Para expresar gustos e intereses personales:
- A mí me encanta(n)…
- A mí me interesa(n)…

Para pedir confirmación:
- …¿verdad?
- …¿no es cierto?

Para expresar deseos:
- Les deseamos mucha suerte.
- Esperamos que lo pasen bien.
- Ojalá aprendan mucho.
- ¡Que se diviertan!

3 ¡Que tengas suerte!

▶ **Relaciona** las expresiones con las fotografías correspondientes.

a. ¡Que sean muy felices!
b. Me interesa mucho este trabajo.
c. Esta es la respuesta correcta, ¿verdad?
d. Espero que les salga bien el examen.

4 Organización

▶ **Escribe** un párrafo ordenando estas acciones de forma lógica. Utiliza las expresiones útiles que sirven para organizar un texto.

Los fans del español… Modelo *Primero, los fans del español…*
1. Van a hacer un proyecto y van a presentarlo.
2. Van a investigar sobre un tema.
3. Tienen que escuchar un mensaje grabado.
4. Van a decidir el tema de investigación.

16 dieciséis

Differentiated Instruction

DEVELOPING LEARNERS

- Display photos of different families. You may choose to include funny pictures from websites or awkward family photos to vary students' responses. Have them comment on the photos using some of the *expresiones útiles* and then identify each family member. Ask them to describe the person in terms of physical appearance and personality traits. If students are having difficulty describing the people in the photo, you may choose to review the vocabulary either using photos or by acting out the word.

EXPANDING LEARNERS

- Ask students to work in groups of three and create a dialogue using as many of the *expresiones útiles* as they can. They may, for instance, have a conversation about the challenges the three pairs will be facing.
  - A. *Primero Michelle y Daniel deben familiarizarse con Mafalda, ¿verdad?*
  - B. *Sí. Me parece una actividad muy divertida.*
  - C. *Entender el humor en otro idioma es difícil. Ojalá puedan hacerlo.*
- Ask groups to practice their lines. Then call on them to come before the class and present their skits.

Antes de empezar

RECUERDA

Relaciones familiares

el padre	la madre
el/la hijo(a)	el/la hermano(a)
el/la abuelo(a)	el/la nieto(a)
el/la tío(a)	el/la sobrino(a)

Características físicas

alto(a)	bajo(a)
gordo(a)	delgado(a)
moreno(a)	rubio(a)

Rasgos de personalidad

perezoso(a)	trabajador(a)
tacaño(a)	generoso(a)
serio(a)	gracioso(a)
optimista	pesimista

Estados de ánimo y sentimientos

aburrido(a)	divertido(a)
contento(a)	triste
frustrado(a)	furioso(a)
tranquilo(a)	nervioso(a)

Información personal

nombre	estado civil
apellidos	domicilio
fecha de nacimiento	número de identidad
lugar de nacimiento	

5 **¿Cuánto sabes?**

▶ **Lee** las palabras del cuadro y escribe otras palabras de cada tema.

Modelo *Relaciones familiares: el/la primo(a), el/la esposo(a)…*

6 **Relaciones personales**

▶ **Completa** un gráfico como este con el vocabulario que sabes del tema de esta unidad. Después, compáralo con el gráfico de un(a) compañero(a) y añade más palabras al tuyo.

primo(a) → Relaciones familiares
esposo(a)
Características físicas
Rasgos de personalidad
Información personal
Estados de ánimo y sentimientos

Activities

3. Before attempting to complete this activity, have students come up with sentences that describe what is happening in each scene. Then ask them to use those sentences to complete the activity and justify their answers.

4. After students complete the activity, have them write some steps in a process, which could be a school project, a recipe, or rules to a game. Be sure they use sequence words to clarify the order in which the steps must be done.

5. Ask students to use their lists from the Independent Starter to assist them in this activity. When they have finished writing additional words, have them describe a person in terms of his or her relationship to other members of the family. Then ask them to describe that relationship to a partner, who must identify the family member. For example: *Magda es la hija de mi tío Carlos. Magda es mi... (prima)*

6. To extend this activity, have student pairs get together with three other pairs of students and create a master chart that displays all of their words. You also may have students bring in a photo of a celebrity, political figure, or sports star and have them complete another chart for this person like the one on the page.

Answer Key

3. 1. a   2. c   3. d   4. b

4. Paragraphs will vary, but the correct sequence of events is: 3, 4, 2, 1.

5. Answers will vary.

6. Answers will vary.

Additional Resources

Fans Online activities
Practice Workbook

HERITAGE LANGUAGE LEARNERS

• In addition to the *expresiones útiles* listed on page 16, ask students to come up with other ways for giving instructions, expressing likes and personal interests, and expressing hopes and wishes. Ask students to make a three-column chart with the expressions under the appropriate heading. After they complete their charts, have them write several sample sentences with the new expressions, read them to the class, and explain what they mean.

TOTAL PHYSICAL RESPONSE (TPR)

• Ask students to get into pairs and to use the *Para dar instrucciones* and *Para expresar gustos e intereses personales* sections of the *Expresiones útiles* to play a game. One student gives an instruction and the other student acts it out. If the student correctly acts out the order, then the first student will say how he or she feels about the action. Students will then switch roles. For example:

A. *¡Toma notas!*

B. (Pretends to take notes in a notebook.)

A. *Correcto. A mí me encanta tomar notas en clase.*

Unit 1

DESAFÍO 1

Describir personas

Presentation

- In *Desafío 1*, Michelle and Daniel become acquainted with the Argentinean comic strip *Mafalda*. Students will preview language used to describe and compare people's personality traits and physical characteristics.

Activities	Standards	Resources
Texto	1.2, 2.1, 2.2	Vis. Pres.
7.	1.2, 1.3, 2.2	
8.	1.1, 1.2, 1.3, 2.2	
9.	1.1, 1.2, 2.2	Audio
10. Cultura	1.1, 1.2, 2.1, 2.2, 3.1, 4.2, 5.1	

Teaching Suggestions

Warm-Up / Independent Starter

- Have students brainstorm some famous comic strip characters they know. How many of these characters are children? What are the topics that are of interest to these characters?

Preparation

- Invite volunteers to share their Independent Starters with the class. Is the class familiar with some of these characters? Then ask for a volunteer to read the introduction to the dialogue. Do students know who Mafalda is?

Texto: Una argentina famosa

- Ask students to observe the characters depicted on this page and mention two physical characteristics for each one. Then have pairs read the dialogue. Now that they have met the characters, do they see any relationship between the characters' appearance and their personality?

- Read aloud the comic strip at the bottom of the page and discuss it as a class. What does the comic strip tell us about Susanita?

Activities

7. After students complete the activity, have them work with a partner and describe another character in the comic strip without revealing his/her name. Partners have to guess who it is.

18

Una argentina famosa

 Michelle and Daniel will write a comic strip, but first they must familiarize themselves with *Mafalda*, a famous comic strip from Argentina, and with other comic heroes.

Mafalda

Libertad

Susanita

Miguelito

Manolito

Felipe

Guille

MICHELLE: Mira, esta es Mafalda. Es una niña argentina de pelo negro. Tiene seis años.

DANIEL: Parece muy inteligente. ¿Y estos son sus amigos?

MICHELLE: Sí. Se llaman Libertad, Susanita, Miguelito, Manolito y Felipe. Y el más pequeño es Guille, su hermano.

DANIEL: ¿Manolito es el niño rubio y alto?

MICHELLE: No, ese es Felipe. Manolito es tan alto como Felipe, pero es más gordo y tiene el pelo corto y castaño.

DANIEL: Ya sé quién es. Entonces el niño pequeño y rubio es Miguelito. ¿Y Susanita?

MICHELLE: Es la niña rubia del pelo rizado.

DANIEL: ¿Y cómo es Mafalda?

MICHELLE: Pues es una niña muy crítica y algo pesimista, pero es muy graciosa. Ella está preocupada por la paz mundial, el futuro del planeta...

DANIEL: ¿Y sus amigos también?

MICHELLE: Cada uno tiene su personalidad. Felipe es muy tímido y pesimista, y está enamorado de una vecina. Manolito, en cambio, es muy ambicioso: siempre piensa en el negocio familiar y en tener muchas tiendas. Y Susanita solo piensa en casarse y tener muchos hijos. Mira, aquí tienes a Susanita.

7 Detective de palabras

▶ **Completa** estas oraciones.

1. Mafalda tiene el pelo ___1___ .
2. El niño ___2___ y alto se llama Felipe.
3. Felipe es tan ___3___ como Manolito.
4. Manolito es más ___4___ que Felipe y tiene el pelo corto y ___5___ .
5. Miguelito tiene el pelo ___6___ .

Differentiated Instruction

DEVELOPING LEARNERS

- Before students read the text, have them look at the pictures of the *Mafalda* characters and brainstorm a list of the physical characteristics and personality traits that they remember. As they read through the dialogue, they should make a note of any words they already knew that are used, or any words that seem like synonyms for words they included in their lists.

EXPANDING LEARNERS

- Ask students to re-read the *Mafalda* characters' physical descriptions and choose the one that most closely matches their own physical description. Then have students read the characters' personality traits and choose the one that is closest to their own personality traits. Is it the same character? Once students have chosen their character or characters, have them get into pairs and read the lines that best describe themselves to their partner.

8 ¿Comprendes?

▶ **Responde** a estas preguntas.

1. ¿Quién es Mafalda? ¿De dónde es?
2. ¿Cómo se llama el hermano de Mafalda?
3. Para Susanita, ¿cómo es el *futuro perfecto*?

▶ **Describe** a un personaje de Mafalda con ayuda del texto y de los dibujos. Habla de sus características físicas y su personalidad.

9 Los amigos de Mafalda

▶ **Escucha** a Michelle y a Daniel, y elige la opción correcta.

1. Mafalda está _____ por las noticias de la radio.
   a. contenta   b. triste   c. preocupada

2. Susanita tiene el pelo _____.
   a. rubio y corto   b. rubio y rizado   c. moreno y largo

3. Susanita siempre está _____ con Manolito.
   a. enojada   b. enamorada   c. contenta

4. Manolito es un niño _____.
   a. perezoso   b. ambicioso   c. optimista

5. Miguelito tiene el pelo en forma de _____.
   a. lechuga   b. almacén   c. cepillo

6. Miguelito es _____.
   a. perezoso   b. creativo   c. divertido

CULTURA
Mafalda

Mafalda es la tira cómica más famosa de Argentina. Su autor es el dibujante Joaquín Salvador Lavado, que firma como Quino. Quino creó este personaje en los años sesenta del siglo pasado para denunciar *(to criticize)* con humor los problemas sociales y la política mundial.

Mafalda vive en Buenos Aires (Argentina), en una familia de clase media. Es una niña idealista y preocupada por la paz mundial que se rebela contra el mundo de los adultos.

Quino
(Argentina).

10 Piensa y explica.
¿Crees que es efectivo usar el humor para criticar la sociedad y la política? ¿Conoces otras formas de arte que sirven para denunciar aspectos negativos de la sociedad?

HERITAGE LANGUAGE LEARNERS

• Ask students to analyze the comic strip presented on page 18. Have them think about what the teacher asked (*¿Futuro perfecto de amar?*) and how Susanita was supposed to respond. If students don't know, ask them to look up the future perfect conjugation of *amar.* (*yo habré amado*) Then have students say what they think Susanita was saying when she answered *¡HIJITOS!* What does this show us about Susanita's personality? Do students think this is typical for someone her age?

CRITICAL THINKING

• Using what they have learned in the dialogue, ask students to write one sentence that each of the *Mafalda* characters would say that would demonstrate their personality traits. Students can write each of these sentences on a separate piece of paper or index card, and trade with a partner. Can their partner infer which person is speaking?

---

8. Have students prepare a description of a famous comic strip character from the information they noted in the Independent Starter activity. Ask them to read their descriptions aloud without revealing the character's identity and ask the class to guess who the *personaje* is.

 AUDIO SCRIPT
See page 11l.

 CULTURA

Mafalda

Argentina, like many other nations in Latin America, has had a turbulent history, marked by military coups, repression, and corruption: ideal material for social and political commentary. A coup d'état brought the military to power in 1976, and from that date until 1983 the military led what has been called *la Guerra Sucia* (the Dirty War) against those who opposed the regime. Because of repression during *la Guerra Sucia*, political and social criticism had to be kept subtle, as in a comic strip. Popular pressure finally restored democracy to the country in 1983.

Answer Key

7. 1. negro   3. alto   5. castaño
    2. rubio   4. gordo   6. rubio

8. 1. Es un personaje de una tira cómica. Es de Argentina.
    2. Se llama Guille.
    3. Es un futuro con *hijitos*. Piensa casarse y tener muchos hijos.
    ▶ Answers will vary.

9. 1. c   2. b   3. a   4. b   5. a   6. b

10. Answers will vary.

Additional Resources

Fans Online activities

DESAFÍO 1

Vocabulario – Características físicas y rasgos de personalidad

Presentation

- In this section, students will learn words that describe physical characteristics and personality traits.

Activities	Standards	Resources
Vocabulario	1.2, 2.2	
11.	1.1, 1.2	
12.	1.1, 1.2, 1.3, 2.2	
13.	1.2, 1.3, 2.2	Audio
14.	1.1, 1.2, 1.3, 4.2, 5.1	
15. Cultura	1.1, 1.2, 2.1, 2.2, 4.2, 5.1	

Teaching Suggestions

Warm-Up / Independent Starter

- Have students describe each of the characters depicted on this page with two adjectives.

Preparation

- Read aloud the words in the *Más vocabulario* feature and have students repeat them after you. Then do the same with the highlighted words on the page. Point out that many of these new words are defined in the reading (e.g., *amistoso = con muchos amigos*). For those words that are not defined in the text, use body language or point to images on the page that will help students comprehend their meaning.

Activities

13. Before playing the audio, give students a couple of minutes to look at the pictures and think of words that describe each of the characters. Then play the audio and have students complete the activity. Were their descriptive words used in the audio? Which ones?

14. If students have no favorite comic book character, ask them to invent one. This fictitious character should have a name, some special personality traits, and be accompanied by an illustration that shows other students what he or she looks like. Then have students use this as their model and complete the activity.

20

Vocabulario

Características físicas y rasgos de personalidad

Este es Condorito, el personaje de tira cómica más famoso de Chile. Tiene los ojos muy grandes. Es un personaje **amistoso**, con muchos amigos. Te los voy a presentar.

Yayita es la novia de Condorito. Es muy bonita: tiene los ojos **almendrados** y el pelo **lacio** y **castaño**. Es muy risueña, siempre se está riendo. Y es muy **bondadosa**, siempre ayuda a los demás.

La madre de Yayita es doña Tremebunda. Ella es **chismosa**, siempre critica a otras personas. Su esposo es don Cuasimodo, que es **calvo** y tiene **bigote**. Don Cuasimodo es muy **egoísta**, solo piensa en sí mismo.

Y este es Pepe Cortisona, rival de Condorito. Es **apuesto**, es decir, bastante guapo, y **seguro de sí mismo**.

Condorito

Yayita   Doña Tremebunda   Don Cuasimodo   Pepe Cortisona

Más vocabulario

Rasgos físicos

la barba	beard
el bigote	mustache
la cicatriz	scar
el lunar	mole
las pecas	freckles
pelo lacio	straight hair
pelo rizado	curly hair

Cualidades

amable, cortés	kind, nice
cariñoso(a)	warm, affectionate
comprensivo(a)	understanding
fiel	faithful
reservado(a), tímido(a)	shy
travieso(a)	mischievous

11 **Definiciones**

▶ **Une** las dos columnas.

Ⓐ
1. apuesto
2. amistoso
3. chismoso
4. egoísta
5. bondadoso
6. travieso

Ⓑ
a. No piensa en los demás.
b. Es bueno y generoso.
c. Es muy atractivo.
d. No le gusta estar quieto.
e. Tiene muchos amigos.
f. Le gusta hablar de los demás.

20 veinte

Differentiated Instruction

DEVELOPING LEARNERS

- Have students use the vocabulary to describe the following celebrities. If students don't know who the celebrities are, then allow students to look them up on the Internet.
  – Matt Damon
  – Lady Gaga
  – Justin Timberlake
  – Beyoncé

EXPANDING LEARNERS

- Have students play a game of "Guess Who" in Spanish. They will use the *Mafalda* characters and the characters on these pages as their list of characters. In pairs, both students will choose one character. Then they take turns to ask and answer yes/no questions about the physical characteristics or personality traits of the character. For example:

  A. ¿Es mujer?
  B. *No.*
  A. ¿Tiene bigote?
  B. *Sí.*

  A. ¿Es egoísta?
  B. *Sí.*
  A. ¿Es don Cuasimodo?
  B. *¡Sí!*

12 Describelos

▶ **Mira** las ilustraciones de la ficha de Vocabulario (página 20) y escribe.

1. ¿Cómo es la novia de Condorito? ¿Cómo va vestida?
2. ¿Cómo es doña Tremebunda? ¿Cómo va vestida?

13 ¿Quién es?

▶ **Escucha** a Michelle y a Daniel y ordena las ilustraciones.

 Ⓐ   Ⓑ    Ⓒ    Ⓓ

| Don Quijote y Sancho Panza | Zipi y Zape | Rompetechos | Mortadelo y Filemón |

▶ **Escucha** otra vez y escribe. ¿Qué características físicas y qué rasgos de personalidad mencionan Michelle y Daniel de cada personaje?

14 Mis estrellas del cómic

▶ **Escribe** un párrafo sobre tus personajes de cómic favoritos y explica cómo son. Después, lee las descripciones de tu compañero(a) y pregúntale por sus personajes favoritos.

Modelo *Mi personaje de cómic favorito es Calvin. Es pelirrojo y muy travieso. Me gusta porque...*

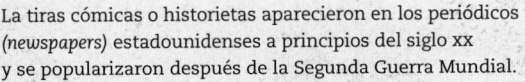

CULTURA

Las tiras cómicas

La tiras cómicas o historietas aparecieron en los periódicos *(newspapers)* estadounidenses a principios del siglo xx y se popularizaron después de la Segunda Guerra Mundial.

Una de las primeras tiras cómicas de América Latina fue *Condorito*, creada en 1949 por el artista chileno René *Pepo* Ríos. El personaje principal es un cóndor que vive en un pueblo imaginario llamado Pelotillehue.

Como en otros cómics, en *Condorito* los personajes y las situaciones son estereotipos que reflejan diversos aspectos de la sociedad.

15 **Habla.** ¿Qué tiras cómicas de tu país conoces? ¿Cómo muestran la sociedad?

DESAFÍO 1

Vocabulario – Características físicas y rasgos de personalidad

 AUDIO SCRIPT
See page 11I.

 CULTURA

Las tiras cómicas

The Spanish cartoon characters Zipi and Zape are the creation of José Escobar Saliente. These twins love soccer, and are always getting into trouble. Spain's Mortadelo and Filemón, and Rompetechos are the invention of Francisco Ibáñez, and all three are capable of bungling anything put before them. Rompetechos is the cartoonist's favorite, and in Spain this character has had a stamp issued in his honor.

Answer Key

11. 1. c   2. e   3. f   4. a   5. b   6. d

12. Answers will vary. Sample answers:
1. Es guapa, bondadosa y risueña. Tiene los ojos almendrados y el pelo lacio y castaño. Lleva un pantalón verde y una blusa amarilla.
2. Doña Tremebunda es chismosa y gorda. Lleva un vestido rosado y un bolso.

13. A, C, B, D
▶ Don Quijote es alto, delgado e idealista. Sancho Panza es bajo, gordo y fiel. Rompetechos es calvo y lleva gafas; es optimista. Zipi y Zape son gemelos y traviesos; uno es rubio y el otro moreno. Mortadelo y Filemón son detectives; Mortadelo es divertido y creativo; Filemón es el jefe y es muy serio.

14. Answers will vary.

15. Answers will vary.

Additional Resources

Fans Online activities
Practice Workbook

HERITAGE LANGUAGE LEARNERS

• There are several expressions used to describe people that vary in different parts of the Spanish-speaking world. For example, *pelo chino* is used in Mexico to describe curly hair. Ask students to come up with a list of the words from their region of origin to describe someone's physical characteristics. Make a class list and encourage students to use both the vocabulary words and the regional words as they apply throughout the chapter.

MULTIPLE INTELLIGENCES:
Visual-Spatial Intelligence

• Have students work in pairs. Provide a photo of a person to one partner, who then has thirty seconds to study the photo. Collect the photos and display all of them. Then have the partner who studied the photo describe the person in the photo to his or her partner. The partner must then select the photo out of the line-up that best fits with the description. Then have the partners switch roles using different photos.

DESAFÍO 1

Gramática – *Ser y estar*

Presentation

- In this section, students will review the uses of the verbs *ser* and *estar*.

Activities	Standards	Resources
Gramática	1.2, 3.1	
16.	4.1	
17.	1.2, 1.3	
18.	1.1	
19.	1.1, 1.3, 5.1	
20.	1.1, 1.2, 5.1, 5.2	
21. Conexiones	1.2, 2.1, 2.2, 3.1, 4.2	

Teaching Suggestions

Warm-Up / Independent Starter

- Have students read the grammar presentation silently. Then write the following sentences on the board and ask students to complete them:
  1. *Nosotros ... cansados. (estamos)*
  2. *¿De quién ... este libro? (es)*
  3. *¿Dónde ... el concierto? (es)*
  4. *¿Qué ... haciendo ustedes? (están)*
  5. *Esos zapatos ... de moda. (están)*

Preparation

- Review students' Independent Starters and then call on volunteers to explain how each verb was used. Then have different volunteers list on the board the rest of the uses of *ser* and *estar* not covered by the sentences in the Independent Starter. Work with students to come up with sentences for each use listed on the board.

Activities

17. After students have completed the activity, ask them to cite the rule for using these verbs. For example, *están de moda*: idiomatic expression; *son muy divertidos*: identifies a characteristic.

18. There are several possible descriptions. For instance, to describe the young man, students may say: *Está dormido / cansado / enfermo.* To extend this activity, ask pairs to come up with two descriptions for each photo.

Gramática

Ser y estar

- The verbs *ser* and *estar* are equivalent to the verb *to be*. In order to review the conjugation of *ser* and *estar*, see page R10.
- The use of *ser* and *estar* is sometimes complex. In general:
  - The verb *ser* is used mainly to identify people, places, and things, and to describe physical characteristics and personality traits.

    La señora Flores **es** mi profesora de Español. **Es** joven y muy inteligente.

  - The verb *estar* is used to express feelings and conditions.

    Javi **está** aburrido porque **está** enfermo.

Otros usos de *ser* y *estar*

USOS DEL VERBO SER

origin and nationality	Yo soy de Costa Rica.	date and time	Hoy es lunes y son las 10.
profession	Mi padre es profesor.	possession	Esta mochila no es mía.
membership	Ese político es republicano.	material	El reloj es de oro.
location of events	La fiesta es en mi casa.	price	Son 40 dólares.

USOS DEL VERBO ESTAR

location of people and things	Mis padres están en casa.
states	La puerta está cerrada.
ongoing actions (estar + present participle)	Estoy estudiando, ahora no puedo salir.
with bien and mal	Este ejercicio no está bien.
idiomatic expressions with de	estar de acuerdo, estar de moda, estar de viaje

- To describe someone or something, use *ser* when referring to inherent and permanent qualities, and *estar* when talking about the result of a process.

    María **es** muy guapa.   Ana **está** muy guapa con ese vestido.

16 **Compara.** ¿Qué verbos, además de *to be*, hay en inglés para los usos de *ser* y *estar*?

17 **¿Ser o estar?**

▶ **Completa** estas oraciones con la forma correcta de los verbos *ser* o *estar*.

1. Los cómics de Mafalda no ___1___ de moda en mi país, pero ___2___ muy divertidos.
2. El examen de Español ___3___ mañana, a las nueve y media.
3. Ana ___4___ preocupada porque su ejercicio ___5___ mal y tiene que repetirlo.

22 veintidós

Differentiated Instruction

DEVELOPING LEARNERS

- For students exhibiting difficulty determining whether to use *ser* or *estar*, provide sentences for them to complete with the appropriate verb. As you review the answers with students, point out the reason for using each verb. Use these sentences to begin the activity:
  1. *Yo ... de Colombia. (soy)*
  2. *Miriam ... en el parque. (está)*
  3. *Ellos ... arquitectos. ... trabajando en un proyecto. (son, Están)*
  4. *Esa blusa ... de seda. (es)*
  5. *Yo no ... de acuerdo contigo. (estoy)*

EXPANDING LEARNERS

- Have students work with a partner or in groups of three. Provide a die to each pair or group. Tell students that they will roll the die, which will determine whether they will work with *ser* or *estar*. If they roll an odd number, they must say a sentence using a form of the verb *ser*. If they roll an even number, they will use a form of the verb *estar*. Explain that they must vary the uses of the verbs. Then play the game as a class.

18 ¿Cómo están? ¿Cómo son?

 ▶ **Habla** con tu compañero(a). ¿Cómo son estas personas? ¿Cómo están?

Modelo   1. *Este hombre está dormido. Es joven y apuesto. Es moreno y...*

 ① 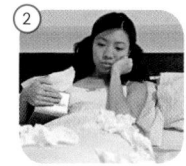 ②  ③  ④

19 Ahora mismo

▶ **Escribe** un correo electrónico a tus padres describiendo tu salón de clase. Incluye la fecha, la hora y describe el lugar y a tus compañeros.

Modelo
¡Hola! Hoy es lunes, 15 de septiembre. Ahora mismo estoy en la escuela...

20 El personaje misterioso

 ▶ **Juega** con tu compañero(a).

Tú

Imagina que eres un personaje famoso.
Tu compañero(a) debe hacerte preguntas para descubrir tu identidad. Tú solo puedes responder sí o no.

Tu compañero(a)

Tu compañero(a) es un personaje famoso.
Hazle preguntas para descubrir su identidad. Debes usar los verbos *ser* y *estar*.

Modelo   A. ¿Eres una mujer?
          B. Sí.
          A. ¿Estás casada?

CONEXIONES: LITERATURA

Don Quijote

Don Quijote es uno de los personajes más famosos de la literatura en español. Es el protagonista de la novela *Don Quijote de la Mancha*, escrita por Miguel de Cervantes en el siglo XVII. En ella el autor critica la sociedad de la época a través de las aventuras de don Quijote, un hombre que se vuelve loco *(goes mad)* y cree que es un caballero *(knight)* medieval.

21 **Investiga.** ¿Qué personajes ficticios de tu cultura son más famosos?

veintitrés 23

HERITAGE LANGUAGE LEARNERS

• Ask students to create a quiz that uses the verbs *ser* and *estar*. Their quiz must include ten multiple-choice questions and ten matching questions. Once students have finished, have them exchange their quizzes with a partner and take their partner's quiz. They must correct the other student's quiz and correct any mistakes made.

COOPERATIVE LEARNING

• Divide the class into groups of no more than four. Be sure to include students with different learning abilities in each group. Tell the class that they must create original example sentences for each of the uses of *ser* and *estar*. Students may illustrate their sentences. Then have the groups present their sentences to the class.

---

20. You might play this as a game, with the class divided into two teams competing against each other. Set a timer and see which team has the most correct answers in the time allowed.

CONEXIONES: LITERATURA

Don Quijote

More than four hundred years after its publication, *El ingenioso hidalgo don Quijote de la Mancha* continues to have universal appeal. Don Quijote has spent so much time reading books of chivalry that he becomes mad and is convinced that he is a knight. With a suit of old armor, his nag Rocinante, and the help of his neighbor, Sancho Panza (who becomes his squire), Don Quijote seeks adventures and aims to help the downtrodden.

Answer Key

16. Answers will vary. Sample answer:
Look → *You look very beautiful tonight.* (Estás guapísima esta noche.) *Taste* → *The soup tastes delicious.* (La sopa está deliciosa.) *Belong* → *This book belongs to Juan.* (Este libro es de Juan.)

17. 1. están   3. es   5. está
     2. son   4. está

18. Answers will vary. Sample answers:
     2. Esta chica está enferma. Es joven. Tiene el pelo negro y largo.
     3. Este señor es serio. Tiene el pelo rubio y corto. Lleva gafas y tiene bigote.
     4. Esta chica es guapa. Tiene el pelo rubio y largo. Está contenta.

19. Answers will vary.

20. Answers will vary.

21. Answers will vary.

Additional Resources

Fans Online activities
Practice Workbook

DESAFÍO 1

Gramática – Las comparaciones y el superlativo

Presentation

- In this section, students will review comparisons of equality, superiority, and inferiority, as well as comparative adjectives and the superlative.

Activities	Standards	Resources
Gramática	1.2, 3.1	
22.	4.1	
23.	1.2	Audio
24.	1.1, 1.2	
25.	1.1, 1.2, 1.3, 2.2, 5.1	

Teaching Suggestions

Warm-Up / Independent Starter

- Have students read the grammar presentation silently. Encourage them to take notes on any material they have trouble understanding.

Preparation

- Encourage students to ask questions about any explanations they did not understand in the presentation and clarify this information for them.
- To help students practice the material, ask them to complete the following sentences:
  1. *Manolo y Miguel miden dos metros. Manolo es … alto como Miguel. (tan)*
  2. *Marta lee tres libros cada semana y María lee cinco. María lee … que Marta. (más)*
  3. *Tengo cinco dólares y tú tienes veinte. Yo tengo … dinero que tú. (menos)*
  4. *Pedro tiene dieciséis años y su hermana tiene veinte. Ella es … que él. (mayor)*
  5. *Esta película es mala, pero la que vi la semana pasada fue aún … (peor)*

Activities

23. After students finish this activity, play the audio one more time. Then ask them to write two new sentences: one true and one false. Have students read their sentences to a partner, who must say which statement is true and which is false and then correct the false one.

Gramática

Las comparaciones y el superlativo

Las comparaciones

- Comparisons are used to show that two or more people or things share the same quality or characteristic in equal, greater, or lesser degree.

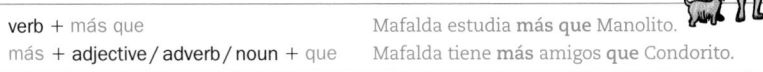

COMPARACIONES DE IGUALDAD

verb + **igual que**	Mi hermana es **igual que** Susanita.
igual de + adjective / adverb + **que**	Felipe es **igual de** alto **que** Manolito.
verb + **tanto como**	Manolito habla **tanto como** Felipe.
tanto(a)(os)(as) + noun + **como**	Condorito tiene **tanta** fama **como** Mafalda.
tan + adjective / adverb + **como**	Yo bailo **tan** bien **como** mi hermano.

COMPARACIONES DE SUPERIORIDAD

verb + **más que**	Mafalda estudia **más que** Manolito.
más + adjective / adverb / noun + **que**	Mafalda tiene **más** amigos **que** Condorito.

COMPARACIONES DE INFERIORIDAD

verb + **menos que**	Nosotros viajamos **menos que** tú.
menos + adjective / adverb / noun + **que**	Yo hablo **menos** rápido **que** tú.

- Some adjectives and adverbs have comparative forms:

bueno → mejor	grande → mayor	bien → mejor
malo → peor	pequeño → menor	mal → peor

Mafalda es **mayor** que Guille.   Yo hablo español **mejor** que tú.

El superlativo

- The superlative is used to express an extreme degree of an adjective. Remember that the superlative is formed with the ending -ísimo (see page R3).

  Esta ciudad es **famosísima**.

- The relative superlative is used to describe a noun in comparison with a larger group.

  el / la / los / las + noun + **más** / menos + adjective + de / que

  Este es **el lugar más bonito del mundo** para vivir.

22 **Compara.** ¿Hay algún adjetivo en inglés que cambie de forma cuando se usa en una comparación?

Differentiated Instruction

DEVELOPING LEARNERS

- Have students make comparative statements between two animals of their choice, such as an elephant and a mouse or a cat and a dog. You may display photos to generate comparisons. Then have students make superlative sentences about the animals, such as the most dangerous, biggest, smallest, or smartest. If students have difficulty making comparative and superlative statements, model the process for them. Point out the parts of the sentence that indicate a comparison. Then have students write their sentences independently.

EXPANDING LEARNERS

- Have students use the Internet to find a Peanuts comic strip. Ask students to use the picture of the *Mafalda* characters on page 12 to compare their physical characteristics and personality traits with those of the Peanuts characters. Tell students to pay special attention to the main characters of the comic strips, Charlie Brown and Mafalda. Ask students to compare and contrast their physical characteristics and personality traits.

23 Los vecinos

 ▶ **Escucha** la conversación entre Michelle y su hermano y decide si estas oraciones son ciertas o falsas. Después, corrige las oraciones falsas.

1. David es más alto que Xavi.
2. Xavi es menor que David.
3. David es tan optimista como Xavi.
4. Xavi es menos amistoso que David.
5. Xavi es tan cortés como David.
6. David habla tanto como Xavi.

24 ¿Quién es el más...?

▶ **Responde** a estas preguntas. Usa las comparaciones o el superlativo.

Modelo *Janet tiene el pelo más largo de la clase.*

En tu clase...

1. ¿Quién tiene el pelo más largo? ¿Y el más corto?
2. ¿Quién es el/la mayor? ¿Y el/la menor?
3. ¿Quién es tan alto(a) como tú?
4. ¿Quién es el/la más estudioso(a)?
5. ¿Quién estudia tanto como tú?
6. ¿Y quién es el/la menos chismoso(a)?

25 Comparando personajes

▶ **Lee** este texto y escribe oraciones comparando a Mafalda y a Susanita.

Modelo *Susanita no está tan preocupada por el mundo como Mafalda.*

> **Mafalda y Susanita**
>
> Mafalda dice que la sociedad está llena de problemas. Por eso ella quiere trabajar para las Naciones Unidas y crear programas para ayudar a los pobres. En cambio, Susanita quiere casarse con un hombre rico, vivir en una casa grande, tener muchos hijos, vestirse siempre a la moda y hablar sobre los demás.

▶ **Escribe** oraciones comparando a personajes de las tiras cómicas de Mafalda o de otras que conozcas. Puedes referirte a su aspecto físico o a su personalidad.

Modelo *Mafalda no es tan ambiciosa como Manolito. Ella es más...*

 ▶ **Lee** las oraciones de tu compañero(a). ¿Estás de acuerdo con todo? ¿Por qué? Coméntalo con él/ella.

veinticinco 25

Gramática – Las comparaciones y el superlativo

24. Ask students to work with a partner and have each one make up additional questions that the partner must answer using comparisons. Tell students that the comparisons do not need to be limited to classmates, but can include newsmakers and even characters from literature, film, or music.

25. To extend this activity, have students draw two figures that may be of people, animals, or things. There should be obvious differences between the two. Based on their drawings, ask students to write a brief description, comparing the figures. Call on volunteers to share their drawings and descriptions with the class.

 AUDIO SCRIPT
See page 111.

Answer Key

22. Sí, por ejemplo: *good → better, best*; *bad → worse, worst.*

23. 1. Falso. Xavi es más alto que David.
   2. Cierto.
   3. Falso. Xavi es más optimista que David.
   4. Falso. Xavi es tan amistoso como David.
   5. Cierto.
   6. Falso. David habla más que Xavi.

24. Answers will vary.

25. Answers will vary. Sample answers:
   – Susanita es más materialista que Mafalda.
   – Mafalda es más generosa que Susanita.
   – Susanita es tan joven como Mafalda.
   ▶ Answers will vary.
   ▶ Answers will vary.

Additional Resources

Fans Online activities
Practice Workbook

HERITAGE LANGUAGE LEARNERS

• Ask students to use celebrities from their culture of origin to make comparisons and use superlatives. Have students find pictures of two men, two women, and two child stars to make comparisons and use superlatives. Have them put the pictures on a sheet of paper and write the comparisons and superlatives between the pictures. Have students share their work with the class.

MULTIPLE INTELLIGENCES:
Bodily-Kinesthetic Intelligence

• Ask four students to line up by height in front of the class. Ask volunteers to make comparisons based on their height. Then have the students rearrange themselves by age. Ask volunteers to make comparisons based on their age. Then have students rearrange themselves based on the color of the shirt they are wearing, from lightest to darkest. Ask volunteers to make comparisons based on their shirt color. Finally, have students rearrange themselves by their athletic ability. Ask volunteers to make comparisons based on their athletic ability.

LECTURA: TEXTO DIALOGADO

Presentation

- In this section, students will read a dialogue, decode cognates, and identify place names contained within, as well as answer comprehension questions based on the reading.

Activities	Standards	Resources
Lectura: texto dialogado	1.1, 1.2, 2.2, 3.1, 3.2, 5.1	Vis. Pres.
26.	1.2	
27.	1.2, 1.3	
28.	1.1, 1.2	
29.	1.1, 5.1	

Teaching Suggestions

Warm-Up / Independent Starter

- Have students read the *Antes de leer* strategies silently. Then ask them to think about possible answers to the questions.

Preparation

- Call on a volunteer to answer the first question in the *Antes de leer* section. Sample response: *Una historia es la narración de un suceso. Una historieta es una historia contada por medio de dibujos.* Clarify that the word *historia* in this case means "story." Ask students if they know another meaning for the word *historia*. (history)

- In addition to the cognates cited, ask pairs of students to identify other cognates in the dialogue. (*perfecto, interesante, inventar, reservado, serio, teatro, público, actores, criminal, motivos, importantes, difícil*) Explain that about 30 to 40% of all the words in Spanish have a related word in English. Remind students that cognates facilitate vocabulary learning and enhance comprehension.

- In addition to having students find words in the dialogue that refer to places, ask them to make a list of other nouns, some naming people and others naming things.

- Read the dialogue aloud to students, modeling correct pronunciation and intonation. Then call on several pairs of students to alternate reading the dialogue aloud.

Antes de leer: estrategias

1. Lee el título del texto. ¿Cuál es la diferencia entre *historia* e *historieta*?
2. Busca los cognados. ¿Reconoces las palabras *historia*, *crimen* y *detective*? ¿Cuál va a ser el tema del diálogo?
3. Busca palabras que se refieren a lugares. ¿Sabes qué es un teatro? ¿Dónde está ese teatro? ¿Qué va a pasar?

Una historieta de detectives

DANIEL: Oye, Michelle, ¿cómo vamos a hacer nuestra historieta?

MICHELLE: ¿Qué te parece si escribimos la historia de un crimen?

DANIEL: Me parece perfecto, eso siempre es interesante. Podemos inventarnos a un detective divertido.

MICHELLE: ¡Ya lo tengo! Un detective un poco reservado y cortés, tan alto como Mortadelo, pero con barba y bigote, como don Quijote.

DANIEL: Bueno, pero que no sea muy serio… Y debe tener un ayudante muy fiel, como Sancho Panza.

MICHELLE: ¿Y dónde es el crimen?

DANIEL: En un teatro de Buenos Aires, durante una función de teatro muy exitosa. ¿Qué te parece? El teatro está lleno de público, los actores están vestidos para la función…

MICHELLE: … y entonces un actor aparece muerto en el escenario y nuestro detective debe encontrar al criminal.

DANIEL: ¡Eso! El detective pregunta a los actores. Uno estaba enojado con el actor muerto, otro estaba celoso de él… Todos tienen motivos importantes para cometer el crimen.

MICHELLE: ¡Qué difícil! ¡Espero que nuestro detective encuentre una buena pista!

26 veintiséis

Differentiated Instruction

DEVELOPING LEARNERS

- If students find the reading passage difficult, go through each line with them and restate the sentence in your own words to aid with comprehension. For example: *¿Qué te parece si escribimos la historia de un crimen?* → *¿En tu opinión, es una buena idea escribir un cuento sobre un crimen?*

EXPANDING LEARNERS

- Have students make a three-column chart with the following headings: *El detective, El crimen, Los actores.* Ask students to review the dialogue together with a classmate. As they get to information they need to complete their chart, allow students time to make notes in the appropriate columns. They should include descriptions, details of the crime, and motives for the crime.

LECTURA: TEXTO DIALOGADO

26 Definiciones

▶ **Une** las dos columnas.

Ⓐ

1. divertido
2. cortés
3. reservado
4. fiel
5. celoso

Ⓑ

a. Es gentil y educado.
b. Quiere lo que tiene otro.
c. Es buen amigo.
d. Es cómico. Tiene buen humor.
e. No le gusta mucho hablar de sí mismo.

27 Última noticia

▶ **Completa** esta noticia del periódico. Pon las palabras del cuadro en la forma correcta.

vestido
lleno
sospechoso
teatro
crimen
muerto

Crimen en el teatro

Un actor aparece ___1___ antes de la función de ___2___ del jueves. El teatro estaba ___3___ de público. Los actores estaban ___4___ para salir al escenario. El detective encuentra varios ___5___. Parece que un actor cometió el ___6___.

28 Cuéntalo tú

▶ **Describe** lo que pasa en estas escenas con tus compañeros. Usa expresiones de la lectura.

29 Con tus palabras

▶ **Responde** a estas preguntas con tu compañero(a).

1. ¿Conoces a algún detective? ¿Cómo es físicamente? ¿Y su personalidad?
2. ¿Qué crimen recuerdas? ¿Qué pasó?

Activities

26. To expand this activity, have students think of other words or phrases that define the words in column A. For example: *divertido: gracioso; cortés: con buenos modales, considerado; reservado: tímido; fiel: leal, alguien en el que puedes confiar; celoso: envidioso.*

27. After finishing this activity, have students work with a partner. Each partner will create a similar exercise: a descriptive paragraph with key words left out, and a list of these words (but not all in the correct form). Partners will exchange papers and complete each other's paragraph.

28. Have students work in small groups and role-play what is being depicted in the illustrations. Allow groups to rehearse their lines and have them come in front of the class and represent their drama.

Answer Key

26. 1. d   2. a   3. e   4. c   5. b

27. 1. muerto   4. vestidos
2. teatro   5. sospechosos
3. lleno   6. crimen

28. Answers will vary. Sample answers:

1. El lujoso teatro, en la ciudad de Buenos Aires, está lleno de público. La gente está esperando a los actores. La función va a comenzar.

2. La función comenzó y los actores están muy sorprendidos porque un actor apareció muerto en el escenario.

3. El detective debe encontrar al criminal, así que tiene que interrogar a los actores. Primero habla con uno de los actores mientras su ayudante habla con una actriz.

29. Answers will vary.

Additional Resources

Fans Online activities

HERITAGE LANGUAGE LEARNERS

• Have students create a dialogue between the detective and the murder suspects. Students should include questions the detective would ask and answers appropriate for the suspects. Remind students to keep in mind what has been said about the actors (i.e., one is jealous, the other is angry), and any other reason someone might have for killing the actor. Then have students present their dialogues to the class.

SPECIAL-NEEDS LEARNERS

• For students with difficulties staying focused while reading long passages, copy the conversation between Michelle and Daniel onto copy paper and cut the conversation into five parts: one part for each exchange. Then pair up students to read the parts together, exchange for exchange. Once students have finished, have them mix up the exchanges and try to put the conversation back together into one single piece of paper. You can leave these students in pairs as they complete the rest of the activities on this page.

DESAFÍO 1

Comunicación

Presentation

- In this section, students will integrate the vocabulary and grammar skills from *Desafío 1* in order to describe physical characteristics and personality traits, as well as to make comparisons.

Activities	Standards	Resources
30.	1.1, 1.2, 1.3, 2.2	
31.	1.1, 1.2, 2.2, 3.1, 3.2	
32.	1.1, 1.2	Audio
33. Final del desafío	1.1, 1.2, 1.3, 5.1	
Tu desafío	1.1, 1.2	

Teaching Suggestions

Warm-Up / Independent Starter

- Have students think about their best friend and how he or she is like and unlike them. Ask them to write as many sentences as they can in the time allowed. They should compare not only physical characteristics and personality traits, but also address habits and personal possessions. For example: *José es tan alto como yo, pero es más delgado. Él viaja más que yo. Tiene tantos libros como yo.*

Preparation

- To apply vocabulary from this *Desafío* and to practice making comparisons, have students create a fictitious and unlikely pair of best friends whose physical characteristics, personality traits, and likes and dislikes are diametrically opposed to each other.
- Ask students to share their descriptions with the class to see who is the most unlikely pair. Pose the following question to students: Do they think that lasting friendships are built on common interests or is it true that opposites attract? Hold a classroom discussion on this topic.

Activities

31. Have volunteers research both theaters. Then ask them to make an oral presentation to the class.

Comunicación

30 **Un diálogo de Mafalda**

 ▶ **Escribe** con tu compañero(a) un diálogo entre dos personajes de Mafalda. Después, represéntenlo. Usen estas ideas.

> Susanita dice que ama a Felipe.

> Mafalda dice que oyó más noticias sobre guerras.

> Manolito tiene una idea nueva para abrir otra tienda.

> Felipe está enamorado, pero no le dice nada a la chica porque es muy tímido.

31 **El mejor teatro**

▶ **Lee** las palabras de Michelle y Daniel sobre el teatro de Buenos Aires en el que van a localizar su historieta y responde a las preguntas.

1. El Teatro Nacional Cervantes abrió en 1921, es tradicional y clásico, y está a cinco cuadras de la plaza de la República.

Teatro Nacional Cervantes (Buenos Aires).

2. Yo encontré el Teatro Gran Rex. Está en la avenida Corrientes, a una cuadra de esa plaza. Abrió en 1937 y me gusta su estilo: es moderno y sencillo.

3. ¿Y qué capacidad tiene el Gran Rex? En el Nacional hay plazas para más de 800 personas. No está mal, ¿no?

4. El Gran Rex es mucho más grande: tiene espacio para 3.000 espectadores. Y siempre tiene los mejores espectáculos internacionales.

5. Bueno, pero el Nacional es un teatro muy popular, con mucho encanto.

6. Michelle, recuerda que necesitamos un teatro con mucho público para nuestra historieta. Creo que es más apropiado el Gran Rex...

Teatro Gran Rex (Buenos Aires).

1. ¿Qué teatro está más cerca de la Plaza de la República?
2. ¿Cuál es el teatro más antiguo? ¿Y el más grande?
3. ¿Qué diferencias hay entre los dos teatros? ¿Cuál es más tradicional?
4. En tu opinión, ¿cuál de los dos teatros es mejor para localizar la historieta? ¿Por qué?

Differentiated Instruction

DEVELOPING LEARNERS

- Have students divide a piece of paper into three parts. Then have them write one of the themes of the *Desafío* in each space (i.e., 1. physical characteristics and personality traits; 2. the verbs *ser* and *estar*; 3. comparisons and superlatives). As students go through the activities, have them write two or three examples from each activity in the corresponding space below the theme. Students can use this piece of paper to see each theme broken down and also as a review for the unit quiz and test.

EXPANDING LEARNERS

- Ask students to use the *Final del desafío* to write the opposites of each statement. For example: *¡Yo soy la mejor actriz, la más elegante, la más guapa...!* → *Yo soy la peor actriz, la menos elegante, la más fea. Y la más egoísta.* → *Y la más generosa.*

32 **¿Quién es el ladrón?**

 ▶ **Escucha** las descripciones de los sospechosos de un robo en el parque y haz un retrato robot de cada uno para ayudar a la policía.

▶ **Habla** con tu compañero(a). ¿Quién es el principal sospechoso según las descripciones?

Modelo *Creo que la chica de la bici es la principal sospechosa porque...*

Final del desafío

¡Yo soy la mejor actriz, la más elegante, la más guapa...!

1

Ese actor es muy agresivo.

2

Ese actor es más cortés que el otro.

3

Yo soy muy sincera: mis compañeros son muy celosos, y...

4

33 **¿Quién dijo qué?**

▶ **Lee** la historieta y relaciona estos bocadillos con la viñeta correspondiente.

¡Usted es un poco chismosa!

Sí, ¡está de muy mal humor!

Y la más egoísta.

¡Ya lo creo! Es mucho más bondadoso.

▶ **Completa** con tu compañero(a) la historieta de Michelle y Daniel.

 **→ TU DESAFÍO** Visita la página web. Escucha las preguntas de tu *Minientrevista Desafío 1* y escribe las respuestas.

veintinueve **29**

---

32. Ask students to work with their partners and create a dialogue in which one will play the suspect, and the other, the detective. The suspect must answer the detective's questions about his or her whereabouts at the time of the crime. It will be up to the detective to make an arrest or not, but it must be justified.

33. Call on volunteers to role-play Michelle and Daniel's comic in front of the class. Ask students to vote on the most likely suspect and justify their choice.

 AUDIO SCRIPT
See page 11l.

Answer Key

30. Answers will vary.

31. 1. El Teatro Gran Rex está más cerca.
2. El Teatro Nacional Cervantes es el más antiguo. El Teatro Gran Rex es el más grande.
3. El Teatro Nacional Cervantes es más pequeño y antiguo que el Gran Rex. También es más tradicional y clásico. El Teatro Gran Rex es moderno y sencillo.
4. Answers will vary. Sample answer: El Teatro Gran Rex es mejor porque es mucho más grande y cabe más público.

32. Answers will vary.
▶ Answers will vary.

33. 1. Y la más egoísta.
2. Sí, ¡está de muy mal humor!
3. ¡Ya lo creo! Es mucho más bondadoso.
4. ¡Usted es un poco chismosa!

Additional Resources

Fans Online activities
Practice Workbook

HERITAGE LANGUAGE LEARNERS

• Have students use the Internet to find the two most famous theaters from their country of origin. Then ask them to write five comparisons and superlatives based on the information they found and the information presented on this page. Students may talk about the exterior and/or the interior of the theaters and some of the types of theatrical acts presented there. Ask volunteers to share their sentences with the class.

CRITICAL THINKING

• The detective and his assistant need to solve the crime, but they have to use their interrogation skills to interview potential witnesses and suspects. Ask students to think of the three most important questions that need to be asked and the three key witnesses/suspects who need to be interviewed to solve this case. Have students also think about what other techniques are available due to the advancements in technology and how they can be used to solve the crime.

Unit 1

DESAFÍO 2

Hablar de acciones pasadas

Presentation

- In *Desafío 2*, Eva y Ethan share information about three Hispanic painters and their family portraits. Students will preview language used to define family relationships and to describe actions in the past.

Activities	Standards	Resources
Texto	1.2, 2.1, 2.2, 3.1, 3.2	Vis. Pres.
34.	1.2, 1.3, 2.2, 3.1	
35.	1.1, 2.1, 2.2, 3.1	
36.	1.1, 1.2, 1.3, 2.2, 3.1	Audio
37. Conexiones	1.1, 1.2, 2.1, 2.2, 3.1, 3,2, 4.2	

Teaching Suggestions

Warm-Up / Independent Starter

- Have students study the paintings on page 30 and write their impressions of the similarities and differences among all three.

Preparation

- Discuss the differences between a portrait and a photograph of a family. Suggest that artists often reflect something about the subjects' nature that a camera cannot capture.

- Ask students to imagine that an artist is going to paint a portrait of them and their family. Who would be included? What would they wear and where would they pose?

Texto: Retratos de familia

- Invite volunteers to share their Independent Starters. Then ask the class to try to guess the time period in which the portraits were painted.

- Read the introduction to the text. Then ask for volunteers to read Eva and Ethan's lines. Did students guess the time period correctly? Discuss as a class the main characters of each portrait.

Activities

36. Call on volunteers to read their descriptions aloud and ask the class to guess which painting is being described.

30

Retratos de familia

Eva and Ethan must find information about three important paintings to prepare an audio guide for the art department's webpage at their school.

EVA: Este cuadro es de Diego Velázquez, un pintor español del siglo XVII. Sus retratos *(portraits)* del rey y de su familia son muy famosos. Aquí está la princesa Margarita con sus criadas *(maids)*. Sus padres están reflejados en el espejo y el pintor también está en el cuadro.

Diego Velázquez (España). *Las Meninas.*

ETHAN: Este cuadro es de Francisco de Goya, un pintor español del siglo XVIII. En el cuadro están el rey Carlos IV y su familia: su esposa María Luisa, sus hermanos, sus hijos y su yerno *(son-in-law)* Luis de Borbón.

Francisco de Goya (España). *La familia de Carlos IV.*

Fernando Botero (Colombia). *La familia presidencial.*

EVA: Este cuadro es de Fernando Botero, un pintor colombiano actual. También representa a una familia: la abuela, el padre, la madre y una niña.

ETHAN: A mí me recuerda al cuadro de Velázquez. Detrás está el pintor... ¡Y hay un gato!

34 **Detective de palabras**

▶ **Completa** estas oraciones.

1. Los ___1___ de la princesa Margarita están reflejados en un espejo.
2. María Luisa era la ___2___ de Carlos IV.
3. Luis de Borbón era el ___3___ de Carlos IV y María Luisa.
4. La ___4___ del cuadro de Botero está formada por la ___5___, el ___6___, la ___7___ y una ___8___.

30 treinta

Differentiated Instruction

DEVELOPING LEARNERS

- Ask students to use the reading strategies from *Desafío 1* to assist them in the reading of this text. First have students read the title and the introduction to the task. Then have them skim the text for cognates and familiar words. Finally have students look for the instances of the verbs *ser* and *estar* to check for verb tense and uses of the verb. Once students have finished, ask them which of the reading strategies worked the best to aid them in this passage, and remind them to continue to use the strategy in future passages.

EXPANDING LEARNERS

- Have students answer the following questions about the art presented on this page. Then have them use the answers to write a paragraph about the work of art they like the most and why.
  1. *Compara las características físicas de las familias en los tres cuadros de esta página.*
  2. *¿Cuál de las obras es más realista?*
  3. *¿Cuál te gusta más? ¿Por qué?*

35 **¿Comprendes?**

▶ **Responde** a estas preguntas.

1. ¿Quién era Diego Velázquez? ¿En qué época vivió? ¿De quiénes hacía retratos?

2. ¿Quién era Francisco de Goya? ¿En qué época vivió?

3. ¿Quién es Fernando Botero? ¿En qué país nació?

36 **Descripciones**

 ▶ **Escucha** y decide. ¿Cuál de estos cuadros de Botero se describe?

Familia.

Una familia.

Escena familiar.

▶ **Elige** otro cuadro de estas dos páginas y escribe una descripción: qué personajes aparecen, qué relación crees que hay entre ellos, cómo son, etc.

CONEXIONES: ARTE

Los pintores de la corte

Antiguamente los reyes y las personas ricas contrataban a los pintores durante años. En ese tiempo los artistas pintaban para sus mecenas *(patrons)*. El rey Felipe IV, por ejemplo, nombró a Velázquez pintor de la corte en 1623. Y Velázquez pintó muchas veces al rey y a su familia. Su retrato más famoso de la familia real *(royal family)* es *Las Meninas.*

Goya fue también pintor de la corte durante algunos años. Uno de los retratos que hizo para los reyes es *La familia de Carlos IV.*

Diego Velázquez (España). *La infanta Margarita de Austria.*

37 **Explica.** ¿Por qué crees que los reyes encargaban *(commissioned)* retratos de sus familias? ¿Crees que ser pintor de la corte era una ventaja para los artistas? ¿Por qué?

treinta y uno **31**

---

37. Have volunteers research some of the portraits that Velázquez and Goya painted of the Spanish Court. Ask them to compare and contrast their styles and explain how each painter represented his subject. They may present their findings in a written report or make an oral presentation to the class.

 AUDIO SCRIPT
See page 11I.

 CONEXIONES: ARTE

Los pintores de la corte

Velázquez painted during Spain's glorious Golden Age, when "the sun never set on the Spanish empire." The richness of princess Margarita's clothes reflect the country's prosperous economy.

Goya was also a painter of Spain's aristocracy, but at a more turbulent time in Spanish history. Many critics believe that *La familia de Carlos IV* reflects the artist's sense of satire. By placing the queen in the center of the painting, she becomes the central figure—more important than the king.

Answer Key

34. 1. padres 4. familia 7. madre
2. esposa 5. abuela 8. niña
3. yerno 6. padre

35. 1. Era un pintor español del siglo XVII. Hacía retratos de la familia real.
2. Era un pintor español del siglo XVIII.
3. Es un pintor colombiano.

36. Describe *Una familia.*
▶ Answers will vary.

37. Answers will vary.

Additional Resources

Fans Online activities

HERITAGE LANGUAGE LEARNERS

• We are presented with three famous Hispanic painters in this *Desafío*. Have students research American painters who have made portraits of past presidents and their families. Ask students to compare the painters and paintings to the ones presented on this page. Have students include the qualities both the American and Hispanic paintings have in common as well as how the paintings differ. Ask students to consider whether the painters were communicating a message or making a social commentary. Have them explain what the message is and how the painter communicates that message.

MULTIPLE INTELLIGENCES:
Visual-Spatial Intelligence

• As students can see, the artist's interpretation of a scene is what makes his or her painting style unique. Ask students to draw a picture of their families in their own unique style. Tell students they may draw inspiration from the more realistic Diego Velázquez or Francisco de Goya, or they can make their own interpretation, like Fernando Botero. Ask volunteers to share their pictures with the class. Have students explain what they wanted to communicate with their drawings.

DESAFÍO 2

Vocabulario – Relaciones familiares

Presentation

- In this section, students will learn and use featured vocabulary to define extended family relationships.

Activities	Standards	Resources
Vocabulario	1.2	
38.	1.2, 1.3	
39.	1.1, 1.2, 1.3	
40.	1.2, 1.3	Audio
41. Cultura	1.1, 1.2, 2.1, 2.2, 3.1, 3.2, 4.2	

Teaching Suggestions

Warm-Up / Independent Starter

- Have students write a list of family relationships they know from previous levels.

Preparation

- Ask students to use the lists from their Independent Starters and create a family tree showing these relationships for a girl named Marta, her siblings, parents, two sets of grandparents, and her parents' brothers and sisters and their children.
- Have students read the words in the *Más vocabulario* feature and the highlighted words in the text. Then call on three students to each read aloud one of the paragraphs on page 32. After each paragraph is read aloud, call on volunteers to define some of the family relationships.

Activities

38. To expand this activity, ask students to make a family tree for José, showing not only his family but also his in-laws.

39. Bring in some photos of celebrities who have been in the news because of their recent engagement, marriage, or divorce and ask students to identify their *estado civil*.

40. Have students work with a partner and create a description of family relationships modeled on the audio. Partners will read their descriptions to one another and then create a family tree.

Vocabulario

Relaciones familiares

Mi familia

Me llamo José y esta es mi familia. Mi madre se llama Ana y su **esposo** se llama Juan. Él es mi **padrastro**. Estos son mis hermanos, Leo e Isabel. En realidad son hijos de mi **padrastro** y **hermanastros** míos. Mi abuelo **materno** es **viudo** y mi abuela **paterna** está **divorciada**.

La boda

Mi hermana Isabel está **casada** con Luis. **Se casaron** el mes pasado. Mi hermano está **prometido** con Marta, su **novia**. No **me parezco** a mis hermanos, pero nos llevamos muy bien.

La familia de Luis

Aquí está mi hermana con su **familia política**. El hombre y la señora son sus **suegros**, los padres de Luis. Ahora Luis es mi **cuñado**.

Más vocabulario

Relaciones familiares

ahijado(a)	*godson / goddaughter*
hijo(a) adoptivo(a)	*adopted son / daughter*
pareja	*partner*
yerno	*son-in-law*
nuera	*daughter-in-law*

Estado civil

casado(a)	*married*
divorciado(a)	*divorced*
separado(a)	*separated*
soltero(a)	*single*
viudo(a)	*widower / widow*

38 **Detective de palabras**

▶ **Elige** la opción correcta según el texto.

1. El padre de mi madre es mi abuelo _____. a. político b. materno
2. Los padres de Luis son los _____ de mi hermana. a. cuñados b. suegros
3. Marta es la _____ de mi hermano. a. novia b. nuera
4. El esposo de mi madre es mi _____. a. padrino b. padrastro
5. El padre de mi madre está _____. a. divorciado b. viudo
6. Luis y yo somos _____. a. cuñados b. hermanos

Differentiated Instruction

DEVELOPING LEARNERS

- Have students make flashcards to help them identify the vocabulary. On one side of the flashcard, students draw or paste a picture of the family member, and his or her position in the family tree. On the other side, students write the Spanish word for the family member. Once students have finished, have them use their flashcards to review with other students. The more they switch, the more students can practice, so have students switch partners frequently.

EXPANDING LEARNERS

- Have students choose a well-known family from a fairy tale, television program, or film to describe, such as Cinderella or the Simpsons. They should include the family relationship, personality traits, and physical appearance in the description. Then have students share their descriptions with the class, leaving out the names of the characters. Have the class guess the identity of the family described.

39 **¿Quién es quién?**

▶ **Lee** los comentarios de José en la página anterior y escribe oraciones siguiendo el modelo.

Modelo   Juan/José → *Juan es el padrastro de José.*

1. Leo/Isabel   2. Juan/Ana   3. Isabel/Luis   4. Marta/Leo   5. Luis/José

▶ **Contesta.** ¿Cuál es el estado civil de cada personaje?

1. Isabel   2. Leo   3. Marta   4. Luis   5. Ana

▶ **Escribe** una definición para cada palabra.

Modelo   abuelo materno → *El abuelo materno es el padre de la madre.*

1. nieto   2. suegro   3. nuera   4. yerno   5. cuñado

 40 **¡Adivina!**

▶ **Escucha** a Eva y completa su árbol genealógico.

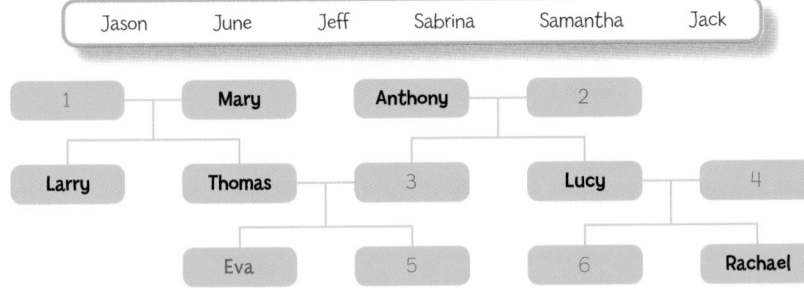

Jason   June   Jeff   Sabrina   Samantha   Jack

1	Mary		Anthony	2
Larry	Thomas	3	Lucy	4
	Eva	5	6	Rachael

 **CULTURA**

Estereotipos familiares

En la cultura hispana hay varios estereotipos familiares generalmente alejados de la realidad. La literatura, el cine, la publicidad, los cómics y los chistes (*jokes*) suelen presentar a la suegra como una persona autoritaria e indiscreta (*tactless*) que siempre discute con su nuera o su yerno. Tampoco las madrastras tienen buena fama; a veces se las presenta como personas con un carácter frío y distante.

41 **Compara.** ¿Existen estereotipos similares a estos en tu cultura? ¿Qué otros estereotipos familiares hay?

HERITAGE LANGUAGE LEARNERS

• Have students write about their extended family, including step-parents, in-laws, nieces and nephews, and first cousins. Ask them to describe the family members they are closest to and explain why they are close to them. They may also discuss family members who live in other countries. Students may not know these relatives personally, but they have perhaps seen pictures or heard about them. If there are students who feel uncomfortable talking about their family, suggest that they describe another family they know from their country of origin.

TOTAL PHYSICAL RESPONSE (TPR)

• Read the following excerpt from *Romeo y Julieta* (Act 1, Scene II) to students. Have them raise their left hands when they hear a male family member and their right hands when they hear a female family member.

ROMEO. *Espera, amigo, claro que sé leer.* [Lee]

«El señor Martino, esposa e hijas; el conde Anselmo y sus bellas hermanas; la señora viuda de Vitruvio; el señor Placencio y sus encantadoras sobrinas; Mercucio y su hermano Valentino; mi tío Capuleto, su esposa e hijas; mi hermosa sobrina Rosalina; Livia; el señor Valentio y su primo Teobaldo […]».

 AUDIO SCRIPT
See page 111.

 CULTURA

Estereotipos familiares

It can be difficult to understand other cultures or perspectives, and creating stereotypes—whether of the interfering mother-in-law, the cruel and unfeeling stepmother, or the neighbor with a different religion or accent—does away with the challenges of understanding those who hold views, customs, and interests that differ from ours. We can laugh at some stereotypes in fiction and film, but perpetuating stereotypes in our lives is a way to keep separating "them" from "us."

Answer Key

38. 1. b   2. b   3. a   4. b   5. b   6. a

39. 1. Leo es el hermano de Isabel.
2. Juan es el esposo de Ana.
3. Isabel es la esposa de Luis.
4. Marta es la novia de Leo.
5. Luis es el cuñado de José.

▶ 1. casada   3. soltera   5. casada
2. soltero   4. casado

▶ Answers will vary. Sample answers:
1. El nieto es el hijo de tu hijo(a).
2. El suegro es el padre de tu esposo(a).
3. La nuera es la esposa de tu hijo.
4. El yerno es el esposo de tu hija.
5. El cuñado es el esposo de tu hermana.

40. 1. Jeff   3. Samantha   5. Sabrina
2. June   4. Jack   6. Jason

41. Answers will vary.

Additional Resources

Fans Online activities
Practice Workbook

DESAFÍO 2

Gramática – El imperfecto y el pasado continuo

Presentation

- In this section, students will use the imperfect and past progressive tenses in order to talk about customary and ongoing actions in the past.

Activities	Standards	Resources
Gramática	1.2, 3.1	
42.	4.1	
43.	1.2, 1.3	
44.	1.2, 1.3	
45.	1.1, 1.2, 5.1	
46. Cultura	1.1, 1.2, 2.1, 3.2, 4.2	Video

Teaching Suggestions

Warm-Up / Independent Starter

- Ask students to think of three things they used to do when they were young children.

Preparation

- Go over the grammar presentation. Remind students that the use of the imperfect to talk about actions that happened repeatedly in the past is often expressed by "used to" in English.

- Ask for volunteers to share their Independent Starters. You may want to write some of their sentences on the board and circle the verb in the imperfect. Be sure to point out the regularity of the imperfect tense endings and the fact that there are only three verbs that are irregular.

- Remind students that the past progressive is used much more often in English than in Spanish, when often the simple imperfect suffices.

Activities

44. Ask students to identify the verbs in the preterite and explain why this tense was used. (*Tuve, pude, llamó, dio, vino, dijo, fuimos, se puso, llegó, salí, llegué.* These verbs describe actions that were completed in the past.)

45. Have students work in small groups and compare answers. Have each group designate a spokesperson who will make a report to the class summarizing the group's responses.

Gramática

El imperfecto y el pasado continuo

El imperfecto

- Use the imperfect tense to talk about actions that happened repeatedly in the past.

  De niña **jugaba** mucho con mis hermanos.

- The imperfect is very regular (see conjugation on page R14):

  | -ar verbs | Add the endings -aba, -abas… |

  | -er and -ir verbs | Add the endings -ía, -ías… |

- There are only three irregular verbs in the imperfect tense:

SER

era	éramos
eras	erais
era	eran

VER

veía	veíamos
veías	veíais
veía	veían

IR

iba	íbamos
ibas	ibais
iba	iban

El pasado continuo

- Use the past progressive to talk about ongoing actions in the past. The past progressive is formed with the verb estar conjugated in the imperfect, plus the present participle (gerundio):

  —¿Qué **estabas haciendo** cuando te llamé?

  —**Estaba dibujando** el árbol genealógico de nuestra familia.

- Remember: regular verbs form the present participle with the endings -ando (hablando) and -iendo (comiendo, escribiendo).

42 **Compara.** ¿Cómo se forma el pasado continuo en inglés? ¿Tiene los mismos usos que en español?

43 **¿Qué hacías?**

▶ **Completa** estas oraciones. Usa el imperfecto.

| preparar |
| hablar |
| jugar |
| pasar |
| ir |
| estar |

1. Antes yo siempre _____ al baloncesto.
2. Mi hermanos y yo siempre _____ las vacaciones con mis primos.
3. Mi familia y yo _____ a la playa todos los veranos, pero ahora preferimos ir a la montaña.
4. Cuando me llamaste, _____ haciendo la tarea.
5. Mientras mis padres _____ la cena, yo puse la mesa.
6. Ayer, mientras tú _____ con tus amigas, mamá llamó por teléfono.

▶ **Escribe** tres oraciones usando el imperfecto de los verbos ser, ver e ir.

Differentiated Instruction

DEVELOPING LEARNERS

- Ask students to make an imperfect tense conjugation table for the following verbs: *estar, ir,* and *jugar.* Then have them write three sentences about their childhood experiences using each verb. For example:

ESTAR

yo estaba	nosotros(as) estábamos
tú estabas	vosotros(as) estabais
usted él estaba ella	ustedes ellos estaban ellas

Cuando estaba en el tercer grado…

EXPANDING LEARNERS

- Ask students to think about the toys they used to play with as children. Have students describe the toy(s), the person or people they used to play with, and in what conditions they used to play. For example: *Cuando era niña, jugaba con mi Rock'em Sock'em Robot™. Siempre jugaba con mi hermana. Yo era el azul y mi hermana era el rojo, y peleábamos por horas…*

44 **El museo de arte**

▶ **Completa** el correo electrónico de Eva. Usa el imperfecto.

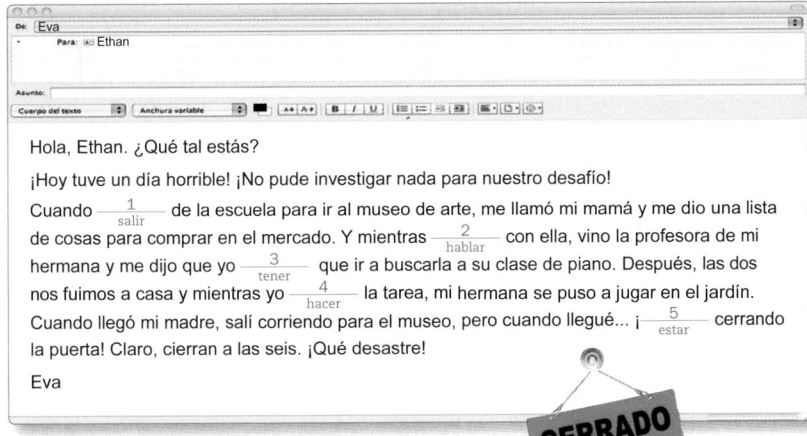

De: Eva
Para: Ethan
Asunto:

Hola, Ethan. ¿Qué tal estás?

¡Hoy tuve un día horrible! ¡No pude investigar nada para nuestro desafío!

Cuando ___1___ (salir) de la escuela para ir al museo de arte, me llamó mi mamá y me dio una lista de cosas para comprar en el mercado. Y mientras ___2___ (hablar) con ella, vino la profesora de mi hermana y me dijo que yo ___3___ (tener) que ir a buscarla a su clase de piano. Después, las dos nos fuimos a casa y mientras yo ___4___ (hacer) la tarea, mi hermana se puso a jugar en el jardín. Cuando llegó mi madre, salí corriendo para el museo, pero cuando llegué... ¡ ___5___ (estar) cerrando la puerta! Claro, cierran a las seis. ¡Qué desastre!

Eva

CERRADO

45 **Cuando era pequeño(a)...**

▶ **Responde** a estas preguntas.

1. ¿Adónde ibas de vacaciones con tu familia cuando eras pequeño(a)?
2. ¿Cuál era tu programa favorito de televisión? ¿Por qué?
3. ¿Practicabas algún deporte? ¿Cuál?

▶ **Compara** tus respuestas con las de tu compañero(a). ¿Era tu vida similar a la suya? ¿Por qué?

Modelo *Mi vida y la de mi compañero eran bastante similares porque los dos...*

CULTURA

Fiestas familiares

La Nochebuena es una fiesta de origen religioso que se celebra en muchos países el 24 de diciembre. Por lo general, en los países hispanos las familias se reúnen esa noche para cenar juntos. Y también es habitual reunirse al día siguiente, el 25 de diciembre, para la comida de Navidad.

46 **Explica.** ¿En tu país se reúnen las familias en Nochebuena y en Navidad? ¿Qué fiestas se suelen celebrar en familia?

Gramática – El imperfecto y el pasado continuo

46. Have volunteers research other holidays that are celebrated in December (e.g., Kwanzaa, Hanukkah, Boxing Day) or during other times of the year (e.g., New Year's Day, Ramadan), and make a short presentation to the class on how these holidays are celebrated.

 **CULTURA**

Fiestas familiares

Unlike Christmas traditions in countries that feature Santa Claus, most children in the Hispanic world receive their gifts from *los Reyes Magos* (the Three Wise Men) on the morning of January 6. In Spain, children write letters to *los reyes,* asking for what they would like to receive. In Peru, children leave their shoes to be filled with the gifts. In Puerto Rico, children leave a little box filled with straw next to their bed, hoping it will be filled with gifts.

Answer Key

42. Se forma con el pasado del verbo *to be* y la forma *-ing* del verbo principal. Tiene los mismos usos que en español, pero se usa con más frecuencia en inglés.

43.
1. jugaba   4. estaba
2. pasábamos   5. preparaban
3. íbamos   6. hablabas
▶ Answers will vary.

44.
1. salía   3. tenía   5. estaban
2. hablaba   4. hacía

45. Answers will vary.
▶ Answers will vary.

46. Answers will vary.

Additional Resources

Fans Online activities
Practice Workbook

HERITAGE LANGUAGE LEARNERS

• We learn about what has shaped our present by the experiences of others in the past. Tell students to write three paragraphs about the childhood experiences of an older family member. Have students include information about where and when this person grew up, typical childhood activities, and any major events that occurred during his or her childhood. Have volunteers share their work with the class. Ask students to compare their childhood with this relative's childhood. Have students talk about what things they wish they could do that their relative did.

MULTIPLE INTELLIGENCES:
Intrapersonal Intelligence

• Have students write about what they were like in elementary school. Have them write about their impressions of school, their activities, their friends, people who were important in their lives, their likes and dislikes, and what they wanted to do when they were older. They should also include a physical description, as well as a description of their personality.

DESAFÍO 2

Gramática – Expresar posesión

Presentation

- In this section, students will review possessive adjectives and pronouns as well as the preposition *de* plus the name of the possessor to indicate possession.

Activities	Standards	Resources
Gramática	1.2, 3.1	
47.	4.1	
48.	1.2	
49.	1.2, 1.3	Audio
50.	1.2, 1.3	
51.	1.1, 1.2, 1.3, 5.1	
52.	1.1, 1.3, 5.1	

Teaching Suggestions

Warm-Up / Independent Starter

- Ask students to make a two-column chart and list all the different forms of possessive adjectives and possessive pronouns they remember. Ask them to label the chart *Expresar posesión* and the columns *Adjetivos posesivos* and *Pronombres posesivos*. If time permits, have them write sentences using some of these forms.

Preparation

- Call on individual students to read aloud one bulleted item each in the *Gramática* feature. Help students to see the difference in meaning in the first example: *Carlos es mi primo. Carlos es primo mío.* (Carlos is my cousin. Carlos is a cousin of mine.)

- You might point out the ambiguity of the possessive adjective *su*. To clarify meaning, write the following on the board: *la maleta de mis tíos.* Explain that *su maleta* is correct, but they could also say *la maleta de ellos* to clear up ownership since *su* can also mean his, her, its, or your.

Activities

47. To expand this activity, have students write more relationships modeled on the *Compara* feature and then ask them to exchange papers with a partner who must translate them into Spanish.

36

Gramática

Expresar posesión

Los adjetivos posesivos

- Possessive adjectives (mi, tu, su...) are used to show ownership. They can be placed before or after the noun they accompany, but some forms change depending on their position. In order to review the forms of possessive adjectives, see page R2.

  Carlos es **mi** primo. Carlos es primo **mío**.

- Possessive adjectives agree in number with the noun they accompany. They agree with the thing possessed, not with the owner. Nuestro and vuestro also agree in gender with the item possessed.

  Estas son **nuestras** hijas, María y Susana.

Los pronombres posesivos

- Possessive pronouns (mío, tuyo, suyo...) are used instead of a noun. The forms are the same as those of the possessive adjectives after the noun (see page R2).

  Estas fotos son **mías** y esas son **tuyas**.

- When the possessive pronoun is used to identify, it is preceded by el, la, los, las (el mío, la tuya, los suyos...).

  Esta es mi familia y aquella es **la suya**.

La preposición *de*

- In Spanish you may also express possession with the preposition de where you would put 's in English. The following structure is used:

thing possessed + de + possessor

  Marta es la **hermana de Ricardo**.

  Remember: de + el → del

47 **Compara.** ¿Cómo se dice en español?

    a. *Laura's stepmother*   **c.** *your brother's fiancée*
    b. *my father's sister-in-law* **d.** *her godson's partner*

48 **¿De quién?**

▶ **Une** las dos columnas.

    Ⓐ   Ⓑ

   1. un disco - de ella   a. suya
   2. un libro - de ti y de mí   b. suyo
   3. una casa - de Victoria y de Álex c. nuestro
   4. una mochila - de ti   d. suyas
   5. unas fotos - de ustedes   e. tuya

Differentiated Instruction

DEVELOPING LEARNERS

- In small groups, have students talk about their family pets. If they do not have a pet, they can speak about one they would like to have or a pet they know. Have them describe the animal's physical appearance and character traits. Ask them to consider what things make the pet happy, sad, or angry. They may also discuss any tricks the pet can do.

EXPANDING LEARNERS

- Have students write descriptions of their immediate family members on a piece of paper. Tell students not to put their names on their papers. Then have students exchange their papers several times to ensure that the paper received by each student is not the one he or she wrote. Then, one by one, have students read the family description aloud for the class to guess whose family fits the description. If a student guesses correctly, then he or she is the next one to read a description.

49 **¿De quién es?**

▶ **Escucha** a Eva y relaciona los objetos con la persona correspondiente.

| su abuelo | su hermana | su ahijado | sus padres |

①  ②  ③  ④

▶ **Escribe** oraciones siguiendo el modelo.

Modelo   *El monopatín no es suyo, es de su hermana.*

50 **Mi familia y la tuya**

▶ **Completa** la conversación entre Michelle y Ethan con los posesivos correctos.

Eva: ___1___ familia es mediana, no tengo muchos primos. ¿Cómo es la ___2___?
Ethan: La ___3___ es muy grande. Tengo veinte primos.
Eva: ¿Y viven todos en los Estados Unidos?
Ethan: No. ___4___ tíos maternos y sus hijos viven en Colombia.
Eva: ¡Qué suerte! Si vas a Colombia puedes alojarte en casa de ___5___ tíos.
Ethan: Sí, claro. Oye, ¿tus abuelos viven con ustedes?
Eva: No. ___6___ abuelos paternos están divorciados, pero siempre vienen
        a las reuniones familiares. ¿Y los ___7___?
Ethan: Los ___8___ llevan casados 45 años. Viven muy cerca de mi casa.

51 **Familias famosas**

▶ **Escribe** oraciones sobre la relación entre personajes de familias famosas. Después, léeselas a tu compañero(a). Él / Ella tiene que adivinar el nombre del personaje.

Modelo   A. *Es la hermana menor de Bart Simpson.*
            B. *Lisa Simpson.*
            A. *No, la hermana menor es Maggie. Lisa es mayor que Maggie.*

52 **Comparen sus familias**

▶ **Habla** con tu compañero(a) sobre tu familia y hazle preguntas sobre la suya. Después, escribe un texto comparándolas.

Modelo

La familia de Sally es mayor que la mía. Ella tiene cuatro hermanos y yo solo tengo uno. Sus hermanos viven en los Estados Unidos y el mío vive en Canadá.

treinta y siete **37**

HERITAGE LANGUAGE LEARNERS

• Have students consider why they might choose to use *de* to show possession instead of a possessive adjective. Ask them to come up with suggestions of when a possessive adjective is used rather than *de* and when they might use the possessive adjective after the noun instead of in front of it. Ask volunteers to share their ideas with the class.

CRITICAL THINKING

• In Spanish, each noun is assigned a gender. Ask students why they think this is necessary in the Spanish language. Ask students how they believe new inventions and technology get their names in Spanish, and once they have a name, how they are assigned a gender. Have volunteers discuss their opinions with the class.

Gramática – Expresar posesión

48. Call on volunteers to identify the possessive pronoun needed to express the following: *una computadora – de mí (mía); una tira cómica – de ellos (suya); la familia – de nosotros (nuestra); unos amigos – de usted (suyos).*

50. To expand this activity, ask students to work in groups of three and write a dialogue based on their imaginary families. Call on volunteer groups to come before the class and read their dialogues.

51. You might turn this into a game and have two teams play against each other. The winner is the team with the most correct guesses in the shortest amount of time.

 AUDIO SCRIPT
See page 111.

Answer Key

47. a. la madrastra de Laura
       b. la cuñada de mi padre
       c. la prometida de tu hermano
       d. la pareja de su ahijado / la pareja del
           ahijado de ella

48. 1. b   2. c   3. a   4. e   5. d

49. 1. su hermana   3. su abuelo
       2. sus padres   4. su ahijado
       ▶ 2. La cámara no es suya, es de sus
             padres.
          3. Las revistas no son suyas, son de su
             abuelo.
          4. El libro no es suyo, es de su ahijado.

50. 1. Mi   4. Mis   7. tuyos
       2. tuya   5. tus   8. míos
       3. mía   6. Mis

51. Answers will vary.

52. Answers will vary.

Additional Resources

Fans Online activities
Practice Workbook

37

LECTURA: TEXTO INFORMATIVO

Presentation

- In this section, students will read a short biography of another famous artist, recognize how the imperfect and the past progressive tenses are used, and identify nouns and verbs that have to do with the family and family relationships.

Activities	Standards	Resources
Lectura: texto informativo	1.2, 1.3, 2.1, 2.2, 3.1, 3.2	
53.	1.1, 1.2, 2.2, 3.1	
54.	1.1, 1.2, 1.3, 2.2, 3.1	
55.	1.1, 1.2, 2.2, 3.1	
56.	1.1, 1.3, 2.2, 3.1	

Teaching Suggestions

Warm-Up / Independent Starter

- Have students read the *Antes de leer* strategies silently. Ask them to scan the biography and write all the nouns and verbs they can find that have to do with the family or family relationships.

Preparation

- Call on volunteers to explain the difference between *biografía* and *autobiografía* and between *retrato* and *autorretrato*. Which of these two do students think reflects a person's life story better: a *biografía* or an *autobiografía*? How do they think a person is best represented, by a *retrato* painted by someone else or by their own *autorretrato*?
- Read the biography aloud to students to model pronunciation and intonation. Then have students alternate reading several lines or a paragraph. You may want to pause after every paragraph and call on a volunteer to paraphrase the content.
- Ask students to take out the lists of nouns and verbs they wrote in their Independent Starters. Now have them read *Una breve biografía* silently and add to their lists. Review these words with students.
- Ask students to cite the uses of the imperfect (*era, se recuperaba*) and the past progressive (*estaba viajando*) in the reading.

Antes de leer: estrategias

1. Lee el título. ¿Qué significa la palabra *biografía*? ¿Qué diferencia hay entre una biografía y una autobiografía? ¿Y entre un retrato y un autorretrato?
2. Mira el autorretrato de Frida Kahlo y descríbelo. ¿Cómo es Frida físicamente? ¿Puedes adivinar algo sobre su origen, su personalidad, su estado de ánimo o sus gustos?
3. Señala todas las palabras que se refieren a la familia y a las relaciones familiares. Clasifícalas en nombres *(nouns)* y en verbos *(verbs)*.

Frida Kahlo (México). *Autorretrato con chango*[1] *y loro.*

1. *monkey*
2. *Amerindian*
3. *giving birth*
4. *crashed*
5. *streetcar*
6. *she suffered injuries*
7. *while she was recovering*
8. *dreams*

Una breve biografía

Frida Kahlo es una de las pintoras más famosas de México. Nació en 1907. Su padre era de origen alemán, y su madre era mexicana, de origen español y amerindio[2]. Su padre se casó dos veces. Su primera esposa murió al dar a luz[3]. Con su segunda esposa tuvo cuatro hijas, y Frida Kahlo fue la tercera de ellas.

Frida pasó su infancia entre mujeres, con su madre, sus hermanas y sus dos hermanastras. Tuvo una vida muy difícil. A los seis años tuvo polio, una enfermedad muy común entonces. En su adolescencia, estaba viajando en un autobús cuando este chocó[4] con un tranvía[5]. Sufrió heridas[6] terribles en las piernas y la espalda, y nunca pudo tener hijos.

Mientras se recuperaba[7], Frida empezó a pintar. Luego conoció a Diego Rivera, el famoso muralista mexicano, y se casaron en 1929. Los dos artistas se divorciaron en 1939, pero volvieron a casarse en 1940.

Frida pintó muchos autorretratos. En ellos refleja aspectos de su vida, sus obsesiones y sus sueños[8], mezclados con elementos de la mitología mexicana.

Frida Kahlo murió a los 47 años. Sus cuadros se hicieron famosos mucho tiempo después. La casa donde vivió es hoy un museo; está en Coyoacán (Ciudad de México) y se llama la Casa Azul.

Differentiated Instruction

DEVELOPING LEARNERS

- Before students begin reading the text, build on prior knowledge by tapping into what they already know about Frida Kahlo. Show students some of Frida's self-portraits (you will find them online) and ask them if she looks familiar. Then ask students questions about things they probably know, such as *¿De qué país es Frida? ¿Cómo fue la vida de Frida: fácil o difícil? ¿Todavía está viva Frida o ya murió?* Ask students to help each other answer your questions. Invite students to add other information they know about Frida.

EXPANDING LEARNERS

- Frida Kahlo lived a very interesting life. Ask students to come up with ten interview questions they would ask Frida if she were still living. Then have students exchange papers and research the answers to their classmates' questions on the Internet. Once students have found some or most of the answers, have them pretend to be an interviewer and Frida Kahlo. The original author asks the questions and the researcher answers the questions. Record the interviews if possible, so students can critique their Spanish.

53 ¿Qué recuerdas?

▶ **Elige** la opción correcta.

1. Su padre se casó...
   a. una vez   b. dos veces   c. tres veces
2. Cuando era niña, Frida vivía con...
   a. tres mujeres   b. cuatro mujeres   c. seis mujeres
3. Frida tuvo polio cuando...
   a. era niña   b. era adolescente   c. era adulta
4. Frida empezó a pintar cuando se recuperaba de...
   a. un accidente   b. una enfermedad   c. su divorcio
5. Los cuadros de Frida Kahlo se hicieron famosos...
   a. antes de su muerte   b. cuando murió   c. muchos años después de su muerte

54 Organización

▶ **Ordena** estas oraciones sobre la biografía de Frida Kahlo.

a. Se casó con Diego Rivera.
b. A los seis años tuvo polio.
c. Nació en 1907.
d. Tuvo un accidente en su adolescencia.
e. Su talento fue reconocido años después de su muerte.
f. Murió a los 47 años.

▶ **Sitúa** los acontecimientos más importantes de la vida de Frida en una línea del tiempo.

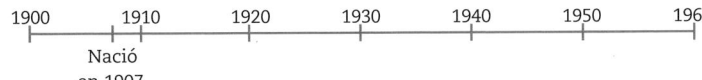

```
1900      1910      1920      1930      1940      1950      1960
           Nació
           en 1907.
```

55 Resúmenes

▶ **Lee** estos textos y decide. ¿Cuál resume mejor la lectura de Frida Kahlo? ¿Por qué?

① Frida Kahlo fue una pintora mexicana. En su vida sufrió mucho porque de niña tuvo polio y de adolescente sufrió un grave accidente. Se casó dos veces con Diego Rivera. Pintó muchos autorretratos donde muestra aspectos de su vida. Su pintura fue reconocida después de su muerte. Hoy su casa de Coyoacán es un museo.

② Frida Kahlo tuvo una vida difícil porque durante su adolescencia el autobús en el que viajaba tuvo un accidente. Sufrió muchas heridas y nunca pudo tener hijos. Frida Kahlo pasó su infancia con su madre, sus dos hermanastras y sus otras tres hermanas. Se casó con Diego Rivera, el famoso muralista mexicano, en 1929. La casa donde vivió se llama la Casa Azul y es un museo.

56 Con tus propias palabras

▶ **Explica.** ¿Cómo era la familia de Frida? ¿Cómo fue su vida? ¿Cómo son sus cuadros?

treinta y nueve **39**

LECTURA: TEXTO INFORMATIVO

Activities

53. To expand this activity, have students work in small groups and imagine that they are reporters wanting to know more about the life of Frida Kahlo. Have them come up with a list of questions they would like to ask her.

55. Call on volunteers to come in front of the class and explain why they selected the paragraph.

56. Have students research more of Kahlo's paintings and bring printouts to class. They should be prepared to talk about the theme of each painting and any other pertinent details.

Answer Key

53. 1. b   2. c   3. a   4. a   5. c

54. c, b, d, a, f, e

▶ Tuvo polio en 1913.
   En 1925 tuvo un accidente.
   Se casó con Diego Rivera en 1929.
   Se divorció en 1939.
   Se volvió a casar en 1940.
   Murió en 1954.

55. Párrafo 1, porque menciona los detalles principales de la vida de Frida Kahlo.

56. Answers will vary. Sample answer:

En la familia de Frida Kahlo había muchas mujeres: su madre, tres hermanas y dos hermanastras. Su vida fue muy difícil. Tuvo polio de niña y en la adolescencia sufrió un accidente muy grave mientras viajaba en autobús.

Tuvo muchos problemas en su matrimonio con Diego Rivera y murió joven.

Muchos de sus cuadros son autorretratos que muestran aspectos de su vida, de sus obsesiones y de sus sueños. En sus cuadros también son comunes diversos elementos de la mitología mexicana.

Additional Resources

Fans Online activities

HERITAGE LANGUAGE LEARNERS

• Ask students to review each sentence in the text and classify the verb and tense. Have students make a list of all of the verbs and their tenses on a separate sheet of paper. For example:

Students read: *Frida Kahlo es una de las pintoras más famosas de México. Nació en 1907.*

Students write: *es → ser, presente*
   nació → nacer, pretérito

SPECIAL-NEEDS LEARNERS

• For students with vision problems, first ask them what they remember from previous classes about Frida Kahlo. Then copy the reading passage onto copy paper, and enlarge the print until it is the size of the full page. If students still have problems with the print, then have them pair up to read the passage aloud together.

Unit 1

DESAFÍO 2

Comunicación

Presentation

- In this section, students will integrate the vocabulary and grammar skills from *Desafío 2* in order to describe family relationships and talk about customary and ongoing actions in the past.

Activities	Standards	Resources
57.	1.2, 1.3, 2.1, 2.2, 3.1, 5.1, 5.2	
58.	1.1, 1.2, 1.3, 2.1, 4.2, 5.1	
59.	1.1, 1.2	Audio
60. Final del desafío	1.1, 1.2, 1.3, 2.2, 3.1, 5.1	
Tu desafío	1.1, 1.2	

Teaching Suggestions

Warm-Up / Independent Starter

- Ask students to think about their relationship with a member, or members, of their family. Then have them write a short paragraph describing what they and the family member(s) used to do or how they were in the past, and describe some of the possessions both had. For example: *Mis abuelos siempre me invitaban a su casa en el campo durante los veranos. Yo pasaba los días allí muy feliz. Montaba a caballo y pescaba en el lago. Mis abuelos tenían dos perros muy simpáticos...*

Preparation

- Spend some time reviewing the grammar topics of this *Desafío* and answer any questions the students may have.

- To apply vocabulary and grammar from this *Desafío*, ask students to write a brief biography of a family member. Students should include a description of the family member and make proper use of the imperfect and past progressive tenses, as well as of possessive adjectives or pronouns.

- Call on volunteers to read their biographies aloud. As students read, write on the board some of the vocabulary and grammar structures from this *Desafío* that they used in their narratives. Were these structures used correctly?

40

Comunicación

57 **Una telenovela**

▶ **Imagina** que eres el guionista *(scriptwriter)* de una nueva telenovela. Dibuja el árbol genealógico de la familia protagonista. Incluye las relaciones familiares del cuadro.

esposo	hijo	nuera	abuela	suegra

▶ **Escribe** una descripción de los dos personajes más importantes de la telenovela.

 ▶ **Presenta** el árbol genealógico a tus compañeros. Explica las relaciones familiares y los rasgos de personalidad más importantes de cada miembro.

Modelo
Esta es la familia de Selena. Ahora viven en México, pero antes vivían en los Estados Unidos. Su abuela era una mujer muy rica...

58 **Familias de ayer y de hoy**

 ▶ **Habla** con tus compañeros(as). En pequeños grupos, escriban una lista de diferencias en la forma de vivir en estas épocas.

Familia Pérez, 1950.   Familia Rodríguez, 2010.

Familias en el año 1950	Familias en el año 2010
Las fotos eran en blanco y negro y no había celulares.	Todos tenemos un celular y podemos hacer videos en color.

▶ **Escribe** un párrafo para resumir *(summarize)* la información de la tabla anterior.

 ▶ **Presenta** a tus antepasados *(ancestors)* comparándolos con tu familia de hoy. Busca fotografías y prepara un póster o una presentación.

40 cuarenta

Differentiated Instruction

DEVELOPING LEARNERS

- Ask students to make up a mini-story about what the families in activity 58 were doing when the photographer called them over to take a picture. Have students think of the times and technology that would have been present in both scenes as they make up their mini-stories. For example: *En 1950, los niños estaban montando en bicicleta con sus amigos...*

EXPANDING LEARNERS

- Tell students to imagine that they were chosen as the winner of a family trip for three. The problem is, they are only allowed to take two other family members. Have students choose two family members and tell what from the past has made this family member special. For example: *Siempre jugaba al dominó con mi prima Mónica. Ella guardaba mis secretos y nunca me fallaba. Por eso, es mi prima favorita y muy amiga mía.*

59 **Recuerdos de infancia**

▶ **Escucha** a Ethan hablando de su infancia y decide si estas oraciones son ciertas o falsas.

1. De pequeño vivía en Boston con su familia.
2. A Ethan no le gustaba mucho el apartamento donde vivían.
3. Sus abuelos vivían con ellos.
4. Ethan se llevaba bien con sus hermanos.
5. Sus primos los visitaban en verano.

Final del desafío

¿Dónde está la información sobre el cuadro de Velázquez?

A ver... aquí: «Velázquez pintó este cuadro en el siglo XVII. En el centro está la princesa Margarita con sus hermanas. Sus tíos están reflejados en el espejo...»

Aquí está la información de *La familia de Carlos IV*, de Goya. «El rey está con su esposa, sus hermanos, sus hijos y su nuera...»

«En este cuadro de Botero, pintor colombiano, vemos a una familia tradicional, con el padre, la madre, los abuelos y una niña.»

60 **¡Qué confusión!**

▶ **Busca** los errores en la audioguía de Eva y Ethan, y corrígelos.

Modelo   *En el cuadro de Velázquez, la princesa Margarita está con sus criadas. Y...*

▶ **Haz** una ficha de este cuadro de Frida Kahlo. Incluye esta información.

– Título de la obra
– Autora de la obra
– Descripción detallada del cuadro

Frida Kahlo (México). *Frida y Diego Rivera.*

**→ TU DESAFÍO**   Visita la página web. Escucha las preguntas de tu *Minientrevista Desafío 2* y escribe las respuestas.

HERITAGE LANGUAGE LEARNERS

• Have students look at the three family paintings from the beginning of the *Desafío*. Ask them to imagine what the conversation between the family members was like prior to posing for the portrait. Tell students to look carefully at the facial expressions of the people in the paintings to help them get an idea of what kind of person he or she was and the family dynamics at the time their portrait was painted. Encourage students to be creative as they come up with their dialogues. Ask volunteers to present their dialogues to the class.

MULTIPLE INTELLIGENCES:
Musical-Rhythmic Intelligence

• Ask students to come up with a freestyle rap to help them remember the family vocabulary from this unit. It doesn't necessarily have to rhyme, but it has to make sense. Ask one student to start a beat and another student to start the freestyle. Have other students add to the freestyle. Make sure to record this freestyle session to replay at a later date.

Activities

57. To extend this activity, ask pairs of students to rehearse a brief soap opera scene in which two of their main characters interact with each other. Then ask students to role-play their scene in front of the class. You may want to hold a class vote to choose the best script and the best actors.

58. Ask students why they think the family shown from 1950 is not smiling and seems so serious. Students could offer realistic explanations, or they might make up a little story about the lives of these family members.

59. Have students correct the false statements in order to make them true. Then call on volunteers to read their corrected statements aloud.

 AUDIO SCRIPT
See page 11 J.

Answer Key

57. Answers will vary.
   ▶ Answers will vary.
   ▶ Answers will vary.
58. Answers will vary.
   ▶ Answers will vary.
   ▶ Answers will vary.
59. 1. Cierto   4. Cierto
   2. Falso   5. Cierto
   3. Falso
60. En el cuadro de Velázquez, Margarita no está con sus hermanas, está con sus criadas. Sus padres están reflejados en el espejo. En el cuadro de Goya, no está la nuera del rey; está el yerno. En el cuadro de Botero, no están los abuelos, solo está la abuela.
   ▶ Answers will vary.

Additional Resources

Fans Online activities
Practice Workbook

DESAFÍO 3

Narrar y describir en pasado

Presentation

- In *Desafío 3*, Asha and Lucas will research well-known Hispanic legends and then write one. Students will preview vocabulary that deals with the life cycle and see how the preterite and imperfect tenses are used to tell a story.

Activities	Standards	Resources
Texto	1.2, 2.2, 3.1, 3.2	Vis. Pres.
61.	1.3, 3.1	
62.	1.1, 1.2, 1.3, 2.1, 2.2, 3.2	
63.	1.1, 1.2, 1.3, 2.2, 3.1	Audio
64. Conexiones	1.1, 1.2, 2.1, 2.2, 3.1	

Teaching Suggestions

Warm-Up / Independent Starter

- Ask students to write the titles of some legends they have read or heard. If they don't know the title, ask them to write the names of the main characters or a line or two to summarize the plot.

Preparation

- Have students share their Independent Starters. Discuss some of these legends, including the characters, the plots, and the countries of origin.

Texto: Flor de leyendas

- Read the introduction to the text and ask the class to observe the illustrations. Invite students to speculate on a possible plot for each legend.
- Call on volunteers to role-play Asha, Tess, Lucas, and Andy and read their parts in front of the class. Had students heard of any of these legends before? Were any of their plot predictions correct?

Activities

62. Ask students to write some sentences that describe what takes place in one of the two legends they finished reading, but tell them to write the sentences out of order. Then ask them to exchange papers with a partner who must put the events in the correct order.

42

Flor de leyendas

Asha and Lucas must investigate some famous Hispanic legends that portray the cycle of life and make up their own to narrate to the class. They are chatting online with Tess and Andy about the legends they learned while traveling through Latin America.

ASHA: Tess, ¿conoces alguna leyenda hispana?

TESS: En México me contaron la historia de la Llorona, pero es muy triste. Es una mujer que existió hace muchos años. Ella era muy linda. Se casó con un hombre muy rico y tuvieron tres hijos. Pero el hombre se separó de ella y, enojada, ella mató a sus hijos.

ASHA: ¿Y por qué la llaman la Llorona?

TESS: Porque después ella se arrepintió (*regretted it*), y ahora llora todas las noches.

LUCAS: Andy, ¿escuchaste alguna leyenda en tus viajes?

ANDY: Sí, la leyenda que motivó la llegada de los españoles a la Florida. Cuando estaban en Puerto Rico, los españoles oyeron hablar de la fuente de la eterna juventud. La leyenda decía que el agua de la fuente convertía a los viejos en jóvenes. Entonces viajaron en barcos para buscarla y llegaron a la península de la Florida. Nunca encontraron la fuente, pero fundaron San Agustín, la ciudad más antigua de los Estados Unidos.

LUCAS: ¡Qué interesante!

61 **Detective de palabras**

▶ **Escribe** en una tabla como esta las formas verbales del pretérito y del imperfecto que hay en el texto.

Pretérito	Imperfecto
contaron	era

42 cuarenta y dos

Differentiated Instruction

DEVELOPING LEARNERS

- Have students look through the dialogue and identify how the previous grammar and vocabulary lessons have made their way into the third *Desafío*. This will show students the importance of progression, and also show them how each *Desafío* is interconnected. The themes of the previous two *Desafíos* are: Vocabulary → physical characteristics, personality traits, and family.
Grammar → the verbs *ser* and *estar*, comparisons and superlatives, the imperfect and the past progressive, and expressing possession.

EXPANDING LEARNERS

- Ask students to explain what happened in the two legends. Have students write a paragraph to summarize what they have just read and indicate from whom they got the information. Ask students to use the preterite and imperfect tenses to tell what happened. For example: *Mientras hablaba con Tess, Asha escuchó una leyenda de México. La leyenda era sobre una mujer muy linda que…*

¿Comprendes?

▶ **Responde** a estas preguntas.

1. ¿Dónde se originó la leyenda de la Llorona?
2. ¿Quién era ella? ¿Por qué llora todas las noches?
3. Según la leyenda, ¿qué buscaban los españoles en la Florida?
4. ¿Cuál fue la primera ciudad que fundaron en la Florida?

▶ **Explica.** ¿Cuál de las dos leyendas te gusta más? ¿Por qué?

63 **La leyenda de las cataratas del Iguazú**

▶ **Escucha** la leyenda que le cuenta Asha a Lucas y relaciona los nombres de los personajes con la ilustración.

1. Naipí
2. Boi
3. Tarobá

▶ **Escucha** otra vez la leyenda y ordena estas oraciones.

a. Un joven muy valiente llamado Tarobá llegó a la zona.
b. Tarobá se transformó en los árboles de las cataratas.
c. Los indígenas eligieron a Naipí para sacrificarla.
d. Naipí se convirtió en una catarata.
e. Tarobá y Naipí escaparon por la noche en una canoa.
f. En el río Iguazú vivía una serpiente muy grande.
g. La serpiente se enojó y dividió el río en dos partes, formando las cataratas.

▶ **Escribe** un resumen de la leyenda de las cataratas del Iguazú.

CONEXIONES: LITERATURA

Las leyendas tradicionales

Las leyendas son historias fantásticas o maravillosas que se presentan como hechos reales. Generalmente, las leyendas tienen un origen antiguo y van pasando de padres a hijos, de generación en generación.

Casi todas las culturas del mundo crearon leyendas para contar sus creencias (*beliefs*) y tradiciones. En muchos casos, estas historias explican el origen de elementos naturales mediante historias que reflejan los valores y la forma de pensar de esa cultura.

CUENTOS Y LEYENDAS DE — AMÉRICA LATINA

64 **Habla.** ¿Qué leyendas tradicionales conoces? Cuenta una a tu compañero(a).

Narrar y describir en pasado

64. Have a classroom discussion on the popularity of legends and why this genre has endured over so many years. Explore with students why they think many legends are similar even though they come from different areas of the world.

AUDIO SCRIPT
See page 11 J.

CONEXIONES: LITERATURA

Las leyendas tradicionales

Legends, myths, folktales, fables, and fairy tales are all fictionalized accounts of events. A legend is a story that often explains the origin of something. A myth is usually an ancient story that deals with supernatural beings, ancestors, or heroes and explains some beliefs. Folktales are part of the oral tradition of a people. Fables are stories that teach a lesson and often involve animals that talk. Fairy tales are stories written for children and describe fantastic forces and beings.

Answer Key

61. Pretérito: contaron, existió, se casó, tuvieron, se separó, mató, se arrepintió, escuchaste, motivó, oyeron, viajaron, llegaron, encontraron, fundaron.
Imperfecto: era, estaban, decía, convertía.

62. 1. Se originó en México.
2. Era una mujer muy linda que se arrepintió de haber matado a sus hijos.
3. La fuente de la eterna juventud.
4. Fundaron San Agustín.
▶ Answers will vary.

63. 1. la joven 2. la serpiente 3. el joven
▶ f, c, a, e, g, b, d
▶ Answers will vary.

64. Answers will vary.

Additional Resources

Fans Online activities

HERITAGE LANGUAGE LEARNERS

• Legends are very important in any society. Have students ask a family member or use the Internet to find a legend from their country of origin. Then ask them to retell it in their own words. Sometimes legends change as they pass from generation to generation. Ask students to tell it however they see fit. For example, if the ending or the moral of the story seems too unrealistic, then have students tell the story the way they would like to hear it.

MULTIPLE INTELLIGENCES:
Intrapersonal Intelligence

• Have students look at the illustrations for *Flor de leyendas* and pay close attention to each person's body language. Ask students to answer in writing the following questions about what they observed:

1. Describe and compare the people in each illustration.
2. What is the relationship between the people in the illustrations?
3. What is the time period?
4. What were the people doing?

Unit 1
DESAFÍO 3

Vocabulario – Biografías

Presentation

- In this section, students will learn key words to describe the life cycle and events, and practice this vocabulary while reading a biography.

Activities	Standards	Resources
Vocabulario	1.2, 2.1, 2.2, 3.2	
65.	1.2, 1.3	
66.	1.2	
67.	1.2, 1.3	
68.	1.1, 1.2	Audio
69. Conexiones	1.1, 1.2, 2.1, 2.2, 3.2, 5.1	

Teaching Suggestions

Warm-Up / Independent Starter

- Ask students to list some words they might expect to see in a biography.

Preparation

- Read aloud the words in the *Más vocabulario* feature and have students repeat them after you. Ask students which ones are easily decodable because they are cognates.
- Call on volunteers to read the highlighted words in *Biografías* and explain what each word means. You may want to first read the biography aloud to model pronunciation, and then have students take turns reading paragraphs.

Activities

65. To expand this activity, have students work with a partner and come up with definitions (in Spanish) for other words in the biography or in the *Más vocabulario* feature.

67. Students can each make up their own logical or illogical sentence and read it aloud to the class. The other students compete against one another and try to be the first to correctly label the sentence and, if it is illogical, make the necessary corrections.

69. Have students think of people they have read about or known who have emigrated to another country. Ask them to describe this person's experience.

44

DESAFÍO 3

Vocabulario

Biografías

Esmeralda Santiago

Esmeralda Santiago **nació** en 1948 en San Juan (Puerto Rico), donde pasó su **niñez**. En su **adolescencia**, a los trece años, se trasladó a Nueva York con su madre y sus diez hermanos. Estudió teatro y baile en la New York City's Performing Arts High School y **se graduó** de la universidad de Harvard en 1976. Actualmente vive en Nueva York con su marido, el director de cine Frank Cantor, y tiene dos hijos.

Esmeralda escribió tres libros autobiográficos. El primero, *Cuando era puertorriqueña*, cuenta su **infancia** en Puerto Rico. El segundo, *Casi una mujer*, se centra en su **juventud** en Nueva York. Y el tercero, *El amante turco*, trata sobre los años de juventud hasta su **graduación** en Harvard. Todos han recibido excelentes críticas y varios premios.

Su primera novela de ficción se titula *America's Dream*. Fue un gran éxito y se tradujo *(was translated)* a seis idiomas. Trata de la vida de una **joven** puertorriqueña que sale de la isla en busca de una vida nueva.

Esmeralda Santiago es también autora de varios artículos, cuentos infantiles y documentales, y colabora como voluntaria en varias asociaciones.

Esmeralda Santiago (Puerto Rico).

Más vocabulario

Etapas y acontecimientos de la vida

el embarazo	pregnancy
el nacimiento	birth
la juventud	youth
la madurez	adulthood
la vejez	old age
la muerte	death

Ritos y celebraciones

el aniversario	anniversary
el bautizo	baptism
la jubilación	retirement
el matrimonio	marriage

Religiones

el budismo	Buddhism
el cristianismo	Christianity
el hinduismo	Hinduism
el islamismo	Islam
el judaísmo	Judaism

65 **Definiciones**

▶ **Escribe** oraciones para definir estas palabras.

Modelo la niñez ⟶ *La niñez es*
la primera etapa de la vida.

1. el nacimiento
2. la adolescencia
3. la vejez
4. la graduación
5. la jubilación

Differentiated Instruction

DEVELOPING LEARNERS

- Have students read Esmeralda Santiago's biography in small groups. Each student in the group reads one sentence at a time until all the sentences have been read. Ask students: Do you think Esmeralda Santiago's life and works are important? Would you like to do some of the things she has done in her life? What would you need to do in order to accomplish what she has accomplished?

EXPANDING LEARNERS

- Ask students to go on the Internet and to look for pictures of Esmeralda Santiago. On most search engines, you can find an option for "Images." There are many photos of the author from her childhood to adulthood. Have students describe Santiago at each stage in her life and explain what they believe she was doing or going through at the time of the picture. For example: *En esta foto, Esmeralda era una adolescente. Creo que estaba en Puerto Rico. Seguramente iba a la escuela y le gustaba escribir.*

66 Asociaciones

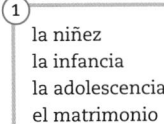

▶ **Busca** el intruso en cada grupo.

1
la niñez
la infancia
la adolescencia
el matrimonio

2
el bautizo
la jubilación
el judaísmo
el matrimonio

3
la vejez
el aniversario
la juventud
la madurez

67 El ciclo de la vida

▶ **Decide** si estas oraciones son lógicas o no. Después, corrige las que no lo son.

1. Cuando Inés terminó sus estudios, invitó a todos sus amigos a su nacimiento.
2. Los novios celebraron su graduación en la iglesia.
3. El embarazo de Ana fue bien. Ayer nació su hijo, Carlitos.
4. Mis padres llevan veinte años casados y mañana celebran su juventud con una fiesta.
5. Lucía trabajó veinticinco años en el hospital y, por fin, se jubiló.

68 Conversaciones

▶ **Escucha** y elige la pregunta o el comentario que corresponde a cada intervención.

a. Seguro que estará muy elegante en su fiesta de aniversario.

b. ¿Dónde celebraron su boda?

c. ¿Cuántos años hacía que trabajaban en esa escuela?

d. ¡Enhorabuena! ¿Dónde quieres trabajar?

e. ¡Qué bien! ¿Es su primer hijo?

f. ¿Fue un niño o una niña?

CONEXIONES: LITERATURA

Cuando era puertorriqueña

La escritora puertorriqueña Esmeralda Santiago empezó escribiendo novelas autobiográficas. *Cuando era puertorriqueña* es la primera parte de sus memorias. En este libro, la autora narra su infancia en Puerto Rico y su llegada a Nueva York, donde tuvo que acostumbrarse a una nueva cultura.

69 **Explica.** ¿Qué dificultades crees que tuvo Esmeralda Santiago cuando emigró?

 AUDIO SCRIPT
See page 11 J.

CONEXIONES: LITERATURA

Cuando era puertorriqueña

Many autobiographies inspire readers, and *Cuando era puertorriqueña* does not fail to do so. It tells the story of a girl of modest means who comes to New York with her family at the age of 13 and goes on to graduate from Harvard *magna cum laude* and become a successful author. In writing her life story, Santiago said she wanted to explain to her children what her life was like in Puerto Rico.

Answer Key

65. Answers will vary. Sample answers:
1. El nacimiento es cuando llegamos al mundo.
2. La adolescencia es el período entre los 13 y 19 años.
3. La vejez es el período a partir de los 65 o 70 años.
4. La graduación es cuando terminamos los estudios.
5. La jubilación es cuando dejamos de trabajar en la vejez.

66. 1. el matrimonio 3. el aniversario
2. el judaísmo

67. 1. Invitó a sus amigos a su graduación.
2. Celebraron su matrimonio.
3. Es lógica.
4. Celebran su aniversario.
5. Es lógica.

68. 1. b 2. e 3. a 4. f 5. c 6. d

69. Answers will vary.

Additional Resources

Fans Online activities
Practice Workbook

HERITAGE LANGUAGE LEARNERS

• When Esmeralda Santiago wrote her autobiography, she chose the most interesting and influential periods in her life. Ask students to choose a time period in their lives that would make the best story. Have students use a web similar to the one below to brainstorm the main ideas of their autobiographies.

COOPERATIVE LEARNING

• Pair expanding learners with developing learners. Have developing learners read the biography of Esmeralda Santiago aloud to their partner. Have expanding learners check their partner's comprehension by asking yes/no questions throughout the reading. For example:

A. *¿Esmeralda nació en Nueva York?*
B. *No. Esmeralda nació en Puerto Rico.*

45

DESAFÍO 3

Gramática – El pretérito y el imperfecto

Presentation

- In this section, students will review the preterite and the imperfect, compare the uses of these verb tenses to one another, and learn how certain verbs change meaning according to whether the preterite or imperfect is used.

Activities	Standards	Resources
Gramática	1.2, 3.1	
70.	4.1	
71.	1.1, 1.2, 3.1	
72.	1.1, 1.2, 2.2	Audio
73.	1.2, 1.3, 2.2, 3.1, 3.2	

Teaching Suggestions

Warm-Up / Independent Starter

- Ask students to write a few sentences, some explaining something they used to do, and others describing something they started and completed in the past.

Preparation

- Have students read the grammar explanations silently, take notes on any material they do not understand, and review the conjugations noted if they need to refresh their memory. Ask them to focus their attention on those verbs that change meaning.

- Ask students to share their Independent Starters with the class and have the class correct each student's work to make sure that they made proper use of the tenses. Review the uses of each tense if students made errors.

- Call on volunteers to read aloud the examples of those verbs that change meaning according to whether they are in the imperfect or the preterite. Ask other students to give another example with each of these verbs in both tenses.

Activities

71. Ask students to write one sentence for each of the verbs that change meaning and exchange papers with a partner who will translate them into English.

46

Gramática

El pretérito y el imperfecto

Los tiempos del pasado

- You already know that in Spanish we use two tenses to talk about the past: the preterite tense (canté) and the imperfect tense (cantaba).

  Cuando **estaba** en la universidad, **conocí** a mi esposo.

  In order to review the conjugations of the preterite and the imperfect, see page R12.

El pretérito y el imperfecto en la narración

- In general, use the **preterite tense** to talk about past actions that are presented as completed actions. And use the **imperfect tense** to talk about past actions that lasted a certain time, without mentioning the end.

  El verano pasado **estuvimos** en Lima.   De pequeña yo no **hablaba** español.

- When telling a story in the past, we use both the preterite and the imperfect tenses:
  – Use the **preterite** to talk about past actions or events that happened in the story.
  – Use the **imperfect** to describe characters and setting and, in general, to explain the circumstances surrounding an event.

  Yo **llegué** a esta escuela en el año 2009. **Era** muy tímida y no **hablaba** inglés. Pero después **aprendí** la lengua e **hice** muchos amigos.

- Some verbs express a different meaning in the preterite than they do in the imperfect.

VERBOS CON DIFERENCIAS DE SIGNIFICADO

	PRETÉRITO	IMPERFECTO
conocer	Conocí a John. (*I met John.*)	Conocía a John. (*I knew John.*)
poder	Ayer pude ir. (*Yesterday I succeeded in going.*)	Ayer podía ir. (*Yesterday I was able to go.*)
querer	No quise llamarte. (*I refused to call you.*)	No quería llamarte. (*I didn't want to call you.*)
saber	Supe la verdad. (*I found out the truth.*)	Sabía la verdad. (*I knew the truth.*)
tener	Tuve fiebre. (*I got a fever.*)	Tenía muchos amigos. (*I had many friends.*)

70 **Compara.** ¿Hay equivalentes al pretérito y al imperfecto en inglés? ¿Cómo se expresa la diferencia entre una acción y una descripción en pasado?

71 **Lo que pasaba y lo que pasó**

 ▶ **Responde.** ¿Por qué se usa el pretérito o el imperfecto en cada caso?
1. a. Beto **conoció** a Chela durante su adolescencia.
   b. Beto **conocía** a Chela desde que eran muy jóvenes.
2. a. Cuando Eva me mintió, **supe** que no era una buena amiga.
   b. Yo no **sabía** que Eva no era sincera.

46 cuarenta y seis

Differentiated Instruction

DEVELOPING LEARNERS

- Review the legend of Popocatépetl with students. Tell them to imagine that they are watching a movie. Without conjugating the verbs, have students classify which parts of the story are background or details and which parts are a main action. Then have students conjugate the background/detail verbs in the imperfect and the main action verbs in the preterite tense. Have volunteers read the completed story aloud.

EXPANDING LEARNERS

- Have students describe a memorable birthday. They should describe where they were, what they did, how they were feeling at the time, and anything else that made the birthday memorable. Tell students to illustrate their writing either by drawing a picture or by making a collage. Once students have finished, have volunteers share their birthday memories with the class.

72 La investigación

▶ **Escucha** la conversación de Asha y Lucas, y responde a estas preguntas.

1. ¿Adónde fue Lucas para encontrar información sobre leyendas hispanas?
2. En su opinión, ¿cómo eran esas leyendas?
3. ¿Dónde buscó más información?
4. ¿Con quién habló Asha para buscar información?
5. ¿Y adónde fue después?
6. Según Asha, ¿cómo era la leyenda que le contaron?

73 Una leyenda volcánica

▶ **Completa** la leyenda que le contaron a Asha poniendo los verbos en la forma correcta del pretérito o del imperfecto.

Leyenda de Popocatépetl e Iztaccíhuatl

Cuenta la leyenda que hace mucho tiempo Popocatépetl, un joven guerrero (*warrior*) que ___1___ (ser) muy valiente, se ___2___ (enamorar) de Iztaccíhuatl, la hija del cacique (*chief*). El joven le ___3___ (decir) al cacique que ___4___ (querer) casarse con su hija. El cacique le ___5___ (prometer) celebrar la boda si Popocatépetl ___6___ (ir) a la guerra y ___7___ (volver) victorioso.

El joven Popocatépetl ___8___ (ir) a la guerra. Y mientras ___9___ (estar) luchando (*fighting*), el cacique ___10___ (mandar) decir a Iztaccíhuatl que Popocatépetl ___11___ (estar) muerto. Ella se puso muy triste y ___12___ (morir). Cuando Popocatépetl ___13___ (volver) victorioso, ___14___ (oír) la noticia de la muerte de su amada y también murió de pena (*grief*).

Volcanes Popocatépetl e Iztaccíhuatl (México).

Para recordar ese gran amor, los dioses cubrieron de nieve los cuerpos de Iztaccíhuatl y Popocatépetl, y los ___15___ (transformar) en dos altas montañas que hoy podemos ver cerca de Ciudad de México: los volcanes Popocatépetl e Itztaccíhuatl. Así, los jóvenes ___16___ (quedar) unidos para siempre, como eternos enamorados.

▶ **Dibuja** una historieta sobre esta leyenda y preséntala a la clase.

cuarenta y siete **47**

Gramática – El pretérito y el imperfecto

72. Ask students to write both true and false statements based on the audio. Ask them to exchange papers with a partner who will indicate if the statements are true or false, and correct the false ones.

73. Have volunteers research other versions of this legend and present these versions to the class.

 AUDIO SCRIPT
See page 11J.

Answer Key

70. En inglés se usa *used to* o *would* en situaciones habituales o que se repetían. (*I would spend all my summers with my aunt.* Pasaba todos los veranos con mi tía.) Generalmente, en inglés no hay diferencia entre las descripciones y las acciones en el pasado. (*Esmeralda was 13 years old when she arrived in New York.* Esmeralda tenía 13 años cuando llegó a Nueva York.)

71. 1. a. *Beto met Chela for the first time.*
　　　b. *Beto has known Chela for years.*
　　2. a. *I found out something.*
　　　b. *I didn't know something about her.*

72. 1. Fue a la biblioteca.
　　2. Eran muy largas y muy difíciles.
　　3. Buscó más información en Internet.
　　4. Habló con un profesor de Español.
　　5. Fue a un restaurante mexicano.
　　6. Era muy bonita.

73. 1. era　　7. volvía　　13. volvió
　　2. enamoró　8. fue　　　14. oyó
　　3. dijo　　9. estaba　　15. transformaron
　　4. quería　10. mandó　　16. quedaron
　　5. prometió 11. estaba
　　6. iba　　12. murió
　　▶ Answers will vary.

Additional Resources
Fans Online activities
Practice Workbook

HERITAGE LANGUAGE LEARNERS

• Have students play a game of charades. Each student writes five sentences on strips of paper about the past where one action was interrupted by another. Students should use a verb in the preterite and a verb in the imperfect tense in each sentence. Once students have finished, have them fold their sentence strips and place them in a bag. Ask volunteers to pick a clue out of the bag and act it out for the class to guess the complete sentence.

SPECIAL-NEEDS LEARNERS

• For students with Asperger's Syndrome, it is very important to present the material in a clear manner and to give them time to absorb what is said. A student with Asperger's Syndrome will often have problems "reading between the lines," as well as understanding word play or figurative language, so make sure to present information using clear, consistent, and straightforward language for these students. You may also want to provide additional worksheets and material before the class so that students can internalize the information ahead of time.

DESAFÍO 3

Gramática – Expresiones temporales para la narración

Presentation

- In this section, students will use time expressions in their narratives.

Activities	Standards	Resources
Gramática	1.2, 3.1	
74.	4.1	
75.	1.1	
76.	1.2, 1.3	
77.	1.2, 1.3	
78. Cultura	1.1, 1.2, 2.2, 3.1, 5.1	Video

Teaching Suggestions

Warm-Up / Independent Starter

- Have students read the grammar presentation silently. Then ask them to think of other time expressions they know and make a list of these words.

Preparation

- Ask students to share their Independent Starters with the class and help them to categorize each time expression with the corresponding tense. Call on two students to compose a class list, showing time expressions used with the preterite and other expressions used with the imperfect. Display this master list in the classroom. Encourage students to refer to this list as they work on the activities on pages 48–49.

Activities

75. Ask students to compare and contrast their partner's responses with theirs. For example: *Pedro vio una película ayer con unos amigos, pero yo fui al cine la semana pasada con mi hermana.*

76. To extend this activity, ask students to write three or four sentences based on the model, exchange papers with a partner, and have them write a related question and answer, again following the model.

77. Ask students to explain why they chose each of the verb tenses.

Gramática

Expresiones temporales para la narración

Marcadores de pasado

- Some time expressions indicate that the action has been completed, and they are usually paired with verbs in the **preterite tense**. Others indicate that the action continued and / or was repeated in the past and they usually go with verbs in the **imperfect tense**.

  El año pasado estuvimos en Canadá. Todos los días hacíamos excursiones.

Acción terminada (pretérito)	Acción no terminada o acción habitual (imperfecto)	
anoche	antes	generalmente
ayer	de niño, de pequeño, de joven…	muchas veces
anteayer	cuando era niño/pequeño…	normalmente
el martes/mes/año pasado	a menudo	siempre
el 2 de enero de 2010	frecuentemente	todos los días

Otras expresiones de pasado

- Remember that you can use the word *hace* to express the amount of time elapsed since an action was completed.

preterite tense + hace + time expression	*Llegué a casa hace dos horas.*

hace + time expression + que + preterite tense	*Hace dos horas que llegué a casa.*

- You can use the word *hacía* with the imperfect tense to describe an action or event that began in the past and continued for some time.

imperfect tense + desde hacía + time expression	*Estudiaba español desde hacía dos años.*

hacía + time expression + que + imperfect tense	*Hacía dos años que estudiaba español cuando viajé a México.*

74 **Compara.** ¿Qué expresiones se usan en inglés para hablar de algo que empezó y continuó en el pasado?

75 **¿Cuándo…?**

▶ **Pregunta** a tu compañero(a). ¿Cuándo hizo estas cosas por última vez?

> ir a una boda   ver una película   estar en la biblioteca   hacer un viaje

Modelo   A. *¿Cuándo fue la última vez que fuiste a una boda?*
B. *Hace dos años. Fui a la boda de mi prima en Boston. ¿Y tú?*

Differentiated Instruction

DEVELOPING LEARNERS

- Provide students with the following sentence starters: *Ayer…, Cuando era joven…, Anoche…, A menudo…, Siempre…, El verano pasado…* and have them complete the sentences about themselves or family members. Have students share their sentences with the class. Remind them to consider whether they are talking about a habitual action or a specific, completed action in the past. If students continue to exhibit difficulty with choosing the correct tense, review the time expressions and discuss how they do or do not refer to specific moments in time.

EXPANDING LEARNERS

- Have students use the word *hace* to describe their morning routine today. Tell students to provide a detailed account of how they spent their morning from the time they woke up until the time they reached this class. Have volunteers share their routines with the class. Then have students compare their routine with that of a partner. For example:

  1. *Hace tres horas que me levanté. No me duché porque me duché por la noche, hace once horas…*

  2. *Fernando y yo nos levantamos hace tres horas y…*

76 **La vida de Lucas**

▶ **Escribe** preguntas y respuestas siguiendo el modelo.

Modelo   Lucas y su familia se fueron a vivir a la Florida hace cuatro años.
   → ¿*Cuánto tiempo hace que Lucas y su familia se fueron a vivir a la Florida?*
   Hace cuatro años que Lucas y su familia se fueron a vivir a la Florida.

1. Lucas empezó a estudiar Español en la escuela hace tres años.
2. Lucas comenzó su clase de Francés hace un mes.
3. Lucas no ganaba un partido de baloncesto desde hacía tres meses.
4. Lucas no veía a sus amigos de la infancia desde hacía un año.

77 **Un mensaje de correo**

▶ **Completa** el mensaje de correo de Lucas poniendo los verbos en imperfecto o en pretérito.

De: | Lucas
• Para: ▶ Asha
Asunto:
Cuerpo del texto | Anchura variable | | A+ A+ | B I U |

Hola, Asha. ¿Qué tal? Estoy otra vez en la biblioteca. Hace solo dos días que ___1___ aquí,
(estar)
pero esta mañana ___2___ volver para buscar más información.
(decidir)
___3___ hace una hora. ___4___ mirando en los estantes cuando ___5___ la bibliotecaria
(Llegar)   (Estar)   (venir)
para ayudarme. Rápidamente ella ___6___ un libro de leyendas mayas. Me ___7___ en una
(encontrar)   (sentar)
mesa y empecé a leer. Las historias son muy interesantes y no son muy largas. Hace diez
minutos ___8___ el libro. ¡Lo leí entero! Mientras lo ___9___ , ___10___ muchas notas para
(terminar)   (leer)   (tomar)
escribir nuestra propia leyenda. ¿Quieres que nos veamos esta tarde?

Lucas

CULTURA

Leyendas de Guatemala

El escritor guatemalteco Miguel Ángel Asturias (1899-1974)
escribió *Leyendas de Guatemala* en 1930. Esta obra es
una selección de tradiciones y mitos de las Américas.
Miguel Ángel Asturias siempre estuvo interesado en la cultura
maya. Estudió y tradujo *(translated)* el *Popol Vuh*, el libro sagrado
de los mayas que explica el origen del mundo y del hombre.

Acuarela de Diego Rivera
(México). *La creación del hombre.*

78 **Investiga.** Busca más información sobre la vida y la obra de Miguel Ángel Asturias.
Comparte los datos con tu compañero(a).

HERITAGE LANGUAGE LEARNERS

• Parents and grandparents often talk about
how much more difficult their life growing up
was compared to young people today. Have
students think about these family "legends"
they may have heard. Ask them to write about
one of these family stories. Remind students
to include both descriptive and main actions
in their stories. Ask volunteers to share their
family legends with the class.

CRITICAL THINKING

• Our society today is shaped by the
contributions of others in the past. Have
students think about the things we have
today and what had to happen for this to be
possible. For example, President Abraham
Lincoln freed the slaves in 1865, which led
to Dr. Martin Luther King Jr. proclaiming his
dream for equality in 1963, which helped
make it possible for Barack Obama to
become president of the United States in
2008. Ask students to think about similar
events and to create a timeline to show the
progression. Have them share these events
with the class.

Gramática – Expresiones temporales para la narración

CULTURA

Leyendas de Guatemala

In addition to being a poet, novelist,
playwright, journalist, and diplomat, Miguel
Ángel Asturias was also the recipient of the
Nobel Prize in Literature (1967). It was while
living on his grandparents' farm that he first
encountered indigenous culture. His nanny
used to tell him stories about the myths and
legends of the country's native peoples, and
these tales influenced his work.

Answer Key

74. Se usan expresiones como: *When I was a child, every summer, often, generally,* etc.

75. Answers will vary. Sample answers:
   2. ¿Cuándo fue la última vez que viste una película? Ayer. Fui con unos amigos.
   3. ... que estuviste en la biblioteca? Esta mañana. Saqué una novela.
   4. ... que hiciste un viaje? El verano pasado. Fuimos a Nueva York.

76. 1. ¿Cuánto tiempo hace que Lucas empezó a estudiar Español? Lucas empezó a estudiar Español hace tres años.
   2. ... hace que Lucas comenzó su clase de Francés? Hace un mes que Lucas comenzó su clase.
   3. ... hacía que Lucas no ganaba un partido de baloncesto? Hacía tres meses que Lucas no ganaba.
   4. ... hacía que Lucas no veía a sus amigos? Hacía un año que Lucas no veía a sus amigos.

77. 1. estuve   5. vino   9. leía
   2. decidí   6. encontró   10. tomé
   3. Llegué   7. senté
   4. Estaba   8. terminé

78. Answers will vary.

Additional Resources

Fans Online activities
Practice Workbook

49

LECTURA: TEXTO LITERARIO

Presentation

- In this section, students will read a legend about the origin of the Inca Empire. As they read, they will be aware of how the preterite and imperfect tenses are used in retelling the legend, and will also recognize how time expressions determine verb tense.

Activities	Standards	Resources
Lectura: texto literario	1.2, 2.2, 3.1, 3.2	
79.	1.1, 1.2, 2.2	
80.	1.2, 1.3, 3.1	
81.	1.1, 1.2, 2.2, 3.2	
82.	1.2, 1.3, 2.2, 3.1	

Teaching Suggestions

Warm-Up / Independent Starter

- Ask students to observe the picture, read the caption, and think about possible topics for the reading. They should not read the title or any other text on this page.

Preparation

- Call on individual students to share their responses from the Independent Starter. Do they have similar predictions regarding the topic of the reading? What led them to their particular prediction? Ask students what role they think pictures have in enhancing reading comprehension.

- Have students work with a partner to read the *Antes de leer* strategies. Then ask pairs to write the answers to the questions posed. Discuss the answers as a class.

- Read the legend aloud to model pronunciation and have students follow along in their books. Then call on individual students to each read a paragraph aloud. Offer assistance with pronunciation of the proper nouns in the story.

- After students have finished reading, ask them to find other cognates in the legend. Examples include: *leyenda, origen, imperio, devastó, decidieron, familias, resto, descubrieron, continuaron, fundó, capital.*

Antes de leer: estrategias

1. Lee el título. ¿Qué significa la palabra *imperio*? ¿Qué sabes sobre los incas?
2. ¿Qué información suelen ofrecer las leyendas?
3. Busca los cognados. ¿Qué significan las palabras *fértil, arrogante, caverna, grupo, ídolo, petrificado* y *estatua*?
4. Lee las tres primeras líneas. ¿Qué piensas que significa la palabra *diluvio*? ¿Es algo negativo o positivo? ¿Cómo lo sabes?

Los hermanos Ayar: una leyenda sobre el origen del imperio inca

Guerrero inca en Ollantaytambo (Perú).

Hace mucho tiempo un gran diluvio devastó las tierras de Pacariqtambo, en los Andes peruanos. Los hermanos Ayar vieron el mal estado de los cultivos y la pobreza[1] de la gente y decidieron buscar otro lugar más fértil y mejor para vivir. Eran cuatro hermanos: Ayar Manco, Ayar Cachi, Ayar Uchu y Ayar Auca. Los cuatro salieron de su ciudad con sus esposas y con otras familias y caminaron hacia el sureste.

Unos días después, hubo una pelea[2] entre Ayar Cachi, que era un joven fuerte y arrogante, y los demás. Sus hermanos estaban celosos y querían matarlo. Entonces lo enviaron[3] a la caverna de Pacarina a buscar semillas[4] y agua. Ayar Cachi entró en la caverna y su sirviente cerró la entrada con una gran piedra. Ayar Cachi no pudo salir nunca más.

Los otros hermanos y el resto del grupo siguieron caminando y llegaron a las tierras de Huanacauri. Allí descubrieron un ídolo de piedra. Ayar Uchu tuvo miedo y atacó al ídolo, pero quedó[5] petrificado para siempre.

Los hermanos y sus familias continuaron viajando, pero en el camino Ayar Auca se convirtió[6] también en estatua de piedra.

Por fin, Ayar Manco llegó con su familia a unas tierras muy buenas y decidieron quedarse allí. Ayar Manco fundó entonces una ciudad. Esta ciudad fue Cuzco (ombligo[7] en quechua), la capital del imperio inca.

1. *poverty*	3. *sent him*	5. *remained*	7. *navel*
2. *fight*	4. *seeds*	6. *became*	

Differentiated instruction

DEVELOPING LEARNERS

- Provide students with a sequence graphic organizer and display one on the board. Have students review the story with a partner and complete the graphic organizer with the events of the story in the right sequence. Tell students that they may add more boxes to the organizer as needed. Then review the sequence of events, writing them into the graphic organizer displayed on the board for students to check with their own work. Explain to students that they may use this graphic organizer to help them with the writing activities at the end of the section.

EXPANDING LEARNERS

- In small groups, have students talk about the events in the story. Ask them which elements of the story are reasonable, and what elements of the plot seem hard to believe. Then have each group rewrite the story according to what they believed happened. Once the groups have finished, have them read their story aloud to the class. Then take a class vote as to which story seems the most believable. Have the class compare the most believable story to the original story. How much of the story changed and how much stayed the same?

LECTURA: TEXTO LITERARIO

79 **Un orden lógico**

▶ **Ordena** estas oraciones según la lectura.

a. Ayar Cachi se peleó con sus hermanos.

b. Ayar Uchu se convirtió en piedra en la tierra de Huanacauri.

c. Todos caminaron hacia el sureste.

d. Ayar Manco fundó la ciudad de Cuzco.

e. Los hermanos Ayar salieron de Pacariqtambo porque la lluvia destrozó las tierras cultivadas.

f. Los hermanos lo metieron en una caverna.

80 **Expresiones equivalentes**

▶ **Escribe** una definición para estas palabras de la lectura.

1. diluvio
2. cultivo
3. fértil
4. caverna
5. ídolo
6. petrificado

Valle sagrado de los incas (Andes peruanos).

81 **Comprensión**

▶ **Lee** de nuevo el texto y responde a estas preguntas.

1. ¿Dónde vivían los hermanos Ayar?
2. ¿Por qué decidieron buscar otro lugar?
3. ¿Qué le pasó a Ayar Cachi?
4. ¿Qué encontraron en las tierras de Huanacauri?
5. ¿Qué hizo Ayar Manco?
6. ¿Cuál era la capital del Imperio inca?

82 **¡A dibujar!**

▶ **Escribe** un resumen del texto.

 ▶ **Dibuja** una tira cómica para ilustrar tu resumen y preséntala a la clase.

Activities

79. To extend this activity, have students write other events that took place in the legend, but write them out of order. Ask them to exchange papers with a partner, who should put them in the correct sequence.

80. Have students write an original sentence with each of these words. Then invite different volunteers to share their sentences.

81. Call on volunteers to come up with different questions to test comprehension.

Answer Key

79. 1. e   3. a   5. b
    2. c   4. f   6. d

80. Answers will vary. Sample answers:
    1. diluvio: lluvia excesiva
    2. cultivo: cosecha, plantación
    3. fértil: productivo
    4. caverna: cueva; un gran hueco en la piedra
    5. ídolo: figura de un dios
    6. petrificado: algo que se convirtió en piedra

81. 1. Vivían en Pacariqtambo, en los Andes peruanos.
    2. Un gran diluvio devastó sus tierras; los cultivos estaban en mal estado y la gente vivía en la pobreza.
    3. Sus hermanos lo metieron en una caverna y su sirviente cerró la entrada con una gran piedra. Ayar Cachi no pudo salir.
    4. Encontraron un ídolo de piedra.
    5. Fue el único hermano que llegó con su familia a unas tierras muy buenas.
    6. Cuzco era la capital del Imperio inca.

82. Answers will vary.
    ▶ Answers will vary.

Additional Resources

Fans Online activities

HERITAGE LANGUAGE LEARNERS

• Many myths and legends have a message or a lesson to teach. Have students discuss what message this legend is trying to teach. Ask them to think about the personalities of the characters and what happens to them. Then have students write about the message and explain how they arrived at that conclusion. Ask volunteers to share their ideas with the class.

MULTIPLE INTELLIGENCES:
Body-Kinesthetic Intelligence

• Have students work in groups to act out the legend of the Ayar brothers. They must decide the best way to communicate the story without using words. Then have the groups act out the story as volunteers in the class provide the narration based on what the actors are doing.

DESAFÍO 3

Comunicación

Presentation

- In this section, students will integrate the vocabulary and grammar skills from *Desafío 3* in order to talk about the cycle of life and tell a story in the past.

Activities	Standards	Resources
83.	1.1, 1.2, 1.3, 2.1, 5.1	
84.	1.2, 5.1	Audio
85. Final del desafío	1.1, 1.2, 1.3	

Teaching Suggestions

Warm-Up / Independent Starter

- Ask students to think about a romantic relationship that exists between some of their friends, family, or celebrities. Ask them to write a brief paragraph explaining who the couple is, and where and how they met. If their relationship ended in marriage, ask students to give the place and date of their union.

Preparation

- Go over the grammar topics from this *Desafío* and review the vocabulary related to the cycle of life. Clarify any doubts students may have regarding the use of the preterite and imperfect tenses to narrate an event or tell a story.

- Have students take out their paragraphs from the Independent Starter, add more details, make sure they have used both the preterite and imperfect correctly, and write a final draft. Call on students to read their paragraphs aloud. Make corrections and suggestions as needed, and ask the class comprehension questions at the end of each narrative.

Activities

83. After students have role-played their interviews for the class, take a class vote on the best interview. Criteria should include the most interesting and/or penetrating questions, the most original and/or insightful answers, and the most convincing acting while conducting the interview and answering the questions.

Comunicación

83 **Una historia de amor**

▶ **Lee** el reportaje y responde a estas preguntas.

Penélope y Javier: la pareja de moda

Los famosos actores españoles Javier Bardem y Penélope Cruz se conocieron el año 1992 durante el rodaje *(filming)* de la película *Jamón, Jamón*. Años después, en 2007, trabajaron en la película *Vicky Cristina Barcelona* y fue entonces cuando empezaron su relación amorosa. Bardem fue elegido mejor actor en el Festival de Cine de Cannes y al aceptar el premio *(prize)* dijo:

«Comparto esta alegría con mi amiga, mi compañera y mi amor, Penélope: te debo muchas cosas y te quiero mucho».

Javier Bardem y Penélope Cruz se casaron en las Bahamas el año 2010 y unos meses después anunciaron que Penélope estaba embarazada. El 22 de enero de 2011 nació Leo Encinas Cruz, el primer hijo de la pareja. Penélope y Javier celebraron el nacimiento del niño con sus familias, que viajaron a los Estados Unidos desde Madrid para conocer al recién nacido. Cuando le preguntaron por su experiencia como madre, Penélope explicó:

«Todas las experiencias que vives te enriquecen». Y añadió: «Ser madre es algo tan maravilloso...».

1. ¿Cuándo se conocieron Javier Bardem y Penélope Cruz?
2. ¿En qué película trabajaban cuando empezaron su relación?
3. ¿Dónde celebraron su boda?
4. ¿Cuánto tiempo hacía que se conocían cuando se casaron?
5. ¿Con quién celebraron el nacimiento de su primer hijo? ¿Qué nombre le dieron?
6. ¿A quién se refiere la expresión *recién nacido*?

▶ **Escribe** con dos compañeros(as) una entrevista para Penélope Cruz y Javier Bardem. Pregunten sobre su vida, su familia, sus aficiones...

Modelo   *Penélope, ¿dónde vivías de niña?*

▶ **Representa** la entrevista con tus compañeros(as).

Differentiated Instruction

DEVELOPING LEARNERS

- Have students make a timeline of their life so far. Ask them to think of major events in their life, such as when they met their best friend, started playing a sport they still play, memorable trips they took, or anything else they feel is significant. You may choose to limit the number of events on the timeline to ten. Then have students write a sentence that accompanies each event on the timeline. Finally, have them write a summary paragraph of their life so far. Encourage students to use time marker phrases, such as *hace ... años que..., desde hace...*

EXPANDING LEARNERS

- A century from now, people will look back on our times and write about our lives. Tell students to pretend it is the year 2112, and write a presentation about what was going on in what is now our present time. Tell them to talk about the clothing, schools, family dynamics, sports, and anything else they think will be significant knowledge a century from now. Once students have finished, have them share their presentation with the class.

84 Los momentos de la vida

▶ **Escucha** y relaciona cada oración con la fotografía correspondiente.

 Ⓐ
 Ⓑ
 Ⓒ
 Ⓓ
 Ⓔ

Final del desafío

Asha, creo que tengo una idea fabulosa para nuestra leyenda. Escucha. Es la historia de un hombre viejo que murió. Pero después de su muerte se sintió mejor y empezó a ser más y más joven. Poco a poco vivió su juventud, más tarde su infancia y, por último, nació otra vez.

¡Lucas, no inventaste nada! Esa es la historia del cuento *Viaje a la semilla*, del escritor cubano Alejo Carpentier.

¡No me digas! Bueno, no pasa nada. Yo soy muy creativo y tengo muchas más ideas para nuestra leyenda. Imagina que hay una fuente donde el agua te mantiene siempre joven...

¡Ay, ay, ay, Lucas! Ya lo veo. Eres muy imaginativo...

85 Una leyenda nueva

▶ **Lee** el diálogo y responde a estas preguntas.
1. ¿Por qué las ideas de Lucas no sirven para hacer una leyenda nueva?
2. ¿Existe una leyenda sobre una fuente con agua que mantiene joven? ¿De dónde viene?

▶ **Escribe** un párrafo para ayudar a Asha y a Lucas con otra idea para una leyenda.

cincuenta y tres 53

HERITAGE LANGUAGE LEARNERS

• Have students compare and contrast a couple they actually know with Penélope and Javier. Have them discuss similarities and differences in the way they met, their courtship, details of their marriage (if they married), and any children they had. Have students share their work with the class. Ask the class to discuss similarities between the couples they just heard about and the celebrity couple they read about.

CRITICAL THINKING

• Discuss with students events that are very life-changing, such as the first day of school ever, births, graduations, first jobs. Write a list of these events on the board and discuss how they can change someone's life. Encourage students to use real examples from their life or from what they have observed in the behavior of other people who have experienced these events. Then have students pick the three most life-changing events and write a few sentences explaining how and why they are such significant events.

Unit 1

DESAFÍO 3
Comunicación

84. To expand this activiy, ask students to find photos or illustrations from magazines or newspapers that depict life events. Then ask them to work with a partner; each one will display the events to the other and read statements out of order that describe these events. Partners must associate the correct event with each statement.

85. Have students work in small groups of three. Ask groups to research the life and works of Alejo Carpentier. Have them summarize their findings in a four-paragraph biography. They may use the biography of Esmeralda Santiago on page 44 as a model. Invite volunteers to share their biography of Carpentier with the class.

AUDIO SCRIPT
See page 11 J.

Answer Key

83. 1. Se conocieron en 1992 durante el rodaje de una película.
2. Trabajaban en *Vicky Cristina Barcelona*.
3. Celebraron su boda en las Bahamas.
4. Hacía 18 años que se conocían.
5. Celebraron el nacimiento con sus familias. Lo llamaron Leo.
6. Se refiere al hijo de Penélope y Javier: Leo Encinas Cruz.
▶ Answers will vary.
▶ Answers will vary.

84. 1. B   2. D   3. E   4. C   5. A

85. Answers will vary. Sample answers:
1. Las ideas de Lucas no son originales. Estas historias ya son leyendas muy conocidas.
2. Sí, existe una leyenda así. Esta leyenda viene de Puerto Rico, donde los españoles, durante la época colonial, oyeron hablar de ella.
▶ Answers will vary.

Additional Resources

Fans Online activities
Practice Workbook

53

Para terminar

Presentation

- In this section, students will review the unit objectives and put them into practice. They will talk about special events in people's lives, conduct an interview using the imperfect tense, and select one of the following *desafíos* to develop: write and draw a comic strip, prepare an audio guide that describes a work of art, or invent and write a legend.

Activities	Standards	Resources
86.	1.1, 1.2, 1.3, 5.1	
87.	1.1, 1.2, 1.3, 3.1, 5.1	
88. Tu desafío	1.1, 1.2, 1.3, 2.1, 2.2, 3.1, 5.1, 5.2	

Teaching Suggestions

Warm-Up / Independent Starter

- Have students go back and review the vocabulary and grammar sections in this unit. Ask them to imagine that they are going to interview someone who has recently celebrated a major life event. Have students write five or more questions, incorporating both the preterite and imperfect tenses and suitable time expressions into these questions that they would ask the person who is celebrating this event.

Preparation

- Have students work with a partner and read aloud their questions from the Independent Starter. Then ask the partner to answer the questions as if he or she were the celebrant. Call on volunteer pairs to present their questions and answers in front of the class.

- Ask students to identify each of the three events shown on this page and brainstorm some words and phrases associated with each one. For example: *boda → novios, casarse, banquete, matrimonio, felicidad; graduación → fin del curso, celebración, prepararse para la universidad, nuevos desafíos; quinceañera → celebrar el cumpleaños, regalos, decoraciones, pastel, fiesta.* Then ask students if they have taken part in any of these kinds of celebrations. Invite volunteers to share their experiences with the class.

54

Todo junto

ESCRIBIR Y LEER

86 **Una experiencia inolvidable**

▶ **Elige** una de estas ilustraciones e imagina que asististe a ese evento. Escribe sobre esa experiencia para compartirla con tus amigos en tu red social.

Modelo   *Ayer asistí a la boda de mi prima Ana. Hacía muy buen tiempo…*

 ▶ **Lee** el texto de tu compañero(a) y hazle preguntas para saber más cosas de su evento.

ESCRIBIR Y HABLAR

87 **Una entrevista**

▶ **Escribe** seis preguntas para tu profesor(a) de Español sobre su vida cuando tenía quince años. Puedes tratar estos temas:

1. Descripción física.
2. Lugar donde vivía y estudiaba.
3. Personalidad.
4. Diversiones y pasatiempos.

 ▶ **Habla** con tu compañero(a) y elijan cinco preguntas. Después, hagan la entrevista y tomen notas para preparar un informe sobre su profesor(a).

 ▶ **Hagan** un cartel o una presentación comparando la vida de ustedes con la de su profesor(a) cuando tenía quince años. Preséntenla a la clase.

Modelo   *Cuando nuestra profesora de Español tenía quince años, vivía con su familia en…*

Differentiated instruction

DEVELOPING LEARNERS

- Have students work with a partner to complete *Tu desafío*. You may provide graphic organizers to help them with their writing. For A, use a sequence graphic organizer to help students map out their story. For B, have students consider questions that their *audioguía* should answer. Then have them do the research. For C, have students use a two-column graphic organizer for their legend. In one column they will write the main actions in the legend and in the other, the background actions and descriptions. Remind students to consider which tense applies to which kind of action.

EXPANDING LEARNERS

- Ask students to think about a significant event that happened in their lifetime. The event could be something political such as a presidential election, a milestone in science or technology, a sporting event such as the World Cup, the Olympics, or the Red Sox winning the World Series. Have students write about how old they were, what they were doing when the event occurred, how family and friends reacted to the event, and whatever else they remember about the event. Ask volunteers to share their work with the class.

Tu desafío

88 **Los desafíos**

¿Recuerdas los desafíos que Andy y Tess les plantearon a los personajes? ¿Cuál te gusta más? Elige una de estas opciones y resuelve tu desafío.

DESAFÍO Ⓐ

Escribe y dibuja una historieta gráfica. Incluye adjetivos de descripción física o de personalidad. Si quieres, puedes hacerla sobre uno de estos personajes de autores hispanos.

Mot (Nacho y Azpiri)

Este simpático monstruo, capaz de viajar a otras dimensiones, apareció en 1988 en un suplemento para niños del diario español *El País*. Sus historietas se adaptaron después a la televisión y a los videojuegos.

Máximo Chambónez (Themo Lobos)

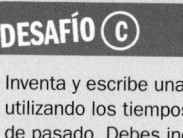

Según el diccionario, Chambón significa «persona de poca habilidad en el juego». Esta definición retrata bien a este personaje inocente y de buenas intenciones, al que nada le sale bien.

DESAFÍO Ⓑ

Elige uno de estos dos cuadros, busca información en Internet y elabora una audioguía. Debes describir el cuadro e incluir algo de información sobre el pintor.

Pablo Picasso (España).
La familia de saltimbanquis.

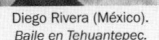

Diego Rivera (México).
Baile en Tehuantepec.

DESAFÍO Ⓒ

Inventa y escribe una leyenda utilizando los tiempos de pasado. Debes incluir alguno de estos elementos:

• **Personajes:** una princesa, un rey, un monstruo, un mago.

• **Acontecimientos:** una boda, una muerte, un viaje, una mentira.

• **Lugares:** un bosque, una selva, un desierto, un país muy lejano.

cincuenta y cinco **55**

Activities

86. Ask students to work with a partner to complete the first part of this activity. Explain that they both must choose the same event, but write about opposite experiences. For instance, if one of the partners writes about how much he liked the food at the wedding reception, the other partner should express the opposite. Once pairs have finished writing about their experiences at the event, have them get together with another pair for the second part of this activity. Have pairs ask each other about the reasons for such different experiences at the same event. For example:

A. *¿Por qué no te gustó la comida del banquete? Tu compañero dice que la comida estaba muy rica.*

B. *No me gustó porque era comida tailandesa y estaba muy picante. Pero a mi compañero le encanta el picante.*

87. For large classes, you may want to ask students to work in small groups rather than in pairs so that you will not have to endure so many interviews. Remind students to use the *usted* form when they address their teacher.

88. Display students' work in the classroom and have the class vote on the best entry in each category.

Answer Key

86. Answers will vary.
▶ Answers will vary.

87. Answers will vary.
▶ Answers will vary.
▶ Answers will vary.

88. Answers will vary.

Additional Resources

Fans Online activities

HERITAGE LANGUAGE LEARNERS

• Students have received several pieces of advice over their lifetimes. Ask them to describe the situations in which they received very useful advice, the advice given, and the outcome. For example: *Cuando era niña, tenía muchos problemas de la piel. Mi mamá me llevó al médico. Él me dijo que no debía tomar refrescos ni comer comida grasosa. También me mandó una pomada. A los tres o cuatro meses mi piel mejoró mucho.*

COOPERATIVE LEARNING

• Hold elections for Spanish class president. Select four students as your candidates, and have them choose a presidential election committee. Students must develop a campaign speech to detail the experiences and qualifications from their past that make them the ideal candidate. The committee must also create a list of questions to ask the other candidates to try to discredit their candidacy. Once students have finished writing their speeches and questions, have the candidates give their speeches and the committees ask their questions. Finally, through secret ballot, hold your class elections.

MAPA CULTURAL

La población latinoamericana

Presentation

- This section presents facts about the diverse origins and history of the population of the Spanish-speaking countries of Latin America. The map and images serve as a reference point for additional cultural readings and activities that expand on the skills students learned in this unit.

Activities	Standards	Resources
Mapa cultural	1.2, 2.1, 2.2, 3.1, 3.2	Video
89.	1.1, 1.2, 1.3, 2.1, 2.2, 3.1	

Cultural Topics

- **Los kuna: un pueblo indígena.** Most of Latin America's population is of mixed ancestry, but there are still some small groups of indigenous people who have preserved their traditional way of life. The Kuna are one of these groups. Located mainly along Panama's northeastern Caribbean coast, the San Blas Islands, and the Darien province, the Kuna resisted assimilation into the Spanish culture of the conquistadors. In 1925, the Kuna rebelled against the Panamanian government and were subsequently granted a special, semi-autonomous status.

- **Colombia: una muestra del mestizaje.** Colombia has a very diverse population and is, for this reason, a good example of Latin America's ethnic diversity. Colombia's population is a reflection of the intermingling of Amerindians, Europeans, and Africans. This intermingling has become so extensive that much of Latin America's population is multiracial. Colombia, like most countries in Latin America, does not record ethnicity information. In fact, most Latin Americans do not identify themselves as belonging to a particular ethnic ancestry and prefer to identify themselves in terms of their national origin.

Teaching Suggestions

Warm-Up / Independent Starter

- Ask students to jot down what they know about the different groups and peoples who have contributed to the creation of the United States' diverse population.

La población latinoamericana

En la antigüedad, las Américas estaban habitadas por distintos pueblos indígenas. Algunos alcanzaron un gran desarrollo, como los aztecas, los mayas y los incas, y se convirtieron en civilizaciones muy avanzadas.

A partir de 1492 empezó la colonización española. Durante la época colonial la población indígena se mezcló con los habitantes llegados de Europa, y este mestizaje se enriqueció aún más con la llegada de africanos a partir del siglo XVI.

La sociedad latinoamericana actual es una sociedad multicultural y multirracial, el resultado de la rica historia del continente.

Tres culturas

La cultura indígena

Algunos países de Latinoamérica tienen importantes minorías indígenas que conservan su lengua y sus costumbres: los mayas en México y Guatemala, los quechuas en Perú, Ecuador y Bolivia, y los guaraníes en Paraguay.

¿Sabías que...?

La mayor parte de la inmigración a Latinoamérica procedía de España, Portugal y Francia. Pero entre 1850 y 1950 llegaron a Latinoamérica numerosos inmigrantes de otras procedencias.

Libaneses, palestinos y sirios se establecieron en México, Colombia, Chile y Centroamérica.

La migración en América entre 1850 y 1950

En Argentina y Uruguay se estableció un gran número de italianos.

Muchos judíos de Europa del este emigraron a Argentina. También hubo emigración alemana hacia Argentina, Uruguay, Chile y Paraguay.

56 cincuenta y seis

Differentiated Instruction

DEVELOPING LEARNERS

- Ask pairs to read and analyze together the information presented in the *Mapa cultural*. Remind students that cognate words enhance their reading comprehension. Point out that most country names and the names given to people from a particular place are cognate words (e.g., *Caribe* → Caribbean, *chino(a)* → Chinese, *azteca* → Aztec).

- Then have pairs work together on a summary of the information in this *Mapa cultural*. These summaries do not necessarily have to be written. Students may, for instance, choose to summarize the information using a graphic organizer or pictures.

EXPANDING LEARNERS

- Ask students to work in small groups to research the history of the population of their state. Encourage them to use a variety of online sources (e.g., the U.S. Census Bureau, genealogical records, immigration records, vital statistics) as well as local library sources.

- Have groups organize their findings on chart paper. Alternatively, they may choose to do a PowerPoint™ or other digital presentation. Encourage the use of visual aids, such as graphic organizers, images, maps, etc. The presentation should be done entirely in Spanish.

La cultura europea

La presencia europea en el continente americano empezó con la llegada de los españoles en 1492. Durante siglos se establecieron en América muchos colonos procedentes de España. Y durante los siglos XIX y XX muchos europeos cruzaron el Atlántico en busca de una vida mejor.

La cultura africana

Los africanos llegaron a América como esclavos en la época colonial. Esta población se extendió desde las Antillas hacia Centroamérica y Suramérica.

La cultura africana tuvo gran influencia en los ritmos musicales latinos.

Algunos chinos y japoneses emigraron a Perú. Sus descendientes constituyen (make up) cerca del 5% de la población actual de este país.

Fisonomía latinoamericana

El mestizaje está patente tanto en la cultura como en las características físicas de la población latinoamericana.
Podemos encontrar rasgos asiáticos en algunos habitantes de Perú, personas afroamericanas con ojos claros en los países caribeños o gente rubia y con ojos azules en muchos países de Latinoamérica.

89 **Sociedades multiculturales y multirraciales**

▶ **Habla** con tu compañero(a) sobre las similitudes y diferencias entre la población latinoamericana y la estadounidense. Creen un diagrama de Venn y preséntenlo a la clase.

▶ **Investiga** uno de los siguientes temas y comparte la información con tus compañeros(as).

1. La comida chifa de Perú.
2. El género musical bomba, de Puerto Rico.
3. Los indígenas mapuches de Chile.
4. Los menonitas mexicanos.

Unit 1
MAPA CULTURAL
La población latinoamericana

Preparation

- Invite students to share their Independent Starters. You may want to create a transparency of the map on this page and add arrows for the different migrations of people to the United States. Remind students of the Native American nations for whom America was already home when the first Europeans arrived, as well as the African slaves who were forcibly brought from Africa, and include these groups in your map. Ask students to take notes during this discussion, since they will need this information for the first part of activity 89.

- Explain that the population of Latin America is the result of similar migrations and intermingling of people from different ethnic and cultural backgrounds. Then go over the *Mapa cultural* as a class.

Activities

89. For the second part of this activity, ask students to prepare a five-question true/false quiz based on the information they researched. As students present their information, ask the class to take notes. Then, at the end of all the presentations, distribute students' quizzes and see if the class is able to answer the questions correctly. If time allows, you may want to hold a class vote to select the most informative presentation.

Answer Key

89. Answers will vary.
▶ Answers will vary.

Additional Resources

Fans Online activities
Practice Workbook

HERITAGE LANGUAGE LEARNERS

- Ask students to research the history of the population of their heritage country. In addition to using reputable online and library sources, encourage them to interview family members as well as other people they know from their country of origin.

- Encourage creativity in the presentation of the information to the class. Students may, for instance, assemble a collection of pictures that showcases their country's population and let the pictures do the talking. If time allows, facilitate a question-and-answer session after each presentation.

CRITICAL THINKING

- Explain that some Latinos are puzzled by the demand for racial self-identification on nearly every application form they have to fill out in the United States. They sometimes feel that they don't really fit in any of those ethnic categories. Why might this be? Ask students to think of possible reasons for most countries in Latin America not to record ethnicity. Why might Latin Americans prefer to identify themselves in terms of their national origin rather than ethnic ancestry? Hold a class discussion to talk about these questions.

ESCRITURA

Un personaje interesante

Presentation

- In this section, students will practice and extend their writing skills, and apply the vocabulary and grammar they have learned in this unit. The writing objective for this unit is to create a character sketch. Students will follow a step-by-step guide consisting of four steps:

  – *Piensa*. Students will plan and develop their writing project, taking into account the type of text, their purpose for writing, and the audience.
  – *Escribe*. Students will write their first draft, striving to create an engaging and appropriate text, and following writing conventions.
  – *Revisa*. Students will evaluate their text. They will look at it critically to see if they have fulfilled their goals.
  – *Comparte*. Students will write the final draft, incorporating the necessary corrections and paying attention to the design and appearance of the text. They will then share their writing.

Activities	Standards	Resources
Escritura	1.1, 1.2, 1.3, 2.2, 3.1	

Teaching Suggestions

Warm-Up / Independent Starter

- Ask students to take a look back at all of the characters introduced in this unit and list them.

Preparation

- Explain to students that they will work on a writing project. First, they will be given the topic, the goal of the text, and an explanation of the type of text they will write. Then they will be guided through the writing process, which is divided into four steps. You may want to share with students the description of each step as explained in the Presentation section.

- Ask for a volunteer to read the Character Sketch box aloud. Explain that a character sketch is like a snapshot that highlights the most distinguishing characteristics and personality traits of the character. A good character sketch paints a picture of the character using words and supports it with strong and vivid details.

58

Un personaje interesante

Character sketch

One of the ways that authors, playwriters, and scriptwriters prepare realistic, three-dimensional characters is by creating a **character sketch** before they write the final work.

A character sketch introduces a character through a collection of significant details, so that the audience gets to know the person's appearance, personality, values, and motivation.

Not as complete as a **biography**, a character sketch gives a basic idea about what to expect from the character—and what *not* to expect.

Un autor famoso está escribiendo una nueva novela sobre uno de los personajes presentados en esta unidad, y quiere tu ayuda para crear un bosquejo (*sketch*) biográfico. Elige el personaje que te parece más interesante.

Piensa

- Piensa en el personaje que vas a describir. ¿Qué idea quieres dar de él o de ella? ¿Es un personaje principal o un personaje secundario? ¿Qué hace en la novela y por qué?

- Piensa en todos los aspectos que pueden ser útiles para describir detalles importantes del personaje: rasgos físicos, personalidad, experiencias significativas, etc. Crea una red para organizar estos puntos importantes.

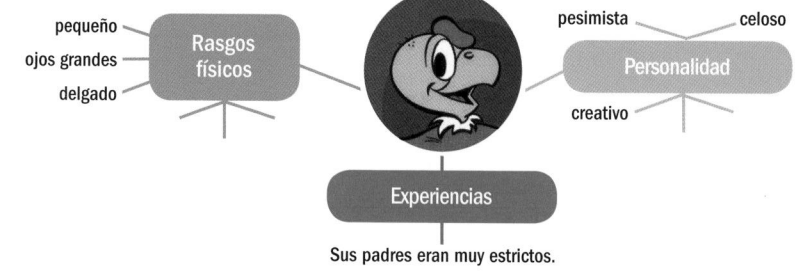

Rubric for Evaluation

	Content	Organization	Conventions
1 point	Limited relevance or significance. Does not capture reader's interest. Limited vocabulary. The main idea is not clear.	Focus on topic is not sustained. Details are not in a logical order. Few or no transitions between ideas.	Many errors in spelling, punctuation, grammar, and usage. Errors obscure meaning.
3 points	Most details are relevant and significant. Vivid images but some inaccurate word choices. Main idea is clear.	Mostly clear focus. Details may not be in the most effective order. Transitions used, but some don't work well.	Some errors in spelling, punctuation, grammar, and usage. Errors don't interfere with meaning.

Escribe

■ Utilizando la red de ideas, redacta el bosquejo del personaje. Escribe por lo menos tres párrafos: uno para cada tema de la red. Recuerda que debes dar detalles significativos para que el lector cree su propia idea del personaje y no olvides usar las Expresiones útiles para dar más fluidez (*fluidity*) al texto.

Expresiones útiles

Al principio.../Primero...	*At first ...*
Luego.../Después...	*Then ...*
Finalmente...	*Finally ...*
Entonces...	*Then ...*
De niño(a)...	*As a child ...*

Revisa

■ Intercambia tu texto con tu compañero(a).

■ Analiza el texto de tu compañero(a):

– ¿Qué opinas de esa descripción? ¿Es una descripción clara y ordenada? ¿Se utilizan los adjetivos necesarios para describir al personaje? Anota los cambios que creas que hay que hacer para mejorar el texto.

– ¿Cómo está escrito el texto? ¿Las oraciones están bien construidas? ¿Las palabras son correctas y están bien escritas? Subraya las palabras o las frases que crees que hay que corregir.

■ Devuelve el texto a su autor(a) con tus sugerencias y analiza las sugerencias que él/ella te propone para mejorar tu texto.

■ Corrige tu texto para que la descripción sea interesante y correcta.

Comparte

■ Reescribe tu texto con buena letra, incorporando todas las correcciones.

■ Dibuja una ilustración para acompañar tu texto. Incluye colores y un escenario que ayuden a comprender la idea general que quieres transmitir.

■ Presenta tu texto a la clase. ¡Buena suerte!

	Content	Organization	Conventions
5 points	Relevant and significant details bring character to life. Precise and vivid word choices. Main idea stands out.	Distinct focus and clear order. Effective use of transitions and logical flow of ideas.	Few, if any, errors in spelling, punctuation, grammar, and usage. Excellent command of the Spanish language.

ESCRITURA

Un personaje interesante

Step-by-Step Instructions

Piensa

■ Students will generate ideas and plan and organize their text. Have them use their Independent Starters to assist them in deciding on a character to write about. Ask students to review the vocabulary. A good command of descriptive adjectives will help them in choosing precise and vivid words. Explain that the reader should be able to get a clear mental image of the character.

Escribe

■ Students will write their first draft following the web they created in *Piensa*. Emphasize that they should show the character instead of just telling about him or her. The details should bring the character to life and the reader should be able to draw his or her own conclusions about the character.

■ Have students read their completed first draft aloud to themselves to see how it flows. Then ask them to make the necessary corrections and changes before they exchange it with a classmate.

Revisa

■ Have students read their partner's text through before they mark anything. Then ask them to read the text again, looking at the content and organization. After this first evaluation, have students read the text one more time, looking for spelling, punctuation, grammar, vocabulary, and usage errors.

Comparte

■ Explain that text-relevant illustrations have powerful effects on comprehension and appreciation of the text. Good illustrations and a fluid presentation will greatly enhance a well-written text.

Evaluation

■ Distribute copies of the rubric to students and discuss the evaluation criteria. Ask students to refer to the rubric as they prepare their projects and as they evaluate their classmates' texts.

REPASO

Vocabulario

Presentation

- In this section, students will review all key vocabulary from the unit, organized by themes, to prepare for an assessment. Students will complete practice activities for each of the three *Desafíos*.

Activities	Standards	Resources
1.	1.2, 1.3	
2.	1.1, 1.2	
3.	1.2, 1.3	

Teaching Suggestions

Warm-Up / Independent Starter

- Give students two or three minutes to draw a family tree of their own family—or a family they know well—similar to the tree in activity 2. Ask students to omit the names of the different family members, except for two. Have students leave blank spaces to write the rest of the names later on. The tree should have three branches and eight blank spaces.

Preparation

- Go over the *Repaso* presentation with the class. You may want to model pronunciation for words that cause students difficulties. Then ask students to make a separate list of the vocabulary words that are cognates. Remind them that cognate words enhance their comprehension and help them learn Spanish. Point out that there are also some false cognates and that they should be aware of these as well (e.g., *comprensivo* doesn't mean "comprehensive"; *embarazo* doesn't mean "embarrassment"; *familia política* doesn't mean "political family").

- Ask students to get together with a partner and exchange the family trees they drew for their Independent Starters. Have partners interview each other to fill out the missing names and complete the family tree. For example:

  A. *¿Cómo se llama el abuelo paterno de Tom?*
  B. *Bill.*
  A. *¿Y cómo se llama la nuera de Bill?*
  B. *Karen.*

Características físicas

la barba	beard
el bigote	mustache
la cicatriz	scar
el lunar	mole
las pecas	freckles

Tener...

ojos almendrados	almond-shaped eyes
pelo lacio	straight hair
pelo rizado	curly hair
pelo castaño	chestnut / brown hair

Ser...

calvo	bald
apuesto	handsome

Relaciones familiares

la madrastra	stepmother
el padrastro	stepfather
el/la hermanastro(a)	step-brother / step-sister
el/la hijo(a) adoptivo(a)	adopted son / daughter
el/la ahijado(a)	godson / goddaughter
materno(a)	maternal
paterno(a)	paternal
la pareja	partner, couple
el/la novio(a)	boyfriend / girlfriend
el/la esposo(a)	husband / wife
la familia política	family-in-law
el/la suegro(a)	father- / mother-in-law
el/la cuñado(a)	brother- / sister-in-law
el yerno	son-in-law
la nuera	daughter-in-law

Estar...

casado(a)	married
divorciado(a)	divorced
prometido(a)	engaged
separado(a)	separated
soltero(a)	single
viudo(a)	widower / widow
casarse	to marry

Rasgos de personalidad

amable	kind, nice
amistoso(a)	friendly
bondadoso(a)	kind
cariñoso(a)	warm, affectionate
chismoso(a)	gossipy
comprensivo(a)	understanding
cortés	kind, nice
egoísta	selfish
fiel	faithful
reservado(a), tímido(a)	shy
risueño(a)	cheerful
seguro(a) de sí mismo(a)	self-assured
travieso(a)	mischievous

Biografías

Etapas y acontecimientos de la vida

el embarazo	pregnancy
nacer	to be born
el nacimiento	birth
la infancia / niñez	childhood
la adolescencia	adolescence
la juventud	youth
la madurez	adulthood
la vejez	old age
la muerte	death
el/la niño(a)	child, boy / girl
el/la joven	young person
el/la adulto(a)	adult

Ritos y celebraciones

el aniversario	anniversary
el bautizo	baptism
la graduación	graduation
la jubilación	retirement
el matrimonio	marriage

Religiones

el budismo	Buddhism
el cristianismo	Christianity
el hinduismo	Hinduism
el islamismo	Islam
el judaísmo	Judaism

Differentiated Instruction

DEVELOPING LEARNERS

- Explain to students that to make new words a permanent part of their Spanish vocabulary, they need to continue reviewing beyond the point of familiarity to achieve true mastery. Have students think about their learning style (i.e., visual, auditory, kinesthetic) and assist them in devising word-learning strategies that work for them.

- Visual learners will benefit from the creation of illustrated flashcards. For students who are auditory learners, saying the words aloud and using a recording device to record themselves will help them. Kinesthetic learners will do well acting out the words.

EXPANDING LEARNERS

- Ask students to create an activity to quiz their classmates on the vocabulary. They may, for instance, list the definitions of vocabulary words and have their classmates fill in the word. For example: *Esta persona no tiene pelo. Es... (calva).* Another option would be to create a true/false quiz. For example: *Alguien chismoso no habla mal de los demás. (Falso)*

- Have students proofread their quiz before they administer it to a classmate. Then have them take each other's quizzes. How did they do? Do they know the unit vocabulary well?

DESAFÍO 1

1 **Mi primo favorito.** Lee el texto y escribe una descripción de Alberto usando otras palabras.

> **Mi primo favorito**
>
> Mi primo Alberto es un chico sensacional. No tiene el pelo lacio, como yo. ¡Qué suerte! Y tampoco es bajo. Siempre está sonriendo y le gusta compartir sus cosas con todos. Es muy cortés con su familia, pero no le gusta hablar en público. Alberto siempre saca buenas notas y no le gusta hablar mal de sus compañeros. ¡Él tiene muchos amigos!

Modelo   *Mi primo Alberto es un chico sensacional. Tiene el pelo rizado y...*

DESAFÍO 2

2 **¿Quién es quién?** Completa estas oraciones.

1. Mónica es la _____ de Manuela.
2. Pablo es el _____ de Beatriz.
3. Daniel es el _____ de Mónica.
4. Pablo y Mónica están _____.
5. Gabriel es el _____ de Daniel y de Manuela.
6. Pablo es el _____ de Tomás y de Laura.

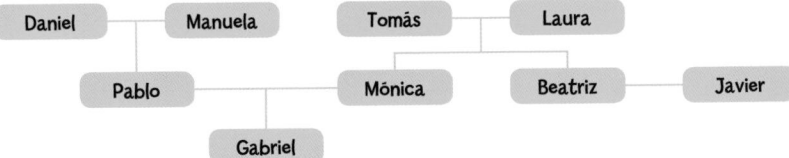

DESAFÍO 3

3 **La vida de Tania.** Relaciona cada etapa vital de Tania con un evento. Después, escribe su biografía.

1. la madurez
2. el nacimiento
3. la juventud
4. la adolescencia
5. la vejez

a. la jubilación
b. la quinceañera
c. el matrimonio
d. el bautizo
e. la graduación

HERITAGE LANGUAGE LEARNERS

- Have students think of a celebration, rite of passage, religious ceremony, etc. that is important for people in their country of origin. Then ask them to list, in a word web, the vocabulary related to this event. For example, if they choose the *quinceañera* as a significant event, they may list related words such as *chambelán* (honor escort), *damas* (maids of honor), *padrinos* (sponsors), etc.
- Ask students to present to the class their chosen event and the related vocabulary. Encourage them to explain the significance of the event and what it entails.

MULTIPLE INTELLIGENCES:
Verbal-Linguistic Intelligence

- Explain to students that they can guess the meaning of many Spanish words by thinking of a more formal way of saying something in English. For example: pharmacy (instead of drugstore) → *farmacia*; enter (instead of come in) → *entre*.
- Ask students to analyze the vocabulary and come up with alternative English translations of some of the words. Students' answers may include: *cortés* → courteous; *egoísta* → egotistical; *reservado* → reserved; *tímido* → timid; *infancia* → infancy; *madurez* → maturity; *matrimonio* → matrimony.

- Once students have completed the activity, have them return the family tree to their partner. Did they get the names and family relationships right? Then have students share with each other some of the physical characteristics and personality traits of the people in their family tree.

Activities

1. To expand this activity, have students write a paragraph that expresses the opposite. For example: *Mi primo Alberto es un chico muy antipático. Tiene el pelo lacio, como yo...* Invite two or three volunteers to read their versions to the class. Did they come up with different descriptions of Alberto?

3. Ask students to work with a partner to complete this activity. Have pairs consider other events in Tania's life, such as children, a divorce, a death in the family, etc. Ask pairs to include these events in their narrative. Invite volunteers to share their paragraphs with the class.

Answer Key

1. Answers will vary. Sample answer:
   Mi primo Alberto es un chico sensacional. Tiene el pelo rizado y es alto. Es risueño y bondadoso. Es muy amable con su familia, pero es reservado. Alberto es estudioso y no es chismoso. ¡Él es amistoso!

2. 1. nuera   4. casados
   2. cuñado   5. nieto
   3. suegro   6. yerno

3. 1. c   2. d   3. e   4. b   5. a
   Answers will vary. Sample answer:
   Tania fue bautizada poco después de su nacimiento. Cuando era adolescente tuvo su fiesta de quinceañera. En su juventud se graduó y poco después, en su madurez, se casó. En la vejez, Tania se jubiló.

Additional Resources

Fans Online activities
Practice Workbook

61

REPASO

Gramática

Presentation

- Students will review grammatical structures presented in the unit. Each grammar point is cross-referenced to the corresponding page on which it was introduced. The activities here provide systematic practice by *Desafío*.

Activities	Standards	Resources
4.	1.2, 1.3, 3.1	
5.	1.3	
6.	1.1, 1.2, 5.1	
7. Cultura	1.1, 1.2, 2.1, 2.2, 3.1	

Teaching Suggestions

Warm-Up / Independent Starter

- Have students answer the following questions in writing about the last time they went out with their friends:
  1. *¿Adónde fueron?*
  2. *¿Qué tiempo hacía ese día?*
  3. *¿Cómo te sentías? ¿Cómo se sentían tus amigos?*
  4. *¿Qué hicieron?*

Preparation

- Ask students to use the questions in the Independent Starter to interview a classmate. Then ask partners to summarize and compare their answers in a paragraph. For example: *Mis amigos y yo fuimos a una pizzería. Mi compañera Lisa fue al cine con sus amigos y después…*

- Go over the *Repaso* with the class. Reassure students that mastering the grammatical structures presented here takes time and practice. Then ask them to check their answers from the Independent Starter and identify the different grammar structures reviewed in this *Repaso*.

Activities

4. Before attempting to complete the text, ask students to read it through. Then have students analyze each sentence and decide if it refers to origin, profession, location, etc. This will tell them whether to use *ser* or *estar*. The first sentence, for instance, refers to an emotional state and requires the use of the verb *estar*.

62

Ser y estar (pág. 22)

SER
- origin and nationality
- profession
- membership
- location of events
- date and time
- possession
- material
- price

ESTAR
- location of people and things
- states
- ongoing actions (estar + present participle)
- with bien and mal
- idiomatic expressions with de (estar de acuerdo, estar de moda, estar de viaje…)

El imperfecto y el pasado continuo (pág. 34)

Imperfecto: actions that happened repeatedly in the past:
De niña jugaba con mis hermanos.

Pasado continuo: ongoing past actions:
Estábamos leyendo cuando llegaste.

Expresar posesión (pág. 36)

ADJETIVOS Y PRONOMBRES POSESIVOS

mi(s) / mío(a)(os)(as)
tu(s) / tuyo(a)(os)(as)
su(s) / suyo(a)(os)(as)
nuestro(a)(os)(as)
vuestro(a)(os)(as)
su(s) / suyo(a)(os)(as)

Aquí están mis fotos. ¿Dónde están las tuyas?
LA PREPOSICIÓN DE
Ese libro es de Carlos.

Expresiones temporales para la narración (pág. 48)

Pretérito: ayer, anoche, el martes pasado, el año pasado, el 2 de enero de 2010…

Imperfecto: antes, de pequeño(a), cuando era joven, a menudo, frecuentemente…

Las comparaciones (pág. 24)

COMPARACIONES DE IGUALDAD

verb + igual que
igual de + adjective / adverb + que
verb + tanto como
tanto(a)(os)(as) + noun + como
tan + adjective / adverb + como

COMPARACIONES DE SUPERIORIDAD E INFERIORIDAD

verb + más que
más + adjective / adverb / noun + que
verb + menos que
menos + adjective / adverb / noun + que

El superlativo (pág. 24)

Add -ísimo(a)(os)(as)
el / la / los / las + noun + más / menos + adjective + de / que

El pretérito y el imperfecto (pág. 46)

PRETÉRITO
- Past actions presented as completed actions:
  El año pasado estuvimos en Lima.

IMPERFECTO
- Past actions that lasted a certain time, without mentioning the end:
  De pequeña yo no hablaba español.
- Descriptions and circumstances surrounding an event in the past:
  De pequeña era muy tímida.

OTRAS EXPRESIONES

preterite tense + hace + time expression
hace + time expression + que + preterite tense
hacía + time expression + que + imperfect tense
imperfect tense + desde hacía + time expression

62 sesenta y dos

Differentiated Instruction

DEVELOPING LEARNERS

- Ask students to look through old magazines to find photos or illustrations of different people. Have them cut out and paste several of the images on sheets of paper. Then ask students to write sentences on each sheet comparing the people's heights, ages, physical appearance, emotional states, etc. Have students use comparisons of inequality or equality, absolute superlatives, or relative superlatives, as appropriate for each set of images. Then ask them to read their sentences aloud.

EXPANDING LEARNERS

- Show students Vincent van Gogh's *Self-Portrait with Bandaged Ear* (1889). You can search for it online. In small groups, have students observe the painting for a few seconds and think of a possible story behind it. What might have prompted van Gogh to do this to himself and then paint a self-portrait?

- Ask groups to come up with a short narrative telling the story behind this picture as they imagine it. For example: *Van Gogh estaba deprimido, y en un momento de desesperación se cortó la oreja. Después…* Invite groups to read their texts to the class.

DESAFÍO 1

4 **Una fiesta de cumpleaños.** Completa el texto con los verbos *ser* y *estar*.

El cumpleaños de Teresa

Mi hermana ___1___ emocionada. ¡Hoy ___2___ su cumpleaños y lo celebramos con una gran fiesta! Hay comida, bebida, flores... Todo ___3___ muy bien.

La fiesta ___4___ en el jardín. Toda mi familia ___5___ aquí. Y Teresa invitó a sus amigos, así que el jardín ___6___ lleno de gente.

En la fiesta hay música en directo porque mi tío ___7___ músico y toca en una orquesta. Todo el mundo ___8___ bailando. ¡Qué divertido!

DESAFÍO 2

5 **¿Qué hacías en ese momento?** Escribe oraciones siguiendo el modelo. Incluye una expresión de tiempo y las palabras *cuando* o *mientras*.

Modelo Tu amiga te llamó.
→ *Yo estaba cenando cuando mi amiga me llamó ayer por la noche.*

1. Pasó una tormenta por tu ciudad.
2. Tus amigos fueron al cine.
3. Tu madre estaba cortando el césped.
4. Tu hermano mayor llegó a casa.
5. Tu padre preparaba la cena.
6. Tu amiga te mandó un mensaje.

DESAFÍO 3

6 **Haz memoria.** Responde a estas preguntas.

1. ¿Adónde iba tu familia de vacaciones cuando eras niño(a)?
2. ¿Qué actividades hiciste con tu clase el año pasado?
3. ¿Qué hacías los fines de semana cuando eras más pequeño(a)?
4. ¿Qué es lo que más te gustó de tus últimas vacaciones? ¿Por qué?

CULTURA

7 **Personajes importantes.** Responde a estas preguntas.

1. ¿Quién pintó el cuadro *Las Meninas*?
2. ¿De dónde es la escritora Esmeralda Santiago?
3. ¿Quién es el autor de la novela *Don Quijote de la Mancha*?

sesenta y tres 63

---

6. Convert this activity into an interview. Have students think of two additional questions they would like to ask their partner. Then have them pair up with another student and interview each other. They should take notes of the answers. After the interview, students will write a paragraph summarizing their partner's responses.

Answer Key

4.
1. está	4. es	7. es
2. es	5. está	8. está
3. está	6. está	

5. Answers will vary. Sample answers:
1. Yo estaba durmiendo cuando pasó anoche una tormenta por mi ciudad.
2. Anteayer, mientras yo estudiaba en la biblioteca, mis amigos fueron al cine.
3. Mi madre estaba cortando el césped cuando llegué a casa ayer por la tarde.
4. Yo estaba viendo la tele cuando mi hermano mayor llegó a casa anoche.
5. El martes por la noche, mi padre preparaba la cena mientras yo estudiaba.
6. Cuando mi amiga me mandó un mensaje esta mañana, yo estaba duchándome.

6. Answers will vary. Sample answers:
1. Íbamos de vacaciones a la playa.
2. Fuimos de viaje de fin de año a Disney World.
3. Iba al parque a jugar con mis amigos. También montaba bicicleta y jugaba a los videojuegos.
4. Me gustó mucho la comida. Fuimos a México y la comida era muy variada.

7.
1. Diego Velázquez.
2. Es de Puerto Rico.
3. Miguel de Cervantes.

Additional Resources

Fans Online activities
Practice Workbook

HERITAGE LANGUAGE LEARNERS

- Ask students to look through an online newspaper from their country of origin. Have them choose a short piece of news that interests them. If there is no access to the Internet in the classroom, you may want to assign this part of the activity as homework the day before.
- Once students have chosen a news article, ask them to identify all of the preterite and imperfect verb forms they find in the text. Then have them analyze the sentences where these verbs are used and explain why each tense was used.

TOTAL PHYSICAL RESPONSE (TPR)

- Divide the class into two teams and play "Charades" with the sentences from activity 5. Agree on how many rounds to play before beginning the game. Without speaking, team members will take turns acting out the missing part of each sentence in activity 5 (i.e., what they were doing when something else happened). They will tell which one of the six sentences they are pantomiming and the other team members must guess the missing part of the sentence.

Unit 1
PROYECTO
Fotos de tu vida

Presentation

- In this section, students will apply the vocabulary, grammar, and cultural information they have learned in this unit to create a photo album of the most important moments in their lives.

Activities	Standards	Resources
Paso 1	1.1, 5.1, 5.2	
Paso 2	1.2, 1.3, 5.1	
Paso 3	1.1, 1.2, 3.1	
Paso 4	1.1, 3.1, 5.1, 5.2	
Paso 5	1.1, 1.2, 1.3, 5.2	

Teaching Suggestions

Warm-Up / Independent Starter

- Have students read the introduction to the project silently. Then ask them to think about important moments in their life and reasons for their importance.

Preparation

- Invite volunteer students to share their Independent Starters. Then discuss as a class the events we tend to perceive as important or life changing. Are there common elements in some of these events (e.g., they relate to family or religion, they are rites of passage)? Are there differences in the kinds of events different cultures consider important? You may want to mention that events that have to do with the cycle of life (e.g., birth, adulthood, death) are important for most cultures. Then ask students to think about the role of photography. Why would we want to capture and keep images of these events?

Step-by-Step Instructions

Paso 1

- Assign this step as homework the day before. You may also have the class discussion that is suggested in the Preparation section in advance to get students thinking about the events and pictures they will include in their album. If there are students who do not have photos or whose religious beliefs forbid taking pictures, allow them to draw or paint images of the events.

Un álbum de
fotos de tu vida

In this project you will create a photo album. Your album will show photos of the most important moments of your life, describe the family members pictured, and tell anecdotes about the people and events pictured.

PASO 1 Elige las fotos más importantes de tu vida

- Busca fotos de los eventos más importantes para ti y tu familia: nacimientos, bautizos, cumpleaños, bodas, vacaciones, celebraciones familiares, días de fiesta, etc.
- Elige las diez fotos más especiales para ti.

PASO 2 Describe las imágenes

- Escribe una descripción para cada una de las fotos. Incluye la siguiente información:
  - ¿Quiénes son las personas de la foto?
  - ¿Qué relación familiar tienen?
  - ¿Por qué es especial esa foto para ti?
  - ¿Qué están haciendo?
  - ¿Cómo se sentían?

Modelo

En esta foto estoy yo con mi hermana Ana. Era el día de mi cumpleaños. De pequeño siempre celebrábamos los cumpleaños en el campo. Mis padres preparaban muchos juegos y lo pasábamos muy bien. Me acuerdo mucho de esta fiesta porque mis abuelos maternos me regalaron una bicicleta.

Rubric for Evaluation

	Content	Organization	Presentation
1 point	Limited relevance. Information is incomplete or not focused. Little Spanish is used.	Inefficient use of time. Descriptions are disorganized, unclear, and difficult to follow.	Unclear communication, not fluent. Many errors in vocabulary and grammar.
3 points	Relevant and focused information, but some of it lacks significance. Spanish is used most of the time.	Time is used well. Descriptions are mostly organized but lack some clarity. Relatively easy to follow.	Clear communication, mostly fluent. Mostly correct vocabulary and grammar.

PASO 3 Corrige los textos

- Intercambia tus textos con tu compañero(a).
- Hazle sugerencias a tu compañero(a) para mejorar su texto. Fíjate en estas cuestiones:
  - – Si ha escrito bien todas las palabras.
  - – Si ha utilizado bien las mayúsculas.
  - – Si ha puesto bien los signos de puntuación.
  - – Si hay palabras que se repiten.
  - – Si el texto se entiende con claridad.
- ¿Te gustaría saber más cosas sobre algunas de las fotos? Pregunta a tu compañero(a) y completen los textos.

PASO 4 Diseña tu álbum de fotos

- Organiza las fotos.
- Decide cómo quieres hacer tu álbum. Puedes hacerlo en papel, en una cartulina o hacer una presentación con la computadora.

  ¡Usa tu imaginación y sé creativo!

PASO 5 Presenta tu álbum

- Enseña tus fotos a tus compañeros(as) y descríbelas. Usa los textos que escribiste, pero intenta no leerlos.
- Contesta las preguntas de tus compañeros(as).

  ¿Cuántos años cumplías?

  ¿Se hicieron daño cuando cayeron al río?

- Mira las presentaciones de tus compañeros(as) y anota los aspectos que más te gustan de cada uno de los álbumes. Decide cuál es el mejor álbum y di por qué.

5 points	Content	Organization	Presentation
	Relevant, focused, and interesting information. Many details and significance are highlighted. Spanish is used exclusively.	Time is used wisely. Descriptions are well organized, clear, and very easy to follow.	Clear communication. Fluent delivery. Correct and complete vocabulary and grammar.

Unidad 1

Autoevaluación

¿Qué aprendiste en esta unidad?

Evalúa tus habilidades. Para cada punto di Muy bien, Bien o Necesito practicar más.

Do these activities to evaluate how well you can manage in Spanish.

a. Can you describe people?

▶ Describe your favorite television or movie character. Include physical and personality characteristics.

▶ Compare your description with one of your classmates'. Which character do you think is better? Why?

b. Can you talk about family relationships and past actions?

▶ Describe your extended family. What are the relationships between them?

▶ With a classmate, tell a real or imaginary story about something that happened to one of your family members.

c. Can you narrate and describe past experiences?

▶ Imagine that you are a famous writer that needs to write his/her biography for an important magazine. Write a paragraph telling your personal history.

▶ Talk with a partner about activities you used to do when you were younger. How long has it been since you did these pastimes?

PROYECTO

Fotos de tu vida

Paso 2

- Before they begin this step, ask students to observe each picture and reminisce silently. Encourage them to jot down, in English, their memories and feelings as they look at each picture. Then have students review the vocabulary and grammar structures studied in this unit. They should now be prepared to begin writing the description for each photo.

Paso 3

- Suggest that students circle the spelling, punctuation, and grammar errors they find in their partner's text, instead of correcting them. Then have partners correct their own text.

Paso 4

- Emphasize the importance of making their albums visually appealing and organizing them in a logical way. Remind students that clear organization helps audiences understand ideas.

Paso 5

- Rehearsals should enable students to present confidently and fluently. If possible, allow for rehearsal time.

Evaluation

- Distribute copies of the rubric to students. Discuss the evaluation criteria and explain how this project will be graded. Encourage students to refer to the rubric as they prepare their projects.

Content

- Ask students to focus their picture descriptions and stories. They should select information that is relevant and interesting.

Organization

- Students may organize their photo presentation chronologically or by order of event importance for them, but the organization they choose should be clear for their audience.

Presentation

- Encourage students to interact with their audience as they present their albums. Emphasize the importance of maintaining eye contact with their listeners as a way of keeping them all interested.

Objectives

- To express feelings.
- To talk about personal relationships.
- To learn and use pronouns for direct and indirect objects.
- To learn pronominal reflexive and reciprocal verbs.
- To express wishes, likes, and preferences.
- To introduce people.

- To extend an invitation and to respond to an invitation.
- To conduct telephone calls.
- To express necessity or obligation.
- To talk about future actions.
- To write a love or friendship card, an invitation, or a descriptive electronic message.

- To identify main ideas and significant details in a variety of texts.
- To know and apply the different stages of the writing process: planning, writing, revising, and sharing.
- To explore cultural aspects of traditional Latin American and Spanish festivities.

Contents

Vocabulary

- Useful expressions to express likes and preferences, to evaluate things, and to express a hypothesis.
- Review: Words for family and personal relationships, for introducing people, and for hobbies, leisure activities, and entertainment.
- Personal relationships.
- Introductions.
- Expressions used to invite, accept, and decline an invitation.
- Telephone calls.

Grammar

- Direct object and indirect object pronouns.
- Pronominal reflexive and reciprocal verbs.
- To express wishes, likes, and preferences: The verbs *gustar, encantar, apetecer*, and *importar*; and the subjunctive mood.
- Non-reflexive pronominal verbs.
- To express necessity or obligation using *deber, tener que, haber que* + infinitive.
- To talk about the future.

Culture

- *La leyenda de san Jordi.*
- Social networks.
- *Gustavo Adolfo Bécquer.*
- *El juego de pelota.*
- Physical contact among Hispanics.
- *El pueblo mixteco.*
- *Juegos precolombinos.*
- *El baile en el mundo latino.*
- *El lenguaje SMS.*
- *Juan Luis Guerra:* A singer from the Dominican Republic.
- Traditional Latin American and Spanish festivities.

Evaluation Criteria

- Express feelings and relate actions to specific feelings.
- Talk about personal relationships.
- Use object pronouns to replace the direct object and the indirect object.
- Recognize and use pronominal reflexive and reciprocal verbs.
- Use expressions to introduce people, extend an invitation, and to accept or decline an invitation.

- Express wishes, likes, and preferences.
- Compare and contrast celebrations.
- Recognize the meaning of verbs depending on their use with pronouns.
- Recognize and use non-reflexive pronominal verbs to express emotions and changes in condition.
- Use *deber, tener que, haber que* + infinitive to express a necessity or obligation.

- Simulate or make telephone calls.
- Use the future tense, adverbs, time expressions, and *cuando* + the present subjunctive.
- Write a *caligrama,* or concrete poem.
- Read different types of texts and identify main ideas and significant details.
- Write a love or friendship card, an invitation, or an informational e-mail.
- Organize and write a plan for a celebration.

Unit Plan

Las tareas/Antes de empezar

Estimated time: 1 session.

Text: ¡Vamos a divertirnos!

Functions & forms:
- Useful expressions to express likes and preferences, to evaluate things, and to express a hypothesis.
- Review of known vocabulary about family and personal relationships, introducing people, hobbies, leisure activities, and entertainment.

DESAFÍO 1

Estimated time: 5 sessions.

Text: El Día de san Jordi.

Functions & forms:
- To express feelings.
- Personal relationships.
- Direct and indirect object pronouns.
- Pronominal reflexive and reciprocal verbs.

Culture:
- La leyenda de san Jordi.
- Las redes sociales.
- Gustavo Adolfo Bécquer.

Reading: Del amor… y del olvido.

DESAFÍO 2

Estimated time: 5 sessions.

Text: Un juego milenario.

Functions & forms:
- To express wishes, likes, and preferences.
- Introductions and invitations.
- The verbs gustar, encantar, apetecer, and importar, and the subjunctive mood to express wishes, likes, and preferences.
- Non-reflexive pronominal verbs.

Culture:
- El juego de pelota.
- El espacio personal.
- El pueblo mixteco.

Reading: Juegos precolombinos.

DESAFÍO 3

Estimated time: 6 sessions.

Text: Un concurso de baile.

Functions & forms:
- To express necessity or obligation.
- Telephone calls.
- The verbs deber, tener que, haber que + infinitive.
- The simple future tense.

Culture:
- El baile en el mundo latino.
- El lenguaje SMS.
- Juan Luis Guerra.

Reading: El mensaje.

Para terminar

Estimated time: 1 session.

Todo junto: Review of Desafíos 1–3.

Tu desafío:
- Desafío A: Write a love or friendship card.
- Desafío B: Write an invitation for a party.
- Desafío C: Write an e-mail explaining a favorite Latin dance.

MAPA CULTURAL

Estimated time: 1 session.

Mapa cultural: La fiesta: expresión comunitaria.

ESCRITURA

Estimated time: 1 session.

Writing: ¿Un poema o un dibujo? ¡Un caligrama!

PROYECTO/EVALUACIÓN

Estimated time: 2 sessions.

Project: Un plan de actividades con tus amigos.

Self-evaluation: Autoevaluación.

Unit 2 **Entre amigos**

Standards for Learning Spanish

 COMMUNICATION

1.1. Interpersonal mode
- Compare and contrast information with a partner.
- Prepare and conduct an interview.
- Engage in oral conversations using personal experience and knowledge.
- Introduce people to partners.
- Talk about future plans with a partner.
- Ask and answer questions on different topics orally.
- Write a proposal to a school principal.
- Write a card to a friend.
- Write a text message with a partner.
- Write an invitation and reply to an invitation.
- Write an inscription / dedication.

1.2. Interpretive mode
- Demonstrate understading of oral and written expressions.
- Understand and obtain information from audio or video recordings.
- Demonstrate understanding of questions related to familiar and less familiar topics.
- Identify main ideas and details and draw conclusions from a variety of texts orally and in writing.

1.3. Presentational mode
- Illustrate and present an advertisement.
- Present personal preferences.
- Present ideas about future technologies.
- Write a *caligrama*.
- Organize and present a plan for a celebration.

CULTURE

2.1. Practices and perspectives
- Read about celebrations related to friendship and love in Hispanic cultures.
- Read about the use of social networks in Latin America and Spain.
- Practice introducing people.
- Learn about practices related to physical contact (personal space) among Hispanics.
- Practice inviting, and accepting or declining an invitation.
- Learn about traditional celebrations in Hispanic countries.

2.2. Products and perspectives
- Read about a Spanish legend.
- Read about ball games that originated in pre-Hispanic cultures.
- Learn about a renowned Romantic Spanish poet and other renowned Latin American writers.
- Learn about the influence of Latin American music in the United States and compare dancing traditions in both cultures.
- Read about a representative singer / composer of the musical culture of the Dominican Republic.

CONNECTIONS

3.1. Interdisciplinary connections
- Understand the similarities and differences between some aspects of grammar in English and in Spanish.
- Learn about renowned writers and poets from Latin America and Spain.
- Read about the importance of games in pre-Hispanic cultures.
- Learn about the Mixteco people and analyze the impact of immigrating to other lands.
- Write a *caligrama*.

3.2. Viewpoints through language / culture
- Read about celebrations to commemorate love and friendship.
- Learn about the use of language in social networks.
- Read about the origins of different games in pre-Hispanic cultures.
- Learn about Latin music and dancing as cultural manifestations.

COMPARISONS

4.1. Compare languages
- Compare the use of object pronouns in English and in Spanish.
- Compare the way to express reciprocal actions in English and in Spanish.
- Compare non-reflexive pronominal verbs in English and in Spanish.
- Compare ways of expressing future time in English and in Spanish.

4.2. Compare cultures
- Compare celebrations in Hispanic countries and in the United States.
- Compare dancing traditions and traditional festivals in Hispanic countries and in the United States.
- Compare pre-Hispanic games and modern games.

COMMUNITIES

5.1. Spanish within and beyond the school setting
- Use language to express feelings and wishes.
- Use language to exchange ideas and opinions, and to talk about future plans.

5.2. Spanish for lifelong learning
- Use technology to learn about cultural traditions in Hispanic countries.
- Learn about the use of social networks in Hispanic countries.
- Learn to respect personal space in social contacts.
- Research the different cultural influences that have shaped the population of Latin America.

Communicative Skills

Interpersonal Mode

		Activities
Speaking	• Engage in conversation with a classmate.	• 3, 11, 23, 27, 42, 61, 70, 76, *Proyecto*
	• Compare and contrast information with a partner.	• 8, 25, 44, 57
	• Ask and answer questions on different topics.	• 5, 70, 83, 84, 85, 86
	• Introduce people.	• 39
Writing	• Write love or friendship inscriptions.	• 12, 31
	• Write a text message with a partner.	• 83, 85
	• Write an invitation or a reply to an invitation.	• 37, 58
Listening	• Understand vocabulary and expressions related to personal relations and feelings.	• 11, 34
	• Understand vocabulary and expressions related to wishes, likes, and preferences.	• 44, 47
Reading	• Understand a variety of messages.	• 35, 39, 83

Interpretive Mode

		Activities
Listening	• Obtain information from conversations.	• 11, 30, 34, 46
	• Listen to audio recordings and identify information.	• 8, 43
Reading	• Demonstrate comprehension of written exchanges, dialogues, or written messages.	• 7, 17, 31, 57, 58, 59, 82
	• Obtain information and draw conclusions from an informative text.	• 9, 18, 40, 49, 50, 62, 66
	• Demonstrate comprehension of a literary story, a poem, or literary quotations.	• 18, 25, 77, 78
	• Reflect on and explain cultural topics in relation to personal knowledge and experience.	• 9, 62, 66, 71
	• Investigate and explain information.	• 13, 36, 49
Viewing	• Connect expressions or information to images.	• 4, 15, 38, 60, 85
	• Create a dialogue based on images.	• 26

Presentational Mode

		Activities
Speaking	• Present an original creation to the class.	• 28, *Escritura*, *Proyecto*
	• Present information, preferences, ideas, and opinions to the class.	• 44, 56, 76, 84, 88
Writing	• Write a poem.	• *Escritura*
	• Write a plan for an event.	• *Proyecto*
Visually Representing	• Draw an advertisement.	• 28
	• Create a *caligrama*.	• *Escritura*

Cross-Curricular Standards

Subject	Standard	Activities
Language Arts	• Compare elements of Spanish grammar with English equivalents.	• 14, 19, 41, 45, 72
	• Write personal cards, invitations, e-mails, or an inscription/dedication.	• 12, 31, 37, 57, 82, 84, 87
Literature	• Read about and research Hispanic writers and poets.	• 18, *Lectura D1*
	• Read about concrete poems and write a poem.	• *Escritura*
Music	• Read about music and dancing traditions in Latin America.	• 62, 71
Social Studies	• Read about a traditional legend from Spain.	• 9
	• Organize and write a plan to celebrate Hispanic Heritage Month.	• *Proyecto*

Lesson Plans (50-Minute Classes)

Day	Objectives	Sessions	Activities	Time	Standards	Resources / Homework
1	To introduce social life and the characters' challenges, and to review learned vocabulary	**Entre amigos / Las tareas / Antes de empezar** (66–71) • Warm-Up: Topic orientation • Presentation: ¡Vamos a divertirnos! • Expresiones útiles and Recuerda	 1–2 3–5	 10 m. 20 m. 20 m.	1.1, 1.2, 1.3, 2.1, 2.2, 3.1, 5.1	Visual Presentation Video Practice Workbook
2	To express feelings	**Desafío 1 – El Día de san Jordi** (72–73) • Warm-Up: Independent Starter • Texto: El Día de san Jordi • Cultura: La leyenda de san Jordi	 6–8 9	 5 m. 35 m. 10 m.	1.1, 1.2, 1.3, 2.1, 2.2, 3.2, 4.2, 5.1	Visual Presentation Audio
3	To talk about personal relationships	**Desafío 1 – Vocabulario** (74–75) • Warm-Up: Independent Starter • Vocabulary: Relaciones personales • Comunidades: Las redes sociales	 10–12 13	 5 m. 35 m. 10 m.	1.1, 1.2, 1.3, 2.1, 3.1, 4.2, 5.1, 5.2	Audio Practice Workbook
4	To learn direct and indirect object pronouns	**Desafío 1 – Gramática** (76–77) • Warm-Up: Independent Starter • Grammar: Los pronombres de objeto directo e indirecto • Conexiones: Gustavo Adolfo Bécquer	 14–17 18	 5 m. 35 m. 10 m.	1.1, 1.2, 1.3, 2.1, 2.2, 3.1, 4.1, 5.1	Audio Practice Workbook
5	To learn pronominal reflexive and reciprocal verbs	**Desafío 1 – Gramática** (78–79) • Warm-Up: Independent Starter • Grammar: Verbos pronominales reflexivos y recíprocos	 19–23	 5 m. 45 m.	1.1, 1.2, 3.1, 4.1, 5.1	Practice Workbook
6	To understand a dialogue and to integrate vocabulary and grammar	**Desafío 1 – Lectura / Comunicación** (80–83) • Warm-Up: Independent Starter • Lectura: Del amor… y del olvido • Comunicación: Review • Final del desafío	 24–26 27–30 31	 5 m. 20 m. 15 m. 10 m.	1.1, 1.2, 1.3, 2.1, 2.2, 3.1, 3.2, 4.2, 5.1, 5.2	Visual Presentation Audio Practice Workbook Tu desafío Quiz on Desafío 1
7	To express wishes, likes, and preferences	**Desafío 2 – Un juego milenario** (84–85) • Warm-Up: Correct quiz on Desafío 1 • Texto: Un juego milenario • Cultura: El juego de pelota	 32–35 36	 5 m. 35 m. 10 m.	1.2, 2.2, 1.3, 2.1, 2.2, 3.1, 3.2, 4.2	Visual Presentation Audio Video
8	To introduce people and to make and respond to an invitation	**Desafío 2 – Vocabulario** (86–87) • Warm-Up: Independent Starter • Vocabulary: Presentaciones • Cultura: El espacio personal	 37–39 40	 5 m. 35 m. 10 m.	1.1, 1.2, 2.1, 3.2, 4.2, 5.1	Audio Practice Workbook
9	To express wishes, likes, and preferences	**Desafío 2 – Gramática** (88–89) • Warm-Up: Independent Starter • Grammar: Expresar deseos, gustos y preferencias	 41–44	 5 m. 45 m.	1.1, 1.2, 1.3, 3.1, 4.1, 5.1, 5.2	Audio Practice Workbook
10	To learn non-reflexive pronominal verbs	**Desafío 2 – Gramática** (90–91) • Warm-Up: Independent Starter • Grammar: Verbos pronominales no reflexivos • Conexiones: El pueblo mixteco	 45–48 49	 5 m. 35 m. 10 m.	1.1, 1.2, 1.3, 2.2, 3.1, 4.1, 5.1	Audio Practice Workbook

Day	Objectives	Sessions	Activities	Time	Standards	Resources / Homework
11	To understand an informational text and to integrate vocabulary and grammar	**Desafío 2 – Lectura/Comunicación** (92–95) • Warm-Up: Independent Starter • *Lectura: Juegos precolombinos* • *Comunicación:* Review • *Final del desafío*	 50–53 54–56 57	5 m. 20 m. 15 m. 10 m.	1.1, 1.2, 1.3, 2.1, 2.2, 3.1, 3.2, 4.2, 5.1, 5.2	Practice Workbook *Tu desafío* Quiz on *Desafío 2*
12	To express necessity or obligation	**Desafío 3 – Un concurso de baile** (96–97) • Warm-Up: Correct quiz on *Desafío 2* • *Texto: Un concurso de baile* • *Cultura: El baile en el mundo latino*	 58–61 62	5 m. 35 m. 10 m.	1.1, 1.2, 2.2, 4.2, 5.1	Visual Presentation Audio Video
13	To conduct telephone calls	**Desafío 3 – Vocabulario** (98–99) • Warm-Up: Independent Starter • Vocabulary: *Llamadas telefónicas* • *Cultura: El lenguaje SMS*	 63–65 66	5 m. 35 m. 10 m.	1.1, 1.2, 2.1, 3.2, 5.1	Audio Practice Workbook
14	To express necessity or obligation	**Desafío 3 – Gramática** (100–101) • Warm-Up: Independent Starter • Grammar: *Expresar necesidad u obligación* • *Cultura: Juan Luis Guerra*	 67–70 71	5 m. 35 m. 10 m.	1.1, 1.2, 1.3, 2.2, 3.1, 4.2, 5.1	Audio Practice Workbook
15	To talk about the future using the simple future tense	**Desafío 3 – Gramática** (102–103) • Warm-Up: Independent Starter • Grammar: *Hablar del futuro*	 72–76	5 m. 45 m.	1.1, 1.2, 1.3, 3.1, 4.1, 5.1	Audio Practice Workbook
16	To understand a short story	**Desafío 3 – Lectura** (104–105) • Warm-Up: Independent Starter • *Lectura: El mensaje*	 77–80	5 m. 45 m.	1.1, 1.2, 1.3, 3.1, 5.1	
17	To integrate vocabulary and grammar	**Desafío 3 – Comunicación** (106–107) • Warm-Up: Independent Starter • *Comunicación:* Review • *Final del desafío*	 81–83 84	5 m. 30 m. 15 m.	1.1, 1.2, 1.3, 5.1	Audio Practice Workbook Quiz on *Desafío 3* **Para terminar – Tu desafío** (109)
18	To integrate language in context	**Para terminar** (108–109) • Warm-Up: Correct quiz on *Desafío 3* • *Todo junto* • *Tu desafío* presentations	 85–86 87	5 m. 20 m. 25 m.	1.1, 1.2, 1.3, 2.1, 2.2, 5.1	Practice Workbook
19	To assess student proficiency and to learn about traditional Hispanic festivities	**Evaluación/Mapa cultural** (110–111) • Warm-Up: Independent Starter • Quiz on *Desafíos 1–3* • *Mapa cultural: La fiesta: expresión comunitaria*	 88	5 m. 15 m. 30 m.	1.1, 1.2, 1.3, 2.1, 2.2, 3.1, 4.2, 5.1, 5.2	Video Practice Workbook
20	To write a *caligrama,* or concrete poem	**Escritura** (112–113) • Warm-Up: Independent Starter • *Escritura: ¿Un poema o un dibujo? ¡Un caligrama!*	 	5 m. 45 m.	1.1, 1.2, 1.3, 3.1, 5.2	Project work
21	To plan a day of activities for a celebration	**Proyecto** (118–119) • Warm-Up: Prepare project presentations • Project presentations		10 m. 40 m.	1.1, 1.2, 1.3, 2.1, 2.2, 5.1, 5.2	**Repaso – Vocabulario** (114–115) **Repaso – Gramática** (116–117)
22	To assess student proficiency	**Assessment** • *Autoevaluación* (119) • Test		10 m. 40 m.	1.1, 1.2, 1.3, 2.1, 2.2, 5.1, 5.2	

Unit 2 Entre amigos

Lesson Plans (90-Minute Classes)

Day	Objectives	Sessions	Activities	Time	Standards	Resources / Homework
1	To introduce social life and the characters' challenges, and to review learned vocabulary	(See Day 12 Unit 1) **Entre amigos/Las tareas/Antes de empezar** (66–71) • Warm-Up: Topic orientation • Presentation: *¡Vamos a divertirnos!* • *Expresiones útiles* and *Recuerda*	 1–2 3–5	(45 m.) 10 m. 20 m. 15 m.	1.1, 1.2, 1.3, 2.1, 2.2, 3.1, 5.1	Visual Presentation Video Practice Workbook
2	To express feelings and to talk about personal relationships	**Desafío 1 – El Día de san Jordi/Vocabulario** (72–75) • Warm-Up: Independent Starter • *Texto: El Día de san Jordi* • *Cultura: La leyenda de san Jordi* • Vocabulary: *Relaciones personales* • *Comunidades: Las redes sociales*	 6–8 9 10–12 13	 5 m. 30 m. 10 m. 35 m. 10 m.	1.1, 1.2, 1.3, 2.1, 2.2, 3.1, 3.2, 4.2, 5.1, 5.2	Visual Presentation Audio Practice Workbook
3	To learn direct and indirect object pronouns, and to learn pronominal reflexive and reciprocal verbs	**Desafío 1 – Gramática** (76–79) • Warm-Up: Independent Starter • Grammar: *Los pronombres de objeto directo e indirecto* • *Conexiones: Gustavo Adolfo Bécquer* • Grammar: *Verbos pronominales reflexivos y recíprocos*	 14–17 18 19–23	 5 m. 35 m. 10 m. 40 m.	1.1, 1.2, 1.3, 2.1, 2.2, 3.1, 4.1, 5.1	Audio Practice Workbook
4	To understand a dialogue, to integrate vocabulary and grammar, and to assess student proficiency	**Desafío 1 – Lectura/Comunicación/Evaluación** (80–83) • Warm-Up: Independent Starter • *Lectura: Del amor… y del olvido* • *Comunicación:* Review • *Final del desafío* • Quiz on *Desafío 1*	 24–26 27–30 31	 5 m. 35 m. 25 m. 10 m. 15 m.	1.1, 1.2, 1.3, 2.1, 2.2, 3.1, 3.2, 4.2, 5.1, 5.2	Visual Presentation Audio Practice Workbook *Tu desafío*
5	To express wishes, likes, and preferences, to introduce people, and to make and respond to an invitation	**Desafío 2 – Un juego milenario/Vocabulario** (84–87) • Warm-Up: Independent Starter • *Texto: Un juego milenario* • *Cultura: El juego de pelota* • Vocabulary: *Presentaciones* • *Cultura: El espacio personal*	 32–35 36 37–39 40	 5 m. 30 m. 10 m. 35 m. 10 m.	1.1, 1.2, 2.1, 2.2, 3.1, 3.2, 5.1, 5.2	Visual Presentation Audio Video Practice Workbook
6	To express wishes, likes, and preferences and to learn non-reflexive pronominal verbs	**Desafío 2 – Gramática** (88–91) • Warm-Up: Independent Starter • Grammar: *Expresar deseos, gustos y preferencias* • Grammar: *Verbos pronominales no reflexivos* • *Conexiones: El pueblo mixteco*	 41–44 45–48 49	 5 m. 35 m. 10 m. 40 m.	1.1, 1.2, 1.3, 2.2, 3.1, 4.1, 5.1, 5.2	Audio Practice Workbook

Day	Objectives	Sessions	Activities	Time	Standards	Resources / Homework
7	To understand an informational text and to integrate vocabulary and grammar	**Desafío 2 – Lectura/Comunicación/Evaluación** (92–95) • Warm-Up: Independent Starter • _Lectura: Juegos precolombinos_ • _Comunicación:_ Review • _Final del desafío_ • Quiz on _Desafío 2_	 50–53 54–56 57	 5 m. 35 m. 25 m. 10 m. 15 m.	1.1, 1.2, 1.3, 2.1, 2.2, 3.1, 3.2, 4.2, 5.1, 5.2	Practice Workbook _Tu desafío_
8	To express necessity or obligation and to conduct telephone calls	**Desafío 3 – Un concurso de baile/Vocabulario** (96–99) • Warm-Up: Independent Starter • _Texto: Un concurso de baile_ • _Cultura: El baile en el mundo latino_ • _Vocabulary: Llamadas telefónicas_ • _Conexiones: El lenguaje SMS_	 58–61 62 63–65 66	 5 m. 30 m. 10 m. 35 m. 10 m.	1.1, 1.2, 2.1, 2.2, 3.2, 4.2, 5.1	Visual Presentation Audio Video Practice Workbook
9	To express necessity or obligation and to talk about the future using the simple future tense	**Desafío 3 – Gramática** (100–103) • Warm-Up: Independent Starter • Grammar: _Expresar necesidad u obligación_ • _Cultura: Juan Luis Guerra_ • Grammar: _Hablar del futuro_	 67–70 71 72–76	 5 m. 40 m. 10 m. 35 m.	1.1, 1.2, 1.3, 2.2, 3.1, 4.1, 4.2, 5.1	Audio Practice Workbook
10	To understand a short story, to integrate vocabulary and grammar, to integrate language in context, and to assess student proficiency	**Desafío 3 – Lectura/Comunicación/Evaluación/ Todo junto** (104–108) • Warm-Up: Independent Starter • _Lectura: El mensaje_ • _Comunicación:_ Review • _Final del desafío_ • _Todo junto_ • Quiz on _Desafío 3_	 77–80 81–83 84 85–86	 5 m. 25 m. 20 m. 10 m. 15 m. 15 m.	1.1, 1.2, 1.3, 3.1, 5.1	Audio Practice Workbook **Para terminar – Tu desafío** (109)
11	To learn about traditional Hispanic festivities and to write a _caligrama,_ or concrete poem	**Tu desafío/Mapa cultural/Escritura** (109–113) • Warm-Up: Independent Starter • _Tu desafío_ presentations • _Mapa cultural: La fiesta: expresión comunitaria_ • _Escritura: ¿Un poema o un dibujo?_ _¡Un caligrama!_	 87 88	 5 m. 15 m. 30 m. 40 m.	1.1, 1.2, 1.3, 2.1, 2.2, 3.1, 4.2, 5.1, 5.2	Video Practice Workbook **Repaso – Vocabulario** (114–115) **Repaso – Gramática** (116–117) Quiz on _Desafíos 1–3_ Project work
12	To plan a day of activities for a celebration and to assess student proficiency	**Proyecto/Assessment** (118–119) • Warm-Up: Correct quiz on _Desafíos 1–3_ • Project presentations • _Autoevaluación_ • Test (See Day 1 Unit 3)		 5 m. 15 m. 10 m. 15 m. (45 m.)	1.1, 1.2, 1.3, 2.1, 2.2, 3.1, 5.1, 5.2	

Unit 2 Entre amigos

8 Las fiestas del amor

1. Se celebra el 23 de abril en Cataluña (España).
2. Los novios les regalan rosas a sus novias.
3. Se celebra el 14 de febrero.
4. Las chicas les regalan a sus novios, a sus amigos o a sus familiares un libro.
5. Se venden muchos chocolates y otros dulces.
6. Los pasteleros preparan chocolates con forma de caballeros y dragones.
7. Se celebra también el Día del Libro porque en esta fecha murieron dos escritores muy famosos.
8. Los novios se regalan tarjetas de amor.

11 Donde hay amor, hay dolor

—Estoy triste, Miguel.

—¿Qué te pasa, mi amor?

—No lo sé. Creo que miento si te digo que estoy enamorada de ti.

—Pero Ana, ¿qué es lo que me dices? Yo te quiero mucho. No te entiendo…

—¿De verdad? Nunca me llamas cuando me lo prometes. No llegas a tiempo a nuestras citas y no me dices que me amas. Es obvio que no me quieres. Debemos romper.

—Ay, Ana, no me hables así. Perdóname, por favor. No me dejes. Podemos resolver nuestros problemas.

—Además, no sé si puedo confiar en ti. Ayer te vi abrazar a Lupe, mi mejor amiga. Me dolió tanto… Si estabas aburrido conmigo, ¿por qué no me lo dijiste?

—Ana, por favor, no te pongas celosa. Lupe y yo solo somos amigos.

—No, Miguel. Si no hay confianza entre los novios, no hay nada.

—Pero Ana…

15 ¿Lo ves o no lo ves?

1. Las compré en un mercadillo, en la calle.
2. Me la regalaron mis padres por mi cumpleaños.
3. ¿Quiere que se lo firme?
4. ¿Los quieres? Es que a mí no me gustan…

30 Paso a paso

—Mañana es el Día de san Jordi. Voy a enviarle a mi novia una rosa con una tarjeta, pero no sé qué dedicatoria escribir. ¿Puedes ayudarme?

—¡Claro que sí! ¿Por qué no lees algún poema romántico, como los del escritor español Gustavo Adolfo Bécquer o los del poeta chileno Pablo Neruda?

—¡Qué buena idea! Voy a buscar los poemas de Pablo Neruda en Internet. ¡Qué maravilla! Encontré un sitio web fenomenal. ¿Sabes que Pablo Neruda le escribió cien sonetos de amor a su esposa?

—¿Cien? ¡Uau! ¡Sí que estaba enamorado!

—Estos poemas son muy románticos. Él la quería mucho. Escucha, Asha, estos versos son perfectos para mi dedicatoria: «Te amo sin saber cómo, ni cuándo, ni de dónde…»

—¡Qué romántico! Pero debes pensar en algo más personal.

—Claro. Y también tengo que elegir el color de la rosa que le voy a enviar.

—Eso no es difícil. Cada color simboliza un sentimiento. Una rosa roja significa amor, una rosada significa aprecio y una amarilla, amistad.

—Entonces voy a regalarle una rosa roja. ¡Gracias, Asha!

34 Desacuerdo

—¡Qué emocionante! Quiero ir a ver el juego de pelota mixteca.

—Pero tenemos que jugar y no sabemos nada. ¿Tú quieres hacerlo?

—Sí, me gustan los deportes. Ojalá no sea muy difícil.

—Pero, Ethan, ¿oíste que hay que darle a la pelota con la mano?

—Claro, tranquila. ¿No juegas tú al voleibol?

—Sí, pero creo que no es lo mismo.

—No te preocupes ahora por eso. El señor Ramírez nos va a explicar todo lo necesario.

—Ojalá tengas razón.

—Ahora debemos preocuparnos por las invitaciones.

—Es verdad. ¿A quiénes vamos a invitar?

—Yo quiero invitar a todos nuestros amigos del club de Español.

—¿A todos?

—Sí, ¿por qué? ¿Qué te pasa?

—Prefiero no invitar a Mario…

—¿Por qué?

—Porque no me cae bien. Prefiero que no venga.

—No estoy de acuerdo, Eva. A mí Mario me parece muy simpático. Creo que debemos invitar a todos.

38 Llámame, por favor

1. Hola, Eva. Recibí tu mensaje para ir al concierto esta noche. Lo siento mucho, pero estoy muy ocupada y no voy a poder ir. Pásalo bien. Te llamo otro día. Un beso.
2. Gracias por la invitación, Eva. ¡Me parece un plan estupendo! Nos vemos allí esta noche. Adiós.
3. ¡Qué sorpresa, Eva! Tengo muchas ganas de verte, pero el concierto es esta noche, ¿verdad? No sé si puedo ir. Es que hoy tengo que terminar un proyecto. Te llamo más tarde, ¿de acuerdo? Adiós.
4. Hola, Eva… Lo siento mucho, pero no me apetece salir. Necesito descansar. ¿Nos vemos el fin de semana que viene? Un beso.

43 Los gustos de Eva

¿Quieren conocer mis gustos? Primero les voy a hablar de mis aficiones. Yo no soy muy deportista, pero me encanta que mis amigos me llamen para ir con ellos al parque; ellos juegan al voleibol y yo… tomo el sol. Me gustan mucho las computadoras y me encanta que mis amigos puedan comunicarse conmigo. Siempre nos mandamos mensajes y fotos. Pero lo que más me gusta es viajar. Cada año voy con mi familia a un lugar diferente. Este año me apetece ir a México porque quiero practicar mi español. Y también por la comida. Me gusta que sea picante. ¿Qué más? Ah, sí. Me gusta mucho la música y, sobre todo, me gusta bailar. Y la moda no me interesa mucho, pero no me importa que mi madre me regale una camisa o unos pantalones de vez en cuando, claro. Bueno, ojalá que tengan gustos parecidos a los míos para poder compartir experiencias y comentarios.

46 ¡Vámonos!

–Es muy tarde, Ethan. Me voy al concierto. ¿Vienes?

–No sé, estoy cenando todavía. Además, estoy muy cansado porque ayer no me dormí hasta las cuatro de la mañana.

–¡Vaya, no te pareces a tu hermano! Tú me dijiste que él siempre va a todos los eventos de la escuela.

–Sí, es cierto, a él le gusta mucho salir. Bueno, me como el arroz en un minuto y nos vamos, ¿vale?

–¡Estupendo!

–Tú tienes la dirección del auditorio, ¿verdad?

–Creo que la tengo aquí... No la encuentro.

–¿Te la aprendiste antes de perderla?

–No, pero sé que el auditorio está cerca del estadio.

–Ay, ay, ay...

–¡Mira, aquí está! Vámonos ya, no quiero que lleguemos tarde al concierto.

60 Los bailes latinos

1. A mí me encanta la cumbia de Colombia. Es un baile con mucha influencia africana. Los hombres llevan camisa blanca y un sombrero. Las mujeres llevan blusa y falda larga. Es un baile muy alegre.

2. Para mí, el baile más romántico y serio es el tango. Hay muchos movimientos lentos, pero es un baile muy difícil. Los movimientos del hombre y de la mujer son diferentes, pero ellos nunca se sueltan, siempre bailan agarrados.

3. Mi baile favorito es la salsa. Es un baile rápido, alegre y divertido. Los bailarines hacen muchos giros y figuras.

65 La publicidad del concurso

–¿Diga?

–Hola, Michelle. Soy Daniel. ¿Qué tal va todo?

–Muy bien. Ayer llamé a varias emisoras de radio.

–¿Conseguiste hablar con alguien?

–No. Dejé recados en todas las emisoras y por la tarde el director de una emisora latina me devolvió la llamada.

–¡Qué bien! ¿Qué te dijo?

–Que mañana tenemos una entrevista en la radio para anunciar el concurso.

–¡Fenomenal! Yo llamé a una escuela de baile y el director me dio los números de teléfono de los estudiantes. Les envié un mensaje de texto a todos. Son ochenta personas en total.

–¡Perfecto! Oye, Daniel, tengo que colgar. Es que tengo poca batería y quiero llamar a un periódico local para poner un anuncio en la página web.

–Buena idea. Hablamos mañana, entonces.

–De acuerdo. Hasta mañana.

–Adiós.

69 Consejos

1. Tienes que estudiar más para sacar buenas notas.

2. Tienes que responder para decir si vas a ir o no.

3. Pues hay que ir a la biblioteca y buscar información para elegir a alguien importante.

4. Tienes que participar. Debes hacer muchas fotografías y elegir la mejor.

73 ¿Qué hará?

¡Hola, mamá! ¿Dónde estás? Ah, hoy es domingo, así que estás con la abuela. Bueno, solo quería contarte mis planes para el desafío, a ver qué te parecen. El lunes voy a trabajar todo el día en Internet. Creo que será muy útil para promocionar el concurso de baile. El martes Michelle y yo veremos a los estudiantes de una escuela de baile. Vamos a seleccionar a los mejores para el concurso. El miércoles voy a hablar con algunos periódicos locales para que anuncien el concurso. La gente tiene que saber cuándo es y dónde se celebra. El jueves me reuniré con el director del concurso. El viernes, a las siete, tendremos un ensayo con todos los participantes antes del concurso. ¿Quieres venir? Espero hablar contigo mañana. Un beso.

81 Necesitan más publicidad

–Hola, Michelle.

–¿Qué tal va todo, Daniel?

–Pues no muy bien, la verdad. ¿Y tú?

–Igual. Escuché mi buzón de voz y el director del concurso me llamó para decirme que vendió pocos boletos. ¡Pero tenemos que vender quinientos para lograr nuestro desafío!

–Sí, lo sé, él me escribió un mensaje de texto diciendo lo mismo. Voy a llamarlo después de hablar contigo. La entrevista en la radio es esta tarde, ¿verdad?

–Al final, no. Me dejaron un recado diciendo que la haremos mañana.

–¡Qué lástima, porque entonces hoy no habrá publicidad del evento!

–Sí, pero todavía podemos llamar a algún periódico para poner un anuncio. Voy a ponerme en contacto con algunos periodistas.

–De acuerdo. ¿Y qué puedo hacer yo?

–Pues... ¿Pusiste la información en las redes sociales? Tenemos que invitar a todos nuestros amigos.

–No, ahora mismo lo hago. Perdona, Michelle, pero tengo otra llamada. Creo que es el director del concurso. Hablamos luego, ¿de acuerdo?

–Vale. Hasta luego.

Unit 2
Entre amigos

The Unit

- The theme for Unit 2 is social interactions. The participants will learn how people express feelings, wishes, and preferences. They will also learn to make plans, invite friends, and express obligation.

- Tim, a veteran of *Fans del español*, will chat with the participants and give them their tasks.
  - *Desafío 1.* Asha and Lucas will research the celebration of Saint Jordi (Saint George), which takes place on April 23rd in Catalonia, Spain. They will then write a card for a special someone in order to commemorate this holiday.
  - *Desafío 2.* Eva and Ethan will participate in a match of *pelota mixteca*, a pre-Hispanic ball game that is still practiced in some Mexican and American cities. They also have to send an invitation to their friends to attend the game.
  - *Desafío 3.* Michelle and Daniel have to design a multimedia ad campaign for a Latin dance competition that will be held in Miami. They must prove their ability to use social media by selling at least 500 tickets to the show.

Activities	Standards	Resources
Entre amigos	1.2, 2.1, 2.2, 3.1	Video

Teaching Suggestions

Warm-Up / Independent Starter

- Have students look at the photos. Then ask them to answer the following questions in writing:
  - Photo 1: ¿Qué hacen estas personas? ¿Dónde están probablemente? ¿Qué venden en ese mercadillo?
  - Photo 2: ¿Sabes qué es la pelota mixteca? ¿Qué significa D.F.? ¿Qué representa la figura del logotipo (logo)?
  - Photo 3: ¿Qué bailes latinos conoces? ¿Sabes qué es la cumbia? ¿De qué país es típica la cumbia?

66

Entre amigos
Vida social

DESAFÍO 1

▶ **Expresar sentimientos**

Vocabulario
Relaciones personales

Gramática
Los pronombres de objeto directo e indirecto

Verbos pronominales reflexivos y recíprocos

DESAFÍO 2

▶ **Expresar deseos, gustos y preferencias**

Vocabulario
Presentaciones

Invitar, aceptar y rechazar una invitación

Gramática
Expresar deseos, gustos y preferencias

Verbos pronominales no reflexivos

PELOTA MIXTECA D F

Celebración del Día de san Jordi en Barcelona (España)

Pelota mixteca (México)

66 sesenta y seis

The Challenge

⚑ DESAFÍO 1

Celebración del Día de san Jordi en Barcelona
A unique celebration takes place in the region of Catalonia (Spain) on April 23rd. The celebration is known in Catalan—the language of this region—as *Diada de Sant Jordi*, or *Día de san Jorge* in Spanish. A legend talks about a village in Catalonia where the villagers were sacrificed to appease a dragon. When it was the turn of the king's daughter to be sacrificed, a pious knight, who happened to be Saint Jordi, killed the dragon. Red roses grew from the dragon's blood, and on the day of Saint Jordi, people exchange books and roses.

⚑ DESAFÍO 2

Pelota mixteca
This game, which is played in some regions of Mexico and in some cities of the United States, consists of five-player teams that strike a small solid ball made of rubber. This ball game is a descendant of one of the numerous pre-Hispanic ball games that were played in Mesoamerica as far back as 3,000 years ago. The original *juego de pelota* had important ritual and religious components. Pre-Hispanic ball courts of different sizes have been found all over Mesoamerica, which attest to the popularity of these types of games.

Entre amigos

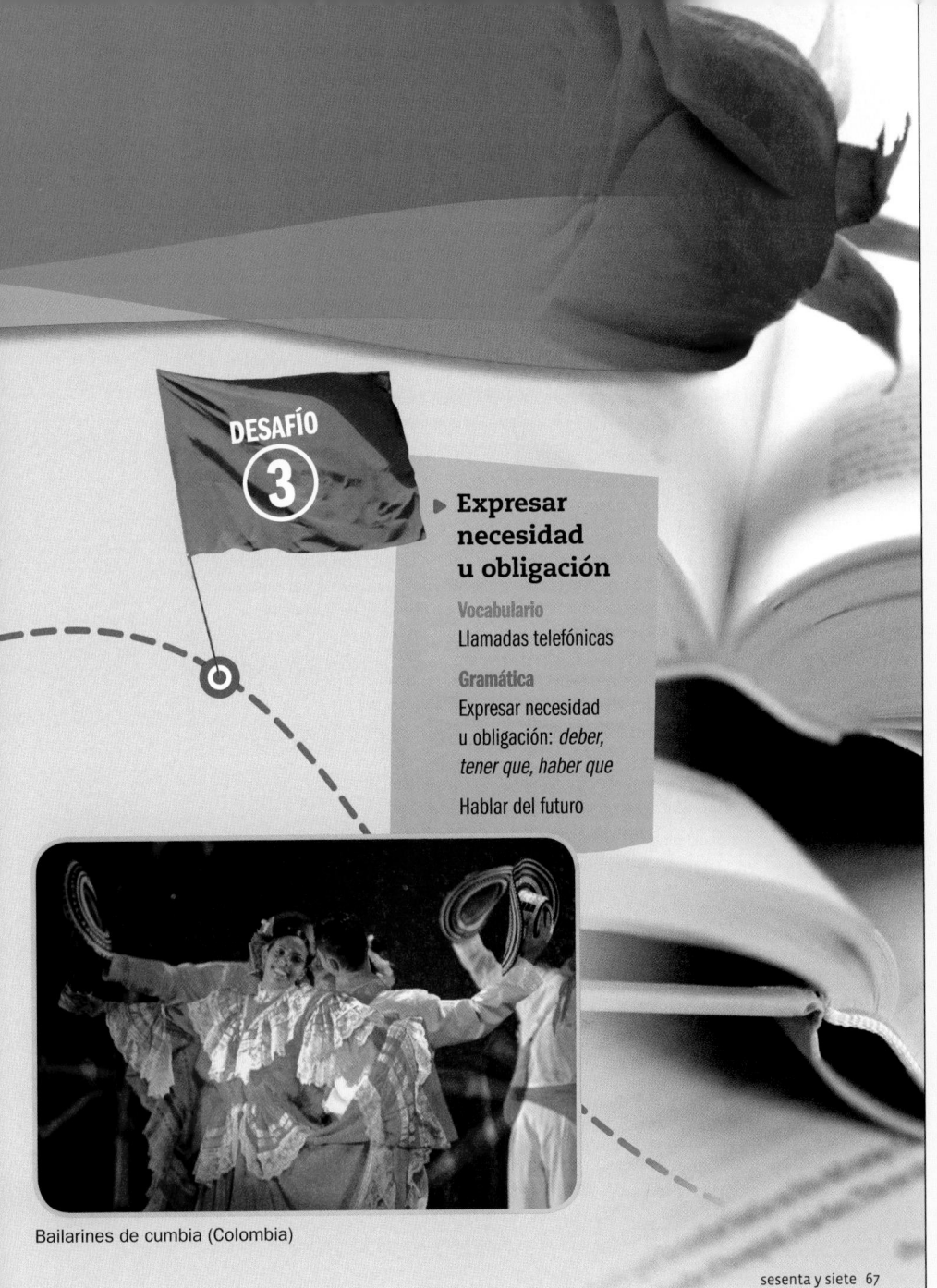

DESAFÍO 3

▶ **Expresar necesidad u obligación**

Vocabulario
Llamadas telefónicas

Gramática
Expresar necesidad u obligación: *deber, tener que, haber que*

Hablar del futuro

Bailarines de cumbia (Colombia)

sesenta y siete **67**

DESAFÍO 3

Bailarines de cumbia

The Latin American region exhibits an amazing variety of dances. Among the most widely known is *cumbia*, which originated on the Caribbean coast of Colombia. It combines elements of African, Spanish, and indigenous traditions. In its beginnings—during the colonial period in Colombia—the *cumbia* was a courtship dance and music. It later spread to urban areas and musicians added more instruments to the traditional drums and flutes. This dance and music genre has also been adopted and adapted in other countries, particularly in Mexico, where it is very popular.

Preparation

- Have students read the captions and brainstorm to reactivate previously learned vocabulary. Create a three-column chart on the board (*celebraciones, juegos y deportes, bailes*) and have students tell you names of celebrations, sports, and dances that they remember.
- Have students read each *Desafío's* objective, as well as the vocabulary and grammar goals, then discuss how each picture might relate to these objectives and goals.

Picture Discussion

- Have students share their Independent Starters.

Celebración del Día de san Jordi en Barcelona (España)

- Ask students to describe the physical characteristics of some of the people pictured and then predict what they think their personalities might be like. Students should use both *ser* and *estar* in their descriptions. Ask them also about their actions (e.g., *El señor de bigote y gafas mira un libro*). As a preview to the unit's grammar topic, you may introduce some questions that require an answer with a direct object: *¿Creen que el señor quiere comprar el libro?*

Pelota mixteca (México)

- Focus students' attention on the word *pelota*. Do they remember what it means? What other sports or games require a *pelota*? Can students guess where the game of *pelota mixteca* is played? How do they know?

Bailarines de cumbia (Colombia)

- Have students describe the people in the photo. Ask them if they know how to dance *cumbia* or other Latin dances. You may want to show a short video of a *cumbia* dance, or bring the music and lyrics of a *cumbia* song to class to introduce students to this type of music.

Objectives

- By the end of Unit 2, students will be able to
  - Express feelings.
  - Talk about personal and social relationships.
  - Make introductions and invitations.
  - Express wishes and likes.
  - Make phone calls.
  - Express needs and obligations.
  - Make future plans.
  - Talk about some holidays, sports, and dances of the Spanish-speaking world.

67

Las tareas

Presentation

- In this section, some of the participants chat with Tim, a former participant in *Fans del español*, who describes the challenges that lie ahead. Students will preview useful expressions for discussing likes and interests, expressing value judgments, and for making assumptions.

Activities	Standards	Resources
Texto	1.2, 2.1, 2.2, 3.1	Vis. Pres.
1.	1.1, 1.2	
2.	1.2, 1.3	

Teaching Suggestions

Warm-Up / Independent Starter

- Have students list, in a two-column chart, all of the expressions they know in Spanish for discussing likes and interests and for expressing value judgments. You may want to get them started with these expressions.

Gustos e intereses	Valoraciones
Me gusta... Me encanta...	¡Qué bien!

Preparation

- Acquaint or reacquaint students with Tim. Explain that he is from San Francisco, CA, and that he used to travel with his grandfather, Mack.

- Invite volunteers to share their Independent Starters. Discuss the uses of the expressions students mention and make corrections where needed. After reading through the text on this page, ask students to point out and classify in the previous chart the expressions they find for discussing likes and interests and for expressing value judgments.

- You may want to review the constructions *deber* + infinitive and *tener* + *que* + infinitive as ways to indicate obligation. Ask students to point out this use in the text. Examples include: *Ahora les explico lo que tienen que hacer. Tendrán que escribir unas tarjetas de amor. Deben enviar invitaciones a todos sus amigos. Tendrán que organizar un concurso de baile latino.*

68

Las tareas

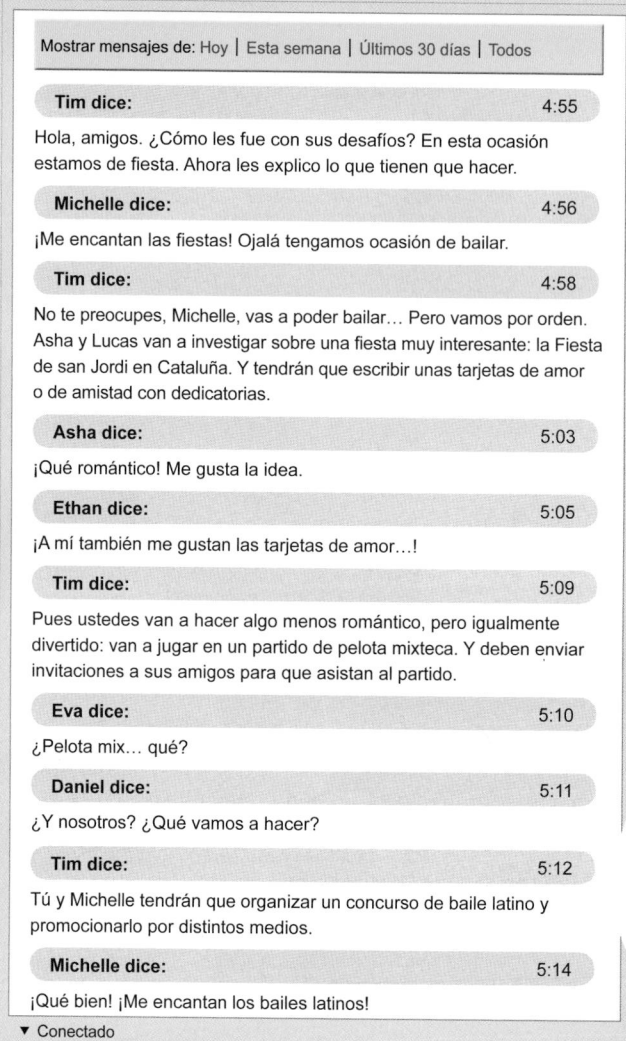

¡Vamos a divertirnos!

The characters want to learn more about Hispanic customs related to social life. Read the chat and find out what their challenges consist of.

Mostrar mensajes de: Hoy | Esta semana | Últimos 30 días | Todos

Tim dice: 4:55

Hola, amigos. ¿Cómo les fue con sus desafíos? En esta ocasión estamos de fiesta. Ahora les explico lo que tienen que hacer.

Michelle dice: 4:56

¡Me encantan las fiestas! Ojalá tengamos ocasión de bailar.

Tim dice: 4:58

No te preocupes, Michelle, vas a poder bailar... Pero vamos por orden. Asha y Lucas van a investigar sobre una fiesta muy interesante: la Fiesta de san Jordi en Cataluña. Y tendrán que escribir unas tarjetas de amor o de amistad con dedicatorias.

Asha dice: 5:03

¡Qué romántico! Me gusta la idea.

Ethan dice: 5:05

¡A mí también me gustan las tarjetas de amor...!

Tim dice: 5:09

Pues ustedes van a hacer algo menos romántico, pero igualmente divertido: van a jugar en un partido de pelota mixteca. Y deben enviar invitaciones a sus amigos para que asistan al partido.

Eva dice: 5:10

¿Pelota mix... qué?

Daniel dice: 5:11

¿Y nosotros? ¿Qué vamos a hacer?

Tim dice: 5:12

Tú y Michelle tendrán que organizar un concurso de baile latino y promocionarlo por distintos medios.

Michelle dice: 5:14

¡Qué bien! ¡Me encantan los bailes latinos!

▼ Conectado

Differentiated Instruction

DEVELOPING LEARNERS

- Read or write the following false statements and ask students to correct them:
  1. *Michelle y Daniel van a organizar un concurso de flamenco. (de baile latino)*
  2. *A Michelle no le gustan las fiestas. (le encantan las fiestas)*
  3. *Asha piensa que escribir tarjetas de amor es aburrido. (es romántico)*
  4. *Ethan tiene que jugar un partido de béisbol. (de pelota mixteca)*
  5. *Ethan y Eva deben enviar tarjetas de amistad. (invitaciones)*

EXPANDING LEARNERS

- Ask students to work with a partner and assign one of the pairs of participants to each pair of students. Explain that they will need to expand their pair's conversation shown on page 69, and that these conversations should be approximately two to three minutes in duration. Give students time to rehearse their lines and call on some pairs to present their conversations in front of the class.

Me pregunto qué es la Fiesta de san Jordi...

Me suena que es parecida a san Valentín.

Me interesa mucho aprender sobre la pelota mixteca.

A mí también, ¡pero no me apetece jugar!

Daniel, hay que enviar muchas invitaciones para que la fiesta sea un éxito.

Tranquila, Michelle, enviaremos mensajes de texto y pondremos un anuncio en línea.

1 ¿Comprendes?

▶ **Responde** a estas preguntas.

1. ¿Qué le gusta a Michelle?
2. ¿Qué tienen que hacer Daniel y Michelle?
3. ¿Qué le parece romántico a Asha?
4. ¿Qué le interesa a Ethan?
5. ¿Cuál de los tres desafíos te gusta más? ¿Por qué?

▶ **Une** la información de las cuatro columnas y escribe tres oraciones completas explicando los desafíos de los personajes.

(A)	(B)	(C)	(D)
tienen que	escribir	tarjetas	de baile
tendrán que	enviar	invitaciones	con dedicatorias
deben	promocionar	un concurso	para un partido

1. Lucas y Asha...   2. Ethan y Eva...   3. Daniel y Michelle...

2 Investiga

▶ **Escribe** el significado de las palabras *anuncio*, *tarjeta*, *dedicatoria* e *invitación*. Puedes usar un diccionario.

sesenta y nueve **69**

Unit 2

Las tareas

👁 **Texto: ¡Vamos a divertirnos!**

- Point out the exclamation marks in the title of the text. Have students guess what they may mean. Ask students to scan the text to find other expressions that have exclamation marks and have them guess their meaning.

- Read the introduction to the text aloud, and then ask for six volunteers to read the chat aloud. Write down the following words on the board and ask students to associate a participant pair with each of these words according to their tasks: *concurso*, *celebración*, *partido*. (Michelle and Daniel, Asha and Lucas, Eva and Ethan)

Activities

1. Encourage students to express themselves by asking related questions. For example: *A Michelle le gustan las fiestas, ¿y a ustedes les gustan? ¿Por qué? ¿Qué hacen normalmente en las fiestas? ¿En qué ocasiones le envían tarjetas de amor o de amistad a alguien? ¿A quién se las envían? ¿Qué deportes les gustan? ¿Cuáles practican?*

Answer Key

1. 1. Le gustan las fiestas.
   2. Organizar un concurso de baile.
   3. Escribir tarjetas de amor.
   4. Aprender sobre la pelota mixteca.
   5. Answers will vary.
   ▶ Answers will vary. Sample answers:
   1. Lucas y Asha tienen que escribir tarjetas con dedicatorias.
   2. Ethan y Eva deben enviar invitaciones para un partido.
   3. Daniel y Michelle tendrán que promocionar un concurso de baile.
2. Answers will vary.

Additional Resources

Fans Online activities
Practice Workbook

HERITAGE LANGUAGE LEARNERS

- Explain to students that *hay que, tener que,* and *deber* are three ways to express obligation, but there are many more. Have students make a list of such verbs or expressions. Suggestions include: *es necesario, es menester, es imprescindible, es obligatorio.* Students should then write or say sentences using each of these expressions. Remind students that when using impersonal expressions with a change of subject, they must use the subjunctive mood (e.g., *Es menester que ustedes hagan la tarea.*). Call on volunteers to share their lists and sentences with the rest of the class.

CRITICAL THINKING

- Enable a class discussion on the pros and cons of handwritten invitations sent through the regular mail service and those that are electronically generated. Before the discussion, ask for a show of hands to see which of these methods students usually use when they want to invite their friends or family to a celebration, and have them explain why they prefer doing this. After the classroom discussion, take another vote to see if any students have changed their mind. If so, have them explain what made them switch to the other method.

69

Unit 2
Antes de empezar

Presentation

- In this section, students will learn a variety of useful expressions for discussing likes and interests, expressing value judgments, and for making assumptions.
- Students will also review nouns and verbs that name social relationships, expressions used in social contexts, and verbs that refer to actions related to leisure activities and free time.

Activities	Standards	Resources
Expresiones útiles	1.2, 2.1	
3.	1.1, 5.1	
4.	1.2	
Recuerda	1.2	
5.	1.1, 1.2, 1.3, 5.1	

Teaching Suggestions

Warm-Up / Independent Starter

- Have students write six complete sentences expressing the following: two things they like to do in their free time, two things they don't like to do, and two things in which they are interested. You may give them the following examples: *Me encanta montar en bicicleta los domingos. No me gusta ver la televisión. Me interesa la música.*

Preparation

- Go over the *expresiones útiles* by using them in personalized contexts. Ask students about their interests and preferences. Then write down sentences on the board and have students react to them with value statements and assumptions. For example: *Josh tiene un coche nuevo.* Possible reaction: *¡Qué suerte!* Possible assumption: *Tengo la impresión de que sus padres se lo compraron.*
- Go over the *Recuerda* expressions by practicing introductions in small groups. Then ask students questions about their relationships: *¿Tienen muchos amigos? ¿Con quién(es) se llevan mejor? ¿Por qué?* Finally, ask students questions about what they like to do in their free time: *¿Les gusta ir al cine? ¿Tocan algún instrumento?*

70

EXPRESIONES ÚTILES

Para expresar gustos e intereses:

¡Me encantan las fiestas!   Me interesa aprender.

Me gusta la idea.   No me apetece jugar.

Para valorar:

¡Qué suerte!   ¡Qué romántico!

¡Qué mala suerte!   ¡Qué lindo!

Para hacer suposiciones:

Me suena que es un juego interesante.

Tengo la impresión de que es parecida a san Valentín.

3 Me gusta, no me gusta

▶ **Escribe** tres cosas para cada categoría según tus gustos e intereses.

No me gusta(n)	Me interesa(n)	Me gusta(n)	Me encanta(n)

 ▶ **Habla** con tu compañero(a). ¿Coinciden sus gustos e intereses?

4 Reacciones

▶ **Relaciona** las expresiones con las fotografías correspondientes.

| a. ¡Qué suerte! | b. ¡Qué lindo! | c. ¡Qué mala suerte! | d. ¡Qué romántico! |

70 setenta

Differentiated Instruction

DEVELOPING LEARNERS

- Ask students to find images in old magazines that would correspond to each of the *expresiones para valorar* on the page as well as to some of the following expressions: *¡Qué problema! ¡Qué maravilla! ¡Qué desastre! ¡Qué guapo(a)! ¡Qué dolor! ¡Qué alegría! ¡Qué simpático(a)!* Have them share their images with a partner, without revealing the expression. Partners must identify the chosen expression or come up with a suitable one.

EXPANDING LEARNERS

- Give students more practice with the expressions in the *Recuerda* feature by having them describe the activities they currently do and sports they practice. Ask them to tell a partner how many times a day, a week, or a month they do each of the activities mentioned. They should also indicate when they did some of these activities the last time. Encourage them to go beyond the vocabulary presented on the page, and to use words from previous lessons.

Antes de empezar

RECUERDA

Relaciones familiares y personales

el/la amigo(a)	discutir
el/la esposo(a)	llevarse bien
el/la novio(a)	llevarse mal

Presentaciones

Me llamo...	Encantado(a).
Soy...	Mucho gusto.
Este(a) es...	

Aficiones, actividades y espectáculos

bailar	escuchar música	ir a un concierto	montar en bicicleta
cantar	escuchar la radio	ir al teatro	pasear/dar un paseo
coleccionar monedas	hacer crucigramas	jugar al ajedrez	pintar
coleccionar sellos	hacer picnic	jugar a los naipes	tocar el piano
dibujar	ir a una exposición	jugar a los videojuegos	tomar/sacar fotos
escribir mensajes	ir al cine	leer un libro	ver una película

5 Tiempo libre

▶ **Escribe.** ¿Qué actividades hacen estas personas?

▶ **Habla** con tu compañero(a). Proponle una de las actividades anteriores. Él/Ella debe aceptar o rechazar tu invitación.

Modelo A. ¿Vamos a una exposición este fin de semana?
B. ¿A qué tipo de exposición?
A. ...

▶ **Haz** una lista de las aficiones y actividades de tiempo libre que te gustan.

setenta y uno 71

Activities

3. Ask students to refer to their Independent Starters to complete this activity. You may also help them focus by suggesting a context (e.g., school, free time, family life).

4. As a follow-up, you may ask students to work on some silent scenes in pairs. Then have students act out the scenes. The other students will react to them with one of the expressions in the box.

5. For the second part of this activity, encourage students to practice accepting or rejecting invitations by asking them to create a brief dialogue and act it out for the class. Remind them to include details, such as where and at what time the event is, how they get there, who else is invited, etc. If they reject the invitation, they should give good reasons for doing so.

Answer Key

3. Answers will vary.
▶ Answers will vary.

4. 1. d   3. a
2. b   4. c

5. Answers will vary. Sample answers:
1. Las niñas tocan el piano.
2. La chica baila.
3. Los señores juegan al ajedrez.
4. Los chicos montan en bicicleta.
5. Él ve una exposición en un museo.
▶ Answers will vary.
▶ Answers will vary.

Additional Resources

Fans Online activities
Practice Workbook

HERITAGE LANGUAGE LEARNERS

• Ask students to review the activities mentioned in the *Recuerda* feature and think of others they know. Then have them work with a partner to make a list of those activities they believe everyone should take part in, and explain why. Next, ask students to get together with another pair to compare and contrast their suggestions and their reasons for participating in these activities.

MULTIPLE INTELLIGENCES:
Bodily-Kinesthetic Intelligence

• One of the activities mentioned in the *Recuerda* feature is *bailar*. Ask students who are familiar with salsa or other dances popular in Spain or Latin America to bring some of this music to class for appreciation and to demonstrate, if possible, how these dances are done. Students might include a brief summary of the history of the music and dance. You could also encourage them to teach the class—and even the teacher— some steps.

Unit 2
DESAFÍO 1

Expresar sentimientos

Presentation

- In *Desafío 1*, Asha and Lucas learn how the holiday of Saint Jordi is celebrated in Catalonia. Students will preview language used to describe personal relationships.

Activities	Standards	Resources
Texto	1.2, 2.1, 2.2, 3.2	Vis. Pres.
6.	1.1, 1.2	
7.	1.1, 1.2, 2.1, 2.2	
8.	1.1, 1.2, 1.3, 2.1, 2.2, 4.2, 5.1	Audio
9. Cultura	1.1, 1.2, 2.1, 3.2, 4.2, 5.1	

Teaching Suggestions

Warm-Up / Independent Starter

- Have students list two of their favorite celebrations. Then ask them to create a vocabulary list related to these celebrations.

Preparation

- Have students work in small groups to share their Independent Starters. Groups will use vocabulary generated by their partners to write ten sentences describing one of the celebrations. Collect and redistribute the sentences among all groups. Ask each new group to read and correct the use of vocabulary. Then return the sentences to the original groups.

Texto: El Día de san Jordi

- Read the introduction to the dialogue. Then show students a map of Spain and point to the region of Cataluña and the city of Barcelona on the map. Explain that the name Jordi is Catalan—the language spoken in Cataluña—for Jorge, and is pronounced *Yordi*.

- Have students work in groups of three to read the dialogue. As they read, ask them to identify five to ten words that the group considers "essential" for retelling the dialogue. Then have groups take turns reenacting the conversation for the class. In their reenactment, students must include the "essential" words generated previously.

72

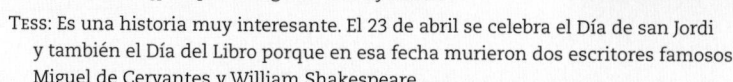

El Día de san Jordi

Asha and Lucas will write a note for a "special someone" in order to commemorate the holiday of Saint Jordi in Cataluña, Spain. First, they decide to interview one of the *Fans del español* who recently traveled to Barcelona.

ASHA: Tess, ¿qué sabes sobre el Día de san Jordi? ¿Cómo se celebra en Cataluña?

TESS: Es una fiesta muy importante. Se celebra el 23 de abril. Ese día los amigos y los enamorados se regalan una rosa o un libro.

LUCAS: Me recuerda al Día de san Valentín. Nosotros normalmente nos regalamos chocolates y tarjetas de amor. Pero... ¿por qué se regalan rosas y libros?

TESS: Es una historia muy interesante. El 23 de abril se celebra el Día de san Jordi y también el Día del Libro porque en esa fecha murieron dos escritores famosos: Miguel de Cervantes y William Shakespeare.

ASHA: ¡Qué coincidencia!

TESS: Sí. El Día de san Jordi los amigos y los enamorados se escriben dedicatorias. Además, los pasteleros preparan caballeros y dragones de chocolate, y los panaderos hacen deliciosos panes de queso con los colores de la bandera catalana.

LUCAS: Libros, rosas, dragones de chocolate... Todavía no entiendo la conexión.

TESS: Es por san Jordi, un caballero (*knight*) antiguo muy romántico. La fiesta recuerda sus hazañas (*feats*).

ASHA: Ah, claro. Cuéntanos su historia, por favor.

6 Detective de palabras

▶ **Completa** estas oraciones.

1. El 23 de abril los amigos y los enamorados ___1___ una rosa o un libro.
2. Nosotros en san Valentín ___2___ tarjetas de amor.
3. El Día de san Jordi los amigos y los enamorados ___3___ dedicatorias.

▶ **Escribe.** ¿Quién realiza las acciones en las oraciones anteriores?

1. Regalar una rosa o un libro.
2. Regalar tarjetas de amor.
3. Escribir dedicatorias.

Differentiated Instruction

DEVELOPING LEARNERS

- Read or write the following questions and ask students to answer them in complete sentences:

  1. ¿Con quién hablan Asha y Lucas? (con Tess)
  2. ¿Qué escritores murieron el 23 de abril? (Cervantes y Shakespeare)
  3. ¿De qué son los caballeros y dragones que preparan los pasteleros? (de chocolate)
  4. ¿Qué productos tienen los colores de la bandera catalana? (los panes de queso)
  5. ¿Quién fue un caballero medieval muy romántico? (san Jordi)

EXPANDING LEARNERS

- Ask students to imagine a conversation between two giants of world literature: Miguel de Cervantes and William Shakespeare. Then have students work with a partner in order for each to role-play one of the writers. Students should describe the setting: Did Shakespeare travel to Spain, did Cervantes go to England, or did the two meet somewhere else? Other than their writing, what did the two men discuss: topics of the day, their future, the future of literature? Allow students to rehearse their lines and call on volunteers to present their conversations before the class.

7 **¿Comprendes?**

▶ **Responde** a estas preguntas.

1. ¿Qué fiesta se celebra el 23 de abril en Cataluña?
2. ¿Qué se regalan los amigos y los enamorados?
3. ¿Son similares esta fiesta y la del 14 de febrero? ¿Por qué?
4. ¿Qué preparan los pasteleros y los panaderos para la fiesta?
5. ¿Crees que puede ser interesante visitar Cataluña el 23 de abril? ¿Por qué?

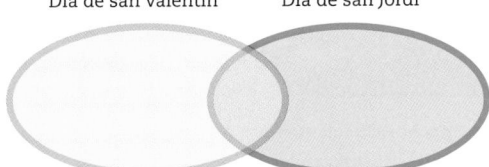

 8 **Las fiestas del amor**

 ▶ **Escucha** y decide. ¿A qué fiesta se refiere cada oración: a la Fiesta de san Valentín, a la de san Jordi o a las dos?

Día de san Valentín   Día de san Jordi

▶ **Escribe** un párrafo describiendo cómo celebras la Fiesta de san Valentín.

 ▶ **Habla** con tu compañero(a). ¿Cómo celebra él o ella la Fiesta de san Valentín? ¿Cuáles son las semejanzas y las diferencias entre lo que hacen ustedes para esa fiesta?

CULTURA

La leyenda de san Jordi

La costumbre de regalar rosas el 23 de abril tiene su origen en la leyenda de san Jorge (Jordi en catalán), patrón de Cataluña.

La leyenda dice que hace mucho tiempo vivía en un lago un terrible dragón. Los habitantes de los pueblos cercanos le daban corderos (*lambs*) para evitar su ataque, pero pronto se acabaron los corderos y empezaron a ofrecerle personas. El propio rey ofreció a su hija al dragón. Y cuando el dragón iba a comerse a la princesa, apareció un valiente caballero para salvarla. Era Jorge. Él luchó contra el dragón y lo mató con su espada (*sword*). De la sangre del dragón salió una rosa roja, que el caballero le dio a la princesa.

San Jorge.

9 **Explica.** ¿Conoces otras leyendas de princesas y dragones? ¿Y alguna leyenda que dio origen a una costumbre o tradición?

setenta y tres 73

Activities

8. Project the lyrics of a love song, such as "Si tú te vas" by Enrique Iglesias. Remove some of the words that refer to feelings, and ask students to fill in the blanks as they listen to the song.

9. Ask students to create some type of artistic representation of the legend, and have them use these pictures to retell the story.

 AUDIO SCRIPT
See page 65I.

 CULTURA

La leyenda de san Jordi

In 1995, the UNESCO declared April 23rd World Book Day. This coincides with Saint Jordi's Day, so on April 23rd book stalls line Barcelona's main boulevard, couples stroll through the streets, book lovers attend readings, and all may visit the roses on display at the Generalitat—a government building.

Answer Key

6. 1. se regalan   3. se escriben
   2. nos regalamos
   ▶ 1. los amigos y los enamorados
      2. nosotros
      3. los amigos y los enamorados

7. 1. Se celebra el Día de san Jordi.
   2. Se regalan una rosa o un libro.
   3. Answers will vary.
   4. Hacen caballeros y dragones de chocolate y panes de queso.
   5. Answers will vary.

8. San Valentín: 3. San Jordi: 1, 4, 6, 7.
   Las dos: 2, 5, 8.
   ▶ Answers will vary.
   ▶ Answers will vary.

9. Answers will vary.

Additional Resources

Fans Online activities

Unit 2

DESAFÍO 1

Vocabulario – Relaciones personales

Presentation

- In this section, students will learn vocabulary to express feelings and describe personal relationships.

Activities	Standards	Resources
Vocabulario	1.2	
10.	1.2	
11.	1.1, 1.2, 5.1	Audio
12.	1.1, 1.2, 1.3, 2.1, 3.1, 5.1	
13. Comunidades	1.1, 1.2, 4.2, 5.1, 5.2	

Teaching Suggestions

Warm-Up / Independent Starter

- Have students create a list of *Las cinco características de un(a) amigo(a) o novio(a) ideal*.

Preparation

- Ask students to share their Independent Starters and create a class list of the most popular characteristics mentioned. Then divide the class in two and ask one half to read the TV conversation, and the other half to read the letter written by *Desesperada*. Working in pairs, have students list the highlighted words. Remind them to write the infinitive of the conjugated verbs. Given the context or related words that students recognize, ask them to try to guess the meaning of the words they listed (e.g., *enamorarse* is a verb related to *amor)*. Then, pair one student from each reading assignment and ask them to create a list of synonyms and antonyms for the highlighted vocabulary.

Activities

11. After finishing the first part of the activity, ask students to provide additional information. For example: *¿Por qué no está contenta Ana con su novio? ¿Es Miguel un novio ideal? ¿Por qué?* Next, ask students to write an e-mail that Ana would send to Lupe and ask a classmate to respond in writing as if they were Lupe.

74

Vocabulario

Relaciones personales

> Te quiero mucho, Isa. Me enamoré de ti en el momento en que te vi.

> Tú, al principio, eras solo un amigo. Me apoyabas y me respetabas. Pero esa amistad se convirtió en un amor verdadero.

> Claro, mi amor, eres mi vida. Cada vez que me abrazas, siento cómo el tiempo se detiene.

> Raúl, ¡estoy tan enamorada de ti!

ASHA: Lucas, ¡me aburre mucho esta telenovela!
LUCAS: Pues este sitio web no es mucho mejor...

Querido doctor Amor:

Hace un año que tengo novio, pero últimamente discutimos con frecuencia. Me echa la culpa de todos los conflictos. Piensa que siempre tiene razón, que nunca se equivoca, y nunca me pide perdón. Él no me aprecia. Y creo que me miente cuando me dice que está con sus amigos. No sé si puedo confiar en él. En cambio, se pone muy celoso cuando yo salgo con mis amigos. Ellos me dicen que «donde hay amor, hay dolor». Sin embargo, no estoy contenta. ¿Debo reconciliarme con él o romper definitivamente?

Desesperada

Más vocabulario

Sentimientos

el abrazo	hug
el beso	kiss
la confianza	trust
la fidelidad	faithfulness

Acciones

disculparse	to apologize
perdonar	to forgive

10 **Palabras relacionadas**

▶ **Completa** estas oraciones con el nombre apropiado.

Modelo Ellos <u>se besan</u>. Es un <u>beso</u> romántico.

1. Mis papás <u>se aman</u> mucho. Es un _____ verdadero.
2. Carmen se siente <u>culpable</u>, pero la _____ no es suya.
3. Hace años que ellos son <u>amigos</u>. Es una larga _____.
4. Los amigos <u>se abrazan</u> al despedirse con un _____ muy grande.
5. Los buenos amigos <u>confían</u> el uno en el otro. Hay mucha _____ entre ellos.

74 setenta y cuatro

Differentiated Instruction

DEVELOPING LEARNERS

- Ask students to make a three-column chart and label the columns *Verbo, Nombre, Adjetivo*. Pair each student with another who has superior language skills or is a heritage learner. Working together, ask students to use the highlighted words and those in the *Más vocabulario* feature to complete the chart with word families. For example, they might include: *discutir* (verb), *discusión* (noun), *discutido* (adjective). Explain that some word families will not include all parts of speech. See which pair comes up with the most words.

EXPANDING LEARNERS

- After students have completed activity 12, give them more practice writing *dedicatorias*, but this time with the following unlikely pairs:
  1. *Ebenezer Scrooge y Santa Claus*.
  2. *Kim Kardashian y Stephen Hawking*.
  3. *Lord Voldemort y Lady Macbeth*.
  4. *George Washington y el rey Jorge III del Reino Unido*.
  5. *Los tres cerditos y el lobo feroz*.

- After students have written their *dedicatorias*, invite them to share some with the class.

11 **Donde hay amor, hay dolor**

 ► **Escucha** la conversación entre una pareja de novios y decide si estas oraciones son ciertas o falsas.

1. Ana está contenta con su novio Miguel.
2. Ana ya no está enamorada de Miguel.
3. Miguel dice que quiere mucho a Ana.
4. Miguel quiere resolver sus problemas con Ana.
5. Ana no confía en Miguel.
6. Miguel quiere romper con Ana.

 ► **Habla** con tu compañero(a). Decidan cómo pueden reconciliarse Ana y Miguel. Describan los cambios necesarios en esta relación.

Modelo   *Miguel debe apreciar más a Ana.*

12 **Poesía... eres tú**

► **Escribe** las dedicatorias de amor o de amistad que estos personajes famosos se envían para celebrar el Día de san Jordi.

Modelo   Bert y Ernie → *Nuestra amistad es muy especial. Siempre puedo confiar en ti. Gracias por ser mi amigo.*

1. Los tres mosqueteros.
2. Romeo y Julieta.
3. Harry Potter y Hermione.
4. Don Quijote y Sancho Panza.
5. La Bella Durmiente y el Príncipe Azul.

COMUNIDADES

LAS REDES SOCIALES

El impacto de las redes sociales (*social networks*) es cada vez más fuerte en Latinoamérica. México, Argentina, Colombia, Brasil, Chile y Venezuela, por ejemplo, estaban entre los 20 países con mayor número de usuarios de Facebook en 2011. Además, cada vez hay más redes sociales en español que se emplean para contactar con amigos, para buscar trabajo, para encontrar personas con aficiones comunes o para poner en contacto a las personas de una misma nacionalidad que viven en otro país.

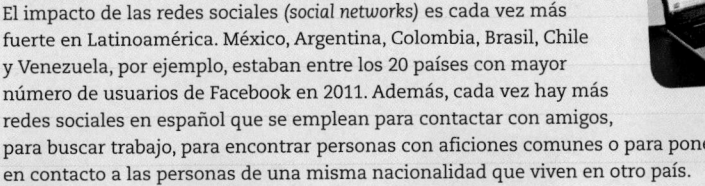

13 **Investiga y explica.** ¿Qué redes sociales son más populares en tu comunidad? ¿Las utilizas? ¿Conoces alguna red social en español?

 setenta y cinco 75

---

12. Ask students to exchange their *dedicatorias* with a classmate without mentioning who wrote it (Romeo, Harry Potter, etc.). Students should try to guess the pair for whom the *dedicatoria* was written. Then give partners a couple of minutes to create a conversation between one of the pairs regarding their relationship. Ask students to present the conversations to the class.

 AUDIO SCRIPT
See page 65I.

COMUNIDADES

Las redes sociales

Just as there are many differences between cultures, it is important for students to understand that they also have many things in common with their peers in Spanish-speaking countries, including those that pertain to social networking. Based on statistics collected in June 2011, 114.5 million people in Latin America had logged onto a social networking site. The participation in social networks is strongest among people aged 15–24 years.

Answer Key

10. 1. amor   3. amistad   5. confianza
      2. culpa   4. abrazo
11. 1. F   2. C   3. C   4. C   5. C   6. F
      ► Answers will vary.
12. Answers will vary.
13. Answers will vary.

Additional Resources

Fans Online activities
Practice Workbook

HERITAGE LANGUAGE LEARNERS

• Ask students to imagine that they have gone to live abroad with their family. They are feeling a bit homesick and want to connect with students from their home country, and would like to use some social media to do this. Ask them to choose a social network and write a post describing themselves and their interests, explaining where they are from, why they are living abroad, what problems they have encountered while living in a foreign country, and other relevant details. Be sure they include what they hope to learn from this experience.

SPECIAL–NEEDS LEARNERS

• Distribute large index cards to students who may be experiencing problems with their vision and ask them to write the highlighted words as well as those in the *Más vocabulario* feature on one side. Then, on the other side, ask them to use their dictionaries, or work with a heritage learner, to write the English-language equivalent. Ask them to read aloud the words in both languages. Finally, have students work with a partner and test each other on this vocabulary.

DESAFÍO 1

Gramática – Los pronombres de objeto directo e indirecto

Presentation

- In this section, students will review the direct and indirect object pronouns.

Activities	Standards	Resources
Gramática	1.2, 3.1	
14.	3.1, 4.1	
15.	1.2	Audio
16.	1.3, 3.1	
17.	1.2, 2.1, 3.1	
18. Conexiones	1.1, 1.2, 2.2, 3.1, 5.1	

Teaching Suggestions

Warm-Up / Independent Starter

- Write the following sentences on the board and ask students to label the direct and the indirect objects in each sentence:
  1. *Ana me compró un libro.*
  2. *Carlos te dio una docena de rosas.*
  3. *¡Envía unas rosas amarillas a tu novia!*
  4. *Tess explica la leyenda a Lucas y a Asha.*

Preparation

- Call on volunteers to share their Independent Starters. Remind students that it is easier to identify the object pronouns if they begin by identifying the verb. They can find the direct object of the verb by asking *what?* or *whom?* For example: What did Ana buy? (a book) They can find the indirect object by asking *to whom?* or *for whom?* For example: For whom did she buy it? (for me)

Activities

16. To extend this activity, create six to eight jumbled sentences that students must unscramble. Warn them to pay close attention to pronoun placement.

18. Assign Bécquer's "Rima xxiii" for homework. Ask students to summarize the author's feelings and imagine how they might feel if someone wrote this *rima* for them. Finally, ask students to combine this lesson's vocabulary and grammar to write their own *rima*.

Gramática

Los pronombres de objeto directo e indirecto

- Remember: sometimes the direct object and the indirect object can be replaced with object pronouns to avoid repetition.

  Ayer compré **un regalo**. **Lo** encontré en el centro comercial.

- The direct object pronoun lo can refer to objects or people, but it can also refer to situations or facts which are neither masculine nor feminine.

  Álex rompió conmigo el verano pasado. ¿Puedes creer**lo**?

- The indirect object pronoun must appear in the sentence when the indirect object is stated as a mí, a ti, a usted, a él, a ella, a nosotros(as), a vosotros(as), a ustedes, a ellos(as):

  Les dieron un premio **a ellas**.

PRONOMBRES DE OBJETO DIRECTO	
me	nos
te	os
lo, la	los, las

PRONOMBRES DE OBJETO INDIRECTO	
me	nos
te	os
le	les

Posición de los pronombres de objeto

- Usually, object pronouns go before the conjugated verb. However, object pronouns may be attached to the end of the verb in the case of:
  – infinitives: Juan me las va a dar. / Juan va a dár**melas**.
  – present participles: Juan me las está dando. / Juan está dándo**melas**.
  – affirmative commands: ¡Dá**melas**!

- When both a direct object pronoun and an indirect object pronoun are used with the same verb, the indirect object pronoun goes before the direct object pronoun. Note that le and les become se when placed in front of a direct object pronoun.

  Pedro **le** dio un abrazo. ⟶ Pedro **se** lo dio.

14 **Compara.** ¿Cómo se dicen estas oraciones en inglés? ¿Cómo se traduce el pronombre lo en cada caso?

  a. Me gusta este libro, lo voy a comprar.
  b. Mañana es el Día de san Valentín. ¿Lo celebramos?

15 **¿Lo ves o no lo ves?**

 ▶ **Escucha** y relaciona cada oración con la fotografía correspondiente.

Differentiated Instruction

DEVELOPING LEARNERS

- Ask students to rewrite these sentences using both direct and indirect object pronouns:
  1. *Quiero leerle el cuento a Juan. (Se lo quiero leer. Quiero leérselo.)*
  2. *¿Quién le dio una rosa a Ana? (¿Quién se la dio?)*
  3. *Quieren traducirme las cartas. (Quieren traducírmelas. Me las quieren traducir.)*
  4. *¿Van ustedes a regalarles libros a sus padres? (¿Van a regalárselos? ¿Se los van a regalar?)*
  5. *Nos están leyendo un poema. (Están leyéndonoslo. Nos lo están leyendo.)*
  6. *¡Firma la carta! (¡Fírmala!)*

EXPANDING LEARNERS

- Ask students to write five sentences that use nouns as direct and indirect objects. Encourage students to write some sentences with infinitives, present participles, and affirmative commands so they can later practice proper placement of the pronouns. Then ask students to exchange papers with a partner, who will rewrite the sentences using direct and indirect object pronouns. Partners will check each other's work.

16 Usa los pronombres

▶ **Transforma** y escribe estas oraciones. Usa pronombres de objeto directo e indirecto.

Modelo   Marisa envió <u>un regalo</u> a <u>Javier</u>. → *Marisa se lo envió.*

1. ¡No des <u>tantos dulces</u> <u>a los niños</u>!
2. Nosotros estamos leyendo <u>los poemas</u> <u>a nuestros amigos</u>.
3. Los chicos querían dar <u>las rosas</u> <u>a sus novias</u>.
4. Mi hermana le regaló <u>un libro</u> <u>a su novio</u>.
5. Hay que enviar <u>las invitaciones</u> <u>a todos los familiares</u>.

17 ¿Lo sabes?

▶ **Lee** este mensaje y escribe. ¿A qué o a quién se refiere cada pronombre destacado?

De: Lucas
Para: Asha
→ *Se refiere a que san Jorge nació en el siglo IV.*
Asunto:

Cuerpo del texto   Anchura variable

Hola, Asha. ¿Qué tal?

Estuve buscando información en Internet. ¿Sabes que san Jorge nació en el siglo IV? **Lo** leí en un blog. Y averigüé que la fiesta se celebra también en Valencia, al sur de Cataluña. ¿Tú **lo** sabías? Como necesitábamos saber más cosas sobre la fiesta, busqué en varias páginas y tomé algunas notas. Luego te **las** mando.

Leí que es típico comer el pan de san Jordi. No sé cómo **lo** preparan, pero seguro que está muy rico. Lo que más me gustó fueron las celebraciones relacionadas con el Día del Libro. En muchas ciudades **lo** celebran con una feria. La gente va allí a comprar libros y a veces los autores **se los** firman. ¿Te imaginas? Yo una vez vi a Isabel Allende firmando libros. **La** reconocí enseguida, pero había mucha gente y no pude pedir**le** un autógrafo…

Ahora te mando más información.
Lucas

CONEXIONES: LITERATURA

Gustavo Adolfo Bécquer

El escritor español Gustavo Adolfo Bécquer (1836-1870) es autor de varias leyendas, pero su obra más conocida son sus *Rimas*, gran ejemplo del Romanticismo español. Las *Rimas* son breves poemas que tratan, sobre todo, del amor y los sentimientos.

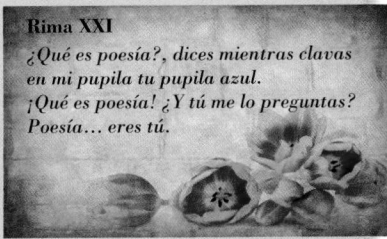

Rima XXI

*¿Qué es poesía?, dices mientras clavas
en mi pupila tu pupila azul.
¡Qué es poesía! ¿Y tú me lo preguntas?
Poesía… eres tú.*

18   **Lee** la Rima XXI. ¿Qué sentimientos expresa el autor? Habla con tu compañero(a).

HERITAGE LANGUAGE LEARNERS

• Ask students to think about a special gift that they received or that they gave to someone. Have them write a few paragraphs to describe the gift, the gift giver or recipient, the occasion or holiday on which the gift was presented, how it was given or presented, and why it was so special. If possible, some students may choose to bring the gift to class. Call on volunteers to read their compositions aloud.

MULTIPLE INTELLIGENCES:
Intrapersonal Intelligence

• Ask students to imagine that they have a *novio* or *novia*, or a special close friend, and have them write a poem that expresses their love for or deep friendship with that person. In addition to conveying these feelings toward the person, students should also communicate what this love or friendship means to them. Encourage students to illustrate their poetry and exhibit their work in the classroom.

Gramática – Los pronombres de objeto directo e indirecto

 AUDIO SCRIPT
See page 651.

 CONEXIONES: LITERATURA

Gustavo Adolfo Bécquer

Gustavo Adolfo Bécquer was born in Seville and died in Madrid. Bécquer is a famous figure in Spanish literature. One of his most celebrated works is called *Leyendas*, which is a collection of supernatural tales. Bécquer's *Rimas* are rather short, simple, but beautiful verses in which he struggles to make sense of life and love.

Answer Key

14. a. *I like this book. I'm going to buy* <u>*it*</u>.
   b. *Tomorrow is Valentine's Day. Are we celebrating* <u>*it*</u>?

15. 1. 3   2. 4   3. 1   4. 2

16. 1. ¡No se los des!
   2. Nosotros se los estamos leyendo. / Nosotros estamos leyéndoselos.
   3. Los chicos se las querían dar. / Los chicos querían dárselas.
   4. Mi hermana se lo regaló.
   5. Se las hay que enviar. / Hay que enviárselas.

17. lo – La fiesta se celebra en Valencia.
   las – algunas notas
   lo – el pan de san Jordi
   lo – qué le gustó más
   lo – el Día del Libro
   se – a la gente; los – los libros
   la – Isabel Allende
   le – a Isabel Allende

18. Answers will vary.

Additional Resources

Fans Online activities
Practice Workbook

DESAFÍO 1

Gramática – Verbos pronominales reflexivos y recíprocos

Presentation

- In this section, students will review and practice reflexive pronouns and verbs, as well as reciprocal verbs.

Activities	Standards	Resources
Gramática	1.2, 3.1	
19.	3.1, 4.1	
20.	1.2, 3.1	
21.	1.1, 1.2	
22.	1.1, 5.1	
23.	1.1, 5.1	

Teaching Suggestions

Warm-Up / Independent Starter

- Have students read the grammar presentation silently. Then ask them to give examples of the following:
  1. reflexive verbs
  2. a reflexive pronoun
  3. reciprocal verbs
  4. a reciprocal action

Preparation

- Review with students the examples they produced for their Independent Starter. Ask the class how each example could be improved. Encourage students to ask questions about any explanations they do not understand and clarify this information for them, referring back to the examples.

- In order to check students' comprehension of the concept of an "action that reflects back on the subject" and one that is done "to one another," show them pictures of the following, or similar, situations: a mom dressing her child and a child dressing himself; someone washing his hands and someone washing his car; someone looking at herself in the mirror and two people looking at each other; two friends hugging one another, etc. Ask students to articulate their observations. Clarify any misconceptions using the previous examples.

Gramática

Verbos pronominales reflexivos y recíprocos

Verbos pronominales

- Pronominal verbs are conjugated with a pronoun that agrees with the subject.

VERBO PRONOMINAL LAVARSE. PRESENTE

Singular		Plural	
yo	me lavo	nosotros(as)	nos lavamos
tú	te lavas	vosotros(as)	os laváis
usted, él, ella	se lava	ustedes, ellos(as)	se lavan

- Pronominal verbs have the pronoun se in the infinitive: lavarse, bañarse, comerse…

Verbos reflexivos y verbos recíprocos

- Use **reflexive verbs** when an action reflects back on the subject. Reflexive verbs are pronominal verbs and are always conjugated with a reflexive pronoun (me, te, se, nos, os, se).

  Yo me visto. *(I get dressed.)*   Mi madre se maquilla. *(My mother makes herself up.)*

  Note that the reflexive pronoun is equivalent to *myself, yourself, himself,* etc.

- Some pronominal verbs may express reciprocal actions *(each other, one another).*

  Nosotros nos escribimos. *(We write to each other.)*

- **Reciprocal verbs** are conjugated like reflexive verbs, but always in the plural forms: nosotros(as) nos…, vosotros(as) os…, ellos(as) / ustedes se…

VERBOS RECÍPROCOS

abrazarse	*to hug*	contarse	*to tell*	pelearse	*to fight*
apoyarse	*to support*	entenderse	*to understand*	perdonarse	*to forgive*
ayudarse	*to help*	hablarse	*to talk*	quererse	*to love*
conocerse	*to know*	odiarse	*to hate*	verse	*to see*

19 **Compara.** ¿Cuál es la diferencia entre levantar y levantarse? ¿Cómo se expresan las acciones recíprocas en inglés?

20 **Diferencias**

▶ **Escribe** oraciones para mostrar la diferencia entre estos verbos.

Modelo   querer/quererse → Yo lo quería, pero él a mí no. Él y yo nos queríamos mucho.

1. ayudar/ayudarse
2. hablar/hablarse
3. escribir/escribirse
4. perdonar/perdonarse

Differentiated Instruction

DEVELOPING LEARNERS

- Ask students to choose one of the verb forms to correctly complete each sentence.
  1. *Miguel y yo conocimos / nos conocimos el año pasado.* (nos conocimos)
  2. *Magda llamó / se llamó a Jorge para ir al cine.* (llamó)
  3. *El perro y el gato se odian / odian.* (se odian)
  4. *Ella maquilla / se maquilla antes de salir.* (se maquilla)
  5. *Mis hermanas siempre bañan / se bañan por la noche.* (se bañan)

EXPANDING LEARNERS

- Ask students to create a short story about two people who are in love, but who are having some problems in their relationship. Students should use as many of the pronominal verbs presented in this lesson as they can while they describe how the couple met, how long they have been dating, what they feel and do for each other, and what their relationship problems are. Students should also offer some suggestions for improving how the couple might get along in the future.

21 Amor compartido

▶ **Completa** estos textos poniendo los verbos en la forma correcta.

| conocerse | llamarse | escribirse | verse | contarse | quererse |

Modelo   *Nacho y Lola se dan libros para el Día de san Jordi.*

Nacho y Lola se quieren

Nacho y Lola están muy enamorados.
___1___ mucho. Cuando no están
juntos, ___2___ para hablar de sus actividades
diarias. Y son muy románticos: el Día
de san Valentín ___3___ poemas de amor.

Nos queremos mucho

Hace mucho tiempo que somos novios. ___4___
desde que teníamos cinco años. Nos encanta
estar juntos; por eso, ___5___ todos los días
después del trabajo. Es importante que ___6___
todos nuestros secretos y sueños.

22 Quiero conocer los detalles

▶ **Escribe.** Imagina que tu compañero(a) tiene un(a) nuevo(a) novio(a). Prepara seis preguntas para saber más sobre su relación.

Modelo   *¿Dónde se conocieron?*
         ¿Se llevaron bien desde el primer momento?

▶ **Habla.** Túrnense para hacerse las preguntas y responder.

23 Por mí y por ti

▶ **Habla** con tu compañero(a) de lo que tú y tus amigos hacen normalmente para mantener su amistad.

Modelo   *Nos contamos nuestras experiencias.*

Gramática – Verbos pronominales reflexivos y recíprocos

Activities

21. Before completing this activity, ask students to read through both paragraphs. Then have them note the differences between the subjects in each paragraph.

22. Model your expectations for the students' completion of this activity by showing them pictures of famous couples (e.g., Bella and Edward, Penélope Cruz and Javier Bardem, Michelle and Barack Obama). Have students generate questions for the couples and write them on the board. Then ask for three volunteers to reenact an imaginary conversation between one of the famous couples and a journalist, by asking and answering the questions posted on the board.

23. Have small groups compile a list of the top five things they recommend in order to have a good relationship with their friends. Have groups report to the class. Which recommendations does the class find most useful?

Answer Key

19. *Levantar* es elevar algo. *Levantarse* es ponerse de pie. En inglés se usan expresiones como *each other* y *one another* para indicar que una acción es recíproca.

20. Answers will vary. Sample answers:
 1. Ella lo ayuda a él. Ellos se ayudan.
 2. Ella no le habla. Ellos no se hablan.
 3. Ana escribió un mensaje. Ana y Tom se escriben mensajes.
 4. Él la perdonó. Ellos se perdonaron.

21. 1. Se quieren   4. Nos conocemos
   2. se llaman   5. nos vemos
   3. se escriben   6. nos contemos

22. Answers will vary.
   ▶ Answers will vary.

23. Answers will vary.

Additional Resources

Fans Online activities
Practice Workbook

HERITAGE LANGUAGE LEARNERS

- After students have said what friends usually do to maintain a strong friendship, ask them to think about what good friends should *not* do in order to uphold that friendship. You may want to get them started by suggesting the following examples: *No nos mentimos. No nos engañamos.* Ask them to list their suggestions. When they finish, have students compare this list with the suggestions they discussed in activity 23 to see whether they came up with more positive or negative suggestions.

CRITICAL THINKING

- Hold a debate on how people should behave in their personal relationships. Ask students to come up with their statements on behavior, such as *las personas deben ayudarse, deben perdonar a sus amigos, los novios no deben verse todos los días.* One student will debate in favor of what is stated, and the other will be opposed. The student in favor will start the debate and speak for a predetermined amount of time, alternating with the student of the opposing view. After a few minutes, call time and take a class vote to see who made the most convincing argument.

LECTURA: TEXTO DIALOGADO

Presentation

- In this section, students will read a dialogue, decode cognates, and discuss some quotes about love made by two famous writers: Gabriel García Márquez and Pablo Neruda. Students will also answer comprehension questions based on the reading.

Activities	Standards	Resources
Lectura: texto dialogado	1.1, 1.2, 2.2, 3.1, 3.2	Vis. Pres.
24.	1.2	
25.	1.1, 1.2, 3.1, 5.1	
26.	1.1, 1.3, 5.1	

Teaching Suggestions

Warm-Up / Independent Starter

- Have students read the *Antes de leer* strategies silently. Then ask them to think about possible answers to the questions.

Preparation

- Ask a student to find a context in the dialogue in which the word *amor* is used. Do the same with the word *olvido*. Use gestures to explain the meaning if students don't understand the words. Ask them to come up with a sentence for each of the two verbs, *amar* and *olvidar*.

- In addition to the cognates cited (i.e., *frase, modelo, dedicatoria*), ask pairs of students to identify other cognates in the dialogue. (*servir, colombiano, poeta, chileno, persona, única, especial*) Remind students that cognates facilitate vocabulary learning and enhance comprehension.

- Have students read silently the three quotes they copied. Then ask them to explain the meaning in their own words. Ask students to think of other famous quotes about love and relationships that they know. Invite volunteer students to share some of these quotes with the class. If they only know the quote in English, help them translate it into Spanish. Then discuss some of these quotes as a class.

Antes de leer: estrategias

1. Lee el título del diálogo. ¿Adivinas el significado de esas palabras? ¿Conoces algún verbo relacionado con la palabra *amor*? ¿Y con la palabra *olvido*?
2. Busca los cognados en el texto. ¿Reconoces las palabras *frase, modelo* y *dedicatoria*?
3. Busca palabras en itálicas. ¿Por qué crees que van así? Copia las citas (*quotes*). ¿Cuál es el tema de estas citas?

Del amor... y del olvido

LUCAS: Asha, ¿dónde conseguiste estas frases de amor?

ASHA: En una página de Internet. Seguro que algunas pueden servirnos de modelo para escribir la dedicatoria. Por ejemplo, mira esta frase del escritor colombiano Gabriel García Márquez:

> *Si alguien llama a tu puerta y estás triste,*
> *abre, que es el amor, amiga mía.*

LUCAS: Sí, me gusta mucho. Claro, es que Gabriel García Márquez es un escritor muy bueno. No es fácil escribir así.

ASHA: Aquí hay una frase más sencilla. Es del poeta chileno Pablo Neruda.

> *A nadie te pareces desde que yo te amo.*

LUCAS: Me encanta... pero ¿qué significa?

ASHA: Pues que la persona amada es única y especial para el amante.

LUCAS: Estoy de acuerdo. Mira, esta también es de Neruda:

> *Es tan corto el amor, y es tan largo el olvido...*

ASHA: ¡Lucas, eso no puedes decírselo a tu novia! ¡Va a pensar que ya no la quieres!

Differentiated Instruction

DEVELOPING LEARNERS

- Ask students to draw a picture to accompany the quote from activity 25 that most appeals to them. Have them label their illustration with the quote. Then ask students to explain why they chose the images and colors they did to illustrate the quote. Display their drawings in the classroom.

EXPANDING LEARNERS

- Ask students to work with a partner and expand the dialogue presented on page 80. Encourage them to find another suitable quote on love from a well-known Hispanic writer, add it to the dialogue, and include its interpretation. Encourage students to add some biographical information about the new author and an anecdote about his or her life. Allow partners time to rehearse their lines and call on some to present their dialogues in front of the class.

24 Opuestos

▶ **Une** las palabras con sus opuestos.

(A)

1. olvido
2. alguien
3. largo
4. sencillo
5. amor
6. fácil

(B)

a. corto
b. recuerdo
c. odio
d. difícil
e. complicado
f. nadie

25 ¿Qué significa?

▶ **Lee** estas citas y elige la mejor explicación.

1. «Si alguien llama a tu puerta y estás triste, abre, que es el amor, amiga mía.»
   a. Cuando estás triste te enamoras de alguien.
   b. Tienes que estar abierto(a) al amor.
   c. El amor siempre llega en el peor momento.

2. «A nadie te pareces desde que yo te amo.»
   a. Me parece que ya no te amo.
   b. Te pareces a mí porque te amo.
   c. Desde que te amo, me pareces única.

3. «Es tan corto el amor, y es tan largo el olvido...»
   a. El amor tiene poca duración y se olvida fácilmente.
   b. Olvidar el amor es difícil.
   c. Recordar el amor es difícil.

▶ **Compara** tus respuestas con las de tu compañero(a) y elijan la cita que más les gusta. Expliquen por qué.

26 Con tus propias palabras

▶ **Escribe** un diálogo para cada fotografía. Puedes usar expresiones de la lectura.

ochenta y uno **81**

- Read the dialogue aloud to students, modeling correct pronunciation and intonation. Then call on several pairs of students to alternate reading the dialogue aloud. Offer suggestions to improve their oral reading.

- Now that students have read the dialogue, discuss as a class the meaning of the title, *Del amor... y del olvido*. What emotions are expressed by the words *amor* and *olvido*? You may want to discuss this quote by Libbie Fudim: *Ámame u ódiame, pero no me olvides.* Is fading away into oblivion worse than being hated?

Activities

24. After students have finished this activity, ask them to write a short definition for each of the words in Column A. For example: *olvido → omisión*; *alguien → alguno, algún*; *largo → extenso*, etc.

26. To expand this activity, have students work in small groups to combine their dialogues and role-play what is being depicted in the pictures. Allow groups to rehearse their lines and have them come in front of the class and represent their scene. Encourage them to be creative.

Answer Key

24.
1. b	3. a	5. c
2. f	4. e	6. d

25. 1. b 2. c 3. b
▶ Answers will vary.

26. Answers will vary.

Additional Resources
Fans Online activities

HERITAGE LANGUAGE LEARNERS

- Ask students to write their own original sentence on the meaning of love. The love described could be between two people, or it could describe love of country, of family, or of an ideal, such as knowledge, integrity, or kindness. Students must be prepared to read their sentences aloud and explain their meanings to the rest of the class.

TOTAL PHYSICAL RESPONSE (TPR)

- Assign the task of finding opposite words from this *Desafío*, as well as from previous lessons, to two students. The two students will make a list of such words and later read one from each pair to each of two opposing teams that will be standing in opposite corners of the room. As each word is read to the teams, players take turns answering with a word of opposite meaning. For example: *amor → odio; mayor → menor*. Players who answer incorrectly are out. The winning team is the one with more players standing when you call time.

81

Comunicación

Presentation

- In this section, students will integrate the vocabulary and grammar skills from *Desafío 1* in order to express feelings and describe different aspects of personal relationships, as well as to use the direct and indirect object pronouns and the pronominal verbs.

Activities	Standards	Resources
27.	1.1, 5.1	
28.	1.2, 1.3, 2.1, 2.2, 3.2, 5.2	
29.	1.1, 1.3, 4.2, 5.1	
30.	1.2, 2.1, 2.2	Audio
31. Final del desafío	1.1, 1.2, 1.3, 2.1, 5.1	
Tu desafío	1.1, 1.2	

Teaching Suggestions

Warm-Up / Independent Starter

- Write the following proverb on the board: *El amor hace girar el mundo.* Set a timer for three minutes and ask students to use the vocabulary and verb structures they learned in this *Desafío* to write as many sentences as they can to describe their reactions to the proverb.

Preparation

- Have students share their Independent Starters in small groups and then discuss how various famous figures would respond to the same proverb (e.g., a character in their favorite book, don Quijote, Lady Gaga).

Activities

28. Before reading the text, ask students to read the title of the selection. Next, have students read the comprehension questions and then read the text. For the second part of this activity, ask students to work together to create a list of three to four evaluation criteria on which their artistic representations will be judged. Put these criteria on a worksheet and distribute to students before the class vote.

82

Comunicación

27 **Vamos a celebrar**

 ▶ **Habla** con tu compañero(a). ¿Con quién te relacionas más? ¿Cómo son las relaciones con familiares y amigos?

28 **¡Participa en el concurso!**

▶ **Lee** el texto y responde a las preguntas.

1. ¿De qué es el concurso?
2. ¿Cómo se va a elegir al ganador?
3. ¿Dónde se podrán ver las ilustraciones favoritas?
4. Esta es una de las ilustraciones que se presentan al concurso. Ponle un título.

Concurso de san Jordi

Los invitamos a participar en el concurso de ilustraciones con motivo del Día del Libro. Los dibujos deben incluir rosas y dragones.

El público votará para elegir la mejor ilustración. Los dibujos más votados serán incluidos en los folletos informativos de la fiesta. Además, los enamorados podrán usar estas ilustraciones para felicitar a sus parejas a través de la página web del ayuntamiento.

La ilustración ganadora del año pasado se titula *Leyendo haces amigos*. El artista quiso representar la rosa como algo que puede encantar al más horrible dragón, además de mostrar el aspecto romántico que posee la leyenda de san Jordi.

¡Anímense y participen!

▶ **Dibuja** tu propio anuncio para el Día de san Jordi. Ponle un título.

 ▶ **Presenta** tu anuncio a la clase. Tus compañeros(as) votarán para decidir qué ilustración representa mejor la Fiesta de san Jordi.

29 **Te toca a ti**

▶ **Escribe.** Vas a proponer un nuevo día de fiesta al director de tu escuela. Explícale cuándo, por qué y cómo se celebrará. No olvides darle un nombre a la fiesta.

Differentiated Instruction

DEVELOPING LEARNERS

- Distribute index cards to students and ask them to make flashcards for any words they do not understand on these pages. Have them write the Spanish word on one side and the English word on the opposite side. Encourage students to work with a partner and take turns quizzing each other with the cards. Remind them to look for cognates to facilitate understanding. Monitor their pronunciation of these cognates, making sure they are not influenced by how these words are pronounced in English.

EXPANDING LEARNERS

- After they complete activity 29, call on students to come in front of the class and make a convincing argument on behalf of the celebration they are proposing. After each presentation, the other students will grade speakers on how well they presented the material and how completely and correctly they addressed the when, why, and how of the proposal by awarding them points ranging from 1 to 10. Call on a few students to tabulate the results and name a winner and two runners up.

30 **Paso a paso**

 ▶ **Escucha** la conversación entre Asha y Lucas mientras se preparan para el Día de san Jordi y decide cuáles de estas afirmaciones son ciertas.

a. Lucas busca poemas en Internet.
b. Lucas tiene que decidir a quién manda la rosa.
c. Lucas le pide ayuda a Asha y ella acepta.
d. Asha encuentra un soneto de Neruda y se lo lee a Lucas.
e. Asha le sugiere a Lucas que lea poemas de Bécquer y de Neruda.
f. A Lucas le encantan los versos de Neruda.
g. Lucas decide regalar una rosa roja a su novia.

▶ **Escucha** de nuevo y ordena las oraciones ciertas del apartado anterior.

Final del desafío

LUCAS: Asha, escucha mi dedicatoria:

> ¡Las rosas son rojas,
> las violetas son azules;
> el azúcar es dulce,
> y también lo eres tú!

ASHA: Lucas, no es una dedicatoria muy original. ¿No aprendiste nada de Bécquer y de Neruda? Hay que ser más romántico...

LUCAS: Vale, trataré de ser más romántico. Escucha esta otra:

> Es el mes de ___1___, el día veintitrés.
> Soy tu humilde ___2___ barcelonés.
> Como la rosa nació de la sangre del ___3___,
> este ramo de ___4___ nace de mi corazón.
> Rescátame de esta prisión de ___5___
> y si este poema no te gusta te pido ___6___.
> ¡Feliz Día de san Jordi!

ASHA: Esa dedicatoria me gusta más. ¿Para quién es?

31 **Una tarjeta con dedicatoria**

▶ **Completa** la dedicatoria de Lucas.

| dragón | caballero | rosas |
| amor | perdón | abril |

▶ **Escribe** una tarjeta para enviársela a alguien especial. Incluye una dedicatoria describiendo la amistad que les une.

 **TU DESAFÍO** Visita la página web. Escucha las preguntas de tu *Minientrevista Desafío 1* y escribe las respuestas.

ochenta y tres **83**

HERITAGE LANGUAGE LEARNERS

• Ask students to rewrite the legend of Saint Jordi. This time, students may focus on describing a kind dragon whose only "crime" is not returning books to the library on time, or perhaps a dragon that exists on a diet of red roses. Give students time to create their legends. You may want to assign this as homework. When students have finished, ask them to read their legends aloud to the rest of the class.

MULTIPLE INTELLIGENCES:
Verbal-Linguistic Intelligence

• Ask students to write a *folleto informativo* that describes the celebration of Saint Jordi. Students should describe what the celebration is, how it has become synonymous with *el Día del Libro*, where it takes place, along with dates and time. Students should also include the activities that are planned for the day, what contests will take place and a description of the prizes that will be awarded. Encourage students to use the Internet to search for more information.

---

29. Call on volunteers to role-play the conversation between a student and the principal of the school.

30. Before listening to the audio selection, ask students to read the true/false statements. After the audio is played for the second time, have students work in pairs to dramatize the scene in which Lucas presents the red rose and his *dedicatoria* to his special someone. Each group will present to the class. Award prizes for "best use of pronouns," "best use of vocabulary," "most dramatic," "funniest," "most romantic," etc.

 AUDIO SCRIPT
See page 65I.

Answer Key

27. Answers will vary.
28. 1. Es de ilustraciones para el Día del Libro.
2. El público votará para elegir al ganador.
3. Se podrán ver en los folletos informativos de la fiesta y en la página web del ayuntamiento.
4. Answers will vary.
▶ Answers will vary.
▶ Answers will vary.
29. Answers will vary.
30. Afirmaciones ciertas: a, c, e, f, g.
▶ c, e, a, f, g
31. 1. abril 4. rosas
2. caballero 5. amor
3. dragón 6. perdón
▶ Answers will vary.

Additional Resources

Fans Online activities
Practice Workbook

83

Unit 2
DESAFÍO 2

Expresar deseos, gustos y preferencias

Presentation

- In *Desafío 2*, Eva and Ethan will learn how to play *pelota mixteca* and will send an invitation to their friends to attend the game. Students will preview language used to introduce people and to express wishes, likes, and preferences.

Activities	Standards	Resources
Texto	1.2, 2.1, 2.2	Vis. Pres.
32.	1.1, 1.2, 3.1	
33.	1.1, 1.2, 3.1	
34.	1.2, 2.2	Audio
35.	1.2, 1.3, 2.1, 2.2	
36. Cultura	1.1, 1.2, 2.1, 2.2, 3.1, 3.2, 4.2	Video

Teaching Suggestions

Warm-Up / Independent Starter

- Ask students to write a list of sports in which hands are essential to play, and describe the equipment needed to play those sports.

Preparation

- Ask several students to talk about one sport from their Independent Starter. Then have them look at the picture on page 84 and ask them what is different from the sports they mentioned.

Texto: Un juego milenario

- Read the introduction aloud. Then ask the class about the last time they sent or received an invitation to attend a game and how they sent or received it (e.g., e-mail, postcard, friend's blog).
- Call on four volunteers to read the dialogue convincingly in front of the class. What do students know now about *pelota mixteca*?

Activities

34. Have students add two more lines to the dialogue between Eva and Ethan. How did students solve the disagreement between Eva and Ethan?

35. After students complete this activity, have them write a comment to send to Eva's blog.

84

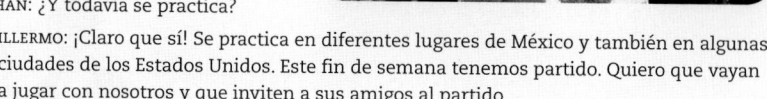

Un juego milenario

Eva and Ethan must learn how to play *pelota mixteca*, a pre-Hispanic game that is still played in Mexico and in some American cities, such as Los Angeles and Fresno. They also have to send an invitation to their friends to attend the game.

TIM: Quiero que conozcan al señor Guillermo Ramírez. Es mexicano y un experto jugador de pelota mixteca.

ETHAN: Encantado.

EVA: Mucho gusto, Guillermo.

ETHAN: Nunca oí hablar de este juego. ¿Cómo se juega?

GUILLERMO: Es un juego originado hace muchísimo tiempo. Tiene muchas reglas, pero lo fundamental es darle a la pelota con la mano.

ETHAN: ¿Y todavía se practica?

GUILLERMO: ¡Claro que sí! Se practica en diferentes lugares de México y también en algunas ciudades de los Estados Unidos. Este fin de semana tenemos partido. Quiero que vayan a jugar con nosotros y que inviten a sus amigos al partido.

EVA: Me parece una idea fantástica.

ETHAN: ¡De acuerdo! Tenemos que darnos prisa y enviar pronto las invitaciones. Pero necesitamos más información.

GUILLERMO: Vale, pero primero... ¿les apetece jugar? ¿Quieren que les enseñe?

ETHAN: Sí, ¿por qué no?

EVA: ¿Tenemos que jugar nosotros? No sé...

32 Detective de palabras

▶ **Completa** estas oraciones.

1. Quiero que ___1___ a Guillermo Ramírez.
2. Quiero que ___2___ a jugar y que ___3___ a sus amigos.
3. ¿Quieren que les ___4___?

▶ **Contesta.** ¿A qué infinitivos corresponden esas formas verbales? ¿Recuerdas qué modo verbal es?

Differentiated Instruction

DEVELOPING LEARNERS

- After students complete activity 32, give them more practice with the subjunctive following the verb *querer* by having them complete these sentences:
  1. *Quiero que los chicos aprendan/aprenden a jugar a la pelota mixteca. (aprendan)*
  2. *El entrenador quiere que yo practico/practique más. (practique)*
  3. *Los aficionados quieren que su equipo gana/gane. (gane)*
  4. *Guillermo quiere que Ethan y Eva jueguen/juegan. (jueguen)*
  5. *Mi hermano quiere que yo haga/hago su tarea. (haga)*

EXPANDING LEARNERS

- After students explain the meaning of *milenario*, ask them to define *centenario (de cien años)* and *bicentenario (de doscientos años)*. Explain that both Spanish and English have words that define age beyond simply stating "in his or her 60s or 70s." For vocabulary enrichment in both languages, write the following words on the board, ask students to repeat each one and then use them in a sentence: *sexagenario* (sexagenarian), *septuagenario* (septuagenarian), *octogenario* (octogenarian), *nonagenario* (nonagenarian). Point out that a fifty-year-old is a *quincuagenario* (no equivalent in English).

33 ¿Comprendes?

▶ **Responde** a estas preguntas.

1. ¿Qué significa *milenario*?
2. ¿Cuál es la característica fundamental del juego?
3. ¿Dónde se practica hoy en día ese juego?
4. ¿Qué deben hacer Eva y Ethan?

34 Desacuerdo

 ▶ **Escucha** la conversación entre Eva y Ethan y decide si estas oraciones son ciertas o falsas. Después, corrige las oraciones falsas.

1. Eva piensa que este juego es similar al voleibol.
2. Ethan espera que el señor Ramírez les dé toda la información sobre el juego.
3. Ethan quiere invitar a sus amigos del club de Español.
4. Eva prefiere no invitar a Mario al partido.
5. Ethan está de acuerdo con Eva.

35 El blog de Eva

▶ **Lee** la entrada del blog de Eva, localiza los errores y escríbela de nuevo.

Un juego milenario

PUBLICADO POR EVA, 20 DE OCTUBRE

¿Oyeron hablar alguna vez de la pelota mixteca? Es un juego moderno que solo se practica en México.

Hoy conocí a un experto jugador de Colombia que me explicó algunas cosas. El juego tiene muy pocas reglas. Lo más importante es no tocar la pelota con las manos. Este experto jugador va a dar una conferencia para hablar de este juego y quiero invitarlos. Ojalá que puedan ir; será muy interesante. ¡Hasta la próxima!

COMENTARIOS (0)   ENVIAR UN COMENTARIO

 **CULTURA**

El juego de pelota

El juego de pelota es un deporte de origen prehispánico que se practicaba en muchas culturas de Mesoamérica. Para estos pueblos, el juego tenía un significado religioso, ya que estaba relacionado con el culto al Sol.

De este antiguo juego derivaron otros, como la pelota mixteca o el ulama, que todavía se practican en algunas zonas de México y del sur de los Estados Unidos.

36 **Investiga.** ¿Conoces otras culturas con tradiciones parecidas?

ochenta y cinco 85

Expresar deseos, gustos y preferencias

 AUDIO SCRIPT
See page 651.

 CULTURA

El juego de pelota

Ulama, which is played in the state of Sinaloa, is another example of an enduring pre-Hispanic ball game. In the most common variation, players use their hips to hit the ball. *Pelota purépecha* is another game of pre-Hispanic origin. In its most spectacular version, a ball is set ablaze and then hit with a stick.

Answer Key

32.
1. conozcan	3. inviten
2. vayan	4. enseñe
▶ 1. conocer	3. invitar
2. ir	4. enseñar

Modo verbal: subjuntivo

33.
1. Que tiene miles de años.
2. Hay que darle a la pelota con la mano.
3. En diferentes lugares de México y en algunas ciudades de los EE. UU.
4. Deben enviar las invitaciones.

34.
1. Falso. Que no es lo mismo que el voleibol.
2. Cierto.
3. Cierto.
4. Cierto.
5. Falso. Ethan no está de acuerdo con Eva.

35. Es un juego milenario que se juega en algunas ciudades de México y de los EE. UU. Hoy conocí a un experto jugador de México. El juego tiene muchas reglas. Lo importante es darle a la pelota con la mano. Este experto jugador va a jugar un partido.

36. Answers will vary.

Additional Resources

Fans Online activities

85

Unit 2
DESAFÍO 2

Vocabulario – Presentaciones. Invitar, aceptar y rechazar una invitación

Presentation

- In this section, students will learn words and expressions to introduce and invite people, to accept or decline an invitation, and to talk about social relationships.

Activities	Standards	Resources
Vocabulario	1.2, 2.1	
37.	1.1, 1.2, 2.1, 5.1, 5.2	
38.	1.2, 2.1	Audio
39.	1.1, 1.2, 2.1, 5.1, 5.2	
40. Cultura	1.1, 1.2, 2.1, 3.2, 4.2, 5.1	

Teaching Suggestions

Warm-Up / Independent Starter

- Provide students with the following items and ask them to separate them in two columns (formal and informal), according to how they will address each of these people:
  1. *Ricardo García, compañero de clase.*
  2. *Isabel Allende, escritora chilena.*
  3. *Arturo Jiménez, profesor de Música.*
  4. *Juana Serrano, amiga.*

Preparation

- Have students read the speech bubbles for *Presentaciones.* Be sure that they understand that *don* and *doña* are used with a first name, whereas *señor* and *señora* are used with a last name. Then have students decide with whom from their Independent Starters they would use these formal titles.
- Read aloud the words in the *Más vocabulario* feature to model correct pronunciation and have students repeat them after you. Call on volunteers to read the expressions in *Invitar, aceptar y rechazar una invitación.* You may then provide some plans to elicit agreement or disagreement (e.g., *¿Les apetece ir a un partido de tenis? ¿Vamos a hacer la tarea?*).

86

Vocabulario

Presentaciones

Buenos días, doña Carmen. Quiero presentarle a don Pedro. Es el profesor de Arte.

Encantada.

Permítanme que les presente a la señora Matos. Es la nueva directora.

Mucho gusto. Yo soy el señor Rivera.

Invitar, aceptar y rechazar una invitación

¿Te apetece...?
¿Vamos a...?
Te invito a...
¿Estás ocupado(a)? / ¿Tienes planes para hoy?

De acuerdo. / Vale.
Sí, ¿por qué no?
Con mucho gusto.
Me parece un buen plan.

No, no me apetece.
Gracias, pero no puedo.
Lo siento, pero estoy ocupado(a).
No sé... Tengo mucho que hacer.

Más vocabulario

Relaciones sociales

el/la anfitrión(a) *host, hostess*
el/la invitado(a) *guest*
la fiesta *party*
la reunión *meeting*

Acciones

llegar tarde *to arrive late*
llegar temprano *to arrive early*
llegar a tiempo *to arrive on time*

37 ¿Sí o no?

▶ **Escribe** una respuesta para cada propuesta aceptando o rechazando la invitación.

1. ¿Estás ocupado(a)? ¿Te apetece venir a cenar a mi casa?
2. ¿Te apetece venir a un concierto conmigo esta noche?
3. Te invito a mi fiesta de cumpleaños el sábado.
4. ¿Quieres tomar un café esta tarde?
5. ¿Vamos al cine?

Differentiated Instruction

DEVELOPING LEARNERS

- Ask students to work with a partner and a heritage learner to practice introducing students to one another. Have them use the following scenarios:
  1. Introduce your boy/girlfriend to one of your parents.
  2. Introduce your younger sibling to your best friend.
  3. Introduce your classmates to a visiting teacher from Mexico.
  4. Introduce your older neighbor to an older newcomer in the neighborhood.
- Ask students to make some of their introductions in front of the class.

EXPANDING LEARNERS

- Give students more practice with making introductions, greeting people, and saying good-bye by having them work in small groups to present two scenes: one set in a Spanish-speaking country and another set here. Ask students to describe who is being introduced, then have them make the customary introduction, complete with either a handshake (or none), a kiss (or two or none) on the cheek, a hug (or none), and the customary way people stand and use body language. Ask them to reenact their introductions for the rest of the class.

38 **Llámame, por favor**

 ▶ **Escucha** los mensajes de los amigos de Eva y relaciona cada uno con una fotografía.

39 **Presentaciones**

 ▶ **Habla** con dos compañeros(as). Inventen diálogos cortos para presentar a estas personas.

Modelo   **1.** A. *Thomas, te presento a Marcos Pérez. Es mi entrenador de baloncesto.*
                B. *Mucho gusto, señor Pérez.*
                C. *Encantado, Thomas.*

1. Marcos Pérez, entrenador de baloncesto.
2. Ana Sanz, doctora de familia.
3. Mar Vega, tu mejor amiga.
4. El alcalde *(mayor)* de tu ciudad.
5. Luis López, un compañero de clase.
6. Laura Gee, tu profesora de Inglés.

 **CULTURA**

El espacio personal

El contacto físico forma parte de las relaciones sociales entre hispanos. En los países hispanos muchas personas se saludan y se despiden con un beso en la mejilla (en España dos), especialmente las mujeres. Los hombres generalmente se estrechan la mano *(shake hands)*.

Además, en los países hispanos suele haber menos distancia física entre las personas cuando hablan o cuando esperan en una fila, por ejemplo, aunque esto depende también del grado de confianza *(intimacy)* y de la situación.

40 **Explica.** ¿Alguna vez has entrado en contacto con una cultura con más o con menos espacio personal que la tuya? ¿Cómo te sentiste?

HERITAGE LANGUAGE LEARNERS

- Ask students to share other ways of making introductions, extending invitations, and accepting or declining invitations that are common in their family's country of origin. Differences may include how *usted, ustedes, vosotros(as),* and *tú* are used, along with other expressions that show polite acceptance or turning down an invitation. Have students share these expressions with the rest of the class.

COOPERATIVE LEARNING

- Ask students to work in small groups and explain that they are going to generate a crossword puzzle, based on the words from this lesson and other related vocabulary that has to do with making introductions and accepting or declining invitations. After students have worked together to generate ten to fifteen words and clues, direct them to a suitable crossword puzzle generator online. Have them print a blank puzzle, which they will exchange with another group, along with their clues to the words. Give groups a set time in which to solve each other's puzzles.

Vocabulario – Presentaciones. Invitar, aceptar y rechazar una invitación

Activities

37. To extend this activity, invite different pairs of students to role-play a question (invitation) and their response for the class.

38. Before listening to the audio, ask students to describe each picture and try to guess whether the people in the pictures are going to accept a prospective invitation or not.

39. As a follow-up, ask several groups of students to present their dialogues in front of the class. Be sure students also practice *don* and *doña*.

 AUDIO SCRIPT
See page 651.

 CULTURA

El espacio personal
Language and culture are inseparable when learning a foreign language. To establish good intercultural communication it is essential to learn, respect, and follow cultural practices. For instance, Latinos seem to have smaller personal space barriers than non-Latinos. When a Latino and a non-Latino meet for the first time, it is frequent to see the non-Latino trying to keep a bigger distance and the Latino getting closer. In this situation, neither person needs to interpret the pattern as rude behavior, but as a cultural difference.

Answer Key

37. Answers will vary.
38. 1. D   2. B   3. C   4. A
39. Answers will vary.
40. Answers will vary.

Additional Resources

Fans Online activities
Practice Workbook

DESAFÍO 2

Gramática – Expresar deseos, gustos y preferencias

Presentation

▪ In this section, students will review verbs used to express wishes, likes, and preferences. They will also review when to use the subjunctive mood with these verbs.

Activities	Standards	Resources
Gramática	1.2, 3.1	
41.	3.1, 4.1	
42.	1.1, 1.3, 5.1	
43.	1.1, 1.2, 1.3, 5.2	Audio
44.	1.1, 1.2, 1.3, 5.1	

Teaching Suggestions

Warm-Up / Independent Starter

▪ Have students write one wish, like, or preference for themselves, their parents, their best friend, and their Spanish classmates and teacher.

Preparation

▪ Have students read the grammar explanations silently, take notes on any material they do not understand, and review the subjunctive verb forms if they need to refresh their memory.

▪ Ask students to share their Independent Starters with the class and have the class correct each student's work to make sure that they made proper use of the contrast between singular and plural (*gusta* vs. *gustan*) and between infinitive and subjunctive (*quiero ir* vs. *quiero que vayas*).

Activities

42. Remind students to take notes about their classmates' wishes for them. Have students share their reactions with the class, encouraging them to explain why they agree or disagree with their classmates' wishes.

43. Introduce the activity by asking students to say what their likes, dislikes, and preferences are regarding the six categories listed. For the third part of this activity, have students compare and contrast their paragraphs with a classmate's paragraph. Ask them to share with the class their similarities and differences.

Gramática

Expresar deseos, gustos y preferencias

Los verbos *gustar, encantar, interesar, apetecer* e *importar*

● Use the verbs gustar, encantar, interesar, apetecer, and importar to express wishes, likes, and preferences. These verbs are paired with an indirect object pronoun: me, te, le, nos, os, les.

A mis hermanos y a mí **nos encanta** celebrar fiestas en casa.

● Generally, these verbs are used in the third person (singular or plural).

Nos encantan los deportes, pero no **nos interesa** nada el fútbol.

However, sometimes couples use these verbs in the first and second person. Notice that the verb agrees in number with the subject:

¿Te gusto (yo)? *(Do you like me?)*   Me gustas (tú). *(I like you.)*

● To express agreement, use the words también and tampoco.

—Me apetece hacer deporte.   —No me gustan los juegos de naipes.
—A mí también.   —A mí tampoco.

El subjuntivo para expresar deseos, gustos y preferencias

● To express wishes, you can also use ojalá (que) followed by the subjunctive.

Ojalá (que) María **visite** México pronto.

Regular verbs form the present subjunctive this way (see conjugation on page R16):

| -ar verbs | Add the endings -e, -es, -e, -emos, -éis, -en. |

| -er and -ir verbs | Add the endings -a, -as, -a, -amos, -áis, -an. |

● You can also use verbs like querer, esperar, preferir, and desear. Use the **subjunctive** in the dependent clause when there are two subjects, and the **infinitive** if there is no subject change.

Quiero conocer a tu mejor amigo.   Prefiero que tú conozcas a mi mejor amigo.

41 **Piensa.** ¿Cómo se dice en inglés a mí también? ¿Y a mí tampoco?

42 **Deseos**

▶ **Habla** con cinco compañeros(as) sobre lo que les deseas después de graduarse. Usa *ojalá (que)* y estos verbos.

Modelo   *Ojalá John pueda ser un jugador de béisbol profesional.*

estudiar	trabajar	vivir	ser
conocer	poder	tener	querer

▶ **Escribe** un párrafo sobre lo que tus compañeros(as) desean para ti. Añade tu reacción: ¿estás de acuerdo con lo que dijeron?

88 ochenta y ocho

Differentiated Instruction

DEVELOPING LEARNERS

● Give students more practice with the present subjunctive by having them complete these sentences with the correct form of the verb in parentheses:

1. *Prefiero que tú (ir) al partido con tu hermano. (vayas)*
2. *¿Desea usted que nosotros solo (hablar) español en la clase? (hablemos)*
3. *¡Ojalá que nuestro equipo (ganar) el partido! (gane)*
4. *¿Qué quieres que (hacer) yo: terminar la tarea o limpiar mi cuarto? (haga)*
5. *Me encanta que te (interesar) estos libros del abuelo. (interesen)*

EXPANDING LEARNERS

● Ask students to expand the paragraph they wrote about their classmates for activity 42, this time including what they wish for their community, their country, or for the entire world in the current year. Get them started with such openers as: *Me interesa que haya más seguridad en mi comunidad. Me importa que el desempleo baje en el país. Ojalá que no haya más guerras. Deseo que los líderes mundiales resuelvan los problemas. Quiero que los científicos encuentren una cura contra el cáncer.*

43 **Los gustos de Eva**

▶ **Escucha** el mensaje que Eva tiene en su página web y decide si estas cosas le gustan o no.

1. los deportes
2. la comida
3. las computadoras
4. la música
5. viajar
6. la ropa de moda

 ▶ **Escucha** de nuevo y completa estas oraciones.

1. A Eva le encanta que sus amigos la ———— para ir con ellos al parque.
2. Le gustan las computadoras y le encanta que sus amigos ———— comunicarse con ella.
3. Le apetece ———— a México con su familia.
4. Prefiere que la comida ———— picante.
5. Le gusta mucho ————.
6. No le importa que su madre le ———— ropa de vez en cuando.

▶ **Escribe** un texto similar al de Eva.

Modelo

> ¿Quieren conocerme mejor? Voy a hablarles de mis gustos. Mi afición favorita es hacer deporte. Me interesan especialmente los deportes de equipo. También...

 44 **Tu amigo ideal**

▶ **Escribe.** ¿Qué gustos debe tener tu amigo(a) ideal? Usa los verbos *querer, preferir, gustar, encantar, interesar*...

Modelo   *Quiero que mi amigo(a) vaya a teatros y museos.*

a. tiempo libre
b. deportes
c. comida
d. música
e. viajes
f. tecnología

 ▶ **Habla** con tu compañero(a) y comparen sus respuestas. Después, presenten los resultados a la clase.

Modelo   *Yo quiero que mi amigo vaya a museos y teatros, pero Sarah prefiere que su amiga practique muchos deportes.*

ochenta y nueve 89

HERITAGE LANGUAGE LEARNERS

• Ask students to talk to the class about sports and social activities in their family's country of origin that may not be known or popular here. Sports or spectacles might include: *corridas de toros, jai alai* or *pelota vasca, charreadas, etc.* Students may also mention the long-standing tradition of the afternoon *siesta* and the *merienda*. Encourage students to include a description of family dynamics when attending social events: many parents expect their children to accompany them to even an informal family gathering, rather than going out with their friends.

CRITICAL THINKING

• Ask students to make up a conversation between two cousins who haven't seen each other in years and have planned a weekend together. The only problem is that they have completely opposite interests and tastes. One cousin could be a sports fanatic, and the other may show interest in reading and hiking. One might like to stay out late dancing, while the other prefers a quiet evening at home. Encourage students to use their imagination to create these differences and also use their critical thinking skills to find middle ground so both cousins will enjoy their time together.

Gramática – Expresar deseos, gustos y preferencias

44. To prepare students for this activity, ask them the following questions about their best friend: *¿Quién es tu mejor amigo(a)? ¿Cómo es? ¿Por qué es tu mejor amigo(a)? ¿Tienen gustos semejantes? ¿Es tu mejor amigo(a) un amigo ideal?*

 AUDIO SCRIPT
See page 651.

Answer Key

41. Se dice *me too* y *me neither*.

42. Answers will vary. Sample answers:
Ojalá que Michelle estudie Medicina.
Ojalá Carlos conozca personas interesantes.
Ojalá que Jill trabaje en una compañía grande.
Ojalá Rita viva en California.
Ojalá que Mike tenga muchos amigos.
Ojalá que Sam sea muy feliz.
Ojalá Silvia quiera vivir en un país hispano.
▶ Answers will vary.

43. 1. No le gustan los deportes.
2. Le gusta la comida.
3. Le gustan las computadoras.
4. Le gusta la música.
5. Le gusta viajar.
6. No le gusta la ropa de moda.
▶ 1. llamen   4. sea
  2. puedan   5. la música
  3. ir   6. regale
▶ Answers will vary.

44. Answers will vary.
▶ Answers will vary.

Additional Resources

Fans Online activities
Practice Workbook

89

DESAFÍO 2

Gramática – Verbos pronominales no reflexivos

Presentation

- In this section, students will learn and practice pronominal verbs which are neither reflexive nor reciprocal.

Activities	Standards	Resources
Gramática	1.2, 3.1	
45.	3.1, 4.1	
46.	1.2	Audio
47.	1.2, 1.3, 3.1	
48.	1.1, 1.2	
49. Conexiones	1.1, 1.2, 2.2, 3.1, 3.2, 5.1	

Teaching Suggestions

Warm-Up / Independent Starter

- Have students read the grammar presentation silently. Ask them to choose one verb from each chart and write a complete sentence.

Preparation

- Start by reviewing the reflexive and reciprocal verbs taught on pages 78–79. Then contrast those verbs with the pronominal verbs introduced on this page.
- Ask for volunteers to write on the board their sentences from the Independent Starter. Use the sentences to provide a battery of examples.

Activities

46. Have students tell the corresponding infinitive for each conjugated verb in Column A. Ask them to write a complete sentence for each one in a different context. If time allows, ask students to give examples for 1, 2, 3, 5, and 6 without using pronominal verbs to emphasize the change of meaning.

48. Have students compare their answers with those of a classmate, and write a paragraph summarizing their comparisons. For example: *Tania y yo somos parecidas porque vamos a la escuela a las ocho de la mañana y dormimos ocho horas. Pero somos diferentes porque…*

90

DESAFÍO 2

Gramática

Verbos pronominales no reflexivos

- Besides reflexive and reciprocal verbs, there are many verbs that are conjugated with reflexive pronouns. Many of them refer to emotions, changes in condition, or processes that happen to the subject.

VERBOS PRONOMINALES

Personas	acordarse	to remember	dormirse	to fall asleep
	alegrarse	to be glad	enterarse	to find out
	atreverse	to dare	olvidarse	to forget
	despertarse	to wake up	preocuparse	to worry
Cosas	abrirse	to open	cerrarse	to close
	arrugarse	to wrinkle	enfriarse	to get cold
	caerse	to fall	mancharse	to get dirty
	calentarse	to warm	romperse	to break

Verbos con cambio de significado

- There are many verbs that can be used with or without pronouns, but with meaning differences. These are the most common:

VERBOS CON CAMBIO DE SIGNIFICADO

acordar	to agree	vs.	acordarse	to remember
aprender	to learn	vs.	aprenderse	to memorize
beber	to drink	vs.	beberse	to drink up
comer	to eat	vs.	comerse	to eat up
dormir	to sleep	vs.	dormirse	to fall asleep
estudiar	to study	vs.	estudiarse	to learn
ir	to go	vs.	irse	to leave
parecer	to seem	vs.	parecerse	to look like
quedar	to arrange to meet	vs.	quedarse	to stay
salir	to leave	vs.	salirse	to go beyond the limits

45 **Compara.** ¿Existe en inglés una forma de expresar la diferencia entre María bebió un refresco y María se bebió un refresco?

46 ¡Vámonos!

▶ **Escucha** el diálogo entre Ethan y Eva, y une las dos columnas.

(A)
1. Eva se va…
2. Ayer Ethan se durmió…
3. Ethan no se parece a su hermano…
4. El hermano de Ethan siempre va…
5. Eva no se aprendió…
6. Eva quiere irse…

(B)
a. porque a él le gusta mucho salir.
b. porque no quiere llegar tarde.
c. la dirección del lugar del concierto.
d. a un concierto.
e. a las cuatro de la mañana.
f. a todos los eventos de la escuela.

Differentiated Instruction

DEVELOPING LEARNERS

- Explain to students that they are going to play "Memory." Distribute index cards on which you have previously written each of the verbs that appear in the *Verbos con cambio de significado* box. Then ask students to shuffle the cards and place them facedown on a desk. Have students play against a partner and try to match the verb pairs. If they make a match, students will say a sentence with each verb; if the sentences are incorrect, or if no match is made, students will place the cards facedown and the partner takes a turn.

EXPANDING LEARNERS

- Explain that many of the verbs in *Verbos pronominales* can also be transitive (e.g., *La puerta se abrió. / Karen abrió la puerta.*). Ask students to work in small groups and review the verbs listed. Then have them collaborate to write a sentence with each of the verbs as they are listed and then, where possible, as either transitive verbs or verbs with the non-pronominal form. Examples include: *Nos calentamos al lado de la estufa. / Calentamos la sopa. Me olvidé de tu cumpleaños. / Olvida a tu exnovio.* Ask students to share their sentences.

47 **Cada oveja con su pareja**

▶ **Elige** la opción correcta.

1. _____ a la biblioteca los jueves por la tarde.
   Voy / Me voy

2. Son casi las seis y tengo una cita a las seis. _____
   ¡Voy! / ¡Me voy!

3. _____ a las once de la noche.
   Duermo / Me duermo

4. Normalmente _____ ocho horas.
   duermo / me duermo

5. _____ el café de un trago (*gulp*).
   Bebí / Me bebí

6. _____ un café después de cenar.
   Bebieron / Se bebieron

7. El estudiante de Chile _____ muy simpático.
   parece / se parece

8. Daniel _____ mucho a su padre.
   parece / se parece

▶ **Escribe** otros ejemplos con verbos que cambian o modifican su significado. Elige cuatro verbos de la ficha de Gramática.

48 **Y ahora tú**

▶ **Responde** a estas preguntas.

1. ¿A qué hora vas a la escuela?
2. ¿Cuántas horas duermes?
3. ¿A qué hora te duermes generalmente?
4. ¿A qué familiar te pareces más? ¿En qué cosas?
5. ¿Te aprendes los números de teléfono de tus amigos(as)? ¿Cuántos recuerdas?
6. ¿Te comes siempre toda la comida del plato?

CONEXIONES: HISTORIA

El pueblo mixteco

La cultura mixteca es una cultura prehispánica que ocupaba los territorios de los actuales estados mexicanos de Puebla, Oaxaca y Guerrero, al sur del país. Los mixtecos fueron muy buenos artesanos y desarrollaron un sistema de escritura con figuras y símbolos gracias al cual hoy conocemos aspectos de su historia y de sus creencias.

Muchos mixtecos emigraron y actualmente viven fuera de sus comunidades de origen, principalmente en ciudades de México y de los Estados Unidos.

49 **Piensa y explica.** ¿Por qué crees que emigraron tantos mixtecos?

Gramática – Verbos pronominales no reflexivos

49. To expand this activity, ask students to share with the class the origin of their family and why they immigrated to the United States. Alternatively, you may ask students to work in groups and make a list of the main groups of immigrants that came to the United States and why they immigrated.

 AUDIO SCRIPT
See page 65 J.

 CONEXIONES: HISTORIA

El pueblo mixteco

The Mixtecs were one of the most influential pre-Hispanic civilizations of Mesoamerica. Today, they are the fourth largest indigenous group in Mexico. They call themselves *Ñuu Savi*, which means "people of the rain." Farming used to be their most important activity, but soil erosion, deforestation, and soil exhaustion have forced many Mixtecs to migrate. There are large Mixtec communities in the western U.S. states of California, Arizona, Oregon, and Washington.

Answer Key

45. Sí. Por ejemplo: *María drank a soda* vs. *María drank the soda* up.

46. 1. d   2. e   3. a   4. f   5. c   6. b

47. 1. Voy   4. duermo   7. parece
2. ¡Me voy!   5. Me bebí   8. se parece
3. Me duermo 6. Bebieron
▶ Answers will vary.

48. Answers will vary.

49. Answers will vary.

Additional Resources

Fans Online activities
Practice Workbook

HERITAGE LANGUAGE LEARNERS

- Explain that there are many verbs that can be used with both the pronominal and non-pronominal forms. In addition to those listed in the *Gramática* feature, some common verbs include *acabarse, acostarse, enamorarse, perderse, presentarse.* Ask pairs of students to write a list of as many of these verbs as they can. Suggest that they use their dictionaries or a good grammar reference book. Ask students to include the shades of meaning between the two forms of these verbs and provide a model sentence for each one. Display their work in the classroom and encourage other students to study these verbs.

CRITICAL THINKING

- Have students think about how they would portray their generation to future generations. What are some key characteristics of their generation? Ask groups of three students to write a description of their generation. You may want to use these sentences to get students started: *Somos una generación que se atreve a probar cosas nuevas. Nos preocupamos por el futuro del planeta y...* Ask groups to share their descriptions with the class. Then have a class discussion to agree on a final description they would want to leave in a time capsule for future generations to study.

LECTURA: TEXTO INFORMATIVO

Presentation

- In this section, students will read a short essay about pre-Hispanic games and sports. They will learn some vocabulary related to the topic of games and sports.

Activities	Standards	Resources
Lectura: texto informativo	1.1, 1.2, 3.1, 3.2	
50.	1.2, 2.1, 2.2	
51.	1.2, 1.3, 2.2, 3.1, 4.2, 5.2	
52.	1.2, 2.1, 2.2, 3.1, 3.2	
53.	1.1, 1.2, 4.2, 5.2	

Teaching Suggestions

Warm-Up / Independent Starter

- Have students read the *Antes de leer* strategies silently. Ask them to scan the text and make a list in their notebooks of all the verb forms in the past that they find. Then have them classify these verbs into imperfect or preterite.

Preparation

- Call students' attention to the prefix *pre-* in contrast to its opposite *pos-* or *post-*. Ask them to give you some examples of their use in English, and then in Spanish. If they cannot think of words in Spanish, you may want to provide these examples: *prehistoria, prefabricado, prepagado, posmeridiano, posmoderno, posguerra*. Make sure that students understand the meaning of the title and of the word *prehispánico(a)*.

- Ask students to share their Independent Starter lists with the class. Review the verb classifications students made and discuss with the class the reason for this text having more verbs in the imperfect than in the preterite. (The text describes pre-Hispanic games. It does not focus on past actions, but rather on descriptions of the past.)

Antes de leer: estrategias

1. Lee el título. ¿Qué significa el prefijo *pre-* de la palabra *precolombinos*? Haz una lista de otras palabras que conoces con este prefijo y explica su significado.
2. Identifica las palabras en negrita *(bold)*. ¿Qué pistas te dan sobre el contenido de la lectura?
3. Haz una lista de juegos en los que se usan balones o pelotas. ¿Cuáles se juegan en equipo? ¿Cuáles se juegan individualmente?
4. Fíjate en los verbos. ¿Qué tiempo verbal predomina: el presente, el pretérito o el futuro? ¿Hay más verbos en pretérito o en imperfecto? ¿Por qué?

Juego de patolli (México).

Juegos precolombinos

Las culturas prehispánicas tenían un componente religioso que se reflejaba en casi todos los aspectos de la vida; desde el trabajo y la comida, hasta los juegos y las diversiones. Por esta razón, se desarrollaron una gran variedad de juegos.

Uno de los juegos precolombinos más conocidos es el **juego de pelota**, un juego de equipo que se jugaba con una pelota de caucho[1]. El objetivo de este juego era pasar la pelota por unos aros[2] de piedra. Para los pueblos prehispánicos, el juego de pelota representaba la lucha[3] de los dioses.

Otros juegos muy populares entre los aztecas eran el totoloque y el patolli. El objetivo del totoloque era darle a unas marcas[4] con bolitas de oro. El patolli era un **juego de mesa** en el que había que mover unas piedras por el tablero[5]. Para indicar los números, en lugar de dados[6] utilizaban unos frijoles con dibujos.

Muchos pueblos eran grandes aficionados a los **juegos competitivos** de destrezas[7] y resistencia, como las carreras a pie o en canoa, la lucha y las competencias de arco y flechas[8].

En América del Norte, los indígenas practicaban otro juego de equipo con pelota que sirvió de base para el actual *lacrosse*.

Con pelota, tablero o dados, lo cierto es que los juegos precolombinos inspiraron varios de los deportes y juegos que practicamos hoy.

1. *rubber*	3. *struggle*	5. *board*	7. *skills*
2. *hoops*	4. *targets*	6. *dice*	8. *bow and arrows*

Differentiated Instruction

DEVELOPING LEARNERS

- Help students to better comprehend the reading passage by first having them read each line aloud, followed by you paraphrasing that line. For example, you might paraphrase the first line as: *La religión tenía un papel muy importante para las culturas prehispánicas.*

EXPANDING LEARNERS

- Give students a chance to edit the reading selection for their local newspaper. The information presented is correct, so students will not have to do any research, but their editor has told them that they must shorten the article by almost half, while still keeping the most relevant facts. Allow students time to complete this assignment and then ask them to turn in the article for "publication" (display in the classroom).

50 ¿Qué recuerdas?

▶ **Elige** la opción correcta.

1. En muchas culturas precolombinas, la religión se relacionaba con…

   a. los juegos   b. la guerra   c. unas pocas actividades

2. En el juego de pelota había que pasar la pelota por…

   a. un tablero   b. unos aros de piedra   c. una carrera a pie

3. En las culturas prehispánicas se desarrollaron juegos de…

   a. tablero y dados   b. contacto   c. estrategia

4. El patolli era un juego de…

   a. contacto   b. mesa   c. destrezas y resistencia

5. Un juego de los antiguos habitantes de Norteamérica es el antecedente del…

   a. béisbol   b. baloncesto   c. *lacrosse*

51 Conexiones

▶ **Relaciona** estos juegos con otros de hoy y escribe un texto explicando las semejanzas y las diferencias.

> juego de pelota

> totoloque   patolli

Juego de pelota (México).

52 Resúmenes

▶ **Lee** estos textos. ¿Cuál expresa mejor la importancia de los juegos en las culturas precolombinas?

1. Las culturas precolombinas, como muchas otras, desarrollaron juegos y diversiones. En algunos de sus juegos favoritos usaban pelotas y en otros usaban tableros y dados para mover fichas. Un juego de pelota muy importante es el *lacrosse*, originario de Norteamérica.

2. Los juegos en las culturas precolombinas tenían una gran importancia debido a su contenido religioso o ritual, como se ve en el juego de pelota, por ejemplo. Otros juegos desarrollaban destrezas importantes para la cultura, tales como la fuerza física o la habilidad para manejar las armas.

53 Con tus propias palabras

▶ **Responde** a estas preguntas.

1. ¿Qué importancia tienen los juegos y deportes en la sociedad de hoy?

2. ¿Qué actividades de tu cultura reflejan creencias religiosas, rituales o tradiciones?

noventa y tres 93

HERITAGE LANGUAGE LEARNERS

• Explain to students that in addition to *pre-*, there are many more prefixes that are commonly used in Spanish. Have students research some, and find words that contain these prefixes to enrich their vocabulary. Ask them to come up with as many prefixes as they can, list their meaning, indicate whether they are of Latin or Greek origin, and include at least one word with each prefix. You may want to get students started with some examples: *tele-: a distancia, del griego, teléfono; sub-: debajo de, del latín, subterráneo.*

SPECIAL-NEEDS LEARNERS

• Help students who have difficulty staying focused when they are reading or listening to long passages by copying the reading selection onto copy paper and cutting it into six parts, one for each paragraph. Then have students work with a partner and take turns reading each paragraph in order. After students finish reading, mix up the parts and ask students to put the reading back together by placing the paragraphs in the correct order on a sheet of paper.

LECTURA: TEXTO INFORMATIVO

■ Ask students to read *Juegos precolombinos* silently and have them share three important ideas from the text (e.g., sports/games and religion were intermingled in pre-Hispanic societies; games and sports were very important; pre-Hispanic games have influenced some of the games we play today).

Activities

51. Ask students if they play board games. Write on the board the words *ajedrez* (chess) and *damas* (checkers). Explain that both games probably have a Persian origin, and were introduced in Europe by the Arabs in the Middle Ages. Another popular game is *dominó* (dominoes), which has a Chinese origin and was introduced in Italy in the 18th century.

52. Before doing this activity, have students work on their summarizing skills. Divide the class in small groups and have them explain the main idea of each paragraph of the reading. Write those ideas on the board. Then have groups complete this activity.

53. As homework, ask students to write a paragraph in response to each of these questions.

Answer Key

50. 1. a   2. b   3. a   4. b   5. c

51. Answers will vary.

52. Párrafo 2, porque resume mejor las funciones que los juegos tenían en las sociedades prehispánicas: valor religioso, desarrollo de destrezas y entrenamiento para la guerra.

53. Answers will vary.

Additional Resources

Fans Online activities

93

DESAFÍO 2

Comunicación

Presentation

- In this section, students will integrate the vocabulary and grammar from *Desafío 2* in order to invite, accept or reject an invitation, and talk about wishes, likes, and preferences.

Activities	Standards	Resources
54.	1.1, 1.2, 1.3, 2.2, 5.1	
55.	1.1, 1.2, 1.3	
56.	1.1, 1.2, 1.3, 5.1	
57. Final del desafío	1.1, 1.2, 1.3, 5.1	
Tu desafío	1.1, 1.2	

Teaching Suggestions

Warm-Up / Independent Starter

- Have the following questions on the board so that students can answer them individually:
  1. *¿Te acuerdas de la última vez que recibiste una invitación a un evento?*
  2. *¿La aceptaste o rechazaste? ¿Por qué?*
  3. *¿Te gusta recibir invitaciones o prefieres enviarlas?*

Preparation

- Go over the vocabulary and grammar topics from this *Desafío*. Clarify any doubts students may have regarding expressing wishes, likes, and preferences, as well as using pronominal verbs.

- As you go over students' answers to the questions in the Independent Starter, you may expand this activity by adding more questions. For example: *¿Dónde fue el evento? ¿Cuánta gente había? ¿Te gusta este tipo de eventos?*

Activities

54. Ask students to exchange their written invitations with a classmate. Then, ask them to write an answer back accepting or rejecting the invitation. Finally, ask for volunteers to explain to the class the invitation they received and whether they accepted or rejected it and why.

94

Comunicación

54 **¿Puedes venir?**

▶ **Lee** el programa de actividades organizadas por tu escuela para celebrar la «Semana Internacional» y selecciona tres eventos a los que te gustaría asistir.

 ▶ **Habla** con tu compañero(a). Por turnos, háganse propuestas y acepten o rechacen las sugerencias.

Modelo

A. *¿Quieres que vayamos juntos a ver el documental sobre las tradiciones españolas?*

B. *No me apetece mucho. Prefiero ir a ver el partido.*

▶ **Escribe.** Selecciona tu evento favorito y escribe una invitación para enviársela a tu mejor amigo(a).

> **PROGRAMA DE LA SEMANA INTERNACIONAL**
>
> **Viernes 3**
> 4:00 p. m. Bailes populares de Chile
> 5:00 p. m. Documental «España y sus tradiciones»
> 6:00 p. m. Japón y las artes marciales
> 7:00 p. m. Cena: sabor de México
>
> **Sábado 4**
> 11:00 a. m. Deportes populares del mundo
> 3:00 p. m. Clase de salsa cubana
> 5:00 p. m. Película: *La vita è bella* (Italia)
> 7:00 p. m. Feria
>
> **Domingo 5**
> 11:00 a. m. Mercado al aire libre
> 5:00 p. m. Fútbol: Europa vs. Latinoamérica
> 7:00 p. m. Cena internacional

55 **Estudiante de intercambio**

▶ **Lee** este fragmento de una solicitud para un programa de intercambio que escribió Ethan. Anota lo que él considera importante.

Quiero vivir con una familia que me muestre la cultura y las costumbres del país. Me interesa que en la familia haya un chico o una chica de mi edad. Soy vegetariano y por eso espero que a la familia no le importe cocinar platos diferentes para mí.

Quiero tomar clases de Ciencias porque este tema me interesa mucho, pero también me apetece aprender algo de Historia y de Arte.

Espero que mis profesores sean simpáticos y no pongan mucha tarea porque quiero tener tiempo libre para visitar los lugares típicos y divertirme.

Ojalá que acepten mi solicitud y pueda estudiar en el extranjero el próximo año.

▶ **Escribe** un párrafo similar expresando tus gustos y preferencias como estudiante extranjero.

94 noventa y cuatro

Differentiated Instruction

DEVELOPING LEARNERS

- Ask students to develop their own *Programa de la Semana Internacional*. Suggest that they review the list of *Aficiones, actividades y espectáculos* on page 71 in order to create a diverse and interesting calendar of events. Remind them to include times for meals with foods from around the Hispanic world.

EXPANDING LEARNERS

- Have students imagine that they have been given the opportunity to apply to a one-semester program in a Spanish-speaking country in order to perfect their language skills. First, they will need to decide where they would like to go, and convince the director of the program that they are worthy candidates and serious students of Spanish. Then, they will need to explain, in a letter to the director, their objectives for spending a semester abroad, including what they plan to do with their Spanish-language skills after they complete their studies.

56 La escuela ideal

▶ **Escribe** una lista de los aspectos que te gustan y los que no te gustan de la escuela. Utiliza estos verbos.

querer	preferir	encantar	interesar
importar	apetecer	desear	gustar

▶ **Presenta** la lista a tus compañeros(as).

Modelo *No me gusta que los estudiantes tiren papeles al suelo.*

Final del desafío

57 La invitación

 ▶ **Escribe.** Eva y Ethan no se ponen de acuerdo. Ayúdalos tú a terminar de escribir la invitación para sus amigos. Hazla colorida y bonita.

▶ **Habla** con tus compañeros(as). Comparen sus invitaciones y seleccionen las más originales.

▶ **Escribe** dos posibles respuestas a la invitación, una aceptándola y otra rechazándola. Da excusas originales.

 **→ TU DESAFÍO** Visita la página web. Escucha las preguntas de tu *Minientrevista Desafío 2* y escribe las respuestas.

noventa y cinco 95

---

55. Ask students to work in groups of three and share their paragraphs. Then, ask them to list the five most important things for an exchange student. Have groups compete with each other using the format of "Family Feud." Alternatively, you can organize this game as a whole class with two groups.

56. Divide the class in two groups and ask half of the class to write a list with the aspects they like about their school. The other half of the class will write a list with the things they do not like about their school. Finally, ask students to create a nice poster to post in the classroom. Alternatively, they can create a slide presentation.

Answer Key

54. Answers will vary.
▶ Answers will vary.
▶ Answers will vary.

55. Answers will vary. Sample answer: Ethan quiere vivir con una familia que le muestre la cultura del país. También quiere que en esa familia haya un(a) chico(a) de su edad y que no les importe cocinar platos vegetarianos. A Ethan le interesa tomar clases de Ciencias y le apetece aprender algo de Historia y de Arte. Por último, Ethan considera importante que los profesores sean simpáticos y no pongan mucha tarea.
▶ Answers will vary.

56. Answers will vary.
▶ Answers will vary.

57. Answers will vary.
▶ Answers will vary.
▶ Answers will vary.

Additional Resources

Fans Online activities
Practice Workbook

HERITAGE LANGUAGE LEARNERS

• Have students use the Internet or the local newspaper to explore a *Semana Internacional* or other international events that take place in their community or in cities nearby. Ask them to take notes and report back to the class as to what the festivities are, why they are being celebrated, who is taking part in them, and other details about the venue and time.

MULTIPLE INTELLIGENCES:
Intrapersonal Intelligence

• Ask students to imagine that they have been selected to take part in an exchange program and have spent the first day and night with a family in their host country. Have students write an entry in their journals that reflects their impressions of their new home and country, their reactions to cultural differences, and their emotions at possibly being away from their family and friends for the first time. You may assign this as homework and have students read their journals aloud the next day.

Unit 2
DESAFÍO 3

Expresar necesidad u obligación

Presentation

- In *Desafío 3*, Daniel and Michelle have to design a multimedia advertisement campaign for a Latin dance competition. They must sell 500 tickets to the show using their knowledge of social media. Students will preview vocabulary related to making phone calls and using mobile phones.

Activities	Standards	Resources
Texto	1.2, 2.2	Vis. Pres.
58.	1.1, 1.2	
59.	1.1, 1.2, 2.2	
60.	1.2, 2.2	Audio
61.	1.1, 5.1	
62. Cultura	1.1, 1.2, 2.2, 4.2	Video

Teaching Suggestions

Warm-Up / Independent Starter

- Ask students to list all of the forms of communication they know and explain which ones they use the most and why.

Preparation

- Have students share their Independent Starters with the class. Ask students which forms of communication are appropriate for various contexts, such as communicating with a friend or announcing a party to a group of people.

Texto: Un concurso de baile

- Call on a volunteer to read the introduction to the dialogue. Ask students to pay attention to and take notes on the ideas that Daniel and Michelle have to promote the dance competition.
- Have students read the dialogue silently. Then ask them which ideas they think will work the best and why.

Activities

59. After students complete this activity, ask them if they think that Daniel and Michelle have a good plan to promote the contest. Have students work with a partner to come up with two more ideas to promote the contest.

96

Un concurso de baile

Daniel and Michelle have to design a multimedia ad campaign for a Latin dance competition to be held in Miami. They must prove their ability to use social media by selling at least 500 tickets to the show! Fernando, the director of the competition, will help them.

¡Qué divertido! Quiero que bailen salsa y rumba, mis bailes favoritos.

Ustedes deben usar varios medios de comunicación para promover el concurso.

Como mi celular tiene acceso a Internet, podemos poner un anuncio en línea.

Voy a escribir un mensaje de texto para enviárselo a todos mis contactos.

Buena idea. También hay que usar las redes sociales.

Parece que tienen un buen plan. Si necesitan ayuda, aquí tienen mi número de teléfono. ¡Suerte!

Y también podemos llamar a las emisoras de radio y a todos nuestros amigos de Miami.

58 Detective de palabras

▶ **Completa** estas oraciones.

1. Michelle y Daniel tienen que usar varios _____ para promocionar el concurso.
2. El _____ de Michelle tiene acceso a Internet.
3. Michelle y Daniel tienen que usar las _____.
4. Michelle va a escribir un _____.
5. Daniel sugiere llamar a las _____ de radio.
6. Michelle y Daniel tienen el _____ del director del concurso.

96 noventa y seis

Differentiated Instruction

DEVELOPING LEARNERS

- Distribute index cards to students and ask them to write those words or phrases from the dialogue that they have trouble either understanding or pronouncing on one side of each card. Pair students with others of superior language skills or with a heritage learner and have them review the meaning and pronunciation of the words on the cards. The developing learners may make notes on the cards. Then, on the opposite side of each card, ask students to write an original sentence using the key word or phrase. Have their partners check their work.

EXPANDING LEARNERS

- Ask students to analyze Michelle and Daniel's approach to organizing the multimedia ad campaign for the dance contest. Do students feel that this pair is prepared to take on the *Desafío*, or do the students think that they would do a better job? Have students work with a partner and rewrite the speech bubbles to reflect how they would go about organizing this campaign. Ask pairs to share their approach by reading their dialogues in front of the class.

59 **¿Comprendes?**

▶ **Responde** a estas preguntas.

1. ¿Cuáles son los bailes que quiere incluir Daniel en el concurso?
2. ¿Qué sugiere Michelle para promocionar el concurso? ¿Y Daniel?
3. ¿A quién va a enviar Daniel un mensaje de texto?
4. ¿Con quiénes quiere comunicarse Michelle?

60 **Los bailes latinos**

▶ **Escucha** y relaciona cada baile con la fotografía correspondiente.

 tango   cumbia   salsa

61 **¿Cuál es tu plan?**

▶ **Habla** con tu compañero(a). Cuando planeas una fiesta u otro evento, ¿cómo comunicas la información a los invitados? ¿Qué formas crees que son más efectivas?

 CULTURA

El baile en el mundo latino

El baile es un elemento importante de la cultura de los países latinos. Cada país o cada región tiene sus bailes típicos. Muchos son tan populares que se han extendido por todo el mundo. Este es el caso de la salsa, la cumbia, el merengue, el mambo, la rumba o el chachachá, por ejemplo, que suelen formar parte de los concursos de baile internacionales.

62 **Compara.** ¿Hay un baile típico de tu cultura? ¿Cuál es? ¿Sabes bailarlo?

noventa y siete 97

Expresar necesidad u obligación

60. Before students listen to the audio, have them describe each picture. What emotions are the dancers communicating? If there are students who are familiar with any of the three dances shown, invite them to share their knowledge with the class.

 AUDIO SCRIPT
See page 65 J.

 CULTURA

El baile en el mundo latino

Most of the dances from Latin America have Amerindian, Spanish, and African influences. The musical instruments that are used in some Latin rhythms also reflect these influences: guitars and violins from Europe, various types of drums from Africa, and maracas and flutes of Amerindian origin. These Latin rhythms and dances continue to evolve, incorporating elements from and contributing to other music genres.

Answer Key

58. 1. medios de comunicación
2. celular
3. redes sociales
4. mensaje de texto
5. emisoras
6. número de teléfono

59. 1. Quiere incluir la salsa y la rumba.
2. Michelle: poner un anuncio en línea. Daniel: usar las redes sociales.
3. A todos sus contactos.
4. Con las emisoras de radio y con sus amigos de Miami.

60. 1. B (cumbia)   2. A (tango)   3. C (salsa)

61. Answers will vary.

62. Answers will vary.

Additional Resources

Fans Online activities

HERITAGE LANGUAGE LEARNERS

• Ask students to describe both the traditional and the contemporary music that is popular in their family's country of origin. Students should describe the instruments that are used in this music and how they differ from those used in traditional or contemporary music in this country. Students should also address the materials used in making the instruments and how they are made. Encourage students to bring in an audio sample and ask them if they prefer listening to this type of music or to something from this country, and why.

MULTIPLE INTELLIGENCES:
Musical-Rhythmic Intelligence

• Ask students to research some dances that are popular in Spain and Latin America. They should address the history of the dance, including its origins and where it is popular today, the instruments used, and the musicians who played a significant role in making this music popular. Students should also bring in some samples of the music and video featuring the dance. Ask students to make an oral presentation to the rest of the class and then have students discuss what they liked most about each dance presented.

DESAFÍO 3

Vocabulario – Llamadas telefónicas

Presentation

- In this section, students will learn key vocabulary to describe making phone calls and using mobile phones.

Activities	Standards	Resources
Vocabulario	1.2, 2.1	
63.	1.2	
64.	1.1, 1.2	
65.	1.2	Audio
66. Cultura	1.1, 1.2, 2.1, 3.2, 5.1	

Teaching Suggestions

Warm-Up / Independent Starter

- Ask students to list some words they already know in Spanish relating to phone calls, cellular phones, and social networks.

Preparation

- Read aloud the words in the *Más vocabulario* feature to model correct pronunciation and have students repeat them after you. Ask for volunteers to represent the verbs by mimicking the actions. Call on students to guess which action the volunteer is representing.

- Have students write out a list of the steps involved in making a phone call and leaving a message. Then ask students to list the steps involved in answering a phone call and taking a message.

Activities

63. To expand this activity, ask students to brainstorm ways to end a phone conversation.

64. After completing this activity, have students act out each dialogue in pairs. Have advanced learners create their own short telephone conversations.

65. After completing this activity, have students quiz each other on the conversation by creating true/false statements. After students have completed their classmate's quiz, ask them to exchange it with a different classmate, who will correct it.

Vocabulario

Llamadas telefónicas

No me queda batería en el celular. ¿Llamamos desde un **teléfono público**?

Claro. ¿Tienes una **tarjeta telefónica** o usamos monedas?

¿Diga?

Hola, ¿está Fernando, por favor?

No, no está. ¿De parte de quién?

Soy Daniel.

Puedes dejarle un recado o llamarlo a su celular.

Es que no tengo batería. ¿Puedo llamar más tarde?

Claro. Yo le digo que lo llamaste.

Más vocabulario

Acciones

colgar el teléfono	to hang up
descolgar el teléfono	to pick up
marcar un número	to dial a number
comunicar	to be busy
devolver una llamada	to call back
ponerse al teléfono	to answer the phone

El celular

el buzón de voz	voice mailbox
la llamada perdida	missed call
quedarse sin saldo	to run out of minutes

63 Detective de palabras

▶ **Une** las dos columnas.

Ⓐ
1. ¿Está Juan?
2. ¿De parte de quién?
3. ¿Diga?
4. ¿Puedo hablar con Ana?

Ⓑ
a. Para contestar una llamada.
b. Para preguntar por alguien.
c. Para preguntar quién llama.

Differentiated Instruction

DEVELOPING LEARNERS

- Ask students to make two lists and label them *Los que hacen la llamada* and *Los que reciben la llamada*. Have students review the words and expressions in *Llamadas telefónicas* and in the *Más vocabulario* feature and write each one under the corresponding list. Be sure to explain that some words will be omitted (e.g., *teléfono público*), while others may appear in both lists (e.g., *colgar el teléfono*). Encourage students to add any other relevant words or expressions they know.

EXPANDING LEARNERS

- In one of the dialogues on page 99, one speaker uses the expression *Ahora se pone* to mean that the person is coming to the phone. Explain to students that there are many more expressions that use the verb *ponerse*. Ask students to use their dictionaries or a grammar reference book and make a list of at least six of these expressions. Then have students write or say an original sentence using *ponerse*.

64 Una llamada al centro cultural

▶ **Ordena** las dos conversaciones telefónicas de Michelle y de Daniel.

—Muy bien, yo se lo digo.
—¿Diga?
—Pues no está en este momento. ¿Quiere dejarle un recado?
—Hola, buenos días. ¿Está Fernando, por favor?
—Sí, por favor. Dígale que llamó Michelle.

—¿Diga?
—¿De parte de quién?
—Soy Daniel.
—Hola, buenas tardes. ¿Puedo hablar con Fernando, por favor?
—Un momento. Ahora se pone.

65 La publicidad del concurso

▶ **Escucha** la conversación entre Daniel y Michelle y elige la opción correcta.

1. Michelle llamó a algunas emisoras de radio y _____.
   a. dejó mensajes   b. habló en la radio   c. nadie contestó

2. El director de una emisora latina _____ la llamada.
   a. contestó   b. devolvió   c. olvidó

3. Daniel se comunicó con los estudiantes de una escuela de baile _____.
   a. por correo electrónico   b. con mensajes de texto   c. con llamadas de teléfono

4. Michelle quiere llamar a un periódico para _____.
   a. dejar un recado   b. poner un anuncio   c. hacer una entrevista

5. Michelle tiene que _____.
   a. recargar su celular   b. recibir una llamada   c. dejar un recado

 **CULTURA**

pq? (¿Por qué?)
qndo (cuando)
dnd (donde)
q (que)
m da = (Me da igual.)
q hcs? (¿Qué haces?)
aora (ahora)
nd (nada)
tmb (también)
tpco (tampoco)
bno (bueno)
+ o − (más o menos)

El lenguaje SMS

Muchas personas utilizan los celulares para enviar mensajes de texto. Los jóvenes, especialmente, han creado un código para comunicarse más rápidamente. Este código consiste en utilizar emoticonos y abreviar algunas palabras, suprimiendo las vocales o las letras mudas.

66 **Explica.** ¿Crees que el uso de estas abreviaturas tiene consecuencias en el uso correcto de la ortografía y la gramática? ¿Por qué?

noventa y nueve 99

---

66. Ask students which abbreviations they most commonly use. Have them make comparisons with the abbreviations listed.

 AUDIO SCRIPT
See page 65 J.

 CULTURA

El lenguaje SMS

SMS language refers to the abbreviations that are used while text messaging on cellular phones or the Internet. Many commonly used words and expressions have a widely accepted abbreviation among cellular phone users, but it is also acceptable to eliminate vowels to shorten a word. Emoticons are symbols that are used to represent emotions, such as a smiley face. Not only does this language speed up the time required to type the message, it also allows users to communicate their message without exceeding the text character limit.

Answer Key

63. 1. b   2. c   3. a   4. b
64. 1. —¿Diga?
    —Hola, buenos días…
    —Pues no está…
    —Sí, por favor…
    —Muy bien, …
  2. —¿Diga?
    —Hola, buenas tardes…
    —¿De parte de quién?
    —Soy Daniel.
    —Un momento…
65. 1. a   2. b   3. b   4. b   5. a
66. Answers will vary.

Additional Resources

Fans Online activities
Practice Workbook

HERITAGE LANGUAGE LEARNERS

• Ask students to describe how people answer the telephone, ask to speak to someone, or ask who is calling in their family's country of origin. Have students work with another heritage learner and imagine that one is making a call and the other is answering. Give them time to rehearse their dialogue and then present it in front of the class. If students are familiar with making calls from a public phone in a Spanish-speaking country, ask them to describe how to do this.

MULTIPLE INTELLIGENCES:
Verbal-Linguistic Intelligence

• Ask students to work with a partner and explain that their task is to write messages to the other, who must answer. Students may select the topic of their messages and how they choose to reply, but both must use *el lenguaje SMS*. You might remind students that the acronym SMS stands for "short message (or messaging) service" *(servicio de mensajes cortos)*. Then ask students to write the same messages, but this time spelled completely and correctly in longhand.

99

DESAFÍO 3

Gramática – Expresar necesidad u obligación

Presentation

- In this section, students will review expressions of necessity or obligation and apply them in the present, past, and future.

Activities	Standards	Resources
Gramática	1.2, 3.1	
67.	1.1, 3.1, 5.1	
68.	1.2	
69.	1.1, 1.2, 1.3	Audio
70.	1.1, 1.2, 5.1	
71. Cultura	1.1, 1.2, 2.2, 4.2	

Teaching Suggestions

Warm-Up / Independent Starter

- Have students read the grammar explanation silently. Then ask them to write a few sentences explaining what they need to do today.

Preparation

- Ask for three volunteers to read the grammar explanation aloud. Then have students take their sentences from the Independent Starter and rewrite them using a different tense. For example: *Tengo que estudiar para el examen de Biología.*
  → *Tenía que estudiar para el examen de Biología.*
  Ask volunteers to share their examples.

Activities

69. Turn the first part of this activity into a game by asking students to create as many statements for each situation as possible. The group with the most statements for each wins. You can make it more challenging by not allowing students to repeat the same verb after *deber*, *tener*, or *haber*.

70. Before beginning this activity, have students look at the three situations listed and brainstorm two additional ones. Write their ideas on the board, so that they can use them as part of the activity. After completing the activity, ask volunteers to present an example to the class.

Gramática

Expresar necesidad u obligación

Deber, tener que, haber que

- Instead of using a direct command, you can use these constructions to express obligation or necessity:

deber + infinitive	**Debemos invitar** a todos nuestros amigos.
tener que + infinitive	**Tenemos que enviar** un mensaje de texto a todo el mundo.
haber que + infinitive	**Hay que poner** un anuncio en la radio.

- Remember: deber + *infinitive* and tener que + *infinitive* are used to say that someone in particular must do something. Thus, you must conjugate the verbs deber and tener to make them agree with the subject.

  Yo **debía llamar** a Fernando.

  Tú y yo **teníamos que enviar** los mensajes.

- On the other hand, haber que + *infinitive* is an impersonal expression, so it is always used in the third person singular (in any tense):

  Hay que promocionar el concurso.

  Había que vender quinientos boletos para conseguir el desafío.

  Habrá que utilizar varios medios de comunicación.

67 **Piensa.** ¿En qué situaciones crees que es más apropiado usar estas construcciones en lugar del imperativo? ¿Por qué?

68 **¿Qué tienen que hacer?**

▶ **Une** las dos columnas.

 A

1. Michelle quiere hablar con sus amigos sobre el concurso de baile.
2. Daniel tiene tres llamada perdidas.
3. A Michelle no le queda mucha batería.
4. Daniel tiene mensajes en su buzón de voz.
5. Michelle llamó a Fernando al centro cultural, pero solo pudo hablar con la secretaria.

 B

a. Tuvo que dejarle un recado.
b. Debe escucharlos.
c. Tiene que recargar su celular.
d. Debe devolver las llamadas.
e. Tiene que llamarlos o mandarles un mensaje.

100 cien

Differentiated Instruction

DEVELOPING LEARNERS

- Ask students to focus their attention on one verb at a time. Write or read the sentence *Debemos invitar a todos nuestros amigos.* Then have students say or write the sentence with the following changes of subject: *yo, tú, Michelle, los chicos,* and *ustedes.* Remind students to make any other necessary corrections. Do the same with the expression *tener que.* Remind students that *haber que* is always conjugated in the third person singular. Then ask students to write or say a sentence with *haber que* in the present, in the imperfect, and in the future.

EXPANDING LEARNERS

- Ask students to write a set of suggestions using *tener que, deber,* and *hay que* that offer advice to Michelle and Daniel that will help them prepare their multimedia campaign for the dance competition. The suggestions should go beyond the preparation of the campaign and offer ideas that will enhance the selection of the judges, the performance of the dancers, the presentation of the prizes, and a follow-up article in the local media.

69 Consejos

▶ **Escribe.** ¿Qué hay que hacer en estas situaciones? Usa *deber*, *tener* o *haber*.

> **a.** Ayer recibí una invitación para asistir a una fiesta de cumpleaños.

> **b.** La escuela organiza un concurso de fotografía. ¡El premio es un viaje!

> **c.** Para la clase de Historia, hay que hacer un trabajo sobre un personaje histórico de nuestro país.

> **d.** No hice bien el examen de Ciencias...

 ▶ **Escucha** y relaciona cada comentario con una de las situaciones anteriores.

▶ **Escucha** de nuevo. ¿Algún comentario coincide con lo que tú escribiste?

70 Ideas para tener éxito

▶ **Habla** con un(a) compañero(a). Por turnos, hagan preguntas y respondan con ideas para tener éxito en estas situaciones.

Modelo   mantenerse en forma

> A. *¿Qué puedo hacer para mantenerme en forma?*
> B. *Debes comer cosas sanas y hacer ejercicio.*

> aprender bailes latinos

> sacar buenas notas

> mantener una relación positiva con los padres

 CULTURA

Juan Luis Guerra

El dominicano Juan Luis Guerra es uno de los cantantes latinos más populares en el mundo. Combina distintos géneros musicales, como el merengue, la salsa o el bolero, en un estilo de fusión afrolatino único. Las letras de sus canciones no solo son de amor; muchas reflejan sus ideas y aspectos de su cultura.

Juan Luis Guerra (República Dominicana).

71 **Piensa y habla.** ¿Hay cantantes representativos de tu cultura? ¿Qué canciones suyas conoces?

ciento uno   101

HERITAGE LANGUAGE LEARNERS

- Ask students to think of another type of competition that interests them. It could be an academic, athletic, or talent competition, or one of another kind, but the event should reflect their Hispanic heritage. Ask students to write a composition that describes this competition and how they would go about promoting it. Call on volunteers to read their compositions aloud.

MULTIPLE INTELLIGENCES:
Intrapersonal Intelligence

- Ask students to write a journal entry that focuses on how they hope to become more successful as a student, as a friend, as a son or daughter, or as a sibling. They might start with their faults or bad habits and then make suggestions to themselves on how they might correct these negative tendencies and be a more productive person.

Gramática – Expresar necesidad u obligación

 AUDIO SCRIPT
See page 65J.

CULTURA

Juan Luis Guerra

Juan Luis Guerra has been the recipient of numerous music awards in the three decades that he has been active as a songwriter and singer. He is known for his unique style, and makes it a personal goal to have each album be original. Jazz, pop, rock and roll, merengue, salsa, and bachata are some of the numerous influences one can hear in his music. While the rhythm of many of his songs is upbeat, his lyrics focus on social messages, criticizing the inequities and failures of our social system.

Answer Key

67. Answers will vary. Sample answer: Estas construcciones se usan para dar un mandato de forma indirecta, en situaciones más formales o corteses que cuando usamos el imperativo.

68. 1. e   2. d   3. c   4. b   5. a

69. Answers will vary. Sample answers:
   a. Debes responder y aceptar la invitación.
   b. Hay que tomar buenas fotos y participar en el concurso.
   c. Tienes que buscar información en Internet.
   d. Debes estudiar más.
   ▶ 1. d   2. a   3. c   4. b
   ▶ Answers will vary.

70. Answers will vary.

71. Answers will vary.

Additional Resources

Fans Online activities
Practice Workbook

DESAFÍO 3

Gramática – Hablar del futuro

Presentation

- In this section, students will review regular and irregular verb forms of the future tense. They will also use time expressions to refer to the future, and learn to use the subjunctive in subordinate clauses referring to the future.

Activities	Standards	Resources
Gramática	1.2, 3.1	
72.	1.2, 4.1	
73.	1.1, 1.2	Audio
74.	1.3	
75.	1.1, 1.3, 5.1	
76.	1.1, 1.3, 3.1, 5.1	

Teaching Suggestions

Warm-Up / Independent Starter

- Ask students to write a few sentences explaining what they are going to do tomorrow, next week, and next year. Tell students not to look at the grammar explanation in their textbook. They should activate prior knowledge and use the verb forms and expressions to talk about the future that they remember.

Preparation

- Ask students to read the grammar explanation silently, and then ask a volunteer to read it aloud. Have students take their sentences from the Independent Starter and rewrite them using the future tense. Ask volunteers to share their examples.

- Have students work in pairs to write two statements using *cuando* + present subjunctive to talk about what they will do when they graduate from high school. Ask volunteers to share their examples.

Activities

73. To extend this activity, have students complete the same table about their schedule for this week. Then have students compare their schedule to that of a classmate and write a brief paragraph contrasting and comparing their schedules.

102

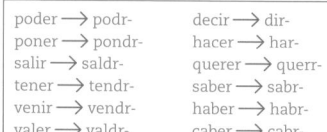

Gramática

Hablar del futuro

El futuro imperfecto

- Remember that to refer to future events, you can use these structures:

ir a + infinitive	Nosotros **vamos a invitar** a todos nuestros amigos.
future	Nosotros **invitaremos** a todos nuestros amigos.

- Regular verbs form the future tense by adding the endings -é, -ás, -á, -emos, -éis, -án to the infinitive (see conjugation on page R15).

- There are some verbs with irregular stem changes in the future tense.

En el futuro **habrá** más coches eléctricos.

FUTURO. VERBOS IRREGULARES

poder ⟶ podr-	decir ⟶ dir-
poner ⟶ pondr-	hacer ⟶ har-
salir ⟶ saldr-	querer ⟶ querr-
tener ⟶ tendr-	saber ⟶ sabr-
venir ⟶ vendr-	haber ⟶ habr-
valer ⟶ valdr-	caber ⟶ cabr-

Marcadores de futuro

- You can use these adverbs and expressions to refer to the future:

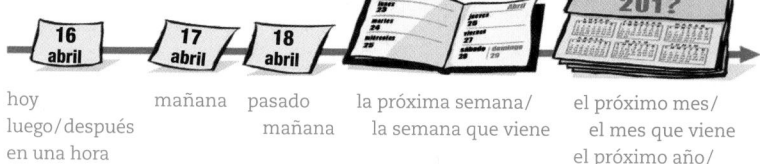

hoy
luego/después
en una hora
esta tarde/
  esta noche

mañana

pasado
mañana

la próxima semana/
la semana que viene

el próximo mes/
  el mes que viene
el próximo año/
  el año que viene

Cuando + presente de subjuntivo

- Use cuando + *present subjunctive* when referring to situations and events that have not yet occurred.

Cuando **estemos** en Miami, **vamos a ver** un concurso de baile latino.
Cuando **tenga** 30 años, seguramente no **existirán** los teléfonos públicos.

72 **Compara.** ¿De qué maneras diferentes se expresa el futuro en inglés?

73 ¿Qué hará?

 ▶ **Escucha** a Daniel y escribe sus planes para esta semana en una tabla como esta.

lunes	martes	miércoles	jueves	viernes

Differentiated Instruction

DEVELOPING LEARNERS

- Give students additional practice with the verbs that have an irregular future tense. Place strips of paper with the infinitives of the irregular verbs listed on this page in a bag. Prepare a cube with the subject pronouns *yo, tú, usted/él/ella, nosotros(as), vosotros(as), ustedes/ellos(as)* on each side. Students will pick up an infinitive, roll the cube, and then, according to the subject, say the corresponding verb form. Encourage them to say a sentence with this verb.

EXPANDING LEARNERS

- Ask students to use the future tense to write at least one paragraph predicting what current technology will be obsolete in fifty years. Students should include supporting details that justify why they think that this technology will not be needed. They will also need to describe the objects that will replace this old technology. Encourage creativity and the use of humor in their compositions.

Gramática – Hablar del futuro

 74 Eventos futuros

▶ **Escribe** oraciones utilizando las tres columnas para contar lo que harán estas personas en el futuro.

Modelo *En diez años, mi mejor amiga tendrá hijos.*

Ⓐ	Ⓑ	Ⓒ
en diez años	mi profesor(a)	jubilarse
esta tarde	yo	hacer la tarea
la semana que viene	mi mejor amigo(a)	graduarse
en el año 2050	mis padres	hacer un largo viaje
dentro de tres años	mis amigos(as) y yo	ir al cine
el próximo año	mi hermano(a)	tener hijos

75 Mis metas para el año que viene

▶ **Escribe** cinco metas *(goals)* que quieres conseguir el próximo año.

▶ **Escribe.** ¿Qué cosas podrás hacer cuando consigas tus objetivos?

Modelo *El año que viene me sacaré la licencia de conducir.*
Cuando tenga mi licencia, podré ir a la universidad en coche.

76 La tecnología de 2050

 ▶ **Habla** con dos compañeros(as). ¿Cómo será el mundo en el año 2050? Piensa en estos objetos y servicios:

• los celulares
• los reproductores de música
• los electrodomésticos

• los coches y el transporte
• las computadoras
• Internet

▶ **Presenta** tus ideas a la clase y compartan sus opiniones.

Modelo

 En el año 2050, los bolígrafos no existirán porque usaremos computadoras para todo.

 Sí. Y las pantallas de las computadoras serán tan grandes como la pared.

ciento tres **103**

74. To expand this activity, ask students to add three statements to each column. For the statements in the third column, have students use irregular verbs (e.g., *salir de viaje, saber los resultados del examen, poder hablar español*).

75. Ask students to write a list of steps they will need to take in order to achieve their goals. Have students present their ideas to the class and chart the common themes.

 **AUDIO SCRIPT**
See page 65 J.

Answer Key

72. Se usan estructuras como *going to* y *will*. Por ejemplo: *I'm going to travel next summer. We'll graduate in two years.*

73. Lunes: va a trabajar todo el día en Internet para promocionar el concurso de baile.
Martes: Michelle y Daniel verán a los estudiantes de una escuela de baile. Van a seleccionar a los mejores para el concurso.
Miércoles: va a hablar con algunos periódicos locales.
Jueves: se reunirá con el director del concurso.
Viernes: tendrán un ensayo con todos los participantes.

74. Answers will vary. Sample answers:
Esta tarde yo haré la tarea.
La semana que viene mi profesora irá al cine.
En el año 2050 mis padres se jubilarán.
Dentro de tres años mis amigos y yo haremos un largo viaje.
El próximo año mi hermano se graduará.

75. Answers will vary.
▶ Answers will vary.

76. Answers will vary.
▶ Answers will vary.

Additional Resources

Fans Online activities
Practice Workbook

HERITAGE LANGUAGE LEARNERS

• Ask students to write a science fiction short story about the future. Students may describe what they think their community, their country, or the world will be like two hundred years from now. Students might address what they think people will look like, how they will dress and spend their leisure time, the jobs they might have, how they will travel and study, what languages they will speak, what foods they will eat, and how the Earth might look to a visitor from outer space.

TOTAL PHYSICAL RESPONSE (TPR)

• Give students practice with *cuando* and both the future tense and the present subjunctive by reading sentences to them that use one of these verb forms, but omitting the verb. Explain to students that they need to listen carefully and, when the future tense should be used, raise their right hand (or give them a colored piece of paper to hold up). Then, when the subjunctive should be used, ask them to raise their left hand (or hold up a sheet of paper of another color). For example: *Cuando me gradúe, [ir] a la universidad.* (future) *Compraré un coche cuando [tener] la licencia.* (subjunctive)

LECTURA: TEXTO LITERARIO

Presentation

- In this section, students will read a short story, or *microcuento*. As they read, they will review vocabulary related to communication and phone calls. Students will also be aware of how descriptions and actions are intertwined in the text through the use of the different past tenses.

Activities	Standards	Resources
Lectura: texto literario	1.1, 1.2, 3.1	
77.	1.1, 1.2	
78.	1.2	
79	1.2, 1.3, 3.1	
80.	1.1, 1.2, 5.1	

Teaching Suggestions

Warm-Up / Independent Starter

- Ask students to observe the illustration, read the title, and make two possible guesses in writing of what may happen in the story.

Preparation

- Call on individual students to share their responses from the Independent Starter. What lead them to their particular prediction? Then have students work with a partner to read the *Antes de leer* strategies. Ask pairs to write the answers to the questions posed and discuss the answers as a class.

- Read the story aloud to model pronunciation and have students follow along in their books. Then call on individual students to each read one paragraph aloud. Offer assistance with the pronunciation of the proper nouns in the story. In two cases (i.e., Martín, Luis), the stress in Spanish falls on a different syllable than in English.

- Use gestures to represent some of the actions in the story. Avoid direct translations as much as possible, although students may find it useful to look at some of the glosses. Revisit the predictions students made in the Independent Starter. How accurate were they?

104

LECTURA: TEXTO LITERARIO

Antes de leer: estrategias

1. Lee el título del cuento. Echa un vistazo *(scan)* al texto para averiguar el tipo de mensaje al que se refiere. ¿Es un mensaje escrito o hablado? ¿Qué palabras te lo indican?
2. Anota las palabras que se refieren a la comunicación. ¿Puedes adivinar de qué trata el texto?
3. Lee la primera y la última línea de cada párrafo. Explica con tus propias palabras lo que ocurre.
4. Busca en el texto las oraciones entre comillas (« »). ¿Son diferentes del resto de la narración? ¿Por qué?

El mensaje

Como cada tarde, Martín llegó a su apartamento después de un largo día de trabajo. El apartamento estaba ordenado y limpio. Martín dejó sobre la mesa de la cocina una pequeña bolsa de plástico con su cena, se fue a su habitación y se quitó la corbata.

En ese momento vio que en el teléfono de la mesita de noche brillaba[1] una luz intermitente. Se quitó la chaqueta mientras miraba el teléfono con un gesto de curiosidad. Pensó en su madre. «¿Por qué no me llama al celular?»

Pasado el breve momento de duda[2] continuó quitándose la ropa. Colgó la chaqueta en una silla, guardó los pantalones en el armario y dobló los calcetines metódicamente. Miró de nuevo hacia el teléfono. «Juan me iba a enviar un mensaje de texto para confirmar la hora del concierto del viernes.» Se puso una sudadera vieja.

Por fin escuchó el mensaje del contestador. Al principio pensó en un anuncio de *telemarketing*. Una voz femenina desconocida repetía un nombre. «Luis... Luis...», creyó entender. El mensaje se interrumpía. Martín se acercó al teléfono para borrar el mensaje pero, indeciso[3], se quedó quieto[4] y escuchó. La mujer lloraba. Martín se sentó en la cama y subió el volumen del contestador. «Luis...», decía una voz angustiada[5]. «Luis..., tengo miedo. Estoy en peligro. ¡Llámame al celular!» Entonces Martín miró el registro de llamadas por primera vez. La mujer gritó[6]. El grito fue horrible.

Confundido por unos minutos, Martín se repuso[7]. «Debe de ser una broma[8]», pensó. Pero no borró el mensaje. Fue a la cocina. Sacó su cena de la bolsa de plástico y se sentó frente al televisor. Puso las noticias: «Una mujer asesinada en circunstancias extrañas... bla, bla, bla». El teléfono sonó. Era la policía.

---

1. *was shining*	3. *undecided*	5. *anguished*	7. *composed himself*
2. *doubt*	4. *still*	6. *screamed*	8. *joke*

Differentiated Instruction

DEVELOPING LEARNERS

- Lead students in a guided reading of the story. Call on students to alternate reading each sentence aloud. After students read, ask them questions to test their comprehension. For example, after the first sentence: *¿Cuándo llegó Martín a su apartamento? (Llegó después de un largo día de trabajo.)*

- If students answer incorrectly, have them read the sentence again. If they still have trouble answering correctly, simplify the Spanish for them: *Como siempre, Martín llegó a su apartamento después de trabajar mucho.*

EXPANDING LEARNERS

- Ask students to think about the conversation Martín might have with the police and what could happen after the call. Ask students to write an ending to the story based on Martín's interaction with law enforcement officers. Do students think that he will be accused of a crime? Do they think that he will cooperate with the police? Who do they think the woman and Luis are? Encourage students to read their stories aloud to the rest of the class.

77 Comprensión y análisis

▶ **Responde** a estas preguntas.

1. ¿Quién es el protagonista del cuento? ¿Hay otros personajes (characters)? ¿Quiénes son?
2. ¿Hay alguna descripción física de Martín en el texto? ¿Y de su personalidad? ¿Cómo piensas que es Martín?
3. ¿Qué hace normalmente Martín después de trabajar?
4. ¿Qué hay en el contestador de Martín?
5. ¿Qué sabemos de la mujer del mensaje: su nombre; su personalidad; su estado de ánimo?
6. ¿Qué piensas que le pasó a la mujer?

78 ¿Quién lo dice?

▶ **Decide.** ¿Quién dice o piensa las siguientes oraciones?

	Martín	La mujer
1. «¿Por qué no me llama al celular?»		
2. «Estoy en peligro.»		
3. «¡Llámame al celular!»		
4. «Juan me iba a enviar un mensaje de texto.»		
5. «Debe de ser una broma.»		

79 ¿Descripciones o acciones?

▶ **Escribe** al menos tres oraciones del cuento que se refieren a descripciones y tres que se refieren a acciones.

Descripción	Acción
Brillaba una luz intermitente.	Se quitó la corbata.

▶ **Escribe** un resumen del texto.

80 Con tus propias palabras

▶ **Responde** a estas preguntas.

1. ¿Alguna vez recibiste un mensaje de voz que era para otra persona? ¿Qué hiciste?
2. ¿Quién crees que es Luis?
3. En tu opinión, ¿qué debió hacer Martín? ¿Por qué?

ciento cinco 105

Activities

77. Ask students to first read the questions and then read the short story again. As they read the story, have students take notes that will help them answer the questions.

79. As they do this activity, point out to students that the imperfect tense is generally used for descriptions and the preterite for completed actions.

80. You may want to assign these questions as homework. Alternatively, you may want to hold a class discussion for question 3.

Answer Key

77. Answers will vary. Sample answers:
1. El protagonista es Martín. Los otros personajes son: la mujer que dejó el mensaje; Juan, que parece ser un amigo de Martín; Luis, el hombre al que llamaba la mujer. También se menciona a la madre de Martín y a la policía.
2. No hay una descripción física de Martín, pero se dice que es ordenado, limpio y metódico.
3. Lleva la cena a casa, se quita la ropa del trabajo y se pone ropa de casa. Después cena frente al televisor mientras ve las noticias.
4. Hay un mensaje de una mujer desconocida.
5. No sabemos su nombre ni cómo era su personalidad, pero sabemos que estaba en peligro y que le pedía auxilio a un hombre llamado Luis. Estaba muy asustada y angustiada.
6. La mujer fue asesinada por un conocido, tal vez un vecino.

78. Martín: 1, 4, 5. La mujer: 2, 3.

79. Answers will vary. Sample answers:
Descripción: El apartamento estaba ordenado.
Acción: El teléfono sonó.
▶ Answers will vary.

80. Answers will vary.

Additional Resources

Fans Online activities

HERITAGE LANGUAGE LEARNERS

• Ask students to imagine that they are the police. How would they organize the investigation of this crime? Who would they interview? What analyses would they make? What equipment would they use for their investigation? Encourage students to work with a partner to plan their investigation strategies. Then have partners present their plan to the class. If time allows, hold a class discussion to decide on a course of action regarding the investigation of this crime.

MULTIPLE INTELLIGENCES:
Visual-Spatial Intelligence

• Explain to students that images can complement a text and give additional meaning to a story. Ask students to make illustrations for *El mensaje* that clarify what they have just read, or what they perceive as what could have happened to the woman, or what will happen when the police and Martín talk. Remind students that their illustrations should add something to the general understanding of what took place or will occur. Display students' illustrations for the entire class to see and comment.

Unit 2
DESAFÍO 3
Comunicación

Presentation

- In this section, students will integrate the vocabulary and grammar skills from *Desafío 3* in order to express needs and actions in the future relating to different forms of phone communication.

Activities	Standards	Resources
81.	1.1, 1.2, 1.3	Audio
82.	1.1, 1.2	
83.	1.1, 1.2, 1.3, 5.1	
84. Final del desafío	1.1, 1.2, 1.3, 5.1	

Teaching Suggestions

Warm-Up / Independent Starter

- Ask students to think about an event that is approaching, such as a holiday, birthday party, or even a school event. Have them write a paragraph about what needs to be done for the event, who will take care of these tasks, and what will happen at the event. For example: *La semana que viene mi familia y yo vamos a celebrar el aniversario de mis abuelos. Yo tengo que pedir el pastel y mi hermano tiene que comprar el regalo. Debemos limpiar la casa. Mis tíos y primos vendrán a mi casa para la cena. Después de la cena habrá música y baile.*

Preparation

- Ask students to share their Independent Starters. Review as a class the expressions of necessity or obligation and the future tense structures that students used in their paragraphs.
- Review the use of *cuando* + present subjunctive to refer to situations and events that have not yet occurred. Ask students to add two statements to their paragraph explaining what will happen when the event they described takes place. For example: *Cuando mis abuelos vean el pastel, se emocionarán.* Call on volunteers to share their sentences with the class.

Activities

82. Ask pairs to share their messages with the class and vote on the best.

106

Comunicación

81 **Necesitan más publicidad**

 ▶ **Escucha** la conversación entre Michelle y Daniel y decide si las siguientes afirmaciones son ciertas o falsas. Después, corrige las oraciones falsas.

1. El director llamó para decir que está muy feliz con la venta de boletos.
2. Daniel va a devolver la llamada al director en unos minutos.
3. Michelle y Daniel tuvieron hoy su entrevista en la radio.
4. Michelle piensa que deben escribir un artículo en algún periódico.
5. Michelle y Daniel creen que tienen que usar las redes sociales para darle publicidad al concurso.
6. Daniel quiere colgar el teléfono porque tiene que escribir un mensaje de texto.

▶ **Escribe** tres ideas para ayudarlos a promocionar el concurso.

82 **Mensajes de texto**

▶ **Lee** los mensajes de texto entre Daniel y su amigo Tony y responde a estas preguntas.

1. ¿Dónde está Daniel?
2. ¿Qué le propone Daniel a su amigo?
3. ¿Su amigo acepta la invitación?

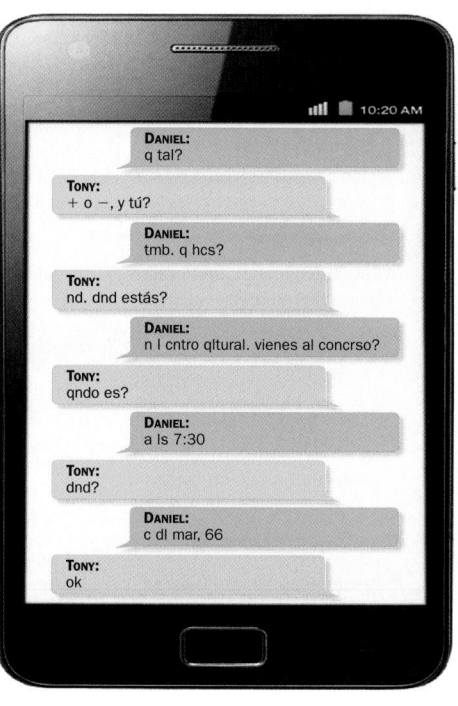

DANIEL: q tal?
TONY: + o −, y tú?
DANIEL: tmb. q hcs?
TONY: nd. dnd estás?
DANIEL: n l cntro qltural. vienes al concrso?
TONY: qndo es?
DANIEL: a ls 7:30
TONY: dnd?
DANIEL: c dl mar, 66
TONY: ok

▶ **Escribe** los mensajes usando palabras completas y signos de puntuación.

▶ **Escribe** con tu compañero(a) una cadena de mensajes entre Daniel y otro amigo suyo al que él invita al concurso.

Differentiated Instruction

DEVELOPING LEARNERS

- Ask students to read the following sentences and change the underlined verbs to the future tense:
  1. *Tengo tiempo para hablar contigo. (Tendré)*
  2. *Puedo hablar español perfectamente. (Podré)*
  3. *¿Cabemos todos en el coche? (Cabremos)*
  4. *Marcos viene mañana. (vendrá)*
  5. *¿Cuánto vale el cuadro? (valdrá)*
  6. *Salgo a las dos. (Saldré)*
  7. *Me dicen lo mismo. (dirán)*
  8. *¿Qué quieres hacer? (querrás)*

EXPANDING LEARNERS

- Have students imagine that they are planning a special event and need to make sure that everything is on track and on schedule. Students will make a checklist of all the steps that need to be taken and details that need to be ironed out before their special event. First, they will need to identify the special event they are planning. Then, they should list their objectives and the tasks that need to be completed for each one, including who is to do them. Students should use the verbs *tener que, deber,* and *hay que.*

83 **Mis preferencias**

▶ **Habla** con tu compañero(a) y presenten sus conclusiones a la clase.

1. ¿Debes dejar siempre un recado en el buzón de voz si la persona no contesta al teléfono?
2. ¿Cuándo y con quién es apropiado usar mensajes de texto?
3. ¿Cuál es tu forma de comunicación preferida?
4. ¿Cuáles son algunas ventajas de la comunicación tradicional? ¿Y de la comunicación moderna?

Final del desafío

¿Enviaron el mensaje de texto con su celular?

Sí, mire. Aquí está.

Concrso de ble latno. A ls 7:30 n l cntro qltural

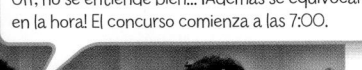

Uff, no se entiende bien... ¡Además se equivocaron en la hora! El concurso comienza a las 7:00.

¡Qué desastre! ¿Qué hacemos?

No se preocupen. Vamos a escribir otro mensaje rápidamente.

 84 **Problemas de comunicación**

▶ **Habla** con un(a) compañero(a) y presenten sus ideas a la clase.

1. ¿Cuáles son los problemas del mensaje de texto que enviaron Daniel y Michelle?
2. ¿Cómo piensan resolver el problema?

▶ **Escribe** un nuevo mensaje anunciando el concurso de baile para ayudar a Daniel y a Michelle.

HERITAGE LANGUAGE LEARNERS

- Students often have trouble spelling words with s, soft c, and z, and words with b and v. Ask students to write the following sentences that you will dictate to them:
  1. *¿Vas a vender los cinco boletos?*
  2. *Tengo un mensaje en el buzón de voz del celular.*
  3. *¿Aceptas mi invitación a la celebración?*
  4. *Mi amiga Cecilia no devuelve las llamadas.*
  5. *Vicente le envía un mensaje a Victoria Valdés.*
  6. *¿Viste el anuncio publicitario del baile?*

COOPERATIVE LEARNING

- Explain to students that many successful advertising campaigns have a slogan and they are going to create one for the Latin dance competition. Have students work in small groups and brainstorm an appealing slogan. Be sure that every member of the group contributes an idea. Groups will discuss all suggestions and vote on their final choice. Encourage them to accompany the slogan with some additional informational text and an image. If possible, have them make a video of their completed ad.

---

83. Have students work in small groups. Ask groups to come up with a "Phone Etiquette" document in which they address some of the questions posed in this activity. Encourage students to add information about appropriate use of communication technologies in more formal contexts, such as business situations.

 AUDIO SCRIPT
See page 65 J.

Answer Key

81. 1. Falso. Que vendió pocos boletos.
2. Cierto.
3. Falso. Tiene su entrevista mañana.
4. Falso. Deben poner un anuncio.
5. Cierto.
6. Falso. Porque tiene otra llamada.
▶ Answers will vary.

82. 1. Está en el centro cultural.
2. Le propone que venga al concurso.
3. Sí, acepta.
▶ Daniel: ¿Qué tal?
   Tony: Más o menos, ¿y tú?
   Daniel: También. ¿Qué haces?
   Tony: Nada. ¿Dónde estás?
   Daniel: En el centro cultural. ¿Vienes al concurso?
   Tony: ¿Cuándo es?
   Daniel: A las 7:30.
   Tony: ¿Dónde?
   Daniel: Calle del Mar, 66.
   Tony: Okay.
▶ Answers will vary.

83. Answers will vary.

84. Answers will vary. Sample answers:
1. No se entiende bien y Michelle y Daniel se equivocaron en la hora.
2. Piensan escribir otro mensaje de texto.
▶ Answers will vary.

Additional Resources

Fans Online activities
Practice Workbook

Para terminar

Presentation

- In this section, students will review the unit objectives and put them into practice. They will use expressions of obligation and direct and indirect object pronouns. They will also select one of the following *desafíos* to develop: write a love or friendship card, write an invitation for a party, or write an e-mail giving instructions on how to learn a Latin dance.

Activities	Standards	Resources
85.	1.1, 1.2, 1.3, 5.1	
86.	1.1, 1.2, 1.3, 5.1	
87. Tu desafío	1.1, 1.2, 1.3, 2.1, 2.2, 5.1	

Teaching Suggestions

Warm-Up / Independent Starter

- Have students go back and review the vocabulary and grammar sections in this unit. Then ask them to think about the tasks they need to do this week and write five sentences, incorporating verbs that express necessity or obligation (i.e., *deber, tener que, haber que*).

Preparation

- Have students work with a partner and read aloud their sentences from the Independent Starter. Then have them ask each other questions to obtain further details on when, with whom, or where those tasks must be done. Call on pairs to come before the class and present their tasks. Have the class take notes. When all pairs have presented, ask the class to determine, based on their notes, who has the busiest schedule.

- Prepare or get some fake money to bring to class and distribute among groups or pairs of students. Have them think of gifts that they could get for their classmates with this money. Then have students come up with a list of sentences in which they describe the gifts they bought, where they bought them, and for whom they bought these gifts. For example: *A John le compramos una tarjeta para bajarse música. La compramos en Internet.*

108

Todo junto

ESCRIBIR Y HABLAR

85 **¡Menuda agenda!**

▶ **Escribe.** Mira las ilustraciones y escribe cinco oraciones sobre lo que Eva tiene que hacer la semana que viene.

Modelo   *El lunes por la tarde Eva tiene que ir a clase de Gimnasia en la escuela. El martes...*

el lunes por la tarde

el martes a las 3:00 p. m.

el miércoles por la tarde

el jueves a las 10:00 a. m.

el viernes a las 5:00 p. m.

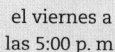 ▶ **Habla.** Prepara tu agenda para la semana que viene y explícale a tu compañero(a) algo que tienes que hacer cada día. Túrnense para hacerse preguntas.

ESCRIBIR Y HABLAR

86 **Muy generoso**

▶ **Escribe** seis oraciones explicando a quién(es) vas a dar estos regalos:

Modelo   *El libro se lo voy a regalar a mi madre.*

1. un libro
2. una rosa
3. un celular
4. un CD de tu grupo favorito
5. unos boletos para un concierto
6. un balón de fútbol

▶ **Habla** con tu compañero(a) y pregúntale a qué compañeros(as) de la clase va a dar estos mismos regalos.

108   ciento ocho

Differentiated Instruction

DEVELOPING LEARNERS

- Ask students to work with a partner and refer to their partner's list of things they have to do next week. Then, in response to each activity or errand, have students state a reason, using the future tense, why their partner cannot comply. For example:

A. *Tengo que ir al museo el jueves.*
B. *No puedes ir porque el museo estará cerrado ese día.*

EXPANDING LEARNERS

- Ask students to review the sentences they wrote for activity 86 and then explain why they are going to give the gifts to the people mentioned. For each gift, ask students to write one sentence that explains their decision. Ask students to think of another gift, explain to whom they plan to give it, and why. Call on volunteers to read their sentences aloud.

Tu desafío

87 **Tarjetas y mensajes**

¿Recuerdas los desafíos que Tim les propuso a los personajes? ¿Cuál te gusta más? Elige una de estas opciones y resuelve tu desafío.

DESAFÍO (A)

Escribe una tarjeta de amor o amistad a una persona que te guste o con quien tengas una buena relación.
No olvides:

- Expresarle a esa persona tus sentimientos.
- Decirle a esa persona lo que vas hacer por ella.
- Explicarle lo que quieres que hagan el uno por el otro.

DESAFÍO (B)

Escribe una invitación para una fiesta en tu casa. Incluye todos los datos necesarios: lugar, día, hora, si hay que llevar algo, etc.

DESAFÍO (C)

Escribe un correo electrónico explicándole a un(a) compañero(a) todo lo que tiene que hacer para aprender tu baile latino favorito.

ciento nueve 109

Para terminar

Activities

85. Ask students to work with a partner to complete the first part of this activity. They both must take turns writing a sentence about Eva's agenda for the week. After they complete the second part of this activity individually, have students exchange their schedules with a classmate. Call on volunteers to explain what his or her partner has planned for the week ahead.

87. Display students' work in the classroom and have the class vote on the best entry in each category.

Answer Key

85. Answers will vary. Sample answers:
El martes a las 3:00 p. m. Eva debe hacer la tarea en la biblioteca.
El miércoles por la tarde Eva y Ethan tienen que estudiar.
El jueves a las 10:00 a. m. Eva tiene que llamar a su madre.
El viernes a la 5:00 p. m. Eva y Ethan deben jugar a la pelota.
▶ Answers will vary.

86. Answers will vary. Sample answers:
2. La rosa se la voy a regalar a mi hermana.
3. El celular se lo voy a dar a mi padre.
4. El CD se lo voy a regalar a la profesora.
5. Las entradas se las voy a dar a mi mejor amigo.
6. El balón de fútbol se lo voy a regalar a mi hermanito.
▶ Answers will vary.

87. Answers will vary.

Additional Resources

Fans Online activities

HERITAGE LANGUAGE LEARNERS

- Ask students to bring to class and share with the other students an invitation to a party or other celebration, such as Saint Jordi or *Día de la Amistad*, from their family's country of origin. Encourage students to explain what differences there are between these celebrations and similar ones in this country. Students should point out if it is customary to bring gifts or food, and if it is more common to celebrate with family or friends. Invite the non-heritage learners to ask questions about these celebrations.

CRITICAL THINKING

- For as long as there has been music in the world, there has been dance. Enable a classroom discussion on the popularity of dancing and why students think this is so. Ask students what they think can be expressed by dancing that cannot be expressed by any of the other arts. You might also discuss dance contests. Ask students if they have ever watched one or participated in one. Ask them why they think dance contests have become so popular.

Unit 2

MAPA CULTURAL

La fiesta: expresión comunitaria

Presentation

- This section presents information about different festivities from the Spanish-speaking world. The images serve as a reference point for additional cultural readings and activities that expand on the skills students learned in this unit.

Activities	Standards	Resources
Mapa cultural	1.2, 2.1, 2.2, 3.1	Video
88.	1.1, 1.2, 1.3, 2.1, 2.2, 3.1, 4.2, 5.1	

Cultural Topics

- **Las comparsas.** The carnival clubs, or *comparsas*, are groups of dancers and musicians who take part in a carnival parade. Each *comparsa* has its own costume, theme, dance routine, and music. In most carnivals, the *comparsas* compete for prizes for best costume, choreography, band, etc. Each *comparsa* meets throughout the year to decide on a theme for their performance, design their costumes, and practice their routines. There are usually strong links among the *comparsa* members. They may be from the same neighborhood or school, share a profession, or have the same ethnic or cultural background.

- **Fiestas latinas en los Estados Unidos.** Latinos in the United States celebrate their identity and contributions to American culture through a variety of festivals. Some of the largest and most well known are the Calle Ocho Festival, a street festival that takes place in March along 23 blocks in Miami's Little Havana area; the Cinco de Mayo holiday to celebrate the 1862 Mexican victory over the occupying French forces in the city of Puebla; and the National Puerto Rican Day Parade, which takes place on the second Sunday in June along Fifth Avenue in New York City, celebrating the Puerto Rican heritage in the United States.

Teaching Suggestions

Warm-Up / Independent Starter

- Ask students to think of a festivity or holiday they like and in which they participate. Why do they like this particular festivity? Do their families or people in their community also participate?

110

La fiesta: expresión comunitaria

Las personas somos seres sociales. Continuamente nos relacionamos con otras personas a las que nos sentimos unidos por razones familiares, étnicas, religiosas, deportivas, etc. Y las fiestas ayudan con frecuencia a reforzar esas relaciones personales. Las fiestas permiten dar identidad y cohesión social al grupo.

La tradición de las comparsas: el Desfile de Llamadas

Las comparsas (*carnival clubs*) son grupos de personas que tocan música y bailan en determinadas fiestas, especialmente en carnaval.

En los carnavales de Montevideo (Uruguay) tiene lugar el Desfile de Llamadas. En este desfile unas cuarenta comparsas bailan por la calle mientras tocan tambores al ritmo del candombe, un género musical de origen africano.

Las comparsas se reúnen durante todo el año para preparar el Desfile de Llamadas.

¡Viva México!

Una fiesta nacional: el Grito de Dolores

La noche del 15 de septiembre el pueblo mexicano conmemora el Grito de Dolores, con el que comenzó la Guerra de la Independencia (1810). Miles de personas se congregan (*gather*) en el Zócalo, en el centro de la Ciudad de México. A las 11:00 p. m. el presidente de México toca la Campana de Dolores y desde el balcón del Palacio Nacional grita tres veces: «¡Viva México!». La multitud (*crowd*) grita de alegría y canta el himno nacional. La ceremonia se repite a la misma hora en todas las plazas mayores del país y la nación entera se une a la celebración.

110 ciento diez

Differentiated Instruction

DEVELOPING LEARNERS

- Ask students to expand on their Independent Starters. Have them list some facts about the festivity they chose for their Independent Starters in a five-column chart. Ask students to use these headings for their chart: *Fiesta; ¿Cuándo es?; ¿Qué se celebra?; ¿Quiénes participan?; ¿Cómo se celebra?*

- Then have students research the origins or history of this festivity and the reason people celebrate it.

EXPANDING LEARNERS

- Ask students to use the information they and their classmates researched for the first part of activity 88, as well as the information included in this *Mapa cultural*, to compare in detail one of the festivities from the Spanish-speaking world with one of the festivities in which they participate. What are the common elements in these festivities? What are the differences? Do students think there are more similarities than differences? Encourage them to organize their information in a graphic organizer, such as a Venn diagram or a comparison-contrast chart.

Los tambores del candombe

Para tocar candombe hacen falta tres tipos de tambor: *piano*, *repique* y *chico*. El *piano* es el más grave y el *chico* es el más agudo.

Cuando llega el último *casteller* a lo alto, levanta la mano. Tradicionalmente es un niño, que lleva casco.

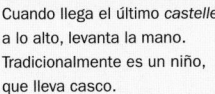

La tradición de las *collas* y los *castells*

En Cataluña (España) es tradicional levantar torres humanas durante las fiestas. Estas torres se llaman *castells* (*castillos* en catalán), y las personas que participan en ellos (los *castellers*) forman una *colla*.

Los miembros de la colla practican durante todo el año para levantar esos castillos.

El lema (*motto*) de las *collas* es: «Fuerza, equilibrio, valor y cordura».

En la base no solo hay miembros de la *colla*. También pueden participar amigos, familiares y espectadores.

---

88 **¿Qué nos une?**

▶ **Investiga** sobre una de estas fiestas. Después, descríbesela a tu compañero(a) y explica qué lazos unen a sus participantes.

El carnaval de Oruro (Bolivia)   El Desfile de Silleteros (Colombia)   Navidad (Puerto Rico)

▶ **Piensa** en tu fiesta favorita y responde a estas preguntas.

1. ¿Participas en ella? ¿Cómo?
2. ¿Qué te une al resto de los participantes?

La fiesta: expresión comunitaria

Preparation

- Invite students to share their Independent Starters. You may want to start a list on the board with the festivities they mention. Discuss as a class what the participants in these festivities have in common, some of the symbols, and how people celebrate. For instance, people who participate in Saint Patrick's Day festivities may have Irish ancestry. Some symbols include the shamrock, the leprechaun, and the color green. There are Saint Patrick's Day parades in many American cities and towns.

- Ask students to think about how these celebrations serve to reinforce cultural identity and promote a renewed sense of self. Then go over the *Mapa cultural* as a class.

Activities

88. You may want to convert the second part of this activity into an interview. Ask students to add five or six questions about the festivity, its origins or history, its symbols, participants, typical ways to celebrate, etc. Then have students get together with a classmate and interview each other. Invite pairs to share their interviews with the class. Are there some festivities and traditions students didn't know about?

Answer Key

88. Answers will vary.

▶ Answers will vary.

Additional Resources

Fans Online activities
Practice Workbook

HERITAGE LANGUAGE LEARNERS

- Ask students to choose one festivity from their heritage country and thoroughly research the topic. Suggest that they organize the information on poster paper to do a class presentation. Encourage students to include visuals. They may also include a brief recording or video containing a sampling of the music or events that are part of the festivity they researched. Have students explain the significance of the celebration and the role the community plays. If time allows, you may want to hold a question-and-answer session at the end of each presentation.

CRITICAL THINKING

- Explain to students that festivals and communal celebrations are probably as old as humankind itself. All cultures have feasts, so there seems to be an innate human need to celebrate with those with whom we have a particular relationship or bond.

- Discuss as a class the festivities in which students participate and the holidays they celebrate. Are there some common elements in all of those celebrations? What are these elements? What do these common elements tell them about our need for communal expression? Hold a class discussion to answer these questions.

Unit 2
ESCRITURA

¿Un poema o un dibujo? ¡Un caligrama!

Presentation

- In this section, students will practice and extend their writing skills. They will apply the vocabulary and grammar they have learned in this unit to create a concrete poem.

Activities	Standards	Resources
Escritura	1.1, 1.2, 1.3, 3.1, 5.2	

Teaching Suggestions

Warm-Up / Independent Starter

- Give students a couple of minutes to draw whatever comes to mind on a blank sheet of paper. They may draw a scene, random pictures, geometric figures, etc. Then ask students to write four or five words they associate with the images they have just drawn.

Preparation

- Discuss as a class a few poetic genres students know. For example: epic poetry (Homer's *Odyssey*), lyric poetry (Shakespeare's poems), dramatic poetry (Greek tragedies), narrative poetry (Chaucer's *Canterbury Tales*), etc. Discuss some of the basic elements of poetry, such as rhythm, rhyme, and figures of speech. You may want to invite volunteer students to recite a poem they know and point out the poetic genre and some poetic elements.

- Ask for a volunteer to read the *Caligrama* box aloud. Explain that concrete poetry is a poetic genre that portrays its subject through its form. Show students two or three of these *caligramas* (you will find them online): "Girándula" by Guillermo de Torre, "El puñal" by Juan José Tablada, "Texto que se encoge" by Guillermo Cabrera Infante, "Triángulo armónico" by Vicente Huidobro. Display each caligrama individually and read it aloud as students observe it. Then read each poem a second time without displaying it. Discuss with students how the shape of these poems reflects the topic and how it enhances comprehension.

112

¿Un poema o un dibujo? ¡Un caligrama!

Caligrama

A concrete poem (in Spanish *caligrama*, from the French *calligramme*) is a visual poem in which the words "draw" or show a person, animal, landscape, or any other object imaginable.

This type of visual poem is credited to the avant-garde poet Guillaume Apollinaire, whose book *Calligrammes* was published in 1918.

Poets from many languages and cultures have been influenced by this genre of poetry.

Existen muchas formas de expresar nuestros sentimientos o nuestras ideas relacionadas con el mundo.

A lo largo de la historia, los poetas han buscado nuevas formas para expresarse. El caligrama es una de ellas.

Elige el tema que prefieras y crea un caligrama.

Piensa

- Busca una idea, una persona, un sentimiento o un tema sobre el que quieras escribir. Trata de elegir un tema al que puedas asociar una imagen.

Temas posibles	Dibujos posibles
La noche	Una estrella
La paz	Una paloma
El amor	Un corazón
La tristeza	Una lágrima
El tiempo	Un reloj

- Escribe las ideas que te sugiere la persona, el sentimiento o el tema elegido. Puedes utilizar un diccionario o un diccionario de sinónimos (*thesaurus*) en español para crear un banco de nombres, adjetivos y verbos que puedes usar cuando escribas tu poema.

Modelo *La noche es oscura.*
Por la noche hay estrellas.
Las estrellas brillan en el cielo.

- Dibuja el contorno de una imagen que represente la idea principal de tu poema. No olvides que luego vas a sustituirlo por palabras.

Rubric for Evaluation

	Content	Organization	Conventions
1 point	Topic of poem and main idea are not clear. Poem doesn't create images in reader's mind. Limited or inappropriate word choice.	Shape is not recognizable or meaning doesn't match shape. No rhyming verses and no apparent rhythm.	Many errors in spelling, punctuation, grammar, and usage. Errors obscure meaning.
3 points	The poem relates to the topic. Main idea is clear. A few vivid images, but some inaccurate word choices.	Shape is recognizable and meaning matches shape for the most part. Poem has a few rhyming verses and some rhythm.	Some errors in spelling, punctuation, grammar, and usage. Errors don't interfere with meaning.

Escribe

■ Redacta unos versos con las ideas que desarrollaste sobre el tema elegido. Si es posible, incorpora palabras que rimen. La rima es un recurso muy utilizado en la poesía, ya que le aporta musicalidad al poema.

Modelo

> La noche es un carro oscuro,
> siempre cargado de estrellas.
> Yo las miro sin apuro
> brillar como una centella
> y no sé cuál es más bella.

Expresiones útiles

la literatura	literature
la poesía	poetry
el poeta, la poetisa	poet
el poema	poem
el verso	line
la estrofa	verse
la rima	rhyme
escribir	to write
crear	to create
componer	to compose
rimar	to rhyme

■ Cuando tengas listo el texto de tu caligrama, escríbelo siguiendo las líneas del dibujo o completando los espacios en blanco. Los versos de tu poema no deben salirse del espacio dibujado. Debes escribir en el sentido de las agujas del reloj, de izquierda a derecha, para que sea más fácil de leer.

Revisa

■ Después de escribir tu caligrama, intercámbialo con tu compañero(a).

■ Lee el caligrama de tu compañero(a). ¿La disposición de las letras representa el contenido del poema? ¿Qué te gustaría añadir o cambiar? Revisa la redacción y la ortografía y escribe tus comentarios.

■ Devuelve el caligrama a tu compañero(a) y corrige tu propio texto. ¿Qué opinas de los cambios propuestos por tu compañero(a)? ¿Crees que entendió bien tu caligrama? Si es necesario, reescríbelo incorporando las correcciones. No olvides borrar las líneas del dibujo antes de entregar tu trabajo.

Comparte

■ Presenta tu trabajo a la clase. ¿Qué opinan tus compañeros(as)? ¿Qué caligramas les gustan más? ¿Por qué? ¡Buena suerte, poeta!

	Content	Organization	Conventions
5 points	The poem clearly relates to the topic. Main idea stands out. Precise and clear word choices create vivid images in reader's mind.	Shape is easily recognizable and meaning matches shape perfectly. Poem has rhyming verses and a clear rhythm.	Few, if any, errors in spelling, punctuation, grammar, and usage. Excellent command of the Spanish language.

ESCRITURA

¿Un poema o un dibujo? ¡Un caligrama!

Step-by-Step Instructions

Piensa

■ Ask students to use their drawings and words from the Independent Starter as a source of inspiration for a topic for their *caligrama*. Once they have decided on a topic, ask students to jot down in English any words or phrases that come to mind when they think of this topic. Then, have them work on a word bank in Spanish.

Escribe

■ Encourage students to write from personal experience about aspects of their chosen topic. Explain that even though the visual pattern of their *caligrama* is important, they should not neglect the language of their poem. Encourage students to add literary devices and use words that appeal to our senses.

■ Thinking of rhyming words in Spanish may be difficult for some students. Suggest that they focus on the general musical quality, or rhythm, of their poem rather than on rhyming individual words. Have students read their completed poem aloud to themselves and ask them to answer these questions: Does the poem express what I want it to say? Does the shape match the subject?

Revisa

■ Have students look at the shape and then read through the poem to determine whether the shape is consistent with the meaning. Does the shape of the poem enhance meaning? Then, ask students to evaluate the content and organization of the poem following the rubric for evaluation. Finally, have students look at the grammar, punctuation, and spelling.

Comparte

■ The visual aspect of a concrete poem is as important as the poem itself. Therefore, encourage students to memorize their poem so that they can recite it as they show it to their classmates.

Evaluation

■ Distribute copies of the rubric to students and discuss the evaluation criteria. Ask students to refer to the rubric as they prepare their writing and as they evaluate their classmates' poems.

REPASO

Vocabulario

Presentation

- In this section, students will review all key vocabulary from the unit, organized by themes, to prepare for an assessment. Students will complete practice activities for each *Desafío*.

Activities	Standards	Resources
1.	1.1, 1.2	
2.	1.1, 1.2, 2.1	
3.	1.2	

Teaching Suggestions

Warm-Up / Independent Starter

- Give students a few minutes to review the vocabulary on their own. Then have them think of the steps that two people who fall in love, become a couple, break up, and then reconcile go through. Ask students to list ten steps in order. For example: *Se enamoran, se llaman por teléfono, se dejan recados, se dan el primer beso...*

Preparation

- Ask pairs to share their lists from the Independent Starter and use each other's lists to flesh out the details of the story of a couple's stormy relationship. If time allows, ask students to illustrate their text. Then invite volunteers to share their stories with the class. After each presentation, you may want to review the vocabulary the presenters used in their story.

- Read over the *Repaso* presentation with students and have them choose three words or phrases that describe their last experience receiving or making a phone call. Ask for volunteers to share their three words, then have the rest of the class try to reconstruct the experience.

Activities

1. Before completing the text, ask students to classify the words in the word bank into verbs, nouns, and adjectives. Then have them read the text through and answer these questions: Who are the characters? What is their relationship like? What challenges are they facing? Finally, ask students to complete the paragraph.

114

REPASO Vocabulario

Relaciones personales

el abrazo	hug
la amistad	friendship
el amor	love
el beso	kiss
la confianza	trust
el dolor	pain
la fidelidad	faithfulness
abrazar	to hug
apoyar	to support
apreciar	to appreciate
confiar en	to trust
disculparse	to apologize
enamorarse de	to fall in love with
estar enamorado(a)	to be in love
pedir perdón	to apologize
perdonar	to forgive
querer	to love
reconciliarse	to make up
respetar	to respect
tener razón	to be right
discutir	to argue
echar la culpa	to blame
equivocarse	to make a mistake
estar/ponerse celoso	to be jealous
mentir	to lie
romper	to break up

Presentaciones

Don/Doña	Mr./Mrs. (first name)
Señor(a)	Mr./Mrs. (last name)
Quiero presentarle a...	I want to introduce you to ...
Permítanme que les presente a...	Allow me to introduce you to ...

Relaciones sociales

el/la anfitrión(a)	host, hostess
el/la invitado(a)	guest
la fiesta	party
la reunión	meeting

Acciones

llegar tarde	to arrive late
llegar temprano	to arrive early
llegar a tiempo	to arrive on time

Invitar, aceptar y rechazar una invitación

¿Te apetece...?	Do you feel like ...?
¿Vamos a...?	Let's go to ...
Te invito a...	I invite you to ...
¿Estás ocupado(a)?	Are you busy?
¿Tienes planes para hoy?	Do you have plans for today?
De acuerdo./Vale.	I agree./OK.
Sí, ¿por qué no?	Yes, why not?
Con mucho gusto.	With pleasure.
Me parece un buen plan.	It seems like a good plan.
No, no me apetece.	No, I don't feel like it.
Gracias, pero no puedo.	Thank you, but I can't.
Lo siento, pero estoy ocupado(a).	I'm sorry, but I'm busy.
No sé... Tengo mucho que hacer.	I don't know ... I have a lot to do.

Llamadas telefónicas

la tarjeta telefónica	phone card
el teléfono público	public phone

El celular

el buzón de voz	voice mailbox
el celular	cell phone
la llamada perdida	missed call
mandar/enviar un mensaje de texto	to send a text message
quedarse sin batería	to run out of battery
quedarse sin saldo	to run out of minutes

Acciones

colgar el teléfono	to hang up the phone
comunicar	to be busy
dejar un recado	to leave a message
descolgar el teléfono	to pick up the phone
devolver una llamada	to call back
llamar más tarde	to call later
marcar un número	to dial a number
ponerse al teléfono	to answer the phone

Hablar por teléfono

¿Diga?	Hello?
¿Está...? / ¿Puedo hablar con...?	May I speak with ...?
¿De parte de quién?	Who's calling?

Differentiated Instruction

DEVELOPING LEARNERS

- Explain to students that for a given verb, there is often a related noun made from the same root. For example: *perdonar → perdón*, *mentir → mentira*. Have students analyze the vocabulary list and classify all the related verbs and nouns in a two-column chart like the one below.

Verbo	Nombre
abrazar	abrazo
enamorarse	amor

- Then ask students to write sentences with six of the verb-noun pairs. For example: *Cuando dos personas se enamoran sienten amor.*

EXPANDING LEARNERS

- Ask pairs of students to create the script for a scene of a *telenovela* (soap opera). The scene could be about two people meeting and falling in love, a couple fighting and breaking up, or a couple reconciling after a fight. Have pairs incorporate into their script as many words and phrases from the vocabulary list as possible.

- Allow for rehearsal time and invite pairs to act out their *telenovela* scenes for the class. Hold a class vote to decide on two winning pairs for "Best Script" and "Best Acting."

DESAFÍO 1

1 **Como el perro y el gato.** Completa el texto. Pon las palabras del cuadro en la forma verbal correspondiente.

enamorado(a)	celoso(a)	quererse	perdón
respetar	romper	discutir	razón

¿Una relación perfecta?

María y Tomás son novios desde el año pasado. Al principio estaban muy ___1___ y ___2___ mucho. Pero ahora no tienen una buena relación. Se llevan muy mal y ___3___ todo el tiempo. ¡Siempre están como el perro y el gato!

María es bastante ___4___ y no confía en Tomás. Piensa que él no la ___5___. En cambio, él cree que María no tiene ___6___ y que debe pedirle ___7___.

¿Crees que pueden reconciliarse o piensas que van a ___8___?

 DESAFÍO 2

2 **¿Voy o no voy?** Escribe la respuesta de Juan aceptando y rechazando las invitaciones. Añade un comentario o una excusa apropiada en cada situación.

1. —¡Hola, Juan! ¡Mañana es mi cumpleaños! Te invito a mi fiesta.
   _____

2. —¡Hola! ¿Qué tal, Juan? Oye, ¿quieres venir conmigo al cine esta tarde?
   _____

3. —¿Qué tal, Juan? ¿Te apetece tomar un helado?
   _____

 DESAFÍO 3

3 **¿Qué debes hacer?** Une las dos columnas.

(A)

1. Cuando llamas desde un teléfono público...
2. Para llamar a una amiga, primero...
3. Si tu amiga no responde a la llamada...
4. Si tu celular no tiene batería...
5. Si tienes una llamada perdida...

(B)

a. necesitas recargarlo.
b. tienes que marcar su número.
c. debes devolver la llamada.
d. puedes usar monedas.
e. puedes dejarle un recado en su buzón de voz.

ciento quince **115**

---

2. Ask students to work with a partner to complete this activity. Once they have finished the activity, ask them to act out the dialogues. They should switch roles. Invite volunteer pairs to present their dialogues to the class.

3. Once students have finished this activity, have them work in small groups and ask them to come up with a story using the sentences from this activity. For example: *Iba a llamar a Azucena, pero mi celular no tenía batería. Dejé recargando el celular y fui a llamarla desde un teléfono público. Puse monedas en el teléfono y marqué el número de Azucena...* Invite groups to read their stories to the class and hold a vote to choose the most entertaining story.

Answer Key

1.
1. enamorados	5. respeta
2. se querían	6. razón
3. discuten	7. perdón
4. celosa	8. romper

2. Answers will vary. Sample answers:
1. De acuerdo. Será un placer celebrar contigo.
   Lo siento, pero estoy ocupado. Es el aniversario de mis padres.
2. Sí, ¿por qué no? No tengo otros planes.
   No, no me apetece. Prefiero quedarme en casa escuchando música.
3. Vale. Ya sabes que me gustan mucho los helados.
   No sé... Tengo mucho que hacer. Mis padres están pintando la casa y tengo que ayudarlos.

3. 1. d 2. b 3. e 4. a 5. c

Additional Resources

Fans Online activities
Practice Workbook

HERITAGE LANGUAGE LEARNERS

• Ask students to look at the vocabulary under *Presentaciones* and *Llamadas telefónicas* and think of regional variants they know. People in Colombia, for instance, often use the titles *señor* and *señora* with a person's first name (e.g., *la señora Isabel*). In some countries, it is common to refer to an older woman as *doñita*. There are also different phrases to answer the phone and other vocabulary related to phone etiquette. Have students compile a list of the vocabulary used in their country of origin, then ask them to get together with other heritage learners and compare their lists.

MULTIPLE INTELLIGENCES:

Interpersonal Intelligence

• Stress the importance of being able to use language in a contextually appropriate fashion. Using the dialogue in activity 2 as a model, ask pairs of students to come up with an invitation for a party or a similar social event. Then ask two pairs to get together and invite each other to their event. First, they should make up excuses for not attending, but the other pair should insist, explaining how great and interesting their event will be. Finally, they accept. Encourage students to be creative in their dialogues.

REPASO

Gramática

Presentation

- Students will review grammatical structures presented in the unit. Each grammar point is cross-referenced to the corresponding page on which it was introduced. The activities here provide systematic practice by *Desafío*.

Activities	Standards	Resources
4.	1.1, 1.2	
5.	1.2	
6.	1.1, 1.2	
7. Cultura	1.1, 1.2, 2.1, 2.2	

Teaching Suggestions

Warm-Up / Independent Starter

- Ask students to write down a pronominal verb that reflects a reaction to or a consequence of each of the following situations:

  1. *Te olvidaste del cumpleaños de tu mamá.*
  2. *Tu novio(a) o mejor amigo(a) no te llama.*
  3. *Te quedaste dormido y no fuiste a una entrevista de trabajo.*

Preparation

- Ask students to get together with a classmate and share their Independent Starters. Are their reactions similar? Then have pairs think of things their partner should do to solve the situation. For example:

  A. *No debes pelearte con tu novia si no te llama. Tienen que verse, hablar y perdonarse.*

  B. *Ojalá pueda perdonarla, pero…*

  Invite pairs to share some of their dialogues with the class and encourage students to add their own advice.

- Go over the *Repaso* presentation with the class. Reassure students that mastering the grammatical structures presented in this *Repaso* takes time and practice. Then ask students to check their dialogues from the Preparation activity and identify the different grammar structures being reviewed in this *Repaso*. Finally, have students provide sample sentences for any grammar topic that was not practiced in their dialogues.

Los pronombres de objeto directo e indirecto (pág. 76)

PRONOMBRES DE OBJETO DIRECTO	
me	nos
te	os
lo, la	los, las

PRONOMBRES DE OBJETO INDIRECTO	
me	nos
te	os
le(se)	les(se)

Expresar deseos, gustos y preferencias (pág. 88)

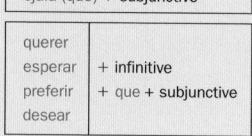

me te le nos os les	+ gustar/encantar/ interesar/apetecer/ importar

EL SUBJUNTIVO

ojalá (que) + subjunctive

querer esperar preferir desear	+ infinitive + que + subjunctive

Expresar necesidad u obligación (pág. 100)

deber + infinitive

tener que + infinitive

haber que + infinitive

Hablar del futuro (pág. 102)

ir a + infinitive

future

cuando + present subjunctive

Verbos pronominales reflexivos y recíprocos (pág. 78)

VERBOS REFLEXIVOS
Mi madre se maquilla.

VERBOS RECÍPROCOS

abrazarse	conocerse	hablarse	perdonarse
apoyarse	contarse	odiarse	quererse
ayudarse	entenderse	pelearse	verse

Nosotros nos escribimos.

Verbos pronominales no reflexivos (pág. 90)

VERBOS PRONOMINALES

Personas		Cosas	
acordarse	dormirse	abrirse	cerrarse
alegrarse	enterarse	arrugarse	enfriarse
atreverse	olvidarse	caerse	mancharse
despertarse	preocuparse	calentarse	romperse

VERBOS CON CAMBIO DE SIGNIFICADO

acordar	vs.	acordarse	estudiar	vs.	estudiarse
aprender	vs.	aprenderse	ir	vs.	irse
beber	vs.	beberse	parecer	vs.	parecerse
comer	vs.	comerse	quedar	vs.	quedarse
dormir	vs.	dormirse	salir	vs.	salirse

Marcadores de futuro (pág. 102)

hoy	today
luego/después	later
en una hora	in an hour
esta tarde/esta noche	this afternoon/this evening
mañana	tomorrow
pasado mañana	the day after tomorrow
la próxima semana/ la semana que viene	next week
el próximo mes/ el mes que viene	next month
el próximo año/ el año que viene	next year

Differentiated Instruction

DEVELOPING LEARNERS

- To practice using the subjunctive to express wishes, ask students to complete these sentences with the correct subjunctive form of the verb in parentheses:

  1. *Mi novio desea que yo lo (acompañar) a los partidos de fútbol.* (acompañe)
  2. *Ojalá que (empezar) el buen tiempo pronto.* (empiece)
  3. *Mis padres quieren que yo (practicar) deportes.* (practique)
  4. *Los profesores prefieren que nosotros (llegar) a tiempo a clase.* (lleguemos)
  5. *Mi madre desea que yo (comer) más frutas y verduras.* (coma)

EXPANDING LEARNERS

- Have students work with a partner to create a short dialogue in which they use direct and indirect object pronouns. Then invite pairs to act out their dialogues in front of the class. For example:

  A. *En San Valentín le escribí un poema a mi novia.*
  B. *¡Qué romántico! ¿Y cómo se lo diste?*
  A. *Lo escribí en una tarjeta y la puse en un ramo de rosas rojas.*
  B. *¿Y le gustó?*
  A. *Pues no mucho. Las flores le dan alergia y los poemas le parecen aburridos.*

DESAFÍO 1

4 **¿Reflexivos o recíprocos?** Completa estas oraciones poniendo los infinitivos en la forma verbal correcta.

1. Manuel y yo ___1___ desde la niñez.
   (conocerse)
2. Mi padre ___2___ temprano para llegar puntual a la oficina.
   (levantarse)
3. A mis amigas y a mí nos encanta ___3___ .
   (maquillarse)
4. Alina y su novio ___4___ todos los días.
   (verse)
5. Mi hermano pequeño y yo ___5___ con frecuencia.
   (pelearse)

DESAFÍO 2

5 **¿Cuál de todos?** Elige la respuesta correcta.

1. Sabrina _____ de la cita y llegó a las 8 de la mañana.
   a. acordó   b. acuerda   c. se acordó
2. Dicen que yo _____ muchísimo a mis hermanos.
   a. me parezco   b. parezco   c. nos parecemos
3. Gloria y su prima _____ a las 10 de la noche.
   a. durmieron   b. se duerme   c. se durmieron
4. Nosotros _____ el jugo de tomate en un minuto.
   a. nos bebimos   b. se bebieron   c. se beben

DESAFÍO 3

6 **En el futuro...** Escribe lo que hará cada persona. Usa los verbos del cuadro.

tener
venir
limpiar
ir
poder

1. Mi hermano y yo _____ nuestro dormitorio mañana.
2. En diez días yo _____ a un concierto de Maná, mi grupo favorito.
3. Esta semana Mario _____ que estudiar mucho para sus exámenes.
4. ¿Crees que nosotras _____ ir al cine esta tarde?
5. La semana que viene daré una fiesta y _____ todos mis amigos.

CULTURA

7 **De aquí y de allá.** Responde a estas preguntas.

1. ¿Qué se regalan los amigos y los enamorados el Día de san Jordi?
2. ¿Dónde se practica actualmente el juego de pelota mixteca?
3. ¿Qué bailes latinos conoces? ¿Cuál te gusta más? ¿Por qué?

REPASO
Gramática

Activities

4. Before attempting to complete this activity, ask students to read each sentence and jot down the subject for each. Next, have students analyze each subject and decide if it refers to one or more than one person. Then have students complete the sentences.

5. To extend this activity, ask students to add three more sentences using pronominal verbs that have not been used. Then have students exchange their activity with another student and complete each other's activity.

6. Once students have completed this activity, ask them to get together with a classmate and select one of the statements to make up a brief story about what else will happen. Have them use the three future structures they have learned in this unit. For example: *La semana que viene daré una fiesta y vendrán todos mis amigos. Voy a tener música latina y habrá baile. Cuando lleguen los invitados les ofreceré un refresco...* Invite pairs to share their stories with the class.

Answer Key

4. 1. nos conocemos   4. se ven
   2. se levanta   5. nos peleamos
   3. maquillarnos

5. 1. c   2. a   3. c   4. a

6. 1. limpiaremos   4. podremos
   2. iré   5. vendrán
   3. tendrá

7. 1. Se regalan una rosa o un libro.
   2. Se practica en diferentes lugares de México y también en algunas ciudades de los Estados Unidos.
   3. Answers will vary. Sample answer: Conozco la salsa, el merengue, la cumbia y el tango. El baile que más me gusta es el tango porque es muy elegante y exige mucha coordinación.

Additional Resources

Fans Online activities
Practice Workbook

HERITAGE LANGUAGE LEARNERS

- Explain to students that there are many verbs in Spanish that are conjugated with reflexive pronouns. In fact, they probably use these verbs often. Ask students to come up with a list of ten pronominal verbs not listed in this *Repaso*. You may get them started with these verbs: *arrepentirse, quejarse, avergonzarse*. Then have students write one sentence for each verb. For example: *Ayer discutí con mi novio, pero después me arrepentí y le pedí perdón*. Invite students to share their sentences with the class and have the class try to guess the meaning of the verbs.

SPECIAL-NEEDS LEARNERS

- Students with learning disabilities benefit from the incorporation of multi-sensory support. Distribute three large index cards and red, purple, and green stickers to students. Have them place a sticker on each index card and label each card with a *Desafío* (i.e., red – *Desafío 1*, purple – *Desafío 2*, green – *Desafío 3*).

- Have students copy examples of the grammar topics for each *Desafío* on the appropriate card. Then ask them to use the cards as a reference when they complete the activities on page 117.

Unit 2
PROYECTO
Actividades con tus amigos

Presentation

- In this section, students will apply the vocabulary, grammar, and cultural information they have learned in this unit to plan a day of activities to celebrate Hispanic Heritage Month.

Activities	Standards	Resources
Paso 1	1.1, 2.1, 2.2	
Paso 2	1.3, 2.1, 2.2, 5.1	
Paso 3	1.1, 1.2, 1.3, 2.1, 2.2, 5.1, 5.2	

Teaching Suggestions

Warm-Up / Independent Starter

- Ask students to think about the type of activities both they and other students their age enjoy. Have them think of at least five activities (e.g., going to a concert, attending a sports event).

Preparation

- Explain to students that most of Central America celebrates its independence from Spain on September 15. Mexico's Independence Day is celebrated the following day, on September 16, and Chile's Independence Day is on September 18. These national celebrations during the month of September account for the timing of Hispanic Heritage Month. Hispanic Heritage Week was first celebrated in 1968. Then, in 1988, President Reagan expanded the celebrations to a thirty-day period. During Hispanic Heritage Month, we celebrate the cultures and contributions of Americans whose ancestors came from the Spanish-speaking world.

- Invite students to share their Independent Starters with the class. You may want to list the most popular activities on the board. Then ask students to think of ways in which some of these activities could be adapted to celebrate Hispanic heritage. For instance, if one of the students' favorite activities is dancing, they will probably enjoy a Latin dance competition or exhibition. Discuss several of these ideas as a class. If your community celebrates Hispanic Heritage Month, you may want to discuss some of the activities that are typically included in the celebrations.

118

Un plan de

actividades con tus amigos

In many cities in the United States, Hispanic Heritage Month is celebrated between September 15 and October 15. In your project, you are going to plan a day of activities to celebrate Hispanic Heritage Month. You will invite your friends to celebrate with you.

PASO 1 Decide qué actividades vas a proponer

- Piensa qué actividades se pueden realizar para celebrar el Mes de la Herencia Hispana. Puedes inventártelas o buscar ideas en Internet.

> Lectura de los poemas más conocidos de la escritora nicaragüense Gioconda Belli.

> Dramatización bilingüe de la leyenda de *El Dorado* presentada por EnCuentos y EnCantos, el grupo de cuentacuentos de la biblioteca.

> Participe en el concurso Salsa con salsa: prepare su receta de salsa y traiga su CD de salsa favorito. ¡Se van a divertir mucho!

> Proyección de una película basada en la vida de Frida Kahlo y discusión, en inglés, sobre la artista y sobre la forma de vida en la primera mitad del siglo XX.

> Manualidades para aprender a hacer artesanías del mundo hispano.

- Elige las actividades más interesantes y divertidas para proponérselas a tus compañeros(as).
- Decide la hora y el lugar de celebración de cada una de las actividades.

Rubric for Evaluation

	Content	Organization	Presentation
1 point	The activities are not relevant. Information is incomplete or not based on research. Little Spanish is used.	Inefficient use of time. Information is disorganized or unclear. The plan is not well designed and organized.	Unclear communication. Delivery is not fluent. Many errors in vocabulary and grammar.
3 points	The activities are relevant. Information is correct but some of it lacks significance. Spanish is used most of the time.	Time is used well. Information is mostly organized but lacks some clarity. The plan is mostly well designed and organized.	Clear communication and fluent delivery. Mostly correct vocabulary and grammar.

PASO 2 Prepara la información

- Busca en Internet información y fotos sobre las actividades que has elegido.
- Escribe en una hoja el plan que vas a proponer a tus compañeros(as). Debes incluir estos datos:
  - Tipo de actividades y breve descripción de cada una.
  - Lugar y hora en que se realizará cada actividad.

MES DE LA HERENCIA HISPANA

De 10:30 a 11:30 a. m., Biblioteca North Regional. Demostraciones de cocina, bailes (salsa, cumbia, vallenato, etc.) y juegos tradicionales precolombinos (patolli y totoloque).

12:00 p. m., Plaza Showers de City Hall.
Cine español ¡GRATIS! Proyección de la película española *Los otros (The Others)*. La película se proyectará en español con subtítulos en inglés.

PASO 3 Invita a tus compañeros(as)

- Habla con tus compañeros(as) y proponles tu plan. Tienes que conseguir atraer al máximo número de ellos(as).

Modelo

A. *¿Quieres que vayamos el sábado por la mañana a ver demostraciones de cocina y bailes típicos mexicanos?*
B. *No sé... El sábado tengo que estudiar.*
A. *Va a ser muy divertido. También habrá juegos tradicionales.*
B. *Vale, ¿a qué hora quedamos?*

- ¿Cuál ha sido el plan que más gustó? ¿Y si lo hacemos?

Unidad 2

Autoevaluación

¿Qué has aprendido en esta unidad?

Do these activities to evaluate how well you understood this unit's concepts.

> Evalúa tus habilidades. Para cada punto, di Muy bien, Bien o Necesito practicar más.

a. Can you express feelings?

▶ Write a letter to a real or imaginary friend or relative to tell him or her how you feel about your relationship.

b. Can you express wishes, likes, and preferences?

▶ Write an invitation to a party for one of your classmates and answer his or her invitation.

▶ What do you prefer to do on the weekends? Ask your partner about his or her preferences, too.

c. Can you express necessity or obligation?

▶ Make an imaginary call to one of your classmates to tell him/her all the things that need to be done for your birthday party. Together, write a list of who must do each task.

PROYECTO

Actividades con tus amigos

Step-by-Step Instructions

Paso 1

- In addition to the activities mentioned in the Preparation section, encourage students to look for other ideas. Good online sources include the Library of Congress Hispanic Heritage Month web page, the Smithsonian Hispanic Heritage Month calendar of events, or the calendar of events of American cities with large Hispanic populations. Remind students to include activities for different types of audiences.

Paso 2

- Encourage students to be creative in their presentation and organization of their plan. They may, for example, create a brochure, a large poster on chart paper, a digital presentation, etc.

Paso 3

- Emphasize to students that they will be attempting to influence their classmates' decisions. Their presentation should therefore be upbeat and enticing. They should have several convincing arguments ready in case their classmates don't accept their invitation.

Evaluation

- Distribute copies of the rubric to students. Discuss the evaluation criteria and explain how this project will be graded. Encourage students to refer to the rubric as they prepare their projects.

Content

- Ask students to consider these questions about their plan: Are the activities balanced? Are they including activities that showcase different aspects of the Hispanic cultures? Are their descriptions of the activities vivid and interesting enough to encourage attendance?

Organization

- Explain to students that they will not have much time to present their plan and try to convince their audience. Efficient use of time is of the utmost importance.

Presentation

- Encourage students to memorize their calendar of events so that they can deliver a fluent presentation and keep eye contact with their audience at all times.

	Content	Organization	Presentation
5 points	The activities are relevant, varied, and interesting. The descriptions are vivid and convincing. Spanish is used exclusively.	Time is used wisely. Information is clearly organized visually and logically. The plan is very well designed and organized.	Clear and fluent communication. Very motivating, upbeat delivery. Correct and complete vocabulary and grammar.

Unit 3 Tus cosas

Objectives

- To identify articles of clothing.
- To describe clothing and traditional costumes of Latin American populations.
- To talk about recent events.
- To describe the appearance and location of objects.
- To use the impersonal pronoun se.

- To use indefinite adjectives and pronouns properly.
- To talk about past experiences.
- To describe past actions using the past perfect.
- To identify and describe domestic tasks and jobs.

- To identify main ideas and significant details in a variety of texts.
- To write descriptive, narrative, or informative texts.
- To know and apply the different stages of the writing process: planning, writing, revising, and editing.

Contents

Vocabulary

- Useful expressions to ask for favors, and to ask for and offer help.
- Review: Words for clothing, footwear, and accessories, material, places in the home, and items in the home.
- Articles of clothing, fabric, and fit.
- Color, texture, and makeup of clothing and objects.
- Domestic chores and jobs.

Grammar

- The past participle.
- To talk about recent events: The present perfect tense.
- Indefinite adjectives and pronouns.
- The use of the impersonal pronoun se.
- The past perfect tense.
- Demonstrative adjectives and pronouns.

Culture

- Traditional and regional Latin American costumes.
- Latin American fashion and style.
- Recycling with clothing.
- Cultural symbols: The wiphala.
- El mercado de Otavalo (Ecuador).
- Colonial farms in Latin America.
- Hotels and tourism in Latin American countries.
- Flamenco dance and music.
- Superstitions.
- The Andalusian patio in Cordoba, Spain.
- Colonial architecture and cities in Latin America.

Evaluation Criteria

- Describe modern and traditional clothing.
- Describe objects using past participles.
- Speak about recent events using the present perfect tense.
- Identify synonyms of adjectives.
- Explore ways populations can maintain cultural traditions and customs.
- Compare and contrast images.
- Identify and describe cultural symbols.
- Describe the shape, texture, and makeup of clothing and objects.

- Use indefinite articles and pronouns to talk about the existence and quantity of nouns.
- Express an action using the impersonal pronoun se.
- Express understanding of the origin, history, and tradition of Spanish music: flamenco.
- Identify chores and jobs performed in the home.
- Describe past actions using the past perfect tense.

- Describe the location and quantity of objects using demonstrative adjectives and pronouns.
- Describe the function and appearance of different types of historic architecture in Latin American cities.
- Write an essay.
- Read different types of texts and identify main ideas and significant details in them.
- Write guided texts giving information, describing, or narrating events.

Unit Plan

Las tareas/Antes de empezar

Estimated time: 1 session.

Text: *Tradiciones con mucho estilo.*

Functions & forms:
- Useful expressions to ask for favors or help, or to offer help.
- Review of known vocabulary about clothing, footwear and accessories, material, places in the home, and objects in the home.

DESAFÍO 1

Estimated time: 5 sessions.

Text: *Un traje muy especial.*

Functions & forms:
- To talk about recent events.
- Articles of clothing, fabric, and fit.
- The past participle.
- The present perfect tense.

Culture:
- *Los trajes regionales.*
- *La moda hispana.*
- *El reciclaje.*

Reading: *Un traje tradicional.*

DESAFÍO 2

Estimated time: 5 sessions.

Text: *En busca del símbolo perdido.*

Functions & forms:
- To describe objects.
- Color, texture, and makeup of clothing and objects.
- Indefinite adjectives and pronouns.
- The impersonal pronoun *se.*

Culture:
- *La wiphala.*
- *El mercado de Otavalo (Ecuador).*
- *Las haciendas coloniales.*

Reading: *Guía de viajeros: un hotel inolvidable.*

DESAFÍO 3

Estimated time: 6 sessions.

Text: *Un festival de flamenco.*

Functions & forms:
- To talk about past experiences.
- Household chores and jobs.
- The past perfect tense.
- Demonstrative pronouns and adjectives.

Culture:
- *El flamenco.*
- *Las supersticiones.*
- *Los patios cordobeses (España).*

Reading: *La casa de muñecas.*

Para terminar

Estimated time: 1 session.

Todo junto: Review of *Desafíos 1–3.*

Tu desafío:
- *Desafío A:* Research and adapt a traditional Hispanic costume.
- *Desafío B:* Design a flag symbolic of all the cultures in the United States and explain its significance.
- *Desafío C:* Design an Andalusian patio and describe it.

MAPA CULTURAL

Estimated time: 1 session.

Mapa cultural: La ciudad colonial.

ESCRITURA

Estimated time: 1 session.

Writing: *Un ensayo de moda.*

PROYECTO

Estimated time: 1 session.

Project: *Una feria sobre ciudades coloniales hispanas.*

Standards for Learning Spanish

COMMUNICATION

1.1. Interpersonal mode
- Exchange personal opinions and experiences.
- Engage in oral conversations using personal knowledge and experience.
- Exchange assignments with a partner and evaluate each other's work.
- Create a visual and describe it with a partner.
- Write a dialogue with a partner.
- Compare and contrast information with a partner.
- Ask and answer questions on different topics orally.
- Ask a partner questions and take notes.

1.2. Interpretive mode
- Demonstrate understanding of oral and written idiomatic expressions.
- Demonstrate understanding of questions relating to familiar and less familiar topics.
- Understand and obtain information from audio or video recordings.
- Understand written exchanges.
- Extract information from a text in a hotel guide.
- Identify main ideas and significant details from a literary story.
- Draw conclusions and make judgments from oral and written texts.
- Interpret texts on topics of other cultures and relate them to personal knowledge and experience.

1.3. Presentational mode
- Dramatize a situation.
- Produce and present an original creation orally.
- Describe objects and clothing with detail.
- Write a descriptive and informative paragraph about an architectural structure.
- Narrate recent events.
- Write an optional ending to a literary text.
- Write a descriptive paragraph comparing or summarizing information.
- Write an essay.
- Present information about a colonial city.

COMPARISONS

4.1. Compare languages
- Compare the formation of past participles in English and in Spanish.
- Compare the indefinites and the demonstratives in English and in Spanish.
- Compare how to express an anonymous action in English and in Spanish.
- Compare the use of the present perfect and past perfect tenses in English and in Spanish.

4.2. Compare cultures
- Compare music in Hispanic countries and in the United States.
- Compare cultural symbols in Hispanic countries and in the United States.

CULTURE

2.1. Practices and perspectives
- Learn about cultural traditions and discuss the importance of maintaining such practices.
- Discover some celebrations in Hispanic countries.
- Learn about hand-crafted objects and goods being sold at open-air markets in various Latin American countries.
- Read about some fashion designers from Latin American countries and their influence on their country's culture and economy.

2.2. Products and perspectives
- Learn about some types of Spanish music and compare them to music in the students' culture.
- Reflect on the origin and influence of various cultural symbols and compare them to cultural symbols in the students' culture.
- Learn about and describe traditional and regional costumes.
- Learn about and describe colonial architecture in Latin America.

COMMUNITIES

5.1. Spanish within and beyond the school setting
- Promote a positive attitude toward other cultures.
- Discuss possibilities for cultural celebrations in the students' school.
- Reflect on the role of symbols of national identity.
- Imagine various scenarios taking place in Hispanic cultures or situations in which Spanish could be used.

5.2. Spanish for lifelong learners
- Appreciate the preservation of traditional costumes and symbols and cultural practices.

CONNECTIONS

3.1. Interdisciplinary connections
- Understand the similarities and differences between some aspects of grammar in English and in Spanish.
- Read and research about how colonization influenced the city development and architecture in Latin American countries.
- Learn about recycling and initiatives to protect the environment.
- Learn about the history and origin of some Spanish music and dance.

3.2. Viewpoints through language/culture
- Read dialogues, informative text, and literary texts in Spanish that provide insight into Hispanic cultures.

Communicative Skills

Interpersonal Mode

		Activities
Speaking	• Exchange opinions or experiences. • Identify and describe articles of clothing, places, or objects to a partner. • Compare information with a classmate. • Ask and answer questions with a partner.	• 7, 29, 32, 50, 74, 75 • 7, 26, 35, 78, 79, 81 • 20, 71, 74, 78 • 24, 41, 59, 79
Writing	• Write a list of items or aspects related to an image or topic. • Write a dialogue with a partner.	• 3, 36, 45 • 2, 11
Listening	• Obtain information from a conversation. • Understand descriptions or clues from a partner.	• 20, 41, 50, 71, 74 • 44, 46
Reading	• Understand descriptive sentences or paragraphs.	• 1, 11

Interpretive Mode

		Activities
Listening	• Obtain information from dialogues. • Understand oral descriptions or narrations.	• 2, 10, 16, 19, 32, 39, 56, 67 • 44, 50, 60
Reading	• Demonstrate comprehension of written exchanges and longer written dialogues. • Reflect on cultural topics in relation to personal knowledge and experience. • Demonstrate comprehension of an informative text. • Understand and obtain information from an e-mail.	• 5, 6, 11, 22, 23, 29, 30, 31, 45, 54, 55, 69, 77 • 12, 21, 33, 37, 42, 57, 61, 70 • 1, 27, 47, 48 • 40, 65
Viewing	• Connect information or descriptions to images. • Obtain information from an image.	• 2, 19, 32, 44, 54, 60 • 3, 7, 16, 24, 26, 28, 36, 56, 75

Presentational Mode

		Activities
Speaking	• Act out a dialogue or short skit aloud. • Present a description or a story to the class. • Present an original creation to the class.	• 2, 11 • 49, 73 • 52, 73, 76, *Escritura, Proyecto*
Writing	• Write sentences or a paragraph to describe clothing. • Write sentences or a paragraph to describe objects or places. • Retell a story or write the end of a story. • Write an essay and present it to the class.	• 3, 7, 16, 78, 80 • 36, 44, 49, 50, 51, 52, 79, 80 • 72, 73 • *Escritura*
Visually Representing	• Present information related to the unit using visuals. • Draw a plan, design clothing, or illustrate a story. • Create a poster, a collage, or a brochure.	• 4, 24, 73, 76, 80, 81 • 4, 24, 73 • 52, 76, *Proyecto*

Cross-Curricular Standards

Subject	Standard	Activities
Language Arts	• Compare elements of Spanish grammar with English equivalents. • Use the writing process to create an essay.	• 13, 17, 38, 43, 62, 66 • *Escritura*
Social Studies	• Read and talk about some types of Spanish architecture. • Read about and research colonial cities in Latin America.	• 42, 70, 80, *Mapa cultural, Proyecto* • *Mapa cultural, Proyecto*
Art	• Create drawings or illustrations.	• 24, 73, 80
Science	• Demonstrate awareness of environmental preservation.	• 21
Music	• Learn about the origin of flamenco music.	• 56, 57

Unit 3 Tus cosas

Lesson Plans (50-Minute Classes)

Day	Objectives	Sessions	Activities	Time	Standards	Resources/Homework
1	To introduce clothing, housing, and the characters' challenges, and to review learned vocabulary	**Tus cosas/Las tareas/Antes de empezar** (120–125) • Warm-Up: Topic orientation • Presentation: *Tradiciones con mucho estilo* • *Expresiones útiles* and *Recuerda*	 1 2–4	 10 m. 20 m. 20 m.	1.1, 1.2, 1.3, 2.1, 2.2, 3.1, 3.2, 5.1	Visual Presentation Audio Video Practice Workbook
2	To talk about recent actions	**Desafío 1 – Un traje muy especial** (126–127) • Warm-Up: Independent Starter • *Texto: Un traje muy especial* • *Cultura: Los trajes regionales*	 5–7 8	 5 m. 35 m. 10 m.	1.1, 1.2, 1.3, 2.1, 2.2, 3.1, 3.2, 4.2	Visual Presentation Audio Video
3	To describe how clothing looks and fits	**Desafío 1 – Vocabulario** (128–129) • Warm-Up: Independent Starter • Vocabulary: *La ropa* • *Cultura: La moda hispana*	 9–11 12	 5 m. 35 m. 10 m.	1.1, 1.2, 1.3, 2.2, 3.1, 5.1	Audio Practice Workbook
4	To learn and use forms of past participles	**Desafío 1 – Gramática** (130–131) • Warm-Up: Independent Starter • Grammar: *El participio*	 13–16	 5 m. 45 m.	1.1, 1.2, 1.3, 2.2, 3.1, 4.1	Audio Practice Workbook
5	To talk about recent events using the present perfect tense	**Desafío 1 – Gramática** (132–133) • Warm-Up: Independent Starter • Grammar: *Hablar de acciones recientes. El presente perfecto* • *Conexiones: El reciclaje*	 17–20 21	 5 m. 35 m. 10 m.	1.1, 1.2, 1.3, 2.1, 3.1, 4.1, 4.2, 5.1, 5.2	Audio Practice Workbook
6	To understand a dialogue and to integrate vocabulary and grammar	**Desafío 1 – Lectura/Comunicación** (134–137) • Warm-Up: Independent Starter • *Lectura: Un traje tradicional* • *Comunicación:* Review • *Final del desafío*	 22–25 26–28 29	 5 m. 20 m. 15 m. 10 m.	1.1, 1.2, 1.3, 2.1, 2.2, 3.1, 3.2, 5.1	Visual Presentation Practice Workbook *Tu desafío* Quiz on *Desafío 1*
7	To describe objects	**Desafío 2 – Describir objetos** (138–139) • Warm-Up: Independent Starter • *Texto: En busca del símbolo perdido* • *Cultura: La wiphala*	 30–32 33	 5 m. 35 m. 10 m.	1.1, 1.2, 2.2, 3.2, 4.2	Visual Presentation Audio
8	To use words to describe the shape, texture, and makeup of objects	**Desafío 2 – Vocabulario** (140–141) • Warm-Up: Independent Starter • Vocabulary: *Describir objetos* • *Cultura: El mercado de Otavalo (Ecuador)*	 34–36 37	 5 m. 35 m. 10 m.	1.1, 1.2, 1.3, 2.1, 2.2, 3.2, 5.1, 5.2	Audio Practice Workbook
9	To learn indefinite adjectives and pronouns	**Desafío 2 – Gramática** (142–143) • Warm-Up: Independent Starter • Grammar: *Los indefinidos* • *Cultura: Las haciendas coloniales*	 38–41 42	 5 m. 35 m. 10 m.	1.1, 1.2, 1.3, 2.1, 2.2, 3.1, 4.1, 4,2, 5.1	Audio Practice Workbook
10	To learn the construction of the impersonal pronoun *se*	**Desafío 2 – Gramática** (144–145) • Warm-Up: Independent Starter • Grammar: *Construcciones impersonales. El pronombre 'se'*	 43–46	 5 m. 45 m.	1.1, 1.2, 1.3, 3.1, 4.1, 5.2	Audio Practice Workbook

Day	Objectives	Sessions	Activities	Time	Standards	Resources / Homework
11	To understand information in a hotel guide and to integrate vocabulary and grammar	**Desafío 2 – Lectura/Comunicación** (146–149) • Warm-Up: Independent Starter • *Lectura: Guía de viajeros: un hotel inolvidable* • *Comunicación:* Review • *Final del desafío*	47–49 50–52 53	5 m. 20 m. 15 m. 10 m.	1.1, 1.2, 1.3, 2.2, 3.1, 3.2, 4.2, 5.1	Audio Practice Workbook *Tu desafío* Quiz on *Desafío 2*
12	To talk about past experiences	**Desafío 3 – Un festival de flamenco** (150–151) • Warm-Up: Correct quiz on *Desafío 2* • *Texto: Un festival de flamenco* • *Cultura: El flamenco*	54–56 57	5 m. 35 m. 10 m.	1.1, 1.2, 1.3, 2.1, 2.2, 3.1, 3.2, 4.2, 5.2	Visual Presentation Audio
13	To identify domestic tasks and jobs	**Desafío 3 – Vocabulario** (152–153) • Warm-Up: Independent Starter • Vocabulary: *Tareas domésticas y oficios* • *Cultura: Las supersticiones*	58–60 61	5 m. 35 m. 10 m.	1.1, 1.2, 1.3, 2.1, 3.2, 4.2, 5.1	Audio Practice Workbook
14	To learn the past perfect tense	**Desafío 3 – Gramática** (154–155) • Warm-Up: Independent Starter • Grammar: *El pluscuamperfecto*	62–65	5 m. 45 m.	1.1, 1.2, 1.3, 2.1, 3.1, 4.1	Audio Practice Workbook
15	To learn and use demonstrative adjectives and pronouns	**Desafío 3 – Gramática** (156–157) • Warm-Up: Independent Starter • Grammar: *Los demostrativos* • *Comparaciones: Los patios cordobeses (España)*	66–69 70	5 m. 35 m. 10 m.	1.1, 1.2, 1.3, 2.1, 2.2, 3.1, 4.1, 5.1	Audio Video Practice Workbook
16	To understand a literary text	**Desafío 3 – Lectura** (158–159) • Warm-Up: Independent Starter • *Lectura: La casa de muñecas*	71–73	5 m. 45 m.	1.1, 1.2, 1.3, 3.1	
17	To integrate vocabulary and grammar	**Desafío 3 – Comunicación** (160–161) • Warm-Up: Independent Starter • *Comunicación:* Review • *Final del desafío*	74–76 77	5 m. 30 m. 15 m.	1.1, 1.2, 1.3, 2.1, 2.2, 3.1, 5.1	Practice Workbook Quiz on *Desafío 3* **Para terminar –** **Tu desafío** (163)
18	To integrate language in context	**Para terminar** (162–163) • Warm-Up: Correct quiz on *Desafío 3* • *Todo junto* • *Tu desafío* presentations	78–79 80	5 m. 20 m. 25 m.	1.1, 1.2, 1.3, 2.1, 2.2, 3.1, 4.2, 5.1	Practice Workbook
19	To assess student proficiency and to learn about Spanish colonial cities in Latin America	**Evaluación/Mapa cultural** (164–165) • Warm-Up: Independent Starter • Quiz on *Desafíos 1–3* • *Mapa cultural: La ciudad colonial*	81	5 m. 15 m. 30 m.	1.1, 1.2, 2.1, 3.1	Video Practice Workbook
20	To create an essay or expository text	**Escritura** (166–167) • Warm-Up: Independent Starter • *Escritura: Un ensayo de moda*		5 m. 45 m.	1.1, 1.2, 1.3, 3.1, 5.1, 5.2	Project work
21	To design promotional materials	**Proyecto** (172–173) • Warm-Up: Prepare project presentations • Project presentations		10 m. 40 m.	1.1, 1.2, 1.3, 2.1, 2.2, 3.1, 5.1, 5.2	**Repaso – Vocabulario** (168–169) **Repaso – Gramática** (170–171) **Autoevaluación** (173)

Lesson Plans (90-Minute Classes)

Day	Objectives	Sessions	Activities	Time	Standards	Resources/ Homework
1	To introduce clothing, housing, and the characters' challenges, and to review learned vocabulary	(See Day 12 Unit 2) ***Tus cosas/Las tareas/Antes de empezar*** (120–125) • Warm-Up: Topic orientation • Presentation: *Tradiciones con mucho estilo* • *Expresiones útiles* and *Recuerda*	 1 2–4	(45 m.) 10 m. 20 m. 15 m.	1.1, 1.2, 1.3, 2.1, 2.2, 3.1, 3.2, 5.1	Visual Presentation Audio Video Practice Workbook
2	To talk about recent actions, and to describe how clothing looks and fits	***Desafío 1 – Un traje muy especial/Vocabulario*** (126–129) • Warm-Up: Independent Starter • *Texto: Un traje muy especial* • *Cultura: Los trajes regionales* • Vocabulary: *La ropa* • *Cultura: La moda hispana*	 5–7 8 9–11 12	 5 m. 30 m. 10 m. 35 m. 10 m.	1.1, 1.2, 1.3, 2.1, 2.2, 3.1, 3.2, 4.2, 5.1	Visual Presentation Audio Video Practice Workbook
3	To learn and use forms of past participles, and to talk about recent events using the present perfect tense	***Desafío 1 – Gramática*** (130–133) • Warm-Up: Independent Starter • Grammar: *El participio* • Grammar: *Hablar de acciones recientes. El presente perfecto* • *Conexiones: El reciclaje*	 13–16 17–20 21	 5 m. 35 m. 40 m. 10 m.	1.1, 1.2, 1.3, 2.1, 2.2, 3.1, 4.1, 4.2, 5.1, 5.2	Audio Practice Workbook
4	To understand a dialogue and to integrate vocabulary and grammar	***Desafío 1 – Lectura/Comunicación/Evaluación*** (134–137) • Warm-Up: Independent Starter • *Lectura: Un traje tradicional* • *Comunicación:* Review • *Final del desafío* • Quiz on *Desafío 1*	 22–25 26–28 29	 5 m. 35 m. 25 m. 10 m. 15 m.	1.1, 1.2, 1.3, 2.1, 2.2, 3.1, 3.2, 5.1	Visual Presentation Audio Practice Workbook *Tu desafío*
5	To describe objects and to use words to describe the shape, texture, and makeup of objects	***Desafío 2 – Describir objetos/Vocabulario*** (138–141) • Warm-Up: Independent Starter • *Texto: En busca del símbolo perdido* • *Cultura: La wiphala* • Vocabulary: *Describir objetos* • *Cultura: El mercado de Otavalo (Ecuador)*	 30–32 33 34–36 37	 5 m. 30 m. 10 m. 35 m. 10 m.	1.1, 1.2, 1.3, 2.1, 2.2, 3.2, 4,2, 5.1, 5.2	Visual Presentation Audio Practice Workbook
6	To learn indefinite adjectives and pronouns and to learn the construction of the impersonal pronoun se	***Desafío 2 – Gramática*** (142–145) • Warm-Up: Independent Starter • Grammar: *Los indefinidos* • *Cultura: Las haciendas coloniales* • Grammar: *Construcciones impersonales. El pronombre 'se'*	 38–41 42 43–46	 5 m. 35 m. 10 m. 40 m.	1.1, 1.2, 1.3, 2.1, 2.2, 3.1, 4.1, 5.1, 5.2	Audio Practice Workbook

Day	Objectives	Sessions	Activities	Time	Standards	Resources / Homework
7	To understand a text in a hotel guide and to integrate vocabulary and grammar	**Desafío 2 – Lectura/Comunicación/Evaluación** (146–149) • Warm-Up: Independent Starter • *Lectura: Guía de viajeros: un hotel inolvidable* • *Comunicación:* Review • *Final del desafío* • Quiz on *Desafío 2*	 47–49 50–52 53	 5 m. 35 m. 25 m. 10 m. 15 m.	1.1, 1.2, 1.3, 2.2, 3.1, 3.2, 4.2, 5.1	Audio Practice Workbook *Tu desafío*
8	To talk about past experiences and to identify domestic tasks and jobs	**Desafío 3 – Un festival de flamenco/ Vocabulario** (150–153) • Warm-Up: Independent Starter • *Texto: Un festival de flamenco* • *Cultura: El flamenco* • Vocabulary: *Tareas domésticas y oficios* • *Cultura: Las supersticiones*	 54–56 57 58–60 61	 5 m. 30 m. 10 m. 35 m. 10 m.	1.1, 1.2, 1.3, 2.1, 2.2, 3.1, 3.2, 4.2, 5.1, 5.2	Visual Presentation Audio Practice Workbook
9	To learn the past perfect tense and to learn demonstrative adjectives and pronouns	**Desafío 3 – Gramática** (154–157) • Warm-Up: Independent Starter • Grammar: *El pluscuamperfecto* • Grammar: *Los demostrativos* • *Comparaciones: Los patios cordobeses (España)*	 62–65 66–69 70	 5 m. 40 m. 35 m. 10 m.	1.1, 1.2, 1.3, 2.1, 2.2, 3.1, 4.1, 5.1	Audio Video Practice Workbook
10	To understand a literary text, to integrate vocabulary and grammar, to integrate language in context, and to assess student proficiency	**Desafío 3 – Lectura/Comunicación/Evaluación/ Todo junto** (158–162) • Warm-Up: Independent Starter • *Lectura: La casa de muñecas* • *Comunicación:* Review • *Final del desafío* • *Todo junto* • Quiz on *Desafío 3*	 71–73 74–76 77 78–79	 5 m. 25 m. 20 m. 10 m. 15 m. 15 m.	1.1, 1.2, 1.3, 2.1, 2.2, 3.1, 5.1	Practice Workbook **Para terminar – Tu desafío** (163)
11	To learn about Spanish colonial cities in Latin America and to create an essay or expository text	**Tu desafío/Mapa cultural/Escritura** (163–167) • Warm-Up: Independent Starter • *Tu desafío* presentations • *Mapa cultural: La ciudad colonial* • *Escritura: Un ensayo de moda*	 80 81	 5 m. 15 m. 30 m. 40 m.	1.1, 1.2, 1.3, 2.1, 2.2, 3.1, 4.2, 5.1, 5.2	Video Practice Workbook **Repaso – Vocabulario** (168–169) **Repaso – Gramática** (170–171) Quiz on *Desafíos 1–3* Project work
12	To design promotional materials	**Proyecto/Assessment** (172–173) • Warm-Up: Correct quiz on *Desafíos 1–3* • Project presentations • *Autoevaluación* • Test (See Day 1 Unit 4)		 5 m. 15 m. 10 m. 15 m. (45 m.)	1.1, 1.2, 1.3, 2.1, 2.2, 3.1, 5.1, 5.2	

Unit 3 Tus cosas

2 **¿Me haces un favor?**

1. –¿Me haces un favor?
   –Dime.
   –¿Me ayudas a ordenar mi habitación? Es que tengo que estudiar mucho y no me da tiempo.
   –Vale, está bien.
2. –¿Puedes hacerme un favor?
   –Claro.
   –¿Me planchas esta camisa? Es que tengo que arreglarme y no quiero llegar tarde.
   –Lo siento, pero no puedo. Tengo muchas cosas que hacer. ¿Por qué no te pones otra?
3. –¿Puedes ayudarme?
   –¿Qué te pasa?
   –Pues que me han invitado a una fiesta y necesito comprarme un vestido. ¿Puedes venir conmigo de compras para ayudarme a elegir uno?
   –Claro. ¿Vamos esta tarde?
   –Sí, qué bien. Muchas gracias.

10 **De compras**

1. –Lola, este vestido es precioso. ¿Quieres que lo compremos para el baile de la semana que viene?
   –No sé... Es que no me gusta la tela. El terciopelo me parece demasiado formal.
2. –¿Te queda bien la camisa? ¿Te la vas a comprar?
   –No, no me gusta nada. Las mangas son muy largas.
3. –¿Me puedes traer otra falda, por favor?
   –¿Más pequeña o más grande?
   –De la misma talla. Es que a esta le falta un botón.
4. –Mamá, ¿me puedes ayudar?
   –Claro, hija. ¿Qué te pasa?
   –La cremallera de este vestido no cierra, creo que está rota.
5. –¿Qué tal le quedan los zapatos?
   –Me aprietan un poco. ¿Puedo probarme una talla más, por favor?
   –Claro, ahora se los traigo.

16 **En la tienda de artesanía**

–Buenos días. ¿En qué puedo ayudarlo?
–Buenos días, señor. Estoy buscando ropa tradicional de algún país de la zona andina.
–Pues tenemos unos ponchos muy coloridos.
–¿Están hechos de forma artesanal?
–Sí, claro. Todos están tejidos con lana y están diseñados con los colores y los dibujos típicos de su región.
–¿Y ese sombrero que está puesto en el maniquí? ¿También es de la zona andina?
–No, es un sombrero de Panamá. Bueno, se llama así, pero realmente es típico de Ecuador.
–¡Qué curioso! ¿Y tiene otros complementos?
–Claro. Mire, en ese estante hay guantes y bufandas traídos de Chile. Y allí hay bolsos y zapatos fabricados con cuero.
–Muchas gracias, voy a verlos.

19 **¿Qué ha hecho hoy Clara?**

Esta mañana he estado de compras en unos grandes almacenes. Primero he entrado en una zapatería y me he comprado unas botas de tacón. Después he ido a una tienda de ropa y me he probado un vestido, pero no lo he comprado porque no me quedaba bien. Luego he almorzado en una cafetería. Y, finalmente, he ido a una tienda de artesanía a comprar un regalo para mi esposo porque mañana es su cumpleaños.

32 **El símbolo perfecto**

–Mira, Asha, tengo algunos símbolos antiguos. ¿Me ayudas a elegir uno?
–Claro, a ver qué encontraste.
–Este es de Ecuador, está en su escudo y en su bandera.
–Ah, claro. Es el cóndor, el símbolo del país. Es muy bonito. ¿Y este? Es muy parecido.
–Es la bandera de México. Tiene un águila y una serpiente. Pero no sé si es una buena idea...
–¿Y este? Parece una bandera. Me encanta, es muy colorido.
–Sí, déjame ver cómo se llama. ¡Es perfecto! Es la wiphala y representa a los pueblos indígenas de los Andes.
–¿Y qué significa?
–No lo sé. Vamos a seguir leyendo.

34 **Las compras**

–Gracias por avisarme de este evento. No sabía que el museo de arte indígena de la ciudad organizaba un mercado de artesanía.
–De nada. Seguro que encontramos algún símbolo interesante.
–Es posible. Además yo quiero comprar algunas cosas. La semana que viene es el cumpleaños de mi abuela y a ella le encanta la artesanía.
–¿Qué te parece ese bote de cuero?
–¿El cuadrado o el redondo?
–El cuadrado. Es perfecto para poner mis lápices y bolígrafos.
–Ah, sí. Es muy bonito. ¿Te lo vas a llevar?
–No sé... No estoy seguro. Oye, Asha, ¿no crees que esta mesa pequeña de café le gustará a tu abuela? Aquí dice que es de madera natural y de muy buena calidad.
–¡Qué buena idea! Pero es demasiado cara... no puedo comprarla. Creo que voy a buscar algo más personal.
–¿Qué tal alguna joya?
–Sí... Esta pulsera de piedras verdosas es muy elegante y es bastante barata. Me la voy a llevar.
–Pues yo voy a comprar este plato de cerámica. Me gustan mucho los dibujos y es muy colorido. Lo puedo poner en la pared.
–Vamos a pagar. ¡Venir hoy aquí ha sido una gran idea, Lucas!

39 **La habitación de Lucas**

–Asha, ¿me echas una mano?
–Claro, ¿qué quieres?
–No sé dónde poner estos libros que compré, mi habitación es un desastre...
–A ver, en la estantería no los puedes poner porque ya hay demasiados libros y no hay espacio para ninguno más. ¿Por qué no los pones en tu escritorio?

–No, ahí es donde estudio y ya tengo muchos cuadernos y papeles.

–¡Ya sé! Ponlos en la mesa redonda del pasillo.

–No, es que ahí hay algunos floreros y muchos adornos de mi madre. Creo que voy a poner los libros en el suelo, entre la estantería y el escritorio.

–Pero ahí tienes los videojuegos.

–Ya, pero tengo pocos. Los voy a guardar en el armario.

–¡Oye, Lucas! ¿Pero cuántos zapatos tienes?

–Pues, bastantes, pero los uso todos.

44 Adivina, adivinanza

1. Se hacen de cristal y normalmente se colocan en las paredes.
2. Se fabrican con diversos materiales, como plata, piedras, cristal o incluso plástico. Se pueden comprar en mercados, almacenes y tiendas especializadas.
3. Generalmente se hacen de cuero o de tela y se pueden comprar en tiendas de muebles.
4. Se hacen con lana y algunos se fabrican a mano.

50 ¡Vamos al mercado!

1. Quiero vender esta lámpara de cristal. El estilo no es muy moderno, pero es muy bonita. ¿Dónde puedo venderla?
2. Yo hago alfombras al estilo tradicional, con una lana muy suave de colores brillantes. ¿Dónde las puedo vender?
3. Mi abuela y yo somos de una familia indígena. Hacemos objetos de cerámica de estilo tradicional: bandejas y vasos muy coloridos con imágenes de animales y plantas. ¿Dónde podemos venderlos?
4. Necesito vender unos adornos que encontré en mi desván. Están muy bien conservados y son muy elegantes. ¿Qué mercado me recomiendan?

56 ¿Qué sabes del flamenco?

–Antes me contaste algunas cosas sobre el flamenco, Eva. ¿Qué más sabes?

–Ya te dije que no sé mucho, pero me gusta. Es un tipo de música que nació hace mucho tiempo en Andalucía y que hoy se conoce en todo el mundo.

–¿El flamenco es lo mismo que las sevillanas?

–Bueno, las sevillanas son un baile folclórico típico de Sevilla relacionado con el flamenco. Pero el flamenco es un estilo musical y tiene muchos bailes.

–Se baila y se canta, ¿no es cierto?

–Sí. Eso es.

–¿Y conoces a algún cantante o bailarín de flamenco?

–Sí. Pero no se llaman cantantes ni bailarines, se llaman cantaores y bailaores.

–Ah, no lo sabía.

60 ¿A quién llamamos?

1. La lámpara no funciona, está estropeada.
2. Quiero pintar la pared de la sala porque no me gusta el color.
3. ¡Hay agua saliendo del lavaplatos!
4. Este armario tiene las puertas rotas, hay que cambiarlas.

64 Oraciones lógicas

1. No puse el lavaplatos porque no había comprado lavavajillas.
2. Sequé los platos porque mi padre los había lavado.
3. Tuve que lavar de nuevo la ropa porque había llovido.
4. Coloqué la ropa en el armario porque mi madre la había planchado.
5. Tendí la ropa en el tendedero porque había dejado de llover.
6. Hice la cama de mi hermano porque él me había ayudado a limpiar.

67 En la florería

–¡Cuántas plantas! ¿Qué compramos?

–A mí me gustan estas rosas.

–Son muy bonitas, pero es una flor muy delicada.

–Ay, mira aquellos tulipanes. Son muy coloridos. Pero Ethan, recuerda que la decoración tiene que tener un estilo andaluz. Y los tulipanes no son típicos de Andalucía.

–Tienes razón.

–Mi compañera me dijo que en los patios y en los balcones de las casas de Andalucía hay muchos geranios.

–¿Y cuáles son los geranios, estos?

–No, son esos de ahí, ¿los ves?

–Ah, sí. ¡Cuántos colores! De acuerdo, pues compramos unos geranios.

Unit 3
Tus cosas

The Unit

- The theme for Unit 3 is personal belongings. The participants will learn how to express recent and past actions, and how to describe objects and talk about domestic chores.

- Tess, a veteran of *Fans del español*, will give the participants their tasks.

  - *Desafío 1.* Michelle and Daniel have to choose a traditional costume from a Spanish-speaking country and adapt the design to their personal taste.

  - *Desafío 2.* Asha and Lucas must choose an indigenous symbol and incorporate it into the décor of an *hacienda* in Ecuador.

  - *Desafío 3.* Eva and Ethan will organize a flamenco festival, but first they must clean up and decorate the room where the festival will take place.

Activities	Standards	Resources
Tus cosas	1.2, 2.1, 2.2, 3.1, 5.1	Video

Teaching Suggestions

Warm-Up / Independent Starter

- Ask students to look at the photos and come up with a description for one of the images. They may reactivate the vocabulary they have previously learned about clothes in a short paragraph in which they describe what people are wearing.

Preparation

- Ask students to read the captions and predict what the topic for each challenge might be. For example, they may answer that the first image is about wearing or making a traditional dress; the second is about national symbols (e.g., flags) or indigenous cultures; and the last image may be about participating in a flamenco show.

- Have students read each *Desafío's* objective, as well as the vocabulary and grammar goals, then discuss how each picture might relate to these objectives and goals.

120

UNIDAD 3
Tus cosas
La ropa y la vivienda

DESAFÍO 1

Mujer con la wiphala (Bolivia)

DESAFÍO 2

▶ **Hablar de acciones recientes**

Vocabulario
Ropa

Gramática
El participio

Hablar de acciones recientes. El presente perfecto

▶ **Describir objetos**

Vocabulario
Describir objetos

Gramática
Los indefinidos

Construcciones impersonales. El pronombre *se*

Traje regional (Guatemala)

120 ciento veinte

The Challenge

DESAFÍO 1

Traje regional

Most regions of the world have a traditional dress that, if no longer worn in everyday life, is likely still used in ceremonies or regional festivities. The variety of these costumes in Latin America is enormous, depending on the climate, the materials found in the region, and local customs and traditions. Some of the garments that make up these costumes are well known internationally, such as the Peruvian *poncho*, the Argentinean *bombachas* (gaucho pants), or the *bombín*, a bowler hat typical of Bolivian outfits.

DESAFÍO 2

Mujer con la wiphala

A symbol is something that is used to represent something else. A flag, for instance, may symbolize a country, a state, a city, or even a sports team. Native peoples of the Americas use a variety of symbols on buildings, artwork, and even in clothing. Some of these symbols identify a tribe, clan, or family. Others represent religious beliefs, geographical features, animals, natural phenomena, etc. The Wiphala—a seven-color flag—is an example of a recognizable Amerindian symbol used by several indigenous communities of the Andes.

Tus cosas

Picture Discussion

- Have students look at the images again and review their predictions about each topic. Then ask them to read the descriptions from their Independent Starter and share their predictions and any information they may have on these topics in a class discussion.

Traje regional (Guatemala)

- Ask students to explain where the country of Guatemala is located and what ethnic group is predominant there. Ask them questions about the colors, patterns, and shapes of the garments shown in the picture. Write the word *huipil* on the board and explain that it is a type of blouse, like the one shown in the photo, worn by Maya women.

Mujer con la wiphala (Bolivia)

- Focus students' attention on the people in the photo and their clothes. Where might they be from? Ask students to locate the country of Bolivia on a map of Latin America. Call their attention to the fact that these people carry a flag. Compare its colors with those of the Bolivian flag. If it is not the official Bolivian flag, what people could this flag be a symbol for? Explain that they will learn about the Wiphala, a flag that is used by the native people of the Andes region.

Espectáculo de flamenco (España)

- Ask students if they know about flamenco dance and music. Do they know where it originated and where it is still performed? Have students describe the clothes that the dancers are wearing. Ask they if they know what instruments are used to accompany flamenco, and explain that the guitar, and different types of percussion—such as hand clapping and foot tapping—are often used to accompany the voices and the dance.

Objectives

- By the end of Unit 3, students will be able to
  - Discuss clothes.
  - Talk about recent actions.
  - Describe objects.
  - Describe past experiences.
  - Talk about chores.
  - Talk about some regional costumes and symbols from the Spanish-speaking world, haciendas in Latin America, and flamenco dance and music.

DESAFÍO

3

▶ **Hablar de experiencias pasadas**

Vocabulario
Tareas domésticas y oficios

Gramática
El pluscuamperfecto

Los demostrativos

Espectáculo de flamenco (España)

DESAFÍO 3

Espectáculo de flamenco

Flamenco is a musical art that originated in the southern Spanish region of Andalusia. It manifests itself through singing, guitar playing, and dancing. Its richness and expressivity derives from the fusion of the many cultures that, for centuries, made this Spanish region home for the Romani people (gypsies), the Arabs, the Christians, and the Sephardic Jews. In recent times, flamenco has been open to other types of fusion that include a variety of musical genres, such as jazz, bossa nova, and samba.

Presentation

- In this section, Lucas listens to a message left in his voicemail by Tess, a former participant, who informs him of the challenges that lie ahead. He must then inform the others. Students will preview useful expressions for asking for a favor, asking for help or further information, and offering help or further information.

Activities	Standards	Resources
Texto	1.2, 2.1, 2.2, 3.2	Vis. Pres.
1.	1.1, 1.2	

Teaching Suggestions

Warm-Up / Independent Starter

- Have students list, in a three-column chart, all of the expressions they know in Spanish for asking for a favor, asking for help, and offering help. For example:

Pedir un favor	Pedir ayuda	Ofrecer ayuda
¿Me haces un favor?	¿Puedes ayudarme?	¿Necesitas ayuda?

Preparation

- Invite volunteers to share their Independent Starters. Discuss the uses of the expressions students mention and make corrections where needed. Help them write complete sentences with these expressions. Then ask students to read through the text on this page and classify, in the same chart, the expressions they find for asking for a favor, asking for help, and offering help. (¿Puedes hacerme un favor? ¿Puedes explicárselas a tus compañeros? No duden en enviarnos cualquier pregunta.) You may also have students choose three people in the class to practice asking for a favor, asking for help with something, and offering help.

- You may want to preview the construction used to express recent actions: haber + participle. Ask students to point out this use in the text. (he hablado, hemos decidido) Invite students to try to guess the meaning of these two phrases. (I have spoken, we have decided)

122

Tradiciones con mucho estilo

 Lucas has a message from Tess in his voicemail explaining the new tasks for each pair. He will have to inform his friends. Read the text in order to discover what each one will have to do.

Hola, Lucas. ¿Qué tal? Espero que estén todos bien.

¿Puedes hacerme un favor? Es que tengo que salir de viaje y tengo mucha prisa. Esta mañana he hablado con Diana sobre las nuevas tareas para ustedes. ¿Puedes explicárselas a tus compañeros? Esto es lo que hemos decidido:

Daniel y Michelle tienen que elegir un traje regional de un país hispano y adaptarlo, dándole un toque personal.

El desafío para Asha y para ti es muy emocionante porque pueden ganar un concurso: deben elegir un símbolo indígena para integrarlo en la decoración de una hacienda en Ecuador. Y si ganan… ¡podrán alojarse allí un fin de semana! Anímense.

Por último, la tarea de Ethan y Eva es un poco diferente. Van a organizar un festival de flamenco.

Diana y yo les deseamos mucha suerte. Y, por favor, no duden en enviarnos cualquier pregunta. ¡Hasta pronto!

Differentiated Instruction

DEVELOPING LEARNERS

- Ask students to work with a partner and role-play the characters in the dialogue on page 123. Ask them to pay special attention to each character's tone, so that it mirrors his or her point of view. For example, Daniel shows some apprehension, perhaps even a bit of fear, about the task put before him. As students reenact the dialogues, monitor their intonation and pronunciation and make suggestions as to improvement. Allow pairs to practice their roles and then call on some to present their dialogues before the class.

EXPANDING LEARNERS

- Have students create new dialogues between the pairs for all of the challenges. This time around, ask them to reverse the roles of the participants, so those who previously showed apprehension are now the more positive of the two. Be sure that students understand that completely new dialogues are needed. For example:

  Michelle: ¡Ay, esto va a ser imposible! Ninguno de los dos sabemos coser y no sé nada de los trajes regionales.

  Daniel: No te preocupes. No vamos a coser. Simplemente vamos a añadir algún detalle nuestro al traje.

¿Tenemos que diseñar un traje? ¡Eso es dificilísimo!

No, hombre, solo tenemos que cambiarle algún detalle para hacerlo más moderno.

Explícame qué son las haciendas, por favor.

Son unas casas de campo muy grandes, de estilo colonial. Son típicas de Ecuador, Perú, Colombia y otros países hispanos.

¿Un festival de flamenco? ¡Yo no sé nada de eso! Espero que alguien nos ayude.

Seguro que lo conseguimos. Hay mucha gente a la que le encanta el flamenco.

1 ¿Comprendes?

▶ **Responde** a estas preguntas.

1. ¿Qué tienen que hacer Michelle y Daniel? ¿Qué opina Daniel sobre esa tarea?

2. ¿Qué tienen que hacer Asha y Lucas? ¿Qué sabe Asha sobre las haciendas?

3. ¿Qué tienen que hacer Eva y Ethan? ¿Qué saben Eva y Ethan sobre el flamenco?

▶ **Lee** los textos y busca el significado de tres palabras que no entiendas. Después, explica su significado en un ejemplo usando tus propias palabras.

Modelo   concurso

→ *Es una competencia donde participan varias personas para conseguir un premio.*

▶ **Lee** las oraciones de tu compañero(a). ¿A qué palabras corresponden sus oraciones?

ciento veintitrés 123

Texto: Tradiciones con mucho estilo

- Have students scan the text, looking for these three elements that relate to the photos they have previously discussed: *traje regional*, *símbolo indígena*, and *festival de flamenco*. In order to help them focus on the challenges, ask students to write down the verbs that relate to those elements. (*traje → elegir, adaptarlo*; *símbolo indígena → elegir, integrarlo*; *festival de flamenco → organizar*)

- After reading the text individually, have students write down the three challenges. Then discuss them with the class, asking further comprehension questions: *¿Qué deben hacer Daniel y Michelle después de elegir el traje regional? ¿Para qué necesitan Asha y Lucas un símbolo indígena? ¿Cómo es la tarea de Michelle y Daniel?*

Activities

1. Explore the vocabulary further by writing expressions or words on the board that may be unfamiliar to students or that they may not remember. For example: *tener prisa, dar un toque personal, alojarse, animarse*. Do not translate them into English. Instead, explain their meaning with gestures and by using them in other contexts.

Answer Key

1. 1. Tienen que elegir un traje regional de un país hispano y adaptarlo. Daniel piensa que es dificilísimo.

   2. Deben elegir un símbolo indígena para integrarlo en la decoración de una hacienda en Ecuador. Asha sabe que las haciendas son casas de campo de estilo colonial.

   3. Tienen que organizar un festival de flamenco. Eva y Ethan no saben nada sobre el flamenco.

   ▶ Answers will vary.

   ▶ Answers will vary.

Additional Resources

Fans Online activities
Practice Workbook

HERITAGE LANGUAGE LEARNERS

- Ask students to work in groups of three and imagine that a TV reporter is going to interview the participants in this unit's *Desafíos*. Have them role-play the reporter and each of the student pairs. The reporter will ask each pair what their challenge is and how confident they feel about completing it. The participating pairs will answer the reporter's questions and add any other information they can share on the topic of their challenge. Allow students time to practice their interviews and call on volunteer groups to make a presentation before the class.

CRITICAL THINKING

- Now that students know more about the participating pairs, ask them which one they think will complete their challenge the most successfully and why. Remind students to base their opinions on what the pairs have accomplished in the first two units, and how well they work together. Students also have the option of having the pairs change partners so that they might best achieve their goal. When students have come to a decision, discuss their predictions and their changes to the participating pairs, tally the results, and see which team is the class favorite.

123

Unit 3
Antes de empezar

Presentation

- In this section, students will learn a variety of useful expressions, some for asking for a favor or help and others for offering help. They will practice these expressions in brief dialogues.

- Students will also review vocabulary they already know related to clothes and the household.

Activities	Standards	Resources
Expresiones útiles	1.2, 2.1	
2.	1.1, 1.2, 1.3	Audio
Recuerda	1.2	
3.	1.1	
4.	1.1, 1.3, 3.1	

Teaching Suggestions

Warm-Up / Independent Starter

- Give students two minutes to list objects and pieces of clothes that they have in their bedrooms. Challenge students to list as many things as they can in the time allotted. To get them started you may suggest: *computadora, libros, mesita de noche, lámpara, cama, pantalones, calcetines, zapatos, suéter, camisa.*

Preparation

- Go over the *expresiones útiles* by using them in personalized contexts. For example, you might ask a student for a favor or help by telling him or her the following: 1. *¿Me haces un favor, Carla? ¿Puedes abrir la ventana?* 2. *John, ¿le echas una mano a Paul con esta actividad?* 3. *Karen, ¿puedes ayudarme a dividir la clase en grupos?*

- Go over the *Recuerda* vocabulary as a class and clarify any words that students might not remember. Then ask students to share their Independent Starter lists with a partner. Have them ask each other at least three questions about the objects they listed. For example: *¿Es la computadora portátil o de mesa? ¿De qué color son los pantalones? ¿De qué material son los zapatos?* They may add more objects to their lists. Have students share their lists with the class and have the class vote on who has more things in his or her room.

124

Antes de empezar

EXPRESIONES ÚTILES

Para pedir un favor:

¿Puedes hacerme un favor?
¿Me haces un favor?

Para pedir ayuda:

¿Puedes ayudarme?
¿Me echas una mano?

Para ofrecer ayuda:

¿Te ayudo? / ¿Puedo ayudarte?
¿Te echo una mano? / ¿Quieres que te eche una mano?
Déjame ayudarte. / Déjame que te ayude.
No dudes en ponerte en contacto con nosotros.

2 ¿Me haces un favor?

▶ **Escucha** y relaciona cada diálogo con la fotografía correspondiente.

Ⓐ  Ⓑ  Ⓒ

▶ **Escucha** de nuevo y completa una tabla como esta.

	¿Qué favor pide?	¿Recibe ayuda?
1	ordenar su habitación	sí
2		
3		

▶ **Escribe** dos diálogos similares con tu compañero(a). Después, memorícenlos y represéntenlos.

124 ciento veinticuatro

Differentiated Instruction

DEVELOPING LEARNERS

- Give students more practice with the words in the *Recuerda* feature by having them find images of people who are wearing some of the clothes mentioned and other images of rooms and furniture in a house or apartment. Have students use these images as they work with a partner and describe to one another what each person is wearing, which rooms are shown, and what furniture is in each room. Then ask the pairs to take turns reading their descriptions aloud.

EXPANDING LEARNERS

- Ask students to make a list of homework assignments and household chores they usually have to do. Then have them work with a partner and come up with several short dialogues that include an expression from the *Expresiones útiles* feature. For example:
  A. *Tengo que escribir un poema para la clase de Español. ¿Me echas una mano?*
  B. *¡Por supuesto! Luego, ¿puedes ayudarme a limpiar mi cuarto?*
  A. *Sí, déjame que te ayude.*

- See which pairs can come up with the most substantial dialogues.

RECUERDA

La ropa
el abrigo	el impermeable
la blusa	los pantalones
la camisa	la sudadera
la camiseta	el suéter
la chaqueta	el traje
la falda	el vestido

El calzado y los complementos
las botas	la bufanda
las sandalias	la corbata
los tenis	las gafas (de sol)
las zapatillas	los guantes

Materiales
el algodón	la lana

La vivienda
el ascensor	el dormitorio
la cocina	el garaje
el comedor	el jardín
el cuarto de baño	el pasillo
la despensa	la sala
el desván	el sótano

Muebles, accesorios y electrodomésticos
la alfombra	el lavaplatos
la cortina	la mesita de noche
el espejo	el microondas
la estantería	la plancha
el horno	el refrigerador
la lámpara	el sillón
la lavadora	el sofá

 3 **¿Cuánto sabes?**

▶ **Describe** las prendas de vestir que hay en este dormitorio.

Modelo   *Hay una camisa blanca, un…*

 4 **Tu casa**

▶ **Dibuja y escribe.** Con tu compañero(a), dibuja el plano de una casa y escribe el nombre de cada parte.

HERITAGE LANGUAGE LEARNERS

• There are many regional variants for the vocabulary reviewed in the *Recuerda* feature. For example, many Spanish speakers use *elevador* and not *ascensor*. Ask students to review the list of words on page 125 and write a regional variant from their family's country of origin (or from another Hispanic country they know) for as many of the words as they can. Ask them to prepare a list of these words and share them with the rest of the class.

TOTAL PHYSICAL RESPONSE (TPR)

• Write the following words in large block letters on separate sheets of paper: *ropa; calzado y complementos; vivienda; muebles, accesorios y electrodomésticos*. Post these headings around the room. As you read the words from page 125, as well as any others that are part of the students' known vocabulary, have them move to stand near the corresponding sheet of paper and say aloud the group to which the word belongs. You may want to work in small groups and secretly assign a "mole" to purposely mislead the others.

Antes de empezar

Activities

2. Before listening to the dialogues, have students look at the photos and describe the images. Ask them questions about the clothes and the objects displayed: *¿Qué es esto? ¿De qué color es? ¿De qué material es? ¿Qué hay en este cuarto? ¿Es un cuarto ordenado o desordenado?* Then ask students to think of possible problems or situations for each photo that may require somebody's help. For example, the shirt seems to be wrinkled, so it probably needs to be ironed; the room is very untidy, so it probably needs to be tidied up, etc. After this discussion, play the audio and ask students to complete the activity.

3. To further review the vocabulary for clothing items, ask volunteers to come up to the front and have the others describe their clothes. You may also bring to class some fashion magazines and have students choose images to describe.

4. Before doing this activity, review the vocabulary of the house by asking students to describe their home to a partner. Model the descriptions by giving them a detailed description of your own home or of an imaginary one.

AUDIO SCRIPT
See page 119 I.

Answer Key

2. 1. A   2. B   3. C
   ▶ 2. Planchar su camisa. No.
      3. Ayudarla a elegir un vestido de fiesta. Sí.
   ▶ Answers will vary.

3. Answers will vary.

4. Answers will vary.

Additional Resources

Fans Online activities
Practice Workbook

Unit 3

DESAFÍO 1

Hablar de acciones recientes

Presentation

- In *Desafío 1*, Michelle and Daniel will choose a traditional costume from a Hispanic country and adapt it to a more modern style. Students will preview language used to describe clothing.

Activities	Standards	Resources
Texto	1.2, 2.2, 3.2	Vis. Pres.
5.	1.1, 1.2, 3.1	
6.	1.1, 1.2	
7.	1.1, 1.2, 1.3	
8. Cultura	1.1, 1.2, 2.1, 2.2, 3.1, 4.2	Video

Teaching Suggestions

Warm-Up / Independent Starter

- Ask students to write a few sentences describing their favorite article(s) of clothing. Ask students to also address these questions in their response: How do they feel when they wear it? When and where do they wear it?

Preparation

- Call on several volunteers to share their Independent Starters with the class. Then ask for a different volunteer to read the introduction to the dialogue. Brainstorm ideas relating to what this "traditional clothing" might be. Do students know what an alpaca looks like? If possible, share photographs of an alpaca and various pictures of clothing made from alpaca wool.

Texto: Un traje muy especial

- Ask for volunteers to read the roles of Michelle and Ana. Then have students write any words that they can't identify or any constructions they don't understand. Ask them to work in pairs to see if they can answer any of their partners' questions. Finally, discuss these questions as a class.

- Have students write a four-sentence paragraph summarizing the conversation between Michelle and her classmate. Ask students for their impressions. How might Michelle and Daniel "adapt" a traditional costume?

126

Un traje muy especial

Michelle and Daniel will have to choose a traditional costume from a Hispanic country and adapt it. In order to do this, they will have to research information about traditional clothing and fashion.

Me encanta el suéter que llevas puesto, Ana. Te queda muy bien.

Gracias. Yo creo que me queda un poco ancho, pero es tan suave... Tócalo.

Es cierto. ¿De qué está hecho?

Está fabricado con lana de alpaca. Mi tía me lo compró en Perú. Allí lo llaman chompa.

¿Y tienes más ropa de Perú, algo típico de allí?

Sí, tengo algunas cosas en casa. ¿Quieres venir a verlas?

Claro. Daniel y yo necesitamos información sobre ropa tradicional.

Pues tengo una muñeca vestida con un traje regional. ¿Les interesa?

5 **Detective de palabras**

▶ **Completa** estas oraciones.

1. A Michelle le encanta el suéter que lleva _____ Ana.
2. Michelle pregunta de qué está _____ el suéter.
3. Ana le dice que está _____ con lana de alpaca.
4. Ana tiene una muñeca _____ con un traje regional.

▶ **Escribe.** ¿Con qué infinitivos relacionas las palabras que has escrito?

126 ciento veintiséis

Differentiated Instruction

DEVELOPING LEARNERS

- Help students identify the cognates in the cultural note, and assist them to see how recognizing cognates and exploring their meaning can enhance their vocabulary, in both Spanish and English. Cognates include: *regionales, típicos, variar, región, signo, identidad, cultural, función, sexo, clase, social, forman, parte, utilizan, celebraciones, especiales, zonas, rurales.* Encourage students to add these words to their notebooks for vocabulary enrichment.

EXPANDING LEARNERS

- Ask students to work with a partner and describe to each other what they are wearing today. Then, have them take turns describing to their partners what they would wear to a special event, without naming the occasion. Partners will guess what the special event is. For example:
  A. *Llevo un vestido elegante.*
  B. *¿Vas a una entrevista de trabajo?*
  A. *No. Llevo tacones altos.*
  B. *¿Vas a una fiesta?*
  A. *Sí.*

6 ¿Comprendes?

▶ **Responde** a estas preguntas.

1. ¿De dónde es originario el suéter de Ana?
2. ¿De qué material está hecho?
3. ¿Cómo es?
4. ¿Por qué van a ir Michelle y Daniel a casa de Ana?

7 Tu estilo

▶ **Escribe** una descripción completa de la ropa que llevan estas personas.

 ①  ②  ③  ④

 ▶ **Habla** con tu compañero(a). ¿Qué estilo te gusta más? ¿Qué tipo de ropa sueles llevar tú?

 CULTURA

Los trajes regionales

Todos los países del mundo tienen trajes típicos que son signo de identidad cultural. Los trajes suelen variar de una región a otra y también en función del sexo o la clase social.

Los trajes regionales ya no forman parte de la vestimenta diaria en las ciudades, pero todavía se utilizan en fiestas y celebraciones especiales, sobre todo en las zonas rurales.

Niño con poncho (Perú).

8 **Habla.** ¿Piensas que es importante mantener los trajes típicos como signo de identidad cultural? ¿Por qué?

Hablar de acciones recientes

Activities

6. To expand this activity, ask students to work in groups of three and imagine the conversation that takes place when Daniel and Michelle arrive at their classmate's house to look at the doll wearing a traditional costume. Have groups write a brief script for this conversation.

7. After students complete this activity, have them compare and contrast their style with that of their partner. Do they have similar tastes in clothes?

 CULTURA

Los trajes regionales

Ponchos and chullos are examples of traditional garments that have become known outside the region where they originated (i.e., the Andes). A poncho is a rectangular sheet of fabric with an opening for the head in the center. Hoods are added to some ponchos to ward off wind and rain. A chullo is a wool hat with earflaps. Today, ponchos and chullos have become fashion items in many countries throughout the world.

Answer Key

5. 1. puesto   3. fabricado
     2. hecho   4. vestida
     ▶ 1. poner   3. fabricar
     2. hacer   4. vestir

6. 1. Es de Perú.
     2. Es de lana de alpaca.
     3. Es muy suave.
     4. Van a ir a casa de Ana porque ella tiene una muñeca vestida con un traje regional.

7. Answers will vary.
     ▶ Answers will vary.

8. Answers will vary.

Additional Resources

Fans Online activities

HERITAGE LANGUAGE LEARNERS

• Ask students to describe or bring in to the class a traditional garment from their family's country of origin and explain what it is, its purpose, and when it is worn. Students may also bring in photos or other images of these garments. Encourage students to describe the festivals or celebrations in which these articles of clothing are worn. In addition to clothes, you may have students bring in some objects or accessories that are associated with the garments or the celebrations described.

MULTIPLE INTELLIGENCES:
Interpersonal Intelligence

• Have students imagine that they are advice columnists and have received the following letter: *Soy un chico boliviano que vive en los EE. UU. desde que tenía dos años de edad. No conozco bien la cultura de Bolivia. Mi dilema es que para el Día Nacional de Bolivia mis padres quieren que me vista con un traje típico de su región y que participe en las festividades vestido así, pero yo no quiero. ¿Qué debo hacer? Gracias. Rafael.*

• Ask students to write an appropriate response.

127

DESAFÍO 1

Vocabulario – Ropa

Presentation

- In this section, students will learn vocabulary related to articles of clothing, shopping, clothing materials, how clothing fits, and verbs that describe actions related to clothing.

Activities	Standards	Resources
Vocabulario	1.2, 3.1, 5.1	
9.	1.2	
10.	1.2	Audio
11.	1.1, 1.2, 1.3, 3.1	
12. Cultura	1.1, 1.2, 2.2, 3.1	

Teaching Suggestions

Warm-Up / Independent Starter

- Ask students to write a description of what they are wearing today on a piece of paper. For example: *Llevo una camiseta azul de algodón, unos pantalones largos, unos zapatos...*

Preparation

- Collect the Independent Starter from each student and read the descriptions aloud. Have students look around the class and identify classmates wearing the clothing described. Write three categories on the board: *Ropa, Calzado,* and *Complementos.* Ask students to place the clothing described in the Independent Starter in the correct category. Then, go over the *Vocabulario* presentation as a class.

Activities

10. Before playing the audio, give students one minute to read the directions and to review the categories for which they will be listening.

11. For the second part of this activity, ask students to create a five-column table with the following headings: *Nombre de mi compañero(a); ¿Qué prenda de vestir?; ¿Se la prueba?; ¿Le queda bien?; ¿La compra?* They will then be able to fill in the answers quickly and efficiently as they listen to their classmates' dialogues. After listening to the dialogues, students should compare and contrast their tables with a partner's.

128

Vocabulario

Ropa

OFERTAS ESPECIALES

Ropa

Chaqueta de lana con **cremallera**
$ 35

Suéter de lana de **manga larga**
$ 36

Camisas de caballero con **bolsillo**
$ 28
el **cuello**
los **botones**

Calzado

los **cordones**

Zapatos planos de señora
$ 65

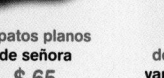
Zapatos de **tacón** de varios colores
$ 50

Zapatos de caballero
$ 49

Complementos

Cinturón de cuero **marrón** o negro
$ 20

Pañuelos de seda de varios diseños
$ 39

Paraguas **liso** en 5 colores
$ 19

Más vocabulario

¿Cómo te queda?

amplio(a)/ajustado(a)	loose/tight
ancho(a)/estrecho(a)	wide/tight
bien/mal	well/badly
largo(a)/corto(a)	long/short
pequeño(a)/grande	small/big

Comprar ropa

el número	shoe size
la talla	size

Acciones

(des)abrocharse	to (un)fasten
(des)atarse	to (un)tie
ponerse	to put on
quitarse	to take off

Materiales

poliéster	polyester
terciopelo	velvet

9 **Asociaciones**

▶ **Busca** el intruso en cada grupo.

1	
algodón	talla
seda	terciopelo

2	
bolsillo	paraguas
manga	cremallera

3	
pañuelo	ajustado
estrecho	ancho

128 ciento veintiocho

Differentiated Instruction

DEVELOPING LEARNERS

- Ask students to look through old magazines and cut out images of articles of clothing and accessories similar to those pictured on this page. Have them glue the images on a large sheet of paper and create their own ads to promote the products. They need to come up with the name of the store, the clothing or accessory item, the old and new prices, and any other special offer, such as 1 for $10, 2 for $15. Have volunteers come before the class and describe their ads.

EXPANDING LEARNERS

- Give students more practice with the new vocabulary by having them work with a partner and take turns creating a dialogue between a disgruntled customer and the store manager. The customer purchased one of the articles advertised but has encountered problems with it (e.g., a pair of shoes in two different sizes, a jacket whose zipper doesn't work, an umbrella that doesn't open). The store manager tries to placate the customer and offer solutions. Then have partners switch roles. Call on some pairs to present their skits to the class.

10 De compras

 ► **Escucha** los diálogos. ¿Qué problema tienen estas personas?

      Ⓐ   Ⓑ

1. Lola
2. Javier   a. la talla o el número
3. Mónica   b. la tela de la prenda de vestir
4. Paloma   c. una parte de la prenda de vestir
5. Carlos

11 En los grandes almacenes

► **Ordena** esta conversación entre Michelle y su amiga Ana.

> MICHELLE: De acuerdo. ¿Qué te parece? ¿Me queda bien?

> ANA: Sí, es muy linda. ¿Por qué no te la pruebas?

> ANA: Pero ahora está rebajada. ¡Pruébatela! Los probadores están por allí.

⓵ MICHELLE: Mira esta falda de rayas, qué bonita. Está de moda y es perfecta para el verano.

> ANA: Creo que te queda un poco estrecha. Voy a buscar otra talla.

> MICHELLE: No sé… Es que es un poco cara, porque es de una marca *(brand)* famosa.

► **Escribe** un diálogo similar con tu compañero(a). Después, memorícenlo y represéntenlo. Sus compañeros(as) tendrán que responder a estas preguntas.

- ¿Qué prenda de vestir se menciona?
- ¿El/La cliente(a) se la prueba?
- ¿Le queda bien?
- ¿La compra?

 **CULTURA**

La moda hispana

Varios de los diseñadores de moda más famosos del mundo son de origen hispano. La venezolana Carolina Herrera, el dominicano Oscar de la Renta o el cubano americano Narciso Rodríguez son solo algunos de los nombres más conocidos. Y cada vez hay más diseñadores hispanos que triunfan en las pasarelas *(catwalks)* de todo el mundo.

Narciso Rodríguez, diseñador cubano americano.

12 **Piensa.** ¿Qué efectos puede tener la cultura de un país sobre el trabajo de sus diseñadores?

ciento veintinueve 129

---

12. Ask students to research well-known Hispanic designers and their famous clients, and choose their favorite outfit or red carpet moment and bring photos to class. Share these in small groups as students describe the outfits worn by the celebrities. The class may then vote on the "best dressed" and "worst dressed" celebrity.

 AUDIO SCRIPT
See page 119I.

 CULTURA

La moda hispana

The fashion and designers of the Spanish-speaking world have had great success on international catwalks in Milan, London, New York, and Paris. Some of the leading Spanish fashion designers who have revolutionized the international fashion industry include: Amaya Arzuaga, Agatha Ruiz de la Prada, Cristóbal Balenciaga, Paco Rabanne, Mariano Fortuny, and Manolo Blahnik. Isabel Toledo is a Cuban-American who designed the outfit worn by Michelle Obama during the 2008 inauguration of President Obama.

Answer Key

9. 1. talla   2. paraguas   3. pañuelo

10. 1. b   2. a   3. c   4. c   5. a

11. 2. Sí, es muy linda…
    3. No sé… Es que es un poco cara…
    4. Pero ahora está rebajada…
    5. De acuerdo. ¿Qué te parece? …
    6. Creo que te queda un poco estrecha…
    ► Answers will vary.

12. Answers will vary.

Additional Resources

Fans Online activities
Practice Workbook

HERITAGE LANGUAGE LEARNERS

- Ask students to research one of the designers mentioned in the culture note, or any other designer from Spain or Latin America. Students should present a brief biographical sketch and include how the designer got his or her start in the business, and name other designers who have been, or continue to be, a source of inspiration. Have students bring some images of the designer's clothes to class and be prepared to explain his or her innovations in style, color, and materials used.

TOTAL PHYSICAL RESPONSE (TPR)

- Students will play a game called *¿Es una ganga?* Prepare some prices for vocabulary items students will know and write them on slips of paper, along with the name of the item. Some should be bargains, but others should be outrageously priced (e.g., *un par de zapatos: $2,000*). Have students take turns reading a slip of paper aloud. Depending on the text, students will stand and shout *¡Es una ganga!* or crouch down and say *¡No es una ganga!* If it is not a bargain, ask students to name a suitable price.

DESAFÍO 1

Gramática – El participio

Presentation

- In this section, students will review the formation of the past participle and how it may be used as an adjective.

Activities	Standards	Resources
Gramática	1.2, 3.1	
13.	1.1, 3.1, 4.1	
14.	1.2	
15.	1.1, 1.2, 3.1	
16.	1.1, 1.2, 1.3, 2.2, 3.1	Audio

Teaching Suggestions

Warm-Up / Independent Starter

- Have students read the grammar presentation silently. Then write the following groups of verb forms on the board and ask students to translate them into Spanish:

  1. To cover: you cover; you covered; the covered dish. (*Cubrir: tú cubres; tú cubriste; el plato cubierto.*)

  2. To break: I break; I broke; the broken plate. (*Romper: yo rompo; yo rompí; el plato roto.*)

  3. To write: he writes; he wrote; the written letter. (*Escribir: él escribe; él escribió; la carta escrita.*)

Preparation

- Review the Independent Starter as a class and ask volunteers to explain the differences in each verb form. Then ask students to translate the following sentences into Spanish: 1. The dish is covered. (*El plato está cubierto.*) 2. The plate is broken. (*El plato está roto.*) 3. The letter is written. (*La carta está escrita.*)

Activities

14. After students have completed the activity, ask them to write a complete sentence with each of the noun/adjective pairs. For example: *Quiero comprarme una falda nueva porque esta falda me queda un poco ajustada. Hay que llevar los zapatos atados para no caerse.*

DESAFÍO 1

Gramática

El participio

El participio como adjetivo

- The past participle (participio) is a verb form that can be used as an adjective to describe a noun.

  El pantalón **lavado** está en la secadora.

- Like other Spanish adjectives, the past participle must agree in number and gender with the noun described.

  Las camisas **planchadas** están en el armario.

Formación del participio

- The past participle is formed this way:

  PARTICIPIO. VERBOS REGULARES

-ar verbs → add -ado	hablar → hablado
-er and -ir verbs → add -ido	comer → comido

- The following verbs have irregular past participles:

  PARTICIPIO. VERBOS IRREGULARES

abrir → abierto	poner → puesto	hacer → hecho	ver → visto
cubrir → cubierto	resolver → resuelto	decir → dicho	escribir → escrito
morir → muerto	volver → vuelto	romper → roto	describir → descrito

- Remember the written accent in the past participle of these -er and -ir verbs.

  caer → caído   leer → leído   oír → oído   traer → traído   creer → creído

La construcción *estar* + participio

- Estar + *past participle* is used to express the state or condition of a subject as a result of a previous action. The past participle must agree with the subject in number and gender.

  María se sentó en el tren. María está **sentada**.

13 **Compara.** ¿Cómo se forma el participio pasado en inglés? ¿Hay irregulares?

14 **¡A vestirse!**

▶ **Une** las dos columnas.

(A)	(B)
1. los cinturones	a. atados
2. la falda	b. cerrada
3. la cremallera	c. abiertas
4. las cajas	d. abrochados
5. los zapatos	e. ajustada

Differentiated Instruction

DEVELOPING LEARNERS

- Give students more practice by having them complete the following phrases with the correct form of the past participle:

  1. *las palabras [decir] (dichas)*
  2. *las cosas [ver] (vistas)*
  3. *los capítulos [leer] (leídos)*
  4. *los problemas [resolver] (resueltos)*
  5. *las canciones [oír] (oídas)*
  6. *los papeles [romper] (rotos)*
  7. *la mesa [poner] (puesta)*

EXPANDING LEARNERS

- Ask students to work with a partner and take turns writing or saying five or six pairs of sentences using the verb *estar* plus a past participle. The pairs must refute what is being described in the first sentence. Sentences may be declarative or interrogative. For example:

  A. *Todos tus problemas están resueltos.*
  B. *¡Qué va! Ningún problema está resuelto.*
  A. *¿Está abierta la puerta?*
  B. *No, la puerta está cerrada.*

- Call on volunteer pairs to present their best dialogues to the rest of the class.

15 Del dicho al hecho

▶ **Completa** estas oraciones poniendo los verbos del cuadro en la forma correspondiente del participio.

| hacer |
| romper |
| abrir |
| desatar |
| ajustar |

1. El almacén está _____ desde las diez de la mañana.
2. Necesito otra talla; esta blusa me queda muy _____.
3. ¡Cuidado, tienes los zapatos _____!
4. Esos pantalones están _____ de algodón.
5. La cremallera no se puede cerrar, está _____.

16 En la tienda de artesanía

▶ **Escucha** la conversación entre Daniel y el vendedor de una tienda de artesanía y decide si estas oraciones son ciertas o falsas. Después, corrige las falsas.

1. Daniel busca ropa tradicional andina en la tienda.
2. Algunos ponchos no están tejidos a mano.
3. Los ponchos están diseñados según el estilo tradicional.
4. Daniel está interesado en un tipo de sombrero fabricado en Panamá.
5. En la tienda hay complementos hechos de cuero.

▶ **Escribe.** Daniel compra estas prendas en la tienda para enseñárselas a Michelle. Escribe una descripción de cada una.

Modelo 1. *Este gorro está hecho de lana. Es muy colorido…*

① ② ③ ④ ⑤

Gramática – El participio

16. Ask further questions regarding Daniel's shopping experience in the market. If possible, ask students to research some of the famous markets in Central or South America and make a list of articles of clothing that they would like to buy. Have them explain their preferences.

 AUDIO SCRIPT
See page 119I.

Answer Key

13. El participio pasado de los verbos regulares se forma añadiendo *-ed* al verbo (e.g., *close → closed*). Hay participios pasados irregulares, como por ejemplo: *see → seen*; *break → broken*.

14. 1. d   2. e   3. b   4. c   5. a

15. 1. abierto   4. hechos
2. ajustada   5. rota
3. desatados

16. 1. Cierto.
2. Falso. Todos están tejidos a mano.
3. Cierto.
4. Falso. El sombrero es típico de Ecuador.
5. Cierto.
▶ Answers will vary. Sample answers:
2. Este bolso es de cuero. Fue diseñado por un diseñador muy conocido.
3. Esta camisa es de algodón. Es ideal para el verano porque es de manga corta. Fue hecha en Guatemala.
4. Esta chaqueta es de lana de alpaca. Está decorada con motivos indígenas de Perú.
5. Este poncho está tejido con lana de llama. Es muy colorido y abrigado.

Additional Resources

Fans Online activities
Practice Workbook

HERITAGE LANGUAGE LEARNERS

• Challenge students to make a list of verbs that have two acceptable forms of the past participle. To get them started, suggest some of the following verbs: *bendecir → bendecido, bendito; confundir → confundido, confuso; despertar → despertado, despierto; elegir → elegido, electo; soltar → soltado, suelto; imprimir → imprimido, impreso*. Students should be prepared to explain that the first form (i.e., the form that ends in *-ado* or *-ido*) is used as a verb and the second form is used as an adjective. For example: *Tu explicación me ha confundido. La explicación es confusa.*

TOTAL PHYSICAL RESPONSE (TPR)

• Tell students that they will play a game to practice the past participles. Ask students to stand and, going by rows, ask the first student to say a past participle. The next student must say a meaningful sentence with that participle. For example: *abierta → La puerta está abierta*. If the sentence is incorrect, the student must sit down, and the following student gets a turn. Upon a correct response, that student says another participle and the next student uses it in a sentence. The winners are those students who are still standing when you call time.

131

DESAFÍO 1

Gramática – Hablar de acciones recientes. El presente perfecto

Presentation

- In this section, students will learn and practice the present perfect.

Activities	Standards	Resources
Gramática	1.2, 3.1	
17.	1.1, 3.1, 4.1	
18.	1.1, 1.2, 3.1	
19.	1.1, 1.2, 3.1	Audio
20.	1.1, 1.3, 5.1, 5.2	
21. Conexiones	1.1, 1.2, 2.1, 3.1, 4.2, 5.1	

Teaching Suggestions

Warm-Up / Independent Starter

- Have students read the grammar presentation silently. Create the following grid on the board or on a worksheet, and ask students to complete it:

ABRIR (to open)

yo *he abierto*	nosotros(as)
tú	vosotros(as)
usted, él, ella	ustedes, ellos(as)

Preparation

- Review students' grids from the Independent Starter. Encourage them to ask questions about any explanations they did not understand in the grammar presentation and clarify this information for them. Ask students to brainstorm when they last used the present perfect in English. Point out that it is common for English speakers to say, "I've closed the door," "We've seen that movie," etc. It is also typical to use the equivalent of *acabar de*: "I just closed the door," "We just saw that movie," etc.

Activities

18. Once students have finished this activity, have them summarize Michelle's actions in a four-sentence paragraph. Ask for volunteers to write their paragraph on the board. Correct each sentence together as a class.

132

Gramática

Hablar de acciones recientes. El presente perfecto

- The present perfect tense (presente perfecto) is the same as *to have + past participle*. In Spanish this tense has two uses:
  - To describe actions that already happened at the time we consider to be the present. That's why we often use time expressions like esta mañana, esta semana, este año, etc. These actions can be continuing actions in the present.

    Hemos vivido en esta ciudad durante muchos años y seguimos viviendo aquí.

  - To describe actions that have recently ended. In these cases, we can also use the expression acabar de.

    He **comprado** una chaqueta.   Acabo de comprar una chaqueta.

Formación del presente perfecto

- The present perfect is conjugated with the helping verb haber and the past participle:

VERBO HABLAR. PRESENTE PERFECTO

Singular		Plural	
yo	he **habl**ado	nosotros(as)	hemos **habl**ado
tú	has **habl**ado	vosotros(as)	habéis **habl**ado
usted, él, ella	ha **habl**ado	ustedes, ellos(as)	han **habl**ado

- The past participle always ends in an -o and does not agree with the subject.

  Nosotras nos **hemos puesto** unos tenis.

- The helping verb and the past participle are never separated. Thus, negative words, object pronouns, and reflexive pronouns go before haber.

  Yo **no me he comprado** nada.

17 **Compara.** ¿Cuándo se usa el presente perfecto en inglés?

18 **Las notas de Michelle**

▶ **Escribe** las palabras de Michelle. ¿Qué ha hecho para preparar el desafío?

Modelo   Hablar con su profesor de Español → *He hablado con mi profesor de Español.*

1. Ver prendas típicas de Perú en casa de su amiga Ana.
2. Ir de compras con su amiga Ana.
3. Llamar a Tess para pedirle más información sobre el desafío.
4. Buscar información en Internet sobre diseñadores hispanos.
5. Ver fotografías de trajes regionales de distintos países.
6. Hacer una lista de tareas pendientes.

132 ciento treinta y dos

Differentiated Instruction

DEVELOPING LEARNERS

- Give students more practice with the present perfect by having them answer the following questions affirmatively:
  1. *¿Han hablado ellos con el profesor?* (Sí, ellos han hablado con el profesor.)
  2. *¿Ha vuelto a casa tu perro?* (Sí, mi perro ha vuelto a casa.)
  3. *¿Han hecho ustedes la cena?* (Sí, hemos hecho la cena.)
  4. *¿Han leído ustedes el poema?* (Sí, hemos leído el poema.)
  5. *¿Has roto el paraguas?* (Sí, he roto el paraguas.)

EXPANDING LEARNERS

- Ask students to complete the following sentences with the present perfect:
  1. *Ellos (traer) los cordones.* (han traído)
  2. *¡Este suéter te (quedar) perfecto!* (ha quedado)
  3. *Ustedes (leer) el libro esta mañana.* (han leído)
  4. *Ana y yo (ver) esta película dos veces.* (hemos visto)
  5. *¿(tú – romper) el paraguas?* (Has roto)
- Then ask students to talk with a partner about what they have done this morning, today, this week, and this month.

132

¿Qué ha hecho hoy Clara?

 ▶ **Escucha** y ordena las ilustraciones.

 ▶ **Escucha** de nuevo y responde a estas preguntas.

1. ¿A qué tiendas del centro comercial ha ido Clara?
2. ¿Qué cosas ha comprado?

 Un repaso de tu vida

 ▶ **Imagina** que tienes 30 años y habla con tu compañero(a). ¿Qué has hecho en tu vida? Después, escribe una comparación.

Modelo *Mi compañero Mike y yo nos hemos graduado y hemos empezado a trabajar. Mike se ha casado, pero yo…*

CONEXIONES: CIENCIAS

El reciclaje

Las Naciones Unidas establecieron en 1973 el día 5 de junio como Día Mundial del Medio Ambiente, con el objetivo de sensibilizar a la población sobre los temas medioambientales.

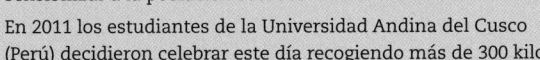
Indradhanush (2008).
Fuente: http://www.guerradelapaz.com

En 2011 los estudiantes de la Universidad Andina del Cusco (Perú) decidieron celebrar este día recogiendo más de 300 kilos de papel y bolsas de plástico. Con estos materiales reciclables crearon más de 25 vestidos que presentaron en un desfile.

Los artistas cubanos Alain Guerra y Neraldo de la Paz, que trabajan juntos con el nombre Guerra de la Paz, utilizan ropa reciclada para realizar esculturas.

 Piensa. ¿Qué actividades piensas que pueden hacer en tu escuela para reciclar materiales?

ciento treinta y tres **133**

Gramática – Hablar de acciones recientes. El presente perfecto

21. If possible, show students photos of some of the recycled dresses created by the students at the university in Cusco. As a follow-up, have students design their own article of clothing using recyclable materials and share these artistic representations with a partner.

 AUDIO SCRIPT
See page 119I.

 CONEXIONES: CIENCIAS

El reciclaje

Participating in World Environment Day events allows us to become actively involved in cleaning up our community and becoming agents for a greener environment. The activities promoted foster awareness of the enviroment, which will hopefully translate into action.

Answer Key

17. Se usa para hablar de acciones que comenzaron en el pasado y aún continúan, acciones pasadas que tienen un efecto en el presente y acciones que ocurrieron en algún momento del pasado sin decir cuándo.

18. 1. He visto…   4. He buscado…
2. He ido…   5. He visto…
3. He llamado…   6. He hecho…

19. 3, 1, 4, 2
▶ 1. Ha ido a una zapatería, a una tienda de ropa y a una de artesanía.
2. Ha comprado unas botas de tacón y un regalo para su esposo.

20. Answers will vary.

21. Answers will vary.

Additional Resources

Fans Online activities
Practice Workbook

HERITAGE LANGUAGE LEARNERS

• Ask students to find information on how *el Día Mundial del Medio Ambiente* is observed in their family's country of origin or in any other Spanish-speaking country. Students may address the impact that protecting or harming the environment has on the target country's economy and people's health. Other days that students may research include *Día Mundial del Agua, Día de la Tierra,* and *Día Mundial del Reciclaje.*

COOPERATIVE LEARNING

• Ask students to work in small groups and create a new *Día Mundial* that focuses on helping to protect our planet. Students will first need to identify the topic, which may range from a campaign to control pollution, stop littering, or enhance people's physical or emotional health. Once the topic has been decided, members of the group will need to explain the impact of their World Day, create a slogan, design a campaign poster, and name a spokesperson who will present their project to the class.

Unit 3

LECTURA: TEXTO DIALOGADO

Presentation

- In this section, students will read a dialogue, review vocabulary, and identify adjectives, as well as answer comprehension questions based on the reading.

Activities	Standards	Resources
Lectura: texto dialogado	1.1, 1.2, 2.2, 3.1, 3.2	Vis. Pres.
22.	1.1, 1.2, 2.2	
23.	1.2, 1.3, 3.1	
24.	1.1, 1.3, 3.1, 5.1	
25.	1.1, 1.2, 2.1, 2.2	

Teaching Suggestions

Warm-Up / Independent Starter

- Have students read the *Antes de leer* strategies silently. Then ask them to write down the answers to the questions.

Preparation

- Call on a volunteer to answer the first question in the *Antes de leer* section. Sample response: *Hay trajes tradicionales de una chica y de un chico.* Ask students to define what it is meant by *traje tradicional.* Then have students answer the following questions regarding the traditional costumes depicted: *¿Qué características tienen? ¿Cuándo creen ustedes que se llevan? ¿Tienen algún significado sus colores y formas?*

- Read the dialogue aloud to students, modeling correct pronunciation and intonation. Then call on several pairs of students to alternate reading the dialogue aloud. Offer suggestions to improve their oral reading.

- Ask pairs of students to explain the meaning of some words in the reading that are also used in English (i.e., *poncho, suéter, sombrero*). Explain to students that these words are loans. *Poncho* comes originally from an indigenous language in Chile, Araucanian; *suéter* is originally an English word; and *sombrero* a Spanish one. Remind students that recognizing loans facilitates vocabulary learning and enhances comprehension.

134

Antes de leer: estrategias

1. Mira las fotos y descríbelas. Los elementos visuales ayudan a comprender un texto. ¿Qué hay en estas fotos?
2. Lee el título del diálogo y adivina la situación. ¿De qué van a hablar los personajes?
3. Busca los adjetivos que se emplean para describir la ropa. ¿Hay más adjetivos positivos o negativos? ¿Qué te dicen del tono de la lectura?

Un traje tradicional

DANIEL: Hola, Michelle. ¿Has elegido un traje regional?

MICHELLE: Sí, esta mañana he encontrado esta foto de un traje guatemalteco. ¿Qué te parece?

DANIEL: Es muy colorido, me gusta mucho. ¿Qué lleva la chica, un poncho de lana?

MICHELLE: No, lleva un huipil. Es un tipo de blusa larga de algodón que se usa en muchos pueblos indígenas. Está tejido a mano, siguiendo las técnicas tradicionales.

DANIEL: El diseño de los bordados[1] es muy original, pero no sé si es fácil adaptarlo.

MICHELLE: Yo creo que sí. Podemos cambiar las mangas y hacerlas más estrechas. Así es más cómodo y práctico.

Chica de la etnia cakchiquel (Guatemala).

DANIEL: Es una buena idea. Te voy a enseñar la foto que he elegido yo. También es de Guatemala. Me gusta esta especie[2] de suéter sin mangas que lleva el chico encima de la camisa.

MICHELLE: ¿Y has pensado algo para adaptarlo?

DANIEL: Sí, quiero darle un toque[3] más moderno: podemos quitar el sombrero de paja[4] y la banda,[5] y cambiar el cuello de la camisa.

MICHELLE: No sé... La banda es lo más auténtico, yo creo que no debemos quitarla.

DANIEL: Lo mejor es empezar a trabajar: voy a hacer unos bocetos[6], a ver qué te parecen.

MICHELLE: De acuerdo. Yo mientras voy a ver si se me ocurre algún diseño original para los bordados del huipil. ¡Manos a la obra!

Chico con ropa tradicional (Guatemala).

| 1. *embroidery* | 2. *kind* | 3. *touch* | 4. *straw* | 5. *sash* | 6. *sketches* |

134 ciento treinta y cuatro

Differentiated Instruction

DEVELOPING LEARNERS

- To reinforce students' comprehension of the dialogue, have them work with a partner or in small groups and read Michelle and Daniel's lines aloud. After they read each role, ask them to summarize what they have just read. If students have difficulty expressing their summaries in Spanish, they may want to simply present a list of things they understood. Once students have completed reading the entire dialogue and have made their summaries, ask them to write a couple of paragraphs that describe the conversation.

EXPANDING LEARNERS

- Ask students to write an antonym for each of the words in boldface in activity 23. They may use a dictionary to look for these words. Then have them write an original sentence using these antonyms. For example:
  1. *colorido: monocromático, de un solo color*
  2. *tradicional: moderno, nuevo*
  3. *original: normal, corriente, copia*
  4. *práctico: poco práctico, incómodo*
  5. *moderno: viejo, antiguo, anticuado*
  6. *auténtico: falso, artificial*
- Sentence: *No me gustan las camisas coloridas; prefiero las de un solo color.*

22 Comprensión

▶ **Responde** a estas preguntas.

1. ¿De dónde son los trajes que han elegido Daniel y Michelle?
2. ¿Cómo se llama la prenda tradicional que ha elegido Michelle?
3. ¿Qué idea propone Michelle para adaptar la prenda?
4. ¿Qué idea propone Daniel para cambiar el traje del chico?
5. ¿Qué opina Michelle al respecto?

23 Sinónimos

▶ **Escribe** estas oraciones del texto sustituyendo las palabras destacadas por otras que signifiquen lo mismo. Puedes usar un diccionario.

	Sinónimos
1. Es muy **colorido**, me gusta mucho.	Es muy vistoso.
2. Está tejido a mano, siguiendo las técnicas **tradicionales**.	
3. El diseño de los bordados es muy **original**.	
4. Así es más cómodo y más **práctico**.	
5. Quiero darle un toque más **moderno**.	
6. La banda es lo más **auténtico**.	

24 Un boceto

▶ **Elige** una de las fotografías y piensa. ¿Cómo puedes adaptar esas prendas para darles tu toque personal? Haz un boceto.

① ② ③ ④

 ▶ **Habla** con tu compañero(a). Muéstrale tu boceto y pregúntale por el suyo.

25 Con tus propias palabras

▶ **Responde** a estas preguntas.

1. ¿Crees que es positivo mantener elementos tradicionales como los trajes, la música, etc. como símbolo de identidad cultural? ¿Por qué?
2. ¿Cómo se puede ayudar a mantener esos elementos tradicionales?

- In addition to having students find adjectives in the dialogue that refer to clothes, ask them to make a list of the words related to clothing items and accessories that they recognize.

Activities

22. To expand this activity, ask additional questions. For example: *¿De qué material es el huipil? ¿Por qué quiere Michelle cambiar las mangas? ¿Qué va a hacer ahora Daniel? ¿Qué quiere hacer Michelle para empezar?*

23. You may do this as a whole-class activity. Provide students with a Spanish synonym dictionary or, if you have access to the Internet in class, with a website such as www.wordreference.com. Then ask individual students to look up the words and choose the most appropriate meaning for the given context.

24. As a follow-up activity, have students write a short description of their drawing, including all the clothes vocabulary.

Answer Key

22. 1. Son de Guatemala.
 2. Se llama *huipil*.
 3. Propone hacer las mangas más estrechas.
 4. Propone quitar el sombrero de paja y la banda, y cambiar el cuello de la camisa.
 5. Opina que no deben quitar la banda.

23. Answers will vary. Sample answers:
 2. típicas, antiguas
 3. único, insólito
 4. funcional, útil
 5. actual, fresco
 6. genuino, puro

24. Answers will vary.
 ▶ Answers will vary.

25. Answers will vary.

Additional Resources

Fans Online activities

HERITAGE LANGUAGE LEARNERS

- Ask students to research one of the garments pictured on page 135. They should name the articles of clothing, including any accessories usually associated with the garment, name the country where the item is worn, describe the celebrations when wearing these clothes would be appropriate, and add some anecdotal information about the history of these clothes (e.g., how they came to be, who generally wears them, why they are important to the country's culture). Students may also make comparisons and contrasts among the garments pictured.

SPECIAL-NEEDS LEARNERS

- For those students who have difficulty staying focused when they are reading or listening to long passages, copy the dialogue between Michelle and Daniel onto copy paper and cut the conversation into six parts, one for each exchange between the two. Then have students work with a partner and role-play their lines. After students finish reading the parts, mix up the exchanges and ask students to put the conversation back together by placing the exchanges in the correct order on a sheet of paper.

DESAFÍO 1

Comunicación

Presentation

- In this section, students will integrate the vocabulary and grammar skills from *Desafío 1* in order to describe clothing and shopping experiences, as well as to use the past participle as an adjective and to form the present perfect.

Activities	Standards	Resources
26.	1.1, 5.1	
27.	1.1, 1.2, 3.1	
28.	1.1, 1.3, 3.1	
29. Final del desafío	1.1, 1.2, 2.2	
Tu desafío	1.1, 1.2	

Teaching Suggestions

Warm-Up / Independent Starter

- Provide students with crayons, colored pencils, or markers. Have them design a "uniform" to be worn by all students and teachers at your school. Ask them to carefully consider the colors and styles chosen, and the aspects of your school culture or your region that these colors and styles symbolize. Students should also keep in mind the climate in your area and take that into consideration when deciding on the materials they would use for their uniform.

Preparation

- Ask students to form small groups and to share the drawings produced in the Independent Starter. Ask each group to nominate one uniform from the group to be presented to the class. Post each of the uniforms that were nominated and ask students to place a sticky note on their top three choices for best representation of the "traditions" of your school.

- Based on students' choices, select the winning design. Then discuss the students' choice as a class. What were the deciding factors? What characteristics do they find most attractive about the design? What could be improved or altered to make the design even better? You may also want to discuss accessories that could be worn with the uniform.

Comunicación

26 **De compras**

▶ **Habla.** Imagina que tú y tu compañero(a) están buscando estas prendas en una tienda. Por turnos, actúen como cliente(a) y vendedor(a).

Modelo   A. *Buenos días. Estoy buscando un suéter de lana.*
B. *¿De qué color y de qué talla lo quiere?*

27 **Un desfile de moda**

▶ **Lee** este artículo y complétalo con las palabras del cuadro.

pasarela	diseñadora	colores	colección	perfección	geométricos

Semana de la moda de Nueva York 2011: Carolina Herrera

El quinto día de desfiles en la semana de la moda de Nueva York se llenó de elegancia y feminidad de la mano de la ___1___ venezolana Carolina Herrera. La creadora, que sigue expandiendo su imperio por todo el mundo, nos presentó una ___2___ para la primavera / verano 2012 llena de ___3___ rojos, verdes, azules y amarillos, con estampados lineales y ___4___.

Desde que Carolina Herrera debutó en la ___5___ de Nueva York

en 1981, no ha faltado a su cita con la ciudad que nunca duerme.

La diseñadora latinoamericana, símbolo de ___6___ y siempre impecable en su look, nos mostró una colección para el próximo verano inspirada en la pureza de las líneas de la Escuela Bauhaus.

El desfile estuvo rodeado de personalidades y caras conocidas, como la actriz René Zellweger o la cantante Nicki Minaj.

Fuente: http://www.ellahoy.es
(texto adaptado)

▶ **Busca** en el texto los adjetivos que equivalen a estos otros.

basado(a)	famoso(a)	acompañado(a)

Differentiated Instruction

DEVELOPING LEARNERS

- Ask students to find a color image of an article of clothing. Have them work with a partner and, without showing or identifying the clothing item, describe it to their partners. Students should mention whether it is for men or women, when it might be worn, its color and fabric, etc. Partners will make a drawing of the garment based on this description. After the partners have described their garment and drawn their partner's clothing, ask them to display the original images and compare them to the drawings. How accurate were their drawings?

EXPANDING LEARNERS

- Ask students to imagine that they are the "fashion police" and are on the lookout for those who infringe on current fashion dos and don'ts. Ask students to write a description—real or imaginary—of how some celebrities or characters students have invented have failed to look their best. Students should describe the clothes and accessories in as much detail as possible, include an image or make their own illustration, and offer some much-needed fashion advice. Invite students to read their descriptions to the rest of the class. Does the class agree with them?

28 **Secciones de moda**

▶ **Habla** con tu compañero(a). Imaginen que van a comprar estas prendas por Internet. ¿En qué sección de la página web las pueden encontrar?

Final del desafío

Daniel, creo que hicimos un gran trabajo. Esta falda tradicional de ___1___ combinada con una blusa de seda me parece muy elegante.

¡Ay, no, eso no está de ___4___!

Y es una combinación bastante innovadora. ¿Crees que deberíamos hacer la blusa de ___2___ corta? ¿O hacerla de ___3___?

Quizás la ___5___ es una tela demasiado formal, pero la experta eres tú...

 29 **Un diseño innovador**

▶ **Completa** los bocadillos del final del desafío.

| moda | lana | seda | manga | terciopelo |

 ▶ **Habla** con tu compañero(a). ¿Les gusta la idea de Daniel y Michelle para el traje regional?

→ TU DESAFÍO Visita la página web. Escucha las preguntas de tu *Minientrevista Desafío 1* y escribe las respuestas.

ciento treinta y siete 137

Activities

26. To expand this activity, ask students to create dialogues that take place in different scenarios. For example: two students who are deciding what to wear to a special dance, two friends (one male and one female) who are preparing their suitcases for a trip to the Caribbean, etc.

27. Before they attempt to complete this activity, have students read the article quickly to get the gist. Then, on a second and more detailed reading, they may start to fill in the blanks.

29. As a closing activity for this *Desafío*, you may want to prepare a fashion show to be presented in the classroom. Each student must write a description of the outfit to be worn. Some students might choose to model the "uniform" created in the Independent Starter. Ask for two or three volunteers who will narrate the show. Ask a colleague if your class can present their fashion show to his or her students.

Answer Key

26. Answers will vary.

27. 1. diseñadora   4. geométricos
2. colección   5. pasarela
3. colores   6. perfección
▶ basado(a): inspirada
famoso(a): conocidas
acompañado(a): rodeado

28. Answers will vary.

29. 1. lana / terciopelo
2. manga
3. terciopelo / lana
4. moda
5. seda
▶ Answers will vary.

Additional Resources

Fans Online activities
Practice Workbook

HERITAGE LANGUAGE LEARNERS

• Ask students to describe the current fashion trends in their family's country of origin. How has fashion there evolved during the '70s, '80s, '90s, and beyond? Encourage them to speak to a family member to get answers. What, if any, were the status symbols in fashion? Are there any current status symbols? What is considered a huge fashion mistake? Are the clothes among students their age similar to those worn in this country? Ask students to share this information with the rest of the class for cross-cultural awareness.

COOPERATIVE LEARNING

• Have students work in small groups and explain that they will be participants in a design contest. Their objective is to come up with an original garment or accessory for a woman, man, or child. Each member of the group will have a specific task to do, but all will have input as to the final article of clothing. One student may choose the fabric, another the colors, someone else the fashion ad that will need to accompany the product, and another will make a drawing of the item.

Unit 3
DESAFÍO 2
Describir objetos

Presentation

- In *Desafío 2*, Asha and Lucas have to select an indigenous symbol to participate in a contest to decorate an *hacienda* in Ecuador. Students will preview language used in describing objects and in referring to nouns using nonspecific terms.

Activities	Standards	Resources
Texto	1.2, 2.1, 3.2	Vis. Pres.
30.	1.1, 1.2	
31.	1.1, 1.2	
32.	1.1, 1.2, 2.2	Audio
33. Cultura	1.1, 1.2, 2.2, 3.2, 4.2	

Teaching Suggestions

Warm-Up / Independent Starter

- Have students make a list of different house styles in the United States. What are the main characteristics of these styles?

Preparation

- Invite volunteers to share their Independent Starters with the class. How many different house styles can they identify? Are those styles related to the history of each region of the United States? Then, ask for a volunteer to read the dialogue's introduction. Do students know what an *hacienda* is?

Texto: En busca del símbolo perdido

- Ask students to get together with a partner and read the dialogue. Have them write any words they can't identify or any constructions they don't understand. Review their lists as a class.

- Ask students to compare the house styles they described in their Independent Starters with the description of an *hacienda* in the dialogue. Is there something similar to an *hacienda* in the United States?

Activities

31. After students complete the activity, have them work with a partner and think of an object that could represent several indigenous cultures.

138

En busca del símbolo perdido

Asha and Lucas are going to participate in a contest hosted by the owners of an *hacienda* in Ecuador. They must choose an indigenous symbol to incorporate into the *hacienda's* décor. The prize is … an all-expense-paid stay at the *hacienda*! Will they win?

ASHA: Lucas, ven, vamos a ver en Internet las fotos de la hacienda para ver cómo está decorada. Mira, es esta. ¿Te gusta?

LUCAS: Sí, me encanta el color de las paredes. Pero… ¿es una hacienda o un hotel?

ASHA: Es una hacienda, una casa de campo típica de Ecuador. Pero algunas se usan hoy como hoteles.

LUCAS: Ah, claro. ¿Y hay algún símbolo indígena en la decoración?

ASHA: Creo que no. A ver…, en la sala hay una chimenea, muebles de madera natural, un cuadro…, pero no veo ningún símbolo.

LUCAS: También se ven algunos adornos de cerámica y de cristal. Parecen muy antiguos. ¿Crees que son indígenas?

ASHA: No, no lo creo, pero ahí se puede poner el símbolo indígena, es el lugar perfecto. ¿Qué te parece?

LUCAS: Yo creo que es mejor ponerlo en el comedor, así lo verán todos los huéspedes. Y como es de estilo rústico, quedará muy bien.

ASHA: De acuerdo. Ahora solo tenemos que encontrar un símbolo indígena. Podemos elegir uno que represente a todas las culturas.

LUCAS: ¡Pero hay tantas culturas indígenas…! ¡Qué difícil!

30 Detective de palabras

▶ **Completa** estas oraciones.

1. _____ haciendas se usan hoy como hoteles.
2. Lucas pregunta si hay _____ símbolo indígena en la decoración.
3. Asha dice que ella no ve _____ símbolo.
4. Hay _____ adornos de cerámica en la sala.
5. Asha quiere elegir un símbolo que represente a _____ las culturas.

Differentiated Instruction

DEVELOPING LEARNERS

- Ask students to work with a partner and take turns reading the dialogue. After they read each part, ask them to describe in their own words what each speaker said. For example, in the first two exchanges, students might say: *Asha usa el Internet para buscar fotos de haciendas y encontró una que le gusta. A Lucas le gusta el color, pero no sabe si es una hacienda o un hotel.*

EXPANDING LEARNERS

- Explain to students that they are going to work with a partner and research what certain colors symbolize. Assign a color to each pair of students. Ask them to explore what emotions and personality traits their color typically represents. For example, red often denotes energy and love. Ask students to describe how other cultures view this color, and what holidays or natural phenomena are associated with it. Have pairs who are working on the same colors get together after their initial research and prepare a joint report for the rest of the class.

31 **¿Comprendes?**

▶ **Responde** a estas preguntas.

1. ¿Qué muebles y objetos de decoración hay en la sala?
2. ¿Dónde quiere poner Asha el símbolo?
3. ¿Por qué Lucas prefiere ponerlo en el comedor?
4. ¿Dónde deciden colocar el símbolo finalmente?
5. ¿Por qué piensa Lucas que será difícil encontrar un símbolo?

32 **El símbolo perfecto**

▶ **Escucha** la conversación de Asha y Lucas. ¿A qué símbolos se refieren?

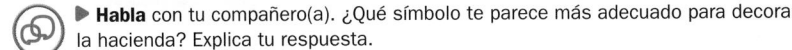

▶ **Habla** con tu compañero(a). ¿Qué símbolo te parece más adecuado para decorar la hacienda? Explica tu respuesta.

CULTURA

La wiphala

La wiphala es un emblema de tela que se usa en la región andina desde hace siglos. Está formada por 49 cuadrados y los 7 colores del arco iris, y se utiliza como bandera de los pueblos nativos de los Andes.

Cada color tiene un significado. Por ejemplo, el rojo representa el mundo y el azul, el espacio cósmico. Y cada *suyu* o región tiene su propia versión de la wiphala.

33 **Compara.** ¿Cómo es la bandera de tu país? ¿Qué significado tienen los elementos que hay en ella?

HERITAGE LANGUAGE LEARNERS

• Ask students to research the words that are related to *símbolo*, such as *emblema, lema, insignia, mascota, representación, escudo de armas,* and *icono* and explain the differences between them, when they might typically be used, and include an example of each one. Students should prepare this information in a short written report. You may want to call on some students to explain these differences to the rest of the class.

MULTIPLE INTELLIGENCES:
Intrapersonal Intelligence

• Ask students to explain what symbols they would choose for themselves, their family, their best friends, and their Spanish class, and what they would choose as a new symbol for their school or favorite sports team. Ask them to draw each symbol and explain its design, its meaning, why they used the colors they did, what each color means, and how they would like to display this symbol.

• Have the class vote on the best symbol for the Spanish class and commission a student volunteer to draw it.

---

32. Before students listen to the audio recording, have them describe each of the symbols depicted. After listening to the audio, ask them to describe each symbol in terms of colors and shapes to review vocabulary they already know and to introduce some new words if needed.

33. If possible, ask students to search on the Internet to learn more about the Wiphala.

AUDIO SCRIPT
See page 119I.

CULTURA

La wiphala

The Wiphala is a square-shaped flag combining the seven colors of the rainbow arranged as patchwork. The square arrangement and colors vary from region to region. The Wiphala is used as a recognizable Amerindian symbol in Bolivia, Peru, Ecuador, Chile, and parts of Argentina and Colombia. It is often present in social and cultural activities, such as marriages, births, funerals, traditional ceremonies, festivities, and games.

Answer Key

30. 1. Algunas   4. algunos
     2. algún   5. todas
     3. ningún

31. 1. Hay una chimenea, muebles de madera natural y un cuadro.
     2. Lo quiere poner en la sala.
     3. Porque así lo verán todos los huéspedes.
     4. Deciden colocarlo en el comedor.
     5. Porque tiene que representar a todas las culturas indígenas.

32. 2, 4, 1
    ▶ Answers will vary.

33. Answers will vary.

Additional Resources

Fans Online activities

139

DESAFÍO 2

Vocabulario – Describir objetos

Presentation

- In this section, students will learn words that describe objects in terms of shapes, textures, materials, and colors.

Activities	Standards	Resources
Vocabulario	1.2, 2.2	
34.	1.1, 1.2, 2.2	Audio
35.	1.1, 5.2	
36.	1.1, 1.3, 2.2, 5.1	
37. Cultura	1.1, 1.2, 2.1, 2.2, 3.2	

Teaching Suggestions

Warm-Up / Independent Starter

- Ask students to write a description of the last object they bought for their room.

Preparation

- Have students look at the pictures on page 140 and ask them the following questions: *¿Dónde están Asha y Lucas: en un centro comercial o en un mercado al aire libre? ¿Qué están mirando? ¿Qué hay en la segunda fotografía? ¿De qué material creen que están hechos?*

- Ask two volunteers to read the first dialogue on page 140. Then go over the highlighted words to emphasize pronunciation. Ask two more volunteers to read the second dialogue and use the same technique to introduce the vocabulary.

- If possible, bring objects with different textures, shapes, and materials to class to ensure that students understand the meaning of the new vocabulary words. Use these objects to introduce the words from the *Más vocabulario* feature.

Activities

34. To extend this activity, ask students the following questions after listening to the conversation: *¿Dónde están Asha y Lucas? ¿Por qué quiere comprar algo Asha? ¿Por qué compra Asha la pulsera en lugar de la mesa? ¿Qué objeto pensó comprar Lucas en primer lugar? ¿Dónde va a colocar Lucas el plato de cerámica que decide comprar?*

DESAFÍO 2

Vocabulario

Describir objetos

ASHA: Lucas, ¿crees que en este mercadillo vamos a encontrar algún símbolo?

LUCAS: Claro, Asha. Hay mucha artesanía indígena. Mira estas alfombras. Son de lana auténtica de alpaca. ¡Qué suaves, tócalas!

ASHA: Son caras, pero de muy buena calidad. Me gusta aquella rectangular, la de colores rojizos.

LUCAS: A mí me gusta más esta. Es muy elegante.

ASHA: Mira, Lucas. Estos platos de cerámica son muy prácticos para la casa, los puedes usar todos los días. Y qué colores tan bonitos: azul oscuro, amarillo limón, rojo brillante, verdoso...

LUCAS: Además, son muy baratos: solo cuestan 15 pesos. Y tienen símbolos...

ASHA: Vamos a ver ese puesto de adornos de madera natural.

Más vocabulario

Formas		Textura		Materiales	
cuadrado(a)	*square*	áspero(a)	*rough*	de hierro	*iron*
ovalado(a)	*oval*	blando(a)	*soft*	de metal	*metal*
redondo(a)	*round*	duro(a)	*hard*	de plástico	*plastic*

34 Las compras

▶ **Escucha** y decide. ¿Qué objetos compraron Asha y Lucas en la exposición del museo de arte indígena?

① 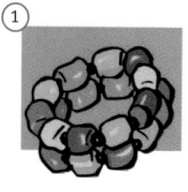 ②  ③ 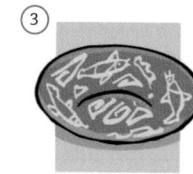 ④

▶ **Escribe** una descripción detallada de cada objeto.

Differentiated Instruction

DEVELOPING LEARNERS

- Ask students to work with a partner and take turns describing objects in the classroom to one another. Students should give their partners one clue at a time, by mentioning the shape of the object, along with its texture, the material it is made of, its color, and any other relevant details. Partners must guess what the object is. After every incorrect answer, the partner must offer another clue. For example:
  A. *Es redondo.*
  B. *¿Es tu pulsera?*
  A. *No. Es de metal.*
  B. *¿Es el reloj?*
  A. *Sí.*

EXPANDING LEARNERS

- Have students work with a partner and imagine that they are at a *mercadillo* in Latin America. One student will be searching for the perfect gift for a family member, a friend, or their teacher, and the other will be the owner of a stand that sells a variety of products. The "customers" do not know what they want, but they have some ideas and will express them to the seller. The seller, however, might have some of his or her own ideas for the "perfect" gift for the customer. Remind students to bargain!

35 **El objeto misterioso**

▶ **Habla.** Por turnos, seleccionen un objeto y descríbanselo a su compañero(a) sin decir su nombre. Él/Ella tiene que adivinar cuál es.

Modelo A. *Es de cristal.*
B. *¿Es la lámpara?*
A. *No. Es rectangular y…*

36 **Eligiendo regalos**

▶ **Escribe** con tu compañero(a) una lista de los aspectos positivos y negativos de estos dos regalos.

Modelo *La alfombra es de lana, pero los colores son demasiado brillantes…*

▶ **Escribe** un correo electrónico a alguien de tu familia dándole buenas razones para comprar uno de esos regalos.

 **CULTURA**

El mercado de Otavalo (Ecuador)

Los mercados indígenas de Latinoamérica son una atracción turística muy importante. Situado a unas horas de Quito, el mercado de Otavalo es uno de los mayores y de los más conocidos. En él se puede comprar ropa, tapices (*tapestries*), textiles, joyas y adornos de piedra, madera o jade. Normalmente todos estos productos están hechos a mano, con los materiales y diseños tradicionales. Pasear por este mercado es una forma de conocer las costumbres y tradiciones de Ecuador.

37 **Piensa y explica.** ¿Qué objetos de artesanía se pueden comprar en la región donde vives?

---

35. Turn this activity into a game. Have flashcards with pictures of these or other objects. Divide the class in two groups. Assign numbers for each student in both groups; if you have twenty students, assign numbers 1 to 10 to each group. Give a flashcard to each student. Student 1 in group A will describe the object on his or her flashcard to student 1 in group B. A team will gain a point if the student guesses the object described.

36. Collect students' e-mails and give each student an e-mail written by another classmate. Ask them to write an answer to the e-mail, explaining why they do not agree and why their own object is better than the classmate's.

 AUDIO SCRIPT
See page 119I.

 CULTURA

El mercado de Otavalo (Ecuador)

Otavalo is located about 60 miles north of Quito. Otavalo is known for its historical importance, its market, and its festivities. The festivity of Yamor is one of the most famous. This celebration coincides with the autumn equinox, when Otavalo's population thanks Mother Earth for the corn harvest. This festivity is a time of gathering between relatives and old friends living far away.

Answer Key

34. 1, 3
▶ Answers will vary.

35. Answers will vary.

36. Answers will vary.
▶ Answers will vary.

37. Answers will vary.

Additional Resources

Fans Online activities
Practice Workbook

HERITAGE LANGUAGE LEARNERS

• Ask students to describe some typical yet unique objects that might be found at a market in their family's country of origin. The products could include food, and also clothes, jewelry, souvenirs, and assorted handicrafts. Encourage students to bring some of these products (or images of them) to class, explain what they are, how and when they are used, what they are made of, and the importance they have for the target culture.

COOPERATIVE LEARNING

• Ask students to work in small groups and open a *mercadillo* in the classroom. Students will need to create a name for their market, bring in or draw images of the products they want to sell, and establish the currency of the country where the transactions take place, along with the prices for the goods. Students from other groups will be the customers and will try to get the best buy. Remind all participants to bargain (*regatear*) over the prices.

• You may want to invite other Spanish classes to come "shop" in your *mercadillo*.

DESAFÍO 2

Gramática – Los indefinidos

Presentation

- In this section, students will review the use of indefinite adjectives and pronouns.

Activities	Standards	Resources
Gramática	1.2, 3.1	
38.	1.1, 4.1	
39.	1.1, 1.2, 1.3	Audio
40.	1.1, 1.2	
41.	1.1, 1.2, 1.3, 5.1	
42. Cultura	1.1, 1.2, 2.1, 2.2, 3.1	

Teaching Suggestions

Warm-Up / Independent Starter

- Write the following phrases and indefinite choices on the board. Ask students to choose the right indefinite for each phrase.
  1. *Mochila llena de libros: pocos / muchos. (muchos)*
  2. *Cine con diez personas: pocas / muchas. (pocas)*
  3. *Salón de clase vacío: alguien / nadie. (nadie)*
  4. *Mesa con tres libros: algunos / ninguno. (algunos)*
  5. *Refrigerador vacío: algo / nada. (nada)*

Preparation

- Have students read the grammar explanation silently and take notes on any material they do not understand.

- Ask volunteers to give the answers for the Independent Starter. During the correction you may point out examples on page 142 to emphasize gender and number agreement when needed as well as the use of *ningún* or *algún* instead of *ninguno* or *alguno* before masculine nouns.

Activities

39. You may want to change the writing part into an oral presentation. Ask students to prepare a poster or sketch of their room and describe it.

41. For the written part, instead of just writing a description of their classmate's house, you may ask students to write a description of their classmate's house comparing it with their own.

Gramática

Los indefinidos

- Use indefinite adjectives or pronouns to refer to nouns using nonspecific terms.

  Hay **algunas** artesanías en la sala y **muchos** muebles.

PRINCIPALES INDEFINIDOS

EXISTENCIA			
Positivos		Negativos	
algo	¿Hay algo en esa caja?	nada	No hay nada en la caja.
alguien	Creo que hay alguien en casa.	nadie	No hay nadie en la calle.
algún, alguno(a)(os)(as)	Tengo algunos discos antiguos.	ningún, ninguno(a)	No tengo ninguna moneda.

CANTIDAD				
poco(a)(os)(as)	varios(as)	mucho(a)(os)(as)	demasiado(a)(os)(as)	todo(a)(os)(as)

- Other indefinites are otro *(another)* and cualquier(a) *(whichever)*. These indefinite adjectives and pronouns must change to show agreement.

  He comprado una joya en este mercado y **otra** en ese **otro** mercado.

Uso de los indefinidos

- When alguno and ninguno precede a masculine singular noun, use algún and ningún.

  En mi casa hay **algún** florero moderno, pero no hay **ningún** florero antiguo.

- Unlike in English, negative indefinites are often used with a verb in the negative.

  No hay **nadie** en la cocina.   No sé **nada** de cocina.

- Remember: there is no variation of gender or number when the words poco, mucho, and demasiado go before an adjective or with a verb, because they are adverbs.

  Los muebles antiguos cuestan **mucho**. Esas mesitas son **demasiado** caras.

38 **Compara.** ¿Cómo se dice en inglés No compré nada en el mercado?

39 **La habitación de Lucas**

▶ **Escucha** la conversación entre Asha y Lucas, y completa estas oraciones.
1. Hay ___1___ libros en la estantería.
2. En el pasillo hay ___2___ floreros y ___3___ adornos.
3. En su habitación hay ___4___ videojuegos.
4. Tiene ___5___ zapatos en el armario.

▶ **Escribe** oraciones similares sobre tu habitación. Usa los indefinidos.

Differentiated Instruction

DEVELOPING LEARNERS

- Ask students to complete the following sentences by choosing the correct indefinite:
  1. *Miguel lee mucho / algún, pero Susi no lee nada / algo. (mucho, nada)*
  2. *No compro nada / algo en esa tienda porque todo es carísimo. (nada)*
  3. *La sopa está demasiado / demasiada caliente. (demasiado)*
  4. *¿Tienes algún / ningún cinturón rojo? (algún)*
  5. *¿Hay alguien / nadie en la biblioteca? No, no hay nadie / alguien. (alguien, nadie)*

EXPANDING LEARNERS

- Ask students to write a response from Sara to Andrea's e-mail. In her reply, Sara should express pleasure at knowing that her friend and her friend's family will be in her country. Sara should also include suggestions as to the *haciendas* where Andrea and her family might stay. She should recommend two suitable *haciendas* and describe the accommodations, prices, location, and activities the guests may participate in. Sara should also mention that she would be happy to make a reservation for her friend. Students should include indefinite adjectives and pronouns in their replies.

40 Las próximas vacaciones

▶ **Completa** el mensaje que la madre de Asha le envía a una amiga mexicana.

> toda   alguna   mucho   demasiada   todas   nada

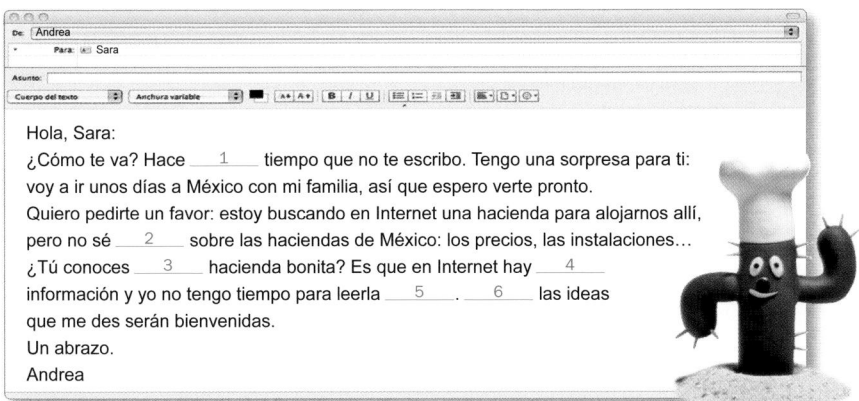

De: Andrea
Para: Sara
Asunto:

Cuerpo del texto   Anchura variable   A+ A+   B I U

Hola, Sara:
¿Cómo te va? Hace ___1___ tiempo que no te escribo. Tengo una sorpresa para ti:
voy a ir unos días a México con mi familia, así que espero verte pronto.
Quiero pedirte un favor: estoy buscando en Internet una hacienda para alojarnos allí,
pero no sé ___2___ sobre las haciendas de México: los precios, las instalaciones…
¿Tú conoces ___3___ hacienda bonita? Es que en Internet hay ___4___
información y yo no tengo tiempo para leerla ___5___. ___6___ las ideas
que me des serán bienvenidas.
Un abrazo.
Andrea

41 ¿Qué casa es mejor?

▶ **Habla.** Tu compañero(a) quiere vender su casa. Pregúntale y toma notas.

1. ¿Hay muchos dormitorios en su casa? ¿Tiene muchos muebles o pocos?
2. ¿Alguien de su familia ha hecho modificaciones en la casa?
3. ¿Hay algo de su casa que le gusta especialmente?

▶ **Escribe** una descripción de la casa de tu compañero(a).

 **CULTURA**

Las haciendas coloniales

Las haciendas son fincas agrícolas que se construyeron
en la época colonial siguiendo el modelo español.
Contaban con una casa principal, una gran extensión
de tierra y viviendas para los trabajadores.

Muchas de estas haciendas se utilizan hoy como hoteles
o como museos y están decoradas con muebles y artesanía locales.

42 **Piensa.** ¿Qué ventajas y desventajas crees que tenía vivir en una hacienda
en la época colonial?

HERITAGE LANGUAGE LEARNERS

- Ask students to research other words that
  may be used in place of farm or *hacienda*.
  Examples include: *finca, granja, cortijo,
  quinta, rancho, chacra, estancia, alquería,* and
  fundo. Students should explain which
  countries or regions use these words, and
  describe the differences between them, and
  perhaps some of their history. For example:
  *Una alquería es una casa con una huerta.
  Este término se usa en España, en la zona de
  Valencia. Hace siglos se refería a una
  pequeña comunidad agrícola al lado de una
  ciudad.*

TOTAL PHYSICAL RESPONSE (TPR)

- Divide the class in half: one team will be *los
  positivos,* the other, *los negativos.* Prepare
  several sentences, leaving out the indefinite,
  and read each sentence aloud. If the
  sentence is to be completed by an
  affirmative indefinite, *los positivos* must stand
  up and complete it. In the case of a negative
  indefinite, *los negativos* will stand and
  answer. For example:
  1. No hay … en la clase. *(nadie)*
  2. No tienes … símbolo para tu escuela.
     (ningún)
  3. Veo a … en la hacienda. *(alguien)*
  4. ¿Quieres tomar…? *(algo)*

Gramática – Los indefinidos

42. Divide the class into two groups. Ask them
to imagine that they are living during colonial
times. Have half of the class write a list of
the advantages of living in an *hacienda*; have
the other half of the class write a list of the
disadvantages. After each group has a list, ask
them to contrast their opinions.

 AUDIO SCRIPT
See page 119I.

 CULTURA

Las haciendas coloniales

The presence of both indigenous and colonial
heritage is important in the architecture of
Latin America. The Spanish colonial style is
often found in religious and civil architecture,
such as churches and government buildings.
Haciendas, which mean "estates" in Spanish,
became the basis of an economic system in
the 16th century that spread all over Latin
America. Although *haciendas* vary from region
to region, they remind us of the architecture
of southern Spain.

Answer Key

38. Se dice, *I bought nothing in the market*
o *I did not buy anything in the market.*

39. 1. demasiados   4. pocos
2. algunos   5. bastantes
3. muchos
▶ Answers will vary.

40. 1. mucho   4. demasiada
2. nada   5. toda
3. alguna   6. Todas

41. Answers will vary.
▶ Answers will vary.

42. Answers will vary.

Additional Resources

Fans Online activities
Practice Workbook

DESAFÍO 2

Gramática – Construcciones impersonales. El pronombre *se*

Presentation

- In this section, students will review and practice how to use the pronoun *se* in impersonal constructions.

Activities	Standards	Resources
Gramática	1.2, 3.1	
43.	1.1, 3.1, 4.1	
44.	1.1, 1.2, 5.2	Audio
45.	1.1, 1.2, 1.3, 2.2	
46.	1.1, 1.2, 1.3, 5.2	

Teaching Suggestions

Warm-Up / Independent Starter

- Have students write a list of things they can and cannot do in their Spanish class. Provide them with the following example: *En la clase de Español no se puede usar teléfonos celulares.*

Preparation

- Have two volunteers read the grammar presentation aloud. Encourage students to ask questions about any explanations they do not understand and clarify this information for them.

- Draw a two-column chart on the board and add these headings: *Se puede... No se puede...* Have volunteers write examples from their Independent Starters under the appropriate column.

- Then have students rewrite the above statements using *se* and a verb in the third person. For example: *No se usan teléfonos celulares en la clase de Español. Se habla solo español.* Make sure that they make proper use of the singular and plural third person.

Activities

45. Before starting the activity, ask students to look at the picture and describe the objects they see in terms of shape, colors, materials, etc. After the activity, have students work in pairs to come up with a geometrical design, inspired by the picture, to be used as an indigenous symbol. Have them explain their design.

144

Gramática

Construcciones impersonales. El pronombre *se*

El pronombre *se* impersonal

- Remember: we can use a construction with the word *se* and the verb in the third person to express an action without emphasizing the person who performs the action.

se + verb in the 3rd person

—¿Cómo **se dice** *apple* en español?
—**Se dice** *manzana.*

Uso de *se* + verbo en tercera persona con valor impersonal

- When the impersonal *se* construction is followed by an infinitive or a clause that begins with *que*, the verb will always be in the third person singular form.

  Se prohíbe hablar por teléfono.
  Se ve que esta ropa es de buena calidad.

- However, when speaking about a noun, the verb will agree in number with the noun. In these cases, the construction *se + verb in the 3rd person* acts as the passive voice:

  Se vende pescado aquí.
  Se venden zapatos aquí.

43 **Compara.** ¿Cómo se dice en inglés Se alquilan casas de madera? ¿Qué diferencia hay entre esta estructura en español y la del inglés?

44 **Adivina, adivinanza**

▶ **Escucha** y relaciona cada pista *(clue)* con el objeto correspondiente.

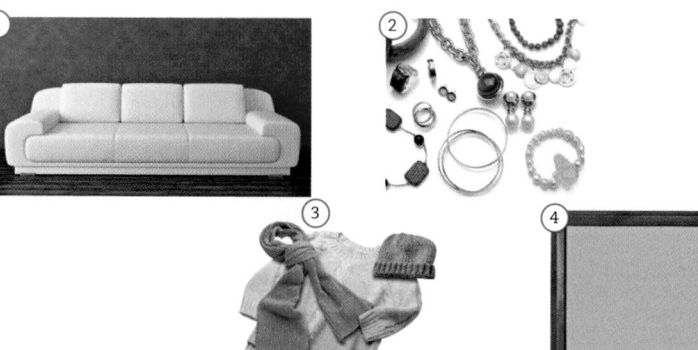

▶ **Escribe** pistas sobre dos objetos de tu casa siguiendo el modelo anterior. Léeselas a tu compañero(a) para que adivine a qué objeto corresponden.

Differentiated Instruction

DEVELOPING LEARNERS

- To give students more practice with the pronoun *se* when referring to a noun, write the following sentences and ask students to rewrite them by using *se* plus a verb in the third person:
  1. *Venden muchos libros. (Se venden muchos libros.)*
  2. *Compran comida en el mercado. (Se compra comida en el mercado.)*
  3. *Hacen recuerdos de cuero. (Se hacen recuerdos de cuero.)*
  4. *Estudian idiomas. (Se estudian idiomas.)*
  5. *Usan la hacienda como hotel. (Se usa la hacienda como hotel.)*

EXPANDING LEARNERS

- Ask students to think about what people should or should not do in order to be a better citizen, student, friend, son or daughter, or sibling. Then ask them to write a list or a paragraph in which they explain what individuals should or should not do, and use the *construcciones impersonales con se* to express this. When students finish, ask them to share their advice with the rest of the class and engage them in a discussion about these recommendations. Explore with students if there is a common thread running through these suggestions.

45 **De compras**

▶ **Lee.** ¿Qué objetos del mercado mencionan Asha y Lucas? Escríbelo.

Un día en el mercado

LUCAS: En este mercado se venden alfombras típicas de Ecuador. ¡Qué lindas!

ASHA: Sí, son increíbles. Se dice que cada alfombra lleva un trabajo de muchos meses.

LUCAS: ¿Con qué material se fabrican?

ASHA: Se hacen de lana de alpaca, creo.

LUCAS: Esos platos son muy interesantes. ¿También se hacen a mano?

ASHA: Sí, aquí se venden muchos objetos artesanales. Ay, mira esas pulseras y esos aretes. ¿No te parecen impresionantes? Creo que me voy a comprar algo.

LUCAS: De acuerdo, pero recuerda que estamos aquí para buscar símbolos indígenas…

ASHA: Ay, Lucas, tranquilo. Tenemos tiempo. Oye, ¿aquí se paga en efectivo o con tarjeta de crédito?

LUCAS: Se paga en efectivo y creo que se puede regatear *(bargain)*.

▶ **Decide** si estas oraciones son ciertas o falsas. Después, corrige las falsas.

1. En el mercado se venden alfombras de cuero.
2. Las alfombras se hacen a mano.
3. En el mercado se puede comprar mucha artesanía.
4. En el mercado no se puede regatear.
5. En el mercado se puede pagar con tarjeta de crédito.

46 **Se hace, no se hace**

▶ **Escribe.** ¿Qué se permite hacer en estos lugares? ¿Y qué se prohíbe?

Modelo   *En el cine se prohíbe hablar. Pero se permite comer palomitas y beber refrescos.*

1. En el cine.
2. En la escuela.
3. En un centro comercial.
4. En un mercado al aire libre.
5. En un avión.

▶ **Habla** con dos compañeros(as). Piensen en dos lugares más y en lo que se permite y se prohíbe hacer allí. Escríbanlo y lean su lista a otro grupo para que adivinen los lugares.

HERITAGE LANGUAGE LEARNERS

- Ask students to work with a partner, or in groups of three, and create a dialogue in which they will use all of the *construcciones impersonales con se* mentioned in the *Gramática* feature. Students may model their dialogues on the one from activity 45, but should use new characters, a new setting, and different content. Allow them time to rehearse their lines and invite some students to present their dialogues in front of the class.

CRITICAL THINKING

- Ask students to make a list of what they can and cannot do in three different areas of their school (e.g., the cafeteria, the gym, the principal's office). To get them started, share these examples: *No se puede correr en la cafetería. Pero se puede hablar con los compañeros en la cafetería.*
- Call on some students to read their rules aloud. Then enable a discussion on whether rules stating what one can do are more or less effective than rules stating what one cannot do.

Gramática – Construcciones impersonales. El pronombre *se*

46. You may turn this activity into a game similar to "Family Feud." Divide the class in two or three groups. Give each group a flashcard containing names of places: *el cine, la escuela, un centro comercial, un mercado al aire libre,* and *un avión.* Ask them to write a list of four things you can or cannot do in these places in order of importance.

 AUDIO SCRIPT
See page 119 J.

Answer Key

43. Se dice, *We rent wooden houses.* En inglés se dice quién alquila las casas: *we.*

44. 1. 4   2. 2   3. 1   4. 3
▶ Answers will vary. Sample answer: Se hacen de madera, de formica, de mármol, etc. Se colocan en los comedores y a veces en las cocinas. (mesas)

45. Alfombras de lana de alpaca, platos, joyas (pulseras y aretes), símbolos indígenas.
▶ 1. Falso. Son de lana de alpaca.
2. Cierto.
3. Cierto.
4. Falso. En el mercado se puede regatear.
5. Falso. Se paga en efectivo.

46. Answers will vary. Sample answers:
2. En la escuela se prohíbe usar teléfonos celulares. Pero se permite practicar deporte en el gimnasio.
3. En un centro comercial se compran muchas cosas diferentes. Pero no se puede regatear.
4. En un mercado al aire libre se puede regatear. Pero normalmente no se puede pagar con tarjeta de crédito.
5. En un avión se permite leer. Pero se prohíbe escuchar música sin auriculares.
▶ Answers will vary.

Additional Resources

Fans Online activities
Practice Workbook

145

LECTURA: TEXTO INFORMATIVO

Presentation

- In this section, students will read the description of a hotel. Students will recognize the use of descriptive adjectives and they will review vocabulary related to architecture and décor.

Activities	Standards	Resources
Lectura: texto informativo	1.1, 1.2, 2.2, 3.1, 3.2	
47.	1.1, 1.2	
48.	1.1, 1.2	
49.	1.3, 4.2, 5.1	

Teaching Suggestions

Warm-Up / Independent Starter

- Have students read the *Antes de leer* strategies silently. Ask them to jot down some notes and prepare to share their answers.

Preparation

- Remind students that *haciendas* are colonial estates found in some areas of Latin America. They were traditionally used as farmhouses, but some of them have been converted into hotels.

- Call on volunteers to explain what type of text this is. Make sure they understand the word *guía*. Brainstorm with students about the type of information that we may expect to find in a travel guide.

- Read the description aloud to students to model pronunciation and intonation. Then have students alternate reading several lines or a paragraph. You may want to pause after every paragraph and call on a volunteer to paraphrase the content.

- Ask students to take out the list of adjectives they wrote in their Independent Starters. In their opinion, is this a positive description or not? Ask related questions: *¿Creen que este es un buen hotel? ¿Por qué? ¿Qué les parece la arquitectura? ¿Y la decoración? ¿Qué características prefieren en un hotel?*

- Call students' attention to the last sentence of the text. What does the expression *hacen de* mean? What is the subject? Can they create a similar sentence with the same expression?

LECTURA: TEXTO INFORMATIVO

Antes de leer: estrategias

1. Lee el título. ¿Qué tipo de texto es? ¿Dónde podemos encontrar un texto como este?
2. Mira la foto y la información. ¿Para qué se usa esta hacienda? ¿Cómo es? ¿De qué materiales crees que está hecha?
3. Busca este dato sin leer todo el texto: ¿Dónde está la hacienda?
4. Fíjate en los adjetivos. ¿Describen la hacienda positiva o negativamente? Escribe algunos ejemplos.

Guía de viajeros: un hotel inolvidable

Hacienda Abraspungo
ECUADOR
42 habitaciones
Categoría: * * * *
Servicios: restaurante, bar, sauna, excursiones.

La Hacienda Abraspungo es una de las más hermosas haciendas de Ecuador. Está situada en la ciudad de Riobamba, a 2.754 metros sobre el nivel del mar[1], en la región del volcán Chimborazo (Ecuador). Su situación excepcional y excelente servicio garantizan[2] una experiencia inolvidable[3] para el huésped.

La hacienda tiene 42 habitaciones decoradas con objetos auténticos de artesanía local y antigüedades[4], como fotografías antiguas, armarios de madera, etc. Cada habitación tiene el nombre de un volcán de la región y está decorada con fotografías y cuadros de ese volcán.

En el restaurante se usan productos naturales de los mercados de Abraspungo, y su cocina es una combinación de la alta gastronomía internacional y de las técnicas tradicionales de la cocina ecuatoriana.

Los jardines y el entorno[5] hacen de esta hacienda un lugar perfecto para descansar.

---

1. *above sea level*   2. *guarantee*   3. *unforgettable*   4. *antiques*   5. *setting*

Differentiated Instruction

DEVELOPING LEARNERS

- Ask students to read the article again, and then have them close their books. Write the following false sentences on the board and ask students to correct them:
  1. *La hacienda está en la región de los terremotos. (volcanes)*
  2. *Todas las habitaciones tienen arte moderno. (tienen antigüedades)*
  3. *No hay jardines, pero hay dos piscinas. (hay jardines)*
  4. *El restaurante es francés. (es internacional)*
  5. *La hacienda es perfecta para reuniones de negocios. (para descansar)*

EXPANDING LEARNERS

- Tell students to imagine that they are travel editors for a leading tourism magazine. As part of their job, they visit and stay at hotels around the world. Students have just spent a few days at the Hacienda Abraspungo and need to write a review of the hotel. Tell students to write their reviews, favorable or negative, and to be sure to include comments on the service, the accommodations, the restaurants, the amenities, and the price.

47 Comprensión

▶ **Responde** a estas preguntas.

1. ¿Cuántas habitaciones tiene la hacienda?
2. ¿Cómo están decoradas?
3. ¿Qué es específico de cada habitación?
4. ¿Qué tipo de comida se sirve en el restaurante?
5. ¿Cómo es el entorno?

▶ **Elige** la opción correcta y explica tu respuesta.

1. El entorno de la hacienda es…   a. urbano   b. rural
2. El estilo de la decoración es…   a. moderno   b. tradicional
3. Las habitaciones tienen cuadros…   a. iguales   b. diferentes
4. Los platos se hacen con productos…   a. internacionales b. locales
5. Probablemente el precio de la hacienda es… a. caro   b. barato

48 Descripciones

▶ **Escribe** los adjetivos del texto que se corresponden con estas definiciones. Después, escribe otra oración con cada uno.

1. Excelente, extraordinario.
2. Memorable.
3. Real, verdadero.
4. Distinto, que no es igual.
5. Que no es artificial.
6. Que no es moderno.

Modelo 1. *excepcional*
→ *El concierto de anoche me pareció excepcional, el mejor que he visto.*

49 Con tus propias palabras

▶ **Escribe** la descripción de un hotel distinto a la Hacienda Abraspungo y presenta tu descripción a la clase.

Modelo

El hotel Wynn está situado en la ciudad de Macao. Su situación es…

ciento cuarenta y siete 147

Activities

47. To expand this activity, ask further comprehension questions.
1. *¿En qué región de Ecuador está esta hacienda?*
2. *¿Qué es lo particular de esta región?*
3. *¿Qué tipo de clima creen que tiene esta región?*
4. *¿Qué servicios se ofrecen en esta hacienda?*

48. Although some of the adjectives are used in their plural or feminine forms in the text, ask students to list these adjectives in their singular, masculine form. However, they can use any form of the adjective in their sentences. For example: 3. *auténtico → Solo compro antigüedades auténticas.*

49. Encourage students to write about hotels they know or they have been to. You may also assign the activity as homework or do it in the computer lab to give them the opportunity to look up the information online. Make sure they look for information in Spanish.

Answer Key

47. 1. Tiene 42 habitaciones.
2. Están decoradas con objetos de artesanía y antigüedades.
3. Cada habitación tiene el nombre de un volcán diferente y está decorada con fotos de ese volcán.
4. Se sirve alta gastronomía internacional.
5. El entorno es montañoso.
▶ 1. b   2. b   3. b   4. b   5. a

48. 2. inolvidable
3. auténtico
4. diferente
5. natural
6. tradicional

49. Answers will vary.

Additional Resources

Fans Online activities

HERITAGE LANGUAGE LEARNERS
• Ask students to imagine that they have just spent the past week at the Hacienda Abraspungo, but have had a horrible time. It was, in fact, the worst vacation they have ever had. Encourage their creativity and ask them to write a scathing letter to the Hacienda's general manager, complaining about everything: the service, the room, the food, the amenities, the weather, the annoying neighbors, the price, and anything else they can think of. Call on students to read their complaints aloud to see who had the worst vacation.

MULTIPLE INTELLIGENCES:
Verbal-Linguistic Intelligence
• Ask students to imagine that they are owners of an *hacienda* which has just opened to the public. Students will prepare a few paragraphs describing their *hacienda*, including its location, how many guests it accommodates, what the rooms are like, what activities are offered, what kind of food is served, and what other amenities it offers. Encourage students to find a suitable image for their *hacienda* to include in their report. Have students read their "guide" to the class. Then take a vote to see which *hacienda* students find most appealing.

147

Unit 3

DESAFÍO 2

Comunicación

Presentation

- In this section, students will integrate the vocabulary and grammar skills from *Desafío 2* in order to describe objects, refer to nouns using nonspecific terms, and use impersonal constructions.

Activities	Standards	Resources
50.	1.1, 1.2, 2.1, 5.1	Audio
51.	1.3, 3.1, 5.1	
52.	1.1, 1.3, 3.1	
53. Final del desafío	1.1, 1.2, 2.2, 3.1	
Tu desafío	1.1, 1.2	

Teaching Suggestions

Warm-Up / Independent Starter

- Have two or three unusual objects on your table and ask students to describe them in detail.

Preparation

- Ask for volunteers to share their Independent Starters in front of the class. Ask each one to take a different object from the table and share with the class the description of that object. After each description, you may ask students to describe the texture of the object.

Activities

50. After finishing this activity, have students work in pairs or small groups to write about the differences between a traditional market and a modern shopping center. You may want to organize this discussion as a debate in which half of the class defends traditional markets and the other half a shopping center.

51. Collect students' descriptions and post them in the classroom. Have students choose one object to buy in order to replace a similar one in their own house. Ask them to explain why they want to replace the one in their house. For example: *Voy a comprar la mesa de trabajo cuadrada porque la mía es redonda y ocupa mucho espacio.*

Comunicación

50 **¡Vamos al mercado!**

▶ **Escribe.** ¿Cómo son estos mercados? ¿Qué crees que se vende en ellos? Escribe un párrafo comparándolos.

Modelo *En el primer mercado hay muchas personas, pero en el otro no hay casi nadie.*

 ▶ **Escucha** las descripciones de varios productos y decide en qué mercado se pueden vender mejor.

Modelo *Yo creo que podemos vender la lámpara en este mercado porque…*

 ▶ **Habla** con tu compañero(a). Imagina que vas a visitar uno de esos mercados. ¿Cuál te gusta más? ¿Por qué?

Modelo A. *A mí me gusta más el primer mercado porque me gusta comprar ropa.*
B. *Pues yo prefiero el segundo porque es más auténtico.*

51 **Se vende**

▶ **Escribe.** Elige dos objetos de tu casa que puedas vender. Escribe una descripción detallada de cada uno para poner un anuncio en Internet.

- ¿Qué es?
- ¿Qué forma tiene?
- ¿De qué color es?
- ¿De qué está hecho?
- ¿Para qué se usa?

148 ciento cuarenta y ocho

Differentiated Instruction

DEVELOPING LEARNERS

- Much of the vocabulary in this *Desafío* has centered on words with opposite meanings (e.g., *blando → duro; alguien → nadie*). Ask students to go through the *Desafío* and review the dialogues, vocabulary, grammar, and reading. Have them find as many pairs of opposites as they can and take note of these words. Encourage them to also include words that might not appear in the *Desafío*, but which are of opposite meaning to those that do appear. For example, they might write *imperfecto* for the word *perfecto* in Asha's fourth exchange on page 138.

EXPANDING LEARNERS

- Have students role-play Asha and Lucas and write a convincing letter to the sponsors of the contest in order to win an unforgettable weekend at the *hacienda*. Students will work with a partner and will need to mention why they have chosen the Wiphala as a symbol for the *hacienda* and why they chose to place it where they did. They should also mention why they believe they deserve to win this trip.

52 **La casa del futuro**

▶ **Escribe** una descripción de la casa del futuro. Debes explicar:

- ¿Cómo es la casa?
- ¿De qué materiales está hecha?
- ¿Qué objetos (muebles, electrodomésticos, adornos) hay en ella y cómo son?
- ¿Qué se puede y qué no se puede hacer en la casa?

 ▶ **Haz** una presentación digital o un póster sobre la casa del futuro y preséntala a la clase.

Final del desafío

Entonces, definitivamente, el símbolo que elegimos es la wiphala, ¿cierto?

Sí. Los dueños de la hacienda pueden ponerla en la pared del comedor.

Pues vamos a escribir la nota. Podemos empezar así: «Estimados señores: Somos dos estudiantes...»

 53 **La nota de Asha y Lucas**

▶ **Escribe.** Con tu compañero(a), ayuda a Asha y a Lucas a escribir la nota para los dueños de la hacienda.

 **TU DESAFÍO** Visita la página web. Escucha las preguntas de tu *Minientrevista Desafío 2* y escribe las respuestas.

HERITAGE LANGUAGE LEARNERS

- Ask students to imagine that they are the judges who will be deciding whether Asha and Lucas are the winners of the *hacienda* weekend. Have students read the letters submitted by all the contestants and evaluate them as to content and originality. They should write their comments on the letters, including corrections to spelling and grammar, and later return the letters to the pairs. Then, they will have a meeting to decide the winners and make their announcement to the class. Students should explain why the lucky pair was chosen.

SPECIAL-NEEDS LEARNERS

- Before students who experience trouble focusing on tasks begin writing their Internet ad for activity 51, help them organize the information they will need to refer to. Help them to select two suitable objects they wish to sell. Be sure they write the questions on a sheet of paper, allowing space for their answers, which should be in complete sentences. Then have them use their answers to create the ads.

52. To prepare students for this activity, you may want to review vocabulary related to houses, such as furniture, appliances, and decorations. Assign different rooms to each student and ask them to write a detailed description of that room in their own house. Then have students work on this activity. During the oral presentation, provide students with a rubric to evaluate their classmates' presentations. After all the presentations, have the class vote for the best house.

 AUDIO SCRIPT
See page 119J.

Answer Key

50. Answers will vary.
▶ Answers will vary. Sample answers:
2. Yo creo que es mejor vender las alfombras en el primer mercado porque se especializa en textiles.
3. Yo creo que es mejor vender los objetos de cerámica en el primer mercado porque hay objetos indígenas.
4. Yo creo que es mejor vender los adornos en el segundo mercado porque van bien con los muebles que se venden en ese mercado.
▶ Answers will vary.

51. Answers will vary. Sample answer:
Es una lámpara de pie de diseño tradicional. Es alta, de color blanco. La parte superior es de tela y la parte inferior es de madera oscura. Se usa para alumbrar.

52. Answers will vary.
▶ Answers will vary.

53. Answers will vary.

Additional Resources

Fans Online activities
Practice Workbook

149

Unit 3
DESAFÍO 3
Hablar de experiencias pasadas

Presentation

- In *Desafío 3*, Eva and Ethan need to organize a flamenco festival in just two days. Students will preview language used to talk about domestic chores and trades and occupations.

Activities	Standards	Resources
Texto	1.2, 2.1	Vis. Pres.
54.	1.1	
55.	1.1	
56.	1.1, 1.2, 1.3, 2.1, 3.2	Audio
57. Cultura	1.1, 1.2, 2.2, 3.1, 4.2, 5.2	

Teaching Suggestions

Warm-Up / Independent Starter

- Ask students to brainstorm what needs to be done to prepare a hall to host an event.

Preparation

- Have students share their Independent Starters with the class. You may want to start a list of tasks on the board. Based on what they like doing or the things they are good at, have students select one or two tasks they can help with.

Texto: Un festival de flamenco

- Read the introduction to the text. Invite students to consider how many days of preparation would be necessary. Do they think two days is a reasonable time?
- Ask students to first read the dialogue silently. Then call on volunteers to role-play Eva and Ethan and read their parts convincingly in front of the class. Ask students to pay attention to and take notes on chores that Eva and Ethan will have to complete. Which tasks are the most challenging in order to get the room ready?

Activities

55. After students complete this activity, have them discuss what else Eva and Ethan should do, besides just preparing the room.

150

Un festival de flamenco

 Eva and Ethan must organize a flamenco festival. They will also have to clean and decorate the hall for the festival, but they only have two days to do it! Do you think they will make it in time?

EVA: Este desafío es muy interesante, tenemos que hacerlo muy bien.

ETHAN: Pero es un poco difícil, ¿no? ¿Tú sabes algo del flamenco?

EVA: No mucho... Solo sé que es un tipo de música típico de Andalucía, en España, que se hace con guitarras españolas, se canta y se baila.

ETHAN: Pues sí que sabes cosas. Vamos a ver la sala donde se celebrará el festival.

* * *

EVA: ¿Esta es la sala?

ETHAN: Me temo que sí...

EVA: ¡Qué desastre! ¡Y solo tenemos dos días!

ETHAN: Sí, hay mucho que hacer. Tenemos que ordenarla, limpiar el suelo, pintar las paredes... ¿Por dónde empezamos?

EVA: A ver... ¿Y si hacemos primero una lista? Después decidiremos quién se ocupa de cada cosa.

ETHAN: ¿Conoces a algún electricista? Hay que reparar las luces.

EVA: Pues sí. Mi tío es electricista y trabaja preparando conciertos de cantantes famosos.

ETHAN: ¿En serio? Nunca me habías hablado de tu tío.

54 **Las tareas**

▶ **Busca** en el diálogo las tareas relacionadas con estas fotografías y escríbelas.

① 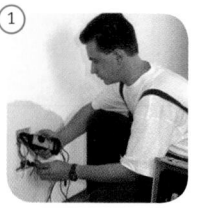 ②  ③  ④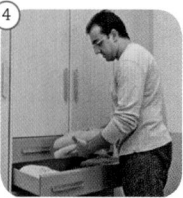

150 ciento cincuenta

Differentiated Instruction

DEVELOPING LEARNERS

- To confirm comprehension of the dialogue, ask students the following questions. Encourage them to reply with complete sentences.
  1. *¿Quién sabe más del flamenco: Eva o Ethan? (Eva)*
  2. *¿Cuál es el instrumento musical más típico del flamenco? (la guitarra)*
  3. *¿Cuántos días tienen Eva y Ethan para ordenar la sala? (dos)*
  4. *¿Qué tienen que pintar? (las paredes)*
  5. *¿Cómo está el suelo? (sucio)*
  6. *¿Quién sabe reparar las luces? (el tío de Eva)*

EXPANDING LEARNERS

- Ask students to read the conversation between Eva and Ethan again and then write a summary of it. Students should describe where the characters are, what challenge they are facing, their reaction at seeing the disorderly room, and the tasks they must complete. Have students pay special attention to the verb tenses. Give them the option of placing all the action in the present, or write a summary in the past tense. The summary should be written in the third person.

Hablar de experiencias pasadas

55 **¿Comprendes?**

▶ **Responde** a estas preguntas.

1. ¿En qué consiste el desafío?
2. ¿Cuánto tiempo tienen Eva y Ethan para hacerlo?
3. ¿Qué piensa Ethan que hay que hacer para preparar la sala?
4. ¿Para qué necesita Ethan a un electricista?

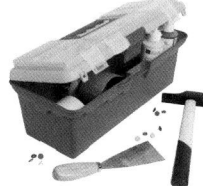

56 **¿Qué sabes del flamenco?**

▶ **Escucha** la conversación entre Eva y Ethan y elige la opción correcta.

1. El flamenco es un…	a. estilo musical	b. baile
2. El flamenco nació en…	a. Sevilla	b. Andalucía
3. Las sevillanas son un tipo de…	a. baile	b. guitarra
4. Las personas que cantan flamenco se llaman…	a. cantantes	b. cantaores
5. Las personas que bailan flamenco se llaman…	a. bailaores	b. bailarines

▶ **Habla** con tus compañeros(as). ¿Sabes algo más del flamenco? Estas fotografías pueden ayudarte.

CULTURA

El flamenco

El flamenco es un estilo musical que nació hace siglos en Andalucía, en el sur de España. Está íntimamente relacionado con el pueblo gitano, pero tiene influencia de otras culturas, como la árabe o la judía.

Hoy esta manifestación artística es conocida en todo el mundo y la UNESCO lo ha declarado Patrimonio Cultural Inmaterial de la Humanidad.

El guitarrista Paco de Lucía (España).

57 **Piensa.** ¿Conoces otros estilos musicales relacionados con alguna etnia o comunidad? ¿Qué tipo de música crees que representa mejor a tu cultura?

HERITAGE LANGUAGE LEARNERS

• Ask students to research flamenco music styles, assigning songs, dances, and instruments played to individual students or to small groups, who will then make a presentation to the rest of the class. Students should include a brief history of the origins of songs and dances and include the role that *las castañuelas, la guitarra,* and *el cajón* play, and perhaps include something about the origin of these instruments. The flamenco musical styles may include *sevillanas, alegrías, seguidillas, bulerías,* and *rumba flamenca.* Encourage students to accompany their presentation with audio or video.

MULTIPLE INTELLIGENCES:
Musical-Rhythmic Intelligence

• If any students are familiar with the music, songs, or dances of flamenco, ask them to share that knowledge with the rest of the class. Students may make a presentation about the history and traditions of this musical genre, or share recordings and DVDs. If students know some dance steps, or can play the guitar or castanets (*castañuelas*), they can first give a demonstration and later teach the other students.

• If students have no knowledge of flamenco, you may bring to class some of this music for students' enjoyment.

---

56. Before students listen to the audio script, have them look at the sentence starters and potential answers to make sure that they understand the vocabulary used. Ask them to look at the options for 4 and 5 and pronounce them. Remind them that they will have to listen for the word that is used in the conversation.

AUDIO SCRIPT
See page 119J.

CULTURA

El flamenco

It is believed that flamenco originated with the Romani people (gypsies) who arrived in Spain between the 9th and 14th centuries. Their music intermingled with the music and instruments of the inhabitants of Spain at that time, and flamenco was born. It is a style of music that began with deep, profound music created only by voice, called *cante jondo*. Percussion sounds and the guitar were later incorporated, and finally, dance. Flamenco is performed in *tablaos*, which are small, intimate cafés.

Answer Key

54. 1. reparar las luces   3. pintar las paredes
2. limpiar el suelo   4. ordenar

55. 1. Consiste en planear un festival de flamenco. También tienen que decorar.
2. Solo tienen dos días.
3. Piensa que tienen que ordenar la sala, limpiar el suelo y pintar las paredes.
4. Lo necesita para reparar las luces.

56. 1. a   2. b   3. a   4. b   5. a
▶ Answers will vary.

57. Answers will vary.

Additional Resources

Fans Online activities

151

DESAFÍO 3

Vocabulario – Tareas domésticas y oficios

Presentation

- In this section, students will learn key words to describe domestic chores, as well as vocabulary to talk about trades and occupations.

Activities	Standards	Resources
Vocabulario	1.2	
58.	1.1	
59.	1.1, 5.1	
60.	1.2, 1.3	Audio
61. Cultura	1.1, 1.2, 2.1, 3.2, 4.2	

Teaching Suggestions

Warm-Up / Independent Starter

- Ask students to list some words they already know relating to household chores. You may want to start the list with these words: *lavar la ropa, barrer, limpiar el dormitorio, sacar la basura.*

Preparation

- Invite students to share their Independent Starters. How many words do students know already? Then read aloud the words in the *Más vocabulario* feature to model correct pronunciation, and have students repeat them after you.

- Ask students to organize the highlighted words from the dialogue into the same three categories as the *Más vocabulario* feature. Encourage students to refer to these lists as they work on the activities on these pages.

Activities

58. To expand this activity, add more items, such as *la pintura, el recogedor, el limpiacristales.* You can also ask students to present short dialogues. For example:

   A. *¿Para qué se usa la plancha?*

   B. *Se usa para planchar la ropa.*

59. Ask student pairs to present their dialogues to the class. Which of the six chores listed in this activity do students do more often? Is there any chore that no one in the class does?

152

Vocabulario

Tareas domésticas y oficios

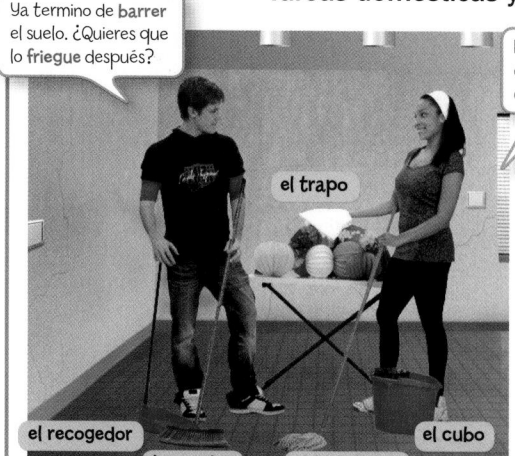

> Ya termino de **barrer** el suelo. ¿Quieres que lo **friegue** después?

> No, yo lo hago. Prefiero que **limpies el polvo**. Y mientras, yo puedo **colgar los adornos**.

el trapo

el recogedor

la escoba

el trapeador

el cubo

EVA: ¡Por fin terminamos!

ETHAN: Sí, trabajamos muy duro. Pero ahora necesitamos ayuda profesional. Hay que llamar a un **albañil** para **reparar** la pared.

EVA: También necesitamos un **electricista** para arreglar las luces y un **pintor**.

ETHAN: ¿Por qué no **pintamos** nosotros las paredes?

EVA: ¿Tú crees que nos da tiempo?

Más vocabulario

Tareas domésticas

doblar la ropa	*to fold the clothes*
hacer la cama	*to make the bed*
lavar los platos	*to wash the dishes*
planchar	*to iron*
secar los platos	*to dry the dishes*
tender la ropa	*to hang out the clothes*

Productos y objetos

el detergente	*laundry detergent*
el lavavajillas	*dishwashing liquid*
el limpiacristales	*window cleaner*
el tendedero	*clothesline*

Oficios

el carpintero	*carpenter*
el jardinero	*gardener*
el plomero	*plumber*

58 **¿Para qué se usa?**

▶ **Escribe** oraciones explicando para qué se usan estos objetos y productos.

Modelo la plancha

→ *La plancha se usa para planchar la ropa.*

1. el tendedero
2. la escoba
3. el trapo
4. el detergente

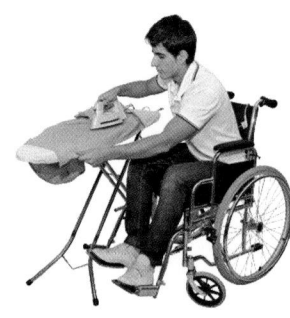

Differentiated Instruction

DEVELOPING LEARNERS

- Read the following statements to students and ask them whether they are *lógicos* or *ilógicos*. Ask them to correct the illogical ones.
  1. *Barro el suelo con el detergente.* (ilógico; con la escoba)
  2. *Tiendo la ropa después de lavarla.* (lógico)
  3. *Llamo al albañil para planchar la pared.* (ilógico; reparar la pared)
  4. *Plancho los platos con la plancha.* (ilógico; plancho la ropa)
  5. *Cuelgo adornos en la pared.* (lógico)
  6. *Uso la cama para limpiar el polvo.* (ilógico; uso el trapo)

EXPANDING LEARNERS

- Read or write the following groups of words and ask students to identify the one word that does not belong:
  1. *fregar   barrer   reparar* (reparar)
  2. *el albañil   el trapo   el plomero* (el trapo)
  3. *limpiar   ordenar   planchar* (planchar)
  4. *barrer   doblar   tender* (barrer)
  5. *el cubo   el trapeador   el tendedero* (el tendedero)
  6. *pintar   tender   lavar* (pintar)

152

59 Las tareas domésticas

▶ **Habla** con tu compañero(a). ¿Quién hace estas tareas domésticas en tu casa?

¿Tú barres el suelo?

No, normalmente barre mi hermano.

1. lavar los platos
2. hacer la cama
3. limpiar el polvo
4. poner la lavadora
5. tender la ropa
6. planchar

60 ¿A quién llamamos?

▶ **Escucha** y relaciona cada oración con una fotografía.

①  ②  ③  ④

▶ **Escribe.** ¿A quién se debe llamar para pedir ayuda en cada caso?

Modelo   1. *Se debe llamar al electricista.*

 **CULTURA**

Las supersticiones

Las supersticiones han existido siempre y en todas las culturas. Muchas son universales y otras son propias de una determinada zona.

En España, hay algunas supersticiones muy conocidas relacionadas con la casa, como poner una escoba detrás de la puerta para evitar visitas inoportunas (*unwelcome*) o colgar una herradura (*horseshoe*) detrás de la puerta para atraer la buena suerte. Romper un espejo, abrir el paraguas dentro de casa o tirar la sal, en cambio, son signos de mala suerte.

61 **Explica.** ¿Conoces otras supersticiones? ¿Eres supersticioso(a)?

ciento cincuenta y tres 153

Vocabulario – Tareas domésticas y oficios

60. To expand the activity, have students create new situations in which help would be required to make a repair.

 AUDIO SCRIPT
See page 119J.

 CULTURA

Las supersticiones

Superstitions are the belief in supernatural occurrences controlling people's fates. While there are some superstitions that are shared by many cultures, certain regions also have their own. Some common superstitions in Western societies go back to ancient Greek and Roman times. Others, like the use of mistletoe, are connected to Norse mythology. But even in our modern-day society, superstitions are still arising. During the 2010 soccer World Cup, it was believed that an octopus by the name of Paul was able to predict the outcome of soccer matches.

Answer Key

58. 1. El tendedero se usa para tender la ropa.
2. La escoba se usa para barrer el suelo.
3. El trapo se usa para limpiar el polvo.
4. El detergente se usa para lavar la ropa.

59. Answers will vary.

60. 1. 4   2. 2   3. 1   4. 3
▶ Answers will vary. Sample answers:
2. Se debe llamar al pintor.
3. Se debe llamar al plomero.
4. Se debe llamar al carpintero.

61. Answers will vary.

Additional Resources

Fans Online activities
Practice Workbook

HERITAGE LANGUAGE LEARNERS

• Ask students to consult with their relatives and make a list of superstitions known in their family's country of origin. Some common superstitions include eating twelve grapes at the stroke of midnight on New Year's Eve for good luck throughout the coming year, and avoiding travel or marriage on a Tuesday the thirteenth, which is a bad luck day throughout the Spanish-speaking world. Ask students to share these superstitions with the class and have all students compare and contrast these superstitions with those in this country.

TOTAL PHYSICAL RESPONSE (TPR)

• Have students stand by their desks and play a vocabulary game. Select one student to start the game by saying a word from the vocabulary. The student who is standing behind the first student, will say a sentence using that vocabulary word, followed by another word for the next student, who must form a sentence with it. For example, *el detergente: Necesito detergente para lavar la ropa.*

• If students cannot form sentences, or if they fail to name a vocabulary word, they are out and must sit down.

153

DESAFÍO 3

Gramática – El pluscuamperfecto

Presentation

- In this section, students will learn the past perfect as well as common adverbs that are used with the past perfect.

Activities	Standards	Resources
Gramática	1.2, 3.1	
62.	1.1, 3.1, 4.1	
63.	1.2	
64.	1.1, 1.2	Audio
65.	1.2, 1.3, 2.1	

Teaching Suggestions

Warm-Up / Independent Starter

- Ask students to write five sentences about actions they have already completed today. For example: *Me he duchado. He desayunado.*

Preparation

- Ask students to read the grammar explanation silently, and then call on different volunteers to read each bullet aloud. Ask students to form the past participles of some of the vocabulary words. For example: *doblar → doblado; hacer → hecho; secar → secado.* You may want to review some of the common irregular past participles.

- Have students take their sentences from the Independent Starter and rewrite them using *Antes de llegar a la clase de Español ya* + past perfect. For example: *Antes de llegar a la clase de Español ya me había duchado. Antes de llegar a la clase de Español ya había desayunado.* Ask volunteers to share their examples.

Activities

64. Before completing this activity, ask students to look at column B and write the past particle of each verb.

65. Have students read the text silently. Then ask them to make a list of the chores completed and who completed them. Have students create a two-column chart to record the information. Once you have reviewed the chores completed, have students write the sentences. You may choose to allow students to work with a partner.

Gramática

El pluscuamperfecto

- The past perfect (pluscuamperfecto) is used to describe an action that was completed before another action in the past.

barrer · fregar · Ahora

Yo **había barrido** el suelo antes de fregarlo.

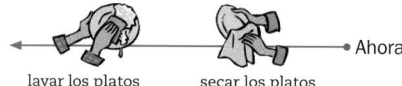

lavar los platos · secar los platos · Ahora

Ayer mi madre secó los platos que yo **había lavado**.

- Observe the difference between the present perfect and the past perfect:

  El artículo **dice** (*present*) que el festival **ha empezado** (*present perfect*).
  El artículo **dijo** (*preterite*) que la familia Gómez **había ganado** (*past perfect*) el año pasado.

Formación del pluscuamperfecto

- To form the past perfect, combine the imperfect of the verb *haber* with a past participle.

VERBO PLANCHAR. PLUSCUAMPERFECTO

Singular		Plural	
yo	había **planch**ado	nosotros(as)	habíamos **planch**ado
tú	habías **planch**ado	vosotros(as)	habíais **planch**ado
usted, él, ella	había **planch**ado	ustedes, ellos(as)	habían **planch**ado

Past perfect with *ya* and *todavía*

- The word *already* can be expressed by two different words: ya and todavía. Ya is used when an action was completed, and todavía is used when the action has not happened or has not been completed. Frequently, todavía is used in a negative sentence, similar to the word *still*.

  Cuando ella llegó, él había comido **ya**.
  Cuando ella llegó, él no había comido **todavía**.

62 **Compara.** ¿Cuándo se usa el pluscuamperfecto en inglés? ¿Es parecido al español?

63 **Por primera vez**

▶ **Escribe** oraciones siguiendo el modelo.

Modelo   Eva pintó la pared. → *Nunca había pintado una pared.*

1. Ethan hizo los adornos para el techo.
2. Ethan y Eva plancharon las cortinas.
3. Eva contrató a un electricista.
4. Ethan y Eva ayudaron al albañil.

Differentiated Instruction

DEVELOPING LEARNERS

- For further practice, have students complete the following sentences with the correct form of the past perfect:
  1. *Sequé los platos porque mi hermana los (lavar). (había lavado)*
  2. *Limpié el polvo porque nadie (limpiar) la casa. (había limpiado)*
  3. *Llamamos al electricista porque (romperse) las luces. (se habían roto)*
  4. *Felipe no podía ayudarme porque (irse) a trabajar. (se había ido)*
  5. *Fregué el suelo porque (caerse) la leche. (se había caído)*

EXPANDING LEARNERS

- Ask students to work with a partner and write a dialogue that describes how they were spared from doing certain chores because another member of the family had already done them. For example:
  A. *¿Lavaste la ropa?*
  B. *No, no la lavé porque Ana ya la había lavado.*
  A. *¿Secaste los platos?*
  B. *No, no los sequé porque Miguel los había secado ya.*

- Call on volunteer pairs to present their dialogues to the rest of the class.

64 **Oraciones lógicas**

▶ **Une** las dos columnas para formar oraciones lógicas. Después, escríbelas usando el pluscuamperfecto.

Ⓐ

1. No puse el lavaplatos...
2. Sequé los platos...
3. Tuve que lavar de nuevo la ropa...
4. Coloqué la ropa en el armario...
5. Tendí la ropa en el tendedero...
6. Hice la cama de mi hermano...

Ⓑ

a. porque mi madre la ___1___.
   planchar
b. porque no ___2___ lavavajillas.
   comprar
c. porque ___3___.
   llover
d. porque mi padre los ___4___.
   lavar
e. porque él me ___5___ a limpiar.
   ayudar
f. porque ___6___ de llover.
   dejar

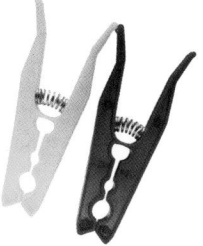

 ▶ **Escucha** y comprueba los resultados.

65 **¿Qué habían hecho?**

▶ **Lee** el mensaje de Ethan y escribe. ¿Que habían hecho ya estas personas cuando salieron de la escuela?

1. Ethan   2. Eva   3. Eva y Ethan   4. el albañil   5. el electricista

Modelo   *Cuando salió de la escuela, Ethan ya había barrido el suelo y...*

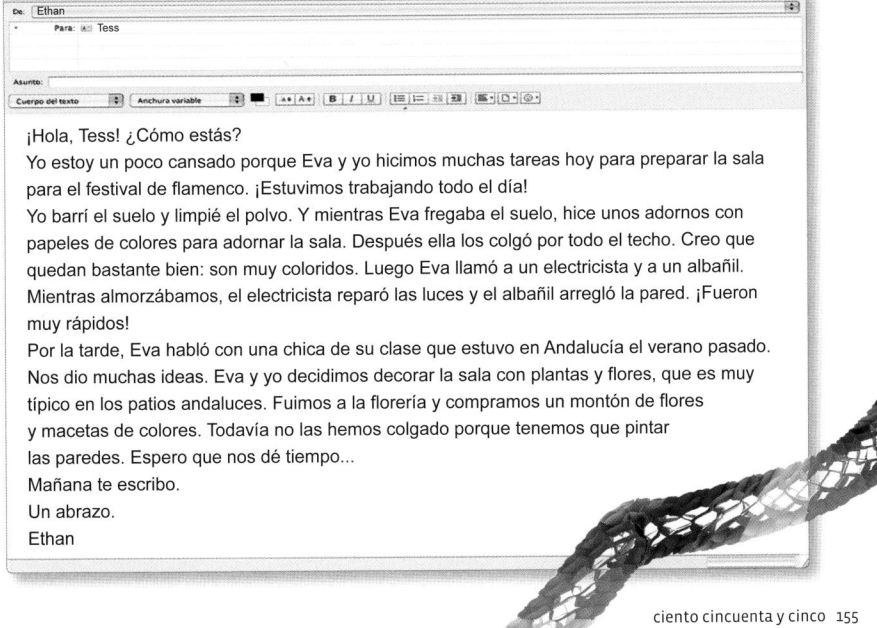

De: Ethan
Para: Tess
Asunto:

¡Hola, Tess! ¿Cómo estás?
Yo estoy un poco cansado porque Eva y yo hicimos muchas tareas hoy para preparar la sala para el festival de flamenco. ¡Estuvimos trabajando todo el día!
Yo barrí el suelo y limpié el polvo. Y mientras Eva fregaba el suelo, hice unos adornos con papeles de colores para adornar la sala. Después ella los colgó por todo el techo. Creo que quedan bastante bien: son muy coloridos. Luego Eva llamó a un electricista y a un albañil. Mientras almorzábamos, el electricista reparó las luces y el albañil arregló la pared. ¡Fueron muy rápidos!
Por la tarde, Eva habló con una chica de su clase que estuvo en Andalucía el verano pasado. Nos dio muchas ideas. Eva y yo decidimos decorar la sala con plantas y flores, que es muy típico en los patios andaluces. Fuimos a la florería y compramos un montón de flores y macetas de colores. Todavía no las hemos colgado porque tenemos que pintar las paredes. Espero que nos dé tiempo...
Mañana te escribo.
Un abrazo.
Ethan

 AUDIO SCRIPT
See page 119J.

Answer Key

62. Por lo general, el pluscuamperfecto en inglés se usa de la misma manera que se usa en español. Por ejemplo: *I had done the laundry already when you called.* (Yo ya había lavado la ropa cuando llamaste.)

63. 1. Nunca había hecho...
2. Nunca habían planchado...
3. Nunca había contratado...
4. Nunca habían ayudado...

64. 1. (b) No puse el lavaplatos porque no había comprado lavavajillas.
2. (d) Sequé los platos porque mi padre los había lavado.
3. (c) Tuve que lavar de nuevo la ropa porque había llovido.
4. (a) Coloqué la ropa en el armario porque mi madre la había planchado.
5. (f) Tendí la ropa en el tendedero porque había dejado de llover.
6. (e) Hice la cama de mi hermano porque él me había ayudado a limpiar.

65. 1. Ethan había barrido el suelo, limpiado el polvo y hecho unos adornos.
2. Eva había fregado el suelo, colgado los adornos y llamado a un electricista y a un albañil. También había hablado con una chica de su clase.
3. Eva y Ethan habían almorzado y habían comprado flores y macetas.
4. El albañil había arreglado la pared.
5. El electricista había reparado las luces.

Additional Resources

Fans Online activities
Practice Workbook

HERITAGE LANGUAGE LEARNERS

• Ask students to write a suitable reply to Ethan's e-mail from former participant Tess. The reply should comment on all the tasks Ethan and Eva have completed so far, complimenting them on their hard work, and asking questions about the premises where the festival will take place, the decorations, the lighting, and why the wall needed to be repaired. Tess might also offer some ideas to make the room look more like *un patio andaluz.*

• After you review their work, ask students to read their compositions aloud.

COOPERATIVE LEARNING

• In groups of four, have students create a story that describes the chores they completed before their parents came home and that also describes something they did before completing this chore, in order to use the *pluscuamperfecto.* For example, the first student might say: *Planché la blusa que había comprado el mes pasado.* The second student will continue the story-chain and say: *Doblé la ropa que habíamos lavado.* Students continue making up sentences. The winning group is the one that has created the largest number of correct sentences when you call time.

155

DESAFÍO 3

Gramática – Los demostrativos

Presentation

- In this section, students will review the demonstratives and learn the neutral forms.

Activities	Standards	Resources
Gramática	1.2, 3.1	
66.	1.1, 3.1, 4.1	
67.	1.1, 1.2	Audio
68.	1.1, 1.2, 3.1	
69.	1.1, 3.1	
70. Comparaciones	1.1, 1.2, 2.1, 2.2, 3.1, 5.1	Video

Teaching Suggestions

Warm-Up / Independent Starter

- Ask students to make a list of a few items that they see in the classroom. Have them choose two things that are very close, two things that are a distance away, and two things that are even farther away.

Preparation

- Ask students to read the grammar explanation silently, and then ask a volunteer to read it aloud. Have students take their vocabulary words from the Independent Starter and add the appropriate demonstrative adjectives to refer to the objects. Have volunteers share their examples as they point to each object.

- Ask students some questions applying the neutral pronouns while pointing to objects that are close to, near, or far away from you. Model for students to respond using the neutral pronoun.

   —¿Qué es esto/eso/aquello?

   —Esto/Eso/Aquello es la bandera de los Estados Unidos.

Activities

67. After listening to the audio recording and answering the question, ask students what influenced Eva and Ethan's decision. Before listening to the recording again, tell students to pay attention to and write down the demonstratives that Eva and Ethan use when referring to the three types of flowers.

Gramática

Los demostrativos

Adjetivos y pronombres demostrativos

- To indicate where something or someone is located in relation to the person speaking, use demonstrative adjectives or pronouns. Demonstrative pronouns are used to avoid repeating the noun.

   —¿Quieres usar **esta** manguera?
   —No, quiero usar **aquella** de allí.

- Demonstrative adjectives and pronouns show gender and number.

   En **este** patio hay una fuente y en **aquel** hay un árbol de azahar.

ADJETIVOS Y PRONOMBRES DEMOSTRATIVOS

Distance from speaker	Singular		Plural	
	Masculino	Femenino	Masculino	Femenino
Near	este	esta	estos	estas
At a distance	ese	esa	esos	esas
Far away	aquel	aquella	aquellos	aquellas

- The neutral forms esto, eso, and aquello are always pronouns. They are used to refer to a general idea, a statement, or an object whose gender is unknown.

   ¿Qué piensas de **esto**?   ¿Qué es **eso**?   **Aquello** es un geranio.

Adverbios demostrativos

- Some adverbs are used to indicate location.

Near	At a distance	Far away
aquí/acá	ahí	allí/allá

66 **Compara.** ¿Hay diferencias de género y de número entre los adjetivos y pronombres demostrativos en inglés?

67 **En la florería**

▶ **Escucha** a Eva y a Ethan en la florería.
¿Qué flores compran para decorar la sala de la escuela?

▶ **Escucha** de nuevo y une las columnas.
¿A qué distancia de Eva y Ethan están estas flores?

   (A)   (B)

   1. las rosas   a. ahí
   2. los tulipanes   b. aquí
   3. los geranios   c. allí

rosas

geranios

tulipanes

Differentiated Instruction

DEVELOPING LEARNERS

- Arrange some objects around the classroom to practice demonstrative adjectives and pronouns with students. Some objects should be close to the students, others farther away, and some in the opposite corner of the classroom. As you point to the objects, ask students questions such as, *¿Ves aquel mapa* (pointing to a map far away)? Elicit the response: *Sí, veo aquel mapa. ¿De quién es esa mochila* (pointing to another student's backpack)? Elicit: *Esa mochila es de* [name of student]. Continue with other questions to give students a chance to practice all forms of the demonstratives.

EXPANDING LEARNERS

- Ask students to work with a partner and, using the conversation in activity 69 as a model, create a dialogue in which they will put into practice the demonstrative adjectives and pronouns as well as the neutral forms *esto, eso,* and *aquello.* Allow students to choose the topic of their conversation. Give them time to practice their dialogues and then call on volunteer pairs to present their dialogues in front of the class.

68 **Una respuesta lógica**

▶ **Une** cada oración con la respuesta más lógica.

Ⓐ

1. ¿Me puedes explicar algo sobre el flamenco?
2. ¿Qué es esto?
3. Voy a terminar todas las tareas para ir luego al cine.
4. ¿Recuerdas cuando viajamos a Chile?

Ⓑ

a. Sí, me encantó todo aquello. Fue increíble.
b. Eso es una buena idea.
c. No sé nada de eso...
d. Es un recogedor. Lo usas cuando barres.

▶ **Escribe** tres oraciones con los pronombres *esto*, *eso* y *aquello*.

69 **Fotos de Andalucía**

▶ **Completa** la conversación con la opción correcta.

ETHAN: ¿Qué tienes ahí, Eva? ¿Qué es ___1___ que miras con tanta atención?
           aquello /eso

EVA: ¿___2___? Son unas fotos que me trajo mi compañera, de su viaje a Andalucía.
        Esto /Aquellas

ETHAN: ¿A ver? ¿Qué es ___3___ de aquí, un jardín?
           aquello /esto

EVA: No, hombre, es un patio. Muchas casas andaluzas los tienen.

ETHAN: Qué bonito. Me gusta ___4___ pared de allí, la del fondo, con las flores.
           aquella /esta

EVA: Sí. Y mira esta otra. ___5___ patio es también muy bonito. Podemos poner
        Este /Aquel
unos platos de cerámica como estos en la sala. ¿Qué te parece?

ETHAN: Creo que ___6___ no es una buena idea, Asha. Se rompen muy fácilmente.
           esta /eso

COMPARACIONES

Los patios cordobeses (España)

Los antiguos habitantes de Córdoba construyeron las viviendas en torno a un patio central para adaptarlas a la climatología seca y calurosa de la ciudad. Normalmente los patios tenían el suelo de piedra, una fuente en el centro y plantas y flores para disminuir la sensación de calor.

En Córdoba se celebra en el mes de mayo el Festival de los Patios, con numerosas actividades y actuaciones folclóricas. Los participantes en el concurso adornan los patios y abren sus casas para que el jurado y los visitantes puedan admirar su hermosa decoración.

70 **Piensa.** ¿Hay alguna conexión entre el clima de tu zona y la arquitectura?

Gramática – Los demostrativos

69. Before beginning this activity, ask students to think about which two pieces of information will affect which demonstratives need to be used. (location and gender) Have students scan the dialogue and point out clues that will help them to determine the correct demonstrative.

AUDIO SCRIPT
See page 119 J.

COMPARACIONES

Los patios cordobeses (España)

Because of the warm, dry climate in the inland region of southern Spain, early inhabitants designed buildings with an interior, open space called *patio*. Many homes have multiple *patios*, but there is typically one in the center. They incorporate natural elements, such as water and plants, in order to create an interior oasis. The city of Córdoba is famous for its well-decorated *patios* and holds an annual competition among homeowners in the month of May.

Answer Key

66. En inglés no hay diferencias de género, pero sí hay diferencias de número. Por ejemplo: *that* girl, *that* boy, *those* girls, *those* boys.

67. Eva y Ethan compran los geranios.
▶ 1. b   2. c   3. a

68. 1. c   2. d   3. b   4. a
▶ Answers will vary.

69. 1. eso   3. esto   5. Este
2. Esto   4. aquella   6. eso

70. Answers will vary.

Additional Resources

Fans Online activities
Practice Workbook

HERITAGE LANGUAGE LEARNERS

• Ask students to describe some homes in their family's country of origin. Encourage them to bring in images of homes that are found in a cross section of the country, including those from both rural and urban areas. Ask them to explain what building materials are used, how the rooms are usually arranged, how weather and altitude impact these structures, and how residents make use of vegetation. Then ask students to compare and contrast these homes to the one pictured from Córdoba. They may present a report to the rest of the class.

CRITICAL THINKING

• Ask students to compare and contrast the typical house or apartment building in their neighborhood with those that have a *patio cordobés*. Ask students to think about the advantages to having a patio in the middle of their home rather than in the back or front yard, or not having one, as is the case with many apartment buildings. Ask them to consider any disadvantage, too. Have students consider how the weather conditions affect this type of home design. Would students or their families have the patience to decorate their homes in a similar way?

LECTURA: TEXTO LITERARIO

Presentation

- In this section, students will read a story about a little girl and the dollhouse that she receives as a gift. As they read, they will review vocabulary for parts of the house and household objects, and they will recognize words that have a positive and a negative meaning. Students will also have the opportunity to recognize the uses of the past perfect and the imperfect tenses while reading about a past experience.

Activities	Standards	Resources
Lectura: texto literario	1.1, 1.2, 3.1	
71.	1.1, 1.2	
72.	1.3	
73.	1.2, 1.3	

Teaching Suggestions

Warm-Up / Independent Starter

- Ask students to observe the illustration and read the title of the story. Have them write a brief paragraph describing the dollhouse in the image.

Preparation

- Call on individual students to share their paragraphs from the Independent Starter. Ask students related questions to help them add details to their descriptions: *¿Cuántas habitaciones tiene la casa? ¿Qué hay en el comedor? ¿Qué hay en el último piso? ¿Falta algo en esta casa?*, etc.

- Have students work with a partner to read the *Antes de leer* strategies and work on the four questions. Once pairs have finished working on these questions, discuss the answers as a class. You may want to ask partners to make a list of all of the words related to parts of the house, furniture, and decorations that they find in the second paragraph.

- Clarify the meaning of some words in the text by pointing out cognates (e.g., *cortinas, terraza, ocupados, respetaban, domésticas*). Also point out the false cognate *discutían*, which in this case means "argued."

Antes de leer: estrategias

1. Lee el título. ¿Conoces la palabra *muñeca*? Si no la conoces, búscala en el diccionario. ¿Qué es una casa de muñecas? ¿Cómo son las que conoces?
2. Lee el primer párrafo. ¿Cuántos personajes hay? ¿Quién es el / la protagonista?
3. Lee el segundo párrafo y responde: ¿Qué se describe? ¿Cómo lo sabes?
4. Lee los dos últimos párrafos y responde: ¿Dónde está María al final de la historia?

La casa de muñecas

María tenía 8 años y era hija única. Sus padres no se llevaban bien y discutían siempre. A María no le gustaba verlos discutir y se escondía[1] en su cuarto cuando esto sucedía.

Unas navidades los reyes magos[2] le trajeron a María una casa de muñecas. ¡Ella siempre había soñado[3] con una casa así! Era la casa de muñecas más bonita del mundo. Tenía tres pisos. En el primer piso había una cocina con una mesa y varias sillas, y un salón de donde partía una escalera de madera. En el segundo piso había cuatro habitaciones, cada una con su cama, su mesita de noche y sus cortinas. Por último, en el piso superior había un desván y una terraza con un columpio[4]. María pasaba horas y horas en su habitación jugando con su casa de muñecas. Parecía que sus padres se habían olvidado de ella por estar ocupados con sus peleas[5].

María pobló[6] la casa de muñecas con unos muñecos de plastilina[7]. Eran una familia numerosa y feliz. Los padres se querían y se respetaban, compartían las tareas domésticas y jugaban con sus hijos. Los niños pasaban de una habitación a otra, subían por las escaleras, encontraban tesoros[8] en el desván y se columpiaban en la terraza.

Un día, María llamó a la puerta de ese pequeño mundo que había creado. Y le abrieron. Entonces María reconoció el vestíbulo, subió por las escaleras y llegó a la terraza. Desde el columpio vio a sus padres buscándola en su habitación. Pero ellos no la vieron en la casa de muñecas…

1. *she hid*	3. *dreamt*	5. *fights*	7. *modeling clay*
2. *the three wise men*	4. *swing*	6. *populated*	8. *treasures*

Differentiated Instruction

DEVELOPING LEARNERS

- Ask students to describe the ideal family. Students may do this by making a list of characteristics and relationships among family members they consider positive and describing activities the family members share with one another. Students may also choose to take the information from their lists and write a few paragraphs to describe their ideal family. Students may also express their opinion by finding images or making illustrations that reflect these qualities and relationships. Invite students to share their work with the class.

EXPANDING LEARNERS

- Ask students to work with a partner. One will role-play María, who is very upset about the situation in her family. The other will role-play an advice columnist. María confides her feelings in a letter she will write to the advice columnist, who must answer her with sound guidance and recommendations for help. When student pairs complete their letters, have them read each one aloud and ask the class to vote on the letter that best describes María's feelings and the one that offers the best advice.

Comprensión

▶ **Completa** estas oraciones con la información del texto.

1. María vivía con…
2. Los padres de María siempre…
3. De regalo, María recibió…
4. La casa tenía…
5. En la casa de muñecas vivían…
6. Un día, María…

 ▶ **Responde** a estas preguntas. Después, compara tus respuestas con dos compañeros(as) y coméntenlas.

1. ¿Cómo eran los padres de María? Descríbelos.
2. ¿Cómo crees que era el ambiente en casa de María? ¿Por qué?
3. ¿María era feliz con su familia? ¿Por qué?
4. ¿Cómo era la familia de los muñecos de plastilina? Descríbela.
5. ¿A qué puerta llamó María? ¿Por qué?
6. ¿Piensas que lo que se cuenta en la historia es posible? ¿Por qué?

72 **Puntos de vista**

▶ **Escribe** la historia desde uno de estos puntos de vista.

• La perspectiva de la madre de María.
• La perspectiva de María.
• La perspectiva de los muñecos de la casa.

73 **Con tus propias palabras**

▶ **Escribe** el final del cuento. Incluye las reacciones de María y de sus padres. ¿Qué aprendió cada uno?

▶ **Dibuja** o recorta ilustraciones para tu cuento y preséntalo a la clase. ¿Quién escribió el final más creativo?

ciento cincuenta y nueve **159**

■ Read the short story aloud to model pronunciation and have students follow along in their books. Then call on individual students to each read a paragraph aloud. After students have finished reading, ask them to compare their descriptions from the Independent Starter with the descriptions of the dollhouse in the text.

Activities

71. As a follow-up to this activity, give students the following related topic to talk about: *un sueño que se hizo realidad* (a dream that came true). Ask them to work together with a partner and exchange their stories of a personal experience they had. Then call on volunteers to share with the class.

72. Make sure that there are at least three students in the class working on each of the perspectives listed in this activity. Have students work individually on their stories. Then have those who worked on the same perspective form a group, share their stories, and come up with one that combines elements from all the members in the group. Have groups share their stories with the class.

73. You may assign this activity as homework and have students share their story endings in class the next day.

Answer Key

71. 1. … sus padres.
2. … discutían.
3. … una casa de muñecas.
4. … tres pisos.
5. … unos niños con sus padres.
6. … llamó a la puerta y entró en la casa de muñecas.
▶ Answers will vary.

72. Answers will vary.

73. Answers will vary.
▶ Answers will vary.

Additional Resources

Fans Online activities

HERITAGE LANGUAGE LEARNERS

• Ask students to talk to family members to see what toys were popular when they were children. Relatives might include *una casa de muñecas*, but they might also mention some toys that are unique to their culture. Have students ask their family members to describe these toys. Relatives should also explain the purpose of the toy: Was it for make-believe play, for educational purposes, or perhaps to improve athletic abilities? Students may bring in the toys or images of them and explain their uses and popularity to the rest of the class.

MULTIPLE INTELLIGENCES:
Intrapersonal Intelligence

• Ask students to think about their gifts from childhood. Then have them write a description of their favorite one and explain why it was their favorite. They should include as many details as they can remember, describe the special occasion on which it was given to them, who gave it to them, and where this gift is now. Was it passed on to a younger sibling? Was it given away, did it break, or do students still have it? Ask students to describe the special meaning this gift had, and might still have, for them.

159

Unit 3
DESAFÍO 3
Comunicación

Presentation

- In this section, students will integrate the vocabulary and grammar skills from *Desafío 3* to express the steps that were completed in order to prepare for an event.

Activities	Standards	Resources
74.	1.1, 1.3	
75.	1.1, 2.2	
76.	1.3, 2.1, 2.2, 3.1, 5.1	
77. Final del desafío	1.1, 1.2, 1.3, 2.1	

Teaching Suggestions

Warm-Up / Independent Starter

- Ask students to make a list of their chores at home. Then have them mark the ones that they have done at least once in the past week or couple of weeks.

Preparation

- Ask students to share with the class their lists of household chores from the Independent Starter. Do most students have similar chores? Have students add to their list chores that other members of their household usually do. They should also include the family member who does each chore. For example: *mamá → lavar los platos; papá → cocinar; mi hermano → barrer la casa; mi hermana → doblar la ropa.*
- Review the use of the past perfect with the class. Then have students take their lists and write six or seven statements about what they and their family have done in the past week or couple of weeks. For example: *Antes de limpiar el polvo, yo había lavado la ropa. Sequé los platos que mi madre había lavado. Mi hermana dobló la ropa que yo había lavado.*

Activities

74. Have each student pair tell the class who completed the most tasks before arriving at school today. At the end of all the presentations, choose a "class champion."

160

DESAFÍO 3
Comunicación

 74 **¿Quién había hecho más cosas?**

▶ **Escribe** una lista de todas las cosas que hiciste hoy antes de venir a la escuela.

 ▶ **Habla** con tu compañero(a). ¿Quién de ustedes había hecho más cosas antes de llegar a la escuela?

Modelo *Cuando llegué a la escuela, yo ya había hecho mi cama, había desayunado, me había duchado…*

75 **El concurso de patios**

▶ **Habla** con tu compañero(a). Comparen estos tres patios cordobeses.

Modelo *Aquel patio tiene una fuente, pero este y ese no.*

aquí

allí

ahí

 ▶ **Habla** con tu compañero(a). ¿Cuál de los tres patios creen que debe ganar el concurso de patios? ¿Por qué?

Differentiated Instruction

DEVELOPING LEARNERS

- Ask students to make a two-column chart. They should label the first column *Lo que hice ayer* and the second column *Lo que había hecho antes*. Ask students to write what they did yesterday in the first column. Then, in the second column, they should write something they had done before doing the activity mentioned in the first column. For example, if they write *Desayuné a las siete* in column one, they might write *Me había duchado antes de desayunar* in column two.

EXPANDING LEARNERS

- Ask students to imagine that they are the owners of one of the beautiful patios shown on the page, and they have done their best to prepare it for the *Festival de los patios*. They are going to write a letter to a friend of theirs who has never visited Córdoba and has never seen a *patio cordobés*. Students must describe their patios, explain what purpose they serve, detail how they have decorated them, and then express hope that they might win a prize for the most beautiful patio of Córdoba!

76 **Un cartel**

▶ **Investiga** más sobre los patios de Córdoba y diseña un cartel para el concurso de patios del próximo año.

▶ **Presenta** el cartel a tus compañeros(as) de clase y elijan el que más les gusta.

Final del desafío

PROFESORA: Bueno, chicos, ¿terminaron su trabajo?

EVA: Sí, señora Clark.

PROFESORA: Estupendo. Cuéntenme qué hicieron.

EVA: Lo primero, tuvimos que ___1___ la sala y hacer algunos arreglos. Eso fue lo más complicado. Y también la pintamos.

PROFESORA: ¿No contrataron a un ___2___ profesional?

ETHAN: No, lo hicimos nosotros.

EVA: Pero sí contratamos a un ___3___ para reparar la pared y a un ___4___ para arreglar las luces.

ETHAN: Lo más divertido fue decorarla. Como es para un festival de flamenco, nos inspiramos en los patios cordobeses.

PROFESORA: ¡Qué buena idea! ¿Y cómo lo hicieron?

ETHAN: Colgamos ___5___ de colores por el techo.

EVA: Y pusimos un montón de plantas y ___6___ con geranios en el suelo y por las paredes.

PROFESORA: ¿Pensaron también en las sillas?

ETHAN: ¿Las sillas? ¿Qué sillas?

PROFESORA: Bueno, habrá un concierto de flamenco y necesitamos poner sillas para el público.

EVA: Eso no lo habíamos pensado…

PROFESORA: Dense prisa, tenemos muy poco tiempo. ¡Necesitamos al menos cien sillas!

77 **¿Lograron el desafío?**

▶ **Completa** la conversación de Eva y Ethan con su profesora.

 electricista   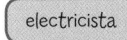 pintor   macetas   albañil   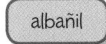 adornos   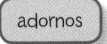 limpiar

▶ **Escribe.** ¿Qué detalle olvidaron Eva y Ethan? ¿Crees que lograron el desafío? ¿Cómo lo solucionaron?

---

75. Before asking students to compare the patios, have them brainstorm words that can be used to describe the patios, such as *fuente, geranios, plantas, columnas, macetas, arcos*. You may also want to review comparative and superlative constructions.

76. Ask students to search on the Internet for previous years' posters to get some ideas. An alternative to creating the poster can be creating a three-dimensional model of a traditional *patio cordobés*. Remind students to incorporate the typical elements.

Answer Key

74. Answers will vary.
▶ Answers will vary.

75. Answers will vary. Sample answers:
Este patio tiene macetas azules, pero esos dos no.
Ese patio y aquel tienen columnas, pero este no.
Ese patio tiene tantas flores como aquel.
▶ Answers will vary.

76. Answers will vary.
▶ Answers will vary.

77. 1. limpiar   4. electricista
2. pintor   5. adornos
3. albañil   6. macetas
▶ Answers will vary. Sample answer:
Eva y Ethan se olvidaron de las sillas para el público. Creo que sí van a lograr el desafío porque son muy trabajadores e inteligentes. Seguramente encontrarán un lugar de alquiler de sillas.

Additional Resources

Fans Online activities
Practice Workbook

HERITAGE LANGUAGE LEARNERS

• Ask students to rewrite the dialogue as a narrative in the past tense in order to use the past perfect tense wherever possible. To get students started, you might read the following: *La señora Clark les preguntó a los chicos si habían terminado su trabajo. Los chicos le contestaron que sí, que lo habían terminado. Antes de ver el resultado, la señora Clark quería saber qué habían hecho.*

• When students finish their narratives, call on volunteers to read them aloud.

MULTIPLE INTELLIGENCES:
Naturalistic Intelligence

• Students have now read about the patios in Córdoba and how they beautify homes and entire neighborhoods. Ask students to work in small groups and come up with a project to beautify a natural area in your city or town. Students must first agree on the area they want to beautify and why. Then all members of the group must contribute their ideas on how to make the area more attractive, and how these improvements will benefit the environment. Finally, they may accompany their ideas with illustrations of the finished project.

161

Unit 3
Para terminar

Presentation

- In this section, students will review the unit objectives and put them into practice. They will describe household objects, and use the present perfect to talk about clothes and accessories. They will also select one of the following *desafíos* to develop: choose a traditional costume from a Spanish-speaking country and adapt the design to their personal taste, design a flag that represents all of the cultures of the United States, or design an Andalusian patio to participate in a contest.

Activities	Standards	Resources
78.	1.1, 1.3, 5.1	
79.	1.1, 1.3, 5.1	
80. Tu desafío	1.2, 1.3, 2.1, 2.2, 3.1, 4.2	

Teaching Suggestions

Warm-Up / Independent Starter

- Have students go back and review the vocabulary and grammar sections in this unit. Encourage them to take notes on any material that they have trouble remembering. Then ask them to close their textbooks and make a list of the clothes and other items that they have recently acquired. Have them include in their list a brief description of each item. For example: *una falda roja de algodón, un espejo redondo de pared, un par de zapatos de cuero de color marrón claro.*

Preparation

- Invite students to share their Independent Starters with the class. Then use the present perfect to ask students details about the items they have recently acquired. For example: *¿Cuándo has comprado esa falda? ¿Dónde la has comprado? ¿Cuánto has pagado por ella?*

- Then ask students to work with a partner to identify and describe several objects in the classroom. They should also mention what each item is used for. For example:

  A. *¿Qué es eso azul que está encima de esa mesa?*

  B. *Eso es una carpeta.*

  A. *¿Y para qué sirve?*

  B. *Se usa para guardar papeles.*

162

Todo junto

ESCRIBIR Y HABLAR

 ¿Qué ropa les has comprado?

▶ **Escribe.** Imagina que esta mañana has ido a comprar ropa para Michelle y Daniel. ¿Qué has comprado para cada uno? Describe las prendas y los complementos con detalle.

Modelo *Para Michelle he comprado unos pantalones negros de algodón, una blusa blanca de seda y unos zapatos planos negros.*

 ▶ **Habla** con tu compañero(a). ¿Qué ropa han comprado para cada personaje? ¿Han elegido estilos muy distintos?

ESCRIBIR Y HABLAR

79 **Una venta de garaje**

▶ **Escribe.** Elige diez objetos de tu habitación para venderlos en una venta de garaje y descríbelos. Incluye esta información.

- ¿Qué objeto es?
- ¿Para qué sirve?
- ¿De qué forma, material y color es?
- ¿Cuánto cuesta?

 ▶ **Habla** con tus compañeros(as). ¿Te interesa alguno de sus objetos? Pide más información y háblales también de los objetos que tú vendes.

162 ciento sesenta y dos

Differentiated Instruction

DEVELOPING LEARNERS

- Ask students to use their information from activity 79 to play a guessing game with a partner. Partners will take turns describing their objects to one another without naming them. Partners will try to guess what it is by asking no more than four questions. For each correct answer, students get one point. If one partner fails to guess what the object is after four questions, the other partner is awarded a point.

EXPANDING LEARNERS

- Explain to students that they are going to make the argument for a school uniform or, for those schools that have uniforms, a new design. Students should decide on the style (one for boys and another for girls), fabric, colors, and appropriate accessories. Students should also define some fashion "don'ts." For example: no baggy pants, no piercings, no tattoos, no T-shirts. After students describe their uniforms and their reasons for the fashion don'ts, have them make their arguments in front of the class. Take a vote for the most convincing argument.

Tu desafío

80 **Desafíos y diseños**

¿Recuerdas los desafíos que Tess les dio a los personajes? ¿Cuál te gusta más? Elige una de estas opciones para completar tu desafío.

DESAFÍO Ⓐ

Adapta un traje regional de un país hispano.
- Elige un traje regional, busca una fotografía y descríbelo con detalle.
- Decide cómo vas a adaptarlo (diseño, tela, etc.) y dibuja un boceto.
- Escribe una descripción del traje y presenta tu adaptación a la clase.

DESAFÍO Ⓑ

Dibuja una bandera que represente simbólicamente todas las culturas de los Estados Unidos.
- Elige el símbolo o símbolos que colocarás en la bandera.
- Prepara una presentación para la clase explicando el significado de los elementos que usaste para diseñar la bandera.

DESAFÍO Ⓒ

Dibuja un patio andaluz y haz una descripción sobre él para presentarlo al concurso de patios.
- Dibuja o busca una fotografía del patio que vas a presentar.
- Escribe la descripción que presentarás al jurado. No olvides describir todos los elementos del patio, los adornos, etc.
- Presenta tu patio a la clase.

ciento sesenta y tres **163**

Activities

78. In order to help students diversify the verbs they use in this activity, write down some infinitives that may be useful: *comprar, elegir, pagar, seleccionar, decidirse por, dar, regalar…* After they finish the activity, ask further questions to have students give more details: *¿Cuánto has pagado por esos pantalones? ¿Dónde has comprado la camisa para Daniel? ¿Qué le ha regalado John a Michelle?*

79. To expand this activity, distribute some photos of objects among students and have them write a description of these objects in order to sell them on the Internet.

80. Display students' work in the classroom and have the class vote on the best entry in each category.

Answer Key

78. Answers will vary.
  ▶ Answers will vary.

79. Answers will vary. Sample answer:
  Quiero vender una mesita de noche. Va a un lado de la cama y sirve para poner una lámpara, libros, el reproductor de música, etc. La mesita es cuadrada y tiene dos cajones. Es de madera de pino y está pintada de blanco. Cuesta $20.
  ▶ Answers will vary.

80. Answers will vary.

Additional Resources

Fans Online activities

HERITAGE LANGUAGE LEARNERS

- Ask students to write a blog entry about a fashion show they attended. The entry can be a serious comment on the clothes shown, or it can be humorous and reflect the student's total lack of fashion sense. The clothes shown might be contemporary, but could also be retro (perhaps from the '50s or '60s) or even regional dresses from other countries and cultures. Invite students to share their blog entry with the rest of the class.

CRITICAL THINKING

- Ask students to think about each of the three tasks the characters have completed in this unit. Then ask them which of the pairs they think executed their task most successfully and why. Students will need to analyze the participants' strengths as well as their weaknesses, and also consider the participants' ability to work together as a team, all of which they have observed from previous units.
- Initiate a classroom discussion and encourage all students to participate.

MAPA CULTURAL

La ciudad colonial

Presentation

- This section presents information about a prototypical Spanish colonial city in the Americas. The images serve as a reference point for additional cultural readings and activities that expand on the skills students learned in this unit.

Activities	Standards	Resources
Mapa cultural	1.2, 2.1, 3.1	Video
81.	1.1, 3.1	

Cultural Topics

- **San Agustín, Florida.** This northeastern Florida city is the oldest continually occupied European settlement in the United States. It was founded in 1565 by the Spanish explorer Pedro Menéndez de Avilés. During the Spanish colonial period, St. Augustine was mainly a military outpost, but it had many of the characteristics of other Spanish colonial towns in the Caribbean: a fort (Castillo de San Marcos), the layout and cobblestone streets, the balconied houses, etc. The city preserves several of its Spanish-era buildings, including the Castillo de San Marcos.

- **Las misiones de California.** Between 1769 and 1823, Spanish missionaries founded a chain of twenty-one missions along California's Camino Real—from San Diego to Sonoma. Missions were, for the most part, self-sufficient villages that followed established settlement and building criteria. The main building consisted of a large square, or quadrangle, with a fountain in the middle. The church, priests' living quarters, kitchen, workshops, and soldiers' barracks were grouped around this quadrangle. The *pueblos* (villages) and the fields for growing crops were located outside the mission walls. All of California's missions have been restored and can be visited today.

Teaching Suggestions

Warm-Up / Independent Starter

- Ask students to sketch a street map of the area surrounding their school. Have them include and label some of the main buildings, streets, and public areas.

164

La ciudad colonial

La colonización española de América se realizó en un período relativamente corto de tiempo. En cien años se fundaron muchas ciudades y la mayor parte de ellas siguió un diseño que identifica a numerosas ciudades coloniales de América: Santo Domingo, La Habana, Ciudad de México, Cartagena de Indias, Lima, Arequipa (Perú)…

Las ciudades coloniales de América tienen un trazado en cuadrícula. En el centro está la plaza mayor y de ella salen varias calles rectas. Conforme la ciudad va creciendo se trazan nuevas calles paralelas y perpendiculares a las existentes. Este trazado permite que la ciudad crezca de manera ordenada. Y también ayuda a la ventilación de la ciudad.

Alrededor de la plaza mayor están el palacio del gobernador, la catedral, el ayuntamiento… Todas las parcelas que rodean la plaza se reservan para edificios públicos de uso religioso, civil y militar.

Plano de Lima en 1687.

Palacio de Gobierno

En las capitales, era la residencia del gobernador o del virrey. En la actualidad suele ser la residencia del presidente del país.

> En España se publicaron distintas ordenanzas con instrucciones para construir las nuevas ciudades.

Art. 113
La grandeza de la plaza sea proporcionada a la cantidad de los vecinos.

Art. 116
Las calles en lugares fríos sean anchas y en los calientes sean angostas.

Ordenanzas de Nueva Población, 1573

164 ciento sesenta y cuatro

Differentiated Instruction

DEVELOPING LEARNERS

- Have pairs of students look for a map of modern-day Lima, Peru, on the Internet. Then ask them to look for the historic district of Lima and trace the map of this historic zone onto a blank sheet of paper.
- As students go over the *Mapa cultural*, ask them to label on their map the buildings, main square, street blocks, etc., mentioned in the *Mapa cultural*. Were they able to find all of these structures on their map of Lima? Do they understand the layout of colonial cities better now?

EXPANDING LEARNERS

- Ask pairs of students to research one of the first English colonial towns in America, such as Jamestown, Williamsburg, or Yorktown in the state of Virginia. Have students look at the layout of the city, architecture, housing, its main public buildings, and any fortifications or defense structures the city might have had.
- Then ask students to compare and contrast this English colonial city with the prototypical Spanish colonial city portrayed in the *Mapa cultural*. Invite volunteer pairs to present their comparisons to the class.

Las viviendas

Las calles delimitan áreas cuadradas para viviendas que en América se llaman cuadras y en España, manzanas.

Las fortificaciones

Casi todas las ciudades coloniales tenían una fortificación o una muralla que servía para defender la ciudad de los ataques enemigos.

El palacio arzobispal

Era la sede de la mayor autoridad religiosa de la ciudad.

La Iglesia Mayor o Catedral

Es el edificio más importante de la ciudad. Destaca de los demás por su altura y su arquitectura.

La Plaza Mayor o de Armas

La plaza es el centro de la ciudad. En este espacio cuadrado y abierto están los principales edificios de la ciudad. Es el lugar de reunión del pueblo y donde se celebran las fiestas más importantes.

El Cabildo o Ayuntamiento

Aquí están las oficinas administrativas de la ciudad. (fuera de la imagen)

Plaza de Armas de Lima.

81 **Ciudades planificadas**

▶ **Observa** el plano de la página 164 y señala dónde crees que está la Plaza de Armas.

▶ **Haz** un plano de tu ciudad con tu compañero(a). Luego describan el trazado y las edificaciones.

HERITAGE LANGUAGE LEARNERS

- Ask students to research the history, architecture, and layout of a colonial city in their country of origin. It could be the capital city of the country, a port city, or a provincial town, but it must be a colonial city that still preserves its old quarter and some of the original colonial buildings.
- Have students organize their information in a visually appealing way and present it to the class. After the presentation, ask the class to compare the city presented by their classmates with the prototypical colonial city presented in the *Mapa cultural*.

MULTIPLE INTELLIGENCES:
Intrapersonal Intelligence

- Ask students to reflect on the type of city or town they like. What kind of layout do they prefer? Do they favor a compact, high-density city or a spread-out, low-density one? Do they prefer a rural town or setting, a medium-sized city, or a large city? What infrastructures are essential to students? Why do they prefer this particular type of city or town?
- Have students reflect on these questions by writing a three-paragraph essay.

Preparation

- Invite students to share their Independent Starters. You may want to create a transparency with a map of the area, and add the buildings, streets, and public areas that students mention. Discuss with students some of these features.

- Discuss the history of your city or town as a class. When was it settled? Who founded it? Have the original layout and buildings been preserved? If so, discuss the history of some of these buildings. Encourage students to think of the reasons behind some of the earliest settlers' decisions. Why did they choose that specific site? Was it a strategic point, an area with abundant water and good soil, the end point of a railway line, etc.? What functions did the main buildings have? Where did the early settlers live? Ask students to take notes during this discussion, since they will need this information for the second part of activity 81.

- Explain to students that cities have been and continue to be developed in response to different functions and influences. This accounts for the large variety of types of cities around the world. Then go over the *Mapa cultural* as a class.

Activities

81. You may want to convert the second part of this activity into a class activity. Students may, for instance, create a scale model of their city. They can use LEGO™ pieces or small blocks for the buildings. Have them label the main buildings, parks, plazas, and other important structures. Alternatively, they may prepare a digital presentation that includes pictures, maps, and historical records.

Answer Key

81. Answers will vary.

▶ Answers will vary.

Additional Resources

Fans Online activities
Practice Workbook

165

Unit 3

ESCRITURA

Un ensayo de moda

Presentation

- In this section, students will practice and extend their writing skills. They will apply the vocabulary and grammar they have learned in this unit to write an essay.

Activities	Standards	Resources
Escritura	1.1, 1.2, 1.3, 3.1, 5.1, 5.2	

Teaching Suggestions

Warm-Up / Independent Starter

- Ask students to think about the concept of fashion (*moda*). What comes to their minds? Encourage students to jot down their thoughts.

Preparation

- Invite students to share their Independent Starters. You may want to create a word web on the board for the word *moda*. Do most students have similar ideas about fashion or are there marked differences in their opinions? Are their opinions about fashion mostly positive, negative, or neutral?

- Ask for a volunteer to read the Essay box aloud. Explain that the word essay comes from the Latin word *exigere*, which means "to examine or test." An essay is a nonfiction piece of writing that examines and argues a subject in a clear and concise manner. Explain to students that in their essays they will set forth a thesis, and will then use evidence and reasoning to prove their thesis.

Step-by-Step Instructions

Piensa

- Ask for a volunteer to read aloud the three topics for the essay. Invite students to explain each of these topics in their own words. Then give them a couple of minutes to decide on a topic for their essay.

- Once students have chosen a topic, ask them to get together with a classmate who has chosen the same topic to brainstorm ideas. Encourage each partner to take opposite points of view. This will assist students in coming up with well-reasoned arguments.

166

Un ensayo de moda

Essay

An **essay** is an expository text that explains thoughts, reflections, or an author's thesis about a topic such as politics, economics, or cultural or social matters.

Essays are commonly used in the American educational system as a way to demonstrate linguistic ability and organization of ideas. However, the genre was developed in the 16th century by writers like Michel de Montaigne and Francis Bacon.

Utiliza lo que has aprendido en esta unidad para escribir un ensayo sobre uno de estos temas:

El uso del uniforme escolar. Ventajas y desventajas.

La importancia cultural de mantener vivos los trajes regionales.

La influencia de los medios de comunicación en la moda.

Debes expresar tus ideas y tus opiniones sobre el tema elegido.

Piensa

- Elige uno de los tres temas presentados y decide la opinión que vas a defender en tu texto. Esa es la **tesis**.

Modelo

El uso del uniforme escolar es importante para el desarrollo de los alumnos.

- Piensa en tres razones con las que puedes defender el tema elegido y escríbelas. Esos son los **argumentos**.

Modelo

Los alumnos no se distraen en clase.

- Piensa en una **conclusión** directamente relacionada con los argumentos elegidos.

- Organiza tus ideas y escribe un guion (*outline*) de acuerdo a cómo vas a presentar tu texto. Recuerda que al escribir un ensayo debes establecer tres partes:

  – Una **introducción** donde presentes el tema y la tesis que vas a defender.

  – Un **desarrollo** en el que expongas los argumentos o razones que apoyan tu tesis.

  – Una **conclusión** que refuerce la tesis expuesta.

> #### Tesis
> El uso del uniforme escolar es importante para el desarrollo de los alumnos.
>
> #### Argumentos
> A. No se distraen en clase.
>   1. Están cómodos...
>
> B. Es menos caro.
>   1. En vez de 5 conjuntos por semana...
>
> C. No se valora a la persona por la ropa que usa.
>   1. No sigue la moda actual...
>
> #### Conclusión
> Todas las escuelas deben exigir el uso de uniformes.

166 ciento sesenta y seis

Rubric for Evaluation

	Content	Organization	Conventions
1 point	Thesis is not clear. No supporting arguments or they lack substance. Limited vocabulary. Main points are not clear.	Focus on topic is not sustained. Details are not in a logical order. Few or no transitions between ideas.	Many errors in spelling, punctuation, grammar, and usage. Errors obscure meaning.
3 points	Thesis is clear but some supporting arguments are weak. Some inaccurate word choices. Main points are clear.	Mostly clear focus. Details are not in the most effective order. Transitions used, but some don't work well.	Some errors in spelling, punctuation, grammar, and usage. Errors don't interfere with meaning.

Escribe

- Utiliza el guion que elaboraste y escribe la primera versión de tu ensayo. No olvides que:

  – La **tesis** que vas a defender en tu ensayo debe ser clara y responder al tema elegido.

  – Los **argumentos** deben ser lógicos y reforzar la tesis expuesta. Evita los argumentos particulares.

    Modelo

    Los alumnos no se distraen en clase. ✓
    Mi primo lleva uniforme y siempre está distraído. ✗

  – La **conclusión** tiene que ser un resumen de la exposición que refuerce la tesis expuesta.

Expresiones útiles

Para comenzar...	To begin …
En primer lugar...	In the first place …
Dado que...	Given that …
Debido a esto...	Because of this …
Teniendo en cuenta que...	Keeping in mind that …
Por esta razón...	For this reason …
En resumen...	In summary …

Revisa

- Cuando termines de escribir, revisa tu texto.

  – ¿Expresa claramente tus ideas? ¿Has organizado bien la información?

  – ¿Has empleado un vocabulario y unas construcciones gramaticales correctas? ¿Es correcta la ortografía?

- Pasa a limpio tu ensayo con las correcciones necesarias e intercámbialo con tu compañero(a). Revisa su ensayo y completa una tabla como esta con valores del 1 al 5.

Criterio	Guía de preguntas	Puntos
Organización de las ideas	¿La estructura del ensayo es apropiada?	
Claridad y coherencia del texto	¿Es evidente la idea principal? ¿Hay argumentos que la apoyan?	
Gramática y ortografía	¿Está bien redactado el texto? ¿Tiene errores ortográficos o gramaticales?	
Comentarios generales	¿Crees que tu compañero(a) debe quitar o agregar texto, cambiar el orden de los párrafos...?	

- Para terminar, devuelve el texto a su autor(a) y revisa los comentarios del tuyo. Modifica lo que consideres necesario y reescribe tu ensayo. Presta atención a la limpieza y legibilidad del documento final.

Comparte

- Presenta tu ensayo a la clase. Tus compañeros(as) deberán tomar notas para hacerte preguntas al final. ¡Buena suerte!

	Content	Organization	Conventions
5 points	Strong thesis followed by substantive supporting arguments. Precise word choices. Main points stand out.	Distinct focus and clear structure that enhance the thesis. Effective use of transitions and logical sequencing.	Few, if any, errors in spelling, punctuation, grammar, and usage. Excellent command of the Spanish language.

ESCRITURA

Un ensayo de moda

- Emphasize to students the importance of an outline as an effective tool to organize their thoughts. The outline will help them keep a clear focus and direction throughout their essay.

- A common structure is the five-paragraph essay, as shown in the graphic. The first paragraph introduces the theme and contains the thesis. The next three paragraphs, or body, of the essay present arguments supporting the thesis. The fifth paragraph is a conclusion, which restates the thesis in light of the arguments provided.

Escribe

- Remind students that their essays should be concise. They should utilize their outlines to avoid going off on tangents within their writing. Transitions such as those in the *Expresiones útiles* box are used to link ideas and paragraphs.

Revisa

- As students read their own text, ask them to try to look at it from an opposite point of view. This will help them discover loopholes in their arguments.

- As students evaluate their classmates' essays, ask them to provide a brief explanation for their scoring. For instance, if they awarded their classmate three points for *Claridad y coherencia del texto*, their explanation might be: "The main idea is clear, but the second and third supporting arguments are weak and limited." These comments will help students to focus their corrections.

Comparte

- Encourage students to deliver a lively reading of their essay. If time allows, you may want to hold a class debate on one of the topics at the end of all of the presentations.

Evaluation

- Distribute copies of the rubric to students and discuss the evaluation criteria as a class. Ask students to refer to the rubric as they prepare their projects and as they evaluate their classmates' essays.

Additional Resources

Fans Online activities

REPASO

Vocabulario

Presentation

- In this section, students will review all key vocabulary from the unit, organized by themes, to prepare for an assessment. Students will complete practice activities for each of the three *Desafíos*.

Activities	Standards	Resources
1.	1.2	
2.	1.2	
3.	1.1, 1.2	

Teaching Suggestions

Warm-Up / Independent Starter

- Ask students to look around and focus on different objects. Have them write in their notebooks whatever descriptive words or phrases come to their minds as they look at each object. For instance, as students look at the classroom door, they may write down in their notebooks *de madera, rectangular,* and *verdosa.* Have students do this with at least six different objects.

Preparation

- Ask students to get together with a classmate to share their Independent Starters. Pairs will take turns reading their descriptions for each object and their partner will try to guess which object is being described. Additional descriptions may be necessary if a partner doesn't guess correctly. For example:

  A. *Es de madera, rectangular y verdosa.*

  B. *La mesa de la profesora.*

  A. *No. Es una cosa muy práctica porque la podemos abrir y cerrar.*

  B. *La puerta.*

- Read over the *Repaso* presentation with students. Then describe what different students in the class are wearing, including details about some of the accessories they are wearing. As you finish describing each person, ask students whom you are describing. Did they guess correctly? For an additional challenge, ask students to add two details about their classmates' outfits.

REPASO Vocabulario

Ropa

el bolsillo	pocket
el botón	button
los cordones	shoelaces
la cremallera	zipper
el cuello	collar
la manga	sleeve
el cinturón	belt
el pañuelo	handkerchief
el paraguas	umbrella
los zapatos de tacón	high-heeled shoes
los zapatos planos	low-heeled shoes
el número	shoe size
la talla	size

Materiales

el cuero	leather
el poliéster	polyester
la seda	silk
el terciopelo	velvet

¿Cómo te queda?

amplio(a)/ajustado(a)	loose/tight
ancho(a)/estrecho(a)	wide/tight
bien/mal	well/badly
largo(a)/corto(a)	long/short
pequeño(a)/grande	small/big

Acciones

(des)abrocharse	to (un)fasten
(des)atarse	to (un)tie
ponerse	to put on
quitarse	to take off

Describir objetos

auténtico(a)	real, authentic
de muy buena calidad	top-quality, high quality
elegante	elegant
natural	natural
práctico(a)	practical, useful

Colores

amarillo limón	lemon yellow
azul oscuro	dark blue
rojizo	reddish
rojo brillante	bright red
verdoso	greenish

Formas

cuadrado(a)	square
ovalado(a)	oval
rectangular	rectangular
redondo(a)	round

Materiales

de cerámica	ceramics
de hierro	iron
de lana	woolen
de madera	wooden
de metal	metal
de plástico	plastic

Textura

áspero(a)	rough
suave	smooth, soft
blando(a)	soft
duro(a)	hard

Tareas domésticas

barrer	to sweep
colgar la ropa	to hang the clothes
doblar la ropa	to fold the clothes
fregar	to scrub
hacer la cama	to make the bed
lavar los platos	to wash the dishes
limpiar el polvo	to dust
planchar	to iron
secar los platos	to dry the dishes
tender la ropa	to hang out the clothes

Productos y objetos

el cubo	bucket
el detergente	laundry detergent
la escoba	broom
el lavavajillas	dishwashing liquid
el limpiacristales	window cleaner
el recogedor	dustpan
el tendedero	clothesline
el trapeador	mop
el trapo	cloth

Oficios

el/la albañil	bricklayer, building worker
el/la carpintero(a)	carpenter
el/la electricista	electrician
el/la jardinero(a)	gardener
el/la pintor(a)	(house) painter
el/la plomero(a)	plumber
arreglar, reparar	to fix
pintar	to paint

Differentiated Instruction

DEVELOPING LEARNERS

- Ask students to write the words from the first column of *La ropa*, and leave several blank lines between the words. Then have them think of different clothing items and accessories they have that relate to each word. For example: *el bolsillo → los pantalones; el botón → la camisa.* Once students have completed this list, ask them to use the vocabulary under *La ropa* and *Describir objetos* to describe each item in their list. For example: *el bolsillo → los pantalones: son de algodón, de color verdoso. La tela es suave y me quedan bien.*

EXPANDING LEARNERS

- Ask students to work in pairs. Have each partner take turns describing a classroom item or object. As one of the partners describes the object, the other partner will draw a picture to try to match the description. Then the artist will reveal his or her drawing. Did the artist draw the correct object? Did he or she capture the description? If time allows, ask students to repeat the activity with clothing items and accessories, cleaning products, etc.

DESAFÍO 1

1 **La ropa.** Une las dos columnas.

      Ⓐ   Ⓑ

1. Se me ha desabrochado…   a. los cordones.
2. Juan, átate…   b. otra talla.
3. Marta siempre lleva…   c. estrecho.
4. Este suéter me queda muy…   d. la chaqueta.
5. Estos pantalones me quedan…   e. zapatos de tacón.
6. Me voy a probar…   f. pequeños.

 DESAFÍO 2

2 **Regalos.** Lee el diálogo entre Belén y Sara y señala el collar que compran.

De compras

—A mí me gusta el collar de cristal con las piedras redondas de colores brillantes.
—Pues a mí me gusta más ese. Me parece muy elegante.
—¿Cuál?
—El collar de las cuentas *(beads)* verdes.
—Sí, es muy bonito y parece de muy buena calidad. A ver… Uy, qué caro.
—¿Y el collar de jade verde?
—¿Cuál? ¿Este?
—No, no, el collar verde y negro.
—¡Ah, sí! ¡Qué bonito! Me encanta el color verdoso de las cuentas cuadradas.
—Además no es muy caro. Sí, este es el collar perfecto para Susana.

  ①
  ②
  ③
  ④

 DESAFÍO 3

3 **Tareas compartidas.** Completa el texto con las palabras del cuadro.

limpio	friega	lava	tiende	barre	planchar	seca	hace

Las tareas de la casa

En mi casa los sábados limpiamos la casa entre todos. Cada uno ___1___ su cama y limpia su dormitorio. Mi padre pone la lavadora y ___2___ la ropa en el tendedero. Cada semana nos toca a uno ___3___. ¡Todos odiamos esa tarea!

Mi madre cocina y, después de comer, ___4___ y ___5___ los platos. Mi hermana mayor ___6___ y ___7___ el suelo de toda la casa. Yo ___8___ el polvo y los cristales.

Activities

2. Ask students to work with a partner to complete this activity. Have partners read aloud the dialogue between Belén and Sara before they work on the activity. Then ask them to list, on a separate sheet of paper, all of the words and phrases used to describe each necklace and the number of the necklace being described (e.g., *de cristal, piedras redondas, colores brillantes*: collar 2).

3. Once students have finished filling in the blanks, ask them to get together with a classmate and check their answers. Then ask them to share information about who does what at home. Have them add details about the tools and products used to complete the chores. For example:

A. *¿Quién limpia el polvo en tu casa?*
B. *Pues a veces yo y otras veces mi hermana.*
A. *¿Y qué usan: un trapo?*
B. *No, usamos una aspiradora.*
A. *¿Una aspiradora?*
B. *Sí. Es una aspiradora que tiene accesorios para limpiar el polvo.*

Answer Key

1. 1. d   3. e   5. f
     2. a   4. c   6. b

2. 3

3. 1. hace   5. seca
     2. tiende   6. barre
     3. planchar   7. friega
     4. lava   8. limpio

Additional Resources

Fans Online activities
Practice Workbook

HERITAGE LANGUAGE LEARNERS

- Ask students to look at the words under *La ropa: ¿Cómo te queda?* What do they notice? (The words are antonyms.) Have students analyze the rest of the vocabulary and provide an antonym for as many adjectives and verbs as they can. Remind students that they can sometimes make antonyms by adding a prefix (e.g., *colgar → descolgar; hacer → deshacer*).

- Invite volunteers to share their antonym lists with the class. Can the class tell which vocabulary word corresponds to each antonym their classmates mention?

COOPERATIVE LEARNING

- Ask students to get together in small groups. Have them imagine that a friend let them stay at his beach house for the weekend. When they get to the house, they find out that the house is a mess: there is a pile of dirty dishes in the kitchen sink, the furniture is covered with dust, the sheets and towels are dirty, etc. Ask groups to come up with a cleaning schedule. They should agree on what needs to be done and assign the different chores. Have groups present their plans to the class.

REPASO

Gramática

Presentation

- Students will review grammatical structures presented in the unit. Each grammar point is cross-referenced to the corresponding page on which it was introduced. The activities here provide systematic practice by *Desafío*.

Activities	Standards	Resources
4.	1.1, 1.2, 3.1	
5.	1.1, 1.2, 3.1	
6.	1.1, 1.2, 3.1	
7. Cultura	1.1, 2.1, 2.2, 3.1	

Teaching Suggestions

Warm-Up / Independent Starter

- Ask students to answer the following questions in writing:
  - ¿Qué has hecho hoy al llegar a la escuela?
  - ¿Qué habías hecho antes de llegar a la escuela?

Preparation

- Invite students to share their Independent Starters with the class. Draw a timeline on the board and write some of the students' answers on the timeline. The sentences that answer the second question should have a verb in the *pluscuamperfecto* (past perfect) and they should be placed before the sentences in the present perfect in the timeline. Be sure students understand the sequence of tenses. If necessary, you may invite volunteers to translate a couple of sentences from each tense into English so that the class can see that the use of these tenses in Spanish generally corresponds to their use in English.

- Divide the class into six groups and assign each group one of the grammar topics on this page. Have groups summarize, in their own words, their assigned topic and come up with four original examples to illustrate it. Then ask groups to present their grammar point to the class. You may want to verbally quiz the class after each presentation to ensure comprehension of these grammar points.

REPASO Gramática

El participio (pág. 130)

PARTICIPIO. VERBOS REGULARES

-ar verbs → add -ado	hablar → hablado
-er and -ir verbs → add -ido	comer → comido vivir → vivido

PARTICIPIO. VERBOS IRREGULARES

abrir → abierto	hacer → hecho
cubrir → cubierto	decir → dicho
morir → muerto	romper → roto
poner → puesto	ver → visto
resolver → resuelto	escribir → escrito
volver → vuelto	describir → descrito

LA CONSTRUCCIÓN ESTAR + PARTICIPIO

María se sentó en el tren. María **está sentada**.
Cerraron el mercado. Los quioscos **están cerrados**.

Los indefinidos (pág. 142)

EXISTENCIA

Positivos		Negativos	
algo	something	nadie	nobody
alguien	someone	nada	nothing
algún,	a few, any,	ningún,	no, (not)
alguno(a)(os)(as)	one, some	ninguno(a)	any, none

CANTIDAD

poco(a)(os)(as)	some, few
varios(as)	several
mucho(a)(os)(as)	many, a lot of
demasiado(a)(os)(as)	too much, too many
todo(a)(os)(as)	all, every, throughout

OTROS INDEFINIDOS

otro(a)(os)(as)	another
cualquier(a)	whichever

Hablar de acciones recientes. El presente perfecto (pág. 132)

yo	he hablado	nosotros nosotras	hemos hablado
tú	has hablado	vosotros vosotras	habéis hablado
usted él ella	ha hablado	ustedes ellos ellas	han hablado

Construcciones impersonales. El pronombre *se* (pág. 144)

EL PRONOMBRE SE IMPERSONAL

¿Cómo se dice *apple* en español?

USO DE SE + VERBO EN TERCERA PERSONA CON VALOR IMPERSONAL

Se puede hablar por teléfono.
Se ve que esta ropa es de buena calidad.
Se vende pescado aquí.
Se venden zapatos aquí.

El pluscuamperfecto (pág. 154)

yo	había planchado	nosotros nosotras	habíamos planchado
tú	habías planchado	vosotros vosotras	habíais planchado
usted él ella	había planchado	ustedes ellos ellas	habían planchado

Los demostrativos (pág. 156)

Distance from speaker	Singular		Plural	
	Masculino	Femenino	Masculino	Femenino
Near	este	esta	estos	estas
At a distance	ese	esa	esos	esas
Far away	aquel	aquella	aquellos	aquellas

Formas neutras: esto, eso, aquello.　　**Adverbios demostrativos:** aquí / acá, ahí, allí / allá.

Differentiated Instruction

DEVELOPING LEARNERS

- For further practice with irregular participles and gender and number agreement, have students complete these sentences:
  1. *Estas cartas ya están (escribir). (escritas)*
  2. *¡Qué horror! La gatita está (morir). (muerta)*
  3. *Los problemas de matemáticas están (resolver). (resueltos)*
  4. *Los muebles están (cubrir) de polvo. (cubiertos)*
  5. *¿Está (abrir) la tienda? (abierta)*
  6. *Ya está (decir) todo lo que había que decir. (dicho)*
  7. *Ese poncho fue (hacer) a mano. (hecho)*

EXPANDING LEARNERS

- For further practice with the present perfect and the *pluscuamperfecto*, have students complete these sentences:
  1. *Este año mi familia y yo no (tomar) vacaciones. (hemos tomado)*
  2. *Tú ya te (despertar) cuando te llamé, ¿verdad? (habías despertado)*
  3. *Yo no (terminar) esta actividad todavía. (he terminado)*
  4. *Mis amigos (venir) a verme esta mañana. (han venido)*
  5. *Tenía sueño porque no (dormir) bien la noche anterior. (había dormido)*

DESAFÍO 1

4 **¿Qué has hecho?** Mira la agenda de María y completa una tabla como esta siguiendo el modelo.

¿Qué cosas ha hecho hoy María?	¿Qué cosas no ha hecho hoy María?
Ha ido al dentista.	

31 de octubre

- Ir al dentista. ✓
- Hacer la compra. ✓
- Llevar a Juan al médico.
- Escribir un e-mail a Rosa para invitarla al cumpleaños. ✓
- Cambiar los pantalones.
- Llamar al plomero. ✓
- Comprar un regalo a Pedro.
- Ver los adornos para el cumpleaños. ✓

 DESAFÍO 2

5 **Se vende.** Lee estas oraciones y elige la opción correcta.

1. En este mercado se venden _____ adornos de artesanía indígena.
   1 cualquiera/muchos

2. No compré la alfombra azul, compré _____ en tonos rojizos.
   2 alguna/otra

3. _____ quiere venir al mercado con nosotras. Están todos muy cansados.
   3 Nadie/Alguien

4. No hay _____ de cerámica en este puesto.
   4 algo/nada

5. En este mercado no se puede comprar _____ recuerdo de México.
   5 ningún/ninguno

DESAFÍO 3

6 **Pluscuamperfecto.** Completa estas oraciones con la forma correcta del pluscuamperfecto. Usa los verbos del cuadro.

| reparar |
| regalar |
| invitar |
| tender |
| hacer |

1. Cuando Felipe llegó, yo todavía no _____ la tarea.
2. Cuando llamé a José, ya _____ la ropa.
3. Ayer me puse el vestido que mi madre me _____ para mi cumpleaños.
4. No llamé al plomero porque mi padre ya _____ el grifo.
5. No fui a la fiesta porque nadie me _____.

 **CULTURA**

7 **Lugares.** Responde a estas preguntas.

1. ¿Qué material producen las alpacas?
2. ¿Qué se puede comprar en el mercado de Otavalo?
3. ¿Cómo se decoran los patios de Córdoba?

ciento setenta y uno 171

HERITAGE LANGUAGE LEARNERS

- Students may have difficulty distinguishing between adjectives and adverbs and say things like, *Ella estaba *media dormida.* Have them complete these sentences with the correct form of the word in parentheses.
  1. *Los zapatos de tacón me gustan (bastante).* (bastante)
  2. *Vinieron (bastante) personas a la fiesta.* (bastantes)
  3. *Esa carne está (poco) cocinada.* (poco)
  4. *Tenemos (poco) días festivos.* (pocos)
  5. *La puerta está (medio) abierta.* (medio)
  6. *¿Quieres (medio) naranja?* (media)

MULTIPLE INTELLIGENCES:
Visual-Spatial Intelligence

- Have pairs work together to draw a house floor plan on poster paper. Ask them to include different areas of the house, both indoors and outdoors. Encourage students to also draw furniture and appliances. Then ask them to list, on a separate sheet of paper, common household chores using the impersonal se. For example: *Se lavan los platos aquí.* Have pairs exchange their floor plans and lists of chores with another pair, and ask them to match the chore with the area of the house where it is usually done.

REPASO
Gramática

Activities

4. After students have completed this activity, have them get together with a classmate and interview each other about what they have and have not done today. For example:
A. *¿Ya has hecho la tarea de Geometría?*
B. *No, no he tenido tiempo. ¿Y tú ya has almorzado?*
A. *No. ¡Son las 10:30 a. m.!*
B. *Es que como no he desayunado, ya tengo hambre.*

7. Before students begin this activity, ask them to get together in groups of three. Have groups look through all of the cultural readings in this unit and come up with three additional questions. Ask them to write their questions legibly on an index card—one question per card. Collect the cards and add three cards with the questions from activity 7. Then organize a trivia game or a similar class competition.

Answer Key

4. Ha hecho la compra. Ha escrito un e-mail a Rosa. Ha llamado al plomero. Ha visto los adornos para el cumpleaños.
No ha llevado a Juan al médico. No ha cambiado los pantalones. No le ha comprado un regalo a Pedro.

5. 1. muchos   4. nada
    2. otra   5. ningún
    3. Nadie

6. 1. había hecho   4. había reparado
    2. había tendido   5. había invitado
    3. había regalado

7. Answers will vary. Sample answers:
1. Producen lana.
2. Se puede comprar ropa, tapices, textiles, joyas y adornos de distintos materiales.
3. Se decoran con suelo de piedra, una fuente en el centro y plantas y flores en todo el patio.

Additional Resources

Fans Online activities
Practice Workbook

171

Unit 3
PROYECTO
Ciudades coloniales hispanas

Presentation

- In this section, students will apply the vocabulary, grammar, and cultural information they have learned in this unit to create materials to promote tourism to colonial cities in Latin America.

Activities	Standards	Resources
Paso 1	1.1, 2.1, 5.2	
Paso 2	1.1, 1.2, 2.1, 3.1, 5.1	
Paso 3	1.1, 1.3, 2.1, 3.1	
Paso 4	1.1, 1.3, 2.1, 3.1, 5.1	

Teaching Suggestions

Warm-Up / Independent Starter

- Ask students to review the *Mapa cultural* on pages 164–165 and imagine that they are visiting a colonial city. What would they like to see and do?

Preparation

- Invite students to share their Independent Starters. Is there a pattern regarding the kinds of things students would like to see and do in a colonial city? If so, they may want to focus on some of those things in their promotional materials.

- Explain that tourism is an important source of revenue for many cities in Latin America. Great efforts have been made to preserve, protect, and restore the heritage of cities across the region. Some of these efforts have the backing of UNESCO and many cities have been included in the list of World Heritage Sites. Encourage students to look up a list of Latin American cities that have been awarded this distinction.

Step-by-Step Instructions

Paso 1

- To assist students in their selection of a city, suggest that they create an index card for each candidate city, listing the top ten reasons to visit it. They may consider the city's architecture, history, food, ambience, location, culture, shopping, climate, etc. Once they have their index cards, encourage a discussion and a group vote to select their city.

Una feria sobre
ciudades coloniales hispanas

Your city will be hosting a Travel Fair to promote tourism in Latin America. Your class will be participating in the festival with stands to promote colonial cities in Latin America. You will need to research the city your group chooses and design promotional materials to attract and inform international visitors.

PASO 1 Elige una ciudad

- Reúnete con tres o cuatro compañeros(as) para seleccionar la ciudad que les interese. Aquí tienen como ejemplo algunas ciudades coloniales hispanas muy conocidas:

Cholula (México).

Cuzco (Perú).

Cartagena de Indias (Colombia).

La Habana (Cuba).

Quito (Ecuador).

PASO 2 Reúne información sobre el centro de la ciudad

- Investiga para obtener información e imágenes sobre la ciudad elegida. Puedes utilizar revistas de turismo, libros, enciclopedias o Internet.
  Aquí tienes algunas ideas:
  - Historia de la ciudad: cuándo fue fundada, quién la fundó, qué importancia tuvo la ciudad, por qué alcanzó esa importancia…
  - Un mapa del centro de la ciudad donde se vea el trazado de las calles.
  - Imágenes de la plaza principal y de los edificios importantes situados en la plaza.
  - Información histórica de la plaza y de sus edificios.
  - La ciudad hoy.

Rubric for Evaluation

	Content	Organization	Presentation
1 point	Limited relevance. Information is incomplete or not focused. Little Spanish is used.	Inefficient use of time. Descriptions are disorganized, unclear, and difficult to follow.	Unclear communication. Delivery is not fluent. Many errors in vocabulary and grammar.
3 points	Relevant and focused information, but some of it lacks significance. Spanish is used most of the time.	Time is used well. Descriptions are mostly organized but lack some clarity. Relatively easy to follow.	Clear communication and fluent delivery. Mostly correct vocabulary and grammar.

PASO 3 Organiza y estructura la información

- Reúnan toda la información conseguida y organícenla. Piensen si es suficiente para su proyecto o si creen que necesitan profundizar en algo más.

- Piensen qué documentos pueden elaborar para presentar la información y elijan dos de ellos. Aquí tienen algunas ideas:
  - Un póster con información adicional.
  - Un folleto turístico.
  - Un *collage* con textos e imágenes.
  - Una presentación virtual.
  - Un video.

- Desarrollen los documentos elegidos. Recuerden que van a presentar la ciudad en una feria de turismo, así que la información tiene que ser muy atractiva y visual para atraer al mayor número de visitantes.

CIUDADES COLONIALES HISPANAS

¡VEN A CONOCERLAS!

PASO 4 Monta tu *stand*

- Reúnan los documentos desarrollados por toda la clase y monten su feria de turismo sobre ciudades coloniales hispanas.

- Muestren la información a los visitantes y contesten sus preguntas.

Unidad 3

Autoevaluación

¿Qué has aprendido en esta unidad?

Do these activities to evaluate how well you understood this unit's concepts.

Evalúa tus habilidades. Para cada punto, di Muy bien, Bien o Necesito practicar más.

a. Can you talk about recent actions?

▶ Talk with a partner about places that you have never been to that you want to visit.

▶ Imagine that you are at a winter fashion show. Describe the clothes and accessories that the models are wearing.

b. Can you describe objects?

▶ Describe three objects that are in your classroom or house. Give details about shapes, colors, and materials. Use indefinites to indicate how many of them there are and explain their use. Your classmate needs to guess what the objects are.

c. Can you talk about past household activities?

▶ Saturday was cleaning day in your house. Write a paragraph about the different chores that your family had already done when it suddenly started raining.

PROYECTO

Ciudades coloniales hispanas

Paso 2

- Explain that most tourist attractions are concentrated in the historic center of the city. This area can be referred to as *centro histórico*, *casco viejo/antiguo*, or *zona colonial*. Students will find good sources of reliable information online by searching the official website for the city (*Ayuntamiento de...* or *Municipalidad de...*). There, they will find links to *Conoce* [city name], *La/Tu ciudad/municipio*, or *Turismo*, which contain information about the city.

Paso 3

- In their promotional materials, encourage students to answer questions a typical first-time visitor might ask, beginning with: Why would I want to visit that place? Students may want to use their index cards from *Paso 1* to list some top reasons to visit their city.

Paso 4

- Encourage students to decorate their booth with crafts, posters, pictures, etc. from their city. They may also wear traditional clothes, a typical hat, or the colors of the city.

Evaluation

- Distribute copies of the rubric to students and encourage them to refer to the rubric as they prepare their projects.

Content

- Explain that the promotional materials should not overwhelm potential tourists with information, but rather make them curious about the city. The goal is to get people to visit the place.

Organization

- Encourage students to experiment with different types of organization. They may, for instance, organize their information thematically (e.g., history, architecture) or do a before and after presentation in which they show the city in the past and now.

Presentation

- Remind students that they are selling their destination, so they should sound enthusiastic, engaged, and authentic. Their audience is their prospective customers.

	Content	Organization	Presentation
5 points	Relevant, focused, and interesting information. Many details and significance are highlighted. Spanish is used exclusively.	Time is used wisely. Descriptions are well organized, clear, and very easy to follow.	Clear and fluent communication. Very motivating, upbeat delivery. Correct and complete vocabulary and grammar.

Unit 4 Vida sana

Objectives

- To identify traditional dishes and foods of the Spanish-speaking world.
- To talk about nutrition.
- To identify personal hygiene practices.
- To name parts of the body.
- To state affirmative and negative commands.
- To use the conditional verb tense properly.

- To use different verbs that express a change.
- To make value statements.
- To give advice and make recommendations.
- To identify main ideas and significant details in a variety of texts.
- To write descriptive, narrative, or informative texts.

- To know and apply the different stages of the writing process: plan, write, revise, and share.
- To explore cultural aspects of food and dishes in Hispanic countries.
- To discuss historical landmarks and tourist locations in Latin American countries.

Contents

Vocabulary

- Useful expressions to show surprise, to ask about someone's ability to do something, and to explain one's own ability to do something.
- Review: Words for food flavors and preparation, and personal hygiene products and practices.
- Food and nutrition.
- Healthy habits and personal hygiene objects and products.
- The doctor's office, parts of the body, and medical specialists.

Grammar

- Affirmative and negative commands.
- Verbs that express change of state.
- The prepositions *para* and *por.*
- To make value statements.
- The conditional tense.
- To give advice or make recommendations.

Culture

- Traditional Latin dishes. *La ropa vieja.*
- Agriculture and staple foods used in Hispanic countries. *La quinua.*
- Traditional Latin American recipes and food preparation.
- Tourist sites and resorts in Latin American countries.
- Cities and geographic locations in Latin America. Punta del Este.
- Medicinal and therapeutic practices in Hispanic countries.
- *El Hospital de Jesús.*
- *El marcapasos.*
- The Aztec legend about the origin of corn.

Evaluation Criteria

- Identify traditional Latin American dishes and their ingredients.
- Identify ways to maintain good health, hygiene, and nutrition.
- Explain how to prepare different dishes.
- Describe the taste, smell, and ingredients of several foods and dishes.
- Identify and describe agriculture and staple foods from the Hispanic world.
- Use commands to tell others what to do or not to do.

- Use verbs and expressions to tell about permanent and temporary changes.
- Express opinions and make value statements using the infinitive and subjunctive verb forms.
- Differentiate between the uses of the prepositions *para* and *por.*
- Express present desires and wishes for the future using the conditional tense.
- Give advice and make recommendations using different expressions and verb forms.

- Compare and contrast dishes from different Hispanic countries.
- Follow and write a recipe for a traditional Hispanic dish.
- Identify and describe historic sites and tourist areas in different Hispanic countries.
- Identify parts of the body.
- Identify different medical professionals, products, and practices.
- Read different types of texts and identify main ideas and significant details in them.

Unit Plan

Las tareas / Antes de empezar

Estimated time: 1 session.

Text: *Nos cuidamos.*

Functions & forms:
- Useful expressions to show surprise, to ask about someone's ability to do something, and to explain one's own ability to do something.
- Review of known vocabulary about foods, food flavors and preparation, and personal hygiene products and practices.

⚑ DESAFÍO 1

Estimated time: 5 sessions.

Text: *La ropa vieja*

Functions & forms:
- To talk about nutrition.
- Food and nutrition.
- Affirmative and negative commands.
- Verbs that express change of state.

Culture:
- *La ropa vieja.*
- *La quinua.*

Reading: *La ropa vieja.*

⚑ DESAFÍO 2

Estimated time: 5 sessions.

Text: *Un balneario uruguayo.*

Functions & forms:
- To make value statements.
- Healthy habits. Personal hygiene objects and products.
- Prepositions *para* and *por*.
- Expressions to make value statements.

Culture:
- *Punta del Este.*
- *Tratamientos alternativos.*
- *Las aguas termales.*

Reading: *El blog personal de Sara.*

⚑ DESAFÍO 3

Estimated time: 6 sessions.

Text: *El hospital más antiguo de las Américas.*

Functions & forms:
- To give advice and make recommendations.
- The doctor's office. Body parts.
- Conditional tense.
- Verbs and expressions to give advice and make recommendations.

Culture:
- *El Hospital de Jesús.*
- *La donación de órganos.*
- *El marcapasos.*

Reading: *La leyenda del maíz.*

Para terminar

Estimated time: 1 session.

Todo junto: Review of *Desafíos 1–3.*

Tu desafío:
- *Desafío A:* Create a presentation about a traditional Hispanic dish.
- *Desafío B:* Design a webpage about a spa.
- *Desafío C:* Prepare an interview of a doctor, conduct the interview, and present the results.

MAPA CULTURAL

Estimated time: 1 session.

Mapa cultural: Alimentos básicos en el mundo hispano.

ESCRITURA

Estimated time: 1 session.

Writing: *Una receta típica.*

PROYECTO/EVALUACIÓN

Estimated time: 2 sessions.

Project: *Elaborar una guía para una vida saludable.*

Self-evaluation: *Autoevaluación.*

Standards for Learning Spanish

COMMUNICATION

1.1. Interpersonal mode

- Exchange personal opinions and experiences.
- Engage in oral conversations using personal knowledge and experience.
- Exchange assignments with a partner and evaluate each other's work.
- Create a visual and describe it with a partner.
- Discuss hypothetical situations with a partner.
- Compare and contrast information with a partner.
- Ask and answer questions on different topics.
- Ask a partner questions and take notes.

1.2. Interpretive mode

- Demonstrate understanding of oral and written expressions.
- Demonstrate understanding of questions relating to familiar and less familiar topics.
- Understand and obtain information from audio or video recordings.
- Understand written exchanges.
- Identify main ideas and significant details from a literary text.

- Extract information from an informative text.
- Draw conclusions and make judgments from oral and written texts.
- Interpret texts on topics of other cultures and relate them to personal knowledge and experience.

1.3. Presentational mode

- Produce and present an original creation orally.
- Design and present a webpage.
- Write sentences or paragraphs comparing or summarizing information.
- Write a blog entry.
- Use graphic organizers to present information.
- Write sentences that express opinions or make value statements about a given situation.
- Write a letter defending a position on a given topic.
- Write a process essay and present it to the class.
- Write an interview and present the results.
- Describe how foods look and taste.

CULTURE

2.1. Practices and perspectives

- Learn how traditional foods are prepared.
- Learn about some traditional and alternative medicinal products and practices in Latin America.
- Learn about ways people maintain good health in Latin America.
- Read and understand an ancient Hispanic legend.

2.2. Products and perspectives

- Learn about some Spanish dishes and compare them to dishes in the students' culture.
- Learn about and describe agricultural crops and staple foods used in Hispanic countries.
- Learn about tourist areas and sites in Hispanic countries.
- Learn about some Latin American inventors and how their inventions changed our way of life.

CONNECTIONS

3.1. Interdisciplinary connections

- Understand the similarities and differences between some aspects of grammar in English and in Spanish.
- Use the writing process to produce a written work.
- Understand MyPlate and identify healthy foods and practices.
- Learn about medical equipment and practices.
- Learn about geographic locations with natural spas and thermal waters.

- Design a guide to healthy living.
- Learn about parts of the body.
- Read and understand a cultural legend.

3.2. Viewpoints through language/culture

- Read dialogues, informative texts, and literary texts in Spanish that provide insight into Hispanic cultures.
- Learn about traditional Hispanic recipes and cooking and eating habits.

COMPARISONS

4.1. Compare languages

- Compare the uses of commands in English and in Spanish.
- Compare the uses of verbs to indicate changes of state in English and in Spanish.
- Compare some prepositions used in English and in Spanish.
- Compare how to express opinions or make value statements in English and in Spanish.
- Compare how to give advice or make recommendations in English and in Spanish.

4.2. Compare cultures

- Compare foods and dishes in Hispanic countries and in the United States.
- Compare medicinal practices in Hispanic countries and in the United States.

COMMUNITIES

5.1. Spanish within and beyond the school setting

- Research and obtain information on the Internet or in a library.
- Discuss activities and services performed in the students' community.
- Imagine situations in which Spanish could be used.
- Write a letter in Spanish.
- Conduct an interview.

5.2. Spanish for lifelong learning

- Promote a positive attitude toward other cultures.
- Discuss future professions and actions.

Communicative Skills

Interpersonal Mode

		Activities
Speaking	• Exchange opinions or experiences. • Engage in conversation with a classmate. • Contrast answers or compare information with a classmate. • Talk to a partner about different topics based on images.	• 4, 18, 22, 35, 55, 58, 61, 81, 83 • 27, 28, 35, 40, 55, 68, 72, 76 • 6, 25, 31, 67, 78, *Proyecto* • 27, 35, 40, 72, 81
Writing	• Write a list of recommendations. • Write questions for an interview or write notes from an interview. • Write a letter or a message for a website asking for or giving recommendations.	• 17, 81 • 36, 79 • 45, 76
Listening	• Understand and obtain information from simple oral exchanges.	• 18, 27, 35, 36, 40, 55, 58, 61, 68, 72, 76, 78
Reading	• Understand a list of items. • Understand the information in a letter or a message in a website.	• 6, 78 • 45, 76

Interpretive Mode

		Activities
Listening	• Understand and obtain information from a conversation. • Understand oral descriptions or narrations. • Listen to a recording and apply information to a task.	• 9, 39, 52, 61, 70, 80 • 20, 31, 58 • 9, 11, 16, 31, 34, 58, 61
Reading	• Demonstrate comprehension of written exchanges and longer written dialogues. • Infer meanings based on a text. • Reflect on cultural topics in relation to personal knowledge and experience. • Demonstrate understanding of a descriptive or narrative text. • Obtain information and draw conclusions from an informative text.	• 1, 8, 23, 24, 28, 30, 55, 56, 57, 79 • 1, 2, 23, 49, *Lectura D3* • 10, 14, 32, 41, 59, 73, 83 • 21, 47, 48, 74, 75 • 10, 14, 31, 32, 41, 46, 53, 59, 73
Viewing	• Connect words, expressions, events, or information to images. • Obtain information from an image.	• 3, 33, 58, 75 • 9, 13, 35, 40, 72, 75, 80

Presentational Mode

		Activities
Speaking	• Present a description or information to the class. • Present an original creation to the class. • Present a dialogue or a skit to the class.	• 22, 36, 78, 82 • 27, 51, 76, 82, *Escritura, Proyecto* • 50, 79
Writing	• Create a list or write an informative paragraph. • Create a poster or an original text. • Write a descriptive paragraph or a response to a letter. • Make value statements or recommendations in written form. • Write a recipe.	• 6, 13, 17, 76, 80, 82 • 27, 51, 76, 82, *Proyecto* • 35, 45, 54, 80 • 13, 17, 27, 43, 44, 67, 70, 71, 76 • 25, *Escritura*
Visually Representing	• Present information in a Venn diagram, chart, graph, or table. • Present information using visuals related to the unit.	• 11, 24, 63 • 27, *Tu desafío, Proyecto*

Cross-Curricular Standards

Subject	Standard	Activities
Language Arts	• Compare elements of Spanish grammar and language with English equivalents. • Use the writing process to write a process essay.	• 15, 19, 37, 42, 64, 69 • *Escritura*
Social Studies	• Read about destinations of interest in Hispanic countries. • Read about and research traditional dishes and foods in Hispanic countries.	• *Texto D2*, 31, 32, 53, *Texto D3*, 59 • 10, *Lectura D1, Mapa cultural*, 82
Art	• Create a poster or an illustrated guide.	• 27, *Proyecto*
Science	• Identify foods in the different categories of MyPlate.	• 6, 14, 27

Lesson Plans (50-Minute Classes)

Day	Objectives	Sessions	Activities	Time	Standards	Resources / Homework
1	To introduce healthy living and the characters' challenges, and to review learned vocabulary	**Vida sana / Las tareas / Antes de empezar** (174–179) • Warm-Up: Topic orientation • Presentation: *Nos cuidamos* • *Expresiones útiles* and *Recuerda*	 1–2 3–6	 10 m. 20 m. 20 m.	1.1, 1.2, 1.3, 2.1, 2.2, 3.1, 3.2, 5.2	Visual Presentation Video Practice Workbook
2	To talk about nutrition	**Desafío 1 – La ropa vieja** (180–181) • Warm-Up: Independent Starter • Texto: *La ropa vieja* • Cultura: *La ropa vieja*	 7–9 10	 5 m. 35 m. 10 m.	1.1, 1.2, 2.1, 2.2, 3.2, 4.2	Visual Presentation Audio Video
3	To identify and describe healthy foods	**Desafío 1 – Vocabulario** (182–183) • Warm-Up: Independent Starter • Vocabulary: *Alimentación* • Conexiones: *La quinua*	 11–13 14	 5 m. 35 m. 10 m.	1.2, 1.3, 2.2, 3.1, 5.2	Audio Practice Workbook
4	To learn commands	**Desafío 1 – Gramática** (184–185) • Warm-Up: Independent Starter • Grammar: *Los mandatos*	 15–18	 5 m. 45 m.	1.1, 1.2, 1.3, 3.1, 4.1, 5.1	Practice Workbook Audio
5	To learn verbs that express a change of state	**Desafío 1 – Gramática** (186–187) • Warm-Up: Independent Starter • Grammar: *Los verbos de cambio*	 19–22	 5 m. 45 m.	1.1, 1.2, 1.3, 2.2, 3.1, 4.1, 5.2	Audio Practice Workbook
6	To understand a dialogue and to integrate vocabulary and grammar	**Desafío 1 – Lectura / Comunicación** (188–191) • Warm-Up: Independent Starter • Lectura: *La ropa vieja* • Comunicación: Review • Final del desafío	 23–25 26–27 28	 5 m. 20 m. 15 m. 10 m.	1.1, 1.2, 1.3, 2.2, 3.1, 3.2, 5.1, 5.2	Visual Presentation Practice Workbook *Tu desafío* Quiz on *Desafío 1*
7	To make value statements	**Desafío 2 – Un balneario uruguayo** (192–193) • Warm-Up: Correct quiz on *Desafío 1* • Texto: *Un balneario uruguayo* • Conexiones: *Punta del Este*	 29–31 32	 5 m. 35 m. 10 m.	1.1, 1.2, 1.3, 2.1, 2.2, 3.1, 4.1	Visual Presentation Audio Video
8	To identify fitness activities and hygiene objects and products	**Desafío 2 – Vocabulario** (194–195) • Warm-Up: Independent Starter • Vocabulary: *Hábitos saludables*	 33–36	 5 m. 45 m.	1.1, 1.2, 1.3, 3.1, 5.2	Audio Practice Workbook
9	To learn the uses of the prepositions *para* and *por*	**Desafío 2 – Gramática** (196–197) • Warm-Up: Independent Starter • Grammar: *'Para' y 'por'* • Conexiones: *Tratamientos alternativos*	 37–40 41	 5 m. 35 m. 10 m.	1.1, 1.2, 1.3, 2.1, 3.1, 3.2, 4.1, 5.2	Practice Workbook
10	To learn how to make value statements	**Desafío 2 – Gramática** (198–199) • Warm-Up: Independent Starter • Grammar: *Hacer valoraciones* • Conexiones: *Las aguas termales*	 42–45 46	 5 m. 35 m. 10 m.	1.1, 1.2, 1.3, 3.1, 4.1, 5.1	Practice Workbook
11	To understand a blog entry and to integrate vocabulary and grammar	**Desafío 2 – Lectura / Comunicación** (200–203) • Warm-Up: Independent Starter • Lectura: *El blog personal de Sara* • Comunicación: Review • Final del desafío	 47–51 52–54 55	 5 m. 20 m. 15 m. 10 m.	1.1, 1.2, 1.3, 2.1, 3.1, 3.2, 5.1	Audio Practice Workbook *Tu desafío* Quiz on *Desafío 2*

Day	Objectives	Sessions	Activities	Time	Standards	Resources / Homework
12	To learn how to give suggestions and make recommendations	**Desafío 3 – El hospital más antiguo de las Américas** (204–205) • Warm-Up: Correct quiz on *Desafío 2* • *Texto: El hospital más antiguo de las Américas* • *Cultura: El Hospital de Jesús*	56–58 59	5 m. 35 m. 10 m.	1.1, 1.2. 1.3, 2.2, 3.1, 3.2	Visual Presentation Audio
13	To talk about medical conditions and practices	**Desafío 3 – Vocabulario** (206–207) • Warm-Up: Independent Starter • Vocabulary: *La consulta médica* • *Comunidades: La donación de órganos*	60–62 63	5 m. 35 m. 10 m.	1.1, 1.2, 1.3, 2.1, 3.1, 4.2, 5.1, 5.2	Audio Practice Workbook
14	To learn the conditional tense to express wishes for the future	**Desafío 3 – Gramática** (208–209) • Warm-Up: Independent Starter • Grammar: *El condicional*	64–68	5 m. 45 m.	1.1, 1.2, 1.3, 3.1, 4.1	Practice Workbook
15	To learn how to give advice or recommendations to others	**Desafío 3 – Gramática** (210–211) • Warm-Up: Independent Starter • Grammar: *Dar consejos y hacer recomendaciones* • *Conexiones: El marcapasos*	69–72 73	5 m. 35 m. 10 m.	1.1, 1.2, 1.3, 2.2, 3.1, 4.1	Audio Practice Workbook
16	To understand a cultural legend	**Desafío 3 – Lectura** (212–213) • Warm-Up: Independent Starter • *Lectura: La leyenda del maíz*	74–75	5 m. 45 m.	1.1, 1.2, 1.3, 2.2, 3.1, 3.2	
17	To integrate vocabulary and grammar	**Desafío 3 – Comunicación** (214–215) • Warm-Up: Independent Starter • *Comunicación:* Review • *Final del desafío*	76–78 79	5 m. 30 m. 15 m.	1.1, 1.2, 1.3, 3.1, 5.1, 5.2	Practice Workbook Quiz on *Desafío 3* **Para terminar – Tu desafío** (217)
18	To integrate language in context	**Para terminar** (216–217) • Warm-Up: Correct quiz on *Desafío 3* • *Todo junto* • *Tu desafío* presentations	80–81 82	5 m. 20 m. 25 m.	1.1, 1.2, 1.3, 2.1, 2.2, 3.1, 5.2	Practice Workbook
19	To assess student proficiency and to learn about staple foods consumed in Hispanic countries	**Evaluación / Mapa cultural** (218–219) • Warm-Up: Independent Starter • Quiz on *Desafíos 1–3* • *Mapa cultural: Alimentos básicos en el mundo hispano*	83	5 m. 15 m. 30 m.	1.1, 1.2, 1.3, 2.1, 2.2, 3.2, 4.2, 5.1, 5.2	Video Practice Workbook
20	To write a process essay (a recipe)	**Escritura** (220–221) • Warm-Up: Independent Starter • *Escritura: Una receta típica*		5 m. 45 m.	1.1, 1.2, 1.3, 2.2, 3.1, 4.1, 5.1, 5.2	Project work
21	To create a guide	**Proyecto** (226–227) • Warm-Up: Prepare project presentations • Project presentations		10 m. 40 m.	1.1, 1.2, 1.3, 2.1, 2.2, 3.1, 3.2, 5.1, 5.2	**Repaso – Vocabulario** (222–223) **Repaso – Gramática** (224–225)
22	To assess student proficiency	**Assessment** • *Autoevaluación* (227) • Test		10 m. 40 m.	1.1, 1.2, 1.3, 2.1, 2.2, 5.1, 5.2	

Unit 4 Vida sana

Lesson Plans (90-Minute Classes)

Day	Objectives	Sessions	Activities	Time	Standards	Resources/Homework
1	To introduce healthy living and the characters' challenges, and to review learned vocabulary	(See Day 12 Unit 3) **Vida sana/Las tareas/Antes de empezar** (174–179) • Warm-Up: Topic orientation • Presentation: *Nos cuidamos* • *Expresiones útiles* and *Recuerda*	 1–2 3–6	(45 m.) 10 m. 20 m. 15 m.	1.1, 1.2, 1.3, 2.1, 2.2, 3.1, 3.2, 5.2	Visual Presentation Video Practice Workbook
2	To talk about nutrition and to identify and describe healthy foods	**Desafío 1 – La ropa vieja/Vocabulario** (180–183) • Warm-Up: Independent Starter • *Texto: La ropa vieja* • *Cultura: La ropa vieja* • Vocabulary: *Alimentación* • *Conexiones: La quinua*	 7–9 10 11–13 14	 5 m. 30 m. 10 m. 35 m. 10 m.	1.1, 1.2, 1.3, 2.1, 2.2, 3.1, 3.2, 4.2, 5.2	Visual Audio Video Practice Workbook
3	To learn commands and to learn verbs that express a change of state	**Desafío 1 – Gramática** (184–187) • Warm-Up: Independent Starter • Grammar: *Los mandatos* • Grammar: *Los verbos de cambio*	 15–18 19–22	 5 m. 40 m. 45 m.	1.1, 1.2, 1.3, 2.2, 3.1, 4.1, 5.1, 5.2	Audio Practice Workbook
4	To understand a dialogue and to integrate vocabulary and grammar	**Desafío 1 – Lectura/Comunicación/Evaluación** (188–191) • Warm-Up: Independent Starter • *Lectura: La ropa vieja* • *Comunicación:* Review • *Final del desafío* • Quiz on *Desafío 1*	 23–25 26–27 28	 5 m. 35 m. 25 m. 10 m. 15 m.	1.1, 1.2, 1.3, 2.2, 3.1, 3.2, 5.1, 5.2	Visual Presentation Practice Workbook *Tu desafío*
5	To make value statements and to identify fitness activities and hygiene objects and products	**Desafío 2 – Un balneario uruguayo/Vocabulario** (192–195) • Warm-Up: Independent Starter • *Texto: Un balneario uruguayo* • *Conexiones: Punta del Este* • Vocabulary: *Hábitos saludables*	 29–31 32 33–36	 5 m. 40 m. 10 m. 35 m.	1.1, 1.2, 1.3, 2.1, 2.2, 3.1, 4.1, 5.2	Visual Presentation Audio Video Practice Workbook
6	To learn the uses of the prepositions *para* and *por* and to learn how to make value statements	**Desafío 2 – Gramática** (196–199) • Warm-Up: Independent Starter • Grammar: *'Para' y 'por'* • *Conexiones: Tratamientos alternativos* • Grammar: *Hacer valoraciones* • *Conexiones: Las aguas termales*	 37–40 41 42–45 46	 5 m. 35 m. 10 m. 30 m. 10 m.	1.1, 1.2, 1.3, 2.1, 3.1, 3.2, 4.1, 5.1, 5.2	Audio Practice Workbook
7	To understand a blog entry and to integrate vocabulary and grammar	**Desafío 2 – Lectura/Comunicación/Evaluación** (200–203) • Warm-Up: Independent Starter • *Lectura: El blog personal de Sara* • *Comunicación:* Review • *Final del desafío* • Quiz on *Desafío 2*	 47–51 52–54 55	 5 m. 35 m. 25 m. 10 m. 15 m.	1.1, 1.2, 1.3, 2.1, 3.1, 3.2, 5.1	Audio Practice Workbook *Tu desafío*

Day	Objectives	Sessions	Activities	Time	Standards	Resources / Homework
8	To learn how to give suggestions and make recommendations and to talk about medical conditions and practices	**Desafío 3 – El hospital más antiguo de las Américas / Vocabulario** (204–207) • Warm-Up: Independent Starter • *Texto: El hospital más antiguo de las Américas* • *Cultura: El Hospital de Jesús* • Vocabulary: *La consulta médica* • *Comunidades: La donación de órganos*	 56–58 59 60–62 63	5 m. 30 m. 10 m. 35 m. 10 m.	1.1, 1.2, 1.3, 2.1, 2.2, 3.1, 3.2, 4.2, 5.1, 5.2	Visual Presentation Audio Practice Workbook
9	To learn the conditional verb tense to express wishes for the future and to learn how to give advice or recommendations to others	**Desafío 3 – Gramática** (208–211) • Warm-Up: Independent Starter • Grammar: *El condicional* • Grammar: *Dar consejos y hacer recomendaciones* • *Conexiones: El marcapasos*	 64–68 69–72 73	 5 m. 40 m. 35 m. 10 m.	1.1, 1.2, 1.3, 2.2, 3.1, 4.1	Audio Practice Workbook
10	To understand a cultural legend, to integrate vocabulary and grammar, to integrate language in context, and to assess student proficiency	**Desafío 3 – Lectura / Comunicación / Evaluación / Todo junto** (212–216) • Warm-Up: Independent Starter • *Lectura: La leyenda del maíz* • *Comunicación:* Review • *Final del desafío* • *Todo junto* • Quiz on *Desafío 3*	 74–75 76–78 79 80–81	 5 m. 25 m. 20 m. 10 m. 15 m. 15 m.	1.1, 1.2, 1.3, 2.1, 2.2, 3.1, 3.2, 4.2, 5.1, 5.2	Practice Workbook **Para terminar – Tu desafío** (217)
11	To learn about staple foods consumed in Hispanic countries and to write a process essay (a recipe)	**Tu desafío / Mapa cultural / Escritura** (217–221) • Warm-Up: Independent Starter • *Tu desafío* presentations • *Mapa cultural: Alimentos básicos en el mundo hispano* • *Escritura: Una receta típica*	 82 83	 5 m. 15 m. 30 m. 40 m.	1.1, 1.2, 1.3, 2.1, 2.2, 3.1, 3.2, 4.1, 4.2, 5.1, 5.2	Video Practice Workbook **Repaso – Vocabulario** (222–223) **Repaso – Gramática** (224–225) Quiz on *Desafíos 1–3* Project work
12	To create a guide	**Proyecto / Assessment** (226–227) • Warm-Up: Correct quiz on *Desafíos 1–3* • Project presentations • *Autoevaluación* • Test (See Day 1 Unit 3)		5 m. 15 m. 10 m. 15 m. (45 m.)	1.1, 1.2, 1.3, 2.1, 2.2, 3.1, 3.2, 5.1, 5.2	

Unit 4 Vida sana

9 Una conversación con el dependiente

–Gracias por ayudarnos con nuestra tarea. ¿Usted sabe cómo se prepara la ropa vieja?

–Sí. Es un plato muy típico de la cocina caribeña tradicional. Mi abuela lo hacía mucho y me enseñó a cocinarlo.

–¿Y cuáles son los ingredientes?

–Los ingredientes básicos son carne de res, cebolla, ajo, tomate, salsa de tomate y especias.

–¿Y no se puede usar pollo o carne de cerdo?

–Sí. Tradicionalmente se hace con carne de res, pero también se puede hacer con pollo. Y hay recetas que añaden papas, chiles, garbanzos, frijoles o zanahorias.

–¿Y cómo se sirve?

–Depende de la receta, pero lo típico es servirla con arroz y plátano frito.

–Gracias. Vamos a buscar varias recetas para elegir la mejor.

–Que tengan suerte.

11 ¿Consejos para una alimentación sana?

1. Es importante consumir frutas y verduras porque contienen una gran cantidad y variedad de vitaminas.
2. Si estás gordo, come más carne roja que carne blanca.
3. No comas alimentos con mucho azúcar porque tienen muchas calorías y no son saludables.
4. Es muy bueno echar bastante sal a las comidas.
5. Si tienes hambre entre comidas, come un poco de chocolate.
6. Bebe agua o infusiones en vez de refrescos.

16 ¿A quién se lo dice?

1. No bebas refrescos o jugos con mucho azúcar.
2. ¡Comamos más legumbres!
3. No fría la comida con mucha grasa y use siempre aceite de oliva.
4. No preparen la comida con mucha sal. Pueden usar especias.
5. No se olvide de tomar varias piezas de fruta todos los días.
6. No tomemos demasiados dulces.

20 Cambios

1. Mis abuelos nacieron en México, pero después se mudaron a los Estados Unidos.
2. Cuando era niña, mis padres me llevaban a los museos en Chicago. Al principio no me gustaba ir porque me aburría, pero después me empezó a gustar.
3. La semana pasada tuve una prueba para tocar la guitarra en un festival de música, pero toqué muy mal. ¡Qué desastre!
4. Cuando mi padre me regaló dos boletos para el fútbol, empecé a gritar y a saltar de alegría.
5. Cuando pienso en el futuro, sé que quiero ayudar a la gente. Por eso quiero estudiar medicina en la universidad.

31 De vacaciones

1. Voy a pasar un fin de semana con mis amigos en este balneario. Solo hay un problema: hay tantas actividades que no podemos decidir qué hacer… ¿Tomamos el sol? ¿Hacemos surf? ¿Vamos de compras? ¿Visitamos alguna galería de arte?
2. ¡Qué estresado estoy! Siempre trabajando… No tengo tiempo para relajarme. Esto no es la buena vida. Vengo al balneario por las aguas curativas y los baños medicinales. Dicen que estas aguas son buenas contra el estrés. Espero que sea verdad.
3. ¡Qué hermoso es este balneario! ¿Qué playa vamos a visitar? Tenemos que decidir entre las dos: la Playa Brava tiene las olas grandes y fuertes del océano Atlántico; la Playa Mansa tiene olas más pequeñas y las aguas tranquilas del Río de la Plata.
4. Se ofrecen tantos tratamientos en este balneario… Me gustaría pasar aquí una semana para probarlos todos. Además de las piscinas, hay masajes terapéuticos y todo tipo de tratamientos para la piel.

34 Gimnasio En forma

¿Trabajas demasiado? ¿Estás siempre nervioso y estresado? ¿Quieres ponerte en forma y bajar de peso? Si te importa el bienestar y quieres cambiar tu estilo de vida, ven a visitar el gimnasio En forma. En En forma puedes entrenar con máquinas, asistir a clases de yoga y pilates o hacer ejercicios aeróbicos. Nuestro equipo de profesionales te ayudará a ponerte en forma. También tenemos un servicio de fisioterapia para dar masajes relajantes y terapéuticos. Recuerda: estamos abiertos desde las cinco de la mañana hasta la medianoche.

39 ¡Qué fuerza de voluntad!

–¿Adónde vas, Lourdes? Es muy temprano.

–Voy al gimnasio. Normalmente voy a esta hora.

–¿Para qué vas?

–Para hacer bicicleta y yoga.

–¿Y no terminas muy cansada?

–Qué va. Me siento menos estresada después de hacer ejercicio.

–¿Cuál es tu actividad favorita?

–El yoga. Es muy relajante. Pero también me gusta correr. ¿Sabes que me entreno para participar en un maratón en julio?

–¡No me digas! ¡Vas a correr 42 kilómetros! ¡Yo no puedo correr ni un kilómetro!

–¿Por qué no vienes al gimnasio conmigo? Puedes empezar a ponerte en forma hoy mismo.

–Ay, gracias, pero no puedo… Tengo que ir… eh… al mercado… porque mi mamá necesita que compre algunas cosas.

52 Es importante relajarse

–Bienvenidos a clase. Vamos a empezar. Relájense… Respiren profundamente y cierren los ojos…

–Michelle, yo no pienso cerrar los ojos. ¿Por qué estamos aquí?

–Shhh, Daniel. Es importante relajarse. El yoga es muy bueno para estirar el cuerpo y relajarse.

–Ya, pero yo no soy tan flexible como tú; me parece bien que hagas yoga, pero a mí no me gusta.

–Imagínense que están en la playa tumbados al sol, escuchando las olas…

–Michelle, ¿por qué no nos vamos? Yo no quiero estar aquí, no me estoy relajando.

–¡Cálmate, Daniel!

–Pero no puedo pasar la pierna por encima de mi cabeza… ¡Ay!

–¿Pero qué haces? Ay, Daniel, es necesario que escuches a la monitora. No tienes que pasar la pierna por encima de tu cabeza…

58 Síntomas

1. Se siente mal. Ayer comió demasiado y hoy le duele mucho el estómago.
2. Hoy me levanté con la cara llena de granos. Creo que es una alergia. Ayer tomé de postre torta de chocolate y creo que llevaba frutos secos.
3. Toso mucho y no puedo respirar bien. Creo que tengo gripe.
4. No me siento bien; tengo fiebre y me duele la garganta.

61 Asha va al médico

–Buenos días, doctora Márquez.

–Buenos días, Asha. ¿Cómo estás?

–Pues no me encuentro muy bien.

–¿Te duele algo?

–Sí, la cabeza.

–Creo que tienes fiebre. Ponte el termómetro. Sí, tienes un poco de fiebre. Te voy a examinar. Voy a escuchar tus pulmones. ¿Puedes toser otra vez? Veamos cómo está tu garganta. Di «ah». Está un poco roja.

–Me duele un poco cuando como, pero no demasiado.

–¿Te molestan los oídos?

–No, creo que no.

–¿Y si te toco aquí, justo debajo de la oreja?

–¡Ay! Sí, me duele un poco.

–Tienes una infección de garganta y de oídos. Voy a darte una receta para que tomes antibióticos durante cinco días, ¿de acuerdo?

–Gracias, doctora.

–Adiós y cuídate.

70 Los problemas de Lucas

–Estoy desesperado. Hace una semana que solo me ocurren cosas malas.

–¿Qué te pasa?

–Pues que esta semana tengo un partido de baloncesto muy importante y me duele mucho la mano derecha.

–Déjame ver. Uy, sí, la tienes hinchada. Te sugiero que vayas al médico lo antes posible.

–Sí, ya fui ayer.

–¿Y qué te dijo el médico?

–Me recomendó tomar unas píldoras para el dolor y ponerme hielo en la mano.

–Entonces seguramente podrás jugar.

–No creo, porque el partido es mañana.

–¡Vaya! Pues te aconsejo que llames al entrenador y le digas que no puedes jugar.

–¡Pero es un partido muy importante!

–No deberías jugar, Lucas.

–¿Qué puedo hacer?

–Yo en tu lugar descansaría y me olvidaría del partido.

–¡Eso nunca!

Unit 4
Vida sana

UNIDAD 4
Vida sana
La alimentación y la salud

The Unit

- The themes for Unit 4 are personal health and nutrition. The participants will learn the relationship between the two as they talk about food and healthy habits. They will also learn to give advice, and make value statements and recommendations.
- Diana, a veteran of *Fans del español*, will give the participants their tasks.
  - *Desafío 1*. Eva and Ethan will have to find the best recipe for *ropa vieja*, a typical Caribbean dish, prepare it, and share it with the other *Fans del español*.
  - *Desafío 2*. Michelle and Daniel will create a website to promote a spa in the seaside resort town of Punta del Este, Uruguay.
  - *Desafío 3*. Asha and Lucas will interview a famous medical specialist who works in the oldest hospital in the Americas.

Activities	Standards	Resources
Vida sana	1.2, 2.1, 2.2	Video

Teaching Suggestions

Warm-Up / Independent Starter

- Have students look at the foods depicted on these pages and ask them to list all the ingredients that they recognize.

Preparation

- Ask students to share their Independent Starters. Help them with the names of foods and ingredients that they may not know yet (e.g., *plátano*, *col*, *habichuela*, *coliflor*, *cereza*, *higo*). Then ask students questions about their preferences. For example: *¿Les gustan las cerezas? ¿Cuál es su fruta preferida? ¿Qué verdura les gusta más?*
- Have students look at the other photos. You may want to ask them these, or similar, questions: *¿Qué creen que significa la palabra baños en este contexto? ¿Para qué van las personas a unos baños? ¿Quién trabaja en una consulta médica? ¿Para qué vamos a una consulta médica?*

DESAFÍO 1

► **Hablar sobre nutrición**

Vocabulario
Alimentación

Gramática
Los mandatos
Los verbos de cambio

DESAFÍO 2

► **Hacer valoraciones**

Vocabulario
Hábitos saludables

Gramática
Para y por
Hacer valoraciones

Baños del Inca (Perú)

Ropa vieja (Cuba)

The Challenge

DESAFÍO 1

Ropa vieja

Ropa vieja is a dish that originated in the Canary Islands, Spain, and is very popular in Cuba, Puerto Rico, the Dominican Republic, and Panama. Depending on the region, it is served with rice or chickpeas. It was originally made with leftovers, and it contains meat that is cooked for a long time and then shredded. The name of this dish, which means "old clothes," has an uncertain origin, although some legends say that one day, in a very poor household where there was nothing to eat, a stew was cooked out of old clothes, which ended up tasting delicious.

DESAFÍO 2

Baños del Inca

The word *baños* (used in plural) refers to a spa, usually located in an area where there are hot springs. For example, Baños del Inca is a natural hot spring, located in Peru, which has been used since Incan times. Another word for this kind of spa is *balneario* but, in this case, it may also refer to a hotel spa located in a beach resort town, such as Punta del Este, Uruguay. These different meanings of the word *balneario* are used in this *Desafío* to make it a bit more challenging.

Vida sana

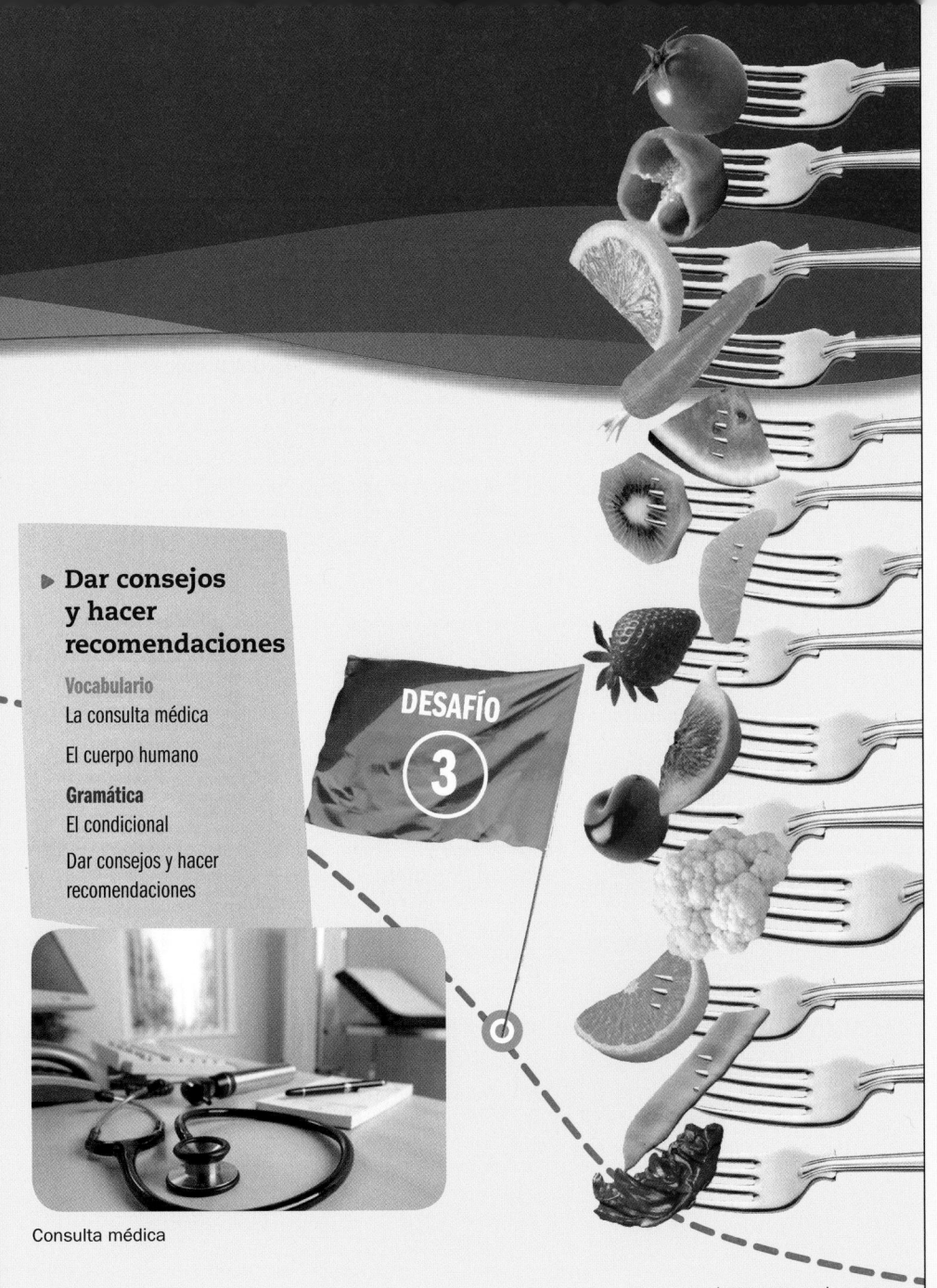

▶ **Dar consejos y hacer recomendaciones**

Vocabulario
La consulta médica

El cuerpo humano

Gramática
El condicional

Dar consejos y hacer recomendaciones

DESAFÍO 3

Consulta médica

ciento setenta y cinco 175

DESAFÍO 3

Consulta médica

Hospitals and medical facilities have existed since antiquity. The Romans, for instance, built *valetudinaria*—hospital-like buildings—which were probably used to treat soldiers injured in battle. In the Americas, the Hospital of Jesús Nazareno, founded in 1524 by Hernán Cortés in Mexico City, claims to be the oldest. Allegedly, Cortés, the Spanish conqueror of Mexico, and Moctezuma, the ruler of the Aztecs, met there for the first time. The hospital hosts some important artworks and cultural relics. Currently it is still in use, and it provides health care to thousands of people every day.

■ Have students read each *Desafío's* objective, as well as the vocabulary and grammar goals, then discuss how each picture might relate to these objectives and goals.

Picture Discussion

■ Have students look at the images again and ask them to write a sentence reacting to each of the photos. For example: *Desafío 1 – Este plato me gusta porque tiene arroz. Desafío 2 – Nadar es bueno para la salud. Desafío 3 – Voy al médico cuando estoy enfermo*. Then ask them to read their sentences. Expand with related questions and provide them with feedback as needed.

Ropa vieja (Cuba)

■ Have students identify the ingredients of this dish. Ask them to guess if the meat used for this dish is beef (*carne de res*), lamb (*cordero*), or pork (*cerdo*). Explain that *ropa vieja* is usually made with beef. Are any students in the class familiar with this dish? Invite them to describe the dish, its flavors, textures, etc.

Baños del Inca (Perú)

■ Ask students to describe this photo. To help students with the description, write related words on the board (e.g., *piscina, aguas termales, baños medicinales*), and ask them if they have ever been to a spa. Call on volunteers to describe the experience. For those students who have not been to a spa, ask them whether they would like to go to one and why.

Consulta médica

■ Brainstorm with students the types of illnesses or conditions that motivate someone to go to a doctor. Write down some of their responses. Examples include: *gripe, problemas de estómago, un hueso roto*, etc. Have students come up with a list of specialists. Call their attention to the fact that many of these words are cognates (e.g., *dentista, internista, radiólogo, pediatra*).

Objectives

■ By the end of Unit 4, students will be able to
  – Talk about food and nutrition.
  – Give commands and orders.
  – Express change.
  – Talk about healthy habits.
  – Make value statements.
  – Talk about the human body.
  – Give recommendations and advice.
  – Talk about some dishes, seaside resorts, and hospitals of the Spanish-speaking world.

175

Las tareas

Presentation

- In this section, the three pairs read a message sent by Diana, a former participant in *Fans del español*. The message contains three riddles that the pairs will have to solve in order to learn about their tasks. Students will preview useful expressions for reacting to something that sounds intriguing or strange and for asking about or expressing the ability to do certain things.

Activities	Standards	Resources
Texto	1.2, 2.1, 2.2, 3.2	Vis. Pres.
1.	1.1, 1.2, 2.2	
2.	1.3	

Teaching Suggestions

Warm-Up / Independent Starter

- Write the word *adivinanza* (riddle) on the board and give students the following examples. Ask them to try to solve the riddles.
  1. *Oro parece, <u>plata no</u> es, el que no lo adivine bien tonto es. (plátano)*
  2. *Por un caminito <u>va caminando</u> un bicho, y el nombre del bicho ya te lo he dicho. (vaca)*

Preparation

- Acquaint or reacquaint students with Diana. Explain that she is from Lawrenceville, NJ, and that she used to travel with her aunt, Rita.

- Call on volunteers to share their Independent Starters. Did students guess correctly? What tipped them in the right direction? Ask students to think of riddles they know in English and invite them to share some of these riddles with the class. Discuss as a class some of the characteristics of both the Spanish and the English riddle-poems that they have just mentioned in this discussion. (They are rhythmic and witty. They rhyme and have a double meaning.)

- Have students scan the text on this page and the dialogue on the following page, and find expressions used to ask about or express the ability to do something. (*¿Se les da bien resolver advinanzas? Soy muy buena para las adivinanzas.*) Then ask students to find an expression used for reacting to something that sounds strange. (*¡Qué raro!*)

176

Las tareas

Nos cuidamos

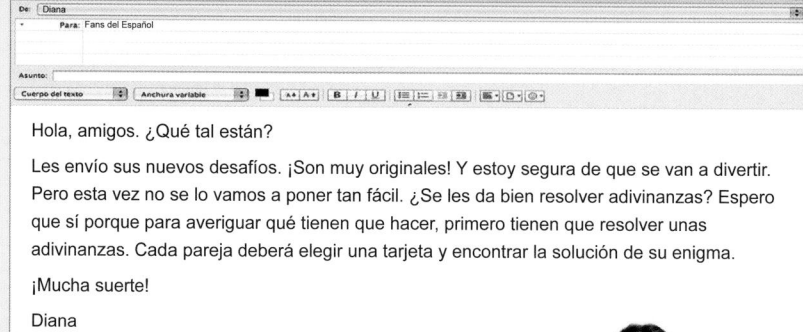 The characters receive the new challenges Diana sent them. But this time, they are pretty mysterious ... Each team will have to solve a riddle in order to find out what their challenge will be. Help them solve the mysteries!

De: Diana
Para: Fans del Español
Asunto:

Hola, amigos. ¿Qué tal están?

Les envío sus nuevos desafíos. ¡Son muy originales! Y estoy segura de que se van a divertir. Pero esta vez no se lo vamos a poner tan fácil. ¿Se les da bien resolver adivinanzas? Espero que sí porque para averiguar qué tienen que hacer, primero tienen que resolver unas adivinanzas. Cada pareja deberá elegir una tarjeta y encontrar la solución de su enigma.

¡Mucha suerte!

Diana

DESAFÍO 1

Es ropa, pero no se pone,
aunque se puede probar.
Es vieja, rica y se come.
Pruébenla. ¡Les va a gustar!

Tarea: Busquen la mejor forma de hacer esta ropa y compártanla.

DESAFÍO 2

Es un balneario al este
y entre dos playas.
Una se llama Mansa
y la otra, Brava.

Tarea: Hagan una página web para promocionar ese lugar.

DESAFÍO 3

Hernán Cortés fundó este hospital,
el primero de América.
¿Qué hospital es? ¿Dónde está?

Tarea: Entrevisten a una especialista del lugar.

176 ciento setenta y seis

Differentiated Instruction

DEVELOPING LEARNERS

- To check students' comprehension, ask them to choose the correct answer for each question.
  1. *Cada pareja tiene que ... una adivinanza. (b)*
     a. *escribir*   b. *resolver*
  2. *¿Quién es buena para las adivinanzas? (b)*
     a. *Asha*   b. *Eva*
  3. *Una pareja hará una página web de... (b)*
     a. *un hospital*   b. *un balneario*
  4. *La especialista trabaja en... (a)*
     a. *un hospital*   b. *un balneario*
  5. *Eva y Ethan deben ... la ropa vieja. (a)*
     a. *compartir*   b. *probarse*

EXPANDING LEARNERS

- Guide students in identifying the clues in *Desafío 1* that indicate that *ropa* is, indeed, a dish. (*se puede probar, rica, se come, hacer, compártanla*) Then ask them the following questions: *¿Qué hacen para ver si les gusta una comida? (La probamos.) ¿Qué adjetivo describe el sabor de la comida en la adivinanza? (rica) ¿Qué se hace con la comida? (Se come.) ¿De qué otra forma se puede decir "preparar la comida"? (hacer la comida) ¿Qué hacen con la comida si tienen invitados? (La compartimos.)*

Las tareas

¿Podemos probar esa ropa, pero no podemos ponérnosla? ¡Qué raro!

Vamos a buscar la palabra *balneario* en el diccionario.

¡Buena idea! Eso nos va a ayudar...

¿Crees que la especialista es una doctora del hospital?

Déjame pensar un minuto... Soy muy buena para las adivinanzas.

Sí, pero no sabemos dónde está.

1 ¿Comprendes?

▶ **Responde** a estas preguntas.

1. ¿Qué significa la palabra *adivinanza*?
2. ¿Conoces alguna ropa que se coma?
3. ¿Qué es un balneario?
4. ¿Qué es un(a) especialista? ¿Qué especialistas hay en un hospital?

▶ **Habla** con tu compañero(a). Hagan hipótesis sobre los enigmas que tienen que resolver los personajes.

Modelo   A. *Yo creo que el primer desafío está relacionado con la comida.*
B. *¿Crees que hay alguna comida que se llame ropa?*

1. ¿En qué crees que consiste el primer desafío? ¿Qué tienen que hacer los personajes?
2. ¿Qué lugar van a promocionar los personajes en el segundo desafío?
3. ¿A quién van a entrevistar los personajes en el tercer desafío? ¿Dónde piensas que está esa persona?

▶ **Compartan** sus hipótesis con otros(as) compañeros(as). ¿Creen que han resuelto las adivinanzas?

2 Palabras

▶ **Escribe** tres palabras del texto que sean nuevas para ti. ¿Qué crees que significan?

ciento setenta y siete 177

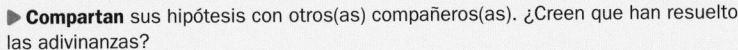

Texto: Nos cuidamos

■ Before reading the text you may prepare students for the fact that the riddles they will be reading contain some words that rhyme. Explain that when the vowels and consonants coincide beginning with the last stressed vowel (e.g., *cabeza* – *pereza*), it is called *rima consonante*. If only the vowels coincide (e.g., *espejo* – *cordero*), it is called *rima asonante*. Ask students to give you more examples of words in Spanish that rhyme.

■ Call on a volunteer to read Diana's e-mail. Then model reading the riddles and ask students to pay attention to the rhyme and rhythm. Give them a few minutes to reread the text and then ask comprehension questions. Some questions you might ask include: *¿Qué nos podemos probar? ¿Qué podemos probar? ¿Cómo van a promocionar el balneario? ¿En qué país creen que está el hospital?*

Activities

1. By now, students should be able to answer these questions without consulting the text, but you may still give them the option.

Answer Key

1. Answers will vary. Sample answers:
   1. Significa *riddle*.
   2. No. La ropa no se come.
   3. Es un *spa*.
   4. Es un médico que practica una rama específica de la Medicina. En los hospitales hay, por lo general, cirujanos, pediatras, médicos de familia, cardiólogos, internistas, etc.
   ▶ Answers will vary.
   ▶ Answers will vary.
2. Answers will vary.

Additional Resources

Fans Online activities
Practice Workbook

HERITAGE LANGUAGE LEARNERS

• Ask students to write a riddle in Spanish and, since this unit has to do with a healthy lifestyle, the answers to their riddles should name a food or a healthy activity. Read these examples to give students ideas: *Blanco por dentro, verde por fuera, si quieres que te diga lo que es, espera.* (la pera) *De bello puedo presumir, soy blanco como la cal, todos me saben abrir, pero nadie me sabe cerrar.* (el huevo) Have students read their riddles to the rest of the class and explain any unknown words. See how fast the other students can solve them.

CRITICAL THINKING

• Ask students to recall the role Hernán Cortés had in the history of the Americas and to name the country that he conquered. (Mexico) Enable a discussion about why Cortés might have established a hospital in Mexico. What medical needs would there have been? What kinds of diseases and injuries would the doctors have treated? Do students think that there would have been cooperation between the Spaniards and the indigenous people? Would they have shared their knowledge of medicine with one another? Ask students to justify their answers.

177

Unit 4

Antes de empezar

Presentation

- In this section, students will learn a variety of useful expressions, some to react to something that sounds intriguing or strange, others for asking about or expressing the ability to do certain things.

- Students will also review words for talking about food and personal hygiene.

Activities	Standards	Resources
Expresiones útiles	1.2, 2.1	
3.	1.2	
4.	1.1	
Recuerda	1.2	
5.	1.3	
6.	1.1, 1.3, 3.1, 5.2	

Teaching Suggestions

Warm-Up / Independent Starter

- Have students write a list of things that they consider themselves to be good at. They can include school subjects, sports, or leisure activities, for example.

Preparation

- Ask students to share their abilities as you use the *expresiones útiles* in personalized contexts. For example, if a student tells you that he or she is good at playing a certain videogame, you may want to react by saying, *¡Qué curioso!* You may also ask direct questions. For example: *¿Se te dan bien las Matemáticas? ¿Eres bueno en Ciencias?* Make sure that students respond in complete sentences, either by mimicking your wording or by using a different expression from the list.

- Have students read the words in the *Recuerda* box and make sure they remember them. Use gestures or context to explain their meaning. You may put students in pairs to take turns at guessing words by asking yes/no questions. To get pairs started, model how to guess the word *sandía* by using the following questions: *¿Es una fruta? ¿Es grande? ¿Es roja por dentro? ¿Es la sandía?*

178

Antes de empezar

EXPRESIONES ÚTILES

¿Que tal se te da el español?

Para expresar extrañeza:
¡Qué raro!
¡Qué extraño!
¡Qué curioso!

Para preguntar por la habilidad para hacer algo:
¿Se te dan bien las adivinanzas?
¿Qué tal se te da la Geografía?
¿Eres bueno(a) en Matemáticas?

Para expresar habilidad para hacer algo:
Se me dan muy bien los idiomas.   Se me dan muy mal los idiomas.
Soy muy bueno(a) en Ciencias.   Soy muy malo(a) en Historia.
Soy un genio para las adivinanzas.   Soy un desastre para las adivinanzas.

3 ¡Qué raro!

▶ **Relaciona** cada oración con la fotografía correspondiente.

1. ¡Qué raro! No consigo terminar el crucigrama...
2. ¡La Física se me da fatal, no entiendo nada!
3. ¡Qué fácil! Esta asignatura se me da muy bien.

▶ **Escribe** un ejemplo con cada expresión.

¡Qué raro!   ¡Qué extraño!   ¡Qué curioso!

4 Preguntas

▶ **Responde** a estas preguntas.

1. ¿Se te da bien cocinar algún plato?
2. ¿En qué deporte eres bueno(a)?
3. ¿Eres bueno(a) en Matemáticas?
4. ¿Qué tal se te da el Español?
5. ¿Se te dan bien las Ciencias?
6. ¿Qué asignatura se te da mejor?

178 ciento setenta y ocho

Differentiated Instruction

DEVELOPING LEARNERS

- Have students work with a partner and think of situations in which they would use one of the following expressions: *¡Qué raro! ¡Qué extraño!* or *¡Qué curioso!* Then have students create short dialogues in which one partner describes the situation, and the other responds with an appropriate expression. Get students started with the following example:
A. *Miguel siempre se levanta a las siete, pero ya son las diez y todavía está durmiendo.*
B. *¡Qué raro!*

EXPANDING LEARNERS

- Ask students to work with a partner and create a dialogue in which they will take turns asking and answering questions about how good they are at certain school subjects and at various tasks and activities. They should choose from among the expressions in the *Expresiones útiles* feature. You may read them the following examples:
A. *¿Qué tal se te da la Historia?*
B. *¡Uf! Se me da muy mal. Pero soy un genio para las computadoras. ¿Y tú?*
A. *A mí también se me dan muy bien las computadoras.*

RECUERDA

Alimentos

el aceite	las lentejas
el ajo	la mayonesa
el atún	el melón
los camarones	la mostaza
la cebolla	la pera
las espinacas	la piña
los guisantes	la sandía
la lechuga	el vinagre

Sabores

agrio(a)	picante
amargo(a)	salado(a)
dulce	soso(a)

Preparación

a la plancha	hervido(a)
asado(a)	empanado(a)
cocido(a)	frito(a)

Acciones

asar	hervir
batir	mezclar
cocer	pelar
echar	picar
freír	probar

Higiene personal

el cepillo	la pasta de dientes
el champú	el secador
el gel	las tijeras
el jabón	la toalla

Acciones

afeitarse	cortarse las uñas
bañarse	lavarse las manos
ducharse	peinarse
cepillarse los dientes	ponerse desodorante

5 **¿Cuánto sabes?**

▶ **Escribe.** Lee las palabras del cuadro Recuerda. ¿Conoces más vocabulario sobre esos temas? Escríbelo.

Modelo   *Alimentos: flan, torta…*

6 **Categorías**

▶ **Escribe** alimentos para cada una de estas categorías. Después, compara tu lista con la de tu compañero(a) y añade más palabras.

 lácteos

 verduras

 legumbres

 fruta

 carne y pescado

ciento setenta y nueve 179

Activities

3. Before starting this activity, ask students to look at the pictures and have them guess if these people are good or bad at what they are doing. To expand this activity, you may ask students to mime the things that they are good or bad at and have the other students guess.

4. After students have written their answers, you may turn this activity into a speaking assignment. Students can share their answers in pairs or small groups, and then present the information about their partner(s) to the class.

5. Ask students to organize the additional words they know by heading, as in the *Recuerda* box. Then ask them to find a new way to organize the words; for example, by letter of the alphabet or by making other correlations (e.g., *el huevo: freír, cocer, hervir, batir*).

6. As an alternative to this activity, you may ask students to write down what they prefer to eat for breakfast, lunch, and dinner, or you may ask them to create an ideal menu.

Answer Key

3. 1. B   2. C   3. A
   ▶ Answers will vary.

4. Answers will vary.

5. Answers will vary.

6. Answers will vary. Sample answers:
   Lácteos: la leche, el queso, el yogur.
   Verduras: las espinacas, la lechuga, el brócoli.
   Legumbres: los guisantes, las lentejas, los frijoles.
   Fruta: la naranja, la piña, la manzana.
   Carne y pescado: la carne de res, el salmón.

Additional Resources

Fans Online activities
Practice Workbook

HERITAGE LANGUAGE LEARNERS

• Ask students to make a list of other words they know for some of the foods shown on the page, as well as other foods they know. Have them explain in which countries these words are commonly used. For example, some Spanish speakers say *gambas*, not *camarones*; others say *ananás* for *piña*, and *arvejas* or *chícharos* for *guisantes*. There are also several variants for the many types of *plátanos,* including *bananas* and *cambures*. Ask students to collaborate and, together, make a master list and share these words with the rest of the class.

CRITICAL THINKING

• Ask students to create a multi-column chart of the food groups (these can be found online) and label each column accordingly. Under each food group ask students to list the foods they have eaten in the past two days. Then have them analyze their eating habits and state whether or not they have been eating a balanced diet. If they have not, ask them to explain what they need to eat in order to have a more nutritious diet. If they are not interested in improving their eating habits, ask them to explain why.

179

DESAFÍO 1

Hablar sobre nutrición

Presentation

- In *Desafío 1*, Eva and Ethan must find out what *ropa vieja* is, make it, and share it with the other *Fans del español*. Students will preview language used to talk about food.

Activities	Standards	Resources
Texto	1.2, 2.2, 3.2	Vis. Pres.
7.	1.2	
8.	1.1, 1.2, 2.2	
9.	1.1, 1.2, 2.2, 3.2	Audio
10. Cultura	1.2, 2.1, 2.2, 3.2, 4.2	Video

Teaching Suggestions

Warm-Up / Independent Starter

- Have students brainstorm dishes from the Spanish-speaking world that they have heard of or have tried before. Ask them to identify the country or countries of origin of the dish and if they know any of the ingredients.

Preparation

- Ask volunteers to share their responses to the Independent Starter. If a student was unable to identify the origin of the food or dish, ask if anyone else knows the information. As students discuss the ingredients, take the opportunity to review some food vocabulary.

Texto: La ropa vieja

- Have students read the dialogue silently. Once they are finished, ask for three volunteers to play the roles of the characters and read the dialogue aloud.
- Ask students to point out parts of the dialogue that contain humor. Do students understand the wordplay?

Activities

7. Remind students to watch for noun/adjective agreement as they complete this activity.

9. Ask students to identify the vocabulary for each picture before deciding if the item is an ingredient in *ropa vieja*.

La ropa vieja

 Eva and Ethan must make *ropa*, and share it with the other *Fans del español*, but first they must figure out exactly what it is!

EVA: Me pregunto qué quiere decir Diana: dice que se puede probar y que es vieja. Humm... La ropa se puede probar... Pero también se puede probar la comida.

ETHAN: Yo creo que el desafío tiene que ver con la comida. La ropa no se come...

EVA: ¿No te quieres comer tu ropa vieja con un poquito de sal y de pimienta, Ethan? ¡Es muy nutritiva!

ETHAN: Muy graciosa, Eva... Ropa vieja... Pues a mí me suena que *ropa vieja* es el nombre de un plato. Vamos al supermercado, a ver si encontramos alguna pista. Allí tienen productos latinos.

* * *

EVA: Perdone, señor. ¿Tienen ustedes algún alimento que se llame *ropa vieja*?

HOMBRE: Pues... sí, hay un plato que se llama ropa vieja. Aquí no lo tenemos, pero puedo decirles los ingredientes necesarios para prepararlo.

ETHAN: Entonces es un plato...

HOMBRE: Y muy sabroso. El ingrediente principal es la carne de res.

ETHAN: ¡Lo sabía! ¡Estaba seguro!

7 **Detective de palabras**

▶ **Completa** estas oraciones. Pon las palabras en la forma correcta.

| carne |
| ingrediente |
| nutritivo(a) |
| sabroso(a) |
| plato |

1. La pasta es muy _____ y aporta mucha energía.
2. Te voy a preparar mi _____ favorito: una lasaña.
3. En una receta hay que dar todos los _____ y las cantidades exactas.
4. Me encanta esta sopa, es muy _____.
5. ¿Prefieres la empanada de _____ o de atún?

Differentiated Instruction

DEVELOPING LEARNERS

- Ask students to rewrite the following false statements to make them true:
  1. *Ethan piensa que el desafío tiene que ver con la ropa.* (con la comida)
  2. *Eva bromea con Ethan y le dice que su ropa es muy vieja.* (nutritiva)
  3. *Ethan sugiere ir a la biblioteca a buscar pistas.* (al supermercado)
  4. *Los chicos le piden información a una señora.* (a un señor)
  5. *El ingrediente principal de la ropa vieja es la carne de cerdo.* (la carne de res)

EXPANDING LEARNERS

- Ask students to review the dialogue and then to write their version of it, but as a narrative written from Eva's or Ethan's point of view. They may use the same sequence of events, or they may choose to create an entirely different scenario. Encourage creativity and humor in their writing. When they finish, call on volunteers to read their compositions aloud.

8 ¿Comprendes?

▶ **Responde** a estas preguntas.

1. ¿Qué tienen que hacer Eva y Ethan?
2. ¿Por qué están confundidos?
3. ¿Para qué van al supermercado?
4. ¿Qué les explica el dependiente sobre la ropa vieja?

9 Una conversación con el dependiente

 ▶ **Escucha** la conversación y decide si estas oraciones son ciertas o falsas. Después, corrige las falsas.

1. La ropa vieja es un plato moderno, típico de la gastronomía caribeña actual.
2. Hay varias recetas para preparar la ropa vieja.
3. La ropa vieja se prepara con pescado y marisco.
4. Algunas personas le añaden zanahorias o papas.
5. En el Caribe este plato se sirve con espinacas y plátano.

▶ **Decide.** ¿Qué ingrediente no sirve para preparar un plato de ropa vieja tradicional?

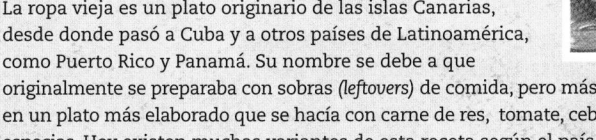

 CULTURA

La ropa vieja

La ropa vieja es un plato originario de las islas Canarias, desde donde pasó a Cuba y a otros países de Latinoamérica, como Puerto Rico y Panamá. Su nombre se debe a que originalmente se preparaba con sobras (leftovers) de comida, pero más tarde se convirtió en un plato más elaborado que se hacía con carne de res, tomate, cebolla, ajo y varias especias. Hoy existen muchas variantes de esta receta según el país o región, con distintos ingredientes como garbanzos o papas.

10 **Piensa.** ¿Hay un plato típico de tu cultura con un nombre curioso? ¿Y algún plato que se prepare con sobras?

DESAFÍO 1
Hablar sobre nutrición

 **AUDIO SCRIPT**
See page 173I.

 CULTURA

La ropa vieja

Ropa vieja is a dish that originated in the Canary Islands. Since the islands were a typical stop for explorers traveling to and from the Caribbean, this dish has become a traditional part of the Caribbean diet. While it was once cooked using leftovers, it is now typically prepared with fresh ingredients. Beef stewed in tomato sauce is the base of the dish, with vegetables and chickpeas added depending on the region.

Answer Key

7. 1. nutritiva   4. sabrosa
2. plato   5. carne
3. ingredientes

8. 1. Tienen que preparar un plato llamado *ropa vieja* y compartirlo con los *Fans del español*.
2. Porque piensan que *ropa vieja* es ropa usada.
3. Van para encontrar alguna pista. Buscan ayuda.
4. Les explica que la ropa vieja es un plato, y que el ingrediente principal es la carne de res.

9. 1. F. Es un plato tradicional.
2. C.
3. F. Con carne de res, de cerdo o pollo.
4. C.
5. F. Se sirve con arroz y plátano frito.
▶ 3

10. Answers will vary.

Additional Resources

Fans Online activities

HERITAGE LANGUAGE LEARNERS

• Ask students to contribute other dishes from Spanish-speaking countries whose names are not immediately thought of as foods. For example, in Spain there is a stew that is called *olla podrida* (literally, rotten pot), and sweets called *huesos de santo* (saint's bones) and *tocino de cielo* (bacon from heaven). Cubans have a beans and rice dish called *moros y cristianos* (Moors and Christians). Students might have to consult with family members who can describe these dishes. Ask students to share this information in a written or oral report to the class.

TOTAL PHYSICAL RESPONSE (TPR)

• Tell students that they are going to play a game. Ask them to stand up and have the first student say a letter. The next player must name a food, cooking method, or a word related to food that starts with that letter. Then, he or she will say a letter and the following player must mention a food-related word that starts with that letter. If students cannot say an appropriate word, they are out and must sit down. Winners are the last students standing when you call time.

DESAFÍO 1

Vocabulario – Alimentación

Presentation

- In this section, students will learn vocabulary related to diet and nutrition.

Activities	Standards	Resources
Vocabulario	1.2, 3.1	
11.	1.2	Audio
12.	1.2, 1.3	
13.	1.3, 5.2	
14. Conexiones	1.2, 2.2, 3.1	

Teaching Suggestions

Warm-Up / Independent Starter

- Ask students to create a two-column chart and label the columns with these headings: *Es saludable*, *No es saludable*. Then have them list five healthy and five unhealthy foods in the appropriate columns.

Preparation

- Read the list of eight rules aloud. For words that are not defined in the text, such as *fritos*, use actions or draw pictures on the board to help students with the meaning. After you have introduced the vocabulary, have students use the charts they created in the Independent Starter to classify all of the foods and drinks mentioned in this vocabulary presentation (including those in the speech bubbles). Once they have finished, have students compare their charts with those of a classmate.

Activities

11. After completing this activity, ask students to listen again to the audio recording and correct the bad advice. To extend this activity, ask students to write three additional statements to read aloud to a partner. The partner has to decide whether the advice is good or bad.

12. Before completing this activity, review the *Más vocabulario* feature. As students complete this activity, ask them to identify the key words that helped them to determine the answer (e.g., *demasiadas especias – picante*).

> **Vocabulario**

Alimentación

OCHO REGLAS PARA MANTENER UNA ALIMENTACIÓN SALUDABLE Y NUTRITIVA

1. Reduzca el consumo de carne roja y aumente el de pescado y carne blanca, que tienen menos grasa.

2. Coma legumbres: tienen muchas proteínas.

3. Coma verduras y hortalizas a diario. Las espinacas, por ejemplo, aportan mucho hierro.

4. Coma varias piezas de fruta cada día. Son ricas en fibra y tienen muchas vitaminas.

5. Evite la comida basura y los alimentos fritos porque son muy grasosos.

6. Cocine con aceite de oliva en vez de usar mantequilla.

7. Sustituya los jugos con azúcar por agua mineral (con gas o sin gas) o infusiones.

8. No coma dulces. Entre horas, coma fruta o frutos secos.

Estoy a dieta. Mi médico me recomendó reducir las calorías de mis comidas y usar poca sal.

Claro, porque la sal no es saludable. Es mejor cocinar con especias.

Yo no como carne, soy vegetariana. Cocino platos ligeros y sin grasa porque son más sanos y se digieren mejor.

11 **¿Consejos para una alimentación sana?**

▶ **Escucha** varios consejos y completa una tabla como esta.

	Buenos consejos	Malos consejos
1		
2		
3		
4		
5		
6		

Más vocabulario

Preparación de los alimentos

crudo(a)	*raw*
poco hecho(a)	*underdone*
al punto	*just right*
muy hecho(a)	*well done*
jugoso(a)	*juicy*
sabroso(a)	*tasty*

Differentiated Instruction

DEVELOPING LEARNERS

- Establish a time limit in which students must complete the following activity. Have them write the first four words from the *Más vocabulario* feature on a sheet of paper. Next to each one, ask them to write as many foods as they can that are usually eaten as described by the word. For example: *crudo – las zanahorias, el melón; poco hecho – la carne de res, el atún; al punto – el pavo, los camarones; muy hecho – los huevos, la hamburguesa.* Ask them to exchange papers with a classmate and check each other's work.

EXPANDING LEARNERS

- Ask students to give examples of the highlighted words on the page, or to provide synonyms or definitions for each one. Students many also state the purpose of each one. For example:
  - *nutritiva: sana, de buena alimentación*
  - *reduzca: disminuya*
  - *carne roja: carne de res*
  - *aumente: incremente*
  - *carne blanca: pollo*
  - *grasoso: con mucha grasa*
  - *sustituya: reemplace*

12 **¿Cómo está la comida?**

▶ **Escribe** los comentarios de los clientes de este restaurante usando las palabras del cuadro.

> poco hecho(a)   jugoso(a)   soso(a)   picante   grasoso(a)

Modelo   «Este filete está perfecto: no está crudo ni tampoco muy hecho.»
   → *Este filete está al punto.*

1. «Este chile con carne tiene demasiadas especias.»
2. «Mi salmón a la plancha tiene muy poca sal.»
3. «Esta carne no me gusta, está poco cocinada.»
4. «Las papas tienen demasiada grasa.»
5. «El pollo en salsa está muy bien cocinado, me encanta.»

13 **Mis recomendaciones**

▶ **Escribe** cinco recomendaciones sobre alimentación a partir de estas fotografías. Explica por qué se deben o no se deben comer estos alimentos.

Modelo

Se deben comer frutos secos porque tienen muchas proteínas.
Pero no se deben comer demasiados porque tienen muchas calorías.

1 2 3 4 5

CONEXIONES: CIENCIAS

La quinua

La quinua es un cereal presente en la dieta de los países andinos desde hace mucho tiempo. Este producto era la base de la alimentación de los incas. Actualmente se considera un *superalimento* y la NASA recomienda su consumo en misiones especiales por su alto contenido en aminoácidos, proteínas, hidratos de carbono y vitaminas.

14 **Piensa y explica.** ¿Por qué se dice que la quinua es un *superalimento*? Busca información sobre sus propiedades y compáralas con las de otros cereales.

HERITAGE LANGUAGE LEARNERS

- Ask students to research other foods that are indigenous to the Americas. You may want to suggest that they start with one or more from this list: avocados, chocolate, corn, chili peppers, papayas, peanuts, pineapples, potatoes, tomatoes, and vanilla. Ask students to address some of the food's history, as well as some information on its nutritional value. Did anyone discover a food that was surprising?

MULTIPLE INTELLIGENCES:
Interpersonal Intelligence

- Have students work with a partner to create a dialogue in which one will play the part of a diner and the other, a server in a restaurant. Using activity 12 as a guide, the diners must express their displeasure with every food served. The servers will use their imagination and try to placate the diners by offering them another dish, treating them to an extra course, or perhaps offering them a big discount. Allow students to work out their dialogues and ask some pairs to present their skits in front of the class.

Vocabulario – Alimentación

 AUDIO SCRIPT
See page 173I.

CONEXIONES: CIENCIAS

La quinua

Quinoa is one of the most powerful foods of the Andean region. It was domesticated about 4,000 years ago on Bolivia's arid high mountain plateaus, and it was considered to be more valuable than gold, as the Incas relied on quinoa to feed their soldiers. They considered it a sacred food, and held ceremonies to ensure a good harvest.

Answer Key

11. Buenos consejos: 1, 3, 6.
Malos consejos: 2, 4, 5.

12. 1. Este chile con carne está picante.
2. Mi salmón está soso.
3. Esta carne está poco hecha.
4. Las papas están grasosas.
5. El pollo en salsa está jugoso.

13. Answers will vary. Sample answers:
1. Se debe comer pescado porque tiene muchas proteínas, pero no se debe freír.
2. No se deben comer demasiadas hamburguesas porque tienen muchas calorías. Tampoco se deben comer demasiadas papas fritas porque son muy grasosas.
3. Se deben comer legumbres porque tienen muchas proteínas, hierro y fibra.
4. Se deben comer verduras porque tienen muchas vitaminas y pocas calorías, y son muy saludables.
5. No se deben comer pasteles porque tienen mucho azúcar y muchas calorías.

14. Answers will vary.

Additional Resources

Fans Online activities
Practice Workbook

DESAFÍO 1

Gramática – Los mandatos

Presentation

▪ In this section, students will learn the *nosotros* commands. They will then review both the regular and irregular negative command forms to tell someone what not to do.

Activities	Standards	Resources
Gramática	1.2, 3.1	
15.	4.1	
16.	1.2, 1.3	Audio
17.	1.2, 1.3, 3.1	
18.	1.1, 5.1	

Teaching Suggestions

Warm-Up / Independent Starter

▪ Have students read the grammar presentation silently. Then write the following sentences on the board and ask students to complete them with the correct form of the verb in parentheses:

1. *Marta, no (comer) dulces todos los días. (comas)*
2. *Señora Castillo, (comprar) hortalizas todas las semanas. (compre)*
3. *Tenemos hambre, pero ¡no (comer) comida basura! (comamos)*
4. *Tomás y Roberto, (hacer) ejercicio todos los días. (hagan)*
5. *Señor Martínez, no (ir) a restaurantes de comida rápida todos los días. (vaya)*

Preparation

▪ When students finish the Independent Starter, review their work and then call on volunteers to explain how they arrived at each conjugation. Remind students that the conjugation of formal (*usted, ustedes*) and negative commands is the same as the present subjunctive conjugation (e.g. *tú comas → no comas*).

Activities

16. Have students listen to the audio recording twice. The first time, ask students to write the doctor's advice (e.g., *no bebas, comamos, no fría*). The second time, have students check their work and identify to whom the doctor is speaking.

Gramática

Los mandatos

Los mandatos afirmativos. La forma *nosotros(as)*

● Use the nosotros(as) command to say what we have to do or to suggest something that we will participate in.

Hagamos un sancocho.

● The command for nosotros(as) uses the same forms as the present subjunctive.

Cocinar	Comer	Consumir
cocinemos (nosotros(as))	comamos (nosotros(as))	consumamos nosotros(as))

● The only irregular nosotros(as) affirmative command is the verb ir.

¡Vamos al supermercado!

● When attaching a reflexive pronoun to the affirmative nosotros(as) commands, drop the final -s.

¡Lavémonos las manos antes de comer!

Los mandatos negativos

● Use negative commands when telling someone what not to do. To give negative commands, we use the same forms as the present subjunctive.

MANDATOS NEGATIVOS REGULARES

Cocinar	Comer	Consumir	
no cocines	no comas	no consumas	tú
no cocine	no coma	no consuma	usted
no cocinemos	no comamos	no consumamos	nosotros(as)
no cocinéis	no comáis	no consumáis	vosotros(as)
no cocinen	no coman	no consuman	ustedes

MANDATOS NEGATIVOS IRREGULARES

Dar	Estar	Ser	Ir	
no des	no estés	no seas	no vayas	tú
no dé	no esté	no sea	no vaya	usted
no demos	no estemos	no seamos	no vayamos	nosotros(as)
no deis	no estéis	no seáis	no vayáis	vosotros(as)
no den	no estén	no sean	no vayan	ustedes

15 **Piensa.** ¿Cómo se expresan los mandatos para *nosotros(as)* en inglés?

Differentiated Instruction

DEVELOPING LEARNERS

● Write a verb in the infinitive (be sure to include reflexive verbs) on each of several index cards and place them in a bag. Then, on strips of paper, write the personal pronouns *tú, usted, nosotros(as),* and *ustedes.* Place the strips of paper in another bag. Ask students to pick from both bags, say the infinitive aloud (e.g., *despertarse*) and the personal pronoun (e.g., *tú*). Then have them give the negative command: *¡No te despiertes!* Be sure students have multiple chances at giving negative commands.

EXPANDING LEARNERS

● Ask students to imagine that they and a friend have been invited to dine with the King and Queen of Spain. They know that they must exhibit their best table manners, but they are worried that their friend might not be so polite. Ask students to write four *nosotros* commands that both of them will need to follow, and at least five negative *tú* commands for their occasionally impolite dinner partner. For example: *Vistámonos con traje y corbata. ¡No te limpies la boca con la corbata!*

16 **¿A quién se lo dice?**

 ▶ **Escucha** estos consejos. ¿A quién se dirige el doctor Suárez?

A ti	A usted	A nosotros(as)	A ustedes

1. _____ 3. _____ 5. _____

2. _____ 4. _____ 6. _____

17 **Un consultorio de salud**

▶ **Lee** la respuesta a una lectora en una revista de salud y escribe una lista con las recomendaciones que le dan para llevar una vida sana.

> **Consejos para una vida sana**
>
> Estimada Jane:
>
> En respuesta a su consulta, lo primero es cambiar sus hábitos alimenticios. No coma tantas grasas ni dulces, no compre alimentos precocinados y no consuma «comida basura». Aumente el consumo de frutas y verduras, prepare platos ligeros y equilibrados, y beba al menos dos litros de agua al día.
>
> Practique, además, algún deporte y busque actividades que requieran salir de casa y hacer algo de ejercicio.
>
> No es bueno pasar demasiado tiempo sentada frente al televisor, por ejemplo. Y no se desanime. No olvide que nunca es demasiado tarde para empezar a llevar una vida más sana.
>
>
>
> El equipo de Vida Sana

▶ **Escribe** cinco recomendaciones más para Jane. Usa la forma *usted* del imperativo.

Modelo *No coma dulces entre horas.*

18 **Nuestros deseos**

▶ **Habla** con tu compañero(a). ¿Qué quieren hacer este fin de semana? Usen el imperativo.

- jugar a los videojuegos
- ir de compras
- asistir a un concierto
- levantar pesas
- cenar en una hamburguesería
- estudiar para el examen de Matemáticas
- ir a montar en bici al parque

Quiero jugar a los videojuegos.

¡No, mejor vayamos a correr por el parque!

ciento ochenta y cinco 185

---

17. To expand this activity, have students draw what Jane was doing before and a picture of what she should be doing. In the "before" picture, have students write negative commands about what she should not do. In the "after" picture, have students write affirmative commands about what she should do.

18. Remind students that the verbs listed are only suggestions and that they may add their own original ideas. Have volunteers present examples of their dialogue to the class.

 AUDIO SCRIPT
See page 173I.

Answer Key

15. Se expresan con *Let's* (e.g., *Let's eat!*).

16. 1. A ti 4. A ustedes
2. A nosotros(as) 5. A usted
3. A usted 6. A nosotros(as)

17. Answers will vary. Sample answers:
Cambie sus hábitos alimenticios.
No coma tantas grasas ni dulces.
No compre alimentos precocinados.
No consuma «comida basura».
Aumente el consumo de frutas y verduras.
Prepare platos ligeros y equilibrados.
Beba al menos dos litros de agua al día.
Practique algún deporte.
Busque actividades que requieran salir de casa y hacer algo de ejercicio.
No pase demasiado tiempo sentada frente al televisor.
No se desanime.
No olvide que nunca es demasiado tarde para empezar a llevar una vida más sana.
▶ Answers will vary.

18. Answers will vary.

Additional Resources

Fans Online activities
Practice Workbook

HERITAGE LANGUAGE LEARNERS

- Ask students to talk about eating habits by having them first compare a "typical" diet in their family's country of origin to a "typical" diet in this country. How are they similar? How do they differ? Which diet do they prefer? Why? Then have them address meal times: When do they usually have dinner here, and when would they have dinner in their family's country of origin? Which schedule do they think is better, and why? What other similarities and differences are there in mealtime customs between the two countries?

MULTIPLE INTELLIGENCES:
Visual-Spatial Intelligence

- Ask students to make a poster to promote good eating habits and to offer other tips for healthful living among their classmates. Students should be guided by the rules for healthy eating listed on page 182 and use common sense when making suggestions for exercise, reducing stress, getting proper rest, and avoiding a sedentary lifestyle. The suggestions should make use of both affirmative and negative informal commands, and students should illustrate their posters. When they finish, display their work in the classroom and discuss their suggestions.

Unit 4
DESAFÍO 1

Gramática – Los verbos de cambio

Presentation

▪ In this section, students will learn and practice several verbs that express change.

Activities	Standards	Resources
Gramática	1.2, 3.1	
19.	4.1	
20.	2.1	Audio
21.	1.2, 2.2	
22.	1.1, 1.2, 1.3, 5.2	

Teaching Suggestions

Warm-Up / Independent Starter

▪ Have students read the grammar presentation silently. Encourage them to take notes on any material that they have trouble understanding. They should make a list of some adjectives and nouns that come to mind as possible aspects of change for each situation (e.g., *ponerse enfermo, quedarse mudo, volverse antipático, hacerse famosa, convertirse en hielo*).

Preparation

▪ Encourage students to ask questions about any explanations they did not understand in the grammar presentation and clarify this information for them. Call on volunteers to share their Independent Starters and discuss and correct students' answers as a class. Point out the part of speech that is used after the verb of change. Clarify that these verbs are frequently used in the preterite tense because, when change is expressed, it has typically already occurred.

▪ Have students complete the following sentences:
1. *La rana ... príncipe.* (b)
   a. *se puso*   b. *se convirtió en*
2. *Mi madre estudió y ... doctora.* (a)
   a. *se hizo*   b. *se volvió*
3. *Cuando perdí el partido, ... triste.* (a)
   a. *me puse*   b. *me convertí en*
4. *Jorge ... sorprendido con la noticia.* (b)
   a. *se hizo*   b. *se quedó*
5. *Pablo no sabía qué decir, así que ... callado.* (b)
   a. *se volvió*   b. *se quedó*

Gramática

Los verbos de cambio

▪ There are several verbs that express a change of state, which can usually be translated as *to become*.

ponerse + adjective	This expresses a physical or emotional change that is generally involuntary, sudden, and temporary. Roberto **se puso** contento cuando perdió 3 kilos. Mi hermano **se pone** rojo cuando tiene que hablar en clase.
quedarse + adjective	This expresses a physical or emotional change that is often lasting and a consequence of another occurrence. Mi tío **se quedó** delgado por estar a dieta un año. María **se quedó** dormida porque estaba cansadísima.
volverse + adjective volverse + noun	This expresses a change that usually happens suddenly. This is applied frequently to changes in a person's behavior or personality. Los jóvenes **se volvieron** locos durante el concierto. El restaurante **se volvió** un buen negocio.
hacerse + adjective	This expresses a gradual change that is the result of the passage of time. This can often be used in the same situations as *volverse + adjective*. Mi prima **se hizo** mayor. Ana **se hizo** muy responsable.
hacerse + noun	This expresses a voluntary change in thinking, social status, or profession. Mi prima **se hizo** budista. Tomás va a la universidad para **hacerse** médico.
convertirse en + noun	This expresses a permanent and dramatic change. Mi padre **se convirtió en** vegetariano. La tienda de ropa **se convirtió en** un supermercado.

19 **Piensa.** ¿De qué forma se expresan los cambios temporales y permanentes en inglés? ¿Cómo se expresa que es un cambio voluntario o inesperado?

20 **Cambios**

▸ **Escucha** y ordena estas oraciones.
a. Se hizo muy aficionada al arte.
b. Se volvió loca con el regalo de su padre.
c. Sus abuelos se convirtieron en ciudadanos estadounidenses.
d. Piensa ir a la universidad para hacerse médica.
e. Se puso nervioso durante la prueba.

Differentiated Instruction

DEVELOPING LEARNERS

• Give students more practice with the various ways to express change in Spanish by having them complete these sentences:
1. *Andrés se hizo / quedó abogado.* (hizo)
2. *Mi vecino se convirtió en / quedó solo después del divorcio.* (quedó)
3. *Lola se hizo / puso triste cuando supo la verdad.* (puso)
4. *¡Ay! Me convierto en / vuelvo loca con esa música.* (vuelvo)
5. *Con el calor, el agua se quedó / convirtió en vapor.* (convirtió en)

EXPANDING LEARNERS

• Ask students to imagine that they are Diana and have them write a response to Ethan's e-mail. Students should answer Ethan's first question, then go on to express pleasure that the pair has discovered what *ropa vieja* is, and how they went about making this discovery. Students should also congratulate the pair for learning more about food from the Spanish-speaking world. Encourage students to use some of the verbs that express change and to add other comments that reflect Diana's satisfaction with the results.

21 **Expertos en cocina caribeña**

▶ **Lee** el mensaje que le manda Ethan a Diana y complétalo. Pon los verbos en la forma correcta.

quedarse   volverse   hacerse   convertirse   ponerse

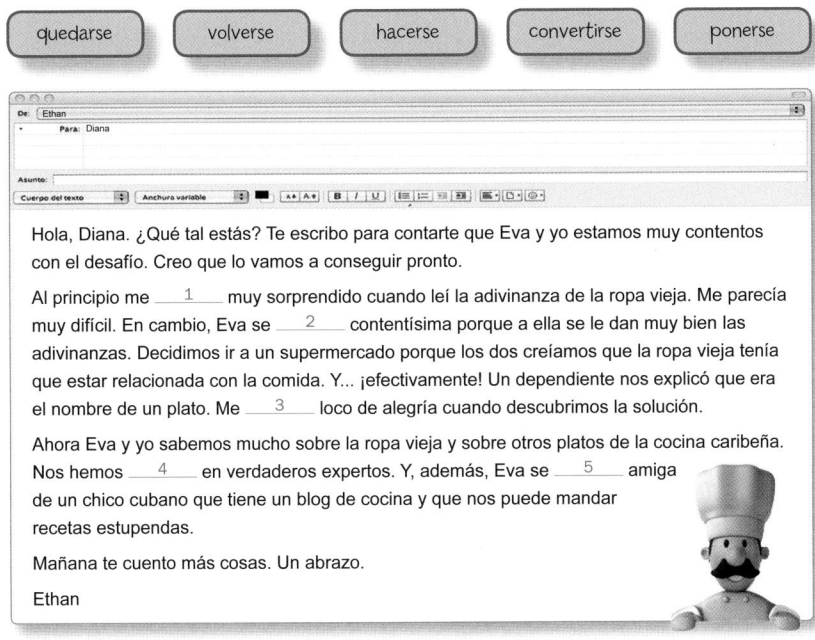

Hola, Diana. ¿Qué tal estás? Te escribo para contarte que Eva y yo estamos muy contentos con el desafío. Creo que lo vamos a conseguir pronto.

Al principio me ___1___ muy sorprendido cuando leí la adivinanza de la ropa vieja. Me parecía muy difícil. En cambio, Eva se ___2___ contentísima porque a ella se le dan muy bien las adivinanzas. Decidimos ir a un supermercado porque los dos creíamos que la ropa vieja tenía que estar relacionada con la comida. Y... ¡efectivamente! Un dependiente nos explicó que era el nombre de un plato. Me ___3___ loco de alegría cuando descubrimos la solución.

Ahora Eva y yo sabemos mucho sobre la ropa vieja y sobre otros platos de la cocina caribeña. Nos hemos ___4___ en verdaderos expertos. Y, además, Eva se ___5___ amiga de un chico cubano que tiene un blog de cocina y que nos puede mandar recetas estupendas.

Mañana te cuento más cosas. Un abrazo.

Ethan

22 **Nuestros cambios**

▶ **Responde** con tu compañero(a) a estas preguntas. Después, presenten una selección de sus mejores ideas a la clase.

1. ¿Qué profesión quieren tener en el futuro?
2. ¿Qué hay que hacer para convertirse en un buen profesional?
3. ¿Qué hay que hacer para no ponerse nervioso(a) en los exámenes?
4. ¿Qué hay que hacer para convertirse en un(a) deportista de élite?
5. ¿Qué dieta hay que seguir para hacerse más fuerte?

David y yo queremos hacernos abogados en el futuro. Para eso, los dos vamos a estudiar en una buena universidad y...

HERITAGE LANGUAGE LEARNERS

• Ask students to create their own "blog" on food from the Caribbean. Explain that they will not write a real blog, but rather a series of short articles about topics related to the food from this part of the world. Students may include something on the history and evolution of the food in general or about a specific dish, or they may review a restaurant where this kind of food is served. Ask students to read or post their "blogs" for the rest of the class.

SPECIAL-NEEDS LEARNERS

• You may want to modify activity 20 for students with hearing impairments. Instead of having them listen to the audio, allow them to read the script and then have them put the events in the correct sequence. You may wish to have the whole class read the script as well, to convert a listening activity into a reading activity.

Gramática – Los verbos de cambio

Activities

20. To expand this activity, have students write about their own changes using the audio as an example. Then ask students to exchange sentences with a partner. The partner should write the change that occurred, applying the verbs of change.

21. After students complete this activity, ask them these comprehension questions: *¿Cuándo se quedó sorprendido Ethan? (Cuando leyó la adivinanza de la ropa vieja.) ¿Por qué se puso contenta Eva? (Porque a ella se le dan bien las adivinanzas.) ¿Cuándo se volvió loco Ethan? (Cuando descubrieron la solución.)*

22. After partners share a response, ask the class to write them two commands on how to achieve the change they desire. For example (to correspond with the model): *Estudien mucho y saquen buenas notas.*

 AUDIO SCRIPT
See page 173l.

Answer Key

19. Estos son algunos de los verbos que se usan en inglés para expresar cambio: *to become, to convert, to transform.* Cuando se quiere comunicar un cambio voluntario, se usa *to become.* Cuando es un cambio involuntario se puede usar *was left* o *went.* Por ejemplo: *I was left dumbfounded.* (Me quedé estupefacto.) *I went mad.* (Me volví loco.)

20. c, a, e, b, d

21. 1. quedé   4. convertido
     2. puso   5. hizo
     3. volví

22. Answers will vary.

Additional Resources

Fans Online activities
Practice Workbook

187

Unit 4

LECTURA: TEXTO DIALOGADO

Presentation

- In this section, students will read a dialogue, identify food vocabulary and place names contained within, and answer comprehension questions based on the reading.

Activities	Standards	Resources
Lectura: texto dialogado	1.2, 2.2, 3.1	Vis. Pres.
23.	1.1, 1.2	
24.	1.3, 2.2, 3.2	
25.	1.1, 1.3, 2.2, 3.2, 5.1	

Teaching Suggestions

Warm-Up / Independent Starter

- Have students write five affirmative commands and five negative commands for Eva and Ethan as they find and prepare their recipes. You may want to get students started with the following examples: *Hablen con un cocinero. No se desanimen si no encuentran información inmediatamente.*

Preparation

- Have students read the *Antes de leer* strategies silently. Then ask them to think about possible answers to the questions.

- Call on a volunteer to answer the first question in the *Antes de leer* section. Have students add words to their lists (e.g., *aceite, tomates, cebolla, ajo, pimiento, papas, pollo, carne de res, garbanzos, arroz, plátanos fritos*). Then, discuss the answers to questions 2 and 3 as a class.

- Ask students to share the commands from their Independent Starter. Have pairs compare their notes. Did anyone come up with the same commands? As a class, chosse the top five most useful recommendations.

- Read the dialogue aloud to students, modeling correct pronunciation and intonation. Then call on several pairs of students to alternate reading the dialogue aloud. Offer suggestions to improve their oral reading.

188

Antes de leer: estrategias

1. Mira las fotos y descríbelas. ¿Qué ingredientes ves en la primera foto? ¿Qué acompañamientos tiene la carne en la segunda foto?

2. Busca en el texto las palabras que se refieren a alimentos. ¿Son los que nombraste al describir las fotos? ¿Hay otros?

3. Busca palabras que se refieren a lugares. ¿Cuáles son? ¿Por qué piensas que se nombran estos lugares en el texto?

La mejor receta

EVA: Tengo una receta fantástica de ropa vieja.

ETHAN: ¿Es la original, la de las islas Canarias?

EVA: No estoy segura... Me la mandó mi amigo cubano, el que tiene un blog de cocina.

ETHAN: Bueno, la ropa vieja es un plato que se prepara en España y en muchos países de América: Cuba, Puerto Rico, Argentina... ¿Qué ingredientes lleva la receta de tu amigo?

EVA: Carne de res o de pollo cocinada en una salsa con tomate, cebollas, pimiento verde, ajo...

ETHAN: ¿Y no lleva plátano?

EVA: No, ¿por qué lo preguntas?

ETHAN: Porque en el Caribe la ropa vieja se sirve con plátano frito y arroz blanco. Y hay gente que también le pone frijoles.

EVA: Es cierto. Esta receta lleva garbanzos y papas. Seguramente es la receta canaria.

ETHAN: Lo importante es que ya tenemos la receta. ¿La preparamos?

EVA: No sé si tenemos tiempo. Aquí dice que hay que cocinar la carne durante tres horas.

ETHAN: ¡Tres horas! Yo creo que para que la carne quede jugosa debemos cocinarla solo una hora.

EVA: ¿Estás seguro?

188 ciento ochenta y ocho

Differentiated Instruction

DEVELOPING LEARNERS

- Verify students' comprehension of the dialogue by asking them to correct the following false statements:

  1. *Una amiga española le mandó la receta a Eva. (un amigo cubano)*
  2. *El ingrediente principal de la ropa vieja es el arroz blanco. (la carne de res)*
  3. *La salsa de la ropa vieja se hace con chiles picantes. (con tomate, cebollas, pimiento verde y ajo)*
  4. *La ropa vieja canaria lleva plátanos y frijoles. (garbanzos y papas)*
  5. *Hay que cocinar la carne una hora. (tres horas)*

EXPANDING LEARNERS

- Have students imagine that they have just learned about the dish called *ropa vieja* and tasted it. They were so impressed with its flavor and its origins that they write a letter to a friend telling him or her all about it, even explaining its unusual name. Ask students to write their letter, describing the food, how it is prepared, where they ate it, and with whom they shared their meal. They should also indicate that their friend needs to try this dish!

23 Comprensión

▶ **Responde** a estas preguntas.

1. ¿Qué es la ropa vieja?
2. ¿De dónde proviene esta receta?
3. ¿Qué ingredientes se necesitan para cocinar la receta de Eva y Ethan?
4. ¿Cómo consiguieron Eva y Ethan la receta?
5. ¿Qué significa *plato* en este texto? ¿Qué otros significados de la palabra *plato* conoces?
6. ¿Qué significa *salsa* en este texto? ¿Qué otros significados de la palabra *salsa* conoces?

24 Un diagrama

▶ **Completa** este diagrama de Venn colocando los ingredientes en el lugar correcto.

Receta de Canarias   Receta de Cuba

carne de res

papas

frijoles

tomates

garbanzos

cebollas

arroz

plátanos

25 Investigación

▶ **Busca** una receta de ropa vieja y escríbela.

▶ **Compara** tu receta con la de tu compañero(a). ¿Hay muchas diferencias entre las dos recetas? Coméntenlo.

■ Ask students to note the word *jugosa*. What does it mean? What is the opposite? Have them read the context, and then ask: *¿Piensan que la carne va a quedar jugosa cocinándola tres horas?*

Activities

23. To extend this activity, ask additional comprehension questions. For example: *¿En qué países se prepara la ropa vieja? ¿Cuánto tiempo piensa Ethan que debe cocinarse la carne? ¿Qué opina Eva?*

24. Write the word *acompañamiento* on the board, and explain that it is the equivalent to a side dish. To prepare students for this activity, ask the following questions: *¿Con qué acompañamientos se sirve la ropa vieja en Canarias? ¿Y en el Caribe?*

25. Have students post their recipes on the wall. Make sure they make a note of the country that the recipe comes from, as well as the book or website in which they found it. Students may vote for the best and most elaborate recipe.

Answer Key

23. 1. Es un plato que se prepara en España y en varios países de Latinoamérica.
2. Es la receta de las islas Canarias.
3. Necesitan carne de res o de pollo, salsa de tomate, cebollas, pimiento verde, ajo, garbanzos y papas.
4. Se las mandó un amigo cubano.
5. Significa "dish", es decir una comida. La palabra *plato* también se refiere al recipiente donde se sirve la comida.
6. *Salsa* significa un puré de tomate, cebollas, ajo y pimiento. También puede ser un tipo de música y de baile.

24. Receta de Canarias: garbanzos, papas. Las dos: carne de res, cebollas, tomates. Receta de Cuba: arroz, frijoles, plátanos.

25. Answers will vary.

Additional Resources

Fans Online activities

HERITAGE LANGUAGE LEARNERS

• Explain to students that the Chilean poet Pablo Neruda wrote several odes in honor of various vegetables (e.g., "Oda al tomate," "Oda a la cebolla," "Oda a la alcachofa," "Oda a la papa"). Clarify that an ode is a lyric poem that expresses appreciation or praise for someone or something. Ask students to think of a food that they thoroughly appreciate. Then have them search for some of Neruda's odes to analyze his style and have them write an original ode to their favorite food. Ask volunteers to read their poetry aloud.

COOPERATIVE LEARNING

• Ask students to work in small groups and tell them that they are going to have their own cooking show, but they must first make an ad for their show. Students will choose a name for the show, the dishes they are going to prepare, and if they are going to focus on one Spanish-speaking country, or an entire region. They will need to describe when the show will appear on TV, create a slogan for it, and accompany their ad with images of the foods they plan to cook. Display their ads in the classroom.

189

Unit 4
DESAFÍO 1
Comunicación

Presentation

- In this section, students will integrate the vocabulary and grammar skills from *Desafío 1* in order to read a recipe for *ropa vieja,* talk about nutrition, give advice, and express change.

Activities	Standards	Resources
26.	1.1, 1.2, 1.3, 2.2	
27.	1.1, 1.2, 1.3, 3.1, 5.1, 5.2	
28. Final del desafío	1.2, 1.3, 2.2, 3.1, 5.1	
Tu desafío	1.1, 1.2	

Teaching Suggestions

Warm-Up / Independent Starter

- Have students think about a friend or family member who does not live a healthy lifestyle and write a brief e-mail with five commands that he or she would say to that person. Students should include both affirmative and negative commands in their e-mail. Ask advanced learners to also write to their friend or family member about changes they would experience if they followed the advice. For example: *Querida tía: Coma menos comida grasosa. Consuma alimentos nutritivos como las verduras y el pescado. Se va a poner contenta porque bajará de peso y...*

Preparation

- Ask students to share their Independent Starters. Discuss some of the vocabulary and verb constructions students used in their answers. Then have students revisit their sentences and try to apply more vocabulary words from this *Desafío.* As a competition, have students count the number of vocabulary words that they have applied and see who has the most!

- Ask students if they know anyone who has changed his or her lifestyle and discuss the changes they have seen in that person. Encourage students to consider emotional as well as physical changes, and sudden as well as gradual changes.

190

DESAFÍO 1

Comunicación

26 **¡Cocinemos ropa vieja!**

▶ **Lee** esta receta de ropa vieja y complétala con estas palabras.

> ajo   cebolla   aceite   agua   arroz   pimiento   carne   tomate

Ropa vieja

Ingredientes

1 kg de carne de res
3 cucharadas de ___1___ de oliva
1 cebolla
1 ___2___ rojo
1 pimiento verde
aceitunas verdes

3 dientes de ajo
1 cucharadita de orégano
1 cucharadita de pimienta
un poco de pimentón
1 taza de salsa de ___3___

Preparación

- Cueza la carne en un litro de ___4___ durante dos horas o hasta que esté hecha.
- Guarde ½ taza del agua donde ha cocido la carne (el caldo).
- Cuando se enfríe la carne, córtela en trozos pequeños.
- Pique los pimientos, la cebolla y el ___5___.
- Fría los pimientos y la ___6___. Cuando estén hechos, añada el ajo, el orégano, la pimienta, el pimentón, la salsa de tomate, las aceitunas y el caldo.
- Eche toda esta mezcla sobre la ___7___.
- Cocine todo a fuego medio hasta que se evapore el agua. Sirva con ___8___ blanco como acompañamiento.

▶ **Lee** de nuevo la receta y responde a estas preguntas.

1. ¿Qué verduras y hortalizas lleva esta receta?
2. ¿Cuáles son las especias que se necesitan para prepararla?
3. ¿Cuál es el ingrediente que contiene más proteínas?
4. ¿Cuánto tiempo se necesita para preparar el plato?

▶ **Piensa** y contesta. ¿Crees que la ropa vieja es un plato sano para alguien que está a dieta? ¿Por qué?

Differentiated Instruction

DEVELOPING LEARNERS

- Ask students to write five statements based on the recipe in activity 26. Some of these statements will be false. Then have them exchange papers with a partner who has to guess which are the false statements and correct them. To get students started, offer these examples:

1. *Hay que cocer la carne en salsa de tomate.* (*Falso. Hay que cocer la carne en agua.*)
2. *Debes cortar la carne en trozos pequeños.* (*Cierto*)

EXPANDING LEARNERS

- Ask students to imagine that they are school dietitians and their job is to counsel students to lead a healthy lifestyle, including proper nutrition, exercise, and rest. Ask students to work with a partner and create a dialogue between the dietitian and a student who has horrid eating habits, never exercises, and sleeps only a few hours a day. The dietitian must explain to the student why it is vital to change his or her habits. The student should present some arguments against these proposed changes. Have students present their dialogues in front of the class.

27 **Mi plato**

▶ **Habla** con tu compañero(a) sobre la imagen de Mi Plato. Creen una comida equilibrada según sus gustos y las proporciones sugeridas.

▶ **Escribe** cinco recomendaciones afirmativas o negativas basadas en la imagen. Usa la forma *nosotros*.

Modelo *¡Comamos proteínas todos los días!*

▶ **Investiga** sobre Mi Plato en Internet y crea un cartel con consejos para una de las categorías alimenticias.

Final del desafío

DIANA: ¿Qué tal, chicos? ___1___ sobre su desafío. ¿Cómo les fue?

ETHAN: Bueno, bien... Estuvimos buscando varias recetas y preparamos dos, pero no nos pusimos de acuerdo. A cada uno nos gusta una versión distinta de la ropa vieja y realmente no sabemos cuál es la mejor.

DIANA: Seguro que las dos son deliciosas.

EVA: No ___2___, tengo una idea. ¡___3___ las dos recetas! Los Fans del español pueden decidir cuál es la mejor.

DIANA: Esa es una buena idea, Eva.

ETHAN: Pues no ___4___ tiempo. ¡Manos a la obra!

28 **¿Qué pasó?**

▶ **Completa** el diálogo poniendo los verbos en la forma *nosotros* del imperativo.

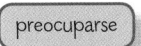 preocuparse   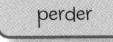 perder   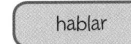 hablar   enviar

▶ **Habla** con tu compañero(a). ¿Crees que Eva y Ethan lograron el desafío? ¿Por qué?

→ TU DESAFÍO Visita la página web. Escucha las preguntas de la *Minientrevista Desafío 1* y escribe las respuestas.

HERITAGE LANGUAGE LEARNERS

• Ask students to describe their favorite dish from their family's country of origin, including any anecdotal information they may have about its origin. Have students write the recipe for this dish and, if they have the opportunity, make a video of themselves preparing the dish as if they were hosts of a cooking show. Ask them to share the video with the rest of the class and, if possible, bring their favorite dish to share with classmates.

MULTIPLE INTELLIGENCES:
Logical-Mathematical Intelligence

• Have students assume that the recipe shown for *ropa vieja* is for eight servings. Ask them to imagine that they are the owners of a small restaurant and need to prepare the same recipe, but for twenty-four servings. Ask students to rewrite the recipe accordingly. Which parts of the process will remain the same? (The time needed to cook the dish.) Then ask them to pare it down to four servings. How much of each ingredient is needed? Which recipe—four, eight, or twenty-four servings—do they think is the most time-effective to make?

Activities

26. Once students have finished this activity, have them rewrite the recipe using *nosotros* commands. If necessary, assist students with difficult conjugations (e.g. *cocer – cozamos; picar – piquemos*). Then ask students to get together with a classmate and compare their recipes.

27. As an alternative to creating a poster, have students work in groups to create commercials promoting *Mi Plato*, using both affirmative and negative *ustedes* commands. Then ask groups to present their commercials to the class. Whose commercial is the most convincing? Hold a class vote.

Answer Key

26. 1. aceite   4. agua   7. carne
      2. pimiento   5. ajo   8. arroz
      3. tomate   6. cebolla

▶ 1. Lleva cebolla, pimiento rojo, pimiento verde, aceitunas verdes, ajo y tomate.
      2. Se necesita orégano, pimienta y pimentón.
      3. La carne de res.
      4. Unas tres horas porque se necesitan dos horas para cocer la carne y luego hay que añadir el resto de los ingredientes y cocinar a fuego medio.

▶ Answers will vary. Sample answer: No es un plato muy sano para alguien que esté a dieta porque tiene carne roja y se fríen las verduras.

27. Answers will vary.
▶ Answers will vary.
▶ Answers will vary.

28. 1. Hablemos   3. Enviemos
      2. nos preocupemos 4. perdamos
      ▶ Answers will vary.

Additional Resources

Fans Online activities
Practice Workbook

191

DESAFÍO 2
Hacer valoraciones

Presentation

- In *Desafío 2*, Michelle and Daniel will learn about a seaside resort in Uruguay and will create a website to encourage tourists to visit a spa in this resort. Students will preview language used to talk about healthy habits and hygiene products, and to make value statements.

Activities	Standards	Resources
Texto	1.2, 2.2	Vis. Pres.
29.	1.1, 1.2, 1.3	
30.	1.1, 2.1	
31.	1.1, 1.2, 2.2	Audio
32. Conexiones	1.2, 2.1, 3.1, 4.1	Video

Teaching Suggestions

Warm-Up / Independent Starter

- Show students a map of South America and ask them to make a list of five "fast facts" about Uruguay. For example: *Uruguay está en América del Sur. La capital es Montevideo...*

Preparation

- Invite volunteers to share their Independent Starters. Encourage them to note the geographical features of Uruguay (e.g., the access to both the Río de la Plata and the Atlantic Ocean).

Texto: Un balneario uruguayo

- If possible, show students pictures of Punta del Este and the spa in Peru. After viewing these images, ask students to complete a "Think-Pair-Share." *¿Cuáles son las características de los dos lugares? ¿Dónde prefieren pasar sus vacaciones? ¿Por qué?*
- Call on several pairs of volunteers to alternate reading the dialogue aloud. Then discuss the different meanings of the word *balneario*. Does the word "spa" in English convey these different meanings?

Activities

29. Ask students if they have ever created a website. What difficulties might Michelle and Daniel face in their task?

Un balneario uruguayo

Michelle and Daniel will learn about the seaside resort town of Punta del Este, Uruguay. They must create a website to encourage tourists to visit a spa in this beach resort.

Playa Brava (Punta del Este, Uruguay).

MICHELLE: Busqué *playa Mansa* y *playa Brava* en Internet y averigüé que son playas de Punta del Este, una ciudad balneario de Uruguay.

DANIEL: Uff... Me parece dificilísimo crear una página web sobre una ciudad.

MICHELLE: Sí, es un poco extraño que tengamos que hacer eso.

DANIEL: Yo busqué *balneario* en el diccionario y dice que también es un edificio con baños medicinales. Por ejemplo, el balneario Baños del Inca.

MICHELLE: ¿Baños del Inca? ¿Dónde está?

DANIEL: Vamos a buscarlo. Mira, ya lo tengo. Está al norte de Perú. Aquí dice que es famoso por sus baños medicinales y por las propiedades del agua.

MICHELLE: Pero según el mapa no está en el mar. ¿Cómo es posible que sea un balneario?

DANIEL: Yo creo que un balneario no está necesariamente en una playa. Por ejemplo, las aguas de Baños del Inca vienen de un manantial *(spring)*.

MICHELLE: Ah, entonces en ese balneario ofrecen tratamientos de salud con el agua del manantial.

DANIEL: Eso es. Y lo que nosotros tenemos que hacer es promocionar un hotel con *spa* en Punta del Este. Me parece más razonable que escribamos sobre eso.

MICHELLE: Sí, tienes razón.

Balneario Baños del Inca (Perú).

29 **Detective de palabras**

▶ **Completa** estas oraciones.

1. Me parece dificilísimo _____ una página web sobre una ciudad.
2. Es extraño que _____ que hacer eso.
3. Me parece más razonable que _____ sobre un hotel en Punta del Este.

Differentiated Instruction

DEVELOPING LEARNERS

- To verify that students understand the information presented, ask the following questions:
  1. *¿Cuál es el desafío de Michelle y Daniel?* (*Hacer una página web para promocionar un balneario.*)
  2. *¿Dónde está el balneario?* (*en Punta del Este, Uruguay*)
  3. *¿Dónde está el balneario de Baños del Inca?* (*en Perú*)
  4. *¿Están todos los balnearios cerca de playas?* (*no*)
  5. *¿Qué ofrecen en Baños del Inca?* (*tratamientos con aguas de manantial*)

EXPANDING LEARNERS

- Ask students to write a narrative that explains what is going on in the dialogue. Remind them that narratives are often written from a third-person point of view, but may also be written from a first-person point of view. Students will decide how they want to focus the point of view of their narratives. Encourage students to include additional information in their paragraphs, such as descriptions of the setting and people involved.

30 **¿Comprendes?**

▶ **Responde** a estas preguntas.

1. ¿En qué país está Punta del Este?
2. Según Daniel, ¿por qué va la gente al balneario Baños del Inca, en Perú?
3. ¿Cuál es la diferencia entre el balneario de Perú y el de Uruguay?

31 **De vacaciones**

▶ **Lee** estas opiniones de usuarios de una página de turismo. ¿Cuál de los dos lugares prefieres visitar? Coméntalo con tus compañeros(as).

Baños del Inca   15 comentarios Puntuación

Baños del Inca es el destino perfecto para relajarse y descansar. En este complejo turístico se puede disfrutar de los baños de aguas termales a distintas temperaturas en sus pozas y manantiales. Además ofrecen otros tratamientos terapéuticos, como masajes, baños sauna con hierbas medicinales y programas para combatir el estrés.

Punta del Este   20 comentarios Puntuación

Punta del Este es uno de los destinos turísticos más famosos del mundo. Tiene hermosísimas playas con aguas tranquilas y otras con grandes olas, perfectas para la práctica de deportes acuáticos como el surf, el windsurf y la navegación a vela (*sailing*). Pero también se pueden practicar otros deportes y visitar sus museos, tiendas y restaurantes, como hacen miles de turistas cada año.

▶ **Escucha** y decide. ¿Qué balneario describe cada persona?

 **CONEXIONES: GEOGRAFÍA**

Punta del Este

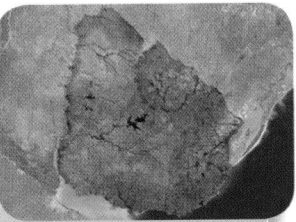

Vista satélite de Uruguay.

Punta del Este es una ciudad costera situada entre el Río de la Plata y el océano Atlántico, muy famosa por sus fantásticas playas.

La playa Mansa (*gentle*) recibe este nombre por sus aguas tranquilas, ya que está situada junto al Río de la Plata y está protegida de las corrientes y vientos del océano. En cambio, la playa Brava (*angry*), situada al oeste, tiene olas (*waves*) mucho más fuertes y peligrosas.

32 **Piensa.** ¿Conoces otros lugares con nombres adecuados a sus características?

ciento noventa y tres **193**

---

31. As students read the descriptions of each place, have them answer these questions: *¿Qué tratamientos se ofrecen en Baños del Inca? ¿Por qué son buenos esos tratamientos para la salud? ¿Qué actividades se ofrecen en Punta del Este?*

 AUDIO SCRIPT
See page 173l.

 CONEXIONES: GEOGRAFÍA
Punta del Este

Punta del Este is a beach resort located approximately an hour and a half from Montevideo, Uruguay. This seaside resort is actually formed by several towns, which used to be fishing villages, located where the Río de la Plata meets the Atlantic Ocean. Together these towns have over twenty miles of pristine beaches. The most popular season is right after Christmas, when the resort is filled with tourists and celebrities.

Answer Key

29. 1. crear   2. tengamos   3. escribamos

30. 1. Está en Uruguay.
2. La gente va por sus baños medicinales.
3. Punta del Este es una ciudad balneario en una playa. Baños del Inca está en el interior del país y sus aguas no son del mar, sino de un manantial.

31. Answers will vary.
▶ Baños del Inca: 2, 4.
Punta del Este: 1, 3.

32. Answers will vary.

Additional Resources

Fans Online activities

HERITAGE LANGUAGE LEARNERS

• Ask students to describe orally or in writing *un balneario* or a well-known vacation spot in their family's country of origin, or in another Spanish-speaking country they know or would like to research. Students should include a brief history and physical description of the place, the features and points of interest that make it popular for vacationers, the activities that can be practiced there, and how visitors to this city or town might travel to the destination.

COOPERATIVE LEARNING

• Ask students to work in small groups to prepare a travel poster for a seaside resort in a Spanish-speaking country. Students in the group will each investigate a different place and take notes. Then they will get together, discuss the selections, and choose a final destination. All members will work collaboratively and contribute to writing a draft for the text. One or two students will review the text and write the final draft. Other students will illustrate the poster with original drawings or with images taken from the Internet.

DESAFÍO 2

Vocabulario – Hábitos saludables

Presentation

- In this section, students will learn vocabulary related to healthy habits and hygiene products.

Activities	Standards	Resources
Vocabulario	1.2, 3.1	
33.	1.3	
34.	1.2	Audio
35.	1.1, 1.3	
36.	1.1, 1.2, 1.3, 5.2	

Teaching Suggestions

Warm-Up / Independent Starter

- Have students look at the highlighted vocabulary words and ask them to generate a list of infinitives, nouns, and adjectives. For example:

verbos	nombres	adjetivos
estirar	músculos	estresado

Preparation

- Review the Independent Starter as a class. For each word, see if students can extrapolate any previously learned words or other related vocabulary (e.g., *estresado – estrés; gimnasio – hacer gimnasia*).

- Write the following questions on the board:
  - ¿Qué hace Daniel en el gimnasio? ¿Por qué va? ¿Para qué se entrena?
  - ¿Quién practica yoga? ¿Por qué? ¿Qué hace mientras practica yoga?

- Give students a few minutes to answer the questions independently, then discuss the answers as a class to ensure comprehension of the content as well as the individual vocabulary words.

Activities

33. To extend this activity, ask students to write sentences with the rest of the words in the *Más vocabulario* feature, as well as the verbs, nouns, and adjectives produced in the Independent Starter. Ask volunteers to write sentences on the board. Review these together as a class, asking students to identify and correct any errors that they find.

Vocabulario

Hábitos saludables

Es necesario **estirar los músculos** antes de hacer ejercicio para **evitar calambres** (*cramps*).

Daniel **se entrena** en un **gimnasio** para una carrera de 5 kilómetros. Hace **ejercicios aeróbicos**. Además, le gusta **cuidarse** para no **aumentar** ni **bajar de peso**.

Es importante que **respires** profundamente...

Michelle se siente un poco **estresada**. Para **relajarse**, practica **yoga** y **pilates**, y a veces se da un **masaje**. Su **monitora** dice que es bueno practicar **ejercicios de relajación** y **descansar**.

Más vocabulario

Objetos y productos de higiene

el albornoz	*bathrobe*
el cortaúñas	*nail clippers*
la crema solar	*sunscreen*
la esponja	*sponge*
la espuma de afeitar	*shaving foam*
el gorro de ducha	*shower cap*
el hilo dental	*dental floss*
la maquinilla de afeitar	*safety razor*

33 ¿**Para qué se usa?**

▶ **Escribe** oraciones para explicar cómo se usan los siguientes objetos.

Modelo *Me pongo el gorro de ducha cuando quiero ducharme sin lavarme el pelo.*

① ② ③ 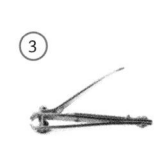 ④  ⑤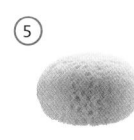

Differentiated Instruction

DEVELOPING LEARNERS

- To help students comprehend the new vocabulary, ask them to make a five-column chart and label the columns as follows: *Cosas, Personas, Lugares, Acciones, Descripciones*. Have students read the vocabulary presentation silently, and place all of the highlighted words, along with those in the *Más vocabulario* feature, under the corresponding header. Help students form sentences with some of these words.

EXPANDING LEARNERS

- Divide the class into two teams and tell students that they will play "Hangman" to practice the new vocabulary. On index cards, prepare definitions for the words or write sentences that can be completed with the new vocabulary. As players from each team pick a card, you will write a line for each letter of the answer on the board. Players call out the letters for the word and get four chances to correctly identify it. If they cannot guess the word, the other team gets a chance to play.

34 **Gimnasio En forma**

 ▶ **Escucha** el anuncio publicitario de un gimnasio y decide. ¿A quiénes les puede interesar visitarlo?

   a. Ramón, 20 años. Está estudiando en la universidad. Quiere ir a clases de pilates.
   b. Ángela, 25 años. Quiere ponerse en forma para correr un maratón.
   c. Mario, 18 años. Le gusta bailar salsa y otros ritmos latinos.
   d. Carlota, 30 años. Quiere un tratamiento de baños medicinales para calmar su dolor de espalda.
   e. Ana, 68 años. Busca un lugar para ir a nadar con sus nietos.
   f. Marina, 40 años. Tiene un trabajo muy estresante y necesita relajarse.

35 **Actividades**

▶ **Escribe** un pie de foto para describir estas imágenes. Después, habla con tu compañero(a) sobre cuáles de estas actividades prefieres hacer y por qué.

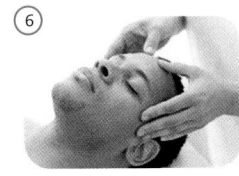

 36 **¡Vamos a conocernos mejor!**

▶ **Pregunta** a tu compañero(a) y toma nota de sus respuestas. Después, presenta la información a la clase.

   1. ¿Estás en forma?
   2. ¿Te gusta hacer ejercicio? ¿Por qué?
   3. ¿Prefieres las actividades en grupo o las que puedes hacer individualmente?
   4. ¿Prefieres ir a un gimnasio o a un balneario?
   5. ¿Cuál es tu actividad favorita en un gimnasio?
   6. ¿Prefieres hacer ejercicio dentro del gimnasio o al aire libre?

ciento noventa y cinco **195**

Vocabulario – Hábitos saludables

34. Before playing the audio, ask students to read the descriptions provided of each person so that they will be prepared to identify who might be interested in visiting the gym. After completing the activity, ask students if they would be interested in visiting this gym and to explain why.

35. After students have finished this activity, have pairs choose one of the photos and, using ten vocabulary words from page 194, come up with a conversation that would take place between two of the people in the photo. For example:
   A. *¿Te gusta hacer ejercicios aeróbicos?*
   B. *Sí, vengo al gimnasio todos los días. Trato de llevar una vida sana…*

36. Ask students to prepare a short, written summary of the healthy (or not-so-healthy) habits of their partners. Collect and provide students with feedback on how well they are able to use this lesson's vocabulary.

 AUDIO SCRIPT
See page 173l.

Answer Key

33. Answers will vary. Sample answers:
   1. Uso el hilo dental para quitar los restos de comida entre los dientes.
   2. Me pongo crema solar cuando hace sol y quiero proteger la piel del sol.
   3. Uso el cortaúñas para cortarme las uñas.
   4. Uso el albornoz después de ducharme.
   5. Uso la esponja para enjabonarme cuando me ducho.

34. a, b, f

35. Answers will vary.

36. Answers will vary.

Additional Resources

Fans Online activities
Practice Workbook

HERITAGE LANGUAGE LEARNERS

• Ask students to imagine that they are the owners of a new gym that has just opened to the public. Have students choose a name and slogan for their gym, and then write an ad for it, explaining the services it provides, the location and hours of operation, some special offers for the first fifty clients, and how to contact the gym for more information. Students should accompany their ad with images they have drawn or cut out from magazines or the Internet.

CRITICAL THINKING

• Ask students to imagine that they are coaches for healthy lifestyles. Their task is to advise three people who have come to them looking to improve their eating habits and their exercise regimen, as well as to reduce stress. Ask students to create profiles for these three individuals and then come up with a fitness plan that will improve their overall health. Ask students to share their clients' situation and their improvement plans for them with the rest of the class.

DESAFÍO 2

Gramática – *Para* y *por*

Presentation

- In this section, students will review and practice the different uses of *para* and *por*.

Activities	Standards	Resources
Gramática	1.2, 3.1	
37.	4.1	
38.	1.2	
39.	1.2, 1.3	Audio
40.	1.1, 2.1	
41. Conexiones	1.2, 2.1, 3.1, 3.2, 5.2	

Teaching Suggestions

Warm-Up / Independent Starter

- Based on previous knowledge, ask students to write an explanation for the use of *por* or *para* in each of the following sentences:
  1. *Vamos a la playa para descansar.* (purpose)
  2. *Ahora mismo salgo para la escuela.* (destination)
  3. *Esta tarea es para el martes.* (deadline)
  4. *Llegué tarde por tu culpa.* (reason)

Preparation

- Ask students to share their Independent Starters with one another. Have them read the uses of *para* and *por* on page 196. They should then compare these rules to the explanations they gave in their Independent Starter.

- Write each use of *por* and *para* on a separate index card and ask pairs of students to pull a card from a bag. Ask each pair to write one original sentence that demonstrates the indicated use of *por* or *para*. Collect these sentences and redistribute them to different pairs. Ask them to explain the use of *por* or *para* as demonstrated in each sentence.

Activities

38. To extend this activity, ask students to write an original sentence in which the meaning of the sentence is changed based on the use of *por* or *para*. Ask several volunteers to write their sentences on the board, and have the class explain the meaning of each sentence.

Gramática

Para y *por*

- *Para* and *por* are often translated as *for* in English, although they have differences in meaning. In many cases it might be grammatically correct to use either *para* or *por*, but the meaning of the sentence will change depending on which preposition you choose.

Usos de *para*

purpose/"in order to"	Hago yoga **para** relajarme. **Para** hacer una paella, necesitamos arroz.
"directed to"/"for the benefit of"	Esta crema solar es **para** Lourdes. Ese escritor trabaja **para** un periódico importante.
destination, direction	Salimos **para** Punta del Este ahora mismo.
deadline, future date	Hay que terminar el trabajo **para** mañana.
comparison, "considering"	Está muy bien **para** ser un hombre tan mayor.
opinion	**Para** mí, este libro es muy bueno.

Usos de *por*

reason, motive, "because of"	María se casó **por** amor.
"in exchange for"	Pagamos quince dólares **por** el desayuno.
ratio, proportion, "per"	Yo manejo a cincuenta millas **por** hora.
movement: through, "via", along, by	Paseamos **por** la playa.
general location	Está **por** aquí.
general time/part of the day	Mi hermano vendrá **por** primavera. **Por** la tarde hacemos deporte.
mode of communication or transportation	Consulté al entrenador **por** teléfono. Envié el paquete **por** barco.
"on behalf of"	Ana estaba enferma y Elena fue a la tienda **por** ella.
object of an errand	Luis se cayó y Ana fue **por** el médico.
agent of an action	*Don Quijote* fue escrito **por** Miguel de Cervantes.

37 **Compara.** ¿Cómo cambia el significado de estas oraciones? Tradúcelas al inglés.

    a. Ana trabajó para su hermano.   **b.** Ana trabajó por su hermano.

38 **¿Para o por?**

▶ **Lee** estas oraciones y explica la diferencia de significado de cada una.

1. a. ¿Quieres dinero <u>para</u> la moto?   2. a. Hay que hacer el informe <u>por</u> la tarde.
   b. ¿Quieres dinero <u>por</u> la moto?   b. Hay que hacer el informe <u>para</u> esta tarde.

Differentiated Instruction

DEVELOPING LEARNERS

- To give students more practice, have them complete the following sentences with *por* or *para*:
  1. *Esta carta es … Juan.* (para)
  2. *Voy a la tienda … pan.* (por)
  3. *Debemos pintar la casa … mañana.* (para)
  4. *… ser extranjero, hablas español muy bien.* (Para)
  5. *Me encanta viajar … barco.* (por)
  6. *¿Cuándo sales … Perú?* (para)
  7. *El gato entró … la ventana.* (por)

EXPANDING LEARNERS

- Divide the class into two teams. Prepare sentences or phrases that require *por* or *para*, but omit them as you read the sentences to students. Players from both teams will take turns trying to identify the correct preposition. As teams answer correctly, they receive one point. If a player answers incorrectly, the other team gets a chance to play.

39 **¡Qué fuerza de voluntad!**

 ▶ **Escucha** la conversación entre dos amigas. Después, completa estas oraciones de forma lógica, utilizando *por* o *para*.

1. Lourdes sale temprano...
2. Lourdes va al gimnasio...
3. Lourdes corre y entrena...
4. Juanita no acompaña a Lourdes; tiene que ir al mercado...

40 **Un balneario para todos**

▶ **Habla** con tu compañero(a). ¿Para qué van estas personas a un balneario? Usen *para* y *por* para describir las actividades.

Modelo *Van a un balneario para relajarse.*

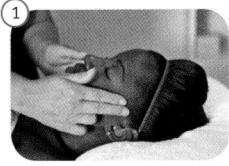 ①  ②  ③

 ④  ⑤

 **CONEXIONES: SALUD**

Tratamientos alternativos

La medicina tradicional se utiliza desde hace miles de años en todo el mundo para prevenir o curar enfermedades. Se basa en el uso de plantas medicinales y en prácticas como la acupuntura o las terapias manuales.

Hoy en día los tratamientos alternativos están muy extendidos. La OMS (Organización Mundial de la Salud) afirma que en algunos países de Asia y África el 80% de la población recibe una atención primaria basada en este tipo de medicina.

41 **Explica.** ¿Conoces algún remedio natural para tratar alguna enfermedad? ¿Crees que este tipo de tratamientos alternativos son efectivos?

HERITAGE LANGUAGE LEARNERS

• Ask students to explore the role medicinal plants have had in the culture of their family's country of origin, or in another Hispanic country. Ask them to use the Internet or talk to members of their family who have used, or continue to use, these natural cures. Students should be prepared to describe the plants, where they are found, and what ailments they are purported to cure or alleviate.

CRITICAL THINKING

• Enable a classroom discussion on the pros and cons of alternative medicine. Why do students think that in some industrialized countries, alternative medicine is looked upon less favorably than standard medical practices? Have students research an alternative medical practice and compare patients' success rates with those of patients who received standard care.

---

40. After students have finished this activity, ask them to choose one photo. They should then write a short blog entry in which the person in the photo talks about his or her healthy habits.

 AUDIO SCRIPT
See page 173I.

 CONEXIONES: SALUD

Tratamientos alternativos

Alternative medicine is defined as any healing treatment that does not fall within the realm of conventional medicine. It is based on historical or cultural traditions rather than scientific evidence. Such alternatives include: acupuncture, herbal and plant treatments, homeopathy, medicinal baths, and mind-body medicine.

Answer Key

37. a. *Ana worked for her brother.* Su hermano era su jefe.
b. *Ana worked in place of her brother.* Ana sustituyó a su hermano en el trabajo.

38. 1. a. *in order to buy*; b. *in exchange for*
2. a. *during the afternoon*; b. *time limit, by*

39. Answers will vary. Sample answers:
1. ... por la mañana.
2. ... para hacer ejercicio.
3. ... para participar en un maratón.
4. ... para comprar unas cosas para su mamá.

40. Answers will vary.

41. Answers will vary.

Additional Resources

Fans Online activities
Practice Workbook

Unit 4

DESAFÍO 2

Gramática – Hacer valoraciones

Presentation

- In this section, students will review and practice how to use the infinitive and the present subjunctive to make value statements.

Activities	Standards	Resources
Gramática	1.2, 3.1	
42.	4.1	
43.	1.2, 1.3	
44.	1.1, 1.2	
45.	1.1, 1.2, 1.3, 5.1	
46. Conexiones	1.2, 3.1, 5.1	

Teaching Suggestions

Warm-Up / Independent Starter

- Ask students to read the following pairs of sentences and compare the use of the infinitive and the subjunctive:
  1. a. *Es aconsejable que María nade con cuidado.*
     b. *Es aconsejable nadar con cuidado.*
  2. a. *Es importante que te relajes.*
     b. *Es importante relajarse.*

Preparation

- Review the Independent Starter, discussing the differences between the use of the subjunctive and the infinitive. Go over the grammar presentation as a class and point out the expressions commonly used to express opinions and make value statements. Can students list any others?

Activities

43. If possible, distribute individual white boards and markers to students. Read a few sentences aloud and ask students to complete each one with the infinitive or the present subjunctive. After each sentence, ask students to hold up the white boards with their answers written. For example: *(hacer) Para vivir una vida sana, es importante que todos ... ejercicio. (hagamos)*

44. To extend this activity, ask students to write four additional statements that they might hear in their Spanish class. Have students work in pairs and react to their partner's statements.

198

Gramática

Hacer valoraciones

Expresiones para hacer valoraciones

- To express opinions and make value statements, we can use impersonal expressions like these:

Es aconsejable... Es conveniente...	It is advisable ...	Es necesario... Es preciso...	It is neccessary ...
Es importante...	It is important ...	Es mejor...	It is better ...
Es bueno...	It is good ...	Es sorprendente...	It is surprising ...

- You can also use the expression me parece, usually followed by a word to express judgment: bien, mal, fatal, horrible, maravilloso, extraordinario...

  Me parece bien que comamos juntos mañana.

El infinitivo y el subjuntivo con expresiones de valoración

- Use the **infinitive** in general statements that do not refer to anyone in particular.

  Es preciso hacer ejercicio cada día.

- Use the **subjunctive** when the dependent clause refers to someone in particular.

  Es preciso que tú hagas ejercicio cada día.

42 **Compara.** ¿Cómo expresas las valoraciones en inglés?

43 **¿Adónde vamos?**

▶ **Une** las columnas para formar oraciones lógicas y escribe las oraciones.

A
1. Es necesario que todos...
2. Es bueno...
3. No es aconsejable...
4. Me parece mal que tú...
5. Nos parece bien que ustedes...
6. Es conveniente que tú...

B
a. vayan a un balneario.
b. hagamos ejercicio.
c. no practiques ningún deporte.
d. beber dos litros de agua al día.
e. cuides tu salud.
f. tomar el sol sin una crema solar.

▶ **Completa** estas oraciones.

1. Para relajarse es bueno...
2. Para estar en forma es necesario que...
3. Para llevar una vida sana es preciso...
4. Para tener una buena salud es aconsejable...

198 ciento noventa y ocho

Differentiated Instruction

DEVELOPING LEARNERS

- Dictate ten sentences using the infinitive to make value statements. For example: *Es importante estudiar para el examen.* Then ask students to rewrite each sentence, using the subjunctive: *Es importante que estudies para el examen.* Remind students that the subjunctive is required after such expressions when there is a change of subject and that the relative pronoun *que* always follows the impersonal expression when there is a change of subject.

EXPANDING LEARNERS

- Ask students to imagine that they are giving advice to a friend who wants to lead a more healthful lifestyle. Ask students to make a list of at least eight suggestions that will help their friend improve his or her lifestyle. The suggestions must be made using the subjunctive mood. Examples might include: *Es aconsejable que duermas por lo menos ocho horas cada noche. No es bueno que bebas tantos refrescos. Es mejor que bebas agua.*

44 **¿Qué te parece?**

▶ **Escribe.** Reacciona a estas afirmaciones con una valoración.

Modelo «No hago nunca ejercicio.»
→ *Me parece mal que no hagas ejercicio. Es necesario estar en forma.*

1. «No voy a estudiar para el examen de Matemáticas.»
2. «Quiero aprender muchas lenguas y viajar por el mundo.»
3. «Voy a tomar clases de yoga.»
4. «Como en restaurantes de comida rápida todos los días.»
5. «Compro muchísima ropa en las tiendas de moda.»

45 **Doctora Sabelotodo**

▶ **Lee** las dos cartas. Luego, escribe una respuesta para cada una.
Usa expresiones para valorar.

Modelo *Es importante que Raúl haga deporte.*

Estimada doctora Sabelotodo:

Tengo 18 años y me llamo Ana. Soy una buena estudiante, pero me siento muy estresada y a veces me duele el estómago. Cada día llego a mi casa a las cuatro de la tarde y me pongo a estudiar. Sigo estudiando hasta la una o las dos de la mañana y me levanto temprano para volver a leer mis tareas. Mis padres están muy preocupados por mí y me dicen que es necesario que salga más y me divierta. ¿Qué debo hacer?

Ana

Estimada doctora Sabelotodo:

Me llamo Raúl y tengo 16 años. Le escribo porque quiero ponerme en forma. Mi vida es muy sedentaria: no hago ejercicio, paso muchas horas frente a la computadora y lo que más me gusta es jugar a los videojuegos. Quiero más actividad en mi vida, pero no sé por dónde empezar. ¡Por favor, deme algún consejo!

Raúl

CONEXIONES: CIENCIAS

Las aguas termales

Las aguas termales son aguas subterráneas que salen a la superficie *(surface)* en forma de vapor o agua caliente. Se suelen encontrar a lo largo de las líneas de fallas *(faults)*.

Géiser en el desierto de Atacama (Chile).

Debido a su alto nivel de mineralización, las aguas termales se utilizan desde hace miles de años como medida terapéutica, especialmente para tratar enfermedades de la piel.

En Latinoamérica hay muchos balnearios, la mayoría situados en zonas volcánicas.

46 **Investiga.** ¿Por qué se calienta el agua debajo de la tierra? ¿Para qué otros problemas de salud suelen emplearse los baños termales?

Gramática – Hacer valoraciones

45. Collect the responses written by the class. Redistribute them and have students work in pairs to write the script for a conversation between Ana and Dra. Sabelotodo or Raúl and Dra. Sabelotodo. Call on volunteers to role-play their conversations for the class.

CONEXIONES: CIENCIAS

Las aguas termales

Hot springs are produced by heat from the Earth's volcanic activity. Due to the high mineral content of these springs, they are considered by many to have health benefits. Therefore, sites with hot springs have become popular tourist destinations. The name *spa* comes from the town of Spa, in Belgium, which has attracted people who like to soak in the healing waters of its hot springs since the 14th century.

Answer Key

42. Se expresan de manera parecida al español. En algunos casos también se usa el subjuntivo, pero generalmente se usa el indicativo. Por ejemplo: *It's important that he exercise.* (Es importante que él haga ejercicio.) *I think it's wonderful that she is my friend.* (Me parece maravilloso que ella sea mi amiga.)

43. 1. b   2. d   3. f   4. c   5. a   6. e
▶ Answers will vary. Sample answers:
1. ... ir a un balneario.
2. ... hagamos mucho ejercicio.
3. ... comer bien y descansar.
4. ... llevar una vida sana.

44. Answers will vary.

45. Answers will vary.

46. Answers will vary.

Additional Resources

Fans Online activities
Practice Workbook

HERITAGE LANGUAGE LEARNERS

• Even though heritage learners may be using the subjunctive correctly, they may not know why they must use this verb mood. Write at least six sentences that state a fact or make value statements. The sentences that state a fact should have a verb in the indicative and the ones that make a value statement, a verb in the subjunctive. Ask students to first identify the verb in each sentence and then explain why each verb mood was used.

MULTIPLE INTELLIGENCES:
Verbal-Linguistic Intelligence

• Ask students to imagine that they have a friend who seems to confuse bad advice with sound counsel. For example, this classmate thinks it is logical to recommend: *Es preciso que duermas solo tres horas.* Have students make a list of this friend's poorly worded suggestions and then offer more logical and helpful advice. To counter the advice above, students might write: *Es malo que duermas tan solo tres horas; es aconsejable que duermas por lo menos ocho horas.*

LECTURA: TEXTO INFORMATIVO

Presentation

- In this section, students will read a young lady's blog entry about her vacation in Punta del Este, Uruguay. Students will identify nouns and verbs that refer to health and exercise.

Activities	Standards	Resources
Lectura: texto informativo	1.2, 1.3, 2.1, 3.1	
47.	1.1, 1.2	
48.	1.2, 1.3	
49.	1.2	
50.	1.1, 1.3	
51.	1.3, 5.1, 5.2	

Teaching Suggestions

Warm-Up / Independent Starter

- Have students think about the title of this text. Ask them to write a list of things that they associate with *la buena vida*.

Preparation

- Call on volunteers to explain what a blog is. You may want to ask these follow-up questions: *¿Alguien en esta clase escribe un blog? ¿Para qué sirven los blogs? ¿Quién participa en los blogs? ¿Qué temas prefieren leer en un blog?*

- Have students work on the *Antes de leer* strategies individually. Then, ask them to share the answers with a partner. Finally, discuss the answers as a class.

- Ask students to scan the text and cite the uses of the present (e.g., *nos bañamos, hacemos surf*), the preterite (e.g., *prometí, llegué, me deprimí*), and the imperfect (e.g., *quería, prefería*) in the reading.

- Read the text aloud to model pronunciation and intonation. Then ask for three volunteers to each read a paragraph. You may want to ask students to pause after each paragraph, and call on a different volunteer to paraphrase the content.

- Brainstorm with students what the expression *la buena vida* means for the author of the blog. Ask students to share their Independent Starters and compare what it means for them.

Antes de leer: estrategias

1. Lee los títulos. ¿Qué tipo de texto es? ¿Qué significa *La buena vida*? ¿Con qué asocias tú esta expresión?

2. Mira las fotos. ¿Te dicen algo sobre la autora del blog? ¿Qué crees que es para ella la buena vida?

3. Lee la primera oración. ¿Cuál va a ser el tema de esta entrada de blog? ¿A quién escribe Sara?

4. Identifica las palabras precedidas por *mi(s)* en el primer párrafo. ¿Qué información te dan sobre Sara?

El blog personal de Sara

La buena vida

Les prometí que les iba a contar mis vacaciones en Punta del Este; bueno, aquí va.

El día que llegué con mis padres a Montevideo llovía. Como ustedes saben, yo no quería venir. Prefería quedarme en Buenos Aires y pasar sola las vacaciones en el apartamento con mi mascota[1] Lula. Mi mamá, obviamente, no me lo permitió: ella dice que 16 años no son suficientes para quedarse sola en la casa. Por eso, cuando llegamos aquí y vi que el tiempo era horrible, me deprimí[2] aún más.

Afortunadamente, el tiempo mejoró y la verdad es que el balneario es extraordinario. Paso el día en la playa leyendo y hablando con unos chicos que conocí. Nos bañamos, hacemos surf y pasamos la tarde tranquilamente.

El hotel La Sirena tiene piscina y un gimnasio para hacer ejercicio. Ofrecen clases gratis[3] (bueno, están incluidas en el precio del hotel, que lo pagan mis papás, claro) de yoga, pilates y de relajación. El otro día entré en la sauna (¡¡¡qué calor!!!) y después me dieron un masaje fantástico. En fin, ¡que esto es la buena vida!

COMENTARIOS (0)   ENVIAR UN COMENTARIO

1. *pet*   2. *I got depressed*   3. *free*

Differentiated Instruction

DEVELOPING LEARNERS

- Conduct a guided reading of Sara's blog. Have students read the text aloud, sentence by sentence. As students read, ask them yes/no questions to check their comprehension. For example: *¿Se fue Sara a Punta del Este de vacaciones? (Sí)* If students cannot answer the question, ask them to read the sentence again. If they continue to have difficulty, rephrase the sentence for them, using simpler language, or breaking a long sentence into two.

EXPANDING LEARNERS

- Ask students to imagine that they, too, are staying at a *balneario* in Punta del Este. Ask them to write an e-mail to a friend at home, describing their trip to Uruguay, their general impressions of the area and the hotel, the activities offered and those they especially enjoy, any day trips they have taken or plan to take, and comments on people they have met along the way. Students might also include some advice to their friend who is thinking of taking the same trip next year.

47 Comprensión

▶ **Responde** a estas preguntas.

1. ¿Cuántos años tiene Sara? ¿Dónde vive?
2. ¿Con quién fue de vacaciones? ¿Adónde fue?
3. ¿Cómo prefería Sara pasar sus vacaciones? ¿Por qué no pudo?
4. ¿Por qué se deprimió el primer día de sus vacaciones?
5. ¿Qué opinión tiene ahora sobre el balneario?
6. ¿Cómo pasa Sara el tiempo en sus vacaciones?

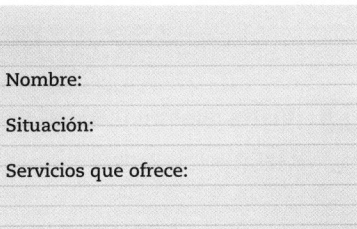

48 Una ficha del balneario

▶ **Completa** una ficha como esta con los datos del balneario.

Nombre:

Situación:

Servicios que ofrece:

49 Definiciones

▶ **Busca** en el texto las palabras que corresponden a estas definiciones.

1. Lugar donde se puede hacer ejercicio.
2. Lugar donde se puede nadar.
3. Lugar donde se puede tomar un baño de vapor.
4. Animal de compañía.
5. Terapia basada en la presión sobre el cuello, la espalda o las piernas.

50 ¿Qué hago?

▶ **Escribe** con tu compañero(a) una conversación entre Sara y una amiga de Argentina.

> No quiero pasar todo el día en el hotel.

> No, es importante que salgas y...

▶ **Representen** la conversación para la clase.

51 Con tus propias palabras

▶ **Elige** uno de estos títulos y escribe una entrada de blog similar a la de Sara.

1. Mis mejores vacaciones   2. Un hotel extraordinario   3. La buena vida

doscientos uno **201**

Activities

47. To expand this activity, personalize questions while relating them to the reading. For example: *Sara no quería ir con sus padres de vacaciones. ¿A ustedes les gusta ir de vacaciones con sus padres o prefieren quedarse solos en casa? ¿Por qué? A Sara le gusta el yoga. ¿Les gusta a ustedes el yoga?*

49. Ask students to work individually, then have them share their answers with a partner. If they find other difficult vocabulary words, they can write similar definitions and ask their partner to find the word they refer to.

50. Ask students to include at least two value statements in their dialogues.

51. As an alternative, ask students to write a comment as a response to Sara's blog entry. Have them include at least two value statements.

Answer Key

47. 1. Tiene 16 años y vive en Buenos Aires.
2. Fue de vacaciones con sus padres a Punta del Este, Uruguay.
3. Prefería estar con su mascota, Lula, en Buenos Aires. Pero su madre no se lo permitió.
4. Se deprimió porque hacía mal tiempo.
5. Ahora le parece extraordinario.
6. Sara realiza diferentes actividades en la playa y en el hotel.

48. Nombre: Hotel La Sirena.
Situación: Punta del Este, Uruguay.
Servicios: playa, piscina, gimnasio, sauna, clases de yoga, de pilates y de relajación.

49. 1. gimnasio   3. sauna   5. masaje
2. piscina   4. mascota

50. Answers will vary.
▶ Answers will vary.

51. Answers will vary.

Additional Resources

Fans Online activities

HERITAGE LANGUAGE LEARNERS

• Ask students to rewrite Sara's blog, but this time have them imagine that Sara is writing it from home. She has convinced her parents that she is responsible and will stay home alone for a week. Students may choose to show a very responsible and mature Sara, or someone who is asking for trouble and courting disaster. Encourage students to use humor in writing about Sara's week alone with her pet, Lula, and to be creative in describing events that take place.

CRITICAL THINKING

• In her blog, Sara mentions that her mother will not allow her to stay home alone because she is only sixteen. Do students agree with this and, if so, at what age do they think this would be acceptable? Or do they think that Sara could have been allowed to stay home alone? Students should support their opinions. What do students think about the age for getting a driver's license in their community? Enable a classroom discussion on age and responsibility.

DESAFÍO 2

Comunicación

Presentation

- In this section, students will integrate the vocabulary and grammar skills from *Desafío 2* in order to describe healthy habits and make value statements.

Activities	Standards	Resources
52.	1.2, 1.3	Audio
53.	1.1, 1.2, 2.1, 3.2	
54.	1.3, 5.1	
55. Final del desafío	1.1, 1.2, 1.3, 2.1, 5.1	
Tu desafío	1.1, 1.2	

Teaching Suggestions

Warm-Up / Independent Starter

- Have students write five value statements for practicing *hábitos saludables*. Ask students to follow this model: *Para vivir una vida sana, es preciso que hagas ejercicio cada día.*

Preparation

- Ask students to share their Independent Starters. Request that students explain the use of the subjunctive or infinitive in each of their statements. Hold a class vote on the top ten recommendations and post them in the classroom.

Activities

52. Ask students to react to the title of this activity (i.e., *Es importante relajarse*). Ask them: *¿Están de acuerdo? ¿Cuándo es importante relajarse? ¿Por qué? ¿Cómo se relajan ustedes?*

53. After completing this activity, and if time allows, ask students to work in small groups to research a *balneario* in a Spanish-speaking country. They should provide pictures and a short written description of the place, modeled on this activity. Have each group present their *balneario* to the class. At the end of all the presentations, students can vote on the *balneario* that they would most like to visit. What were the deciding factors?

DESAFÍO 2

Comunicación

52 **Es importante relajarse**

 ▶ **Escucha** la conversación entre Michelle y Daniel, y decide si estas oraciones son ciertas o falsas. Después, corrige las falsas.

1. Es necesario que Daniel y Michelle cierren los ojos.
2. La monitora les pide a Michelle y a Daniel que hagan bien los ejercicios.
3. Para Michelle es importante relajarse.
4. A Daniel le parece mal que Michelle haga yoga.
5. A Daniel no le relaja hacer yoga.
6. Michelle cree que es necesario que Daniel la escuche.

53 **¡Visita nuestro balneario!**

▶ **Lee** este folleto y responde a las preguntas.

Un paraíso para disfrutar

Aguasclaras es un complejo situado en la costa atlántica de Uruguay, en un entorno tranquilo, el lugar perfecto para descansar. Desde 1960, Aguasclaras ofrece interesantes propuestas turísticas para todos los gustos.

En Aguasclaras encontrará una gran variedad de alojamientos. Puede elegir uno de nuestros fantásticos hoteles, alojarse en el cámping o alquilar una cabaña en el bosque.

En sus hermosas playas de arenas blancas, podrá practicar numerosos deportes acuáticos y disfrutar del paisaje.

En el club deportivo hay gimnasio, piscina e instalaciones para practicar voleibol, fútbol y tenis. Además, el club cuenta con un grupo de monitores profesionales que organizan actividades para niños.

Además, en Aguasclaras podrá disfrutar de buenos restaurantes, locales de moda y tiendas de todo tipo.

¡Venga a visitarnos!

1. ¿Qué es Aguasclaras?
2. ¿Dónde está situado?
3. ¿Cuándo se inauguró?
4. ¿Qué tipo de alojamientos ofrece?
5. ¿Qué deportes se pueden practicar allí?
6. ¿Te gustaría pasar unas vacaciones en Aguasclaras o prefieres un hotel con *spa*? ¿Por qué?

Differentiated Instruction

DEVELOPING LEARNERS

- Ask students to complete these sentences:
  1. *¿Te parece bien que Miguel llamarte / te llame tan tarde?* (te llame)
  2. *Es un lugar perfecto para / por descansar.* (para)
  3. *Por / Para mí, es importante hacer / que haga ejercicio.* (Para, hacer)
  4. *Es conveniente que llegas / llegues a tiempo.* (llegues)
  5. *Me parece mal que perder / pierdas la clase de yoga por / para llegar tarde.* (pierdas, por)
  6. *Me parece bien que te relajas / relajes en un balneario.* (relajes)

EXPANDING LEARNERS

- Ask students to imagine that they are the principal of the school and will write a response to the student-generated letters from activity 54. They will need to justify the reasons for eliminating the physical education program and all the sports in which the school participates. Explain to students that the letters may state rational reasons for eliminating these programs, or the reasons may be illogical and humorous. Encourage students to use the subjunctive with value statements.

54 **Exprésate**

▶ **Imagina** que tu escuela piensa reducir los programas de Educación Física y todos los deportes. Escríbele una carta al director(a) explicándole la importancia de estos programas.

Modelo

> Estimado señor Director:
>
> Los programas de Educación Física son muy importantes para la salud de los alumnos. Por eso me parece sorprendente que los quieran reducir. Es necesario que...

Final del desafío

—¿Miramos las fotos del hotel? Podemos seleccionar las mejores y escribir sobre ellas.

—Yo creo que es mejor que los dos __1__ antes las secciones de la página web.
    (pensar)

—¿Tienes algo pensado?

—Podemos poner una sobre las instalaciones, otra sobre las actividades, otra sobre las tarifas...

—Espera, espera, no tan deprisa. ¿Ponemos algo sobre los tratamientos terapéuticos?

—Sí, claro. Es importante que __2__ sobre los servicios terapéuticos que ofrecen.
    (escribir)

¿Te parece bien que __3__ esta foto de la piscina?
    (poner)

—Prefiero esta de los masajes, es más bonita. Además, ¿no te parece sorprendente que en el balneario __4__
    (dar)
masajes con piedras calientes?

—Sí, es muy original. También es necesario __5__
    (informar)
sobre las instalaciones del hotel.

—¿Por ejemplo?

—Pues las habitaciones, el restaurante, la piscina...

—Ah, bien. ¿Y qué más?

55 **Te toca a ti**

▶ **Completa** la conversación entre Michelle y Daniel. Presta atención a los tiempos de los verbos.

 ▶ **Habla** con tu compañero(a). ¿Qué secciones de la página web consideras más importantes para promocionar el balneario? ¿Por qué te parecen necesarias?

⚑→ **TU DESAFÍO** Visita la página web. Escucha las preguntas de la *Minientrevista Desafío 2* y escribe las respuestas.

doscientos tres 203

HERITAGE LANGUAGE LEARNERS

- Ask students to imagine that they are reporters for a local paper and have gone to the grand opening of a *balneario*. Their job is to write a review of the hotel, describing where it is, what special services it offers, what accommodations are available and their prices, and how to go about making a reservation or requesting more information. Of course, they will also need to include their personal opinion.

MULTIPLE INTELLIGENCES:
Musical-Rhythmic Intelligence

- Explain to students that to complement the web page for their spa, Michelle and Daniel have asked them to create a song that promotes it. Have students review the descriptions of the *balnearios* they have read about in this *Desafío,* and ask them to work with two or three classmates to come up with the words and the melody. Give them time to rehearse their song and then call on volunteer groups to sing it in front of the class.

---

54. Before starting this activity, assign one of the following roles to each of the students: *un profesor de educación física, un atleta, un padre, un estudiante.* Ask each student to represent this perspective in his or her letter to the principal. After writing the letter, assign students to groups of four (with each perspective represented in each group). Have students debate the pros and cons of the cancellation of physical education classes. They should represent the opinions and perspectives presented in their letters.

🎧 **AUDIO SCRIPT**
See page 173I.

Answer Key

52. 1. Cierto.
2. Falso. Les pide que respiren profundamente y cierren los ojos.
3. Cierto.
4. Falso. A Daniel le parece bien que Michelle haga yoga.
5. Cierto.
6. Falso. Es necesario que Daniel escuche a la monitora.

53. 1. Es un balneario.
2. En la costa atlántica de Uruguay.
3. Se inauguró en 1960.
4. Ofrece hoteles, cámping y cabañas en el bosque.
5. Deportes acuáticos, voleibol, fútbol y tenis.
6. Answers will vary.

54. Answers will vary.

55. 1. pensemos   4. den
2. escribamos   5. informar
3. pongamos
▶ Answers will vary.

Additional Resources

Fans Online activities
Practice Workbook

203

Unit 4

DESAFÍO 3

Dar consejos y hacer recomendaciones

Presentation

- In *Desafío 3*, Asha and Lucas will interview a medical specialist who works at the oldest hospital in the Americas. Students will preview vocabulary to talk about health, and structures to give recommendations.

Activities	Standards	Resources
Texto	1.2, 2.2	Vis. Pres.
56.	1.2, 1.3	
57.	1.1, 1.2	
58.	1.1, 1.2	Audio
59. Cultura	1.2, 2.2, 3.1, 3.2	

Teaching Suggestions

Warm-Up / Independent Starter

- Have students write a short paragraph describing what they imagine a hospital would have been like in the year 1524. Who would it serve? What ailments would it treat? What would medical treatment be like?

Preparation

- Invite volunteers to share their Independent Starters. List the main points and see if anyone came up with a unique historical perspective.
- You may want to prepare a short list of well-known hospitals in the United States (e.g, Mayo Clinic, Johns Hopkins Hospital, Massachusetts General Hospital) and some basic information about them, in order to compare them with *Hospital de Jesús*.

Texto: El hospital más antiguo de las Américas

- Read the introduction aloud. Then have students read the dialogue silently. Have them write any words they can't identify or any constructions they don't understand. Review students' lists as a class. Then have two volunteers read the dialogue in front of the class.
- Ask students to brainstorm ways in which Asha and Lucas can approach Dr. Sánchez and ask for an interview. Will the doctor agree to do the interview? Poll the class.

204

El hospital más antiguo de las Américas

 A famous medical specialist is in town for a conference. Her name is Dr. Lucía Sánchez, and she works at the oldest hospital in the Americas. Asha and Lucas must interview her and write a brief biography for the local newspaper. But where will they find her?

LUCAS: ¿Ya averiguaste cuál es el hospital más antiguo de las Américas?

ASHA: Sí, es el Hospital de Jesús. Está en la Ciudad de México.

LUCAS: ¿Y cómo vamos a entrevistar a una especialista de ese hospital? ¿Tenemos que ir a México?

ASHA: No, estamos de suerte. Leí en el periódico que la doctora Lucía Sánchez da una conferencia aquí, en la ciudad. Ella trabaja en el Hospital de Jesús.

LUCAS: ¿En serio?

ASHA: Sí. La conferencia termina en media hora. Yo que tú me daría prisa.

LUCAS: Sí, sí. Vamos para allá.

ASHA: Mira, ahí está. ¡Cuánta gente!

LUCAS: ¿Sabes a qué se dedica?

ASHA: Sí, es pediatra. Antes trabajó como médica de familia, pero ahora se dedica exclusivamente a tratar a niños. ¿Por qué lo preguntas?

LUCAS: Porque últimamente me duele bastante la cabeza y quizá ella me pueda diagnosticar o recetar algún medicamento.

ASHA: ¡Pero no hemos venido aquí para una consulta, hemos venido para hacerle una entrevista!

LUCAS: Ya, ya. Oye, Asha, creo que la doctora Sánchez ya está terminando. Deberíamos acercarnos y presentarnos, ¿no crees?

ASHA: Claro.

56 · Detective de palabras

▶ **Completa** estas oraciones.

1. La doctora Sánchez es una ___1___ del Hospital de Jesús.
2. Antes trabajaba como ___2___ de familia, pero ahora es ___3___.
3. A Lucas le duele la ___4___.
4. Lucas piensa que quizás la doctora le pueda ___5___ o recetar algún ___6___.

▶ **Decide.** ¿Estas oraciones se refieren al pasado o al futuro?

1. Yo que tú me daría prisa.   2. Deberíamos acercarnos y presentarnos.

Differentiated Instruction

DEVELOPING LEARNERS

- Read the following false statements to students and ask them to make the statements true, according to the conversation.
  1. *El Hospital de Jesús está en Guadalajara, México.* (en Ciudad de México)
  2. *La especialista se llama Lucinda Gómez.* (Lucía Sánchez)
  3. *La doctora está aquí para ver a un paciente.* (para dar una conferencia)
  4. *La doctora es médica de familia.* (es pediatra)
  5. *A Lucas le duele bastante el estómago.* (le duele la cabeza)

EXPANDING LEARNERS

- Ask students to work in groups of three. Two will play the roles of Asha and Lucas, and the third student will be Dr. Sánchez, who has just finished giving her conference. Explain to students that they will role-play the first time the two participants meet the specialist. Have students imagine how they introduced themselves to her, how they explained what their *desafío* was, and how they were able to persuade her to do an interview. Dr. Sánchez may show some reluctance, but eventually agrees to the interview.

57 ¿Comprendes?

▶ **Responde** a estas preguntas.

1. ¿Dónde trabaja la doctora Lucía Sánchez?
2. ¿Qué está haciendo en la ciudad?
3. ¿Cuál es su especialidad?
4. ¿Qué tienen que hacer Asha y Lucas?

58 Síntomas

▶ **Escucha** y relaciona cada oración con la fotografía correspondiente.

▶ **Pregunta** a tu compañero(a). ¿Alguna vez tuvo esos síntomas? ¿Qué hizo?

CULTURA

El Hospital de Jesús

El Hospital de Jesús está en la Ciudad de México y es el más antiguo de las Américas. Fue fundado en 1524 por Hernán Cortés. Se dice que se construyó en el mismo lugar donde se encontraron por primera vez Cortés y Moctezuma, el emperador de los aztecas. Desde 1904 funciona como institución de beneficencia privada y atiende a personas sin recursos económicos.

59 Piensa. ¿Qué crees que hacía la gente si necesitaba cuidados médicos cuando no existían los hospitales? ¿Qué tipo de cuidados médicos crees que había en la época de Hernán Cortés?

HERITAGE LANGUAGE LEARNERS

- Ask students to research *el Hospital de Jesús* and to share this information with the rest of the class. For example, they will learn that the hospital was originally called *Hospital de la Purísima Concepción de Nuestra Señora* and that it was built to offer medical services to poor Spanish soldiers and the indigenous people of Mexico. The hospital also has a mural by José Clemente Orozco that depicts *el encuentro* between the Spaniards and the native peoples of Mexico.

SPECIAL-NEEDS LEARNERS

- Help students who have difficulties staying focused while reading a dialogue of some length by copying portions of the dialogue onto copy paper and then cutting it into four or five parts. Have students work with a partner and first take turns reading the parts as they appear in the text. Then, mix up the parts you have copied and cut, and have students put them in the correct order and role-play the conversation again. Guide them as they are putting the conversation in the proper order.

Activities

58. In order to prepare students for this activity, have them work in pairs to review vocabulary to talk about illnesses. Ask them to list as many words as they remember. For example: *alergia* (allergy), *resfriado* (cold), etc.

59. Ask volunteers to share their answers and write the main ideas on the board.

 AUDIO SCRIPT
See page 173J.

 CULTURA

El Hospital de Jesús

The *Hospital de Jesús* has been helping low-income patients for almost five centuries. The building has been designated a World Heritage Site. Inside the building there are many important and valuable art and cultural works. The hospital was the site of some of the first autopsies and organ dissections performed in the Americas.

Answer Key

56.
1. especialista	4. cabeza
2. médica	5. diagnosticar
3. pediatra	6. medicamento

▶ Se refieren al futuro.

57.
1. En el Hospital de Jesús, en la Ciudad de México.
2. Está dando una conferencia.
3. Su especialidad es pediatría.
4. Entrevistar a la doctora Sánchez.

58. 1. A   2. C   3. D   4. B

▶ Answers will vary.

59. Answers will vary.

Additional Resources

Fans Online activities

205

DESAFÍO 3

Vocabulario – La consulta médica. El cuerpo humano

Presentation

- In this section, students will learn words to talk about health, the human body, medical procedures, and medical specialties.

Activities	Standards	Resources
Vocabulario	1.2, 3.1	
60.	1.2, 3.1	
61.	1.1, 1.2, 1.3	Audio
62.	1.2, 1.3	
63. Comunidades	1.2, 1.3, 2.1, 3.1, 4.2, 5.1, 5.2	

Teaching Suggestions

Warm-Up / Independent Starter

- Have students draw the outline of a human body and ask them to tag as many review body parts as they can remember.

Preparation

- Have a volunteer share his or her Independent Starter. After this presentation, ask students to add any additional body parts that they can remember.

- Ask students to read the text on page 206 and divide the highlighted words in two groups: 1. words related to a doctor's work (e.g., *análisis de sangre, diagnóstico*); 2. words related to a patient's symptoms (e.g., *escalofríos, mareos*). Have two volunteers read their lists and make sure they understand the meaning of the words. Use extra pictures, drawings, and gestures if needed. Emphasize pronunciation.

- Read the words in the *El cuerpo humano* and *Más vocabulario* sections aloud to model correct pronunciation and have students repeat them after you.

Activities

60. To expand this activity, prepare flashcards with one body part on each one. Pair students and ask them to describe the body part they have on their flashcard to a partner. Partners should try to guess the body part.

Vocabulario

La consulta médica

Me llamo Adriana y soy médica. Cada día vienen a la consulta muchos pacientes. Algunos solo quieren hacerse una **revisión** o unos **análisis de sangre**. Otros vienen porque tienen alguna enfermedad. Yo les pregunto cuáles son sus **síntomas**, les hago un **examen físico** y hago un **diagnóstico** de lo que les pasa.

> Estoy mareado (*dizzy*) y tengo escalofríos (*chills*).

> Le voy a tomar el pulso.

Cuando alguien se hace daño, le hacemos una **radiografía** para ver si tiene algún hueso roto. Si tiene una herida, la enfermera se encarga de **darle puntos** para cerrarla. Y si hay infección, le damos un **antibiótico**.

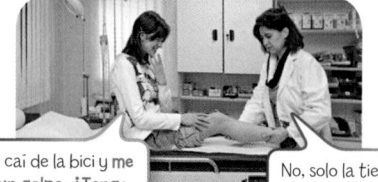

> Me caí de la bici y me di un golpe. ¿Tengo la pierna rota?

> No, solo la tienes hinchada (*swollen*). Te voy a recetar unas píldoras para el dolor.

El cuerpo humano

los músculos
el cerebro
el corazón
los pulmones
el hígado
el estómago
el intestino
los huesos

Más vocabulario

Especialistas médicos

el/la dentista	*dentist*
el/la oculista	*ophthalmologist*
el/la pediatra	*pediatrician*
el/la psicólogo(a)	*psychologist*

60 **Anatomía**

▶ **Une** las dos columnas.

(A)

1. Son blancos y duros. Forman el esqueleto del cuerpo.
2. Tenemos dos y los usamos para respirar.
3. Es el motor del cuerpo humano.
4. Es el órgano donde se reciben los alimentos.
5. Es un líquido de color rojo. Es vital para distribuir oxígeno.

(B)

a. el corazón
b. la sangre
c. el estómago
d. los huesos
e. los pulmones

206 doscientos seis

Differentiated Instruction

DEVELOPING LEARNERS

- To help students learn the vocabulary presented, have pairs play "Memory." Prepare two sets of index cards for each new word or phrase. Distribute the cards so that each student pair receives no more than ten, making sure there are two sets for each word. Place the cards facedown on a desk and have students try to match as many pairs as they can, saying each word or phrase along with its definition as they uncover cards. To make the game more challenging, you may ask students to use the word or phrase in a sentence.

EXPANDING LEARNERS

- Have students work with a partner and create a dialogue between a patient and his or her doctor. The patient is suffering from a series of "imaginary" ailments and explains them in detail to the doctor, who must listen patiently and try to convince the patient that there is nothing seriously wrong with him or her. Encourage students to use humor in both the description of their maladies as well as in their medical advice, and to use as many new vocabulary words and expressions as they can.

61 **Asha va al médico**

 ▶ **Escucha** y decide si estas oraciones son ciertas o falsas. Después, corrige las falsas.

1. Asha va al médico porque le duele el estómago.
2. Primero, la doctora le pone el termómetro.
3. Después, la doctora le examina la garganta.
4. Asha tiene una infección de garganta y de estómago.
5. La doctora le receta un jarabe.

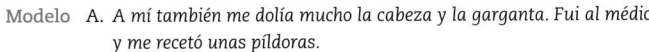 ▶ **Habla** con tu compañero(a). ¿Alguna vez tuviste los mismos síntomas que Asha? ¿Fuiste al médico? ¿Qué te recetó?

Modelo A. *A mí también me dolía mucho la cabeza y la garganta. Fui al médico y me recetó unas píldoras.*

 B. *¿Y qué clase de píldoras te recetó?*

 A. *Antibióticos.*

62 **Experiencias personales**

▶ **Responde** a las preguntas y escribe un párrafo para describir tu última visita al médico.

1. ¿Cuándo fuiste al médico por última vez?
2. ¿Por qué fuiste al médico?
3. ¿Qué síntomas tenías?
4. ¿Qué hizo el/la médico(a) en la consulta?
5. ¿Qué diagnosticó el/la médico(a)?
6. ¿Qué te recomendó hacer? ¿Te dio una receta para tomar algún medicamento?

 **COMUNIDADES**

LA DONACIÓN DE ÓRGANOS

España es líder mundial en el número de donantes de órganos. En 2011 las cifras se situaban en 35,3 donantes por millón de habitantes, muy por encima de la media europea y nueve puntos más que en los Estados Unidos. Los trasplantes que más se realizan son los de riñón, hígado, corazón y pulmón.

63 **Investiga.** ¿Cuál es el número de donantes de órganos en tu comunidad? ¿Esta cifra está aumentando en los últimos años? Haz un gráfico para mostrar los resultados.

Cualquiera de ellos podría salvarte la vida. ¿No harías tú lo mismo?

Donación sin Fronteras ONT

HERITAGE LANGUAGE LEARNERS

• Ask students to research the number of organ donors in proportion to the population in this country and in their family's country of origin (or another Spanish-speaking country they know). Also ask students to list the organs that are most frequently donated. Have them compile this information in a chart or graph and compare the statistics. Ask them how this information compares to what is stated in the *Comunidades* feature on the page.

MULTIPLE INTELLIGENCES:
Visual-Spatial Intelligence

• Ask students to make a poster that promotes the benefits of organ donation and blood donation. Students can invent a name for an organization that sponsors this endeavor and a title or slogan that will get viewers' attention, or they can research local organizations that are actively involved in the topic. They may model their posters after the one pictured on page 207, but they should be creative and come up with new ideas.

Vocabulario – La consulta médica. El cuerpo humano

61. Encourage students to imagine a different health problem if they did not have Asha's symptoms. For example:

A. *A mí no me dolía la cabeza, pero me dolía mucho el estómago, y fui al médico.*

B. *¿Y qué te dijo el médico?*

A. *Me dijo que debía descansar.*

62. For privacy reasons, suggest to students that they talk about a fictitious visit to a doctor.

 AUDIO SCRIPT
See page 173J.

 COMUNIDADES

La donación de órganos

Organ donation is the process of giving biological tissue, an organ, or part of an organ to be transplanted into another person. Experts note that one person's organs can help up to fifty people. Organ donation can occur with a deceased donor or with a living donor. Unfortunately, the need for organs is still greater than the supply.

Answer Key

60. 1. d   2. e   3. a   4. c   5. b

61. 1. Falso. Le duele la cabeza.
2. Cierto.
3. Falso. Escucha los pulmones de Asha.
4. Falso. Tiene una infección de garganta y de oídos.
5. Falso. Le receta antibióticos.
▶ Answers will vary.

62. Answers will vary.

63. Answers will vary.

Additional Resources

Fans Online activities
Practice Workbook

DESAFÍO 3

Gramática – El condicional

Presentation

- In this section, students will learn the conjugation and uses of the conditional tense.

Activities	Standards	Resources
Gramática	1.2, 3.1	
64.	1.3, 4.1	
65.	1.2, 1.3	
66.	1.2, 1.3	
67.	1.3	
68.	1.1, 1.2	

Teaching Suggestions

Warm-Up / Independent Starter

- Have students conjugate the following verbs in the future tense:

  1. *nosotros – decir*
  2. *ella – poner*
  3. *ellas – tener*
  4. *ustedes – hacer*
  5. *usted – saber*
  6. *tú – salir*
  7. *yo – querer*
  8. *eso – valer*
  9. *ellos – venir*
  10. *él – poder*

Preparation

- Ask a volunteer to read aloud the uses of the conditional listed on page 208. To clarify that this verb structure can refer to the present or the future, contextualize some examples.

PRESENTE	FUTURO
A. *¿Qué quieres comer?*	A. *¿Adónde irás este verano?*
B. *Me comería una pizza.*	B. *Me gustaría visitar París.*

- Have different volunteers share their Independent Starters. If necessary, correct students' responses and let them know that the conditional tense has the same irregular verbs. Then, ask students to conjugate the Independent Starter examples in the conditional forms.

Activities

66. After students finish this activity, give them the following sentence starters and have students complete them with verbs in the conditional:

  1. *Si me tocara la lotería…*
  2. *Si viajar en el tiempo fuera posible…*

Gramática

El condicional

El condicional

- To express wishes for the future, we can use the conditional. The conditional tense is equivalent to the English construction *would + verb*, when referring to the present or the future, not to the past.

  Me **gustaría** cenar en un restaurante.

- This tense is called *conditional* because it is used to talk about the things that could occur in the present or future if certain conditions are met.

  Iría a la fiesta (si me invitaran/si me diera tiempo/si tuviera un vestido adecuado…).
  I would go to the party (if they invited me/if I had the time/if I had the right dress …).

Formación del condicional

- The conditional is formed by adding the endings -ía, -ías, -ía, -íamos, -íais, -ían to the infinitive:

CONDICIONAL. VERBOS REGULARES

	Hablar	Comer	Escribir
yo	hablaría	comería	escribiría
tú	hablarías	comerías	escribirías
usted, él, ella	hablaría	comería	escribiría
nosotros(as)	hablaríamos	comeríamos	escribiríamos
vosotros(as)	hablaríais	comeríais	escribiríais
ustedes, ellos(as)	hablarían	comerían	escribirían

- The twelve verbs that have changes in their stems in the future tense have the same change in the conditional tense.

CONDICIONAL. VERBOS IRREGULARES

poder → podr-	decir → dir-
poner → pondr-	hacer → har-
salir → saldr-	querer → querr-
tener → tendr-	saber → sabr-
venir → vendr-	haber → habr-
valer → valdr-	caber → cabr-

64 **Compara.** ¿Cómo se traduce al español la oración *When we were young, we would get a cold every winter?* ¿Qué tiempo se usa en español?

65 **Mensaje de texto**

▶ **Completa** el mensaje de texto que le envía Lucas a un amigo. Usa el condicional.

llegar   pedir   saber   poder

¿ ___1___ venir a buscarme a la escuela? Tengo una cita con el médico. Se lo ___2___ a mi hermano, pero él no ___3___ a tiempo. ¿Tú ___4___ cómo llegar al Hospital San Juan?

Differentiated Instruction

DEVELOPING LEARNERS

- Ask students to complete the following sentences with the conditional of the verb in parentheses:

  1. *Hace mucho frío. Yo no (salir) esta noche.* (saldría)
  2. *¿(Nosotros – poder) hacerte una pregunta?* (Podríamos)
  3. *En un coche más grande, (nosotros – caber) todos.* (cabríamos)
  4. *¿Qué (decir) tus padres?* (dirían)
  5. *No sé qué (hacer) yo sin ti.* (haría)
  6. *Yo (saber) qué hacer.* (sabría)

EXPANDING LEARNERS

- Ask students to write at least one paragraph in which they describe what they would like to do in the future, after they graduate from high school. Their plans could be rational and thoughtful (e.g., *iría a la universidad, compartiría un apartamento con dos compañeros*) or they could be extravagant (e.g., *pasaría un año viajando por el mundo, me compraría un coche deportivo*). After they complete their paragraphs, ask students to read them aloud to the rest of the class.

66 Un viaje alrededor del mundo

▶ **Une** las dos columnas para formar oraciones lógicas. Pon los verbos en condicional y escribe las oraciones.

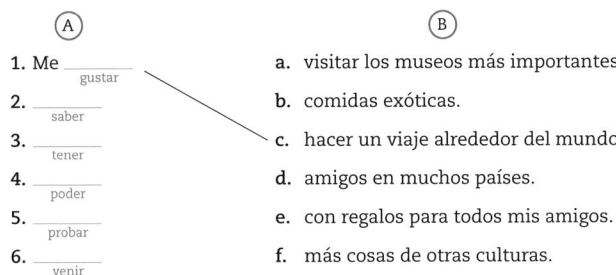

A		B
1. Me _____ (gustar)		a. visitar los museos más importantes.
2. _____ (saber)		b. comidas exóticas.
3. _____ (tener)		c. hacer un viaje alrededor del mundo.
4. _____ (poder)		d. amigos en muchos países.
5. _____ (probar)		e. con regalos para todos mis amigos.
6. _____ (venir)		f. más cosas de otras culturas.

Modelo 1. *Me gustaría hacer un viaje alrededor del mundo.*

67 ¿Qué haría?

▶ **Escribe.** Piensa en tu mejor amigo(a). ¿Qué haría en estas situaciones?

Modelo Me duele el pie, pero quiero jugar al fútbol.
→ *Jessie en mi lugar no jugaría y se pondría hielo en el pie.*

1. No me encuentro bien, pero voy a subir a la pirámide de Cuicuilco.
2. Me siento un poco débil, pero quiero hacer ejercicio.
3. Me duelen los oídos y estoy mareado.
4. Ayer me di un golpe en la muñeca y hoy no la puedo mover bien.
5. Me duele el estómago, pero tengo hambre.
6. Mi médico se muda a otro estado la semana próxima.

▶ **Elige** las oraciones más originales y compártelas con la clase.

68 ¿Qué harían ustedes?

▶ **Habla** con tu compañero(a). ¿Qué harían ustedes en estas situaciones? Intenten llegar a un acuerdo.

1. Estás planeando ir de viaje al extranjero.
2. Tienes fiebre.
3. Tu mejor amigo(a) se traslada a vivir a otro país.
4. Estás en un hospital en México y el médico no habla inglés.
5. Tu mejor amigo se da un golpe en la cabeza y está mareado.
6. Ves que una persona se cae al cruzar la calle y no se levanta.

Buscaríamos una buena oferta y elegiríamos un país interesante.

HERITAGE LANGUAGE LEARNERS

• Ask students to describe what their life would be like if they moved back to live in their family's country of origin. Ask them to describe where they would live, what they would study in school, what language or languages they might speak, what their meals would be like and when would they have them, what sports they would play, and how they would spend their free time. Call on volunteers to read their compositions to the other students.

MULTIPLE INTELLIGENCES:
Interpersonal Intelligence

• Ask students to work in groups of three and role-play friends who cannot decide what to do or where to go this weekend. One student will be a negotiator who will try to settle the friends' differences. You can get students started by giving them the following example:

A. *Yo iría al cine.*
B. *Pues, yo no. A mí me gustaría ir de compras.*
C. *Bueno, podríamos ir al cine el sábado por la noche, y el domingo podríamos ir de compras. ¿Qué les parece?*

DESAFÍO 3
Gramática – El condicional

68. While students are working on the activity, draw a six-column chart with the following headings on the board: *Viaje al extranjero, Fiebre, Amigo en otro país, Médico no habla inglés, Golpe en la cabeza, Persona en el suelo.* Have volunteers write their recommendations under the appropriate category.

Answer Key

64. Se traduce: Cuando éramos jóvenes nos resfriábamos todos los inviernos. En español se utiliza el imperfecto en este contexto.

65. 1. Podrías   3. llegaría
     2. pediría   4. sabrías

66. 2. (f) Sabría más cosas de otras culturas.
     3. (d) Tendría amigos en muchos países.
     4. (a) Podría visitar los museos más importantes.
     5. (b) Probaría comidas exóticas.
     6. (e) Vendría con regalos para todos mis amigos.

67. Answers will vary. Sample answers:
     1. Toni en mi lugar no subiría y llamaría a un médico.
     2. Lucía en mi lugar no haría ejercicio y descansaría.
     3. Sara en mi lugar iría al médico.
     4. Luis en mi lugar iría a urgencias.
     5. Sam en mi lugar no comería nada y tomaría un té caliente.
     6. Carmen en mi lugar buscaría otro médico lo antes posible.
    ▶ Answers will vary.

68. Answers will vary.

Additional Resources

Fans Online activities
Practice Workbook

DESAFÍO 3

Gramática – Dar consejos y hacer recomendaciones

Presentation

- In this section, students will learn and practice how to give advice and make recommendations.

Activities	Standards	Resources
Gramática	1.2, 3.1	
69.	4.1	
70.	1.2, 1.3	Audio
71.	1.3	
72.	1.1	
73. Conexiones	1.2, 2.2, 3.1	

Teaching Suggestions

Warm-Up / Independent Starter

- Ask students to write six recommendations to people they know in order to help them improve their health. Have them use these expressions: *hay que, tener que, deber, necesitar.*

Preparation

- Ask students to read the grammar presentation and clarify any questions they might have. Then have students rewrite the examples from their Independent Starters using the grammar structures on page 210. For example:

Tienes que hacer deporte. → *Te aconsejo que hagas deporte.*

Activities

70. After finishing this activity, ask students to get together with a classmate and read their recommendation for Lucas. Have partners integrate their recommendations to come up with just one recommendation for Lucas.

72. Ask students to write three or four recommendations for a famous person without mentioning his or her name. Have volunteers read their recommendations and the rest of the class guess whom the recommendations are for.

73. Write on the board the list of inventions that students came up with. If possible, have students work in small groups and ask each group to research one of the inventions.

Gramática

Dar consejos y hacer recomendaciones

- To give advice or to make recommendations to others, you may use the following verbs:

  aconsejar *(to advise)*   recomendar (e > ie) *(to recommend)*   sugerir (e > ie) *(to suggest)*

  These three verbs can be used with either the infinitive or the subjunctive:

  El médico le **recomienda beber** agua.
  El médico le **recomienda** que **beba** agua.

- You can also use deber + *infinitive* in the present (debes) or in the conditional (deberías). The verb deber suggests a certain amount of obligation:

  Debes beber agua.   **Deberías** beber más agua.

Expresiones coloquiales para dar consejos y hacer recomendaciones

- It is common to give advice by putting yourself in the place of the other person. In this case, the conditional is used:

  Yo lo llamaría.

- Sometimes these colloquial expressions are used to show that the speaker is putting himself or herself in the other person's place.

Yo en tu lugar + conditional	Yo en tu lugar lo llamaría.
Yo que tú + conditional	Yo que tú iría a su casa.

69 **Compara.** ¿Cómo se construyen en inglés las recomendaciones dirigidas a una persona? ¿Y las recomendaciones generales? ¿Es similar este contraste en español?

70 **Los problemas de Lucas**

 ▶ **Escucha** la conversación entre Lucas y Asha y decide si estas oraciones son ciertas o falsas. Después, corrige las falsas.

1. Lucas está triste porque le duele la pierna y no puede jugar al fútbol.
2. Asha le recomienda a Lucas que vaya a urgencias.
3. El médico le recomendó tomar unas píldoras para el dolor.
4. Asha le sugiere a Lucas que avise al entrenador de baloncesto.
5. Asha le recomienda que juegue con cuidado para no ponerse peor.

▶ **Escribe** una recomendación para Lucas.

210 doscientos diez

Differentiated Instruction

DEVELOPING LEARNERS

- Ask students to rewrite the following recommendations and advice by changing the verb to the subjunctive:

1. *Me aconseja dormir más horas. (Me aconseja que duerma más horas.)*
2. *Te sugiero estudiar. (Te sugiero que estudies.)*
3. *Nos recomiendan esperar una hora. (Nos recomiendan que esperemos una hora.)*
4. *El médico me recomienda comer más verduras. (El médico me recomienda que coma más verduras.)*
5. *Le aconsejamos viajar a Chile. (Le aconsejamos que viaje a Chile.)*

EXPANDING LEARNERS

- Ask students to make a list of what they should do and what they should not do in these places: *la escuela, la casa, la calle, la biblioteca.* Have students use a different verbal structure for each category. Use the following examples to get them started:

  – *En la escuela: No deben comer en clase.*
  – *En casa: Aconsejamos que ayuden con las tareas domésticas.*
  – *En la calle: Yo no montaría en monopatín.*
  – *En la biblioteca: Deberían hablar en voz baja.*

71 **Recomendaciones para todos**

▶ **Escribe** recomendaciones apropiadas para cada situación.

Modelo Montar en bicicleta
→ *Recomiendo llevar un casco para proteger la cabeza.*

1. Tener síntomas de alergia.
2. Darse un golpe muy fuerte en la cabeza.
3. Sufrir dolor de estómago con frecuencia.
4. Romperse un tobillo.
5. Sentirse débil.

72 **¡Hay que cuidarse!**

▶ **Habla** con tu compañero(a). Decidan la mejor recomendación para cada persona.

Modelo A. *Le sugiero a Eva que descanse y no estudie más hasta mañana.*
B. *Estoy de acuerdo. Yo en su lugar dormiría.*

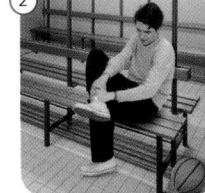

CONEXIONES: TECNOLOGÍA

El marcapasos

El marcapasos es un aparato que regula el latido *(beat)* del corazón por impulsos eléctricos. Lo inventó Jorge Reynolds Pombo, un ingeniero colombiano, en 1958. Esta máquina revolucionaria era tan grande que había que llevar la batería en una carretilla *(wheelbarrow)*. Hoy en día tiene el tamaño de un reloj *(watch)* y se coloca dentro del cuerpo del enfermo.

73 **Piensa.** ¿Puedes pensar en otros inventos que revolucionaron la medicina?

Gramática – Dar consejos y hacer recomendaciones

 AUDIO SCRIPT
See page 173 J.

 CONEXIONES: TECNOLOGÍA

El marcapasos

The first pacemaker made by Jorge Reynolds Pombo weighted about 100 lbs., and had to be recharged from an automobile every 72 hours! With time, pacemaker designs became lighter and wearable, and eventually were implanted directly into the body.

Answer Key

69. Se usa el infinitivo en las recomendaciones a alguien en concreto y el gerundio en las recomendaciones generales. Por ejemplo: *The doctor advises Jenn to exercise.* (El doctor le aconseja a Jenn que haga ejercicio.) *The doctor advises exercising.* (El doctor recomienda hacer ejercicio.)

70. 1. Falso. Le duele la mano y no puede jugar al baloncesto.
2. Falso. Le sugiere que vaya al médico.
3. Cierto.
4. Cierto.
5. Falso. Le recomienda que descanse y se olvide del partido.
▶ Answers will vary.

71. Answers will vary. Sample answers:
1. Sugiero tomar medicamentos.
2. Aconsejo ir a urgencias lo antes posible.
3. Recomiendo cuidar la dieta.
4. Aconsejo tener el pie quieto y no moverse.
5. Sugiero descansar y tomar vitaminas.

72. Answers will vary.

73. Answers will vary.

Additional Resources

Fans Online activities
Practice Workbook

HERITAGE LANGUAGE LEARNERS

• There are several idiomatic expressions that use words for parts of the body. For example, to indicate that one must be careful, Spanish speakers say *¡Ojo!* Ask students to make a list of such expressions, explain what they mean, and share them with the class. Other examples include: *tener mano para algo* (to be good at something), *en boca cerrada no entran moscas* (if you keep your mouth shut, you won't put your foot in it), *ser un cerebro* (to be brainy), *costar un riñón* (to cost an arm and a leg).

MULTIPLE INTELLIGENCES:
Interpersonal Intelligence

• Ask students to work with a partner and have both write a letter to an advice columnist with a problem they are having. For privacy reasons, student may invent the problem. Ask partners to exchange letters and write a suitable reply, using the verbs that have been presented in this lesson. Call on volunteers to read both the letter asking for advice and the reply aloud to the rest of the class.

Unit 4
LECTURA: TEXTO LITERARIO

Presentation

- In this section, students will read an Aztec legend about the origins of corn in Mexico. As they read, they will recognize cognates and expressions that refer to nutrition and food.

Activities	Standards	Resources
Lectura: texto literario	1.2, 2.2, 3.1, 3.2	
74.	1.1, 1.2	
75.	1.2, 1.3, 2.2	

Teaching Suggestions

Warm-Up / Independent Starter

- Ask students to read the title of the reading. Then have them answer these questions related to their prior knowledge about corn: *¿Dónde se originó el maíz? ¿Dónde se cultiva en la actualidad? ¿Cómo se come? ¿Qué usos tiene el maíz?*

Preparation

- Have students work with a partner to read the *Antes de leer* strategies. Then ask pairs to write the answers to the questions posed. Once pairs have finished, discuss the answers as a class.

- Call on individual students to share their responses from the Independent Starter. Discuss their knowledge about corn. Are they familiar with the origins of corn? Do they know that corn was not known in Europe before the 15th century? Are students aware that corn is the most widely grown crop in America? Discuss some of the uses of corn (e.g., for human consumption, for animal feed, to produce ethanol).

- Read the legend aloud to model pronunciation and have students follow along in their books. Then call on individual students to each read a paragraph aloud. Offer assistance with pronunciation of the proper nouns in the story.

- Make sure that students understand the word *hormiga* (ant). With what qualities do students associate this insect? Why do they think Quetzalcóatl chooses the form of an ant? What other legends do students know in which ants have an important role?

212

LECTURA: TEXTO LITERARIO

Antes de leer: estrategias

1. Lee el título. ¿De qué crees que trata? ¿Qué sabes sobre el maíz?
2. Busca los cognados. ¿Qué significan las palabras *acceso, colosal, dificultades, esfuerzos, grano* y *preciado*?
3. Busca las palabras que se refieren a la alimentación. Clasifícalas en nombres, adjetivos y verbos.

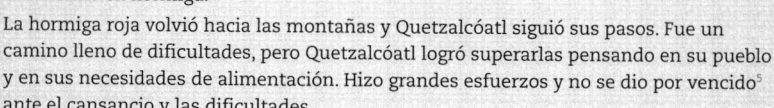

La leyenda del maíz

Cuentan las historias antiguas que, antes de la llegada del dios Quetzalcóatl, los aztecas se alimentaban de raíces y de los animales que cazaban[1]. En aquellos tiempos no tenían maíz porque este cereal estaba escondido[2] detrás de las montañas y ellos no tenían acceso a él.

Algunos dioses intentaron separar las montañas con su colosal fuerza, pero no lo lograron. Entonces los aztecas le plantearon[3] el problema a Quetzalcóatl.

—Yo les traeré el maíz —les respondió el dios.

Quetzalcóatl no intentó separar las montañas con su fuerza, sino que empleó su astucia[4]. Vio a una pequeña hormiga roja que descendía de la montaña llevando un trocito de maíz y se transformó en hormiga.

La hormiga roja volvió hacia las montañas y Quetzalcóatl siguió sus pasos. Fue un camino lleno de dificultades, pero Quetzalcóatl logró superarlas pensando en su pueblo y en sus necesidades de alimentación. Hizo grandes esfuerzos y no se dio por vencido[5] ante el cansancio y las dificultades.

Quetzalcóatl llegó hasta donde estaba el maíz, tomó un grano maduro[6] entre sus mandíbulas[7] y emprendió el regreso. Al llegar, entregó el prometido grano de maíz a los hambrientos[8] indígenas.

Los aztecas plantaron la semilla y así consiguieron el maíz que desde entonces sembraron y cosecharon. El preciado grano aumentó sus riquezas y ellos se volvieron más fuertes y construyeron ciudades, palacios, templos… Y desde entonces vivieron felices.

Desde ese momento, los aztecas veneraron al generoso Quetzalcóatl, el dios amigo de los hombres, el dios que les trajo el maíz.

Fuente: http://letrasparavolar.org/la-leyenda-del-maiz (texto adaptado)

1. *hunted*	3. *posed*	5. *didn't give up*	7. *jaws*
2. *hidden*	4. *astuteness*	6. *ripe*	8. *starving*

212 doscientos doce

Differentiated Instruction

DEVELOPING LEARNERS

- To help students better comprehend the legend, ask them to put the following events in order:

1. *Quetzalcóatl se transformó en una hormiga.* (5)
2. *Los aztecas sembraron el maíz.* (7)
3. *Los aztecas se alimentaban de raíces.* (1)
4. *Quetzalcóatl vio una hormiga roja.* (4)
5. *Algunos dioses intentaron separar las montañas.* (2)
6. *Quetzalcóatl llegó hasta donde estaba el maíz.* (6)
7. *Los aztecas le plantearon el problema a Quetzalcóatl.* (3)

EXPANDING LEARNERS

- Ask students to read the legend again, but this time they should define or provide a synonym for as many of the words that appear in the text as they can. Examples might include: *historias (cuentos), se alimentaban (comían), intentaron (trataron), respondió (contestó), se transformó en (se convirtió en), volvió (regresó), siguió (continuó), dificultades (problemas), superar (conquistar), el regreso (la vuelta), plantaron (sembraron), aumentó (incrementó), construyeron (hicieron).* After students compile their lists, check them for accuracy and see who has the most words.

74 **Comprensión**

▶ **Responde** a estas preguntas.

1. ¿Quién era Quetzalcóatl?
2. ¿Por qué los aztecas no se alimentaban de maíz?
3. ¿Quién llevó el maíz a los aztecas?
4. ¿Cómo lo consiguió?
5. ¿Qué consecuencias positivas tuvo el maíz para los aztecas?

▶ **Une** estos verbos que aparecen en la lectura con sus sinónimos.

Ⓐ

1. lograr
2. emplear
3. descender
4. entregar
5. venerar

Ⓑ

a. bajar
b. conseguir, obtener
c. adorar, honrar
d. usar, utilizar
e. dar

75 **Cuéntalo tú**

▶ **Ordena** estas ilustraciones según la lectura. Después, descríbelas.

Ⓐ

Ⓑ

Ⓒ

Ⓓ

▶ **Escribe** un resumen del texto.

doscientos trece 213

Activities

74. You may ask students to work in pairs to answers these questions. One partner can, for instance, look for each answer in the text and read the corresponding section aloud. The other partner listens to what his or her partner is reading and then writes the answer to the question.

75. As an alternative to the second part of this activity, you may ask students to research the legends surrounding the origins of another food or dish and write a summary. Some examples include: the potato and the pre-Incan god Viracocha; cocoa and Quetzalcóatl; coffee and an Ethiopian shepherd called Kaldi; the sandwich and John Montagu, 4th Earl of Sandwich. Encourage students to do the research in Spanish by providing them with appropriate websites in Spanish.

Answer Key

74. 1. Era el dios de los aztecas.
   2. Porque el maíz estaba escondido detrás de las montañas.
   3. El dios Quetzalcóatl.
   4. Se convirtió en una hormiga y siguió a una hormiga roja hasta el lugar donde estaba el maíz, y trajo una semilla.
   5. Aumentó sus riquezas y se volvieron fuertes y poderosos.
   ▶ 1. b   2. d   3. a   4. e   5. c

75. A, C, D, B
   ▶ Answers will vary.

Additional Resources

Fans Online activities

HERITAGE LANGUAGE LEARNERS

• There is a rich tradition of legends from across the American continents. Ask students to research some of these stories from their family's country of origin, or another Spanish-speaking country, and select one to retell to the rest of the class. Students may find legends about the origins of things, especially those products that are linked to the country's culture, like corn, or those that have to do with the creation of the Earth and sky.

SPECIAL-NEEDS LEARNERS

• Enlarge the images for activity 75 so that students with visual impairment can understand what is going on in the illustrations. You may also want to have students practice describing the contents of the images aloud before beginning the activity as a way to review vocabulary. Some students might benefit from responding orally rather than in writing to all the activities posted.

DESAFÍO 3

Comunicación

Presentation

- In this section, students will integrate the vocabulary and grammar skills from *Desafío 3* in order to talk about medical symptoms and procedures, give advice and recommendations, and talk about what they would do with a million-dollar inheritance.

Activities	Standards	Resources
76.	1.1, 1.2, 1.3, 5.1	
77.	1.1, 5.2	
78.	1.1, 1.3, 3.1, 5.1	
79. Final del desafío	1.1, 1.2, 1.3, 3.1	

Teaching Suggestions

Warm-Up / Independent Starter

- Ask students to write as many words as they remember under the following categories:
  1. *Partes del cuerpo y órganos.*
  2. *Problemas de salud.*

Preparation

- Divide the class into small groups. Have students share their Independent Starter lists in their group and create a common group list. Give each group different colored sticky notes and ask them to write each word for body parts and organs from their list on a sticky note.

- Draw or post a large picture of the human body on the board. Ask students to go one by one to the board and post a sticky note in the right place on the human body picture (they cannot repeat words). Make sure that every group has the same number of opportunities to go to the board. At the end, count the number of sticky notes from each team to find the winning team.

- Discuss as a class which *problemas de salud* are associated with each body part or organ. For example: *mareado → la cabeza; tos → los pulmones.* Use the same picture of the human body on the board and have students post sticky notes with the different health problems.

Comunicación

76 **El consultorio de Sonia**

▶ **Lee** la entrada de Asha en una página web de consultas. Habla con tu compañero(a) sobre las recomendaciones que puede darle Sonia a Asha.

Modelo   A. *Pienso que Sonia le puede recomendar a Asha que haga yoga antes de dormir.*

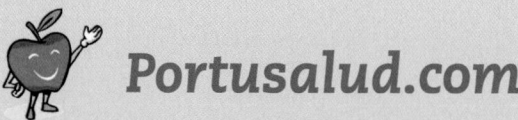

Salud	Enfermedades	Alergias	Medicamentos	Consultorio

Consultas

Querida Sonia:

Me llamo Asha y tengo diecisiete años. Tengo dos problemas de salud y me gustaría saber qué me recomienda. El primero es que tengo insomnio. No puedo dormir por las noches y por eso me siento mal durante el día. Además estoy de mal humor y no me puedo concentrar. ¿Qué podría hacer?

Mi segundo problema es un poco diferente. Tengo una nueva amiga. Se llama Gloria. Me encanta ir a su casa, pero cuando estoy allí comienzo a estornudar y a toser sin parar. En su casa hay muchas flores frescas. Yo creo que tengo alergia a alguna de esas flores, pero no sé cómo decírselo. A mí me gustaría visitarla más, pero me siento mal. Por eso prefiero no ir. ¿Qué me recomienda?

Asha

▶ **Escribe** tu propia entrada para la página web de consultas e intercámbiala con tu compañero(a). Puedes escribir sobre algo ficticio.

▶ **Lee** la entrada de tu compañero(a) y escribe recomendaciones para solucionar su problema.

77 **La herencia**

▶ **Escribe.** Imagina que recibes una herencia *(inheritance)* de un millón de dólares. Escribe qué harías:

| por tu familia | por tu escuela | por tu mejor amigo(a) | por tu comunidad |

Differentiated Instruction

DEVELOPING LEARNERS

- Ask students to complete these sentences:
  1. *El médico recomienda que tomes / tomas una aspirina.* (tomes)
  2. *Miguel debe / deberías dormir más horas.* (debe)
  3. *Yo que tú iría / iré a la fiesta.* (iría)
  4. *El profesor sugiere que estudiamos / estudiemos la lección.* (estudiemos)
  5. *¿Me aconsejas que vaya / voy de vacaciones?* (vaya)
  6. *Yo en tu lugar compraría / compre ese coche.* (compraría)
  7. *Debemos / Debamos comer más verduras.* (Debemos)

EXPANDING LEARNERS

- Ask students to imagine that the year is 1524 and they are in Mexico City. They are about to interview Hernán Cortés on the completion of the *Hospital de Jesús*. Have students work with a partner who will role-play Cortés. Students will ask Cortés questions regarding this hospital: why he decided to build it, who it is going to serve, how it was built, how Cortés obtained the funds needed, and how he feels seeing this work completed. Call on volunteer pairs to present their interviews in front of the class.

78 Más vale prevenir

▶ **Escribe.** Tu escuela va a publicar un folleto con recomendaciones para prevenir enfermedades y accidentes frecuentes. Haz una lista de recomendaciones.

▶ **Habla** con dos compañeros(as) y comparen sus listas. Escriban una lista común y preparen un folleto para presentarlo en la clase.

Final del desafío

1. Tengo una amiga que quiere ser pediatra, como usted. ¿Qué le aconsejaría?

2. ¿Qué les sugeriría a nuestros lectores para tener buena salud?

3. ¿Por qué eligió esta profesión?

4. ¿Cómo es el hospital donde trabaja usted?

a. Es un lugar con mucha historia. Es emocionante trabajar allí.

b. Siempre me ha gustado ayudar a la gente, y quería estudiar Ciencias.

c. Pues le recomendaría estudiar Biología, Química y Psicología.

d. Que se alimenten bien, hagan ejercicio y descansen. ¡Ah, y que visiten al médico de vez en cuando!

79 La entrevista

▶ **Relaciona** cada pregunta con la respuesta correspondiente. ¿Crees que las preguntas de Asha y Lucas son interesantes? ¿Por qué? Escríbelo.

▶ **Escribe** cuatro preguntas más con dos compañeros(as) para entrevistar a la doctora Sánchez. Después, representen la entrevista.

doscientos quince 215

HERITAGE LANGUAGE LEARNERS

• Ask students to describe some medical professions in their family's country of origin. They may address careers for physicians, nurses, dentists, pharmacists, or other healthcare workers. Ask them to talk to the class about the educational requirements, any other special training or residency, and the careers that are available to them after completing their education. Students might compare and contrast the roles pharmacists have in this country and in some Spanish-speaking countries, where they often have more authority in dispensing medicine.

CRITICAL THINKING

• Ask students to research other medical equipment, devices, or procedures that have revolutionized healthcare. Students may choose to investigate a centuries-old apparatus or explore the most recent medical innovations. Ask students to take notes from their research, and to prepare a written report with their findings. Be sure students select different devices or procedures so that there will be a variety of topics under investigation. Display students' work or call on volunteers to read their reports to the class.

Activities

77. You may turn this activity into a "Family Feud" game.

78. Bring large colored paper, markers, and magazine pictures to the classroom. Encourage students to create colorful and original brochures. When they are finished, post the brochures around the classroom and ask students to vote for the best one. If possible, post the winning brochure in a visible place in the school, such as the library or the cafeteria.

79. If possible, videotape the interviews. Show all or some interviews to the class and review any problems related to the unit vocabulary and grammar.

Answer Key

76. Answers will vary. Sample answer:
Para el insomnio, Sonia puede recomendarle a Asha que no tome café o bebidas con cafeína por la noche. Para el problema con su amiga, le puede sugerir que le explique que tiene alergia.
▶ Answers will vary.
▶ Answers will vary.

77. Answers will vary. Sample answers:
Por la familia: Los ayudaría a comprar una casa más grande y los invitaría a un crucero por el Caribe.
Por la escuela: Donaría dinero para mejorar la biblioteca y la sala de computación.
Por el mejor amigo: Lo invitaría a un viaje conmigo por Latinoamérica.
Por la comunidad: Ayudaría con un donativo a la creación de zonas verdes y a la construcción de una piscina comunitaria.

78. Answers will vary.
▶ Answers will vary.

79. 1. c   2. d   3. b   4. a
▶ Answers will vary.

Additional Resources

Fans Online activities
Practice Workbook

215

Unit 4
Para terminar

Presentation

- In this section, students will review the unit objectives and put them into practice. They will talk about their favorite dish, and will practice making recommendations. Students will also select one of the following *desafíos* to develop: research a typical dish from a Hispanic country, create a website for a *balneario*, or write an interview for a physician.

Activities	Standards	Resources
80.	1.1, 1.3, 3.1	
81.	1.1	
82. Tu desafío	1.2, 1.3, 2.1, 2.2, 3.1, 5.2	

Teaching Suggestions

Warm-Up / Independent Starter

- Have students go back and review the vocabulary and grammar sections in this unit. Then ask them to write a list of recommendations for a healthy lifestyle for people in the class.

Preparation

- Have students share their Independent Starters. You may have four students write their lists on the board at a time, or ask them to read their lists aloud. Those that have the most varied, accurate, and creative recommendations will be the winners. Call on a panel of volunteers to act as judges for the contest. Have students justify their choices for a winner or winners. Then discuss as a class some of the changes that people in the class would undergo if they followed these recommendations for a healthy lifestyle. For example: *Si hacemos ejercicio regularmente, nos haremos más fuertes. Si practicamos yoga nos convertiremos en personas más relajadas.*

- Ask students to think about what they had for lunch or dinner and to identify the ingredients of their meal. Call on volunteer students to share the information with the class. Then ask the class to suggest ways to improve these meals. For example: *Sugiero que no bebas un refresco con la comida. Yo en tu lugar acompañaría la comida con agua.*

216

Para terminar

Todo junto

ESCRIBIR

80 **Los mejores platos**

▶ **Escribe.** Mira las fotos y responde a las preguntas.

1. ¿Qué ingredientes ves en cada plato? Haz una lista.
2. ¿Cómo está cocinado cada uno: al horno, frito, hervido, en salsa…?
3. ¿Qué plato te parece más nutritivo? ¿Por qué?
4. ¿Qué plato crees que tiene menos calorías?
5. ¿Qué plato te gusta más? ¿Por qué?

▶ **Escribe** un párrafo describiendo tu plato preferido. Explica:

- ¿Qué ingredientes tiene?
- ¿Por qué te gusta?
- ¿Cuándo lo comes?
- ¿Quién lo prepara normalmente?
- ¿Cómo se prepara?

HABLAR Y ESCRIBIR

81 **Tus recomendaciones**

▶ **Habla** con tu compañero(a) y escriban dos recomendaciones para cada persona.

Modelo   *Es necesario que prepares un horario de estudio. Te recomiendo que…*

216 doscientos dieciséis

Differentiated Instruction

DEVELOPING LEARNERS

- Ask students whether the following statements are true (*cierto*) or false (*falso*):
  1. *Los pediatras les hacen exámenes físicos a la gente mayor. (falso)*
  2. *Si te das un golpe muy fuerte, puedes romperte un hueso. (cierto)*
  3. *Si te duelen los ojos, vas al oculista. (cierto)*
  4. *No necesitas una receta para los antibióticos. (falso)*
  5. *Si tu médico te recomienda algo, deberías hacerlo. (cierto)*
  6. *Es bueno tener escalofríos. (falso)*
  7. *Tengo dos corazones y un pulmón. (falso)*

EXPANDING LEARNERS

- Ask students which word does not belong and explain why it doesn't belong.
  1. oculista   píldoras   antibióticos (oculista)
  2. recomendar   sugerir   recetar (recetar)
  3. dentista   huesos   psicólogo (huesos)
  4. tomar el pulso   recetar   escalofríos (escalofríos)
  5. recomendado   mareado   hinchado (recomendado)
  6. radiografía   respirar   dar puntos (respirar)

Tu desafío

82 **Alimentación, salud e higiene**

¿Recuerdas los desafíos que Diana les dio a los personajes? ¿Cuál te gusta más? Elige una de estas opciones y resuelve tu desafío.

DESAFÍO (A)

Investiga sobre la comida tradicional de un país hispano y haz una presentación sobre uno de los platos típicos y sus ingredientes. Utiliza alguna fotografía.

DESAFÍO (B)

Diseña una página web para un balneario o un lugar de vacaciones. Incluye información sobre las instalaciones, las actividades que se pueden hacer y los lugares que se pueden visitar.

DESAFÍO (C)

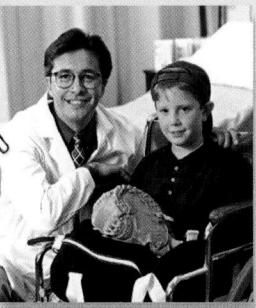

Prepara una entrevista a un(a) médico(a). Si es posible, hazle la entrevista y presenta los resultados. Si no, escribe una presentación del personaje y el cuestionario con tus preguntas.

doscientos diecisiete 217

Para terminar

Activities

80. To expand the second part of this activity, ask students to write a description of their favorite meal. This meal should include a starter (*primer plato*), an entree (*segundo plato*), a side dish (*acompañamiento*), a drink (*bebida*), and a dessert (*postre*). Invite volunteer students to share their descriptions with the class. Does the class find this meal appealing?

81. You may want to ask students to write a short paragraph from the point of view of the person in each photo, describing their health and lifestyle situation. Afterward, have students exchange their papers to see if they imagined similar situations for each person. Then, ask them to discuss the recommendations for each person.

82. Display students' work in the classroom and have the class vote on the best entry for each category.

Answer Key

80. Answers will vary. Sample answers:
1. La hamburguesa tiene pan, carne, lechuga, tomate y queso, y de acompañamiento papas fritas con salsa de tomate. El segundo plato tiene pescado, y de acompañamiento verduras y una ensalada. El tercer plato tiene pasta, salsa de tomate y queso. El cuarto plato tiene pollo y verduras.
2. La hamburguesa es frita. El pescado es al horno. La pasta es hervida y luego en salsa. El pollo es al horno.
3. El plato de pescado me parece que es más nutritivo porque el pescado tiene proteínas y minerales.
4. Creo que el plato de pescado tiene menos calorías porque está hecho al horno.
5. Answers will vary.
▶ Answers will vary.

81. Answers will vary.

82. Answers will vary.

Additional Resources

Fans Online activities

HERITAGE LANGUAGE LEARNERS

- Ask students to compare and contrast the typical diet from their family's country of origin to the typical diet of this country. Encourage them to describe the foods that are usually eaten in their heritage country, and ask them to explain why they think the diet from there is more healthful than, the same as, or less healthful than the diets here. Students should justify their opinions with facts about the foods they are describing.

MULTIPLE INTELLIGENCES:
Verbal-Linguistic Intelligence

- Ask students to review the *desafíos* in this unit and to write a conclusion to one of them. They may write a happy ending in which the participants successfully complete their challenge, or they may choose to describe a disastrous ending. As students describe how their chosen *desafío* ends, remind them to keep in mind the personalities of the participants and how successful they have been in the past. Invite students to share their compositions with the rest of the class.

217

Unit 4

MAPA CULTURAL

Alimentos básicos en el mundo hispano

Presentation

- This section presents information about different staple foods of the Spanish-speaking world. The images serve as a reference point for additional cultural readings and activities that expand on the skills students learned in this unit.

Activities	Standards	Resources
Mapa cultural	1.2, 2.1, 2.2, 3.2, 4.2	Video
83.	1.1, 1.3, 2.1, 2.2, 4.2, 5.1, 5.2	

Cultural Topics

- **La milpa.** A sophisticated land used evolved in Mesoamerica during the pre-Hispanic period. The ancient Mayas, Zapotecs, Aztecs, and other Mesoamerican peoples developed the *milpa*, a crop-growing system. These Mesoamerican farmers cleared a plot of land and planted corn, beans, and squash, which were their staple crops. They cultivated the milpa plot for two or three years. By then the soil had been depleted, so they let the plot lie fallow for about eight years to allow for natural renewal of soil fertility. This field rotation allowed farmers to produce enough food without using fertilizers and pesticides—neither of which existed at the time.

- **El arroz.** Rice is the most important staple food in the world. Though not native to the Americas, rice has become a staple food in many countries in Latin America, especially in the Caribbean basin and South America. There are many staple dishes that contain rice, such as *arroz con frijoles* (rice and beans), *arroz con gandules* (rice and pigeon peas), and *arroz con pollo* (chicken and rice). Rice is also important in Spain, since it is the main ingredient of *paella*, a well-known dish.

Teaching Suggestions

Warm-Up / Independent Starter

- Ask students to think about what they eat in a typical week. Is there a grain, root vegetable, legume, or fruit that they eat regularly?

Alimentos básicos en el mundo hispano

Desde hace siglos, productos como los cereales (el maíz, el arroz, el trigo) o las papas son alimentos básicos de la Humanidad. Estos productos proporcionan nutrientes esenciales y crecen abundantemente en distintas zonas del planeta, donde se han adaptado a distintas condiciones climatológicas. Muchos de esos alimentos son originarios de las Américas y desde aquí se extendieron al resto del mundo.

El maíz

El maíz es un alimento muy característico de la cocina latinoamericana. Fue un producto esencial para la alimentación de los mayas y los aztecas y está presente en sus creencias religiosas y en sus celebraciones. Se consume principalmente en México y en Centroamérica: las tortillas de maíz acompañan todas las comidas.

> Hay muchos tipos de maíz y mazorcas *(corncobs)* con diferentes tamaños y colores. El grano *(grain)* también puede tener distintas formas. Son curiosas las tortillas negras que se hacen en México con maíz negro.

El trigo

En España el trigo es el cereal más importante y se consume de distintas formas: con él se hace harina, pan, pasta o copos *(flakes)* para el desayuno.

> En Castilla, la región central de España, son frecuentes los paisajes llanos con campos de trigo y molinos *(mills)* de viento, donde antiguamente se molía el grano para hacer harina.

Differentiated Instruction

DEVELOPING LEARNERS

- Have pairs consisting of developing and heritage learners conduct a guided reading of the *Mapa cultural*. Have the developing learners take turns reading the text, sentence by sentence. As they pause between sentences, have the heritage learners say a true/false statement to check their comprehension. The developing learners must say whether the statement is true or false, and correct it if it is false. For example:

A. *El maíz es típico de la cocina española.*

B. *No, eso es falso. El maíz es típico de la cocina latinoamericana.*

EXPANDING LEARNERS

- Explain that the center of origin for a plant is also the part of the world where one can find the greatest genetic variation. Mexico is a center of genetic diversity for corn, and Peru for potatoes. Ask students to research a couple of heirloom varieties of Mexican corn and Peruvian potatoes. Have them compile information regarding the origin of the variety, the places where it grows, why it is appreciated, how it is used in dishes, etc. Ask students to summarize the information and present it to the class. Encourage them to include pictures.

La papa y la yuca

La papa y la yuca son tubérculos (*tubers*), es decir, crecen dentro de la tierra, junto con las raíces (*roots*) de la planta. Los dos alimentos tienen usos parecidos en la cocina, aunque sus sabores son diferentes.

La papa

La papa es un cultivo que se adapta con facilidad a una gran variedad de suelos (*soils*) y climas. Este hecho y su gran valor nutritivo han convertido a la papa en uno de los alimentos más consumidos en el mundo. Actualmente hay 5.000 tipos de papa, de los cuales 3.000 se producen en Perú.

La yuca

La yuca, también llamada mandioca, es el segundo tubérculo en consumo y producción mundial. En América se produce especialmente en Brasil y en Paraguay. La yuca se puede comer asada, frita o hervida en platos como el sancocho.

83 **Nuevos sabores**

▶ **Habla** con tu compañero(a).

1. ¿Qué alimento comen más?
2. ¿De qué forma lo cocinan?
3. ¿Cuántos tipos de maíz hay en su estado?

▶ **Investiga.** Busca información sobre uno de los siguientes alimentos. Escribe un texto con los datos más importantes: dónde se cultiva, cómo se cocina, etc. Después, comparte tu información con tus compañeros(as). ¿Qué alimento es más importante? ¿Por qué?

- El arroz
- Los frijoles
- El chile o ají
- El tomate

HERITAGE LANGUAGE LEARNERS

- Ask students from different cultural backgrounds—not just Spanish speakers—to think of a staple food associated with their heritage culture. Ask them to think of typical dishes prepared with this food, the history of this food in their culture, and any legends or myths associated with this food.

- Then have students do a brief presentation. Encourage them to include visuals in their presentation. If appropriate, they may bring a sample of the food or a snack made with the food (e.g., popcorn, rice cakes, potato chips) to share with the class.

CRITICAL THINKING

- Explain that corn was domesticated in Mexico's central valleys about 8,700 years ago. From there, corn spread and by the time the first Europeans arrived in the Americas, corn was a staple food on the continents. Today, corn is cultivated throughout the world.

- Have students trace *La ruta del maíz* (the corn route) on a world map (i.e., the route they imagine the spread of corn took after the arrival of the Europeans in 1492). Once students have traced their corn route, ask them to research the topic. How accurate was their route?

MAPA CULTURAL

Alimentos básicos en el mundo hispano

Preparation

- Invite students to share their Independent Starters. Write the foods they mention on the board and classify them according to food groups (i.e., grains; fruits; vegetables; dairy products; meat, poultry, and seafood; nuts, seeds, and legumes). Is there a particular food that students eat in a larger proportion? As a class, discuss the availability of certain foods in their community and the dishes people eat frequently.

- Explain to students that a staple food is one that constitutes the dominant part of a population's diet. These foods are eaten very regularly and they supply a large proportion of a person's nutritional needs. Staple foods vary from place to place, depending on what crops grow well in the area, local culinary customs, etc. Cereal grains and starchy root vegetables are the most common staple foods. Animal products have also become a staple food for some countries in the past fifty years.

- Go over the *Mapa cultural* as a class. Then divide the class into small groups to work on activity 83.

Activities

83. For the second part of this activity, ask each group to research a different food. You may want to add the following foods to the four listed in this activity: *la calabaza* (squash), *el boniato o camote* (sweet potato), and *el aguacate* (avocado). Ask groups to prepare a five-minute presentation. At the end, hold a class vote to choose the most important food, according to the class.

Answer Key

83. Answers will vary.
▶ Answers will vary.

Additional Resources

Fans Online activities
Practice Workbook

ESCRITURA

Una receta típica

Presentation

- In this section, students will practice and extend their writing skills. They will apply the vocabulary and grammar they have learned in this unit to write a recipe to share their community's culinary traditions.

Activities	Standards	Resources
Escritura	1.1, 1.2, 1.3, 2.2, 3.1, 4.1, 5.1, 5.2	

Teaching Suggestions

Warm-Up / Independent Starter

- Ask students to think about a special meal they have had at home or in their community to celebrate an important event.

Preparation

- Ask students to share their Independent Starters. What dishes were served at this meal? Are some of these dishes typical of a particular festivity (e.g., turkey during Thanksgiving) or a specific cultural tradition (e.g., *pan de muerto* to celebrate *Día de Muertos* in Mexico)? Discuss as a class the cultural significance of food and how what we eat speaks about who we are. Encourage students to think about the role food plays in their families and communities.

- Ask for a volunteer to read the Process Essays and Prescriptive Texts box aloud. Explain that in a process essay the writer explains steps or stages that lead to a result. These steps should be easy to visualize and follow a logical order. When the readers finish reading this type of essay, they will know how to do something that they didn't know how to do before.

Step-by-Step Instructions

Piensa

- You may want to assign part of this step as homework prior to working on this project, since students may not know how to prepare the dish and would probably need to ask a family member. Encourage students to choose dishes that have a special significance for their family or community.

Una receta típica

Process essays and prescriptive texts

Prescriptive texts have the goal of telling the reader how to do something. They are often referred to as "process essays" because they explain the steps required to complete a process. For that reason, they are usually written directly addressing the reader, using commands rather than third person narration or description.

Recipes are one of the most common examples of prescriptive writing. Recipes are texts that explain how to create a certain dish. They tell you the ingredients required and the order of steps to follow in preparing the dish.

Las recetas de cocina son textos en los que se explica cómo se elabora un plato. Con frecuencia, las recetas forman parte de la tradición cultural y familiar y se transmiten de una generación a otra.

Para compartir la tradición culinaria de tu comunidad, vas a escribir una receta de cocina.

Ten en cuenta que una buena receta tiene que tener tres elementos:

1. Nombre del plato

2. Ingredientes

3. Preparación

Piensa

- ¿Qué plato típico sabes preparar? Debe ser un plato típico de tu comunidad o de tu país.

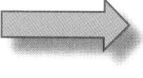 Sopa de espinacas

- ¿Qué ingredientes necesitas para prepararlo? Haz una lista y escribe la cantidad que necesitas.

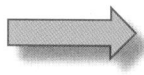 1 bolsa de espinacas 1 cebolla...

- ¿Cómo se prepara el plato? Busca información y anota los pasos en el orden en el que se realizan. Indica si es preciso el tiempo de elaboración.

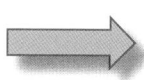 Fríe la cebolla con la mantequilla durante 3 minutos...

- ¿Qué otra información valiosa puedes aportar? Por ejemplo, dónde se pueden comprar los ingredientes, con qué se puede acompañar el plato, etc.

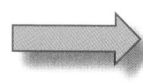 La sopa de espinacas puede servirse acompañada de...

Rubric for Evaluation

	Content	Organization	Conventions
1 point	Process is not clear or not explained. Few pieces of necessary information. Limited or inappropriate word choice.	Organization is confusing. Recipe is hard to follow. Writing is confusing. Transitions are not present.	Many errors in spelling, punctuation, grammar, and usage. Errors obscure meaning.
3 points	Mostly clear process but some steps are not specific. Includes most necessary information. Some inaccurate word choices.	Organization is clear, but some steps may not be in the proper order. Writing is clear. Some transitions are present.	Some errors in spelling, punctuation, grammar, and usage. Errors don't interfere with meaning.

Escribe

■ Utiliza las ideas que anotaste y escribe tu receta. No olvides delimitar bien las distintas fases del proceso de preparación y colocarlas en orden.

Puedes escribir las instrucciones en infinitivo, en imperativo o con la forma impersonal se.

Modelo   *Freír la cebolla.*
          Fríe la cebolla.
          Se fríe la cebolla.

■ Dibuja o saca fotos de los ingredientes, de los distintos pasos para preparar el plato y del resultado final para ilustrar la receta.

Vocabulario útil

añadir	*to add*
cortar	*to cut*
escurrir	*to drain*
dejar	*to leave*
freír	*to fry*
hornear	*to bake*
hervir	*to boil*
pelar	*to peel*
picar	*to chop*
poner	*to put*
rallar	*to shred*
remover	*to stir*

Revisa

■ Intercambia tu receta con tu compañero(a).

■ Lee la receta de tu compañero(a). ¿Entiendes bien todos los pasos? Identifica los errores gramaticales u ortográficos que haya.

■ Devuelve la receta a su autor(a) con alguna sugerencia y revisa la tuya. Vuelve a escribir tu receta incorporando las correcciones necesarias.

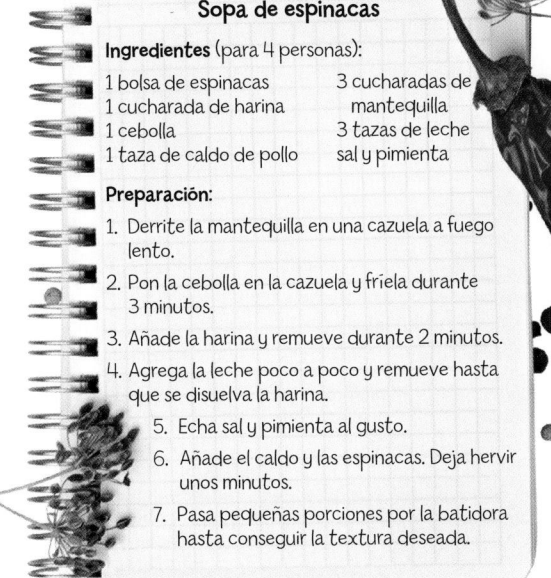

Sopa de espinacas

Ingredientes (para 4 personas):

1 bolsa de espinacas
1 cucharada de harina
1 cebolla
1 taza de caldo de pollo

3 cucharadas de mantequilla
3 tazas de leche
sal y pimienta

Preparación:

1. Derrite la mantequilla en una cazuela a fuego lento.
2. Pon la cebolla en la cazuela y fríela durante 3 minutos.
3. Añade la harina y remueve durante 2 minutos.
4. Agrega la leche poco a poco y remueve hasta que se disuelva la harina.
5. Echa sal y pimienta al gusto.
6. Añade el caldo y las espinacas. Deja hervir unos minutos.
7. Pasa pequeñas porciones por la batidora hasta conseguir la textura deseada.

Comparte

■ Presenta tu receta a la clase. ¿Qué opinan tus compañeros(as)? ¿Qué receta les gusta más? ¿Por qué?

■ Creen un libro de cocina con todas sus recetas para la clase.

doscientos veintiuno 221

	Content	Organization	Conventions
5 points	Clear and focused process. Includes all necessary information. Precise and clear word choices.	Logical progression of steps. Writing is smooth and coherent. Uses appropriate transitions when needed.	Few, if any, errors in spelling, punctuation, grammar, and usage. Excellent command of the Spanish language.

■ Ask students to use ingredients that are relatively easy to find in local supermarkets. In the instructions section, encourage students to add tips and tricks that would help the cook, as well as precautions that need to be taken.

Escribe

■ Emphasize to students that they should consider the knowledge their readers need to have in order to succeed at preparing the dish. In other words, they should write from the perspective of their readers. Have students define any terms that may not be clear to their readers. It is important, however, that students do not overwhelm their readers with directions.

■ If students choose to include pictures, suggest that they include pictures of a family or community gathering where the dish was being served. This will allow their readers to see the dish in a cultural context.

Revisa

■ Before students exchange their recipe with a classmate, have them address these questions: Am I being consistent in the way I'm addressing the reader? Am I overwhelming the reader with too many steps? If so, could I merge some of the steps? Is there a logical link between the steps? Am I getting the readers involved and interested? Then have students exchange their texts and evaluate each other's recipes using the rubric.

Comparte

■ Encourage students to begin their presentation by showing images of the dish. This will give their audience a general idea about the dish. Then ask students to explain the steps in their own words, instead of just reading the instructions.

Evaluation

■ Distribute copies of the rubric to students and discuss the evaluation criteria. Ask students to refer to the rubric as they prepare their writings and as they evaluate their classmates' recipes.

221

REPASO

Vocabulario

Presentation

- In this section, students will review all key vocabulary from the unit, organized by themes, to prepare for an assessment. Students will complete practice activities for each of the three *Desafíos*.

Activities	Standards	Resources
1.	1.3, 3.1	
2.	1.2, 1.3	
3.	1.2, 1.3	

Teaching Suggestions

Warm-Up / Independent Starter

- Ask students to think of their favorite dish and list the ingredients. Then have them think of the reasons they like this dish and write down a description of the flavors, texture, and the way the dish is cooked and served. Finally, ask students to list some nutritional information for this dish.

Preparation

- Ask students to work with a classmate and share their Independent Starters. Do they have similar taste in food or not? Then have pairs analyze the nutritional value of their favorite dishes. Are these dishes healthy or do they contain too much fat, sugar, or other unhealthy ingredients? Encourage pairs to think of both positive and negative health consequences of having these dishes often. For instance, if one of the dishes they mentioned was pizza, they may say, *El queso de la pizza tiene calcio, y ese mineral es bueno para los huesos. Pero la pizza tiene mucha grasa, que es mala para el corazón.*

- Have pairs share their discussions with the class. What are the most popular foods in your class? Based on this information, does the class seem to have healthy eating habits? What could be improved? Hold a class discussion to address these questions and invite students to come up with a list of activities to promote a healthier lifestyle. Remind students to include in their recommendations a wide range of activities to make them appealing to a wider audience. Then read over the *Repaso* presentation with students.

222

REPASO Vocabulario

Alimentación

el aceite de oliva	olive oil
el agua mineral	mineral water
las especias	spices
las infusiones	infusions
la carne blanca	white meat
la carne roja	red meat
la comida basura	junk food
los frutos secos	dried fruits and nuts
nutritivo(a)	nutritional
vegetariano(a)	vegetarian

Preparación de los alimentos

crudo(a)	raw
poco hecho(a)	underdone
al punto	just right
muy hecho(a)	well done
jugoso(a)	juicy
sabroso(a)	tasty
ligero(a)	light
grasoso(a)	greasy

Nutrición

las calorías	calories
la fibra	fiber
la grasa	fat
el hierro	iron
las proteínas	proteins
las vitaminas	vitamins

Acciones

aumentar	to increase
digerir	to digest
estar a dieta	to be on a diet
evitar	to avoid
reducir	to reduce
sustituir	to substitute

Especialistas médicos

el/la dentista	dentist
el/la oculista	ophthalmologist
el/la pediatra	pediatrician
el/la psicólogo(a)	psychologist

Hábitos saludables

aumentar de peso	to gain weight
bajar de peso	to lose weight
cuidarse	to take care of oneself
darse un masaje	to get a massage
descansar	to rest
entrenar	to train
estirar los músculos	to stretch one's muscles
evitar calambres	to avoid cramps
hacer ejercicios aeróbicos	to do aerobics
hacer ejercicios de relajación	to do relaxation exercises
practicar pilates/yoga	to practice pilates/yoga
relajarse	to relax
respirar	to breathe
sentirse estresado(a)	to feel stressed
el gimnasio	gym
el/la monitor(a)	(sports) instructor

Objetos y productos de higiene

el albornoz	bathrobe	el gorro de ducha	shower cap
el cortaúñas	nail clippers	el hilo dental	dental floss
la crema solar	sunscreen	la maquinilla de afeitar	safety razor
la esponja	sponge		
la espuma de afeitar	shaving foam		

La consulta médica

el análisis de sangre	blood test
el antibiótico	antibiotic
el diagnóstico	diagnosis
el examen físico	physical exam
las píldoras	pills
la radiografía	X-ray
la revisión médica	medical checkup
los síntomas	symptoms
dar puntos	to give stitches
darse un golpe	to bump
estar hinchado(a)	to be swollen
estar mareado(a)	to be dizzy
estar roto(a)	to be broken
recetar	to prescribe
tener escalofríos	to have chills
tomar el pulso	to take one's pulse

El cuerpo humano

el cerebro	brain
el corazón	heart
el estómago	stomach
el hígado	liver
los huesos	bones
el intestino	intestines
los músculos	muscles
los pulmones	lungs

222 doscientos veintidós

Differentiated Instruction

DEVELOPING LEARNERS

- Ask students to close their books and draw a large stick figure on a sheet of paper. Then have them label the figure with as many body parts as they can. Next, ask students to think of eight symptoms and the body parts associated with them (e.g., *tos → los pulmones; brazo roto → los huesos*), and write these associations on a separate sheet.

- Pair students up and have one partner read the symptoms while the other identifies the body parts associated with each symptom on the stick figure. Then have partners switch roles.

EXPANDING LEARNERS

- Ask students to imagine that they are going on a fifteen-day vacation to an isolated tropical island and they are only allowed five personal care items. Ask them to list what they would take.

- Pair students with a classmate of the opposite sex and tell them that the two of them can only take five items. Have them decide which items they will take.
  A. *Yo necesito la maquinilla de afeitar.*
  B. *Eso no es esencial. Tenemos que llevar pasta de dientes.*
  A. *Sí, eso es necesario. Y también hilo dental.*

DESAFÍO 1

1 **Expertos en nutrición.** ¿Qué alimentos son ricos en fibra? ¿Y en hierro? Completa la tabla.

Fibra	Grasa	Hierro	Proteínas	Vitaminas
la lechuga				

DESAFÍO 2

2 **Campeón de natación.** Lee cómo es la rutina diaria de este nadador y completa el texto con las palabras del cuadro.

entrenar	estresado	ejercicios
evitar	masaje	estirar

La vida de un campeón

Me llamo Daniel Meco y soy campeón de natación. Empecé a competir a los diez años. Todos los días, antes de meterme en el agua, hago __1__ para __2__ los músculos. Esto es muy bueno para __3__ calambres. Después nado durante cuatro o cinco horas. Algunos días, después de __4__, me doy un __5__. Gracias al deporte, nunca estoy __6__. Bueno, excepto los días que tengo competición, ¡como hoy!

DESAFÍO 3

3 **Asociaciones.** Relaciona cada acción con el sujeto al que corresponde lógicamente.

MÉDICO
1. _____
2. _____
3. _____
4. _____

recetar
tener escalofríos
estar enfermo
diagnosticar
estar mareado
tener fiebre
dar puntos
tomar el pulso

PACIENTE
1. _____
2. _____
3. _____
4. _____

doscientos veintitrés 223

Activities

1. Ask students to look at the list under *Alimentación* and classify the foods by the type of nutrient they think is more abundant in each type of food. For example: *la comida basura*: *grasa*; *la carne roja*: *proteínas*; *las legumbres*: *hierro*, etc. Then ask students to think of three examples for each food group (e.g., *la comida basura*: *hamburguesas*, *papas fritas*, *donas*; *la carne roja*: *carne de res*, *carne de cerdo*, *carne de cordero*). Once students have compiled these lists, they are ready to complete the activity.

2. Ask students to work with a partner. Have one partner read each sentence aloud. When they get to a blank, they should say the word "blank" and continue to read the sentence. Once they have finished reading the sentence, their partners should fill in the blank. Once students have completed the text, the partner who filled in the blanks should now read the whole paragraph aloud while his or her partner decides whether the answers are correct.

Answer Key

1. Answers will vary. Sample answers:
   Fibra: los frijoles, la avena, el brócoli.
   Grasa: la carne roja, el aceite, la mantequilla.
   Hierro: las espinacas, las lentejas, el salmón.
   Proteínas: la carne de res, los garbanzos, los huevos.
   Vitaminas: la naranja, el aguacate, la zanahoria.

2. 1. ejercicios   4. entrenar
   2. estirar   5. masaje
   3. evitar   6. estresado

3. Médico: recetar, diagnosticar, dar puntos, tomar el pulso.
   Paciente: tener escalofríos, estar enfermo, estar mareado, tener fiebre.

Additional Resources

Fans Online activities
Practice Workbook

HERITAGE LANGUAGE LEARNERS

- Ask students to research homemade remedies from their country of origin, as well as foods recommended for certain aliments. For example: *Para el dolor de estómago lo mejor es una infusión de manzanilla. Para el dolor de garganta, haz gárgaras de agua con sal. ¿Sabías que el ajo es un antibiótico natural?* Suggest that they also interview family members.

- Have students organize their findings in a brochure decorated with images. Ask students to share their "Good Health Brochure" with the class. Does the class know other remedies?

MULTIPLE INTELLIGENCES:
Musical-Rhythmic Intelligence

- Discuss the importance of music and songs in spreading a message. Ask students to think of the most frequent health and lifestyle issues in their community. Have them work in small groups to create a catchy tune and clever lyrics to promote a healthier lifestyle. Ask them to pay particular attention to the chorus, since they will ask their audience to join them in singing the chorus. For example: *Cuida tu alimentación / para una mejor nutrición. / Y no olvides que el ejercicio frecuente / ayuda al cuerpo y la mente.*

REPASO

Gramática

Presentation

- Students will review grammatical structures presented in the unit. Each grammar point is cross-referenced to the corresponding page on which it was introduced. The activities here provide systematic practice by *Desafío*.

Activities	Standards	Resources
4.	1.2, 1.3	
5.	1.2	
6.	1.2, 1.3	
7. Cultura	1.1, 2.1, 2.2	

Teaching Suggestions

Warm-Up / Independent Starter

- Give students a couple of minutes to review the grammar topics on this page silently.

Preparation

- Ask students to get together with a classmate. Then have them close their textbooks and answer the following questions in writing:

1. Use a negative command to tell a friend not to go to the park today.
2. Translate this sentence into Spanish: The pumpkin (*calabaza*) turned into a carriage (*carruaje*).
3. Translate this sentence into Spanish: I like traveling by train.
4. Give a friend a recommendation regarding his or her lifestyle.
5. Tell your partner what you would do in his or her place to get better grades.
6. What would you do if your stomach hurt?

Ask students to open their textbooks and check their answers. Are most of their answers correct? Do they need more practice in a particular area? Provide additional practice to those students who need it.

- Go over the *Repaso* presentation with the class. Then invite volunteer pairs to share some of their answers to the Preparation activity with the class and identify the different grammar structures being reviewed in this *Repaso*.

REPASO Gramática

Los mandatos. La forma *nosotros(as)* (pág. 184)

MANDATOS REGULARES

Cocinar	Comer	Consumir
(no) cocinemos	(no) comamos	(no) consumamos

MANDATOS IRREGULARES

Dar	Estar	Ser	Ir
(no) demos	(no) estemos	(no) seamos	(no) vayamos

Los verbos de cambio (pág. 186)

- ponerse + adjective
- quedarse + adjective
- volverse + adjective
- volverse + noun
- hacerse + adjective
- hacerse + noun
- convertirse en + noun

Para y por (pág. 196)

PARA

- purpose / "in order to"
- "directed to" / "for the benefit of"
- destination, direction
- deadline, future date
- comparison, "considering"
- opinion

POR

- reason, motive, "because of"
- "in exchange for"
- ratio, proportion, "per"
- movement: through, "via," along, by
- general location
- general time / part of the day
- mode of communication
- mode of transportation
- "on behalf of"
- object of an errand
- agent of an action

Hacer valoraciones (pág. 198)

Es aconsejable… Es conveniente… Es importante… Es bueno… Es necesario… Es preciso… Es mejor… Es sorprendente… Me parece bien/mal/fatal…	+ infinitive + que + subjunctive

Dar consejos y hacer recomendaciones (pág. 210)

Aconsejar Recomendar (e → ie) Sugerir (e → ie)	+ infinitive + que + subjunctive
Debes… Deberías…	+ infinitive
Yo… Yo en tu lugar… Yo que tú…	+ conditional

El condicional (pág. 208)

VERBOS REGULARES

	Hablar	Comer	Escribir
yo	hablaría	comería	escribiría
tú	hablarías	comerías	escribirías
usted, él, ella	hablaría	comería	escribiría
nosotros(as)	hablaríamos	comeríamos	escribiríamos
vosotros(as)	hablaríais	comeríais	escribiríais
ustedes, ellos(as)	hablarían	comerían	escribirían

VERBOS IRREGULARES

- poder → podr-
- poner → pondr-
- salir → saldr-
- tener → tendr-
- venir → vendr-
- valer → valdr-
- decir → dir-
- hacer → har-
- querer → querr-
- saber → sabr-
- haber → habr-
- caber → cabr-

Differentiated Instruction

DEVELOPING LEARNERS

- Ask students to think of three negative commands that they are likely to find on a sign in each of the following places. Then have students write these commands on a sheet of paper using the command form for the pronoun in parentheses.
  - In a hospital waiting room. (*ustedes*)
  - In a restaurant kitchen. (*nosotros*)
  - In a gym. (*tú*)
  - In a diet clinic. (*usted*)
- Invite students to share their commands with the class without telling the class the place. Can the class guess the place?

EXPANDING LEARNERS

- Ask students to write a quiz to test a partner on the use of different expressions to give advice and make recommendations. Have students come up with five different statements using the structures listed on page 224. They should leave two blank lines between the statements so that their partner can write two alternative ways of expressing the same thing. For example: *Te aconsejo comer más verduras.* Possible answers: *Debes comer más verduras. Yo en tu lugar comería más verduras.* Have partners take each other's quiz. How did they do?

DESAFÍO 1

4 **¡Cómo cambió Lidia!** Escribe oraciones para expresar los cambios de Lidia. Utiliza los verbos de cambio.

Modelo *Lidia se ha quedado delgada.*

ANTES	AHORA
1. Lidia pesaba 70 kilos.	Lidia pesa 55 kilos.
2. Lidia no dejaba propina.	Lidia deja una buena propina.
3. Lidia trabajaba en un hospital.	Lidia trabaja en una escuela.
4. Lidia comía mucha carne.	Lidia no come nunca carne.

DESAFÍO 2

5 **Por y para ti.** Completa estas oraciones con *por* o *para*.

1. Pasé toda la tarde haciendo una torta _____ ti.
2. Este hotel no es muy bueno _____ ser tan caro.
3. Consiguió el premio _____ ser el mejor candidato.
4. No pude ir a la boda y mi hermana fue _____ mí.
5. Estas tareas son _____ el viernes.

DESAFÍO 3

6 **Los consejos de mi suegra.** Completa los consejos que Carmen le da a su nuera María. Pon los verbos en la forma correcta.

| llevarse |
| poner |
| cocinar |
| hacer |
| venir |

1. María, yo que tú _____ flores en la sala.
2. María, yo en tu lugar no _____ esa comida para Acción de Gracias.
3. María, deberías _____ a mi casa más a menudo.
4. María, yo me _____ otro corte de pelo.
5. María, te recomiendo que _____ bien conmigo.

CULTURA

7 **Alimentación y salud.** Responde a estas preguntas.

1. ¿Qué es la ropa vieja?
2. ¿Dónde está el hospital más antiguo de las Américas?
3. ¿Qué alimentos son básicos en la cocina latinoamericana?

doscientos veinticinco 225

HERITAGE LANGUAGE LEARNERS

- Ask pairs to compile a list of idiomatic expressions with the verbs on page 186. You may want to get them started with these expressions: *Ponerse como un tomate* (to blush), *quedarse de piedra* (to be stunned), *hacerse el sordo* (to pretend not to hear).
- Have students write a sentence for each expression to show how it is used. Then invite pairs to read five of their sentences to the class. While one of the partners reads, the other pantomimes the sentence. Can the class guess the meaning of the idiomatic expression?

TOTAL PHYSICAL RESPONSE (TPR)

- Have students count off from 1 to 5 and assign each number the following categories of negative commands: 1s → *tú*, 2s → *usted*, 3s → *nosotros(as)*, 4s → *vosotros(as)*, 5s → *ustedes*. Then say a verb in the infinitive form and call out a number from 1 to 5. Be sure to include verbs that have irregular forms. The first student to stand up and give the corresponding command is the winner of that round and is awarded 1 point. Keep a tally of students' scores and continue playing until you call time. You may also require the class to pantomime the command.

Unit 4

REPASO

Gramática

Activities

5. Have students explain the uses of *por* and *para* for each of the blanks. The first sentence, for instance, refers to something (*una torta*) that is directed to someone (*tú*), so *para* is the right preposition.

6. Ask students to work with a partner to complete this activity. Once they have finished, have pairs use some of the sentences to write a dialogue between Carmen and María. For example:
A. *María, deberías venir a mi casa más a menudo.*
B. *Sí, Carmen, yo te visitaría más a menudo, pero vives muy lejos.*
Invite pairs to act out their dialogues for the class. You may want to hold a class vote to choose the best or most entertaining dialogue.

Answer Key

4. Answers will vary. Sample answers:
2. Lidia se ha vuelto generosa.
3. Lidia se hizo maestra.
4. Lidia se convirtió en vegetariana.

5.
1. para	4. por
2. para	5. para
3. por	

6.
1. pondría	4. haría
2. cocinaría	5. te lleves
3. venir	

7. Answers will vary. Sample answers:
1. Es un plato de las islas Canarias, desde donde pasó a varias zonas del Caribe y de Latinoamérica. Se hace con carne de res, tomates, pimientos, ajos y especias. En algunas versiones este plato también lleva garbanzos y papas.
2. En la Ciudad de México.
3. El maíz, la papa y la yuca. También son importantes el arroz, los frijoles, los tomates y los chiles o ajíes.

Additional Resources

Fans Online activities
Practice Workbook

225

PROYECTO

Guía para una vida saludable

Presentation

- In this section, students will apply the vocabulary, grammar, and cultural information they have learned in this unit to create a guide for their classmates with recommendations for healthy living.

Activities	Standards	Resources
Paso 1	1.1, 1.2, 1.3, 2.1, 2.2, 3.1, 3.2, 5.1, 5.2	
Paso 2	1.1, 1.2	
Paso 3	1.3, 3.1, 5.1, 5.2	
Paso 4	1.1, 3.1, 5.1, 5.2	
Paso 5	1.3, 3.1, 5.1, 5.2	

Teaching Suggestions

Warm-Up / Independent Starter

- Ask students to think about their eating habits, exercise routines, outdoor activities, and family life. Have students jot down what they do in each of these four areas.

Preparation

- As a class, discuss this paradox: as countries get wealthier, their obesity rates increase. Why might this be? Discuss that we seem to be making poor food choices and leading a more sedentary lifestyle. What other factors might impact our weight and well-being? Students may mention stress, genetics, certain illnesses, the higher cost of fruits and vegetables compared with processed foods, the convenience of fast food, etc. Ask for a volunteer to read the project introduction. Then divide the class into groups of three.

Step-by-Step Instructions

Paso 1

- Ask students to share their Independent Starters. Have groups designate one student to list the group's habits in each of the four areas.

Paso 2

- Have groups analyze their list from *Paso 1* and determine which habits are healthy and which are not. Then ask groups to think of good lifestyle choices they can make to have a healthier life.

226

PROYECTO

Elaborar una

guía para una vida saludable

The Chilean government has created a program for living a healthy life that is called Choose to Live Healthy *(Elige vivir sano: www.eligevivirsano.cl)*. This program gives recommendations in four areas:

Eat healthy — Move your body — Get fresh air — Enjoy your family

In this project you will work in groups of three to create a guide for your classmates with recommendations and information about getting fresh air, moving your body, eating healthy, and spending more quality time with your family.

PASO 1 Describe tus hábitos

- Piensa cuáles son tus hábitos relacionados con estas áreas y escríbelos.

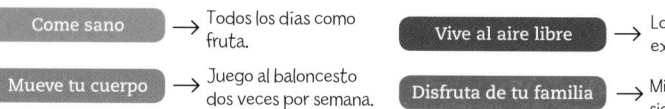

Come sano → Todos los días como fruta.

Mueve tu cuerpo → Juego al baloncesto dos veces por semana.

Vive al aire libre → Los fines de semana hacemos excursiones al campo.

Disfruta de tu familia → Mi familia y yo cenamos siempre juntos.

- Comenta tus hábitos con tus compañeros(as).

Modelo

A. *Yo evito comer alimentos con muchas calorías.*

B. *Pues yo como hamburguesas dos o tres veces por semana.*

A. *Deberías comer menos hamburguesas porque tienen mucha grasa.*

PASO 2 Analiza los hábitos de tu grupo

- Contesten a estas preguntas para recoger los hábitos del grupo.

 ¿Cuáles son los hábitos más saludables del grupo?

– ¿Cuáles son los hábitos que tienen que cambiar?
– ¿Qué pueden hacer para cambiar los malos hábitos?

- Con la información anterior, hagan una lista con los hábitos más recomendables para cada una de las cuatro áreas.
- Pueden buscar más información en Internet para ampliar la lista.

Rubric for Evaluation

	Content	Organization	Presentation
1 point	The recommendations are not relevant. Information is incomplete or incorrect. Little Spanish is used.	The guide's formatting is minimal or unattractive. The organization of the material is confusing.	Unclear communication. Delivery is not fluent. Many errors in vocabulary and grammar.
3 points	The recommendations are relevant. Information is correct but some of it lacks significance. Spanish is used most of the time.	The guide has attractive formatting and the images go well with the text. The information is well organized.	Clear communication and fluent delivery. Mostly correct vocabulary and grammar.

PASO 3 Decide los hábitos más importantes

- Con toda la información que tienen, decidan cuáles son las cinco recomendaciones más importantes para cada una de las áreas.

Come sano	Vive al aire libre
Mueve tu cuerpo	Disfruta de tu familia

PASO 4 Elabora la guía

- Diseñen la guía.
- Escriban los textos que van a poner en la guía.
- Busquen fotos o dibujos en Internet para decorar la guía.

Elige vivir sano

¡Mueve tu cuerpo!

1. Es bueno dar un paseo de una hora todos los días.

2. Es importante que hagas ejercicios de relajación cuando estés estresado.

3. ...

PASO 5 Presenta la guía

- Presenten la guía a sus compañeros(as).
- Durante la presentación de tus compañeros(as), anota los hábitos que vas a seguir para llevar una vida más sana.
- Elijan la guía que más les gusta para repartirla a los(as) alumnos(as) de su escuela.

Unidad 4

Autoevaluación

¿Qué has aprendido en esta unidad?

Do these activities to evaluate how well you can manage in Spanish.

Evalúa tus habilidades. Para cada punto, di Muy bien, Bien o Necesito practicar más.

a. Can you talk about food and nutrition?
   ▶ Explain what you need in order to prepare a complete healthy meal.
   ▶ Imagine that you are going to a friend's house for dinner. Write him or her some recommendations of things he or she should do—and not do—to have a successful dinner.

b. Can you make judgments?
   ▶ Explain which health and hygiene habits are the most important for a healthy mind and body, in your opinion, and why.

c. Can you give advice and make recommendations?
   ▶ Imagine that a member of your family is not feeling well. Describe which symptoms he or she has. Give recommendations of what he or she should do to feel better.
   ▶ If it were you who had these symptoms, what would you do?

PROYECTO

Guía para una vida saludable

Paso 3

- Good sources of information include Nutrition.gov and the Healthy Lifestyle link on the Mayo Clinic website. Remind students to list their sources.

- Ask students to take their audience into consideration. Some recommendations may be more appropriate for older adults or for children. They should consider the typical schedule and lifestyle of students their age and tailor their advice accordingly.

Paso 4

- If access to computers with brochure creation software is available to all of the students, you may want to ask them to use this software for their guide layout. Remind students that visuals enhance what they are saying.

Paso 5

- Encourage students to interact with their audience as they present their plan. Emphasize the importance of engaging the audience.

Evaluation

- Distribute copies of the rubric to students. Discuss the evaluation criteria and explain how this project will be graded. Encourage students to refer to the rubric as they prepare their projects.

Content

- Students should carefully consider which recommendations to include. They may want to research the effectiveness of some of these recommendations in order to make well-informed decisions. Have them proofread their work carefully and include a list of sources.

Organization

- Explain that the guide should have an attractive format. Emphasize the importance of having a good mix of text and graphics or pictures.

Presentation

- Ask students to strive to motivate and inspire their audience, as they are trying to persuade their listeners to make lifestyle changes. Encourage students to memorize their text as much as possible so that they sound fluent and self-confident.

	Content	Organization	Presentation
5 points	The recommendations are relevant, varied, and interesting. The information is well researched. Spanish is used exclusively.	The guide has very attractive formatting. There is a good mix of text and images. The information is clearly organized, visually and logically.	Clear and fluent communication. Very motivating, engaging delivery. Correct and complete vocabulary and grammar.

Unit 5 ¿Trabajas?

Objectives

- To identify different professions.
- To talk about abilities and qualifications of professionals and workers.
- To discuss employment opportunities and volunteerism.
- To express certainty and doubt.
- To talk about past actions.

- To refer to something that is unknown.
- To describe someone or something.
- To talk about the gender of nouns.
- To express feelings and emotions.
- To express an obstacle or difficulty.
- To identify main ideas and significant details in a variety of texts.

- To write descriptive, narrative, or informative texts.
- To know and apply the different stages of the writing process: planning, writing, revising, and sharing.
- To discuss historical and influential figures from Latin American countries.

Contents

Vocabulary

- Useful expressions to tell ability or inability to do something, to encourage or to console someone, and to express agreement or disagreement.
- Review: Words for professions and employment locations.
- Professions and employment positions
- Jobs and technology, attributes of different professionals, and actions performed by professionals.
- Volunteerism and community service.

Grammar

- To express certainty and doubt.
- The imperfect subjunctive.
- To give details: The relative pronoun *que*.
- Noun gender.
- To express feelings or emotions.
- To express difficulty.

Culture

- César Chávez and other Hispanic civil rights leaders.
- *El Día del Trabajo.*
- *Astronautas hispanos.*
- Mass communication used in Hispanic communities: *El Diario La Prensa* and television in Spanish.
- Successful Hispanic professionals: María Elena Salinas.
- Organizations and individuals that assist people in Hispanic communities.
- *Turismo sostenible.*
- Human rights and environmental concerns in Hispanic communities: *Frente de Defensa de la Amazonía.*
- Universities in Hispanic countries.

Evaluation Criteria

- Identify historical Hispanic figures and describe their actions.
- Identify different professions, employment positions, and places of work.
- Describe the qualifications and attributes of, and the actions performed by various professionals.
- Explain ways to find and secure employment opportunities.
- Identify different charitable organizations and describe ways in which they assist people.

- Express certainty and doubt using the indicative and subjunctive moods.
- State feelings and emotions using various verb choices and expressions.
- Understand the formation and use of the imperfect subjunctive verb tense.
- Use adjective clauses to provide more information about a noun.
- Identify and form masculine and feminine nouns.

- Express difficulty by providing information about a difficulty in a given action.
- Identify forms of mass communication used in Hispanic communities.
- Identify community service and volunteer opportunities.
- Discuss ways in which the environment is being protected in Hispanic countries.
- Write a formal letter.
- Identify institutions of higher learning and areas of study in Hispanic countries.

Unit Plan _____

Las tareas/Antes de empezar

Estimated time: 1 session.

Text: *Ciudadanos responsables.*

Functions & forms:
- Useful expressions to tell ability or inability to do something, to encourage or to console someone, and to express agreement or disagreement.
- Review of known vocabulary about professions and places of work.

DESAFÍO 1

Estimated time: 5 sessions.

Text: *El Día de César Chávez.*

Functions & forms:
- To express certainty and doubt.
- Professions and employment locations.
- Indicative and subjunctive moods to express certainty and doubt.
- Imperfect subjunctive.

Culture:
- *César Chávez.*
- *El Día del Trabajo.*
- *Astronautas hispanos.*

Reading: *Una vida interesante.*

DESAFÍO 2

Estimated time: 5 sessions.

Text: *El trabajo perfecto.*

Functions & forms:
- To refer to something that is unknown.
- Work and technology.
- To give details: Adjective clauses.
- Noun gender.

Culture:
- *El Diario La Prensa.*
- *María Elena Salinas.*
- *Televisión en español.*

Reading: *Manuel Jalón, un inventor humanista.*

DESAFÍO 3

Estimated time: 6 sessions.

Text: *Por el bien común.*

Functions & forms:
- To express feelings and difficulty.
- Volunteer work and community service.
- Verbs, verb moods, and verb tenses to express feelings and emotions.
- Conjunctions followed by indicative or subjunctive to express difficulty.

Culture:
- *Hispanos solidarios.*
- *Turismo sostenible.*
- *Frente de Defensa de la Amazonía.*

Reading: *Música.*

Para terminar

Estimated time: 1 session.

Todo junto: Review of *Desafíos 1–3.*

Tu desafío:
- *Desafío A:* Prepare a presentation about a Hispanic leader who has fought for human rights.
- *Desafío B:* Choose an employment want ad and write a letter to the potential employer.
- *Desafío C:* Create a presentation about volunteering in your community.

MAPA CULTURAL

Estimated time: 1 session.

Mapa cultural: *Universidades hispanas.*

ESCRITURA

Estimated time: 1 session.

Writing: *Una carta formal.*

PROYECTO

Estimated time: 1 session.

Project: *Un proyecto de una organización solidaria.*

Standards for Learning Spanish

COMMUNICATION

1.1. Interpersonal mode
- Exchange personal opinions and experiences.
- Engage in oral conversations using personal knowledge and experience.
- Exchange assignments with a partner and evaluate each other's work.
- Create a visual and describe it with a partner.
- Discuss hypothetical situations with a partner.
- Compare and contrast information with a partner.
- Ask and answer questions on different topics.
- Ask a partner questions and take notes.

1.2. Interpretive mode
- Demonstrate understanding of oral and written expressions.
- Demonstrate understanding of questions relating to familiar and less familiar topics.
- Understand and obtain information from audio or video recordings.
- Understand written exchanges.
- Extract information from an informative text.
- Identify main ideas and significant details from a literary text.
- Draw conclusions and make judgments from oral and written texts.
- Interpret texts on topics of other cultures and relate them to personal knowledge and experience.

1.3. Presentational mode
- Produce and present an original creation.
- Write and present a formal letter.
- Write sentences or paragraphs comparing or summarizing information.
- Complete sentences with relevant information or correct verb tenses.
- Write a descriptive paragraph.
- Write questions for an interview and present the results.
- Create a list of information and present it to the class.

COMPARISONS

4.1. Compare languages
- Compare doubt and certainty expressions in English and in Spanish.
- Compare the use of indicative and subjunctive in English and in Spanish.
- Compare the gender of nouns for professions in English and in Spanish.

4.2. Compare cultures
- Compare celebrations in Hispanic countries and in the United States.
- Compare mass media used in Hispanic countries and in the United States.

CULTURE

2.1. Practices and perspectives
- Learn about cultural traditions and discuss the importance of such practices.
- Learn about what people in Hispanic populations do in their jobs or professions.
- Learn how people use mass media to stay informed or to communicate in Hispanic cultures.
- Learn about and use various expressions.
- Discuss the effect tourism can have on Hispanic cultures and economies.
- Learn how working in agriculture has played an important role in Hispanic culture and history.

2.2. Products and perspectives
- Learn about some products created by Hispanic inventors.
- Learn about universities built in Hispanic countries.

COMMUNITIES

5.1. Spanish within and beyond the school setting
- Research and obtain information on the Internet.
- Discuss services provided in one's own community.
- Imagine situations in which Spanish could be used.
- Write a letter in Spanish to a potential employer.
- Learn about charitable organizations in the community.

5.2. Spanish for lifelong learners
- Discuss ways in which Spanish can be used in future life experiences and careers.
- Discuss attributes, education, and training needed for future careers.

CONNECTIONS

3.1. Interdisciplinary connections
- Understand the similarities and differences between some aspects of grammar in English and in Spanish.
- Learn about historical Hispanic figures and their influence on history.
- Discuss professions in Hispanic communities and the United States.
- Learn about mass media used in Hispanic communities.
- Learn about charitable organizations run by Hispanic leaders.
- Use the writing process to produce a written work.

3.2. Viewpoints through language/culture
- Read dialogues, informative texts, and literary texts in Spanish that provide insight into Hispanic cultures.

Communicative Skills

Interpersonal Mode

		Activities
Speaking	• Exchange opinions or experiences. • Engage in conversation with a classmate. • Compare pictures or information with a classmate.	• 3, 27, 28, 55, 56, 59, 62, 78, 79 • 4, 12, 14, 19, 24, 28, 34, 45, 69, 81, 82, 86 • 26, 63, 73
Writing	• Write questions for an interview or take notes from an interview. • Make a list of information about a topic. • Interview a classmate or professional and take notes.	• 9, 80 • 63, 73 • 14, 80
Listening	• Understand simple oral exchanges and react appropriately. • Understand answers or oral exchanges and apply information to a summary task.	• 3, 4, 12, 14, 19, 24, 26, 27, 28, 34, 45, 56, 59, 62, 69, 79, 82, 84 • 9, 26, 63, 73, 80, 81
Reading	• Understand the information in a wide variety of texts and react properly to it or use it to talk with classmates.	• 27, 55, 56, 73, 78, 79, 82, *Escritura*

Interpretive Mode

		Activities
Listening	• Understand and obtain information from a conversation. • Understand oral descriptive or informative sentences or texts. • Listen to a recording and apply information to a task.	• 13, 39, 59, 68, 83 • 8, 18, 44, 53, 62 • 62, 83
Reading	• Demonstrate comprehension of written exchanges and longer written dialogues. • Reflect on cultural topics in relation to personal knowledge and experience. • Understand a news article or an employment announcement. • Understand and obtain information from an informative or narrative text. • Infer meanings based on a text.	• 1, 7, 25, 30, 31, 32, 56, 57, 58, 82 • 10, 15, 20, 35, 40, 49, 85 • 28, 33, 36, 48, 50, 51, 53, 79, 85 • 23, 27, 28, 36, 50, 51, 52, 60, 61, 64, 74, 75, 76, 85, *Mapa cultural* • 2, 52, 76
Viewing	• Connect information to images. • Obtain information from an image.	• 18, 59, • 12, *Mapa cultural*

Presentational Mode

		Activities
Speaking	• Present information and an original creation to the class.	• 29, 81, 85, *Proyecto*
Writing	• Create a poster and present it to the class. • Write a list with items or a descriptive paragraph about job and professions. • Write a formal letter. • Write an ending to a story or a poem. • Write an employment announcement or a newspaper headline.	• 29, 81 • 36, 63, 84 • 85, *Escritura* • 29, 78 • 55, *Proyecto*
Visually Representing	• Present information in a chart, a table, or graphic organizer. • Present information using visuals related to the unit.	• 4, 26, 51 • 85, *Mapa cultural*

Cross-Curricular Standards

Subject	Standard	Activities
Language Arts	• Compare elements of Spanish grammar and language with English equivalents. • Use the writing process to write a formal letter.	• 16, 21, 41, 46, 52, 65, 70 • *Escritura*
Social Studies	• Learn and talk about some historical figures from Hispanic communities. • Learn about some of the history of human and labor rights.	• 7, 8, 10, 20, 23, 40, 50 • 10, 26, 27, 60, 85
Science	• Reflect on and learn about the protection of the environment.	• 64, 74

Lesson Plans (50-Minute Classes)

Day	Objectives	Sessions	Activities	Time	Standards	Resources/ Homework
1	To introduce employment and professions and the characters' challenges, and to review learned vocabulary	**¿Trabajas?/Las tareas/Antes de empezar** (228–233) • Warm-Up: Topic orientation • Presentation: *Ciudadanos responsables* • *Expresiones útiles* and *Recuerda*	 1–2 3–5	10 m. 20 m. 20 m.	1.1, 1.2, 1.3, 2.1, 2.2, 3.1, 3.2, 5.1	Visual Presentation Video Practice Workbook
2	To express certainty and doubt	**Desafío 1 – El Día de César Chávez** (234–235) • Warm-Up: Independent Starter • *Texto: El Día de César Chávez* • *Conexiones: César Chávez*	 6–9 10	5 m. 35 m. 10 m.	1.1, 1.2, 1.3, 2.1, 2.2, 3.1, 5.1	Visual Presentation Audio
3	To identify different professionals and employment positions	**Desafío 1 – Vocabulario** (236–237) • Warm-Up: Independent Starter • Vocabulary: *Profesiones y cargos* • *Conexiones: El Día del Trabajo*	 11–14 15	5 m. 35 m. 10 m.	1.1, 1.2, 1.3, 2.1, 3.1, 4.2, 5.1, 5.2	Audio Practice Workbook
4	To express certainty and doubt	**Desafío 1 – Gramática** (238–239) • Warm-Up: Independent Starter • Grammar: *Expresar certeza y duda* • *Cultura: Astronautas hispanos*	 16–19 20	5 m. 35 m. 10 m.	1.1, 1.2, 1.3, 2.1, 2.2, 3.1, 4.1, 5.1, 5.2	Audio Practice Workbook
5	To learn the imperfect subjunctive	**Desafío 1 – Gramática** (240–241) • Warm-Up: Independent Starter • Grammar: *El imperfecto de subjuntivo*	 21–24	5 m. 45 m.	1.1, 1.2, 1.3, 2.1, 3.1, 3.2, 4.1, 5.1	Practice Workbook
6	To understand a dialogue and to integrate vocabulary and grammar	**Desafío 1 – Lectura/Comunicación** (242–245) • Warm-Up: Independent Starter • *Lectura: Una vida interesante* • *Comunicación:* Review • *Final del desafío*	 25–27 28–29 30	5 m. 20 m. 15 m. 10 m.	1.1, 1.2, 1.3, 2.1, 2.2, 3.1, 3.2, 5.1	Visual Presentation Practice Workbook *Tu desafío* Quiz on *Desafío 1*
7	To refer to something that is unknown	**Desafío 2 – El trabajo perfecto** (246–247) • Warm-Up: Correct quiz on *Desafío 1* • *Texto: El trabajo perfecto* • *Comunidades: El Diario La Prensa*	 31–34 35	5 m. 35 m. 10 m.	1.1, 1.2, 1.3, 2.2, 3.1, 5.1, 5.2	Visual Presentation
8	To identify abilities and qualifications of different professionals	**Desafío 2 – Vocabulario** (248–249) • Warm-Up: Independent Starter • Vocabulary: *Trabajo y tecnología* • *Cultura: María Elena Salinas*	 36–39 40	5 m. 35 m. 10 m.	1.1, 1.2, 1.3, 2.1, 3.1, 4.2, 5.1, 5.2	Audio Practice Workbook
9	To learn how to describe nouns using adjective clauses	**Desafío 2 – Gramática** (250–251) • Warm-Up: Independent Starter • Grammar: *Dar detalles. El relativo 'que'*	 41–45	5 m. 45 m.	1.1, 1.2, 1.3, 3.1, 4.1, 5.1, 5.2	Audio Practice Workbook
10	To learn how to form masculine and feminine nouns	**Desafío 2 – Gramática** (252–253) • Warm-Up: Independent Starter • Grammar: *El género del nombre* • *Comunidades: Televisión en español*	 46–48 49	5 m. 35 m. 10 m.	1.1, 1.2, 1.3, 2.1, 3.1, 4.2, 5.1, 5.2	Video Practice Workbook

Day	Objectives	Sessions	Activities	Time	Standards	Resources/ Homework
11	To understand a news article and to integrate vocabulary and grammar	**Desafío 2 – Lectura/Comunicación** (254–257) • Warm-Up: Independent Starter • *Lectura: Manuel Jalón, un inventor humanista* • *Comunicación:* Review • *Final del desafío*	 50–52 53–55 56	5 m. 20 m. 15 m. 10 m.	1.1, 1.2, 1.3, 2.2, 3.1, 3.2, 5.1, 5.2	Audio Practice Workbook Quiz on *Desafío 2*
12	To express feelings and difficulty	**Desafío 3 – Por el bien común** (258–259) • Warm-Up: Correct quiz on *Desafío 2* • *Texto: Por el bien común* • *Comunidades: Hispanos solidarios*	 57–59 60	 5 m. 35 m. 10 m.	1.1, 1.2. 1.3, 2.1, 2.2, 3.1, 3.2, 5.1, 5.2	Visual Presentation Audio
13	To talk about volunteer work and environmental preservation in a community	**Desafío 3 – Vocabulario** (260–261) • Warm-Up: Independent Starter • Vocabulary: *Voluntariado y trabajo comunitario* • *Comunidades: Turismo sostenible*	 61–63 64	 5 m. 35 m. 10 m.	1.1, 1.2, 1.3, 2.1, 3.1, 4.2, 5.1, 5.2	Audio Video Practice Workbook
14	To learn how to express feelings and emotions	**Desafío 3 – Gramática** (262–263) • Warm-Up: Independent Starter • Grammar: *Expresar sentimientos*	 65–69	 5 m. 45 m.	1.1, 1.2, 1.3, 3.1, 4.1	Audio Practice Workbook
15	To learn how to provide information about an obstacle or difficulty in a given action	**Desafío 3 – Gramática** (264–265) • Warm-Up: Independent Starter • Grammar: *Expresar dificultad* • *Comparaciones: Frente de Defensa de la Amazonía*	 70–73 74	 5 m. 35 m. 10 m.	1.1, 1.2, 1.3, 2.1, 2.2, 3.1, 4.1, 5.1	Practice Workbook
16	To understand a literary text	**Desafío 3 – Lectura** (266–267) • Warm-Up: Independent Starter • *Lectura: Música*	 75–78	 5 m. 45 m.	1.1, 1.2, 1.3, 2.2, 3.1, 3.2	
17	To integrate vocabulary and grammar	**Desafío 3 – Comunicación** (268–269) • Warm-Up: Independent Starter • *Comunicación:* Review • *Final del desafío*	 79–81 82	 5 m. 30 m. 15 m.	1.1, 1.2, 1.3, 2.2, 3.1, 5.1, 5.2	Practice Workbook *Tu desafío* Quiz on *Desafío 3* **Para terminar – Tu desafío** (271)
18	To integrate language in context	**Para terminar** (270–271) • Warm-Up: Correct quiz on *Desafío 3* • *Todo junto* • *Tu desafío* presentations	 83–84 85	 5 m. 20 m. 25 m.	1.1, 1.2, 1.3, 2.1, 2.2, 3.1, 4.2, 5.1, 5.2	Audio Practice Workbook
19	To assess student proficiency and learn about higher education institutions in Hispanic countries	**Evaluación/Mapa cultural** (272–273) • Warm-Up: Independent Starter • Quiz on *Desafíos 1–3* • *Mapa cultural: Universidades hispanas*	 86	 5 m. 15 m. 30 m.	1.1, 1.2, 1.3, 2.1, 2.2, 3.1, 3.2, 5.2	Video Practice Workbook
20	To write a formal letter	**Escritura** (274–275) • Warm-Up: Independent Starter • *Escritura: Una carta formal*		 5 m. 45 m.	1.1, 1.2, 1.3, 3.1, 5.1	Project work
21	To develop a project for a non-profit organization	**Proyecto** (280–281) • Warm-Up: Prepare project presentations • Project presentations		 10 m. 40 m.	1.1, 1.2, 1.3, 2.1, 2.2, 3.1, 3.2, 5.1, 5.2	**Repaso – Vocabulario** (276–277) **Repaso – Gramática** (278–279) **Autoevaluación** (281)

Lesson Plans (90-Minute Classes)

Day	Objectives	Sessions	Activities	Time	Standards	Resources/ Homework
1	To introduce employment and professions and the characters' challenges, and to review learned vocabulary	(See Day 12 Unit 4) **¿Trabajas?/Las tareas/Antes de empezar** (228–233) • Warm-Up: Topic orientation • Presentation: *Ciudadanos responsables* • *Expresiones útiles* and *Recuerda*	 1–2 3–5	(45 m.) 10 m. 20 m. 15 m.	1.1, 1.2, 1.3, 2.1, 2.2, 3.1, 4.2, 5.1	Visual Presentation Video Practice Workbook
2	To express certainty and doubt and to identify different professionals and employment positions	**Desafío 1 – El Día de César Chávez/ Vocabulario** (234–237) • Warm-Up: Independent Starter • *Texto: El Día de César Chávez* • *Conexiones: César Chávez* • Vocabulary: *Profesiones y cargos* • *Conexiones: El Día del Trabajo*	 6–9 10 11–14 15	 5 m. 30 m. 10 m. 35 m. 10 m.	1.1, 1.2, 1.3, 2.1, 2.2, 3.1, 3.2, 4.1, 5.1, 5.2	Visual Presentation Audio Practice Workbook
3	To express certainty and doubt and to learn the imperfect subjunctive	**Desafío 1 – Gramática** (238–241) • Warm-Up: Independent Starter • Grammar: *Expresar certeza y duda* • *Cultura: Astronautas hispanos* • Grammar: *El imperfecto de subjuntivo*	 16–19 20 21–24	 5 m. 35 m. 10 m. 40 m.	1.1, 1.2, 1.3, 2.1, 3.1, 4.1, 5.1, 5.2	Audio Practice Workbook
4	To understand a dialogue and to integrate vocabulary and grammar	**Desafío 1 – Lectura/Comunicación/ Evaluación** (242–245) • Warm-Up: Independent Starter • *Lectura: Una vida interesante* • *Comunicación:* Review • *Final del desafío* • Quiz on *Desafío 1*	 25–27 28–29 30	 5 m. 35 m. 25 m. 10 m. 15 m.	1.1, 1.2, 1.3, 2.1, 2.2, 3.1, 3.2, 5.1	Visual Presentation Practice Workbook *Tu desafío*
5	To refer to something that is unknown and to identify abilities and qualifications of different professionals	**Desafío 2 – El trabajo perfecto/Vocabulario** (246–249) • Warm-Up: Independent Starter • *Texto: El trabajo perfecto* • *Comunidades: El Diario La Prensa* • Vocabulary: *Trabajo y tecnología* • *Cultura: María Elena Salinas*	 31–34 35 36–39 40	 5 m. 35 m. 10 m. 30 m. 10 m.	1.1, 1.2, 1.3, 2.1, 2.2, 3.1, 4.2, 5.1, 5.2	Visual Presentation Audio Practice Workbook
6	To learn how to describe nouns using adjective clauses and to learn how to form masculine and feminine nouns	**Desafío 2 – Gramática** (250–253) • Warm-Up: Independent Starter • Grammar: *Dar detalles. El relativo 'que'* • Grammar: *El género del nombre* • *Comunidades: Televisión en español*	 41–45 46–48 49	 5 m. 40 m. 35 m. 10 m.	1.1, 1.2, 1.3, 2.1, 3.1, 4.1, 4.2, 5.1, 5.2	Audio Video Practice Workbook

Day	Objectives	Sessions	Activities	Time	Standards	Resources/ Homework
7	To understand a news article and to integrate vocabulary and grammar	**Desafío 2 – Lectura/Comunicación/Evaluación** (254–257) • Warm-Up: Independent Starter • *Lectura: Manuel Jalón, un inventor humanista* • *Comunicación:* Review • *Final del desafío* • Quiz on *Desafío 2*	 50–52 53–55 56	 5 m. 35 m. 25 m. 10 m. 15 m.	1.1, 1.2, 1.3, 2.2, 3.1, 3.2, 5.1, 5.2	Audio Practice Workbook
8	To express feelings and difficulty and to talk about volunteer work and environmental preservation in a community	**Desafío 3 – Por el bien común/Vocabulario** (258–261) • Warm-Up: Independent Starter • *Texto: Por el bien común* • *Comunidades: Hispanos solidarios* • Vocabulary: *Voluntariado y trabajo comunitario* • *Comunidades: Turismo sostenible*	 57–59 60 61–63 64	 5 m. 30 m. 10 m. 35 m. 10 m.	1.1, 1.2. 1.3, 2.1, 2.2, 3.1, 3.2, 4.2, 5.1, 5.2	Visual Presentation Audio Video Practice Workbook
9	To learn how to express feelings and emotions and to learn how to provide information about an obstacle or difficulty in a given action	**Desafío 3 – Gramática** (262–265) • Warm-Up: Independent Starter • Grammar: *Expresar sentimientos* • Grammar: *Expresar dificultad* • *Comparaciones: Frente de Defensa de la Amazonía*	 65–69 70–73 74	 5 m. 40 m. 35 m. 10 m.	1.1, 1.2, 1.3, 2.1, 2.2, 3.1, 4.1, 5.1	Audio Practice Workbook
10	To understand a literary text, to integrate vocabulary and grammar to integrate language in context, and to assess student proficiency	**Desafío 3 – Lectura/Comunicación/Evaluación/ Todo junto** (266–270) • Warm-Up: Independent Starter • *Lectura: Música* • *Comunicación:* Review • *Final del desafío* • *Todo junto* • Quiz on *Desafío 3*	 75–78 79–81 82 83–84	 5 m. 25 m. 20 m. 10 m. 15 m. 15 m.	1.1, 1.2, 1.3, 2.2, 3.1, 3.2, 5.1, 5.2	Practice Workbook **Para terminar – Tu desafío** (271)
11	To learn about higher education institutions in Hispanic countries and to write a formal letter	**Tu desafío/Mapa cultural/Escritura** (271–275) • Warm-Up: Independent Starter • *Tu desafío* presentations • *Mapa cultural: Universidades hispanas* • *Escritura: Una carta formal*	 85 86	 5 m. 15 m. 30 m. 40 m.	1.1, 1.2, 1.3, 2.1, 2.2, 3.1, 3.2, 5.1, 5.2	Video Practice Workbook **Repaso – Vocabulario** (276–277) **Repaso – Gramática** (278–279) Quiz on *Desafíos 1–3* Project work
12	To develop a project for a non-profit organization	**Proyecto/Assessment** (280–281) • Warm-Up: Correct quiz on *Desafíos 1–3* • Project presentations • *Autoevaluación* • Test (See Day 1 Unit 6)		 5 m. 15 m. 10 m. 15 m. (45 m.)	1.1, 1.2, 1.3, 2.1, 2.2, 3.1, 3.2, 5.1, 5.2	

Unit 5 ¿Trabajas?

8 Dedicado a su gente

El famoso líder sindicalista César Chávez nació en Yuma (Arizona) el 31 de marzo de 1927 en una familia humilde de origen mexicano. Cuando era muy joven, tuvo que abandonar los estudios y empezar a trabajar como agricultor en los campos de Arizona para ayudar a su familia. Pronto comprobó que los agricultores no recibían salarios adecuados ni atención médica. Por eso formó la Asociación Nacional de Agricultores, que trabajaba de forma pacífica para defender los derechos laborales de los trabajadores agrícolas. Esta asociación agrupó a los campesinos inmigrantes, la mayoría de origen hispano. Con Chávez a la cabeza, organizaron varias huelgas y manifestaciones para llamar la atención sobre su causa, y consiguieron el reconocimiento de sus derechos. Chávez murió en 1993, a los 66 años. El 31 de marzo, día de su nacimiento, se celebra en los Estados Unidos el Día de César Chávez en su honor.

13 ¿Qué quiere ser Asha?

–¿Ya sabes lo que quieres hacer después de graduarte?

–Qué va, me está costando mucho decidirlo.

–Te aconsejo que consideres tu personalidad, tus habilidades y tus gustos. Puedes hacer una prueba de aptitud o ir a una feria informativa de las que organizan las universidades.

–Sí, no es mala idea… Tengo que pensarlo porque casi todos nuestros amigos saben ya qué quieren hacer con su futuro.

–¿Qué te contaron?

–Pues, mira, a Carlos le encanta hablar y discutir, así que piensa ser abogado.

–Ja, ja, ja. Sí, va mucho con su personalidad.

–A Ana le encanta viajar y estudiar idiomas; creo que va a trabajar como guía turística o como traductora.

–Buena idea.

–Y a Manuela le gusta mucho el arte y dibuja muy bien, así que va a estudiar diseño gráfico.

–Tú eres muy buena con las computadoras y te encantan los videojuegos. ¿Qué te parece programadora informática?

–Hum, puede ser… ¡Ojalá que una computadora tome esta decisión por mí!

18 ¿Vivir para trabajar o trabajar para vivir?

1. Yo tengo un restaurante. Es verdad que trabajo muchas horas, pero me gusta mi trabajo y ser mi propio jefe.

2. Yo soy abogada y trabajo para gente sin recursos económicos. Es cierto que el salario no es alto, pero tengo la oportunidad de mejorar la sociedad y de ayudar a los demás.

3. Mi trabajo es estupendo. Soy arquitecto y diseño edificios eficientes desde el punto de vista energético. Es obvio que tengo mucha responsabilidad, pero vale la pena.

4. Soy secretaria y trabajo en una oficina. Llego muy temprano por la mañana y nunca salgo antes de las nueve de la noche. Me gusta mi trabajo, pero dudo que me quede aquí mucho más… Necesito tener más tiempo libre.

5. Yo me dedico a enseñar Español. En clase tengo la oportunidad de compartir experiencias con jóvenes estudiantes. Y estoy convencida de que aprender un idioma los ayudará a encontrar un buen trabajo.

39 Buscando un puesto

–Buenos días. ¿En qué puedo ayudarlo?

–Buenos días. Llamo por el anuncio. Estoy interesado en el puesto de técnico.

–¿Tiene usted formación en computación?

–No tengo formación especializada, pero me siento cómodo usando las computadoras. Se me dan bien.

–¿Y sabe instalar una impresora y conectarla a una computadora?

–Sí, claro. Y también puedo arreglar problemas básicos.

–Perfecto. También tendrá que usar la fotocopiadora.

–Muy bien, no hay ningún problema.

–El puesto es a media jornada. ¿Le parece bien?

–Sí. Prefiero trabajar solo media jornada porque estoy estudiando.

–Muy bien. ¿Podría venir a la oficina para una entrevista el martes a las tres y media?

–Por supuesto. Muchas gracias.

44 La universidad

1. Voy a graduarme en seis meses y voy a ir a la universidad, pero no quiero estar lejos de mi casa.

2. Me encanta la universidad que elegí porque tiene un programa muy bueno de Derecho. Es que quiero hacerme abogada.

3. Cuando empecé a buscar universidad, quería que estuviera en Nueva York, pero finalmente me decidí por una universidad de California.

4. Estuve mucho tiempo buscando una universidad con unos buenos cursos de Tecnología. Por fin la encontré y ahora estoy muy contenta.

5. Cuando pienso en la universidad, me imagino una escuela pequeña donde todos se conocen. Eso es lo que busco.

6. Desde que estaba en el colegio quería hacerme médica. Por eso solo buscaba universidades que tuvieran facultad de Medicina. Al final encontré una muy buena.

53 Buscando trabajo

1. Me encanta cocinar, siempre estoy probando recetas nuevas. Además conozco platos de muchos países.

2. No tengo mucha experiencia, pero ayudaba a mi padre con su negocio. Me encargaba de las fotocopias y a veces también hacía llamadas a los clientes. Eso sí, no puedo trabajar a jornada completa porque todavía estoy estudiando.

3. Soy el mayor de cinco hermanos y por eso tengo mucha experiencia con niños. Pero no puedo trabajar los fines de semana…

4. El año pasado tomé un curso de diseño gráfico y ahora estoy buscando trabajo. Necesito un buen sueldo, pero mi horario es flexible.

59 ONG

–En la página web de esta ONG hay muchas fotos, mira. Hay jóvenes que ayudan a construir una escuela. Y también tienen un proyecto para fomentar la lectura. ¡Qué buena idea! Podríamos organizar una biblioteca. ¿Qué te parece?

–La verdad es que no me apetece mucho, Eva. Ayer vi una organización que tiene un proyecto muy interesante. Quieren ideas para convencer a la gente de que no arroje basura en el parque. Podríamos hacer carteles y ponerlos en los parques de toda la ciudad.

–Es que yo prefiero hacer algo que ayude a la gente.

–¿Por ejemplo?

–Pues organizar actividades para personas mayores que no tienen familia. Aquí hay una ONG que se dedica a eso.

–No es mala idea. También podríamos colaborar con esta organización que ayuda a personas que no tienen casa. Les ofrecen ropa, comida, atención médica…

–Ethan, tenemos que decidirnos pronto porque no tenemos mucho tiempo para pensar…

–Sí, tienes razón.

62 Un anuncio

¿Le preocupa la situación de los inmigrantes en su comunidad? Un País para Todos es una organización internacional que lucha por los derechos de los inmigrantes desde 1990. Nuestra misión es mejorar la convivencia entre las diferentes culturas. Para más información sobre los programas solidarios en su comunidad, llame al 800-555-2222 o envíe un correo electrónico a unpaisparatodos@ong.org. Necesitamos su ayuda. ¡Hágase voluntario!

68 Las experiencias de Andy

–Y cuéntame, Andy. ¿Qué es lo que más te sorprendió en tus viajes por Latinoamérica?

–¡Uf! No es fácil contestar a esa pregunta. Déjame pensar… Me sorprendió mucho que hubiera tantas organizaciones benéficas en todos los países que visité.

–Sí, es que hay demasiados problemas en el mundo. ¿A ti qué es lo que más te preocupa?

–¿Lo que más me preocupa? Que los niños sufran. Y también me enoja que haya compañías que destruyan los bosques para conseguir beneficios económicos.

–Sí, es una lástima. Andy, me alegra que tengas experiencias tan extraordinarias para contar.

–Y a mí me emociona que Ethan y tú vayan a colaborar con una organización benéfica. Seguro que después también tendrán muchas cosas que contarme.

–Gracias, Andy. Te llamaremos pronto.

83 Profesionales

1. –Señor Pons, usted es abogado. Díganos, ¿qué le gusta y qué no le gusta de su trabajo?

   –Bueno, me encanta mi trabajo. Me permite tener contacto con la gente, resolver problemas, defender casos importantes… Es un trabajo muy interesante. Gano bastante dinero, pero es un trabajo muy duro porque trabajo muchas horas.

2. –Señora Castro, ¿puede decirnos cuáles son las ventajas y desventajas de su trabajo?

   –Las ventajas… A mí me conviene mucho este trabajo porque tiene horarios fijos y yo tengo una familia, así que necesito una rutina. Otra ventaja es que tengo mucho contacto con la gente. La verdad es que no veo desventajas en mi trabajo. Me gusta mucho lo que hago.

3. –Ángela, usted trabaja en esta empresa desde hace tres meses. ¿Es su primer trabajo?

   –Sí, este es mi primer trabajo.

   –¿Y cuáles son las ventajas y los inconvenientes de su trabajo?

   –Cuando terminé la universidad, decidí hacer un máster en Ingeniería Industrial. El trabajo que hago es bueno y, aunque no me pagan mucho, tengo posibilidades de desarrollar mi carrera y de aprender. Además, trabajo en proyectos que tienen un impacto positivo en la comunidad.

4. –Usted, señor Collado, tiene un trabajo muy peligroso. ¿Qué es lo que más le gusta de lo que hace?

   –Hay muchas cosas que me gustan. Es verdad que es peligroso, pero es emocionante salvar vidas y ayudar a la gente. Para mí es muy positivo que la comunidad tenga confianza en mí y poder participar en casos de emergencia.

Unit 5
¿Trabajas?

The Unit

- The themes for Unit 5 are work and professions, including volunteer work.
- Tim, a veteran of *Fans del español*, will give the participants their tasks.
  - *Desafío 1.* Asha and Lucas have to conduct research on the life and work of César Chávez, a famous civil rights leader, and make a presentation on his life.
  - *Desafío 2.* Michelle and Daniel must answer job ads in the oldest Spanish-language newspaper in the United States.
  - *Desafío 3.* Eva and Ethan must find a non-profit organization and write a proposal for a project to help the less fortunate.

Activities	Standards	Resources
¿Trabajas?	1.2, 2.1, 2.2, 3.1, 5.1	Video

Teaching Suggestions

Warm-Up / Independent Starter

- Prepare a short questionnaire for students to answer in writing.
  1. ¿Qué líder político o social te gusta o te inspira? ¿Por qué?
  2. ¿Qué periódicos o revistas lees? ¿Por qué?
  3. ¿Qué organización benéfica te parece importante? ¿Por qué?

Preparation

- Ask volunteers to read their Independent Starters and initiate a class discussion on these topics. To expand the discussion, you may want to ask some of these questions: ¿Qué cualidades les parecen importantes en un líder? ¿Cómo se informan de lo que ocurre? ¿Qué noticias les interesan? ¿Conocen a personas famosas que trabajen por alguna causa justa? ¿Hacen ustedes trabajo de voluntariado?
- Have students read each *Desafío's* objective, as well as the vocabulary and grammar goals, then discuss how each picture might relate to these objectives and goals.

228

UNIDAD 5
¿Trabajas?
El trabajo y las profesiones

DESAFÍO 1

El Diario La Prensa (Nueva York)

EL DIARIO

Expresar certeza y duda

Vocabulario
Profesiones y cargos

Gramática
Expresar certeza y duda

El imperfecto de subjuntivo

DESAFÍO 2

Referirse a lo desconocido

Vocabulario
Trabajo y tecnología

Gramática
Dar detalles. El relativo *que*

El género del nombre

El activista César Chávez (Estados Unidos)

The Challenge

DESAFÍO 1

El activista César Chávez
César Estrada Chávez—born in 1927 in Yuma, Arizona—was a civil rights leader and activist who became an important historical icon in the Hispanic community. Of Mexican background, he founded the United Farm Workers Association in support of fair wages and better working conditions for farm workers in the United States. César Chávez Day is celebrated on March 31st in many parts of the United States, including the states of California, Arizona, Colorado, Michigan, New Mexico, Texas, Utah, and Wisconsin.

DESAFÍO 2

El Diario La Prensa
El Diario La Prensa, based in New York, is the most widely read Spanish-language newspaper in New York and the third largest in the country. This newspaper is the result of a merger that combined the oldest Spanish-language newspaper, *La Prensa*, founded in 1913, and *El Diario de Nueva York*, founded in 1947. As is the current situation with most newspapers, *El Diario La Prensa* has suffered a decrease in sales in recent years. However, the online version has an increasing number of readers and it is quite influential among Spanish speakers in this country.

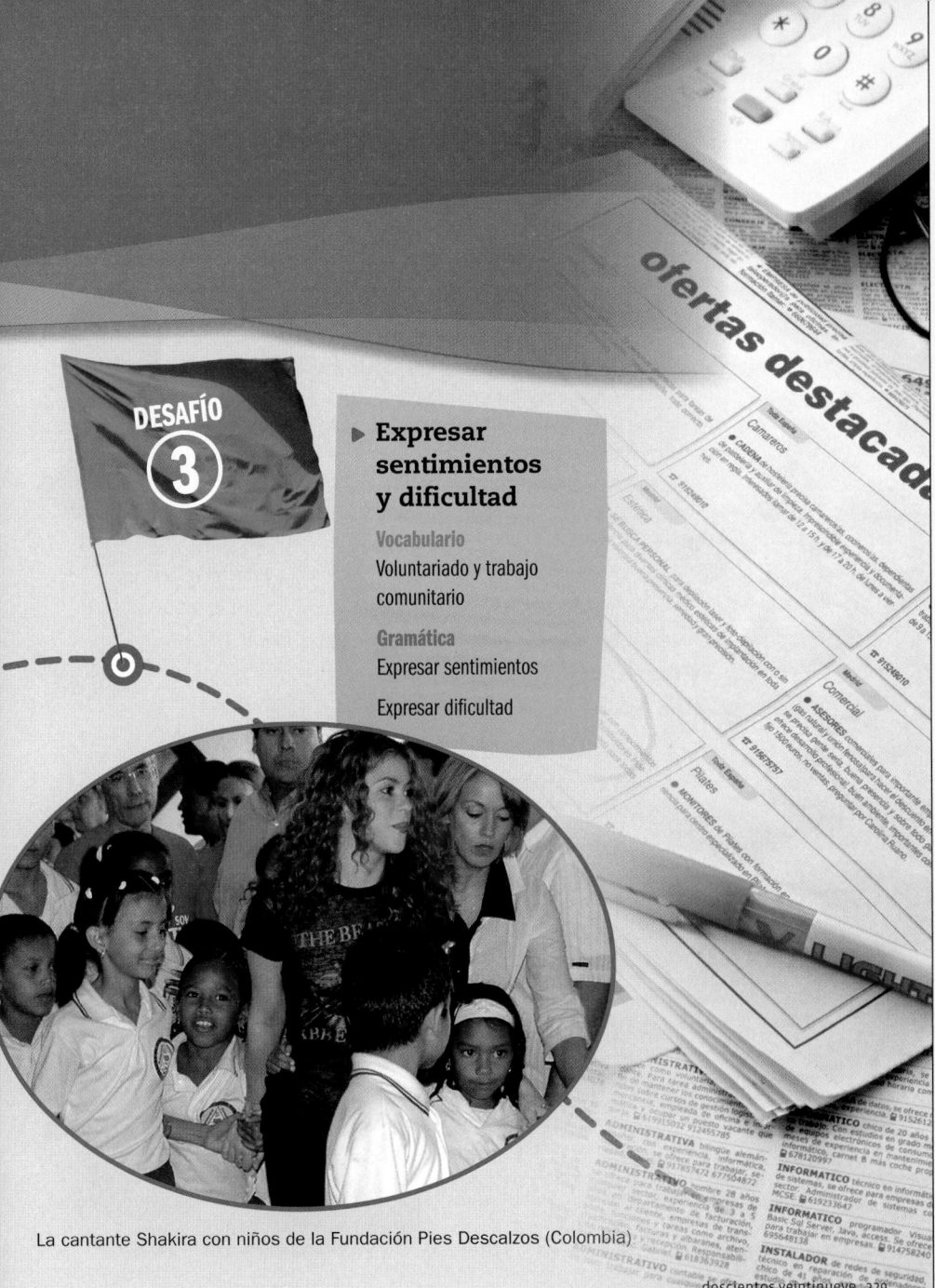

¿Trabajas?

DESAFÍO 3

▶ **Expresar sentimientos y dificultad**

Vocabulario
Voluntariado y trabajo comunitario

Gramática
Expresar sentimientos

Expresar dificultad

La cantante Shakira con niños de la Fundación Pies Descalzos (Colombia)

doscientos veintinueve 229

Picture Discussion

▪ Ask students to look at the photos and check their knowledge. Do they know the leader, the newspaper, and the foundation depicted in the photos? If they don't, you may wish to have small groups do some brief research, then share their findings.

El activista César Chávez (Estados Unidos)

▪ Ask students to describe this photo. Can they guess what these people are doing? Why do they think they carry a photo of César Chávez? Ask students to brainstorm celebrations, marches, or events in which people might carry or display a photo of their leader or favorite personality. Examples include a parade celebrating Martin Luther King Day, a political convention, a sports event, etc.

El Diario La Prensa (Nueva York)

▪ Have students discuss foreign-language media that they are familiar with in this country, such as radio stations, television channels, magazines, and newspapers. How might the content of the media change depending on the language? (e.g., different celebrities in the news, more or less world news coverage) What can one learn by reading or viewing media in other languages?

La cantante Shakira con niños de la Fundación Pies Descalzos (Colombia)

▪ Ask students to list some well-known charitable NGOs (i.e., non-governmental organizations), also called non-profit organizations, or NPOs, in the United States. Examples include the American Red Cross, Greenpeace, and the United Way. Do some of these organizations have celebrity sponsors and spokespeople? What types of causes do these organizations support? How might these causes be similar or different in other countries?

Objectives

▪ By the end of Unit 5, students will be able to
  – Talk about professions and job titles.
  – Express certainty and doubt.
  – Talk about work and technology.
  – Provide details and talk about unknown things or people.
  – Talk about volunteering and community work.
  – Express feelings and difficulty.
  – Talk about an influential Hispanic civic rights leader and some well-known Hispanic professionals, as well as some of the media and NGOs of the Spanish-speaking world.

▶ DESAFÍO 3

La cantante Shakira con niños de la Fundación Pies Descalzos

Non-governmental organizations (ONGs in Spanish) operate independently of specific governments, and pursue charity causes or social, global, or cultural interests. Famous Hispanics have become sponsors of foundations that operate in Latin America and Spain. Some examples are *Pies Descalzos,* a foundation created by Shakira, a Colombian singer, to improve the education and quality of life of disadvantaged children, and *Mi Sangre,* sponsored by Juanes, another Colombian singer, to support children affected by civil unrest.

229

Unit 5
Las tareas

Presentation

- In this section, the three pairs will participate in a videoconference with Tim, who describes their next challenges to them. Students will preview ways to express whether they are capable of doing something or not, and they will also preview expressions of encouragement.

Activities	Standards	Resources
Texto	1.2, 2.1, 2.2, 3.1, 3.2, 5.1	Vis. Pres.
1.	1.1, 1.2, 1.3, 2.1	
2.	1.3	

Teaching Suggestions

Warm-Up / Independent Starter

- Give students the following expressions and ask them to write three sentences that would prompt these expressions as a reaction:
  1. ¡Anímate! (Come on!)
  2. ¡Claro! (Of course!)
  3. No se rindan. (Don't give up.)

Preparation

- Ask students to share their sentences from the Independent Starter with the class. Who came up with the most interesting or clever sentence for each expression? Take a class vote to decide.

- Write the following phrases on the board and make sure students understand the meaning: derechos laborales (work or labor rights), anuncios de trabajo (job ads), and organización no gubernamental (non-governmental organization). Have students find these expressions in the text on page 230 and the dialogue on page 231 and associate them with each of the Desafíos.

- Discuss the word trabajo and its different meanings (i.e., job, work, task, employment, effort). Ask students to find the word in the text and have them derive the meaning through the context.

- Have students identify the following command forms in the text: No se preocupen, dinos, anímate, no se rindan. Remind students of the relationship between the ustedes commands and the present subjunctive forms (i.e., they are the same).

230

Las tareas

Ciudadanos responsables

 Tim gets in touch with the Fans del español in order to inform them about their new challenges. Read the conversation to find out what they will have to do.

TIM: Hola, amigos. ¿Cómo les va? Esta vez voy a darles yo las tareas. Van a tener que trabajar mucho, pero no se preocupen. Seguro que todo saldrá bien.

EVA: Hola, Tim, estamos preparados. Por favor, dinos lo que hay que hacer.

TIM: Asha y Lucas tienen que investigar sobre un líder hispano muy famoso, César Chávez, y preparar una presentación sobre su vida.

LUCAS: Suena interesante. Si no me equivoco, se celebra un festival en su honor...

ASHA: Sí, es en marzo, creo. Pero a mí me cuesta mucho trabajo hablar en público.

TIM: ¡Anímate! Estoy seguro de que lo conseguirás.

LUCAS: ¡Claro, Asha! Puedes hacerlo.

ASHA: Está bien...

MICHELLE: Y nosotros, ¿qué tenemos que hacer?

TIM: Daniel y tú van a contestar anuncios de trabajo.

DANIEL: ¿Cooooómo? ¿Seremos capaces?

MICHELLE: Claro, ¿por qué no?

TIM: Y, por último, Ethan y Eva van a elegir una ONG para proponerle un proyecto de voluntariado.

ETHAN: ¿Una ONG?... ¿Qué es una ONG?

EVA: Creo que ONG significa Organización No Gubernamental.

TIM: Exacto. ¿Tienen alguna pregunta? Bien, pues adelante. Y si tienen algún problema, no se rindan. Yo estaré aquí para ayudarlos.

230 doscientos treinta

Differentiated Instruction

DEVELOPING LEARNERS

- Ask students to make a four-column chart. The heading of each column will correspond to the names of the student pairs, plus Tim. Have students organize the information presented on this page. Students should describe the task each pair must complete, and include any lines that reflect the doubts or certainties the pairs may have about the successful completion of their task, as well as Tim's words of encouragement. Ask students why they think Tim is the one giving encouragement.

EXPANDING LEARNERS

- After students have read the dialogue, ask them to write the words or expressions that show encouragement and those that show doubt, and to indicate who says them. For example: Encouragement → Seguro que todo saldrá bien. ¡Anímate! (Tim) Doubt → A mí me cuesta mucho trabajo hablar en público (Asha); ¿Seremos capaces? (Daniel). Then ask students to provide other words or expressions that communicate similar feelings. For example, Tim might say: ¡No te rindas! Asha could state: Esto va a ser muy difícil. Daniel's line might be: ¡Pero si no estamos preparados!

¿Qué sabes de César Chávez?

Pues sé que fue un líder hispano que trabajó en favor de los derechos laborales.

¿Dónde buscamos los anuncios de trabajo?

En el periódico hispano más antiguo de los Estados Unidos.

¿Hay muchas organizaciones no gubernamentales hispanas?

Sí. Muchos hispanos famosos colaboran activamente con alguna organización no gubernamental.

1 **¿Comprendes?**

▶ **Contesta.** ¿Qué tiene que hacer cada pareja?

1. Asha y Lucas   2. Daniel y Michelle   3. Eva y Ethan

▶ **Escribe** la respuesta a estas preguntas.

1. ¿Quién fue César Chávez?
2. ¿Dónde van a buscar los anuncios de trabajo Daniel y Michelle?
3. ¿Qué es una ONG?

▶ **Explica.** ¿Qué desafío te parece más interesante? ¿Por qué?

2 **Investiga**

▶ **Escribe** tres expresiones del texto que sean nuevas para ti. ¿Qué crees que significan?

 Texto: Ciudadanos responsables

- To help students focus on the gist of the dialogue, have them read what Tim says in order to identify the three *desafíos*. Then ask students to skim over the reading to identify key words that catch their attention about the dialogue. What do these key words tell them about the theme of the dialogue?

- Read the text aloud in order to model correct intonation and pronunciation. Then have students read the dialogue aloud in small groups. Make them repeat the exclamatory and interrogative sentences with the appropriate emphasis in order to practice colloquial language.

Activities

1. To expand this activity, ask additional questions. These are some questions you may want to ask: *¿Qué problema tiene Asha? ¿Qué le preocupa a Daniel? ¿Qué opina Tim sobre estos problemas o preocupaciones de los participantes?*

Answer Key

1. 1. Tienen que investigar y preparar una presentación sobre César Chávez, un líder hispano muy famoso.
   2. Tienen que contestar anuncios de trabajo.
   3. Tienen que proponer un proyecto de voluntariado a una ONG.
   ▶ 1. Fue un líder hispano que trabajó en favor de los derechos laborales.
   2. Van a buscarlos en el periódico hispano más antiguo de los Estados Unidos.
   3. Es una organización no gubernamental.
   ▶ Answers will vary.
2. Answers will vary.

Additional Resources

Fans Online activities
Practice Workbook

HERITAGE LANGUAGE LEARNERS

- Ask students to bring a Spanish-language newspaper to class. The paper could be from a community in this country or from around the Spanish-speaking world. Have students share the paper with the rest of the class and point out the similarities and differences between it and a national or local paper. Ask the heritage learners to read, or translate, some headlines. Ask them to address the paper's approach to both international and national news. Then ask all students to discuss the most distinguishing features of the Spanish-language paper.

COOPERATIVE LEARNING

- Ask students to work in small groups and imagine that they have been given the chance to select one of the *desafíos* to complete. Which one would they choose and why? How would they go about gathering information? Who would the group like as a partner and why? Have them discuss this among themselves, making sure that all members contribute their ideas. Then, after students reach an agreement, ask them to explain their approach to the rest of the class.

Las tareas

231

Antes de empezar

Presentation

- In this section, students will learn a variety of useful expressions, some to express whether they feel capable of doing something or not, and others for encouraging or consoling others.
- Students will also review words that refer to professions and work locations.

Activities	Standards	Resources
Expresiones útiles	1.2, 2.1	
3.	1.1, 5.1, 5.2	
Recuerda	1.2	
4.	1.1, 1.2, 1.3	
5.	1.3	

Teaching Suggestions

Warm-Up / Independent Starter

- Have students list words they know that describe professions and trades. Then ask them to create a separate list of verbs that are associated with the professions they listed.

Preparation

- Go over the *expresiones útiles* by using them in personalized contexts. For instance, you might express your doubts about your ability to do something. Then have students react by using expressions to encourage you. Model the activity with a student in front of the class.

  A. *Me cuesta trabajo ir al gimnasio todos los días.*
  B. *No se rinda.*

- You may ask students to write down a list of things that they consider difficult about learning a language. Then brainstorm solutions with them and use some of the *expresiones útiles* to encourage them.

- To practice the expressions for telling whether someone is capable of doing something or not, you may write some statements or opinions on the board and have students react to them. In order not to hurt anybody's feelings, make sure that the statements are not controversial but instead are humorous. For example: *Creo que a ustedes les cuesta trabajo levantarse temprano porque tienen cara de dormidos.*

232

EXPRESIONES ÚTILES

Para expresar si puedes o no puedes hacer algo:

(No) **Puedo** hacerlo.
(No) **Soy capaz de** terminar las tareas pronto.
(No) **Me resulta fácil/difícil** leer en español.
(No) **Me cuesta trabajo** levantarme pronto.

Para animar:

¡Anímate!
No te rindas.
Lo conseguirás.
Seguro que todo saldrá bien.

3 ¿Eres capaz?

▶ **Ordena** estas palabras y escribe oraciones.

1. trabajo/escribir/Me/en/cuesta/español
2. patinar/No/capaz/soy/de
3. resulta/manejar/fácil/Me/bastante
4. cuesta/No/trabajo/me/cocinar

 ▶ **Habla.** ¿Piensas que puedes hacer estas cosas? Díselo a tu compañero(a). Él / Ella debe reaccionar a tu comentario.

- cantar en público
- tocar un instrumento
- manejar un coche
- cocinar
- sacar buenas notas en tus exámenes
- jugar a algún deporte: béisbol, baloncesto, fútbol...

No soy capaz de cantar en público, me da vergüenza.

¡Anímate! Tienes una voz muy bonita.

Differentiated Instruction

DEVELOPING LEARNERS

- Read some statements or questions to students that describe both everyday tasks and other actions that are nearly impossible to complete. Then ask students to answer if they can or cannot do them. Encourage students to use as many of the expressions on the page as they can. For example:

  A. ¿Puedes leer 100 páginas en 10 minutos?
  B. No puedo hacerlo.
  A. ¿Te resulta fácil contestar en español?
  B. Sí, me resulta fácil contestar en español.

EXPANDING LEARNERS

- Have students work with a partner and create some conversations using the expressions on the page, or others they may know. Students will take turns stating that they cannot do something, and partners will respond with some encouraging words. The first student will then make either a positive or a negative response to the partner's comment. For example:

  A. No soy capaz de escribir este informe.
  B. Seguro que el informe saldrá bien.
  A. ¡Qué va! Estás equivocado. / ¡Por supuesto! Tienes razón.

RECUERDA

Profesiones

el/la abogado(a)	el/la bombero(a)	el/la director(a)	el/la policía
el/la arquitecto(a)	el/la cajero(a)	el/la ingeniero(a)	el/la secretario(a)
el/la auxiliar de vuelo	el/la cocinero(a)	el/la maestro(a)	el/la técnico(a)
el/la bibliotecario(a)	el/la dependiente(a)	el/la mesero(a)	el/la telefonista

Lugares de trabajo

el aeropuerto	la escuela	la oficina	la tienda
la biblioteca	la fábrica	el restaurante	el supermercado

4 **¿Cuánto sabes?**

▶ **Habla** con tu compañero(a). ¿Conocen a personas con las profesiones del cuadro Recuerda?

Modelo A. *Dos de mis tíos son abogados, pero no conozco a ningún arquitecto.*
 B. *Yo sí. La hermana mayor de mi mejor amiga es arquitecta.*

▶ **Completa.** ¿Conoces más vocabulario sobre esos temas? Escríbelo.

Modelo *el/la recepcionista...*

▶ **Organiza** el vocabulario en una red de ideas.

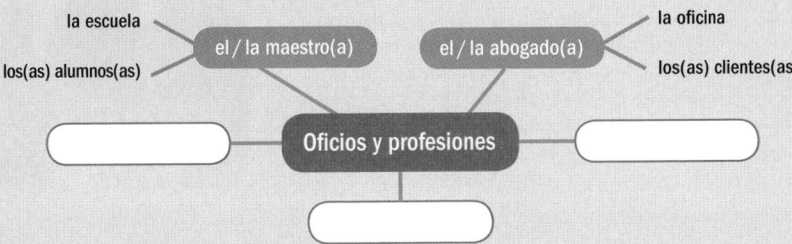

5 **¿Qué hacen en su trabajo?**

▶ **Escribe** oraciones con elementos de las tres columnas.

Modelo *El profesor enseña a los estudiantes.*

profesor(a)	enseñar	cereales y frutas
abogado(a)	curar	clientes
agricultor(a)	arreglar	edificios
veterinario(a)	diseñar	coches
mecánico(a)	cultivar	estudiantes
arquitecto(a)	defender	animales

doscientos treinta y tres **233**

HERITAGE LANGUAGE LEARNERS

• Ask students to interview a Spanish speaker who practices one of the professions listed on page 233. Students might ask about the requirements for this job, including any educational requirements, how long the person has been at this position and in this field, what studies he or she has completed, and how he or she became interested in this field. Students should also give an example of a typical day at work, and conclude with describing opportunities for their own generation in this job.

MULTIPLE INTELLIGENCES:

Verbal-Linguistic Intelligence

• Write the names of professions on cards and place them in a bag. Do the same with names of places where these people might work. Ask students to pick one card from each bag and, using a verb of their choice and any other descriptive phrases, make up a sentence with these elements. For example, if a student picks *el/la cajero(a)* and *el aeropuerto*, the sentence might be: *El cajero llega al aeropuerto a las nueve.* The sentences may be humorous, but they must be grammatically correct.

Antes de empezar

■ When reading through the *Recuerda* box, ask students to share any additional words they had in their Independent Starters for professions. For each profession listed, ask students to share any related verb that they had listed as well.

Activities

3. Before doing the second part of this activity, ask a couple of volunteers to read the dialogue in the photo, then place students in pairs. Monitor them as they practice their dialogues, then select a few pairs to present one of their dialogues in front of the class.

4. To make the activity more engaging, have pairs share their dialogues with the class and ask further questions. For example: *¿Cómo se llama la arquitecta que conoces? ¿Dónde trabaja? ¿Qué hace en su trabajo?*

5. To extend this activity, you may want to ask additional questions. For example: *¿Qué hacen los agricultores? ¿Dónde trabajan los mecánicos? ¿Quiénes son los clientes de los veterinarios?*

Answer Key

3. 1. Me cuesta trabajo escribir en español.
 2. No soy capaz de patinar.
 3. Me resulta bastante fácil manejar.
 4. No me cuesta trabajo cocinar.
 ▶ Answers will vary.

4. Answers will vary.
 ▶ Answers will vary.
 ▶ Answers will vary.

5. Answers will vary. Sample answers:
 La abogada defiende a los clientes.
 El agricultor cultiva cereales y frutas.
 El veterinario cura a los animales.
 El mecánico arregla los coches.
 La arquitecta diseña edificios.

Additional Resources

Fans Online activities
Practice Workbook

DESAFÍO 1

Expresar certeza y duda

Presentation

- In *Desafío 1*, Asha and Lucas must make a presentation about César Chávez to be delivered during a celebration in his honor. Students will preview language used for talking about professions as well as some expressions that indicate doubt or certainty.

Activities	Standards	Resources
Texto	1.2, 2.1, 3.1	Vis. Pres.
6.	1.2, 1.3, 2.1	
7.	1.1, 1.2, 2.1, 3.1	
8.	1.2, 3.1	Audio
9.	1.1, 1.3, 2.1, 3.1	
10. Conexiones	1.1, 1.2, 1.3, 2.1, 2.2, 3.1, 5.1	

Teaching Suggestions

Warm-Up / Independent Starter

- Ask students to think of a person that they consider a leader. Have them list five personal qualities that make this person a good leader, and define what it means to be a leader.

Preparation

- Invite students to share their Independent Starters within small groups. Ask each group to come to a consensus on five essential leadership characteristics.

Texto: El Día de César Chávez

- Ask students to read the introduction to the reading silently. Then have them write a "to do list" for Asha and Lucas as they embark up on their research project. For example: 1. *Tienen que ir a la biblioteca.* 2. *También deben buscar información en Internet.*

- Ask for volunteers to read aloud the roles of Asha, Lucas, and Mrs. Wilson. Then have students work in pairs to write sentences summarizing the content. Require that they use the verbs *ayudar, celebrar, defender, hablar, luchar, nacer,* and the nouns *información, libro,* and *líder.* Ask each group to write a sentence on the board.

234

El Día de César Chávez

Asha and Lucas must make a presentation about the life of a famous civil rights leader at a César Chávez Day festival. But first, they will need to do some serious research on the topic!

ASHA: ¿Por dónde empezamos, Lucas?

LUCAS: A ver, sabemos que César Chávez fue un líder estadounidense de origen mexicano y que trabajó por los derechos de los trabajadores.

ASHA: Y también sabemos que se celebra un festival en su honor en marzo. Pero yo nunca he asistido. ¿Y tú?

LUCAS: No, yo tampoco. ¡Tengo una idea! Vamos a hablar con la señora Wilson. Es mi profesora de Historia.

ASHA: ¿Ahora?

LUCAS: Sí. Es probable que esté en su despacho.

* * *

LUCAS: Buenos días. ¿Podemos hablar con usted un momento?

SEÑORA WILSON: Claro, Lucas.

LUCAS: Asha y yo necesitamos información sobre César Chávez y estoy seguro de que usted nos puede ayudar.

SRA. WILSON: Por supuesto. ¿Qué quieren saber?

ASHA: Pues cómo fue su vida, qué hizo para defender a los trabajadores, cómo luchó por sus derechos…

SRA. WILSON: Podría contarles algunas cosas, pero dudo que me dé tiempo. Esperen, puedo dejarles un libro que tengo por aquí. En él encontrarán mucha información sobre César Chávez.

LUCAS: Muchas gracias, señora Wilson.

SRA. WILSON: De nada. Si necesitan algo más, vengan a verme.

6 **Detective de palabras**

▶ **Lee** estas oraciones. ¿Cuáles expresan certeza *(certainty)*? ¿Y cuáles expresan duda *(doubt)*?

1. Sabemos que César Chávez fue un líder de origen mexicano.
2. Es probable que la señora Wilson esté en su despacho.
3. Estoy seguro de que usted nos puede ayudar.
4. Dudo que me dé tiempo.

▶ **Observa** en cada oración el verbo de la cláusula dependiente *(dependent clause)* y decide si estas afirmaciones son ciertas o falsas.

1. Las expresiones de certeza *Sabemos* y *Estoy seguro* llevan el verbo en indicativo.
2. Las expresiones de duda *Es probable* y *Dudo* llevan el verbo en subjuntivo.

Differentiated Instruction

DEVELOPING LEARNERS

- After students have read the dialogue at least once, make a copy of each of the two parts of the dialogue and then cut each part into strips, keeping each speaker's lines intact. Give students the lines for the first dialogue out of order and ask them to put the conversation back in the correct sequence. Have them do the same with the lines from the second part of the dialogue. When the conversations are in the correct order, ask students to take turns reading each speaker's lines aloud.

EXPANDING LEARNERS

- Based on what students know about César Chávez from the information on these pages and the audio, plus any additional information they might research, ask them to write a brief summary of his life. Students may choose to do this as a third-person narrative, or as a brief autobiography. Encourage students to accompany their compositions with images from Chávez's life and display their work in the classroom. If this assignment coincides with Chávez's birthday on March 31, you might hold a special César Chávez Day celebration in your classroom.

DESAFÍO 1

Expresar certeza y duda

 7 **¿Comprendes?**

▶ **Responde** a estas preguntas.

1. ¿De dónde era César Chávez?

2. ¿De dónde piensas que eran muchos de los agricultores a los que él defendía?

3. ¿En qué estados crees que se celebra el Día de César Chávez?

4. ¿Cómo crees que luchó Chávez por los derechos laborales? ¿Por qué?

 8 **Dedicado a su gente**

 ▶ **Escucha** un programa de radio sobre César Chávez y elige la opción correcta.

1. ¿De dónde era Chávez?
   a. de Arizona   b. de Ciudad de México   c. de Texas

2. ¿En qué siglo vivió Chávez?
   a. en el siglo XIX   b. en el siglo XX   c. en el siglo XXI

3. ¿A quiénes defendió Chávez?
   a. a los niños   b. a los agricultores   c. a los empresarios

4. ¿Qué quería mejorar Chávez para los agricultores?
   a. el salario   b. la atención médica   c. las dos cosas

5. ¿Qué organizó para conseguir esas mejoras?
   a. un festival   b. una empresa   c. huelgas y manifestaciones

6. ¿A qué edad murió Chávez?
   a. a los 93 años   b. a los 66 años   c. a los 31 años

9 **Una entrevista imaginaria**

 ▶ **Habla** con tu compañero(a) y hagan una lista de cinco preguntas que les gustaría hacer a César Chávez.

CONEXIONES: HISTORIA

César Chávez

César Chávez nació en 1927 en Arizona en una familia de emigrantes de origen mexicano que trabajaba en el campo. A los 13 años dejó la escuela para ayudar a su familia. Más tarde decidió dedicar su vida a luchar de forma pacífica *(peaceful)* por los derechos de los agricultores. En 1964 creó el primer sindicato *(labor union)* de trabajadores agrícolas, el *National Farm Workers Association*.

César Chávez con un agricultor.

10 **Piensa y explica.** ¿Conoces a otros personajes históricos que lucharon de forma pacífica por los derechos laborales? ¿Qué sabes de ellos?

HERITAGE LANGUAGE LEARNERS

• Ask students to research some other Hispanic leaders in this country who fought to improve workers' and minorities' rights. Students may go back in history and cite Junípero Serra, a Spanish missionary who established missions in America's Southwest, or Antonia Novello, who served as Surgeon General in the US government from 1990 to 1993, or labor leaders such as Linda Chávez-Thompson. Or, students may choose to research members of Congress, mayors or governors, entrepreneurs, or celebrities who have been active in the Hispanic community.

MULTIPLE INTELLIGENCES:
Intrapersonal Intelligence

• Ask students to imagine that they are César Chávez at thirteen, when he had to leave school in order to work and help his family. Have students write a journal entry that reveals Chávez's emotions at this time. Students might describe a child who is glad to leave school in order to help his family, or someone who might think that without an education he is doomed to a life of poverty. Then ask students to comment on how this situation might affect what Chávez will do in the future.

Activities

8. Before starting this activity, have students read the questions and list any vocabulary that they don't recognize. Remind them to use previously learned vocabulary, families of words, and cognates to define this unfamiliar vocabulary.

9. Collect students' questions, write them on a worksheet, and distribute to students. Ask them to investigate the life and work of César Chávez and answer the questions generated by the class.

 AUDIO SCRIPT
See page 227l.

 CONEXIONES: HISTORIA

César Chávez

César Chávez worked tirelessly for the rights of farm workers in the southwestern United States. Using nonviolent means, such as marches, strikes, and boycotts, Chávez brought national attention to the struggles of these workers. In recognition of Chávez's contributions, he posthumously received the Presidential Medal of Freedom—the highest civilian award that the United States bestows.

Answer Key

6. Certeza: 1, 3.   Duda: 2, 4.
   ▶ 1. Cierto.   2. Cierto.

7. 1. Era de los Estados Unidos, pero de origen mexicano.
   2. Eran de origen mexicano.
   3. Answers will vary.
   4. Answers will vary.

8. 1. a   2. b   3. b   4. c   5. c   6. b

9. Answers will vary.

10. Answers will vary.

Additional Resources

Fans Online activities

Unit 5
DESAFÍO 1

Vocabulario – Profesiones y cargos

Presentation

- In this section, students will learn vocabulary related to various jobs and professions.

Activities	Standards	Resources
Vocabulario	1.2, 3.1	
11.	1.2, 1.3	
12.	1.1	
13.	1.2, 1.3	Audio
14.	1.1, 1.2, 5.2	
15. Conexiones	1.1, 1.2, 2.1, 3.1, 4.2, 5.1	

Teaching Suggestions

Warm-Up / Independent Starter

- Ask students to think about these questions: *¿Has pensado en tu futuro profesional? ¿Qué piensas hacer? ¿Por qué?*

Preparation

- Review the Independent Starter with the class. Take a poll of the professions in which students are interested. Do several students share a future profession?

- Ask students to review the vocabulary on page 236 and to notice the cognate words. Do any of these professions listed interest them? Which ones? Why?

- Ask students to create a three-column chart and list the professions given on this page in the first column. Then, in the second column, ask them to list one verb that is best associated with each profession. In the third column, ask them to list an adjective for each profession as well. This is a good opportunity to review previously learned vocabulary or expand new vocabulary terms.

Activities

12. Ask students to role-play a conversation between two of the professionals represented. Have them discuss what their responsibilities are and how they spend their days. Why do they like their jobs?

236

DESAFÍO 1

Vocabulario

Profesiones y cargos

Me cuesta mucho trabajo decidir qué hacer en el futuro, Asha.

Eres muy bueno con los números. ¿No te interesa ser **contador**? Podrías ganar un buen salario.

Pero me gustaría hacer algo por los demás. Sería fascinante ser **científico** y **descubrir** el remedio de alguna enfermedad.

Los **periodistas** también son importantes. **Investigan** qué pasa en el mundo y nos **informan**.

Hay muchas posibilidades... Los bomberos son héroes porque **apagan incendios** y **salvan vidas**. Pero también me gusta mucho viajar y soy muy extrovertido. Podría ser **comerciante** internacional y dedicarme a comprar y vender mercancías. ¿Tú sabes qué profesión quieres tener?

Más vocabulario

Profesiones

el/la banquero(a)	banker	el/la funcionario(a)	government employee
el/la diseñador(a) gráfico(a)	graphic designer	el/la juez(a)	judge
el/la empresario(a)	businessman/ businesswoman	el/la obrero(a)	(blue collar) worker
		el/la programador(a)	
el/la escritor(a)	writer	informático(a)	computer programmer
el/la farmacéutico(a)	pharmacist	el/la traductor(a)	translator

Cargos

el/la coordinador(a)	coordinator	el/la gerente	manager
el/la director(a)	director	el/la jefe(a)	boss
el/la empleado(a)	employee	el/la presidente(a)	president

11 **¿Dónde trabajan?**

▶ **Escribe.** ¿Dónde trabajan estos(as) profesionales? ¿Cuáles deben ser sus habilidades?

Modelo *El profesor trabaja en la escuela. Debe ser organizado y paciente.*

1. el profesor
2. la empresaria
3. el banquero
4. la periodista
5. la farmacéutica
6. el comerciante

236 doscientos treinta y seis

Differentiated Instruction

DEVELOPING LEARNERS

- To reinforce the vocabulary presented, ask students to complete the following sentences:

1. *Si eres bueno con los números, puedes ser... (contador/a)*
2. *Los ... investigan qué sucede en el mundo. (periodistas)*
3. *Si sabes dos idiomas muy bien, puedes ser... (traductor/a)*
4. *Los ... pueden descubrir remedios de enfermedades. (científicos)*
5. *Las personas que trabajan para el gobierno son... (funcionarios)*
6. *Los ... trabajan en las fábricas. (obreros)*

EXPANDING LEARNERS

- Ask students to make a word web that associates at least five professions with adjectives that describe them, as well as the tools, equipment, and education that are needed to carry them out, places where people usually work, and qualities that a person should have in order to practice the profession successfully. Students may use the word web on page 233 as a model. For example: *escritor → independiente; computadora, bolígrafo, papel; en casa; ser creativo*. Then have students use the words in the web to describe each profession in detail.

12 **Cada cual en su puesto**

 ▶ **Habla** con tu compañero(a). ¿Qué profesión podrían tener estos jóvenes?

 ①  ② 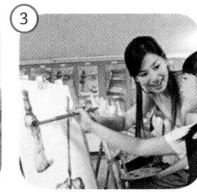 ③  ④

Modelo *De mayor esta chica podría ser veterinaria porque…*

13 **¿Qué quiere ser Asha?**

 ▶ **Escucha** la conversación y decide si estas oraciones son ciertas o falsas. Después, corrige las falsas.

1. Asha está preocupada por su futuro.
2. Lucas le recomienda a Asha que hable con un consejero profesional.
3. Según Asha, Manuela va a elegir una carrera artística.
4. A Asha le encanta la tecnología.
5. Lucas le aconseja a Asha que sea ingeniera.

14 **Tu futuro**

 ▶ **Pregunta** a tu compañero(a). Después, recomiéndale una profesión para su futuro.

1. ¿Qué clase te gusta más? ¿Te gustaría estudiar esa asignatura en la universidad? ¿Por qué?
2. ¿Cuáles son tus habilidades?
3. ¿Con qué prefieres trabajar: con personas, con animales, con computadoras…?
4. ¿Qué te importa más: ganar un buen salario o disfrutar del trabajo?

CONEXIONES: HISTORIA

El Día del Trabajo

Desde el siglo XIX, en muchos países se celebra el primero de mayo el Día Internacional del Trabajo. Esta celebración nació en recuerdo de los obreros de las fábricas de Chicago que en 1886 pidieron la reducción de la jornada laboral a ocho horas.

15 **Investiga.** ¿Cuándo y cómo se celebra el Día del Trabajo en los Estados Unidos?

HERITAGE LANGUAGE LEARNERS

- Ask students to research the history of Labor Day in the United States and in their family's country of origin, or in another Spanish-speaking country of their choice. Also ask them to describe how this holiday is celebrated, the social importance it has, and the role it has played in advocating workers' rights, fair wages, and retirement benefits. Then enable a discussion on how effective this celebration has been in preserving these benefits.

MULTIPLE INTELLIGENCES: Logical-Mathematical Intelligence

- Ask students to research statistics on average starting wages for at least five of the professions or jobs mentioned on the page. Students should include careers that require university or graduate degrees, as well as jobs that may require only a high school diploma. Have students make a chart or graph that shows the relationship between wages and educational degrees. Ask students how this information might affect their decisions regarding education and their career choices.

---

14. Prepare a four-column table with these headers: *Clase favorita; Habilidades; Personas, animales* o *computadoras; Buen salario o disfrutar.* Rather than having students work with only one partner, ask them to fill in the table for three classmates, and then make comparisons between them.

 AUDIO SCRIPT
See page 227l.

 CONEXIONES: HISTORIA

El Día del Trabajo

In many parts of the Spanish-speaking world, Labor Day is celebrated on May 1st. The events that inspired this day took place in Chicago, in 1886. Factory workers went on strike in support of the eight-hour workday. This labor conflict resulted in parades, protests, and fiery speeches. During the course of one of these events, violence erupted between the workers and the police, resulting in several deaths. The details of this incident have never been fully clarified.

Answer Key

11. Answers will vary.

12. Answers will vary.

13. 1. Cierto.
2. Falso. Que haga una prueba de aptitud o que vaya a una feria informativa.
3. Cierto.
4. Cierto.
5. Falso. Le aconseja que sea programadora informática.

14. Answers will vary.

15. Answers will vary.

Additional Resources

Fans Online activities
Practice Workbook

DESAFÍO 1

Gramática – Expresar certeza y duda

Presentation

- In this section, students will review the use of the indicative or the subjunctive when expressing certainty and doubt.

Activities	Standards	Resources
Gramática	1.2, 3.1	
16.	4.1	
17.	1.2, 1.3	
18.	1.2, 1.3	Audio
19.	1.1, 5.1, 5.2	
20. Cultura	1.1, 1.2, 2.1, 2.2, 3.1, 5.1, 5.2	

Teaching Suggestions

Warm-Up / Independent Starter

- Ask students to write an explanation for the use of the subjunctive or the indicative in each of the following pairs of sentences:
    1. a. *Es evidente que el contador es organizado.*
       b. *Es dudoso que el contador sea organizado.*
    2. a. *Es cierto que a Asha le gusta la tecnología.*
       b. *Es probable que a Asha le guste la tecnología.*

Preparation

- Call on volunteers to share their Independent Starters with the class. Help them articulate the rule to explain why the subjunctive or the indicative is used in each case.
- Have students read the grammar presentation on page 238. They should then compare the rules they created for the Independent Starter with the explanation provided in the text.

Activities

18. Before listening to the audio, ask students to think of one or two professions associated with each photo.

19. Ask students to talk with four classmates and then use the expressions of certainty and doubt to draw some conclusions from their conversations. For example: *Es evidente que muchos estudiantes desean ganar mucho dinero, pero dudo que eso sea posible...*

Gramática

Expresar certeza y duda

El indicativo y el subjuntivo en expresiones de certeza y duda

- In general, verbs or expressions that indicate **certainty** require a verb in the indicative in the dependent clause.

  <u>Es evidente</u> que Ana **trabaja** mucho.
  <u>Sé</u> que el jefe **es** justo.

EXPRESIONES DE CERTEZA CON INDICATIVO

Es verdad / Es cierto / Es evidente / Es obvio + que
Estar convencido(a) / Estar seguro(a) + de que
Saber + que
No dudar + que

- On the other hand, most verbs or expressions that indicate **doubt** require a verb in the subjunctive.

  <u>Es posible</u> que Ana **trabaje** mucho.
  <u>Dudamos</u> que el jefe **sea** justo.

EXPRESIONES DE DUDA CON SUBJUNTIVO

Es dudoso / Es improbable + que
Es posible / Es probable + que
Dudar + que

El subjuntivo en oraciones negativas de certeza y duda

- Many **negative expressions** require a verb in the subjunctive.

  <u>No es verdad</u> que Ana **trabaje** mucho.
  <u>No estoy seguro</u> de que el jefe **sea** justo.

EXPRESIONES NEGATIVAS CON SUBJUNTIVO

No es verdad / No es cierto
No es evidente / No es obvio   + que
No es posible / No es probable
No estar convencido(a) / No estar seguro(a) + de que

16 **Compara.** ¿Cómo se puede expresar duda en inglés? ¿Cómo se expresa certeza en forma negativa?

17 **¿Certeza o duda?**

▶ **Decide** si estas oraciones expresan certeza o duda. Después, elige las formas verbales correctas.

1. Es evidente que la directora _____ muy cansada.
   _{está/esté} — está/esté

2. Dudo que el nuevo ingeniero _____ español.
   hable/habla

3. No estamos seguros de que los bomberos _____ apagar el incendio.
   pueden/puedan

4. Es posible que el comerciante _____ las necesidades de sus clientes.
   entienda/entiende

5. Estoy convencido de que los abogados _____ los derechos de los pobres.
   defienden/defiendan

6. Es probable que los farmacéuticos _____ los efectos de estos medicamentos.
   estudien/estudian

Differentiated Instruction

DEVELOPING LEARNERS

- Ask students to choose the correct verb to complete each statement.
    1. *Estoy segura de que tú puedes / puedas hacerlo.* (puedes)
    2. *No es cierto que esa clase es / sea difícil.* (sea)
    3. *Es obvio que tú quieres / quieras a tus padres.* (quieres)
    4. *Es posible que llueve / llueva esta noche.* (llueva)
    5. *No es verdad que el presidente visita / visite esta escuela.* (visite)
    6. *Estamos convencidos de que Juan va / vaya a ganar el concurso.* (va)

EXPANDING LEARNERS

- Explain to students that they are going to generate several short exchanges with a partner in order to practice using both the subjunctive and the indicative with expressions of doubt or certainty. Taking turns, one student will make a statement that expresses either certainty or doubt. Then, the other student will make a statement with a verb or an expression that contradicts this. For example:
  B. *Dudo que la profesora nos dé tarea hoy.*
  A. *Estoy seguro de que sí nos va a dar tarea.*

18 **¿Vivir para trabajar o trabajar para vivir?**

 ▶ **Escucha** a varios(as) empleados(as). ¿A qué se dedican? Relaciona sus palabras con la fotografía correspondiente.

 ▶ **Escucha** otra vez y decide si estas oraciones son ciertas o falsas. Después, corrige las falsas.

1. Es cierto que trabaja muchas horas, pero le gusta mucho su trabajo.
2. Está convencida de que tiene un buen salario.
3. Duda que valga la pena tener tanta responsabilidad en su trabajo.
4. Es posible que cambie de trabajo porque le dedica demasiadas horas.
5. No está segura de que aprender un idioma ayude a sus alumnos en el futuro.

19 **Profesiones interesantes**

 ▶ **Habla** con tu compañero(a). ¿Qué profesiones te parecen interesantes? ¿Qué sabes con certeza sobre ellas? ¿De qué cosas no estás seguro(a)?

Modelo A. *A mí me parece muy interesante ser banquero. Estoy seguro de que se gana mucho dinero.*
B. *No dudo que se gana mucho dinero, pero sé que se trabaja muchas horas.*

 CULTURA

Astronautas hispanos

Franklin R. Chang-Díaz, de San José (Costa Rica), fue el primer astronauta hispano que ingresó en la NASA, en 1980. En la siguiente década fueron seleccionados otros muchos astronautas hispanos, como el argentino Fernando Caldeiro, el peruano Carlos Noriega, la estadounidense de origen mexicano Ellen Ochoa o el español Pedro Duque.

Franklin R. Chang-Díaz.

20 **Investiga y explica.** ¿Cuáles son los conocimientos y habilidades necesarios para hacerse astronauta? ¿Te gustaría ser astronauta? ¿Por qué?

doscientos treinta y nueve 239

HERITAGE LANGUAGE LEARNERS

- Ask students to research one of the Hispanic astronauts mentioned in the *Cultura* feature and gather their biographical, educational, and professional information. You might assign a different astronaut to each student so there is no duplication of information. After students assemble their data, ask them to make a written report so that you may check their command of written language. If time permits, ask these students to read their work aloud or to make a brief oral summary to the rest of the class.

MULTIPLE INTELLIGENCES:
Intrapersonal Intelligence

- Ask students to imagine that they, too, are astronauts and are embarking on their first voyage to outer space, where they will stay for an extended period of time with astronauts from several countries. Ask students to write entries in their journals, reflecting their doubts about the journey, their thoughts about leaving their family and spending so much time with relative strangers, and possibly their anxiety about what lies ahead, as well as the confidence they show in themselves and their mission.

 AUDIO SCRIPT
See page 227I.

 CULTURA

Astronautas hispanos

The NASA website lists fifteen Hispanic astronauts, all of whom are accomplished individuals. For example, Joseph Acaba has a Master's degree in geology. Fernando Caldeiro served as a member of the President's Advisory Commission on Educational Excellence for Hispanic Americans. Franklin Chang-Díaz has spent more than 1,500 hours in space, including nineteen hours of spacewalks. Sidney Gutierrez is a retired Colonel in the U.S. Air Force.

Answer Key

16. En inglés se usa el modo indicativo en ambos casos. Por ejemplo: *It is possible that he will win the race.* (Es posible que él gane la carrera.) *It is not true that Liz is my friend.* (No es cierto que Liz sea mi amiga.)

17. Certeza: 1, 5.   Duda: 2, 3, 4, 6.
1. está   3. puedan   5. defienden
2. hable   4. entienda   6. estudien

18. 1. B   2. D   3. E   4. C   5. A
▶ 1. Cierto.
2. Falso. El salario no es alto.
3. Falso. Vale la pena.
4. Cierto.
5. Falso. Está segura de que los ayudará.

19. Answers will vary.

20. Answers will vary.

Additional Resources

Fans Online activities
Practice Workbook

239

DESAFÍO 1

Gramática – El imperfecto de subjuntivo

Presentation

- In this section, students will learn how to conjugate the imperfect subjunctive and when to use it rather than the present subjunctive.

Activities	Standards	Resources
Gramática	1.2, 3.1	
21.	4.1	
22.	1.3, 3.1	
23.	1.2, 1.3, 2.1, 3.1, 3.2	
24.	1.1, 1.2, 3.1, 5.1	

Teaching Suggestions

Warm-Up / Independent Starter

- Ask students to write the six preterite forms for each of these verbs: *ganar, vender, descubrir.*

Preparation

- Review and correct the Independent Starter. When students first learn a new tense, it may be difficult for them to conjugate it while at the same time understanding how to use it. In order to help them with this process, stress the importance of identifying the *ellos* form of the preterite so that they will correctly conjugate the imperfect subjunctive. Remind students that there are many verbs that are irregular in the preterite tense, so the more familiar students are with the preterite tense, the easier they will find the formation of the imperfect subjunctive.

- Ask students to make a list of frequently used verbs that are irregular in the preterite tense (e.g., *ser, ir, hacer, tener, querer, poder, buscar, pedir, dar*). Then have students create a three-column chart and complete it with the infinitive, preterite tense, and imperfect subjunctive conjugation of each verb. They can use this chart as a reference.

Activities

22. Ask students to identify the infinitives of the verbs used in the dependent clause in each sentence. This will help them avoid errors when conjugating the imperfect subjunctive.

Gramática

El imperfecto de subjuntivo

El imperfecto de subjuntivo. Formación

- When a sentence in the past tense requires the subjunctive mood, we normally use the imperfect subjunctive.

  Era imposible que **llegara** tarde.

- To form the imperfect subjunctive, start with the *ellos* form of the preterite, drop the -ron ending, and add the following endings: -ra, -ras, -ra, -ramos, -rais, -ran.

IMPERFECTO DE SUBJUNTIVO. VERBOS REGULARES

	Trabajar	Comer	Escribir
yo	trabaja**ra**	comie**ra**	escribie**ra**
tú	trabaja**ras**	comie**ras**	escribie**ras**
usted, él, ella	trabaja**ra**	comie**ra**	escribie**ra**
nosotros(as)	trabajá**ramos**	comié**ramos**	escribié**ramos**
vosotros(as)	trabaja**rais**	comie**rais**	escribie**rais**
ustedes, ellos(as)	trabaja**ran**	comie**ran**	escribie**ran**

Note: The vowel that precedes the nosotros(as) ending is always accented.

- If a verb is irregular in the preterite, it is also irregular in the imperfect subjunctive.

  ir ⟶ ellos fueron ⟶ yo fuera

- There is another set of endings for the imperfect subjunctive: -se, -ses, -se, -semos, -seis, -sen. These two forms are interchangeable.

Uso del imperfecto de subjuntivo

- The imperfect subjunctive is used in the same situations in which you would use the present subjunctive, whenever the verb in the main clause is in the past.

  La profesora me **aconseja** (present) + que estudie más. (present subjunctive)

  La profesora me **aconsejó** (preterite)
  La profesora me **aconsejaba** (imperfect) + que estudiara más. (imperfect subjunctive)
  La profesora me **había aconsejado** (past perfect)

21 **Compara.** ¿Cómo expresarías en inglés los ejemplos anteriores?

22 **En el pasado**

▶ **Escribe** estas oraciones en pasado.

1. Estoy contento de que ganes tanto dinero. ⟶ Estaba contento...
2. Me parece muy mal que el director no hable español. ⟶ Me pareció muy mal...
3. El profesor sugiere que yo busque un trabajo. ⟶ El profesor había sugerido...
4. Es dudoso que el bombero tenga miedo. ⟶ Era dudoso que...

Differentiated Instruction

DEVELOPING LEARNERS

- Help students practice the forms of the imperfect subjunctive by playing a game. Prepare two cubes: one will have six verbs on it, the other will have the six subject pronouns. Students will take turns rolling both cubes, and then saying aloud the corresponding verb form. Give students one point for each correct response. Alternatively, you can put six letters of the alphabet on the cube instead of the verbs. Students will have to think of a verb that begins with that letter and conjugate it in the correct form.

EXPANDING LEARNERS

- Ask students to complete the following sentences with both forms of the imperfect subjunctive of the verbs in parentheses and then read the sentences aloud:

  1. *Luis sugirió que (nosotros – estar) listos a las ocho. (estuviéramos, estuviésemos)*
  2. *Te recomendé que (estudiar). (estudiaras, estudiases)*
  3. *¿Dudaste que (yo – llegar) a tiempo? (llegara, llegase)*
  4. *No era evidente que (él – ser) el jefe. (fuera, fuese)*
  5. *Queríamos que (mejorar) las condiciones de trabajo. (mejoraran, mejorasen)*

23 ¿Qué nos enseñó César?

▶ **Lee** el texto sobre César Chávez y escribe oraciones siguiendo el modelo.

Era evidente que...	No era cierto que...
Era improbable que...	Chávez y los trabajadores
Chávez sabía que...	estaban seguros de que...

Modelo

Era evidente que a Chávez le preocupaba la gente.

Un ejemplo de lucha pacífica

César Chávez quería mejorar las condiciones de trabajo, casa, salud y educación de los trabajadores agrícolas inmigrantes en los Estados Unidos. Se dedicó a su comunidad, a la justicia y a la dignidad de su gente. Pensaba que se podían lograr los derechos laborales a través de huelgas *(strikes)*, manifestaciones *(demonstrations)*, teatro, arte, música, discursos *(speeches)*, diálogo y negociación. Esta acción sin violencia requería mucho trabajo y sacrificio.

24 En una empresa

▶ **Habla** con tu compañero(a). ¿Qué dice cada persona? ¿Por qué dice eso? Usa el vocabulario de las tres columnas.

la directora	pedir	llamar
el coordinador	querer	ser
la secretaria	sugerir	organizar
mi compañero	aconsejar	buscar
la jefa	recomendar	dar
		asistir
		ordenar
		hablar
		aprender

Modelo A. *La directora me pidió que fuera puntual.*
B. *Claro, es evidente que no se puede llegar tarde al trabajo. A mí me sugirió...*

Gramática – El imperfecto de subjuntivo

23. Ask for five volunteers to each write a sentence on the board. Have students identify and correct any errors in the sentences. Provide students with additional practice with the sequence of tenses by giving them several sentence starters in the past tense (e.g., *Chávez no dudaba que..., No era verdad que los trabajadores...*) Ask students to think of verbs they could use to complete these sentences. Then have students repeat the process of identifying the infinitive, the third person plural of the preterite, and the correct conjugation of the imperfect subjunctive.

24. Upon completion of this conversation, call on several volunteer pairs to role-play two of their dialogues in front of the class.

Answer Key

21. Presente: *The teacher advises me to study.* Pasado: *The teacher advised me to study.* Pluscuamperfecto: *The teacher had advised me to study.*

22. 1. Estaba contento de que ganaras tanto dinero.
2. Me pareció muy mal que el director no hablara español.
3. El profesor había sugerido que yo buscara un trabajo.
4. Era dudoso que el bombero tuviera miedo.

23. Answers will vary. Sample answers:
Era improbable que se lograran mejores condiciones de trabajo sin hacer nada.
Chávez sabía que su lucha iba a ser difícil.
No era cierto que Chávez apoyara la violencia.
Chávez y los trabajadores estaban seguros de que iban a lograr sus objetivos.

24. Answers will vary.

Additional Resources

Fans Online activities
Practice Workbook

HERITAGE LANGUAGE LEARNERS

• Ask students to write a brief description of a situation, cause, or controversy that elicits contradictory feelings among the population, and to include facts in their descriptions. Then ask students to write a persuasive paragraph advocating either a peaceful demonstration for or against what they have described, or some other peaceful approach. Ask students to exchange their compositions and proofread their classmate's work. Have students make any necessary corrections and then call on volunteers to read their work aloud.

CRITICAL THINKING

• Enable a class discussion on the effectiveness of different methods of protest. Do students think that peaceful demonstrations, like those that Chávez supported, are more effective than other, perhaps more forceful, forms of protest? What do protestors accomplish by staging sit-ins, hunger strikes, or boycotts? On an international level, do students think that embargoes and imposed sanctions work? Encourage all students to participate in this discussion.

LECTURA: TEXTO DIALOGADO

Presentation

- In this section, students will read a dialogue. They will identify conversation topics, as well as expressions of doubt and certainty. Students will also answer comprehension questions based on the reading, and research some topics related to agriculture and the Mexican population in the United States.

Activities	Standards	Resources
Lectura: texto dialogado	1.2, 2.2, 3.1, 3.2	Vis. Pres.
25.	1.1, 1.2, 2.2, 3.1	
26.	1.1, 1.3, 2.1, 3.1	
27.	1.1, 1.2, 2.2, 3.1	

Teaching Suggestions

Warm-Up / Independent Starter

- Ask students to think of other influential people throughout history who have had a major impact in spite of, or due to, a difficult life full of challenges. Students may choose to include famous people or not-so-famous people who have had an impact on their lives. Ask them to describe the person's main contributions in a short paragraph in Spanish.

Preparation

- Have students read the *Antes de leer* strategies silently. Then ask them to jot down possible answers to the questions.
- Call on volunteers to share their answers to the *Antes de leer* with the class. Sample answers:
  1. *Hablan de César Chávez.*
  2. *Hablan de su infancia y trabajo (trabajó en el campo desde pequeño), de su familia (tenía un pequeño rancho y una tienda de comestibles), de sus ideas (estaba a favor de la protesta pacífica), de sus acciones políticas (fundó la Asociación Nacional de Agricultores, luchó por los derechos de las personas).*
  3. *Certeza: «Porque sabemos que tuvo…»; «Seguro que los salarios… eran muy bajos»; «… estaban convencidos de que la protesta pacífica era más eficaz». Duda: «No sabía que fuera…»; «… es posible que se parezcan».*

242

Antes de leer: estrategias

1. Lee el título del texto y mira las fotos. ¿De quién hablan Lucas y Asha?
2. Mira el texto y decide si Lucas y Asha hablan sobre los siguientes temas relativos a esa persona: su infancia, su familia, sus estudios, su trabajo, sus ideas, sus acciones políticas. Da ejemplos.
3. Señala las expresiones que expresan certeza y las que expresan duda.

Desfile del Día de César Chávez en San Fernando (California).

Una vida interesante

Lucas: Ya tenemos bastante información sobre César Chávez. ¿Preparamos la presentación?

Asha: Sí. Podemos empezar diciendo algo sobre su vida, ¿no? Porque sabemos que tuvo una vida muy interesante. El libro que nos prestó tu profesora dice que la familia de Chávez tenía un pequeño rancho y una tienda de comestibles, y que perdieron todo durante la Gran Depresión.

Lucas: Claro, por eso tuvo que trabajar en el campo desde pequeño. Y en aquella época las condiciones de trabajo en Arizona y California no eran muy buenas para los trabajadores de origen mexicano.

Asha: Seguro que los salarios de los trabajadores del campo eran muy bajos y el trabajo muy duro.

Lucas: Sí, y por eso fundó la Asociación Nacional de Agricultores. ¿Sabes que era vegetariano?

Asha: No, no sabía que fuera vegetariano, pero sí sabía que fue un defensor de los animales.

Lucas: Qué interesante. Yo creo que en algunas cosas César Chávez se parece a Gandhi, ¿no crees?

Asha: Sí, es posible que se parezcan. Los dos lucharon por los derechos de las personas y estaban convencidos de que la protesta pacífica era más eficaz que la violencia.

242 doscientos cuarenta y dos

Differentiated Instruction

DEVELOPING LEARNERS

- Help students understand the cause and effect relationships in the reading. Ask them to create a two-column chart and label the first column *Causas*, and the second *Efectos*. Then ask students to go through the reading to find as many of these relationships as they can. For instance, they may list *Gran Depresión* under *Causa*, and *la familia de Chávez perdió su rancho y su tienda* under *Efectos*.

EXPANDING LEARNERS

- Ask students to find examples of some statements that express certainty and some that express doubt or uncertainty in the text, and write these sentences in their notebooks. Then, ask them to alter these statements so that those that express certainty express doubt or uncertainty, and those that express uncertainty or doubt express certainty. For example:
  – *Sí, es posible que se parezcan. → Es verdad que se parecen.*
  – *No sabía que fuera vegetariano. → Estaba segura de que era vegetariano.*

25 Comprensión

▶ **Responde** a estas preguntas.

1. ¿Cómo afectó la Gran Depresión a la familia de César Chávez?
2. ¿Por qué tuvo César Chávez una infancia muy dura?
3. ¿Para qué fundó la Asociación Nacional de Agricultores?
4. ¿Por qué piensa Asha que César Chávez y Gandhi se parecen?

26 Para saber más

▶ **Investiga** con tu compañero(a) sobre uno de estos temas. Utilicen una tabla como esta.

• La Gran Depresión
• La agricultura en Arizona y California
• La población mexicana en los Estados Unidos

Lo que sabemos	Lo que queremos saber	Lo que hemos aprendido

27 Palabras famosas

▶ **Lee** estas citas de Chávez y de Gandhi. ¿Cuáles crees que corresponden a cada uno? Coméntalo con tu compañero(a) y justifica tu respuesta.

Modelo   A. *Estoy segura de que estas palabras son de Chávez porque habla de la huelga.*
B. *Sí, yo también.*

1. «La huelga y el boicoteo no nos han costado tanto. Lo que no nos han pagado en salarios, mejores condiciones de trabajo y nuevos contratos, nos lo han pagado en respeto propio y dignidad humana.»

2. «Un país, una civilización se puede juzgar por la forma en que trata a sus animales.»

3. «Cuando tienes personas juntas que creen en algo muy fuertemente –ya sea religión o política o sindicatos–, suceden las cosas.»

4. «La diferencia entre lo que hacemos y lo que somos capaces de hacer resolvería la mayoría de los problemas del mundo.»

doscientos cuarenta y tres **243**

■ Read the dialogue aloud to students, modeling correct pronunciation and intonation. Then call on several pairs of students to alternate reading the dialogue aloud. Offer suggestions to improve their oral reading.

■ Write down some cognates and have students explain their meaning within the context of the reading (e.g., *presentación, rancho, salario, vegetariano, protesta pacífica*). Then list other words that are not cognates. Have students guess the meaning through the context (e.g., *comestibles, duro, derechos*).

Activities

25. To expand this activity, ask students additional questions based on the reading. For example: *¿Por qué tuvo que trabajar César Chávez cuando era pequeño? ¿Cómo eran los salarios de los trabajadores del campo? ¿Cómo creen que se puede protestar pacíficamente?*

26. You may want to assign the completion of the first two columns of the chart as homework. The next day, have students get together with a classmate and compare their charts. Then, ask pairs to discuss one of the topics in greater detail and complete the third column of the chart.

Answer Key

25. 1. Perdieron todo lo que tenían: un pequeño rancho y una tienda de comestibles.

2. Porque tuvo que trabajar en el campo desde pequeño.

3. Para luchar por los derechos de los trabajadores del campo.

4. Porque ambos luchaban por los derechos de las personas y estaban convencidos de que la protesta pacífica era más eficaz que la violencia. Además, los dos eran vegetarianos.

26. Answers will vary.

27. 1. Chávez 2. Gandhi 3. Chávez 4. Gandhi

Additional Resources

Fans Online activities

243

HERITAGE LANGUAGE LEARNERS

• Ask students to think about what they would like to improve or change in their community, nation, or the world, and direct them to write one or more lines related to this. Explain that their words should be worthy of being quoted in posterity, so students must take great care in writing them. You may suggest that students use the quotes on the page as models, but the topics they choose and their wording should be their own. When students complete their work, ask them to read their quotes to the rest of the class.

COOPERATIVE LEARNING

• Ask students to work in small groups and assign one of the topics from activity 26 to them. Explain that they will use the information each one had previously gathered, and they will decide what additional information they will need to research in order to make a more detailed and interesting report. Students will decide among themselves which facts each one will investigate, and how to integrate this new information into their final report. All members of the group will work together in preparing the final draft.

Unit 5

DESAFÍO 1

Comunicación

Presentation

- In this section, students will integrate the vocabulary and grammar skills from *Desafío 1* in order to talk about the life and work of important leaders.

Activities	Standards	Resources
28.	1.1, 1.2, 1.3, 2.2, 3.1, 5.1	
29.	1.1, 1.2, 1.3, 2.1, 3.1, 5.1	
30. Final del desafío	1.2, 1.3, 3.1	
Tu desafío	1.1, 1.2	

Teaching Suggestions

Warm-Up / Independent Starter

- Ask students to describe, in a short paragraph, what the American Dream means to them. For example: *Para mí, el sueño americano significa poder estudiar, trabajar y lograr el éxito. El sistema de vida estadounidense me permite lograr eso si me esfuerzo.*

Preparation

- Ask students to share their Independent Starters. Create a list of characteristics on the board that describe the meaning of the American Dream for the students in your class. Discuss people in students' families or communities who embody these characteristics.

- To refresh students' memories, have them brainstorm as many key vocabulary words from this *Desafío* (i.e., *profesiones y cargos*) as they can in two minutes. Then, ask them to use six of the words in sentences that either indicate certainty or doubt, or that employ the imperfect subjunctive. For example: *Es evidente que los comerciantes son extrovertidos. No es cierto que todos los científicos fueran buenos estudiantes.*

- After going over some of students' sentences as a class, ask them to take a few minutes to review the topic that gave them the most trouble before continuing on to the communication activities. Remind students to use the imperfect subjunctive conjugation chart they created as reference for the lesson on pages 240–241.

244

DESAFÍO 1

Comunicación

28 El sueño norteamericano

▶ **Lee** el artículo y responde a las preguntas.

Miércoles, 12 de agosto de 2009

Obama recibe a Sotomayor, primera hispana en la Corte Suprema de los Estados Unidos

El presidente de los Estados Unidos, Barack Obama, recibió hoy en la Casa Blanca a Sonia Sotomayor, la primera jueza hispana que accede a la Corte Suprema de Justicia del país, a quien el mandatario describió como una encarnación del sueño americano que «inspira» a toda la nación.

«Celebramos un momento extraordinario para nuestra nación y celebramos el impacto que Sotomayor ya ha tenido en personas de todo Estados Unidos inspiradas por su excepcional vida», afirmó Obama. El mandatario consideró que, cuando Sotomayor juró su cargo el pasado sábado, el país

La jueza Sonia Sotomayor.

«dio otro paso hacia una unión más perfecta que todos buscamos». Y es que, agregó Obama, Sotomayor es la encarnación de «todos los que en este país afrontan desafíos y luchas en sus vidas

y que oyen la historia de la jueza Sotomayor y piensan para sí mismos, "si ella pudo superar tanto y llegar tan lejos, ¿entonces por qué no puedo hacerlo yo?"».

Al recordar los humildes orígenes de la jueza, nacida hace 55 años en el popular barrio neoyorquino del Bronx, hija de inmigrantes puertorriqueños y que logró graduarse con honores en algunas de las más prestigiosas universidades del país, Obama afirmó que su vida es un «símbolo» de que «perdura la fe en el sueño americano».

Fuente:
http://www.diariocolatino.com
(texto adaptado)

1. ¿Dónde nació Sonia Sotomayor? ¿Cuál es su origen?
2. ¿A qué se dedica? ¿A qué puesto accedió en agosto de 2009?
3. ¿Por qué, según Obama, Sotomayor encarna el sueño americano?

 ▶ **Habla** con tu compañero(a). ¿Qué otras personas piensas que encarnan el sueño americano? ¿Por qué? Justifica tu respuesta. Aquí tienes algunas ideas.

Abraham Lincoln

Oprah Winfrey

Steve Jobs

244 doscientos cuarenta y cuatro

Differentiated Instruction

DEVELOPING LEARNERS

- Explain to students that recognizing cognates is one way to help them decode new words, and is also an effective way to increase their vocabulary in both Spanish and English. Help students identify the cognates in the reading selection for activity 28, and have them write these words in their notebooks. Ask them to write the English-language equivalent and an original sentence in Spanish next to each word. Get students started by pointing out the following cognates: *Corte Suprema, presidente, Justicia, mandatario, encarnación, nación.*

EXPANDING LEARNERS

- Ask students to choose a famous or historical figure who, in their opinion, embodies the American Dream. The person may be one of the individuals shown on the page, or someone of the students' choosing. Then ask students to explain why this person embodies the American Dream. If needed, students may do some research in order to uncover more relevant information about the person they have selected. Have students present a brief written or oral report to the class.

29 Un poema

▶ **Diseña** un cartel con tu compañero(a) para un día festivo en honor a un personaje admirado. Incluyan una fotografía o un dibujo y un lema *(slogan)* que reflejen su filosofía.

▶ **Escribe** un poema dedicado a ese personaje. Sigue las instrucciones para preparar un poema en forma de diamante.

- Su nombre.
- Dos adjetivos que lo describen.
- Tres verbos (en gerundio) sobre su vida.
- Dos adjetivos que lo describen.
- Su apellido.

Un personaje admirado

César
solidario, comprometido
educando, organizando, luchando
humilde, trabajador
Chávez

Final del desafío

No estoy segura de que todos nuestros compañeros ___1___ quién es Chávez, así que podemos empezar hablando de su infancia, de su familia, de su juventud...

Dudo que nos ___2___ tiempo... Es verdad que ___3___ contar algo de su vida, pero lo más importante es explicar su legado *(legacy)*: les aconsejó a los agricultores que ___4___ juntos y que ___5___ sin violencia para lograr sus metas.

30 Una figura impresionante

▶ **Completa** el diálogo con la forma apropiada del indicativo o del subjuntivo de los verbos del cuadro.

trabajar	saber	luchar	dar	deber

 **→ TU DESAFÍO** Visita la página web. Escucha las preguntas de tu *Minientrevista Desafío 1* y escribe las respuestas.

doscientos cuarenta y cinco 245

Activities

28. To expand the second part of this activity, ask students to write a brief biography of one of the people they chose as someone who embodies the American Dream. Then have students get together with a partner and ask pairs to role-play a conversation between the two people that they selected. You may want to model a conversation between the current president of the United States and Abraham Lincoln, or between Oprah Winfrey and Sonia Sotomayor. Encourage students to try to incorporate the vocabulary and the expressions of certainty or doubt, as well as the imperfect subjunctive in their conversations.

29. Ask students to write on an index card the slogan that they created for the person they chose, and then collect the cards. Have pairs share their posters and poems with the class. Encourage students to ask questions. The following day, redistribute the index cards to all students and ask them to name the person whose philosophy is represented on each card. Post the posters and poems around the room.

Answer Key

28. 1. Nació en el barrio del Bronx, en Nueva York. Es hija de inmigrantes puertorriqueños.
2. Es jueza. En agosto de 2009 accedió a la Corte Suprema de Justicia de los Estados Unidos.
3. Porque Sotomayor pudo superar muchos desafíos y llegar muy lejos.
▶ Answers will vary.

29. Answers will vary.
▶ Answers will vary.

30. 1. sepan   4. trabajaran
2. dé   5. lucharan
3. debemos

245

Unit 5
DESAFÍO 2
Referirse a lo desconocido

Presentation

- In *Desafío 2*, Michelle and Daniel will answer job ads in the oldest Spanish-language daily newspaper in the United States. Students will preview language used to talk about jobs and technology.

Activities	Standards	Resources
Texto	1.2, 2.2, 3.1	Vis. Pres.
31.	1.2, 1.3	
32.	1.1, 1.2, 2.2	
33.	1.2, 1.3	
34.	1.1, 1.2, 5.2	
35. Comunidades	1.1, 1.2, 1.3, 2.2, 3.1, 5.1, 5.2	

Teaching Suggestions

Warm-Up / Independent Starter

- Write the following questions on the board and allow students time to prepare a written response: *¿Dónde podemos buscar trabajo? ¿Qué cualidades y habilidades tienes? ¿Qué tipo de trabajo puedes solicitar?*

Preparation

- Have students share their Independent Starters. Ask students if any of them currently has a job and how they obtained the position.

Texto: El trabajo perfecto

- Tell students to pay attention to the characteristics that Daniel and Michelle say that they have that will be useful for their job search.

- Have student predict whether Michelle and Daniel will be able to successfully respond to the job advertisements and obtain jobs.

Activities

33. Before starting this activity, have students identify the part of speech of each of the vocabulary words provided. Then ask students to scan the ads to determine whether a noun or adjective is required. After completing the activity, ask students to decide which job they are most qualified for.

246

El trabajo perfecto

Michelle and Daniel must answer job ads in the oldest Spanish-language daily newspaper in the U.S. They call Tim to ask for some help. Which jobs will they be qualified for?

MICHELLE: ¡Hola, Tim! Soy Michelle. ¿Cómo estás?

TIM: Muy bien. ¿Y tú?

MICHELLE: Bien también. ¿Sabes? Daniel y yo ya averiguamos que *El Diario La Prensa* de Nueva York es el periódico en español más antiguo de los Estados Unidos.

TIM: Así es, Michelle. Tienen que leer la sección de anuncios clasificados, decidir qué trabajos les interesan y responder a una de las ofertas.

DANIEL: ¿Responder a una oferta de trabajo? ¡Pero si todavía estamos estudiando! Y no tenemos experiencia. ¡Es imposible!

TIM: ¿Por qué? Piensen en sus habilidades. Estoy seguro de que hay muchos trabajos que pueden hacer.

DANIEL: ¿Tú crees?

MICHELLE: Tim tiene razón. Los dos somos responsables, buenos estudiantes y hablamos inglés y español.

TIM: ¡Anímense! Y si necesitan que les eche una mano, no duden en llamarme.

DANIEL: Está bien, Tim. Muchas gracias.

31 Detective de palabras

▶ **Elige** la opción correcta.

1. Los personajes deben ver la sección de…	a. español	b. anuncios
2. Daniel dice que él y Michelle no tienen…	a. experiencia	b. tiempo
3. Tim sugiere que piensen en sus…	a. habilidades	b. estudios

32 ¿Comprendes?

▶ **Responde** a estas preguntas.

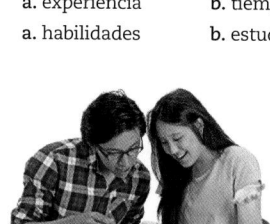

1. ¿Dónde se publica *El Diario La Prensa*?
2. ¿Cuál es el desafío de Michelle y Daniel?
3. ¿Por qué piensa Daniel que es un desafío difícil?
4. ¿Qué opina Tim?

Differentiated Instruction

DEVELOPING LEARNERS

- Have students choose the correct answer to each question.
  1. *¿Qué deben solicitar Michelle y Daniel?* (a)
     a. *trabajo*   b. *experiencia*
  2. *¿Qué sección deben consultar?* (b)
     a. *las novedades*   b. *los anuncios clasificados*
  3. *¿Quién dice que no tienen experiencia?* (b)
     a. *Michelle*   b. *Daniel*
  4. *¿Quién dice que son responsables?* (a)
     a. *Michelle*   b. *Daniel*
  5. *¿Quién ofrece su ayuda?* (b)
     a. *Daniel*   b. *Tim*

EXPANDING LEARNERS

- Make the title of the dialogue, *El trabajo perfecto,* a starting point for elaboration among students. Ask them to think about what would be a "perfect" job for them in the future, when they finish school. Ask students to state the job and describe it, including its requirements and responsibilities, compensation and other benefits, and why they think it is perfect for them. After students write their compositions, call on some to read them aloud to the rest of the class.

33 **Ofertas de empleo**

▶ **Lee** dos anuncios que consultaron Michelle y Daniel y complétalos con estas palabras.

técnico	media	computadoras	información	experiencia	empleo

Se busca periodista con 5 años de _____1_____. Jornada completa, horario flexible.

Rellenar la solicitud de _____2_____ en www.eldiariony.com

Se necesita personal _____3_____ para trabajar con _____4_____, impresoras y fotocopiadoras. _____5_____ jornada, salario negociable.

Para más _____6_____, entrar en www.eldiariony.com

34 **Las cualificaciones necesarias**

 ▶ **Habla** con tu compañero(a) sobre las cualificaciones necesarias para estos trabajos. Usen las sugerencias y piensen en otras ideas.

- gerente de un restaurante
- periodista
- comerciante
- veterinario(a)
- contador(a)

> tener experiencia
> tener formación
> ser responsable
> ser cortés
> tener licencia de conducir

EL DIARIO
WWW.ELDIARIONY.COM EL CAMPEÓN DE LOS HISPANOS
LA PRENSA NUEVA YORK, MARTES 7 DE FEBRERO AÑO 2017

COMUNIDADES

EL DIARIO LA PRENSA

El Diario La Prensa es el periódico en español más antiguo de los Estados Unidos. Actualmente es el diario más leído entre los hispanos de Nueva York, con alrededor de 240.000 lectores diarios y 630.000 los fines de semana. Tiene noticias especialmente orientadas a la comunidad hispana y las secciones habituales de cualquier diario: noticias nacionales e internacionales, economía, opinión, deportes...

35 **Investiga.** ¿Hay algún periódico en español donde tú vives? ¿Qué medio de comunicación prefieres para estar informado(a): televisión, periódicos, Internet...? ¿Por qué?

▶ **Escribe.** Lee un artículo de *El Diario La Prensa* a traves de Internet y escribe un resumen de ese artículo.

HERITAGE LANGUAGE LEARNERS

- Ask students to find *El Diario La Prensa,* or other Spanish-language newspapers from around the world, online. Have students make copies of some sections of these newspapers and share them with the class. Students should point out similarities and differences between these papers and a local English-language paper from their community.

CRITICAL THINKING

- Many people think that paper copies of newspapers may soon disappear and be replaced by online editions. Find out what students think about this by enabling a discussion on the topic. Ask students what media they use for getting the news, and how important it is for them to receive timely updates. Ask students what they think newspapers could do to increase circulation and assure subscribers that newspapers are still a viable means of communication.

Referirse a lo desconocido

34. Turn this activity into a game. Have pairs try to write as many qualifications necessary for each job as they can think of. Partners share their responses and must eliminate any that are repeated by another pair. The pair with the largest number of qualifications not stated by another pair wins. You may use the suggested list of jobs or add in your own.

 COMUNIDADES

El Diario La Prensa

In 1963, *El Diario de Nueva York* and *La Prensa* merged to form *El Diario La Prensa*. This award-wining publication is based in New York City and is the oldest Spanish-language newspaper in the United States. Other influential Spanish-language newspapers in the United States include *La Opinión* (Los Angeles, CA), *El Nuevo Herald* (Miami, FL), and *Hoy* (Chicago, IL).

Answer Key

31. 1. b   2. a   3. a

32. 1. Se publica en Nueva York.
2. Michelle y Daniel tienen que leer los anuncios clasificados, decidir qué trabajos les interesan y responder a una de las ofertas.
3. Daniel piensa que es difícil porque no tienen experiencia.
4. Tim piensa que hay muchos trabajos que pueden hacer.

33. 1. experiencia   4. computadoras
2. empleo   5. Media
3. técnico   6. información

34. Answers will vary.

35. Answers will vary.

Additional Resources

Fans Online activities

247

DESAFÍO 2

Vocabulario – Trabajo y tecnología

Presentation

- In this section, students will learn and use target vocabulary to talk about jobs and technology.

Activities	Standards	Resources
Vocabulario	1.2, 3.1	
36.	1.2, 1.3, 5.2	
37.	1.2	
38.	1.2, 5.2	
39.	1.2, 1.3	Audio
40. Cultura	1.1, 1.2, 1.3, 2.1, 3.1, 4.2, 5.1	

Teaching Suggestions

Warm-Up / Independent Starter

- Have students write a list of qualities that companies want their employees to possess.

Preparation

- Ask three volunteers to play the role of the young professionals in the vocabulary presentation and read their parts aloud. Then have students find context clues that help them to understand the meaning of the vocabulary. For example: *media jornada → unas 20 horas por semana; exigente → le gusta que sus empleados trabajen bien.*

- Ask students to look at the *Más Vocabulario* feature. Have them repeat the words after you to practice correct pronunciation.

- Finally, have students add vocabulary words to the lists they created during the Independent Starter and share their responses with the class.

Activities

36. Have students use their lists from the Independent Starter to help complete this activity.

37. To extend this activity, have students play a vocabulary game with a partner. Have one partner turn to face away from the board. Write four vocabulary words on the board. The partner who is looking at the board needs to describe the words to his or her partner, who must then guess them. Have partners switch roles and write a different list of words.

248

Vocabulario

Trabajo y tecnología

Hoy hablamos con…

JÓVENES PROFESIONALES CON MUCHO FUTURO

«Me considero una persona **emprendedora** y **organizada**. Por eso hace un año creé una empresa, así que soy mi propia jefa. Tengo tres empleados. Soy **exigente** y me gusta que trabajen bien, pero siempre soy **amable** con ellos.»

Liliana, 35 años

«Trabajo como **gerente** en una pequeña empresa. Soy **eficiente** y **responsable**, algo muy necesario para supervisar a mi equipo de empleados.

Trabajo a **jornada completa**, unas 40 horas semanales. Tengo un buen **sueldo** con el que tengo lo suficiente para vivir. Además, tengo por **contrato** dos semanas de **vacaciones**.»

Leonardo, 35 años

«Yo soy diseñadora gráfica en una empresa publicitaria. Ahora solo trabajo **media jornada**, unas 20 horas por semana. Soy muy **creativa** y dicen que también soy **ambiciosa**, porque quiero **ascender** a un puesto con más responsabilidad y llegar lejos en mi carrera profesional.»

Elizabeth, 25 años

la computadora

la pantalla

el reproductor de CD

el teclado

el ratón

Más vocabulario

Tecnología

la fotocopiadora	copier
la impresora	printer

Acciones

abrir un documento	to open a document
bajar un archivo	to download a file
cerrar un programa	to close an application
clicar con el ratón	to click the mouse
colgar/subir una foto	to upload a picture
fotocopiar un informe	to copy a report
guardar un mensaje	to save a message
imprimir un gráfico	to print a graphic
navegar por Internet	to surf the Internet

36 Habilidades

▶ **Escribe.** ¿Qué habilidades se mencionan en el texto de la ficha de Vocabulario? ¿Cuáles tienes tú? ¿Qué otras cualidades tuyas pueden ayudarte a encontrar un empleo?

Modelo *Yo soy ordenado, puntual y muy responsable. Eso es bueno para cualquier trabajo.*

248 doscientos cuarenta y ocho

Differentiated Instruction

DEVELOPING LEARNERS

- Review the highlighted words with students and ask them to categorize these words according to whether they describe terms related to work or to employees. To do this, students will make a two-column chart and label one of the columns *El trabajo,* and the other *Los empleados.* For example, *media jornada* describes *el trabajo,* and *creativa* describes *los empleados.* Then review the remaining terms on the page. Have students point to the parts of a computer and name each part, as well as name the actions they carry out on the computer.

EXPANDING LEARNERS

- Ask students to imagine that they are looking for an after-school or weekend job. Because potential employers will need to know their qualifications and extracurricular activities and interests, as well as a summary of their academic studies before they set up an interview, have students prepare their résumé, including this information in Spanish. Students will need to include personal data such as name, address, and contact phone, as well as any previous work experience. Students should also briefly explain why they are seeking this job.

37 Interpretando los anuncios clasificados

▶ **Une** las dos columnas y averigua qué significan estas expresiones de los anuncios clasificados.

Ⓐ
1. jornada completa
2. ser responsable
3. ser amable
4. media jornada
5. ser ambicioso

Ⓑ
a. un horario de 20 horas semanales
b. ser cortés y agradable
c. tener deseo de ascender
d. cumplir con las obligaciones
e. un horario de 40 horas semanales

38 Para rellenar la solicitud de empleo

▶ **Ordena** estos pasos para completar una solicitud de empleo por Internet.

a. Clicar en el enlace de la solicitud de empleo.
b. Enviar la solicitud completada a la compañía.
c. Bajar la solicitud.
d. Conectar la computadora y abrir Internet.
e. Llenar los formularios y guardar la copia completada.

39 Buscando un puesto

▶ **Escucha** y completa estas oraciones.

1. Daniel responde a un anuncio para un puesto de ___1___ .
2. Daniel no tiene ___2___ en computación.
3. A Daniel se le da muy bien usar las ___3___ .
4. El puesto requiere que Daniel instale una ___4___ y que use una ___5___ .
5. El trabajo es de media ___6___ .
6. Daniel tiene la ___7___ el martes.

CULTURA

María Elena Salinas

Hija de inmigrantes mexicanos, María Elena Salinas es una de las hispanas más influyentes en los Estados Unidos. Empezó a trabajar como periodista en 1981 en Los Ángeles y, seis años después, llegó a ser presentadora del noticiero de Univisión. Además de dedicarse a su carrera, María Elena Salinas trabaja para defender los derechos de los hispanos.

María Elena Salinas.

40 **Explica.** ¿Por qué María Elena Salinas puede ser un modelo para otros hispanos? ¿Qué otros hispanos famosos influyen en tu país?

Vocabulario – Trabajo y tecnología

39. Have students listen to the recording a second time to check their answers. As an alternative to this activity, have students create true/false statements about the conversation and quiz a classmate.

AUDIO SCRIPT
See page 227l.

CULTURA

María Elena Salinas

María Elena Salinas is a news anchor on multiple Univision broadcasts, including the most watched Spanish-language news program in the United States. She began her career working as a radio newsreader in California and now occupies one of the top-ranking positions on Spanish television. Salinas has covered some of the world's major events and interviewed some of the most influential world leaders. She dedicates much of her time to advocating for Hispanics in the United States.

Answer Key

36. Answers will vary.

37. 1. e   2. d   3. b   4. a   5. c

38. d, a, c, e, b

39. 1. técnico   5. fotocopiadora
       2. formación   6. jornada
       3. computadoras   7. entrevista
       4. impresora

40. Answers will vary.

Additional Resources

Fans Online activities
Practice Workbook

HERITAGE LANGUAGE LEARNERS

• Explain to students that they will work with a partner and role-play an employer and an applicant. Both students should be prepared to ask and answer questions about the requirements for the job, including education and experience, responsibilities and hours to be worked, remuneration, and any special benefits or other compensation. Give students time to put together their interviews and have them perform their skits in front of the class.

CRITICAL THINKING

• In many countries, the annual vacation is one calendar month, not a mere two weeks as mentioned in the article on page 248. Do students think that having such a long break from work interferes with a company's efficiency? Or do they think that a long break revitalizes employees? What do students think would be the consequences in the United States if all employees had longer vacations? Would they be willing to forego yearly raises or bonuses in order to take a four- or five-week vacation every year?

DESAFÍO 2

Gramática – Dar detalles. El relativo *que*

Presentation

■ In this section, students will provide details using adjective clauses, the relative pronoun *que*, and both the indicative and subjunctive moods.

Activities	Standards	Resources
Gramática	1.2, 3.1	
41.	4.1	
42.	1.2, 1.3	
43.	1.3	
44.	1.2, 5.2	Audio
45.	1.1, 1.2, 5.1	

Teaching Suggestions

Warm-Up / Independent Starter

■ Write the following sentences on the board and ask students to rewrite them adding an adjective to describe the underlined noun:
1. *Tengo una amiga.*
2. *La empresa busca empleados.*
3. *Yo encontré un libro en la biblioteca.*

Preparation

■ Go over the grammar presentation. Be sure to point out that the verb in the main clause helps determine whether the noun that is being described exists or not. Clarify that in English, we generally use "who" as a relative pronoun when referring to people, whereas in Spanish it is far more common to use *que*, rather than *quien*.

■ Have students rewrite their statements from the Independent Starter, changing the adjective to an adjective clause using the correct form of the verb *ser*. For example: *Tengo una amiga amable.* → *Tengo una amiga que es amable.*

Activities

42. Before starting this activity, have students look at each of the main clauses and determine if the sentence will have to be completed using the indicative or the subjunctive. Then have them work independently to complete the activity.

250

Gramática

Dar detalles. El relativo *que*

El pronombre relativo *que*

● In Spanish, as in English, we use adjectives or adjective clauses to add information about a noun.

Conozco a un <u>escritor</u> <u>muy famoso</u>.
noun   adjective

Conozco a un <u>escritor</u> <u>que es muy famoso</u>.
noun   adjective clause

● In Spanish, we generally use *que* to introduce the adjective clause. *Que* is used for both people and things.

Conozco a un escritor	+	que + es muy famoso.
main clause		adjective clause

In this example, the dependent clause describes the noun and acts as an adjective.

Indicativo y subjuntivo en la cláusula adjetiva

● When the adjective clause describes someone or something that exists or is known, use the indicative.

En esta empresa <u>hay un vendedor</u> que <u>habla</u> japonés.
person exists   indicative mood

● When the adjective clause describes someone or something that doesn't exist, is unknown, or whose existence is in question, use the subjunctive.

En esta tienda <u>no hay nadie</u> que <u>hable</u> japonés.
person doesn't exist   subjunctive mood

¿<u>Hay alguien</u> en esta tienda que <u>hable</u> japonés?
existence in question   subjunctive mood

<u>Busco una impresora</u> que <u>imprima</u> 100 páginas en un minuto.
unclear if the object exists   subjunctive mood

● Remember to maintain the same tense (present or past) in both clauses.

La empresa **quiere** un contador que **tenga** experiencia.
La empresa **quería** un contador que **tuviera** experiencia.

41 **Compara.** ¿Cómo expresarías en inglés los ejemplos anteriores?

42 **En la oficina**

▶ **Une** las dos columnas y escribe oraciones lógicas.

Ⓐ
1. Tengo una fotocopiadora…
2. Conozco a una arquitecta…
3. Hay algunos empleados…
4. La jefa busca un ayudante…
5. Aquí no hay ninguna computadora…

Ⓑ
a. que tenga reproductor de CD.
b. que hace copias en color.
c. que trabajan a media jornada.
d. que sea muy eficiente.
e. que es muy creativa.

Differentiated Instruction

DEVELOPING LEARNERS

● Ask students to complete the following sentences by choosing the correct verb:
1. *Tengo un asistente que es / sea muy responsable.* (es)
2. *Busco un trabajo que ofrece / ofrezca un horario flexible.* (ofrezca)
3. *Aquí no hay ninguna impresora que funcione / funciona.* (funcione)
4. *¿Conoces a alguien que puede / pueda bajar estos archivos?* (pueda)
5. *Necesito empleados que me ayudan / ayuden.* (ayuden)
6. *Hay muchas personas que saben / sepan colgar fotos.* (saben)

EXPANDING LEARNERS

● Ask students to complete these sentences with the correct form of the verb:
1. *No hay nadie aquí que me (entender).* (entienda)
2. *¿Buscas una persona que (poder) traducir este artículo?* (pueda)
3. *La empresa quería una coordinadora que (hablar) francés.* (hablara)
4. *Buscaban a alguien que (saber) arreglar la fotocopiadora.* (supiera)
5. *No había nada que me (interesar) en esa empresa.* (interesara)
6. *El país necesita líderes que (tener) imaginación.* (tengan)

43 Candidatos

▶ **Escribe** oraciones usando el relativo *que*. Presta atención a las formas verbales.

Modelo   *El jefe busca un periodista que sepa manejar computadoras.*

El jefe busca	un empleado	saber manejar computadoras.
El gerente quería	una coordinadora	ser responsable y eficiente.
Los empleados deseaban	un secretario	poder usar la fotocopiadora.
La empresa necesita	una arquitecta	tener diez años de experiencia.
Afortunadamente hay	un periodista	ser creativo.

44 La universidad

▶ **Escucha** a varios estudiantes hablando de la universidad y elige la opción correcta.

1. Él _____ una universidad que esté cerca de donde viven sus padres.
   a. busca   b. va a   c. encontró

2. Ella _____ una universidad que tiene un programa de Derecho.
   a. busca   b. irá a   c. no conoce

3. Antes _____ una universidad que estuviera en Nueva York.
   a. quiere   b. encontró   c. buscaba

4. Después de mucho tiempo _____ una universidad que ofrecía cursos de Tecnología.
   a. busca   b. encontró   c. necesitaba

5. Él _____ asistir a una escuela que sea pequeña.
   a. va a   b. buscaba   c. quiere

6. Ella _____ una universidad que tuviera una facultad de Medicina.
   a. quería   b. necesita   c. conoce

▶ **Escribe.** ¿Qué tipo de universidad vas a buscar? ¿Por qué?

Modelo   *Yo voy a buscar una universidad que tenga una facultad de Ingeniería porque…*

45 ¿A quién conoces?

▶ **Habla** con tu compañero(a) para identificar personas de tu escuela que tengan estas características. ¿Puedes añadir más?

saber francés
cantar bien
jugar al tenis
diseñar páginas web
trabajar a media jornada
manejar un coche
pensar en hacerse abogado(a)

Modelo
¿Conoces a alguien que sepa francés?

No, no conozco a nadie que sepa francés, pero conozco a una chica que habla alemán.

doscientos cincuenta y uno 251

HERITAGE LANGUAGE LEARNERS

• Ask students to write two paragraphs about what they consider to be their ideal job. They should use the relative pronoun *que* whenever possible in their descriptions. To get students started, you might give them this example: *Busco un trabajo que pague muy bien. Quiero tener un jefe que sea amable e inteligente. Quiero tener unos compañeros que me puedan enseñar algo.* When students complete their descriptions, call on volunteers to read their compositions aloud.

MULTIPLE INTELLIGENCES:
Verbal-Linguistic Intelligence

• Have pairs create a dialogue between a person and his or her much younger brother or sister, who is always asking the older sibling questions. The questions should make use of adjective clauses, and the responses will use either the subjunctive or indicative mood. Encourage students to use a variety of tenses. For example:

A. *Oye, Miguel, ¿conoces a alguien que sepa portugués?*

B. *No, no conozco a nadie que sepa portugués.* Or: *Sí, conozco a alguien que sabe portugués.*

Unit 5
DESAFÍO 2

Gramática – Dar detalles. El relativo *que*

43. Before starting this activity, remind students of the sequence of tenses (i.e., present and present subjunctive, past and imperfect subjunctive).

45. After students have completed this activity, ask them to share one of their partner's responses with the class. For example: *Mi compañero no conoce a nadie que sepa hablar francés, pero conoce a una chica que habla alemán.*

AUDIO SCRIPT
See page 227I.

Answer Key

41. *The company wants an accountant who has experience. The company wanted an accountant who had experience.*

42. 1. (b) Tengo una fotocopiadora que hace copias en color.
2. (e) Conozco a una arquitecta que es muy creativa.
3. (c) Hay algunos empleados que trabajan a media jornada.
4. (d) La jefa busca un ayudante que sea muy eficiente.
5. (a) Aquí no hay ninguna computadora que tenga reproductor de CD.

43. Answers will vary. Sample answers:
El gerente quería un secretario que pudiera usar la fotocopiadora.
Los empleados deseaban una coordinadora que tuviera diez años de experiencia.
La empresa necesita un empleado que sea responsable y eficiente.
Afortunadamente hay una arquitecta que es creativa.

44. 1. a   2. b   3. c   4. b   5. c   6. a
▶ Answers will vary.

45. Answers will vary.

Additional Resources

Fans Online activities
Practice Workbook

251

Unit 5
DESAFÍO 2
Gramática – El género del nombre

Presentation

- In this section, students will review and practice the gender of nouns, including the gender of occupational names and job titles. They will also learn exceptions to the agreement rules.

Activities	Standards	Resources
Gramática	1.2, 3.1	
46.	4.1	
47.	1.3, 3.1	
48.	1.2, 1.3	
49. Comunidades	1.1, 1.2, 2.1, 4.2, 5.1, 5.2	Video

Teaching Suggestions

Warm-Up / Independent Starter

- Ask students to write a list of ten items that they see in the classroom along with the definite article that accompanies each noun (e.g., *el escritorio, la puerta*).

Preparation

- Invite students to share their responses to the Independent Starter. Ask students how they know the gender of the nouns they listed. Call on volunteers to read aloud one bulleted item each in the *Gramática* feature. Point out that the examples provided are frequently problematic for students of Spanish.

- You may want to point out the reason singular feminine nouns beginning with an accented *a-* or *ha-* take a masculine article. Have students say the examples aloud, and then try to say them using a feminine article. Note that they are more difficult to pronounce with *la* than with *el*.

Activities

48. Ask students true/false questions based on the online forum. Have them correct the false statements. For example:
    1. *Marta y su hermana se pelearon y por eso ya no trabajan juntas. (falso)*
    2. *Marta necesita alguien que repare computadoras. (cierto)*

Gramática

El género del nombre

Masculino y femenino. Casos especiales

- In Spanish, nouns that end in -o are usually masculine and nouns that end in -a are usually feminine. But there are numerous exceptions:

  el día   el mapa   el planeta   el pijama   el sofá   la mano

- Some words are feminine even though they end in -o, because they are the shortened version of feminine nouns.

  la foto (la fotografía)   la moto (la motocicleta)

- Most nouns of Greek origin ending in -ma are masculine. Most have cognates in English.

  el clima   el drama   el diagrama   el dilema   el diploma   el idioma
  el poema   el problema   el programa   el síntoma   el sistema   el tema

El género en oficios, profesiones y cargos

- There are a lot of nouns ending in -or. To form the feminine, add -a.

  el doctor/la doctora   el profesor/la profesora

  Exception: el actor/la actriz.

- Nouns ending in -ista and -a do not change.

  el/la artista   el/la periodista   el/la poeta   el/la astronauta

- Generally, nouns ending in -e do not change.

  el/la agente   el/la cantante   el/la detective   el/la gerente

  Some exceptions:

  el cliente/la clienta   el jefe/la jefa   el presidente/la presidenta

- Some nouns ending in -o don't change in the feminine form.

  el/la modelo   el/la piloto   el/la soldado   el/la testigo

Excepción a las normas de concordancia

- Feminine nouns that begin with a stressed a- or ha- follow this pattern:
  - In the singular, they take a masculine article.

    el habla   un agua   el ala roja   un área pequeña

  - In the plural, they take a feminine article.

    las hablas   unas aguas   las alas rojas   unas áreas pequeñas

46 **Compara.** ¿Cómo se expresa el género en inglés en los nombres de profesiones?

---

47 **El género**

▶ **Escribe** oraciones con estas palabras.
Usa un adjetivo para describir el sustantivo.

Modelo   *La famosa periodista vino a mi ciudad a recoger un premio.*

periodista	arte
cliente	foto
estudiante	días

Differentiated Instruction

DEVELOPING LEARNERS

- Ask students to close their books and then write or say the correct definite article or articles for the following words:

  1. *sofá (el)*
  2. *periodista (el, la)*
  3. *artista (el, la)*
  4. *poema (el)*
  5. *presidente (el)*
  6. *síntoma (el)*
  7. *detective (el, la)*
  8. *pijama (el)*
  9. *piloto (el, la)*
  10. *agua (el)*
  11. *modelo (el, la)*
  12. *sistema (el)*
  13. *área (el)*
  14. *testigo (el, la)*
  15. *gerente (el, la)*
  16. *moto (la)*

EXPANDING LEARNERS

- Tell students that they are going to play a game in which you will call out nouns and they will have to say aloud the corresponding definite article or articles. After students identify the articles of words such as *cliente, jefe,* and *presidente,* ask them to say the corresponding feminine word, along with the article. Words do not need to be limited to those presented in the *Gramática* feature, and might include: *la pizza, la sauna, el chalet, el eslogan, el fax, el jazz, el módem, el software, el yoga.*

48 Un foro de trabajo

▶ **Lee** este foro sobre profesiones y complétalo con los artículos que faltan (el, la, los, las).

Autor	Mensaje
Marta32 Publicado: 8/03/2013 4:30 p. m.	Hola, amigos del foro. A principios de este año abrí una empresa de *marketing*. Todo empezó bien, pero ___1___ problema es que necesito cubrir varios puestos muy rápido y no encuentro gente. Mi hermana era ___2___ gerente y se ocupaba de buscar personal, pero tuvo que mudarse y ya no trabaja aquí.
LuisaRuiz Publicado: 8/03/2013 5:10 p. m.	Hola, Marta32. Yo soy programadora informática. ¿No necesitas a alguien que controle ___3___ sistema informático de tu empresa?
Marta32 Publicado: 8/03/2013 5:14 p. m.	Gracias, LuisaRuiz, pero ya tengo una persona para eso. Precisamente diseñó ___4___ programa de contabilidad con el que trabajamos. ¿Te interesa trabajar en ___5___ área de instalación y reparación de computadoras? Hay que hablar perfectamente inglés.
LuisaRuiz Publicado: 8/03/2013 5:18 p. m.	___6___ idioma no es un problema. Hablo inglés y francés. Solo me preocupa ___7___ tema de los horarios. Tengo una niña pequeña y solo puedo trabajar media jornada.
Marta32 Publicado: 8/03/2013 5:25 p. m.	No importa. Mándame tu currículum.
LuisaRuiz Publicado: 8/03/2013 5:30 p. m.	Perfecto. Puedo pasarme por la empresa la semana que viene, ___8___ día que prefieras.

 COMUNIDADES

TELEVISIÓN EN ESPAÑOL

Muchas comunidades de los Estados Unidos tienen acceso a la programación de televisión en español. Univisión y Telemundo son dos de las cadenas más populares, muestra de la creciente demanda del español en el país. Telemundo ofrece subtítulos en inglés para atraer a los espectadores que están aprendiendo español.

49 **Habla.** ¿Se puede ver televisión en español donde tú vives? ¿Te gustaría poder ver programas de televisión o películas en español? ¿Por qué?

doscientos cincuenta y tres 253

HERITAGE LANGUAGE LEARNERS

- Students probably know some words that differ in meaning only by their gender, such as *el policía* (policeman), *la policía* (policewoman, police force) and *el cura* (priest), *la cura* (cure). Introduce them to others: *el capital* (capital, money), *la capital* (capital city); *el coma* (coma), *la coma* (comma); *el frente* (front), *la frente* (forehead); *el orden* (order, as opposed to disorder), *la orden* (command, religious order); *el pendiente* (earring), *la pendiente* (slope). Have students write these words in their notebooks, and then come up with a sentence for each word.

MULTIPLE INTELLIGENCES:
Verbal-Linguistic Intelligence

- Ask students to write a paragraph or a dialogue about any job-related topic, but have them leave a blank where the definite or indefinite article would be placed. Then ask students to exchange papers with a classmate, who will add the missing articles. Students will review each other's work and check for errors.

Gramática – El género del nombre

49. If you have Internet access in your classroom, log onto the *Univisión* or *Telemundo* website and have students look at the different programming available. You can also play a news clip and have students list all of the words they are able to comprehend.

 COMUNIDADES

Televisión en español

For almost sixty years, Spanish-language television has existed in the United States. Today, *Univisión* and *Telemundo* are the two most popular networks, continuously competing for viewers. Both channels offer news, soap operas, children's cartoons, movies, and other programming to attract a variety of viewers. More than half of all families of Hispanic or Latino descent have access to Spanish-language television in their homes.

Answer Key

46. Generalmente, las palabras que se refieren a profesiones no tienen género en inglés (e.g., *doctor, lawyer, teacher, lifeguard*). Ciertas profesiones que terminan en –*man*, se cambian a –*woman* (e.g., *businessman → businesswoman*). También hay ciertas profesiones con distintas formas (e.g., *actor → actress*).

47. Answers will vary.

48.
1. el	4. el	7. el
2. la	5. el	8. el
3. el	6. El	

49. Answers will vary.

Additional Resources

Fans Online activities
Practice Workbook

253

LECTURA: TEXTO INFORMATIVO

Presentation

- In this section, students will read a newspaper obituary of a Spanish inventor and businessman. Students will practice vocabulary related to professions and jobs, and they will draw conclusions from given statements.

Activities	Standards	Resources
Lectura: texto informativo	1.1, 1.2, 2.2, 3.1, 3.2	
50.	1.1, 1.2, 2.2	
51.	1.2, 1.3, 2.2	
52.	1.2, 1.3, 2.2, 3.1, 5.1	

Teaching Suggestions

Warm-Up / Independent Starter

- Have students read the *Antes de leer* strategies silently. Ask them to take notes as they scan the text in search of the answers and get ready to share them.

Preparation

- With the class, brainstorm a list of inventions or appliances that have facilitated domestic work. Ask related questions to help students give details. For example: *¿Para qué sirve ese aparato? ¿Cómo funciona? ¿Saben quién lo inventó?* Take a poll on which of those inventions or appliances are the most useful and why. Have students come up with inventions of their own that would facilitate housework even more.

- Call on different volunteers to answer the questions in the *Antes de leer* section. As a class, correct and discuss the answers. Then have students scan the text for vocabulary related to professions and jobs. (*inventor, empresario, ingeniero aeronáutico, técnico*)

Activities

50. To expand this activity, ask additional questions and have students look up the answers. For example: *¿Dónde está Zaragoza? ¿Qué significa ser riojano? ¿Qué es una patente? ¿Qué son los «aviones a reacción»?*

Antes de leer: estrategias

1. Lee el titular *(headline)* y la entradilla *(lead)* de esta noticia. ¿Qué temas crees que se van a tratar?
2. Fíjate en la estructura del cuerpo de la noticia: tiene tres párrafos. ¿En cuál de ellos se habla de los inventos de Manuel Jalón?
3. ¿Cómo imaginas la vida de Manuel Jalón? Busca en el texto algún dato sobre su infancia o su juventud.

EL PAÍS, 18 de diciembre de 2011   SOCIEDAD

Manuel Jalón, un inventor humanista

El ingeniero patentó la popular fregona[1] y la aguja hipodérmica desechable[2]

RAMÓN CASAMAYOR

Manuel Jalón Corominas (Logroño, 1925) era un empresario humanista. Una humanidad caracterizada, entre otras cosas, por una coquetería[3] que le impedía[4] revelar su edad casi desde sus años mozos[5]. Zaragozano[6] de adopción pese a su origen riojano[7], con dos guerras a sus espaldas –la civil española y la segunda mundial– que le marcaron notablemente, se alistó en el ejército del aire, lo que le permitió titularse como ingeniero aeronáutico y ser uno de los primeros técnicos españoles que a principios de los cincuenta se desplazó a los Estados Unidos para traerse desde allí los primeros «aviones a reacción» que utilizaría el ejército español. Pero no solo se trajo los reactores. Como buen observador, se empapó[8] de las formas de vida de una sociedad que terminarían imponiéndose en el mundo entero.

Emprendedor nato, creó en un taller[9] de Zaragoza en 1956 uno de los inventos españoles más famosos: la fregona. Es curioso que dos de los principales inventos comerciales españoles estén basados en un palo[10]: la fregona y el chupachups[11]. En realidad, la fregona era una mejora de los modelos americanos adaptada a las necesidades y los gustos españoles. Era más pequeña, bonita y económica, y en poco tiempo de mucho menor peso por la invasión del plástico de aquellos años.

Manuel Jalón ha muerto este viernes a los 86 años, un año después de publicar su libro *Manual para la otra vida*, fruto de «años y años de razonamiento[12]» según comentaba a finales de 2010, cuando volvía a reconocer su suerte de haber pasado la infancia en el campo, cerca de la naturaleza, contemplando los milagros cotidianos que le llevaban a preguntarse el porqué de las cosas.

Fuente: Diario *El País* (España)
(texto adaptado)

1. *mop*	3. *vanity*	5. *youth*	7. *from La Rioja (Spain)*	9. *workshop*	11. *lollipop*
2. *disposable syringe*	4. *prevented*	6. *from Zaragoza (Spain)*	8. *soaked up*	10. *stick*	12. *reasoning*

Differentiated Instruction

DEVELOPING LEARNERS

- To verify students' comprehension of the reading, ask them the following questions:
  1. *¿Dónde nació Manuel Jalón? (En Logroño, España.)*
  2. *¿Cuándo y dónde inventó la fregona? (En 1956, en Zaragoza.)*
  3. *¿Qué otro invento español también tiene un palo? ¿Qué es? (El chupa-chups. Es un dulce.)*
  4. *¿Por qué eran mejores las fregonas españolas que las americanas? (Eran más pequeñas, bonitas y económicas, y pesaban menos.)*

EXPANDING LEARNERS

- Ask students to write in their notebooks the words and phrases from the reading whose meaning they don't know. Ask students to use the context to try to guess the meaning. As a last option, they can look up the words in a dictionary. Then have students write an original sentence using each word or phrase. For example: *nato (born) → Ese gerente es un líder nato.*

50 Comprensión

▶ **Responde** a estas preguntas.

1. ¿Qué significa «ser zaragozano de adopción»?
2. ¿De qué se graduó Manuel Jalón?
3. ¿Qué le aportó a Manuel su experiencia en los Estados Unidos?
4. ¿Qué inventó Manuel Jalón? ¿La fregona es un invento genuinamente suyo?
5. ¿A qué crees que se refiere la expresión «la invasión del plástico»? ¿Qué consecuencias tuvo esa «invasión»?

51 Evidencias y conclusiones

▶ **Completa** un diagrama como este con información del texto y establece conclusiones sobre la personalidad de Manuel Jalón.

EVIDENCIAS

Manuel Jalón vivió dos guerras.
Se graduó como ingeniero aeronáutico.
Viajó a los Estados Unidos.
Creó varios inventos famosos.
Publicó un libro.

CONCLUSIONES

Manuel Jalón era…

- Una persona fuerte.

52 Con tus propias palabras

▶ **Escribe** con tus palabras el significado de este fragmento del texto. ¿Cómo se dicen en inglés las palabras destacadas? ¿Se parecen a las palabras en español?

Una humanidad caracterizada, entre otras cosas, por una coquetería que le impedía <u>revelar</u> su edad casi desde sus años mozos. Zaragozano de adopción pese a su origen riojano, con dos guerras a sus espaldas –la civil española y la segunda mundial– que le <u>marcaron</u> notablemente, <u>se alistó</u> en el ejército del aire.

▶ **Investiga.** ¿En qué años tuvieron lugar las dos guerras que se mencionan en el texto? ¿Qué edad tenía Manuel Jalón en cada una de ellas?

doscientos cincuenta y cinco **255**

HERITAGE LANGUAGE LEARNERS

- Manuel Jalón considered himself *un empresario humanista* (a humanist businessman), and he was more proud of this than of his inventions. Ask students to think of two achievements that they are proud of. Then have students write a two-paragraph text describing what these achievements are and explaining why they are proud of them.

SPECIAL-NEEDS LEARNERS

- Help those students who experience language-processing difficulties with their reading comprehension by pointing out cognates, allowing students to look up new words in their dictionaries, and asking them to identify the verb tenses. As students read the text aloud, ask them to paraphrase each sentence to verify their understanding of what is being described.

---

51. To facilitate this activity, you may give students other statements as evidence and have them draw their conclusions about Manuel Jalón's personality. For example: *Trajo de los Estados Unidos los primeros aviones a reacción que se utilizaron en España. Pasó la infancia en el campo, cerca de la naturaleza.* Alternatively, you may ask students to find all of the adjectives in the text that describe his personality and correlate these traits to the evidence stated in the text. For example: *Era emprendedor porque creó y patentó varios inventos. Era observador porque estudió la sociedad estadounidense.*

Answer Key

50. 1. No nació en Zaragoza, pero vivió toda su vida en esa ciudad.
2. De ingeniero aeronáutico.
3. Le aportó ideas para sus inventos.
4. Inventó la fregona y la aguja hipodérmica desechable. La fregona no era un invento suyo, sino una adaptación de un invento estadounidense.
5. Significa que muchas cosas empezaron a hacerse de plástico. Los objetos de plástico eran más livianos, pequeños y baratos.

51. Answers will vary.

52. Answers will vary. Sample answer:
Manuel Jalón era un poco vanidoso y no le gustaba decir su edad. Nació en La Rioja, pero se crió en Zaragoza. La guerra civil española y la segunda guerra mundial dejaron en él una profunda huella. Se alistó en la fuerza aérea.
Revelar: *to reveal*; marcaron: *marked*; se alistó: *he enlisted.*
▶ Guerra civil española: 1936–1939 (11–14 años).
Segunda guerra mundial: 1939–1945 (14–20 años).

Additional Resources

Fans Online activities

DESAFÍO 2

Comunicación

Presentation

- In this section, students will integrate the vocabulary and grammar skills from *Desafío 2* in order to talk about jobs and technology.

Activities	Standards	Resources
53.	1.1, 1.2, 1.3, 3.1, 5.2	Audio
54.	1.3, 5.2	
55.	1.1, 1.2, 1.3, 5.1	
56. Final del desafío	1.1, 1.2, 1.3, 3.1	

Teaching Suggestions

Warm-Up / Independent Starter

- Ask students to write a paragraph about the abilities and skills necessary to obtain a job in a company that does all of its work electronically. To assist students, give them the following sentence starters: *La empresa busca empleados que… Los requisitos son… Es necesario que…*

Preparation

- Review adjective clauses that use the indicative or the subjunctive, and ask students to explain how to determine the mood of the subordinate clause. You may also want to review the present and the imperfect subjunctive conjugations, and contrast the use of these two tenses.

- Ask students to exchange their Independent Starters with a partner. Have students peer review each other's work, focusing on the subordinate clause. Then ask pairs to brainstorm differences between these answers and the abilities and skills necessary for a completely manual or non-technological job. Which qualities remain the same no matter what type of job it is? Which qualities differ greatly?

- Ask students how to gain experience in order to obtain a job. What alternative activities (e.g., volunteer work, internships, school projects, clubs) might help a student their age gain experience before entering the workplace?

256

Comunicación

53 Buscando trabajo

▶ **Completa** estos anuncios con la forma correcta de los verbos.

Secretario(a)

Se busca secretario(a) que ___1___ experiencia con computadoras
tener
e impresoras. Se prefiere persona
que ___2___ trabajar media jornada
poder
y con horario flexible.

Diseñador(a) de páginas web

Se busca empleado(a) que ___3___ diseñar
saber
páginas web. Se prefiere a alguien que
___4___ trabajar horas extraordinarias.
querer
Jornada completa y sueldo negociable.

Monitor(a)

Se necesitan personas que ___5___
ser
pacientes para trabajar con niños
de 7 a 10 años. Jornada completa,
de lunes a viernes, y 2 semanas de
vacaciones más los días feriados.

Cocineros(as)

Se buscan cocineros(as) que ___6___
conocer
la cocina criolla. Se solicitan personas que
___7___ disponibles los fines de semana.
estar
Media jornada. Sueldo negociable.

▶ **Responde** a estas preguntas.

1. ¿En qué puestos se requiere que el empleado trabaje al menos 40 horas semanales?
2. ¿Para qué trabajos se necesita tener experiencia?
3. ¿En qué puesto se trabaja solo los sábados y los domingos?
4. ¿Estás cualificado(a) para alguno de estos trabajos? Explica para cuál y por qué.

 ▶ **Escucha** y decide qué puesto debe solicitar cada persona.

54 Mis habilidades

▶ **Escribe.** Piensa en tus habilidades y en un lugar donde te gustaría trabajar. Escribe un texto explicándolo.

> Soy…
> Sé cómo…
> Puedo…
> Si desean más información…

> Me gustaría trabajar en una oficina.

Differentiated Instruction

DEVELOPING LEARNERS

- Ask students to imagine that they are looking for a job, and that one of the positions described in activity 53 interests them. Have students write a response to the ad, making sure that they address all the requirements mentioned affirmatively, including agreement to the terms and conditions described in the ad. They should also state their qualifications for the job. They can use imaginary information. For example: *Soy secretaria y tengo 5 años de experiencia con computadoras e impresoras. Busco un puesto de media jornada porque estoy estudiando informática…*

EXPANDING LEARNERS

- Ask students to work in groups of three. Explain that they are to imagine that a friend of theirs is looking for a job and needs three letters of recommendation from those who have known him or her academically, professionally, or socially. The group must first decide what job this friend is looking for, and who will respond from the academic, professional, and social point of view. After students write their letters, call on some to read them aloud. Take a class vote on the three most influential letters.

55 **Se buscan estudiantes**

▶ **Escribe** dos anuncios para trabajos en tu comunidad. Usa las expresiones del cuadro.

> Se busca...   Se solicita...
> Es preferible que...   Los requisitos son...
> Es necesario que...   Es imprescindible...

▶ **Comparte** los anuncios con tus compañeros(as). ¿Cuáles te parecen más interesantes? ¿Por qué?

Final del desafío

DANIEL: ¿Encuentras algún anuncio interesante?

MICHELLE: Sí, en ___1___ museo de arte del barrio están buscando un guía. Y yo tengo experiencia con ___2___ arte. Pero no estoy segura...

DANIEL: ¿Cuál es ___3___ problema?

MICHELLE: Pues que ___4___ horario no es flexible. Además, conozco a ___5___ gerente y no es muy simpática.

DANIEL: No importa, yo creo que debes llamar.

MICHELLE: Está bien... Voy a llamar.

MICHELLE: Buenos días. Llamo por ___6___ anuncio para ___7___ puesto de guía.

SECRETARIO: ___8___ entrevistas son el jueves por la tarde.

MICHELLE: ¿Este jueves? ¿___9___ día 4?

SECRETARIO: Sí, eso es. ¿Puede usted venir a ___10___ tres?

 56 **El puesto ideal**

▶ **Completa** la conversación con los artículos definidos que faltan (el, la, los, las).

 ▶ **Habla** con tu compañero(a). ¿Debe solicitar Michelle el puesto si no le cae bien la gerente del museo? ¿Por qué?

Modelo A. *Yo pienso que Michelle no debería solicitar el puesto porque es importante que se lleve bien con la gerente.*

B. *Pues yo creo que debe solicitarlo porque...*

doscientos cincuenta y siete 257

Activities

53. After students have finished this activity, have pairs role-play a job interview for one of the jobs listed in this activity. One student plays the role of the manager or boss and the other, the potential applicant.

54. Before starting this activity, have students brainstorm other useful sentence starters. For example: *Prefiero un trabajo que... Busco una empresa que...*

56. After completing the dialogue with the articles, ask for volunteers to present the conversation to the class. Then have students work on the second part of this activity.

 AUDIO SCRIPT
See page 227I.

Answer Key

53. 1. tenga   4. quiera   7. estén
2. pueda   5. sean
3. sepa   6. conozcan

▶ 1. En el puesto de monitor y en el de diseñador de páginas web.
2. Se necesita experiencia en el puesto de secretario, de diseñador de páginas web y de cocinero.
3. En el puesto de cocinero.
4. Answers will vary.

▶ 1. cocinero
2. secretario
3. monitor
4. diseñador de páginas web

54. Answers will vary.

55. Answers will vary.
▶ Answers will vary.

56. 1. el   3. el   5. la   7. el   9. El
2. el   4. el   6. el   8. Las   10. las
▶ Answers will vary.

Additional Resources

Fans Online activities
Practice Workbook

HERITAGE LANGUAGE LEARNERS

• Ask students to bring to class some *anuncios clasificados* from a Spanish-language newspaper from their heritage country. If there are jobs and professions that are unique to that country's culture, have students elaborate on these jobs. Ask students to describe the jobs that are most in demand, and to address the following questions: Are there many jobs that require applicants to know another language? Do the ads mention whether companies are looking for male or female workers? Do the ads require people to call and set up an interview, or to respond by e-mail?

COOPERATIVE LEARNING

• Ask students to work in groups of three or four to discuss the requirements needed for a world leader. Based on a consensus within the group, students will write an *anuncio clasificado* for this job. The ads should include a detailed job description as well as the educational requirements, work experience, and other skills and qualifications (e.g., knowing at least one foreign language) demanded of all the potential candidates. Encourage students to use adjective clauses with the subjunctive when stating the qualifications they are looking for in a candidate.

257

Unit 5
DESAFÍO 3

Expresar sentimientos y dificultad

Presentation

■ In *Desafío 3*, Eva and Ethan must choose a charitable organization led by a famous Latino and write a project proposal. Students will preview language used to talk about volunteering, and structures used to express feelings.

Activities	Standards	Resources
Texto	1.2, 2.1, 2.2, 3.2	Vis. Pres.
57.	1.2, 1.3	
58.	1.1, 1.2	
59.	1.1, 1.2, 1.3, 5.1	Audio
60. Comunidades	1.1, 1.2, 1.3, 2.1, 2.2, 3.1, 5.1, 5.2	

Teaching Suggestions

Warm-Up / Independent Starter

■ Have students brainstorm names of charitable organizations they know. Also ask them to identify the main activities of each organization.

Preparation

■ Have students share their Independent Starters. Write a list of the organizations as well as the main activities of these organizations. Ask students if they have volunteered for any of those organizations and which one they would like to work with.

Texto: Por el bien común

■ Read the introduction to the dialogue aloud. Then have students read the dialogue silently. Once they are finished, ask for three volunteers to play the roles of the characters and read the dialogue aloud.

■ Ask students to describe the characters' feelings in this dialogue. Are they happy? Uncomfortable? Sad? Discouraged?

Activities

59. Before listening to the audio, ask students to look at the pictures, write a brief description, and try to figure out what kind of organization each of the photos relates to.

258

Por el bien común

There are several renowned non-profit organizations whose leaders are famous Latinos. Eva and Ethan must choose one and write a proposal for a project. What a difficult decision!

ANDY: ¡Qué sorpresa, amigos! ¿Cómo les va?

EVA: Estamos un poco desanimados con nuestro desafío. Quizá tú puedas ayudarnos.

ANDY: Sí, cómo no.

EVA: Seguramente estuviste en muchas comunidades durante tus viajes y viste a muchas personas que necesitan ayuda en todo el mundo. ¿No te deprime que haya tanta gente con problemas?

ANDY: Claro, Eva. Pero me alegró mucho poder colaborar en algo, aunque fuera poco. Afortunadamente, hay muchas organizaciones que colaboran en proyectos importantes en casi todos los países.

ETHAN: ¿Pero cómo vamos a elegir solo una? Hay muchísimas. Y cada una tiene un objetivo diferente: unas son para ayudar a niños que no van a la escuela, otras para atender a personas mayores, otras para cuidar el medio ambiente… ¡Me molesta que tengamos que elegir solo una!

ANDY: Tranquilos, chicos. En el futuro, siempre pueden cooperar como voluntarios con otras asociaciones. Por ahora decidan con qué causa quieren colaborar y qué pueden hacer ustedes. Así será más fácil encontrar la organización apropiada.

EVA: De acuerdo, Andy. Muchas gracias.

ANDY: No se rindan. Este puede ser el desafío más importante de todos.

«Contribuimos a que la niñez sea protagonista en la construcción de la paz en Colombia.»

Fuente: http://www.fundacionmisangre.org

57 **Detective de palabras**

▶ **Completa** estas oraciones con palabras del diálogo.

1. En sus viajes Andy vio a muchas personas que ___1___ ayuda.
2. Hay muchas organizaciones que ___2___ en proyectos importantes.
3. Hay organizaciones para ___3___ a niños que no van a la escuela, otras para ___4___ a personas mayores y otras para ___5___ el medio ambiente.
4. Eva y Ethan pueden ___6___ como voluntarios con muchas asociaciones.

258 doscientos cincuenta y ocho

Differentiated Instruction

DEVELOPING LEARNERS

• Explain to students that they are going to keep track of the encouraging and discouraging remarks made in the dialogue. Ask students to make a two-column chart labeled *Comentarios animados* and *Comentarios desanimados*. Then have them read the conversation line by line and decide where to categorize each speaker's comments. For instance, Andy's advice at the end, *No se rindan,* would be an encouraging remark, while Eva's line, *Estamos un poco desanimados,* would be an example of a discouraging remark. Explain that some remarks will not fit either category.

EXPANDING LEARNERS

• Ask students to review the verbs they used to complete activity 57 and write other words that could replace them. For example, students might write the following: 1. *necesitan: requieren;* 2. *colaboran: cooperan;* 3. *ayudar: asistir;* 4. *atender: cuidar;* 5. *cuidar: proteger;* 6. *cooperar: colaborar, trabajar.* Ask students to read the sentences with their new words in place.

58 **Una elección difícil**

▶ **Responde** a estas preguntas.

1. ¿Por qué deciden los personajes hablar con Andy?
2. ¿Qué le deprime a Eva?
3. ¿Qué le dice Andy a Eva al respecto?
4. ¿Qué le molesta a Ethan?
5. Según Andy, ¿qué tienen que hacer antes de elegir una organización?

59 **ONG**

 ▶ **Escucha** la conversación entre Eva y Ethan y ordena las fotografías.

 ▶ **Escucha** de nuevo y escribe. ¿A qué se dedica cada organización?

 ▶ **Habla** con tu compañero(a). ¿A qué organización te gustaría ayudar? ¿Por qué?

Modelo *A mí me gustaría ayudar a la ONG que se ocupa de las personas mayores porque puedo hacerlo aquí, en mi comunidad.*

 **COMUNIDADES**

HISPANOS SOLIDARIOS

Existen varias organizaciones no gubernamentales (ONG) creadas por hispanos que se dedican a ayudar a los más necesitados. Entre ellas están la fundación Pies Descalzos o la fundación Mi Sangre, creadas respectivamente por los cantantes colombianos Shakira y Juanes.

Pau Gasol (España).

Otros famosos colaboran habitualmente con proyectos solidarios, como el jugador de la NBA Pau Gasol, que coopera con UNICEF, organización de las Naciones Unidas que protege los derechos de los niños de todo el mundo.

60 **Piensa y explica.** Imagina que puedes crear una organización benéfica *(charitable)*. ¿Qué causa apoyarías? ¿Por qué?

Expresar sentimientos y dificultad

60. As a follow-up, group students by similar organizations. Ask groups to write a brief description in order to advertise their organization.

 AUDIO SCRIPT
See page 227J.

 COMUNIDADES

Hispanos solidarios

Pies Descalzos and *Mi Sangre* were created to help children in Colombia who suffer directly from war violence and poverty. These organizations offer psychological support and educational opportunities. The actress Eva Longoria is another Hispanic celebrity involved in charity work. She founded Eva's Heroes, an organization that helps young adults with intellectual special needs.

Answer Key

57. 1. necesitan   3. ayudar   5. cuidar
2. colaboran   4. atender   6. cooperar

58. 1. Porque Andy estuvo en muchas comunidades que necesitaban ayuda.
2. Le deprime que haya tanta gente con problemas.
3. Que le alegró haber podido colaborar.
4. Que tenga que elegir solo una organización entre tantas.
5. Decidir con qué causa quieren colaborar.

59. B, A, D, C
▶ A. Convencer a la gente de que no arroje basura en el parque.
B. Fomentar la lectura.
C. Ayudar a personas que no tienen casa.
D. Organizar actividades para personas mayores que no tienen familia.
▶ Answers will vary.

60. Answers will vary.

Additional Resources

Fans Online activities

HERITAGE LANGUAGE LEARNERS

• Ask students to research which NGOs are sponsored by celebrities in their family's country of origin. Have students choose one and prepare a written or oral report. Students should find out something about its history, the sector of the population it serves, a description of the organization's services, what role the celebrity plays in this NGO, and how concerned citizens can find out more information and possibly volunteer or contribute to the cause. If students know of any campaign to promote this organization, have them share this information.

SPECIAL-NEEDS LEARNERS

• Students who experience difficulties with language processing may have trouble listening to the audio and then speaking with a classmate in order to complete activity 59. Help them finish this activity successfully by providing them with the audio script. For the third part of this activity, you may pair these students with those who have superior language skills or are heritage speakers, or you may choose to have students write their answers before explaining their reasons to a classmate.

DESAFÍO 3

Vocabulario – Voluntariado y trabajo comunitario

Presentation

- In this section, students will learn words and expressions used to talk about volunteering and community service.

Activities	Standards	Resources
Vocabulario	1.2, 3.1	
61.	1.2, 1.3	
62.	1.1, 1.2	Audio
63.	1.1, 1.2, 1.3, 5.1, 5.2	
64. Comunidades	1.1, 1.2, 1.3, 2.1, 4.2, 5.1, 5.2	Video

Teaching Suggestions

Warm-Up / Independent Starter

- Ask students to identify the volunteer or community service work depicted in the pictures on page 260.

Preparation

- Ask three volunteers to read the text under each picture aloud. After each text, have students repeat the key words after you. Make sure they understand the new words, pointing out any cognates. In addition, use pictures in the text, or extra pictures, to clarify the meaning of new words.

- Read the words in the *Más vocabulario* feature aloud and have students repeat them after you. You may want to remind them that Spanish words ending in *-cia*, *-ción*, and *–dad* are normally feminine.

Activities

61. After completing this activity, ask students to write a complete sentence using each word in an appropriate context. Alternatively, you may ask students to write a definition for each word.

62. Before playing the audio, have students read each sentence and ask them to take notes on any words they do not understand. Ask them to guess what kind of organization the advertisement is going to be about.

260

Vocabulario

Voluntariado y trabajo comunitario

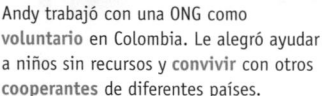

Andy trabajó con una ONG como **voluntario** en Colombia. Le alegró ayudar a niños sin recursos y **convivir** con otros **cooperantes** de diferentes países.

También pasó una semana con un pueblo indígena en la selva amazónica de Ecuador. Para él es importante **proteger los derechos** de estos pueblos y el medio ambiente.

Habitualmente **colabora** con una **organización** que **atiende** a personas mayores en su comunidad. Él es un **ciudadano** muy **comprometido**: le gusta **cooperar** en varios proyectos.

Más vocabulario

Trabajo comunitario

la convivencia	coexistence
la cooperación	cooperation
los deberes	duties
los derechos humanos	human rights
la integración	integration
la solidaridad	solidarity
la tolerancia	tolerance

61 **La decisión de Eva**

▶ **Lee** la entrada de Eva en su diario y complétala con las palabras adecuadas.

derechos
ciudadana
comunidad
cooperante
cooperar
organización

Querido diario: *8 de abril*

Hoy Andy me mostró fotos de su trabajo como __1__ por distintos países de Latinoamérica. Me di cuenta de que en muchos lugares no se respetan los __2__ humanos. He decidido ser una __3__ comprometida y por eso voy a __4__ con alguna __5__ de ayuda a personas con pocos recursos económicos en mi __6__.

260 **doscientos sesenta**

Differentiated Instruction

DEVELOPING LEARNERS

- Give students index cards so they can make flashcards for the new vocabulary. Ask them to write the Spanish word or phrase on one side, and the English on the opposite side. Be sure to point out the cognates and the word families so students will not be overwhelmed by the number of new terms. Then have them work with a partner and quiz each other. Monitor their pronunciation to make sure students are not pronouncing the cognates as if they were words in English.

EXPANDING LEARNERS

- Ask students to make a word web based on the new vocabulary. For each new word, students should write as many words as they can that are related. For example, *voluntario* would include *voluntad, voluntariamente, voluntariado; convivir* would include *convivencia;* and *cooperar* would include *cooperación, cooperante,* and *cooperativa.* Encourage students to use a dictionary to find more terms and to add them to the word families. Ask students to write these new words in their notebooks for vocabulary enrichment.

62 **Un anuncio**

 ▶ **Escucha** el anuncio de una ONG que oyó Ethan en la radio y decide si estas oraciones son ciertas o falsas.

1. El nombre de esta organización es Un Mundo de Todos.
2. Esta organización lucha por los derechos de los inmigrantes.
3. Su principal objetivo es mejorar la convivencia entre diferentes culturas.
4. Solo se puede contactar con la organización por correo electrónico.
5. El anuncio es para recaudar dinero para la organización.

 ▶ **Habla** con tu compañero(a) y decidan. ¿Esta organización es una buena opción para Eva y Ethan? ¿Qué tipos de proyectos relacionados con la inmigración podrían presentar?

Modelo   A. *Yo creo que esta organización es una buena opción para Eva y Ethan porque pueden trabajar en su comunidad.*
B. *Sí, estoy de acuerdo.*

63 **Voluntariado**

▶ **Responde** a estas preguntas.

1. ¿Alguna vez has trabajado como voluntario(a)?
2. ¿Qué hiciste? ¿Cómo fue la experiencia?
3. ¿Qué organizaciones benéficas conoces? ¿A qué se dedican?
4. ¿Qué tipo de organización crees que falta en tu comunidad?

 ▶ **Habla** con tres compañeros(as) y comparen sus respuestas. Entre todos, hagan una lista de los posibles trabajos voluntarios que se pueden hacer en su comunidad.

 **COMUNIDADES**

TURISMO SOSTENIBLE

El turismo es una parte muy importante en la economía de muchos países, pero también puede ser un problema para el medio ambiente. El turismo sostenible es un tipo de turismo que trata de respetar al máximo la naturaleza, la cultura y la sociedad del lugar. Evitar construir en zonas naturales, controlar el uso excesivo de recursos como el agua o conservar el paisaje son algunas de las bases del turismo sostenible.

64 **Piensa.** ¿Cómo crees que se puede promover el turismo sostenible en tu comunidad?

HERITAGE LANGUAGE LEARNERS

- Ask students to imagine that they are journalists for a Spanish-language newspaper. They are going to write a feature story about a group of students who recently returned from abroad where they worked with a non-profit organization as volunteers. Students will need to research a country, find out what non-profit organizations have a presence there, and describe what the work of the volunteers entailed. Students will also need to mention the impact this experience had on the volunteers.

MULTIPLE INTELLIGENCES:
Interpersonal Intelligence

- Ask students to name some non-profit organizations in their community whose objective is to help certain sectors of the population in need of special assistance. Have students choose one of these organizations and present a written or oral report that describes its services, the population it targets, how it has affected the community, and information on how people can volunteer their time for the organization.

---

64. Have students share their answers in small groups and select the five to ten most relevant recommendations. Have them create a poster with the selection they made, and ask each group to present their poster to the class.

 AUDIO SCRIPT
See page 227J.

 COMUNIDADES

Turismo sostenible

Costa Rica is one of the Latin American countries that has most successfully promoted the development of sustainability standards in the tourism industry. The government-supported Certification for Sustainable Tourism Program makes the concept of sustainability practical, helping businesses make choices about natural and social resources and helping them implement standards that foster respect for the environment.

Answer Key

61. 1. cooperante   4. cooperar
2. derechos   5. organización
3. ciudadana   6. comunidad

62. 1. Falso. Es Un País para Todos.
2. Cierto.
3. Cierto.
4. Falso. Se puede contactar por teléfono.
5. Falso. Es para buscar voluntarios(as).
▶ Answers will vary.

63. Answers will vary.
▶ Answers will vary.

64. Answers will vary.

Additional Resources

Fans Online activities
Practice Workbook

261

DESAFÍO 3

Gramática – Expresar sentimientos

Presentation

- In this section, students will review how to express feelings using the infinitive and the subjunctive.

Activities	Standards	Resources
Gramática	1.2, 3.1	
65.	1.3, 4.1	
66.	1.1, 1.2, 1.3	
67.	1.2, 1.3	
68.	1.2, 1.3	Audio
69.	1.1	

Teaching Suggestions

Warm-Up / Independent Starter

- Have students write their feelings about these topics: *las guerras en el mundo*, *las nuevas tecnologías*, *la contaminación*.

Preparation

- Ask students to read the grammar explanation silently, and have them take notes on any material they do not understand. Provide additional examples to emphasize the change of meaning when using present or past subjunctive in the dependent clause. You may want to ask students to do activity 65 at this point.

- Have students take their sentences from the Independent Starter and rewrite them using the subjunctive if they are not already in that format. Call on volunteers to share their examples.

Activities

66. Have students compare their sentences with a partner's. For example: *A Elena y a mí nos alegra que a nuestros amigos les gusten las mismas cosas que a nosotros.*

68. Before playing the audio, ask student to read the title of the activity and the sentences, and ask them to guess some possible answers. Ask volunteers to share their answers to be sure that they understand the grammar structure they will hear in the audio.

262

Gramática

Expresar sentimientos

Expresar sentimientos

- To express feelings or emotions we use many verbs that work just like *gustar*: the verb is conjugated in the third person and it requires an object pronoun.

  Nos alegra ayudar en la comunidad.
  Me preocupa que haya hambre en el mundo.

VERBOS PARA EXPRESAR SENTIMIENTOS		
aburrir	deprimir	extrañar
alegrar	divertir	fascinar
asustar	emocionar	molestar
dar miedo	enfadar	preocupar
dar pena	enojar	sorprender

El infinitivo y el subjuntivo para expresar sentimientos

- The clause that adds information about the verb of emotion, that is, the dependent clause, takes a verb in either the infinitive or the subjunctive:

  – Use the infinitive when the main clause and the dependent clause refer to the same person.

  *Nos alegra **cooperar** con organizaciones no gubernamentales (ONG).*
  a nosotros   nosotros

  – Use *que* + *subjunctive* when the main clause and the dependent clause refer to different people.

  *Nos alegra que **cooperes** con organizaciones no gubernamentales.*
  a nosotros   tú

¿Presente o pasado?

- If the subjunctive mood is required in the dependent clause, look at the verb in the main clause:

  – If the main clause is in the present, use the present subjunctive in the dependent clause.

  Me molesta (present) + que te enfades. (present subjuntive)

  – If the main clause is in the past, use the imperfect subjunctive in the dependent clause.

  Me molestó (preterite)
  Me molestaba (imperfect) + que te enfadaras. (imperfect subjunctive)

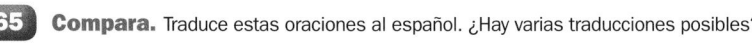

65 **Compara.** Traduce estas oraciones al español. ¿Hay varias traducciones posibles?

   a. *I'm worried that they will forget my birthday.*
   b. *I was worried that they would forget my birthday.*

66 **Tus sentimientos**

▶ **Escribe** los sentimientos que te producen estos hechos.

Modelo *Me fascina que haya gente que se dedique a ayudar a los demás.*

1. … que a mis amigos les gusten las mismas cosas que a mí.
2. … que mi familia me felicite por mi cumpleaños.
3. … que algunas personas no encuentren trabajo.
4. … que exista el hambre en el mundo.

262 doscientos sesenta y dos

Differentiated Instruction

DEVELOPING LEARNERS

- Ask students to choose the correct verb to complete the following sentences:

1. *Nos preocupa que las personas mayores están / estén solas. (estén)*
2. *Me da pena que haya / hay tantos niños sin hogar. (haya)*
3. *Me molesta que no trabajes / trabajas como voluntaria. (trabajes)*
4. *Me deprime que mucha gente no tiene / tenga tolerancia. (tenga)*
5. *Me emociona que la sociedad es / sea solidaria con los pobres. (sea)*
6. *Me alegra que tú colabores / colaboras conmigo. (colabores)*

EXPANDING LEARNERS

- Ask students to select six of the verbs listed in *Verbos para expresar sentimientos* and write a sentence for each one that reflects what is true for them. For example, they may say: *Me aburre que mi vecino siempre hable del mismo tema. Me emocionó que mi amiga Carla trabajara como voluntaria en una organización para la protección del medio ambiente. Me preocupa que haya tanta pobreza en el mundo.* When students finish, ask them to work in groups of no more than three, and compare what triggers their feelings and emotions.

67 ¡Ánimo!

▶ **Lee** el correo electrónico de Tim y complétalo con la forma correcta de los verbos.

De: Tim

Para: Eva; Ethan

Asunto:

Cuerpo del texto | Anchura variable

Queridos Eva y Ethan:

Me alegra que ___1___ una tarea tan importante. Colaborar con una ONG es algo
tengan /tuvieran

maravilloso. Y, sobre todo, me emociona que ustedes ___2___ a presentar un proyecto
vayan/fueran

para colaborar con ellos. No me sorprendió que Andy me ___3___ que les deprime que
diga/dijera

haya tanta gente con problemas en el mundo. A mí me pasa lo mismo. Pero también me dijo

que le preocupaba que ustedes se ___4___ tristes. Afortunadamente, sé que están
sientan/sintieran

ilusionados con el proyecto. Me alegra que ___5___ así. ¡Ánimo!
reaccionen/reaccionaran

Tim

68 Las experiencias de Andy

▶ **Escucha** la conversación entre Andy y Eva y completa estas oraciones.

1. A Andy le sorprendió que...
2. A Andy le preocupa que los niños...
3. A Andy le enoja que algunas compañías...
4. A Eva le alegra que Andy...
5. A Andy le emociona que Eva y Ethan...

69 Cómo hemos cambiado

▶ **Habla** con tu compañero(a). Explica tus sentimientos o los sentimientos de tu familia
ante estos temas. ¿Han cambiado esos sentimientos con el tiempo?

Modelo   A. *Antes no me preocupaba que la gente no reciclara, pero ahora sí. Y me alegra
que cada vez haya más gente que recicle la basura en sus casas.*

               B. *En mi familia pasa lo mismo. Antes no nos preocupaba...*

| ① el reciclaje | ② la medicina | ③ el dinero | ④ la televisión | ⑤ la contaminación |

---

69. To expand this activity, write on the board
Cómo ha cambiado mi vida and have students
write their feelings about the changes that they
have experienced in their lives in the last few
years. Have them share their answers with a
partner. Finally, ask volunteers to share their
answers with the class following the model
in the activity.

> **AUDIO SCRIPT**
> See page 227J.

Answer Key

65. a. Me preocupa que se olviden de mi
cumpleaños.

    b. Me preocupaba / Me preocupó que
se olvidaran de mi cumpleaños.

66. Answers will vary. Sample answers:

    1. Me alegra...   3. Me preocupa...

    2. Me emociona...   4. Me da pena...

67. 1. tengan   4. sintieran

    2. vayan   5. reaccionen

    3. dijera

68. 1. ... hubiera tantas organizaciones
benéficas en los países que visitó.

    2. ... sufran.

    3. ... destruyan los bosques para conseguir
beneficios económicos.

    4. ... tenga experiencias tan extraordinarias
para contar.

    5. ... vayan a colaborar con una
organización benéfica.

69. Answers will vary.

Additional Resources

Fans Online activities
Practice Workbook

HERITAGE LANGUAGE LEARNERS

- Ask students to create a word search puzzle
for some of the vocabulary and grammar
presented in this lesson. Students may write
the clues and use computer software to
generate the puzzle and determine the
placement of the words, or they may create
their own on graph paper. After their clues
and game board are complete, have them
exchange with a partner and see how quickly
they can find the hidden words.

MULTIPLE INTELLIGENCES:
Intrapersonal Intelligence

- Ask students to imagine that they have
signed on as volunteers for a non-profit
organization that will take them to a
developing country for several months. Ask
students to write an entry in their journals on
the eve of their trip that reflects their feelings
and emotions. Students may feel excitement
or apprehension about their journey, or even
a bit of fear. Ask them to ponder both the
pros and cons of such an undertaking and
reflect these feelings in their journal.

DESAFÍO 3

Gramática – Expresar dificultad

Presentation

■ In this section, students will learn and practice words and structures to express difficulties or adversities in completing an action.

Activities	Standards	Resources
Gramática	1.2, 3.1	
70.	4.1	
71.	1.2, 1.3, 3.1	
72.	1.2, 1.3, 3.1	
73.	1.1, 1.2, 1.3	
74. Comparaciones	1.1, 1.2, 1.3, 2.1, 2.2, 5.1	

Teaching Suggestions

Warm-Up / Independent Starter

■ Have students read the grammar presentation silently. Encourage them to take notes on any material that they have trouble understanding.

Preparation

■ Go over the grammar explanations with students and clarify any points they did not understand. To help students understand the difference between *aunque / a pesar de que* + subjunctive and *aunque / a pesar de que* + indicative, write examples on the board and ask students to determine what is being expressed by the underlined parts.

1. *No saco buenas notas, a pesar de que estudio mucho.*
2. *Ayudaré a limpiar el parque, aunque esté cansada.*

■ After checking students' answers, ask them to identify the verbal mood that is used in each case. You may want to point out that, generally, *aunque* is translated as "even if" when followed by the subjunctive mood, and as "even though" when followed by the indicative mood.

Activities

72. Ask students to change the underlined parts from real to unreal or uncertain, and vice versa. Ask them to explain the difference in meaning from the original counterpart.

Gramática

Expresar dificultad

Expresar dificultad

● Use *aunque* (*although, even though, even if*) and *a pesar de que* (*despite, although*) to provide information about an obstacle or difficulty in a given action.

> *Aunque* sea difícil, colaboraré con una ONG.
> *A pesar de que* no tenía tiempo, ayudé a los niños.

● The clause with *aunque* or *a pesar de que* can be at the beginning or at the end of a sentence.

> *Aunque* sea difícil, colaboraré.   Colaboraré, *aunque* sea difícil.

¿Subjuntivo o indicativo?

● *Aunque* can be followed by either the subjunctive or the indicative. Generally, the subjunctive is used after *aunque* when referring to unreal or uncertain situations, probabilities, or unknown outcomes.

	Modo del verbo después de *aunque*	¿Qué dice el hablante?
Seré tolerante, aunque **es** difícil. *I'll be tolerant, even though it is difficult.*	indicative	*Being tolerant is difficult, but I'll still be tolerant.*
Seré tolerante, aunque **sea** difícil. *I'll be tolerant, even if it is difficult.*	subjunctive	*Being tolerant may be difficult, but I'll still be tolerant.*
Marta fue a la ONG, aunque **estaba** cansada. *Marta went to the NGO, even though she was tired.*	indicative	*Marta was tired, but she went to the NGO.*
Marta iba a la ONG, aunque **estuviera** cansada. *Marta went to the NGO, even if she was tired.*	subjunctive	*Marta may have been tired, but she went to the NGO.*

● *A pesar de que* works like *aunque*.

> Carlos puede ir a las reuniones de la ONG, **a pesar de que** no **es** voluntario.
> Carlos puede ir a las reuniones de la ONG, **a pesar de que** no **sea** voluntario.

70 **Compara.** Traduce al inglés los dos ejemplos anteriores. ¿Hay diferencias de sentido en las distintas traducciones que hiciste?

71 **Sea como sea**

▶ **Explica.** ¿Qué diferencia de significado hay entre las dos oraciones de cada grupo?

1. a. Eva y Ethan serán cooperantes, aunque están ocupados.
   b. Eva y Ethan serán cooperantes, aunque estén ocupados.

2. a. Ethan ayudará a personas mayores en una residencia, a pesar de que no las conoce.
   b. Ethan ayudará a personas mayores en una residencia, a pesar de que no las conozca.

Differentiated Instruction

DEVELOPING LEARNERS

● Write the following pairs of sentences on the board and assist students in explaining the difference between each pair:

1. *Aunque yo no quiera, lo haré. / Aunque yo no quiero, lo haré.*
2. *A pesar de que no te conozco, te ayudaré. / A pesar de que no te conozca, te ayudaré.*
3. *Aunque no se encuentre bien, será voluntario. / Aunque no se encuentra bien, será voluntario.*
4. *Aunque llueva, irás al parque. / Aunque llueve, irás al parque.*

EXPANDING LEARNERS

● Ask students to make a list of three things they do not plan to do (e.g., *No iré a la reunión hoy*), and three things that they will or would do despite the circumstances (e.g., *Me dedicaré a proteger el medio ambiente*). Then, have students state an obstacle or difficulty to each action and decide if the indicative or the subjunctive is needed. For example: *No iré a la reunión hoy aunque me lo pidas. Me dedicaré a proteger el medio ambiente, aunque no es un tema muy popular en esta comunidad.*

72 **Superando obstáculos**

▶ **Decide.** ¿La información subrayada se refiere a situaciones reales (R) o a situaciones irreales / dudosas (I)?

1. <u>A pesar de que es muy joven,</u> Tess se preocupa por las personas mayores.

2. <u>A pesar de que Asha y Lucas tienen poco tiempo,</u> colaboran con varias organizaciones.

3. Andy participa en obras benéficas, <u>aunque esté ocupado</u>.

4. <u>Aunque tengan pocos colaboradores,</u> la mayoría de las ONG tienen éxito.

▶ **Escribe** dos oraciones más (una cierta y una incierta) siguiendo los ejemplos anteriores.

73 **Nada es imposible**

 ▶ **Habla** con tu compañero(a). Inventen una lista de obstáculos o dificultades para estos hechos y escriban oraciones.

Modelo   Andy viajó a Machu Picchu.
→ *Andy viajó a Machu Picchu, aunque le diera miedo volar.*

Michelle aprendió a bailar salsa.

Lucas ganó el partido de baloncesto.

Asha sacó muy buenas notas en todas las asignaturas.

COMPARACIONES

Frente de Defensa de la Amazonía

El FDA es una organización ecuatoriana creada en 1994 que lucha por los derechos humanos y medioambientales de la región amazónica de Ecuador. Uno de los objetivos de esta organización es que las compañías petrolíferas no ocupen el bosque ni destruyan la naturaleza para obtener el petróleo.

 74   **Piensa.** ¿Qué organizaciones protegen el medio ambiente donde tú vives? ¿Contra qué problemas luchan?

Gramática – Expresar dificultad

73. Ask students to write about their family or their friends' experiences, following the model in this activity. If possible, ask students to bring pictures. For example: (Picture of one person at the Eiffel Tower) *Mi hermana subió a la Torre Eiffel a pesar de que tenía vértigo.*

 COMPARACIONES

Frente de Defensa de la Amazonía

Given the vast area of the Amazon basin, many organizations in different countries are concerned with its conservation and sustainability. Most of them are attempting primarily to stop big corporations from polluting the Amazon. However, many are also involved in promoting fair trade of forest wood by empowering local organizations to get access to fair profits without compromising sustainability.

Answer Key

70. *Carlos can attend the NGO meetings, even though he is not a volunteer.*

Carlos can attend the NGO meetings, even if he is not a volunteer.

71. 1. La oración «a» indica que están ocupados. En la oración «b» no se sabe si van a estar ocupados.

2. La oración «a» indica que Ethan no conoce a las personas mayores. En la «b» no se sabe si Ethan conoce a las personas.

72. 1. R   2. R   3. I   4. I
▶ Answers will vary.

73. Answers will vary.

74. Answers will vary.

Additional Resources

Fans Online activities
Practice Workbook

HERITAGE LANGUAGE LEARNERS

• Ask students to identify a local, national, or international environmental issue. Then have students write several proposed solutions to this problem. Each solution must be countered by a clause that describes an obstacle or difficulty to it. According to whether the situation is real or unknown, students should use the indicative or the subjunctive. For example:

Problema: Nuestra playa está sucia.
Solución: Vamos a organizar una campaña para limpiarla este fin de semana.
Obstáculo/Dificultad: Aunque algunos se opongan, vamos a organizar...

COOPERATIVE LEARNING

• Have students work in groups of three or four and have each participant come up with a situation that is the result of an action, using those described in activity 73 as models. Then ask students to work together in order to come up with difficulties or obstacles to each of these situations. After students discuss their choices, have them select two such obstacles or difficulties and write a corresponding sentence for each. Invite groups to read some of their sentences aloud.

LECTURA: TEXTO LITERARIO

Presentation

- In this section, students will read a short literary text by Ana María Matute. They will use pre-reading strategies to help them fully comprehend the text. Students will also write a new ending for the story.

Activities	Standards	Resources
Lectura: texto literario	1.2, 2.2, 3.1, 3.2	
75.	1.2, 1.3	
76.	1.1, 1.2	
77.	1.1, 1.2, 1.3	
78.	1.1, 1.2, 1.3	

Teaching Suggestions

Warm-Up / Independent Starter

- Ask students to write a list of professions that may be related to music (e.g., *compositor, violinista, pianista, director de orquesta, profesor de Música, director de coro, cantante*).

Preparation

- Call on individual students to share their responses from the Independent Starter. Ask students to find the profession that is depicted in the text. Then ask students: *¿Qué hacen los compositores? (Componen piezas musicales.) ¿Conocen algún compositor famoso? ¿Qué tipo de música compone o componía? ¿Qué personalidad tienen, por lo general, los compositores? ¿Creen que es una profesión difícil? ¿Por qué?*

- Have students work with a partner to read the *Antes de leer* strategies. Then ask pairs to write the answers to the questions posed. Once pairs have finished working on the *Antes de leer* questions, discuss the answers as a class.

- Read the story aloud to model pronunciation and have students follow along in their books. Then call on individual students to each read a paragraph aloud. Offer assistance with the pronunciation of some long or difficult words (e.g., *acostumbradas, sigilosamente, rendija*). After students have finished reading, ask them to find cognates in the story (e.g., *acostumbradas, silencio, notas, piano, estudio, inventa, música*).

Antes de leer: estrategias

1. Lee superficialmente *(scan)* el texto. Escribe todas las palabras relacionadas con la música que encuentres.

2. Fíjate en la estructura del texto. ¿Cuántos párrafos tiene? Busca el primer verbo de cada párrafo. ¿Qué tiempo verbal es?

3. Busca en el texto las palabras que se refieren a personas. ¿Quiénes son los protagonistas? ¿Qué relación tienen: familiar, de amistad, profesional…?

4. Busca una palabra que se refiere a una profesión. ¿Cuál es? ¿Por qué piensas que esa palabra está escrita con mayúsculas *(capital letters)*?

Música

Las dos hijas del Gran Compositor —seis y siete años— estaban acostumbradas al silencio. En la casa no debía oírse ni un ruido, porque papá trabajaba. Andaban de puntillas[1], en zapatillas, y solo a ráfagas[2] el silencio se rompía con las notas del piano de papá. Y otra vez silencio.

Un día, la puerta del estudio quedó mal cerrada, y la más pequeña de las niñas se acercó sigilosamente[3] a la rendija[4]; y pudo ver cómo papá, a ratos, levantaba[5] notas del piano, y a ratos, se inclinaba sobre un papel, y anotaba algo.

La niña más pequeña corrió entonces en busca de su hermana mayor. Y gritó, gritó por primera vez en tanto silencio:

—¡La música de papá, no te la creas…! ¡Se la inventa!

ANA MARÍA MATUTE (España, 1925).

1. *tip-toeing*   2. *bursts*   3. *silently*   4. *crack*   5. *elicited*

Differentiated Instruction

DEVELOPING LEARNERS

- To verify students' comprehension of the story, ask them to complete the following statements:

1. *El … era normal en la casa.* (b)
   a. *ruido*   b. *silencio*
2. *Las hermanas eran…* (a)
   a. *obedientes*   b. *desobedientes*
3. *El padre trabajaba…* (a)
   a. *en casa*   b. *con la orquesta*
4. *La niña pequeña observó…* (b)
   a. *el piano*   b. *cómo trabajaba su padre*
5. *El padre … la música.* (b)
   a. *leía*   b. *escribía*

EXPANDING LEARNERS

- Ask students to work in small groups and rewrite the story, this time as a play. Remind students that, with the exception of stage directions, there will be no narrative text in their work, only dialogue and sound effects or music. Students will need to use their imagination and create some dialogue between the characters. Give students time to write and finalize their drama and then to rehearse it. When students are ready, call on groups to come in front of the class and put on their play.

LECTURA: TEXTO LITERARIO

75 Comprensión

▶ **Completa** estas oraciones.

1. El padre de las niñas se dedicaba a...
2. Para no hacer ruido, las niñas...
3. Un día, la más pequeña vio...
4. La niña le dijo gritando a su hermana...
5. La niña dijo que su papá inventa la música porque...

▶ **Escribe** un resumen de la historia.

76 Significa que...

▶ **Explica** el significado de estas oraciones con tus propias palabras.

Modelo Las hijas estaban acostumbradas al silencio.
→ *Normalmente las hijas no escuchaban mucho ruido.*

1. En la casa no debía oírse ni un ruido.
2. El silencio se rompía con las notas del piano.
3. Un día, la puerta quedó mal cerrada.
4. El papá levantaba notas del piano.
5. La niña corrió en busca de su hermana.

77 Imagínalo tú

▶ **Lee** de nuevo el texto y escribe tus ideas sobre estas cuestiones. Luego, compártelas con un grupo de compañeros(as).

1. ¿Cómo era el ambiente de la casa? Descríbelo.
2. ¿Cómo era el padre? ¿Por qué?
3. ¿Cómo te imaginas que jugaban las niñas? ¿Por qué?
4. ¿Qué sentimientos tenían las hijas hacia el padre?
5. ¿Qué relación tenían entre ellas? ¿Por qué?
6. ¿Cómo te imaginas a la madre de esta familia? Descríbela.

78 Con tus propias palabras

▶ **Imagina.** ¿Qué ocurre después? Escribe el final del cuento.

▶ **Lee** el final del cuento de tu compañero(a). ¿Cómo es: original, divertido, triste, misterioso...? Dale tu opinión.

doscientos sesenta y siete 267

Activities

75. To help students complete the sentences, ask them related questions. For example:
1. *¿Cuál era el trabajo del padre?*
2. *¿Cómo caminan ustedes para no hacer ruido?*
3. *¿Qué hacía el padre cuando componía su música?*
4. *¿Qué es lo que la hermana no debe creer?*
5. *¿Qué anotaba el padre?*

77. You may want to ask students to rewrite the short story, adding the ideas that they have gathered in this activity from working in pairs or groups. They should add a couple of paragraphs describing the house, the father, and the mother. They should decide where to place these paragraphs within the story to make it flow.

Answer Key

75. Answers will vary. Sample answers:
1. ... componer música.
2. ... andaban de puntillas.
3. ... a su padre tocando el piano y escribiendo algo.
4. ... que su padre se inventaba la música.
5. ... no la lee, sino que la crea.
▶ Answers will vary.

76. Answers will vary. Sample answers:
1. La casa debía estar en silencio.
2. Alguien tocaba de vez en cuando el piano.
3. La puerta quedó un poco abierta.
4. El papá estaba tocando el piano.
5. La niña fue rápidamente a llamar a su hermana.

77. Answers will vary.

78. Answers will vary.
▶ Answers will vary.

Additional Resources

Fans Online activities

HERITAGE LANGUAGE LEARNERS

- Ask students to think about what they were like when they were about the same age as the sisters in "Música." Ask them to think about how they behaved and how they interacted with other members of their family. Then have students write a few paragraphs in narrative form that describe their family dynamics at the time. Students may accompany their narratives with photos or illustrations of their home and family. If students don't feel comfortable writing about their own family, they may write about a family they know.

MULTIPLE INTELLIGENCES: Visual-Spatial Intelligence

- Ask students to imagine what the setting and the characters in the story looked like. Ask students to then draw an image or several images that could accompany this short story. Students may choose to draw the two sisters, including details of their clothes and toys; their father; their house, including the music room; or any other image related to the story. Ask students to talk about why they depicted the images as they did, and display all students' work in the classroom.

DESAFÍO 3

Comunicación

Presentation

- In this section, students will integrate the vocabulary and grammar skills from *Desafío 3* in order to talk about volunteering and community service work, as well as expressing feelings and describing adversities in completing an action.

Activities	Standards	Resources
79.	1.1, 1.2, 1.3	
80.	1.1, 1.3, 5.1, 5.2	
81.	1.1, 1.3, 5.1, 5.2	
82. Final del desafío	1.1, 1.2, 1.3, 2.2, 3.1, 5.1	
Tu desafío	1.1, 1.2	

Teaching Suggestions

Warm-Up / Independent Starter

- Now that students know more about the topic, ask them to summarize their feelings about volunteer and non-profit work in their peer group, in their community, and in their country. For example: *Me sorprende que haya tan pocos estudiantes en mi clase que trabajen como voluntarios. Pero me alegra que en mi comunidad haya varias organizaciones que...*

Preparation

- Invite students to share their Independent Starters with the class. Does the class feel the same or are there different opinions? What are some of the reasons for students' opinions? Are they fully informed about the different non-profit organizations that exist and the work they do? Discuss some of students' feelings regarding volunteer work.

- Ask students to complete the following sentences using the vocabulary from this *Desafío*:
  1. *Me encanta ser voluntario, a pesar de que...*
  2. *Los derechos humanos son muy importantes, aunque...*
  3. *La convivencia entre diferentes culturas es posible, a pesar de que...*
  4. *Aunque mi trabajo como voluntario fue corto, ...*

Comunicación

79 Noticias

▶ **Lee** estos titulares de periódico y escribe oraciones expresando tus sentimientos.

① Un helicóptero que transportaba a cooperantes internacionales sufre un accidente

② Un famoso millonario funda un hospital para niños con cáncer

③ A partir del próximo año todos los transportes públicos serán eléctricos

④ Miles de hectáreas de bosque destruidas para construir apartamentos de lujo

 ▶ **Escribe** dos titulares más, uno positivo y otro negativo, y léeselos a tu compañero(a). Después, comenta con él/ella tus reacciones a sus titulares.

Modelo   A. *Un hombre gana la lotería y dona el dinero para construir un hospital.*
            B. *Me emociona que haya gente tan solidaria.*

80 Trabajo comunitario

▶ **Lee** los resultados obtenidos en un estudio sobre el trabajo comunitario entre los estudiantes estadounidenses de 16 a 19 años y escribe oraciones siguiendo el modelo.

Modelo   *Me da pena que pocos estudiantes atiendan a personas enfermas en su comunidad.*

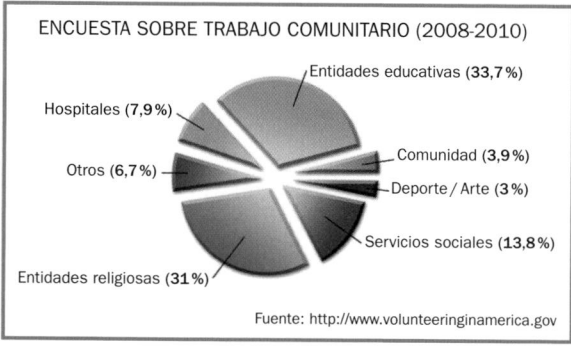

ENCUESTA SOBRE TRABAJO COMUNITARIO (2008-2010)

- Entidades educativas (33,7 %)
- Hospitales (7,9 %)
- Comunidad (3,9 %)
- Otros (6,7 %)
- Deporte / Arte (3 %)
- Servicios sociales (13,8 %)
- Entidades religiosas (31 %)

Fuente: http://www.volunteeringinamerica.gov

 ▶ **Pregunta** a tu compañero(a). ¿Qué trabajo comunitario hace o le gustaría hacer? ¿Por qué? Toma nota de sus respuestas y escribe un resumen.

Differentiated Instruction

DEVELOPING LEARNERS

- Ask students who are still having trouble using the subjunctive or the infinitive to express emotions to write the verbs listed on page 262 in their notebooks, allowing a space between each one for at least two sample sentences. Work with students and help them form two sentences with each of these verbs, one using the infinitive and another the subjunctive. For example: *Me fascina leer libros de ciencia ficción. Me fascina que tú leas libros de ciencia ficción.*

EXPANDING LEARNERS

- Ask students to work with a partner and come up with a dialogue between two students, one who is advocating that the other contribute his or her time as a volunteer on several community projects, only to be countered by the other student, who has endless excuses for not volunteering. Students will work together to create the dialogue and will take turns reading the two parts. They should try to work in the subjunctive to express feelings, emotions, obstacles, or difficulties. Encourage students to be creative and use humor in their excuses.

¡Manos a la obra!

▶ **Haz** una lista con dos compañeros(as) de problemas que afectan a su comunidad.

▶ **Elijan** uno de esos problemas y hagan un cartel para concienciar a la gente. Incluyan un eslogan. Después, presenten el cartel a la clase.

El bosque es de todos

¡Cuídalo!

Final del desafío

Tantas organizaciones, tantas tareas... Me da pena ___1___ solo una.
(elegir)

Sí, lo sé, pero piénsalo así: aunque ___2___ que elegir solo una... ¡una es mejor que ninguna!
(tener)

A mí me gustaría hacer algo por los niños; sobre todo me preocupa que no ___3___ ir a la escuela.
(poder)

Estoy totalmente de acuerdo. Todos los niños del mundo tienen derecho a la educación, aunque ___4___ en países en vías de desarrollo.
(vivir)

Conozco una asociación en Los Ángeles dedicada a los niños inmigrantes. Podemos proponerles un proyecto de voluntarios bilingües para ayudarlos en las clases.

 El proyecto de Eva y Ethan

▶ **Completa** los bocadillos con la forma correcta de los verbos señalados.

▶ **Habla** con tu compañero(a). ¿Qué opinan sobre la idea de Ethan? ¿Les gustaría ser voluntarios en esa organización? ¿Por qué?

 **TU DESAFÍO** Visita la página web. Escucha las preguntas de tu *Minientrevista Desafío 3* y escribe las respuestas.

doscientos sesenta y nueve **269**

HERITAGE LANGUAGE LEARNERS

• Ask students to create their own non-profit organization in a Spanish-speaking country of their choice. They should briefly describe the organization's objectives and identify its target population. Then ask them to create a poster with this information and to state the advantages of volunteering for their organization (e.g., it gives them an opportunity to interact with people from all sectors of society, it teaches them teamwork and leadership skills, and gives them a chance to explore possible careers related to their volunteerism). Invite students to present their organization to the class.

CRITICAL THINKING

• Ask students to write a three-paragraph composition explaining why they think it is important for all residents of a community to contribute their time doing volunteer work. Students should first make their statement and then list and detail at least five reasons that justify their assertion. Students might include the improvements to the community that volunteering would produce.

Activities

79. Ask students to write a brief newspaper entry for one of the headlines they wrote. Encourage students to use vocabulary and grammar structures from this *Desafío*. Collect the news articles, paste them together, and post them in the classroom. Ask students to read them and select the one they like the most. Have them write their feelings about the news article they selected and explain why they feel the way they do.

80. To prepare students for this activity, ask them to brainstorm a list of activities for each category in the graphic.

81. Before starting work on the project, have each group create a list of problems they see in their community. Ask groups to share their answers and write the list on the board. Have each group work on a different problem in order to have a wide variety of posters.

Answer Key

79. Answers will vary. Sample answers:
1. Me da pena que pasara algo así.
2. Me alegra que use parte de su dinero para construir un hospital.
3. Me sorprende mucho que todos los transportes públicos sean eléctricos.
4. Me entristece que el ser humano no cuide la naturaleza.
▶ Answers will vary.

80. Answers will vary. Sample answers:
Me sorprende que tantos estudiantes ayuden a entidades religiosas.
Me preocupa que tan pocos estudiantes apoyen el deporte y el arte.
▶ Answers will vary.

81. Answers will vary.
▶ Answers will vary.

82. 1. elegir   3. puedan
     2. tenemos   4. vivan
▶ Answers will vary.

Additional Resources

Fans Online activities
Practice Workbook

269

Unit 5
Para terminar

Presentation

- In this section, students will review the unit objectives and put them into practice. They will talk about advantages and disadvantages of certain professions, write about a family member's job, and select one of the following *desafíos* to develop: investigate and prepare a presentation about a human rights advocate, write a cover letter to apply for a job of their choice, or prepare a presentation about a volunteer job that can be done in their community and which may require the use of Spanish.

Activities	Standards	Resources
83.	1.2, 1.3, 3.1, 5.2	Audio
84.	1.1, 1.3, 5.1	
85. Tu desafío	1.2, 1.3, 2.1, 2.2, 3.1, 4.2, 5.1, 5.2	

Teaching Suggestions

Warm-Up / Independent Starter

- Have students write a list of things that they consider to be advantages of having a part-time or summer job. You may also want to ask them to write a list of disadvantages.

Preparation

- Have students work with a partner and share their lists from the Independent Starter. Ask students to elaborate on their lists, including details about why each point is an advantage or disadvantage. Call on volunteer pairs to present their lists to the class. Does the class agree with their classmates' opinions? Are there some differences of opinion?

- Ask students to imagine that they are going on a volunteer trip with a non-profit organization. They will be working in a community in a Spanish-speaking country. Have students write a couple of paragraphs on their feelings about the trip. They should give details about the work they will do, explain certainties and doubts they have, tell their feelings about the trip, and describe their plans in case certain difficulties arise. After writing their paragraphs, they should share their work with a partner, correcting any mistakes and highlighting or identifying each grammar topic included.

270

Para terminar

Todo junto

ESCUCHAR Y ESCRIBIR

83 Profesionales

▶ **Escucha** las entrevistas e indica las ventajas e inconvenientes de cada trabajo.

> Hacer cosas interesantes.
> Hacer cosas emocionantes.
> Poder desarrollar su carrera.
> Tener horarios fijos.
> Tener contacto con la gente.
> Tener la posibilidad de aprender.
> Tener impacto en la comunidad.

> Tener un trabajo duro.
> Tener un trabajo peligroso.
> No ganar mucho dinero.
> Trabajar muchas horas.

Mario Pons. Abogado.

Isabel Castro. Farmacéutica.

Ángela López. Ingeniera.

José Luis Collado. Bombero.

▶ **Escribe** un párrafo sobre cada persona con la información anterior.

Modelo   *Mario Pons es abogado.*
          Lo más positivo de su trabajo es...

ESCRIBIR Y HABLAR

84 Un buen trabajo

▶ **Escribe** un párrafo describiendo el trabajo de alguien de tu familia y tu opinión sobre él. Explica:
- En qué consiste su trabajo.
- Qué es lo que más y lo que menos te gusta de ese trabajo.
- Cómo necesitas prepararte para ese trabajo.

Modelo   *Mi tío es diseñador gráfico. Diseña páginas web para empresas. Pienso que es un trabajo divertido y además tiene un horario flexible.*

▶ **Habla** con tu compañero(a). Explícale por qué elegiste ese trabajo y comenten sus opiniones. Usen expresiones de duda y certeza.

Modelo   *Yo también pienso que es un trabajo divertido, pero no es cierto que todos los diseñadores gráficos tengan un horario flexible.*

270 doscientos setenta

Differentiated Instruction

DEVELOPING LEARNERS

- Ask students to review the objectives listed at the beginning of this unit. Have them make a chart and use these objectives as headings. Under each heading, ask students to write at least two sample sentences to verify that they have understood these objectives and are confident in recognizing them and using them in their work. Answer any questions students may have so that they are prepared to be formally assessed.

EXPANDING LEARNERS

- Ask students to imagine that they are the immediate supervisor of one of the professionals mentioned in activity 83. Their task is to write a job evaluation for this employee. Job evaluations should include a description of the employee's responsibilities as well as an assessment of how well the employee carried these out. Evaluations should also describe how well the employee works with others, how well he or she identifies with the policies of the organization, and an assessment of the goals the employee has established for the next twelve months.

Tu desafío

85 El trabajo y las profesiones

¿Recuerdas los desafíos que Tim les dio a los personajes? ¿Cuál te gusta más? Elige una de estas opciones y resuelve tu desafío.

DESAFÍO Ⓐ

Investiga sobre alguno de estos líderes que trabajan o trabajaron en favor de los derechos humanos y prepara una presentación.

Rigoberta Menchú (Guatemala).   Dolores Huerta (Estados Unidos).   Adolfo Pérez Esquivel (Argentina).

DESAFÍO Ⓑ

Busca un periódico o una página web con anuncios de trabajo en español. Selecciona el anuncio que te parece más interesante y escribe una carta presentándote para ese trabajo. Explica:

- Por qué quieres optar a ese puesto.
- Por qué crees que deben elegirte para el trabajo.

Ven a conocernos

VOLUNTARIOS EN LA ACCIÓN SOCIAL Exposición itinerante

DESAFÍO Ⓒ

Haz una presentación sobre uno o dos de los trabajos voluntarios que pueden hacerse en tu comunidad, especialmente los que requieren hablar español.

Explica si hay organizaciones que apoyen esos trabajos y cuáles son los requisitos para trabajar como voluntario(a).

doscientos setenta y uno **271**

Activities

83. Before listening to the audio, have students observe the photos. Then ask them to guess what the advantages and disadvantages of each of the jobs may be.

84. To facilitate students' tasks, provide them with a list of sentence starters that they should include in their conversations for the second part of this activity. For example: *dudo que, es improbable que, no es evidente que, no estoy convencido(a) de que, estoy seguro(a) de que, es verdad que, no dudo que,* etc.

85. Display students' work in the classroom and have the class vote on the best entry in each category.

 AUDIO SCRIPT
See page 227J.

Answer Key

83. 1. Ventajas: tener contacto con la gente, hacer cosas interesantes.
Inconvenientes: tener un trabajo duro, trabajar muchas horas.
2. Ventajas: tener horarios fijos, tener contacto con la gente.
Inconvenientes: ninguno.
3. Ventajas: poder desarrollar su carrera, tener impacto en la comunidad, tener la posibilidad de aprender.
Inconvenientes: no ganar mucho dinero.
4. Ventajas: hacer cosas emocionantes, tener impacto en la comunidad.
Inconvenientes: tener un trabajo peligroso.
▶ Answers will vary.

84. Answers will vary.
▶ Answers will vary.

85. Answers will vary.

Additional Resources

Fans Online activities

HERITAGE LANGUAGE LEARNERS

- Ask students to research a leader from their family's country of origin. This person could be someone from government, the arts, a community organizer, an environmentalist, a doctor or nurse, or someone from virtually any profession or sector of society. Ask students to prepare a brief biography of this person and to include what motivated this individual to take on a leadership role, and the impact his or her involvement has had on the community.

SPECIAL-NEEDS LEARNERS

- Assist students with language-processing difficulties in completing activity 83. These students may find it difficult to listen, process, and encode the information presented in the audio. Provide a written script for these students so they can gather the required information. Students may find it less stressful to write two or three sentences about each professional, rather than try to complete an entire paragraph.

271

MAPA CULTURAL

Universidades hispanas

Presentation

- This section presents information about different universities in the Spanish-speaking world. The images serve as a reference point for additional cultural readings and activities that expand on the skills students learned in this unit.

Activities	Standards	Resources
Mapa cultural	1.2, 2.1, 2.2, 3.1, 3.2	Video
86.	1.1, 1.3, 2.2, 5.2	

Cultural Topics

- **Graduados destacados.** Many graduates of Latin American and Spanish universities have made outstanding contributions to the world. Mario J. Molina, a graduate of the Universidad Nacional de México, received the Nobel Prize in Chemistry in 1995 for his role in recognizing the threat of CFC gases to the ozone layer. Mario Vargas Llosa, a graduate of the Universidad Nacional de San Marcos (Peru), was the recipient of the Nobel Prize in Literature in 2010. Mariana Weissmann, a graduate of the Universidad de Buenos Aires (Argentina), and a pioneer in the use of computers to study the properties of solids, was the recipient of the L'Oréal-UNESCO Award in 2003.

- **Programas de español.** In addition to their regular programs, a significant number of universities in the Spanish-speaking world have programs especially designed for the teaching of Spanish as a second language. These universities also boast a wide network of exchange agreements with American universities. Some well-known Spanish language programs include those offered by the Universidad de Salamanca (Spain), Universidad de Costa Rica, Universidad de Guadalajara (Mexico), Universidad Autónoma de Santo Domingo (Dominican Republic), and Universidad Católica del Perú, among many others.

Teaching Suggestions

Warm-Up / Independent Starter

- Ask students to list five universities they know or have heard about. Then have students write two things they associate with each university.

272

Universidades hispanas

El sistema actual de universidades surgió en Europa durante la Edad Media. La primera universidad fue la de Bolonia, en Italia, fundada a finales del siglo XI. Después se fundaron otras muchas universidades europeas: Oxford, París, Módena, Cambridge, Salamanca, Coímbra…

En América, en el siglo XVI se fundaron varias universidades: la Universidad de Santo Tomás de Aquino, en Santo Domingo; la Universidad de San Marcos, en Lima; la Universidad de México; la Universidad de la Plata, en Sucre… La universidad más antigua de los Estados Unidos es Harvard (1636).

En Latinoamérica y en España hay universidades con mucho prestigio que llevan cientos de años funcionando.

Universidad de Chile

La Universidad de Chile (UCh), ubicada en Santiago de Chile, fue fundada en 1842, aunque en Santiago hubo universidad con otros nombres desde la época colonial. La UCh también es conocida como «la U», «la Chile» o «la Casa de Bello», en honor al humanista Andrés Bello, su primer rector.

La UCh goza de gran prestigio en Latinoamérica. Tiene catorce facultades y otros centros de estudio e investigación asociados.

Alumnos: 35.000 (mujeres: 48%; hombres: 52%)
Profesores: 4.500
Titulaciones:
- 67 carreras
- 157 programas de postgrado

Pablo Neruda

El poeta chileno Pablo Neruda (1904–1973) estudió en la UCh. En su época de estudiante escribió uno de sus libros más conocidos: *Veinte poemas de amor y una canción desesperada.* Pablo Neruda recibió el Premio Nobel en 1971.

272 doscientos setenta y dos

Differentiated Instruction

DEVELOPING LEARNERS

- Have students organize the information in this *Mapa cultural* three different ways: 1. from the oldest to the newest university; 2. from the largest (by number of students) to the smallest; 3. from the one with the lowest student-teacher ratio to the one with the highest ratio (students can calculate this ratio by dividing the number of students by the number of professors). Once they have these three lists, ask students to analyze them and to look at the pictures on these pages. In which one of these three universities would they like to study? Why?

EXPANDING LEARNERS

- Ask students to research the educational options available to high school graduates in their state. For instance, in addition to four-year universities, there are two-year institutions where students can work toward an associate degree in a variety of academic, technical, or occupational fields. Ask students to include both public and private institutions.

- Have students organize the information in a clear manner. You may want to coordinate a sort of "Education Fair" for students to inform their classmates of the educational choices available in their state.

Universidad de Alcalá (España)

La Universidad de Alcalá (UAH) está situada en Alcalá de Henares (Madrid), la ciudad donde nació Miguel de Cervantes. Se fundó en 1499 y actualmente tiene dieciocho facultades y escuelas.

La sede de la UAH es un edificio de gran valor histórico y artístico declarado por la UNESCO Patrimonio de la Humanidad.

Antonio de Nebrija

Por las aulas de la Universidad de Alcalá pasaron profesores y alumnos célebres. Entre los profesores está Antonio de Nebrija (1441–1552), autor de la primera gramática de la lengua española.

Alumnos: 28.700 (mujeres: 57%; hombres: 43%)
Profesores: 2.200
Titulaciones:
• 35 carreras
• 88 programas de postgrado

Universidad Nacional Autónoma de México

En 1551 se fundó en la Ciudad de México la Real y Pontificia Universidad de México, llamada hoy Universidad Nacional Autónoma de México (UNAM).

La UNAM es una de las universidades más grandes de Latinoamérica y de mayor prestigio académico. Cuenta con trece facultades y diversas instituciones y centros de investigación. Su sede central *(main campus)* es Patrimonio de la Humanidad.

Ana María Cetto

Entre los graduados y profesores destacados de la UNAM está la física Ana María Cetto, subdirectora del Organismo Internacional de Energía Atómica.

Alumnos: 316.600 (mujeres: 51%; hombres: 49%)
Profesores: 36.000
Titulaciones:
• 96 carreras
• 73 programas de postgrado

---

86 **Los estudios y el trabajo**

▶ **Escribe**.

1. ¿Qué profesión te gustaría ejercer *(to practice)*? ¿Qué estudios y habilidades son necesarios?
2. ¿En qué centro educativo te gustaría estudiar? ¿Por qué?
3. ¿Te gustaría pasar algunos meses en una universidad latinoamericana? ¿En cuál?

 ▶ **Comenta** tus respuestas con tus compañeros(as).

doscientos setenta y tres **273**

MAPA CULTURAL
Universidades hispanas

Preparation

■ Invite students to share their Independent Starters. Write on the board the top five universities students mention. What are some of the most common associations students made regarding these universities? Are some of these associations related to sports teams, the history of the university, its architecture, etc.? Explain that although we tend to think of a university as a center for learning and research, universities embody many other things. For some students, it may be their first time living away from home. In other cases, the relationships students forge during their university years have a lasting impact on their future personal and professional lives. Universities also influence the life of the communities and towns where they are located.

■ You may want to hold a class discussion about the features that matter most to students when choosing a university or other type of higher learning institution. Have they decided on a place yet? If you consider it appropriate, share some of your own university experiences. Then go over the *Mapa cultural* as a class.

Activities

86. Have students convert this activity into an interview. Ask pairs to interview each other and write down their partner's answers. Then discuss students' answers as a class and compile them in a chart on the board. What are the top four or five professions the class chose? Are students well informed regarding the academic and training requirements for each profession they chose? Invite students to comment on some of their choices.

Answer Key

86. Answers will vary.
▶ Answers will vary.

Additional Resources

Fans Online activities
Practice Workbook

HERITAGE LANGUAGE LEARNERS

• Ask students to research a university from their heritage country. It may be a renowned university or one that is not well known but that has some unique features (e.g., its history, architecture, community service, famous alumni, location). Alternatively, students may choose one of their parents' alma maters and interview them about their university experience.

• Have students organize their findings in an informative and visually appealing presentation to share with the class. Encourage students to also include things such as the university's anthem, motto, mascot, coat of arms, etc.

MULTIPLE INTELLIGENCES:
Verbal-Linguistic Intelligence

• Ask students to work with a partner to create an advertisement for a university of their choosing. Pairs should research the university and include a brief description (e.g., history, number of students, number of degrees offered, famous alumni). Then ask students to come up with a slogan for their ad and a list of the top five reasons prospective students should consider their university. Encourage students to include images in their ad. Ask pairs to present their ads to the class and hold a class vote to choose a university.

Unit 5
ESCRITURA
Una carta formal

Presentation

- In this section, students will practice and extend their writing skills. They will apply the vocabulary and grammar they have learned in this unit to write a formal letter.

Activities	Standards	Resources
Escritura	1.1, 1.2, 1.3, 3.1, 5.1	

Teaching Suggestions

Warm-Up / Independent Starter

- Ask students to read the title of this page silently and have them jot down the first three things that come to their minds upon reading the words *carta formal*.

Preparation

- Ask students to share their Independent Starters. You may want to list on the board the different types of formal letters students mention and discuss the situations in which one would write such a letter. Some examples include: a cover letter for a job application, a letter of recommendation to recommend a person for a job position, an appreciation letter to thank a person or an organization for their work, an inquiry letter to request more information about something.

- Ask for a volunteer to read the Formal Letters box aloud. Discuss as a class the language and style that is expected in these letters. You may want to compare and contrast a formal letter to some other forms of informal communication students use often (e.g., e-mails, postings on forums or social networks). Then read the writing task aloud. You may want to show students examples of the three types of formal letters listed.

Step-by-Step Instructions

Piensa

- Explain that a formal letter should be clear and concise. There is no place in this type of letter for small talk. Therefore, students should limit the scope of their letter. The objective of the letter should be clearly understood by the reader.

274

Una carta formal

Formal Letters

There are many different types of letters, and each one has a different purpose and format. Invitations, acceptance letters, letters of resignation, cover letters, letters of complaint, and informal notes are all letters that are used in everyday communication.

Formal letters, also known as business letters, are often written to someone who is not a personal acquaintance of the writer. They are also generally less personal in nature.

«Nadie es más solitario que aquel que nunca ha recibido una carta.»

ELIAS CANETTI

Las cartas han sido históricamente el principal medio de comunicación a distancia. Hoy existen nuevos medios de comunicación, pero la carta sigue siendo una forma de escritura muy utilizada.

Las cartas pueden ser personales (dirigidas a un familiar o a un amigo) o formales. Ejemplos de cartas formales son las cartas al director en la prensa, las cartas de presentación y las cartas de reclamación.

Vas a escribir una carta formal a una persona de tu comunidad. Puedes utilizar alguna de estas ideas:

- Escribir a un político local, estatal o nacional para explicarle tu opinión sobre un asunto, o para reaccionar ante una decisión suya.
- Escribir al director de un periódico para opinar sobre algo que leíste o para corregir un error.
- Escribir a una empresa para pedir que hagan algo u opinar sobre algo que han hecho.

Piensa

- Define tu proyecto de escritura. Debes dar respuesta a estas preguntas:
  - ¿Para qué voy a escribir? → el **propósito**
  - ¿Qué voy a escribir? → el **género**
  - ¿A quién voy a escribir? → el **destinatario**
  - ¿Qué voy a decir? → las **ideas**

Mi proyecto de escritura

- **Propósito.** ¿Para qué voy a escribir? Para hacer una reclamación.
- **Género.** ¿Qué voy a escribir? Una carta formal.
- **Destinatario.** ¿A quién voy a escribir? A la agencia de viajes.
- **Ideas.** ¿Qué voy a decir? Que quiero que me devuelvan el dinero de la reserva puesto que han cancelado el viaje.

274 doscientos setenta y cuatro

Rubric for Evaluation

	Content	Organization	Conventions
1 point	Main purpose of the letter is not clear. Message has missing information. Word choice and tone are inappropriate for audience.	Does not follow suggested format. No apparent organization. Ideas are hard to follow. Very few or no transitions used.	Many errors in spelling, punctuation, grammar, and usage. Errors obscure meaning.
3 points	Main purpose of the letter is clear. Message is mostly complete. Word choice and tone are mostly appropriate for audience.	Format is close to the suggested model. Organization is clear, but some ideas may not be in the right sequence. Some transitions used.	Some errors in spelling, punctuation, grammar, and usage. Errors don't interfere with meaning.

Expresiones útiles

Saludos:

Querido(a)…	*Dear …*
Estimado(a)…	*Dear …*
Muy señor(a) mío(a)…	*Dear Sir …*

Despedidas:

Afectuosamente.	*Affectionately,*
Un cordial saludo.	*Regards,*
Atentamente.	*Sincerely,*

Escribe

■ Utiliza las ideas que anotaste y escribe la primera versión de tu carta. Puedes escribir este borrador (*draft*) a mano, pero la versión final debe estar escrita con la computadora.

■ Recuerda utilizar la forma *usted* si no conoces a la persona a quien va dirigida la carta.

■ Busca información sobre la persona o la compañía para obtener su dirección y los datos necesarios. Asegúrate de escribir tu carta en el formato apropiado. Abajo tienes un esquema que puede ayudarte.

Revisa

■ Después de escribir tu carta, intercámbiala con tu compañero(a) y revísala.

■ Lee la carta de tu compañero(a) y analiza estas cuestiones:

– ¿El propósito queda claro? ¿El tono es apropiado?

– ¿Sigue el formato indicado?

– ¿Hay errores gramaticales u ortográficos?

■ Devuelve la carta a su autor(a) con tus sugerencias y revisa tu trabajo teniendo en cuenta sus comentarios.

■ Pasa a limpio tu carta con los errores corregidos.

Comparte

■ Lee tu carta a la clase. ¿Qué opinan tus compañeros(as)? Entre todos(as), elijan las cuatro cartas más convincentes.

■ Si lo crees apropiado, envía tu carta. ¿Crees que te van a responder? ¿Por qué?

Diagram labels: membrete · lugar y fecha · línea de saludo · cuerpo · despedida · firma y nombre del firmante

	Content	Organization	Conventions
5 points	Main purpose of the letter stands out. Message is complete, clear, and concise. Word choice and tone are appropriate for audience.	Follows the suggested model. Organization is clear. Ideas are well sequenced. Uses transitions smoothly.	Few, if any, errors in spelling, punctuation, grammar, and usage. Excellent command of the Spanish language.

ESCRITURA

Una carta formal

■ If access to the Internet is available, encourage students to look for samples of their type of letter online. Ask them to rank the letters they found on clarity and conciseness.

Escribe

■ Tell students that format and style are very important in formal letters. In most formal letters it is advisable to address the recipient formally (i.e., using *usted* and appropriate titles) and keep a businesslike tone. A common organization for this type of letter includes a short opening where the writer introduces him or herself, a statement about the reason for writing and relevant details to justify the main point, a statement about the action expected, and information on how the writer can be contacted.

Revisa

■ Before students exchange their letters with a classmate, have them look at the letter format to make sure that they have included all the sections and information needed. Then ask them to read the first paragraph to themselves. Is the purpose of the letter clearly stated in this first paragraph? Then have students exchange their texts and evaluate each other's letters.

Comparte

■ Emphasize the importance of selecting the right tone in formal correspondence. Encourage students to transmit their letter's tone when they read it aloud to their classmates. Ask students to pay attention to their body language and use it to help them convey their message.

Evaluation

■ Distribute copies of the rubric to students and discuss the evaluation criteria. Ask students to refer to the rubric as they prepare their writing and as they evaluate their classmates' letters.

Vocabulario

Presentation

- In this section, students will review all key vocabulary from the unit, organized by themes, to prepare for an assessment. Students will complete practice activities for each of the three *Desafíos*.

Activities	Standards	Resources
1.	1.2	
2.	1.3	
3.	1.2, 1.3	

Teaching Suggestions

Warm-Up / Independent Starter

- Have students write a list of activities they enjoy doing.

Preparation

- Ask students to imagine that they are a career counselor. Have them think of six or seven questions they would ask a classmate to find out the kinds of professions for which their classmate is best suited. You may get students started with these questions: *¿Cuáles son tus tres cualidades más importantes? ¿Qué tecnologías utilizas en tu vida diaria? ¿Cuáles son tus clases favoritas?*

- Then ask students to get together with a classmate and ask him or her their questions. Have students make note of their partners' answers. Then allow students a couple of minutes to decide on two or three professions for their partner. They must be ready to justify their recommendations. What do their partners think of the recommended professions? Then have partners share their Independent Starters with each other. Would students change their recommendations now that they know what their partners like doing?

- Go over the *Repaso* presentation with the class, modeling pronunciation and intonation as necessary. Ask students to go through the vocabulary and make a list of cognates. How many did they find? Then have students look for false cognates. Did they find any? For example: *comprometido* is not "compromised," but "committed."

276

Profesiones y cargos

el/la banquero(a)	banker
el/la científico(a)	scientist
el/la comerciante	vendor
el/la contador(a)	accountant
el/la diseñador(a) gráfico(a)	graphic designer
el/la empresario(a)	businessman/ businesswoman
el/la escritor(a)	writer
el/la farmacéutico(a)	pharmacist
el/la funcionario(a)	government employee
el/la juez(a)	judge
el/la obrero(a)	(blue collar) worker
el/la periodista	journalist
el/la programador(a) informático(a)	computer programmer
el/la traductor(a)	translator

Cargos

el/la coordinador(a)	coordinator
el/la director(a)	director
el/la empleado(a)	employee
el/la gerente	manager
el/la jefe(a)	boss
el/la presidente(a)	president

Acciones

apagar incendios	to put out fires
descubrir	to discover
informar	to inform
investigar	to research
salvar vidas	to save lives

Trabajo

ascender	to be promoted
el contrato	contract
la jornada completa	full-time
la media jornada	part-time
el sueldo	salary
las vacaciones	vacation

Cualidades

amable	friendly	emprendedor(a)	entrepreneurial
ambicioso(a)	ambitious	exigente	demanding
creativo(a)	creative	organizado(a)	organized
eficiente	efficient	responsable	responsible

Tecnología

la computadora	computer	el ratón	mouse
la fotocopiadora	copier	el reproductor de CD	CD player
la impresora	printer		
la pantalla	screen	el teclado	keyboard

Acciones

abrir un documento	to open a document
bajar un archivo	to download a file
cerrar un programa	to close an application
clicar con el ratón	to click the mouse
colgar/subir una foto	to upload a picture
fotocopiar un informe	to copy a report
guardar un mensaje	to save a message
imprimir un gráfico	to print a graphic
navegar por Internet	to surf the Internet

Voluntariado y trabajo comunitario

la convivencia	coexistence	la solidaridad	solidarity
la cooperación	cooperation	la tolerancia	tolerance
los deberes	duties	el/la ciudadano(a)	citizen
los derechos humanos	human rights	el/la cooperante	aid worker
la integración	integration	el/la voluntario(a)	volunteer
la organización	organization	comprometido(a)	committed

Acciones

atender a personas mayores	to attend to the elderly	cooperar	to cooperate
colaborar	to collaborate	proteger	to protect
convivir	to coexist		

276 doscientos setenta y seis

Differentiated Instruction

DEVELOPING LEARNERS

- To reinforce students' comprehension of the vocabulary, ask them to complete the following sentences with the name of a profession and a reason for them liking or disliking said profession:
  1. *Quiero ser ... porque...*
  2. *No quiero ser ... porque...*

- Have students share their sentences with a partner. Then ask pairs to agree on a job they both like and explain why they think they would be suitable for such a job, and a job they both dislike vand the reason it would not be a good job for them.

EXPANDING LEARNERS

- Ask students to imagine that they have already graduated and are looking for a job. Explain that potential employers will ask about their qualifications, abilities, interests, knowledge of technology, experience with community service or volunteer work, salary expectations, etc. Students must first state the job they are hoping to find, and then write at least two paragraphs explaining how they would be an asset to their new employer. Alternatively, students may work with a partner to create a job interview incorporating this information, and then act it out in front of the class.

DESAFÍO 1

1 **Trabajos y cualidades.** Une cada profesión con la cualidad que crees más apropiada para su desarrollo.

(A)
1. cocinero(a)
2. escritor(a)
3. funcionario(a)
4. empresario(a)
5. juez(a)
6. contador(a)

(B)
a. responsable
b. emprendedor(a)
c. amable
d. eficiente
e. organizado(a)
f. creativo(a)

DESAFÍO 2

2 **Iconos.** ¿A qué acciones se refieren estos iconos? Escríbelas.

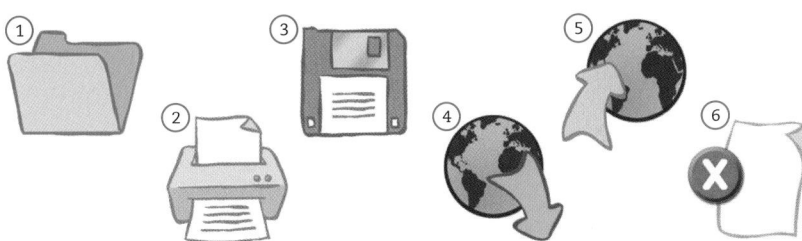

① ② ③ ④ ⑤ ⑥

DESAFÍO 3

3 **Un Mundo de Todos.** Completa el texto con las palabras del cuadro.

> tolerancia   organización   colaborar   integración
> solidaridad   ciudadanos   convivencia

Camisetas solidarias

La ___1___ Un Mundo de Todos, que trabaja por la ___2___ de las personas inmigrantes en la sociedad, ha puesto en marcha una campaña para fomentar la ___3___ y mejorar la ___4___ entre todos los ___5___. Tú puedes ___6___ con Un Mundo de Todos comprando una camiseta con el lema «La ___7___ nos une». El dinero recaudado por la venta de camisetas se invertirá en clases de inglés para los inmigrantes que necesitan mejorar el idioma.

doscientos setenta y siete 277

Activities

1. Explain to students that most of the qualities apply to several professions (e.g., *organizado* → *funcionario, contador, cocinero*). But students should ask themselves: In which profession is this quality absolutely necessary? In other words, if an employee doesn't have this quality, he or she may not be able to perform his or her job. In the above example, an accountant would need to be very organized to perform his or her job well.

2. To extend this activity, ask students to go on the Internet and look for pictures of a toolbar in Spanish. They can, for instance, search for *barra de herramientas de Word* and click the option for "Images" on their search engine. This will show them pictures of different Word™ menus in Spanish. Ask students to try to figure out the English equivalents of this vocabulary. Were they surprised by some of the translations?

3. Ask students to read each sentence through before attempting to complete it. Once they have completed the paragraph, have students work with a partner and write three comprehension questions (e.g., *¿Cuáles son los objetivos de la organización Un Mundo de Todos?*). Then have pairs exchange their questions with another pair and answer each other's questions.

Answer Key

1. Answers will vary. Sample answers:
   1. d   2. f   3. c   4. b   5. a   6. e
2. 1. abrir un documento   4. bajar un archivo
   2. imprimir   5. subir / colgar
   3. guardar   6. cerrar un programa
3. 1. organización   5. ciudadanos
   2. integración   6. colaborar
   3. solidaridad   7. tolerancia
   4. convivencia

Additional Resources

Fans Online activities
Practice Workbook

HERITAGE LANGUAGE LEARNERS

- Ask students to look at the job section of an online newspaper from their heritage country. Then have them read the ads for jobs they like or would be interested in, and choose one of these jobs. Once students have selected a job, ask them to write a cover letter to accompany their résumé. Explain that the letter should highlight their qualifications and background, and should convince the reader to look at their résumé.

- Invite volunteers to read their letters to the class. If time allows, hold a class vote on the most convincing letter.

COOPERATIVE LEARNING

- Have small groups of students imagine that they volunteer at a community service organization and that they need to promote their organization to attract new volunteers. Students will need to design a public relations campaign that includes a brief oral presentation explaining the purpose of the organization, as well as posters or handouts with details such as the organization's name, activities and programs in which they participate, and how to get involved with the organization. Have groups present their organization to the class. Which organization was able to attract the largest number of volunteers?

277

REPASO

Gramática

Presentation

- Students will review grammatical structures presented in the unit. Each grammar point is cross-referenced to the corresponding page on which it was introduced. The activities here provide systematic practice by *Desafío*.

Activities	Standards	Resources
4.	1.2, 1.3	
5.	1.2	
6.	1.2, 1.3	
7. Cultura	1.1, 2.1, 2.2, 3.1	

Teaching Suggestions

Warm-Up / Independent Starter

- Have students write sentences expressing their emotional reaction to each one of the following situations. Ask students to use different verbs from the list of *Verbos para expresar sentimientos*.
  1. *El voluntario atiende a las personas mayores.*
  2. *El empleado no es responsable.*
  3. *Los ciudadanos protegen el medioambiente.*
  4. *El escritor no es creativo y no sabe qué escribir.*

Preparation

- Ask students to get together with a classmate and share their Independent Starters. Are their reactions similar? Then have pairs comment on each other's reactions. For example:
  A. *Me da pena que el empleado no sea responsable.*
  B. *Pues es posible que pierda el trabajo.*
  A. *Sí. Estoy convencido de que perderá el trabajo si no cambia.*

  Invite pairs to share some of their dialogues with the class and encourage students to add their own comments and reactions.

- Divide the class into six groups and assign each group one of the grammar topics. Ask them to come up with three sentences to illustrate their grammar point. Have groups share their sentences with the class. If students need more reinforcement, write some of their examples on the board and explain the grammar point.

REPASO Gramática

Expresar certeza y duda (pág. 238)

EXPRESIONES DE CERTEZA CON INDICATIVO

Es verdad / Es cierto / Es evidente / Es obvio + que
Estar convencido(a) / Estar seguro(a) + de que
Saber + que
No dudar + que

EXPRESIONES DE DUDA CON SUBJUNTIVO

Es dudoso / Es improbable
Es posible / Es probable   + que
Dudar + que

EXPRESIONES NEGATIVAS CON SUBJUNTIVO

No es verdad / No es cierto
No es evidente / No es obvio   + que
No es posible / No es probable
No estar convencido(a) / No estar seguro(a) + de que

El imperfecto de subjuntivo (pág. 240)

VERBOS REGULARES

TRABAJAR	COMER	ESCRIBIR
trabajara	comiera	escribiera
trabajaras	comieras	escribieras
trabajara	comiera	escribiera
trabajáramos	comiéramos	escribiéramos
trabajarais	comierais	escribierais
trabajaran	comieran	escribieran

USO DEL IMPERFECTO DE SUBJUNTIVO

Mi profesor me aconsejaba
Mi profesor me había aconsejado   + que estudiara más.

Dar detalles. El relativo *que* (pág. 250)

EL PRONOMBRE RELATIVO QUE

Voy a tomar un autobús que va al centro.
Conozco a un chico que toca el piano.

INDICATIVO Y SUBJUNTIVO

• person or thing exists	+ indicative
• person or thing doesn't exist • unclear if the person or thing exists • existence in question	+ subjunctive

El género del nombre (pág. 252)

CASOS ESPECIALES

- Masculine nouns that end in -a: el día, el mapa.
- Feminine nouns that end in -o: la foto, la moto.
- Masculine nouns of Greek origin that end in -ma: el clima, el drama.

OFICIOS, PROFESIONES Y CARGOS

- Masculine nouns that end in -or, form the feminine adding -a: el doctor / la doctora.
  Exception: el actor / la actriz.
- Masculine and feminine nouns with the same ending:
  - Ending in -ista and -a: el / la artista, el / la periodista.
  - Ending in -e: el / la agente, el / la cantante.
    Exceptions: el cliente / la clienta, el jefe / la jefa, el presidente / la presidenta.
  - Ending in -o: el / la modelo, el / la piloto.

EXCEPCIÓN A LAS NORMAS DE CONCORDANCIA

- Feminine nouns that begin with a stressed a- or ha-
  - In the singular: el agua.
  - In the plural: las aguas.

Expresar sentimientos (pág. 262)

VERBOS PARA EXPRESAR SENTIMIENTOS

aburrir	dar pena	enfadar	molestar
alegrar	deprimir	enojar	preocupar
asustar	divertir	extrañar	sorprender
dar miedo	emocionar	fascinar	

INFINITIVO Y SUBJUNTIVO

The main clause and the dependent clause refer to the same person.	+ infinitive
The main clause and the dependent clause refer to different people.	+ que + subjunctive

Expresar dificultad (pág. 264)

Aunque	+ indicative (when referring to real situations).
A pesar de (que)	+ subjunctive (when referring to unreal or uncertain situations, probabilities, or unknown outcomes).

Differentiated Instruction

DEVELOPING LEARNERS

- To reinforce students' comprehension of the subjunctive with expressions of doubt and with negative expressions, ask them to complete each of the following sentences. Once they have finished their sentences, discuss with students the use of the subjunctive in each one of these cases.
  - Dudo que…
  - No es cierto que…
  - Es posible que…
  - No estoy seguro(a) de que…
  - Es improbable que…

EXPANDING LEARNERS

- Have pairs come up with an advertisement for a job. First, they must decide the type of employer they are (e.g., *un bufete de abogados*, *una compañía de construcción*). Then, they will decide on the type of position that has become available in their company and the person they are looking for to fill this position. Once they have made these decisions, ask them to design and write their ad. For example: *Prestigioso bufete de abogados busca un abogado que sea bilingüe…* Encourage pairs to post their ad in the classroom. Is anyone interested in this position?

DESAFÍO 1

4 **¿Presente o imperfecto?** Completa estas oraciones.
Pon los infinitivos en presente o en imperfecto de subjuntivo.

1. Mi novia quiere que le _____ flores por su cumpleaños.
   (regalar)
2. El médico me había recomendado que _____ más agua.
   (beber)
3. A mi perro no le gustaba que mi gato _____ a su lado.
   (comer)
4. Los padres aconsejan a sus hijos que _____ todos los días.
   (estudiar)
5. Nos encantó que Shakira _____ sus canciones más famosas.
   (cantar)

 DESAFÍO 2

5 **Interpretando el sentido.** ¿Qué significa cada oración? Elige la opción correcta.

1. Busco un libro de minerales que tiene muchas fotos en color.
   a. Conozco el libro.
   b. No sé si existe un libro con esas características.
2. En mi empresa se necesita a un(a) telefonista que hable chino y japonés.
   a. Mis jefes no saben si encontrarán un(a) empleado(a) con estos conocimientos.
   b. Mis jefes quieren contratar a un(a) telefonista que ya conocen.
3. Quiero comprar una casa que tiene vistas al mar y que es barata.
   a. Todavía tengo que encontrar la casa.
   b. Ya he encontrado una casa barata y con vistas al mar.

 DESAFÍO 3

6 **Dificultades.** Escribe oraciones con *aunque* siguiendo el modelo.

Modelo   No hace mucho frío. Voy a ponerme mi abrigo nuevo.
   → *Aunque no hace mucho frío, voy a ponerme mi abrigo nuevo.*

1. Es posible que llueva esta tarde. Voy a ir a la playa.
2. No sé si a Juan le gusta el chocolate. Voy a regalarle chocolates.
3. Es muy tarde. Voy a llamar a mi amiga Laura por teléfono.
4. Estos zapatos son muy caros. Voy a comprarlos.

 **CULTURA**

7 **Profesionales de Latinoamérica.** Responde a estas preguntas.

1. ¿Recuerdas el nombre de alguno de los astronautas hispanos de la NASA?
2. ¿Cuál es la profesión de María Elena Salinas?
3. ¿Qué personajes célebres estudiaron en universidades de Latinoamérica? Da algún ejemplo.

María Elena Salinas.

doscientos setenta y nueve 279

Activities

4. Ask students to break this activity into steps. First have them focus on the main clause. Then ask students to look at the verb and decide whether it refers to something in the present or something in the past. Remind students that there are several ways to express past tense (e.g., preterite, imperfect, past perfect). If the main verb is in the present tense, they should use present subjunctive in the dependent clause. If the main verb is in the past tense, they should use imperfect subjunctive in the dependent clause.

6. Have students work with a classmate to complete this activity. One of the partners will read the first sentence of each pair of sentences aloud. The other partner will determine whether the sentence expresses doubt or not. The first sentence in 1, for instance, expresses doubt (*Es posible que...*). If the sentence expresses doubt, the verb after *aunque* should be in the subjunctive.

Answer Key

4. 1. regale   4. estudien
     2. bebiera   5. cantara
     3. comiera

5. 1. a   2. a   3. b

6. 1. Aunque llueva, voy a ir a la playa.
     2. Aunque a Juan no le guste el chocolate, voy a regalarle chocolates.
     3. Aunque es muy tarde, voy a llamar a mi amiga Laura por teléfono.
     4. Aunque estos zapatos son muy caros, voy a comprarlos.

7. Answers will vary. Sample answers:
     1. Franklin Chang-Díaz, Fernando Caldeiro, Ellen Ochoa.
     2. Es periodista.
     3. Ana María Cetto, Pablo Neruda.

Additional Resources

Fans Online activities
Practice Workbook

HERITAGE LANGUAGE LEARNERS

- Ask students to work with a partner to come up with a rhyme or a mnemonic device to help their classmates learn the gender of certain nouns. For example:

  El artista habla con el agente,
  que habla con la gerente.
  ¿Cuál es el problema de esa gente?
  Pues parece que el planeta
  desapareció del mapa.

- Check students' work for correct grammar and spelling, and then ask them to share their rhymes or mnemonic devices with the class.

MULTIPLE INTELLIGENCES:

Intrapersonal Intelligence

- Ask students to think about their answers to the following questions:
  – *¿Qué te preocupaba de niño?*
  – *¿Qué te sorprendió en tu cumpleaños?*
  – *¿Qué te emocionó en la última película que viste?*
  – *¿Qué te enojó la última vez que discutiste con un amigo(a)?*

- Ask them to write at least two paragraphs elaborating their answers to these questions. Remind them to use the imperfect subjunctive in the dependent clause when necessary.

Unit 5

PROYECTO

Una organización solidaria

Presentation

- In this section, students will apply the vocabulary, grammar, and cultural information they have learned in this unit to develop a non-profit project and create an ad to find professionals and volunteers for the project.

Activities	Standards	Resources
Paso 1	1.1, 1.2, 3.1, 5.1, 5.2	
Paso 2	1.1, 1.2, 1.3, 2.2, 3.1, 3.2, 5.1, 5.2	
Paso 3	1.1, 1.3, 3.1	
Paso 4	1.1, 1.3, 3.1	
Paso 5	1.3, 2.2, 3.1, 5.1, 5.2	

Teaching Suggestions

Warm-Up / Independent Starter

- Ask students to read the introduction to the project silently. Then have them list all of the non-profit organizations they know of or have heard about.

Preparation

- Have students share their Independent Starters. Write on the board the names of the organizations students mention. As a class, discuss what these organizations do, the places where they usually work, the types of professionals and volunteers who work for these organizations, the advertisement campaigns some of these organizations conduct, etc. Students might mention UNESCO, the Red Cross, United Way, the Bill and Melinda Gates Foundation, the World Wildlife Fund. After this discussion, divide the class into small groups to work on their projects.

Step-by-Step Instructions

Paso 1

- Have groups consider their own interests when deciding on an activity. When deciding on a place, have students narrow down their choices to two or three communities. Then have them research the needs of those communities in the field they have chosen, and select the place where they think their project would be more useful.

280

PROYECTO

Un proyecto de

una organización solidaria

Would you like to develop a project to benefit your community? To create your own non-profit organization? Work with your classmates to develop your own non-profit project and define the profile of your volunteers.

PASO 1 Elijan una actividad

- En grupos, elijan una actividad que les gustaría desarrollar. Les damos algunas ideas.

  - Protección del medio ambiente
  - Ayuda a las personas discapacitadas
  - Ayuda a las personas mayores
  - Cooperación para el desarrollo
  - Ayuda a la infancia
  - Ayuda a los inmigrantes
  - Participación ciudadana

- Decidan el lugar donde quieren desarrollar la actividad elegida.

PASO 2 Elaboren el proyecto

- Infórmense sobre la situación de ese lugar en el campo que hayan elegido.

  – ¿Qué necesidades tiene?   – ¿Qué pueden hacer para ayudar?

- Elaboren un proyecto con algunas acciones concretas. Piensen en posibles fuentes de financiación e incorpórenlas a su proyecto.

  Modelo
  Construcción de una escuela infantil para niños de 0 a 3 años de un barrio de Lima.
  El objetivo es que estos niños y niñas estén cuidados y alimentados mientras sus madres van a trabajar fuera de casa.

280 doscientos ochenta

Rubric for Evaluation

	Content	Organization	Presentation
1 point	The ad is not relevant. Information is incomplete or not based on research. Little Spanish is used.	Inefficient use of time. The ad's formatting is minimal. The organization of the information is confusing.	Unclear communication. Delivery is not fluent. Many errors in vocabulary and grammar.
3 points	The ad is relevant. Information is complete but some of it lacks significance. Spanish is used most of the time.	Time is used well. The ad has attractive formatting. The information is well organized.	Clear communication and fluent delivery. Mostly correct vocabulary and grammar.

PASO 3 Definan el perfil del cooperante

- Anoten las tareas que va a hacer el / la profesional o el / la voluntario(a) que están buscando.
- Hagan una lista con las cualidades que tiene que tener esa persona.

organizado(a)   trabajador(a)

eficiente   amable   creativo(a)

responsable   emprendedor(a)

- Escriban un texto en el que describan cómo deben ser los(as) profesionales o los(as) voluntarios(as) de la organización.

Modelo

Se buscan jóvenes amables, responsables, activos y motivados para conseguir ayuda, y nuevos socios para la construcción de una escuela infantil en Lima.

PASO 4 Decidan las condiciones laborales

- Decidan la duración del proyecto, el salario para los(as) profesionales y el horario.

PASO 5 Hagan los anuncios

- Con toda la información anterior, elaboren un anuncio para buscar a personas ideales para su proyecto.

Nombre de la ONG

Lugar en el que trabaja:

Proyecto que desarrolla:

Se busca:

_____

_____

Se ofrece:

_____

_____

- Graben un anuncio de radio para presentar su organización y pedir algunos(as) voluntarios(as) que colaboren con ella.

Unidad 5

Autoevaluación

¿Qué has aprendido en esta unidad?

Do these activities to evaluate how well you can manage in Spanish.

Evalúa tus habilidades. Para cada punto, di Muy bien, Bien o Necesito practicar más.

a. Can you describe what you know about professions?

▶ Explain two things you know and two doubts you have about your future profession.

▶ Describe three things that your family or teachers advised you in the past.

b. Can you talk about the type of job you want?

▶ Describe the characteristics of the type of job you would like to have, and explain why.

c. Can you express feelings and difficulties?

▶ Express your feelings about the community service projects you or your friends have participated in, or would like to participate in.

▶ Describe the actions you will take to help your community despite difficulties or other situations that may arise.

5 points	Content	Organization	Presentation
	The ad is relevant, complete, and grabs the audience's attention. The information is well researched. Spanish is used exclusively.	Time is used extremely well. The ad has very attractive formatting. The information is clearly organized.	Clear and fluent communication. Very motivating, engaging delivery. Correct and complete vocabulary and grammar.

PROYECTO

Una organización solidaria

Paso 2

- Ask groups to also look at what is already being done by other organizations in their field in the place where they are planning to work so that they don't duplicate services. Explain to students that their project should have a very clear objective and be narrow in scope.

Paso 3

- Have students list, in sequence, the tasks that need to be done in order to accomplish their objective for the project. Then ask them to select the tasks they plan to assign to the new volunteer. This person would not be in charge of everything, but rather of one aspect of their project.

Paso 4

- Ask students to research similar projects online. This would give them a realistic idea of the duration, cost, and commitment of these types of projects.

Paso 5

- Remind students that potential candidates should be able to find information in the ad that will help them determine whether this position is suitable for them.

Evaluation

- Distribute copies of the rubric to students. Discuss the evaluation criteria and explain how this project will be graded. Encourage students to refer to the rubric as they prepare their projects.

Content

- Have students proofread their ad carefully, paying close attention to verbal mood. Remind students that for *Se busca*, they don't know if the person exists, whereas for *Se ofrece*, they know for certain what they are offering.

Organization

- Due to the space limitations of an ad, format and organization are of utmost importance. Every single word counts! Encourage students to choose a name for their non-profit organization that very clearly reflects its goals and the type of work it does.

Presentation

- Encourage students to show enthusiasm for their project and the kind of work their non-profit organization does. They should aim at making prospective candidates feel needed and appreciated.

Unit 6 Tus aficiones

Objectives

- To state opinions.
- To identify different leisure activities.
- To use expressions of courtesy in Spanish.
- To state the probability or purpose of an action.
- To identify traditional and popular sports and pastimes.

- To describe cultural events and sporting competitions.
- To quote someone directly or indirectly.
- To indicate location or origin.
- To plan a trip or excursion.
- To identify main ideas and significant details in a variety of texts.

- To write descriptive, narrative, or informative texts.
- To know and apply the different stages of the writing process: planning, writing, revising, and sharing.
- To explore cultural aspects of traditional sports in Spain and Latin America.

Contents

Vocabulary

- Useful expressions to show doubt and skepticism, and to express agreement or disagreement.
- Review: Words for sports, travel, and modes of transportation.
- Leisure time and entertainment performances. Film genres.
- Sports and competitions.
- Trips and accommodations, the airport, and traveling by plane.

Grammar

- To express opinion.
- To use expressions of courtesy.
- To express probability of an action.
- To express purpose.
- Indirect speech.
- To express location.

Culture

- *El Festival de Cine de San Sebastián*.
- Watching foreign movies.
- A culture night: *La Noche en Blanco*.
- Hispanic actors and movie directors, and Spanish-language films.
- The pre-Hispanic Moche culture.
- The best places for water sports in Latin America: *La Libertad*, El Salvador.
- History of the Pan American Games.
- The Ruta Quetzal cultural and adventure program.
- *Hoteles con encanto*.
- *El Hotel de Sal (Bolivia)*.
- Literary texts by Hispanic authors: *Galletitas*, by Jorge Bucay.
- Popular and traditional sports among Spanish-speaking populations.

Evaluation Criteria

- Identify sports, games, pastimes, and leisure activities done in Hispanic communities and one's own community.
- Identify and compare different genres and elements of motion pictures.
- Express one's opinion in the affirmative and negative using various structures.
- Show respect for people in social situations by using courteous phrases.
- Describe regional and international sporting competitions.

- Name and describe traditional sports that are an essential part of some Hispanic cultures.
- Express the possibility or probability of an action taking place.
- Express the purpose of an action using infinitives or the subjunctive mood.
- Describe some cultural festivals and excursions.
- Describe a typical travel experience and compose a trip itinerary.

- Differentiate between direct and indirect speech.
- Indicate a destination, origin, location, or movement using the subjunctive or indicative mood.
- Describe a character from a literary text.
- Write a short narrative text.
- Classify related words into categories.
- Use future tense verbs to explain events that may occur in the near future.

Unit Plan _____

Las tareas/Antes de empezar

Estimated time: 1 session.

Text: *Viajes por el mundo hispano.*

Functions & forms:
- Useful expressions to show doubt and skepticism, and to express agreement or disagreement.
- Review of known vocabulary about sports, travel, and modes of transportation.

⚐ DESAFÍO 1

Estimated time: 5 sessions.

Text: *Un cartel de cine.*

Functions & forms:
- To state opinions.
- Leisure time and entertainment performances, film genres, and elements of cinema and theatre.
- Verbs and verb moods to express opinion.
- Expressions of courtesy.

Culture:
- *El Festival de Cine de San Sebastián.*
- *Las películas extranjeras.*
- *La Noche en Blanco.*

Reading: *De cine.*

⚐ DESAFÍO 2

Estimated time: 5 sessions.

Text: *Un deporte extremo.*

Functions & forms:
- To express probability of an action.
- Sports, sportsmen and women, and sport competitions.
- Certain expressions and the future tense to express probability.
- To express purpose of an action.

Culture:
- *¿Surfistas prehispánicos?*
- *El triángulo olímpico.*
- *La Libertad.*

Reading: *Historia de los Juegos Panamericanos.*

⚐ DESAFÍO 3

Estimated time: 6 sessions.

Text: *Colaboradores en la Ruta Quetzal.*

Functions & forms:
- To convey someone else's words.
- Trips and accommodations, the airport, and expressions related to traveling by plane.
- Indirect speech.
- To indicate location.

Culture:
- *La Ruta Quetzal.*
- *Hoteles con encanto.*
- *El Hotel de Sal (Bolivia).*

Reading: *Galletitas*, by Jorge Bucay.

Para terminar

Estimated time: 1 session.

Todo junto: Review of *Desafíos 1–3.*

Tu desafío:
- *Desafío A:* Organize a Spanish and Latin American film festival and make a poster to promote it.
- *Desafío B:* Write and conduct an interview of the best athletes in your school and write a report with this information.
- *Desafío C:* Research and choose one of the Ruta Quetzal expeditions, write a card with the information and present it to the class.

MAPA CULTURAL

Estimated time: 1 session.

Mapa cultural: *Deportes con tradición.*

ESCRITURA

Estimated time: 1 session.

Writing: *Un cuento.*

PROYECTO/EVALUACIÓN

Estimated time: 2 sessions.

Project: *Un plan para un viaje de estudios.*

Self-evaluation: *Autoevaluación.*

Standards for Learning Spanish

COMMUNICATION

1.1. Interpersonal mode

- Exchange personal opinions and experiences.
- Engage in oral conversations using personal knowledge and experience.
- Exchange assignments with a partner and evaluate each other's work.
- Create a visual and describe it with a partner.
- Discuss hypothetical situations with a partner.
- Compare and contrast information with a partner.
- Ask and answer questions on different topics.
- Ask a partner questions and take notes.

1.2. Interpretive mode

- Demonstrate understanding of oral and written expressions.
- Demonstrate understanding of questions relating to familiar and less familiar topics.
- Understand and obtain information from audio or video recordings.
- Understand written exchanges.
- Extract information from an informative text.

- Identify main ideas and significant details from a literary text.
- Draw conclusions and make judgments from oral and written texts.
- Interpret texts on topics of other cultures and relate them to personal knowledge and experience.

1.3. Presentational mode

- Produce and present an original creation.
- Write and present an original story.
- Write sentences or paragraphs comparing information.
- Complete sentences with relevant information or correct verb tenses.
- Write questions for an interview and present the results.
- Create a list of information and present it to the class.
- Write sentences or a paragraph summarizing information.

CULTURE

2.1. Practices and perspectives

- Learn about cultural traditions and discuss the importance of such practices.
- Learn about activities people in Hispanic populations do in their leisure time.
- Learn about sports and competitions played in Hispanic countries.
- Identify types of artistic performances in Hispanic countries.
- Discuss famous actors and directors of Spanish-language films.

- Learn about and use various expressions to show courtesy and to state agreement.

2.2. Products and perspectives

- Learn about various genres of Spanish-language films produced in Hispanic countries.
- Learn about costumes and equipment used in traditional sporting events.
- Learn about hotels and tourist destinations in Hispanic countries.

CONNECTIONS

3.1. Interdisciplinary connections

- Understand the similarities and differences between some aspects of grammar in English and in Spanish.
- Learn about some types of artistic and musical performances in Hispanic communities.
- Describe the unique construction materials or design of some buildings.
- Identify different angles and geometric shapes used in elements of various sports and pastimes.

- Learn about different geographical locations in some Hispanic countries.

3.2. Viewpoints through language / culture

- Read dialogues, informative texts, and literary texts in Spanish that provide insight into Hispanic cultures.
- Learn about how sports join countries and strengthen the friendship among them.

COMPARISONS

4.1. Compare languages

- Compare how to state opinions in English and in Spanish.
- Compare how expressions of courtesy are used in English and in Spanish.
- Compare how to state direct and indirect speech in English and in Spanish.

4.2. Compare cultures

- Compare types of cultural festivals and events in Hispanic countries and in the United States.
- Compare leisure activities and sporting events in Hispanic countries and in the United States.
- Compare travel accommodations and tourist attractions in Hispanic countries and in the United States.

COMMUNITIES

5.1. Spanish within and beyond the school setting

- Research and obtain information on the Internet.
- Discuss activities in one's own community.
- Imagine situations in which Spanish could be used.
- Discuss leisure activities and sports that take place in one's own community.

5.2. Spanish for lifelong learning

- Discuss ways in which Spanish can be used in future life experiences.
- Discuss one's preferred movies, music, and artistic performances in Spanish.

Communicative Skills

Interpersonal Mode

		Activities
Speaking	• Exchange opinions, ideas, preferences, or experiences.	• 3, 9, 12, 18, 35, 62, 71, 77, 78, 83, 85, *Proyecto*
	• Compare pictures or information with classmates.	• 5, 30, 52, 56, 83
	• Interview a classmate.	• 39, 80
	• Engage in a conversation with a classmate.	• 3, 9, 12, 18, 26, 58, 71, 77, 83
Writing	• Write descriptive sentences or dialogues.	• 22, 55, 65, 81, 82
	• Use personal information to respond to an e-mail or a blog.	• 45, 55
Listening	• Understand a classmate's answers.	• 39, 52, 62, 71
	• Extract pertinent information from a classmate's oral description or opinions.	• 3, 26, 52, 56, 77, 83, *Proyecto*
Reading	• Understand simple descriptive or informative texts.	• 49, 75
	• Understand an informative text and use the information to talk with classmates.	• 18, 80

Interpretive Mode

		Activities
Listening	• Obtain information from short dialogues or a longer conversation.	• 3, 8, 13, 29, 34, 42, 61, 70, 76
	• Understand questions, opinions, or simple oral descriptions.	• 17, 20, 48, 57
Reading	• Understand and make inferences from descriptive, narrative, or informative texts.	• 10, 14, 18, 28, 36, 38, 40, 49, 50, 52, 63, 67, 72,
	• Understand a literary story or a narrative text.	• 55, 78, *Escritura*
	• Use visuals or context clues to understand unfamiliar words and concepts.	• 2, 11, 25
	• Reflect on cultural topics in relation to personal knowledge and experience.	• 10, 14, 36, 50, 67, 72
Viewing	• Connect information to images.	• 3, 83
	• Obtain information from an image.	• 12, 22
	• Interpret information from a graph, table, or graphic organizer.	• 5, *Escritura*

Presentational Mode

		Activities
Speaking	• Present information, a description, or an original creation to the class.	• 84, *Escritura, Proyecto*
	• Present the results of an interview or a debate.	• 30, 83
	• Create and act out a dialogue.	• 22, 65, 81, 82
Writing	• Summarize information in written form.	• 30, 54, 83, 84
	• Write descriptions or narratives based on a picture, a topic, or a text.	• 54, 66, 77, 79, *Escritura*
	• Write sentences or a paragraph about personal experiences.	• 38, 45, 66
Visually Representing	• Create a poster to promote a product.	• 57, 84
	• Organize information in a graph, table, or chart.	• 2, 3, 5, 25, 27, 37, 48, 53, 78

Cross-Curricular Standards

Subject	**Standard**	**Activities**
Language Arts	• Compare elements of Spanish grammar and language with English equivalents.	• 15, 19, 41, 46, 68, 73
	• Use the writing process to write an original story.	• *Escritura*
Social Studies	• Learn about cultural practices and products of the Spanish-speaking world.	• 8, 10, 23, 51, 59, 63, *Mapa cultural*
Geography	• View a map and make inferences.	• 50
Math	• Identify the use of geometric shapes and angles in some sports.	• 40

Lesson Plans (50-Minute Classes)

Day	Objectives	Sessions	Activities	Time	Standards	Resources/ Homework
1	To introduce leisure time activities and vacations and the characters' challenges, and to review learned vocabulary	**Tus aficiones/Las tareas/Antes de empezar** (282–287) • Warm-Up: Topic orientation • Presentation: *Viajes por el mundo hispano* • *Expresiones útiles* and *Recuerda*	 1–2 3–5	 10 m. 20 m. 20 m.	1.1, 1.2, 1.3, 2.1, 2.2, 3.1, 3.2, 5.1	Visual Presentation Audio Video Practice Workbook
2	To express opinions	**Desafío 1 – Un cartel de cine** (288–289) • Warm-Up: Independent Starter • *Texto: Un cartel de cine* • *Cultura: El Festival de Cine de San Sebastián*	 6–9 10	 5 m. 35 m. 10 m.	1.1, 1.2, 1.3, 2.1, 2.2, 3.1, 4.2, 5.2	Visual Presentation Audio
3	To identify genres and elements of cinema, theatre, and other entertainment performances	**Desafío 1 – Vocabulario** (290–291) • Warm-Up: Independent Starter • Vocabulary: *Ocio y espectáculos* • *Comparaciones: Las películas extranjeras*	 11–13 14	 5 m. 35 m. 10 m.	1.1, 1.2, 1.3, 2.1, 2.2, 4.2	Audio Practice Workbook
4	To express opinions	**Desafío 1 – Gramática** (292–293) • Warm-Up: Independent Starter • Grammar: *Expresar opinión*	 15–18	 5 m. 45 m.	1.1, 1.2, 1.3, 2.1, 2.2, 3.1, 3.2, 4.1, 5.1, 5.2	Audio Practice Workbook
5	To express courtesy and politeness	**Desafío 1 – Gramática** (294–295) • Warm-Up: Independent Starter • Grammar: *Fórmulas gramaticales de cortesía* • *Cultura: La Noche en Blanco*	 19–22 23	 5 m. 35 m. 10 m.	1.1, 1.2, 1.3, 2.1, 3.1, 4.1, 4.2, 5.1	Audio Practice Workbook
6	To understand a dialogue and to integrate vocabulary and grammar	**Desafío 1 – Lectura/Comunicación** (296–299) • Warm-Up: Independent Starter • *Lectura: De cine* • *Comunicación:* Review • *Final del desafío*	 24–27 28–30 31	 5 m. 20 m. 15 m. 10 m.	1.1, 1.2, 1.3, 2.1, 2.2, 3.1, 3.2, 5.1, 5.2	Visual Presentation Audio Practice Workbook Quiz on *Desafío 1*
7	To express probability	**Desafío 2 – Un deporte extremo** (300–301) • Warm-Up: Correct quiz on *Desafío 1* • *Texto: Un deporte extremo* • *Cultura: ¿Surfistas prehispánicos?*	 32–35 36	 5 m. 35 m. 10 m.	1.1, 1.2, 1.3, 2.1, 2.2, 3.1, 4.2	Visual Presentation Audio
8	To identify sports and to talk about sports competitions	**Desafío 2 – Vocabulario** (302–303) • Warm-Up: Independent Starter • Vocabulary: *Deportes* • *Conexiones: El triángulo olímpico*	 37–39 40	 5 m. 35 m. 10 m.	1.1, 1.2, 1.3, 2.1, 3.1, 5.1	Practice Workbook
9	To express the possibility or probability of an event taking place	**Desafío 2 – Gramática** (304–305) • Warm-Up: Independent Starter • Grammar: *Expresar probabilidad*	 41–45	 5 m. 45 m.	1.1, 1.2, 1.3, 3.1, 4.1, 5.1	Audio Practice Workbook
10	To indicate the purpose of an action	**Desafío 2 – Gramática** (306–307) • Warm-Up: Independent Starter • Grammar: *Expresar finalidad* • *Conexiones: La Libertad*	 46–49 50	 5 m. 35 m. 10 m.	1.1, 1.2, 1.3, 2.1, 3.1, 4.1	Audio Video Practice Workbook

Day	Objectives	Sessions	Activities	Time	Standards	Resources/ Homework
11	To understand an informative text and to integrate vocabulary and grammar	**Desafío 2 – Lectura / Comunicación** (308–311) • Warm-Up: Independent Starter • *Lectura: Historia de los Juegos Panamericanos* • *Comunicación:* Review • *Final del desafío*	51–54 55–57 58	5 m. 20 m. 15 m. 10 m.	1.1, 1.2, 1.3, 2.1, 3.1, 3.2, 4.2, 5.1	Audio Practice Workbook *Tu desafío* Quiz on *Desafío 2*
12	To convey someone else's words	**Desafío 3 – Colaboradores en la Ruta Quetzal** (312–313) • Warm-Up: Correct quiz on *Desafío 2* • *Texto: Colaboradores en la Ruta Quetzal* • *Cultura: La Ruta Quetzal*	59–62 63	5 m. 35 m. 10 m.	1.1, 1.2. 1.3, 2.1, 2.2, 3.2, 5.1, 5.2	Visual Presentation Audio Video
13	To describe how to prepare and plan for a trip	**Desafío 3 – Vocabulario** (314–315) • Warm-Up: Independent Starter • *Vocabulary: Viajes y alojamiento* • *Cultura: Hoteles con encanto*	64–66 67	5 m. 35 m. 10 m.	1.1, 1.2, 1.3, 2.2, 4.2, 5.1, 5.2	Practice Workbook
14	To differentiate between direct and indirect speech	**Desafío 3 – Gramática** (316–317) • Warm-Up: Independent Starter • *Grammar: El estilo indirecto* • *Conexiones: El hotel de Sal (Bolivia)*	68–71 72	5 m. 35 m. 10 m.	1.1, 1.2, 1.3, 2.2, 3.1, 4.1, 4.2, 5.1	Audio Practice Workbook
15	To indicate a destination, origin, location, or movement	**Desafío 3 – Gramática** (318–319) • Warm-Up: Independent Starter • *Grammar: Expresar lugar*	73–77	5 m. 45 m.	1.1, 1.2, 1.3, 2.2, 3.1, 4.1, 5.1, 5.2	Audio Practice Workbook
16	To understand a literary text	**Desafío 3 – Lectura** (320–321) • Warm-Up: Independent Starter • *Lectura: Galletitas*	78–79	5 m. 45 m.	1.1, 1.2, 1.3, 2.2, 3.1, 3.2	
17	To integrate vocabulary and grammar	**Desafío 3 – Comunicación** (322–323) • Warm-Up: Independent Starter • *Comunicación:* Review • *Final del desafío*	80–81 82	5 m. 30 m. 15 m.	1.1, 1.2, 1.3, 5.1, 5.2	Practice Workbook *Tu desafío* Quiz on *Desafío 3* **Para terminar – Tu desafío** (325)
18	To integrate language in context	**Para terminar** (324–325) • Warm-Up: Correct quiz on *Desafío 3* • *Todo junto* • *Tu desafío* presentations	83 84	5 m. 20 m. 25 m.	1.1, 1.2, 1.3, 2.1, 2.2, 5.1, 5.2	Practice Workbook
19	To assess student proficiency and identify traditional sports played in Hispanic countries	**Evaluación / Mapa cultural** (326–327) • Warm-Up: Independent Starter • Quiz on *Desafíos 1–3* • *Mapa cultural: Deportes con tradición*	85	5 m. 20 m. 25 m.	1.1, 1.2, 1.3, 2.1, 2.2, 3.1, 3.2, 5.2	Video Practice Workbook
20	To write a short story	**Escritura** (328–329) • Warm-Up: Independent Starter • *Escritura: Un cuento*		5 m. 45 m.	1.1, 1.2, 1.3, 3.1, 5.1	Project work
21	To plan a trip and create a travel itinerary	**Proyecto** (334–335) • Warm-Up: Prepare project presentations • Project presentations		10 m. 40 m.	1.1, 1.2, 1.3, 2.1, 2.2, 3.1, 5.1, 5.2	**Repaso – Vocabulario** (330–331) **Repaso – Gramática** (332–333)
22	To assess student proficiency	**Assessment** • *Autoevaluación* (335) • Test		10 m. 40 m.	1.1, 1.2, 1.3, 2.1, 2.2, 5.1, 5.2	

Lesson Plans (90-Minute Classes)

Day	Objectives	Sessions	Activities	Time	Standards	Resources/ Homework
1	To introduce leisure time activities and vacations and the characters' challenges, and to review learned vocabulary	(See Day 12 Unit 5) ***Tus aficiones/Las tareas/Antes de empezar*** (282–287) • Warm-Up: Topic orientation • Presentation: *Viajes por el mundo hispano* • *Expresiones útiles* and *Recuerda*	 1–2 3–5	(45 m.) 10 m. 20 m. 15 m.	1.1, 1.2, 1.3, 2.1, 2.2, 3.1, 3.2, 5.1	Visual Presentation Audio Video Practice Workbook
2	To express opinions and to identify genres and elements of cinema, theatre, and other entertainment performances	***Desafío 1 – Un cartel de cine/Vocabulario*** (288–291) • Warm-Up: Independent Starter • *Texto: Un cartel de cine* • *Cultura: El Festival de Cine de San Sebastián* • Vocabulary: *Ocio y espectáculos* • *Comparaciones: Las películas extranjeras*	 6–9 10 11–13 14	 5 m. 30 m. 10 m. 35 m. 10 m.	1.1, 1.2, 1.3, 2.1, 2.2, 3.1, 4.2, 5.2	Visual Presentation Audio Practice Workbook
3	To express an opinion and to express courtesy and politeness	***Desafío 1 – Gramática*** (292–295) • Warm-Up: Independent Starter • Grammar: *Expresar opinión* • Grammar: *Fórmulas gramaticales de cortesía* • *Cultura: La Noche en Blanco*	 15–18 19–22 23	 5 m. 35 m. 40 m. 10 m.	1.1, 1.2, 1.3, 2.1, 2.2, 3.1, 3.2, 4.1, 4.2, 5.1, 5.2	Audio Practice Workbook
4	To understand a dialogue and to integrate vocabulary and grammar	***Desafío 1 – Lectura/Comunicación/Evaluación*** (296–299) • Warm-Up: Independent Starter • *Lectura: De cine* • *Comunicación:* Review • *Final del desafío* • Quiz on *Desafío 1*	 24–27 28–30 31	 5 m. 35 m. 25 m. 10 m. 15 m.	1.1, 1.2, 1.3, 2.1, 2.2, 3.1, 3.2, 5.1, 5.2	Visual Presentation Audio Practice Workbook
5	To express probability, to identify sports, and to talk about sports competitions	***Desafío 2 – Un deporte extremo/Vocabulario*** (300–303) • Warm-Up: Independent Starter • *Texto: Un deporte extremo* • *Cultura: ¿Surfistas prehispánicos?* • Vocabulary: *Deportes* • *Conexiones: El triángulo olímpico*	 32–35 36 37–39 40	 5 m. 35 m. 10 m. 30 m. 10 m.	1.1, 1.2, 1.3, 2.1, 2.2, 3.1, 4.2, 5.1	Visual Presentation Audio Practice Workbook
6	To express the possibility or probability of an event taking place and to indicate the purpose of an action	***Desafío 2 – Gramática*** (304–307) • Warm-Up: Independent Starter • Grammar: *Expresar probabilidad* • Grammar: *Expresar finalidad* • *Conexiones: La Libertad*	 41–45 46–49 50	 5 m. 40 m. 35 m. 10 m.	1.1, 1.2, 1.3, 2.1, 3.1, 4.1, 5.1	Audio Video Practice Workbook

Day	Objectives	Sessions	Activities	Time	Standards	Resources/ Homework
7	To understand an informative text, and to integrate vocabulary and grammar	***Desafío 2 – Lectura/Comunicación/Evaluación*** (308–311) • Warm-Up: Independent Starter • *Lectura: Historia de los Juegos Panamericanos* • *Comunicación:* Review • *Final del desafío* • Quiz on *Desafío 2*	 51–54 55–57 58	 5 m. 35 m. 25 m. 10 m. 15 m.	1.1, 1.2, 1.3, 2.1, 3.1, 3.2, 4.2, 5.1	Audio Practice Workbook *Tu desafío*
8	To convey someone else's words and to describe how to prepare and plan for a trip	***Desafío 3 – Colaboradores en la Ruta Quetzal/ Vocabulario*** (312–315) • Warm-Up: Independent Starter • *Texto: Colaboradores en la Ruta Quetzal* • *Cultura: La Ruta Quetzal* • Vocabulary: *Viajes y alojamiento* • *Cultura: Hoteles con encanto*	 59–62 63 64–66 67	 5 m. 30 m. 10 m. 35 m. 10 m.	1.1, 1.2. 1.3, 2.1, 2.2, 3.2, 4.2, 5.1, 5.2	Visual Presentation Audio Video Practice Workbook
9	To differentiate between direct and indirect speech, and to indicate a destination, origin, location, or movement	***Desafío 3 – Gramática*** (316–319) • Warm-Up: Independent Starter • Grammar: *El estilo indirecto* • *Conexiones: El hotel de Sal (Bolivia)* • Grammar: *Expresar lugar*	 68–71 72 73–77	 5 m. 40 m. 10 m. 35 m.	1.1, 1.2, 1.3, 2.2, 3.1, 4.1, 4.2, 5.1, 5.2	Audio Practice Workbook
10	To understand a literary text, to integrate vocabulary and grammar, to integrate language in context, and to assess student proficiency	***Desafío 3 – Lectura/Comunicación/Evaluación/ Todo junto*** (320–324) • Warm-Up: Independent Starter • *Lectura: Galletitas* • *Comunicación:* Review • *Final del desafío* • *Todo junto* • Quiz on *Desafío 3*	 78–79 80–81 82 83	 5 m. 25 m. 20 m. 10 m. 15 m. 15 m.	1.1, 1.2, 1.3, 2.1, 2.2, 3.1, 3.2, 5.1, 5.2	Practice Workbook *Tu desafío* **Para terminar – Tu desafío** (325)
11	To identify traditional sports played in Hispanic countries and to write a short story	***Tu desafío/Mapa cultural/Escritura*** (325–329) • Warm-Up: Independent Starter • *Tu desafío* presentations • *Mapa cultural: Deportes con tradición* • *Escritura: Un cuento*	 84 85	 5 m. 15 m. 30 m. 40 m.	1.1, 1.2, 1.3, 2.1, 2.2, 3.1, 3.2, 5.1, 5.2	Video Practice Workbook **Repaso – Vocabulario** (330–331) **Repaso – Gramática** (332–333) Quiz on *Desafíos 1–3* Project work
12	To plan a trip and create a travel itinerary	***Proyecto/Assessment*** (334–335) • Warm-Up: Correct quiz on *Desafíos 1–3* • Project presentations • *Autoevaluación* • Test (See Day 1 Unit 7)		 5 m. 15 m. 10 m. 15 m. (45 m.)	1.1, 1.2, 1.3, 2.1, 2.2, 3.1, 5.1, 5.2	

Unit 6 Tus aficiones

3 Estamos de acuerdo

1. –Me divierte muchísimo patinar sobre hielo. ¿A ti no?
   –Sí, a mí también.
2. –Yo creo que el béisbol es el deporte más popular del mundo.
   –Bueno, según se mire. En la televisión hay partidos de fútbol a todas horas.
3. –Me encantaría aprender a montar a caballo.
   –A mí no, me da miedo.
4. –Me encanta viajar, es la mejor forma de aprender cosas sobre otras culturas.
   –Yo pienso lo mismo.
5. –En Hollywood hay muy pocos actores latinos famosos.
   –Si tú lo dices...

8 El festival de cine

–Estoy leyendo un artículo sobre el Festival de Cine de San Sebastián. Creo que nos puede ayudar a resolver nuestro desafío.

–¿San Sebastián? ¿Dónde está? ¿En México?

–No, San Sebastián es una ciudad española. Está al norte, en la costa.

–Ah. ¿Y qué dice el artículo?

–Pues que allí se celebra todos los años en septiembre un festival de cine y que ponen muchísimas películas en varias salas de la ciudad para que el público pueda verlas.

–¿Es un festival muy famoso?

–Sí, parece ser que todos los años van actores y directores de cine muy importantes.

–Pero solo compiten películas españolas, ¿no?

–¡No, qué va! Es un festival de cine internacional con mucho prestigio. Mira, en esta foto está Glenn Close recogiendo un premio.

–Ah, sí. Y estos son Antonio Banderas y Julia Roberts. Pues sí que van famosos, sí.

–Y aquí está Gael García Bernal. ¡Me encanta este actor mexicano! Es guapísimo.

–Pero, ¿te gusta porque es buen actor o porque es guapísimo?

–Por las dos cosas. ¿Has visto *Babel*? Es una película que estuvo nominada para siete premios Oscar: como mejor película, mejor director...

–No, no la he visto. Oye, no sabía que eras tan aficionada al cine.

13 Los mejores fans del mundo

–¿Qué hiciste anoche, Diego? ¿Al final fuiste al cine?

–¡Qué va! Cambié de idea. Estuve con mi hermano en uno de los mejores conciertos de mi vida. Fuimos a ver a los Reyes del Rock.

–¿En serio? Es increíble que consiguieran boletos porque leí que se agotaron una hora después de ponerse a la venta.

–Sí, pero tuvimos mucha suerte.

–¿Dónde fue el concierto?

–En el auditorio. Cantaron todas las canciones de su nuevo disco. Pero lo mejor es que la música no era el único espectáculo; los efectos especiales eran geniales. Había fuegos artificiales, juegos de luces, confeti...

–¡Qué suerte! Seguro que fue un gran concierto.

–¡Sí! El público se volvió loco. Todos aplaudimos mucho y nadie quería que terminara. Al final el cantante dijo que éramos los mejores fans del mundo. Ahora te enseño las fotos.

17 De acuerdo

1. ¿Qué te parece si vamos al concierto de Coldplay?
2. ¿Qué tal si vamos al cine con tu hermano pequeño? Hoy estrenan una película de animación muy divertida.
3. Me gustaría ir al circo. Dicen que hay un espectáculo increíble con elefantes.
4. En el Teatro Real hay un espectáculo fabuloso: el Ballet Folclórico de México va a interpretar danzas tradicionales de varias regiones mexicanas.
5. ¿Qué prefieres hacer: ir a la ópera o a una conferencia del escritor Gabriel García Márquez? Es que son a la misma hora...

20 La cortesía no cuesta nada

1. ¿Querrías acompañarme al teatro?
2. ¿Me das el periódico? Es que quiero ver la cartelera.
3. No quiero ir al cine contigo porque no me gustan las películas de ciencia ficción.
4. Lo siento, pero hoy no puedo, tengo mucho trabajo. ¿Podríamos ir otro día al cine?
5. ¡Es el mejor concierto del año! ¡Compra ya los boletos!
6. El teatro está un poco lejos... Llama a un taxi.

29 ¡Nos encanta el cine!

–Aunque hemos llegado muy temprano, ya hay una fila muy larga.

–Es que es una película con mucho éxito. Pero creo que no ha ganado ningún premio...

–Ya, aunque puede ganar un premio muy especial: estar en nuestro festival de cine hispano.

–Sí, eso es un gran honor.

–Me interesa el título: *Ladrón que roba a ladrón*. ¿Por qué se llama así?

–Es la historia de unos ladrones que intentan robar a otro hombre y resulta que ese hombre también es un ladrón.

–Ah, ya entiendo. Parecido al Zorro...

–No exactamente. El Zorro robaba a los ricos para ayudar a los pobres. Pero, como la película del Zorro, *Ladrón que roba a ladrón* tiene acción y drama, y dicen que es bastante divertida.

–La película es en versión original con subtítulos en inglés, ¿verdad?

–No creo que sea subtitulada, Daniel. Pero no vamos a tener ningún problema.

–Si tú lo dices...

34 La competencia de surf

–¡Hola! Usted es uno de los jueces de la competencia, ¿verdad?

–Así es.

–¿Podemos hacerle unas preguntas?

–Claro. ¿Qué quieren saber?

–¡Muchas cosas! Es que tenemos que escribir un reportaje. Y aunque somos muy aficionados al surf, es la primera vez que asistimos a una competencia.

–Pues es muy interesante. Empezó ayer. Hoy es el segundo día y los surfistas ya conocen bien las olas. Quédense a verlos. Y vengan también mañana, que es el último día.

–¿Cuántos participantes hay?

–Bueno, este año hay unos treinta surfistas, pero hace tres o cuatro
años participaron casi cien.

–¿Todos los surfistas son hispanos?

–No, vienen deportistas de todo el mundo.

–¿Y qué otras actividades hay hoy?

–En esta ciudad hay mucha afición al deporte. Pueden ir a correr o a
montar en bici por el parque; o practicar deportes acuáticos en la playa...

–No, quiero decir si hay algún espectáculo, algún evento...

–Ah, sí. Esta noche, a las diez, hay un concierto al aire libre.

–Qué bien. Pues muchas gracias.

–De nada. Que lo pasen bien.

42 ¿Qué estarán haciendo?

1. –¿Sabes dónde está Eva hoy?
   –No, pero mañana tiene un examen de Matemáticas. Supongo que
   está estudiando.

2. –Quiero que Michelle vaya al cine con nosotros esta noche, pero
   no contesta al teléfono.
   –Sé que su padre le compró unos boletos para un concierto...

3. –Hoy Daniel y yo íbamos a correr juntos, pero él no vino al parque.
   –Creo que sus padres querían que los ayudara con las tareas
   domésticas.

4. –¿Diga?
   –Hola, señora Thomas. Soy Johnny. ¿Está Ethan, por favor?
   –Lo siento, Johnny, pero no está. Creo que se fue a la playa a
   hacer surf.

5. –Hace unos días que no veo a Asha.
   –Yo tampoco, pero recuerdo que estaba algo estresada porque
   tiene que hacer un trabajo de Ciencias y necesitaba encontrar
   información.

6. –¿Sí?
   –Hola, Tomás. ¿Sabes dónde está Lucas?
   –Ni idea... Pero sé que le gusta practicar tenis todas las tardes.

48 ¿A quién le afecta?

1. Fui a la playa para hablar con uno de los jueces de la competencia.

2. Tomo notas durante la competencia para que Asha tenga toda
   la información.

3. Tomé fotos para ponerlas en el reportaje.

4. Preparé una lista de preguntas para entrevistar a los surfistas.

5. Estuve en el gimnasio para que los surfistas me explicaran cómo
   se preparan.

6. Pasé la tarde en la biblioteca para investigar sobre los deportes
   en la época prehispánica.

57 El anuncio del campeonato

¿Te gusta el surf? Si contestaste que sí, no te pierdas el Campeonato
Panamericano de Surf en la playa de Tamarindo (Costa Rica). Se
celebrará del 4 al 7 de junio y habrá más de setenta participantes
de todo el mundo. Podrás ver a los mejores surfistas de Australia,
los Estados Unidos, Perú, Chile, Argentina, México y, cómo no, de
Costa Rica. ¡Esperamos verte! Recuerda: del 4 al 7 de junio en la
playa de Tamarindo.

61 Los preparativos

–Lucas, ¿buscaste información sobre los vuelos a Madrid?

–Sí. Ayer encontré un boleto de una compañía aérea española, pero
creo que es muy caro. Cuesta mil trescientos dólares.

–Sí, es demasiado caro. ¿Miraste alguna otra compañía?

–Hay una compañía italiana que tiene una buena oferta, pero el horario
es muy malo. Los chicos tendrían que pasar una noche en Barcelona
antes de llegar a Madrid.

–Demasiado complicado. Hay que seguir buscando. ¿Ya sabemos si
los chicos necesitan un visado para el viaje?

–Esta mañana llamé a la embajada, pero salió el buzón de voz y dejé
un mensaje. Todavía no me han respondido. ¿Y tú cómo vas con las
reservas del alojamiento?

–Bastante bien. Envié correos electrónicos a tres cámpings cerca
de Madrid y todos me han contestado ya. Hice una reserva en uno
de ellos para dos noches.

–¡Estupendo!

70 Compañeros de viaje

–Hola, Lucas. ¿Estás con Asha?

–Sí, estamos almorzando.

–Tengo una sorpresa para ustedes. ¡Si quieren pueden ir al viaje con
los chicos!

–¿De veras? ¿Podemos participar en la Ruta Quetzal?

–No exactamente, no se emocionen tanto. No van a participar, pero
pueden acompañar a los chicos estadounidenses hasta Madrid y pasar
una semana con ellos. Después, ustedes tendrán que regresar.

–¿Qué te parece, Asha?

–¡Genial! Pero oye, Lucas, yo no tengo tienda de campaña.

–No te preocupes, de eso me encargo yo.

–Veo que están muy emocionados, pero no se olviden de su desafío.
¿Tienen ya todo organizado para los chicos?

–Estamos casi listos. Tenemos toda la información necesaria y las
reservas hechas.

–No olviden confirmar todos los detalles del viaje.

–No, no. Precisamente anoche hablé con los organizadores y hoy espero
su respuesta para confirmar las reservas.

–¡Excelente trabajo! ¡Y buena suerte!

76 Planes

–Además de conocer Madrid, me gustaría visitar alguna ciudad donde
no tengamos que usar el coche para todo.

–A mí me gustaría estar en un lugar donde haya olas grandes para
practicar surf.

–Quizá podamos ir a Cádiz, en el sur de España. Allí hay varios lugares
donde se celebran competencias de surf.

–¿Y dónde prefieres alojarte? ¿En un hotel, en un cámping...? También
podríamos alojarnos en un parador desde donde se pueda ver el mar.

–Si lo que queremos es disfrutar de la naturaleza, podemos quedarnos
en un cámping.

–Tú eres la experta, Asha. Nos alojaremos donde tú quieras.

–También podemos preguntar a Tim y a Tess. Ellos estuvieron en España
y seguro que nos recomiendan sitios interesantes.

Tus aficiones

UNIDAD 6

The Unit

- The themes for Unit 6 are leisure time, sports, and travel. The participants will learn to express opinions and probability. They will also learn to use indirect speech when they talk about what other people said.

- Tess and Tim send the participants a message with their tasks.
  - *Desafío 1.* Michelle and Daniel have to help organize a film festival that includes Spanish and Latin American movies.
  - *Desafío 2.* Eva and Ethan must interview some Hispanic surfers at an international surfing competition in California.
  - *Desafío 3.* Asha and Lucas will plan the trip that the American students participating in the Ruta Quetzal will take to Madrid, Spain.

Activities	Standards	Resources
Tus aficiones	1.2, 2.1, 2.2, 3.1, 5.1	Video

Teaching Suggestions

Warm-Up / Independent Starter

- Have students make a list of their hobbies, and then describe them and explain when they practice them.

Preparation

- Ask students to look at the photos and read the captions. Have students read each *Desafío's* objective, as well as the vocabulary and grammar goals. Then ask students to formulate a statement that they feel exemplifies the objective, vocabulary, and grammar for each *Desafío*. For example: *Es fantástico que haya festivales de cine.* Afterward, have students share their sentences with each other and discuss which *Desafío* gave them the most difficulty.

Picture Discussion

- Have students look at the images again and describe them. Then ask them to share their lists from the Independent Starter. Can they see themselves participating in any of these activities? Which one(s)? Why?

Tus aficiones

El tiempo libre y los viajes

DESAFÍO 1

▶ **Expresar opiniones**

Vocabulario
Ocio y espectáculos

Gramática
Expresar opinión

Fórmulas gramaticales de cortesía

Festival Internacional de Cine de San Sebastián (España)

DESAFÍO 2

Mascotas de los Juegos Panamericanos de Guadalajara (México)

▶ **Expresar probabilidad**

Vocabulario
Deportes

Gramática
Expresar probabilidad

Expresar finalidad

282 doscientos ochenta y dos

The Challenge

DESAFÍO 1

Festival Internacional de Cine de San Sebastián

The Spanish-language movie industry is reaching an increasingly wider audience. Mexico, Spain, and Argentina are well known in the international film industry, but Cuba, Colombia, Chile, and other Hispanic countries have long traditions of movie-making, and often host international film festivals. The oldest and most prestigious of these festivals are the *Festival de Guadalajara*, in Mexico, and the *Festival de San Sebastián*, in Spain. The *Concha de Oro* (Golden Shell) is the equivalent of the Oscar award in San Sebastián.

DESAFÍO 2

Mascotas de los Juegos Panamericanos de Guadalajara

The first Pan American Games took place in 1951 in Buenos Aires, Argentina. Since then, these games have become one of the most important sports competitions in the world. The Pan American Games have been celebrated every four years since that time in different cities throughout the Americas. The United States holds the largest number of medals, followed by Cuba, Canada, Brazil, Argentina, and Mexico.

Tus aficiones

DESAFÍO 3

▶ **Transmitir las palabras de otros**

Vocabulario
Viajes y alojamiento

Gramática
El estilo indirecto

Expresar lugar

Grupo de participantes
de la Ruta Quetzal

doscientos ochenta y tres **283**

Festival Internacional de Cine de San Sebastián (España)

■ Ask students whether they have attended a film festival. Have they seen any Spanish or Latin American movies? Which one(s)? Invite students to briefly summarize the plot. Explain to them that an important international film festival takes place each September in the city of San Sebastián, in northern Spain.

Mascotas de los Juegos Panamericanos de Guadalajara (México)

■ Have students describe this picture. What are these children doing? What do the three mascots represent? Explain that the Pan American Games are a multi-sport event that takes place somewhere in the Americas every four years. The 2011 games took place in Guadalajara, Mexico, and featured three colorful mascots, Gavo, Leo, and Huichi, which represent the city of Guadalajara and the state of Jalisco.

Grupo de participantes de la Ruta Quetzal

■ Ask students questions in order to help them describe the photo. For example: *¿Qué ven en esta foto? ¿Qué edades creen que tienen estos chicos? ¿De dónde son? ¿Cómo están? ¿Por qué piensan ustedes que están contentos? ¿Han participado ustedes alguna vez en un intercambio cultural para jóvenes? ¿Les interesa hacerlo? ¿Por qué?* Explain to students that the Ruta Quetzal is a trip for Spanish-speaking teenagers to a variety of countries to promote intercultural exchanges.

Objectives

■ By the end of Unit 6, students will be able to
  – Talk about leisure-time activities.
  – Express opinions.
  – Use expressions of courtesy.
  – Talk about sports and sports competitions.
  – Express probability.
  – Talk about the purpose of an action.
  – Talk about travel and lodging.
  – Tell what others have said.
  – Express location.
  – Talk about the film industry of the Spanish-speaking world, surfing and sports competitions, and adventure travel to promote intercultural exchanges among teenage students.

⚑ **DESAFÍO 3**

Grupo de participantes de la Ruta Quetzal

The Ruta Quetzal consists of a trip from Spain to the Americas and back, in which close to three hundred teenagers from more than fifty countries—especially Spanish-speaking countries—participate every year. The students are selected based on merit; they must present an original piece of work or art related to a given topic, as well as complete an interview. The program was founded in 1979 by Miguel de la Quadra-Salcedo, a Spanish reporter and former athlete, and it aims to promote the study of the geography, history, and environment of the Spanish-speaking world.

Las tareas

Presentation

- In this section, the three pairs receive a message from Tess and Tim, who will assign them the new tasks that they must accomplish. Students will preview useful expressions to show agreement, disagreement, and doubt.

Activities	Standards	Resources
Texto	1.2, 2.1, 2.2, 3.1, 3.2	Vis. Pres.
1.	1.1, 1.2, 1.3, 2.1, 2.2	
2.	1.3, 3.1	

Teaching Suggestions

Warm-Up / Independent Starter

- Have students use a three-column chart like the one below to list all of the expressions they know in Spanish for expressing agreement, disagreement, and doubt. You may want to get them started with the following expressions:

Acuerdo	Desacuerdo	Duda
Sí, estoy de acuerdo.	No estoy de acuerdo.	No sé…

Preparation

- Invite volunteers to share their lists of expressions from the Independent Starter. Discuss the uses of the expressions students mention and make corrections where needed. Then ask students to scan the participants' dialogue on page 285 and add to their chart any additional expressions they find for agreeing, disagreeing, or expressing doubt.

- You may want to preview the use of *para* + infinitive to express the purpose for doing something. Ask students to scan the text on page 284 and point out this use (i.e., *para promocionarlo, para hacer las entrevistas, para facilitar la llegada*).

Texto: Viajes por el mundo hispano

- Ask students to read the introduction to the text silently. Then have them look at the photos on this page and come up with two questions about each one.

Las tareas

Viajes por el mundo hispano

 The characters receive a message that Tess and Tim sent them in order to help them in the new tasks. Do you want to know what they will have to do? This is what Tess and Tim say.

Tim: Hola, amigos. ¿Cómo están? Tess y yo vamos a presentarles sus nuevos desafíos. El primero es para Michelle y Daniel. ¿Conocen el cine hispano? ¿Les gusta? Pues tienen que ayudar a organizar un festival de cine con películas españolas y latinoamericanas. Y tendrán que hacer un cartel para promocionarlo. Seguro que lo harán muy bien.

flores de otro mundo

dirigida por icíar bollaín

Tess: El desafío de Ethan y Eva es más dinámico: tienen que entrevistar a unos surfistas sobre las competencias de surf en el mundo hispano. Tal vez tengan que viajar a alguna playa famosa para hacer las entrevistas.

Tim: Por último, Asha y Lucas tienen un desafío muy viajero. Deben colaborar con los organizadores de la Ruta Quetzal para facilitar la llegada de los estudiantes norteamericanos a Madrid, donde comenzará la expedición. Si no saben lo que es la Ruta Quetzal, busquen información en Internet. Estoy seguro de que les va a interesar mucho.

Differentiated Instruction

DEVELOPING LEARNERS

- Have students read the descriptions of the tasks silently before reading them aloud. Ask students to think about the subject matter of each task and the interest they may have in each one. Then have students rank the tasks from most interesting to least interesting and from what they consider to be the most difficult to the least difficult, and explain why they have categorized them this way. Ask students which task they would like to complete, and who they would like to have as a partner.

EXPANDING LEARNERS

- Encourage students to come up with other ways to carry out each task. For example, instead of making a poster to celebrate the film festival, students might prepare an interview with one of the leading directors or actors from the festival, or they might write a review of one of the featured films. Instead of interviewing surfers, students might suggest making a video of the competition. For those participating in the Ruta Quetzal, students might research the history of this cultural exchange. Ask students to work in small groups, discuss alternative activities, and present their ideas to the class.

Me apetece mucho aprender sobre cine hispano.

Sí, a mí también.

La Ruta Quetzal... Hum, suena bien.

¡El surf...! ¡Me encanta el surf! Este desafío es facilísimo.

¿Tú crees?

Yo pienso lo mismo, aunque no sé exactamente qué es la Ruta Quetzal...

 ¿Comprendes?

▶ **Completa** estas oraciones. ¿En qué consisten los desafíos de los personajes?

1. Michelle y Daniel tienen que...　　2. Eva y Ethan van a...　　3. Asha y Lucas deben...

▶ **Responde** a estas preguntas.

1. ¿De dónde son las películas que deben seleccionar Michelle y Daniel?
2. ¿Qué deben hacer para promocionar el festival?
3. ¿Adónde van a viajar Eva y Ethan?
4. ¿Qué crees que es la Ruta Quetzal?

 Investiga

▶ **Completa** una tabla como esta con palabras de la misma familia. Busca en los textos las palabras que faltan.

Acción (verbo)	Concepto (nombre)	Persona (nombre)
competir		competidor(a)
	organización	
		entrevistador(a)

doscientos ochenta y cinco **285**

Unit 6
Las tareas

■ Read the text aloud in order to model correct intonation and pronunciation. Then ask for volunteers to read it aloud. After each paragraph, ask students questions to help them summarize the paragraph. For example: *¿Qué tienen que hacer Michelle y Daniel? ¿Qué desafío tienen Eva y Ethan? ¿Qué van a hacer Asha y Lucas?* Check if they understood the dialogue.

Activities

1. To expand the second part of this activity, ask related questions. For example: *¿Qué es un festival de cine? ¿Qué festivales de cine conocen ustedes? ¿Qué pasa en esos festivales? ¿Qué público asiste? ¿Conocen alguna competencia deportiva famosa? ¿Qué competencias les gustan más? ¿De dónde creen que son los estudiantes que participan en la Ruta Quetzal? ¿Cómo lo saben?*

2. Practice the formation of nouns and verbs in Spanish with other words found in the text, such as *presentar, información*, and *colaborar*. Ask students to identify and relate these words with other nouns, verbs, or adjectives.

Answer Key

1. 1. ... ayudar a organizar un festival de cine y hacer un cartel para promocionarlo.
   2. ... entrevistar a unos surfistas.
   3. ... colaborar con los organizadores de la Ruta Quetzal para facilitar la llegada de los estudiantes norteamericanos a Madrid.

   ▶ 1. Son españolas y latinoamericanas.
   2. Deben hacer un cartel.
   3. Tal vez tengan que viajar a alguna playa famosa.
   4. Answers will vary.

2. Acción: organizar, entrevistar.
   Concepto: competencia, entrevista.
   Persona: organizador.

Additional Resources

Fans Online activities
Practice Workbook

HERITAGE LANGUAGE LEARNERS

• Students may know that the quetzal is a brightly colored and rare bird of Central America, and that it is the national bird of Guatemala. The quetzal has been immortalized in Mesoamerican mythology, and is still considered a symbol of goodness and light. Ask students to explore some of the legends and folklore surrounding the quetzal, and share these tales with the class. If possible, have heritage learners bring in books that retell some of the legends and ask these students to read them aloud, paraphrasing the more difficult passages for the rest of the class.

MULTIPLE INTELLIGENCES:
Interpersonal Intelligence

• Ask students to work in small groups and choose the task which, by group consensus, they would like to complete. Then ask them to discuss how they would go about completing it. Members of the group should take turns making suggestions for carrying out the challenge successfully. The group will discuss everyone's suggestions after all of them have been presented. Based on their decision, the group will then write a description of how they will complete the task. Call on a volunteer from each group to read their description aloud.

Unit 6
Antes de empezar

Presentation

- In this section, students will learn a variety of useful expressions, some for expressing agreement, others for expressing disagreement, and others for showing doubt about something.
- Students will also review vocabulary related to sports, travel, and transportation.

Activities	Standards	Resources
Expresiones útiles	1.2, 2.1	
3.	1.1, 1.2, 1.3, 2.1	Audio
Recuerda	1.2	
4.	1.2, 1.3	
5.	1.1, 1.2, 1.3, 5.1	

Teaching Suggestions

Warm-Up / Independent Starter

- Have students make a list in a two-column chart of nouns and verbs related to travel. You may give them the following examples to get them started:

Nombres	Verbos
avión	viajar
habitación	reservar
boleto	comprar

Preparation

- Read the *expresiones útiles* aloud to model pronunciation and intonation, and have students repeat each expression after you. Clarify that *también* is used in affirmative statements, whereas *tampoco* is used in negative ones. Then, use the *expresiones útiles* in personalized contexts. For example, you may want to ask students to react to certain statements using the given expressions. Encourage them to give you complete answers, justifying their opinion or reaction. For example:
  1. A. *Las películas románticas me parecen aburridas.*
     B. *Bueno, depende. A mí me gustan si los actores son buenos.*
  2. A. *Yo creo que los deportistas sufren mucho en las competencias deportivas.*
     B. *¡Qué va! Creo que ellos disfrutan del esfuerzo que hacen.*

286

Antes de empezar

EXPRESIONES ÚTILES

Para expresar acuerdo:
Yo pienso lo mismo (que tú).
Por supuesto.
Sin duda.
Sí, yo también / tampoco.
Sí, a mí también / tampoco.

Para mostrar duda y escepticismo:
Bueno, depende...
Supongo...
¿Tú crees?
Si tú lo dices...
Bueno, según se mire.

Para expresar desacuerdo:
Creo que te equivocas.
¡Qué va!
En absoluto.
Yo sí / Yo no.
A mí sí / A mí no.

3 Estamos de acuerdo

 ▶ **Escucha** y relaciona cada diálogo con la fotografía correspondiente.

 ▶ **Escucha** de nuevo y completa una tabla como esta.

	Acuerdo	Desacuerdo	Duda
1	✓		
2			
3			
4			
5			

 ▶ **Habla** con tu compañero(a). Expresa tu opinión sobre alguno de los temas anteriores. Él/Ella debe reaccionar usando alguna de las expresiones útiles.

Modelo A. *Este fin de semana hay un partido de béisbol en el estadio.*
B. *Creo que te equivocas... Fue el sábado pasado.*

286 doscientos ochenta y seis

Differentiated Instruction

DEVELOPING LEARNERS

- Ask students to make a three-column chart and title it *Viajes y transporte*. Have students label the columns *Antes del viaje, Durante el viaje,* and *La llegada*. Then ask students to write as many related words from the *Recuerda* feature, as well as others they know, to complete the columns. For example, they could write *Antes del viaje → la agencia de viajes; Durante el viaje → hacer escala;* and *La llegada → hacer turismo*. Give students a time limit in which to complete this task.

EXPANDING LEARNERS

- Give students more practice with the *expresiones útiles* by having them work with a partner to develop a dialogue. In their conversation, students will take turns stating an opinion on a subject of their choosing. Their partner will then make either a statement of agreement or one that expresses doubt or skepticism that is appropriate to the context of the dialogue. Encourage students to go beyond the vocabulary presented on the page, and use words from previous units.

RECUERDA

Deportes

el baloncesto	el balón/la pelota
el béisbol	el bate
el esquí	el casco
el fútbol	el guante
la gimnasia	la raqueta
el golf	
la natación	empatar
el senderismo	entrenar
el tenis	ganar
el voleibol	jugar
	perder

Viajes y transporte

el autobús	la excursión
el avión	la oficina de turismo
el tren	la tarifa
el aeropuerto	las vacaciones
el equipaje	facturar el equipaje
la estación	hacer escala
el horario	hacer turismo
la llegada	perder el avión
la salida	reservar habitación
la agencia de viajes	
el boleto	

4 **¿Cuánto sabes?**

▶ **Lee** las palabras del cuadro Recuerda. ¿Conoces más vocabulario sobre esos temas? Escríbelo.

Modelo *Deportes: el fútbol americano, el alpinismo…*

5 **¡A clasificar!**

▶ **Completa** un gráfico como este. Después, compáralo con el de tu compañero(a) y añade más palabras.

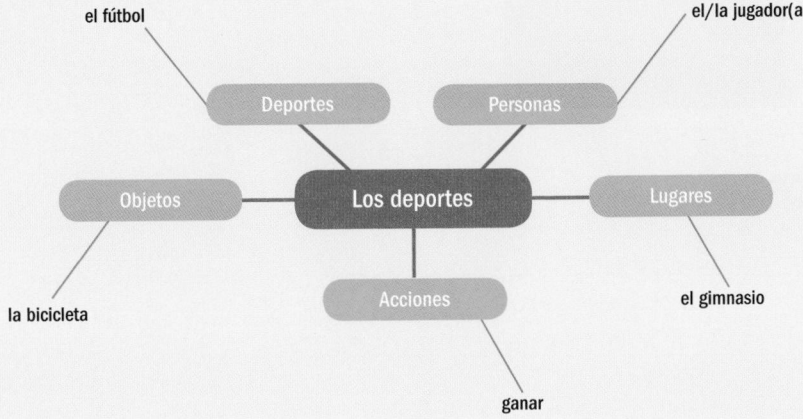

el fútbol — Deportes — el/la jugador(a) — Personas — Los deportes — Lugares — el gimnasio — Objetos — la bicicleta — Acciones — ganar

---

HERITAGE LANGUAGE LEARNERS

• Ask students to make a list of ways they might express agreement or disagreement and doubt or skepticism, in addition to those mentioned on page 286. Have students also include ways to express certainty. Students should then write or say sentences using each of these expressions. Remind students that when expressing doubt, they must use the subjunctive if there is a change of subject in the dependent clause. Be sure that students understand the differences between such constructions as *Creo que van a venir* and *Dudo que vengan.*

MULTIPLE INTELLIGENCES:
Verbal-Linguistic Intelligence

• Write the words and phrases from the *Recuerda* feature on slips of paper and place them in a bag. Ask each student to pick one and, taking turns, ask them to explain what the term means to the rest of the class. Explain to students that they should imagine that their classmates have no knowledge of this word or phrase, so their explanations must be very precise. For some of the sports mentioned, students may explain how to play the game. All explanations must be in Spanish, but body language is allowed.

Antes de empezar

■ Have students write three statements or opinions about a video game, a film, or a sport that they know well. Put them in pairs and have them react to their partner's opinion using the expressions of agreement, disagreement, or doubt. Ask students to continue their conversation in order to defend their position, explain their opinion, or reinforce the point that the students agree upon.

A. *El fútbol americano es el deporte más interesante.*

B. *En absoluto. El fútbol americano tiene demasiadas reglas.*

A. *Bueno, según se mire, puede parecer así. Pero cuando entiendes las reglas, ¡el fútbol americano es pura emoción!*

Activities

3. Before listening to the audio, have students look at the photos and come up with some opinions about each topic pictured. Then have them think of *expresiones útiles* that could be used to react to each of their opinions.

4. Have students use their independent Starters to help complete this activity.

5. As students fill in their word webs, see if they can extrapolate related words for each entry. For example, when they list *la bicicleta*, they could add *ciclismo* to the *Deportes* category and *ciclista* to the *Personas* category.

 AUDIO SCRIPT
See page 281I.

Answer Key

3. 1. D   2. B   3. A   4. C   5. E
▶ 2. Duda   4. Acuerdo
  3. Desacuerdo   5. Duda
▶ Answers will vary.

4. Answers will vary.

5. Answers will vary.

Additional Resources

Fans Online activities
Practice Workbook

287

Unit 6

DESAFÍO 1

Expresar opiniones

Presentation

- In *Desafío 1*, Michelle and Daniel will organize a Hispanic film festival and make a poster to promote the event. Students will preview language used to talk about leisure activities, ways to express personal opinions, and expressions of courtesy.

Activities	Standards	Resources
Texto	1.2, 2.1, 2.2	Vis. Pres.
6.	1.2, 1.3, 2.2	
7.	1.1, 1.2, 2.1, 2.2	
8.	1.2, 1.3, 2.1, 2.2	Audio
9.	1.1, 1.3, 5.2	
10. Cultura	1.1, 1.2, 2.1, 3.1, 4.2	

Teaching Suggestions

Warm-Up / Independent Starter

- Bring in different movie posters or project them from the Internet. Then ask students to write their answers to these questions: *¿Qué información hay en el cartel de una película? ¿Cómo debe promocionar el cartel la película?*

Preparation

- Discuss film festivals that students have heard of or attended. What benefits can they see of film festivals as cultural events?

Texto: Un cartel de cine

- Ask students to read the introduction to the dialogue silently. Then have them refer to their answers to the Independent Starter and list ideas for Michelle and Daniel.

- Ask for volunteers to read the dialogue between Michelle and Daniel aloud. Do students know other Spanish-language movies that they can recommend?

Activities

7. Keep a list of the students' favorite movies and actors. The class can then celebrate their own film festival. Students can vote for *la mejor película, mejor actor, actriz*, etc. Students can role-play their favorite celebrities arriving on the red carpet.

288

Un cartel de cine

 Michelle and Daniel have to organize a film festival by choosing five Hispanic movies. They will need to make a poster to promote the movies and their festival.

MICHELLE: Tenemos que elegir cinco películas para el festival de cine. ¿Podrías ayudarme, por favor?

DANIEL: ¿Cinco películas hispanas? Pero... ¿no podemos poner nuestras películas favoritas de Hollywood?

MICHELLE: ¡Noooo! Hay películas muy buenas hechas en algunos países hispanos. México, Argentina y España, por ejemplo, producen muchas películas cada año.

DANIEL: ¿Tú crees?

MICHELLE: Pues claro. Hace poco vi *Nocturna*, una película española de animación. El protagonista es un niño que intenta evitar que las estrellas se apaguen. Tienes que verla, te va a encantar.

DANIEL: Puede ser. Pero yo no veo muchas películas en español. Y no creo que los estudiantes puedan entenderlas.

MICHELLE: Creo que te equivocas. Ya entendemos bastante español. Además, podemos poner películas con subtítulos.

DANIEL: Si tú lo dices... Oye, además de elegir las películas, necesitamos información del evento para hacer el cartel de promoción.

MICHELLE: Tienes razón. Estoy segura de que tengo los datos en algún lugar... Sí, aquí están. Las funciones serán el próximo sábado en el auditorio.

DANIEL: ¡Perfecto! ¡Manos a la obra!

6 **Detective de palabras**

▶ **Completa** estas oraciones.

1. Michelle y Daniel van a seleccionar cinco ___1___ para un festival de ___2___.
2. Michelle vio hace poco una película española de ___3___.
3. El ___4___ de *Nocturna* es un niño.
4. Michelle sugiere poner películas con ___5___.
5. El festival será el sábado en el ___6___.

288 doscientos ochenta y ocho

Differentiated Instruction

DEVELOPING LEARNERS

- Ask students to read the dialogue silently and to look for any words or expressions that denote agreement *(tienes razón, ¡perfecto!)*, disagreement *(¡noooo!, creo que te equivocas)*, doubt or skepticism *(¿tú crees?, puede ser, si tú lo dices)*, or certainty *(pues claro, estoy segura)*. Have students say these expressions or write them in their notebooks. After students identify these words, ask them to say or write other expressions that could be used in their place.

EXPANDING LEARNERS

- Ask students to work with a partner and rewrite Michelle and Daniel's script. They need to keep the same objective for the *desafío*, but their approach and the information they may have on Spanish-language films will differ. Encourage students to create the roles so that one is the more positive of the two. Give students time to rehearse their lines and call on volunteers to act out their skits in front of the class.

7 **¿Comprendes?**

▶ **Responde** a estas preguntas.

1. ¿Por qué crees que Daniel prefiere elegir películas de Hollywood?
2. ¿Qué problema ve Daniel en poner películas en español en el festival?
3. ¿Qué idea le sugiere Michelle?
4. ¿Qué datos piensas que deben incluir Michelle y Daniel en el cartel de promoción?
5. ¿A ti te gustaría ver la película *Nocturna*? ¿Por qué?

 8 **El festival de cine**

 ▶ **Escucha** y decide si estas oraciones son ciertas o falsas.

1. Michelle y Daniel hablan de un festival de cine que se celebra en México.
2. Este festival tiene lugar en diciembre.
3. En el festival compiten las mejores películas del cine español.
4. La película *Babel* estuvo nominada para siete premios Oscar de Hollywood.
5. Gael García Bernal es un director español de cine.

 ▶ **Escucha** de nuevo y corrige las oraciones falsas.

 9 **Te toca a ti**

 ▶ **Habla** con tu compañero(a) sobre tu película favorita. Dile cuál es, de qué trata, quiénes son los protagonistas y por qué te gusta tanto. Después, informa a la clase sobre la película favorita de tu compañero(a).

 CULTURA

El Festival de Cine de San Sebastián

San Sebastián es una ciudad situada al norte de España, en la costa del mar Cantábrico. En ella se celebra un famoso festival de cine al que acuden importantes directores y actores de todo el mundo. Además de los premios habituales (mejor director, mejor película, mejor guion...), desde 1986 se entrega el premio Donostia como homenaje a grandes figuras del cine. Entre los premiados, por ejemplo, están Susan Sarandon, Robert de Niro, Woody Allen, Antonio Banderas y Julia Roberts.

Antonio Banderas, actor español.

10 **Explica.** ¿Por qué crees que se celebran tantos festivales internacionales de cine? ¿Piensas que una película puede reflejar la cultura de su país? ¿Cómo?

doscientos ochenta y nueve **289**

HERITAGE LANGUAGE LEARNERS

• Michelle and Daniel have to choose five Spanish-language films, but heritage learners will perhaps be familiar with more Hispanic films. Ask students to do some research on leading Hispanic actors, directors, and popular films from the present or the past. Assign different topics to each student to avoid duplication. After students have gathered their information, ask them to share it with the rest of the class in the form of an oral presentation.

MULTIPLE INTELLIGENCES:
Musical-Rhythmic Intelligence

• Ask students to work in small groups and to imagine that they are songwriters. Their challenge is to write an award-winning song for a movie that is sure to be a nominee at a Spanish-language film festival. Group members must combine their talents and come up with a song worthy of an award. Students should determine the film's setting and plot before they start on the lyrics. Give them time to rehearse before performing their song. Then take a class vote to see who gets the award.

Unit 6

DESAFÍO 1

Expresar opiniones

10. Ask students to share examples of movies that they believe reflect "American culture." Ask them to explain why they believe this to be so.

 AUDIO SCRIPT
See page 281I.

 CULTURA

El Festival de Cine de San Sebastián
Every September, the Spanish city of San Sebastián hosts an international film festival. Since 1953, countries from all over the world have been invited to submit films. Some of the various categories in which the films compete are: films made in Spain, Basque films, and films from Latin America. The "Golden Shell" is awarded to the best picture; the "Silver Shell" goes to the best director, actress, and actor.

Answer Key

6. 1. películas   4. protagonista
     2. cine   5. subtítulos
     3. animación   6. auditorio
7. 1. Answers will vary.
     2. Piensa que los estudiantes no van a entenderlas.
     3. Poner películas con subtítulos.
     4. Answers will vary.
     5. Answers will vary.
8. 1. Falso. Hablan de un festival de cine que se celebra en España.
     2. Falso. Tiene lugar en septiembre.
     3. Falso. Compiten películas del cine internacional.
     4. Cierto.
     5. Falso. Gael García Bernal es un actor mexicano.
9. Answers will vary.
10. Answers will vary.

Additional Resources

Fans Online activities

289

Unit 6
DESAFÍO 1

Vocabulario – Ocio y espectáculos

Presentation

- In this section, students will learn vocabulary relating to different entertainment events that people might attend in their free time.

Activities	Standards	Resources
Vocabulario	1.2	
11.	1.1, 1.3	
12.	1.1, 1.2, 2.2	
13.	1.2	Audio
14. Comparaciones	1.1, 1.2, 2.1, 2.2, 4.2	

Teaching Suggestions

Warm-Up / Independent Starter

- Ask students to write their answers to the following questions: *¿Qué espectáculos te gustan? ¿Has asistido alguna vez a un concierto? ¿A cuál? ¿Vas al teatro de vez en cuando? ¿Prefieres ver las película en el cine, en la computadora o en la televisión? ¿Por qué?*

Preparation

- Review students' answers to the questions in the Independent Starter as a class. Then ask students to create a list of categories represented by the examples mentioned by their classmates. Place each entertainment option within one of the categories.

- Ask students to work with a partner to define each of the movie genres listed in the *Más vocabulario* feature. Which is their favorite? Invite students to share with the class their favorite movies from each genre.

Activities

13. After students have finished this activity, have them write a short review of a play, musical, ballet, or concert that they attended. (If they have not attended one of these events, ask them to write about a TV show or sporting event.) Before writing, ask the class what information should be included in such a review. What information would prospective spectators like to know before they attend?

290

Vocabulario

Ocio y espectáculos

¿Te apetece ir esta tarde a un musical?

Podemos reservar los boletos por Internet. Así no tenemos que hacer fila en la taquilla. ¿Reservo boletos para la función de las seis?

Es que no me gustan los musicales... Pero podemos ir al cine. Este fin de semana estrenan muchas películas.

la cartelera

la sala
el telón
el escenario
el público
la butaca
el pasillo
la ópera
el ballet
el circo
el concierto

Más vocabulario

Cine y teatro

aplaudir	to applaud
la audiencia	audience
el auditorio	auditorium
el/la protagonista	main character

la película...
cómica	comedy
de acción/aventura	action/adventure
de ciencia ficción	science fiction
de dibujos animados	animated
de suspenso	thriller
de terror	horror
dramática	drama
policíaca	detective
romántica	romance

11 **El intruso**

 ▶ **Escribe** la palabra que no corresponde en cada grupo. Explícale a tu compañero(a) por qué no pertenece a ese grupo.

1	2	3	4
escenario	cómico	concierto	público
pasillo	dramático	ópera	boleto
sala	circo	protagonista	taquilla
cartelera	romántico	*ballet*	butaca

290 doscientos noventa

Differentiated Instruction

DEVELOPING LEARNERS

- Ask students to choose the correct word or phrase to complete these sentences:
  1. *Compro las entradas en...* (b)
     a. *la función*   b. *la taquilla*
  2. *El público ... si le gusta el espectáculo.* (a)
     a. *aplaude*   b. *estrena*
  3. *Bajan ... al final del ballet.* (a)
     a. *el telón*   b. *el escenario*
  4. *Prefiero ... al lado del pasillo.* (a)
     a. *una butaca*   b. *un telón*
  5. *Vamos a la ... para ver películas.* (b)
     a. *cartelera*   b. *sala de cine*

EXPANDING LEARNERS

- Tell students that they need to explain what each of the new vocabulary words mean, but in Spanish, not English. Ask them to work with a partner and prepare their definitions. You may get them started by giving them these examples: *Estrenar quiere decir representar algo por primera vez. El auditorio es el lugar donde se presentan obras teatrales, películas, óperas o ballet.* Call on volunteers to read their definitions, and have students write the most accurate definitions in their notebooks.

12 Carteles

 Observa estos carteles de películas españolas. ¿A qué género crees que pertenecen?

 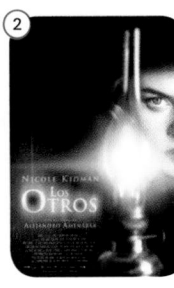 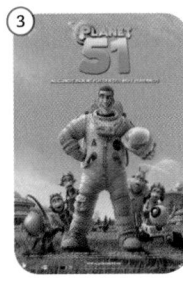

 Habla con tu compañero(a). ¿Cuál de esas películas preferirías ver? ¿Por qué?

Modelo A. *A mí me gustaría ver ¿Para qué sirve un oso? porque parece muy divertida.*
B. *Pues yo prefiero las películas de terror.*

13 Los mejores fans del mundo

 Escucha a dos amigos y elige la opción correcta.

1. Diego fue...
   a. al cine   **b.** al circo   **c.** a un concierto
2. Diego y su hermano tuvieron suerte porque...
   a. consiguieron boletos   **b.** no llovió   **c.** las butacas eran cómodas
3. El evento tuvo lugar...
   a. en el cine   **b.** en el auditorio   **c.** en el teatro
4. A Diego le encantaron...
   a. los fans   **b.** los bailarines   **c.** los efectos especiales
5. Al final del concierto, el público...
   a. aplaudió mucho   **b.** se quejó   **c.** hizo muchas fotos

 **COMPARACIONES**

Las películas extranjeras

En los cines de los Estados Unidos no suelen verse películas extranjeras. En cambio, en otros países suelen proyectar películas americanas o de otros países, a veces en versión original con subtítulos.

Ver películas extranjeras nos puede enseñar mucho sobre otras culturas y hacernos reflexionar sobre la nuestra.

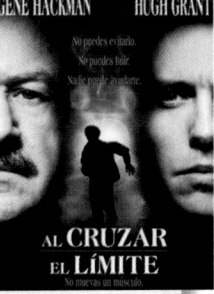

14 **Compara.** Las películas estadounidenses que tienen éxito en otros países suelen ser películas de acción. ¿Por qué piensas que es así? ¿Qué géneros crees que son los más interculturales?

HERITAGE LANGUAGE LEARNERS

• Of course, American films are foreign films in all the other countries around the world, including the students' heritage countries. Ask heritage learners what American films have had an impact on the movie industry in their family's country of origin, and what actors from the United States are especially popular. Ask them if movies are usually dubbed, or if they have subtitles. Have them share with the class the titles of some recent popular films, and see if the class can guess the titles in English.

TOTAL PHYSICAL RESPONSE (TPR)

• Divide the class into two or four teams and have them play "Charades" against each other. Write each of the new words on an index card or strip of paper and place them in a bag (each team will receive a set). Players will take turns picking a word and then pantomiming it so team members can guess what it is. Give students a time limit in which to guess the word. If a team fails to guess correctly, play goes to the other team.

---

14. Ask students to prepare a list of the most popular movies made in the United States. What aspects of American culture are depicted in these movies? Which of these aspects might be a true representation of American culture and which might be stereotypes? How can we distinguish between cultural characteristics and stereotypes? Discuss what we can learn about other cultures from watching their films.

 AUDIO SCRIPT
See page 281I.

 COMPARACIONES

Las películas extranjeras

Foreign-language films in the United States are generally subtitled, whereas in many other countries they are usually dubbed. Subtitles are not popular with the general public; many moviegoers feel that subtitles are distracting when watching a film. But foreign film-friendly audiences prefer the experience of the authentic voices of the actors and they feel that a subtitled film preserves the artistic integrity of the film better than a dubbed film. Notwithstanding some objections to subtitling, there is a growing interest in the United States for foreign films.

Answer Key

11. 1. cartelera   3. protagonista
      2. circo   4. público

12. Answers will vary. Sample answers:
      1. cómica   3. de dibujos animados
      2. de suspenso
      ▶ Answers will vary.

13. 1. c   2. a   3. b   4. c   5. a

14. Answers will vary.

Additional Resources

Fans Online activities
Practice Workbook

Unit 6
DESAFÍO 1

Gramática – Expresar opinión

Presentation

- In this section, students will learn the difference between using the indicative and the subjunctive in order to express a personal opinion.

Activities	Standards	Resources
Gramática	1.2, 3.1	
15.	1.2, 4.1	
16.	1.2, 1.3	
17.	1.2, 1.3	Audio
18.	1.1, 1.2, 2.1, 2.2, 3.1, 3.2, 5.1, 5.2	

Teaching Suggestions

Warm-Up / Independent Starter

- Ask students to complete the following sentences:
  1. *Yo creo que Antonio Banderas…*
  2. *Mi mamá opina que las películas románticas…*
  3. *Me parece que el circo…*
  4. *Mi mejor amigo(a) piensa que la ópera…*
  5. *Los alumnos suponen que las películas de terror…*

Preparation

- Ask for five volunteers to each write their answer to one of the sentences in the Independent Starter on the board. Then go over the grammar presentation as a class. Ask students to correct the sentences they wrote on the board if necessary. Make sure that all of the verbs are in the indicative mood, since the sentences express opinions in the affirmative.

- Review the formation of the present subjunctive so that the conjugation won't be an obstacle to the correct completion of the exercises. Remind students that the present subjunctive is formed by using the *yo* form of the verb in the present indicative and that there are many irregular *yo* forms (e.g., *conozco, digo, hago*). They also need to consider stem-changing verbs. However, there are only six true irregular verbs in the present subjunctive: *ir, ser, dar, estar, saber, haber.* Provide students with a practice worksheet of the present subjunctive. For example: *estrenar (yo), recoger (tú), aplaudir (él),* etc.

Gramática

Expresar opinión

Verbos para expresar opinión

- To express a personal opinion in Spanish, use structures like the following:

OPINION VERB		OPINION
Creo	+ que +	la película **es** divertida.
No creo	+ que +	la película **sea** divertida.

VERBOS DE OPINIÓN

creer	parecer
imaginar	pensar
opinar	suponer

- The verb parecer works like the verb gustar: it is conjugated in the third person and it requires an object pronoun.

  Me parece que este es el mejor director de cine del mundo.

El indicativo y el subjuntivo con los verbos de opinión

- Opinion verbs can be used in affirmative or negative statements.
  - When the verb in the main clause states an opinion in the **affirmative**, use the **indicative mood** in the dependent clause.

    Los críticos <u>piensan</u> que la soprano **canta** bien.
    <u>Me parece</u> que **es** una buena película.

  - When the verb in the main clause states an opinion in the **negative**, use the **subjunctive mood** in the dependent clause.

    Los críticos <u>no piensan</u> que la soprano **cante** bien.
    <u>No me parece</u> que **sea** una buena película.

CONSTRUCCIONES AFIRMATIVAS

creer
imaginar
opinar
parecer + que + indicative
pensar
suponer

CONSTRUCCIONES NEGATIVAS

no creer
no parecer + que + subjunctive
no pensar

15 **Compara.** ¿Se emplean formas verbales distintas en inglés para expresar opiniones afirmativas y negativas?

16 **Yo no lo creo**

▶ **Escribe** la respuesta a estas opiniones usando construcciones negativas.

Modelo   Creo que las butacas de ese teatro son muy cómodas.
  → *Pues yo no creo que sean cómodas, porque es un teatro muy viejo.*

1. Pienso que el parque es el mejor lugar para celebrar el concierto.
2. Yo creo que el teatro es un espectáculo muy aburrido.
3. A mí me parece que todas las películas de terror son malísimas.
4. Creo que ser director de cine es el mejor trabajo del mundo.

292 doscientos noventa y dos

Differentiated Instruction

DEVELOPING LEARNERS

- Ask students to write one sentence that expresses what they believe or think (using *creer* and *pensar*), and one that states what something seems to be to them (using *parecer*). Then have them use these same verbs, but in negative constructions so that they will use the subjunctive mood. Remind students that the subjunctive is always used with these verbs in negative constructions when there is a change of subject. Ask students to share their sentences with the rest of the class.

EXPANDING LEARNERS

- Have students work with a partner and, taking turns, create several short dialogues between an optimist and a pessimist. The optimists will, of course, use the affirmative constructions listed on the page, while the pessimists will counter their partner's remarks with some of the negative expressions, along with the corresponding subjunctive mood. Give students time to practice their dialogues and then call on some pairs to present one or two exchanges before the rest of the class.

Left page

 17 **De acuerdo**

▶ **Completa** estas oraciones poniendo los verbos en el tiempo y modo correctos.

1. No me apetece. Pienso que en esos espectáculos _____ a los animales.
   _{maltratar}

2. Pienso que _____ una idea fenomenal; me encanta ese grupo.
   _{ser}

3. Creo que _____ ir al evento literario; me fascina ese autor.
   _{preferir}

4. No creo que _____ boletos porque es un *ballet* muy famoso.
   _{quedar}

5. No creo que _____ una buena idea ir al cine con Pedrito.
   _{ser}

▶ **Escucha** y relaciona las propuestas con las oraciones correspondientes del apartado anterior.

 18 **Una noche de jazz**

▶ **Lee** estas propuestas de ocio y decide a cuáles te gustaría asistir y a cuáles no.

GUÍA DE OCIO: ESTRENOS

MÚSICA
Orquesta Nacional de Jazz (jueves 7, 8:00 p. m., sala La Luna)
La ONJ interpretará varias canciones de su último disco *Mujeres del jazz*, una recopilación de temas para disfrutar y bailar al ritmo del mejor jazz.

Christina Aguilera en concierto (viernes 8, 10:00 p. m., Palacio de la Música.
Christina Aguilera presenta las canciones de su último disco y recuerda sus grandes éxitos.

CINE
Festival de cine argentino (de jueves 7 a sábado 9, Cine Capitol)
Selección de las mejores películas argentinas de los últimos diez años. Consultar cartelera.

TEATRO-MUSICALES
Cats **(viernes 8, 9:00 p. m., Teatro Sol)**
Representación del famoso musical a cargo de la compañía Pasos.

BALLET
Ballet Nacional de Cuba: *La magia de la danza*
(viernes 8, 7:00 p. m., Teatro Real)
La famosísima compañía de *ballet* ofrece en su último espectáculo una selección de fragmentos de clásicos como *El lago de los cisnes*, *Giselle* o *Don Quijote*.

 ▶ **Habla** con tu compañero(a). Expresa tus preferencias y averigua si quiere ir contigo a ver alguno de esos espectáculos.

Modelo   A. *Pienso que debemos ir al concierto de jazz porque la orquesta es buenísima.*
B. *Yo no, es que no me gusta nada el jazz. Me parece que es mejor ir a...*

doscientos noventa y tres **293**

HERITAGE LANGUAGE LEARNERS

• Ask students to write a descriptive paragraph about a totally pessimistic person. This individual could be real or fictional, but needs to be the voice of gloom. Students should use the negative constructions on page 292, but encourage them to go beyond these expressions to complete their paragraphs and to give life to their character. Call on volunteers to read their compositions aloud and, if the character they are describing is real, see if the other students can guess who it is.

CRITICAL THINKING

• Ask students to consider the genres presented in *Guía de ocio: Estrenos* in activity 18. Ask them to state which one they think best exemplifies the culture of either the United States or a Spanish-speaking country. Encourage students to do some research on the topic in order to support their reasons. After students state their reasons, ask them to write their own short, descriptive paragraph for the event's premiere and be prepared to read their compositions aloud.

Right page

Activities

17. To expand this activity, ask students to give an opinion about each of the following statements:
1. *En el circo maltratan a los animales.*
2. *A los jóvenes no les gusta la ópera.*
3. *La música es la lengua universal.*
4. *Los niños pequeños no deben ir al cine.*

18. As an extension of this activity, ask students to use local newspapers or the Internet to identify five cultural events that are currently happening in your area. Ask them to describe one to a classmate and come to a consensus as to which event they might like to attend.

 AUDIO SCRIPT
See page 281I.

Answer Key

15. No. Por ejemplo: *I think Meryl Streep is a good actress.* (Creo que Meryl Streep es una buena actriz.) *I don't think Meryl Street is a good actress.* (No creo que Meryl Streep sea una buena actriz.)

16. Answers will vary. Sample answers:
1. No pienso que el parque sea el mejor lugar, porque hay mosquitos.
2. No creo que el teatro sea un espectáculo aburrido, porque las actuaciones son en vivo.
3. Pues a mí no me parece que todas las películas de terror sean malísimas.
4. No creo que ser director de cine sea el mejor trabajo del mundo porque tienen muchas responsabilidades.

17. 1. maltratan   4. queden
2. es   5. sea
3. prefiero
▶ 1. 2   2. 5   3. 1   4. 4   5. 3

18. Answers will vary.

Additional Resources

Fans Online activities
Practice Workbook

293

DESAFÍO 1

Gramática – Fórmulas gramaticales de cortesía

Presentation

- In this section, students will learn how to show respect for people in social situations by using expressions of courtesy.

Activities	Standards	Resources
Gramática	1.2, 2.1, 3.1	
19.	2.1, 4.1	
20.	1.1, 1.2, 2.1, 3.1, 5.1	Audio
21.	1.3, 2.1	
22.	1.1, 1.2, 1.3, 2.1	
23. Cultura	1.2, 1.3, 2.1, 4.2, 5.1	

Teaching Suggestions

Warm-Up / Independent Starter

- Ask students to write a list of all of the words and phrases they can think of that indicate politeness or courtesy. These can be as simple as the word *gracias*, or the use of *usted* as opposed to *tú*.

Preparation

- Review the Independent Starter in small groups. Ask each group to report their findings and make a master list for the class.

- Instruct students to read the grammar explanation on page 294. Have them brainstorm two or three examples of social situations that would require them to use these expressions of courtesy. You can use this grammar presentation as an opportunity to review the formation of each verb tense given, as well as any irregular verbs.

Activities

20. Ask students to explain this refrain: *La cortesía no cuesta nada.* Have students give personal examples of their experiences with courtesy and when it has been important.

22. Instruct students to take notes while their classmates present their dialogues. Which expressions of courtesy are used? To facilitate students' note taking, ask them to create a five-column chart with these headings: *Grupo, Por favor, Una pregunta, El condicional, El imperfecto.*

Gramática

Fórmulas gramaticales de cortesía

La cortesía

- All languages have expressions of courtesy, or polite phrases, to show respect for people in social situations. These expressions normally accompany requests or commands.

- Two common ways of making polite requests in Spanish are:
  - Using por favor to soften a direct command: Préstame el libro, **por favor**.
  - Phrasing the request as a question: ¿Me prestas el libro?

- Other polite forms of making requests include using the conditional and the imperfect indicative.

El condicional de cortesía

- In Spanish, as in English, the conditional tense is often used to make polite requests.

  —¿**Podrías** prestarme el libro?　　　—¿Puedo ayudarla?
  —Sí, por supuesto.　　　　　　　　　—Sí, me **gustaría** cambiar estos boletos.

El imperfecto de cortesía

- When purchasing something, it is common to use the imperfect indicative verb forms to make a polite request. In this case, it does not refer to the past; it is simply an expression of courtesy.

  —¿Qué desea?
  —**Quería** reservar dos boletos.
  —¿Para cuándo los quiere?

19 **Compara.** Analiza los ejemplos anteriores. ¿Qué fórmulas de cortesía usarías en inglés en cada caso? ¿Hay fórmulas más corteses que otras?

20 **La cortesía no cuesta nada**

 ▶ **Escucha** cada oración y decide. ¿La persona que habla usa una forma de cortesía?

 ▶ **Piensa** tres cosas que puedes pedir ahora mismo a tu compañero(a). Pídeselas usando formas corteses y responde a sus peticiones.

Modelo　A. ¿Podrías prestarme un lápiz?
　　　　　B. Claro. Toma.
　　　　　A. Gracias.

Differentiated Instruction

DEVELOPING LEARNERS

- Ask students to bring in images from old magazines and, working with a partner, to create short dialogues that relate to the images. Partners will take turns asking one another to do something related to the image, and the other should respond. Both students must use some of the expressions of courtesy presented on the page. For example:
  A. ¿Podrías ayudarme con la tarea de Español?
  B. ¡Por supuesto! Me encantaría ayudarte.

- Ask students to present their dialogues in front of the class.

EXPANDING LEARNERS

- Give students more practice with the expressions of courtesy by having them write a short dialogue between *una persona maleducada* and *una persona muy cortés*. The rude person will give an unending stream of commands to the courteous person, who will respond by rephrasing each gruff command with an expression of courtesy. For example:
  A. ¡Dame ese libro ahora mismo!
  B. ¿Podrías darme ese libro cuando tengas tiempo?

- Invite some students to act out their dialogues in front of the class.

21 **¡No seas maleducado!**

▶ **Escribe** estas oraciones usando otras formas de cortesía.

Modelo Ven conmigo al estreno del espectáculo, por favor.
→ *¿Podrías venir conmigo al estreno?*

1. ¿Puedes averiguar cuándo se ponen a la venta los boletos?
2. Llama a nuestros amigos para ver si quieren ir con nosotros, por favor.
3. ¿Vas tú a la taquilla para comprar los boletos?
4. Compra los boletos más baratos, por favor.
5. Podríamos reunirnos en mi casa antes de salir para ir al teatro.

22 **¡Qué corteses son!**

▶ **Habla** con tu compañero(a). Escriban un diálogo para una de estas escenas y represéntenlo para la clase. Usen expresiones de cortesía.

Modelo A. *¿Me podrías decir a qué hora empieza el concierto?*
B. *Claro. Empieza a las ocho.*

 **CULTURA**

La Noche en Blanco

En varias ciudades del mundo se organizan exposiciones, espectáculos y otros eventos culturales durante una noche específica del año. Es lo que se conoce como la Noche en Blanco. La idea surgió en París en 2002 y se extendió a otras ciudades, como Madrid, Roma, Lima o La Paz. En los Estados Unidos se celebran eventos similares: Luminaria, en San Antonio, y Sleepless Night, en Miami.

La Noche en Blanco (Madrid).

 23 **Investiga.** Averigua qué espectáculos se organizaron en la última edición de la Noche en Blanco en Madrid. Elige los tres que te parezcan más interesantes y explica por qué.

HERITAGE LANGUAGE LEARNERS

• Ask students to give some more examples of polite phrases or constructions, as well as when and with whom these phrases may be used. For example, *Tenga la bondad de… / ¿Tendría la bondad de…?* might be used in a more formal setting, and to a person whom students would address with *usted*. Students might use *quisiera* to express something they would like to do or have (e.g., *Quisiera un té con limón, por favor*). Other expressions include *importar* (e.g., *¿Te importaría ayudarme a limpiar?*). Ask students to share these expressions with the rest of the class.

COOPERATIVE LEARNING

• Ask students to work in small groups and organize their own *Noche en Blanco* for their community. Each member of the group will focus on one event, which could range from theater, film, dance, or music to an art or photography exhibition. First, group members need to discuss the overall theme of the night. Then, students will write a description of their event, and afterward get together with the group to come up with a brief introduction to the *Noche en Blanco* and include their individual descriptions.

 AUDIO SCRIPT
See page 281I.

 CULTURA

La Noche en Blanco

Every September, Madrid celebrates its art and culture. From sunset to sunrise, thousands of *madrileños,* as well as thousands of visitors, have the opportunity to attend more than 150 cultural events. There are different types of exhibitions, interactive art projects, live music, dance, and theatrical performances. The city's parks and major museums stay open late and admission is free.

Answer Key

19. En inglés usamos también la palabra *please* (por favor), el condicional y preguntas con *can, could, may, will* y *would*. Las fórmulas con *could, may* y *would* son las más corteses.

20. 1. sí 2. sí 3. no 4. sí 5. no 6. no
▶ Answers will vary.

21. Answers will vary. Sample answers:
1. ¿Podrías averiguar cuándo…?
2. ¿Llamas tú a nuestros amigos para…?
3. Vete, por favor, a la taquilla para…
4. ¿Podrías comprar los boletos…?
5. ¿Nos reunimos en mi casa antes de…?

22. Answers will vary.

23. Answers will vary.

Additional Resources

Fans Online activities
Practice Workbook

LECTURA: TEXTO DIALOGADO

Presentation

- In this section, students will read a dialogue, identify the Spanish-language movies and Spanish-speaking actors contained within, and answer comprehension questions based on the reading.

Activities	Standards	Resources
Lectura: texto dialogado	1.2, 1.3, 2.1, 2.2, 3.1, 3.2, 5.1	Vis. Pres.
24.	1.2, 1.3, 2.2, 5.1	
25.	1.2, 1.3, 3.1	
26.	1.1, 1.2, 1.3, 2.2, 5.1	
27.	1.3, 5.2	

Teaching Suggestions

Warm-Up / Independent Starter

- Ask students to make a list of foreign movies and actors and actresses they know. Then have students write five sentences stating their opinions about these movies and actors.

Preparation

- In order to prepare students to talk about the topic of movies, ask them related questions. For example: *¿Qué películas les gustan: de acción, románticas, cómicas…? ¿Cuáles son, en su opinión, los mejores actores en la actualidad? ¿Por qué? ¿Y los mejores directores? ¿En qué piensan cuando oyen la palabra Hollywood?*

- Have students read the *Antes de leer* section silently and ask them to work in pairs to complete each question. Then have pairs share their answers with another pair of students.

- Ask students to share the names of the films that they have identified before reading the text. Have they watched these movies? Can they briefly summarize what these movies are about? Ask them if they recognize some of the actors and directors.

- Read the dialogue aloud to students, modeling correct pronunciation and intonation. Then call on several pairs of students to alternate reading the dialogue aloud. Offer suggestions to improve their oral reading.

Antes de leer: estrategias

1. Lee el título y mira las fotos. ¿De qué hablan Michelle y Daniel? ¿Qué piensas que pueden decir sobre ese tema?
2. Lee superficialmente *(scan)* el texto. Identifica los títulos de las películas que están en cursiva *(italics)*. ¿Reconoces alguna? ¿Qué sabes sobre ella?
3. Busca los nombres propios e investiga quiénes son esas personas. Compáralos con directores o actores que ya conoces.

De cine

MICHELLE: Daniel, ¿investigaste sobre el cine en español?

DANIEL: Sí. Y pienso que tiene muy buenos actores y directores. También averigüé que hay bastantes películas que ganaron premios importantes, como *Biutiful*, del director mexicano Alejandro González Iñárritu.

MICHELLE: Es la película que estuvo nominada para los Oscar, ¿no? La que protagoniza Javier Bardem…

DANIEL: Sí, eso es. También estuvo nominado varias veces el director español Pedro Almodóvar.

MICHELLE: Ah, sí. Yo creo que es el director de cine español más famoso en los Estados Unidos. Pero nunca he visto una película suya.

DANIEL: Yo tampoco, pero sé que hizo una con Penélope Cruz que se titulaba *Volver*. Y dime, ¿encontraste alguna comedia latinoamericana para nuestro festival?

MICHELLE: Hay muchísimas comedias de México, Colombia, Chile y Argentina. Me gustó *Nueve reinas*. Es una película argentina de acción muy divertida. Cuenta la historia de dos estafadores *(con men)* que intentan robar medio millón de dólares.

DANIEL: ¿Y participa algún actor famoso?

MICHELLE: Sí, Ricardo Darín.

DANIEL: No sé quién es. Solo conozco a ese actor mexicano que te gusta tanto, Gael García Bernal.

MICHELLE: Piensa un poco, Daniel, conoces a muchos más actores hispanos. No me digas que no sabes quiénes son Salma Hayek, Jennifer López, Eva Mendes, Antonio Banderas o Guillermo del Toro.

DANIEL: Ah, sí, tienes razón. Oye, podríamos invitar a Salma y a Gael a nuestro festival…

Alejandro González Iñárritu, director de cine mexicano.

Gael García Bernal, actor mexicano.

296 doscientos noventa y seis

Differentiated Instruction

DEVELOPING LEARNERS

- Ask students to match the people in the first column with the type of movies in which they would most likely appear.

1. *unos novios* (f)
2. *un payaso* (d)
3. *un detective* (a)
4. *un pez que habla* (b)
5. *un explorador* (c)
6. *un monstruo* (e)

a. *una película policíaca*
b. *dibujos animados*
c. *una película de aventura*
d. *una película cómica*
e. *una película de terror*
f. *una película romántica*

EXPANDING LEARNERS

- Explain to students that titles often "make" a best-selling book or an award-winning movie. Have students write the titles of five or six of their favorite films and then think of other titles that might have made the film even more appealing or, to the contrary, could have squashed it at the box office. After students rewrite their titles, have volunteers share them with the class. Ask the other students to guess what the original titles of these movies were.

24 Comprensión

▶ **Busca** la siguiente información en el diálogo y completa estas fichas. Si no encuentras algún dato, puedes mirar en Internet.

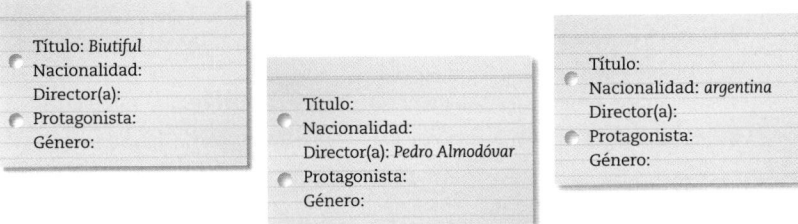

Título: *Biutiful*
Nacionalidad:
Director(a):
Protagonista:
Género:

Título:
Nacionalidad:
Director(a): *Pedro Almodóvar*
Protagonista:
Género:

Título:
Nacionalidad: *argentina*
Director(a):
Protagonista:
Género:

25 Palabras útiles

▶ **Completa** una tabla como esta con palabras del texto. ¿Pudiste aprender muchos términos útiles?

Palabra	Significado posible (hipótesis)	Significado del diccionario	Ejemplo
nominada	*named*	*nominated*	La película fue nominada para un Oscar.

26 Lo que ya sabes

▶ **Habla** con tu compañero(a) sobre el cine hispano. Puedes seguir este guion:

1. ¿Conoces alguna película española o latinoamericana? ¿Cómo se llama? ¿De qué trata?
2. ¿Conoces a algún actor o a alguna actriz hispanos? ¿Cómo se llama? ¿En qué película(s) actúa?
3. ¿Qué tipo de películas te gustan? ¿Por qué?
4. ¿Qué película recomendarías a tu compañero(a)? ¿Por qué? ¿De qué trata?
5. ¿Qué te parece más importante en una película: el director, los actores, la acción...? ¿Por qué?

27 Con tus propias palabras

▶ **Piensa** en tu película favorita y completa una ficha como esta.

Título:
Nacionalidad:
Director(a):
Protagonista:
Género:
Sinopsis:

Unit 6

LECTURA: TEXTO DIALOGADO

- Have students look for cognates in the dialogue (e.g., *nominado, comedia, acción*). Use gestures or context to explain words that they may not be familiar with.

Activities

24. Before working on this activity, test students' knowledge by having them find the following information in the dialogue: *tres títulos de películas* (*Biutiful, Volver, Nueve reinas*); *dos actores mexicanos* (Salma Hayek, Gael García Bernal); *un director español* (Pedro Almodóvar); *un director mexicano* (Alejandro González Iñárritu); *dos actores españoles* (Javier Bardem, Penélope Cruz).

26. To expand this activity, show some posters of Spanish-language movies, and have students guess what they are about. Ask students to discuss if they would like to see each movie, and to explain why or why not.

Answer Key

24. 1. Nacionalidad: mexicana
   Director: Alejandro González Iñárritu
   Protagonista: Javier Bardem
   Género: dramática

   2. Título: *Volver*
   Nacionalidad: española
   Protagonista: Penélope Cruz
   Género: dramática

   3. Título: *Nueve reinas*
   Director: Fabián Bielinsky
   Protagonista: Ricardo Darín
   Género: acción

25. Answers will vary.

26. Answers will vary.

27. Answers will vary.

Additional Resources

Fans Online activities

HERITAGE LANGUAGE LEARNERS

- Ask students to read *De cine* silently and, using words from the dialogue, make a word family chart. Students will need to place each word under the corresponding heading of *Verbo, Nombre,* or *Adjetivo/Participio pasado.* Encourage students to include as many words as they can in their charts and to use their dictionaries if needed. You may want to get them started by providing the following examples: *Verbo → investigaste; Nombre → investigación; Adjetivo/Participio pasado → investigado.*

COOPERATIVE LEARNING

- People in the arts often talk about the ideal or "dream" cast. Ask small groups of students to come up with a dream cast of their own. The participants might be protagonists of a movie, a TV series, or a musical production. First, all members of the group must come to a consensus regarding the type of spectacle they want and describe it in a few words. Then, all must contribute the names of several actors, singers, or musicians. Allow students to discuss these nominees and then have them come to a unanimous decision. Have them describe their "dream cast" to the class.

DESAFÍO 1

Comunicación

Presentation

■ In this section, students will integrate the vocabulary and grammar skills from *Desafío 1* in order to describe various types of entertainment and cultural events.

Activities	Standards	Resources
28.	1.1, 1.2, 2.1, 2.2, 3.1, 3.2	
29.	1.2, 2.2	Audio
30.	1.1, 1.3, 3.1, 5.1	
31. Final del desafío	1.1, 1.2, 1.3, 2.1, 2.2, 5.2	

Teaching Suggestions

Warm-Up / Independent Starter

■ Ask students to read the headline and the lead sentence of the news article in activity 28 and predict the content. Have students identify all of the cognates as well as other words they recognize. What type of event is being described?

Preparation

■ Ask students to share their Independent Starters. If possible, print the lyrics of one of the songs sung by Julieta Venegas. White out some of the words of the song and distribute it to students. While you play the song, instruct students to fill in the missing words. Replay the song and ask students to provide the missing lyrics. Then, have students summarize the "story" sung.

Activities

29. Before listening to the audio, ask students to predict what the following phrase might mean: *Ladrón que roba a ladrón*. After listening, ask students to form pairs and role-play the conversation between Michelle and Daniel after they have seen the film *Ladrón que roba a ladrón*. Ask them to include affirmative and negative opinion statements.

30. As students discuss their favorite songs, have them use expressions of courtesy as they talk with their classmates, and have them include opinion statements as they chat with one another.

Comunicación

28 **Venegas conquista México**

▶ **Lee** este artículo sobre un concierto de Julieta Venegas y responde a las preguntas.

1. ¿Cuándo y dónde se celebró el concierto?
2. ¿Con quién actuó Julieta Venegas?
3. ¿Por qué no va a actuar Julieta Venegas durante un tiempo?

EL UNIVERSAL   Sábado, 10 de diciembre de 2011

Julieta Venegas cierra gira en el Auditorio

La cantautora hizo un dueto con sus colegas y compatriotas Carla Morrison y Natalia Lafourcade

Julieta Venegas cerró el viernes su gira «Otra Cosa», que le ha llevado durante un año por diversos escenarios del mundo, ofreciendo un emotivo concierto en el Auditorio Nacional de la capital mexicana en el que repasó lo mejor de su carrera musical.

Tal como lo anticipó, la cantautora mexicana quiso hacer de esta una presentación muy especial e hizo un dueto con sus colegas y compa-triotas Carla Morrison y Natalia Lafourcade. Venegas interpretó un repertorio muy variado, en el que incluyó canciones de sus cinco discos en estudio, entre las cuales destacaron «Amores platónicos», «Otra cosa», «Limón y sal», «Algún día», «Sería feliz» y «Amores perros».

Venegas planea retirarse algunos meses de los escenarios para enfocarse en la composición de los te-

Julieta Venegas, cantante mexicana.

mas que darán vida a su próxima producción discográfica, prevista para 2012.

Fuente: http://www.eluniversal.com.mx
(texto adaptado)

29 **¡Nos encanta el cine!**

 ▶ **Escucha** el diálogo entre Michelle y Daniel, y decide si estas oraciones son ciertas o falsas.

1. Michelle cree que la película ha ganado muchos premios.
2. El protagonista de la película quiere ayudar a los pobres.
3. *Ladrón que roba a ladrón* es una película de ciencia ficción.
4. Daniel piensa que la película es en inglés con subtítulos en español.

 ▶ **Escucha** de nuevo y corrige las oraciones falsas.

Differentiated Instruction

DEVELOPING LEARNERS

• Remind students that recognizing cognates is one way to help them comprehend new material and increase their vocabulary in both Spanish and English. Before students read the article in activity 28, ask them to scan it and write in their notebooks the cognates they see. Alongside each word, have students write the English-language equivalent. Ask students if any of these words are new to them, including those in English. Then have students use five of these words in sentences.

EXPANDING LEARNERS

• Ask students to work with a partner and imagine that they are at the movies. They are going to create a dialogue in which one will be a courteous and quiet movie patron, while the other does more talking than the actors in the film. Explain that the courteous patron's polite requests of the noise maker are to no avail, and the talking continues to get louder and more annoying. The "courteous" one will finally lose patience and make a very direct command to the bothersome patron.

30 Una lista de éxitos

▶ **Escribe** una lista con tus cinco canciones favoritas.

▶ **Comparte** tu lista con la clase y entre todos(as), preparen otra lista con las diez canciones más votadas.

Final del desafío

MICHELLE: Creo que estamos listos para preparar nuestro cartel. ¿Me das los datos que tienes, por favor?

DANIEL: Claro. El festival es el cuatro de abril en el auditorio a las siete de la tarde.

MICHELLE: Perfecto. No creo que los boletos deban costar mucho. Queremos que todos vengan a nuestro festival sin preocuparse por el precio…

DANIEL: De acuerdo. ¿Qué te parece si hacemos un concurso? Podemos pedir al público que vote la mejor película y sortear (*to raffle off*) una colección de películas hispanas en DVD.

MICHELLE: Me parece una idea estupenda, Daniel. Bueno, y ahora lo más importante: ¿cuáles son las cinco películas que vamos a elegir?

DANIEL: Supongo que estamos de acuerdo en poner *Nocturna* y *Ladrón que roba a ladrón*. Pero las demás… ¿Por qué no preguntamos a los fans del español? Ellos pueden ayudarnos a completar nuestro cartel.

31 El cartel del festival

▶ **Lee** el diálogo y responde a estas preguntas.

1. ¿Dónde y cuándo se celebra el festival?
2. ¿Qué idea propone Daniel para atraer al público?
3. ¿Qué películas hispanas eligen Daniel y Michelle?

▶ **Recomienda** algunas películas para que Michelle y Daniel puedan completar el cartel. Explica las razones de tu elección.

doscientos noventa y nueve **299**

---

31. Ask students to research different Spanish-language films in preparation for their own film festival. Ask them to think of ways in which they could promote the event. If possible, preview some of the films and show selected segments to the class.

 AUDIO SCRIPT
See page 281I.

Answer Key

28. 1. Se celebró el viernes, 9 de diciembre de 2011, en el Auditorio Nacional de la Ciudad de México.
2. Actuó con Carla Morrison y Natalia Lafourcade.
3. Porque va a trabajar en su próximo disco.

29. 1. Falso. No cree que la película haya ganado premios.
2. Falso. Los protagonistas son unos ladrones que intentan robarle a otro hombre, y resulta que ese hombre también es un ladrón.
3. Falso. Es una película que tiene acción y drama.
4. Falso. Piensa que es en español con subtítulos en inglés.

30. Answers will vary.
▶ Answers will vary.

31. 1. Se celebra en el auditorio el cuatro de abril, a las 7:00 p. m.
2. Propone pedirle al público que vote la mejor película y sortear una colección de películas hispanas en DVD.
3. Daniel y Michelle eligen *Nocturna* y *Ladrón que roba a ladrón*.
▶ Answers will vary.

Additional Resources

Fans Online activities
Practice Workbook

HERITAGE LANGUAGE LEARNERS

- Ask students to research a film festival in their family's country of origin, or in any other Spanish-speaking nation, including those mentioned in this *Desafío*. Then ask them to write a short feature article about the festival for a local Spanish-language newspaper. The information should include where the festival will take place, the dates and times when the films will be shown, some of the leading actors and directors who will be present, and a description of the general ambience of the festival.

MULTIPLE INTELLIGENCES:
Intrapersonal Intelligence

- Ask students to imagine that they have been nominated for a prestigious award in the movie industry. This award may be for acting, directing, or producing. It is the eve of the event, and all the nominees are hoping they will be winners, so they need to put the final touches on their acceptance speeches. Ask students to write a short speech that not only thanks some individuals for their support, but also reflects the winner's emotions and opinions at this time.

DESAFÍO 2

Expresar probabilidad

Presentation

■ In *Desafío 2*, Eva and Ethan need to interview some Hispanic surfers who are competing in California in order to write an article about surfing competitions. Students will preview language used to talk about sports competitions, and to express probability and purpose.

Activities	Standards	Resources
Texto	1.2, 2.1	Vis. Pres.
32.	1.2, 1.3	
33.	1.1, 1.2	
34.	1.2	Audio
35.	1.1, 1.3	
36. Cultura	1.1, 1.2, 2.1, 2.2, 3.1, 4.2	

Teaching Suggestions

Warm-Up / Independent Starter

■ Write the following questions on the board and allow students time to prepare a written response: *¿Qué deportes se pueden practicar en la playa? ¿Cuál(es) te gusta(n) más? ¿Por qué?*

Preparation

■ Have students share their responses to the Independent Starter. Do they know if any of these sports are part of the Olympic Games? Why might some sports be included or excluded from major sporting events like the Olympics or the Pan American Games?

Texto: Un deporte extremo

■ Read the introduction to the text aloud. Then have students read the dialogue silently. Ask them to pay attention to the doubts and questions that Eva and Ethan have.

■ Ask students whether they think Eva and Ethan are fans of surfing. Have them justify their answers using the text.

Activities

34. Before beginning this activity, have students predict the answers. Then play the audio recording twice.

Un deporte extremo

 Eva and Ethan are attending a surfing competition in Huntington Beach, California. Their task consists of interviewing some Hispanic surfers and writing an article about surfing competitions.

ETHAN: Tenemos que hacer una buena entrevista y elegir preguntas interesantes. ¿Qué es lo que más nos puede interesar de estos deportistas?

EVA: Principalmente cómo se preparan para las competencias.

ETHAN: También podríamos preguntarles dónde practican y si lo hacen con un entrenador.

EVA: ¿Un entrenador de surf? ¿Eso existe?

ETHAN: Tendrán algo parecido para aprender nuevas técnicas, supongo.

EVA: Puede ser... El surf no es solo para aficionados. Hay campeonatos muy importantes. Es una pena que este deporte no esté incluido en los Juegos Olímpicos.

ETHAN: Sí, pero Tess me contó que hay una asociación de surfistas latinoamericanos que organiza competencias en muchos países: Argentina, Perú, Brasil, Nicaragua, Costa Rica... ¿A cuántas personas debemos entrevistar?

EVA: No sé, pero deberíamos charlar con varios surfistas. A esta competencia vienen participantes y visitantes de todo el mundo.

ETHAN: Vamos a preguntar a ese chico. Seguro que nos puede ayudar.

32 Detective de palabras

▶ **Completa** estas oraciones.

1. Eva y Ethan quieren saber cómo se preparan los ___1___ para las ___2___.
2. Eva y Ethan les van a preguntar si practican con un ___3___.
3. Hay ___4___ de surf muy importantes.
4. Eva opina que es una pena que el surf no esté incluido en los ___5___ Olímpicos.

300 trescientos

Differentiated Instruction

DEVELOPING LEARNERS

• Conduct a guided reading of the dialogue. Call on students to read the two parts, sentence by sentence. As they finish reading each sentence, ask them questions to verify that they have understood. For example, after they read the first sentence, ask: *¿Qué tipo de preguntas tienen que elegir Eva y Ethan? (preguntas interesantes)* If students answer incorrectly, have them read the sentence again and try to answer. For those students who continue to have difficulty understanding, you may want to try rephrasing the sentence or breaking it down into shorter segments.

EXPANDING LEARNERS

• After students have completed activity 35, encourage them to write additional questions they would like to ask surfers. Then have them work with a partner and conduct a mini-interview. Partners will take turns asking and answering each other's questions about this sport. Questions might include how surfers first became interested in surfing, how they felt when they started to surf, places where they have surfed and where they would like to surf, and any dangers involved in this sport. Invite students to present their interviews to the class.

33 ¿Comprendes?

▶ **Responde** a estas preguntas.

1. ¿Cuál es el desafío de Eva y Ethan?
2. ¿A qué evento deportivo van para conseguir su desafío?
3. ¿Qué información quieren obtener acerca de los surfistas?
4. ¿Qué duda tienen sobre la preparación de los surfistas?
5. ¿Qué les contó Tess sobre las competencias de surf?

34 La competencia de surf

▶ **Escucha** la conversación entre Eva, Ethan y uno de los jueces de la competencia, y elige la opción correcta.

1. La competencia de surf dura…
   a. un día   b. dos días   c. tres días

2. Este año participan…
   a. treinta surfistas   b. cuarenta surfistas   c. cien surfistas

3. Los participantes son…
   a. hispanos   b. norteamericanos   c. de varios países

4. Eva quiere saber si ella y Ethan pueden…
   a. bañarse en la playa   b. montar en bici   c. asistir a algún espectáculo

5. Además de la competencia de surf, por la noche se celebra…
   a. un concierto   b. una carrera   c. un concurso

35 Te toca a ti

▶ **Habla** con tu compañero(a). ¿Qué deberían preguntar Eva y Ethan a los surfistas? Escriban tres preguntas interesantes y compártanlas con otros(as) compañeros(as).

CULTURA

¿Surfistas prehispánicos?

La cultura moche o mochica se desarrolló hace más de 2.000 años en el actual territorio de Perú. Los mochicas desarrollaron complejos sistemas de riego y usaron embarcaciones llamadas *caballitos de totora* que todavía se fabrican en la actualidad. En sus cerámicas plasmaban escenas cotidianas, como la escena de pesca que muestra la pieza de la fotografía.

Figura mochica (Perú).

36 **Compara.** ¿Qué sabes del estilo de vida de las culturas indígenas de tu región? ¿Qué nos muestra su artesanía?

trescientos uno 301

---

35. Before completing this activity, refer students to the dialogue on page 300 and the doubts that the characters have. As students share their questions, record them on the board, and hold a class vote to select five questions.

AUDIO SCRIPT
See page 281I.

CULTURA

¿Surfistas prehispánicos?
Ceramics that have been recovered from ruins in northern Peru link the first surfers to fishermen of the Moche culture. The rafts these fishermen used could be considered the first type of surfboard. Because fishing with such strong tides required both courage and skill, the fishermen were considered warriors.

Answer Key

32. 1. deportistas   4. campeonatos
      2. competencias   5. Juegos
      3. entrenador

33. 1. Tienen que entrevistar a unos surfistas y escribir un artículo sobre las competencias de surf.
      2. Van a una competencia de surf en Huntington Beach, California.
      3. Quieren saber cómo se preparan, dónde practican y si tienen un entrenador.
      4. No saben si los surfistas se entrenan con la ayuda de un entrenador.
      5. Les contó que hay una asociación de surfistas latinoamericanos que organiza competencias en varios países.

34. 1. c   2. a   3. c   4. c   5. a

35. Answers will vary.

36. Answers will vary.

Additional Resources

Fans Online activities

301

HERITAGE LANGUAGE LEARNERS

- Ask students to research *los caballitos de totora* and the Moche culture that first produced these rafts thousands of years ago. Students should explain what the *caballitos* are called in the ancient language of the region, the materials used in making these rafts, their practical and recreational uses, and their possible extinction because very few artisans know how to make them. After students research the topic, ask them to make the argument for sponsoring workshops so that younger generations can learn how to make the *caballitos*.

MULTIPLE INTELLIGENCES:
Visual-Spatial Intelligence

- Ask students to make a poster advertising a surfing competition. It may be the one that Eva and Ethan are covering or any other— real or fictitious. Ask students to give the competition a name and decide whether it is local or international. Students should include the place, dates and times, the surfers' categories, and mention the after-surfing activities that are planned. Encourage students to create a logo for the competition and to add their own illustrations on the poster, or find some suitable images from the Internet.

DESAFÍO 2

Vocabulario – Deportes

Presentation

- In this section, students will learn and use featured vocabulary to communicate about sports and sports competitions.

Activities	Standards	Resources
Vocabulario	1.2	
37.	1.2, 1.3, 3.1	
38.	1.2, 1.3, 2.1, 5.1	
39.	1.1, 1.3, 3.1	
40. Conexiones	1.1, 1.2, 3.1	

Teaching Suggestions

Warm-Up / Independent Starter

- Have students write a list of the sports that they can name in Spanish. Ask students who finish before their classmates to also write down where the sport is played or practiced.

Preparation

- Ask two volunteers to play the roles of Eva and Ethan and read the dialogue aloud. Ask for three additional volunteers to read the sports festival sign. If there are any errors with pronunciation, repeat the word, demonstrating the correct pronunciation. Ask students to paraphrase the contents of the poster in their own words. Also make sure they describe each venue listed on the poster. Then have students share their lists of sports from the Independent Starter and add more events to the sports festival poster.

- Direct students' attention to the *Más vocabulario* feature. Say the vocabulary words aloud and ask students to repeat them after you. For each term, ask students to define each word in Spanish, either aloud or in writing. Note key terms that are unfamiliar to students on the board to facilitate their definitions. Emphasize the pronunciation of cognate words whose stress falls on different syllables in each language (e.g., *local, campeón*).

Activities

37. See if students can add more sports and athletes to the list, using the sports they brainstormed in the Independent Starter.

Vocabulario

Deportes

> Ayer vi a un equipo de ciclistas entrenando. ¡Era impresionante!

> Sí, el ciclismo es un deporte muy duro. Pero a mí no me gustan los deportes competitivos.

> A mí sí, es más emocionante que haya ganadores y perdedores... ¡a menos que haya un empate!

¡BIENVENIDOS AL FESTIVAL DEL DEPORTE!

VIERNES 22

 Campeonato de remo
Playa norte

 Finales de atletismo
Estadio municipal

SÁBADO 23

 Competencia de natación
Piscina municipal

 Regata de vela
Playa norte

 Competencia de esquí acuático
Playa sur

DOMINGO 24

 Carrera de ciclismo
Estadio (pista central)

 Partido de baloncesto
Cancha municipal

Más vocabulario

Competencias

los Juegos Olímpicos	Olympics
el / la aficionado(a)	fan, supporter
el/la campeón(a)	champion
el equipo local	home team
el equipo visitante	visiting team
el marcador	scoreboard
el tanteo	score
la victoria	victory
la derrota	defeat

Deportistas

el/la atleta	athlete
el/la esquiador(a)	skier
el/la surfista	surfer
el/la nadador(a)	swimmer
el/la navegante	sailor

37 ¿Qué deporte?

 Completa una tabla como esta.

Deporte	Deportista
ciclismo	
	esquiador
surf	surfista
natación	
	atleta

302 trescientos dos

Differentiated Instruction

DEVELOPING LEARNERS

- Ask students to choose the correct answer.

  1. *El equipo ganador es el...* (a)
     a. *campeón* b. *tanteo*
  2. *El equipo ... no es de aquí.* (a)
     a. *visitante* b. *local*
  3. *La carrera de ciclismo es en...* (b)
     a. *la cancha* b. *la pista*
  4. *... indica el tanteo.* (a)
     a. *El marcador* b. *La carrera*
  5. *... se practica en la cancha.* (a)
     a. *El baloncesto* b. *El atletismo*
  6. *Vamos ... a ver el esquí acuático.* (b)
     a. *al estadio* b. *a la playa*

EXPANDING LEARNERS

- Give students the opportunity to learn more about other aquatic sports—from *la natación sincronizada* to *el kayak,* and *las motos acuáticas.* Ask students to select one of these aquatic sports and do some research on the history of the sport, some of the major competitions, where this sport is especially popular, and any other anecdotal information of interest. Ask students to prepare a written report, complete with images, of their findings. Then have students make an oral presentation to the rest of the class.

38 **La Copa Mundial**

▶ **Completa** el blog de Eva sobre su campeonato deportivo favorito.

empate	
campeón	
partido	
campeonato	
victoria	

Desde Huntington Beach (California)
Publicado por Eva Bishop 28/05/2012

La Copa Mundial de fútbol es mi ___1___ internacional favorito.
¡El ___2___ de la final de 2010 fue muy emocionante! Recuerdo
que jugaban España y los Países Bajos. Al final del segundo
tiempo el marcador estaba en 0-0, había un ___3___. Por eso
los jugadores tuvieron que jugar la prórroga (*overtime*). Finalmente
Iniesta marcó un gol y la selección española consiguió
la ___4___. El equipo salió de Sudáfrica como ___5___ del mundo.
¡Siempre recordaré ese partido!

COMENTARIOS (0)   ENVIAR UN COMENTARIO

▶ **Escribe** un comentario sobre un evento deportivo para el blog de Eva.

39 **Los gustos de la clase**

▶ **Habla** con tu compañero(a) sobre sus gustos y preferencias deportivas, y toma nota de sus respuestas.

1. ¿Qué deportes practicas habitualmente?
2. ¿Dónde prefieres practicar deporte?
3. ¿Prefieres los deportes individuales o de equipo?
4. ¿Admiras a algún(a) deportista en particular?
5. ¿Qué deportes de los Juegos Olímpicos te parecen más emocionantes?

CONEXIONES: MATEMÁTICAS

El triángulo olímpico

En las regatas de vela, los barcos siguen normalmente un recorrido
marcado por boyas (*buoys*) colocadas en forma de triángulo.
Es el llamado «triángulo olímpico». En el diagrama de la ilustración,
por ejemplo, el recorrido tiene forma de triángulo equilátero,
con tres lados iguales y tres ángulos agudos.

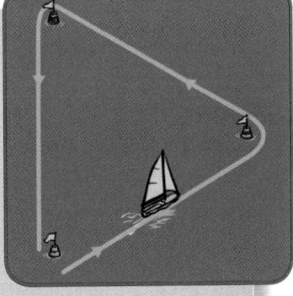

40 **Piensa.** ¿Conoces otros deportes en los que los ángulos y las formas geométricas sean importantes? Pon algunos ejemplos.

---

38. After completing the first part of this activity, ask students if they know when the next *Copa Mundial* will take place and if they ever watch international soccer games. Before starting the second part of this activity, have students brainstorm some of the events about which they could write their comment.

39. As an alternative to this activity, have students research a famous athlete and use the information they find to create skits, pretending that a reporter is interviewing the famous athlete. You may want to have the class generate some sample questions that could be used as part of the role-play.

CONEXIONES: MATEMÁTICAS

El triángulo olímpico
The shape of the racecourse for many regattas is called the Olympic Triangle. The design of an equilateral triangle allows sailors to display their skills facing all directions of the wind and spectators to see the magnificent sails from all angles. The sailors need to be skilled at adjusting the angle of the sails relative to the angle of the wind in order to control direction and speed.

Answer Key

37. Deporte: esquí, atletismo.
Deportista: ciclista, nadador(a).

38. 1. campeonato   4. victoria
2. partido   5. campeón
3. empate
▶ Answers will vary.

39. Answers will vary.

40. Answers will vary.

Additional Resources

Fans Online activities
Practice Workbook

HERITAGE LANGUAGE LEARNERS

• Ask students to think about one of the most memorable sports events they have watched or in which they have participated—it could be an international competition or a local school event. Have students write several paragraphs about the competition or about one of the athletes. Students will need to identify the sport, explain where, when, and with whom they played or watched it, describe how the game or competition progressed, and tell if it ended in victory or defeat. Call on volunteers to read their paragraphs aloud.

TOTAL PHYSICAL RESPONSE (TPR)

• Divide the class into two teams and play "Charades." Previously, you will have written some of the vocabulary from this *Desafío*, plus relevant words from page 287, on slips of paper, and placed them in a bag. Each team will pick a word from the bag and use pantomime so that team members may guess what it is. Set a time for players to guess. Each team scores 1 point for each correct answer. If a team cannot answer correctly, play goes to the other team.

DESAFÍO 2

Gramática – Expresar probabilidad

Presentation

- In this section, students will learn how to express probability by using certain expressions as well as the future tense.

Activities	Standards	Resources
Gramática	1.2, 3.1	
41.	1.3, 4.1	
42.	1.1, 1.2	Audio
43.	1.2, 1.3, 3.1	
44.	1.1, 1.2	
45.	1.2, 1.3, 3.1, 5.1	

Teaching Suggestions

Warm-Up / Independent Starter

- Ask students to think of the different ways in which they know how to express possibility in Spanish or words they know that express probability. They should write five sentences about things that are probably happening right now in their community or will probably happen in the near future using the structures they already know.

Preparation

- Ask for volunteers to share their Independent Starters. They may have recalled the subjunctive with expressions such as, *Es posible que…*, *Es probable que…*, *Puede que…* or they may have written down words such as *probablemente* or *quizás*.

- Have students read the first part of the grammar explanation aloud in small groups. After they are finished, clarify that the indicative mood can also be used with *quizás* and *tal vez* to convey a higher degree of certainty. For example: *Quizás te llamo para salir a cenar. Tal vez vamos mañana al cine.* Point out that the use of one mood or another can convey subtle differences in meaning, rather than one mood being the "correct" one.

- Ask students to read the second part of the grammar explanation in the same small groups. Point out that the future of probability is not a direct translation from English. Review some of the ways this is expressed in English (e.g., I wonder, I suppose, must) so that students understand that this use of the future tense in Spanish does not refer to the future.

Gramática

Expresar probabilidad

Expresiones de posibilidad

- Expressions such as quizá(s), tal vez, and a lo mejor are used to talk about the possibility or probability of an action taking place.
  - Quizá(s) and tal vez are generally followed by the subjunctive mood, especially when the speaker wants to convey a considerable degree of doubt.

    Quizás te **llame** para salir a cenar. Tal vez **vayamos** mañana al cine.
  - A lo mejor is followed by the indicative mood.

    A lo mejor **vamos** mañana al estadio.

  Note that que is not used after these expressions.

El futuro de probabilidad

- The future tense in Spanish generally corresponds to the future tense in English.

  En vacaciones **iremos** de excursión a las montañas.

- But the future tense is also sometimes used idiomatically in Spanish to express conjecture or probability in the present.

  —¡Qué raro! Hoy no vino Luisa. —¿Dónde está el entrenador?
  —**Estará** enferma. —**Estará** en el gimnasio.

  Although there isn't an exact equivalent in English to this use of the future tense, phrases and words such as *I suppose, I wonder, must,* and *probably* convey a similar sense in English. For example: *She's probably sick / I suppose he is at the gym.*

41 **Compara.** Traduce al español de todas las maneras posibles la siguiente oración: *Perhaps she'll come to the party*.

42 **¿Qué estarán haciendo?**

 ▶ **Escucha** y une las columnas.

 Ⓐ   Ⓑ

1. Eva…   a. estará haciendo surf.
2. Michelle…   b. estará limpiando la casa.
3. Daniel…   c. estará buscando información en Internet.
4. Ethan…   d. estará estudiando en la biblioteca.
5. Asha…   e. estará en la cancha.
6. Lucas…   f. estará en el concierto.

304 trescientos cuatro

Differentiated Instruction

DEVELOPING LEARNERS

- Give students more practice with expressing probability by having them complete the following sentences:

1. *A lo mejor … luego.* (b)
   a. *venga*   b. *viene*
2. *Tal vez … el examen hoy, pero no lo creo.* (a)
   a. *tengamos*   b. *tenemos*
3. *¿… Pedro en casa?* (a)
   a. *Estará*   b. *Esté*
4. *… yo tome clases de surf.* (a)
   a. *Quizás*   b. *A lo mejor*
5. *… las dos de la tarde.* (b)
   a. *Sea*   b. *Serán*

EXPANDING LEARNERS

- Ask students to expand their answers to activity 44 by having them work with a partner and create a dialogue based on the answers to questions 2–6.

  A. *Mi mejor amigo estará en clase, o quizá esté en la biblioteca porque tiene un examen mañana.*

  B. *Pues mi mejor amiga estará en la piscina porque entrena para una competencia.*

- Then have students take turns asking their partner at least three more questions similar to those in the activity, and expanding their answers as they did previously.

43 Quizás

▶ **Completa** estas oraciones poniendo el verbo en la forma correcta.

Modelo   Tal vez el equipo contrario *gane* el partido hoy.

1. Quizás mi surfista favorito _____ a su rival.
   derrotar

2. Tal vez nuestros surfistas favoritos _____ .
   empatar

3. Quizás _____ a la competencia más de mil aficionados.
   asistir

4. Tal vez el surf _____ un deporte olímpico algún día.
   ser

5. Quizás Ethan y Eva _____ con algunos surfistas esta tarde.
   hablar

6. A lo mejor yo _____ mañana en una carrera de ciclismo.
   participar

44 Una respuesta lógica

▶ **Responde** a estas preguntas.

1. ¿Qué hora será ahora mismo? (no mires el reloj)
2. ¿Dónde estará ahora mismo tu mejor amigo(a)?
3. ¿Qué estará haciendo tu madre o tu padre en este momento?
4. ¿Qué habrá hoy para cenar?
5. ¿Qué pasarán esta noche por televisión?
6. ¿Cuál será la tarea para hoy?

45 Este fin de semana

▶ **Escribe** un correo electrónico a tu compañero(a) sobre tus planes para este fin de semana. Muestra tu grado de confianza en que los planes se realicen usando el indicativo o el subjuntivo.

Modelo

Hola, Carlos:

¿Cómo estás? No sé qué hacer este fin de semana. Quizá vaya al cine y tal vez venga Raquel también. Si vamos al cine, veremos una comedia porque es lo que más nos gusta. Quizás comamos antes o a lo mejor vemos la película temprano y después vamos a comer algo. ¿Te apetece venir?

▶ **Escribe.** Intercambia tu correo electrónico con tu compañero(a) y escríbele una respuesta.

HERITAGE LANGUAGE LEARNERS

• Students may know some other ways of expressing "perhaps" (e.g., *acaso, igual, lo mismo, posiblemente, probablemente*). In some Spanish-speaking countries, *de repente* or *de pronto* is also used to mean "perhaps." Point out that *de repente te escribe* is equivalent to *a lo mejor te escribe. Igual* and *lo mismo* are used in informal speech (e.g., *igual ganan otro campeonato; lo mismo ganan otra vez*). *Acaso* is more academic (e.g., *acaso llueva hoy*). Ask students to write sentences using each of these phrases.

CRITICAL THINKING

• Divide the class into several teams and explain that they are going to debate whether our society places too much importance on competitive sports in schools. Assign half of the debaters to defend the importance our culture places on these sports. Students should mention the positive effects competitiveness has on individuals, including the values of teamwork that it teaches. Assign the other debaters to defend the position that too much emphasis is placed on sports competition, and this takes time away from academic studies that would better prepare students for the future.

DESAFÍO 2

Gramática – Expresar probabilidad

Activities

42. Play the audio recording twice. Remind students that the statements are referring to the present, not the future.

43. After completing this activity, have students write additional statements about Eva and Ethan, and the probability of them accomplishing their task.

44. You may want to turn this into a communicative activity by having students work with a partner. One partner asks the even-numbered questions and the other asks the odd-numbered ones.

45. Ask students to incorporate at least three statements that indicate a high degree of probability and three that indicate a low degree of probability. You can ask students to write their e-mails on pieces of paper, or to exchange e-mail addresses and send real e-mails, copying you in the cc field or printing them out to bring to class. If you teach more than one section of the same course, you may want to have students exchange with a student of yours from the other class.

> **AUDIO SCRIPT**
> See page 281 J.

Answer Key

41. Quizá(s) / Tal vez ella venga a la fiesta.
Quizá(s) / Tal vez / A lo mejor ella viene a la fiesta.

42. 1. d   2. f   3. b   4. a   5. c   6. e

43. 1. derrote   4. sea
2. empaten   5. hablen
3. asistan   6. participo

44. Answers will vary.

45. Answers will vary.
▶ Answers will vary.

> ### Additional Resources
> Fans Online activities
> Practice Workbook

DESAFÍO 2

Gramática – Expresar finalidad

Presentation

- In this section, students will learn expressions of purpose and how to apply them using the subjunctive or the infinitive.

Activities	Standards	Resources
Gramática	1.2, 3.1	
46.	1.2, 4.1	
47.	1.2, 1.3	
48.	1.2, 3.1	Audio
49.	1.1, 1.2	
50. Conexiones	1.1, 1.2, 2.1, 3.1	Video

Teaching Suggestions

Warm-Up / Independent Starter

- Have students complete a two-column chart like the one below. Provide an example and ask students to think of four more actions and their effects.

Mis acciones	El efecto
Hago la tarea.	Saco buenas notas.

Preparation

- Call on students to read each bullet in the *Gramática* feature. Draw their attention to the examples provided, noting the examples that do not have a change of subject, and those that do.

- Have students use their charts from the Independent Starter and connect the two columns using an appropriate expression of purpose. Provide the following examples: *Hago la tarea para sacar buenas notas. Hago la tarea para que mis profesores estén contentos.* Then call on volunteers to share some of their sentences.

Activities

47. Before completing this activity, have students determine which statements do and do not have a change of subject.

48. Before playing the audio, ask students to list what they need to listen for in order to determine whether the person is completing the action for his or her benefit or to benefit someone else.

306

Gramática

Expresar finalidad

Expresar finalidad

- Expressions such as para (que) and a (que) indicate the purpose of the action that is being taken. This is usually expressed in English by *so that* and *in order to/that*.

El infinitivo y el subjuntivo con expresiones de finalidad

- Para and para que are the most commonly used expressions in Spanish to indicate the purpose of an action.
  - Use para + **infinitive** when the main clause and the dependent clause have the same subject.
  - Use para que + **subjunctive** when the clauses have different subjects.

Pido una pizza **para** cenar.	Pido una pizza **para que** cenes.
yo yo	yo tú

- A and a que can also be used to express the purpose of an action. They are generally used with verbs that express movement, such as ir, venir, subir, bajar, entrar, or salir.
  - Use a + **infinitive** when the main clause and the dependent clause have the same subject.
  - Use a que + **subjunctive** when the clauses have different subjects.

Vengo **a** darte los libros.	Vengo **a que** me des los libros.
yo yo	yo tú

Preguntar sobre la finalidad de una acción

- To ask about the purpose of an action, use ¿para qué...? or ¿a qué...? followed by a verb in the indicative mood.

—**¿Para qué** pides una pizza?   —**¿A qué vienes** hoy por aquí?
—La pido **para que** cenes.   —Vengo **a** darte los libros.

46 **Compara.** Traduce al inglés estas oraciones. ¿Puedes usar *so that* en los dos casos?

    a. Te llamo **para** hablar.   **b.** Te llamo **para que** hablemos.

47 **¿Para qué?**

▶ **Completa** cada oración con una respuesta lógica. Usa el infinitivo o el subjuntivo.

Modelo Mis profesores me dan tareas para que yo... → *estudie en casa.*

1. Por la mañana me levanto temprano para...
2. Ordeno y limpio mi dormitorio para que mis padres...
3. Quiero sacar buenas notas para...
4. Mis amigos me llaman por teléfono para que yo...
5. Trato de dormir ocho horas cada noche para...

Differentiated Instruction

DEVELOPING LEARNERS

- Give students more practice with *para* + infinitive and *para que* + subjunctive by having them complete the following sentences:

1. *Los esquiadores piden nieve (poder) esquiar. (para poder)*
2. *Nado todos los días (estar) en forma. (para estar)*
3. *Mis padres me dan dinero (yo – comprar) el libro. (para que compre)*
4. *Compro dos entradas (tú – venir) conmigo. (para que vengas)*
5. *Los aficionados gritan (animar) a su equipo. (para animar)*

EXPANDING LEARNERS

- Using Eva's status feed as a model, ask students to write at least six entries that describe where they are and what they are doing. Then have them exchange their profiles with a partner, who will ask questions about why they are doing this, using *para, para que, a,* or *a que.* For example:

A. *Estoy en la piscina, entrenándome.*
B. *¿Para qué te entrenas?*
A. *Para competir en el campeonato de la escuela.*

48 ¿A quién le afecta?

▶ **Escucha** a Ethan y decide a quién o a quiénes afectan sus acciones.

	1	2	3	4	5	6
A él mismo (infinitivo)	✓					
A otras personas (subjuntivo)						

49 Un día muy largo

▶ **Lee** lo que Eva escribió hoy en una red social y responde a las preguntas.

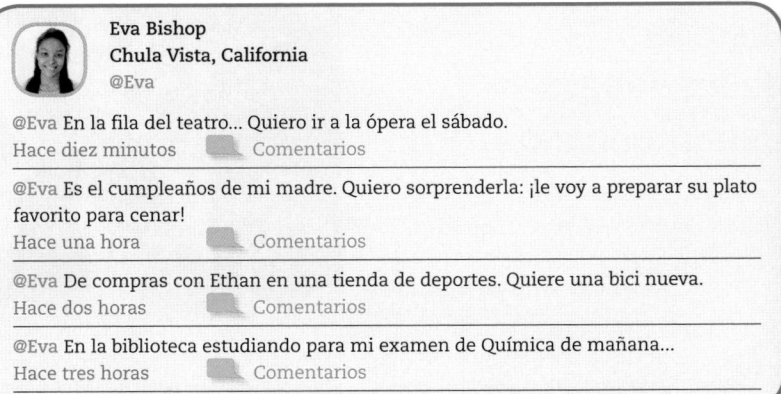

Eva Bishop
Chula Vista, California
@Eva

@Eva En la fila del teatro… Quiero ir a la ópera el sábado.
Hace diez minutos   Comentarios

@Eva Es el cumpleaños de mi madre. Quiero sorprenderla: ¡le voy a preparar su plato favorito para cenar!
Hace una hora   Comentarios

@Eva De compras con Ethan en una tienda de deportes. Quiere una bici nueva.
Hace dos horas   Comentarios

@Eva En la biblioteca estudiando para mi examen de Química de mañana…
Hace tres horas   Comentarios

1. ¿A qué va a la biblioteca?
2. ¿Para qué va a la tienda de deportes?
3. ¿Para qué va a cocinar?
4. ¿Para qué está en la fila?

CONEXIONES: GEOGRAFÍA

La Libertad

La Libertad, en El Salvador, es uno de los mejores sitios para hacer surf y practicar otros deportes acuáticos de riesgo. Su ubicación en la costa del océano Pacífico es perfecta para atraer a los salvadoreños porque está solo a 30 o 40 minutos de la capital, San Salvador.

Golfo de México
Mar Caribe
El Salvador
OCÉANO PACÍFICO

50 Piensa y explica. Observa el mapa y la forma de Centroamérica.
¿Por qué crees que los mejores lugares para hacer surf están en la costa pacífica?

HERITAGE LANGUAGE LEARNERS

• Ask students to research La Libertad, El Salvador, or any other popular surfing area in Latin America. Students should include data on the natural features that make the area an ideal place to practice surfing. Students should gather some general information about the area, some details on the surfing conditions, and perhaps what other aquatic sports are available. Then ask students to use this information and create a travel brochure aimed primarily at surfers and other water sports enthusiasts.

SPECIAL-NEEDS LEARNERS

• Help students with an auditory processing disorder to read aloud the directions to all the activities and then repeat the directions to you. As they repeat the directions, ask that they break them down into small steps. This process will help them reinforce their comprehension of the tasks they need to complete. You might also provide them with the audio script to help them better comprehend any recorded material.

Gramática – Expresar finalidad

49. To extend this activity, have students make a list of what they need to do today and tomorrow. Have them give their list to a partner, who will ask them the purpose of their actions.
A. *¿A qué vas a casa de Helen?*
B. *A verla. Es mi mejor amiga.*

AUDIO SCRIPT
See page 281 J.

CONEXIONES: GEOGRAFÍA

La Libertad
Waves on the beaches of La Libertad can reach to over 12 ft. high and can provide a ride of 300 m. It is one of the best spots for surfing in Latin America, but it is not yet a popular tourist destination. Tourism in El Salvador suffered because of the civil war in the 1980s; however, many predict that this quiet place will become a hot spot for international surfing enthusiasts.

Answer Key

46. a. *I call you in order to talk.*
   b. *I call you so that we can talk.*

47. Answers will vary. Sample answers:
   1. … ir a la escuela.
   2. … no me digan nada.
   3. … ir a una buena universidad.
   4. … vaya con ellos al cine.
   5. … descansar.

48. A él mismo: 1, 3, 4, 6.
   A otras personas: 2, 5.

49. 1. A estudiar para su examen de Química.
   2. Para que Ethan compre una bici nueva.
   3. Para sorprender a su madre en su cumpleaños.
   4. Para comprar entradas para la ópera.

50. Answers will vary.

Additional Resources

Fans Online activities
Practice Workbook

LECTURA: TEXTO INFORMATIVO

Presentation

- In this section, students will read a brief history of the Pan American Games, recognize how grammar structures are used in context, and compare games and sports using learned vocabulary.

Activities	Standards	Resources
Lectura: texto informativo	1.2, 1.3, 2.1, 3.1, 3.2	
51.	1.2, 1.3, 3.1	
52.	1.1, 1.2, 2.1, 3.1, 4.2	
53.	1.2, 1.3, 5.1	
54.	1.3, 5.1	

Teaching Suggestions

Warm-Up / Independent Starter

- Ask students to:
  - Write three statements describing what they think takes place at the Pan American Games.
  - Write three statements describing the purpose of international competitions like the Pan American Games.

Preparation

- Have students read the *Antes de leer* strategies silently. Then ask them to take notes.

- Write down the word *principio* and make sure that students understand what it means. If they don't, explain the meaning in Spanish in relation to *final*, which is a cognate. You may point out that *principio*, in other contexts, also means "principle," like its correlated word in English. Then have students find two dates in the first two paragraphs that refer to the two beginnings of the games.

- Read the text aloud to students to model pronunciation and intonation. Then have students alternate reading several lines or a paragraph. You may pause after every paragraph and call on a volunteer to paraphrase the content.

- Ask students to take out the sentences they wrote for their Independent Starters. Then have them read *Historia de los Juegos Panamericanos* silently and take additional notes. Review these answers with students.

Antes de leer: estrategias

1. Lee el título. ¿Qué crees que habrá en este texto: información, opiniones o la expresión de emociones y sentimientos?

2. Lee superficialmente *(scan)* el texto y haz una lista de los lugares que se mencionan. ¿De qué región geográfica se habla? ¿Qué significa el adjetivo *panamericano(a)*?

3. ¿A qué juegos se refiere el título del texto? ¿Qué sabes de este tipo de juegos? ¿Puedes hacer algunas hipótesis sobre el contenido del texto?

Historia de los Juegos Panamericanos

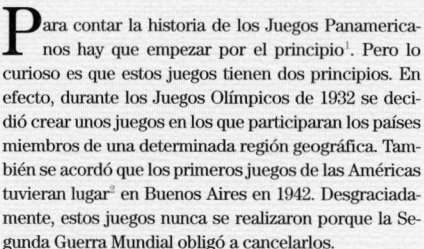

Clausura de los XVI Juegos Panamericanos en Guadalajara (México).

Para contar la historia de los Juegos Panamericanos hay que empezar por el principio[1]. Pero lo curioso es que estos juegos tienen dos principios. En efecto, durante los Juegos Olímpicos de 1932 se decidió crear unos juegos en los que participaran los países miembros de una determinada región geográfica. También se acordó que los primeros juegos de las Américas tuvieran lugar[2] en Buenos Aires en 1942. Desgraciadamente, estos juegos nunca se realizaron porque la Segunda Guerra Mundial obligó a cancelarlos.

Fue necesario esperar hasta 1948, durante los Juegos Olímpicos de Londres, para retomar[3] la idea de crear los Juegos Panamericanos. Allí se acordó mantener Buenos Aires como la sede[4] para los primeros juegos, que se celebraron en 1951. Desde entonces, un año antes de los Juegos Olímpicos, atletas de casi todos los países de las Américas se reúnen para competir en nombre de su país.

El término Panamericano se eligió, precisamente, porque su significado connota la unidad de países, y ayuda de esta manera a expresar los ideales olímpicos de amistad y unidad de los pueblos.

Los Juegos Panamericanos se han celebrado en diferentes países: Canadá (1967 y 1999), Argentina (1951 y 1995), México (1955 y 2011), Estados Unidos (1959 y 1987), Colombia, Puerto Rico, Venezuela, Cuba, República Dominicana y Brasil (1963 y 2007).

Aunque los Juegos Panamericanos se iniciaron con la participación de 21 países, en el año 2011 hubo 42 países participantes. Actualmente se incluyen todos los deportes olímpicos, además de bolos[5], esquí acuático, karate, patinaje artístico[6], patinaje de velocidad, squash y fútbol sala[7]. Los países que más medallas han obtenido en estos juegos son Estados Unidos, Cuba, Canadá, Argentina y Brasil.

1. *beginning*
2. *would take place*
3. *to take up again*
4. *site*
5. *bowling*
6. *figure skating*
7. *indoor soccer*

Differentiated Instruction

DEVELOPING LEARNERS

- Ask students to complete activity 51 as they read the text. Recommend that they read each paragraph once for meaning, and then read it again, focusing on the information contained. Students will determine if this information answers *¿dónde?*, *¿cuándo?*, or *¿para qué?* and write these facts under the corresponding heading. When students complete the activity, call on individuals to read the data they have compiled under one or more of the headings.

EXPANDING LEARNERS

- Have students work in small groups and imagine that one of them is a reporter, and the others are competing in the Pan American Games. The students are at the site of the Games, and the reporter will identify the city and introduce the audience to the athletes. Questions posed to the athletes may include asking them where they are from, which sport they are competing in, how long they have been participating in similar competitions, their opinions about these Games, and any other relevant questions that give the audience some insight into the lives of the athletes.

51 Comprensión

▶ **Responde** a estas preguntas.

1. ¿Cuándo se decidió crear los Juegos Panamericanos?
2. ¿Cuándo se celebraron por primera vez? ¿Dónde?
3. ¿Para qué se decidió crear estos juegos?

52 ¿Qué opinan?

▶ **Lee** de nuevo el texto y responde a estas preguntas.

1. ¿Por qué crees que es una buena idea tener juegos regionales?
2. ¿Por qué crees que los Juegos Panamericanos se celebran un año antes de los Juegos Olímpicos?
3. ¿Cuáles son las cualidades necesarias en una ciudad para ser sede de los Juegos Olímpicos Panamericanos?
4. ¿Qué ciudades de tu país serían ideales para ser la sede de los Juegos Panamericanos?

▶ **Habla** con tu compañero(a). Comparen sus respuestas para ver si están de acuerdo.

53 Compara

▶ **Escribe** las semejanzas y las diferencias entre los Juegos Panamericanos y los Juegos Olímpicos. Puedes utilizar datos que ya sabes e investigar más en Internet.

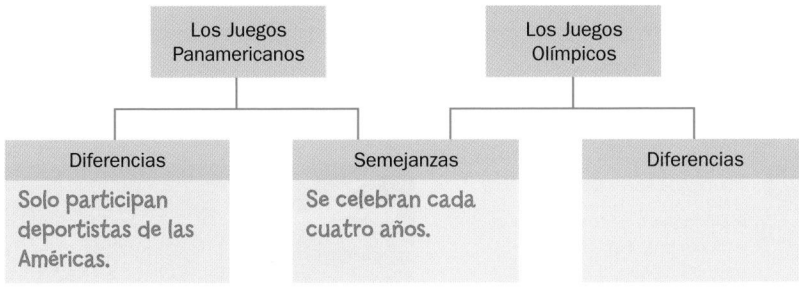

Los Juegos Panamericanos y los Juegos Olímpicos:
semejanzas y diferencias

Los Juegos Panamericanos		Los Juegos Olímpicos	
Diferencias	Semejanzas		Diferencias
Solo participan deportistas de las Américas.	Se celebran cada cuatro años.		

54 Con tus propias palabras

▶ **Escribe** un texto de dos o tres párrafos. Explica cuál es el deporte más popular en tu escuela, cuál es la competencia más importante de ese deporte y cuál es el rival del equipo de tu escuela.

trescientos nueve 309

Activities

52. Have students check their answers with a partner before sharing them with the class. Collect a list of the cities suggested for question 4, and write them on the board. Have a class discussion to identify the best cities on the list. Remind students of factors such as accessibility for international competitors, weather, transportation, etc.

53. Have students research which sports are included in the Olympic Games and which ones are not. They should be prepared to talk about the topic after they complete the activity.

54. After students write about the sports at their school, ask them to find out information about the sporting habits of schools in Spanish-speaking countries. Do the schools have sports teams? How popular are they? Which sports are the most common? What kind of competitions do students participate in?

Answer Key

51. Answers will vary. Sample answers:
   1. Durante los Juegos Olímpicos de 1932.
   2. Se celebraron por primera vez en 1951, en Buenos Aires, Argentina.
   3. Para que participaran los países miembros de una determinada región geográfica y ayudar así a la expresión de los ideales olímpicos de amistad y unidad de los pueblos.

52. Answers will vary.
   ▶ Answers will vary.

53. Answers will vary.

54. Answers will vary.

Additional Resources

Fans Online activities

HERITAGE LANGUAGE LEARNERS

• Ask students to describe orally or in writing the participation of their family's country of origin in the last Pan American Games, or in the Olympics. They might research when and where the country participated, what the competitions were, who the most famous athletes were, how many medals were won, and any other interesting anecdotal information. Students may want to profile one of the outstanding athletes who participated, or one of the exceptional teams. Encourage students to include some images in their presentation.

MULTIPLE INTELLIGENCES:
Logical-Mathematical Intelligence

• Divide the class into small groups and have them conduct some research on the Internet to find out the four most popular team sports in the United States based on attendance numbers. After students gather the information, have them figure out the percentages and make a pie graph that shows these percentages. Ask the different groups to compare their graphs. Did they come up with similar graphs or not?

Unit 6
DESAFÍO 2

Comunicación

Presentation

- In this section, students will integrate the vocabulary and grammar skills from *Desafío 2* in order to communicate probability and purpose in the context of sporting events.

Activities	Standards	Resources
55.	1.1	
56.	1.2, 1.3, 2.1, 3.1	
57.	1.1, 1.2, 1.3, 2.1, 5.1	Audio
58. Final del desafío	1.1, 1.2, 1.3, 3.1, 5.1	
Tu desafío	1.1, 1.2	

Teaching Suggestions

Warm-Up / Independent Starter

- Ask students to think about an event for which they had to prepare. They may choose a sporting event in which they participated or another event that required practice and preparation. Have students write a paragraph about what they did in order to prepare and the final result of their actions. For example: *Mi equipo de baloncesto y yo entrenamos con mucha disciplina para ganar el campeonato. El entrenador nos enseñó técnicas muy útiles para que tuviéramos una ventaja sobre nuestro rival. El día del partido...*

Preparation

- Spend some time reviewing the statements of purpose. Review when a conjugated verb is necessary in the dependent clause and when the verb is left in the infinitive. Then ask students to share their responses to the Independent Starter and analyze their paragraphs as a class.
- Ask students which sports require the most preparation and why. Have students incorporate the expressions of probability in their answers using the vocabulary from this *Desafío*. For example:
  A. *A lo mejor el béisbol requiere más horas de entrenamiento que el fútbol americano, pero en el fútbol hay que tener mayor preparación física.*
  B. *Quizás el surf sea uno de los deportes más difíciles porque son necesarias varias destrezas.*

Comunicación

55 El blog de Juan José

▶ **Lee** la entrada del blog de un surfista y complétala con las formas correctas.

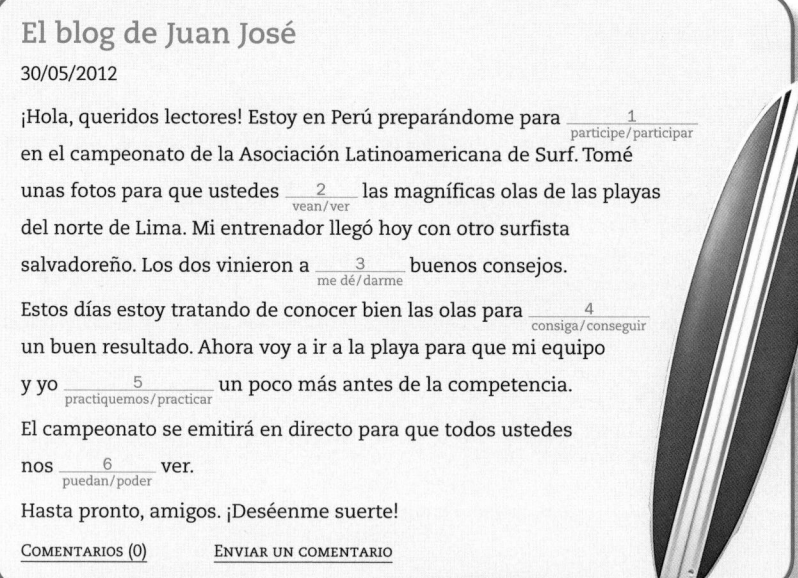

El blog de Juan José
30/05/2012

¡Hola, queridos lectores! Estoy en Perú preparándome para ___1___ (participe/participar) en el campeonato de la Asociación Latinoamericana de Surf. Tomé unas fotos para que ustedes ___2___ (vean/ver) las magníficas olas de las playas del norte de Lima. Mi entrenador llegó hoy con otro surfista salvadoreño. Los dos vinieron a ___3___ (me dé/darme) buenos consejos.

Estos días estoy tratando de conocer bien las olas para ___4___ (consiga/conseguir) un buen resultado. Ahora voy a ir a la playa para que mi equipo y yo ___5___ (practiquemos/practicar) un poco más antes de la competencia.

El campeonato se emitirá en directo para que todos ustedes nos ___6___ (puedan/poder) ver.

Hasta pronto, amigos. ¡Deséenme suerte!

COMENTARIOS (0)   ENVIAR UN COMENTARIO

▶ **Escribe** un comentario para el blog de Juan José. Puedes darle algunas sugerencias para prepararse para la competencia.

56 Un noticiero del partido

▶ **Describe** a tu compañero(a) esta escena. Haz también algunas hipótesis sobre qué estarán haciendo los jugadores y los aficionados y para qué.

Modelo *El partido acaba de terminar. Los fans del equipo ganador lo estarán celebrando porque....*

Differentiated Instruction

DEVELOPING LEARNERS

- Prepare index cards with images or words that represent sports-related vocabulary and explain to students that they will play a game of *¿Qué estará haciendo?* Have students pick a card and say a sentence that states what their friend Pepe might be doing. For example, if students pick *el equipo local*, they might say: *Pepe estará animando al equipo local.* Should students pick *la carrera de ciclismo*, their sentence might be: *Pepe estará participando en la carrera de ciclismo.* Students score a point for every correct sentence.

EXPANDING LEARNERS

- Have students imagine that they have just gone surfing for the first time, and they want to share their impressions of this thrilling experience with their friends. Allow students to choose any means of communication they prefer to express their emotions, descriptions of the beach and the waves, and what they learned from this experience. Encourage students to write at least two sentences with the future to express probability, and two using *para* or *para que* to show the purpose of an action.

310

57 El anuncio del campeonato

 ▶ **Escucha** un anuncio de la radio y responde a estas preguntas.

1. ¿Cómo se llama el campeonato?
2. ¿Dónde y cuándo se celebra?
3. ¿Cuántos surfistas participan?
4. ¿De qué países vienen los participantes?

▶ **Crea** un cartel o un folleto para promocionar esta competencia de surf.

Final del desafío

Eva: Ethan, ¿dónde ___1___ los surfistas?

Ethan: No lo sé, pero me imagino que en la playa. Vamos, la competencia empieza enseguida. ¿Crees que ___2___ olas hoy?

Eva: Seguro que sí, en el Pacífico siempre hay olas. Por cierto, ¿tú ___3___ ahí las preguntas de la entrevista, verdad?

Ethan: Sí, aquí las tengo. Escribí cincuenta preguntas sobre su vida, sus aficiones, su familia, sus entrenamientos y las competencias. ¿___4___ suficiente?

Eva: ¿Suficiente? ¡No van a tener tiempo para responder a todas las preguntas! Anda, vamos a elegir las diez mejores. Luego podremos incluir algunas respuestas interesantes en el reportaje para que sea más entretenido. Ya escribí un borrador del texto.

Ethan: ¡Fantástico, Eva!

58 La entrevista

▶ **Completa** la conversación poniendo estos verbos en la forma correcta del futuro.

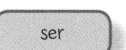 ser   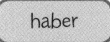 haber   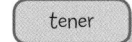 tener   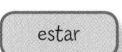 estar

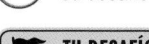 ▶ **Habla** con tu compañero(a). ¿Qué problema tienen Eva y Ethan? ¿Crees que van a lograr su desafío?

🚩→ TU DESAFÍO   Visita la página web. Escucha las preguntas de tu *Minientrevista Desafío 2* y escribe las respuestas.

trescientos once 311

HERITAGE LANGUAGE LEARNERS

• Ask students to name someone in sports from a Hispanic country whom they would like to interview and briefly explain why. Ask students to write at least seven questions that they would like to ask this person. Then have students exchange their questions with a partner, who will do some research on the person named and answer the questions. If time allows, have students conduct their interviews in front of the class as if they were doing a TV interview.

CRITICAL THINKING

• Ask students to think about how a surfing competition is organized. Most likely, a committee would be appointed to explore the site with the most reliable waves and available housing for the participants and their fans. Organizers would have to find sponsors who would be willing to offer prizes to the competitors. There would need to be an energetic public relations and advertising campaign. Have students work in small groups and discuss the tasks that need to be done before, during, and after the competition.

Activities

55. After completing this activity, have students write the script of a conversation between Juan José and Ethan in which Ethan interviews Juan José about his life as a professional surfer.

56. Before starting this activity, review the future of probability with students. Remind them that since they are making suppositions about what is going on in the picture, it is appropriate to use the future of probability. Students may also incorporate *tal vez* and *quizá(s)*.

57. Before students design their posters, have them brainstorm the information that the poster should contain. You can challenge students by requiring them to include both a statement of probability and a statement of purpose.

 AUDIO SCRIPT
See page 281J.

Answer Key

55. 1. participar   4. conseguir
     2. vean   5. practiquemos
     3. darme   6. puedan
     ▶ Answers will vary.

56. Answers will vary.

57. 1. Campeonato Panamericano de Surf.
     2. Se celebra en la playa de Tamarindo, Costa Rica, del 4 al 7 de junio.
     3. Habrá más de 70 participantes.
     4. Los participantes vienen de todo el mundo. Estarán los mejores participantes de Australia, Estados Unidos, Perú, Chile, Argentina, México y Costa Rica.
     ▶ Answers will vary.

58. 1. estarán   3. tendrás
     2. habrá   4. Será
     ▶ Answers will vary.

Additional Resources

Fans Online activities
Practice Workbook

311

DESAFÍO 3

Transmitir las palabras de otros

Presentation

- In *Desafío 3*, Asha and Lucas will organize the trip that American students participating in the Ruta Quetzal will take to Madrid, Spain. Students will preview language used to talk about travel and lodging.

Activities	Standards	Resources
Texto	1.2, 2.1, 3.2	Vis. Pres.
59.	1.2, 1.3	
60.	1.1, 1.2, 2.1	
61.	1.2, 1.3	Audio
62.	1.1, 1.2, 1.3, 2.1, 5.2	
63. Cultura	1.1, 1.2, 2.1, 2.2, 5.1	Video

Teaching Suggestions

Warm-Up / Independent Starter

- Have students read the title and the introduction to the dialogue on page 312 and ask them to describe what they think the Ruta Quetzal is.

Preparation

- Ask volunteers to share their Independent Starters. Write a list of the students' ideas on the board.

Texto: Colaboradores en la Ruta Quetzal

- Show students pictures from previous years' Rutas (you can find them online). Then have volunteers read aloud the roles of Tim, Asha, and Lucas.

- Ask students to compare the information they learned in the dialogue about the Ruta Quetzal with their guesses from the Independent Starter and with the pictures they looked at before reading. Then have students summarize the information they have about the Ruta Quetzal.

Activities

59. After completing this activity, you may ask students what they understand by *viaje cultural* and list the activities they would expect in this trip. You may also ask them if they have ever used a passport or applied for a visa.

60. Discuss with students how easy or difficult this *desafío* will be for Asha and Lucas when comparing it with previous ones they have completed. Ask students to justify their answers.

312

Colaboradores en la Ruta Quetzal

Asha and Lucas are going to help the organizers of the Ruta Quetzal. They will have to plan the trip that the American students will take to Madrid, Spain, the city where the route begins. Tim will provide some help as well.

TIM: ¡Hola, chicos! ¿Ya saben lo que es la Ruta Quetzal?

ASHA: Sí. La Ruta Quetzal es un viaje cultural para jóvenes de 16 y 17 años por España y Latinoamérica.

LUCAS: Y para este desafío nosotros tenemos que ayudar a los chicos estadounidenses que van a participar este año, ¿verdad?

TIM: Eso es. Este año la ruta comienza en España, así que los participantes de todos los países deberán reunirse en Madrid. Ustedes tendrán que ocuparse de reservar los boletos del viaje y el alojamiento.

ASHA: La ruta se realiza en verano, o sea que es temporada alta. No creo que encontremos muchas ofertas de vuelos.

LUCAS: Bueno, trataremos de encontrar el mejor precio para un vuelo directo con destino a Madrid.

TIM: Ya saben que desde allí los participantes volarán a Bolivia.

ASHA: Ufff, espero que el avión no llegue con retraso. Por cierto, Tim, ¿sabes si los chicos necesitan tener visados para viajar a Madrid?

TIM: No, no lo sé. Tendrán que llamar a la embajada o preguntárselo a los organizadores del viaje.

LUCAS: Yo me encargo de eso.

ASHA: Pues yo voy a empezar a buscarles alojamiento. ¡Gracias, Tim!

59 Detective de palabras

▶ **Completa** estas oraciones con palabras del diálogo.

1. La Ruta Quetzal es un ___1___ cultural.

2. Asha y Lucas tienen que ocuparse de reservar los ___2___ del viaje y el ___3___.

3. Lucas intentará encontrar un ___4___ directo hasta Madrid.

4. Asha y Lucas deben averiguar si los estudiantes necesitan tener ___5___ para viajar a España.

312 trescientos doce

Differentiated Instruction

DEVELOPING LEARNERS

- Ask students to choose the correct answer.

1. *Los participantes en la Ruta Quetzal tienen ... años.* (b)
   a. *más de 17*   b. *entre 16 y 17*

2. *Asha cree que habrá ... ofertas de vuelos.* (b)
   a. *muchas*   b. *pocas*

3. *La Ruta Quetzal se realiza en...* (a)
   a. *verano*   b. *mayo*

4. *¿Adónde van los participantes desde Madrid?* (b)
   a. *a casa*   b. *a Bolivia*

5. *¿Quién va a llamar a la embajada?* (a)
   a. *Lucas*   b. *Asha*

EXPANDING LEARNERS

- Ask students to write a persuasive letter to the organizers of the Ruta Quetzal explaining why they would be good candidates for the next trip. Remind students to mention their mastery of the Spanish language and their interest in the geography, history, and archaeology of the Spanish-speaking world. Students should emphasize their fascination with other cultures, and their wish to interact with students from around the world and ultimately forge a career working with the Spanish language or the Foreign Service. Have students read their letters aloud.

60 **¿Comprendes?**

▶ **Responde** a estas preguntas.

1. ¿Quiénes participan en la Ruta Quetzal?
2. ¿Dónde comienza este año la Ruta Quetzal?
3. ¿En qué consiste el desafío de Asha y Lucas?
4. ¿Por qué cree Asha que no encontrarán muchas ofertas de vuelos?
5. ¿Para qué les recomienda Tim que llamen a la embajada o a los organizadores?

61 **Los preparativos**

▶ **Escucha** y decide si estas oraciones son ciertas o falsas.

1. Lucas encontró un boleto muy barato con una compañía aérea española.
2. El problema con la compañía aérea italiana es que tienen que pasar una noche en Barcelona.
3. Lucas envió un correo electrónico a la embajada, pero todavía no tiene respuesta.
4. Asha hizo las reservas en dos cámpings cerca de Madrid.

▶ **Escucha** de nuevo y corrige las oraciones falsas.

62 **Participantes**

▶ **Lee** la ficha de Cultura y hazle estas preguntas a tu compañero(a). Después, compartan sus opiniones con la clase.

1. ¿Te gustaría participar en la Ruta Quetzal? ¿Por qué?
2. ¿Cómo te prepararías para el viaje?

CULTURA

La Ruta Quetzal

La Ruta Quetzal es un programa cultural y de aventura en el que un grupo de jóvenes de 16 y 17 años procedentes de más de 50 países realizan un viaje de un mes y medio de duración por España y Latinoamérica. Este proyecto tiene como objetivo fomentar (to promote) el conocimiento cultural y científico del mundo hispanohablante mediante visitas y conferencias (lectures). También promueve la cooperación internacional con el fin de crear valores de justicia y solidaridad.

63 **Investiga.** ¿Qué tipo de actividades te imaginas que hacen los participantes en la Ruta Quetzal? Investiga en su página web. ¿Cuáles te parecen más interesantes?

trescientos trece 313

Transmitir las palabras de otros

 AUDIO SCRIPT
See page 281 J.

 CULTURA

La Ruta Quetzal

To be selected for the Ruta Quetzal, students produce an original research project on arts or science related to the Hispanic world. Students who are selected take part in a wide range of activities, such as tours of historic towns, hiking and camping, reenactments of historic explorations, and workshops on history, politics, and the environment. An important part of the trip involves attending lectures given by university professors or relevant personalities.

Answer Key

59. 1. viaje   4. vuelo
2. boletos   5. visados
3. alojamiento

60. 1. Participan jóvenes de 16 y 17 años.
2. Comienza en Madrid, España.
3. Consiste en ayudar a los estudiantes estadounidenses que van a participar este año en la Ruta.
4. Porque es temporada alta.
5. Para saber si necesitan visados.

61. 1. Falso. Encontró un boleto barato con una compañía aérea italiana.
2. Cierto.
3. Falso. Dejó un mensaje en el buzón de voz de la embajada.
4. Falso. Hizo una reserva para dos noches en un cámping cerca de Madrid.
62. Answers will vary.
63. Answers will vary.

Additional Resources

Fans Online activities

HERITAGE LANGUAGE LEARNERS

- Ask students to imagine that the Ruta Quetzal is going to spend some time in their family's country of origin and they will be working with the Ruta's organizers to make sure that the participants will have a meaningful trip. Students will select three or four different areas within the country that are worthy of a one- or two-day visit. Have students describe these areas, and the cultural sites located there. Students should also make recommendations for spots where participants can hike and observe natural wonders and where they might find lodging.

SPECIAL-NEEDS LEARNERS

- Provide the script for activity 61 to students with hearing disabilities. Ask them to read the script once or twice before listening to the audio. For some students, it may be appropriate for you to read the script to them before playing the recording. Then play the recording and have students track the text of the script with their fingers.

DESAFÍO 3

Vocabulario – Viajes y alojamiento

Presentation

- In this section, students will learn words related to travel and lodging.

Activities	Standards	Resources
Vocabulario	1.2	
64.	1.3	
65.	1.1, 1.3, 5.1, 5.2	
66.	1.3	
67. Cultura	1.1, 1.2, 2.2, 4.2	

Teaching Suggestions

Warm-Up / Independent Starter

- Ask students to write a list of things they had to do to get ready for their last trip.

Preparation

- Have different volunteers read the speech bubbles aloud. Then have students repeat the highlighted words after you. Explain to students that there isn't an exact equivalent in the United States of a *pensión*. It is an inexpensive hotel-like lodging, similar to a guesthouse or inn.

- Read the text *Consejos útiles: vuelos y reservas* aloud. Have students repeat the highlighted words after you and make sure they understand each word. Show pictures or give students examples. For instance, to explain *vuelo directo* and *vuelo con escalas* you may have a trip route written on the board: Chicago → Madrid vs. Chicago → Nueva York → Madrid.

- After you have introduced the vocabulary, have students review their Independent Starter lists and ask them to incorporate new vocabulary words as needed.

Activities

65. Ask students to bring travel brochures to make the presentation more real. To make sure they are on task, ask students to take notes on the basic data from each presentation.

66. You may want to ask students to prepare a visual presentation based on the text they wrote. Ask them not to read the text during their presentation.

314

Vocabulario

Viajes y alojamiento

> Por favor, ¿se necesita visa para viajar a España?

> Si viaja como turista, puede entrar sin visado.

> Buscamos un hotel en Madrid que esté bien situado. O una pensión.

> Necesito las fechas de entrada y salida para hacer las reservas.

Asha y Lucas consultan con la embajada. Quieren llevar la documentación en orden para el **control de pasaportes**.

Después acuden a la agencia de viajes a comprar sus boletos y reservar alojamiento en Madrid.

Consejos útiles: vuelos y reservas

Antes de comprar un boleto de avión, piense que hay **vuelos directos** y **vuelos con escalas**. Por tanto, considere todas las opciones posibles para elegir la más adecuada de acuerdo con su destino.

Si su viaje coincide con un período de **temporada alta** (normalmente, en verano y en vacaciones), haga la reserva con la antelación suficiente.

Cuando compre el boleto, **confirme la reserva**. Si su viaje es de ida y vuelta, trate de cerrar el vuelo de regreso. Así se evitará el riesgo de no tener **plaza disponible** para su vuelta.

Para **vuelos internacionales**, confirme su reserva de salida o de regreso al menos con 72 horas de antelación. En caso contrario, podría **cancelarse la reserva**.

Más vocabulario

El aeropuerto

la línea aérea	*airline*
el mostrador	*counter*
la tarjeta de embarque	*boarding pass*
la terminal	*terminal*
el vuelo nacional	*domestic flight*
procedente de...	*arriving from ...*
con destino a...	*departing for ...*

Viajes

el retraso/la demora	*delay*
la temporada baja	*low season*
el viaje de negocios	*business trip*
el viaje organizado	*package tour*
el viaje de placer	*personal trip*

64 **Viajes, viajes, viajes**

▶ **Escribe** una oración con cada palabra. Usa un contexto para recordarla.

Modelo la pensión
  → *Nos alojamos en una pensión porque era más barata que un hotel.*

1. la visa	3. el retraso	5. la temporada alta
2. el vuelo	4. la terminal	6. el viaje organizado

Differentiated Instruction

DEVELOPING LEARNERS

- Ask students whether the following statements are true (*cierto*) or false (*falso*). Have them correct the false statements.

1. *Un vuelo directo es un vuelo con escalas.* (falso; sin escalas)
2. *Si el avión sale a tiempo, no hay retrasos.* (cierto)
3. *Si viajas para tu empresa, haces un viaje de placer.* (falso; viaje de negocios)
4. *Si te gusta viajar con otras personas, haz un viaje organizado.* (cierto)
5. *Por lo general, los viajes son más caros en temporada baja.* (falso; en temporada alta)

EXPANDING LEARNERS

- Ask students to research some *paradores* in different regions of Spain and recommend three that cater to travelers with different needs and interests. For example, some travelers might be parents traveling with children, others might be college students, and others might be retired couples. Some might be nature lovers and want to do some hiking, others might want to focus on cultural activities, and others might prefer simply relaxing and dining at upscale restaurants. Students should make up their own travelers' profiles and make their suggestions for the ideal *parador* accordingly.

65 En la agencia de viajes

▶ **Escribe** con tu compañero(a) un diálogo entre un(a) agente de viajes y un(a) cliente(a) que prepara sus vacaciones. Incluyan la siguiente información:

1. ¿Adónde quiere ir? ¿Con quién irá?
2. ¿Cuándo va a ir? En ese lugar, ¿es temporada alta o baja?
3. ¿Cómo quiere ir?
4. ¿Hay vuelos directos a ese destino o tendrá que hacer escala?
5. ¿Dónde se va a alojar?

▶ **Representen** el diálogo para la clase.

66 Mi último viaje

▶ **Escribe** un texto sobre el último viaje que hiciste. Incluye estos datos:

1. Cuándo, adónde y con quién fuiste.
2. Qué medios de transporte usaste.
3. En qué lugares te alojaste.
4. Algún problema relacionado con el viaje.

 **CULTURA**

Hoteles con encanto

Los paradores de turismo son una cadena de hoteles de lujo creada en España en 1929 para proyectar en el exterior una imagen moderna y de calidad del turismo. Muchos paradores están situados en edificios históricos, como castillos, palacios y monasterios restaurados; otros están ubicados en plena naturaleza. Los paradores ofrecen también restaurantes de alta calidad donde se elaboran los platos tradicionales de cada zona.

Comedor del Parador de Sigüenza (España).

67 **Piensa.** ¿Qué edificio histórico de los Estados Unidos crees que podría convertirse en un hotel de lujo? ¿Qué ventajas tendría alojarse allí?

trescientos quince 315

Vocabulario – Viajes y alojamiento

67. Assign this activity for homework and ask students to bring a picture of the building they selected and briefly explain to the class why they made that selection.

 CULTURA

Hoteles con encanto

The most popular *paradores* are located in Granada, León, and Santiago de Compostela, where reservations should be made well in advance. In addition to offering superb service and food, all *paradores* encourage high-quality tourism by arranging activities with local businesses. These activities range from cooking lessons to art, history tours, and outdoor activities.

Answer Key

64. Answers will vary. Sample answers:
  1. El estudiante de intercambio no pudo entrar en el país porque no tenía visa.
  2. El vuelo de Chicago a Nueva York se retrasó dos horas.
  3. Debido a un retraso por una tormenta, perdimos la conexión con el siguiente vuelo.
  4. Al llegar al aeropuerto hay que buscar la terminal donde está la compañía aérea con la que se va a viajar.
  5. En temporada alta los pasajes están muy caros.
  6. En un viaje organizado la agencia de viajes hace todas las reservas.

65. Answers will vary.
  ▶ Answers will vary.

66. Answers will vary.

67. Answers will vary.

Additional Resources

Fans Online activities
Practice Workbook

315

HERITAGE LANGUAGE LEARNERS

• Ask students to research some historic buildings in their family's country of origin and decide which one would make an ideal *parador* to welcome travelers, and why. Have students address the history of the building and describe the accommodations they propose for the new *parador*. Students should also mention some of the *parador's* services, such as the availability of a restaurant, spa, recreational activities, or organized tours, as well as a brief description of the nearby historic and cultural sites.

MULTIPLE INTELLIGENCES:
Verbal-Linguistic Intelligence

• Ask students to select one of Spain's *paradores* and create an ad that promotes this *parador*. The ad should address the *parador's* name, location, and historic importance, the nearby natural sites and cultural attractions, and a description of the *parador's* accommodations, amenities, and prices. Students should include information on how to ask for more information or make a reservation. Encourage students to include images. Display students' work in the classroom and have students vote on the most effective ad.

DESAFÍO 3

Gramática – El estilo indirecto

Presentation

- In this section, students will learn how to use indirect or reported speech to report what another person said.

Activities	Standards	Resources
Gramática	1.2, 3.1	
68.	1.2, 4.1	
69.	1.3	
70.	1.2, 1.3	Audio
71.	1.1, 1.2, 5.1	
72. Conexiones	1.1, 1.2, 2.2, 3.1, 4.2	

Teaching Suggestions

Warm-Up / Independent Starter

- Have students write four things that their parents or siblings said the last time they traveled somewhere. Ask them to use direct speech. For example: *Mi madre dijo: «Tenemos que hacer una reserva».*

Preparation

- Discuss the grammar topic with students. As extra practice, have them convert their Independent Starter sentences into indirect speech. Emphasize that in cases in which a command or request is involved, the subjunctive is needed.

Activities

70. After students have finished, ask them to change these sentences into direct speech to make them aware of the changes in subject, tense, and mood.

71. For the second part of this activity, in order to avoid having many students working with the same situation, you may have several sets of flashcards with numbers 1 to 5. Give every pair of students a flashcard with a number and ask them to work with the corresponding situation.

 AUDIO SCRIPT
See page 281 J.

316

Gramática

El estilo indirecto

Estilo directo y estilo indirecto

VERBOS ÚTILES

> decir
> contar
> comentar
> explicar
> anunciar
> preguntar
> contestar

- In Spanish, as in English, we use **direct speech** to quote word for word what another person said. We use **indirect or reported speech** to relate what another person said.

  Luis **dice**: «No **hablo** inglés». → Luis **dice que** no **habla** inglés.

- In reported speech, the reporting verb (decir, responder…) is followed by que. The subject pronoun changes, and it may be necessary to change the verb tense to match the moment of speaking.

  Luis **dijo**: «No **hablo** inglés». → Luis **dijo que** no **hablaba** inglés.

- With the verb preguntar, in indirect yes / no questions, use si instead of que.

  Luis me preguntó: «¿Tienes hermanos?». → Luis me preguntó **si** tenía hermanos.

El indicativo y el subjuntivo en el estilo indirecto

- If the direct speech relays information, use the **indicative mood** in the dependent clause of the reported speech.

ESTILO DIRECTO	ESTILO INDIRECTO
La línea aérea **anunció**: «**Hay** un retraso».	La línea aérea **anunció** que **había** un retraso.
Los pasajeros **dijeron**: «**Vamos** a reclamar».	Los pasajeros **dijeron** que **iban** a reclamar.

- If the direct speech relays a request or a command, use the **subjunctive mood** in the dependent clause of the reported speech.

ESTILO DIRECTO	ESTILO INDIRECTO
Ana le **dice** a su esposo: «**Compra** los boletos».	Ana le **dice** a su esposo que **compre** los boletos.
El piloto les **dijo** a los pasajeros: «¡**Siéntense**!».	El piloto les **dijo** a los pasajeros que **se sentaran**.

68 **Compara.** ¿Cómo es la estructura verbal en inglés cuando el estilo indirecto expresa información? ¿Y cuando expresa mandato? ¿Hay diferencias?

69 **¿Quién dijo qué?**

▶ **Escribe** estas oraciones usando el estilo indirecto.

1. Asha le comentó a Tim: «En temporada alta no hay ofertas».
2. Lucas le dijo a Asha: «Prefiero un vuelo directo, sin escalas».
3. Lucas le pidió a Asha: «Llama a la embajada para pedir información».
4. Asha le contestó a Tess: «No me gusta viajar en avión, prefiero el tren».

Differentiated Instruction

DEVELOPING LEARNERS

- Ask students to change the direct speech to indirect speech in these sentences:
  1. *Mi amigo me comentó: «No tengo pasaporte». (… que no tenía pasaporte.)*
  2. *La línea aérea anunció: «Hay retraso». (… que había retraso.)*
  3. *El agente de viajes nos dijo: «Lleguen temprano». (… que llegáramos temprano.)*
  4. *Mi madre dice: «Ven conmigo». (… que vaya con ella.)*
  5. *El profesor me dijo: «¡Estudia!». (… que estudiara.)*

EXPANDING LEARNERS

- Working with a partner, ask students to create a dialogue in which students will practice both direct and indirect speech by talking about everyday school and social events. Explain that they should work in examples of indirect speech that include requests in order to use the subjunctive. You might get students started by giving them the following example:
  A. *¿Qué te dijo el profesor de Matemáticas?*
  B. *Me dijo que no aprobé el examen.*
  A. *¿Y qué te recomendó?*
  B. *Me recomendó que estudiara más.*

70 **Compañeros de viaje**

▶ **Escucha** y une las dos columnas. Después, escribe las oraciones poniendo el verbo en la forma correcta.

Ⓐ	Ⓑ
1. Tim le dice a Lucas y a Asha...	a. que ella no _____ tienda de campaña. (tener)
2. Tim les anuncia a Asha y Lucas...	b. que _____ los detalles del viaje. (confirmar)
3. Asha le explica a Lucas...	c. que anoche _____ con los organizadores. (hablar)
4. Lucas le responde a Asha...	d. que _____ pasar una semana en Madrid. (poder)
5. Tim les pide...	e. que no se _____. (preocupar)
6. Asha le dice a Tim...	f. que _____ una sorpresa para ellos. (tener)

71 **Conversaciones**

▶ **Imagina** estas situaciones y responde a las preguntas.

Modelo 1. *Le dije que limpiaría mi cuarto después de estudiar.*

1. Tu padre te pidió que limpiaras tu cuarto. Tú estabas estudiando. ¿Qué le dijiste?
2. Le dijiste a tu amigo(a) que viniera a tu casa para estudiar juntos(as), pero no vino. ¿Qué te dijo?
3. Tu hermano te confesó que le gusta una chica de su clase. ¿Qué le preguntaste?
4. Tu abuela te anunció que acaba de apuntarse a un viaje a Europa. ¿Qué le pediste?
5. El profesor les comentó que hicieron bien el examen. ¿Qué le respondieron?

▶ **Habla** con tu compañero(a) sobre una de esas situaciones. Hazle otras preguntas para saber más cosas.

Modelo A. *Mi abuela me anunció que se va de viaje a Europa este verano.*
B. *¿Y le pediste algo?*
A. *Sí, le pedí que me trajera un recuerdo.*

CONEXIONES: CIENCIAS

El Hotel de Sal (Bolivia)

En el departamento de Potosí (Bolivia) se encuentra el Hotel de Sal, construido casi en su totalidad con bloques de sal. Es un moderno edificio ubicado en un gran salar en los Andes, a unos 3.650 metros de altitud. Solo tiene 27 habitaciones y, entre otros servicios, organiza rutas turísticas por la zona.

72 **Compara.** ¿Conoces otros hoteles o edificios sorprendentes por el material usado en su construcción o por su forma?

HERITAGE LANGUAGE LEARNERS

- Ask students to imagine that they have just interviewed an experienced travel agent who has published a book with practical tips for travelers. Ask students to write a list of these tips they have assembled from this expert. To do this, students should use indirect speech that makes use of both the indicative and the subjunctive. For example:
1. *El agente de viajes les dice a los viajeros que lleguen al aeropuerto dos horas antes del vuelo si es internacional.*
2. *También dice que deben llevar el pasaporte en un lugar seguro.*

MULTIPLE INTELLIGENCES:
Visual-Spatial Intelligence

- Ask students to research some hotels that are unusual not only because of the building materials and their shape, but also because of where they are located. Some examples include cave hotels in Turkey, a former jailhouse in Switzerland, a jumbo jet converted to a hotel in Sweden, an underwater lodge in Florida, treetop hotels in Turkey and China, and the chance to sleep in a shoe or an elephant (referring to hotels that are in these shapes). Ask students to select one of these hotels and make a poster to promote it.

CONEXIONES: CIENCIAS

El Hotel de Sal (Bolivia)

This hotel makes good use of local materials and resources. Not only are the walls made of salt, but the beds and most of the furniture are as well. In addition to local trips to visit the surrounding salt flats and the desolate yet beautiful salt desert surrounding the hotel, guests can relax at the hotel by taking baths in salt-water pools, which is considered good for health purposes.

Answer Key

68. Para expresar información se usa *that* y una cláusula subordinada (e.g., *The travel agent says that he has good fares.*). Para expresar un mandato se usa el infinitivo (e.g., *The captain asked the passengers to sit down.*).

69.
1. Asha le comentó a Tim que en temporada alta no había ofertas.
2. Lucas le dijo a Asha que prefería un vuelo directo, sin escalas.
3. Lucas le pidió a Asha que llamara a la embajada para pedir información.
4. Asha le contestó a Tess que no le gustaba viajar en avión y que prefería el tren.

70.
1. (f) Tim le dice a Lucas y a Asha que tiene...
2. (d) Tim les anuncia a Asha y Lucas que pueden...
3. (a) Asha le explica a Lucas que ella no tiene...
4. (e) Lucas le responde a Asha que no se preocupe.
5. (b) Tim les pide que confirmen...
6. (c) Asha le dice a Tim que anoche habló...

71. Answers will vary.
▶ Answers will vary.

72. Answers will vary.

Additional Resources

Fans Online activities
Practice Workbook

DESAFÍO 3

Gramática – Expresar lugar

Presentation

- In this section, students will learn and practice ways to express location.

Activities	Standards	Resources
Gramática	1.2, 3.1	
73.	1.2, 4.1	
74.	1.2, 1.3	
75.	1.2, 1.3, 2.1, 2.2	
76.	1.1, 1.2	Audio
77.	1.1, 1.2, 1.3, 5.1, 5.2	

Teaching Suggestions

Warm-Up / Independent Starter

- Have students answer the following questions:
  1. ¿Dónde estudias? ¿Cómo es ese lugar?
  2. ¿Adónde vas a practicar deportes? ¿Dónde está ese lugar?
  3. ¿Adónde irás en tus próximas vacaciones?
  4. ¿Por dónde paseas normalmente?

Preparation

- Have students read the grammar presentation silently. Encourage them to ask questions about any explanations they did not understand. Then read the examples of the grammar explanations aloud and point out the part of speech that is used to express location. Discuss the difference in meaning when using the indicative mood versus the subjunctive mood in the dependent clause.

- Have volunteers share their answers from the Independent Starter. After that, ask them to rewrite their sentences using *donde*. Provide them the following example: *Estudio en la biblioteca. Es un edificio muy grande y moderno.* → *La biblioteca donde estudio es un edificio grande y moderno.*

Activities

73. Provide students with more examples to be sure they understand the change of meaning depending on which mood is used. For example: *Comeremos donde hacen las mejores hamburguesas. / Comeremos donde hagan las mejores hamburguesas. Pasearemos hasta donde termina la calle. / Pasearemos hasta donde termine la calle.*

Gramática

Expresar lugar

Expresar lugar

- Use *donde* to introduce a dependent clause that refers to a place. *Donde* is often preceded by a preposition to indicate destination, origin, location, or movement.

> El parador **donde** estamos es muy antiguo.
> Esta es la calle **por donde** pasamos ayer.

EXPRESIONES DE LUGAR	
donde	*where*
adonde	*to where*
de/desde donde	*from where*
por donde	*through where*

El indicativo y el subjuntivo con expresiones de lugar

- When the main clause refers to a known (to the speaker), definite, or real place, use the **indicative mood** in the dependent clause.

> Vamos de vacaciones adonde **fuimos** el año pasado.
> Nos alojaremos en el único hotel desde donde se **ve** el mar.

- When the main clause refers to an unknown (to the speaker), indefinite, or hypothetical place, use the **subjunctive mood** in the dependent clause. In this case *donde* is often translated as *wherever, whatever place,* or *anywhere.*

> Vamos de vacaciones adonde tú **quieras.**
> Nos alojaremos en un hotel desde donde se **vea** el mar.

Preguntar sobre un lugar

- To ask about a place, use *dónde* or a preposition + *dónde* followed by a verb in the indicative mood.

> (?) ¿Dónde está la catedral?   →? ¿Adónde vas?
> ?→ ¿De dónde vienes?   ?→ ¿Por dónde se va al mercado?

73 **Compara.** Analiza y compara estas oraciones. ¿Qué significan?
   a. Iremos de viaje adonde tú **quieres.**   b. Iremos de viaje adonde tú **quieras.**

74 **Direcciones**

▶ **Completa** estas preguntas usando *dónde, por dónde, de dónde* y *adónde.*

1. ¿_____ está el aeropuerto más cercano?
2. ¿_____ vienes, Tim? Es muy tarde...
3. ¿_____ se va al Hotel El Inca?
4. ¿_____ van Asha y Lucas con tanta prisa?
5. ¿_____ son estas fotografías tan bonitas?
6. ¿_____ puedo ir a la estación de autobuses?

318 trescientos dieciocho

Differentiated Instruction

DEVELOPING LEARNERS

- Ask students to complete these sentences:
  1. ¿... está el mostrador? (b)
     a. *Adónde*   b. *Dónde*
  2. ¿... sales hacia la escuela? (b)
     a. *Adónde*   b. *Desde dónde*
  3. Hay que pasar ... está el control de pasaportes. (a)
     a. *por donde*   b. *desde donde*
  4. Voy ... tú me lleves. (a)
     a. *adonde*   b. *de donde*
  5. ¿... viene tanta gente?   (a)
     a. *De dónde*   b. *Adónde*
  6. ¿... se va a la terminal? (b)
     a. *Adónde*   b. *Por dónde*

EXPANDING LEARNERS

- Have students work with a partner and take turns asking and answering each other's questions about real or imaginary vacations, or about everyday activities. Students should include questions that make use of *donde, adonde, por donde,* and *de/desde donde,* as well as using these words as interrogatives when asking questions. For example:
  A. ¿Adónde fueron de vacaciones?
  B. Fuimos a Florida, desde donde salimos para las Bahamas.
  A. ¿Y de dónde en Florida salieron?
  B. De Miami. Es un puerto desde donde salen muchísimos cruceros.

75 Un foro de la ruta

▶ **Completa** este foro sobre la Ruta Quetzal.

| donde | dónde | desde donde | adónde | por donde |

Ruta Quetzal BBVA

Autor	Mensaje
Marcos Publicado: 11/04/2013 12:30 p. m.	Hola, me gustaría participar en la próxima Ruta Quetzal. ¿Alguien sabe ___1___ puedo leer los requisitos?
Gema Publicado: 11/04/2013 3:10 p. m.	Hola, Marcos. Yo participé el año pasado. Tienes toda la información en su página web. Clica con el ratón ___2___ dice «¿Cómo participar?»
Marcos Publicado: 11/04/2013 4:30 p. m.	¡Qué suerte! Seguro que visitaste un montón de países. ¿___3___ fuiste?
Gema Publicado: 11/04/2013 4:50 p. m.	Fuimos a México para conocer los misteriosos Caminos Blancos mayas. Eran los caminos que usaban los mayas para establecer rutas comerciales y ___4___ transportaban el agua y otras mercaderías. Después de recorrer la península de Yucatán, volamos a España y visitamos ciudades como Madrid, Segovia o Ávila. Luego fuimos al sur, a Cádiz, ___5___ salimos para Lisboa (Portugal). Finalmente seguimos hasta Galicia y recorrimos parte del famosísimo Camino de Santiago.

76 Planes

▶ **Escucha** a Asha y a Lucas haciendo planes para su viaje a Madrid y responde a estas preguntas.

1. ¿Adónde le gustaría ir a Asha, además de a Madrid? ¿Y a Lucas?
2. ¿Dónde sugiere Lucas que pueden alojarse?
3. ¿Dónde prefiere alojarse Asha?
4. Según Lucas, ¿dónde se alojarán?

77 El viaje más agradable

▶ **Habla** con tu compañero(a). Planeen un viaje imaginario según sus preferencias.

Modelo   hotel → *Yo quiero alojarme en un hotel donde haya piscina cubierta.*

| **Lugar:** playa / montaña / ciudad | **Alojamiento:** hotel / cámping / pensión / parador |
| **Transporte:** avión / tren / coche | **Temporada:** primavera / verano / otoño / invierno |

▶ **Escribe** el plan de viaje con todos los detalles.

trescientos diecinueve 319

---

76. You may want to change the format of this activity into a "complete the sentence" exercise and add some more questions.

1. *A Asha le gustaría ir de vacaciones a una ciudad…*
2. *A Lucas le gustaría estar en un lugar…*
3. *Cádiz es una ciudad…*
4. *Lucas sugiere alojarse en un parador…*
5. *Asha sugiere quedarse en un cámping…*
6. *Lucas dice que se alojarán…*

 AUDIO SCRIPT
See page 281J.

Answer Key

73. a. *We will take a trip where you want to go.*
   b. *We will take a trip wherever you may want to go.*

74.
1. Dónde	4. Adónde
2. De dónde	5. De dónde
3. Por dónde	6. Por dónde

75.
1. dónde	4. por donde
2. donde	5. desde donde
3. Adónde	

76.
1. A Asha le gustaría ir a una ciudad donde no tenga que usar el coche. A Lucas le gustaría ir a un lugar donde haya olas grandes para practicar surf.
2. En un parador desde donde se vea el mar.
3. Prefiere alojarse en un cámping donde se disfrute de la naturaleza.
4. Se alojarán donde Asha quiera.

77. Answers will vary.
   ▶ Answers will vary.

Additional Resources

Fans Online activities
Practice Workbook

319

LECTURA: TEXTO LITERARIO

Presentation

- In this section, students will read a short story. As they read, students will become aware of how the present tense is used in a scene which emphasizes a mental process over an action.

Activities	Standards	Resources
Lectura: texto literario	1.2, 2.2, 3.1, 3.2	
78.	1.1, 1.2, 1.3	
79.	1.3	

Teaching Suggestions

Warm-Up / Independent Starter

- Ask students to observe the picture, read the title, and think about possible topics for the reading. Have them express their hypotheses in writing.

Preparation

- Call on individual students to share their Independent Starters. Do they have similar predictions regarding the topic of the reading? What led them to their particular predictions? Ask students to read the title again, and make sure they understand that it is the diminutive form of a noun. Do they know the meaning of *galleta*? How might this be connected with the topic of traveling?

- Have students work with a partner to read the *Antes de leer* strategies. Then ask pairs to write the answers to the questions posed. Once pairs have finished working on the *Antes de leer* questions, discuss the answers as a class.

- Read the short story aloud to model pronunciation and have students follow along in their books. Then call on individual students to alternate reading a paragraph aloud. Offer assistance with pronunciation of difficult words.

- After students have finished reading, create a two-column chart on the board and ask them to look for adjectives in the text that describe the woman and the young man, and list them in each column. Examples include: *(mujer) elegante, fastidiada, indignada, irritada, furiosa; (joven) divertido, sonrisa amorosa, angelical.* Have students compare the two columns.

320

Antes de leer: estrategias

1. Lee el título del texto. ¿Qué significa la palabra *galleta*? Fíjate en las ilustraciones. ¿De qué crees que trata el texto?
2. ¿Qué comida llevas contigo cuando vas de viaje? ¿Hablas a veces con otros pasajeros que no conoces en los trenes o en los aviones?
3. Mira el tercer párrafo. Anota las palabras que describen a la mujer.
4. Mira el cuarto párrafo. Anota las palabras que describen al joven. ¿Crees que el joven y la mujer se llevarán bien?

Galletitas
Jorge Bucay (Argentina, 1949)

A una estación de trenes llega una tarde una señora muy elegante. En la ventanilla le informan que el tren está retrasado y que tardará aproximadamente una hora en llegar a la estación. Un poco fastidiada[1], la señora va al puesto de diarios y compra una revista, luego pasa al quiosco y compra un paquete de galletitas y una lata de gaseosa[2].

Preparada para la forzosa[3] espera, se sienta en uno de los largos bancos del andén. Mientras hojea la revista[4], un joven se sienta a su lado y comienza a leer un diario. Imprevistamente la señora ve, por el rabillo[5] del ojo, cómo el muchacho, sin decir una palabra, estira la mano, agarra el paquete de galletitas, lo abre y después de sacar una comienza a comérsela despreocupadamente.

La mujer está indignada. No está dispuesta a ser grosera[6], pero tampoco a hacer de cuenta que nada ha pasado; así que, con gesto ampuloso[7], toma el paquete y saca una galletita que exhibe frente al joven y se la come mirándolo fijamente.

Por toda respuesta, el joven sonríe... y toma otra galletita. La señora gime[8] un poco, toma una nueva galletita y, con ostensibles señales de fastidio, se la come sosteniendo otra vez la mirada en el muchacho. El diálogo de miradas y sonrisas continúa entre galleta y galleta. La señora cada vez más irritada, el muchacho cada vez más divertido.

Finalmente, la señora se da cuenta de que en el paquete queda solo la última galletita. «No podrá ser tan caradura[9]», piensa, y se queda como congelada[10] mirando alternativamente al joven y a las galletitas. Con calma, el muchacho alarga la mano, toma la última galletita y, con mucha suavidad, la corta exactamente por la mitad. Con su sonrisa más amorosa le ofrece media a la señora.

320 trescientos veinte

Differentiated Instruction

DEVELOPING LEARNERS

- Have students read the story silently and write any words they do not understand, including those that are footnoted, in their notebooks. Ask them to use a dictionary to look up the meanings. Pair these students with those who have superior language skills or are heritage learners. Ask the developing learners to read the story aloud, and have their partners help them with their pronunciation and intonation. After students read each paragraph, ask them to summarize it to their partners.

EXPANDING LEARNERS

- After students complete activity 78, ask them to use the information from their charts and write a detailed description of one character, including a profile as if they were psychologists. Explain to students that they do not need to limit themselves to the descriptions found in the story. Encourage them to be creative and to add their own ideas as to the person's behavior. Students might even make assumptions about what this person was like as a young child, or what he or she will be like twenty years from now.

—¡Gracias! —dice la mujer tomando con rudeza la media galletita.

—De nada —contesta el joven sonriendo angelical mientras come su mitad.

El tren llega. Furiosa, la señora se levanta con sus cosas y sube al tren. Al arrancar, desde el vagón ve al muchacho todavía sentado en el banco del andén y piensa: «Insolente». Siente la boca reseca de ira[11]. Abre la cartera para sacar la lata de gaseosa y se sorprende al encontrar, cerrado, su paquete de galletitas… ¡intacto![12]

Fragmento del cuento tradicional «Galletitas», según adaptación
del autor Jorge Bucay, libro *De la autoestima al egoísmo.*

1. *annoyed*	4. *she pages through the magazine*	7. *exaggerated*	10. *frozen*
2. *soda*	5. *corner*	8. *groans*	11. *anger, rage*
3. *obligatory*	6. *rude*	9. *he won't have the nerve*	12. *untouched*

78 Impresiones

▶ **Escribe** las palabras utilizadas en el texto para describir las actitudes, los gestos y las acciones y reacciones de cada personaje. Reflexiona sobre la forma en que este vocabulario establece un contraste entre ellos.

Los personajes de *Galletitas*		
	Señora	**Chico joven**
Actitudes		
Gestos		
Acciones		
Reacciones		

 ▶ **Responde** a estas preguntas y comenta tus respuestas con tus compañeros(as).

1. ¿Qué piensa el lector sobre los dos personajes durante la lectura? ¿Y al final del cuento?
2. ¿Cuál de los dos personajes te despierta mayor simpatía? ¿Por qué?
3. ¿Piensas que esta historia puede ocurrir en la vida real? ¿Cómo reaccionarías tú si fueras la señora? ¿Y si fueras el joven?
4. ¿Crees que tu reacción sería diferente si el joven que «roba» las galletas fuera menos cortés? ¿Por qué?

79 Con tus propias palabras

▶ **Escribe** la escena que sigue al final de este cuento.

Activities

78. To expand this activity, you may want to ask additional comprehension questions. For example: *¿Dónde tiene lugar esta historia? ¿Por qué tiene que esperar la señora? ¿Por qué está indignada? ¿Cómo reacciona el joven? ¿Qué descubre la señora cuando sube al tren?*

Answer Key

78. Answers will vary. Sample answers:
Actitudes: (señora) fastidiada, irritada, furiosa; (joven) despreocupado, cada vez más divertido.
Gestos: (señora) gesto ampuloso, señales de fastidio, se queda como congelada; (joven) alarga la mano con calma, con mucha suavidad.
Acciones: (señora) saca y exhibe una galleta frente al joven, se la come mirándolo fijamente, mira al joven y a las galletitas; (joven) agarra el paquete de galletitas y se come una, toma una nueva galletita, le ofrece media galletita a la señora.
Reacciones: (señora) está indignada, sostiene otra vez la mirada, toma con rudeza la media galleta, tiene la boca reseca de ira; (joven) sonríe por respuesta, contesta sonriendo angelical.

▶ Answers will vary. Sample answers:
1. El lector piensa que el joven es insolente y maleducado porque le roba las galletas a la señora. Al final del cuento se da cuenta de que la señora se equivocó y reaccionó de manera exagerada.
2. El joven, porque es amable.
3. Answers will vary.
4. Sí. Creo que no me caería tan bien y no sentiría simpatía por él.

79. Answers will vary.

Additional Resources

Fans Online activities

HERITAGE LANGUAGE LEARNERS

- Ask students to imagine that they are on a train traveling through a Spanish-speaking country. They are traveling alone, and the trip will take a long time. Ask students to write a short story about their trip, which might include fellow passengers such as a mysterious stranger, an old friend they haven't seen for some time, a group of unruly children, or any other characters they would like to include. Students should decide the point of view they want to use and the plot. Invite students to read their stories aloud.

MULTIPLE INTELLIGENCES:
Visual-Spatial Intelligence

- Ask students to think about what the two characters in the story looked like, what clothes they might have worn, and in what year the story might have taken place. Then ask them to draw one of the scenes in the story. The scene could be of both characters "sharing" *las galletitas*, of the woman alone when she is buying the cookies, of her opening her purse on the train, or of the young man alone on the bench as the woman's train pulls away. Exhibit students' work in the classroom.

DESAFÍO 3

Comunicación

Presentation

- In this section, students will integrate the vocabulary and grammar skills from *Desafío 3* in order to talk about travel and lodging arrangements, as well as to report what a person said, and to express location.

Activities	Standards	Resources
80.	1.1, 1.2, 1.3, 5.1, 5.2	
81.	1.1, 1.2, 1.3, 5.1	
82. Final del desafío	1.1, 1.2, 1.3, 5.1	
Tu desafío	1.1, 1.2	

Teaching Suggestions

Warm-Up / Independent Starter

- Have students complete these sentences following this model: *Siempre como en restaurantes donde usan productos orgánicos.*
  1. *Este año vamos de vacaciones...*
  2. *Me gusta quedarme en hoteles...*
  3. *Prefiero las playas...*
  4. *No me gustan los lugares...*
  5. *No recuerdo...*

Preparation

- Ask volunteers to read their Independent Starter sentences aloud. Make sure all students understand the connotation indicated by the use of the indicative versus the subjunctive mood in these sentences. You may want to change the mood of some of the sentences students shared to demostrate how the meaning changes. For example: *Este año vamos de vacaciones adonde decidan mis padres* (i.e., to whatever place my parents decide). *Este año vamos de vacaciones adonde decidieron mis padres* (i.e., to the place my parents chose).
- Have students work in pairs and write a brief conversation between Asha and Lucas discussing how far they are in their *desafío* right now. They should use two examples for expressing location. Ask a pair of students to write their dialogues on the board.

322

Comunicación

80 Viajeros

 ▶ **Haz** este cuestionario a tu compañero(a) y toma nota de sus respuestas.

¿Qué tipo de viajero eres?

Haz este cuestionario y descúbrelo.

1. Te gustan más las vacaciones...
   a. de aventura
   b. culturales
   c. de relax

2. Prefieres alojarte...
   a. en un cámping
   b. en un apartamento
   c. en un hotel

3. En general, prefieres ir de vacaciones...
   a. al campo
   b. a una ciudad
   c. a la playa

4. En tus viajes, lo que más te interesa es...
   a. la naturaleza
   b. los deportes
   c. la cultura

5. En tu maleta hay siempre...
   a. una brújula
   b. un suéter
   c. unas gafas de sol

6. Cuando estás de viaje, sueles comer...
   a. al aire libre
   b. en un buen restaurante
   c. comida rápida

7. Planificas tus viajes...
   a. nunca
   b. con mucha antelación
   c. con poco tiempo

8. Elegirías un viaje organizado...
   a. nunca
   b. para ir al extranjero
   c. para ir a cualquier lugar

9. Te gustaría ir de viaje...
   a. a Machu Picchu (Perú)
   b. a Buenos Aires (Argentina)
   c. a una playa del Caribe

10. De tus viajes traes...
    a. buenas experiencias
    b. muchos regalos
    c. fotografías

 ▶ **Analiza** las respuestas de tu compañero(a) y dile qué tipo de viajero(a) es. ¿Qué destino del mundo hispano le recomiendas?

 aventurero(a)  urbano(a)  de sol y playa

Modelo *Yo creo que eres un viajero muy aventurero porque te gustan las vacaciones de aventura y prefieres alojarte en un cámping. Pero también dijiste que cuando estás de viaje sueles comer en un buen restaurante...*

Differentiated Instruction

DEVELOPING LEARNERS

- Ask students to rephrase their partners' answers for activity 80 using indirect speech. For example:
  1. *Me dijiste que te gustaban más las vacaciones...*
  2. *Me dijiste que preferías alojarte en...*
  3. *Me dijiste que en general preferías ir de vacaciones...*
  4. *Me dijiste que cuando estabas de viaje, lo que mas te interesaba era...*
  5. *Me dijiste que en tu maleta había siempre...*
  6. *Me dijiste que cuando estabas de viaje solías comer...*

EXPANDING LEARNERS

- Have students think about how this *desafío* might end. Do they think Asha and Lucas will complete their task successfully? Or will they fail? Why do they think so? Ask students to write either a happy or a sad ending to this challenge. Students may do this by writing an additional dialogue to what is presented on page 323, or with a narrative, explaining what the travel agent and the camp director are going to say and what the participants are going to do next.

81 **Problemas en el viaje**

▶ **Escribe** con tu compañero(a) un diálogo para cada una de estas situaciones.

Situación A
Al llegar al hotel, un cliente descubre que no hay una reserva a su nombre, aunque está seguro de que habló con el recepcionista para confirmarla.

Situación B
Un pasajero llega al mostrador de la terminal en el aeropuerto y una empleada le dice que su vuelo no es directo y tendrá que hacer escala.

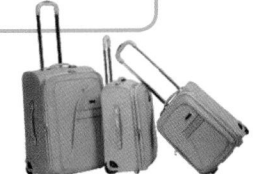

▶ **Representa** uno de los diálogos con tu compañero(a).

Final del desafío

Buenos días. Soy Lucas Cardoso. Llamaba para confirmar las reservas que hice ayer.

¿Cómo? Pero si ustedes me confirmaron que...

¿Que el cámping está completo? ¡No puede ser! Ayer me dijeron que...

82 **¿Y ahora qué?**

▶ **Completa.** Lucas habla con una agente de viajes y Asha con el director del cámping. Completa los bocadillos usando el estilo indirecto.

▶ **Escribe** con tu compañero(a) uno de los diálogos completos. Después, represéntenlo para la clase.

☞ → TU DESAFÍO Visita la página web. Escucha las preguntas de tu *Minientrevista Desafío 3* y escribe las respuestas.

HERITAGE LANGUAGE LEARNERS

• At times, students confuse the letters *b* and *v*. They may also omit the letter *h* in some words. Dictate the following sentences:
1. *Baja a la habitación de Valeria y busca el boleto.*
2. *Héctor hizo las reservas para el viaje y obtuvo el visado.*
3. *¿Ya ha salido el vuelo con destino a Venezuela?*
4. *¿En qué hotel se va a quedar Héctor en Honduras?*
5. *Ya viene el avión donde viaja Bárbara.*
6. *Mi vecino va de vacaciones a Bolivia.*
7. *No hay hospedaje en este vecindario.*

CRITICAL THINKING

• Ask students to think about the qualities a person needs in order to organize a trip of such complexity as that planned by Asha and Lucas and make a list of these attributes. Students might mention such skills as the ability to plan in advance, allow time for unexpected events, exhibit persistence, know how to delegate tasks, and understand people's needs and motivations. Partners must be able to work together harmoniously and know how to equitably divide the tasks. Have students read their lists and assign one student to create a master list with the best ideas.

■ Have students rewrite several of the dialogue lines on the board using indirect speech. If students have difficulties with the grammar or the vocabulary terms in these dialogues, have them refer back to the page on which they were introduced. You may also wish to do a mini-summary of each topic before beginning this activity, in order to demonstrate the forms and functions being used.

Activities

80. Write all three categories (*aventurero*, *urbano*, and *de sol y playa*) on the board. Ask students to go one by one to the board and write the name of their partner under the appropriate category. At the end, count the number of students under each category. Have students work in pairs and, taking into account the results, ask them to plan the best trip for the class, explaining their decisions.

81. You may want to ask students if they or a relative has experienced any of these two situations. If so, ask them to share the experience with the class.

82. In order to avoid repetition, have half of the class work on the dialogue between Lucas and the travel agent, and the other half work on the dialogue between Asha and the director of the camp.

Answer Key

80. Answers will vary.
▶ Answers will vary.
81. Answers will vary.
▶ Answers will vary.
82. Answers will vary. Sample answers: Lucas: Pero si ustedes me confirmaron que tenían plazas suficientes. Asha: Ayer me dijeron que no había problemas, que había lugar en el cámping para todos.
▶ Answers will vary.

Additional Resources

Fans Online activities
Practice Workbook

323

Para terminar

Presentation

- In this section, students will review the unit objectives and put them into practice. They will look at some documents and talk about events that they may include as they organize a week of cultural events at their school. Students will also select one of the following *desafíos* to develop: organize a Spanish-language film festival and create a poster to promote it, write an interview for the best athletes in their school and use the results of the interview to write an article, or do a brief presentation on one of the trips undertaken by the Ruta Quetzal.

Activities	Standards	Resources
83.	1.1, 1.2, 1.3, 2.2, 5.1	
84. Tu desafío	1.1, 1.3, 2.1, 2.2, 5.1, 5.2	

Teaching Suggestions

Warm-Up / Independent Starter

- Have students go back and review the vocabulary and grammar sections in this unit. Then ask them to make a list of the events and activities that they think would be worthy of including in a week of cultural events at their school.

Preparation

- Have students close their textbooks. Then write the following list of tasks on the board and have students complete them in their notebooks:

  1. *Expresa tu opinión sobre una película estrenada recientemente, un concierto de tu grupo musical favorito o un partido de tu equipo preferido.*

  2. *Expresa la probabilidad de que tu equipo o atleta favorito gane la próxima competencia en la que participe.*

  3. *Resume en un párrafo lo que dicen los expertos sobre lo que debemos hacer antes de viajar a otro país.*

  Ask students to share their answers to these questions in small groups and check their work together. They may open their textbooks now and review any vocabulary or grammar topic that they have not yet mastered.

Todo junto

ESCRIBIR Y HABLAR

83 **Una semana cultural**

▶ **Clasifica** estos documentos en las siguientes categorías.

| cine/teatro | música | arte | deportes |

▶ **Haz** una lista de diez actividades interesantes para un festival cultural. Puedes basarte en las propuestas anteriores o buscar otras posibilidades en revistas o en Internet.

▶ **Habla** con tu compañero(a) y decidan cuáles son las diez mejores actividades. Deben argumentar sus opiniones.

Modelo   A. *Yo creo que debemos proponer un concierto de pop porque a la mayoría de los estudiantes les gusta ese tipo de música.*

B. *Me parece muy bien. Quizá podamos invitar a algún grupo de la ciudad.*

▶ **Comenten** su propuesta en pequeños grupos. Después, elaboren una lista definitiva y presenten los resultados a la clase.

Differentiated Instruction

DEVELOPING LEARNERS

- Ask students whether the following statements are true (*cierto*) or false (*falso*):

  1. *El público aplaude si le gusta un concierto.* (cierto)
  2. *El baloncesto es un deporte acuático.* (falso)
  3. *La tarjeta de embarque describe qué películas ponen.* (falso)
  4. *El hotel y la pensión son alojamientos.* (cierto)
  5. *El tanteo indica la cancha.* (falso)
  6. *Hay una regata de vela en la terminal.* (falso)
  7. *Si tienes plaza disponible, tienes asiento en el avión.* (cierto)

EXPANDING LEARNERS

- Have students indicate which word does not belong and explain why.

  1. *tanteo   marcador   regata (regata)*
  2. *estadio   carrera   cancha (carrera)*
  3. *opinar   dudar   creer (dudar)*
  4. *telón   remo   escenario (remo)*
  5. *empate   de terror   cómica (empate)*
  6. *victoria   perdedor   derrota (victoria)*
  7. *retraso   temporada   demora (temporada)*
  8. *público   aficionado   campeón (campeón)*
  9. *remo   atletismo   visado (visado)*
  10. *butaca   navegante   surfista (butaca)*

Tu desafío

84  **El tiempo libre**

¿Recuerdas los desafíos que Tess y Tim les dieron a los personajes? ¿Cuál te gusta más? Elige una de estas opciones y resuelve tu desafío.

DESAFÍO Ⓐ

Organiza un festival de cine español y latinoamericano. Primero elige tres películas y después prepara un cartel para promocionarlo.

DESAFÍO Ⓑ

Escribe una lista de preguntas para hacer una entrevista a los(as) mejores deportistas de tu escuela sobre sus entrenamientos y sus competencias. Con esa información escribe un reportaje.

DESAFÍO Ⓒ

Busca información sobre las expediciones organizadas por la Ruta Quetzal y elige la que te parezca más interesante. Después, escribe una ficha con estos datos y haz una breve presentación en clase:

- Itinerario (países y recorrido) de la expedición elegida.
- Cuándo se celebró.
- Por qué te parece interesante.

trescientos veinticinco 325

Unit 6

Para terminar

- Have students work with a partner and share their Independent Starters. Then ask students to look at the photos on page 324 and see if any of the leisure activities depicted could be included in their week of cultural events at school and why. Call on volunteer pairs to come before the class and present their ideas. Ask the class to take notes since these ideas will help them with activity 83.

Activities

83. For the first part of this activity, ask students to look for clues in the photos that will allow them to identify the events. For instance, in photo 5, the location of the event is *Centro Dramático Nacional*, which indicates that the event may be a play or other type of theatrical event. For the second part of this activity, have students use their Independent Starters and the notes they took during the Preparation activity. This will expedite the completion of this part of the activity. Tell students that if their community does not seem to offer a wide variety of events from which to choose in order to plan their cultural festival, they can go outside their community and propose events that they would like to see and that might be possible to arrange. For example, if a nearby city has a large Puerto Rican population, students may suggest inviting a Puerto Rican music group from that city to come perform at their school.

84. Display students' work in the classroom and have the class vote on the best entry in each category.

Answer Key

83. Cine / teatro: 5, 6.
Música: 3.
Arte: 1, 4.
Deportes: 2.
▶ Answers will vary.
▶ Answers will vary.
▶ Answers will vary.

84. Answers will vary.

Additional Resources

Fans Online activities

HERITAGE LANGUAGE LEARNERS

- Ask students to work with a partner and assess their own skills and their partner's in order to determine which of the three *desafíos* in this unit they are best suited to complete successfully. All the challenges require research, teamwork, and organizational skills. *Desafío 1* requires artistic ability in designing a poster. *Desafío 2* requires excellent verbal and interpersonal skills. *Desafío 3* requires working with a large group of people. Then have students write at least one paragraph that summarizes their skills in completing one of these *desafíos*, and another assessing their partner's.

COOPERATIVE LEARNING

- Ask students to work in small groups and write ten questions that are related to this unit and could be used to take a survey about students' likes, dislikes, and opinions. The questions may be related to the activities that are presented in the *Desafíos*, or the vocabulary, grammar, or *Cultura* features. All members of the group will have input on selecting and finalizing the questions. Then assign groups to interview two or more of the other groups to see what their classmates are thinking. Groups may want to tabulate the results of the opinion poll.

MAPA CULTURAL
Deportes con tradición

Presentation

- This section presents information about different traditional sports of the Spanish-speaking world. The images serve as a reference point for additional cultural readings and activities that expand on the skills students learned in this unit.

Activities	Standards	Resources
Mapa cultural	1.2, 2.1, 2.2, 3.1, 3.2	Video
85.	1.1, 1.2, 1.3, 2.1, 2.2, 5.2	

Cultural Topics

- **Juegos de pelota prehispánicos.** The numerous archaeological remains of pre-Hispanic ball courts unearthed throughout Mexico and Central America are proof of the importance ball games had for Mesoamerican cultures. In most pre-Hispanic societies, ball games had religious significance, but people also played for fun. One of the main contributions of these ball games to modern-day sports is the rubber ball. Rubber was a product of the Americas, unknown in Europe at the time of the colonization. The elasticity of rubber and the bouncing qualities of rubber balls were much appreciated, and soon these rubber balls replaced the balls that had been used in Europe.

- **El fútbol.** Football, or soccer, is not a traditional sport of the Spanish-speaking world. In fact, modern soccer originated in England. However, soccer has become the main sport—and a prominent part of the culture—in most of the Spanish-speaking world. Mexico City's Estadio Azteca, with a capacity of 105,000 spectators, is one of the largest soccer stadiums in the world, and is home to Mexico's national team. The World Cup, an international soccer competition celebrated every four years, is a spellbinding affair in most of Latin America and Spain.

Teaching Suggestions

Warm-Up / Independent Starter

- Ask students to list their top three sports and why they like these sports.

326

Deportes con tradición

El deporte es una práctica saludable y también una de las manifestaciones de la cultura de un pueblo. Algunos países conservan deportes tradicionales con una historia muy antigua.

El tejo (Colombia)

En Colombia se practica desde hace más de 500 años un juego tradicional: el tejo. Cada jugador lanza un disco (el tejo) para introducirlo por un aro *(hoop)* de metal. Hoy este juego es el deporte nacional de Colombia.

El tejo se juega en un campo de 19,5 metros de largo por 2,5 metros de ancho. En cada extremo del campo se coloca una caja con un aro y cuatro mechas triangulares *(gunpowder triangles)*. El objetivo es introducir el tejo en el aro o explotar las mechas.

Antiguamente los indígenas jugaban con un disco de oro.

La charreada (México)

La charreada es el deporte nacional mexicano. En realidad, es una exhibición de las habilidades de los jinetes mexicanos. Cada jinete va vestido con el traje típico mexicano.

Cada charreada consta de diez pruebas o suertes en las que el/la jinete debe demostrar su dominio del caballo y su capacidad para domar a los toros.

326 trescientos veintiséis

Differentiated Instruction

DEVELOPING LEARNERS

- Ask students to summarize the contents of this *Mapa cultural* in a four-column chart. Have them use the following headings for their chart and include the corresponding information in each column: *Nombre del deporte, País de origen, Equipamiento, Objetivo*. Then have them add their top three favorite sports to the chart and fill in the information for the four columns. Invite students to share their charts with a partner and compare and contrast each other's charts.

EXPANDING LEARNERS

- Ask pairs to research ring-toss games, rodeo, polo, and weight lifting. Have them compare and contrast these sports with the four traditional sports in this *Mapa cultural*. Students should list the similarities and differences between these sports. Encourage them to investigate the origins of these sports and mention how some of them have influenced each other. For instance, the American rodeo has some of its roots in the cattle ranching practices of Mexican *vaqueros* in northern Mexico and the western United States during the 19th century. Ask partners to present their findings to the class.

El pato (Argentina)

El pato es el deporte nacional de Argentina. Se juega desde principios del siglo XVII. Dos equipos de cuatro jinetes *(riders)* compiten para meter una pelota especial (el pato) en el aro *(hoop)* del equipo contrario. Los aros tienen un metro de diámetro y están sobre un poste de 2,40 metros de altura que se coloca en los extremos del campo.

> En el pato se usa una pelota de cuero con cuatro asas *(handles)*.

El levantamiento de piedras (España)

En el País Vasco, al norte de España, se practica el levantamiento de piedras. Los atletas compiten por levantar la piedra más pesada desde el suelo hasta el hombro o por levantar una piedra varias veces en dos o tres minutos.

> Las piedras tienen distintas formas (de cilindro, cubo o esfera). Algunas pesan más de 200 kilos.

85 **Deportes para todos**

▶ **Valora** estos aspectos de los deportes anteriores de 1 a 4. Después, comenta tus valoraciones con tu compañero(a) para comprobar si coinciden.

- Nivel de destreza necesaria para practicarlos.
- Grado de diversión.
- Simbolismo nacional o cultural.

▶ **Habla** con tu compañero(a) sobre los deportes favoritos de cada uno(a).

trescientos veintisiete **327**

Preparation

- Have students share their Independent Starters. Create a chart on the board to keep track of the sports students mention and determine the top three class favorites. As a class, discuss what they know about the origins of these sports, their main characteristics and rules, famous teams or players, and possible reasons for the popularity of these sports in this country. Invite students to consider the various roles sports play in our society.

- Explain to students that games and sporting activities have been part of human culture for thousands of years. Some of humanity's early sports were a test of a person's skill and strength. Other sports, such as the pre-Hispanic ball games of the Americas, were team sports. At first, most of these sports were probably ritualistic in nature or they served as preparation for war. But with the passage of time, sports have become a pastime promoting socialization and social integration.

Activities

85. For the second part of this activity, ask partners to choose two of their favorite sports for in-depth research of an aspect of each of these sports. They may focus, for instance, on the sport's history and development, its introduction to their state or community, its early failures or successes, its fans, or its most famous players. Once students have collected the information, have them organize it to do a class presentation. Remind students to use reputable sources of information.

Answer Key

85. Answers will vary.
▶ Answers will vary.

Additional Resources

Fans Online activities
Practice Workbook

327

ESCRITURA

Un cuento

Presentation

- In this section, students will practice and extend their writing skills. They will apply the vocabulary and grammar they have learned in this unit to write a short story.

Activities	Standards	Resources
Escritura	1.1, 1.2, 1.3, 3.1, 5.1	

Teaching Suggestions

Warm-Up / Independent Starter

- Ask students to think about their favorite short story or a story that made quite an impact on them when they first read it.

Preparation

- Invite students to share their Independent Starters. Is there a class favorite short story? Remind students of some of the elements of a short story: limited length and number of characters, clearly defined conflict, focused nature, and precise narration. Some important 19th-century writers who helped popularize this genre include Edgar Allan Poe (United States, 1809–1849), Guy de Maupassant (France, 1850–1893), and Anton Chekhov (Russia, 1860–1904). Poe is particularly known for his mystery tales and is considered to be the father of mystery fiction.

- Ask for a volunteer to read the Narrative Texts and Stories box aloud. Explain that they will be writing a short story. Point out that the plot of a short story may be inspired by a real-life event, but the story is, for the most part, fictional. The topic of the short story determines the type of story it is.

Step-by-Step Instructions

Piensa

- Discuss with students a short story that the majority of them have read. Examples might include, "The Murders in the Rue Morgue" by Edgar Allan Poe, "Heart of Darkness" by Joseph Conrad, or "The Snows of Kilimanjaro" by Ernest Hemingway. This will give students a feel for short story writing.

328

Un cuento

Narrative Texts and Stories

Narrative writing includes texts in which the writer tells a real or fictional series of events, presenting the circumstances and actions of the characters in a specific place and time.

Stories are short narrative texts that, in general, are simple yet relatively intense.

El cuento es uno de los géneros narrativos más antiguos. Se trata de una narración corta y sencilla que con frecuencia se transmite por la tradición oral. Sus temas son muy variados: hay cuentos de misterio, cuentos de terror, cuentos de ciencia ficción, cuentos fantásticos, cuentos realistas...

Grandes escritores de la literatura universal fueron grandes cuentistas. Es el caso del estadounidense Edgar Allan Poe o los argentinos Jorge Luis Borges y Julio Cortázar. Y ahora tú vas a poder imitarlos creando tu propio cuento.

Piensa

- Decide los aspectos clave de tu cuento: el tema, el argumento y los personajes.

El tema — Todo cuento parte de una idea. Explica. ¿Cuál va a ser el tema de tu cuento: un suceso extraño, un hecho mágico, un asunto misterioso, una aventura divertida...? Exprésalo en una oración.

Modelo

Unos científicos descubren que la Estrella Polar ha desaparecido.
Unos niños se quedan encerrados en un parque de atracciones.

El argumento — Escribe un resumen del texto en el que respondas a estas preguntas:
- ¿Cuál es el punto de partida del cuento? ⟶ **situación inicial**
- ¿Qué hecho o qué problema desencadena el cuento? ⟶ **acontecimiento inicial**
- ¿Qué van a hacer los personajes? ⟶ **acciones**
- ¿Cuál va a ser el final del cuento? ⟶ **situación final**

Esquematiza el argumento en un diagrama como este:

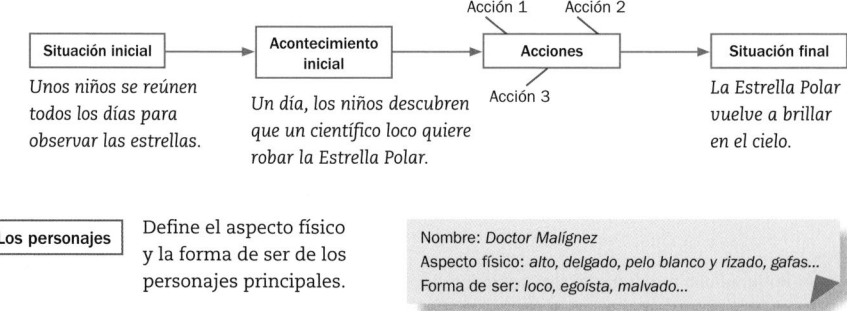

Situación inicial
Unos niños se reúnen todos los días para observar las estrellas.

Acontecimiento inicial
Un día, los niños descubren que un científico loco quiere robar la Estrella Polar.

Acción 1   Acción 2
Acciones
Acción 3

Situación final
La Estrella Polar vuelve a brillar en el cielo.

Los personajes — Define el aspecto físico y la forma de ser de los personajes principales.

Nombre: *Doctor Malígnez*
Aspecto físico: *alto, delgado, pelo blanco y rizado, gafas...*
Forma de ser: *loco, egoísta, malvado...*

328 trescientos veintiocho

Rubric for Evaluation

	Content	Organization	Conventions
1 point	Undeveloped plot. Reader's attention is not grabbed. Unclear or absent conflict. Inappropriate word choices.	The storyline is not logical in places. Story is hard to follow. Ending is confusing. Transitions are not present.	Many errors in spelling, punctuation, grammar, and usage. Errors obscure meaning.
3 points	Mostly well-developed plot. Reader's attention is grabbed, but not held. Clear conflict. Some inaccurate word choices.	Logical storyline. Story is relatively easy to follow. Ending makes sense. Some transitions are present.	Some errors in spelling, punctuation, grammar, and usage. Errors don't interfere with meaning.

Escribe

■ Tomando como punto de partida las ideas que anotaste, escribe el borrador de tu cuento. Puedes seguir estas recomendaciones:

– Piensa que, para motivar al lector, es esencial un buen comienzo y mantener un aire de misterio a lo largo de la historia.

– Presenta los hechos siguiendo un orden lógico e intenta incluir diálogos entre los personajes.

– Utiliza las Expresiones útiles. Evita los estereotipos y las redundancias.

Expresiones útiles

Érase una vez...	*Once upon a time...*
Hace mucho tiempo...	*A long time ago...*
Un día...	*One day...*
Una vez...	*Once...*
Cuando...	*When...*
De pronto / De repente...	*Suddenly.../ All of a sudden...*
Rápidamente...	*Quickly...*
Para colmo...	*To top it off...*
Al final...	*Finally...*

Revisa

■ Después de escribir tu cuento, intercámbialo con tu compañero(a). Para revisar su trabajo, puedes hacerte las siguientes preguntas:

– ¿Hay coherencia y unidad en su texto?

– ¿Los hechos están organizados cronológicamente?

– ¿Es interesante la historia que cuenta?

– ¿Tiene errores gramaticales u ortográficos? ¿Cuáles son?

■ Devuelve el texto a su autor(a) con tus sugerencias y vuelve a revisar tu trabajo. ¿Qué opina tu compañero(a) de tu cuento? Reescríbelo incorporando las correcciones que sean necesarias.

■ Para terminar, dibuja una pequeña ilustración relacionada con tu cuento.

Comparte

■ Lee tu texto a la clase. Pídele a tu profesor(a) y a tus compañeros(as) su opinión. ¿Les gusta tu cuento?

■ Intenta publicar tu cuento en el periódico o en la página web de la escuela. ¡Buena suerte!

	Content	Organization	Conventions
5 points	Well-developed plot that grabs and holds the reader's attention. Clearly established conflict. Word choices add to the storyline and help reveal the theme.	Logical and interesting storyline. Story is very easy to follow. Ending pulls the story together. Uses appropriate transitions when needed.	Few, if any, errors in spelling, punctuation, grammar, and usage. Excellent command of the Spanish language.

■ Remind students that everything in a short story revolves around a conflict. In brainstorming for their story, they must first concentrate on coming up with a conflict or problem that needs to be resolved. The resolution of this conflict is what keeps the readers interested. You may want to point out that in many contemporary stories, the reader is left to decide the resolution.

Escribe

■ Explain to students that each major event in their story should be linked in steps that make sense. Remind them to drop clues that help the reader solve the problem. Students may also want to include some "distracters" to throw the reader off the track, but the solution to the conflict or problem at the conclusion of their story should be credible—the pieces should all fit together.

Revisa

■ As students read their classmates' stories, ask them to try to solve the conflict or problem before they get to the end of the story. Are enough clues provided to help them solve the puzzle? Then ask them to read the conclusion of the story. Does it make sense? Do they, as the readers, feel like saying, "Of course!" or are they confused by the ending?

Comparte

■ Encourage students to think of reading aloud as a performance, and a good performance can enhance the audience's enjoyment of the story. Proper emphasis, rhythm, and intonation are especially important. Ask students to pay attention to their audience as they read. They may find it useful to glance around the room from time to time. Allow for rehearsal time so that students can practice reading their story to themselves aloud at least once.

Evaluation

■ Distribute copies of the rubric to students and discuss the evaluation criteria. Ask students to refer to the rubric as they prepare their writing and as they evaluate their classmates' short stories.

Unit 6

REPASO

Vocabulario

Presentation

- In this section, students will review all key vocabulary from the unit, organized by themes, to prepare for an assessment. Students will complete practice activities for each of the three *Desafíos*.

Activities	Standards	Resources
1.	1.2, 1.3	
2.	1.2	
3.	1.2, 1.3	

Teaching Suggestions

Warm-Up / Independent Starter

- Ask students to review the vocabulary list. Then have them create a three-column chart with the following headings: *Ocio y espectáculos, Los deportes, Viajes y alojamiento*. Have students think of associations among words within each category, and ask them to list these associations in the appropriate column. For example: *la audiencia → el público, la función; el campeón → el ganador, la victoria, el campeonato*.

Preparation

- Have students share their associations from the Independent Starter with a partner. Ask pairs to use their associations to write definitions in Spanish for the vocabulary. For example, *la audiencia: el público que asiste a una función o espectáculo; el campeón: el ganador, o persona que obtiene la victoria, en un campeonato*.

- Have pairs present their definitions to the class. The class will match the vocabulary to the corresponding definition. Then read over the *Repaso* presentation with students.

Activities

1. To expand this activity, ask students to work with a partner to classify the rest of the words under *Ocio y espectáculos*. There may be words that different students classified in different ways. For differences in classification, ask students to explain their choices.

330

REPASO Vocabulario

Ocio y espectáculos

Cine y teatro

la audiencia	audience
el auditorio	auditorium
el boleto	ticket
la butaca	seat
la cartelera	entertainment guide
el escenario	stage
la fila	line
la función	performance
el musical	musical
el pasillo	aisle

el/la protagonista	main character
el público	audience, public
la sala	(movie) theater
la taquilla	box office
el telón	curtain

Otros espectáculos

el ballet	ballet
el circo	circus
el concierto	concert
la ópera	opera

Acciones

aplaudir	to applaud
estrenar	to open

La película...

cómica	comedy
de acción/aventura	action/adventure
de ciencia ficción	science fiction
de dibujos animados	animated
de suspenso	thriller
de terror	horror
dramática	drama
policíaca	detective
romántica	romance

Deportes

Competencias

el/la aficionado(a)	fan, supporter
el/la campeón(a)	champion
el campeonato	championship
la cancha/la pista	court
la carrera	race
la competencia	competition
los deportes competitivos	competitive sports
el equipo local	home team
el equipo visitante	visiting team
el estadio	stadium
los Juegos Olímpicos	Olympics
el marcador	scoreboard
el partido	game, match
la regata	boat race
el tanteo	score
la derrota	defeat
el empate	tie
la victoria	victory
el/la ganador(a)	winner
el/la perdedor(a)	loser

Viajes y alojamiento

Viajes y alojamiento

bien situado(a)	well located
la fecha de entrada/salida	check-in/check-out date
el hotel	hotel
la pensión	rooming house
la plaza disponible	available seat
el retraso/la demora	delay
la temporada alta/baja	high/low season
el viaje de negocios	business trip
el viaje organizado	package tour
el viaje de placer	personal trip
la visa	visa

Viajar en avión

el control de pasaportes	passport control
la línea aérea	airline
el mostrador	counter
la tarjeta de embarque	boarding pass
la terminal	terminal
el vuelo con escala(s)	stopover flight
el vuelo directo	direct flight
el vuelo internacional	international flight
el vuelo nacional	domestic flight
procedente de...	arriving from...
con destino a...	departing for...
cancelar una reserva	to cancel a reservation
confirmar una reserva	to confirm a reservation

Deportes y deportistas

el atletismo	athletics
el baloncesto	basketball
el ciclismo	cycling
el esquí acuático	water-skiing
la natación	swimming
el remo	rowing
la vela	sailing

el/la atleta	athlete
el/la ciclista	cyclist
el/la esquiador(a)	skier
el/la surfista	surfer
el/la nadador(a)	swimmer
el/la navegante	sailor

Differentiated Instruction

DEVELOPING LEARNERS

- Ask students to look at the vocabulary and list on a sheet of paper all of the words that are cognates of English words, paying close attention to the spelling of these words in Spanish. Then have students analyze the remaining vocabulary words and on the back of their sheet of paper list, those words whose meaning they can extrapolate. For example: *dibujos animados* → animated drawings → cartoons. Students are now left with words that are not cognates and whose meanings they can't extrapolate. Ask them to concentrate on reviewing this shorter list.

EXPANDING LEARNERS

- Ask students to work with a partner. They will create a *Consejos útiles* document for a friend who has never traveled abroad. Students should include instructions about how to plan for the trip, what to do at the airport, where to stay at their destination, etc. Encourage students to use as many words and expressions from the vocabulary list as possible. They may also include drawings or pictures of an airport, showing the different areas they mention in their presentation. Have volunteer pairs share their *consejos* with the class. Does the class have anything to add?

330

DESAFÍO 1

1 **Grupos.** Clasifica las palabras del cuadro en una tabla como esta.

| el público | la sala de cine | el circo | el telón |
| el auditorio | el musical | la butaca | el/la protagonista |

Lugares	Personas	Objetos	Espectáculos

DESAFÍO 2

2 **La palabra adecuada.** Completa estas oraciones con las palabras del cuadro.

natación
empate
campeonato
regata
marcador
cancha
derrota
visitante

1. El partido terminó con un resultado de 2-2. Hubo un _____.
2. Podemos ver el tanteo en el _____.
3. Este verano voy a participar en una _____ de vela.
4. Mis amigos y yo reservamos una _____ para jugar al tenis.
5. El equipo perdedor tiene que aceptar su _____.
6. Ya no quedan boletos para ver la final del _____.
7. En el partido había más aficionados del equipo local que del equipo _____.
8. Ese es el nadador que ganó la carrera de _____.

DESAFÍO 3

3 **Pros y contras.** Escribe una ventaja y un inconveniente de cada una de estas acciones.

Modelo   1. *Alojarse en un hotel es más cómodo que alojarse en una pensión, pero también es más caro.*

1. a. Alojarse en un hotel.
   b. Alojarse en una pensión.
2. a. Viajar en temporada alta.
   b. Viajar en temporada baja.
3. a. Hacer un viaje de negocios.
   b. Hacer un viaje de placer.
4. a. Viajar en un vuelo directo.
   b. Viajar en un vuelo con escalas.
5. a. Hacer un viaje organizado.
   b. Hacer un viaje no organizado.

trescientos treinta y uno   331

---

3. Once students finish this activity, ask them to work with a partner and organize a trip. First they must decide on a place, then have them choose one option from each of the five sets of sentences in this activity. Ask pairs to write down their plans. For example: *Vamos a hacer un viaje organizado al Caribe. Nos alojaremos en un hotel, pero viajaremos en temporada baja. El viaje será de placer...* Have pairs read their trip plans to the class.

Answer Key

1. Lugares: el auditorio, la sala de cine.
   Personas: el público, el/la protagonista.
   Objetos: la butaca, el telón.
   Espectáculos: el musical, el circo.

2. 1. empate   5. derrota
   2. marcador   6. campeonato
   3. regata   7. visitante
   4. cancha   8. natación

3. Answers will vary. Sample answers:
   2. Viajar en temporada baja es más barato que viajar en temporada alta, pero algunos sitios cierran en la temporada baja.
   3. Hacer un viaje de placer es más divertido que hacer un viaje de negocios, pero tenemos que pagarnos el viaje.
   4. Viajar en un vuelo directo es más cómodo que viajar en un vuelo con escalas, pero a veces es más caro.
   5. Hacer un viaje no organizado es más emocionante que hacer un viaje organizado, pero si no conocemos el lugar puede ser problemático.

Additional Resources

Fans Online activities
Practice Workbook

HERITAGE LANGUAGE LEARNERS

• Ask students to research a destination (e.g., a city, beach, national park, historic town) in their country of origin and plan a trip there for the Spanish class. Have students think of free-time activities and sports their classmates can enjoy in this place, shows or entertainment activities they can attend, and suitable accommodations and modes of transportation. Encourage students to look for pictures to enhance their presentation. Then have students present their plan to the class. Ask the class to imagine that they will actually visit this place and encourage them to ask relevant questions.

COOPERATIVE LEARNING

• Have students work in groups of three or four. Give each group the same travel budget and tell them to imagine that they will take a two-week trip together. Each group must agree on the places they would like to visit, how they would get there, where they would stay, the activities they would participate in, etc. Ask students to consider their budget carefully as their plans will need to be believable. Once students have finished, ask groups to describe their plans to the class. Then hold a class vote for the best vacation plan.

Unit 6
REPASO
Gramática

Presentation

- Students will review grammatical structures presented in the unit. Each grammar point is cross-referenced to the corresponding page on which it was introduced. The activities here provide systematic practice by *Desafío*.

Activities	Standards	Resources
4.	1.1, 1.2	
5.	1.2, 1.3	
6.	1.2, 1.3	
7. Cultura	1.1, 1.2, 2.1, 2.2	

Teaching Suggestions

Warm-Up / Independent Starter

- Give students a couple of minutes to silently review the grammar topics on this page.

Preparation

- Play several rounds of "Telephone" to practice reported speech. Divide the class into lines of five students each and whisper the same phrase to the first student in each line. The student needs to convert your phrase into reported speech and whisper it to the next student in his or her line. Ask the last player in each of the lines to repeat the phrase as she or he heard it. Has the phrase changed? Be sure to use a variety of phrases that include commands, requests, information, data, etc. For example: *Ustedes hablan muy bien español. Presten atención en clase.*

- Go over the rest of the grammar topics from this *Repaso* with the class. If needed, provide additional examples and practice activities.

Activities

4. You may want to convert this activity into a class debate. Divide the class into five groups and assign a different topic to each group. Then divide each group into two smaller groups consisting of students for each side of the debate. Give each group a few minutes to prepare their arguments and then begin the debate with one of the groups. At the end, have the class choose a winning side for each topic.

332

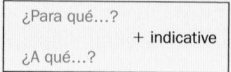

REPASO Gramática

Expresar opinión (pág. 292)

CONSTRUCCIONES AFIRMATIVAS

creer	
imaginar	
opinar	+ que + indicative
parecer	
pensar	
suponer	

CONSTRUCCIONES NEGATIVAS

no creer	
no parecer	+ que + subjunctive
no pensar	

Fórmulas gramaticales de cortesía (pág. 294)

EXPRESIONES DE CORTESÍA
Dame el diccionario, por favor.
¿Me das el diccionario?

EL CONDICIONAL DE CORTESÍA
¿Podrías ayudarme?
Me gustaría salir un poco antes.

EL IMPERFECTO DE CORTESÍA
Quería probarme el abrigo verde.

Expresar probabilidad (pág. 304)

EXPRESIONES DE PROBABILIDAD

Quizá(s)	+ subjunctive (unlikely)
Tal vez	+ subjunctive (unlikely)
A lo mejor	+ indicative

EL FUTURO DE PROBABILIDAD
—¿Qué hora es?
—No sé, serán las doce…

Expresar finalidad (pág. 306)

EXPRESIONES DE FINALIDAD

para a	+ infinitive (when the clauses have the same subject)
	+ que + subjunctive (when the clauses have different subjects)

PREGUNTAR SOBRE LA FINALIDAD

¿Para qué…?	
¿A qué…?	+ indicative

El estilo indirecto (pág. 316)

EL INDICATIVO Y EL SUBJUNTIVO EN EL ESTILO INDIRECTO

- Information → indicative
  - Main clause in the present:
    El periódico dice: «Hoy estrenan dos películas».
    El periódico dice que hoy estrenan dos películas.
  - Main clause in the past:
    El periódico decía: «El partido es a las ocho».
    El periódico decía que el partido era a las ocho.

- Request or command → subjunctive
  - Main clause in the present:
    El profesor me dice: «Haz la tarea».
    El profesor me dice que haga la tarea.
  - Main clause in the past:
    El profesor nos dijo: «Escriban una carta».
    El profesor nos dijo que escribiéramos una carta.

Expresar lugar (pág. 318)

EXPRESAR LUGAR

donde adonde	+ indicative (known, definite, or real place)
de / desde donde por donde	+ subjunctive (unknown, indefinite, or hypothetical place)

PREGUNTAR SOBRE UN LUGAR

¿Dónde…?	
¿De dónde…?	+ indicative
¿Adónde…?	
¿Por dónde…?	

Differentiated Instruction

DEVELOPING LEARNERS

- For further practice with the use of the indicative or the subjunctive after *donde*, have students complete these sentences:
  1. *Esta es la calle donde vive / viva mi tía.* (vive)
  2. *No me importa adonde vamos / vayamos de vacaciones, solo quiero descansar.* (vayamos)
  3. *¿De dónde vienes / vengas, Sonia?* (vienes)
  4. *Vivo en una casa desde donde se ve / vea la escuela.* (ve)
  5. *Cualquier hotel donde nos alojamos / alojemos será más caro en temporada alta.* (alojemos)

EXPANDING LEARNERS

- Ask students to write a postcard to a friend sharing their opinions about a vacation they are taking. This trip could be real or imaginary, but the description should include opinions about the place, the accommodations, the availability of leisure activities, etc. For example: *¡Hola, Carlos! Espero que estés bien. Yo estoy muy contento. Creo que este es el mejor viaje que he hecho. Me parece que las playas son las más limpias de toda esta zona. Mi hermano no piensa que haya mucha variedad de actividades, pero…* Invite volunteers to share their postcards with the class.

DESAFÍO 1

4 **¿Qué opinas?** Habla con tu compañero(a) sobre estas noticias imaginarias y compartan sus opiniones.

1. Las personas que tengan un perro deberán pagar una tasa *(fee)* cada año.
2. Se permitirá que las tiendas abran por la noche todos los días.
3. Las empresas darán cinco días más de vacaciones al año a sus empleados(as).
4. Se prohíbe el uso de bolsas de plástico en los supermercados.
5. Será obligatorio llevar uniforme en todas las escuelas de High School.

 DESAFÍO 2

5 **Conjeturas.** Escribe conjeturas para explicar estas circunstancias. Utiliza el futuro.

1. Llegas a la escuela por la mañana un lunes y no hay nadie.
2. El/la profesor(a) de Español llega a clase con ropa muy elegante.
3. Una de tus compañeras tiene un ramo de rosas rojas.
4. Llegas a tu casa y el suelo está mojado.
5. Llevas media hora esperando a un(a) amigo(a) con quien tienes una cita.

 DESAFÍO 3

6 **Dice, dijo, decía...** Transforma estas oraciones usando el estilo indirecto.

1. Mi jefe me dijo: «Envíe el informe por la mañana».
2. El profesor nos dijo: «El examen de Español es el próximo lunes».
3. Mi madre siempre dice: «Estudia todos los días, no solo antes del examen».
4. Mi novio me dice: «Eres la mejor».
5. El periodista afirmó: «No hay razón para preocuparse».

  **CULTURA**

 7 **Viajes y turismo.** Responde a estas preguntas.

1. ¿Dónde se celebra un famoso festival de cine de España?
2. ¿Qué son los caballitos de totora? ¿Quiénes los utilizaban?
3. ¿Qué es un parador de turismo? ¿Dónde podemos encontrarlo?

trescientos treinta y tres **333**

5. To expand this activity, show students different pictures of a variety of situations (e.g., a student looking happily at the exam in front of him or her, a baby crying, passengers waiting at the terminal), and ask them to express a conjecture about each picture. For example: *El examen será fácil. El bebé tendrá hambre. El vuelo estará retrasado.*

Answer Key

4. Answers will vary.

5. Answers will vary. Sample answers:
1. Será festivo.
2. Irá a una fiesta después de clase.
3. Será su cumpleaños.
4. Habrá llovido.
5. Se habrá olvidado de la cita.

6. 1. Mi jefe me dijo que enviara el informe por la mañana.
2. El profesor nos dijo que el examen de Español era el próximo lunes.
3. Mi madre siempre dice que estudie todos los días, no solo antes del examen.
4. Mi novio me dice que soy la mejor.
5. El periodista afirmó que no había razón para preocuparse.

7. 1. En San Sebastián, una ciudad del norte de España.
2. Son una especie de canoas que utilizaban los indígenas de la cultura moche de Perú.
3. Es una cadena de hoteles de lujo creada en España en 1929. Están situados en edificios históricos o ubicados en plena naturaleza.

Additional Resources

Fans Online activities
Practice Workbook

HERITAGE LANGUAGE LEARNERS

• Spanish differs from English in the use of *usted* as a way to show respect. This may cause difficulty for some native English speakers when using expressions of courtesy. For instance, if they use an appropriate expression of courtesy but don't use *usted* in a context in which they would need to use it, they may sound rude. Asking their teacher *¿Podrías ayudarme con esta tarea?* is an example of this. Have heritage students come up with a list of situations in which we would normally use *usted* in Spanish in order to assist their classmates with this issue.

TOTAL PHYSICAL RESPONSE (TPR)

• Divide the class into two teams: one will be the "positives" and the other, the "negatives." Say several opinion statements, some negative and some affirmative, in the present tense. Do not conjugate the verb in the dependent clause (e.g., *Creo que [ir] llover. No pienso que mi equipo de fútbol [ganar].*). For affirmative opinion statements, the "positives" must stand and say the entire sentence, conjugating the verb in the present indicative. For negative opinion statements, the "negatives" must stand and say the entire sentence, conjugating the verb in the present subjunctive.

PROYECTO

Un viaje de estudios

Presentation

- In this section, students will apply the vocabulary, grammar, and cultural information they have learned in this unit to organize a one-week trip to a Hispanic country for their Spanish class.

Activities	Standards	Resources
Paso 1	1.1, 1.2, 2.1, 2.2, 3.1, 5.1, 5.2	
Paso 2	1.1, 1.2, 2.1, 2.2, 5.1	
Paso 3	1.1, 1.3, 2.1, 2.2, 5.1	
Paso 4	1.1, 1.3, 5.1	
Paso 5	1.3, 3.1, 5.1, 5.2	

Teaching Suggestions

Warm-Up / Independent Starter

- Ask students to think about the last field trip they took. Have them create a two-column chart and list things they liked about the trip in the left column and things they didn't like or that can be improved in the right column.

Preparation

- Invite students to share their Independent Starters with the class. What things did students like most about their field trips? What did they like least? Students may find this information useful when they plan the activities for their projects. Discuss with students some of the purposes of field trips: to broaden students' experiences, to help build community, to conduct research, to give students real-world experiences. Encourage students to keep the goal of their particular field trip in mind as they plan it.

- Ask for a volunteer to read the project introduction aloud. Then divide the class into small groups to work on the project.

Step-by-Step Instructions

Paso 1

- Ask students to first agree on a purpose or goal for their trip. Then, with their goal in mind, have them decide on a place.

PROYECTO

Un plan para

un viaje de estudios

What would you do if your class won an award that consists of a one-week trip to a Hispanic country? In small groups, you have to organize the trip and the activities that you will do at the destination and present the plan to your classmates. The trip with the most votes wins.

PASO 1 Elige el destino

- ¿A qué lugar de Latinoamérica te gustaría viajar? ¿Por qué? Escribe algunos argumentos para convencer a tus compañeros(as). Aquí tienes algunas sugerencias.

Costa Rica.

México.

Chile.

Puerto Rico.

El Salvador.

- En pequeños grupos, discutan cada propuesta y elijan uno de los lugares para ir de viaje.

  Modelo   A. *A mí me gustaría ir a las playas de El Salvador para hacer surf.*
         B. *Me parece muy bien.*
         C. *Pues yo prefiero ir a México porque…*

PASO 2 Busca información

- ¿Qué saben del lugar elegido? Busquen información sobre él.
  - Forma de llegar.
  - Lugares para visitar.
  - Actividades que hacer.

Rubric for Evaluation

	Content	Organization	Presentation
1 point	The activities are not relevant. Information is incomplete or not based on research. Little Spanish is used.	Inefficient use of time. Information is disorganized or unclear. The trip is not well designed and organized.	Unclear communication. Delivery is not fluent. Many errors in vocabulary and grammar.
3 points	The activities are relevant. Information is correct but some of it lacks significance. Spanish is used most of the time.	Time is used well. Information is mostly organized but lacks some clarity. The trip is mostly well designed and organized.	Clear communication and fluent delivery. Mostly correct vocabulary and grammar.

PASO 3 Planifica el viaje

- Define los datos básicos de tu plan de viaje:
  - ¿En qué fechas va a ser?
  - ¿Qué medio(s) de transporte van a utilizar?
  - ¿Dónde se van a alojar?
- Teniendo en cuenta el destino elegido y la época en la que van a viajar, hagan una lista con las actividades que pueden realizar allí para conocer mejor la cultura del país.

Modelo

A. *Yo creo que podemos ir a ver una charreada.*
B. *Sí, sí, a nuestros compañeros les gustará mucho.*
C. *También podemos ir a ver un concierto de mariachis. Estoy segura de que les puede apetecer.*

PASO 4 Prepara la información

- Piensen cómo van a presentar el viaje a sus compañeros(as) y preparen toda la información. Deben presentar un plan de viaje detallado con una descripción breve de cada lugar o de cada actividad. Acompañen su presentación con imágenes.

PASO 5 Presenta el viaje

- Presenten su viaje a toda la clase y contesten las preguntas de sus compañeros(as).
- Elijan el viaje que más les guste y expliquen las razones de su elección.

Unidad 6

Autoevaluación

¿Qué has aprendido en esta unidad?

Do these activities to evaluate how well you understood this unit's concepts.

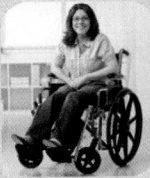

Evalúa tus habilidades. Para cada punto, di Muy bien, Bien o Necesito practicar más.

a. Can you express your opinions and make polite requests about different free-time activities?

▶ Give your opinion about the free-time activities that you and your friends do.

▶ Imagine you and your friends are going to the movies. Make three polite requests that you would ask before or during the outing.

b. Can you express purpose and probability when talking about sports?

▶ Tell two things that are very likely to happen at the next sporting event you attend, as well as two things that are less likely to happen.

▶ Describe three things that an athlete does when training, and the purpose of each action.

c. Can you express location and report what someone else says?

▶ Tell three things that your parents told you to do the last time you traveled.

▶ Describe the type of place you would like to go and the type of accommodations you would like to have the next time you travel.

PROYECTO

Un viaje de estudios

Paso 2

- For larger countries, such as Mexico and Chile, suggest to students that they concentrate on a region or on one or two cities. Ask students to keep in mind that this is a week-long trip. Their trip plan should be very focused and specific so that no time is wasted.

Paso 3

- Ask students to take into consideration high and low season dates, since that will affect the cost of the trip and the availability of accommodations.

Paso 4

- Encourage students to give this *Paso* careful consideration. Remind them that they should focus on convincing their classmates that their trip is the best option.

Paso 5

- Since students will be trying to influence their classmates' decisions, their presentation should be upbeat and enticing. They should research their destination thoroughly to be able to answer their classmates' questions.

Evaluation

- Distribute copies of the rubric to students. Encourage students to refer to the rubric as they prepare their projects.

Content

- Ask groups to consider these questions about their trip: Does our trip reflect the goal we set for it? Are the activities balanced? Do they showcase the country's culture? Are our descriptions of the activities vivid and interesting? Will the travelers find the experience fulfilling?

Organization

- Explain that most researchers agree that excellent organization and enjoyable content are the two most important measures of the effectiveness of a presentation. Therefore, encourage students to consider their presentation's organization carefully.

Presentation

- Tell students that for a successful presentation, they must know their objectives. These objectives drive their presentation and move the audience to their end goal: to vote for their trip.

	Content	Organization	Presentation
5 points	The activities are relevant, varied, and interesting. The descriptions are vivid and convincing. Spanish is used exclusively.	Time is used wisely. Information is clearly organized visually and logically. The trip is very well designed and organized.	Clear and fluent communication. Very motivating, upbeat delivery. Correct and complete vocabulary and grammar.

Por el planeta

Objectives

- To learn about nature and the environment.
- To describe the behavior of some insects and animals.
- To discuss efforts to preserve and protect the environment.
- To state actions if certain conditions are met.
- To describe cultural and environmental celebrations in Hispanic communities.

- To discuss concepts related to meteorology and astronomy.
- To express the time or sequence of events.
- To discuss commerce in Hispanic countries.
- To identify natural disasters and natural resources.
- To express cause and effect.

- To identify some protected ecological areas on Earth.
- To identify main ideas and significant details in a variety of texts.
- To engage in meaningful conversations.
- To know and apply the different stages of the writing process: planning, writing, revising, and sharing.

Contents

Vocabulary

- Useful expressions to show how to do something, to express desires or wants, and to ask for something in a courteous manner.
- Review: Words for geographical features, weather, nature, and the universe.
- Nature and the environment, and fauna.
- Weather and meteorology, and the universe and astronomy.
- Natural disasters and natural resources, natural elements, and economic activities.

Grammar

- To form and use conditional sentences and to express real or likely conditions.
- To express unlikely or hypothetical and impossible or contrary-to-fact conditions.
- To express time or sequence of events.
- The present perfect subjunctive.
- To express cause and consequence.
- The personal preposition *a*.

Culture

- Protected natural areas: *Reserva Especial de la Biosfera*.
- *La región de Magallanes (Chile)*.
- National symbols.
- Seasonal celebrations and festivals: The *Noche de san Juan*, the Inti Raymi and other festivals of the Sun.
- Fair trade activities in some Hispanic countries.
- *La industria en Chile*.
- Products manufactured in Hispanic countries and the most important handicrafts fair in Latin America.
- A short story by the Guatemalan writer Augusto Monterroso.
- Unique ecological areas in Latin American countries.

Evaluation Criteria

- Identify elements in nature and in the environment.
- Describe the migration of the monarch butterfly to Mexico.
- Identify protected ecological areas and endangered animals around the world.
- Identify environmental changes and the causes for environmental problems.
- Discuss ways to preserve and protect the environment.

- Express likely, unlikely, and impossible conditions.
- Describe some cultural festivals and celebrations related to the seasons.
- Describe the weather and talk about the universe.
- Describe fair trade activities in some Hispanic countries.
- Tell when something happens, and place events in the proper sequence.

- Identify different environmental disasters and different natural resources.
- Express the cause and consequence of certain actions.
- Describe economic activities and commerce in some Hispanic countries.
- Identify nature preserves and other ecological areas on Earth.
- Identify the literary elements in a text.
- Write a cause and effect essay.

Unit Plan _____

Las tareas/Antes de empezar

Estimated time: 1 session.

Text: ¡Salvemos el planeta!

Functions & forms:
- Useful expressions to show how something is done, to express desires or wants, and to ask for something in a courteous manner.
- Review of known vocabulary about geographical features, weather, nature, and the universe.

⚑DESAFÍO 1

Estimated time: 5 sessions.

Text: Una maravilla de la naturaleza.

Functions & forms:
- To make hypotheses.
- Nature and the environment.
- To express real or likely conditions.
- To express unlikely and impossible conditions.

Culture:
- Reserva Especial de la Biosfera.
- La región de Magallanes (Chile).
- Símbolos nacionales.

Reading: ¡Ayudemos a las mariposas monarca!

⚑DESAFÍO 2

Estimated time: 5 sessions.

Text: La fiesta del Sol.

Functions & forms:
- To express the time.
- Meteorology and astronomy.
- To express the sequence of events.
- The present perfect subjunctive.

Culture:
- Las fiestas del Sol.
- La festividad del Inti Raymi.
- La Noche de san Juan.

Reading: Las tradiciones del Sol.

⚑DESAFÍO 3

Estimated time: 6 sessions.

Text: Un desafío muy justo.

Functions & forms:
- To express cause and consequence.
- Natural disasters and natural resources.
- Structures to express cause and consequence.
- The personal preposition a.

Culture:
- Comercio sostenible.
- La industria en Chile.
- Una feria de artesanía.

Reading: El eclipse, by Augusto Monterroso.

Para terminar

Estimated time: 1 session.

Todo junto: Review of Desafíos 1–3.

Tu desafío:
- Desafío A: Research and describe an animal in danger of extinction and propose solutions for its survival.
- Desafío B: Create a presentation about a Hispanic celebration related to the equinoxes or solstices.
- Desafío C: Create a poster about handcrafted products from Hispanic countries.

MAPA CULTURAL

Estimated time: 1 session.

Mapa cultural: Espacios naturales singulares.

ESCRITURA

Estimated time: 1 session.

Writing: Un reportaje medioambiental.

PROYECTO

Estimated time: 1 session.

Project: Una campaña publicitaria en favor del medio ambiente.

Unit 7 Por el planeta

Standards for Learning Spanish

COMMUNICATION

1.1. Interpersonal mode
- Exchange personal opinions and experiences.
- Engage in oral conversations using personal knowledge and experience.
- Exchange assignments with a partner and evaluate each other's work.
- Discuss hypothetical situations with a partner.
- Compare and contrast information with a partner.
- Apply personal knowledge or experiences to ask and answer questions on different topics.
- Ask a partner questions and take notes.

1.2. Interpretive mode
- Demonstrate understanding of oral and written expressions.
- Demonstrate understanding of questions relating to familiar and less familiar topics.
- Understand and obtain information from audio or video recordings.
- Understand written exchanges.
- Identify main ideas and significant details from an informative or literary text.
- Draw conclusions and make judgments from oral and written texts.
- Understand new vocabulary presented in Spanish.

1.3. Presentational mode
- Produce and present an original creation.
- Write and present a dialogue.
- Write sentences or paragraphs comparing information.
- Complete sentences with relevant information or correct verb tenses.
- Write answers to given questions.
- Create a list of information and present it to the class.
- Write sentences or a paragraph summarizing information.

CULTURE

2.1. Practices and perspectives
- Learn about Hispanic cultural celebrations related to the equinoxes and to the summer and winter solstices.
- Learn about Hispanic cultural celebrations related to preserving the environment.
- Discuss how Hispanic populations preserve their traditional crafts while protecting the environment.

2.2. Products and perspectives
- Learn about handcrafted and manufactured products produced in and exported from Hispanic countries.

CONNECTIONS

3.1. Interdisciplinary connections
- Understand the similarities and differences between some aspects of grammar in English and in Spanish.
- Identify elements in nature and in the universe.
- Learn about the behavior of some animals.
- Learn about environmental issues and ways to protect the environment.
- Identify natural habitats, nature preserves, and other ecological areas on Earth.
- Learn about endangered animals and protected ecological areas.
- Identify weather patterns and natural disasters.
- Learn about economic activities and commerce in Hispanic countries.
- Use the writing process to produce a written work.

3.2. Viewpoints through language / culture
- Read dialogues, informative texts, and literary texts in Spanish that provide insight into Hispanic cultures.
- Learn about how economic and trade activities respect the environment.

COMPARISONS

4.1. Compare languages
- Compare how to express when certain conditions are met in English and in Spanish.
- Compare the use of the present perfect subjunctive in Spanish and other verb tenses in English.
- Compare how to express the sequence of events in English and in Spanish.
- Compare how to state the cause and effect of actions in English and in Spanish.

4.2. Compare cultures
- Compare types of cultural festivals and events in Hispanic countries and in the United States.
- Compare economic activities in Hispanic countries and in the United States.
- Compare national symbols in Hispanic countries and in the United States.

COMMUNITIES

5.1. Spanish within and beyond the school setting
- Research and obtain information on the Internet.
- Discuss activities in one's own community.
- Imagine situations in which Spanish could be used.

5.2. Spanish for lifelong learners
- Discuss ways in which Spanish can be used in future life experiences.
- Discuss one's preferred motion pictures, music, and artistic performances in Spanish.

Communicative Skills

Interpersonal Mode | Activities

Speaking	• Exchange opinions or experiences. • Ask and answer questions with a partner. • Contrast answers, and compare or share information with a classmate. • Engage in a conversation with a classmate.	• 13, 50, 87 • 25, 41, 46, • 5, 19, *Proyecto* • 31, 46, 41, 50, 58, 62, 64, 73, 83, 85, 87, 89
Writing	• Write suggestions or advice. • Summarize information in written form. • Agree on and write a list of items	• 28, 30 • 19, 50 • 62
Listening	• Understand and obtain information from simple oral exchanges.	• 41, 50, 64, 73
Reading	• Understand descriptive or informative texts. • Understand a list of items.	• 24, *Escritura* • 50

Interpretive Mode | Activities

Listening	• Understand and obtain information from a conversation. • Understand oral descriptions or narrations.	• 9, 12, 19, 23, 36, 61, 76 • 30, 40, 44, 55, 66
Reading	• Demonstrate comprehension of written exchanges and longer written dialogues. • Infer meanings based on a text. • Demonstrate understanding of a descriptive or a narrative text. • Obtain information and draw conclusions from an informative text.	• 1, 7, 10, 26, 32, 33, 34, 58, 60, 85 • 2, 53, 59, 80, 87 • 77, 79, 80 • 8, 11, 15, 18, 20, 29, 37, 42, 51, 52, 59, 63, 68, 78, 86, 88, *Escritura*
Viewing	• Obtain information from an image. • Connect words, expressions, events, or information to images.	• 6, 13, 31, 45, 72, 82 • 4, 40, 55

Presentational Mode | Activities

Speaking	• Present a dialogue or skit to the class. • Present a description or information to the class. • Present an original creation to the class.	• 56 • 62, 82, 88 • *Escritura, Proyecto*
Writing	• Write a descriptive or informative paragraph. • Write an original e-mail or entry for a blog.	• 6, 24, 32, 67, 72, 81, 84 • 54, 57
Visually Representing	• Draw pictures or use photographs to illustrate information. • Present information in a Venn diagram, chart, graph, or table.	• 25, 32, 46, 83, 88, *Proyecto* • 5, 23, 26, 79, 89

Cross-Curricular Standards

Subject	Standard	Activities
Language Arts	• Compare elements of Spanish grammar and language with English equivalents. • Use the writing process to create an article.	• 16, 43, 47, 53, 69, 74 • *Escritura*
Social Studies	• Discuss cultural festivals and celebrations in Hispanic countries. • Learn about commerce and economic activities in Hispanic countries. • Identify national symbols of Hispanic countries.	• 37, 51, 52, 88 • 15, 63, 68, 78, 88 • 20
Science	• Describe the migration of monarch butterflies. • Identify protected ecological areas and endangered animals. • Understand the difference between a solstice and an equinox.	• 7, 10, 26, 28 • 11, 18, 88, *Mapa cultural* • 36, 52

335D

Lesson Plans (50-Minute Classes)

Day	Objectives	Sessions	Activities	Time	Standards	Resources/ Homework
1	To introduce nature, the environment, and the characters' challenges, and to review learned vocabulary	**Por el planeta/Las tareas/Antes de empezar** (336–341) • Warm-Up: Topic orientation • Presentation: *¡Salvemos el planeta!* • *Expresiones útiles* and *Recuerda*	 1–2 3–6	 10 m. 20 m. 20 m.	1.1, 1.2, 1.3, 2.1, 2.2, 3.1, 3.2, 5.1	Visual Presentation Video Practice Workbook
2	To make hypotheses	**Desafío 1 – Una maravilla de la naturaleza** (342–343) • Warm-Up: Independent Starter • *Texto: Una maravilla de la naturaleza* • *Conexiones: Reserva Especial de la Biosfera*	 7–10 11	 5 m. 35 m. 10 m.	1.1, 1.2, 1.3, 2.1, 2.2, 3.1, 5.1	Visual Presentation Audio Video
3	To identify ways to care for the environment and protect nature	**Desafío 1 – Vocabulario** (344–345) • Warm-Up: Independent Starter • Vocabulary: *La naturaleza y el medio ambiente* • *Comunidades: La región de Magallanes (Chile)*	 12–14 15	 5 m. 35 m. 10 m.	1.1, 1.2, 1.3, 2.2, 3.1, 5.1	Audio Practice Workbook
4	To form conditional sentences and to express real or likely conditions	**Desafío 1 – Gramática** (346–347) • Warm-Up: Independent Starter • Grammar: *Expresar condición (I)* • *Cultura: Símbolos nacionales*	 16–19 20	 5 m. 35 m. 10 m.	1.1, 1.2, 1.3, 2.1, 2.2, 3.1, 4.1, 4.2, 5.2	Audio Practice Workbook
5	To express unlikely and impossible conditions	**Desafío 1 – Gramática** (348–349) • Warm-Up: Independent Starter • Grammar: *Expresar condición (II)*	 21–25	 5 m. 45 m.	1.1, 1.2, 1.3, 3.1	Audio Practice Workbook
6	To understand a dialogue and to integrate vocabulary and grammar	**Desafío 1 – Lectura/Comunicación** (350–353) • Warm-Up: Independent Starter • *Lectura: ¡Ayudemos a las mariposas monarca!* • *Comunicación:* Review • *Final del desafío*	 26–28 29–31 32	 5 m. 20 m. 15 m. 10 m.	1.1, 1.2, 1.3, 3.1, 4.2, 5.1, 5.2	Visual Presentation Audio Practice Workbook *Tu desafío* Quiz on *Desafío 1*
7	To express the time	**Desafío 2 – La fiesta del Sol** (354–355) • Warm-Up: Correct quiz on *Desafío 1* • *Texto: La fiesta del Sol* • *Cultura: Las fiestas del Sol*	 33–36 37	 5 m. 35 m. 10 m.	1.1, 1.2, 1.3, 2.1, 3.1, 4.2, 5.1	Visual Presentation Audio
8	To talk about the weather and astronomy	**Desafío 2 – Vocabulario** (356–357) • Warm-Up: Independent Starter • Vocabulary: *El tiempo meteorológico. El universo* • *Cultura: La festividad del Inti Raymi*	 38–41 42	 5 m. 35 m. 10 m.	1.1, 1.2, 2.1, 3.1, 3.2, 5.1, 5.2	Audio Practice Workbook
9	To express the time or sequence of events	**Desafío 2 – Gramática** (358–359) • Warm-Up: Independent Starter • Grammar: *Expresar tiempo*	 43–46	 5 m. 45 m.	1.1, 1.2, 1.3, 3.1, 4.1, 5.1, 5.2	Audio Practice Workbook
10	To learn the present perfect subjunctive	**Desafío 2 – Gramática** (360–361) • Warm-Up: Independent Starter • Grammar: *El presente perfecto de subjuntivo* • *Cultura: La Noche de san Juan*	 47–50 51	 5 m. 35 m. 10 m.	1.1, 1.2, 1.3, 2.1, 3.1, 4.1, 4.2, 5.1	Video Practice Workbook

Day	Objectives	Sessions	Activities	Time	Standards	Resources/Homework
11	To understand an informative text and to integrate vocabulary and grammar	**Desafío 2 – Lectura/Comunicación** (362–365) • Warm-Up: Independent Starter • *Lectura: Las tradiciones del Sol* • *Comunicación:* Review • *Final del desafío*	 52-54 55-57 58	5 m. 20 m. 15 m. 10 m.	1.1, 1.2, 1.3, 2.1, 2.2, 3.1, 3.2, 4.1, 5.1, 5.2	Audio Practice Workbook Quiz on *Desafío 2*
12	To express cause and consequence	**Desafío 3 – Un desafío muy justo** (366–367) • Warm-Up: Correct quiz on *Desafío 2* • *Texto: Un desafío muy justo* • *Conexiones: Comercio sostenible*	 59-62 63	5 m. 35 m. 10 m.	1.1, 1.2. 1.3, 2.1, 2.2, 3.1, 3.2, 5.1	Visual Presentation Audio
13	To learn about natural disasters and natural resources	**Desafío 3 – Vocabulario** (368–369) • Warm-Up: Independent Starter • Vocabulary: *Desastres naturales. Recursos naturales* • *Comunidades: La industria en Chile*	 64-67 68	5 m. 35 m. 10 m.	1.1, 1.2, 1.3, 2.1, 3.1, 4.2, 5.1	Audio Practice Workbook
14	To express cause and consequence	**Desafío 3 – Gramática** (370–371) • Warm-Up: Independent Starter • Grammar: *Expresar causa y consecuencia*	 69-73	5 m. 45 m.	1.1, 1.2, 1.3, 3.1, 4.1	Practice Workbook
15	To use the personal preposition *a* correctly	**Desafío 3 – Gramática** (372–373) • Warm-Up: Independent Starter • Grammar: *La preposición a personal* • *Conexiones: Una feria de artesanía*	 74-77 78	5 m. 35 m. 10 m.	1.1, 1.2, 1.3, 2.1, 2.2, 3.1, 4.1, 4.2, 5.1	Audio Practice Workbook
16	To understand a literary text	**Desafío 3 – Lectura** (374–375) • Warm-Up: Independent Starter • *Lectura: El eclipse*	 79-81	5 m. 45 m.	1.1, 1.2, 1.3, 3.1, 3.2, 5.1	
17	To integrate vocabulary and grammar	**Desafío 3 – Comunicación** (376–377) • Warm-Up: Independent Starter • *Comunicación:* Review • *Final del desafío*	 82-84 85	5 m. 30 m. 15 m.	1.1, 1.2, 1.3, 3.1, 5.1, 5.2	Practice Workbook *Tu desafío* Quiz on *Desafío 3* **Para terminar –** **Tu desafío** (379)
18	To integrate language in context	**Para terminar** (378–379) • Warm-Up: Correct quiz on *Desafío 3* • *Todo junto* • *Tu desafío* presentations	 86-87 88	5 m. 20 m. 25 m.	1.1, 1.2, 1.3, 2.1, 2.2, 3.1	Practice Workbook
19	To assess student proficiency and identify unique ecological areas on Earth	**Evaluación/Mapa cultural** (380–381) • Warm-Up: Independent Starter • Quiz on *Desafíos 1–3* • *Mapa cultural: Espacios naturales singulares*	 89	5 m. 15 m. 30 m.	1.2, 1.3, 2.1, 3.1, 4.2, 5.1	Video Practice Workbook
20	To write an article	**Escritura** (382–383) • Warm-Up: Independent Starter • *Escritura: Un reportaje medioambiental*		5 m. 45 m.	1.1, 1.2, 1.3, 3.1	Project work
21	To prepare a publicity campaign for an environmental awareness celebration	**Proyecto** (388–389) • Warm-Up: Prepare project presentations • Project presentations		10 m. 40 m.	1.1, 1.2, 1.3, 2.1, 2.2, 3.1, 4.2, 5.1, 5.2	**Repaso – Vocabulario** (384–385) **Repaso – Gramática** (386–387) **Autoevaluación** (389)

Lesson Plans (90-Minute Classes)

Day	Objectives	Sessions	Activities	Time	Standards	Resources/ Homework
1	To introduce nature, the environment, and the characters' challenges, and to review learned vocabulary	(See Day 12 Unit 6) **Por el planeta/Las tareas/Antes de empezar** (336–341) • Warm-Up: Topic orientation • Presentation: *¡Salvemos el planeta!* • *Expresiones útiles* and *Recuerda*	 1–2 3–6	(45 m.) 10 m. 20 m. 15 m.	1.1, 1.2, 1.3, 2.1, 2.2, 3.1, 3.2, 5.1	Visual Presentation Video Practice Workbook
2	To make hypotheses and to identify ways to care for the environment and protect nature	**Desafío 1 – Una maravilla de la naturaleza/ Vocabulario** (342–345) • Warm-Up: Independent Starter • *Texto: Una maravilla de la naturaleza* • *Conexiones: Reserva Especial de la Biosfera* • Vocabulary: *La naturaleza y el medio ambiente* • *Comunidades: La región de Magallanes (Chile)*	 7–10 11 12–14 15	 5 m. 30 m. 10 m. 35 m. 10 m.	1.1, 1.2, 1.3, 2.1, 2.2, 3.1, 5.1	Visual Presentation Audio Video Practice Workbook
3	To form conditional sentences and to express likely, unlikely, and impossible conditions	**Desafío 1 – Gramática** (346–349) • Warm-Up: Independent Starter • Grammar: *Expresar condición (I)* • *Cultura: Símbolos nacionales* • Grammar: *Expresar condición (II)*	 16–19 20 21–25	 5 m. 35 m. 10 m. 40 m.	1.1, 1.2, 1.3, 2.1, 2.2, 3.1, 4.1, 4.2, 5.2	Audio Practice Workbook
4	To understand a dialogue and to integrate vocabulary and grammar	**Desafío 1 – Lectura/Comunicación/Evaluación** (350–353) • Warm-Up: Independent Starter • *Lectura: ¡Ayudemos a las mariposas monarca!* • *Comunicación:* Review • *Final del desafío* • Quiz on *Desafío 1*	 26–28 29–31 32	 5 m. 35 m. 25 m. 10 m. 15 m.	1.1, 1.2, 1.3, 3.1, 4.2, 5.1, 5.2	Visual Presentation Audio Practice Workbook *Tu desafío*
5	To express the time and to talk about the weather and astronomy	**Desafío 2 – La fiesta del Sol/Vocabulario** (354–357) • Warm-Up: Independent Starter • *Texto: La fiesta del Sol* • *Cultura: Las fiestas del Sol* • Vocabulary: *El tiempo meteorológico. El universo* • *Cultura: La festividad del Inti Raymi*	 33–36 37 38–41 42	 5 m. 35 m. 10 m. 30 m. 10 m.	1.1, 1.2, 1.3, 2.1, 3.1, 3.2, 4.2, 5.1, 5.2	Visual Presentation Audio Practice Workbook
6	To express the time or sequence of events and to learn the present perfect subjunctive	**Desafío 2 – Gramática** (358–361) • Warm-Up: Independent Starter • Grammar: *Expresar tiempo* • Grammar: *El presente perfecto de subjuntivo* • *Cultura: La Noche de san Juan*	 43–46 47–50 51	 5 m. 40 m. 35 m. 10 m.	1.1, 1.2, 1.3, 2.1, 3.1, 4.1, 4.2, 5.1, 5.2	Audio Video Practice Workbook

Day	Objectives	Sessions	Activities	Time	Standards	Resources/Homework
7	To understand an informative text and to integrate vocabulary and grammar	***Desafío 2 – Lectura/Comunicación/Evaluación*** (362–365) • Warm-Up: Independent Starter • *Lectura: Las tradiciones del Sol* • *Comunicación:* Review • *Final del desafío* • Quiz on *Desafío 2*	 52–54 55–57 58	 5 m. 35 m. 25 m. 10 m. 15 m.	1.1, 1.2, 1.3, 2.1, 2.2, 3.1, 3.2, 4.1, 5.1, 5.2	Audio Practice Workbook
8	To express cause and consequence, and to talk about natural disasters and natural resources	***Desafío 3 – Un desafío muy justo/Vocabulario*** (366–369) • Warm-Up: Independent Starter • *Texto: Un desafío muy justo* • *Conexiones: Comercio sostenible* • Vocabulary: *Desastres naturales. Recursos naturales* • *Comunidades: La industria en Chile*	 59–62 63 64–67 68	 5 m. 30 m. 10 m. 35 m. 10 m.	1.1, 1.2. 1.3, 2.1, 2.2, 3.1, 3.2, 4.2, 5.1	Visual Presentation Audio Practice Workbook
9	To express cause and consequence, and to use the personal preposition *a* correctly	***Desafío 3 – Gramática*** (370–373) • Warm-Up: Independent Starter • Grammar: *Expresar causa y consecuencia* • Grammar: *La preposición a personal* • *Conexiones: Una feria de artesanía*	 69–73 74–77 78	 5 m. 40 m. 35 m. 10 m.	1.1, 1.2, 1.3, 2.1, 2.2, 3.1, 4.1, 4.2, 5.1	Audio Practice Workbook
10	To understand a literary text, to integrate vocabulary and grammar, to integrate language in context, and to assess student proficiency	***Desafío 3 – Lectura/Comunicación/Evaluación/Todo junto*** (374–378) • Warm-Up: Independent Starter • *Lectura: El eclipse* • *Comunicación:* Review • *Final del desafío* • *Todo junto* • Quiz on *Desafío 3*	 79–81 82–84 85 86–87	 5 m. 25 m. 20 m. 10 m. 15 m. 15 m.	1.1, 1.2, 1.3, 2.1, 3.1, 3.2, 5.1, 5.2	Practice Workbook *Tu desafío* ***Para terminar – Tu desafío*** (379)
11	To identify unique ecological areas on Earth and to write an article	***Tu desafío/Mapa cultural/Escritura*** (379–383) • Warm-Up: Independent Starter • *Tu desafío* presentations • *Mapa cultural: Espacios naturales singulares* • *Escritura: Un reportaje medioambiental*	 88 89	 5 m. 15 m. 30 m. 40 m.	1.1, 1.2, 1.3, 2.1, 2.2, 3.1, 4.2, 5.1	Video Practice Workbook ***Repaso – Vocabulario*** (384–385) ***Repaso – Gramática*** (386–387) Quiz on *Desafíos 1–3* Project work
12	To prepare a publicity campaign for an environmental awareness celebration	***Proyecto/Assessment*** (388–389) • Warm-Up: Correct quiz on *Desafíos 1–3* • Project presentations • *Autoevaluación* • Test (See Day 1 Unit 8)		 5 m. 15 m. 10 m. 15 m. (45 m.)	1.1, 1.2, 1.3, 2.1, 2.2, 3.1, 4.2, 5.1, 5.2	

9 La migración de la mariposa monarca

–Hola, Ethan. Encontré un reportaje muy bueno sobre las mariposas monarca. Explican que cada otoño estas mariposas empiezan su viaje hacia el sur para escapar del frío. Pero es un viaje de casi cinco mil kilómetros. ¿No es increíble?

–Sí, ya lo creo.

–Pero lo más curioso es que esta especie es capaz de volver a los mismos sitios de hibernación tras varias generaciones. Aquí dice que, con frecuencia, llegan a los mismos árboles donde estuvieron sus antepasados… ¿Cómo saben adónde ir si nunca hicieron esa ruta?

–Yo leí en Internet que se fijan en la posición del sol en el cielo y también siguen su instinto.

–Y después de hibernar, ¿qué hacen? ¿Se quedan allí o vuelven al norte?

–Comienzan a volar hacia el norte otra vez en primavera. Pero ese viaje es más largo que la vida de las mariposas. Esta especie deposita los huevos durante la migración y son sus descendientes quienes llegan al norte en verano. Esta migración se repite todos los años y es única en el reino de los insectos.

–¡Es increíble!

12 Un museo viviente

–Como saben, el archipiélago de las Galápagos es un grupo de islas volcánicas que se formaron hace millones de años. Aquí viven muchas especies animales únicas. Hay muy pocos lugares del mundo donde se puede encontrar tantas variedades de flora y fauna.

–Es cierto, yo nunca vi tantos tipos de aves, mamíferos, reptiles y peces. ¿Cómo se explica esta diversidad?

–Este archipiélago está a más de mil kilómetros de las costas de Sudamérica. Nunca formó parte del continente. Por eso, sus recursos naturales permanecieron casi intactos durante siglos, hasta que llegó el primer ser humano.

–¿Vamos a ver las famosas tortugas gigantes de las Galápagos?

–Claro. Podrán comprobar que son animales muy grandes; pueden pesar más de 300 kilos y viven entre 100 y 150 años.

–¡Es impresionante! ¿Qué se hace para protegerlas?

–En 1959 se declaró a esta región Parque Nacional. También se estableció la Fundación Charles Darwin para proteger y conservar el hábitat de las islas.

–¿Charles Darwin, el famoso biólogo?

–Sí. Se llama así porque él hizo muchos estudios en las islas.

19 Las tres «R» del reciclaje

–Buenas tardes. Hoy, en nuestro espacio dedicado al medio ambiente, vamos a hablar de reciclaje. ¿Alguna vez han oído hablar de las tres erres del reciclaje? Para explicárnoslo tenemos con nosotros a doña Margarita Cifuentes, experta en estos temas. Díganos, ¿qué son las tres erres?

–Las tres erres del reciclaje son los conceptos básicos de la ecología que todos debemos conocer y poner en práctica para conservar el medio ambiente.

–¿Y cuáles son esos conceptos?

–El primero, reducir. Si queremos conservar los recursos naturales, debemos reducir la cantidad de basura que producimos, el consumo de agua, de energía, etc.

–Muy bien. ¿Y el segundo?

–Reutilizar los envases de vidrio, plástico o metal. Así promoveremos el ahorro ecológico y económico, y no agotaremos los recursos naturales del planeta.

–Entonces, reducir, reutilizar y… ¿cuál es el tercero? ¿Reciclar?

–Efectivamente. Antes de comprar un producto, debemos considerar si es reciclable o no. Si reciclamos más, reduciremos el costo de recogida y eliminaremos varias toneladas de basura.

–Si le parece, vamos a pasar a las llamadas para que nuestros oyentes puedan plantearle preguntas o compartir sus comentarios con todos nosotros.

23 Los temas del día

1. Estoy muy ocupado y no sé dónde depositar los residuos. Si tuviera más tiempo, reciclaría más.

2. Estamos en el Parque Nacional Galápagos y vamos a hacer muchas excursiones. Si vamos a la Fundación Charles Darwin, veremos las tortugas que crían allí.

3. Si las mariposas monarca no conocieran las rutas migratorias, nunca llegarían a México.

4. Yo colaboro con una asociación que defiende a las especies protegidas. Si no hubiera organizaciones como esta, muchos animales desaparecerían.

5. El quetzal busca refugio en el biotopo de Guatemala. Si no hubiera lugares protegidos como este, su existencia correría peligro.

6. ¡Mira, ahí hay un quetzal! Si no está prohibido, le haré una foto.

30 Nuestro planeta

1. Eva, no debes usar bolsas de plástico. ¿Por qué no llevas una bolsa de tela cuando vas a comprar? Además, debes tratar de elegir productos en envases reciclables.

2. El solitario Jorge es probablemente el último ejemplar vivo de la tortuga gigante de Pinta, una de las especies nativas de las islas Galápagos.

3. En 2002, el petrolero Prestige se hundió en las aguas del Atlántico cerca de la costa de Galicia, en el noroeste de España. Las más de 75.000 toneladas de fuel que llevaba se vertieron al mar, provocando una de las peores catástrofes ecológicas de la historia.

4. La situación de la selva amazónica es preocupante. Desde 1992 la selva amazónica brasileña ha perdido más de 230.000 kilómetros cuadrados para explotar la madera de los árboles.

36 En la clase de Ciencias Naturales

–Hoy vamos a estudiar Astronomía. ¿Alguien sabe lo que son los solsticios y los equinoccios?

–Sí. Me parece que los solsticios son los días en los que el Sol alcanza el punto más alto o el punto más bajo en el cielo.

—Muy bien. Efectivamente, los solsticios y los equinoccios tienen que ver con la posición del Sol respecto a la Tierra; concretamente, a la línea del ecuador. Los solsticios tienen lugar el 20 o 21 de junio y el 21 o 22 de diciembre. Son los días con más o con menos horas de sol. En cambio, los equinoccios ocurren al principio de la primavera y del otoño, y los días duran aproximadamente lo mismo que las noches.

—Pero en algunas zonas del planeta hay meses en los que casi todo el tiempo es de día o de noche, ¿no?

—Así es. Cerca de los polos en invierno apenas hay horas de día y, en cambio, en verano hay muy pocas horas de noche.

40 ¿Cómo está el día?

1. El cielo está muy nublado. Seguro que hoy llueve.
2. Hace bastante frío, pero me encanta la nieve. ¿Salimos a dar un paseo?
3. ¡Vaya tormenta! ¿Has visto cuántos relámpagos?
4. ¡Qué bien, hoy está despejado y no hay ni una nube en el cielo!

44 ¿Pasado o futuro?

1. Cuando llegué al trabajo, estaba nevando.
2. Cuando tenga 18 años, Jacobo irá a la universidad.
3. Continuaremos el partido cuando deje de llover.
4. Cuando me acosté, vi la luna llena en el cielo.

55 ¡El clima se vuelve loco!

—A continuación, damos paso al pronóstico del tiempo.

—Hoy lunes tendremos cielos nubosos y lluvias. Para mañana esperamos temperaturas similares y tiempo soleado. Pasado mañana, sin embargo, el tiempo cambiará. Hay muchas posibilidades de lluvia y tormentas, especialmente por la tarde. El jueves esperamos cielos despejados y temperaturas un poco más bajas. El viernes seguirán bajando las temperaturas y hay posibilidades de lluvia.

61 En busca de productos justos

—Hola, Diana. ¿Cómo estás?

—Muy bien, qué sorpresa. ¿Y ustedes?

—Pues un poco decepcionados, la verdad.

—¿Por qué?

—Porque recorrimos todo el centro de la ciudad y hay muy pocos lugares donde vendan productos de comercio justo.

—Bueno, pero veo que ya tienen información sobre los productos que pueden presentar en la feria, ¿verdad?

—Sí... En una tienda especializada en café compramos un café de México importado directamente de la región de Oaxaca.

—Y nos explicaron que gracias a esta iniciativa los productores no se ven obligados a vender el café a los intermediarios a precios tan bajos.

—Claro, a menudo los intermediarios obtienen más beneficios que las propias comunidades productoras y eso no es justo.

—También estuvimos en un supermercado y encontramos una sección de productos de comercio justo procedentes de países hispanos. Tenían muchas cosas, pero lo que más nos llamó la atención fue la quinua orgánica de Perú; compramos varios paquetes.

—Muy bien. ¿Y no encontraron nada de artesanía? Si quieren, puedo enviarles algunos recuerdos que compré durante mis viajes.

—¡Eso sería estupendo!

—Gracias, Diana.

—De nada. Hasta pronto, chicos.

66 Desastres naturales

1. Tal como había anunciado el servicio nacional de meteorología, vientos de más de 200 kilómetros por hora golpearon la costa del país. Los fuertes vientos arrancaron algunos árboles y miles de hogares estuvieron varias horas sin electricidad.

2. La capital de Chile amaneció hoy con temblores que causaron el caos entre la población. Según nos informan nuestros compañeros chilenos, a las cinco de la mañana y durante casi un minuto todo comenzó a temblar. Varios edificios se derrumbaron, pero sin causar víctimas mortales.

3. Todo parece indicar que hay una fuerte actividad volcánica en la zona. Hay una densa nube de polvo y ceniza que se puede ver desde varios kilómetros de distancia. Algunas personas están siendo atendidas en los hospitales por problemas respiratorios.

4. Desde hace dos horas varios grupos de bomberos y voluntarios tratan de apagar el fuego que se originó la noche pasada en el bosque. Varias poblaciones cercanas han sido evacuadas por precaución.

76 En la ONG

—Ya llegamos, allí está la ONG de la que te había hablado.

—¿Tú crees que trabajan en proyectos de comercio justo?

—Creo que sí, porque tienen una tienda. ¿Entramos?

—Claro. ¡Tenías razón, Michelle! Hay muchos productos de alimentación con el sello de comercio justo.

—Anda, hay chocolate mexicano. ¡¡¡Y se puede probar!!! ¿Quieres un trozo?

—¡Claro! Hum, está delicioso. ¿Cuánto cuesta?

—No sé, no pone el precio.

—¿Ves a alguien que trabaje aquí?

—Ese chico lleva una camiseta con las palabras «Por un comercio justo». Seguro que trabaja aquí. Pregúntale, por favor. Yo voy a dar una vuelta por la tienda. Hay objetos de artesanía muy interesantes.

—Ahora vengo. Ah, luego tenemos que llamar a Diana para contarle lo que hemos comprado.

Unit 7
Por el planeta

The Unit

- The themes for Unit 7 are nature and the environment. The participants will learn how to make hypotheses, express time, and express cause and effect related to these topics.

- Diana, a veteran of *Fans del español*, sends the participants a link to a web page that has all the information about their tasks.

  - *Desafío 1.* Eva and Ethan have to study the habitat of the monarch butterfly and create an educational video in collaboration with a group of Mexican students.

  - *Desafío 2.* Asha and Lucas have to investigate different celebrations of the June solstice in Hispanic countries and make a slide show presentation.

  - *Desafío 3.* Michelle and Daniel will organize a festival featuring fair-trade products and handicrafts.

Activities	Standards	Resources
Por el planeta	1.2, 2.1, 2.2, 3.1, 5.1	Video

Teaching Suggestions

Warm-Up / Independent Starter

- Have students look at the photos, and ask them to write three sentences about things that they associate with each of these topics: monarch butterflies, the June solstice celebrations, and fair-trade products.

Preparation

- Introduce the topics of this unit by asking students related questions. For example: *¿Qué les interesa más de la naturaleza? ¿Qué problemas se relacionan con el medio ambiente? ¿Qué evento relacionado con el Sol tiene lugar el 24 de junio? ¿Qué saben del comercio justo* (fair trade)?

- Have students read each *Desafío's* objective, as well as the vocabulary and grammar goals, then discuss how each illustration might relate to these objectives and goals.

336

Por el planeta
La naturaleza y el medio ambiente

DESAFÍO 1

▶ **Hacer hipótesis**

Vocabulario
La naturaleza y el medio ambiente

Gramática
Expresar condición (I): el indicativo

Expresar condición (II): el subjuntivo y el condicional

Desfile del Inti Raymi. Cuzco (Perú)

DESAFÍO 2

▶ **Expresar tiempo**

Vocabulario
El tiempo meteorológico

El universo

Gramática
Expresar tiempo

El presente perfecto de subjuntivo

Mariposa monarca (México)

336 trescientos treinta y seis

The Challenge

DESAFÍO 1

Mariposa monarca

- Monarch butterflies are among the most beautiful and interesting insects, and are best known because they migrate during the winter, often well over 2,000 miles. Males can be recognized by two black spots on their hind wings, and they are slightly bigger than females. Like other butterflies, monarchs go through several stages: egg, larva, pupa or chrysalis, and finally, adult butterfly. Larvae feed exclusively on milkweed, but because of the decimation of milkweed plants due to the construction of roads and other human interventions, their habitat is shrinking.

DESAFÍO 2

Desfile del Inti Raymi. Cuzco

- There are four solar events that are closely related to the calendar: the two solstices and the two equinoxes. The summer solstice, the longest day of the year, happens around June 21 in the Northern Hemisphere, while the winter solstice occurs near December 21. On the two equinoxes, the days are the same length as the nights. Because these events mark the passing of seasons, and seasons are important for agriculture, they have been identified in different cultures as special days. In fact, many cultures around the world attribute special traits to these days.

Por el planeta

DESAFÍO 3

▶ **Expresar causa y consecuencia**

Vocabulario
Desastres naturales

Recursos naturales

Gramática
Expresar causa y consecuencia

La preposición *a* personal

Feria de artesanía (Colombia)

Picture Discussion

- Ask students to share their Independent Starters. Then have them look at the photos again and brainstorm what they know about the topics. Finally, ask students to review their predictions about each topic.

Mariposa monarca (México)

- Have students describe the photo. Ask these questions to get them started: *¿Qué insecto es este? ¿De qué color es? ¿Qué está haciendo?* Explain that monarch butterflies migrate every autumn from Canada and the northern United States to Mexico, where they hibernate, mate, and then return. You may also assign students to do a brief investigation online and then check their knowledge through questions.

Desfile del Inti Raymi. Cuzco (Perú)

- Ask questions about the photo. Then explain that the Inti Raymi, or Festival of the Sun, takes place in Cuzco, Peru, around the winter solstice, on June 24. At this time of year in the Southern Hemisphere, the days are short and the Incas used to prepare banquets to plead for the Sun's return. Today, this celebration attracts thousands of visitors to Cuzco.

Feria de artesanía (Colombia)

- Ask students to observe the picture and read the caption. Then ask them these questions to initiate a discussion: *¿Qué es artesanía? ¿Qué tipo de objetos creen que se venden en las ferias de artesanía? ¿Cómo se fabrican, por lo general, estos objetos?* Explain that these types of fairs aim to preserve traditional craftmanship techniques and foster sustainability for folk artists.

Objectives

- By the end of Unit 7, students will be able to
  - Talk about nature and the environment.
  - Make hypotheses.
  - Talk about the weather and the universe.
  - Express time.
  - Talk about natural disasters and natural resources.
  - Express cause and consequence.
  - Talk about the migration of the monarch butterfly, the different celebrations of the June solstice in Hispanic countries, and fair-trade practices.

⌐DESAFÍO 3

Feria de artesanía

- The concept of fair trade, or *comercio justo,* dates back to the sixties, when some NGOs decided to introduce a type of commerce that would establish fair relations between producers in developing countries and consumers in developed countries. As a result, some shops were created that would import products bought directly from the producers. But it wasn't until 1997 that a global stamp or mark of fair trade was created to label the products that comply with certain requirements based on fairness, sustainability, and human rights.

337

Las tareas

Presentation

- In this section, the three pairs look at a web page sent by Diana, which describes the challenges for the participants. Students will preview useful expressions to talk about how to do things, express wishes, and make polite requests.

Activities	Standards	Resources
Texto	1.2, 2.1, 2.2, 3.1, 3.2	Vis. Pres.
1.	1.2, 1.3	
2.	1.2, 1.3	

Teaching Suggestions

Warm-Up / Independent Starter

- Have students restate the following sentence from the reading using their own words: *Ustedes deben averiguar cómo se celebra el solsticio de junio.*

Preparation

- Invite volunteers to share their Independent Starters. Discuss the use of *cómo* in this sentence and the ways that students found to paraphrase this word. Ask students to scan the reading for another sentence that uses *cómo* in a similar way.

- Divide the class into two groups and ask one group to scan the dialogues on page 339 in order to jot down the sentences that express a wish. (*Me encantaría que nos encargáramos de celebrar una fiesta para el solsticio de junio. Es que a nosotros nos gustaría mucho hacer el de las mariposas.*) The other group will jot down a polite request. (*¿A Daniel y a ti les importaría ocuparse del desafío sobre el comercio justo?*)

- You may want to review the use of the conditional to express wishes or polite requests in different contexts. For example: *Me gustaría probarme esa chaqueta. ¿Me harías un favor?*

Texto: ¡Salvemos el planeta!

- Prepare a three-column chart on the board with the following headings: *Tarea 1, Tarea 2, Tarea 3.* Then ask students to scan the text on page 338 and point out the tasks that the three pairs must do.

¡Salvemos el planeta!

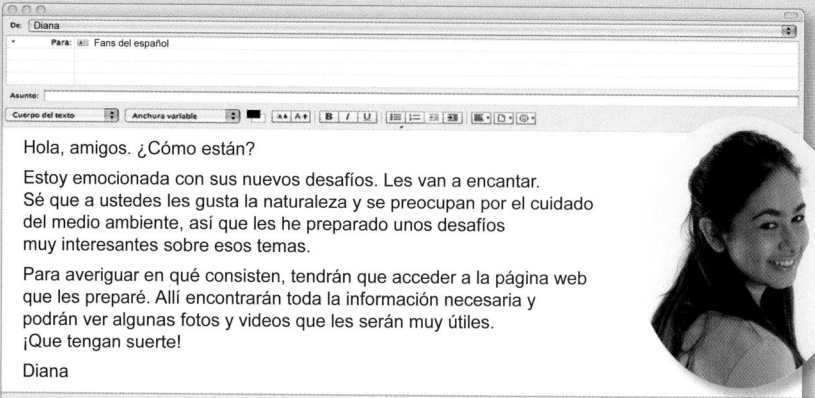

Diana sends an e-mail to the characters with a link to a web page that she made where they will find all the information they need to complete their tasks. Read it to discover what they have to do.

> De: Diana
> Para: Fans del español
> Asunto:
>
> Cuerpo del texto | Anchura variable | B I U
>
> Hola, amigos. ¿Cómo están?
>
> Estoy emocionada con sus nuevos desafíos. Les van a encantar. Sé que a ustedes les gusta la naturaleza y se preocupan por el cuidado del medio ambiente, así que les he preparado unos desafíos muy interesantes sobre esos temas.
>
> Para averiguar en qué consisten, tendrán que acceder a la página web que les preparé. Allí encontrarán toda la información necesaria y podrán ver algunas fotos y videos que les serán muy útiles. ¡Que tengan suerte!
>
> Diana

LasTareas.com

INFORMACIÓN **TAREAS** **RECURSOS** **PREGUNTAS**

TAREA 1
¿Saben que las mariposas monarca migran cada año de Canadá a México? Es un viaje muy largo y difícil, y por eso me gustaría que las ayudaran. Deberán investigar sobre el hábitat de estas mariposas y hacer un video en colaboración con un grupo de estudiantes mexicanos. Aquí pueden ver algunas <u>fotos</u> de estas mariposas.

TAREA 2
¿Alguna vez han oído hablar de la Fiesta del Sol o de la Noche de san Juan? En muchos países hispanos hay celebraciones muy antiguas relacionadas con el cambio de estación. Ustedes deben averiguar cómo se celebra el solsticio de junio en varios lugares y tendrán que hacer una presentación para explicarlo. Pueden ver estas <u>fotos</u> para tomar ideas.

TAREA 3
Supongo que están familiarizados con términos como «comercio justo» o «economía sostenible», pero les he preparado un <u>documento</u> para ayudarlos. Ustedes tendrán que organizar una feria de comercio justo con productos naturales y artesanales para demostrar cómo se puede comerciar de forma justa y respetando la naturaleza.

Differentiated Instruction

DEVELOPING LEARNERS

- Ask students to read the e-mail and the text on page 338 and make a list in their notebooks of any unknown words. Then ask students to try to guess the meaning of these words based on the context in which they are used. Finally, have students look up these words in their dictionaries and write the English-language definitions next to each word. Did they guess some of the meanings correctly? After students do this, have them read the material again and ask them if their comprehension has improved.

EXPANDING LEARNERS

- After students complete activity 2, ask them to make a chart that shows the word families for each of the verbs listed. Then have them go through the text on both pages and find other words that could be included in a *Familia de palabras* chart. For example, they might write *emocionada* from the first line of Diana's e-mail, and then write *emocionarse, emoción, emocionante.* You might want to turn this into a mini-competition to see who has created the largest word families after you call time.

Me parece interesantísimo hacer un video para compartirlo con los estudiantes de México. Entre todos podremos ayudar a las mariposas.

Me encantaría que nos encargáramos de celebrar una fiesta para el solsticio de junio.

A mí también, pero antes tenemos que averiguar cómo lo celebran en otros países.

Hola, Michelle. Quería hacerte una pregunta. ¿A Daniel y a ti les importaría ocuparse del desafío sobre el comercio justo? Es que a nosotros nos gustaría mucho hacer el de las mariposas.

No hay problema, Eva. Voy a decírselo a Daniel.

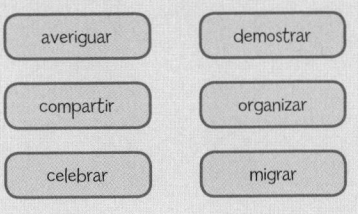

 1 **¿Comprendes?**

▶ **Escribe** la respuesta a estas preguntas.

1. ¿Cuál es la tarea de Eva y Ethan?
2. ¿Qué tienen que hacer Daniel y Michelle?
3. ¿Qué van a hacer Eva y Ethan para ayudar a las mariposas monarca?
4. ¿Qué es el solsticio de junio?
5. ¿Qué significa la expresión *comercio justo*?

 2 **Investiga**

▶ **Busca** el significado de estos verbos que aparecen en los textos. Después, escribe oraciones que te ayuden a recordarlo.

Modelo

compartir → *Mis hermanos y yo compartimos las tareas domésticas.*

averiguar	demostrar
compartir	organizar
celebrar	migrar

HERITAGE LANGUAGE LEARNERS

• Point out the adjective ending in *–ísimo* that Daniel uses on page 339 *(interesantísimo)*. Then have students write the *–ísimo* forms of the following adjectives and use them in a sentence:

1. *rico (riquísimo)*
2. *feliz (felicísimo)*
3. *vago (vaguísimo)*
4. *amable (amabilísimo)*
5. *largo (larguísimo)*
6. *joven (jovencísimo)*
7. *antiguo (antiquísimo)*
8. *fuerte (fuertísimo/fortísimo)*
9. *simpático (simpatiquísimo)*

COOPERATIVE LEARNING

• Not all students will be familiar with *comercio justo* (FT: fair trade) and *economía sostenible*. Ask students to work in pairs, with each person responsible for researching one of the two topics. Encourage students to find examples of fair trade and sustainable economy in their community and share their research and the examples they found with their partner. Call on two groups to give a brief oral presentation to the class on each of these topics.

Las tareas

■ After reading the text on page 338 and the dialogues on page 339, have students add details to the columns on the board. For example: 1. *Van a trabajar en colaboración con estudiantes mexicanos.* 2. *Tienen que ver unas fotos.* 3. *Tienen que demostrar cómo se puede comerciar de forma justa.*

Activities

1. Expand this activity by asking students their opinion about the tasks. For example: *¿Qué tema les interesa más: las mariposas monarca, las celebraciones del solsticio o el comercio justo? ¿Qué preferirían hacer: un video, una presentación o una feria? ¿Por qué creen que Eva prefiere hacer la tarea sobre las mariposas?*

2. Ask students to look at the context in which these verbs appear and guess their meaning before looking up the words.

Answer Key

1. 1. Investigar sobre el hábitat de las mariposas monarca.
   2. Organizar una feria de comercio justo con productos naturales y artesanales.
   3. Harán un video explicativo en colaboración con un grupo de estudiantes mexicanos.
   4. Es el día más largo del año en el hemisferio norte y el más corto en el hemisferio sur.
   5. Answers will vary. Sample answer: Es un sistema de comercio en el que se les pagan precios justos a los productores y se respeta la naturaleza.

2. Answers will vary.

Additional Resources

Fans Online activities
Practice Workbook

339

Unit 7
Antes de empezar

Presentation

- In this section, students will learn a variety of useful expressions to talk about how to do things, express wishes, and express polite requests.
- Students will also review words to talk about geographical features, the environment, the weather, and the universe.

Activities	Standards	Resources
Expresiones útiles	1.2, 2.1	
3.	1.1, 1.2	
4.	1.1, 1.2, 1.3	
Recuerda	1.2, 3.1	
5.	1.1, 1.2, 1.3, 3.1	
6.	1.3	

Teaching Suggestions

Warm-Up / Independent Starter

- Have students write five sentences using words they already know for talking about nature, geographical features, and the environment. To get them started you may want to suggest the following examples: *planta, árbol, mar, río, contaminación, sequía, aire, medio ambiente.*

Preparation

- Go over the *expresiones útiles* by using them in personalized contexts. For example, you might use sentences with *cómo* in the following ways: *Quiero saber cómo estudian ustedes para la clase de Español. John quiere saber cómo puede ahorrar electricidad en su casa.* You may also have students express wishes or make polite requests. Model for them: *Me gustaría que hiciera buen tiempo el sábado. ¿Te importaría escribir la palabra solsticio en la pizarra?*
- Have students read their sentences from the Independent Starter. Add more review vocabulary words on the board as they arise. Identify any review vocabulary words that are not easily recognized by the majority of the students in the class and add them to a separate list. These words can form a "short list" of words to study rather than trying to focus on every review vocabulary word that comes to mind.

340

Antes de empezar

EXPRESIONES ÚTILES

Para expresar el modo de hacer algo:

Hay que averiguar **cómo** se celebra el solsticio de junio.
Van a demostrar **cómo** se puede comerciar de forma justa.

Para expresar deseos:

Me **gustaría** que ayudaran a las mariposas.
Me **encantaría** que nos encargáramos de este desafío.

Para pedir algo cortésmente:

¿**Te importaría** ayudarme?
¿**Serías tan amable de** decírselo a Daniel?
¿**Podrían** ustedes ocuparse del desafío del comercio justo?

3 **Con cortesía**

▶ **Lee** estos mandatos y transfórmalos en peticiones corteses.

Modelo Pásame la sal. *¿Serías tan amable de pasarme la sal?*

1. Ven pronto.   2. Hablen más despacio.   3. Dime cuándo es el examen.

4 **Expresiones**

▶ **Completa** estos diálogos con las expresiones útiles.

1. —¿Sabes _____ se dice *shark* en español?
   —Sí, se dice *tiburón.*

2. —¿Te _____ llevarme en coche a la escuela?
   —No, en absoluto. Vamos.

3. —¿_____ tan amable de enviarme el informe?
   —Por supuesto.

4. —Me _____ mucho saber varios idiomas.
   —Claro, a mí también.

▶ **Escribe** un diálogo para cada fotografía usando las expresiones útiles.

340 trescientos cuarenta

Differentiated Instruction

DEVELOPING LEARNERS

- Review the use of the subjunctive mood with verbs that express a wish (e.g., *Me gustaría que ayudaran a las mariposas*). Then have students complete the following sentences. Answers will vary, but students should use the imperfect subjunctive in the dependent clause.

1. *Me encantaría que el medio ambiente…*
2. *¿Te gustaría que el aire…?*
3. *Nos gustaría que ustedes…*
4. *A mis padres les encantaría que yo…*
5. *Yo querría que mis compañeros…*
6. *Me gustaría mucho que la contaminación…*

EXPANDING LEARNERS

- Give students more practice with the expressions in the *Expresiones útiles* section by having them work with a partner to develop a dialogue. In their conversations, students should make at least two statements using *cómo,* two expressing wishes with verbs like *gustar* in the conditional, and conclude with making several polite requests. Partners' responses to these statements should be logical and the conversation should be natural. Encourage students to go beyond the vocabulary presented on the page, and to use words from previous lessons.

RECUERDA

Geografía

el bosque	el mar
la cascada	la montaña
el continente	el océano
el desierto	la región
la isla	el río
el lago	el valle

El tiempo meteorológico

estar nublado	la lluvia
hacer calor/frío	la nieve
llover	el relámpago
nevar	el viento

La naturaleza

el agua	el águila
el aire	el caballo
el animal	el cerdo
el árbol	el elefante
la contaminación	el mono
el medio ambiente	el oso
la planta	la oveja
la sequía	la vaca

El universo

la estrella	el sistema solar
la Luna	el Sol
el planeta	la Tierra

5 **¿Cuánto sabes?**

▶ **Completa** una tabla como esta con el vocabulario que ya sabes sobre estos temas. Después, compárala con la de tu compañero(a) y añade más palabras a tu tabla.

La naturaleza y el medio ambiente	El tiempo meteorológico	Los desastres naturales
la contaminación la sequía		el tornado

6 **Un paisaje**

▶ **Escribe** una lista de palabras relacionadas con cada fotografía.

▶ **Elige** una de las fotografías y escribe una descripción completa.

HERITAGE LANGUAGE LEARNERS

• After students complete activity 6, ask them to work with a partner and read each other's descriptions of the photographs. Then, ask students to work individually and write another composition, this time comparing and contrasting the photos, based on the two written descriptions and any other insight they may have of what is being depicted. Ask students to include where they think the photos were taken, which location they would prefer to visit and why, and which place would seem to have the more endangered environment. Students should also explain their answers.

MULTIPLE INTELLIGENCES:
Verbal-Linguistic Intelligence

• Tell students that they are going to play a game. On slips of paper, write all the words (except *valle*) that appear under *Geografía*, the word *animal*, and, if students have studied the planets, include the word *planeta*. Place the slips of paper in two or more bags (depending on how many teams you choose), and explain that students will take turns picking a slip. The object of the game is for students to name a geographical feature, animal, or planet depending on the category chosen. Students are not allowed to repeat what their classmates have answered.

Antes de empezar

Activities

3. To extend this activity, add other commands to the list. For example: *Abre el libro en la página 48. Vayan a la pizarra. Muéstrame tu cuaderno. Levántense.*

4. After students have completed the second part of this activity, have them get together with a classmate and select one of the dialogues they wrote. They will have to rehearse and act it out for the class.

6. To expand this activity, bring multiple photos of landscapes that show different parts of the world and different seasons. Distribute them to pairs of students and have the students describe them. Then ask for volunteer pairs to share some of their descriptions with the class. Ask related questions as they present their photos. For example: *¿Qué tiempo hace? ¿Qué animales viven en ese lugar?*

Answer Key

3. Answers will vary. Sample answers:
1. ¿Te importaría venir pronto?
2. ¿Podrían hablar más despacio?
3. ¿Serías tan amable de decirme cuándo es el examen?

4.
1. cómo
2. importaría
3. Serías
4. gustaría

▶ Answers will vary.

5. Answers will vary.

6. Answers will vary. Sample answers:
1. Flores, bosque tropical, árboles, plantas, lluvia, llover, hacer calor.
2. Hacer frío, nevar, montañas, río, lago, isla, valle, árboles altos, estar nublado.

▶ Answers will vary.

Additional Resources

Fans Online activities
Practice Workbook

Unit 7
DESAFÍO 1
Hacer hipótesis

Presentation

- In *Desafío 1*, Eva and Ethan will study the habitat of the monarch butterfly and prepare an educational video with a group of Mexican students. Students will preview language used to talk about nature and the environment and to express condition.

Activities	Standards	Resources
Texto	1.2, 3.1	Vis. Pres.
7.	1.1, 1.2, 3.1	
8.	1.1, 3.1	
9.	1.2, 1.3, 3.1	Audio
10.	1.2, 3.1	
11. Conexiones	1.1, 1.2, 2.1, 2.2, 3.1, 5.1	Video

Teaching Suggestions

Warm-Up / Independent Starter

- Have students write a description of the seasons in their region. Are there four distinct seasons? If so, which is their favorite? Why?

Preparation

- Have students review their Independent Starters. Ask them questions that will prepare them to understand the dialogue that they are about to read. For example: What is migration? Do they know of any birds or animals that migrate due to seasonal changes?

Texto: Una maravilla de la naturaleza

- Read the introduction to the reading aloud and have students predict what they will learn about the migration of the monarch butterflies. Then ask students to read the roles of Ethan, Eva, and Diana in groups of three.

- Ask students to brainstorm a list of steps that Ethan and Eva will have to take in order to create an educational video. What information will they need to discover?

Activities

7. Ask students to define *deforestación*. What types of *contaminación* are students familiar with?

342

Una maravilla de la naturaleza

 Migration of the monarch butterflies is a natural phenomenon that takes place every year in North America. Eva and Ethan have to study the habitat of these insects and create an educational video in collaboration with a group of Mexican students.

ETHAN: Yo he visto las mariposas monarca cada primavera y cada otoño... ¡pero no sabía adónde iban!

EVA: Yo sabía que van a pasar el invierno a México desde el sur de Canadá. Pero no sé a qué zona de México van.

DIANA: Van a los bosques del estado de Michoacán. Es un viaje larguísimo, de más de 4.000 kilómetros.

EVA: ¿Y tardan mucho?

DIANA: Qué va, 30 o 40 días. Lo peor es que a veces no encuentran vegetación para alimentarse a causa de la deforestación y la contaminación.

EVA: Pobrecitas, tenemos que ayudarlas. Hay que conservar el ecosistema para que el ciclo de migración no se destruya.

ETHAN: En el video deberíamos explicar que si cambiara el clima, las plantas que alimentan a las mariposas morirían y ellas también.

EVA: ¿Y cómo vamos a colaborar con los estudiantes de México?

ETHAN: ¡Filmando el hábitat de las mariposas aquí y allá!

DIANA: ¡Qué buena idea, Ethan! Mucha suerte, amigos.

7 **Detective de palabras**

▶ **Completa** estas oraciones.

1. Dos problemas que afectan a las mariposas monarca son la ___1___ y la ___2___.
2. Hay que conservar el ___3___ de las mariposas monarca.
3. Ethan y Eva van a filmar el ___4___ de las mariposas monarca.

▶ **Busca** las palabras del texto que corresponden a estas imágenes.

Differentiated Instruction

DEVELOPING LEARNERS

- To help students understand the dialogue, have them skim the material, identifying cognates and looking up any unfamiliar words as they do this. Help them identify some of the many cognates (e.g., *pasar, zona, kilómetros, vegetación, deforestación, ecosistema, ciclo, migración, explicar, clima, plantas, colaborar, hábitat, idea*). Point out that *larguísimo* (from *largo*) is a false cognate; it means long, not large. Then, have students work in groups of three and assign each one a different character. Ask them to rehearse their lines and then role-play the parts in front of the class.

EXPANDING LEARNERS

- Recap the migration of the monarch butterflies for students and explain that they will write an original account of this migration, but from a butterfly's point of view. Students will use their imagination to describe preparations for the trip, possible alternative routes, scenic "side trips" the butterfly may choose to take, recommendations as to the best food along the way, descriptions of the other butterflies traveling in the group, and any other ideas that occur to them. Ask students to read their accounts aloud.

8 **Comprensión**

▶ **Responde** a estas preguntas.

1. En tu opinión, ¿cómo sabe la mariposa hacia dónde tiene que viajar?
2. ¿Cómo crees que afecta el clima a estos animales?
3. ¿Cómo piensas que se puede ayudar a las mariposas monarca?

9 **La migración de la mariposa monarca**

▶ **Escucha** a Eva y a Ethan, y decide si estas oraciones son ciertas o falsas.

1. Viajan más de cinco mil kilómetros en invierno en busca de temperaturas más frías.
2. Tienen que hibernar para sobrevivir.
3. Siguen a las aves (birds) para llegar a México.
4. Los descendientes de las mariposas completan el viaje hacia el norte.
5. Migran solo una vez durante una década.

▶ **Escucha** de nuevo y corrige las oraciones falsas.

10 **Paso a paso**

▶ **Ordena** estos pasos de la migración de la mariposa monarca.

a. Llegan a Canadá para pasar el verano.
b. Empiezan su viaje hacia el norte en primavera. Mientras vuelan, ponen sus huevos. Así nace otra generación de mariposas para seguir el viaje.
c. Vuelan hacia México. Tardan 30 o 40 días en llegar.
d. Salen de Canadá para empezar su migración.
e. Hibernan en los bosques de Michoacán (México).

CONEXIONES: CIENCIAS

Reserva Especial de la Biosfera

México es un país con una flora y una fauna muy ricas, y cuenta con varias áreas protegidas. Los bosques de Michoacán, en el centro del país, son el destino de las mariposas monarca que migran cada año desde el norte del continente para pasar el invierno. Esta zona, declarada Reserva Especial de la Biosfera, ofrece las condiciones medioambientales ideales para su supervivencia.

Mariposas monarca (México).

11 **Investiga.** ¿Qué zonas protegidas hay en tu país? ¿Qué beneficios aportan a la naturaleza?

HERITAGE LANGUAGE LEARNERS

• Ask students to define the following terms from the dialogue in their own words: *deforestación, contaminación, ecosistema, ciclo, migración, hábitat.* Then have them write an original sentence using each of these words. Call on students to read one or two of their definitions, along with their sample sentences, aloud to the class. Encourage peer review of the accuracy of these definitions. Once these definitions have been approved, the other students may wish to write them in their notebooks.

MULTIPLE INTELLIGENCES:
Logical-Mathematical Intelligence

• Ask students to calculate how many kilometers the monarch butterflies fly each day during their migration to Mexico. Students will need to divide 4,500 km by 40 days to figure out that these tiny insects travel a little more than 112 km a day. Have students figure out the distance between your city and other cities and landmarks. Then, ask students to figure out how long it would take a monarch butterfly to fly the distances mentioned. Finally, have students convert the kilometers to miles (remind them that 1 km equals 0.62 miles).

10. Organize students in small groups and set up "stations" around the room. Each station has to research a step on the monarch's migration route. For example: Station 1 → Research where in Canada the monarch butterflies live. Station 2 → Research their migration routes, etc. Ask groups to share their findings with the class.

AUDIO SCRIPT
See page 335I.

CONEXIONES: CIENCIAS

Reserva Especial de la Biosfera

It is believed that monarch butterflies are guided during their migration by the magnetic pull of the Earth and the position of the Sun. They hibernate in the oyamel fir forests of Michoacán, Mexico. The humidity in this type of forest prevents the monarchs from drying out. Conservation of these forests is crucial, and even though they are protected, illegal logging in the region contributes to deforestation.

Answer Key

7. 1. deforestación   3. ecosistema
  2. contaminación   4. hábitat
  ▶ 1. bosque   3. vegetación/plantas
  2. mariposa

8. Answers will vary.

9. 1. Falso. Viajan casi cinco mil kilómetros para escapar del frío.
  2. Cierto.
  3. Falso. Siguen el sol y su instinto.
  4. Cierto.
  5. Falso. Migran cada año.

10. d, c, e, b, a

11. Answers will vary.

Additional Resources

Fans Online activities

343

DESAFÍO 1

Vocabulario – La naturaleza y el medio ambiente

Presentation

■ In this section, students will learn vocabulary relating to nature and the environment.

Activities	Standards	Resources
Vocabulario	1.2, 3.1	
12.	1.2, 3.1	Audio
13.	1.1, 3.1, 5.1	
14.	1.1, 1.2, 1.3	
15. Comunidades	1.1, 1.2, 2.2, 3.1, 5.1	

Teaching Suggestions

Warm-Up / Independent Starter

■ Write the following questions on the board and ask students to write their answers on an index card: *¿Qué problemas ecológicos encuentran las mariposas durante su migración? ¿Cómo crees que Eva y Ethan van a ayudarlas?*

Preparation

■ Collect the cards prepared in the Independent Starter and redistribute them to different students. Then ask students to read the cards they got aloud. Keep a running list of the answers on the board.

■ Divide students into groups of three. Ask each group to read the description of one of the volunteers (Raúl, Gabriela, or Marta), and identify the type of problem that this volunteer is working to solve. Then, reorganize the groups so that there is an "expert" on each character in each new group. The expert will explain the problem to the group and tell what the character is doing to solve that problem.

■ Have students consult a dictionary and write definitions in Spanish for the highlighted vocabulary. Collect these definitions and post them in the classroom.

Activities

12. Before beginning this activity, ask students to describe what the title *Un museo viviente* might refer to.

344

Vocabulario

La naturaleza y el medio ambiente

GENTE POR LA ECOLOGÍA

Varios voluntarios nos cuentan cómo colaboran en diversas tareas ecológicas para cuidar el medio ambiente y proteger la naturaleza.

«Yo soy Raúl. El año pasado gané un premio por un trabajo sobre los efectos de la **deforestación** en la destrucción de los **ecosistemas**, la flora y la fauna. Debemos **respetar** a las **especies protegidas**».

«Me llamo Gabriela y colaboro con una organización ecologista que realiza campañas para **concienciar** sobre la necesidad de reducir la contaminación. Nos preocupa mucho el **cambio climático**, el **efecto invernadero** y que aumente el **agujero de la capa de ozono** porque **amenazan** el futuro del planeta».

Deforestación.

«Yo soy Marta. Colaboro desde hace años con una organización que **denuncia** las **mareas negras** y otras **catástrofes ecológicas**.

Marea negra.

También realizamos campañas para **fomentar** el ahorro de energía y el uso de **energías alternativas** para que no **se agoten** los recursos naturales».

el papel y el cartón

las pilas

el vidrio

las latas y los envases de plástico

¡NO LOS TIRES A LA BASURA, RECÍCLALOS!

Más vocabulario

Fauna

el anfibio	*amphibian*	el mamífero	*mammal*
el ave (fem.)	*bird*	el reptil	*reptile*
el insecto	*insect*	el pez	*fish*

12 **Un museo viviente**

▶ **Escucha** la conversación y completa estas oraciones.

1. En las islas Galápagos hay una gran variedad de _____ animales.
2. Hay pocos lugares en el mundo con tantas variedades de _____ y fauna.
3. En este archipiélago viven aves, mamíferos, _____ y peces.
4. Los _____ naturales de las islas permanecieron intactos durante siglos.
5. Las _____ gigantes de las Galápagos pesan más de 300 kilos.
6. La Fundación Charles Darwin se estableció para conservar el _____ de las islas.

Differentiated Instruction

DEVELOPING LEARNERS

• Ask students to close their books and make a three-column chart. Have them label the columns as follows: *Efecto positivo, Efecto negativo,* and *Afectado.* Then ask students to open their books, and categorize as many of the new words as they can under these headings. For example, *cuidar el medio ambiente* would fall under the category of *Efecto positivo,* while *la contaminación* belongs under *Efecto negativo,* and *ecosistema, flora,* and *fauna* would be listed under *Afectado.*

EXPANDING LEARNERS

• Have students complete a word search puzzle based on some of the new vocabulary from this lesson. Write sentences, leaving out a key word, and post them on the whiteboard or give photocopies to students. Then find a software program that will allow you to create a puzzle from the answers to your clues. Make copies and distribute. Students must first identify the missing words and then search for them in the puzzle. You might set a time limit to see who is the first to successfully complete the puzzle.

13 Ciudadanos responsables

 ▶ **Habla** con tu compañero(a). Identifiquen cada objeto y decidan en qué contenedor se debe depositar cada uno.

Modelo   *Esto es una botella. Hay que depositarla en el contenedor de vidrio.*

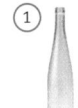 ①  ②  ③  ④  ⑤  ⑥

14 Opiniones

▶ **Lee** estas opiniones y di si estás de acuerdo o no con ellas y por qué.

1. «Yo pienso que los recursos naturales son muy abundantes. No debemos preocuparnos demasiado porque nunca se van a agotar.»
2. «El reciclaje no sirve para nada, es solo un negocio para las empresas.»
3. «Si no hacemos nada para evitarlo, el cambio climático terminará con la vida en el planeta.»
4. «La deforestación es una de las mayores catástrofes ecológicas porque destruye el hábitat de muchas especies.»

 COMUNIDADES

LA REGIÓN DE MAGALLANES (CHILE)

Chile es uno de los principales países productores de tulipanes, que exporta principalmente a Holanda, Canadá y los Estados Unidos. Las condiciones climáticas de la región de Magallanes, al sur del país, permiten cultivar (*grow*) especies de climas fríos en condiciones naturales.

Plantación de tulipanes.

15 Compara. ¿Se producen muchas flores en la zona donde vives? ¿Por qué crees que es así? ¿Qué industrias son importantes en tu comunidad?

HERITAGE LANGUAGE LEARNERS

• Explain to students that deforestation has affected many areas in the Amazon rainforest. Indigenous peoples have been affected adversely and their territory has been reduced. Ask students to research how deforestation may be affecting their family's country of origin, or any other country in the Americas. Ask them to prepare a written report, including statistics on acres lost to deforestation, how it has affected the local population, the organizations responsible for cutting down the forests, and what is being done to stop the destruction. Ask student to cite their sources.

CRITICAL THINKING

• Ask students to work in small groups and prepare to debate the following issue: saving an endangered species whose habitat is in the path of a proposed highway expansion or commercial development vs. supporting the construction. Indicate to each group which argument they are going to defend. Give groups time to prepare and then call on individuals from each group to defend their case against members of the other team. Explain that students will only be allowed a certain number of minutes to make their opening argument, then defend it, and make their rebuttals.

Vocabulario – La naturaleza y el medio ambiente

14. After finishing this activity, have students form pairs and compare and contrast their reactions to these quotes. You may want to select one of the quotes and have a class discussion.

15. Ask students to point out the location of Chile on a map and note some geographical features. If flowers do not grow all year long where you live, ask students to ponder where a florist or a supermarket gets the flowers that they sell during the colder months.

 AUDIO SCRIPT
See page 335I.

 COMUNIDADES

La región de Magallanes (Chile)

Many areas of Chile are separated from the rest of South America by mountain chains, glaciers, and deserts. Consequently, Chile has a large number of plants that do not grow anywhere else in the world. In fact, there are more than 5,000 endemic plant species in Chile. Because it is summer in Chile when it is winter in the Northern Hemisphere, Chilean flower growers can meet demand in northern regions when flowers may be in short supply.

Answer Key

12. 1. especies   4. recursos
     2. flora   5. tortugas
     3. reptiles   6. hábitat

13. 2. periódicos – papel   5. caja – papel
     3. bote – envases   6. lata – envases
     4. tarro – vidrio

14. Answers will vary.

15. Answers will vary.

Additional Resources

Fans Online activities
Practice Workbook

DESAFÍO 1

Gramática – Expresar condición (I)

Presentation

- In this section, students will learn how to use the present indicative and the future to express conditions that refer to real (factual) or likely events.

Activities	Standards	Resources
Gramática	1.2, 3.1	
16.	4.1	
17.	1.2, 1.3, 3.1	
18.	1.2, 1.3, 3.1	
19.	1.1, 1.2, 1.3, 3.1, 5.2	Audio
20. Cultura	1.1, 1.2, 2.1, 2.2, 3.1, 4.2	

Teaching Suggestions

Warm-Up / Independent Starter

- Show students pictures of different problems confronting nature. Ask them to create a two-column chart and list the problems and what will happen if we don't find solutions to these problems.

Preparation

- Ask students to read the grammar explanation on page 346 silently and answer questions that they may have. You may suggest to students that they look at the formula for the formation of conditional sentences as if it were a mathematical formula, where variables are replaced.

- Have students share their charts from the Independent Starter. Then assist them in forming a few sentences using the information in their charts. For example: *Si seguimos usando los recursos naturales sin control, se agotarán.*

Activities

17. To expand this activity, have students come up with a result clause for each of these conditions: *Si continúa la deforestación... Si no ahorramos energía...*

19. Before completing this activity, ask students what and how they recycle in their own homes. Then, after completing the activity, have pairs design a sign that represents their ideas about the three R's. Invite students to share their sign with the class.

Gramática

Expresar condición (I)

Oraciones condicionales con si

- Use conditional sentences with si *(if)* clauses to express what could happen if some condition is met. The si clause expresses the condition; and the main clause, the result. Si clauses can come at the beginning or end of a sentence.

<u>Si tengo dinero</u>, <u>iré de vacaciones</u>.
condition   result

<u>Llámame</u> <u>si puedes</u>.
result   condition

Oraciones condicionales reales. El indicativo

- Use the indicative mood to refer to real (factual) or likely conditions in either the present or the future. Several tense combinations are possible.

<u>Si</u> + present indicative + present indicative / future indicative / command
si clause (condition)   main clause (result)

	SI CLAUSE (condition)	MAIN CLAUSE (result)
To describe what is always true or what happens if the condition is met.	Present indicative Si tengo sed, *If (Whenever) I'm thirsty,*	Present indicative bebo agua. *I drink water.*
	Si estudio, *If I study,*	saco buenas notas. *I get good grades.*
To express what will happen if the condition is met.	Present indicative Si tengo tiempo, *If I have time,*	Future indicative iré al gimnasio. *I'll go to the gym.*
To give an order dependent on a condition being met.	Present indicative Si me duermo, *If I fall asleep,*	Command despiértame. *wake me up.*

16 **Compara.** ¿Cómo se expresa el resultado de una condición en inglés? ¿Se parece al español?

17 **Ayuda al planeta**

▶ **Une** las columnas y escribe las oraciones.

Ⓐ

1. Si usamos más el transporte público...
2. Si reciclamos el papel...
3. Si construimos barcos más seguros...
4. Si protegemos los bosques...
5. Si se produce el cambio climático...

Ⓑ

a. se cortarán menos árboles.
b. no se destruirán los ecosistemas.
c. habrá menos riesgo de marea negra.
d. habrá más inundaciones.
e. habrá menos contaminación.

Differentiated Instruction

DEVELOPING LEARNERS

- Write on the board the following phrases that indicate a result, and ask students to provide the condition. Sentences will vary, but must be logical. For example:

1. *Si ... desaparecerán las playas. (hay marea negra)*
2. *Si ... habrá menos contaminación. (cuidamos el medio ambiente)*
3. *Si ... hay menos basura. (reciclamos)*
4. *Si ... denúnciala. (ves una catástrofe ecológica)*
5. *Si ... desaparecerán muchas especies. (no protegemos los ecosistemas)*

EXPANDING LEARNERS

- Ask students to make a list of five ecological concerns in their community and describe them with a si clause in the present tense, plus the present or future tense in the result clause. The concerns may focus on what is happening in nature or school. For example: *Naturaleza → Si respetamos a las especies protegidas de nuestra región, no desaparecerán. Escuela → Si organizamos una campaña para reciclar, los estudiantes tomarán el tema del reciclaje en serio.*

18 El biotopo del quetzal

▶ **Lee** el texto y completa las oraciones siguiendo el modelo.

El quetzal: una especie protegida

El quetzal es un ave que vive en los bosques montañosos de Chiapas (México), Guatemala y otros países centroamericanos. Para muchos es el pájaro más bonito del mundo porque tiene un plumaje muy vistoso. Su pecho es rojo y tiene una larga cola de plumas verdes y azules muy característica. Actualmente el quetzal se encuentra en peligro de extinción por la destrucción de su hábitat y el tráfico ilegal.

En 1977 la Universidad de San Carlos de Guatemala estableció el biotopo del quetzal para conservar el hábitat de esta ave. Es una zona protegida al norte del país donde se dan las condiciones ambientales adecuadas para el desarrollo de esta especie animal. Allí se puede observar una gran variedad de plantas, aves, insectos y mamíferos.

Modelo Si se permite la deforestación… → *se destruirá el hábitat del quetzal.*

1. Si continúa el tráfico ilegal del quetzal…
2. Si se destruyen los bosques donde vive el quetzal…
3. Si se recrea el ecosistema del hábitat del quetzal…

19 Las tres «R» del reciclaje

 ▶ **Escucha** un fragmento de un programa de radio sobre medio ambiente y toma notas de la información más importante.

 ▶ **Comparte** tus notas con tu compañero(a) y escriban seis resultados de practicar las tres «R» del reciclaje. Después, compartan sus ideas con la clase.

Modelo *Si reutilizamos productos de vidrio, ahorraremos energía.*

CULTURA

Símbolos nacionales

Algunas especies animales y vegetales se han convertido en símbolo de su país y, en muchos casos, aparecen en sus escudos y banderas. El quetzal, por ejemplo, es símbolo de Guatemala; está en su bandera y da nombre a su moneda. Otros ejemplos son el cóndor (Colombia y Ecuador), el águila real (México), la orquídea (Venezuela) o el ceibo (Argentina y Uruguay).

 20 Investiga y habla. ¿Qué ave es el símbolo nacional de los Estados Unidos? ¿Qué representa?

Gramática – Expresar condición (I)

20. Show students pictures of the symbols mentioned in the reading. After reading, ask students to find pictures of these symbols in other forms: coins, flags, etc. How do these symbols represent the countries where they are found?

 AUDIO SCRIPT
See page 335I.

 CULTURA

Símbolos nacionales

The dictionary defines a *symbol* as something used for or regarded as representing something else; consequently, a *national symbol* is something that represents a particular country. National symbols exist to unify a people, and they may originate from a historical event, a celebration, a famous place, an animal or bird that is indigenous to the country, etc. Flags, colors, and songs are common official national symbols.

Answer Key

16. Sí, se parece al español porque en inglés también se usa el presente, futuro e imperativo para expresar el resultado de una condición.

17. 1. e   2. a   3. c   4. b   5. d

18. Answers will vary. Sample answers.

1. … este se extinguirá.
2. … este desaparecerá.
3. … este vivirá sin peligro.

19. Answers will vary.

20. El águila calva. Representa la libertad.

Additional Resources

Fans Online activities
Practice Workbook

HERITAGE LANGUAGE LEARNERS

• Ask students to research the quetzal or another endangered animal or plant species that is from a Spanish-speaking country. Examples might include the jaguar, the Iberian lynx, or the giant anteater. Have students collect data on the species' habitat, its plight, and what is being done to help protect it. Encourage students to incorporate some *si* clauses with the indicative mood in their descriptions. Then ask students to use this information and some images to promote their endangered species in a poster.

MULTIPLE INTELLIGENCES:

Visual-Spatial Intelligence

• Ask students to think about an animal or plant that would represent them and their families on a coat of arms or flag. Then, have them design their family's coat of arms or flag. When their illustrations are complete, students should be prepared to present them to the rest of class. Students should name the animal or plant they have selected, explain its significance to them, and provide some data regarding their choices. Students should also explain why they selected the colors or other symbols on their flag or coat of arms.

DESAFÍO 1

Gramática – Expresar condición (II)

Presentation

- In this section, students will learn how to express unlikely, hypothetical, or contrary-to-fact conditions.

Activities	Standards	Resources
Gramática	1.2, 3.1	
21.	1.1, 1.2, 3.1	
22.	1.2, 1.3, 3.1	
23.	1.2, 1.3, 3.1	Audio
24.	1.1, 1.3	
25.	1.1, 1.2, 1.3	

Teaching Suggestions

Warm-Up / Independent Starter

- Sometimes students do not understand the subtleties of expression in their own language; consequently, they have trouble using them correctly in another. With this in mind, write the following pairs of sentences on the board and ask students to analyze them:
  1. a. If the butterflies migrate south, they will be able to hibernate.
     b. If the butterflies were to migrate south, they would be able to hibernate.
  2. a. If the oil tanker sinks, there will be an oil spill.
     b. If the oil tanker sank (were to sink), there would be an oil spill.

Preparation

- Ask students to read the grammar explanation on page 348. You may want to review the formation of the imperfect subjunctive (i.e., third person plural of the preterite plus the endings -ra, -ras, -ra, -ramos, -rais, -ran), as well as the conditional (i.e., the infinitive plus the endings -ía, -ías, -ía, -íamos, -íais, -ían). Remind students of any irregular verbs.

- Then ask students to try to translate the sentences from the Independent Starter into Spanish.
  1. a. Si las mariposas migran al sur, podrán hibernar.
     b. Si las mariposas migraran al sur, podrían hibernar.
  2. a. Si se hunde el petrolero, habrá una marea negra.
     b. Si se hundiera el petrolero, habría una marea negra.

Gramática

Expresar condición (II)

Oraciones condicionales potenciales. El subjuntivo y el condicional

- Use the imperfect subjunctive in the si clause and the conditional in the main clause to express unlikely, hypothetical, or contrary-to-fact conditions in either the present or the future.

> Si + imperfect subjunctive + conditional
> si clause (condition)   main clause (result)

	SI CLAUSE (condition) Imperfect subjunctive	MAIN CLAUSE (result) Conditional
To express an unlikely or hypothetical condition in the present or in the future.	Si tuviera tiempo, *If I had the time,*	tomaría clases de piano. *I would take piano lessons.*
	Si Ana me invitara a su boda, *If Ana were to invite me to her wedding,*	no iría, *I would not go.*
To express an impossible or contrary-to-fact condition in the present.	Si yo fuera un animal, *If I were an animal,*	sería un águila. *I would be an eagle.*

Note that the conditional tense is used in the main clause, never in the si clause.

21 **Compara.** Transforma la siguiente oración en una oración condicional potencial y compara el significado de las dos oraciones.

Si reciclamos más, ayudaremos al medio ambiente.

22 **Somos ecologistas**

 Transforma estas oraciones en condicionales potenciales. Fíjate en el modelo.

Modelo   Si voy a las islas Galápagos, veré las tortugas.
→ *Si fuera a las islas Galápagos, vería las tortugas.*

1. Si se destruyen los bosques, los animales perderán su hábitat.
2. Si los gobiernos colaboran, evitaremos la deforestación.
3. Si cuidamos su hábitat, las mariposas vivirán sin peligro.
4. Si ustedes visitan el biotopo del quetzal en Guatemala, verán a estas aves.
5. Si denunciamos las catástrofes ecológicas, evitaremos su aumento.
6. Si Eva y Ethan tienen tiempo, investigarán la migración de las mariposas monarca.

Tortuga gigante.
Islas Galápagos (Ecuador).

Differentiated Instruction

DEVELOPING LEARNERS

- Ask students to complete the following sentences with the correct form of the verbs in parentheses:
  1. *Si yo (ir) a Guatemala, (poder) ver un quetzal. (fuera, podría)*
  2. *Si nuestra comunidad (proteger) la naturaleza, nosotros (disfrutar) de las zonas verdes. (protegiera, disfrutaríamos)*
  3. *Si la gente (respetar) las especies protegidas, no (estar) en peligro. (respetara, estarían)*
  4. *Si ustedes (fomentar) el reciclaje, la ciudad (estar) más limpia. (fomentaran, estaría)*

EXPANDING LEARNERS

- Ask students to create a public relations campaign that supports recycling in their community. Students may write an ad for TV, radio, or the printed media, create a web page, or make a poster. Encourage students to use sentences with a *si* clause and the imperfect subjunctive, plus the conditional tense in the main clause to show the hypothetical results of their good advice. Students should come up with a slogan for their recycling campaign and be sure to include images or other graphics from magazines or the Internet.

23 **Los temas del día**

 ▶ **Escucha** a varios jóvenes hablar del medio ambiente y completa una tabla como esta. Fíjate bien en las formas verbales.

	Condicionales reales (si + indicativo)	Condicionales potenciales (si + subjuntivo)
1		✓
2		
3		
4		
5		
6		

▶ **Completa** estas oraciones. Usa el subjuntivo.

1. Yo reciclaría más si...
2. El aire sería más puro si...
3. No habría animales en peligro de extinción si...

24 **Las vacaciones serían perfectas si...**

▶ **Escribe** un párrafo explicando las condiciones que tendrían que cumplirse para tener unas vacaciones perfectas. Después, compáralo con tu compañero(a) para averiguar en qué coinciden.

Modelo

> Las vacaciones serían perfectas si no tuviera que hacer tareas ni estudiar. También serían mejores si pudiera ir con mis amigos a...

25 **Si yo fuera**

▶ **Pregunta** a tu compañero(a) y haz un dibujo sencillo para ilustrar cada una de sus respuestas. Túrnense para preguntar y responder. Al final, presenten sus dibujos a la clase.

Modelo   *Si Larry visitara las islas Galápagos, tomaría un barco para visitar todas las islas.*

1. Si visitaras las islas Galápagos, ¿qué harías?
2. Si pudieras pasar las vacaciones en un país hispano, ¿adónde irías?
3. Si pudieras proteger a una especie en peligro de extinción, ¿cuál elegirías?
4. Si fueras un ave, un insecto o un reptil, ¿qué animal serías?
5. Si pudieras ser otra persona durante un día, ¿quién te gustaría ser?

HERITAGE LANGUAGE LEARNERS

• Ask students to think about a topic related to the environment and explain that they will write a paragraph on this topic. First, have students state some goals they would like to see accomplished regarding their chosen topic. Then, have them write the paragraph and include the conditions that would need to be met in order to accomplish these goals. Remind them to use a *si* clause with the imperfect subjunctive to state the condition and the conditional tense in the main clause to describe the result.

SPECIAL-NEEDS LEARNERS

• Allow visually impaired students to complete activity 23 by working with a partner and, after listening to the audio, telling their partners which conditions are real by using *si* with the indicative mood, and which conditions are unlikely or hypothetical by using *si* and the imperfect subjunctive. Partners will need to make sure that the tenses used in the main clause correspond to the condition stated.

Gramática – Expresar condición (II)

Activities

22. To complete this activity, ask estudents to refer to the sentences translated in the Preparation activity. Then have students answer this question: *¿A qué dedicarías tu tiempo si fueras ecologista?*

24. Collect the descriptions written by the students and redistribute them to the class. Ask students to read the descriptions and to guess the place being described and the student who may have written the description.

> 🎧 **AUDIO SCRIPT**
> See page 335I.

Answer Key

21. Si recicláramos más, ayudaríamos al medio ambiente.

22. 1. Si se destruyeran los bosques, los animales perderían su hábitat.
2. Si los gobiernos colaboraran, evitaríamos la deforestación.
3. Si cuidáramos su hábitat, las mariposas vivirían sin peligro.
4. Si visitaran el biotopo del quetzal en Guatemala, verían a estas aves.
5. Si denunciáramos las catástrofes ecológicas, evitaríamos su aumento.
6. Si Eva y Ethan tuvieran tiempo, investigarían la migración de las mariposas monarca.

23. Condicionales reales: 2, 6.
Condicionales potenciales: 1, 3, 4, 5.
▶ Answers will vary. Sample answers:
1. ... en mi escuela hubiera un programa de reciclaje.
2. ... los coches no fueran tan contaminantes.
3. ... el ser humano fuera respetuoso con el medio ambiente.

24. Answers will vary.

25. Answers will vary.

> ### Additional Resources
> Fans Online activities
> Practice Workbook

349

Unit 7

LECTURA: TEXTO DIALOGADO

Presentation

- In this section, students will read a dialogue, identify vocabulary that refers to seasons and nature, find place names contained within, and descipher the meaning of words. Students will also answer comprehension questions based on the reading.

Activities	Standards	Resources
Lectura: texto dialogado	1.1, 1.2, 3.1	Vis. Pres.
26.	1.2, 1.3, 3.1	
27.	1.2, 3.1	
28.	1.1, 1.2, 1.3, 3.1	

Teaching Suggestions

Warm-Up / Independent Starter

- Have students read the *Antes de leer* strategies silently. Then ask them to take notes as they prepare to answer the questions.

Preparation

- Use a map of North America to help students locate and track the migration routes of monarch butterflies. Have them locate the state of Michoacán in central Mexico. Then ask students to make guesses about weather conditions in this region of Mexico. To facilitate their task, review the seasons of the year and the months. Finally, have students guess the distance that the butterflies travel every year.

- Read the dialogue aloud to students, modeling correct pronunciation and intonation. Then call on several pairs of students to alternate reading the dialogue aloud. Offer suggestions to improve their oral reading.

- To extend the reading activity and practice productive language skills, ask students to "chat" with the characters, either online with each other, or by passing a paper back and forth within a small group. Alternatively, you may want to assign certain students to be Eva, Pedro, Ethan, and Lucía, and have them "chat" with another small group of students to continue the conversation. Call on volunteer groups to share their "chats" with the class.

350

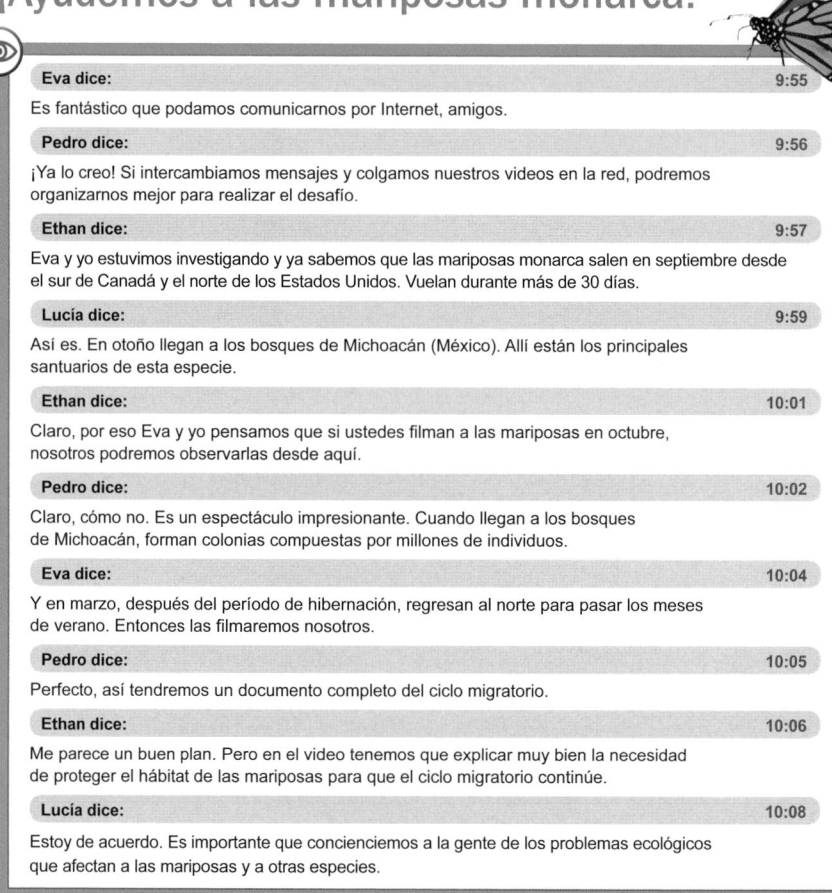

Antes de leer: estrategias

1. ¿Cuántos personajes intervienen en el chat? ¿Quiénes piensas que son Lucía y Pedro? ¿En qué país crees que están?

2. Busca las palabras que se refieren a meses del año y responde: ¿Cuándo migran las mariposas monarca? ¿Cuándo regresan?

3. Busca las palabras que se refieren a lugares. ¿Desde dónde vuelan las mariposas monarca? ¿Adónde van?

¡Ayudemos a las mariposas monarca!

Eva dice: 9:55
Es fantástico que podamos comunicarnos por Internet, amigos.

Pedro dice: 9:56
¡Ya lo creo! Si intercambiamos mensajes y colgamos nuestros videos en la red, podremos organizarnos mejor para realizar el desafío.

Ethan dice: 9:57
Eva y yo estuvimos investigando y ya sabemos que las mariposas monarca salen en septiembre desde el sur de Canadá y el norte de los Estados Unidos. Vuelan durante más de 30 días.

Lucía dice: 9:59
Así es. En otoño llegan a los bosques de Michoacán (México). Allí están los principales santuarios de esta especie.

Ethan dice: 10:01
Claro, por eso Eva y yo pensamos que si ustedes filman a las mariposas en octubre, nosotros podremos observarlas desde aquí.

Pedro dice: 10:02
Claro, cómo no. Es un espectáculo impresionante. Cuando llegan a los bosques de Michoacán, forman colonias compuestas por millones de individuos.

Eva dice: 10:04
Y en marzo, después del período de hibernación, regresan al norte para pasar los meses de verano. Entonces las filmaremos nosotros.

Pedro dice: 10:05
Perfecto, así tendremos un documento completo del ciclo migratorio.

Ethan dice: 10:06
Me parece un buen plan. Pero en el video tenemos que explicar muy bien la necesidad de proteger el hábitat de las mariposas para que el ciclo migratorio continúe.

Lucía dice: 10:08
Estoy de acuerdo. Es importante que concienciemos a la gente de los problemas ecológicos que afectan a las mariposas y a otras especies.

350 trescientos cincuenta

Differentiated Instruction

DEVELOPING LEARNERS

- Help students gain confidence in their comprehension of the dialogue by having them search for cognates. There are many easily recognizable cognates in the dialogue (e.g., *fantástico, comunicar, video, organizar, investigar, septiembre, santuario, especie, filmar, observar, espectáculo, impresionante, millones, individuo, marzo, periodo*). Help students identify the false cognate (*realizar*). Explain that *realizar* means "to accomplish," and that the Spanish-language equivalent for "to realize" is *darse cuenta*. Point out that the word *colonias* has two different meanings: "colonies" and "colognes."

EXPANDING LEARNERS

- After students complete activity 28, ask them to write six true/false statements about the monarch butterfly and exchange their papers with a partner. Partners will answer each other's questions, and rewrite the false statements to make them true. Encourage students to use information not previously stated in the textbook, but found in independent sources such as books, magazines, and the Internet. When students complete this task, call on volunteers to compose a fact sheet on the monarch butterfly, pulling together data from their classmates' statements.

26 El ciclo migratorio

▶ **Completa** este gráfico con la información del texto.

El ciclo migratorio de la mariposa monarca

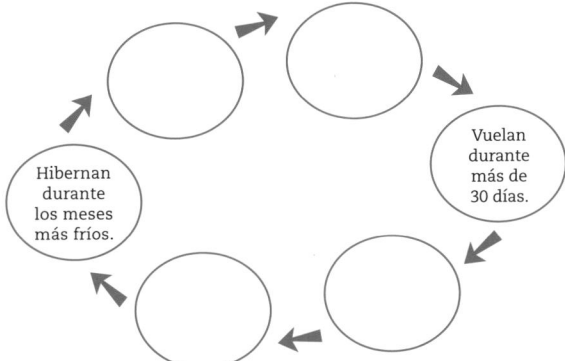

Vuelan durante más de 30 días.

Hibernan durante los meses más fríos.

27 Definiciones

▶ **Lee** estas definiciones del diccionario. ¿A qué palabras del texto corresponden?

1. Lugar de condiciones apropiadas para que viva un organismo.

2. Estado que se presenta en algunos animales como adaptación al invierno y que consiste en un descenso de la temperatura corporal.

3. Grupo de animales de una misma especie que conviven en un territorio limitado.

28 Con tus propias palabras

▶ **Responde** a estas preguntas sobre las mariposas monarca. Puedes buscar información en revistas especializadas, en Internet, etc.

1. ¿De qué colores son las mariposas monarca?
2. ¿Cómo son los bosques de México donde pasan el invierno las mariposas monarca?
3. ¿Qué temperatura necesitan las mariposas monarca para vivir?
4. ¿Cuánto tiempo suele vivir la mariposa monarca?

▶ **Escribe** con tu compañero(a) algunas sugerencias para que los personajes del diálogo hagan mejor el video.

Modelo *Deberían incluir un mapa con la ruta migratoria.*

trescientos cincuenta y uno 351

Activities

26. After students have finished this activity, encourage them to use the graphic organizer to summarize, in their own words, the information they drew from the text.

27. Have students note the cognates when reading these definitions. Words or phrases like *condiciones apropiadas*, *estado*, *adaptación*, *grupo*, or *especie* may be helpful when trying to get the gist of the definitions.

28. Students may have to find some of this information on the Internet. You may want to divide the class in groups of four and assign one question per individual, then have each group prepare a presentation that includes photos and texts or a digital slideshow.

Answer Key

26. Answers will vary. Sample answer:

Salen desde el sur de Canadá y el norte de los Estados Unidos en septiembre. → Vuelan durante más de 30 días. → Llegan a los bosques de Michoacán. → Forman colonias compuestas por millones de individuos. → Hibernan durante los meses más fríos. → En marzo regresan al norte.

27. 1. hábitat   2. hibernación   3. colonia

28. Answers will vary. Sample answers:

1. Son de color naranja y negro.
2. Son principalmente bosques de abeto oyamel (*oyamel fir trees*).
3. Necesitan clima templado.
4. En verano viven de 2 a 6 semanas; en invierno, alrededor de 7 a 8 meses para poder migrar e hibernar.

▶ Answers will vary.

Additional Resources

Fans Online activities

HERITAGE LANGUAGE LEARNERS

• Point out the use of a noun, *monarca*, to define *las mariposas* and have students note that nouns used as adjectives appear in the singular form. Ask students to brainstorm other words that use nouns as adjectives and write the singular and plural forms in their notebooks. For example:

1. *el año luz (los años luz)*
2. *el coche cama (los coches cama)*
3. *el hombre rana (los hombres rana)*
4. *el perro policía (los perros policía)*
5. *la palabra clave (las palabras clave)*

MULTIPLE INTELLIGENCES:

Verbal-Linguistic Intelligence

• Ask students to imagine that they have traveled to the monarch butterfly sanctuary in Michoacán. On arriving, they see the millions of butterflies that have flown in from the north and are preparing for their winter stay. Ask students to write a letter to their friends back home, describing their trip and arrival, the sanctuary, the butterflies' behavior, and, of course, the spectacle of seeing so many butterflies. Students may include recommendations for others to visit or for helping to protect the monarch's habitat.

DESAFÍO 1

Comunicación

Presentation

- In this section, students will integrate the vocabulary and grammar skills from *Desafío 1* in order to describe nature and the environment.

Activities	Standards	Resources
29.	1.1, 1.2, 1.3, 3.1, 5.1	
30.	1.2, 3.1	Audio
31.	1.1, 3.1, 5.1, 5.2	
32. Final del desafío	1.1, 1.2, 1.3, 3.1, 4.2, 5.1	
Tu desafío	1.1, 1.2	

Teaching Suggestions

Warm-Up / Independent Starter

- Ask students to create a list of five statements for protecting the environment. They should use conditional clauses. For example: *Si nosotros reciclamos, generaremos menos basura.*

Preparation

- Have volunteers write the statements from their Independent Starters on the board. Ask the class to correct any errors. Try to get as wide a variety of vocabulary as possible in order to practice the target vocabulary from this lesson.

Activities

29. After students have finished the second part of this activity, have pairs rewrite their advice statements using *si* clauses. For example: *Si separáramos la basura, podríamos reciclarla más fácilmente. Si no imprimiéramos los mensajes, usaríamos menos papel.* Invite pairs to share some of their sentences with the class.

30. Before listening to the audio recording, ask students to predict what types of specific information they might hear pertaining to *la marea negra, la deforestación, una especie protegida,* and *el reciclaje.* Have them take brief notes about each topic before playing the audio. After listening, they can confirm how accurate their predictions were.

Comunicación

29 **¿Qué puedes hacer tú?**

▶ **Lee** este folleto con consejos para proteger el medio ambiente y complétalo con las palabras del cuadro.

energía	transporte	calor	papel	basura	envases

¿Qué puedes hacer?

Proteger el medio ambiente puede ser una actividad diaria. Aquí te decimos cómo.

En la escuela
- Lleva tu almuerzo en ___1___ reutilizables.
- Antes de comprar material escolar, revisa lo que te sobró del curso anterior y úsalo de nuevo.
- Trata de separar y generar menos ___2___ .

En el trabajo
- Escribe o imprime por los dos lados de la hoja de ___3___ .
- En la cafetera usa un filtro permanente hecho de tela en vez de filtros desechables.
- Camina, usa tu bici o el ___4___ público para ir a trabajar. También puedes organizarte para que varios compañeros usen un solo auto.

En la cocina
- Mantén tu refrigerador entre 38 y 41 °F y el congelador entre 1 y 5 °F. No lo coloques cerca de una fuente de calor.
- Usa ollas a presión, pues gastan poca ___5___ .
- No precalientes el horno. Apágalo 15 minutos antes y aprovecha el ___6___ que queda en el horno para terminar la cocción.

Fuente: http://www.eluniversal.com.mx (texto adaptado)

▶ **Escribe** con tu compañero(a) un consejo más para cada categoría.

30 **Nuestro planeta**

▶ **Escucha** a Eva y a Ethan, y decide a qué se refiere cada uno.
a. A la marea negra.
b. A la deforestación.
c. A una especie protegida.
d. Al reciclaje.

352 trescientos cincuenta y dos

Differentiated Instruction

DEVELOPING LEARNERS

- After students complete the first part of activity 29, ask them to choose six suggestions and rewrite them so they use the imperfect subjunctive in the *si* clause and the conditional tense in the main clause. Guide them as they complete the first two statements. For example: *Si llevaras tu almuerzo en envases reutilizables, ayudarías al medio ambiente. Si revisaras los materiales escolares que te sobraron del curso anterior, podrías reutilizarlos.* Explain to students that they will have to reword some of the suggestions in order to use the *si* clauses logically.

EXPANDING LEARNERS

- After students complete the first part of activity 29, ask them to add two (instead of one) pieces of advice for protecting the environment to each of the three categories. Have students use the imperative or a *si* clause with the imperfect subjunctive or the present indicative. You might give them the following examples to get them started: *Para ir a la escuela, camina, toma el autobús o comparte el coche con otros estudiantes. Si usaras una taza de cerámica o de porcelana para tomar café en el trabajo, evitarías el uso de productos desechables.*

31 ¡A explorar!

▶ **Habla** con tu compañero(a). Si pudieran visitar uno de estos lugares, ¿a cuál irían? ¿Qué harían allí para ayudar a proteger el medio ambiente?

Reserva de mariposas monarca (México).

Arrecifes de coral (Puerto Rico).

Parque Nacional Tierra del Fuego (Argentina).

Final del desafío

ETHAN: Todos los animales y las plantas necesitan comida, agua y espacio para sobrevivir. El lugar donde se encuentran estos elementos es su ___1___.

EVA: En invierno la mariposa monarca no puede encontrar comida ni protegerse del frío en el norte. Por eso tienen que ___2___ hacia el sur, a zonas más cálidas.

ETHAN: Si aprendemos más sobre las plantas que sirven de alimento y refugio a estas mariposas, podremos promover programas de ___3___ de su hábitat a lo largo de su ruta de migración.

EVA: Es necesario ___4___ la flora y reducir la ___5___ y el uso de pesticidas que pueden matar a las mariposas y su comida.

32 El ensayo general

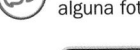 

▶ **Completa** el guion que están ensayando Eva y Ethan para su video.

| deforestación | migrar | conservación | proteger | hábitat |

▶ **Escribe** un guion similar sobre la flora o la fauna de la región donde vives. Ilústralo con alguna fotografía o dibujo y preséntalo a la clase.

→ TU DESAFÍO   Visita la página web. Escucha las preguntas de tu *Minientrevista Desafío 1* y escribe las respuestas.

31. Ask students to think of additional places to visit in Spanish-speaking countries, and the environmental issues that each place faces. You may wish to have them act out their conversations in front of the class.

32. For the first part of this activity, ask for volunteers to play the roles of Eva and Ethan as they prepare their video. For the second part of this activity, you may want to ask students to write the script for a conversation between two animals, birds, or insects. They will chat about their origins, habitats, problems that they experience, and their futures. For instance, they might choose to write about a meeting between a quetzal bird and a bird who has suffered the consequences of an oil spill. Have students illustrate their script and share it with the class. Some volunteers may want to act out their dialogue with a classmate in front of the class.

AUDIO SCRIPT
See page 335I.

Answer Key

29. 1. envases   4. transporte
   2. basura   5. energía
   3. papel   6. calor
   ▶ Answers will vary.

30. 1. d   2. c   3. a   4. b

31. Answers will vary.

32. 1. hábitat   4. proteger
   2. migrar   5. deforestación
   3. conservación
   ▶ Answers will vary.

Additional Resources

Fans Online activities
Practice Workbook

HERITAGE LANGUAGE LEARNERS

• Before the class starts activity 31, ask heritage learners to each research one or more of the places mentioned in the photos (i.e., *la reserva de la mariposa monarca, los arrecifes de coral en Puerto Rico, el Parque Nacional Tierra del Fuego*). Then have them prepare a short oral presentation that addresses the ecological concerns affecting these areas, including some proposed solutions. Display a map so students may show the rest of the class where these places are. Encourage the non-heritage language learners to ask questions.

MULTIPLE INTELLIGENCES:

Logical-Mathematical Intelligence

• Have students research other animals that carry out long migratory cycles. For example, explain that the Arctic tern holds the world record with a 44,000 mile round trip journey from the Arctic to Antarctica. Mammals, including caribou and some whales, migrate thousands of miles, as do certain sea turtles and some insects. Ask students to research some of these long-distance migratory animals and make a chart with the distances tracked (in both miles and kilometers), the number of days taken to reach their destinations, and the average distance traveled per day.

DESAFÍO 2

Expresar tiempo

Presentation

- In *Desafío 2*, Asha and Lucas must find out how the June solstice is celebrated in different Hispanic countries and make a slide show presentation to explain it to their classmates. Students will preview language used to talk about the weather and to express time.

Activities	Standards	Resources
Texto	1.2, 2.1	Vis. Pres.
33.	1.1, 1.2, 1.3, 2.1, 3.1	
34.	1.1, 1.2, 2.1	
35.	1.2, 2.1, 3.1	
36.	1.1, 1.2, 3.1	Audio
37. Cultura	1.1, 1.2, 2.1, 4.2, 5.1	

Teaching Suggestions

Warm-Up / Independent Starter

- Write the following questions on the board and have students prepare a written response: *¿Cuándo cambian las estaciones? ¿Por qué hay cambios climáticos durante el año?*

Preparation

- Have students share their responses to the Independent Starter. Ask students if they know the approximate dates of when the seasons officially change.

- Discuss the way(s) in which the weather in their region changes as a result of the seasons.

Texto: La fiesta del Sol

- Read the title and the introduction to the dialogue aloud. Then ask students to pay attention to the countries and celebrations that are discussed in the dialogue.

- Ask students how Asha and Lucas plan on organizing their presentation and which celebrations they are going to include.

Activities

34. To extend this activity, ask students to write two additional questions about the conversation between Asha and Lucas. Have students ask their partner the two questions.

La fiesta del Sol

Asha and Lucas must find out how the June solstice is celebrated in Hispanic countries. Then they will make a slide show presentation to explain it to their classmates.

ASHA: Me alegra que hayamos elegido un desafío tan interesante. Pero antes de empezar tenemos que investigar sobre el solsticio de junio.

LUCAS: Humm… Estoy pensando que en el hemisferio norte es el solsticio de verano, pero en el hemisferio sur es el solsticio de invierno.

ASHA: Es cierto. Entonces tenemos que averiguar cómo celebran el solsticio de junio en varios países hispanos y elegir lugares que estén en los dos hemisferios.

LUCAS: Eso es.

ASHA: A ver… Yo sé algo del Inti Raymi. Es una fiesta muy importante que celebraban los incas en Cuzco (Perú) desde antes de que llegaran los españoles. Para los incas, el dios del Sol era el más importante. Por eso construyeron varios templos en su honor e hicieron observatorios para estudiar el universo y los astros.

Celebración del Inti Raymi en Cuzco (Perú).

LUCAS: ¿Ah, sí? No sabía que los incas eran buenos astrónomos. ¿Y cuándo era esa celebración?

ASHA: El 24 de junio. ¿Te imaginas hacer una fiesta del Sol en invierno? ¿Y si está nublado o nieva?

LUCAS: Ja, ja, tienes razón. Junio es un mes frío en Perú… Yo también tengo información para ti. Ayer, después de salir de la escuela, hablé con Diana y me contó algo sobre la Noche de san Juan.

ASHA: ¿La Noche de san Juan?

LUCAS: Sí, es una fiesta muy popular en España y en otros países mediterráneos. Se celebra el 24 de junio. En algunos lugares encienden hogueras *(bonfires)* y la gente pide un deseo porque muchos piensan que es una noche mágica.

Noche de san Juan en Alicante (España).

ASHA: ¡Qué bonito! Yo quiero saber más cosas de la Noche de san Juan.

33 Detective de palabras

▶ **Completa** estas oraciones del diálogo.

1. Antes de _____, Asha y Lucas tienen que investigar sobre el solsticio de junio.
2. Los incas celebraban el Inti Raymi desde antes de que _____ los españoles.

Differentiated Instruction

DEVELOPING LEARNERS

- Ask students to say whether the following sentences are true *(cierto)* or false *(falso)*. Have them correct the false statements.

1. *Lucas piensa que en el hemisferio sur el solsticio de invierno es en junio. (cierto)*

2. *Van a elegir lugares solo en el hemisferio sur. (falso; en los dos hemisferios)*

3. *Asha sabe algo sobre el Inti Raymi. (cierto)*

4. *Los incas construyeron templos en honor a Marte. (falso; en honor al dios del Sol)*

5. *Los incas eran buenos astrónomos. (cierto)*

EXPANDING LEARNERS

- Ask students to imagine that they are in Cuzco, Peru, or Alicante, Spain, and they have been chosen to organize either *el Inti Raymi* or *la Noche de san Juan*. Have students make a list of all the tasks they need to complete before the celebrations begin. To make a realistic list, have students do some research on these celebrations. Students should include the traditional activities such as the music, costumes, and food in Cuzco, the preparation of the bonfires in Alicante, and other community activities.

34 ¿Comprendes?

▶ **Responde** a estas preguntas.

1. ¿Cuál es el desafío de Lucas y Asha?
2. ¿Cómo se llama la celebración de los incas en honor al Sol?
3. ¿Qué les parece extraño a Lucas y a Asha de la celebración de la fiesta del Sol en Perú?
4. ¿Cuándo se celebra la Noche de san Juan?

 35 ¿Verano o invierno?

▶ **Decide** si en estos lugares el solsticio de junio corresponde al verano o al invierno.

1. México
2. Chile
3. España
4. Estados Unidos
5. Bolivia
6. Argentina

 **36 En la clase de Ciencias Naturales**

▶ **Escucha** al profesor en la clase de Ciencias Naturales y elige la opción correcta.

1. Los momentos en que el Sol alcanza el punto más alto o más bajo en el cielo son...
   a. los solsticios
   b. los equinoccios

2. Los solsticios tienen lugar...
   a. dos veces al año
   b. cuatro veces al año

3. Los equinoccios se producen...
   a. en verano y en invierno
   b. en primavera y en otoño

4. Durante los equinoccios, las noches...
   a. duran lo mismo que los días
   b. son más largas que los días

CULTURA

Las fiestas del Sol

Los cambios de estación se celebran desde hace miles de años en lugares de todo el mundo, especialmente los solsticios (entre el 20 y el 23 de diciembre y entre el 20 y el 23 de junio). Algunas de las fiestas más conocidas son el Inti Raymi —que se celebra en Perú, Bolivia y Ecuador— y la Noche de san Juan —que se celebra en España y en otros países hispanos.

Hogueras de san Juan. Guipúzcoa (España).

37 Piensa y explica. ¿Por qué crees que tantas culturas y civilizaciones celebraban antiguamente el cambio de estación?

---

35. Ask students to discuss how the differences between the northern and southern hemispheres affect the global economy. For example, tell them to think about agriculture and tourism.

 AUDIO SCRIPT
See page 335I.

 CULTURA

Las fiestas del Sol

Many ancient cultures celebrated the solstices, as many of their religious beliefs were tied to nature. Ancient civilizations were able to identify the days of the year when the days are the shortest and longest. Some of the most well-known solstice celebrations in the Spanish-speaking world happen in South America (*Inti Raymi*) and Spain (*Noche de san Juan*).

Answer Key

33. 1. empezar   2. llegaran

34. 1. Tienen que investigar cómo se celebra el solsticio de junio en el mundo hispanohablante y crear una presentación.
2. Se llama Inti Raymi.
3. Les parece extraño que esta celebración tenga lugar durante el solsticio de invierno, pues piensan que hace frío y nieva en esas fechas.
4. Se celebra el 24 de junio.

35. 1. verano   4. verano
2. invierno   5. invierno
3. verano   6. invierno

36. 1. a   2. a   3. b   4. a

37. Answers will vary.

Additional Resources

Fans Online activities

HERITAGE LANGUAGE LEARNERS

• Ask students to research festivals in their family's country of origin that celebrate the sun, other celestial bodies, or the seasons. Ask students to describe one of these celebrations to the rest of the class, and include a brief history, an explanation of why it is celebrated, who observes the festivity, and when and where the festivity takes place. Students should include any other interesting details along with any printed information or images they may have about the celebration.

MULTIPLE INTELLIGENCES:

Intrapersonal Intelligence

• Explain to students that on *la Noche de san Juan,* in some places in Spain, people might throw something old into the bonfires or they might toss into the flames a paper on which they have written something they would like to change. There is also the custom of throwing three coins into the sea, making a wish for each one. Ask students to follow these customs and explain what old item they would get rid of, what object, circumstance, or situation they would like to change, and what wishes they would make.

DESAFÍO 2

Vocabulario – El tiempo meteorológico. El universo

Presentation

- In this section, students will learn and use featured vocabulary to communicate about the weather and the universe.

Activities	Standards	Resources
Vocabulario	1.2, 3.1	
38.	1.2	
39.	1.2	
40.	1.1, 1.2	Audio
41.	1.1, 1.2, 3.1, 5.1, 5.2	
42. Cultura	1.1, 1.2, 2.1	

Teaching Suggestions

Warm-Up / Independent Starter

- Have students write a list of the weather expressions and seasons that they remember in Spanish. Ask them to briefly illustrate each one.

Preparation

- Ask students to share their Independent Starters. Record the responses on the board. Categorize the terms by expressions with *hacer*, conjugated verbs, and expressions with *estar*.
- Ask for two volunteers to play the roles of Asha and Lucas and read the dialogues aloud. Then direct students' attention to the *Más vocabulario* feature. Say the words aloud and ask them to repeat after you. Have students create a list of weather terms with the new vocabulary, ordering them from the best weather conditions to the worst.

Activities

38. You may want to turn this activity into a game. Write the vocabulary words on cardstock or large note cards. Have four volunteers come to the front of the class and stand side by side. Give each one a note card and instruct the students not to show the card to the class. When you give them the signal, they can turn the cards to the class. Watch for the first hand to be raised and provide the first student with the correct answer a point in the game.

Vocabulario

El tiempo meteorológico

¡Vaya día hace hoy!

Sí, está lloviendo a cántaros. No me gustan nada las tormentas. Me dan miedo los truenos y los relámpagos.

¡Qué bien, por fin se despejó! ¡El sol brilla y ha salido el arco iris!

Todavía llovizna, porque caen gotas.

El universo

¡Me encanta observar las galaxias e imaginar las constelaciones! Me gustaría ser astrónoma.

el telescopio

Creo que estoy viendo un meteorito.

Más vocabulario

Fenómenos meteorológicos

el chubasco	*heavy shower*
la escarcha	*frost*
el granizo	*hail*
la nevada	*snowfall*
la nube	*cloud*
el temporal	*storm*

Acciones

helar	*to freeze*
nublarse	*to cloud over*
soplar el viento	*to blow (wind)*

Adjetivos

despejado(a)	*clear*
lluvioso(a)	*rainy*
soleado(a)	*sunny*
nuboso(a)	*cloudy*

38 El intruso

▶ **Decide** qué palabra no corresponde a cada grupo.

1. nube — nevada — granizo — constelación
2. trueno — relámpago — arco iris — tormenta
3. chubasco — llovizna — despejado — tormenta
4. escarcha — planeta — galaxia — estrella
5. llover — observar — nevar — helar

356 trescientos cincuenta y seis

Differentiated Instruction

DEVELOPING LEARNERS

- Ask students to make a four-column chart and label it *El tiempo meteorológico*. Have them label each column with the name of a season (i.e., *el verano, el otoño, el invierno, la primavera*). After students have studied the new vocabulary that describes the weather, ask them to think about the typical weather in their community during each season. Then have students list these weather-related words under the corresponding season. Point out that some words may belong in more than one category.

EXPANDING LEARNERS

- Have students imagine that they are meteorologists working on a weather channel. Ask them to work in pairs and write their own script for the program. One student might do the national weather outlook, while the other concentrates on current and projected local weather. Students should try to use as much of the weather-related vocabulary as they can. Give students time to rehearse their "programs" and then call on some volunteers to present their weather show to the rest of the class.

39 **Hoy hace buen tiempo**

▶ **Une** las dos columnas y escribe las oraciones.

(A)	(B)
1. Hace	a. el viento.
2. Sopla	b. la lluvia.
3. Cae	c. el sol.
4. Brilla	d. frío.
5. Hay	e. tormenta.

40 **¿Cómo está el día?**

▶ **Escucha** y relaciona cada oración con la fotografía correspondiente.

41 **Te toca a ti**

▶ **Habla** con tu compañero(a). Túrnense para hacerse estas preguntas.

1. ¿Te gustaría ser astrónomo(a)? ¿Por qué?
2. ¿Has visto un eclipse lunar o solar? ¿Cuándo fue y dónde estabas?
3. ¿Alguna vez has mirado por un telescopio? ¿Qué viste?
4. ¿Prefieres el verano o el invierno? ¿Por qué?
5. ¿Te dan miedo las tormentas?

CULTURA

La festividad del Inti Raymi

El Inti Raymi es un rito inca en honor del dios del Sol. Se celebra desde la época precolombina el 24 de junio en Cuzco (Perú), coincidiendo con el solsticio de invierno en el hemisferio sur. Los incas tenían un calendario muy parecido al calendario moderno y celebraban este día con una ceremonia para pedir una buena cosecha al Sol.

Celebración del Inti Raymi en Cuzco (Perú).

42 **Piensa y explica.** ¿Por qué crees que los incas pedían una buena cosecha al dios del Sol? ¿Cómo piensas que una buena o una mala cosecha afectaba a sus vidas?

HERITAGE LANGUAGE LEARNERS

• Explain to students that there are many legends from the Americas that explain the origins of natural phenomena, such as thunder, lightning, rain, or volcanoes. Assign each student a different phenomenon and a country or region, and ask them to research the mythological explanations of the phenomenon. Then, using the information they have gathered, ask students to write their own version of the legend, which may be in the form of a narrative or a dialogue. Call on volunteers to read their legends to the rest of the class.

MULTIPLE INTELLIGENCES:

Verbal-Linguistic Intelligence

• Ask students to research the history of the Inti Raymi. Have them take notes on how the early celebrations were observed. Students should include descriptions of the colorful costumes, the music, the decorations, and the sharing of food and drink. Students might also mention legends surrounding the Incas' belief that if the Sun god was not pleased, he would go farther away from the Earth and it would become cold and their crops would fail. Encourage students to also research the Inca calendars and explain their role in these Sun celebrations.

---

39. Have students create a song or rhyme to remember some of the weather expressions. They can use the pairs of words given in this activity or they can combine the vocabulary in different ways.

40. After completing this activity, have students write statements to describe each photograph.

 AUDIO SCRIPT
See page 335 J.

 CULTURA

La festividad del Inti Raymi

The Incan Empire celebrated the solstice that occurs in June. According to Incan beliefs, the Sun god, Inti, was the creator and most powerful god. In order to receive a good harvest from him, they gathered to plead for his return when the days became shorter. These celebrations, including parades, dances, and ceremonies, continue today in and around the area of Cuzco, the former capital of the Incan Empire.

Answer Key

38. 1. constelación   4. escarcha
      2. arco iris   5. observar
      3. despejado
39. 1. d   2. a   3. b   4. c   5. e
40. 1. D   2. C   3. A   4. B
41. Answers will vary.
42. Answers will vary.

Additional Resources

Fans Online activities
Practice Workbook

357

DESAFÍO 2

Gramática – Expresar tiempo

Presentation

■ In this section, students will learn to express when actions take place in relation to one another in the present, past, and future.

Activities	Standards	Resources
Gramática	1.2, 3.1	
43.	4.1	
44.	1.1, 1.2, 1.3, 3.1	Audio
45.	1.2, 1.3	
46.	1.1, 1.2, 5.1, 5.2	

Teaching Suggestions

Warm-Up / Independent Starter

■ Have students write down five things that they have done this week. You can have them leave the verbs in the infinitive.

Preparation

■ Have students read the grammar explanation silently. Draw their attention to identifying past actions, habitual actions, and future actions. Point out that *antes de que* always requires the subjunctive, whereas *después de que* and *cuando* only require the subjunctive when referring to future events. Have students discuss why they think this might be so.

■ Ask students to turn their Independent Starter lists into a paragraph. Have them apply *antes de (que)*, *después de (que)*, and *cuando* as applicable to tell the sequence of the activities they completed. In order to expand their language use, they may need to add actions that other people in their lives did as well (e.g., *La profesora me felicitó cuando terminé la presentación*).

■ Invite students to share their paragraphs with the class. Ask them in which cases they needed to conjugate the verb, and in which cases they left the verb in the infinitive, and why.

Activities

44. After completing this activity, have students write three original statements using *cuando*: one in the present habitual, one in the past, and one in the future.

Gramática

Expresar tiempo

Expresar tiempo

• Use the conjunction *cuando* and other time expressions to express the time or sequence of events. These expressions are placed either at the beginning or the end of a sentence.

> **Cuando** nieva, hace frío.
> Anoche llovió **después de que** te fueras.

EXPRESIONES DE TIEMPO	
cuando	*when*
antes de (que)	*before*
después de (que)	*after*

• *Cuando* indicates that two events happen at once, or that one event happens slightly after another, and it is used with the indicative or with the subjunctive.

| cuando + indicative (past or habitual event) | Me llamó **cuando llegó** a casa. Siempre me llama **cuando llega** a casa. |
| cuando + subjunctive (future event) | Me llamará **cuando llegue** a casa. Llámame **cuando llegues** a casa. |

Expresar anterioridad o posterioridad

• Antes de (que) or después de (que) are used to express that one event precedes or follows another.

• If the main clause and the dependent clause have the **same subject**, use these structures:

antes de + infinitive	<u>Haré</u> la tarea antes de <u>cenar</u>.
	yo — yo
después de + infinitive	Siempre <u>te acuestas</u> después de <u>cenar</u>.
	tú — tú

• If the main clause and the dependent clause have **different subjects**, use these structures:

antes de que + subjunctive	<u>Haré</u> la tarea antes de que <u>cenes</u>.
	yo — tú
después de que + subjunctive	<u>Me acostaré</u> después de que <u>cenemos</u>.
	yo — nosotros
después de que + indicative	Ayer <u>me acosté</u> después de que <u>cenamos</u>.
	yo — nosotros

43 **Compara.** Traduce al inglés todos los ejemplos de la ficha. ¿Qué forma verbal se usa en inglés cuando no hay un cambio de sujeto?

44 **¿Pasado o futuro?**

 ▶ **Escucha** y completa estas oraciones.

1. Cuando _____ al trabajo, estaba nevando.
2. Cuando _____ 18 años, Jacobo irá a la universidad.
3. Continuaremos el partido cuando _____ de llover.
4. Cuando me _____, vi la luna llena (*full moon*) en el cielo.

▶ **Responde.** ¿Cuáles de las oraciones anteriores se refieren al pasado? ¿Y al futuro?

Differentiated Instruction

DEVELOPING LEARNERS

• Ask students to review their completed sentences from activity 45 and find the common elements that prompted the use of the infinitive or the subjunctive in each case. Guide students by asking them about the subjects, the words that are used in each sentence (*después de, después de que, cuando*), and the tense of the verb in the main clause. Write similar sentences on the board and have students complete them.

EXPANDING LEARNERS

• Give students more practice by having them complete the following sentences with the correct form of the verb in parentheses:

1. *Cuando (llover), siempre hay truenos.* (llueve)
2. *Cuando (empezar) a llover, cierra las ventanas.* (empiece)
3. *Después de (comprar) el telescopio, me matriculé en una clase de Astronomía.* (comprar)
4. *Antes de que (tú – comprar) un telescopio, debes aprender a usarlo.* (compres)
5. *Voy a pasar la aspiradora antes de que (llegar) los invitados.* (lleguen)

45 Un día en la vida de Asha

▶ **Completa** estas oraciones. ¿Qué hará hoy Asha?

Asha irá a la escuela después de…

Asha volverá a clase después de…

Asha saldrá de casa
después de que Lucas…

Asha entrará en la biblioteca
cuando Lucas…

Asha cenará
después de…

46 Momentos importantes

▶ **Elige** tres momentos importantes de tu vida y haz dibujos
sencillos para ilustrarlos.

▶ **Intercambia** tus dibujos con tu compañero(a) y hazle preguntas
para saber más detalles sobre esos momentos.

Modelo   A. *Cuando cumplí quince años, mis padres*
                me organizaron una fiesta.

            B. *¿A cuánta gente invitaron?*

▶ **Pregunta** a tu compañero(a). ¿Cuáles son sus deseos y sueños para el futuro?
¿Qué hará cuando los consiga?

Modelo   A. *¿Qué harás cuando termines la escuela secundaria?*

            B. *Iré a la universidad. Quiero estudiar Historia.*

            A. *¿Y qué harás después de terminar tus estudios?*

            B. *Probablemente trabaje en una escuela. También quiero viajar por Latinoamérica*
                porque me interesa mucho la Historia precolombina.

trescientos cincuenta y nueve 359

---

45. To extend this activity, ask students to rewrite
the statements using the present habitual and
then the past tense.

46. Before beginning this activity, have students
brainstorm some important moments. While
some may be personal, such as scoring the
winning run, other moments will be shared by
other students, such as entering high school.
As an alternative to drawing, you can allow
students to bring in three pictures of special
occasions or events. Have them put a caption
under each drawing or photograph and decorate
a bulletin board or part of the hallway.

 AUDIO SCRIPT
See page 335 J.

Answer Key

43. En inglés se usa el gerundio (*-ing*) cuando
no hay un cambio de sujeto. Por ejemplo: *I'll
do my homework before having dinner.* (Haré
la tarea antes de cenar.) *You always go to
bed after having dinner.* (Siempre te
acuestas después de cenar.)

44. 1. llegué   3. deje
          2. tenga   4. acosté

         ▶ 1. pasado   3. futuro
            2. futuro   4. pasado

45. Answers will vary. Sample answers:

         1. … desayunar.   4. … llegue.
         2. … almorzar.   5. … hacer la tarea.
         3. … la llame.

46. Answers will vary.
         ▶ Answers will vary.
         ▶ Answers will vary.

Additional Resources

Fans Online activities
Practice Workbook

HERITAGE LANGUAGE LEARNERS

• Ask students to name other conjunctions
used to express time, such as *en cuanto,
tan pronto como, mientras,* and *hasta que.*
Remind students that the subjunctive is used
after these conjunctions when the action has
not yet occurred, but the indicative is used
when the action has occurred or takes place
on a regular basis. Ask students to write five
sentences using some of these conjunctions.
Students should write the verb that follows
each conjunction in its infinitive form. Then
have students exchange papers with a
partner to determine which mood is needed
and complete the sentences.

CRITICAL THINKING

• After students complete activity 46, have
each pair join another pair and summarize
their hopes and dreams for the future. Ask
students to tabulate these results in a chart,
labeled with the students' names. Then have
this group get together with another group
and compare the results. Ask students to
identify any common threads running through
the students' expectations. When students
finish, enable a classroom discussion to see
what the students' hopes and dreams have
in common. You might ask them if they think
these are universal expectations, or relevant
only to their culture.

DESAFÍO 2

Gramática – El presente perfecto de subjuntivo

Presentation

- In this section, students will learn the present perfect of the subjunctive and its use.

Activities	Standards	Resources
Gramática	1.2, 3.1	
47.	4.1	
48.	1.2, 1.3, 3.1	
49.	1.2, 1.3	
50.	1.1, 1.2, 1.3, 5.1	
51. Cultura	1.1, 1.2, 2.1, 4.2, 5.1	Video

Teaching Suggestions

Warm-Up / Independent Starter

- Have students conjugate the verbs *hablar, comer,* and *vivir* in the present perfect of the indicative (e.g., *he hablado, he comido, he vivido*).

Preparation

- Review students' Independent Starters and have them write one sentence with each of the verbs (e.g., *Ya he hablado hoy con mi novio. He comido una hamburguesa. He vivido en esta ciudad tres años.*). Then direct students to the grammar feature and have them read it silently.

- Review the list of main clauses that require the subjunctive. Then have students rewrite their sentences, adding a main clause that would trigger the use of the subjunctive (e.g., *Me alegra que ya haya hablado hoy con mi novio. Saldremos cuando te hayas comido la hamburguesa. No creo que hayas vivido en esta ciudad tres años.*).

Activities

47. Use this activity as an opportunity to reinforce the idea that the present perfect subjunctive does not have a direct correspondence in English. If students try to translate directly, it may result in incorrect sentences. Instead, they should focus on the meaning.

48. Before starting this activity, have students form the past participle of the verbs that are listed.

Gramática

El presente perfecto de subjuntivo

El presente perfecto de subjuntivo

- We normally use the present perfect subjunctive in the same types of sentences in which we would use the present subjunctive, when the action in the dependent clause is presented as completed.

  Dudo que **hayan visto** el eclipse.   Avísame cuando **haya pasado** la tormenta.

Formación y uso del presente perfecto de subjuntivo

- The present perfect subjunctive is formed with the present subjunctive of haber and the past participle of the main verb.

PRESENTE PERFECTO DE SUBJUNTIVO. VERBOS REGULARES

	Hablar	Comer	Vivir
yo	haya **habl**ado	haya **com**ido	haya **viv**ido
tú	hayas **habl**ado	hayas **com**ido	hayas **viv**ido
usted, él, ella	haya **habl**ado	haya **com**ido	haya **viv**ido
nosotros(as)	hayamos **habl**ado	hayamos **com**ido	hayamos **viv**ido
vosotros(as)	hayáis **habl**ado	hayáis **com**ido	hayáis **viv**ido
ustedes, ellos(as)	hayan **habl**ado	hayan **com**ido	hayan **viv**ido

- These are some examples of use of the present perfect subjunctive.

Main clause requiring the subjunctive		Present perfect subjunctive (completed action)	
No creo que	I don't think that	hayas terminado la tarea.	you have finished your homework.
Nos alegra que	We are happy that	hayas sacado buenas notas.	you have gotten good grades.
Llámame	Call me	cuando hayas llegado a casa.	when you have gotten home.
Saldremos	We will go out	cuando hayas terminado de comer.	when you have finished eating.

47 **Compara.** Traduce estas oraciones al inglés. ¿Qué tiempos verbales se usan?

a. Ha dejado de llover.   **b.** Estoy contenta de que haya dejado de llover.

48 **Tus impresiones**

▶ **Completa** estas oraciones con la forma correcta del presente perfecto de subjuntivo.

1. Tal vez el profesor de Ciencias _____ a Asha y a Lucas con su desafío.
   ayudar
2. Asha y Lucas prepararán su presentación cuando _____ fotografías adecuadas.
   encontrar
3. No creo que ninguno de mis amigos _____ alguna vez el Inti Raymi.
   celebrar
4. Me sorprende que Lucas y Asha no _____ información sobre la celebración de la Noche de san Juan en Latinoamérica.
   buscar

Differentiated Instruction

DEVELOPING LEARNERS

- Have students choose the correct verb form to complete the following sentences:

1. *Me alegra que hayas hecho / has hecho esta presentación.* (hayas hecho)
2. *Es una lástima que se ha roto / haya roto el vaso.* (haya roto)
3. *No creemos que has dicho / hayas dicho esto.* (hayas dicho)
4. *Es posible que él ha llegado / haya llegado tarde.* (haya llegado)
5. *Es malo que hayan salido / han salido durante el temporal.* (hayan salido)
6. *Estoy contento de que me has escrito / hayas escrito.* (hayas escrito)

EXPANDING LEARNERS

- Ask students to write a dialogue between someone who is very positive and upbeat and a friend who is very pessimistic. The optimist should make statements using verbs such as *creo, me alegra, no dudo, es bueno que, es posible,* while the pessimist counters by using verbs such as *no creo, dudo, es malo que, no es posible.* Students may choose their topic, or you may assign one to them. Give them some time to rehearse their lines and then call on volunteers to role-play their dialogues in front of the class.

49 Avanzando con el desafío

▶ **Escribe** tus reacciones al progreso de Asha y Lucas. Usa las expresiones del cuadro.

Modelo Asha y Lucas terminaron su presentación.
⟶ *No creo que hayan terminado su presentación.*

Es bueno que…
Es una lástima que…
Dudo que…
Es posible que…
Me alegra que…
No creo que…

1. Asha ha investigado las tradiciones de los mayas.
2. Daniel eligió todas las fotografías que quiere usar.
3. Asha y Lucas eligieron cuatro celebraciones para su presentación.
4. Asha perdió sus apuntes sobre la Noche de san Juan.
5. A Lucas se le olvidó buscar información sobre el Inti Raymi.
6. Lucas y Asha se reunieron anoche para comparar ideas.

50 Esta semana

 ▶ **Habla** con tu compañero(a) sobre lo que han hecho esta semana y escríbanlo en una lista. Incluyan una acción falsa.

 ▶ **Intercambien** su lista con la de otra pareja. Comenten sus impresiones sobre las acciones y decidan cuál es la falsa.

Modelo
A. *Dudo que hayan visto un eclipse solar.*
B. *Sí, no es posible que haya habido un eclipse solar y no nos hayamos enterado.*

- estudiar para el examen de Biología
- jugar a un videojuego
- ver a una actriz famosa por la calle
- ir a nuestro restaurante favorito
- ver un eclipse solar
- participar en un chat en español

 **CULTURA**

La Noche de san Juan

La Noche de san Juan es una fiesta de origen muy antiguo que se celebra en España y en otros países europeos el 24 de junio, coincidiendo con la llegada del verano. Por influencia española, esta festividad también se celebra en varios países de Latinoamérica.

En muchos lugares es costumbre encender una hoguera *(bonfire)* y saltar por encima; en otros, existe la tradición de bañarse en el mar. Muchos creen que es una noche mágica y hacen ritos para pedir deseos.

Hoguera de san Juan. Alicante (España).

51 **Piensa y explica.** ¿En tu comunidad hay alguna fiesta similar a la fiesta de la Noche de san Juan? ¿Hay alguna fiesta relacionada con el cambio de estación? ¿En qué consiste?

trescientos sesenta y uno **361**

HERITAGE LANGUAGE LEARNERS

- Ask students to name a special time of the year or an event that they would like to see celebrated. It could be the first day of snow, the first blossom of spring, or the last star to "disappear" from the sky in the morning. After they identify the event, ask them to invent a legend surrounding it. The legend should explain the event's origin and what special significance it has in the students' culture. Remind students to give their legends a title and ask them to read their stories aloud.

TOTAL PHYSICAL RESPONSE (TPR)

- Tell students that they are going to play a game. Prepare twenty-five incomplete sentences and tell students that the sentences may be completed with the subjunctive, infinitive, or indicative form of the verb. Give each student three sheets of colored paper (e.g., white, red, and blue). As you read each sentence aloud, ask students to hold up the white sheet if the subjunctive is correct, the red sheet for the infinitive, and the blue sheet for the indicative. Call on students to repeat the sentence, with the correct verb form in place.

Unit 7

DESAFÍO 2

Gramática – El presente perfecto de subjuntivo

50. As an alternative to this activity, you may want to play the game "Two Truths and a Lie." Each student writes down two activities that he or she really did, and one activity that he or she did not do. Each student reads the activities and the class decides which activity is false.

 CULTURA

La Noche de san Juan

Many celebrations associated with John the Baptist include purification rituals through water and fire. In Puerto Rico, it is customary for people to walk backward into the ocean at exactly midnight on June 23rd. In some states of Venezuela, people celebrate Saint John's wake with drumming throughout the night. In Otavalo, Ecuador, this holiday is celebrated with dances and parades, and people dress in costumes.

Answer Key

47. a. It *has stopped* raining.
   b. *I am glad that it has stopped raining.*
   Se usa el presente perfecto de indicativo en ambas oraciones.

48. 1. haya ayudado   3. haya celebrado
   2. hayan encontrado   4. hayan buscado

49. Answers will vary. Sample answers:
   1. No creo que Asha haya investigado…
   2. Es posible que Daniel haya elegido…
   3. Me alegra que Asha y Lucas hayan elegido…
   4. Es una lástima que Asha haya perdido…
   5. Dudo que a Lucas se le haya olvidado…
   6. Es bueno que Lucas y Asha se hayan reunido…

50. Answers will vary.
   ▶ Answers will vary.

51. Answers will vary.

Additional Resources

Fans Online activities
Practice Workbook

361

Unit 7

LECTURA: TEXTO INFORMATIVO

Presentation

- In this section, students will read an informative text about traditions and celebrations related to the Sun. They will examine conjunctions and transition words, and they will answer comprehension questions.

Activities	Standards	Resources
Lectura: texto informativo	1.2, 1.3, 2.1, 2.2, 3.1, 3.2	
52.	1.2, 1.3, 2.1, 3.1	
53.	1.1, 1.2, 2.1, 3.1, 4.1	
54.	1.3, 3.1	

Teaching Suggestions

Warm-Up / Independent Starter

- Ask students to imagine that they participated in a *Noche de san Juan* celebration last week. Have them write four sentences describing the events surrounding the celebration: what happened before the celebration, during the celebration, and after the celebration. They should use time expressions.

Preparation

- Call on volunteers to share their Independent Starters with the class. Then have students read the *Antes de leer* strategies silently. Ask them to take notes and prepare themselves to share their answers.

- Invite students to share any traditions related to the Sun that they may have experienced or heard about. You may want to prepare some video clips of Inti Raymi, Fallas, or San Juan celebrations. Ask students to take notes as they watch and then discuss what people do, what they wear, when and where the celebrations take place, etc.

- Read the text aloud to model pronunciation and intonation. Then have students alternate reading several lines or a paragraph. Pause after each paragraph and call on a volunteer to paraphrase the content. As an alternative after reading the entire text, you may divide the class into groups and assign each group a paragraph to summarize. Then have them write down the summary.

362

LECTURA: TEXTO INFORMATIVO

Antes de leer: estrategias

1. Fíjate en el título. ¿Qué tradiciones relacionadas con el Sol conoces?
2. Lee la primera oración. ¿Sobre cuáles de estos temas crees que vas a encontrar información en el texto: astronomía, rituales funerarios, recetas de comida, celebraciones tradicionales, mercados populares?
3. Mira las fotografías. ¿Qué relación crees que tienen con el texto? Explícalo.

Las tradiciones del Sol

En su curso anual a través del espacio, la posición relativa del Sol y de la Tierra marca cuatro fechas de importancia especial: los dos equinoccios (cuando el día y la noche tienen la misma duración) y los dos solsticios (el día más largo y el día más corto del año). Los humanos aprendieron a reconocer los equinoccios y los solsticios hace miles de años. Poder predecir[1] estos eventos les permitía saber el mejor momento para cazar[2], sembrar o realizar otras actividades necesarias para su supervivencia[3]. Por lo tanto, no es de extrañar[4] que nuestros antepasados dieran a esas fechas un sentido mágico o religioso.

Hoy sabemos que en muchos lugares del mundo se realizaban ceremonias y ritos relacionados con el Sol. Y actualmente[5] se mantienen muchas tradiciones relacionadas con el cambio de estación.

En la región española de Valencia se celebran el 19 de marzo las Fallas, una festividad en honor a san José. Esta fiesta tiene su origen en las antiguas celebraciones del equinoccio de primavera. Otra fiesta muy conocida es la Noche de san Juan, que tiene lugar el 24 de junio, es decir, el día del solsticio de verano. En las dos fiestas hay muchos ritos relacionados con el fuego, como encender hogueras o lanzar fuegos artificiales[6].

Fiesta de las Fallas en Valencia (España).

362 trescientos sesenta y dos

Differentiated Instruction

DEVELOPING LEARNERS

- Because of its length, reading this text can be a daunting task for some students. Help them first identify the topic sentence of each paragraph, which will give students an idea of what the paragraph is about. In this article, the topic sentence is the first one in each paragraph. Then have students skim the material; if they come across any unfamiliar words, ask them to look for context clues and cognates in order to decode the words. Finally, have them read the text silently once more, and then call on individual students to take turns reading it aloud.

EXPANDING LEARNERS

- After students read the text, ask them to make a four-column chart and label each column *Solsticio de verano, Solsticio de invierno, Equinoccio de primavera,* and *Equinoccio de otoño.* Then ask students to read the article again, and place references to these occurrences accordingly. For example, students will write *las Fallas* under *equinoccio de primavera.* When students finish, ask them to include one event from their community under each of these headings.

En las Américas también encontramos ejemplos de celebraciones relacionadas con los equinoccios y los solsticios. Algunas tienen su origen en antiguas civilizaciones, como los mayas o los aztecas, que realizaron muchos estudios sobre los astros. En efecto, muchos de los edificios de carácter religioso construidos por estos pueblos servían como observatorios solares. En la pirámide de Kukulkán (México) se puede ver la sombra[7] de una serpiente durante los equinoccios. Y en la ciudad maya de Copán (Honduras) el Sol crea curiosos efectos de sombras en los monumentos durante los solsticios y los equinoccios.

Pirámide de Kukulkán (México).

---

 1. *to forecast*   2. *to hunt*   3. *survival*   4. *it is not surprising*   5. *nowadays*   6. *fireworks*   7. *shadow*

52 Comprensión

▶ **Responde** a estas preguntas.

1. ¿Qué información y qué ventajas dio el conocimiento de los equinoccios y los solsticios a nuestros antepasados?

2. ¿Qué lugares se mencionan en el texto? Haz una lista y escribe dónde están situados.

3. ¿Qué consecuencias tienen los equinoccios y los solsticios en la vida actual?

53 Conectores

▶ **Fíjate** en los conectores destacados en estas oraciones del texto. ¿Qué crees que significan? ¿Cuál es su equivalente en inglés?

1. <u>Por lo tanto</u>, no es de extrañar que nuestros antepasados dieran a esas fechas un sentido mágico o religioso.

2. Otra fiesta muy conocida es la Noche de san Juan, que tiene lugar el 24 de junio, <u>es decir</u>, el mismo día del solsticio de verano.

3. <u>En efecto</u>, muchos de los edificios de carácter religioso construidos por estos pueblos servían como observatorios solares.

54 Con tus propias palabras

▶ **Elige** uno de estos títulos y escribe una entrada de blog.

| El día más largo del año | El día más corto del año |

HERITAGE LANGUAGE LEARNERS

• Ask students to research Mayan astronomy and the role it played in Mayan life and culture. Students should address what resulted from these studies (e.g., the Mayan calendar, accurate calculations regarding solar and lunar eclipses), who the astronomers were, what power they held, and how their knowledge helped the Mayan culture survive. Students might wish to investigate the Dresden Codex, which is a book on Mayan astronomy. Ask students to write a short report and then call on some volunteers to make a brief presentation to the class.

CRITICAL THINKING

• Ask students to consider and discuss humankind's fascination with both the Sun and fire. Why do students think the Sun played such an important role in the indigenous cultures of the Americas? Ask students why, after building beautiful and huge figures out of papier-mâché (the *ninots*), these same people would set the figures on fire and destroy them during the *Fallas* and on *la Noche de san Juan* in Spain.

Activities

52. Ask students to use their summaries from the Preparation activity and their own words to answer the comprehension questions. Emphasize that they should not answer word for word what they just read. You may also encourage them to use circumlocution (i.e., restating an idea using different wording) when they don't know a word, as it is a sign of intermediate to advanced level of proficiency.

54. You may want to ask students to try to include in their blog entry some of the connectors from activity 53. Remind them that transitions and connectors help them show the logical relationship between ideas and give their writing cohesiveness.

Answer Key

52. Answers will vary. Sample answers:

1. Conocer estos fenómenos les dio a nuestros antepasados mayor control sobre su hábitat, ya que así sabían cuál era la mejor época para cazar, sembrar o realizar actividades necesarias para su supervivencia.

2. Valencia (España); Kukulkán (México); Copán (Honduras).

3. Mantenemos algunas fiestas y tradiciones relacionadas con el cambio de estación. También se cambia la hora en otoño y en primavera. Y en la agricultura son muy importantes las estaciones.

53. 1. Motivo de algo que se ha dicho: *therefore*.

2. Que se va a explicar de otra manera: *in other words*.

3. Verdad o certeza: *in fact*.

54. Answers will vary.

Additional Resources

Fans Online activities

363

DESAFÍO 2

Comunicación

Presentation

- In this section, students will integrate the vocabulary and grammar skills from *Desafío 2* in order to talk about future events and the weather.

Activities	Standards	Resources
55.	1.2, 1.3	Audio
56.	1.1, 1.2, 1.3, 2.1, 2.2, 5.1, 5.2	
57.	1.1, 1.2, 1.3, 2.1, 5.1	
58. Final del desafío	1.1, 1.2, 1.3, 2.1, 3.1, 5.1	

Teaching Suggestions

Warm-Up / Independent Starter

- Ask students to describe the current weather conditions and what they will do when the weather changes. For example: 1. *Está despejado y soleado. Cuando llegue la tormenta este fin de semana, me quedaré en casa.* 2. *¡Llueve a cántaros! Cuando se despeje, iremos al parque a caminar.*

Preparation

- Have students share their Independent Starters. Review the use of the subjunctive after *cuando* in their statements. Then review the use of the indicative, infinitive, and subjunctive after the conjunctions studied in this *Desafío*.

- Give students some time to review on their own the two grammar explanations as well as the vocabulary presentation. Then ask students to work in small groups to restate each grammar concept and practice using the more difficult vocabulary words. They should find that activities which integrate all three topics, such as those found on these pages, will be easier to complete once they have refreshed their memories about the target words and grammar structures.

- Ask students to recall the challenge that Asha and Lucas were given and have them make predictions about whether or not they think the participants will complete the task.

Comunicación

55 ¡El clima se vuelve loco!

 ▶ **Escucha** la predicción meteorológica y corrige los errores de este gráfico.

Tiempo 1-7 días				8-14 días		
Hoy 05 Mar	Mañana 06 Mar	Miércoles 07 Mar	Jueves 08 Mar	Viernes 09 Mar	Sábado 10 Mar	Domingo 11 Mar
16° 7° 15 km/h N 1.5 mm +info	14° 7° 15 km/h N 2.1 mm +info	15° 6° 15 km/h N 2.1 mm +info	13° 7° 16 km/h N 5.4 mm +info	15° 6° 17 km/h N 2.8 mm +info	14° 6° 13 km/h N 2.3 mm +info	15° 6° 14 km/h N 3.4 mm +info

56 De viaje a Perú

▶ **Lee** este folleto de una agencia de viajes y escribe algunas preguntas que le harías al agente.

VIAJE AL CORAZÓN DEL IMPERIO INCA

20 de junio	Llegada a Cuzco (Perú) y entrada en el hotel.
21 de junio	Visita guiada por Cuzco. Visita opcional al templo de Coricancha y a la catedral de Cuzco.
22 de junio	Viaje en tren a Machu Picchu. Incluye cena tradicional en un restaurante típico.
23 de junio	Presentación de bailes y música tradicionales en la Plaza de Armas de Cuzco.
24 de junio	Excursión al sitio arqueológico de Sacsayhuamán para ver la ceremonia del Inti Raymi.
25 de junio	Viaje de vuelta.

 ▶ **Habla** con tu compañero(a). Representen el diálogo entre el/la agente de viajes y un(a) cliente(a) interesado(a). Usen expresiones de tiempo.

Modelo A. *¿Cuándo tendremos una tarde libre para hacer compras?*
B. *Después de hacer la visita guiada por Cuzco.*

Differentiated Instruction

DEVELOPING LEARNERS

- After students read the dialogue between Asha and Lucas, ask them to say whether the following sentences are true (*cierto*) or false (*falso*). Have them correct the false statements.

1. *Todavía no tienen las fotos de la presentación. (falso; ya las tienen)*
2. *Antes de empezar deberían ensayar. (cierto)*
3. *Van a hablar de la importancia del Sol después de explicar lo que es Inti Raymi. (falso; hablarán de eso antes)*
4. *Parece que se les ha olvidado algo. (falso; no se les ha olvidado nada)*

EXPANDING LEARNERS

- After students read the dialogue on page 365, ask them to write a summary of Lucas and Asha's conversation. Remind them to use the third-person narrative and decide whether they want to place the verbs in the present or the past tense.

- You may want to extend the summary to include Lucas and Asha's conversation on page 354 as well.

57 Fiestas famosas

▶ **Responde.** ¿Qué fiesta te gustaría conocer? Busca información sobre ella.

- El Inti Raymi (Perú).
- Las Fallas (España).
- Las hogueras de san Juan (España).

Final del desafío

Celebración del Inti Raymi
en Cuzco (Perú).

LUCAS: Ya tenemos todas las fotos de la presentación. Yo creo que quedó muy bonita.

ASHA: Sí, ¿verdad? Pues vamos a grabar el texto.

LUCAS: Perfecto. Oye, antes de ____1____ la presentación, deberíamos practicar.

hacer / hacemos

ASHA: De acuerdo. Si quieres, tú puedes empezar con la celebración del Inti Raymi.

LUCAS: Yo creo que antes de que ____2____ en qué consiste esa celebración, deberíamos

explicar / expliquemos
hablar de la importancia del Sol para los incas y otras civilizaciones.

ASHA: Es una idea excelente. Y cuando ____3____ esa parte, yo puedo grabar el texto sobre la Noche

lees / leas
de san Juan y las Fallas en España.

LUCAS: No creo que se nos ____4____ nada...

haya olvidado / olvidara

58 La presentación

▶ **Completa** la conversación entre Asha y Lucas con las formas verbales correctas.

▶ **Habla** con tu compañero(a). ¿Crees que Asha y Lucas han organizado bien su presentación? ¿Piensas que el orden de los contenidos es el adecuado?

Modelo *Yo creo que antes de hablar del Inti Raymi deberían hacer una introducción para explicar qué es el solsticio de verano y el solsticio de invierno. Y después de...*

trescientos sesenta y cinco 365

HERITAGE LANGUAGE LEARNERS

- Ask students to promote tourism to Cuzco and Machu Picchu by preparing a brief travel brochure with fascinating information and details that many other tour guides ignore. Have students go beyond the typical descriptions and find some interesting facts that would entice tourists to spend time in these places. Encourage students to include visuals or their own illustrations.

MULTIPLE INTELLIGENCES:

Verbal-Linguistic Intelligence

- Ask students to imagine that they took the tour that is described in activity 56. They had high expectations that they were going to have a memorable trip. And, in some ways, the trip was memorable because absolutely everything that could go wrong did, and they will always remember this experience! Ask students to write an e-mail message to their family or a friend, describing this terrible trip.

Unit 7

DESAFÍO 2

Comunicación

Activities

55. To extend this activity, have students work in pairs to create a role-play of a weather forecast—modeled on the audio for this activity—for a city of their choice. It should be an accurate forecast that would be appropriate at this time of year.

56. After completing this activity, ask students if they would like to take the trip or make any modifications to the itinerary. As an extension of this activity, have students imagine that they are travel agents who need to create a television advertisement for this trip. The commercial should include what tourists will do while in Cuzco and a little bit of information about the Inti Raymi. Have students incorporate the conjunctions of time with the future tense.

57. To extend this activity, have students work with a partner to research two of the celebrations. Then have students compare the celebrations in a written report. They can pretend that they went to the celebrations, then describe their experience.

 AUDIO SCRIPT
See page 335J.

Answer Key

55. Martes: tiempo soleado.
Miércoles: lluvia y tormentas.
Jueves: cielos despejados.
Viernes: temperaturas más bajas.

56. Answers will vary.
▶ Answers will vary.

57. Answers will vary.

58. 1. hacer   3. leas
2. expliquemos   4. haya olvidado
▶ Answers will vary.

Additional Resources

Fans Online activities
Practice Workbook

365

Unit 7

DESAFÍO 3

Expresar causa y consecuencia

Presentation

- In *Desafío 3*, Michelle and Daniel will have to organize a festival featuring fair-trade handicrafts. Students will preview language used to talk about natural resources and economic activities, and expressions used to talk about cause and consequence.

Activities	Standards	Resources
Texto	1.2, 2.1, 2.2, 3.2	Vis. Pres.
59.	1.1, 1.2, 3.1	
60.	1.1, 1.2	
61.	1.1, 1.2	Audio
62.	1.1, 1.2, 1.3, 2.2	
63. Conexiones	1.1, 1.2, 2.1, 2.2, 3.1, 5.1	

Teaching Suggestions

Warm-Up / Independent Starter

- Ask students to write a list of items from foreign countries that they can buy in a supermarket or in an open-air market in their community.

Preparation

- Ask volunteers to share their responses from the Independent Starter and write them on the board, creating different categories according to students' responses (e.g., *comida*, *artesanía*, *ropa*). Ask students if they can remember the country of origin for each product.

Texto: Un desafío muy justo

- Have students read the title and the introduction. Then ask them: *¿Saben cómo se dice en español "fair trade"? ¿A qué se refiere esta expresión?*

- Have volunteers read the dialogue aloud. Afterward, stress the words or sentences that need pronunciation reinforcement. Ask students to read the dialogue again individually and extract the specific information they now know about *comercio justo*.

Activities

60. After finishing this activity, ask students to work in small groups to discuss which of Daniel's ideas they like most and why.

366

Un desafío muy justo

Daniel and Michelle have to organize a festival featuring fair-trade *artesanía*. First, they will have to find out what fair trade is, how it works, and what kind of products it includes.

MICHELLE: Mira, Daniel, encontré este folleto sobre economía sostenible. Es muy interesante.

DANIEL: ¿A ver?

MICHELLE: Mejor te lo cuento porque tengo que irme a clase enseguida. Aquí explican que el comercio justo tiene que ver con un desarrollo social y económico que respeta el medio ambiente.

DANIEL: Yo también he investigado y creo que debemos trabajar dos ideas.

MICHELLE: ¿Cuáles?

DANIEL: La primera es que la artesanía es muy importante para el desarrollo de las comunidades rurales, y por eso hay que protegerla. Y la segunda, que el uso de materias primas locales ayuda a cuidar el medio ambiente y ahorra energía.

MICHELLE: ¿Tú crees que alguna ONG se dedica a esto?

DANIEL: Yo creo que sí. ¿Por qué me lo preguntas?

MICHELLE: Por conseguir más información. Cerca del parque hay una ONG que tiene una tienda. Supongo que venderán productos de comercio justo. ¿Quieres que vayamos a preguntar? Cierran a las siete, así que podemos ir después de clase.

DANIEL: De acuerdo, luego nos vemos.

59 **Detective de palabras**

▶ **Completa** estas oraciones del diálogo.

1. a. Mejor te lo cuento, ___1___ tengo que irme a clase enseguida.
   b. ___2___ conseguir más información.

2. a. La artesanía es muy importante para el desarrollo de las comunidades rurales y ___3___ hay que protegerla.
   b. Cierran a las siete, ___4___ podemos ir después de clase.

▶ **Observa** las oraciones que has completado y decide. ¿Las oraciones del grupo 1 expresan causa o consecuencia? ¿Y las oraciones del grupo 2?

366 trescientos sesenta y seis

Differentiated Instruction

DEVELOPING LEARNERS

- Before students read the dialogue on their own, ask them to skim it while identifying the main idea of each segment. Help them locate cognates and use context clues to decode unfamiliar words, and ask them to write the definition given in the text of *el comercio justo* in their notebooks, along with Daniel's two ideas for working on this *Desafío*. Remind students that the acronym ONG means *organización no gubernamental*. Then assign students a partner and ask them to role-play the dialogue.

EXPANDING LEARNERS

- Ask students to read the dialogue silently and then close their books. Then have them write a three-paragraph narrative to describe what is going on in the conversation. Students should be sure to include a definition of *comercio justo* and a summary of Daniel's ideas regarding handicrafts and using local materials. Encourage students to add other ideas on how the participants might proceed in order to carry out their *desafío* successfully.

60 **¿Comprendes?**

▶ **Responde** a estas preguntas.

1. ¿En qué consiste el desafío de Michelle y Daniel?
2. ¿Sobre qué es el folleto que le enseña Michelle a Daniel?
3. Según las investigaciones de Daniel, ¿sobre qué ideas pueden trabajar?
4. ¿Qué propone Michelle?
5. ¿Qué les recomendarías a Daniel y a Michelle para comenzar a trabajar en su desafío?

 61 **En busca de productos justos**

 ▶ **Escucha** la conversación y responde a estas preguntas.

1. ¿Por qué están decepcionados Daniel y Michelle?
2. ¿De qué producto de comercio justo habla Daniel? ¿Cuál es su origen?
3. Según Diana, ¿qué desventaja tiene vender este tipo de productos a través de intermediarios?
4. ¿Qué compraron Daniel y Michelle en un supermercado?
5. ¿Qué les va a prestar Diana para la feria de comercio justo?

 62 **Ayuda para Daniel y Michelle**

 ▶ **Escribe** con tu compañero(a) una lista de productos que Daniel y Michelle pueden incluir en la feria de comercio justo. Expliquen brevemente las razones de su selección.

Modelo   A. *Podemos incluir café. Es un producto que se consume en todo el mundo y se cultiva en muchos países de Centroamérica y de Suramérica.*
   B. *De acuerdo. Yo incluiría también el té.*

▶ **Presenten** su selección a la clase.

CONEXIONES: ECONOMÍA

Comercio sostenible

El comercio justo o comercio sostenible es un sistema de comercio promovido por las Naciones Unidas y diversas organizaciones no gubernamentales. Se basa en una relación más justa entre consumidores y productores, reduciendo la diferencia entre lo que ganan los productores y lo que pagan los consumidores. Entre sus principios están la defensa del trabajo digno, el respeto a los derechos humanos, la calidad, la producción sostenible y el cuidado del medio ambiente.

FAIRTRADE
COMERCIO JUSTO

63 **Investiga.** ¿Qué tipo de productos se venden en los establecimientos de comercio justo? ¿Conoces alguna tienda que los venda?

HERITAGE LANGUAGE LEARNERS

• Ask students to look into the history of *el comercio sostenible* in their family's country of origin or another Hispanic country, and make a brief presentation to the class. Ask them to identify the local products that are traded, and the impact this has had on the local economy. If students have any of these products at home, encourage them to bring them to class, explain what they are and their purpose, how and where they were made or cultivated, and by whom.

SPECIAL-NEEDS LEARNERS

• Help hearing-impaired students complete activity 61 by providing them with the script. Ask them to read the conversation once, then look over the questions and refer back to the script to find the answers. Next, ask students to describe any products they or their families customarily buy that are the result of fair trade practices. Ask them to say where they buy these products, who makes them, and identify the country of origin.

---

61. Before playing the audio, have students read the title and the questions, so that they will be able to figure out basic information about the audio.

 AUDIO SCRIPT
See page 335 J.

 CONEXIONES: ECONOMÍA

Comercio sostenible

Sustainable commerce is based upon the ideas of social justice, peace, security, and empowering communities to overcome poverty. There are many international organizations devoted to promoting sustainability by means of educational programs and grants.

Answer Key

59. 1. a. porque   2. a. por eso
       b. Por   b. así que
   ▶ 1. causa   2. consecuencia

60. 1. En organizar una feria de comercio justo.
   2. Es sobre economía sostenible.
   3. Sobre la importancia de la artesanía en las comunidades rurales y el uso de materias primas locales.
   4. Ir a una ONG porque tienen una tienda.
   5. Answers will vary.

61. 1. Porque hay pocos lugares donde vendan productos de comercio justo.
   2. Habla de café de Oaxaca (México).
   3. Los intermediarios pagan precios muy bajos a los productores.
   4. Compraron quinoa orgánica de Perú.
   5. Objetos artesanales.

62. Answers will vary.
   ▶ Answers will vary.

63. Answers will vary.

Additional Resources

Fans Online activities

367

DESAFÍO 3

Vocabulario – Desastres naturales. Recursos naturales

Presentation

- In this section, students will learn words to talk about natural disasters, natural resources, and economic activities.

Activities	Standards	Resources
Vocabulario	1.2, 3.1	
64.	1.1, 1.2, 1.3, 3.1, 5.1	
65.	1.2, 1.3, 3.1	
66.	1.2	Audio
67.	1.3, 5.1	
68. Comunidades	1.1, 1.2, 2.1, 3.1, 4.2, 5.1	

Teaching Suggestions

Warm-Up / Independent Starter

- Ask students to think of two major natural disasters they remember and answer these questions in writing: *¿Qué ocurrió? ¿Dónde y cuándo sucedió? ¿Qué hacías cuando ocurrió?*

Preparation

- Read the highlighted words and have students repeat them after you. Then ask students to briefly describe the pictures showing natural disasters on page 368. Have some volunteers read the descriptions aloud.

- After sharing their answers from the Independent Starter, ask students if any of the disasters they described coincide with the ones described in the text on page 368.

- Read the words in the *Más vocabulario* feature and under *Recursos naturales*, and ask students to repeat them after you. Have students think of natural resources and economic activities that are common in their state or region and list them in their notebooks. Call on volunteers to share their lists with the class.

Activities

66. To extend this activity, play the audio recording a second time and ask students to write their own brief news summaries for two of the headlines.

Vocabulario

Desastres naturales

En octubre de 1998 el **huracán** Mitch causó graves **inundaciones** y hubo grandes pérdidas materiales y humanas. Fue el **ciclón** tropical más poderoso que ha pasado por América Central.

En 1998 ocurrió uno de los **incendios forestales** más graves en Guatemala. El fuego quemó la selva Lacandona, una de las reservas más importantes de nuestro planeta.

En 2010 Chile sufrió un **terremoto** devastador, de 8,8 grados en la escala de Richter. Produjo olas gigantes en el mar, el derrumbe de muchos edificios y varias **erupciones volcánicas**.

Recursos naturales

el carbón

el gas natural

los minerales

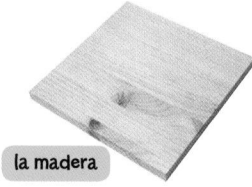
la madera

Más vocabulario

Metales

el acero	*steel*
el bronce	*bronze*
el estaño	*tin*
el hierro	*iron*
el oro	*gold*
la plata	*silver*
el plomo	*lead*

Actividades económicas

la agricultura	*agriculture*
la ganadería	*livestock*
la industria	*industry*
la minería	*mining*
la pesca	*fishing*

64 Buenas definiciones

▶ **Elige** tres palabras de la ficha de Vocabulario y escribe una definición para cada una.

Modelo   *Es un viento muy fuerte.*

 ▶ **Lee** tus definiciones a tu compañero(a) para que adivine de qué palabras se trata. Túrnense.

368   trescientos sesenta y ocho

Differentiated Instruction

DEVELOPING LEARNERS

- Ask students to read the following groups of words and say which one does not belong:

1. *la plata*   *el estaño*   *la pesca (la pesca)*
2. *el carbón*   *el huracán*   *el terremoto* (el carbón)
3. *el hierro*   *el ciclón*   *la minería (el ciclón)*
4. *la industria*   *la erupción*   *la ganadería* (la erupción)
5. *el oro*   *el bronce*   *la inundación* (la inundación)
6. *la sequía*   *la minería*   *la agricultura* (la sequía)
7. *el acero*   *la madera*   *el plomo* (la madera)

EXPANDING LEARNERS

- Ask students to write a brief newspaper article about a natural disaster that occurred in their community, state, or anywhere in the world. Explain that they can write about something that happened recently or many years ago, but they should report it as if it were happening today. Encourage students to do some research on the incident in order to make it more realistic, but to use their imagination if they plan to include eyewitness accounts. Students will also need an attention-grabbing headline. Display their articles in the classroom.

65 **¿Cuál es la relación?**

▶ **Une** los productos con las actividades.

Ⓐ

Ⓑ

1. aparatos eléctricos
2. carne, leche y huevos
3. marisco y pescado
4. frutas y verduras
5. metales y minerales

a. agricultura
b. industria
c. minería
d. ganadería
e. pesca

Parque Fundidora (Monterrey).

 66 **Desastres naturales**

▶ **Escucha** y relaciona cada noticia con su titular.

Ⓐ
Después de varias semanas de espera el volcán se despertó

Ⓑ
Un incendio forestal en México destruye miles de hectáreas de bosque

Ⓒ
Un fuerte terremoto despierta a los ciudadanos de Santiago

Ⓓ
El poderoso huracán golpeó la costa durante más de 12 horas

 67 **Tu experiencia**

▶ **Escribe** sobre un desastre natural que haya afectado fuertemente a tu comunidad o a tu país. ¿Qué ocurrió? ¿Qué consecuencias materiales, humanas y para el medio ambiente tuvo?

 **COMUNIDADES**

LA INDUSTRIA EN CHILE

Chile es un país con grandes reservas de minerales; por ello, la minería es una de sus principales actividades económicas. Chile es un importante productor de hierro, cobre (copper), plomo, oro y plata, entre otros metales.

Mina de cobre (Chile).

68 **Compara.** ¿Qué recursos naturales hay en la zona donde vives? ¿Qué industrias son más importantes?

trescientos sesenta y nueve 369

Vocabulario – Desastres naturales. Recursos naturales

67. Before starting this activity, you may want to ask students to brainstorm natural disasters that have happened in their community or country. Alternatively, you may assign this activity as homework and encourage students to use books, newspapers, and the Internet to find out information and visuals.

68. To extend this activity, ask students to select a local factory. Have them research it to answer the following questions:

1. ¿Qué produce esa fábrica?
2. ¿Desde cuándo está la fábrica en la zona?
3. ¿De dónde es la compañía?
4. ¿Es esa fábrica respetuosa con el medio ambiente?

 AUDIO SCRIPT
See page 335 J.

 COMUNIDADES

La industria en Chile

Chile is currently one of the most developed countries in South America. Chile's economic success stems, in part, from its natural resources. Chile is the second-largest producer of salmon in the world. Another strong industry in Chile is forestry. The Chilean government is actively providing technical support for the development of this industry.

Answer Key

64. Answers will vary.
▶ Answers will vary.
65. 2. d   3. e   4. a   5. c
66. 1. D   2. C   3. A   4. B
67. Answers will vary.
68. Answers will vary.

Additional Resources

Fans Online activities
Practice Workbook

HERITAGE LANGUAGE LEARNERS

• Remind students of the wealth of legends that abound on the American continents, especially the Maya and Aztec legends of Mesoamerica. Some students might be familiar with the legend of Popocatépetl and Iztaccíhuatl, a brave warrior and a beautiful princess, who were turned into the two volcanoes that are near Mexico City. Ask students to research other legends that attempt to explain natural phenomena such as fire, floods, earthquakes, and volcanic eruptions and how they came to be. Have them select one and retell it to the class.

MULTIPLE INTELLIGENCES:

Intrapersonal Intelligence

• Briefly discuss the Chilean mining accident of 2010, when thirty-three miners were trapped 700 meters below the surface for sixty-nine days. Ask students to imagine that they were one of these miners and have them write journal entries expressing their thoughts, fears, and hopes while they were trapped and as they were being rescued. Students should also make comments on the miners' day-to-day lives in the mine, how they interacted with the others, and what they did to alleviate the boredom and uncertainty of those long days.

DESAFÍO 3

Gramática – Expresar causa y consecuencia

Presentation

- In this section, students will learn some expressions to talk about cause and consequence.

Activities	Standards	Resources
Gramática	1.2, 3.1	
69.	1.3, 4.1	
70.	1.2, 3.1	
71.	1.2	
72.	1.3	
73.	1.1, 1.2, 3.1	

Teaching Suggestions

Warm-Up / Independent Starter

- Have students answer these questions in writing: *¿Por qué se agotan los recursos naturales? ¿Por qué se produce la deforestación? ¿Por qué están desapareciendo algunas especies?*

Preparation

- Have students read the grammar presentation with a partner and summarize the main points in their notebooks. Then ask volunteer pairs to explain each section of the grammar presentation aloud to their classmates. Offer additional examples whenever possible, and ask questions to guide the students' presentations.

- Have students rewrite their answers from the Independent Starter using both *porque + indicativo* and *por + infinitivo*. They may need to rearrange some sentences in order to adequately represent both grammatical structures in their answers. For example: *Los recursos naturales se agotan porque se utilizan sin control. Los recursos naturales se agotan por utilizarlos sin control.* Then ask students to write one more consequence for each sentence.

Activities

70. After finishing this activity, ask some volunteers to write several examples on the board without underlining the part that expresses cause or consequence. Have the class decide.

370

Gramática

Expresar causa y consecuencia

Expresiones de causa

- In English, the cause or reason for a situation is usually expressed with *because* or *because of*. The most frequently used structures to express cause in Spanish are these:

| porque + indicative | Hay árboles en el suelo **porque** el huracán los **tiró**. |

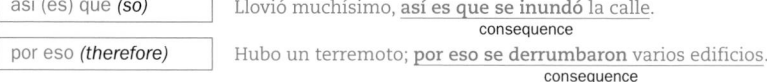

cause

| por + infinitive | Los recursos naturales se destruyen **por no reciclar**. |

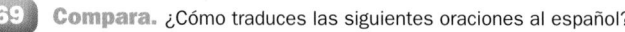

cause

Notice that the cause clause with porque + *indicative* goes after the main clause.

- To ask about the reason why something happens or someone does something, use ¿Por qué…? followed by a verb in the indicative mood.

—¿**Por qué** no **viniste** ayer? —¿**Por qué es** famosa esa tienda?

—**Porque hubo** inundaciones. —**Por vender** productos de comercio justo.

Expresiones de consecuencia

- To introduce the consequence or conclusion of an event previously stated, use these expressions followed by a verb in the indicative mood:

| así (es) que *(so)* | Llovió muchísimo, **así es que se inundó** la calle. |

consequence

| por eso *(therefore)* | Hubo un terremoto; **por eso se derrumbaron** varios edificios. |

consequence

69 **Compara.** ¿Cómo traduces las siguientes oraciones al español?

a. *Because of the hurricane, trains did not work.*

b. *Because the hurricane destroyed everything, trains did not work.*

70 **Causas y consecuencias**

▶ **Lee** estas oraciones y decide si la parte subrayada expresa una causa o una consecuencia.

1. Hubo un fuerte huracán; <u>por eso se destruyeron tantos árboles</u>.

2. Hay una fuerte sequía <u>porque llueve muy poco</u>.

3. La fábrica recibió una multa <u>por no reciclar</u>.

4. Hay peligro de erupción; <u>por eso no podemos visitar el volcán</u>.

5. <u>Por no tener cuidado con las hogueras</u>, se producen muchos incendios forestales.

6. En las noticias dijeron que no podíamos salir de nuestras casas, <u>así que no fui a la escuela</u>.

370 trescientos setenta

Differentiated Instruction

DEVELOPING LEARNERS

- Ask students to look for images of natural disasters in old magazines or newspapers and bring some to class. Ask them to attach each image to a sheet of paper and write a sentence under each one that describes what happened and why, using the expressions of cause and consequence shown on the page. Call on students to read some of their sentences aloud. Display students' work in the classroom.

EXPANDING LEARNERS

- Ask students to write at least five sentences that explain the cause, reason, consequence, or conclusion of an action, but to leave a blank where the corresponding expression *(porque, por, así [es] que, por eso)* belongs. The sentences should focus on the topic of this lesson: natural disasters. Then have students exchange their papers with a partner and have their partners complete each sentence.

DESAFÍO 3

Gramática – Expresar causa y consecuencia

 Expresiones

▶ **Completa** estas oraciones con las expresiones adecuadas.

| por |
| porque |
| por eso |
| así (es) que |

1. Daniel y Michelle están muy contentos _____ les encanta su desafío.
2. Muchas personas están mal pagadas, _____ no viven dignamente.
3. Michelle quiere saber _____ qué hay tanta diferencia entre lo que reciben los productores y el precio final de los productos.
4. Esta ONG es conocida _____ defender los derechos de los animales.
5. El comercio justo favorece el cuidado del medio ambiente; _____ apoya los productos y la agricultura ecológica.
6. Daniel y Michelle tienen bastante información, _____ van a empezar a organizar la feria de comercio justo.

 **Busca las causas**

▶ **Escribe** pies de foto para explicar las causas de estas situaciones. Usa las expresiones *porque* y *por*.

Modelo   1. *El bosque se destruyó porque hubo un incendio.*

 En consecuencia...

 ▶ **Habla** con tu compañero(a). ¿Qué consecuencias tuvieron estos hechos?

Modelo   La erupción del volcán formó una nube de humo gigante.
   → *Por eso los aviones no pudieron volar y cerraron el aeropuerto.*

1. Los medios de comunicación anunciaron que el huracán llegaría a tierra por la tarde.
2. Las lluvias provocaron importantes inundaciones en la capital.
3. Este año se quemaron miles de hectáreas de bosque.
4. He leído que ha aumentado el uso de pesticidas en las explotaciones agrícolas.
5. El otoño pasado no llovió casi nada.
6. La ONG denunció a una fábrica por contaminar el río.

trescientos setenta y uno   371

---

72. To expand this activity, have students add a consequence for each picture. For example:
El bosque se destruyó porque hubo un incendio, así es que muchos animales murieron.

73. Have students think about whether they have experienced any of these problems, and ask them to write what the consequences were for them and their families.

Answer Key

69. a. Los trenes no funcionaron/funcionaban por el huracán.
   b. Los trenes no funcionaron/funcionaban porque el huracán destruyó todo.

70. 1. consecuencia   4. consecuencia
   2. causa   5. causa
   3. causa   6. consecuencia

71. 1. porque   4. por
   2. por eso   5. por eso
   3. por   6. así (es) que

72. Answers will vary. Sample answers:
   2. Los edificios se derrumbaron porque hubo un terremoto.
   3. La vegetación desapareció por la sequía.
   4. Los postes se cayeron porque hubo un huracán.

73. Answers will vary. Sample answers:
   1. Por eso muchas personas compraron provisiones y se fueron a refugios.
   2. Por eso la capital se quedó sin luz.
   3. Por eso los gobiernos hacen campañas publicitarias para concienciar a los ciudadanos de que tengan más cuidado.
   4. Por eso cada vez hay más contaminación en los acuíferos.
   5. Por eso es necesario ahorrar agua.
   6. Por eso es necesario tener leyes de protección del medio ambiente.

Additional Resources

Fans Online activities
Practice Workbook

HERITAGE LANGUAGE LEARNERS

• Ask students to look into the rescue organizations in Latin America and Spain that help out during natural disasters. They will most likely find the International Red Cross, but there are also local associations that are well equipped to handle rescues. Then ask students to search the Internet and find a compelling story about a rescue from a natural disaster in a Hispanic country and provide details. Students may do this in a written report or in an oral presentation to the class.

COOPERATIVE LEARNING

• Ask students to work in small groups and to imagine that they are at the site of a natural disaster. Some members of the group will be TV reporters, others will be witnesses to the disaster. Working together, students will identify where and when the catastrophe occurred. Reporters will describe the scene, witnesses will explain what they were doing at the time and how they are reacting, and the news anchor will coordinate all the accounts of the disaster. Give students time to practice and then call on groups to present their story to the class.

371

DESAFÍO 3

Gramática – La preposición *a* personal

Presentation

- In this section, students will review and practice the use of the personal *a*.

Activities	Standards	Resources
Gramática	1.2, 3.1	
74.	3.1, 4.1	
75.	1.2	
76.	1.1, 1.2	Audio
77.	1.2, 3.1	
78. Conexiones	1.1, 1.2, 2.1, 2.2, 4.2, 5.1	

Teaching Suggestions

Warm-Up / Independent Starter

- Have students translate the following sentences into Spanish:

  1. I have many friends at school.
  2. My grandma loves her grandchildren.
  3. I called my aunt last night.
  4. There are many people in that restaurant.

Preparation

- Have students read the grammar presentation silently, then work with a partner to summarize the main points. Ask students to share their Independent Starters with their partners. They should discuss why they are using the personal *a* or not in each case. Then ask volunteers to write their translations on the board, and discuss their sentences as a class. Students should explain that the personal *a* is not used in sentence 1 because of the verb *tener*, and in sentence 4 because of the verb *haber*.

Activities

75. After finishing this activity, ask students to justify their answers. For example: 1. *a alguien* → the direct object is a pronoun referring to people; 2. *tener más amigos* → the personal *a* is not used with the verb *tener*. If students find out that they made a mistake, ask them to correct their answer.

Gramática

La preposición *a* personal

Uso de la preposición *a* personal

- Spanish labels certain direct objects by placing an *a* before them. This word has no English translation and conveys no meaning in Spanish; it is just a marker. The following are some of the most common uses of this marker:

The direct object refers to a definite or specific person or people.	Vi a Daniel en la biblioteca. *I saw Daniel at the library.*
The direct object refers to a definite pet.	Quiero mucho a mi gato. *I love my cat very much.*
The direct object is a pronoun referring to people, such as alguien (*someone*), nadie (*nobody*), alguno (*some*), ninguno (*none*), todos (*everybody*).	No llamé a nadie anoche. *I didn't call anyone last night.*

- The personal *a* is not used in the following cases:

When the direct object refers to an indefinite person or group of people.	La compañía necesita un gerente bilingüe. *The company needs a bilingual manager.* Veo gente en el parque. *I see people in the park.*
With the verbs tener and haber.	Tengo dos hermanos y una hermana. *I have two brothers and one sister.* Hay alguien en el laboratorio. *There is someone at the lab.*

74 **Compara.** Al traducir al español la oración *Lucas sees Asha*, ¿cómo sabemos a qué parte de la oración hay que asignar la *a* personal?

75 **¿Con *a* o sin *a*?**

▶ **Completa** las oraciones usando la *a* personal cuando sea necesario.

1. Michelle quiere conocer _____ alguien en la ONG que hay cerca del parque.
2. Michelle está decidida a tener _____ más amigos comprometidos con el medio ambiente.
3. Daniel alimenta _____ su gato exclusivamente con comida orgánica.
4. Diana tiene _____ unos vecinos que le venden verduras de su propia granja.
5. Diana cree que hay _____ muchas personas que no saben lo que es el mercado sostenible.
6. Daniel conoce una ONG que necesita _____ un coordinador que hable español para sus proyectos con Latinoamérica.

Differentiated Instruction

DEVELOPING LEARNERS

- Write the following sentences and ask students to write *a* if it is needed and *no* if it is not:

  1. ¿Tienes … novio? (no)
  2. Me parece que hay … muchas víctimas de las inundaciones. (no)
  3. Saco … mi perro a pasear todas las mañanas. (a)
  4. El comercio justo ayuda … los productores. (a)
  5. Esa organización busca … voluntarios. (no)
  6. No veo … nadie en el gimnasio. (a)
  7. El huracán dejó … las personas de la costa sin hogar. (a)

EXPANDING LEARNERS

- Ask students to work with a partner and take turns creating more sentences, some of which will require the personal *a*. Students should say or write at least one sentence that uses the examples shown on this page.

- You may want to give students the following examples to get them started:

  1. Este tren ha traído turistas desde Madrid.
  2. El carnaval tiene una nueva reina.
  3. No conocemos nadie en esta ciudad. (a nadie)

76 En la ONG

▶ **Escucha** la conversación de Daniel y Michelle en una ONG y responde a estas preguntas.

1. ¿A qué se dedica la ONG a la que van Daniel y Michelle?
2. ¿Qué ve Daniel al entrar en la ONG?
3. ¿Qué producto de la tienda menciona Michelle?
4. ¿A quién buscan Michelle y Daniel en la tienda?
5. ¿Qué otros productos hay en la tienda?
6. ¿A quién van a llamar Michelle y Daniel más tarde?

77 Artesanía colombiana

▶ **Lee** el mensaje que les envía Diana a los personajes y busca tres oraciones donde falta la *a* personal.

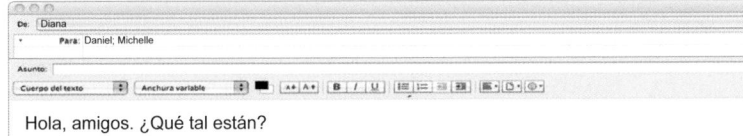

De: Diana
Para: Daniel; Michelle
Asunto:

Cuerpo del texto | Anchura variable | A+ A+ | **B** *I* U | ☰ ☷ ☷ | ☰ ▾ ☐ ▾ ☺ ▾

Hola, amigos. ¿Qué tal están?

Como les prometí, les mando unos recuerdos que compré en Colombia.

Seguramente el producto más famoso de Colombia es el café, pero no compré café porque no me gusta… Sin embargo, compré otras cosas.

En una tienda de objetos de cuero conocí el dueño y me explicó todo sobre la fabricación de sus productos. Después fui a un mercado al aire libre grandísimo. Allí compré bisutería y objetos de decoración para regalárselos a mis amigos.

Yo quería comprarme un cuadro de recuerdo, pero en el mercado no vi nadie que vendiera cuadros. Al final, cerca del hotel encontré una mujer que vendía fotografías de paisajes y me traje una foto enorme de la laguna de Guatavita. Espero que les guste.

Diana

CONEXIONES: ARTE

Una feria de artesanía

La feria de artesanía más importante de Latinoamérica se llama Expoartesanías y se celebra anualmente en Colombia. Su finalidad es favorecer la situación del sector artesanal colombiano, mantener viva la artesanía tradicional y, al mismo tiempo, usar materias primas locales que ayuden a preservar el medio ambiente.

78 **Explica.** ¿En el lugar donde vives hay ferias de artesanía? ¿Qué tipo de productos se venden?

trescientos setenta y tres **373**

HERITAGE LANGUAGE LEARNERS

• Ask students to describe some of the handicrafts from their family's country of origin or from another Spanish-speaking country. If students are able, ask them to bring some of these articles to class, explain where they are from, what they are, their uses, how they are made, and what materials were used in making them. If any of your heritage speakers have family members who are artisans, invite them to come to class to talk about their skills and perhaps to demonstrate how they make their crafts.

COOPERATIVE LEARNING

• Ask students to work in groups of six or seven and set up their own handicrafts fair. They should bring in actual artifacts from home, copy their images, or make their own illustrations. Students should identify each product with its name and purpose, and include labels that indicate country of origin, materials used, and price. Ask students to give their fair a name and display their goods. Invite the groups to mingle and view each other's crafts. You might even give students play money so they may "purchase" something.

---

77. To expand this activity, have students work in pairs and ask each other these questions:

1. *¿Qué va a regalar Diana? ¿A quién?*
2. *¿Qué producto no compró Diana? ¿Por qué?*
3. *¿A quién conoció Diana en el mercado?*
4. *¿Qué trajo Diana de recuerdo?*

After finishing the activity, ask them to explain which answers require the personal *a* and why.

 AUDIO SCRIPT
See page 335J.

 CONEXIONES: ARTE

Una feria de artesanía

Craft fairs play an important role in promoting the craft business and fair trade. In addition to Expoartesanías, other famous craft fairs include Fiesta de la Artesanía in Argentina and Las Manos del Mundo in Mexico. Both fairs help entrepreneurs from those countries and other nations to build a professional international network.

Answer Key

74. Al objeto directo: Lucas ve a Asha.

75. 1. a   2. X   3. a   4. X   5. X   6. X

76. 1. Trabajan en proyectos de comercio justo.
2. Productos de alimentación con el sello de comercio justo.
3. Menciona el chocolate mexicano.
4. A alguien que trabaje en la tienda.
5. También hay objetos de artesanía.
6. Van a llamar a Diana.

77. … conocí al dueño y me explicó…
… en el mercado no vi a nadie que…
… encontré a una mujer que vendía…

78. Answers will vary.

Additional Resources

Fans Online activities
Practice Workbook

373

LECTURA: TEXTO LITERARIO

Presentation

- In this section, students will read a short story by Guatemalan author Augusto Monterroso.

Activities	Standards	Resources
Lectura: texto literario	1.2, 3.1, 3.2	
79.	1.2, 1.3	
80.	1.1, 1.2	
81.	1.3, 3.1, 5.1	

Teaching Suggestions

Warm-Up / Independent Starter

- Ask students to observe the picture and answer the first point in the *Antes de leer* strategies.

Preparation

- Call on individual students to share their responses from the Independent Starter. Contrast their descriptions of an eclipse with definitions found online or in a Spanish-only dictionary. Ask them if they have ever experienced an eclipse. If there are students in class who answer affirmatively, invite them to share their experiences with the class.

- Have students work with a partner to read the rest of the *Antes de leer* strategies. Give students some time to research the names of Carlos Quinto (known in Spain as Carlos I), and of Aristotle (a Greek philosopher and writer). Then ask pairs to write the answers to the questions in their notebooks. Once pairs have finished working on the *Antes de leer* questions, discuss the answers as a class.

- Read the short story aloud to model intonation and pronunciation, and have students follow along in their books. Then call on individual students to each read a paragraph aloud.

- Before having students read the story again individually, discuss with them the meaning of some phrases that may clarify some passages (e.g., *la selva poderosa, su ignorancia topográfica, su labor redentora, indígenas de rostro impasible, su cultura universal, Bartolomé sorprendió la incredulidad en sus ojos*).

374

Antes de leer: estrategias

1. Lee el título. ¿Qué es un eclipse? ¿Qué ocurre cuando hay uno? ¿Se pueden predecir los eclipses?
2. Lee las tres primeras líneas del texto. ¿Quién es el personaje principal? ¿Dónde está? ¿Cómo se siente?
3. Busca los nombres propios del texto. ¿Sabes quién fue Carlos Quinto? ¿Y Aristóteles? Si no lo sabes, investígalo.

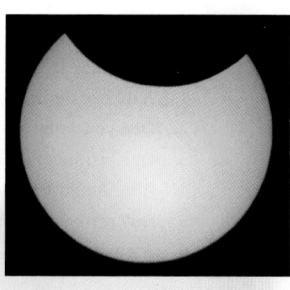

El eclipse

Cuando fray Bartolomé Arrazola se sintió perdido, aceptó que ya nada podría salvarlo. La selva poderosa[1] de Guatemala lo había apresado[2], implacable y definitiva. Ante su ignorancia topográfica se sentó con tranquilidad a esperar la muerte. Quiso morir allí, sin ninguna esperanza, aislado, con el pensamiento fijo[3] en la España distante, particularmente en el convento de los Abrojos, donde Carlos Quinto condescendiera una vez a bajar de su eminencia[4] para decirle que confiaba en el celo religioso de su labor redentora[5].

Al despertar se encontró rodeado por un grupo de indígenas de rostro[6] impasible que se disponían a sacrificarlo ante un altar, un altar que a Bartolomé le pareció como el lecho[7] en que descansaría, al fin, de sus temores[8], de su destino, de sí mismo.

Tres años en el país le habían conferido un mediano dominio de las lenguas nativas. Intentó algo. Dijo algunas palabras que fueron comprendidas.

Entonces floreció[9] en él una idea que tuvo por digna de su talento y de su cultura universal y de su arduo conocimiento de Aristóteles. Recordó que para ese día se esperaba un eclipse total de sol. Y dispuso[10], en lo más íntimo, valerse de[11] aquel conocimiento para engañar a sus opresores y salvar la vida.

—Si me matáis —les dijo— puedo hacer que el Sol se oscurezca en su altura.

Los indígenas lo miraron fijamente y Bartolomé sorprendió la incredulidad en sus ojos. Vio que se produjo un pequeño consejo[12], y esperó confiado, no sin cierto desdén[13].

Dos horas después el corazón de fray Bartolomé Arrazola chorreaba[14] su sangre vehemente sobre la piedra de los sacrificios (brillante bajo la opaca luz de un sol eclipsado), mientras uno de los indígenas recitaba sin ninguna inflexión de voz, sin prisa, una por una, las infinitas fechas en que se producirían eclipses solares y lunares, que los astrónomos de la comunidad maya habían previsto y anotado en sus códices sin la valiosa ayuda de Aristóteles.

AUGUSTO MONTERROSO (Guatemala, 1921–2003). *Obras completas y otros cuentos*

1. *powerful*	5. *that he had confidence in his religious mission*	8. *fears*	12. *meeting*
2. *captured*		9. *flourished*	13. *scorn*
3. *fixed*		10. *decided*	14. *was dripping*
4. *once stepped down from his exalted position*	6. *face*	11. *make use of*	
	7. *bed*		

Differentiated instruction

DEVELOPING LEARNERS

- Before students read the story, ask them to read the first sentence of each paragraph, which is the topic sentence and which will explain what is going on in that paragraph. Students should once more look for context clues if they come across an unfamiliar word, identify cognates (*aceptó, topográfica, tranquilidad,* etc.), and look for word families of familiar vocabulary (*poderoso → poder*). Suggest that they include the footnoted words in their notebooks for vocabulary enrichment. Call on individual students to take turns reading the story aloud.

EXPANDING LEARNERS

- After students read *El eclipse* ask them to write a character profile of Fray Bartolomé Arrazola. Students should be guided by the information and descriptions in the text, but they may also use prior knowledge of the role priests had in the New World. Ask students to read their profiles aloud and conduct a classroom discussion on the similarities and differences that students have described.

79 Comprensión

▶ **Completa** este mapa de la historia.

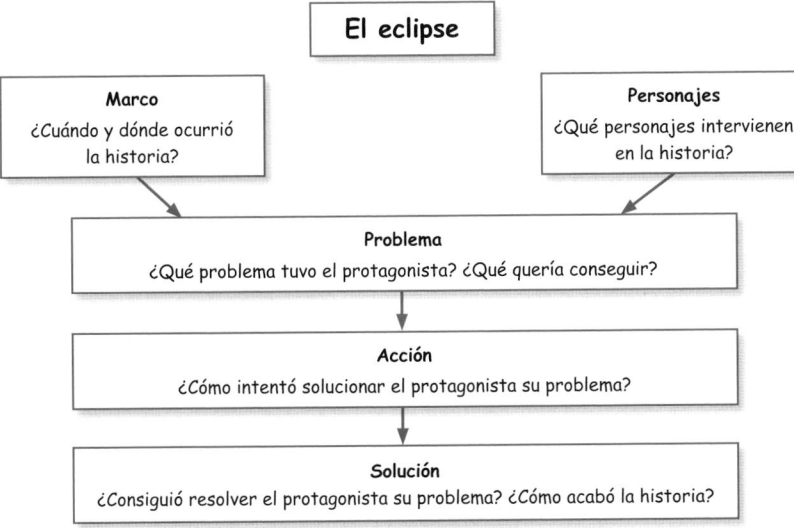

El eclipse

Marco
¿Cuándo y dónde ocurrió
la historia?

Personajes
¿Qué personajes intervienen
en la historia?

Problema
¿Qué problema tuvo el protagonista? ¿Qué quería conseguir?

Acción
¿Cómo intentó solucionar el protagonista su problema?

Solución
¿Consiguió resolver el protagonista su problema? ¿Cómo acabó la historia?

80 Explicaciones

▶ **Relaciona** las siguientes oraciones del texto con la mejor explicación.

1. Ante su ignorancia topográfica se sentó con tranquilidad a esperar la muerte.
   a. Aceptó que iba a morir porque no sabía nada de la selva.
   b. No sabía nada de topografía y por eso estaba tranquilo.
   c. Era tan ignorante que se sentó para morir.

2. Tres años en el país le habían conferido un mediano dominio de las lenguas nativas.
   a. Dominaba el país gracias a la lengua que había aprendido.
   b. Había aprendido a hablar un poco la lengua de los indígenas.
   c. Los nativos le habían dado clases de lengua durante tres años.

3. Los indígenas lo miraron fijamente y Bartolomé sorprendió la incredulidad en sus ojos.
   a. A Bartolomé le sorprendieron los ojos de los indígenas.
   b. Vio que los indígenas no creían lo que decía.
   c. Los indígenas miraron fijamente a Bartolomé y él se asustó.

81 Con tus propias palabras

▶ **Investiga** sobre el escritor Augusto Monterroso y escribe un texto sobre él. Incluye
algunos datos sobre su vida y un resumen de alguna obra importante.

trescientos setenta y cinco **375**

Activities

79. Guide students in finding clues to complete this activity. What time references are there in the story? When was Carlos Quinto the king of Spain? Where is Bartolomé: in Guatemala or in Spain? What does the word *distante* mean? What sentences refer to or describe Bartolomé? What sentences refer to or describe the natives?

80. To further expand the comprehension of the text, have students work in groups to summarize each of the paragraphs in the text with their own words. Emphasize that they should focus on the main actions. For example: Paragraph 1: *Bartolomé estaba perdido en la selva de Guatemala y pensó que iba a morir.*

Answer Key

79. Answers will vary. Sample answers:
Marco: en la selva de Guatemala, durante el reinado de Carlos Quinto, en el siglo XVI.
Personajes: fray Bartolomé; los indígenas.
Problema: los indígenas lo habían hecho prisionero y él quería salvar su vida.
Acción: intentó usar sus conocimientos de Aristóteles para hacer creer a los indígenas que el Sol lo obedecía.
Solución: no resolvió su problema, los indígenas lo sacrificaron.

80. 1. a   2. b   3. b

81. Answers will vary. Sample answer:
Augusto Monterroso (1921–2003) nació en Honduras y se estableció desde muy joven en Guatemala. Estuvo exiliado en México, país donde murió.
Entre los cuentos más conocidos de Monterroso se encuentra el microcuento más corto que se conoce en español: "El dinosaurio".

Additional Resources

Fans Online activities

HERITAGE LANGUAGE LEARNERS

• Ask students to write a new ending to this story. Suggest that students change the mood of the story starting with the second paragraph, where the author states *"se disponían a sacrificarlo."* Remind students that most encounters between Spaniards and the indigenous population did not end in battles or death. Perhaps Fray Bartolomé can talk himself out of being sacrificed, or perhaps the native population wants to welcome him into their community. Encourage students to be creative. Have students read the "happy" ending to the class.

CRITICAL THINKING

• Ask students to imagine that they are among the indigenous population who came across Fray Bartolomé Arrazola in the jungle. Ask them to write their thoughts upon seeing the priest. Students are not limited by the story's final outcome. Remind them that this might have been the first time they were looking at a European, so they would have no idea where he was from or why he was there in their land. The local population might think of this outsider as an enemy, a curiosity, or a possible friend.

Unit 7
DESAFÍO 3
Comunicación

Presentation

- In this section, students will integrate the vocabulary and grammar skills from *Desafío 3* in order to talk about natural disasters and natural resources, as well as to express cause and consequence.

Activities	Standards	Resources
82.	1.3, 3.1, 5.1, 5.2	
83.	1.1, 1.3, 5.1, 5.2	
84.	1.2, 1.3, 3.1, 5.1	
85. Final del desafío	1.1, 1.2, 1.3	
Tu desafío	1.1, 1.2	

Teaching Suggestions

Warm-Up / Independent Starter

- Have students answer the following questions:
  1. *¿Qué recursos naturales forman parte de tu vida diaria?*
  2. *¿Con qué actividad económica se relacionan?*

Preparation

- Have students share their Independent Starters. Ask them to consider resources that might not immediately come to mind, such as air, water, and types of flora and fauna. Then have students work in pairs and discuss how the disappearance of those natural resources would affect their lives or their communities. Finally, ask students to make recommendations to try to avoid those negative consequences.

Activities

82. To enhance their presentations, ask students to bring in photos of the phenomenon they chose to describe. They can take the photos themselves or look at local community resources, such as newspapers and websites, in order to find photos of the local situation. To vary the responses, you can also expand this activity to include ecological situations in Spanish-speaking countries.

DESAFÍO 3

Comunicación

82 **Desastres ecológicos**

▶ **Mira** las fotografías e identifica los problemas ecológicos que ilustran. Después, escribe sobre las causas y las posibles consecuencias de esos problemas.

Modelo 1. *El aire se contamina mucho en las grandes ciudades porque hay demasiados coches. Y por eso hay cada vez más personas con problemas respiratorios.*

▶ **Haz** una presentación del problema ecológico que afecta más al lugar donde vives. Incluye algunas recomendaciones para evitarlo o reducir sus consecuencias.

83 **¡Salvemos el planeta!**

▶ **Habla** con dos compañeros(as) sobre las consecuencias que estas actividades humanas tienen para la Tierra y toma nota de sus ideas.

- No comprar productos locales.
- No usar materias primas locales.
- Usar bolsas y envases de plástico y tirarlos en lugar de reciclarlos.
- No usar bombillas *(lightbulbs)* ecológicas.
- Comprar frutas y verduras que no son de temporada.

▶ **Preparen** un folleto para concienciar a su comunidad de las consecuencias de estas acciones. Dibujen un logo para el folleto que simbolice la salvación del planeta.

Differentiated Instruction

DEVELOPING LEARNERS

- Ask students to look through magazines, newspapers, or the Internet for images of ecological problems. Have them select at least four images and ask them to identify the problem depicted (e.g., *Hay mucho tráfico en esta ciudad*). Then ask students to give a solution (e.g., *Hay que usar el transporte público o compartir el coche*). Next, have students show the cause or consequence between the problem and the solution by using *porque/por* or *así (es) que/por eso*. For example: *Hay mucho tráfico porque la gente no usa el transporte público y no comparte el coche.*

EXPANDING LEARNERS

- Have students work with a partner and prepare a dialogue between someone who is very environmentally conscientious and someone who never gives the environment a second thought. The careless student may start the conversation by making a politically incorrect environmental statement, which the conscientious student will counter with sound advice. For example:
  A. *Nunca apago las luces de la casa.*
  B. *Debes apagarlas porque estás malgastando la electricidad.*

- Allow students to prepare their lines and have them present their skits in front of the class.

84 ¿Recuerdas cuando...?

▶ **Piensa** en desastres naturales que ocurrieron en tu comunidad, en tu país o en el mundo.

- terremotos
- inundaciones
- erupciones volcánicas
- huracanes

▶ **Escribe** una breve noticia sobre uno de ellos. Incluye la siguiente información:

- Cuándo y dónde ocurrió.
- Qué causas lo produjeron (naturales o humanas).
- Qué consecuencias tuvo.

Final del desafío

① ¿Hay alguien que pueda ayudarnos a montar nuestro puesto para la feria?

Claro, tenemos a varios colaboradores especialistas en comercio sostenible. Vengan conmigo.

② Les presento a Mario. Él los ayudará.

Mucho gusto.

③ Aquí encontrarán comida y bebida. En esa otra parte tenemos la ropa, los objetos de decoración y la bisutería. Son productos artesanales, hechos a mano. Espero que encuentren lo que necesitan.

85 En la tienda de comercio justo

▶ **Lee** el diálogo y responde a estas preguntas.

1. ¿Dónde están Daniel y Michelle?
2. ¿Para qué han ido allí?

 ▶ **Habla** con tu compañero(a). ¿Cómo continúa la historia de Daniel y Michelle? ¿Encontrarán lo que buscan en esa tienda? Escriban el diálogo que sigue a estas escenas.

 → **TU DESAFÍO** · Visita la página web. Escucha las preguntas de tu *Minientrevista Desafío 3* y escribe las respuestas.

trescientos setenta y siete 377

---

83. Alternatively, have the class divide into five groups and assign one situation to each group. Then, ask them to create a skit to dramatize their situation.

84. To make the presentations more engaging, you may organize the activity as a local TV news program. Encourage students to set up part of the classroom as a TV studio and prepare visuals to accompany the news presentation. If possible, record the presentations for the students to watch afterward. Depending on the number of students, you may want to consider dividing the class into pairs or small groups.

85. To expand this activity, have students look for examples of the personal direct object in the dialogue. Ask them to explain why the personal *a* is needed or not.

Answer Key

82. Answers will vary. Sample answers:
    2. Hay muchos parques contaminados por la basura que tira la gente, así que hay parques que limitan el número de visitantes.
    3. Los bosques están desapareciendo por la deforestación. Y por eso se está destruyendo el hábitat de muchas especies que pueden llegar a extinguirse.
    ▶ Answers will vary.

83. Answers will vary.
    ▶ Answers will vary.

84. Answers will vary.
    ▶ Answers will vary.

85. 1. Están en una ONG en la que hay una tienda de productos de comercio justo.
    2. Han ido a esa tienda porque necesitan productos para montar su puesto para la feria de comercio justo.
    ▶ Answers will vary.

Additional Resources

Fans Online activities
Practice Workbook

Para terminar

Presentation

- In this section, students will review the unit objectives and put them into practice. They will read a newspaper article about some ecological initiatives that are being taken in Mexico, and will comment on a quote using the vocabulary and the strategies that they have learned in this unit. Students will also select one of the following *desafíos* to develop: research an animal in danger of extinction and make recommendations to protect it, prepare a presentation about a celebration of the solstices or equinoxes in a Hispanic country, or find information about handicrafts from a Hispanic country and create a poster to share with the class.

Activities	Standards	Resources
86.	1.2, 1.3, 2.1	
87.	1.1, 1.2, 3.1	
88. Tu desafío	1.2, 1.3, 2.1, 2.2, 3.1	

Teaching Suggestions

Warm-Up / Independent Starter

- Have students go back and review the vocabulary and grammar sections in this unit. Ask them to write a paragraph explaining why they think it is important to take care of the environment and to include three recommendations (*propuestas ecológicas*) that they may have.

Preparation

- Ask students to share their paragraphs from the Independent Starter. Explain to the class that they will be voting on three paragraphs: the one with the best arguments, the one with the best recommendations, and the one with the best use of language. Suggest that they take notes as their classmates read their paragraphs so that they may cast an informed vote. If possible, give the winners an ecological award (e.g., a notebook made of recycled paper, a pen made of recycled bottles, a recycled bag).

- Then discuss the weather today with the class. What is the weather like in your community? Is today's weather typical for this time of the year?

Para terminar

Todo junto

LEER Y ESCRIBIR

 86 Propuestas ecológicas

▶ **Lee** este artículo de prensa.

México vive con energía renovable

11 de septiembre de 2011

Con el objetivo de tender puentes (*mend the bridges*) entre las empresas dedicadas a las energías renovables y funcionarios de gobierno, investigadores, académicos, organizaciones no gubernamentales y personas interesadas en el tema, la Asociación Nacional de Energía Solar (ANES) organiza la XXXV Semana Nacional de Energía Solar 2011. El tema de la semana es «México vive con Energía Renovable» y tendrá lugar en la ciudad de Chihuahua del 3 al 8 de octubre. Con esto la Asociación cumple con su objetivo fundamental de promover el uso de las fuentes renovables de energía en México de manera ininterrumpida desde su fundación en 1976.

Durante el congreso habrá talleres (*workshops*) de actualización impartidos por expertos en la materia y se hablará de temas de gran importancia para la industria como normas para equipos y sistemas solares, energías renovables en edificios o leyes para el aprovechamiento de la energía renovable, entre muchas otras. También se entregará el premio al Emprendedor Solar, un concurso destinado a inventores, investigadores, ingenieros, estudiantes y emprendedores que presenten una propuesta empresarial original, basada en tecnologías de energía solar o renovable, a un jurado proveniente del sector académico y empresarial. Se premiarán las tres mejores propuestas.

Fuente: http://www.oem.com.mx/elsoldemexico (texto adaptado)

▶ **Responde** a estas preguntas.

1. ¿Qué evento se celebra del 3 al 8 de octubre?
2. ¿Quién lo organiza?
3. ¿Cuál es su tema?
4. ¿Cómo se llama el premio que van a entregar?
5. ¿Qué ventajas crees que tiene este tipo de iniciativas?

LEER Y HABLAR

 87 ¿Somos un problema?

▶ **Lee** estas palabras del científico español Ramón Margalef.

> «El hombre no solo es un problema para sí, sino también para la biosfera en que le ha tocado vivir».

 ▶ **Habla** con tu compañero(a). ¿Qué quieren decir las palabras de Margalef? ¿Por qué los seres humanos somos un problema para la biosfera? Pongan varios ejemplos.

Modelo A. *Yo creo que Ramón Margalef quiere decir que el hombre no cuida la naturaleza ni se preocupa del medio ambiente. Por eso es un problema para la biosfera.*
B. *Estoy de acuerdo. Por ejemplo, el hombre causa la contaminación del aire.*

Differentiated instruction

DEVELOPING LEARNERS

- Ask students which word does not belong and explain why it does not belong.

1. el pez   el ave   la industria (la industria)
2. el anfibio   el estaño   el hierro (el anfibio)
3. la galaxia   el carbón   el meteorito (el carbón)
4. el granizo   el vidrio   las latas (el granizo)
5. la madera   la ecología   los ecosistemas (la madera)
6. lluvioso   soleado   nuboso (soleado)
7. respetar   brillar   fomentar (brillar)

EXPANDING LEARNERS

- Ask students to review the *desafíos* in this unit, select one, and write a conclusion that goes beyond the *Final del desafío* in their texts. Students should state whether they think the participants will complete their challenge successfully or not, and explain why. Students should also comment on the compatibility of the participants. Do they think the tasks could have been accomplished more successfully if there had been different partners? Ask students how they would have handled the *desafío* they selected.

Tu desafío

88 **La naturaleza y el medio ambiente**

¿Recuerdas los desafíos de los personajes? ¿Cuál te gusta más? Elige una de estas opciones y resuelve tu desafío.

DESAFÍO Ⓐ

Investiga sobre un animal en peligro de extinción. Sigue estos pasos:

- Descríbelo: explica cómo es, dónde vive...
- Explica por qué está en peligro de extinción.
- Haz recomendaciones sobre lo que se puede hacer para protegerlo.

DESAFÍO Ⓑ

Busca información sobre una celebración de un país hispano relacionada con los solsticios o los equinoccios.

Haz una breve presentación en clase. Explica dónde se celebra, su origen y en qué consiste.

DESAFÍO Ⓒ

Busca información sobre productos artesanales procedentes de países hispanos.

Haz un póster. Incluye fotografías o dibujos de los productos y esta información:

- Qué producto es y cuál es su origen.
- De qué está hecho y para qué sirve.
- Qué precio tiene.

trescientos setenta y nueve 379

Activities

86. Ask students to scan the article to find the type of renewable energy that is mentioned most. Then, before students start reading the article, have them read the five comprehension questions. After students have read the article, write the word *taller* on the board and make sure students understand it. Then, ask them to identify the topics that will be discussed during the conference. Clarify words like *tema* (topic, theme) or *premio* (award) before students answer the comprehension questions.

87. To expand this activity, you may want to ask students to work in pairs to prepare a sentence that could be used as an ecological quote. Ask them to be creative and display their quotes in the classroom.

88. Display students' work in the classroom and have the class vote on the best entry in each category.

Answer Key

86. 1. Se celebra la XXXV Semana Nacional de Energía Solar 2011.
    2. Lo organiza la Asociación Nacional de Energía Solar (ANES).
    3. El tema de la semana es «México vive con Energía Renovable».
    4. Premio al Emprendedor Solar.
    5. Answers will vary.

87. Answers will vary
    ▶ Answers will vary.

88. Answers will vary.

Additional Resources

Fans Online activities

HERITAGE LANGUAGE LEARNERS

- Ask students to identify some environmental problems in their family's country of origin. Have them explain how these problems are either escalating, under control, or resolved, and which organizations are responsible for trying to solve the problem. Ask students if environmental issues are political issues and whether the local population or the government gives these matters importance. Encourage students to compare how ecological concerns are viewed in this country and in their heritage country.

CRITICAL THINKING

- Ask students to predict what they think the state of planet Earth might be like two hundred years from now. Have students consider the toll of natural disasters and ecological problems such as global warming, deforestation, the greenhouse effect, and the depletion of our natural resources. Students might consider the plight of endangered species and the effects of air and water pollution, as well as a growing population. Ask students to write a few paragraphs describing the future as well as proposing some solutions to these problems.

MAPA CULTURAL

Espacios naturales singulares

Presentation

- This section presents information about some unique natural areas of the Spanish-speaking world. The images serve as a reference point for additional cultural readings and activities that expand on the skills students learned in this unit.

Activities	Standards	Resources
Mapa cultural	1.2, 2.1, 3.1	Video
89.	1.2, 1.3, 3.1, 4.2, 5.1	

Cultural Topics

- **El delta del río Orinoco.** River deltas are land areas that are formed at the mouth of a river. Deltas create expanses of wetlands that are very rich in nutrients, providing a habitat for a large variety of flora and fauna. The Orinoco River, which flows through Venezuela, constitutes one of the major river systems of South America. Its delta, on the Atlantic Ocean, extends for about 275 miles. The swamp forests of this delta provide a unique habitat for several endemic species. Some, such as the Orinoco crocodile, the Amazon River dolphin, and the giant river otter, are endangered.

- **Anfibios en peligro.** Pollution, habitat destruction, and a deadly skin fungus are some of the causes of dramatic declines in the population of amphibians throughout the world. It is believed that about one-third of the world's known amphibian species are threatened or extinct. This decline has been closely documented in the cloud forests of Monteverde, in Costa Rica, where several species of frogs and toads have become extinct in the past thirty years. The scientific community has responded by creating the Amphibian Conservation Action Plan, which aims to coordinate global action for implementing amphibian conservation.

Teaching Suggestions

Warm-Up / Independent Starter

- Ask students to think of a national park or nature preserve that they have visited or know. Have them list some of the flora and fauna typical of this natural area.

Espacios naturales singulares

En nuestro planeta hay numerosas áreas de especial valor ecológico. Pero muchos de estos espacios naturales se encuentran amenazados por la acción del ser humano. Es necesario encontrar el equilibrio entre la conservación de estos espacios tan singulares y el desarrollo económico de nuestra sociedad.

Cabo de Hornos (Chile)

Ubicación: sur de Chile.
Superficie: 4.884.273 hectáreas.
Ecosistemas: bosques lluviosos, tundra, matorral (*scrubland*).

La Reserva del Cabo de Hornos, situada al sur de la Patagonia, alberga el ecosistema forestal más austral del mundo. En esta región hace mucho frío y viento durante todo el año, y por eso allí viven pocas especies. Entre la vegetación hay gran variedad de líquenes (*lichens*) y musgos (*mosses*).

Las aguas de esta zona son muy peligrosas para los barcos por las corrientes, el fuerte oleaje y los icebergs.

El pingüino de Magallanes es una especie característica de la Patagonia.

Lanzarote (España)

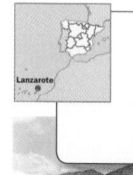

Ubicación: islas Canarias (España).
Superficie: 84.610 hectáreas.
Ecosistemas: volcánico, costero.

La isla de Lanzarote, en el archipiélago español de Canarias, es de origen volcánico. En los siglos XVIII y XIX hubo numerosas erupciones que alteraron el 25% de su superficie: tiene dunas de arena negra volcánica y restos de lava.

En Lanzarote viven muchas especies vegetales y animales que se han adaptado al medio seco, volcánico y hostil de los campos de lava. La isla fue declarada Reserva de la Biosfera en 1993.

380 trescientos ochenta

Differentiated Instruction

DEVELOPING LEARNERS

- Explain to students that they will create an illustrated map of the natural areas mentioned in this *Mapa cultural*. You may want to have students work in pairs or small groups for this activity. Ask them to trace the map of the Americas (i.e., North, Central, and South America), the Atlantic Ocean, and the Canary Islands onto chart paper. Then have students determine the location of the four natural areas covered in this *Mapa cultural* and label them. Next, students will draw icons and other illustrations that represent the unique flora, fauna, and ecosystems of these protected areas.

EXPANDING LEARNERS

- Have students work in small groups and assign to each group one of the animals mentioned in this *Mapa cultural* (i.e., *el pingüino de Magallanes, el ocelote, el jaguar, el tiburón ballena*). Ask groups to research their assigned animal. They should focus their research on the unique adaptations of this animal to the environment where it lives and its conservation status. Ask groups to share their information with the class.

Las Yungas (Argentina)

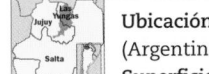

Ubicación: provincias de Salta y Jujuy (Argentina).
Superficie: 1.328.270 hectáreas.
Ecosistemas: selvas y bosques de montaña.

La Reserva de las Yungas, en el norte de Argentina, es la zona de mayor biodiversidad del país. Las Yungas son las selvas de las laderas orientales de los Andes, entre los 400 y los 3.000 metros de altitud. El clima es cálido y húmedo, y las nubes cubren estas selvas gran parte del año.

El ocelote y el jaguar son dos felinos que viven en el ecosistema de las Yungas.

Arrecife Alacranes (México)

Ubicación: Golfo de México.
Superficie: 333.768 hectáreas.
Ecosistemas: arrecifes de coral.

El arrecife Alacranes es el mayor banco de corales del Golfo de México. Sirve de barrera natural en tormentas y huracanes, y protege las costas de la erosión. Desde 2006 forma parte de la Red Mundial de Reservas de la Biosfera de la UNESCO.

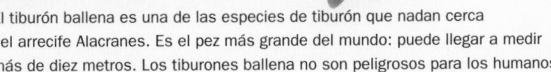

El tiburón ballena es una de las especies de tiburón que nadan cerca del arrecife Alacranes. Es el pez más grande del mundo: puede llegar a medir más de diez metros. Los tiburones ballena no son peligrosos para los humanos.

89 **Un planeta singular**

 ▶ **Resume** la información en una tabla. Incluye estos datos:

1. Nombre del espacio natural y ubicación.
2. Ecosistemas.
3. Elementos singulares.
4. Valor ecológico.

 ▶ **Añade** a la tabla dos espacios naturales singulares de tu país. Comparte la información con la clase.

HERITAGE LANGUAGE LEARNERS

• Ask students to choose a natural area or an ecosystem in their heritage country that is of particular interest to them. Have them focus on a specific issue that needs attention (e.g., a threatened animal or plant species, urban or agricultural encroachment, overexploitation of the resources). Ask students to research the issue thoroughly and find out what is being done, if anything, to address the problem. Then have students come up with a plan of action to help solve or deal with the issue. Encourage students to present to the class.

MULTIPLE INTELLIGENCES:
Naturalistic Intelligence

• Have students work in small groups and assign each group one of the four areas discussed in this *Mapa cultural*. Ask groups to research endemic plants or animals of their assigned area and choose one to investigate further. Have students research the importance in the natural cycle of the particular plant or animal they have chosen. For example, some lichens fix nitrogen to the soil, making it available for trees and larger plants, which in turn serve as refuge and food for animals. Ask each group to present their findings to the class.

Preparation

■ Invite students to share their Independent Starters. You may want to compile a list on the board of the parks and natural areas students mention. As a class, discuss the flora and fauna as well as the ecosystems that are typical of these natural areas. If time allows, ask students to research the challenges some of these areas face. For instance, invasive species, air pollution, urban encroachment, and even direct impact from a large number of visitors are some of the threats many American national parks and nature preserves face.

■ Display a map of the world and guide students to locate the four regions covered in this *Mapa cultural* (i.e., the southern tip of Chile; the island of Lanzarote in the Atlantic Ocean off the coast of Morocco; the provinces of Salta and Jujuy, in northwestern Argentina; the Caribbean coast along Mexico's Yucatan Peninsula).

Activities

89. For the second part of this activity, you may want to divide the class into small groups. Assign each group a different natural reserve or protected area to research. Ask groups to assign different tasks to each group member so that their presentation is as complete and well organized as possible. Encourage students to include images of their assigned natural reserve as well as of its flora and fauna. Then have groups present their information to the class.

Answer Key

89. Answers will vary.
  ▶ Answers will vary.

Additional Resources

Fans Online activities
Practice Workbook

Unit 7

ESCRITURA

Un reportaje medioambiental

Presentation

- In this section, students will practice and extend their writing skills. They will apply the vocabulary and grammar they have learned in this unit to write a cause and effect essay about an environmental issue affecting their community.

Activities	Standards	Resources
Escritura	1.1, 1.2, 1.3, 3.1	

Teaching Suggestions

Warm-Up / Independent Starter

- Have students list in their notebooks two or three environmental issues affecting their community. Then ask them to think about some possible causes for theses issues.

Preparation

- Have students share their Independent Starters with the class. On the board, list the issues students mention. If necessary, bring more issues to light by asking additional questions. For example: Is air or water pollution an issue? Are there enough green areas? Are the ecosystems of these green areas healthy? Does the community have a recycling program? Are the natural resources being exploited in a responsible manner? Then discuss as a class some of the possible causes for these issues.

- Ask for a volunteer to read the Cause and Effect Writing box aloud. Explain to students that in a cause and effect essay they should first distinguish between causes (reasons) and effects (consequences), and then focus their essay on either the causes or the effects.

Step-by-Step Instructions

Piensa

- Have students use their Independent Starters and the class discussion of the Preparation activity to help them select a topic for their essay. As students research their topics, remind them that they should name the sources of their information. You may want to require students to include a bibliography at the end of their essay.

382

ESCRITURA

Un reportaje medioambiental

Cause and effect writing

Most events or situations have a variety of causes that led to their creation. They may, in turn, have an array of effects on future actions, events, or situations.

In a cause and effect **essay**, the writer examines either the different causes that have brought about a particular situation, or the myriad of effects that that situation has had.

El objetivo de los reportajes es informar. A través de la exposición de hechos de interés general, que pueden ser actuales o no, los reportajes presentan la información obtenida mediante una investigación. En ocasiones, el reportaje contiene entrevistas a expertos o se citan fuentes de información reconocidas.

En esta unidad vas a escribir un reportaje sobre algún problema medioambiental de tu ciudad o de tu comunidad, analizando sus causas y sus consecuencias.

Piensa

- Antes de comenzar a escribir, considera qué problemas relacionados con el medio ambiente pueden estar afectando a tu comunidad y elige uno de ellos.

- Busca información sobre las causas y las consecuencias del problema elegido. Puedes ir a la biblioteca, preguntar en distintos centros de tu comunidad relacionados con el cuidado del medio ambiente, buscar en Internet o preguntarle a tu profesor(a) de Ciencias.

- Organiza tus ideas. No olvides que cada causa tiene sus consecuencias.

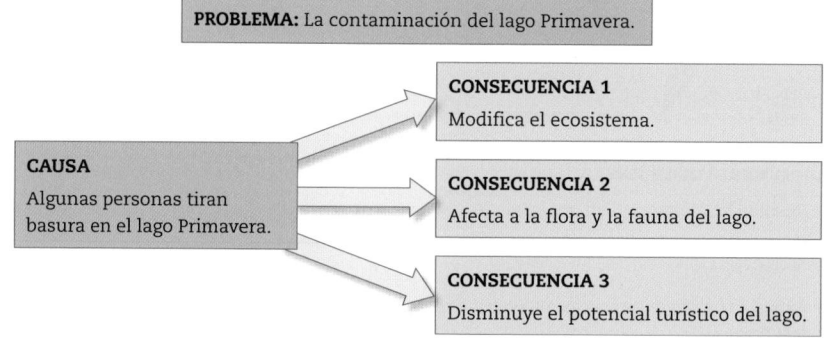

PROBLEMA: La contaminación del lago Primavera.

CAUSA
Algunas personas tiran basura en el lago Primavera.

CONSECUENCIA 1
Modifica el ecosistema.

CONSECUENCIA 2
Afecta a la flora y la fauna del lago.

CONSECUENCIA 3
Disminuye el potencial turístico del lago.

382 trescientos ochenta y dos

Rubric for Evaluation

	Content	Organization	Conventions
1 point	Both the thesis and the essay's purpose are somewhat unclear. Inappropriate and unspecific word choices.	Illogical or very basic organization. Transitions are not present or not used well. Ineffective concluding paragraph.	Many errors in spelling, punctuation, grammar, and usage. Errors obscure meaning.
3 points	Thesis is clear and is supported with some evidence. Essay's purpose is mostly clear. Some inaccurate word choices.	Logical organization of ideas. Some effective transitions are present. Concluding paragraph restates thesis, but is not very effective.	Some errors in spelling, punctuation, grammar, and usage. Errors don't interfere with meaning.

Escribe

■ Tomando como punto de partida las ideas que anotaste, escribe el borrador de tu reportaje.

Intenta que tu texto sea claro, interesante y fácil de comprender. Usa las Expresiones útiles para exponer las causas y consecuencias del problema.

■ Pon un título al reportaje. Ten en cuenta que debe referirse al tema de tu investigación y motivar al lector.

Modelo

Expresiones útiles

A causa de…	Because of …
Dado que…	Given that …
De manera que…	So that …
Debido a…	Due to …
Como…	As …
Por eso…	Therefore …
Por este motivo…	For this reason …
Por tanto…	So …

El lago Primavera: un problema de todos

La contaminación del lago Primavera, situado en las afueras de la ciudad, es un problema de todos.

Una de las causas principales de la contaminación del lago es la basura que algunas personas arrojan en los alrededores. Este comportamiento afecta a la flora y la fauna de la zona. Además causa mal olor y, por tanto, disminuye el potencial del lago como zona turística y de entretenimiento de la comunidad…

Estado actual del lago Primavera.

Revisa

■ Una vez finalizado tu borrador, revisa con cuidado el texto y comprueba que tus ideas estén correctamente enlazadas.

■ Busca una imagen o haz un dibujo para ilustrar tu reportaje. Incluye un pie de foto.

■ Intercambia tu trabajo con tu compañero(a) y revisa su reportaje. Presta atención a los errores gramaticales u ortográficos y anota tus sugerencias para mejorar su reportaje.

■ Devuelve el texto a su autor(a) con algunas sugerencias y reescribe tu trabajo incorporando los cambios necesarios para que cumpla su propósito.

Comparte

■ Lee tu reportaje a la clase. Al final, elijan los mejores trabajos y averigüen cómo publicarlos en un periódico local con ayuda de su profesor(a).

	Content	Organization	Conventions
5 points	Clearly stated and fully supported thesis. Essay's purpose is clear. Accurate, rich, and purposeful word choices.	Logical and effective organization of ideas. Uses appropriate transitions when needed. Concluding paragraph binds essay together.	Few, if any, errors in spelling, punctuation, grammar, and usage. Excellent command of the Spanish language.

ESCRITURA
Un reportaje medioambiental

■ Explain that the essay should begin with an introduction that contains a thesis statement that clearly states the focus of the essay, and a list of the major points the essay will address. It is advisable to limit the number of major points to a maximum of three to be able to provide enough supporting details. Students may choose to organize their major points chronologically, in order of importance, or by categories.

Escribe

■ Explain that a good use of transitions is especially important in a cause and effect essay. Transitions help to bridge ideas and add coherence to the text, but an overuse of transitions can be counterproductive. Therefore, encourage students to consider carefully whether a transition is needed and, if so, analyze which transition would be the best option. Ask students to classify each of the *expresiones útiles* as "transition words for cause" or "transition words for effect."

Revisa

■ Have students read their classmate's essay once without making any comments. Next, have them underline the thesis statement. Then ask students to evaluate the effectiveness of the essay. Suggest the following questions: Is the focus clear? What are the causes? What are the effects? Is it easy to distinguish between a cause and an effect? Is the information presented in an effective order? Explain to students that the answers to these questions should be apparent upon reading the essay.

Comparte

■ Ask students to be prepared to explain or define to the class any unfamiliar terms. They should also be prepared to cite some of their sources as a way of lending validity to their arguments. The tone of students' presentations should be professional and factual, but they should also show that they are truly interested in the subject.

Evaluation

■ Distribute copies of the rubric to students and discuss the evaluation criteria. Ask students to refer to the rubric as they prepare their writing and as they evaluate their classmates' essays.

REPASO

Vocabulario

Presentation

- In this section, students will review all key vocabulary from the unit, organized by themes, to prepare for an assessment. Students will complete practice activities for each of the three *Desafíos*.

Activities	Standards	Resources
1.	1.2, 1.3	
2.	1.1, 1.2	
3.	1.3, 4.2, 5.1	

Teaching Suggestions

Warm-Up / Independent Starter

- Ask students to draw a quick sketch of a forest, park, or nature preserve they know well. Then have students label their drawings with some of the flora and fauna typical of the place.

Preparation

- Pair students up to share their drawings from the Independent Starter and ask them to explain their drawings. Then, on the back of their drawings, have pairs list the following regarding the place they drew: the weather during the different seasons, natural resources, environmental threats, actions that can be taken to protect the place, and possible natural disasters. Allow students to consult their textbooks as they work on this part of the activity.

- Call on volunteers to present their natural area to the class. Then read over the *Repaso* presentation with students.

Activities

2. To extend this activity, ask students to add a paragraph to the text. They could, for instance, explain what happened that night when Carlota used her telescope, or describe a meteorological phenomenon that prevented Carlota from using her telescope. The paragraph should have at least four blank spaces to be completed with vocabulary from *Desafío 2*. Ask students to exchange their paragraphs with a classmate and complete each other's activity.

REPASO Vocabulario

El medio ambiente

el agujero de la capa de ozono	hole in the ozone layer
el cambio climático	climate change
la catástrofe ecológica	ecological catastrophe
la deforestación	deforestation
la ecología	ecology
el ecosistema	ecosystem
el efecto invernadero	greenhouse effect
la energía alternativa	alternative energy
la especie protegida	protected species
la marea negra	oil spill

Acciones

agotarse	to run out
amenazar	to threaten
concienciar	to make aware
denunciar	to report, to denounce
fomentar	to promote, to encourage
reciclar	to recycle
respetar	to respect

El tiempo meteorológico

Fenómenos meteorológicos

el arco iris	rainbow
el chubasco	heavy shower
la escarcha	frost
la gota	drop
el granizo	hail
la nevada	snowfall
la nube	cloud
el temporal	storm
la tormenta	storm
el trueno	thunder

Acciones

brillar	to shine
despejarse	to clear up
helar	to freeze
llover a cántaros	to pour (rain)
lloviznar	to drizzle
nublarse	to cloud over
soplar el viento	to blow (wind)

Adjetivos

despejado(a)	clear
lluvioso(a)	rainy
nuboso(a)	cloudy
soleado(a)	sunny

La naturaleza

Fauna

el anfibio	amphibian	el mamífero	mammal
el ave	bird	el reptil	reptile
el insecto	insect	el pez	fish

Materiales y objetos reciclables

el cartón	cardboard
el envase de plástico	plastic container
la lata	can
el papel	paper
la pila	battery
el vidrio	glass

El universo

el/la astrónomo(a)	astronomer
la constelación	constellation
la galaxia	galaxy
el meteorito	meteorite
el telescopio	telescope

Desastres naturales

el ciclón	cyclone
la erupción volcánica	volcanic eruption
el incendio forestal	forest fire
la inundación	flood
el huracán	hurricane
el terremoto	earthquake

Actividades económicas

la agricultura	agriculture
la ganadería	livestock
la industria	industry
la minería	mining
la pesca	fishing

Recursos naturales

el carbón	coal
el gas natural	natural gas
la madera	wood
los minerales	minerals

Metales

el acero	steel
el bronce	bronze
el estaño	tin
el hierro	iron
el oro	gold
la plata	silver
el plomo	lead

Differentiated Instruction

DEVELOPING LEARNERS

- Ask students to list all of the actions in this *Repaso* (e.g., *agotarse, brillar*) on a sheet of paper. While they do that, prepare index cards with vocabulary words that students can easily associate with the actions they are listing (e.g., *los recursos naturales, el sol*). Then, put the cards facedown on a table and ask students to take one. They have thirty seconds to make an association. Allow them to consult their list of actions. Examples of associations: *el vidrio → reciclar; la naturaleza → proteger; las energías alternativas → fomentar*.

EXPANDING LEARNERS

- Have students imagine that they are producing an exposé for a local TV station about a nature preserve affected by air pollution, urban encroachment, and the neglect of local authorities. Ask students to work with a partner to write the script. They should address the state of the nature preserve, offer some solutions, and encourage the public to take action. Alternatively, students can write a script for an interview between a journalist and a representative of the local authorities, who will try to make up excuses to justify the government's lack of attention to the problem.

DESAFÍO 1

1 **El medio ambiente.** Completa estas oraciones con las palabras del cuadro.

> deforestación
>
> catástrofes
>
> especies
>
> cambio climático
>
> energías
>
> marea negra

1. Yo estoy a favor del uso de _____ alternativas.
2. La _____ en los bosques tropicales ha crecido en los últimos años.
3. El petróleo del barco se extendió por el mar provocando una gran _____.
4. En Puerto Rico hay más de setenta _____ protegidas para evitar su extinción.
5. Para evitar el _____ debemos reciclar y ahorrar energía.
6. El hombre causa muchas de las _____ ecológicas del planeta.

 DESAFÍO 2

2 **Carlota y las estrellas.** Completa el texto con las palabras del cuadro.

> nubes   astrónoma   luna   despejado   telescopio   galaxia   constelaciones

El sueño de Carlota

Carlota quiere ser ___1___. Sus padres le regalaron un ___2___ por su cumpleaños. Todas las noches, Carlota mira las estrellas. Conoce el nombre de todas las ___3___. Le gustaría descubrir una ___4___ nueva. Esta noche hay ___5___ llena (*full moon*) y Carlota quiere estudiar bien cómo es. Quiere verla de cerca. Solo necesita que el cielo esté ___6___. ¡Ojalá no haya ___7___!

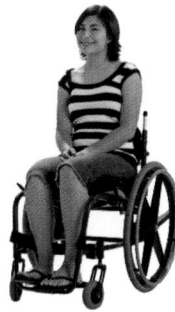

 DESAFÍO 3

3 **Economía nacional.** Escribe. ¿A qué actividades económicas se refiere cada dibujo? ¿En qué zonas o estados de tu país se realiza cada una?

 ①  ② 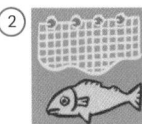 ③  ④ 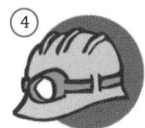 ⑤

---

3. Divide the class into five groups and assign each group one of the icons depicted in this activity. Then have groups research what their state produces in their assigned area. Once they have finished, ask groups to report to the class. Did students know that there were so many different productive activities in their state?

Answer Key

1.
1. energías
2. deforestación
3. marea negra
4. especies
5. cambio climático
6. catástrofes

2.
1. astrónoma
2. telescopio
3. constelaciones
4. galaxia
5. luna
6. despejado
7. nubes

3. Answers will vary. Sample answers:
1. La industria: En el estado de Michigan hay mucha industria relacionada con la fabricación de coches.
2. La pesca: Se realiza en las zonas costeras y en los lagos y ríos.
3. La agricultura: Hay agricultura en casi todos los estados, pero sobre todo en el medio oeste del país y en California.
4. La minería: En los estados de Wyoming y Colorado hay minas de carbón, uranio, oro, etc.
5. La ganadería: Hay mucha ganadería en los estados de Texas, Kansas, Nebraska y Oklahoma.

Additional Resources

Fans Online activities
Practice Workbook

HERITAGE LANGUAGE LEARNERS

• Ask students to compare and contrast *el tiempo meteorológico* and *la naturaleza* in their family's region of origin with those of their community in the United States. Encourage students to use a comparison-contrast chart or a similar graphic organizer to list the similarities and differences. Students should be prepared to present the information to the class and answer any questions their classmates might have.

MULTIPLE INTELLIGENCES:
Visual-Spatial Intelligence

• Divide the class into six groups and assign each group one of these regions of the continental United States: Northeast, Southeast, Southwest, Midwest, West, Pacific Northwest. Have students trace the map of their region onto chart paper and draw illustrations or paste cutout images that represent *la naturaleza, los desastres naturales, los recursos naturales,* and *las actividades económicas* of their region. Students should not label their maps. Have groups present their maps to the class. Can the class "read" the maps?

REPASO

Gramática

Presentation

- Students will review grammatical structures presented in the unit. Each grammar point is cross-referenced to the corresponding page on which it was introduced. The activities here provide systematic practice by *Desafío*.

Activities	Standards	Resources
4.	1.2, 1.3	
5.	1.2	
6.	1.2, 3.1	
7. Cultura	1.1, 1.2, 2.1, 2.2, 3.1	

Teaching Suggestions

Warm-Up / Independent Starter

- Write the following paragraph on the board. Ask students to rewrite it, adding constructions to express the time and sequence of events, and to express cause and consequence.
  No llovía. Los cultivos se secaron. Pasaron varios meses. Se vio una nube en el horizonte. Por fin comenzó a llover. Estuvo lloviendo una semana. Hubo inundaciones. Paró de llover. Salió el sol y se formó un arco iris.

Preparation

- Call on several volunteers to share their Independent Starters. Use students' paragraphs to go over the uses of *cuando, antes de (que), después de (que), porque, por, así (es) que,* and *por eso*. Point out how these expressions are needed to give the paragraph coherence and flow.

- Go over the rest of the grammar topics from this *Repaso* with the class. If needed, provide additional examples and practice activities for some of the topics.

Activities

4. Before students start forming sentences, ask them to read the phrases in the left column and classify them as "real or likely conditions" or "unlikely, hypothetical, or contrary-to-fact conditions." This will tell them what verb mood they should use in the "if" clause.

REPASO Gramática

Expresar condición (I) (pág. 346)
ORACIONES CONDICIONALES REALES.
EL INDICATIVO

si + present indicative + present indicative / future indicative / command

Si tengo tiempo, iré al gimnasio.

Expresar condición (II) (pág. 348)
ORACIONES CONDICIONALES POTENCIALES.
EL SUBJUNTIVO Y EL CONDICIONAL

si + imperfect subjunctive + conditional

Si tuviera tiempo, iría al gimnasio.

Expresar tiempo (pág. 358)

EXPRESAR TIEMPO

cuando + indicative (past or habitual event)
cuando + subjunctive (future event)

Cuando nieva, hace frío.
Llámame cuando llegues.

EXPRESAR ANTERIORIDAD O POSTERIORIDAD

antes de después de	+ infinitive
antes de que	+ subjunctive
después de que	+ subjunctive + indicative

El presente perfecto de subjuntivo (pág. 360)
PRESENTE PERFECTO DE SUBJUNTIVO. VERBOS REGULARES

HABLAR	COMER	VIVIR
haya hablado	haya comido	haya vivido
hayas hablado	hayas comido	hayas vivido
haya hablado	haya comido	haya vivido
hayamos hablado	hayamos comido	hayamos vivido
hayáis hablado	hayáis comido	hayáis vivido
hayan hablado	hayan comido	hayan vivido

Expresar causa y consecuencia (pág. 370)

EXPRESIONES DE CAUSA

porque + indicative

por + infinitive

EXPRESIONES DE CONSECUENCIA

así (es) que + indicative

por eso + indicative

La preposición *a* personal (pág. 372)

- Use *a* with direct objects that:
  - Refer to a definite or specific person or people.
  - Refer to a definite pet.
  - Are pronouns such as *alguien, nadie, alguno, ninguno, todos.*
- Don't use *a* in these cases:
  - When the direct object refers to an indefinite person or group of people.
  - With the verbs *tener* and *haber.*

Differentiated Instruction

DEVELOPING LEARNERS

- For further practice with the present perfect subjunctive, ask students to imagine that they are visiting an earthquake disaster zone and have them complete the following sentences:
  1. *Es una lástima que (ocurrir) esta catástrofe. (haya ocurrido)*
  2. *Espero que los bomberos (rescatar) a las personas atrapadas. (hayan rescatado)*
  3. *No creo que la población (estar) preparada. (haya estado)*
  4. *Dudo que (llegar) todos los equipos de rescate. (hayan llegado)*
  5. *Me alegro de que no (haber) un incendio. (haya habido)*

EXPANDING LEARNERS

- Ask students to select a sentence from activity 5 to serve as the beginning of a story. They should use constructions to express the time and sequence of events, and to express cause and consequence in their story. For example: *Cuando me gradúe, haré una gran fiesta porque es un logro que hay que celebrar. Antes de enviar las invitaciones, haré una lista de las personas que quiero invitar. Cuando ya sepa cuántas personas vendrán, contrataré a...* Invite students to share their stories with a classmate or with the class.

DESAFÍO 1

4 **Si...** Escribe oraciones condicionales.

Condición	Resultado
1. conseguir (yo) un trabajo mejor	comprar (yo) un coche nuevo
2. hacer mucho frío	helarse las carreteras
3. tener (tú) más años	entender (tú) el problema
4. salir (tú) a la calle	ponerse (tú) una bufanda
5. salir (yo) pronto de la escuela	ir (yo) a casa de mi mejor amigo

 DESAFÍO 2

5 **Acierta con los verbos.** Completa las oraciones. Pon los verbos en el modo correcto.

1. Me levanto todos los días antes de que _____ el sol.
   _{salir}
2. Cuando yo _____, haré una gran fiesta.
   _{graduarse}
3. Limpiaré la sala después de que _____ todos.
   _{irse}
4. Cuando yo _____ de limpiar el suelo de la sala, entró el gato.
   _{terminar}
5. Nosotros siempre cenamos después de que el niño _____.
   _{dormirse}

 DESAFÍO 3

6 **Tú corriges.** Completa estas oraciones con la *a* personal si es necesario.

1. Ayer tuve que llevar _____ mi perro al veterinario.
2. Me gusta conocer _____ gente nueva.
3. El café de la plaza necesita _____ meseros.
4. ¿Hay _____ alguien aquí?
5. Tengo _____ un hijo de seis años.

 **CULTURA**

7 **De viaje por Latinoamérica.** Responde a estas preguntas.

1. ¿Qué es la orquídea? ¿Y el cóndor? ¿De qué países son símbolo nacional?
2. ¿Qué es el Inti Raymi?
3. ¿Qué espacios naturales singulares de Latinoamérica conoces? Nombra al menos dos.

HERITAGE LANGUAGE LEARNERS

- Have students write two paragraphs about a contrary-to-fact situation. Ask them to imagine that they live and attend school in their heritage country or in a Spanish-speaking country they know. Have them research what students their age do, the classes they take, their schedule, etc. Then ask students to use that information to write their paragraphs. For example: *Si viviera en México estaría en la preparatoria. No tomaría clases de...* Ask students to share their paragraphs with the class and discuss similarities and differences between their actual life and their hypothetical life.

MULTIPLE INTELLIGENCES:
Verbal-Linguistic Intelligence

- Ask students to imagine that they are members of an environmental organization. Have pairs make a plea to help save an endangered animal or plant. To achieve greater impact, have students ask their audience to put themselves in the endangered species' shoes. For example: *Si fueras un oso panda y vieras desaparecer tu hábitat, tendrías miedo por el futuro de tus hijos. Por eso, te unirías a otros osos panda y...* Ask students to share their pleas with the class and hold a vote on the most heartfelt and touching plea.

Unit 7

REPASO

Gramática

6. To extend this activity, give students the following sentences and ask them to add the personal *a* to those sentences that need it:
   1. *Llamo mi novia diariamente. (a mi novia)*
   2. *La contaminación nos afecta todos. (a todos)*
   3. *La compañía busca biólogos con experiencia.*
   4. *Hay muchas personas que reciclan.*

Answer Key

4. Answers will vary. Sample answers:
1. Si consiguiera un trabajo mejor, me compraría un coche nuevo.
2. Si hace mucho frío, se hielan las carreteras.
3. Si tuvieras más años, entenderías el problema.
4. Si sales a la calle, ponte una bufanda.
5. Si salgo pronto de la escuela, iré a casa de mi mejor amigo.

5. 1. salga   4. terminé
2. me gradúe   5. se duerme
3. se vayan

6. 1. a   3. *X*   5. *X*
2. *X*   4. *X*

7. 1. La orquídea es una flor y es el símbolo de Venezuela. El cóndor es un ave y es el símbolo de Colombia y Ecuador.
2. Es una fiesta en honor al Sol que se celebra el 24 de junio en Cuzco, Perú. Esta celebración es de origen inca y marca el comienzo del solsticio de invierno en el hemisferio sur.
3. Answers will vary. Sample answer: En el extremo sur de Chile se encuentra la Reserva del Cabo de Hornos, que es una región donde hace mucho frío pues está cerca de la Antártida. En las costas del Caribe mexicano se encuentra el arrecife Alacranes, que es el mayor banco de corales del Golfo de México.

Additional Resources

Fans Online activities
Practice Workbook

387

PROYECTO

Medio ambiente

Presentation

- In this section, students will apply the vocabulary, grammar, and cultural information they have learned in this unit to prepare a publicity campaign to promote World Environment Day.

Activities	Standards	Resources
Paso 1	1.1, 1.2, 2.1, 3.1, 5.1	
Paso 2	1.2, 5.1, 5.2	
Paso 3	1.3, 5.1	
Paso 4	1.1, 1.3, 5.1, 5.2	

Teaching Suggestions

Warm-Up / Independent Starter

- Ask students to think of environmental projects or activities in which they have participated or would be interested in participating.

Preparation

- Invite students to share their Independent Starters with the class. Is the class familiar with most of these activities? Which ones do they think are most effective? Which would be most engaging for students their age? Ask students who have participated in some of these environmental campaigns to share their experiences with the class. Ask them to include information about what they think worked well and things they feel that can be improved upon.

- Ask for a volunteer to read aloud the project introduction. Encourage students to visit the website of the United Nations Environment Program (UNEP) to learn more about this initiative.

Step-by-Step Instructions

Paso 1

- Ask students to choose a topic that they care about or feel strongly about. Their campaign will be more effective and they will have more to say if they identify with the topic.

- Students will find additional ideas for their campaign on the Teens for Planet Earth website and on the Students for the Environment link at the U.S. Environmental Protection Agency website.

388

PROYECTO

Una campaña publicitaria en favor del

medio ambiente

WORLD ENVIRONMENT DAY | 05 JUNE
Green Economy: Does it include you?

Every year on June 5, the United Nations celebrates World Environment Day. On this day, environmental awareness and protection activities are organized around the world. The website of the United Nations Environment Programme (UNEP) gives some ideas for celebrating this day:

Llamamos a la acción. Organice una limpieza de su barrio o su localidad; no utilice bolsas plásticas y motive a su comunidad a hacer lo mismo; plante un árbol o mejor organice un movimiento para sembrar árboles en comunidad; camine al trabajo; inicie una jornada de reciclaje… Las posibilidades son ilimitadas.

In this project, you will prepare a publicity campaign in order to promote this initiative.

DÍA MUNDIAL DEL MEDIO AMBIENTE
PNUMA
5 DE JUNIO
Bosques: La Naturaleza a su servicio
En apoyo del Año Internacional de los Bosques de las Naciones Unidas

PASO 1 Planifica tu campaña

- Decide el tema de la campaña. Aquí tienes algunas ideas:
  – Diez acciones para proteger el medio ambiente.
  – Cómo ahorrar energía.
  – Fomentar el reciclaje.
  – Contra el cambio climático.
  – Por la protección de las especies amenazadas.

- Decide cómo vas a difundir tu campaña. Comparte tus ideas con tus compañeros(as).

Yo voy a hacer un póster.

Yo voy a hacer un video y lo subiré a Internet.

También podemos hacer una entrada de blog o poner mensajes en las redes sociales.

Nosotras vamos a crear mensajes para imprimir en camisetas.

388 trescientos ochenta y ocho

Rubric for Evaluation

	Content	Organization	Presentation
1 point	Main idea is not identified. The campaign shows limited original ideas and is not persuasive.	Inefficient use of time. Information is disorganized or unclear. The campaign is not well designed and organized.	Unclear communication. Delivery is not fluent. Many errors in vocabulary and grammar.
3 points	Main idea is partially defined and its importance is somewhat highlighted. The campaign is creative and persuasive.	Time is used well. Information is mostly organized but lacks some clarity. The campaign is mostly well designed and organized.	Clear communication and fluent delivery. Mostly correct vocabulary and grammar.

PASO 2 Define el contenido de la campaña

- Haz un guion con las ideas que quieras transmitir sobre el tema elegido. Ten en cuenta que las campañas publicitarias tienen el objetivo de convencer de algo o animar a hacer algo.

  Modelo

  – Estamos destruyendo los bosques, aunque los necesitamos para respirar y para vivir.
  – Necesitamos los bosques para evitar el cambio climático.

- Piensa en una frase que refleje bien la idea central de tu campaña. Ese será tu eslogan.

  Modelo

  ¡Entre todos podemos!

- Reúne un banco de imágenes adecuado para tu anuncio. Si vas a hacer un video, define qué imágenes vas a utilizar.

PASO 3 Realiza tu anuncio

- Escribe los textos de tu anuncio. Ten en cuenta el medio que vas a utilizar: póster, video, radio...
- Trabaja sobre el documento final:
  – Haz el póster incluyendo las imágenes y los textos definitivos.
  – Diseña el texto y los motivos gráficos para las camisetas.
  – Graba tu video.
  – Graba tu anuncio para la radio.
  – ...

  En todos los casos, el eslogan (la idea central) debe quedar bien destacado.

PASO 4 Comparte tu anuncio

- Muestra tu campaña a tus compañeros(as) y difúndela para que llegue a toda la comunidad.

Unidad 7

Autoevaluación

¿Qué has aprendido en esta unidad?

Do these activities to evaluate how well you can manage in Spanish.

> Evalúa tus habilidades. Para cada punto di Muy bien, Bien o Necesito practicar más.

a. Can you express hypothetical situations related to the environment?
> ▶ Tell how your community will benefit if everyone recycles.
> ▶ If you had the resources, what would you do to help the environment? State three conditions and what you would do about them.

b. Can you relate future actions?
> ▶ Tell two things you will do in the future that are dependent on the actions of other people.
> ▶ Describe three things that your friends will do before and after it rains today.

c. Can you express cause and consequence?
> ▶ Tell three causes of a natural disaster that you know of.
> ▶ Describe three of the consequences of an earthquake.

	Content	**Organization**	**Presentation**
5 points	Main idea is clearly defined and its importance is demonstrated. The campaign is creative, original, and persuasive.	Time is used wisely. Information is clearly organized visually and logically. The campaign is very well designed and organized.	Clear and fluent communication. Very motivating, upbeat delivery. Correct and complete vocabulary and grammar.

PROYECTO

Medio ambiente

Paso 2

- The students' aim is to get their audience involved and prompt them into action. A catchy slogan and powerful images are some of the things that will help students make an impression. They may want to provide a few important statistics and facts to impress upon their audience a sense of urgency to act.

Paso 3

- Discuss with students the value of music in advertisement to help get the message across. They could, for instance, create music for their slogan, or use appropriate background music for their presentation.

Paso 4

- You may want to promote students' ideas in the community by sending their suggestions to local Spanish-language media outlets. Alternatively, you may allow students to promote their campaigns in school.

Evaluation

- Distribute copies of the rubric to students. Discuss the evaluation criteria and explain how this project will be graded. Encourage students to refer to the rubric as they prepare their projects.

Content

- Have students analyze their campaigns and ask themselves these questions: Does my campaign inform the audience about something of interest to them? Is my message clear? Is it persuasive? Does the main point stand out? Is there a differentiating factor that makes my campaign unique?

Organization

- Encourage students to pay special attention to the introduction and the ending. The introduction should set the scene and gain the audience's attention. The ending should drive the point home in one sentence.

Presentation

- Allocate ten-minute time slots (five minutes for larger classes) for students to present their campaigns. They should have rehearsed their presentations so that they use their time wisely. Have the class vote on the best campaign.

Unit 8 En sociedad

Objectives

- To describe and narrate in the past.
- To give factual statements in the indicative.
- To express wishes, opinions, and values.
- To use the passive voice.
- To differentiate between definite and indefinite articles.
- To use the subjunctive mood.
- To learn about the history of some Hispanic cities and countries.

- To learn about the history and culture of ancient civilizations in Latin America.
- To discuss the political systems in some Hispanic countries.
- To learn about the goals and practices of some multinational organizations.
- To describe and compare national symbols.
- To discuss the practices and products of multicultural populations.

- To learn about ways Hispanic populations celebrate and preserve their cultures.
- To identify main ideas and significant details in a variety of texts.
- To engage in meaningful conversations.
- To know and apply the different stages of the writing process: planning, writing, revising, and sharing.

Contents

Vocabulary

- Useful expressions to ask for wants and preferences, to express indifference or lack of preference, and to express resignation.
- Review: Words for politics, society, history, and civilizations.
- Historical figures, historical events, ancient civilizations, and archaeology.
- Politics and government, posts and titles, and ideologies.
- Society and community.

Grammar

- The passive voice.
- To talk about past actions and situations.
- To talk about the different stages of an action.
- To talk about factual events: The indicative mood.
- Definite and indefinite articles.
- Uses of the subjunctive mood.

Culture

- History and culture of the Mayan civilization. Mayan archaeological treasures.
- UNESCO World Heritage Sites.
- *La Organización de los Estados Americanos (OEA)*.
- The meaning of national flags.
- Women political leaders in Hispanic countries.
- *La Orquesta Sinfónica Juvenil de las Américas*.
- Multicultural populations and celebrations.
- *El Museo del Barrio (Nueva York)*.
- A poem by Nicolás Guillén (Cuba).
- *Una ciudad con historia: Barcelona*.
- History of Hispanic cities and countries.

Evaluation Criteria

- State past actions and situations.
- Demonstrate understanding of the formulation and use of the passive voice.
- Describe an important event or time period in the history of a Latin American country.
- Discuss the history and culture of the Mayan civilization.
- Give factual statements using the indicative mood.

- Discuss the different stages of an action.
- Describe the political and governmental systems in various Hispanic countries.
- Describe what some organizations do to help Latin American populations.
- Name important political figures in Latin American history.
- Differentiate between the use of definite and indefinite articles.

- Use the subjunctive mood.
- Discuss the advantages of the cultural diversity in cities and countries.
- Discuss multicultural celebrations.
- Describe and compare the cultural heritage of students in the class.
- Describe the antique or modern characteristics of a city.
- Write a persuasive essay.

Unit Plan _____

Las tareas/Antes de empezar

Estimated time: 1 session.

Text: *Pasado y presente del mundo hispano.*

Functions & forms:
- Useful expressions to ask for wants and preferences, to express indifference or lack of preference, and to express resignation.
- Review of known vocabulary about politics, society, history, and civilizations.

⚑ DESAFÍO 1

Estimated time: 5 sessions.

Text: *Un mapa muy valioso.*

Functions & forms:
- To describe and narrate in the past.
- Historical figures, historical events, and ancient civilizations.
- The passive voice.
- To talk about past events and situations.

Culture:
- *Patrimonio de la Humanidad.*
- *La herencia maya.*
- *La numeración maya.*

Reading: *La Escalinata de los Jeroglíficos.*

⚑ DESAFÍO 2

Estimated time: 5 sessions.

Text: *Una organización multinacional.*

Functions & forms:
- To talk about factual events.
- Politics and government.
- To talk about the stages of an action.
- To state factual statements: The indicative mood.

Culture:
- *La misión de la OEA.*
- *El significado de las banderas.*
- *Mujeres en el poder.*

Reading: *Entrevista a Debra McKeon.*

⚑ DESAFÍO 3

Estimated time: 6 sessions.

Text: *Un calendario multicultural.*

Functions & forms:
- To express wishes, opinions, and values.
- Society.
- Definite and indefinite articles.
- The subjunctive mood (review).

Culture:
- *El corazón de la multiculturalidad.*
- *El Museo del Barrio.*
- *El Festival de Comida Internacional.*

Reading: *La muralla.*

Para terminar

Estimated time: 1 session.

Todo junto: Review of *Desafíos 1–3.*

Tu desafío:
- *Desafío A:* Prepare a presentation about the history of an indigenous population in the Americas.
- *Desafío B:* Prepare a presentation about an international organization that addresses human rights, peace, or equality.
- *Desafío C:* Create a brochure about international celebrations in your community.

MAPA CULTURAL

Estimated time: 1 session.

Mapa cultural: *Una ciudad con historia: Barcelona.*

ESCRITURA

Estimated time: 1 session.

Writing: *Y tú, ¿qué opinas?*

PROYECTO/EVALUACIÓN

Estimated time: 2 sessions.

Project: *Una presentación sobre un país de Latinoamérica.*

Self-evaluation: *Autoevaluación.*

Unit 8 En sociedad

Standards for Learning Spanish

 COMMUNICATION

1.1. Interpersonal mode
- Exchange personal opinions and experiences.
- Engage in oral conversations using personal knowledge and experience.
- Exchange assignments with a partner and evaluate each other's work.
- Discuss hypothetical situations with a partner.
- Compare and contrast information with a partner.
- Apply personal knowledge or experiences to ask and answer questions on different topics.
- Ask a partner questions and take notes.

1.2. Interpretive mode
- Demonstrate understanding of oral and written expressions.
- Demonstrate understanding of questions relating to familiar and less familiar topics.
- Understand and obtain information from audio or video recordings.
- Understand written exchanges.
- Identify main ideas and significant details from an informative or literary text.
- Draw conclusions and make judgments from oral and written texts.
- Understand new vocabulary presented in Spanish.

1.3. Presentational mode
- Produce and present an original creation orally.
- Write and present a dialogue.
- Write sentences or paragraphs comparing information.
- Complete sentences with relevant information or correct verb tenses.
- Write answers to given questions.
- Create a list of information and present it to the class.
- Write sentences or a paragraph summarizing information.

 CULTURE

2.1. Practices and perspectives
- Learn about multicultural events and celebrations.
- Learn about practices and perspectives of ancient civilizations from Latin America.
- Describe multinational organizations that help Latin American populations.
- Discuss how culture can influence the art, music, and food in a community.
- Learn about the political and governmental systems in Hispanic countries.
- Learn about ways that various populations celebrate and preserve their culture.

2.2. Products and perspectives
- Identify some ancient architectural structures in Hispanic countries.
- Learn about hieroglyphics and symbols used by ancient civilizations to communicate.
- Compare the symbolism and significance of national flags.
- Discuss food, art, and other items from various Latin American cultures.

 CONNECTIONS

3.1. Interdisciplinary connections
- Understand vocabulary and some aspects of grammar in Spanish.
- Learn about the history of some ancient civilizations in Latin America.
- Learn about mathematical systems used by ancient civilizations.
- Identify historical and political figures in Latin American countries.
- Learn about politics and government.
- Learn about worldwide organizations that address human rights, peace, and equality.
- Learn about national symbols.
- Discuss important events and time periods in the history of some Latin American countries.

3.2. Viewpoints through language / culture
- Read dialogues, informative texts, and literary texts in Spanish that provide insight into Hispanic cultures.

 COMPARISONS

4.1. Compare languages
- Compare stating past actions in English and in Spanish.
- Compare the structures used in English and in Spanish to talk about the different stages of an action.
- Compare definite and indefinite articles in English and in Spanish.
- Compare the use of the passive voice in English and in Spanish.

4.2. Compare cultures
- Compare places of cultural importance in Hispanic countries and in the United States.
- Compare national symbols and flags used in Hispanic countries and in the United States.
- Compare political and governmental systems in Hispanic countries and in the United States.

 COMMUNITIES

5.1. Spanish within and beyond the school setting
- Research and obtain information on the Internet.
- Discuss activities in one's own community.
- Imagine situations in which Spanish could be used.
- Write an e-mail to a classmate or person in the community.

5.2. Spanish for lifelong learners
- Discuss ways in which Spanish can be used in future life experiences.

Communicative Skills

Interpersonal Mode

		Activities
Speaking	• Exchange opinions or experiences. • Contrast answers or compare information with a classmate. • Engage in a conversation with a classmate. • Play a guessing game with a classmate.	• 47, 48, 64, 74, 80, 84 • 6, 45, 56, 73 • 13, 36, 45, 47, 60, 73, 82 • 40, 69, 83
Writing	• Write brief dialogues. • Write a news report. • Summarize information in a list.	• 4 • 19 • 81
Listening	• Understand and obtain information from simple oral exchanges.	• 40, 48, 57, 81, 82, *Proyecto*
Reading	• Understand a list of items. • Understand a narrative text or a persuasive text.	• 45 • 31, *Escritura*

Interpretive Mode

		Activities
Listening	• Understand and obtain information from brief dialogues or a longer conversation. • Understand oral narrative or informative texts.	• 3, 9, 30, 35, 39, 63 • 12, 17, 44, 78
Reading	• Demonstrate comprehension of written exchanges and longer written dialogues. • Infer meanings based on a text. • Obtain information and draw conclusions from an informative text. • Demonstrate understanding of a poem.	• 7, 8, 26, 32, 34, 58, 59 • 2, 7, 11, 25, 51, 62 • 14, 24, 29, 37, 41, 49, 50, 61, 79 • 75, 76
Viewing	• Obtain information from an image or visual. • Connect words, expressions, events, or information to images.	• 12, 28, 53, 68, 80 • 9, 44, 60, 82

Presentational Mode

		Activities
Speaking	• Present a dialogue or skit to the class. • Present a description or information to the class. • Present an original creation to the class.	• 4, 23 • 28, 64, 84, *Proyecto* • *Escritura*
Writing	• Summarize information in written form. • Write a descriptive or narrative paragraph. • Write an e-mail, a formal letter, or a research report.	• 14, 44, 52, 82, 83 • 31, 53, 56 • 73, 79, *Proyecto*
Visually Representing	• Create a poster or drawing, or use photographs, to present information. • Present information in a Venn diagram, chart, graph, or table.	• 27, 80, *Proyecto* • 3, 6, 45, 55, 64, 76, 78

Cross-Curricular Standards

Subject	Standard	Activities
Language Arts	• Compare elements of Spanish grammar and language with English equivalents. • Use the writing process to write a persuasive essay.	• 15, 20, 42, 46, 66, 71 • *Escritura*
Social Studies	• Learn about the history and historical figures of Hispanic countries. • Discuss multiculturalism and multicultural festivals and celebrations. • Identify and compare flags as national symbols. • Learn about politics and government, and political figures in Hispanic countries. • Learn about international organizations that address issues in Latin American countries.	• 10, 12, 14, 22, 82, 84, *Proyecto* • 61, 70, 84 • 41, 53 • 38, 39, 49, 55 • 10, 34, 37, 84
Math	• Learn about mathematical systems used by ancient civilizations.	• 24

Lesson Plans (50-Minute Classes)

Day	Objectives	Sessions	Activities	Time	Standards	Resources / Homework
1	To introduce history, politics, and societal issues, and the characters' challenges, and to review learned vocabulary	**En sociedad/Las tareas/Antes de empezar** (390–395) • Warm-Up: Topic orientation • Presentation: *Pasado y presente del mundo hispano* • *Expresiones útiles* and *Recuerda*	 1–2 3–6	 10 m. 20 m. 20 m.	1.1, 1.2, 1.3, 2.1, 2.2, 3.1, 3.2, 5.1	Visual Presentation Audio Video Practice Workbook
2	To describe and narrate in the past	**Desafío 1 – Un mapa muy valioso** (396–397) • Warm-Up: Independent Starter • *Texto: Un mapa muy valioso* • *Cultura: Patrimonio de la Humanidad*	 7–9 10	 5 m. 35 m. 10 m.	1.1, 1.2, 1.3, 2.1, 2.2, 3.1, 4.2, 5.1	Visual Presentation Audio Video
3	To talk about archaeology and the history of ancient civilizations in Latin America	**Desafío 1 – Vocabulario** (398–399) • Warm-Up: Independent Starter • Vocabulary: *Personajes, acontecimientos, civilizaciones* • *Cultura: La herencia maya*	 11–13 14	 5 m. 35 m. 10 m.	1.1, 1.2, 1.3, 2.2, 3.1, 5.1, 5.2	Audio Practice Workbook
4	To use and form sentences in the passive voice	**Desafío 1 – Gramática** (400–401) • Warm-Up: Independent Starter • Grammar: *La voz pasiva*	 15–19	 5 m. 45 m.	1.1, 1.2, 1.3, 3.1, 4.1	Audio Practice Workbook
5	To talk about past events within various situations	**Desafío 1 – Gramática** (402–403) • Warm-Up: Independent Starter • Grammar: *Usos de los tiempos de pasado (repaso)* • *Conexiones: La numeración maya*	 20–23 24	 5 m. 35 m. 10 m.	1.1, 1.2, 1.3, 2.2, 3.1, 4.1, 5.1, 5.2	Practice Workbook
6	To understand a dialogue and to integrate vocabulary and grammar	**Desafío 1 – Lectura/Comunicación** (404–407) • Warm-Up: Independent Starter • *Lectura: La Escalinata de los Jeroglíficos* • *Comunicación:* Review • *Final del desafío*	 25–28 29–31 32	 5 m. 20 m. 15 m. 10 m.	1.1, 1.2, 1.3, 2.1, 2.2, 3.1, 3.2, 4.2, 5.2	Visual Presentation Audio Practice Workbook Quiz on *Desafío 1*
7	To talk about factual events	**Desafío 2 – Una organización multinacional** (408–409) • Warm-Up: Correct quiz on *Desafío 1* • *Texto: Una organización multinacional* • *Cultura: La misión de la OEA*	 33–36 37	 5 m. 35 m. 10 m.	1.1, 1.2, 1.3, 2.1, 3.1, 5.1	Visual Presentation Audio Video
8	To talk about politics and government	**Desafío 2 – Vocabulario** (410–411) • Warm-Up: Independent Starter • Vocabulary: *Política y gobierno* • *Cultura: El significado de las banderas*	 38–40 41	 5 m. 35 m. 10 m.	1.1, 1.2, 2.1, 2.2, 3.1, 4.2, 5.2	Audio Practice Workbook
9	To talk about the different stages of an action	**Desafío 2 – Gramática** (412–413) • Warm-Up: Independent Starter • Grammar: *Hablar de las etapas de una acción*	 42–45	 5 m. 45 m.	1.1, 1.2, 1.3, 3.1, 4.1, 5.1	Audio Practice Workbook
10	To talk about factual events using the indicative mood	**Desafío 2 – Gramática** (414–415) • Warm-Up: Independent Starter • Grammar: *Usos del indicativo (repaso)* • *Conexiones: Mujeres en el poder*	 46–48 49	 5 m. 35 m. 10 m.	1.1, 1.2, 2.1, 3.1, 4.1, 4.2, 5.1	Practice Workbook

Day	Objectives	Sessions	Activities	Time	Standards	Resources / Homework
11	To understand an informative text and to integrate vocabulary and grammar	**Desafío 2 – Lectura / Comunicación** (416–419) • Warm-Up: Independent Starter • *Lectura: Entrevista a Debra McKeon* • *Comunicación:* Review • *Final del desafío*	50–52 53–56 57	5 m. 20 m. 15 m. 10 m.	1.1, 1.2, 1.3, 2.1, 2.2, 3.1, 3.2, 4.2, 5.1	Practice Workbook *Tu desafío* Quiz on *Desafío 2*
12	To express wishes, opinions, and values	**Desafío 3 – Un calendario multicultural** (420–421) • Warm-Up: Correct quiz on *Desafío 2* • *Texto: Un calendario multicultural* • *Comunidades: El corazón de la multiculturalidad*	58–60 61	5 m. 35 m. 10 m.	1.1, 1.2, 1.3, 2.1, 2.2, 3.1, 3.2, 5.1	Visual Presentation
13	To learn about cultural diversity in societies	**Desafío 3 – Vocabulario** (422–423) • Warm-Up: Independent Starter • Vocabulary: *Sociedad* • *Cultura: El Museo del Barrio*	62–64 65	5 m. 35 m. 10 m.	1.1, 1.2, 1.3, 2.1, 2.2, 4.2, 5.1	Audio Practice Workbook
14	To refer to known or unknown objects or persons	**Desafío 3 – Gramática** (424–425) • Warm-Up: Independent Starter • Grammar: *Los artículos* • *Cultura: El Festival de Comida Internacional*	66–69 70	5 m. 35 m. 10 m.	1.1, 1.2, 1.3, 2.1, 2.2, 3.1, 4.1, 5.1, 5.2	Practice Workbook
15	To use the subjunctive mood	**Desafío 3 – Gramática** (426–427) • Warm-Up: Independent Starter • Grammar: *Usos del subjuntivo (repaso)*	71–74	5 m. 45m.	1.1, 1.2, 1.3, 3.1, 4.1, 5.1	Practice Workbook
16	To understand a literary text	**Desafío 3 – Lectura** (428-429) • Warm-Up: Independent Starter • *Lectura: La muralla*	75–77	5 m. 45 m.	1.1, 1.2, 1.3, 2.1, 2.2, 3.1, 3.2	
17	To integrate vocabulary and grammar	**Desafío 3 – Comunicación** (430–431) • Warm-Up: Independent Starter • *Comunicación:* Review • *Final del desafío*	78–80 81	5 m. 30 m. 15 m.	1.1, 1.2, 1.3, 2.1, 2.2, 3.1, 5.1	Audio Practice Workbook *Tu desafío* Quiz on *Desafío 3* **Para terminar – Tu desafío** (433)
18	To integrate language in context	**Para terminar** (432–433) • Warm-Up: Correct quiz on *Desafío 3* • *Todo junto* • *Tu desafío* presentations	82–83 84	5 m. 20 m. 25 m.	1.1, 1.2, 1.3, 2.1, 2.2, 3.1, 3.2, 5.1, 5.2	Practice Workbook
19	To assess student proficiency and discuss the history of a Hispanic city	**Evaluación / Mapa cultural** (434–435) • Warm-Up: Independent Starter • Quiz on *Desafíos 1–3* • *Mapa cultural: Una ciudad con historia: Barcelona*	85	5 m. 20 m. 25 m.	1.1, 1.2, 2.1, 2.2, 3.1, 4.2, 5.1	Video Practice Workbook
20	To write a persuasive essay	**Escritura** (436–437) • Warm-Up: Independent Starter • *Escritura: Y tú, ¿qué opinas?*		5 m. 45 m.	1.1, 1.2, 1.3, 3.1, 5.2	Project work
21	To create a report about a historical event or time period of a Latin American country	**Proyecto** (442–443) • Warm-Up: Prepare project presentations • Project presentations		10 m. 40 m.	1.1, 1.2, 1.3, 2.1, 2.2, 3.1, 5.1, 5.2	**Repaso – Vocabulario** (438–439) **Repaso – Gramática** (440–441)
22	To assess student proficiency	**Assessment** • *Autoevaluación* (443) • Test		10 m. 40 m.	1.1, 1.2, 1.3, 2.1, 2.2, 5.1, 5.2	

Lesson Plans (90-Minute Classes)

Day	Objectives	Sessions	Activities	Time	Standards	Resources / Homework
1	To introduce history, politics, and societal issues, and the characters' challenges, and to review learned vocabulary	(See Day 12 Unit 7) **En sociedad / Las tareas / Antes de empezar** (390–395) • Warm-Up: Topic orientation • Presentation: *Pasado y presente del mundo hispano* • *Expresiones útiles* and *Recuerda*	 1–2 3–6	(45 m.) 10 m. 20 m. 15 m.	1.1, 1.2, 1.3, 2.1, 2.2, 3.1, 3.2, 5.1	Visual Presentation Audio Video Practice Workbook
2	To describe and narrate in the past, and to talk about archaeology and the history of ancient civilizations in Latin America	**Desafío 1 – Un mapa muy valioso / Vocabulario** (396–399) • Warm-Up: Independent Starter • Texto: *Un mapa muy valioso* • Cultura: *Patrimonio de la Humanidad* • Vocabulary: *Personajes, acontecimientos, civilizaciones* • Cultura: *La herencia maya*	 7–9 10 11–13 14	 5 m. 30 m. 10 m. 35 m. 10 m.	1.1, 1.2, 1.3, 2.1, 2.2, 3.1, 4.2, 5.1, 5.2	Visual Presentation Audio Video Practice Workbook
3	To use and form sentences in the passive voice, and to talk about past events within various situations	**Desafío 1 – Gramática** (400–403) • Warm-Up: Independent Starter • Grammar: *La voz pasiva* • Grammar: *Uso de los tiempos de pasado (repaso)* • Conexiones: *La numeración maya*	 15–19 20–23 24	 5 m. 35 m. 40 m. 10 m.	1.1, 1.2, 1.3, 2.2, 3.1, 4.1, 5.1, 5.2	Audio Practice Workbook
4	To understand a dialogue and to integrate vocabulary and grammar	**Desafío 1 – Lectura / Comunicación / Evaluación** (404–407) • Warm-Up: Independent Starter • Lectura: *La Escalinata de los Jeroglíficos* • Comunicación: Review • Final del desafío • Quiz on *Desafío 1*	 25–28 29–31 32	 5 m. 35 m. 25 m. 10 m. 15 m.	1.1, 1.2, 1.3, 2.1, 2.2, 3.1, 3.2, 4.2, 5.2	Visual Presentation Audio Practice Workbook
5	To talk about factual events and to talk about politics and government	**Desafío 2 – Una organización multinacional / Vocabulario** (408–411) • Warm-Up: Independent Starter • Texto: *Una organización multinacional* • Cultura: *La misión de la OEA* • Vocabulary: *Política y gobierno* • Cultura: *El significado de las banderas*	 33–36 37 38–40 41	 5 m. 35 m. 10 m. 30 m. 10 m.	1.1, 1.2, 1.3, 2.1, 2.2, 3.1, 4.2, 5.1, 5.2	Visual Presentation Audio Video Practice Workbook
6	To talk about the different stages of an action and to talk about factual events using the indicative mood	**Desafío 2 – Gramática** (412–415) • Warm-Up: Independent Starter • Grammar: *Hablar de las etapas de una acción* • Grammar: *Usos del indicativo (repaso)* • Conexiones: *Mujeres en el poder*	 42–45 46–48 49	 5 m. 40 m. 35 m. 10 m.	1.1, 1.2, 1.3, 2.1, 3.1, 4.1, 4.2, 5.1	Audio Practice Workbook

Day	Objectives	Sessions	Activities	Time	Standards	Resources / Homework
7	To understand an informative text and to integrate vocabulary and grammar	**Desafío 2 – Lectura / Comunicación / Evaluación** (416–419) • Warm-Up: Independent Starter • *Lectura: Entrevista a Debra McKeon* • *Comunicación:* Review • *Final del desafío* • Quiz on *Desafío 2*	50–52 53–56 57	5 m. 35 m. 25 m. 10 m. 15 m.	1.1, 1.2, 1.3, 2.1, 2.2, 3.1, 3.2, 4.2, 5.1	Practice Workbook *Tu desafío*
8	To express wishes, opinions, and values, and to learn about cultural diversity in societies	**Desafío 3 – Un calendario multicultural / Vocabulario** (420–423) • Warm-Up: Independent Starter • *Texto: Un calendario multicultural* • *Comunidades: El corazón de la multiculturalidad* • Vocabulary: *Sociedad* • *Cultura: El Museo del Barrio*	58–60 61 62–64 65	5 m. 30 m. 10 m. 35 m. 10 m.	1.1, 1.2. 1.3, 2.1, 2.2, 3.1, 3.2, 4.2, 5.1	Visual Presentation Audio Practice Workbook
9	To refer to known or unknown objects or persons and to use the subjunctive mood	**Desafío 3 – Gramática** (424–427) • Warm-Up: Independent Starter • Grammar: *Los artículos* • *Cultura: El Festival de Comida Internacional* • Grammar: *Usos del subjuntivo (repaso)*	66–69 70 71–74	5 m. 40 m. 10 m. 35 m.	1.1, 1.2, 1.3, 2.1, 2.2, 3.1, 4.1, 5.1, 5.2	Practice Workbook
10	To understand a literary text, to integrate vocabulary and grammar, to integrate language in context, and to assess student proficiency	**Desafío 3 – Lectura / Comunicación / Evaluación / Todo junto** (428–432) • Warm-Up: Independent Starter • *Lectura: La muralla* • *Comunicación:* Review • *Final del desafío* • *Todo junto* • Quiz on *Desafío 3*	75–77 78–80 81 82–83	5 m. 25 m. 20 m. 10 m. 15 m. 15 m.	1.1, 1.2, 1.3, 2.1, 2.2, 3.1, 3.2, 5.1, 5.2	Audio Practice Workbook *Tu desafío* **Para terminar – Tu desafío** (433)
11	To discuss the history of a Hispanic city and to write a persuasive essay	**Tu desafío / Mapa cultural / Escritura** (434–437) • Warm-Up: Independent Starter • *Tu desafío* presentations • *Mapa cultural: Una ciudad con historia: Barcelona* • *Escritura: Y tú, ¿qué opinas?*	84 85	5 m. 15 m. 30 m. 40 m.	1.1, 1.2, 1.3, 2.1, 2.2, 3.1, 3.2, 4.2, 5.1	Video Practice Workbook **Repaso – Vocabulario** (438–439) **Repaso – Gramática** (440–441) Quiz on *Desafíos 1–3* Project work
12	To create a report about a historical event or time period of a Latin American country	**Proyecto / Assessment** (442–443) • Warm-Up: Correct quiz on *Desafíos 1–3* • Project presentations • *Autoevaluación* • Test • *Actividad de final de curso: ¿Qué proyectos relacionados con el español tienes para el futuro?*		5 m. 20 m. 15 m. 20 m. 30 m.	1.1, 1.2, 1.3, 2.1, 2.2, 3.1, 5.1, 5.2	

3 **¿Te apetece?**

1. –¿Tienes ganas de salir a dar un paseo?
   –Bueno. La verdad es que estoy bastante aburrido.
2. –¿Te apetece conducir o prefieres que lleve yo el coche?
   –Me da lo mismo, la verdad.
3. –¿Te gustaría acompañarme esta tarde a una exposición sobre la cultura maya?
   –Lo siento, pero ya tengo planes.
4. –¿Te gustaría que fuéramos a cenar a un restaurante mexicano?
   –Como quieras. Elige tú.
5. –¿Tienes ganas de ir al cine? Hace mucho que no vamos.
   –Claro, buena idea.
6. –Voy a encargar una pizza para cenar. ¿Te apetece alguna en especial?
   –Me da igual. Pide la que quieras.

9 **Joya de Cerén**

–Aquí tenemos el famoso sitio precolombino conocido como la Pompeya de Centroamérica.

–¿La Pompeya de Centroamérica? ¿Por qué se llama así?

–Porque sus habitantes tuvieron que abandonar este lugar a causa de la erupción de un volcán en el año 600. En aquella época Cerén era un pequeño pueblo agrícola.

–Ah, ya entiendo... Eso es lo que sucedió en la famosa ciudad de Pompeya, en Italia.

–Exacto. La erupción del volcán cubrió todo el pueblo de lava y ceniza.

–¿Y qué les pasó a los habitantes?

–Se cree que todos pudieron salir a tiempo porque no se han descubierto restos humanos. Pero sí se conservan los restos de las casas y numerosos objetos de uso cotidiano.

–Es cierto: hay cuchillos, boles y platos de barro... Me parece que hay algo dentro.

–Sí, son restos de comida: frijoles, cacao y chiles. La ceniza que cubrió el pueblo protegió todos estos restos de los efectos del tiempo. Por eso están tan bien conservados y Cerén es un sitio arqueológico tan importante en El Salvador y en toda Centroamérica. Gracias a su descubrimiento se ha podido estudiar la vida diaria de este pueblo tal y como era en aquel momento, hace 1400 años.

–¡Es fascinante!

12 **El París de los mayas**

Hola, amigos. Escuché su mensaje pidiéndome información. Voy a recomendarles uno de los sitios arqueológicos más importantes de Latinoamérica. Se trata de Copán, en Honduras. Deberían incluirlo en su mapa de los tesoros mayas porque es importantísimo. De hecho, los arqueólogos lo consideran el París de los mayas por su riqueza artística y cultural. Entre las ruinas de esa antigua ciudad se pueden visitar muchos lugares interesantes; el recorrido es bastante largo. Uno de los que más me impresionó fue el Juego de pelota, que está muy bien conservado. Era el centro social de la ciudad. En la Gran Plaza los mayas realizaban sus ceremonias religiosas y también los sacrificios. ¡Qué miedo!

Otro lugar muy famoso es la Escalinata de los Jeroglíficos. Los mayas escribían con jeroglíficos y las escaleras están llenas de jeroglíficos en los que se cuenta la historia de la ciudad. Ah, se me olvidaba. También visité los Túneles, que están bajo las ruinas. Pero solo se pueden visitar dos: el de Rosalila y el de los Jaguares. Allí hay restos de un importante templo y varias tumbas.

17 **La NASA colabora con los arqueólogos**

–Descubren ruinas arqueológicas con tecnología de la NASA.

–En efecto, un grupo de arqueólogos ha descubierto los restos de una antigua ciudad maya en Belice utilizando la tecnología de la NASA para su investigación. Los científicos volaron por toda la región y escanearon la zona con ayuda de tecnología láser de la NASA. Así realizaron un mapa del lugar en tres dimensiones. Unos días más tarde encontraron las ruinas de la antigua ciudad maya de El Caracol en plena selva. El proyecto será publicado próximamente en la revista *Arqueología 2000*.

30 **Un futuro arqueólogo**

–Me encantó estudiar esta civilización precolombina, Asha. Los mayas tenían una cultura muy interesante.

–Estoy de acuerdo. Descubrieron el concepto del cero y usaban los números para organizar el tiempo en forma de calendario. ¿No es increíble?

–Sí. Y hace dos mil años ya habían desarrollado un sistema para escribir. Me gustaría investigar estos jeroglíficos...

–Afortunadamente, y gracias al trabajo realizado por los arqueólogos, tenemos muchísimos restos de la antigua cultura maya.

–Sí, pero todavía hay misterios que no han sido descubiertos. Nadie sabe qué les pasó a los habitantes de Tikal o de Copán... ¡Quizá lo pueda descubrir yo algún día!

–¿Hablas en serio, Lucas? ¿Te interesa ser arqueólogo?

–Posiblemente... Podría pasar mis días excavando, restaurando y reconstruyendo ruinas. Asha, si tuvieras la oportunidad de vivir en la época de los antiguos mayas, ¿lo harías?

–¡Ay, Lucas! ¡Qué pregunta! Pues no lo sé. Aunque fuera una cultura muy adelantada, no sé si podría vivir sin mi computadora, mi teléfono, mi correo electrónico...

35 **Más información**

–Vamos a buscar más información sobre la OEA en Internet.

–Mira, este es el logo. Parecen banderas, ¿no?

–Sí, seguramente son las banderas de los países que forman parte de la organización. ¿Qué pone debajo?

–Es el lema. Dice: «Democracia para la paz, la seguridad y el desarrollo».

–Tenemos que averiguar qué países forman la OEA. Déjame mirar... Aquí está: «Los 35 países independientes de las Américas han ratificado la Carta de la OEA y son miembros de la Organización».

–Entonces los Estados Unidos forman parte de la OEA.

–Sí. Y también casi todos los países de Centroamérica, el Caribe y Suramérica.

–¿Dice algo sobre los proyectos en los que trabajan?

–Sí... ¡Increíble! La organización actúa en 43 áreas diferentes, incluyendo temas políticos, sociales, educativos y económicos.

–Me parece que esta vez tenemos una tarea difícil.

–No te preocupes. Ahora ya sabemos qué es la OEA, qué países la forman y en qué áreas trabaja. Es un buen principio.

39 Política latinoamericana

–¿Sabías que la mayoría de los países latinoamericanos ahora son repúblicas democráticas?

–Sí, ahora casi todos los estados son democráticos. Pero no siempre fue así. Muchos pasaron por dictaduras muy largas.

–¿Por ejemplo?

–Pues Chile. Allí gobernó Pinochet durante casi veinte años.

–Pero seguro que no sabías que en México hubo una monarquía.

–¿En México? ¿Cuándo?

–Después de la independencia de España.

–Ah, pero de eso hace ya mucho tiempo. Ahora voy a preguntarte yo, a ver si sabes esto. ¿Qué país latinoamericano ha tenido más años de democracia?

–Pues... ¿Costa Rica, quizás?

–Sí, eso es. Y además en Costa Rica no hay ejército.

–Qué curioso.

44 Ethan se prepara

Bueno... a practicar. Buenos días, clase. Para mi presentación he seleccionado el tema «Política mexicana contemporánea». Tengo que decir que antes de esta presentación no sabía mucho sobre este tema y lo que he aprendido me ha sorprendido mucho. Empecé a buscar información en nuestro libro de Historia y tomé algunas notas. Después fui a la biblioteca y consulté varios libros. Por la noche, cuando acabé de cenar, estuve buscando imágenes de personajes importantes de la historia de México en Internet. Y entonces empecé a escribir. Pero luego pensé que sería más interesante incluir algunos testimonios reales y pensé en mi amigo Juan Ramón. Él es mexicano, aunque lleva cinco años viviendo en los Estados Unidos. Él y su familia me contaron muchísimas cosas interesantes sobre la política mexicana en los últimos cincuenta años. Empezaré mi presentación mostrándoles una fotografía de...

63 Conversación en un restaurante

–Buenas tardes. Me llamo Ana. ¿Qué van a comer?

–Hola. Queríamos probar las famosas empanadas colombianas.

–Les van a encantar, ya verán. Las hacemos según la receta tradicional.

–¿Es usted de Colombia?

–Sí, pero llevo aquí más de diez años.

–¿Y no echa de menos su país?

–Sí, claro, pero voy a menudo a Colombia a visitar a mi familia y a mis amigos. Alguna vez he pensado en regresar, pero ahora tengo la ciudadanía estadounidense.

–¿Entonces tiene doble nacionalidad?

–Sí, eso es. Me siento totalmente integrada aquí, aunque conservo mis raíces y muchas costumbres de mi país.

–En Nueva York hay gente de todas partes del mundo, supongo que eso ayuda a integrarse.

–Sí, aquí la cultura se respira en la calle. Constantemente se ven celebraciones de distintos países y comunidades.

–Es verdad. Yo asistí este año al desfile del Año Nuevo chino y también al del Día de san Patricio, el patrón de los irlandeses.

–Pues este jueves hay un festival de bailes tradicionales de mi país.

–¿Qué se celebra?

–El Día de la Independencia de Colombia. Es muy divertido, les recomiendo que vayan. Y si les gusta la cocina colombiana tendrán oportunidad de probar las arepas, el arroz con sancocho...

–¡Tenemos que ir! ¡No nos lo podemos perder!

–Bueno, voy a traerles sus empanadas. ¿O ya no tienen hambre?

–¡Sí, sí!

78 Mi desfile favorito

1. Me llamo Estela. Soy puertorriqueña y vivo en Nueva York desde que era niña. El evento cultural que más me gusta es el Desfile Nacional de Puerto Rico, claro. Se celebra en junio y es todo un espectáculo. Cada año participa más de un millón de personas y suelen acudir cantantes o actores famosos, como Marc Anthony o Jennifer López. Pero lo más emocionante es ver a tantas personas orgullosas de su cultura y su identidad nacional.

2. Yo soy Manuel Alejandro y soy dominicano. Como saben, en los Estados Unidos se celebra en enero el Mes de la Herencia Dominicana. Hay multitud de eventos, pero lo que me parece más interesante es la exhibición de pintura y fotografía de artistas dominicanos en el Museo del Parque, en Queens. Yo soy pintor y creo que es muy importante que haya iniciativas como esta para dar a conocer nuestro arte y nuestra cultura a todo el público.

3. Hola, yo soy Mariana y soy mexicana. A mí me gusta mucho el Desfile del Día de la Hispanidad, no me lo pierdo nunca. Se celebra el fin de semana previo al 12 de octubre. Ese día desfilan por la Quinta Avenida muchos hispanos que exhiben los rasgos propios de su cultura: los trajes, los bailes, la música... Lo que más me gusta es el sentimiento de unidad que se respira. Recuerdo que en 2010 se rindió homenaje a la selección española de fútbol y a los mineros chilenos que fueron rescatados de una mina en el desierto de Atacama.

Unit 8
En sociedad

The Unit

- The themes for Unit 8 are history, politics, and society. Students will describe historic events, narrate in the past, and express opinions. They will also review how to talk about real and hypothetical situations.

- Andy, a veteran of *Fans del español*, will present the tasks to the participants.
  - *Desafío 1.* Asha and Lucas must find the Mayan treasures, and provide a map of where these treasures are located.
  - *Desafío 2.* Eva and Ethan will investigate what the OEA is and write a report about the projects that this organization undertakes.
  - *Desafío 3.* Michelle and Daniel will prepare a calendar of multicultural events that take place in New York City.

Activities	Standards	Resources
En sociedad	1.2, 2.1, 2.2, 3.1, 5.1	Video

Teaching Suggestions

Warm-Up / Independent Starter

- Have students associate each of the photos with one of the following topics: history, politics, or society. Ask them to justify their associations in a three-sentence paragraph.

Preparation

- Ask students if they think that the study of history is important. Invite them to justify their opinions. You may want to ask students about their favorite historical period. For example: *¿Qué época del pasado les gustaría haber conocido? ¿Por qué? ¿Cómo se imaginan esa época?* Then ask them if they are interested in politics, and where or how they get informed. For example: *¿Les interesa la política? ¿Leen las noticias de política en los periódicos?* Finally, ask students what type of social events they are interested in and how often they attend these events.

En sociedad
Historia, política y sociedad

DESAFÍO 1

▶ **Describir y narrar en pasado**

Vocabulario
Personajes, acontecimientos, civilizaciones

Gramática
La voz pasiva

Usos de los tiempos de pasado (repaso)

DESAFÍO 2

▶ **Hablar de hechos reales**

Vocabulario
Política y gobierno

Gramática
Hablar de las etapas de una acción

Usos del indicativo (repaso)

Ruinas de Tikal (Guatemala)

Sede de la OEA (Washington DC)

390 trescientos noventa

The Challenge

DESAFÍO 1
Ruinas de Tikal

Mayan cultures—which extended around what is today Guatemala, Honduras, El Salvador, and southern Mexico—left behind a number of cities with outstanding architecture and art. Copán, in Honduras, has a unique staircase with engraved hieroglyphics; Bonampak, in Mexico, is home to a small temple decorated with beautiful mural paintings; and Chichén Itzá, also in Mexico, is probably one of the most complex cities, housing an assortment of temples and palaces. The findings at these sites indicate that the Mayas also had an advanced knowledge of math and astronomy.

DESAFÍO 2
Sede de la OEA

The Organization of American States (OAS or *OEA, Organización de Estados Americanos*) is a multinational, regional association of the governments of thirty-five countries in the Americas. The organization was created to promote democracy, defend human rights, establish a multinational security system, foster economic development and well-being among its members, and support inter-American cooperation. Its headquarters are located in Washington, D.C., and its General Assembly brings together the representatives of all its member states once a year.

En sociedad

DESAFÍO
3

▶ **Expresar deseos, opinar y valorar**

Vocabulario
Sociedad

Gramática
Los artículos

Usos del subjuntivo (repaso)

Desfile Nacional Dominicano (Nueva York)

trescientos noventa y uno 391

- Have students read each *Desafío's* objective, as well as the vocabulary and grammar goals, then have them share their paragraphs from the Independent Starter and discuss how each picture might relate to these objectives and goals.

Picture Discussion

- Have students look at the photos again and brainstorm what they know about the topics.

Ruinas de Tikal (Guatemala)

- Invite students to share what they know about Tikal. You may ask them some of these questions to refresh their memories: *¿Quiénes eran los habitantes de Guatemala antes de la llegada de los españoles? (los mayas) ¿Por qué eran conocidos los mayas? (por sus construcciones, escritura, conocimientos de astronomía) ¿Qué tipo de construcciones hay en esta foto? (pirámides)*

Sede de la OEA (Washington DC)

- Ask students to think of important government buildings located in Washington, D.C. Discuss with students that many international organizations have a presence in Washington, D.C. With this in mind, have students try to guess which international organization the OEA might be. (*Organización de Estados Americanos*) Remind students that the name is in Spanish.

Desfile Nacional Dominicano (Nueva York)

- Ask students to describe the costumes people are wearing in the picture. Does this type of celebration remind students of something? (a carnival) Call students' attention to the fact that this parade is taking place in New York City. Discuss New York City's multiculturalism and its role as the most diverse city in the United States.

Objectives

- By the end of Unit 8, students will be able to
  - Talk about historic facts and events.
  - Talk about how things have been done and by whom.
  - Talk about politics and ideologies.
  - Express the different stages of an action.
  - Review how to talk about facts.
  - Talk about society.
  - Review how to express wishes, opinions, and value judgments.
  - Talk about important times in the history of Latin America and Spain, familiarize themselves with current politics, and talk about social and cultural events.

⚑**DESAFÍO 3**

Desfile Nacional Dominicano

For many people, one of New York City's most attractive traits is the variety of cultures and ethnic groups that have settled in it and made it their own. Well beyond Chinatown and Little Italy, numerous other cultures have left their mark. According to the 2010 Census, 28.6% of New York City's population is of Hispanic origin. Puerto Ricans and Dominicans comprise the largest and second-largest Latino groups in the city, but the Dominican population is increasing at twice the rate of the city's overall Latino population and is projected to surpass Puerto Ricans within the next fifteen years.

391

Las tareas

Presentation

■ In this section, Lucas, Eva, Asha, and Ethan participate in a chat with Andy to find out about their last challenges. Students will preview expressions for asking others about their wishes and preferences. They will also preview some common colloquial ways to express indifference or resignation.

Activities	Standards	Resources
Texto	1.2, 2.1, 3.1, 3.2	Vis. Pres.
1.	1.1, 1.2	
2.	1.1, 1.3	

Teaching Suggestions

Warm-Up / Independent Starter

■ Have students do a recap of the pre-Hispanic civilizations of Latin America that they have studied or heard about. Ask them to create a chart to list the civilizations and four things they know about each one. To help students organize the information, you may want to suggest the following headings for their charts: *Civilización, Región de América Latina, Yacimientos* (sites) *arqueológicos, Elementos culturales, Conocimientos (astronomía, agricultura, etc.).*

Preparation

■ Call on different volunteers to share their charts from the Independent Starter. Display a map of Latin America and ask students to locate the territory on the map that was controlled by, or under the influence of, the different civilizations they mentioned in their Independent Starters. Invite the class to add other information they know about each of the civilizations mentioned.

■ Have students scan the text on this page and the dialogue on the following page, and find expressions used to ask someone for his or her preferences or wishes. (*¿Qué les parece? ¿Tienen ganas de empezar a trabajar? ¿Qué te parece nuestra última tarea?*) Then ask students to find expressions used to express resignation or indifference. (*¡Qué le vamos a hacer! Me da igual, como tú quieras.*)

■ You may also want to review other colloquial expressions in the text (e.g., *Ya, ya…, ¿verdad?, ¡Por supuesto!, No sé, déjame pensar…*).

392

Las tareas

Pasado y presente del mundo hispano

 The characters are very interested in learning more about Hispanic history and society. Read the chat to find out what their last challenges will be.

> Mostrar mensajes de: Hoy | Esta semana | Útimos 30 días | Todos
>
> **Andy dice:** 2:35
> ¿Cómo están, amigos? ¿Están animados para sus últimos desafíos?
>
> **Lucas dice:** 2:36
> Yo estoy un poco triste, es una lástima que estemos terminando.
>
> **Eva dice:** 2:38
> ¡Qué le vamos a hacer! Todo tiene un final… Pero no hay que estar triste, Lucas. Aprendimos muchísimo con los desafíos y lo pasamos muy bien.
>
> **Lucas dice:** 2:40
> Ya, ya…
>
> **Andy dice:** 2:41
> Anímense, ya tenemos preparadas sus nuevas tareas. Algunos de ustedes dijeron que querían saber más sobre historia y política de los países hispanos, ¿verdad?
>
> **Asha dice:** 2:43
> Sí. Yo quiero aprender más sobre las civilizaciones precolombinas.
>
> **Ethan dice:** 2:45
> Y yo quiero saber más cosas sobre la política actual.
>
> **Andy dice:** 2:46
> Muy bien, pues estas son sus tareas: Asha y Lucas tienen que descubrir los tesoros mayas y hacer un mapa con su localización. Eva y Ethan deberán averiguar qué es la OEA y escribir un artículo sobre los proyectos en los que trabaja. Y, finalmente, Michelle y Daniel prepararán un calendario con los eventos multiculturales más interesantes de Nueva York para incluirlo en un folleto turístico. ¿Qué les parece? ¿Tienen ganas de empezar a trabajar?
>
> **Asha dice:** 2:49
> ¡Por supuesto! Eso de los tesoros suena muy bien… ¡Espero que encontremos oro!
>
> ▼ Conectado

392 trescientos noventa y dos

Differentiated Instruction

DEVELOPING LEARNERS

• Ask students to work with a partner and add one more comment to each of the participants' dialogues on page 393. Then have students rehearse their lines and present their extended dialogues to the rest of the class or to several other pairs. You may want to explain that *siglas* means "acronym," an abbreviation that stands for the name of an organization.

EXPANDING LEARNERS

• Ask students to rewrite the chat and the dialogues on these pages in narrative form to explain what the challenges are and the participants' reactions to them. To do this, students may choose to write using the first-person approach, as if they were one of the participants, or use the neutral third-person point of view. Call on some students to read their compositions aloud.

¿Qué te parece nuestra última tarea?

Parece divertida. Me recuerda el mapa del tesoro de los piratas. ja. ja.

¿Qué será la OEA?

Evidentemente, son siglas. Debe de ser la Organización de... No sé, déjame pensar...

Me da igual, como tú quieras.

Yo tengo varios amigos en Nueva York. ¿Hablamos con ellos o miramos primero alguna página web?

1 **¿Comprendes?**

▶ **Escribe.** ¿Qué tiene que hacer cada pareja?

1. Asha y Lucas   2. Eva y Ethan   3. Michelle y Daniel

▶ **Responde** a estas preguntas.

1. ¿Qué crees que son los tesoros mayas?
2. ¿Qué piensas que es la OEA?
3. ¿Qué culturas y grupos étnicos conviven en Nueva York?
4. ¿Qué desafío te parece más interesante? ¿Por qué?

2 **Investiga**

▶ **Busca** el significado de tres palabras o expresiones nuevas y escribe algunos ejemplos que te ayuden a recordarlas.

trescientos noventa y tres **393**

Las tareas

👁 Texto: Pasado y presente del mundo hispano

■ Read the introduction. Then point out the sentences in the text that have question marks or exclamation points. Model the pronunciation and intonation of these sentences and have students repeat after you. Assign the different roles of the dialogue in the chat to five students and remind them to emphasize the intonation and be careful with the pronunciation. Then have them read the dialogue aloud.

■ Work on comprehension through questions. For example: *¿Qué les pregunta Andy a los participantes? ¿Qué opina Lucas? ¿Qué dice Eva? ¿Qué quiere aprender Asha?*

Activities

1. For the second part of this activity, help students make educated guesses. For question 1, you may ask them to point the area of Central America where most of the Mayan influence is found (i.e., southern Mexico, Guatemala, Honduras, El Salvador). For question 2, explain that acronyms change from one language to the other. For question 3, ask students to think about different areas in New York City that are usually associated with some ethnic groups (Chinatown, Spanish Harlem, etc.).

Answer Key

1. 1. Descubrir los tesoros mayas y hacer un mapa con su localización.
   2. Averiguar qué es la OEA y escribir un artículo sobre sus proyectos.
   3. Preparar un calendario con los eventos multiculturales más interesantes de Nueva York para incluirlo en un folleto turístico.
   ▶ Answers will vary.
2. Answers will vary.

Additional Resources

Fans Online activities
Practice Workbook

HERITAGE LANGUAGE LEARNERS

• Ask students to identify some other acronyms *(siglas)* in Spanish for well-known international organizations. Examples include: *ONU (Organización de las Naciones Unidas), OTAN (Organización del Tratado del Atlántico Norte), OPEP (Organización de Países Exportadores de Petróleo), FMI (Fondo Monetario Internacional).* Then ask students to share these acronyms with the class to see if the class can guess what these organizations are called in English.

COOPERATIVE LEARNING

• Ask students to think about cultural or multicultural events that are celebrated at school, in their community, or in their state, and explain that they are going to make a calendar that reflects these celebrations. Have students work in small groups and assign two or three months to each group, depending on class size. Each group should focus on the events that take place in their assigned months. Some group members may write a brief description of the events; other group members may illustrate the calendar. Display students' work in the classroom.

Unit 8
Antes de empezar

Presentation

- In this section, students will learn a variety of useful expressions to ask others about their wishes and preferences, and to express indifference or resignation.
- Students will also review vocabulary to talk about social and historical issues. They will also review some terms associated with politics.

Activities	Standards	Resources
Expresiones útiles	1.2, 2.1	
3.	1.2, 1.3	Audio
4.	1.1, 1.3	
Recuerda	1.2, 3.1	
5.	1.2, 1.3	
6.	1.1, 1.2, 1.3, 3.1	

Teaching Suggestions

Warm-Up / Independent Starter

- Write the following dialogues on the board and ask students to translate them into English:
  1. —¿Te gustaría ir al cine o prefieres ir al teatro?
     —Me da igual.
  2. —No podemos ir a la playa porque está lloviendo.
     —¡Qué le vamos a hacer!

Preparation

- Discuss students' translations for the dialogues in the Independent Starter. Pay special attention to students' translations of *Me da igual* (It's all the same to me) and *¡Qué le vamos a hacer!* (There is nothing we can do about it). Then go over the *expresiones útiles* by using them in personalized contexts. For example: *¿Les apetece probar la comida colombiana? ¿Les gustaría viajar a Perú? ¿Tienen ganas de conocer España?*
- Then give students some prompts and ask them to react by using expressions of indifference or resignation. For example: *Michelle y Daniel van a tener que trabajar mucho para lograr su objetivo.* → *Así es la vida. ¿Qué desafío les gustaría realizar?* → *Nos da igual.*

394

Antes de empezar

EXPRESIONES ÚTILES

Para preguntar por deseos y preferencias:

- ¿Tienes ganas de…?
- ¿Te apetece…?
- ¿Te gustaría…?

Para expresar indiferencia o falta de preferencia:

- Me da igual / Me da lo mismo.
- No me importa.
- Como quieras.

Para expresar resignación:

- ¡En fin!
- ¡Qué le vamos a hacer!
- Así es la vida.

3 ¿Te apetece?

 ▶ **Escucha** los diálogos y completa una tabla como esta. Fíjate en las reacciones de cada persona a las propuestas.

	Acepta la propuesta	Rechaza la propuesta	Expresa indiferencia
1	✓		
2			
3			
4			
5			
6			

4 Resignados

 ▶ **Escribe** con tu compañero(a) tres diálogos cortos que incluyan una expresión de resignación.

Modelo
—¡Oh, no! Olvidé mi celular en casa.
—¿Vas a volver a buscarlo?
—No, es muy tarde. Qué le vamos a hacer…

394 trescientos noventa y cuatro

Differentiated Instruction

DEVELOPING LEARNERS

- Read the following to students and have them answer using one of the *expresiones útiles*. Sample answers are provided.
  1. *No has aprobado el examen. (¡Qué le vamos a hacer!)*
  2. *¿Qué prefieres: té o café? (Me da igual.)*
  3. *¿Te molesto si cambio el canal de la televisión? (No me importa.)*
  4. *Voy a cerrar la ventana porque hace frío. (Como quiera.)*
  5. *Hemos perdido otro partido. (¡En fin!)*
  6. *¿Te apetece ir a la playa? (Me da lo mismo.)*

EXPANDING LEARNERS

- Students will play a word game. Write a word from this lesson on the board vertically. Divide the class into two teams and ask a player from one team to write as many words as possible that start with each of the letters. Players from the other team must face away from the board so they cannot see the word. After you call time, a player from the other team will write additional new words. Tally each team's words, check their spelling, and repeat the process with another word. All verbs must be in the infinitive.

RECUERDA

La política		La historia	
la bandera	el gobierno	el cacique	la guerra
la ciudad	la nación	el conquistador	el imperio
la capital	el país	el emperador	la independencia
el estado	el pueblo		

Las civilizaciones

La sociedad

el ciudadano	la cultura	los aztecas
la comunidad	la población	los incas
		los mayas

5 ¿Cuánto sabes?

▶ **Lee** las palabras del cuadro Recuerda. ¿Conoces más vocabulario sobre esos temas? Escríbelo.

Modelo   La política: votar, el presidente...

6 Historia y política

▶ **Completa** un gráfico como este con el vocabulario que sabes sobre el tema de esta unidad.

La antigüedad   La época moderna

el cacique

▶ **Compara** tu gráfico con el de tu compañero(a) y comenten las similitudes y diferencias. Después, añade más palabras a tu gráfico.

HERITAGE LANGUAGE LEARNERS

• Students may have difficulty with some nouns that have special forms for male and female (e.g., *el emperador, la emperatriz*). Ask students to brainstorm other nouns that share these characteristics. Alternatively, you may read the following words and ask students to say the corresponding feminine form: *el actor (la actriz), el príncipe (la princesa), el rey (la reina), el duque (la duquesa), el marqués (la marquesa), el héroe (la heroína), el marido (la mujer), el yerno (la nuera), el gallo (la gallina), el caballo (la yegua), el toro (la vaca).*

SPECIAL-NEEDS LEARNERS

• Ask students with an auditory processing disorder to read the directions to the activities and then repeat the directions to you. This will reinforce their comprehension of what they are expected to do. Allow these students to read the audio script for activity 3 while the other students are listening to the recording. Do this for all audio portions of this unit to enable students to complete the listening activities with a marked degree of success.

Unit 8

Antes de empezar

■ To review the *Recuerda* vocabulary, ask each student to list on the board a different fact about the United States (e.g., capital city, flag, number of states, independence date, form of government). Students may not repeat facts. You may want to divide that class into groups and convert this activity into a game.

Activities

4. After students complete this activity, have them rehearse their dialogues and ask for volunteers to act them out in front of the class.

5. Ask questions to generate additional vocabulary related to each of the topics. For example: *¿Qué tipo de gobierno tiene los Estados Unidos? (democracia) ¿Qué se hace en las elecciones? (votar) ¿Cómo se llama la persona que gobierna un estado? (gobernador/a)*

6. To expand this activity, you may bring photos of people and places in the past and of people and places in the present. Ask students to work in pairs to describe and compare the photos. For example: *En el pasado las mujeres llevaban vestidos largos; hoy llevan pantalones y faldas cortas. En las calles no había luz eléctrica; ahora todas la calles están iluminadas.* Correct students' use of the past tense as necessary.

AUDIO SCRIPT
See page 389l.

Answer Key

3. 2. indiferencia   5. acepta
  3. rechaza   6. indiferencia
  4. indiferencia

4. Answers will vary

5. Answers will vary.

6. Answers will vary.
  ▶ Answers will vary.

Additional Resources

Fans Online activities
Practice Workbook

Unit 8
DESAFÍO 1

Describir y narrar en pasado

Presentation

- In *Desafío 1*, Asha and Lucas must find out where the Mayan treasures are hidden and make a map. Students will preview language used to talk about historic events and past civilizations.

Activities	Standards	Resources
Texto	1.2, 2.1, 2.2, 3.1	Vis. Pres.
7.	1.2, 1.3, 2.2, 3.1	
8.	1.1, 1.2, 2.2, 3.1	
9.	1.2, 1.3, 2.2, 3.1	Audio
10. Cultura	1.2, 2.2, 3.1, 4.2, 5.1	

Teaching Suggestions

Warm-Up / Independent Starter

- Post pictures of famous ruins from around the world (e.g., Rome, the moai of Easter Island, Machu Picchu, Egyptian pyramids). Then ask students to write the answers to these questions: *¿Dónde están estas ruinas? ¿Quiénes vivían ahí? ¿Cuáles son los tesoros de su civilización?*

Preparation

- Have students compare their Independent Starters in small groups. Then have groups write their information on newsprint and post these large sheets around the room.

Texto: Un mapa muy valioso

- Read the introduction to the text. Then, using a map of Mexico and Central America, have students point out the regions where the Mayas lived and flourished.
- Ask students to work in pairs. Each partner will take the role of Lucas or Asha and read the dialogue aloud to one another.

Activities

7. After students have finished this activity, have them use their answers to recreate the dialogue between Lucas and Asha with a partner.

9. Before listening to the audio selection, have students write down a brief description for each of the three photographs shown.

396

Un mapa muy valioso

Asha and Lucas have to make a map of the Mayan treasures. How difficult! Their first step will be to discover where the Mayan treasures are hidden.

LUCAS: ¿Un mapa de los tesoros mayas? ¿Y cómo vamos a saber dónde están los tesoros?

ASHA: Sabemos que los mayas eran una antigua civilización que vivía en Centroamérica. Y eran muy poderosos.

LUCAS: ¿Sabes si los mayas estuvieron en muchas guerras?

ASHA: No, no tengo ni idea. ¿Por qué lo preguntas?

LUCAS: Pues porque si invadían a otros pueblos, es probable que se llevaran el oro, la plata y las piedras preciosas (*precious stones*). Y esos pueden ser sus tesoros.

ASHA: Es posible, pero tengo una idea: vamos a mi casa. Mis padres tienen un libro con un montón de fotografías sobre las civilizaciones precolombinas. Seguro que nos da alguna pista.

LUCAS: De acuerdo, vamos.

* * *

ASHA: Aquí no habla de ninguna invasión maya. Dice que los mayas construyeron un gran imperio y que tenían muchísimos conocimientos de matemáticas y de astronomía.

LUCAS: Mira estas fotos, Asha. Dice que Copán y Tikal son tesoros escondidos en la selva… Yo creía que eran solo ruinas. ¿Crees que han descubierto algún tesoro allí?

ASHA: ¡Claro, ya lo entiendo! ¡Las ruinas son los tesoros mayas! ¡Ya podemos empezar a hacer el mapa!

Ruinas mayas de Copán (Honduras).

7 **Detective de palabras**

▶ **Completa** estas oraciones.

1. Asha y Lucas van a hacer un mapa de los tesoros _____.
2. Asha y Lucas saben que los mayas eran una _____ muy poderosa.
3. Lucas quiere saber si los mayas participaron en muchas _____.
4. Los mayas construyeron un gran _____.
5. Los tesoros mayas son sus _____.

▶ **Busca** en el diálogo oraciones con estos verbos. ¿Comprendes su significado? Escribe tres ejemplos que te ayuden a recordarlo.

(invadir)   (construir)   (descubrir)

Differentiated Instruction

DEVELOPING LEARNERS

- Ask students to say whether the following sentences are true (*cierto*) or false (*falso*). Have them correct the false statements.
  1. *Los mayas vivían en Suramérica. (falso; vivían en Centroamérica)*
  2. *Asha pregunta si los mayas estuvieron en muchas guerras. (falso; Lucas lo pregunta)*
  3. *Lucas piensa que los tesoros de los mayas eran el oro y la plata. (cierto)*
  4. *Los mayas tenían grandes conocimientos de astronomía y matemáticas. (cierto)*
  5. *Copán y Tikal son pueblos aztecas. (falso; son ruinas mayas)*

EXPANDING LEARNERS

- This might be a good time for students to review some verb tenses and their uses. Ask students to make a four-column chart and label the columns *Imperfecto, Pretérito, Presente perfecto, Imperfecto del subjuntivo.* Then have students go back and find examples of these tenses, write them in the corresponding column, and briefly explain why they were used. For instance, *eran* is in the imperfect and describes the Mayas. *Se llevaran* is in the imperfect subjunctive; it describes an action in the past and follows an expression that indicates doubt (i.e., *es probable*).

8 Comprensión

▶ **Responde** a estas preguntas.

1. ¿En qué consiste el desafío?
2. ¿Qué son los «tesoros» mayas?
3. ¿Qué es una civilización «precolombina»?
4. ¿Dónde vivían los antiguos mayas?
5. ¿Qué más cosas sabes sobre la civilización maya?

9 Joya de Cerén

 ▶ **Escucha** la conversación entre un guía y un turista. ¿En qué lugar están?

 ▶ **Escucha** de nuevo y decide si estas oraciones son ciertas o falsas. Después, corrige las falsas.

1. Cerén está en Italia.
2. Los arqueólogos han descubierto que un terremoto destruyó el pueblo.
3. Se cree que sus habitantes pudieron marcharse antes de que el pueblo desapareciera.
4. Los arqueólogos descubrieron canchas de pelota entre las ruinas.
5. Los visitantes pueden aprender cómo era una casa en Cerén hace 1400 años.

CULTURA

Patrimonio de la Humanidad

Muchos de los lugares declarados Patrimonio de la Humanidad por la UNESCO debido a su gran importancia cultural o natural están en América Latina. Entre los más conocidos están la ciudad prehispánica de Chichén-Itzá (México), las ruinas mayas de Copán (Honduras), el sitio arqueológico Joya de Cerén (El Salvador) y el santuario histórico de Machu Picchu (Perú). El objetivo de la UNESCO es catalogar, preservar y dar a conocer estos lugares.

Machu Picchu (Perú).

10 Investiga.
Averigua qué criterios de selección aplica la UNESCO para elegir un lugar como Patrimonio de la Humanidad.

▶ **Haz** una lista con los lugares de tu país que consideras que podrían ser declarados Patrimonio de la Humanidad. ¿Qué otros lugares se podrían añadir a la lista?

HERITAGE LANGUAGE LEARNERS

• Ask students to write a story that is set in Chichén Itzá, Copán, Joya de Cerén, or Tulum. Explain that they should write from the point of view of one of the pre-Columbian Mayas or from that of one of the first archaeologists to explore these sites. Students should research the site they select so their descriptions are accurate. Encourage students to add images to their compositions. Call on volunteers to read their stories aloud.

MULTIPLE INTELLIGENCES:
Verbal-Linguistic Intelligence

• Ask students to research and prepare a written report on the *Popol Vuh*, a collection of mythological and historical narratives from the Quiché Maya civilization in Guatemala. Explain that this text addresses the creation of this pre-Columbian indigenous group, by tracing the creation of the world, the story of its gods and goddesses, and the formation of the first men and women, who were initially made of mud and then of wood, both without success, and then finally made of corn.

Describir y narrar en pasado

10. Have small groups of students review the previous units in their textbook and find other UNESCO World Heritage Sites that have been described. Ask groups to discuss which sites they would most like to visit and why.

 AUDIO SCRIPT
See page 389I.

 CULTURA

Patrimonio de la Humanidad

UNESCO identifies sites that are of cultural or natural value to all of humanity. In the United States, UNESCO cultural sites include the Statue of Liberty and Independence Hall. Natural sites include the Grand Canyon, Yellowstone, and the Great Smoky Mountains.

Answer Key

7. 1. mayas   4. imperio
2. civilización   5. ruinas
3. guerras
▶ Answers will vary.

8. 1. En encontrar los tesoros mayas y hacer un mapa.
2. Son las ruinas mayas.
3. Una civilización que se estableció antes de la llegada de Cristóbal Colón.
4. Vivían en Centroamérica.
5. Answers will vary.

9. Foto 1: las ruinas de Cerén.
▶ 1. Falso. Está en El Salvador.
2. Falso. Un volcán lo destruyó.
3. Cierto.
4. Falso. Encontraron restos de las casas y objetos de uso diario.
5. Cierto.

10. Answers will vary.

Additional Resources

Fans Online activities

397

DESAFÍO 1

Vocabulario – Personajes, acontecimientos, civilizaciones

Presentation

■ In this section, students will learn vocabulary related to historic figures, events, and civilizations.

Activities	Standards	Resources
Vocabulario	1.2, 2.2, 3.1	
11.	1.2	
12.	1.2, 1.3, 2.2	Audio
13.	1.1, 5.2	
14. Cultura	1.2, 1.3, 2.2, 3.1, 5.1	Video

Teaching Suggestions

Warm-Up / Independent Starter

■ Ask students to scan the text on this page and write the verb that corresponds to each of the following nouns: *explorador (explorar), conquistador (conquistar), invasión (invadir), restaurador (restaurar), descubridor (descubrir), reconstrucción (reconstruir), excavación (excavar).*

Preparation

■ Create a two-column chart on the board with the following column headings: *Nombres, Verbos.* Call on volunteers to complete it with the information from their Independent Starters.

■ Call on three students to read each of the paragraphs of *Las grandes civilizaciones de América.* Help students with the pronunciation of the highlighted words. Then read the vocabulary in the *Más vocabulario* feature and ask students to repeat each word after you.

■ Ask students questions to ensure comprehension of the vocabulary. For example: *¿De dónde vinieron los conquistadores? ¿Qué civilizaciones encontraron? ¿Quién invadió Tenochtitlán?*

Activities

11. To extend this activity, ask students to match the vocabulary to these additional definitions: 1. *un período de cien años;* 2. *una organización política gobernada por un emperador;* 3. *una casa grande, decorada muy lujosamente.*

398

Vocabulario

Personajes, acontecimientos, civilizaciones

Estatua **del conquistador Juan Ponce de León en San Juan (Puerto Rico).**

Palacio **maya en Palenque (México).**

LAS GRANDES CIVILIZACIONES DE AMÉRICA

Cuando los exploradores españoles llegaron a América en el siglo xv, encontraron grandes civilizaciones. Entre las más importantes están las civilizaciones maya, azteca e inca.

Los conquistadores sometieron a los pobladores del territorio americano. En 1521 Hernán Cortés invadió la ciudad de Tenochtitlán y puso fin al poderoso imperio azteca, que dominaba en aquella época la mayor parte del actual México. Y Francisco Pizarro conquistó el imperio inca, que ocupaba la zona andina.

Hoy sabemos mucho sobre aquellas culturas gracias a importantes descubrimientos arqueológicos. Las excavaciones realizadas por los arqueólogos y los trabajos hechos para restaurar las ruinas de las antiguas ciudades continúan en la actualidad y nos siguen dando pistas sobre los grandes avances de aquellas civilizaciones.

Más vocabulario

Hechos históricos		Arqueología	
la batalla	*battle*	descubrir	*to discover*
la conquista	*conquest*	desaparecer	*to disappear*
la guerra	*war*	excavar	*to excavate*
la invasión	*invasion*	reconstruir	*to reconstruct*

11 **¿Quiénes son?**

▶ **Busca** en la ficha de Vocabulario las palabras que corresponden a estas definiciones.

1. Persona que estudia las civilizaciones antiguas a través de sus restos.	2. Persona que somete y controla un territorio mediante la guerra.	3. Persona que examina un territorio lejano o poco conocido.

398 trescientos noventa y ocho

Differentiated Instruction

DEVELOPING LEARNERS

• Ask students to complete the sentences with the correct vocabulary words from page 398.

1. *Colón llegó a América en el … xv. (siglo)*
2. *El … azteca dominaba gran parte de México. (imperio)*
3. *Los arqueólogos esperan … nuevas ruinas. (descubrir/excavar)*
4. *Había importantes … en las Américas. (civilizaciones)*
5. *Los … siempre están buscando lugares nuevos. (exploradores)*
6. *Se han hecho muchos trabajos para restaurar las… (ruinas)*
7. *Los nobles vivían en… (palacios)*

EXPANDING LEARNERS

• Ask students to complete the following analogies:

1. *excavar : la excavación :: … : la invasión (invadir)*
2. *restaurar : destruir :: la paz : … (la guerra)*
3. *luchar : la lucha :: … : el descubrimiento (descubrir)*
4. *el ciudadano : la casa :: el rey : … (el palacio)*
5. *nuevo : antiguo :: aparecer : … (desaparecer)*
6. *descubrir : explorar :: invadir : … (conquistar)*
7. *el control : el dominio :: la lucha : … (la batalla)*

12 El París de los mayas

 ▶ **Escucha** a Andy y une las dos columnas.

Ⓐ   Ⓑ

1. El Juego de pelota

2. La Gran Plaza

3. La Escalinata de los Jeroglíficos

4. Los Túneles

a. Contiene el texto más largo que se conserva de la civilización maya.

b. Están situados bajo el sitio arqueológico.

c. Es el lugar donde se realizaban las ceremonias, incluidos los sacrificios.

d. Era el centro social de la ciudad.

▶ **Escribe.** Asha y Lucas tienen curiosidad después de escuchar a Andy. Mira las fotos y escribe cinco preguntas sobre las ruinas de Copán.

Modelo   *¿Los arqueólogos han podido interpretar los jeroglíficos que descubrieron?*

 13 ¿Te gustaría ser arqueólogo(a)?

 ▶ **Explica.** ¿Te gustaría ser arqueólogo(a)? Habla con tu compañero(a) y explícale tus motivos.

Modelo

A. *A mí no me gustaría ser arqueólogo, me parece una profesión muy aburrida.*

B. *Pues a mí sí porque viajan a lugares increíbles. Y pienso que debe ser muy emocionante.*

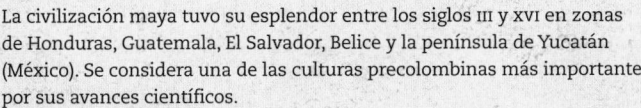 **CULTURA**

La herencia maya

La civilización maya tuvo su esplendor entre los siglos III y XVI en zonas de Honduras, Guatemala, El Salvador, Belice y la península de Yucatán (México). Se considera una de las culturas precolombinas más importantes por sus avances científicos.

Los mayas desarrollaron un completo sistema de escritura y un calendario basado en un año de 365 días, e hicieron numerosos estudios astronómicos y matemáticos.

 14 **Investiga.** ¿Qué sabes de los mayas en la actualidad? Busca información y escribe un breve texto sobre ellos. Puedes mencionar dónde viven, qué aspectos de su cultura conservan, etc.

trescientos noventa y nueve 399

Vocabulario – Personajes, acontecimientos, civilizaciones

12. Before playing the audio, have students read the statements in the exercise and try to guess the answers. Then, as they listen to the audio, ask them to correct their answers.

13. Before completing this activity, ask small groups of students to research different archaeological sites in Central and South America. Have them find out information about some of the archaeologists who have worked (or are working) to restore these sites. Then invite the groups to share their information with the class.

 AUDIO SCRIPT
See page 389I.

 CULTURA

La herencia maya

Historians and archaeologists suggest that several causes contributed to the disappearance of millions of Mayas: foreign invasions, disease, the collapse of key trade routes, and environmental disasters. However, there are still almost seven million Mayas living in southern Mexico and parts of Central America. Many still speak the indigenous languages of the region and keep their culture and traditions alive.

Answer Key

11. 1. arqueólogo   3. explorador
    2. conquistador

12. 1. d   2. c   3. a   4. b
  ▶ Answers will vary.

13. Answers will vary.

14. Answers will vary.

Additional Resources

Fans Online activities
Practice Workbook

HERITAGE LANGUAGE LEARNERS

- After students complete activity 11, ask them to write their own definitions for the rest of the highlighted words and those that appear in the *Más vocabulario* feature. Call on students to read some of their definitions aloud and discuss the accuracy of their definitions with the class. Encourage all students to write some of these definitions in their notebooks.

COOPERATIVE LEARNING

- Ask students to work in small groups and research an ancient *juego de pelota* in Mesoamerica. Each student in the group will write about one aspect of the game. Suggestions include a description of how the game was played, where and when it was played, who the players were, the players' clothing and gear, the cultural symbolism of the game, and the myths and legends associated with *el juego*. Encourage students to add other categories as well as anecdotes that generate interest. Have students gather their reports for display or presentation to the class.

DESAFÍO 1

Gramática – La voz pasiva

Presentation

■ In this section, students will learn how to use the passive voice in order to emphasize the receiver or product of an action rather than the performer.

Activities	Standards	Resources
Gramática	1.2, 3.1	
15.	4.1	
16.	1.2, 3.1	
17.	1.2	Audio
18.	1.2, 1.3, 3.1	
19.	1.1, 1.2, 1.3, 3.1	

Teaching Suggestions

Warm-Up / Independent Starter

■ Ask students to define the terms "active voice" and "passive voice," using their knowledge of English grammar. Then have students read these two pairs of sentences, translate them, and explain how they are different:

1. a. *Los arqueólogos descubrieron las ruinas.*
   b. *Las ruinas fueron descubiertas por los arqueólogos.*
2. a. *Cortés invadió la ciudad.*
   b. *La ciudad fue invadida por Cortés.*

Preparation

■ Divide the class into small groups and ask them to read through the grammar presentation aloud. They should then go back over each point, restating it in their own words and providing additional examples. Then have a whole-class discussion in which students can ask any questions their small group had.

■ Ask students to share their Independent Starters. Have them identify which sentences are written in the active voice and which are written in the passive voice. Point out the importance of adjective agreement in using the passive voice.

Activities

16. After completing this activity, ask students to change sentences 1 and 3 to the active voice. (*Miles de turistas visitan las ruinas cada año. Un famoso periodista escribió la noticia.*)

Gramática

La voz pasiva

- Use the passive voice to emphasize the receiver or product of an action rather than the performer. Note how the passive voice changes the focus of this sentence:

  <u>Los aztecas fundaron Tenochtitlán.</u> → <u>Tenochtitlán fue fundada por los aztecas.</u>
      active voice   passive voice

- Passive sentences usually have this structure:

  > **subject** (receiver) + **verb** (ser + past participle) + **agent** (with por)

  <u>Las ruinas</u> <u>fueron descubiertas</u> <u>por un arqueólogo.</u>
      subject   verb   agent

Formación y uso de la voz pasiva

- The passive voice is formed with the verb *ser* followed by a past participle. The participle must agree in gender and number with the subject.

  fue funda**da** (la ciudad)   fueron descubier**tas** (las ruinas)

- We can use the passive voice in a variety of tenses by conjugating *ser* into that tense.

ACTIVE VOICE	PASSIVE VOICE
La profesora **explica** la lección.	La lección **es explicada** por la profesora.
La profesora **ha explicado** la lección.	La lección **ha sido explicada** por la profesora.
La profesora **explicó** la lección.	La lección **fue explicada** por la profesora.
La profesora **explicará** la lección.	La lección **será explicada** por la profesora.

- The passive voice with *ser* is less common in Spanish than in English. In Spanish it is not normally employed in the following cases:
  – With verbs of perception (ver, oír, sentir…) or emotion (querer, odiar…).
    Sara no **oyó** el timbre.   Carlitos **odia** los frijoles.
  – With an indirect object.
    Ellos le construyeron un templo al emperador.

15 **Compara.** ¿Cómo expresarías en español estas ideas?

  a. *The movie was seen by many people.*   b. *I was given an award.*

16 **¿Activa o pasiva?**

  ▶ **Decide** qué oraciones están en voz pasiva.

  1. Las ruinas son visitadas por miles de turistas cada año.
  2. Los estudiantes estuvieron en clase de Historia.
  3. La noticia fue escrita por un famoso periodista.
  4. No podemos ir de excursión por el mal tiempo.

Differentiated Instruction

DEVELOPING LEARNERS

- Review the irregular past participles by having students complete these sentences:
  1. *La llave fue (devolver) por él. (devuelta)*
  2. *Los vasos serán (romper) por los niños. (rotos)*
  3. *Las tartas fueron (hacer) por mi abuela. (hechas)*
  4. *El poema fue (escribir) por el poeta. (escrito)*
  5. *La tienda fue (abrir) por él. (abierta)*
  6. *Las flores serán (poner) en la mesa por mi madre. (puestas)*
  7. *La frase ha sido (decir) por ella. (dicha)*
  8. *Las ruinas fueron (descubrir) por él. (descubiertas)*

EXPANDING LEARNERS

- Ask students to complete the following sentences using the passive voice. For example: *El radio (descubrir) (Marie Curie).* → *El radio fue descubierto por Marie Curie.*
  1. *Colón (patrocinar) (Reyes Católicos).* (*… fue patrocinado por los Reyes Católicos.*)
  2. *México (conquistar) (Hernán Cortés).* (*… fue conquistado por Hernán Cortés.*)
  3. *El Quijote (escribir) (Cervantes).* (*… fue escrito por Cervantes.*)
  4. *Tenochtitlán (gobernar) (Moctezuma).* (*… fue gobernada por Moctezuma.*)

17 **La NASA colabora con los arqueólogos**

 ▶ **Escucha** una noticia radiofónica y une las dos columnas.

Ⓐ

1. La tecnología de la NASA...
2. Una antigua ciudad maya...
3. La zona...
4. Las ruinas de la ciudad...
5. El proyecto...

Ⓑ

a. fueron encontradas en la selva.
b. ha sido empleada por un grupo de arqueólogos.
c. ha sido descubierta en Belice.
d. fue escaneada con tecnología láser.
e. será publicado en la revista *Arqueología* 2000.

18 **Algunos cambios**

▶ **Decide** qué oraciones se pueden transformar usando
la voz pasiva y escríbelas haciendo los cambios necesarios.

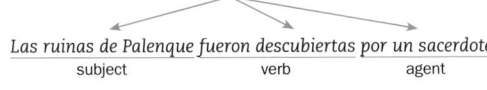

Modelo   Un sacerdote descubrió las ruinas de Palenque.

Las ruinas de Palenque fueron descubiertas por un sacerdote.
subject   verb   agent

Ruinas de Palenque (México).

1. Un sacerdote *(priest)* descubrió las ruinas de Palenque.
2. El guía les dio un plano a los turistas.
3. Los chicos no vieron los monumentos.
4. Los expertos explicarán la historia de la conquista.
5. Los arqueólogos restaurarán los restos del templo.
6. Todos oímos la noticia en la radio.

19 **Noticias impactantes**

▶ **Ordena** estos titulares de prensa.

① fue encontrado/Un extraño / de Salta /
reptil gigante/en / la provincia

② Un/Brasil/delfín albino/
en/fue descubierto

③ fue detenida / por conducir /La/
famosa cantante /demasiado lento

④ afirma/fue secuestrado/Un hombre/
que/por extraterrestres

 ▶ **Habla** con tu compañero(a). Elijan un titular y escriban la noticia añadiendo todos
los detalles que imaginen. Usen la voz pasiva.

 cuatrocientos uno 401

 Unit 8
DESAFÍO 1
Gramática – La voz pasiva

17. Before listening to the audio selection, ask students to brainstorm how NASA may "collaborate" with a group of archaeologists. Then have students read the statements under each column and try to guess the answers.

18. After completing this activity, ask students to explain the reason why numbers 2, 3, and 6 cannot be written in the passive voice.

19. To extend this activity, ask small groups to write a short script for one of the events, and then rehearse quietly before presenting their skit to the class. Have students vote on the most engaging version of each event. These skits can also serve as the basis for the second part of the activity.

AUDIO SCRIPT
See page 389l.

Answer Key

15. a. Mucha gente vio la película.
b. Me dieron un premio.

16. 1, 3

17. 1. b   2. c   3. d   4. a   5. e

18. 4. La historia de la conquista será explicada por los expertos.
5. Los restos del templo serán restaurados por los arqueólogos.

19. 1. Un extraño reptil gigante fue encontrado en la provincia de Salta.
2. Un delfín albino fue descubierto en Brasil.
3. La famosa cantante fue detenida por conducir demasiado lento.
4. Un hombre afirma que fue secuestrado por extraterrestres.
▶ Answers will vary.

Additional Resources

Fans Online activities
Practice Workbook

HERITAGE LANGUAGE LEARNERS

• After students complete activity 19, ask them to make up another headline that uses the passive voice. Then have them write a short newspaper article that relates to the headline. Explain to students that they should use the passive voice as many times as they can in their article. Next, ask them to work with a partner and exchange articles. Partners will rewrite these pieces, but this time they should avoid using the passive voice. Discuss with students which version of the article is more dynamic and effective, and why.

CRITICAL THINKING

• Ask students to imagine that they are archaeologists and that they have come upon what they believe to be some ruins of an ancient civilization that had been considered fictitious. How will they react to this discovery? Will they keep it a well-guarded secret for a while, or will they announce it to the world, and possibly expose themselves to ridicule if the ruins are not authentic? Ask students to ponder this and explain what they would do and why. They should include in their compositions a description of what they have discovered.

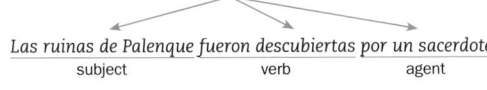

Unit 8

DESAFÍO 1

Gramática – Usos de los tiempos de pasado (repaso)

Presentation

■ In this section, students will review how to use different past tenses to talk about past events and situations.

Activities	Standards	Resources
Gramática	1.2, 3.1	
20.	4.1	
21.	1.2, 1.3	
22.	1.2, 1.3, 2.2, 3.1, 5.1	
23.	1.1, 1.3, 5.2	
24. Conexiones	1.1, 1.2, 2.2, 3.1	

Teaching Suggestions

Warm-Up / Independent Starter

■ Write these sentences on a worksheet or on the board and ask students to compare and contrast the use of the past tenses.

1. *Ayer hablé con el arqueólogo.*
2. *El arqueólogo siempre hablaba con los estudiantes después de clase.*
3. *Mientras los estudiantes hablaban con el arqueólogo, él leía unos textos antiguos.*
4. *He hablado con el arqueólogo muchas veces.*
5. *Ya había hablado con el arqueólogo cuando tú llegaste.*

Preparation

■ Ask students to compare their answers from the Independent Starter with a partner. Then review students' answers with the class. Go over the grammar presentation as a class and then ask students to write five original sentences that reflect the uses of these past tenses. Ask for six to eight volunteers to each write a sentence on the board, and ask the class to identify any errors they may find.

Activities

21. Ask students to identify the tense in the model, then have them review the present perfect before working on this activity.

402

Gramática

Usos de los tiempos de pasado (repaso)

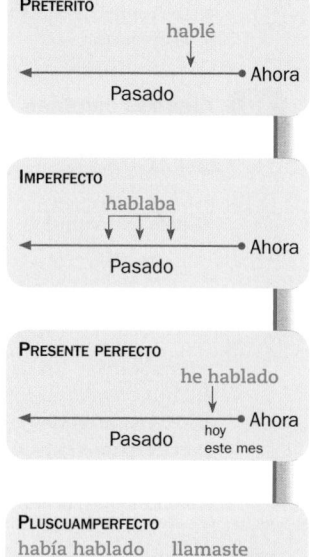

- We use different past tenses to talk about past events, explain the situations that gave rise to those events, and describe the people who took part in them.

- Use the **preterite tense** (hablé) to talk about past actions that are **presented as completed**. Time expressions that indicate that an action has been completed are often paired with verbs in the preterite tense.

  > <u>Anoche</u> **cené**, luego **hice** la tarea de Ciencias y después me acosté.

- Use the **imperfect tense** (hablaba) to talk about past actions that lasted a certain time **without mentioning the end**. This tense is also used to describe characters and setting, and to explain the circumstances surrounding an event. Expressions that indicate a continuing and/or repeated action are often paired with verbs in the imperfect tense.

  > <u>Cuando **era** pequeña</u>, **vivía** cerca de un parque y **jugaba** allí con mis amigos.

- Use the **present perfect tense** (he hablado) to talk about actions that began in the past but which **continue into the present** or to describe actions that have recently ended.

  > **He vivido** en la misma casa <u>durante diez años</u>.
  > <u>Hoy</u> **he llegado** tarde a clase.

- Use the **past perfect tense** (había hablado) to talk about a past action that **was completed before another action** took place. Words such as <u>ya</u> and <u>todavía</u> are often paired with verbs in the past perfect.

  > Cuando me **llamaste**, yo <u>ya</u> **había hablado** con Juan.

20 **Compara.** ¿Qué tiempos del pasado usas en inglés? ¿Qué expresa cada uno?

21 **¡Qué día tan ocupado!**

▶ **Escribe** lo que han hecho hoy Asha y Lucas para avanzar en su desafío.

Modelo (Asha) Leer un reportaje sobre las ruinas de Palenque, en Chiapas (México).
→ *Asha ha leído un reportaje sobre las ruinas de Palenque.*

1. (Asha) Ver un video sobre los jeroglíficos del Templo del Sol (Palenque).
2. (Asha) Buscar fotografías de las ruinas de Palenque.
3. (Lucas) Tomar notas sobre la situación geográfica de las ruinas de Tikal (Guatemala).
4. (Lucas) Hacer una ficha sobre las construcciones del yacimiento arqueológico de Tikal.

402 cuatrocientos dos

Differentiated Instruction

DEVELOPING LEARNERS

- Ask students to complete these statements:

  1. ¿... ustedes en Copán? (e) — a. *habías llegado*
  2. *De joven, yo... en Madrid.* (f) — b. *Empezó*
  3. *Cuando te llamé, todavía no...* (a) — c. *he visto*
  4. *... a llover a las dos en punto.* (b) — d. *había estado*
  5. *Creo que te... esta mañana.* (c) — e. *Han estado*
  6. Yo *nunca... aquí.* (d) — f. *vivía*

EXPANDING LEARNERS

- Ask students to name a project or task they would either like to do or need to complete (e.g., *aprobar el examen de Español*). Then have them list all the steps they have recently completed in order to carry out this project or task successfully. Students should describe these steps by using the present perfect tense. For example: *He repasado todos los verbos irregulares en el pretérito. He estudiado los usos del subjuntivo.* Call on students to read aloud their goals and the steps they have already taken to achieve their goals.

22 **Una civilización muy avanzada**

▶ **Lee** la línea del tiempo y escribe qué habían hecho los mayas antes de la llegada de los europeos.

Modelo *Antes de la llegada de los europeos, los mayas ya habían desarrollado un sistema de escritura.*

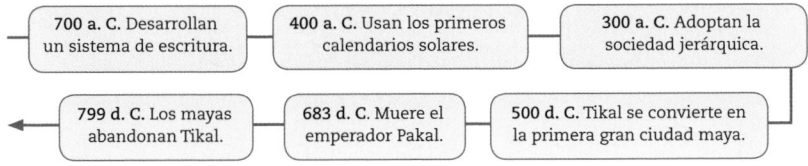

| 700 a. C. Desarrollan un sistema de escritura. | 400 a. C. Usan los primeros calendarios solares. | 300 a. C. Adoptan la sociedad jerárquica. |

| 799 d. C. Los mayas abandonan Tikal. | 683 d. C. Muere el emperador Pakal. | 500 d. C. Tikal se convierte en la primera gran ciudad maya. |

a. C. = antes de Cristo (before Christ); d. C. = después de Cristo (after Christ).

▶ **Escribe** un párrafo sobre lo que habían hecho los pueblos indígenas de tu región antes de la llegada de los europeos.

23 **Eran las cinco de la mañana cuando…**

▶ **Representa** con tu compañero(a) una conversación entre dos arqueólogos(as) que hablan sobre sus últimos viajes. Expliquen adónde fueron, qué descubrieron, qué tiempo hacía, etc.

Modelo *El año pasado viajé con mi equipo al sur de México. Recuerdo que eran las cinco de la mañana cuando llegamos a las ruinas de…*

CONEXIONES: MATEMÁTICAS

La numeración maya

Los mayas crearon un sistema de numeración para medir el tiempo e inventaron el concepto de «cero». Por eso, los números mayas están relacionados con los días, los meses y los años de su calendario. Los tres símbolos básicos de este sistema eran el punto (equivale al uno), la raya (equivale al cinco) y el caracol (equivale al cero). Combinando estos símbolos obtenían los números del 0 al 19.

24 **Piensa.** ¿Cómo podrían representar los mayas los números mayores de 19?

Gramática – Usos de los tiempos de pasado (repaso)

23. You may also want to ask students to imagine that some sort of "obstacle" arose during their day as archaeologists (e.g., horrible weather, the intrusion of a dangerous animal, an injury), and have them incorporate this incident into their conversation.

CONEXIONES: MATEMÁTICAS

La numeración maya

The Mayas discovered the concept of zero around the year 36 BC. We use a base ten, or decimal, numeral system, meaning that we count by ten digits. The Mayas used a base twenty system, assigning symbols to numbers from zero to nineteen. It is possible that they developed this system from counting on fingers and toes. Numbers after nineteen were written vertically in powers of twenty.

Answer Key

20. En inglés se usa el pasado simple (e.g., *It rained last week*), el presente perfecto (e.g., *It hasn't rained since last week)* y el pasado perfecto (e.g., *It had rained before it started to snow*).

21. 1. Asha ha visto un video…
2. Asha ha buscado fotografías…
3. Lucas ha tomado notas sobre…
4. Lucas ha hecho una ficha sobre…

22. Habían usado los primeros calendarios solares y habían adoptado la sociedad jerárquica. Tikal se había convertido en la primera gran ciudad maya. Había muerto el emperador Pakal y los mayas habían abandonado Tikal.
▶ Answers will vary.

23. Answers will vary.

24. Answers will vary.

Additional Resources

Fans Online activities
Practice Workbook

HERITAGE LANGUAGE LEARNERS

• Ask students to imagine a conversation between two indigenous Mayas that takes place when the Spaniards started arriving in the Americas. The Mayas have just seen the first Europeans disembarking from their ship. They had never seen such a sight. Ask students to work with a partner and create a dialogue that reflects their initial emotions: surprise, curiosity, anxiety, fear, or even anger. In their conversations, students might speculate where these visitors have come from, what they want from the population, and how the two cultures might interact.

MULTIPLE INTELLIGENCES:
Logical-Mathematical Intelligence

• Explain to students that the Mayan numerals consisted of only three symbols: a shell shape for the zero, a dot for one, and a bar for five. Ask students to study the Mayan numerals depicted in the *Conexiones* feature on page 403 for a couple of minutes. Then have students close their textbooks and write the answers to the following arithmetic problems using Mayan numerals:

1. 7 + 6   4. 19 − 0
2. 6 × 3   5. 5 × 2
3. 8 − 8   6. 4 + 5

LECTURA: TEXTO DIALOGADO

Presentation

- In this section, students will read a dialogue, identify place names and dates contained within, recognize cognates and definitions of words, and answer comprehension questions based on the reading.

Activities	Standards	Resources
Lectura: texto dialogado	1.1, 1.2, 2.2, 3.1	Vis. Pres.
25.	1.2, 3.1	
26.	1.1, 1.2, 2.2	
27.	1.3, 4.2, 5.2	
28.	1.3, 2.1, 2.2, 3.1	

Teaching Suggestions

Warm-Up / Independent Starter

- Ask students to write five sentences about five different things they know about the Mayan civilization. Have them use these structures:
  - the passive voice
  - the preterite tense
  - the imperfect tense
  - the present perfect tense
  - the past perfect tense

Preparation

- In order to draw on prior knowledge in comprehending the reading, have students share their Independent Starter sentences with a partner. Then ask students to read the *Antes de leer* strategies silently. Ask them to work with a different partner to answer the questions. Discuss the answers as a class.

- Have students locate Copán on a map of Honduras. To help them identify the century in which the staircase was built, call their attention to the fact that centuries are normally expressed in Spanish with Roman numerals, and give them examples to practice decoding them.

- Ask pairs of students to scan the dialogue for cognates. (*Historia, colaborar, identificar, ruinas, tesoros, importante, información, templo, pirámide, usar, ceremonias, cósmico, representar, monumento, signos, narrar, conquistas*)

Antes de leer: estrategias

1. Lee el título del diálogo y mira las fotos. ¿Reconoces la palabra *jeroglífico*? ¿Y la palabra *escalinata*? ¿En qué se diferencia una escalinata de una escalera?

2. Adivina el tema del diálogo. ¿Con quién hablan Asha y Lucas? ¿De qué crees que hablan?

3. Localiza el lugar y la fecha que se mencionan en el texto. Anota dónde está la Escalinata de los Jeroglíficos y cuándo se construyó.

La Escalinata de los Jeroglíficos

ASHA: Lucas, te presento al señor Ángel López. Es profesor de Historia.

LUCAS: Mucho gusto, señor López.

SR. LÓPEZ: Igualmente. Asha me dijo que tienen muchas preguntas para mí.

LUCAS: Así es.

SR. LÓPEZ: Estoy encantado de poder colaborar con ustedes. Díganme, ¿en qué puedo ayudarlos?

ASHA: Hemos identificado las ruinas de Copán, en Honduras, como uno de los tesoros mayas más importantes. Pero nos gustaría tener más información sobre la Escalinata de los Jeroglíficos.

SR. LÓPEZ: ¡Cómo no! Esa escalinata era parte de un templo en forma de pirámide y se usaba para hacer ceremonias. Fue construida en el siglo VIII.

LUCAS: Leímos en Internet que los escalones tenían un significado cósmico...

SR. LÓPEZ: Es cierto. Representan a los dioses del bien y del mal, la vida y la muerte. Pero lo más importante del monumento son los jeroglíficos.

ASHA: ¿Qué representan?

SR. LÓPEZ: Son más de 2500 signos que narran la historia de los gobernantes de Copán, sus logros, sus guerras y sus conquistas.

Differentiated Instruction

DEVELOPING LEARNERS

- Read the following statements and ask students whether they are true (*cierto*) or false (*falso*). Have them correct the false ones.

  1. *Copán está en Yucatán.* (falso; en Honduras)
  2. *Asha quiere tener más información sobre la Escalinata de los Jeroglíficos.* (cierto)
  3. *La escalinata era parte de un templo.* (cierto)
  4. *Los escalones representaban a los gobernantes mayas.* (falso; a los dioses)
  5. *Los jeroglíficos representan la naturaleza maya.* (falso; la historia de los gobernantes de Copán)

EXPANDING LEARNERS

- Ask students to write a persuasive paragraph to recruit fellow students to join an archaeological expedition to Central America as volunteers. Students should include a description of one or two sites that are described in this lesson, or choose an alternative, and also mention something about the history or legends surrounding the site. Students' paragraphs should include an explanation of what the volunteer archaeologists are going to be looking for and what they are going to do, as well as what they will learn from this experience.

LECTURA:
TEXTO DIALOGADO

25 Definiciones

▶ **Une** las dos columnas.

Ⓐ	Ⓑ
1. templo	a. Figura o símbolo que representa una palabra.
2. escalinata	b. Lugar o edificio público destinado al culto.
3. ceremonia	c. Éxito.
4. jeroglífico	d. Acción solemne de honor o respeto.
5. logro	e. Escalera amplia y artística, generalmente de un solo tramo.

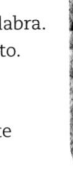

26 Comprensión

▶ **Lee** el diálogo otra vez y responde a estas preguntas.

1. ¿En qué país están las ruinas de Copán?
2. ¿Para qué se usaba la Escalinata de los Jeroglíficos?
3. ¿Cuándo fue construida?
4. ¿Qué representaban los escalones?
5. ¿Qué narran los jeroglíficos?

27 Tu propia escalinata

▶ **Dibuja** una escalinata y añade jeroglíficos para representar tu propia historia. Después, escribe un párrafo explicando los hechos más importantes.

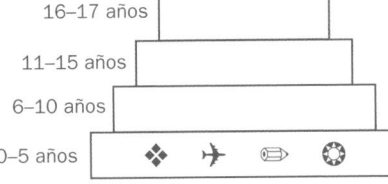

▶ **Presenta** tu escalinata a la clase.

28 Investigación

▶ **Elige** uno de estos temas y, en grupos pequeños, preparen una presentación para la clase.

LAS PIRÁMIDES MAYAS

Pirámide del adivino.
Ruinas de Uxmal (México).

LOS MAYAS EN LA ACTUALIDAD

Vendedora ambulante frente
al Palacio de Gobierno (Guatemala).

■ Read the dialogue aloud to students, modeling correct pronunciation and intonation. Then call on three volunteers to read the dialogue aloud, playing the parts of Lucas, Asha, and Mr. López. Offer suggestions to improve their oral reading.

Activities

25. You may help students find the right associations by asking them which of the words in column A refer to places, actions, or things. You may also have them identify cognates in the definitions (e.g., *figura, símbolo, público, culto, acción, honor, respeto*).

26. Call students' attention to the verb tense that they will be using to answer each question. Although they may vary, these are the most likely tenses: 1 and 5 → present; 2 and 4 → imperfect; 3 → preterite.

28. Make a list of questions that students should cover in their presentations. For example: 1. *Las pirámides mayas: ¿Dónde están? ¿Quién las construyó? ¿Cuándo fueron construidas? ¿Para qué servían?* 2. *Los mayas en la actualidad: ¿Quiénes son? ¿Dónde viven? ¿Cómo son? ¿Qué idioma(s) hablan?*

Answer Key

25. 1. b   2. e   3. d   4. a   5. c

26. 1. Están en Honduras.
   2. Se usaba para hacer ceremonias.
   3. Fue construida en el siglo VIII.
   4. Representaban a sus dioses.
   5. Narran la historia de los gobernantes de Copán.

27. Answers will vary.
   ▶ Answers will vary.

28. Answers will vary.

Additional Resources

Fans Online activities

HERITAGE LANGUAGE LEARNERS

• Ask students if they or anyone in their family has visited any of the ruins described in this *Desafío*. Ask students to provide more images if they are available, and a more personal account of these sites. If students cannot do this, ask them to select one of the sites and make a brief but insightful report or oral presentation. You might encourage students to invite a speaker who has studied the history of the Mayan civilization to come to class and share his or her knowledge with students.

MULTIPLE INTELLIGENCES:
Visual-Spatial Intelligence

• After students complete activity 27, ask them to project what their lives will be like from the ages of 18–22, 23–43, 44–64, and beyond the age of 65. Ask them to draw another *escalinata* and decorate it with new hieroglyphics that describe their life events at these different stages. Have students accompany their *escalinata* with a few paragraphs that detail what they project they will be studying, and where they will be working and living the rest of their lives. Display their artwork and call on volunteers to read their projections.

Unit 8
DESAFÍO 1
Comunicación

Presentation

- In this section, students will integrate the vocabulary and grammar skills from *Desafío 1* in order to describe historic events and civilizations.

Activities	Standards	Resources
29.	1.1, 1.2, 2.2, 3.2	
30.	1.1, 1.2, 2.2	Audio
31.	1.1, 1.3, 5.2	
32. Final del desafío	1.2, 2.2, 3.1	

Teaching Suggestions

Warm-Up / Independent Starter

- Ask students to react to two of the following quotes about time and history. Ask them to be as specific as possible.
  1. *Si el presente trata de juzgar el pasado, perderá el futuro.* (Winston Churchill)
  2. *Ni el pasado ha muerto, ni está el mañana –ni el ayer– escrito.* (Antonio Machado)
  3. *El pasado me ha revelado la estructura del futuro.* (Pierre de Teilhard de Chardin)
  4. *Si no quieres repetir el pasado, estúdialo.* (Baruch de Spinoza)

Preparation

- Review the reactions to the Independent Starter in a roundtable discussion. Be sure to discuss topics one at a time and to encourage equally active participation from all group members.

Activities

29. After students have completed this activity, ask them to work in pairs. Assign one of the four paragraphs of the article to each pair. Ask each pair to read their assigned paragraph aloud and to write one headline that would be generated based on the content (e.g., *Tulum fue el lugar más visitado en 2011*). Then, assign students to groups of four. Make sure that each member of the group has read a different paragraph. They will share their headlines with other members of the group.

30. Before listening to the audio recording, ask students to read the questions for better comprehension of the content.

406

DESAFÍO 1

Comunicación

29 **El mundo maya**

▶ **Lee** este artículo de prensa y responde a las preguntas.

Casi 2 millones de personas visitaron el mundo maya en 2011

Ciudad amurallada de Tulum (México).

El Instituto Nacional de Antropología e Historia de Quintana Roo afirmó que el turismo cultural está aumentando y que cerraron el año con 1.777.320 visitantes en los doce sitios abiertos al público. Tulum sigue siendo el lugar favorito de los extranjeros y el más visitado en México.

Adriana Velázquez Morlet, directora general del INAH, afirmó que el turismo extranjero prefería el sitio prehispánico de Tulum, adonde llegaron 670.064 personas, por encima de Chichén-Itzá,

que recibió 654.415 visitas, y de Teotihuacán, que ocupó el tercer lugar con 510.367 turistas de otras naciones.

«En diciembre, Tulum recibió 100.590 turistas, lo que consideramos un número histórico en el período vacacional de fin de año», señaló.

La funcionaria atribuyó este aumento de visitantes a que han logrado fortalecer la infraestructura y el trabajo de investigación, conservación y mantenimiento por parte del INAH-Conaculta, y también a la difusión de esta enorme riqueza cultural. Y anunció que este año el INAH y la Secretaría de Turismo promoverán diez zonas arqueológicas de la región sureste, donde floreció la cultura maya. Los sitios son Edzná y Calakmul, en Campeche; Izapa y Palenque, en Chiapas; Tulum y Cobá, en Quintana Roo; Comalcalco y Pomoná, en Tabasco; y Chichén-Itzá y Uxmal, en el estado de Yucatán.

Fuente: http://www.eluniversal.com.mx
(texto adaptado)

1. ¿Cuál fue el lugar más visitado por los turistas extranjeros en 2011? ¿En qué país está?
2. ¿Qué significan las siglas INAH?
3. ¿Qué cargo ocupa Adriana Velázquez?
4. ¿Por qué cree Adriana Velázquez que aumentó el número de turistas en Tulum?
5. ¿Qué iniciativas se van a realizar para fomentar el turismo, según Adriana Velázquez?

30 **Un futuro arqueólogo**

▶ **Escucha** a Asha y a Lucas, y responde a estas preguntas.

1. ¿Qué descubrimiento de los mayas menciona Asha? ¿Y Lucas?
2. ¿Qué le gustaría investigar a Lucas?
3. ¿Por qué no ha desaparecido la cultura de los mayas?
4. ¿Qué misterio no se ha resuelto todavía, según Lucas?
5. ¿Le gustaría a Asha vivir en la época de los antiguos mayas? ¿Por qué?

406 cuatrocientos seis

Differentiated Instruction

DEVELOPING LEARNERS

- Ask students to read the article in activity 29 aloud and, as they do this, to identify each of the past tenses used. After they correctly name the tense, ask them to explain why it was used. Refer them back to the *Gramática* feature on page 402 if they have difficulty doing this. Then ask students to rephrase one of the sentences in the passive voice and read it aloud.

EXPANDING LEARNERS

- Have small groups play "Jeopardy" against each other. They must be the first to provide the questions to the answers you give them. For example:
  1. *la astronomía* (¿Qué desarrollaron los mayas?)
  2. *obra que explica el origen del mundo maya* (¿Qué es el *Popol Vuh*?)
  3. *Copán* (¿Qué ruinas mayas hay en Honduras?)
  4. *en Chichén Itzá* (¿Dónde está la pirámide de Kukulcán?)
  5. *los matemáticos mayas* (¿Quiénes inventaron el cero?)

31 Tus descubrimientos

 ▶ **Imagina** que eres un(a) arqueólogo(a) que ha encontrado estas ruinas. Escribe un diario sobre tus descubrimientos. Después, intercambia tu texto con tu compañero(a) y coméntenlos.

Modelo

> Después de excavar el primer sitio, descubrí unas cabezas gigantes de piedra. Se me ocurrieron muchas preguntas...

Final del desafío

> ¡Me gustó mucho aprender más sobre los ___1___! Sobre todo lo que leímos acerca de las ___2___ de Tulum y de Chichén-Itzá.

> Empezaremos por situar las ___4___ excavadas por los arqueólogos en Palenque.

> Ya estamos listos para hacer nuestro mapa de los ___3___ mayas. Corresponde a los territorios de Honduras, El Salvador, Guatemala y México.

> Sí. Y de México vamos a Guatemala, donde están las ruinas ___5___ de Tikal.

> No te olvides de Copán, en Honduras. Es un ___6___ muy importante.

32 El mapa de los tesoros

▶ **Completa** el diálogo con estas palabras.

tesoros	precolombinas
monumento	pirámides
ruinas	mayas

▶ **Localiza** en un mapa de Centroamérica los tesoros mayas que mencionan los personajes.

> Y, por último, Cerén, en El Salvador.

cuatrocientos siete 407

HERITAGE LANGUAGE LEARNERS

- Ask students to describe other ruins that are not mentioned in this *Desafío*. The ruins could be from their family's country of origin, or from any place in the Spanish-speaking world. After students do their research, ask them to describe where these ruins are located, when they were discovered and by whom, the role of these ruins in the country's culture and their impact on world culture, and how they are being preserved. Encourage students to include some legends surrounding the site, and to accompany their reports with images. Ask them to present to the class.

MULTIPLE INTELLIGENCES: Naturalist Intelligence

- Explain to students that many of the ruins described in this unit are near sites of natural beauty and are popular tourist destinations. Ask students to gather information on these spots and design a travel brochure that would appeal to a family or a group of friends with a wide range of interests. Some are amateur archaeologists and would like to spend their time visiting ruins and learning more about them; others want to enjoy the local flora and fauna; still others like aquatic sports and would like to spend time on the beach.

🎧 **AUDIO SCRIPT**
See page 389l.

Answer Key

29. 1. Tulum fue el lugar más visitado. Está en México.
2. Significan Instituto Nacional de Antropología e Historia.
3. Es directora general del INAH.
4. Porque habían logrado fortalecer la infraestructura, el trabajo de investigación, la conservación y el mantenimiento, y habían también promovido la difusión de esta riqueza cultural.
5. Para fomentar el turismo, Adriana Velázquez anunció que el INAH y la Secretaría de Turismo promoverán diez zonas arqueológicas de la región en la que floreció la cultura maya.

30. 1. Asha menciona el concepto del cero y el calendario. Lucas menciona el sistema de escritura.
2. A Lucas le gustaría investigar los jeroglíficos.
3. La cultura de los mayas no ha desaparecido porque los arqueólogos han descubierto muchos restos de esta antigua civilización.
4. Todavía no se ha resuelto qué les pasó a los habitantes de Tikal o de Copán.
5. Asha no sabe si le gustaría vivir en la época de los antiguos mayas porque tendría que vivir sin su computadora, teléfono, correo electrónico, etc.

31. Answers will vary.

32. 1. mayas   4. ruinas
2. pirámides   5. precolombinas
3. tesoros   6. monumento
▶ Answers will vary.

Additional Resources

Fans Online activities
Practice Workbook

Unit 8
DESAFÍO 2
Hablar de hechos reales

Presentation

- In *Desafío 2*, Ethan and Eva will have to find out what the *OEA* is and write a report about this organization. Students will preview vocabulary used to talk about government and politics, and verb constructions that refer to the different stages of an action.

Activities	Standards	Resources
Texto	1.2, 2.1	Vis. Pres.
33.	1.1, 1.2, 3.1	
34.	1.1, 1.2, 2.1	
35.	1.2, 1.3, 2.1	Audio
36.	1.1, 3.1, 5.1	
37. Cultura	1.1, 1.2, 2.1	

Teaching Suggestions

Warm-Up / Independent Starter

- Have students brainstorm a list of international organizations that they know.

Preparation

- Call on several volunteers to share their Independent Starters. If students' answers are limited, provide them with a short list of organizations (e.g., UN, UNESCO, WHO, OECD) and ask students to work in groups to investigate these organizations and their goals.

Texto: Una organización multinacional

- Read the introduction and invite students to try to guess the meaning of *OEA*. Point out that a lot of the vocabulary related to government, economy, and politics is easily recognizable due to the high percentage of cognates.
- Have students read the dialogue silently. Did they guess the meaning of *OEA*? Then call on several pairs of volunteers to read the roles of Eva and Ethan aloud.

Activities

35. Before playing the audio selection, have students read the sentences and look up the words that they do not understand.

408

Una organización multinacional

Ethan and Eva have to decipher information in order to complete their challenge. They have to find out what the OEA is, and write a report about the projects that it undertakes.

EVA: ¿La OEA? No tengo idea de qué puede ser.

ETHAN: Evidentemente son siglas. La O debe de ser *organización*.

EVA: Sí, tiene sentido. También sabemos que realiza proyectos porque nuestra tarea consiste en averiguar en qué proyectos trabaja y escribir sobre ello.

ETHAN: Y como es una organización, es probable que esté relacionada con el gobierno.

EVA: Podría ser el gobierno de un estado…

ETHAN: ¡Estado! ¡Claro! Ese es el significado de la E: *Organización del Estado…* ¿Qué más? Tenemos que seguir pensando.

EVA: No, hombre, vamos a dejar de perder el tiempo. ¿No hay una enciclopedia aquí?

ETHAN: Ah, sí. Aquí está. Te lo leo: *OEA, Organización de Estados Americanos.* ¡Eva, teníamos razón!

EVA: Sí, sí, pero continúa. ¿Qué más dice?

ETHAN: Dice que es una organización supranacional que lleva trabajando desde 1948 y reúne a los países del hemisferio occidental con dos objetivos: fortalecer la cooperación mutua y defender los intereses comunes.

EVA: ¿El hemisferio occidental? ¿Entonces a qué países se refiere?

ETHAN: Quizá sean los Estados Unidos. O los países de las Américas. Debemos seguir buscando información.

33 **Detective de palabras**

▶ **Completa** estas oraciones del diálogo.

1. Tenemos que _____ pensando.
2. Vamos a _____ de perder el tiempo.
3. La OEA _____ trabajando desde 1948.
4. Debemos _____ buscando información.

▶ **Decide.** Entre las oraciones anteriores, ¿cuáles expresan que una acción continúa y cuál expresa que una acción se interrumpe?

Differentiated Instruction

DEVELOPING LEARNERS

- Ask students to read the dialogue in small groups. Help them decode any unfamiliar words by asking them to look for cognates and to analyze the context. After they read each line, have them paraphrase what they have just read to verify their comprehension. Once students have finished, ask them to write a short summary of what has taken place in the dialogue. Call on volunteers to read their summaries aloud.

EXPANDING LEARNERS

- Knowing prefixes will help students decode new words, such as *supranacional*. Have students look up the meaning of these prefixes: *ante-, anti-, dis-, sub-, super-, trans-*. Then ask students to match the following words with their meaning:

  1. *antipático* (f)
  2. *superdotado* (c)
  3. *transformar* (d)
  4. *subalterno* (e)
  5. *antesala* (a)
  6. *discordia* (b)

  a. *espacio delante de la sala*
  b. *desacuerdo*
  c. *tiene un coeficiente intelectual superior*
  d. *cambiar de forma*
  e. *está sujeto a otro*
  f. *sin simpatía*

34 **¿Comprendes?**

▶ **Responde** a estas preguntas.

1. ¿En qué consiste el desafío de Eva y Ethan?
2. ¿Qué es la OEA?
3. ¿Dónde encuentran Eva y Ethan el significado de estas siglas?
4. ¿Cuál es el objetivo de la OEA? ¿Qué tipo de proyectos piensas que realiza?

 35 **Más información**

▶ **Escucha** la conversación entre Eva y Ethan, y completa estas oraciones.

1. Ethan cree que en el logo de la OEA están las _____ de los países que la forman.
2. El lema de la OEA es: «Democracia para la _____, la seguridad y el desarrollo».
3. La OEA está formada por _____ países independientes de las Américas.
4. La OEA trabaja en proyectos _____, sociales, educativos y económicos.

36 **¿Qué proyecto?**

▶ **Habla** con tu compañero(a). ¿En qué áreas de la OEA les gustaría trabajar? ¿Por qué?

- Protección de la infancia.
- Lucha contra la pobreza.
- Desarrollo sostenible.
- Promoción del comercio.
- Protección de los derechos humanos.
- Promoción de la igualdad de género y defensa de la mujer.

Modelo   A. *A mí me gustaría colaborar en el área de desarrollo sostenible porque me interesa la ecología.*
B. *Yo pienso que es más necesario trabajar para luchar contra la pobreza.*

 **CULTURA**

La misión de la OEA

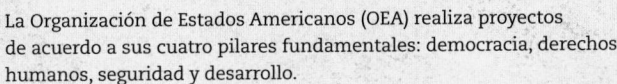

La Organización de Estados Americanos (OEA) realiza proyectos de acuerdo a sus cuatro pilares fundamentales: democracia, derechos humanos, seguridad y desarrollo.
Esta organización tiene su sede en Washington DC y a ella pertenecen 35 estados americanos independientes. La OEA trabaja en proyectos tan variados como la protección de los derechos humanos, el desarrollo sostenible, la consolidación de la paz y la democracia o el desarrollo económico, social y cultural de los estados miembros.

 37 **Piensa.** ¿Qué ventajas y qué dificultades hay cuando los países trabajan en proyectos comunes?

---

37. Before doing this activity, have students discuss in small groups some of the challenges all of the countries of the Americas face (e.g., improving education, protecting the environment). Ask volunteers to share their answers with the class.

 AUDIO SCRIPT
See page 389I.

 CULTURA

La misión de la OEA

This organization has a logo that shows the official flags of the thirty-five members arranged in an arc that conveys the idea of equality among its members. The logo symbolizes the transnational scope of the organization and is available in the four official languages of the organization: English, Spanish, French, and Portuguese.

Answer Key

33. 1. seguir   3. lleva
2. dejar   4. seguir
▶ Continúa: 1, 3, 4.   Se interrumpe: 2.

34. 1. Tienen que averiguar qué es la OEA y escribir un informe sobre esa organización.
2. Es la Organización de Estados Americanos.
3. En una enciclopedia.
4. Fortalecer la cooperación entre los países miembros y defender los intereses comunes. Answers will vary.

35. 1. banderas   3. treinta y cinco
2. paz   4. políticos

36. Answers will vary.

37. Answers will vary.

Additional Resources

Fans Online activities

HERITAGE LANGUAGE LEARNERS

- Ask students to define *supranacional*. Remind them that the prefix *supra-* means *por encima de*. *Supranacional*, according to the Royal Academy of the Spanish Language (*RAE* in Spanish), refers to *una entidad que está por encima del ámbito de los gobiernos e instituciones nacionales y que actúa con independencia de ellos*. Ask students to list some other common prefixes and suffixes, along with their meanings. Have them write an example word for each one, along with a sentence.

CRITICAL THINKING

- Have students review the topics mentioned in activity 36. Then ask them to think about which one of these areas is the most problematic to their own community and how more public awareness would help the problem. Next, have students write a few paragraphs describing how this problem or situation has been affecting their community and how they would go about encouraging the local population to improve the situation. Encourage those students who have selected the same areas to work together and compare their recommendations.

DESAFÍO 2

Vocabulario – Política y gobierno

Presentation

■ In this section, students will learn vocabulary related to politics and government.

Activities	Standards	Resources
Vocabulario	1.2, 2.1, 3.1	
38.	1.2, 3.1	
39.	1.2, 2.1, 3.1	Audio
40.	1.1, 5.2	
41. Cultura	1.1, 1.2, 2.1, 2.2, 4.2	

Teaching Suggestions

Warm-Up / Independent Starter

■ Have students give examples of countries that have these political systems: *monarquía, república democrática, dictadura.*

Preparation

■ Ask students to look at the picture in the vocabulary section, but they should not read the caption. Then ask the class the following questions: *¿Quién creen que es el hombre que firma el documento? ¿Qué tipo de documento puede ser? ¿Quiénes son la mujer y el niño? ¿De qué país creen que son estas personas?*

■ Have a volunteer read the second paragraph aloud. Emphasize pronunciation of the highlighted words. To make sure students understand the meaning, you may ask them these questions: *¿Tenemos una monarquía en este país? ¿Quiénes son el presidente y el vicepresidente? ¿Quiénes son los "ministros" en nuestro sistema político?*

■ Call on three volunteers to read the first, third and fourth paragraphs. Emphasize the pronunciation of the cognates in the vocabulary to minimize any interference from English in students' pronunciation of these words.

■ Ask students to share their Independent Starters. Create a three-column chart on the board and ask students to list the main characteristics of the three political systems mentioned in the Independent Starter (e.g., *monarquía: el rey es el jefe del Estado...*).

Vocabulario

Política y gobierno

La mayoría de los países latinoamericanos son **repúblicas democráticas**. Los(as) **ciudadanos(as)** eligen al jefe o jefa del Estado, que es también el jefe o jefa del Gobierno.

En España hay una **monarquía constitucional**. El jefe del Estado es el **rey**. El rey representa al país, pero no gobierna. El gobierno está formado por el/la **presidente(a)**, los(as) **vicepresidentes(as)** y los(as) **ministros(as)**.

En los países democráticos hay un **Parlamento** que elabora las **leyes**. En España, el Parlamento está formado por el **Congreso de los Diputados** y el **Senado**.

Tanto en España como en Latinoamérica ha habido períodos de **dictadura**, en los que el **poder** está concentrado en una sola persona. En algunos casos el **dictador** es elegido por **votación**. En otros, llega al poder mediante un **golpe de Estado**.

Juan Carlos I, rey de España, firmando la Constitución.

Más vocabulario

Cargos y títulos

el alcalde/la alcaldesa	*mayor*
el/la diputado(a)	*representative*
el/la gobernador(a)	*governor*
el príncipe/la princesa	*prince/princess*
el/la senador(a)	*senator*
la reina	*queen*

Acciones

apoyar	*to support*
aprobar	*to approve*
dirigir	*to direct*
gobernar	*to govern*
rechazar	*to reject*
votar	*to vote*

Ideologías

demócrata	*democrat*	liberal	*liberal*
comunista	*communist*	republicano(a)	*republican*
conservador(a)	*conservative*	socialista	*socialist*

---

38 Gobiernos

▶ **Completa** estas oraciones con los verbos del cuadro en la forma correcta.

> gobernar
> votar
> aprobar
> apoyar

1. Los ciudadanos _____ para elegir a sus representantes.

2. Las leyes se _____ en el Parlamento.

3. ¿Qué presidente _____ ahora en los Estados Unidos?

4. Muchos famosos _____ públicamente a los partidos políticos.

Differentiated Instruction

DEVELOPING LEARNERS

• For many students, the amount of vocabulary presented here may be daunting. To help these students, encourage them to draw five concept webs and organize the vocabulary accordingly. Ask students to write the following in the central circle of each of the five webs: *Tipos de gobierno, Lugares y otros sustantivos, Acciones, Cargos y títulos, Ideologías*. Then ask students to write the vocabulary related to each category in the circles branching out from the central circle in each of the webs.

EXPANDING LEARNERS

• After students review the vocabulary and read *Política y gobierno*, tell them they are going to play a word game. Ask them to pick an index card at random on which you will have written the new words. Students must either give an example with the word (e.g., *El gobernador del estado es...*) or say a sentence (e.g., *Mis padres siempre votan en las elecciones*). Students return the index card to the bag, but if the same card is picked again, new examples must be given.

39 **Política latinoamericana**

▶ **Elige** la opción correcta. Si no estás seguro(a), anota las respuestas que te parecen más probables. Después, escucha la conversación entre Eva y Ethan, y comprueba los resultados.

1. ¿Cuál es la forma de gobierno actual en la mayoría de los países latinoamericanos?
   a. democracia   **b.** dictadura   **c.** monarquía

2. ¿Qué forma de gobierno hubo en Chile de 1973 a 1990?
   a. monarquía   **b.** dictadura   **c.** democracia

3. ¿En qué país hubo una monarquía después de independizarse de España?
   a. en Argentina   **b.** en Cuba   **c.** en México

4. ¿Cuál es el país latinoamericano con más tradición democrática?
   a. Costa Rica   **b.** Chile   **c.** Nicaragua

5. ¿En qué país no hay ejército (*army*)?
   a. en Colombia   **b.** en México   **c.** en Costa Rica

 40 **Descúbrelo**

▶ **Elige** tres palabras o expresiones de la ficha de Vocabulario y escríbelas. Tu compañero(a) deberá adivinar cuáles son haciéndote preguntas. Túrnense.

 ¿Es un cargo o un título?

¿Existe ahora en los Estados Unidos?

 Sí.

No.

CULTURA

El significado de las banderas

La bandera de México está dividida en tres franjas verticales: verde, blanca y roja. El verde simboliza la esperanza; el blanco, la pureza; y el rojo, la sangre de los héroes nacionales. En el centro está el escudo nacional, inspirado en la leyenda azteca sobre la fundación de Tenochtitlán, la antigua capital del imperio. Según la leyenda, los aztecas debían buscar una nueva tierra que les traería riqueza y poder; la encontrarían cuando vieran un águila sobre un nopal (*prickly pear cactus*) devorando una serpiente.

41 **Compara.** Compara la bandera de tu país con la de México. ¿Qué elementos la forman? ¿Qué significado tienen?

Unit 8

DESAFÍO 2

Vocabulario – Política y gobierno

Activities

40. You may want to turn this activity into a game. Prepare a set of flashcards with the words or expressions from the vocabulary section. Divide the class into two teams. Alternating turns, students try to guess the word by asking questions similar to the ones they have in activity 40. The group that gets the answer first will get the point.

41. Bring colored markers and paper in different colors to class. Divide the class into small groups and ask each group to design a flag for their school. They have to decide which colors and motifs they would include and explain why. Ask students to present their flags to the class and then have the class vote on the most original flag.

AUDIO SCRIPT
See page 389 J.

CULTURA

El significado de las banderas

In Mexico, the flag is a respected symbol. Flag Day is a major festivity that takes place on February 24. While the flag's pattern and colors have been consistent since 1821, the present flag is the fourth official design. It was adopted in 1968, coinciding with the celebration of the Olympic Games in Mexico City.

Answer Key

38. 1. votan   3. gobierna
      2. aprueban   4. apoyan
39. 1. a   2. b   3. c   4. a   5. c
40. Answers will vary.
41. Answers will vary.

Additional Resources

Fans Online activities
Practice Workbook

HERITAGE LANGUAGE LEARNERS

• While students may be familiar with nouns that end in -*a* that are invariable (e.g., *el/la comunista, el/la demócrata, el/la socialista*), explain that other words are invariable but end in -*o*. The gender of these nouns is indicated by the article, and include words such as *el/la testigo*. Ask students to brainstorm other words that fit this pattern (e.g., *el/la modelo, el/la piloto, el/la reo, el/la soldado, el/la soprano*). Ask students to write a sentence with each form of these words.

COOPERATIVE LEARNING

• Ask students to work in small groups and design a new state seal. All students will contribute their ideas regarding the colors and symbols, and explain their choices after researching their meaning. Students will also discuss any wording that will appear on their seal. After discussing their choices, the group will take a vote and follow up with a design. Those who are artistically gifted might draw the seal, while others will write the meaning of the colors and symbols. Have groups present their seals to the rest of the class and explain their design.

DESAFÍO 2

Gramática – Hablar de las etapas de una acción

Presentation

- In this section, students will learn how to talk about different moments of an action.

Activities	Standards	Resources
Gramática	1.2, 3.1	
42.	1.2, 4.1	
43.	1.2, 1.3, 3.1	
44.	1.2, 1.3, 3.1	Audio
45.	1.1, 1.3, 5.1	

Teaching Suggestions

Warm-Up / Independent Starter

- Have students list six things they did yesterday. Ask them to use infinitives and to list the actions in the order in which they happened. For example: *desayunar a las 7:00 a. m., asistir a tres clases…*

Preparation

- Have students read the grammar explanation silently and ask them to prepare questions about what they do not understand. Then ask students to work in groups to find any questions they all have in common, and to answer any questions their peers have that they can answer.

- Ask students to do activity 42. Once they finish, discuss their answers as a class. Then have them rewrite three of the actions in their Independent Starters using the verb forms introduced in the grammar presentation. For example: *Empecé a desayunar a las 7:00 a. m. Llevaba estudiando cuatro horas cuando salí a almorzar…* Have volunteers share their sentences.

Activities

43. To expand this activity, write the following information on the board: ONU (1945) – *luchar por la paz;* UNESCO (1946) – *eliminar la pobreza;* OTAN (1949) – *garantizar la seguridad.* Then have students write complete sentences similar to the answers for this activity. For example: *La ONU empezó a luchar por la paz en 1945. La UNESCO sigue trabajando para eliminar la pobreza.*

Gramática

Hablar de las etapas de una acción

Fases de la acción

- These are some of the structures we use in Spanish to talk about the different stages of an action:

empezar a + infinitive	Expresses the **beginning** of an action. *Empezó a llover por la mañana. (It started to rain in the morning.)*
seguir + present participle	Expresses the **continuation** of an action. *El bebé sigue llorando. (The baby continues to cry.)*
dejar de + infinitive	Expresses the **interruption** of a usual or habitual activity. *Juan dejó de trabajar el año pasado. (Juan stopped working last year.)*
acabar de + infinitive	Expresses the **end** of an action. *Isabel acabó de comer y se acostó. (Isabel finished eating and went to bed).* The structure acabar de + *infinitive* is also used to express a recently finished activity. *Acabo de llegar. (I just arrived.)*
llevar + present participle	Expresses an action that has been **going on** for a specific length of time. *Llevo leyendo dos horas. (I have been reading for two hours.)*

Los pronombres de objeto en las construcciones verbales

- In the above verb structures, object pronouns can be placed before the conjugated verb or attached to the end of the infinitive or the present participle.

  Se lo empezó a leer ayer./Empezó a leérselo ayer.
  Le lleva dando clases de piano un mes./Lleva dándole clases de piano un mes.

42 **Compara.** ¿Cómo dices en inglés lo siguiente? ¿Qué formas verbales usas?

a. Dejó de llover.

b. Ayer acabé de pintar mi cuarto.

c. Elsa sigue tomando clases de piano.

d. Hoy empiezo a estudiar para el examen.

43 **¿Cuánto tiempo?**

▶ **Responde** a estas preguntas con oraciones completas.

1. ¿Cuándo empezaste a estudiar Español?
2. ¿A qué hora acabaste de hacer la tarea ayer?
3. ¿Cuánto tiempo llevas viviendo en tu ciudad?
4. ¿Sigues viendo a tus amigos(as) de la infancia?

412 cuatrocientos doce

Differentiated Instruction

DEVELOPING LEARNERS

- Ask students to answer these questions:
  1. ¿A qué hora empezaste a estudiar hoy? (*Empecé a estudiar…*)
  2. ¿Sigues jugando al fútbol? (*Sí, sigo jugando. / No. Dejé de jugar.*)
  3. ¿Cuándo acabaste de almorzar? (*Acabé de almorzar…*)
  4. ¿Cuánto tiempo llevas esperando a tu amigo? (*Llevo esperándolo…*)
  5. ¿Cuándo dejaste de comer carne? (*Dejé de comer carne… / No dejé de comer carne; sigo comiéndola.*)
  6. ¿Cuántos años llevas asistiendo a la escuela? (*Llevo asistiendo a la escuela…*)

EXPANDING LEARNERS

- Ask students to use the structures for the different stages of an action and apply them to their own lives and those of their family or friends. Ask them to name those things they or others have started, continue to do, stopped doing, ended, or have just done, as well as to express how long they have been doing something. Encourage students to combine these actions into a cohesive paragraph or two. Call on volunteers to read their paragraphs to the rest of the class.

44 **Ethan se prepara**

 ▶ **Escucha.** Ethan explica a sus compañeros(as) cómo preparó la presentación para la clase de Ciencias Sociales. Ordena las fotografías.

 ▶ **Escucha** de nuevo y toma notas. Después, escribe un resumen de los pasos que siguió Ethan para preparar su presentación. Usa las estructuras de la ficha de Gramática.

Modelo   *Primero, Ethan empezó a buscar información en el libro de Historia. Después…*

45 **Haz memoria**

▶ **Completa** una tabla como esta.

Cosas que llevo haciendo mucho tiempo	Cosas que he dejado de hacer
Ir a clase de Música. Jugar al béisbol todos los fines de semana.	Tocar la guitarra.

 ▶ **Intercambia** tu lista con tu compañero(a) y hazle preguntas para saber más detalles.

Modelo   A. *No sabía que siguieras estudiando Música.*
B. *Sí, ahora tomo clases de piano.*
A. *¿Y por qué dejaste de tocar la guitarra?*

cuatrocientos trece **413**

Gramática – Hablar de las etapas de una acción

44. After finishing this activity, ask students to write how they prepared their last presentation, following the model given in this activity.

AUDIO SCRIPT
See page 389 J.

Answer Key

42. a. *It stopped raining.*
b. *I finished painting my bedroom yesterday.*
c. *Elsa continues to take piano lessons.*
d. *I'll start to study for the exam today.*

43. Answers will vary. Sample answers:
1. Empecé a estudiar Español hace cuatro años.
2. Acabé de hacer la tarea a las 9:00 p. m.
3. Llevo viviendo en esta ciudad seis años.
4. No, no sigo viendo a mis amigos de la infancia. Dejé de verlos cuando me mudé de ciudad.

44. C, B, D, A
▶ Answers will vary. Sample answer:
… siguió buscando información en libros de la biblioteca. Cuando acabó de cenar empezó a buscar imágenes de personajes importantes de México en Internet. Luego empezó a escribir, pero dejó de escribir porque pensó que sería más interesante incluir testimonios reales. Pensó en un amigo mexicano que lleva viviendo en los Estados Unidos cinco años. El día de la presentación empezó a hablar de una fotografía.

45. Answers will vary.
▶ Answers will vary.

Additional Resources

Fans Online activities
Practice Workbook

HERITAGE LANGUAGE LEARNERS

• Ask students to think about the customs, habits, or other everyday actions that they or members of their family used to do in their country of origin and compare this to what they do now. Perhaps they used to have dinner at 8:00 p.m., but now they dine at 6:00 p.m.—or perhaps they continue to dine at 8:00 p.m. Ask students to list what they or others in their family have either started doing, stopped doing, or continue to do, or how long they have been doing something. After they complete their lists, discuss these cultural adjustments with them.

SPECIAL-NEEDS LEARNERS

• To focus students' attention more effectively, ask them to concentrate on one grammar structure at a time. After they read aloud the first example, ask them to make up another sentence with *empezar a*. Do the same with all the other structures on the page. Then ask students some questions with these structures that generate a response with a direct object pronoun (e.g., *¿Sigues estudiando Ciencias? → Sí, sigo estudiándolas / las sigo estudiando*). Students should answer first by placing the direct object pronouns after the infinitive or participle and then before the conjugated verb.

Unit 8
DESAFÍO 2

Gramática – Usos del indicativo (repaso)

Presentation

- In this section, students will review and practice the use of the indicative mood for expressing real or factual statements.

Activities	Standards	Resources
Gramática	1.2, 3.1	
46.	4.1	
47.	1.1, 5.1	
48.	1.1, 1.2, 2.1	
49. Conexiones	1.1, 1.2, 2.1, 3.1, 4.2	

Teaching Suggestions

Warm-Up / Independent Starter

- Write the following sentence starters on the board, and ask students to complete a sentence for each one:
  1. *Estoy seguro(a) de que…*   4. *Aunque…*
  2. *A lo mejor…*   5. *Cuando…*
  3. *Creo que…*

Preparation

- Have students read the grammar presentation silently. Encourage them to take notes on any material they have trouble understanding and ask questions about what they did not understand.

- Have volunteers share their answers from the Independent Starter. While going over the answers, review the different uses of the indicative mood. If students used the subjunctive for some of the sentences with *aunque* and *cuando*, explain this use as well. Emphasize that *creer que* is used with the indicative while *no creer que* is used with the subjunctive.

Activities

48. Have each student write their classmates' opinions during the conversation. In order to share each group's opinions, select a speaker *(portavoz)* from each group. As a follow-up, or as an alternative to the previous suggestion, ask students to select one of the topics and write a brief note on that topic.

414

Gramática

Usos del indicativo (repaso)

El modo indicativo

- The mood of a verb conveys the speaker's attitude toward a subject. The indicative is the most common verb mood in both English and Spanish, and is primarily used for factual statements. These are some common uses of the indicative mood in Spanish.

  – To express:

certainty	Estoy segura de que **iré** a la universidad.
opinions in the affirmative	Creo que **va** a llover.

  – To ask about:

the purpose of an action	¿Para qué **compraste** ese teléfono?
the reason for something	¿Por qué no me **llamaste**?
a place or location	¿Dónde **está** el hotel?

  – After:

aunque, for real situations or known outcomes	Aunque no **tengo** dinero, soy feliz.
a lo mejor	A lo mejor te **llamo** esta noche.
donde, for known, definite, or real places	Vamos al restaurante donde **cenamos** ayer.
cuando and después de que, for habitual or past actions	Cuando **llueve** mucho, las calles se inundan.

  – In conditional sentences to express factual or likely conditions.

  Si me duele la cabeza, **tomo** una aspirina.

46 **Compara.** ¿Qué modo usas en inglés en los casos anteriores? ¿Hay alguna diferencia entre el inglés y el español en estos casos?

47 **Muchas preguntas**

▶ **Pregunta** a tu compañero(a) sobre sus planes para este fin de semana. Intercambien preguntas y opiniones.

Modelo

A. *¿Qué planes tienes para el fin de semana?*
B. *A lo mejor voy al cine con mis amigas. ¿Y tú?*
A. *Creo que voy a ir de excursión.*
B. *¿En serio?*

Differentiated Instruction

DEVELOPING LEARNERS

- To reinforce the use of the indicative mood with opinion statements in the affirmative, give students the following prompts and have them complete the sentences:
  - *Creo que las dictaduras…*
  - *Pienso que las elecciones…*
  - *Me parece que el presidente…*
  - *Opino que los ciudadanos…*
  - *Creo que la democracia…*

EXPANDING LEARNERS

- After students complete activity 48 using the indicative, ask them to regroup and express their opinions using the subjunctive with *no creo que, no estoy seguro(a) de que, cuando, aunque, antes de que, no pienso que,* and *donde.* The topics of their conversation do not need to be limited to those shown on the page. Ask them to identify additional suitable topics before they exchange their opinions.

48 Opiniones

▶ **Habla** con tus compañeros(as). En pequeños grupos, intercambien sus opiniones sobre estos temas. Usen las palabras y expresiones del cuadro.

estoy seguro(a)	creo	aunque	a lo mejor
cuando	donde	pienso	después de que

Modelo   *Yo creo que algún día todas las dictaduras van a desaparecer porque…*

la paz en el mundo

las dictaduras

la democracia

los símbolos patrióticos

la monarquía

CONEXIONES: CIENCIAS SOCIALES

Mujeres en el poder

Desde el siglo xx el acceso de la mujer a cargos políticos en Latinoamérica es cada vez mayor. Presidentas como Michelle Bachelet (Chile), Cristina Fernández de Kirchner (Argentina) y Laura Chinchilla (Costa Rica) son ejemplos de la creciente igualdad entre hombres y mujeres en la vida política.

49 **Piensa.** ¿Conoces otras mujeres que ocupen cargos políticos importantes en Latinoamérica? ¿Y en otros países?

Michelle Bachelet y Cristina Fernández de Kirchner.

Gramática – Usos del indicativo (repaso)

49. You may want to assign this activity as homework so students can do research on the Internet. As a follow-up, have students work in groups or pairs to prepare a visual presentation about one of these women. If possible, assign a different person to each pair.

CONEXIONES: CIENCIAS SOCIALES

Mujeres en el poder

The patriarchal system in Latin America has been very entrenched in the political system, and women have faced discrimination and oppression. For this reason, the prominence of political women in the last thirty years is remarkable. This success in politics mirrors changes in other areas traditionally reserved for men, like the fields of science, economy, and also university positions.

Answer Key

46. En ingles también se usa el modo indicativo en estos casos.

47. Answers will vary.

48. Answers will vary. Sample answers:
- Estoy seguro de que la paz en el mundo es posible con buena voluntad.
- Después de que la democracia llega a los países, la gente participa más en política.
- Aunque los símbolos patrióticos son muy conocidos, es necesario recordarlos en eventos especiales.
- A lo mejor la institución de la monarquía desaparece con el paso del siglo XXI.

49. Answers will vary.

Additional Resources

Fans Online activities
Practice Workbook

HERITAGE LANGUAGE LEARNERS

- Ask students to research women who are or have been leaders in politics, business, the arts, science, or in humanitarian efforts in the country of origin of their families, or in the local Hispanic community. Ask students to choose one of these women, prepare a biographical sketch, and mention her achievements. If students know a woman who is a leader in the community, encourage them to invite her to class to speak about her organization and achievements. Students should present a brief biography of this person before introducing her to the class.

MULTIPLE INTELLIGENCES:
Verbal-Linguistic Intelligence

- Ask students to research women in Latin America and Spain who have held political power. These leaders can be from the present or the past, and might even include figures from legends or mythology (e.g., Coatlicue, Aztec goddess of life, death, and rebirth). Have students select one of these women and write a personal and professional profile about her. Students should include some biographical data, achievements, and interesting anecdotes about her life and work. Invite students to share their profiles with the rest of the class.

415

Unit 8

LECTURA: TEXTO INFORMATIVO

Presentation

■ In this section, students will read an interview with Debra McKeon, managing director of the YOA (Youth Orchestra of the Americas). Students will learn about this inter-American initiative and its origins and purpose. Students will also work on synonyms, and will answer comprehension questions based on the reading.

Activities	Standards	Resources
Lectura: texto informativo	1.1, 1.2, 2.1, 2.2, 3.1, 3.2	
50.	1.1, 1.2, 2.1, 2.2	
51.	1.2	
52.	1.3, 2.1, 5.1	

Teaching Suggestions

Warm-Up / Independent Starter

■ Have students read the interview questions for comprehension and ask them to make guesses as to the possible answers.

Preparation

■ Have students work on the *Antes de leer* strategies individually. Then, have them share the answers with a partner. Call on volunteer pairs to share answers from the *estrategias* and from their Independent Starters. Make sure that they know what to expect from the interview.

■ Ask students to scan the text again and identify two dependent clauses in the indicative mood (e.g., *Es la única orquesta de jóvenes que representa…*; *Somos conscientes del importante y poderoso papel que juegan…*) and two in the subjunctive mood (e.g., *se anima a los miembros de la YOA a que aprendan…*; *se hace un gran esfuerzo para que participen…*). Depending on your students' level, you may ask them to explain the uses of each verbal mood in these cases, or just to recognize them.

■ Read the text aloud to model pronunciation and intonation. Then have students alternate reading each question and Debra McKeon's answer. Pause after every answer and call on a volunteer to paraphrase the content.

416

Antes de leer: estrategias

1. Lee el título y mira las fotografías. ¿Qué relación crees que tiene Debra McKeon con la Organización de Estados Americanos?

2. Lee superficialmente *(scan)* el texto. ¿Cuándo nació la Orquesta Juvenil de las Américas? ¿Quiénes participan en ella?

3. ¿Qué significa la palabra *orquesta*? Localiza en el texto otras palabras relacionadas con la música.

Entrevista a DEBRA MCKEON

¿Podría hablarnos acerca de la Orquesta Juvenil de las Américas: su historia, su origen, sus objetivos?

La Orquesta Sinfónica Juvenil de las Américas (YOA en inglés) es bastante nueva. Nació en 2002, promovida por la OEA, y está basada en el Sistema de Orquestas Juveniles e Infantiles de Venezuela, de José Antonio Abreu. Es la única orquesta de jóvenes que representa a todo el continente americano. Somos capaces de tocar un repertorio con música de toda América, ya que tenemos miembros de todos los países, lo que hace que siempre haya algún músico para quien «esa sea su música» y puede guiar[1] la interpretación.

Ensayo de la Orquesta Sinfónica Juvenil de las Américas.

¿Cómo se conforma[2] la orquesta cada año?

Los músicos se eligen para participar en la YOA durante un año. En ese tiempo reciben entrenamiento de alto nivel con maestros que vienen de las instituciones más respetadas[3] del continente. Además de sus estudios de perfeccionamiento intensivos, se anima a los miembros de la YOA a que aprendan más sobre las diversas ciudades y países que visitan, y las culturas que representan los mismos músicos.

¿Cómo se elige a los miembros de la orquesta?

Los músicos de la orquesta se seleccionan a través de audiciones que se realizan en cada país. La convocatoria está abierta a ciudadanos de los países participantes. Los músicos se seleccionan sobre todo por sus logros artísticos, y se hace un gran esfuerzo para que participen jóvenes de todos los países americanos. Todos los músicos participan con una beca completa para evitar diferencias económicas en los procesos de selección.

¿Cómo consigue la orquesta los fondos[4] para funcionar durante todo el año?

La YOA se apoya en individuos, fundaciones, corporaciones y gobiernos de toda América que creen en la importancia de su misión. Cada año, la orquesta debe conseguir aproximadamente 1.4 millones de dólares para cubrir los costos relacionados con las presentaciones y las actividades en las comunidades, además de la gestión[5] y otros gastos institucionales.

Differentiated Instruction

DEVELOPING LEARNERS

• Pair developing learners with partners of superior language skills who will monitor them as they read the interview aloud, helping with their pronunciation and offering advice to improve their intonation. As they read, ask the developing learners to identify any words that are not familiar, and encourage them to decode these terms by identifying cognates and looking for context clues. As they finish reading each paragraph, have students summarize its content to their partner.

EXPANDING LEARNERS

• Ask students to write four additional questions they would have liked to ask Debra McKeon. Then have them work with a partner and take turns asking these new questions and answering them as if they were Ms. McKeon. To make both the questions and the responses more meaningful, encourage students to research the *Orquesta Sinfónica Juvenil de las Américas* and respond to the orchestra's motto: "music transforming lives." Encourage students to ask and answer questions regarding the power of music.

¿Cuál es la importancia de un proyecto como este?

Somos conscientes del importante y poderoso papel que juegan los intercambios interculturales entre los jóvenes en el arte. La YOA fue creada para servir como un símbolo internacional del compromiso y la cooperación que hay en América en ámbitos del arte y la educación. Esta orquesta representa a América globalmente a través del alcance[6] musical de sus conciertos y recitales, y de sus programas en radio, televisión, grabaciones y giras.

Fuente: http://www.gestioncultural.org (texto adaptado)

Actuación de la Orquesta Sinfónica Juvenil de las Américas.

1. to guide
2. to form
3. respected
4. funds
5. management
6. scope

---

50 ¿Comprendes?

▶ **Responde** a estas preguntas.

1. ¿Qué ventaja, según Debra McKeon, tiene la Orquesta Juvenil de las Américas respecto a otras?
2. ¿Cuánto tiempo están los músicos en la Orquesta?
3. Además de proporcionarles formación, ¿qué tipo de conocimientos les ofrece la Orquesta a los músicos?
4. ¿Por qué motivo se dan becas completas a los músicos?

51 Sinónimos

▶ **Une** las dos columnas.

(A)	(B)
1. repertorio	a. éxito
2. entrenamiento	b. trabajo, sacrificio
3. logro	c. preparación
4. esfuerzo	d. recopilación, serie
5. costo	e. gasto, valor

52 Con tus propias palabras

▶ **Escribe.**

1. ¿Qué opinas de la importancia de este proyecto? ¿Qué puede aportar a los jóvenes?
2. ¿Conoces otros proyectos similares? ¿En qué consisten?

cuatrocientos diecisiete **417**

■ After finishing the reading, ask students to close their textbooks and then ask them the same questions that were posed to Debra McKeon to test students' comprehension.

Activities

50. You may want to divide the class into small groups and have each group come up with three additional comprehension questions. Collect the questions and redistribute them to different groups. Ask each group to answer all the questions (i.e., the four questions from this activity and the three additional questions you gave them). Then invite groups to share their answers with the class.

51. In order to facilitate comprehension and their association with words of similar meaning, have students reread the sentences in the text in which the terms from column A appear. You may want to have students rewrite each sentence using the synonym from column B.

52. If students are unaware of other organizations for young people, ask them to research some of these organizations online. They may find an organization in which they can participate!

Answer Key

50. 1. Que es capaz de tocar un repertorio musical de todas las Américas con mucha autenticidad porque tiene músicos de todos los países.
2. Están un año.
3. Conocimientos sobre distintas culturas.
4. Para evitar diferencias económicas.

51. 1. d   2. c   3. a   4. b   5. e

52. Answers will vary.

Additional Resources

Fans Online activities

Unit 8
DESAFÍO 2
Comunicación

Presentation

- In this section, students will integrate the vocabulary and grammar skills from *Desafío 2* in order to talk about politics and government.

Activities	Standards	Resources
53.	1.3, 2.2	
54.	1.2, 1.3, 3.1, 5.1	
55.	1.2, 1.3, 2.1, 4.2	
56.	1.1, 1.3, 3.1, 5.1	
57. Final del desafío	1.1, 1.2, 1.3, 2.2, 3.1, 5.1	
Tu desafío	1.1, 1.2	

Teaching Suggestions

Warm-Up / Independent Starter

- Have students read the following headlines and decide what kind of political system each of them refers to:
  1. *Graves problemas sociales por la represión militar.*
  2. *La reina firma un acuerdo muy importante.*
  3. *Millones de personas participaron en las elecciones presidenciales.*

Preparation

- Ask volunteers to share their Independent Starters. Then have students list words they learned in this *Desafío* that are related to each of these three political systems. Allow students to go back and review some of these words if they don't remember them. Then ask students to use the words they listed to write a brief summary of the main characteristics of these political systems. Call on volunteers to share their summaries with the class.

Activities

54. If possible, have students prepare similar questions to ask a community or school leader and write a report about him or her.

418

Comunicación

53 **Banderas**

▶ **Averigua** a qué países hispanos corresponden estas banderas.

▶ **Escribe** un texto describiendo una de las banderas anteriores. Explica qué colores y qué elementos la forman, y qué significado tienen.

54 **Una líder local**

▶ **Lee** las respuestas de una líder comunitaria y escribe las preguntas que le hizo la periodista.

> ### La entrevista
> 1. Empecé a interesarme por la política cuando era adolescente.
> 2. Empecé a estudiar Ciencias Políticas y Economía a los dieciocho años, en la universidad. Lo dejé dos años después.
> 3. Empecé a trabajar porque mi familia necesitaba dinero.
> 4. Seguí estudiando un año después.
> 5. Terminé mi maestría en Ciencias Políticas hace muy poco tiempo.
> 6. Participo en comités locales y proyectos sociales desde hace tres años.

55 **Dos gobiernos**

▶ **Lee** estas notas sobre el sistema de gobierno de Perú. Compáralo con el de tu país y completa un diagrama de Venn.

> ### Sistema de gobierno de Perú
> - Perú es una república democrática con un sistema multipartidario (es decir, con varios partidos políticos).
> - El voto es obligatorio para todos los ciudadanos entre los 18 y los 70 años.
> - Según la Constitución, el presidente de la república es el jefe del Estado y el jefe del Gobierno. Es elegido cada cinco años y no puede ser reelegido inmediatamente.
> - El presidente elige a los ministros y al presidente del consejo de ministros.
> - El Congreso está formado por una sola cámara de 130 miembros, que son elegidos cada cinco años.

418 cuatrocientos dieciocho

Differentiated Instruction

DEVELOPING LEARNERS

- Pair students with those who possess superior language skills. Ask developing learners to use the indicative mood and write sentences that express the following: certainty and opinions in the affirmative; questions to ask about the purpose of an action, the reason for something, and a place or location. Ask their partners to check their work and to guide them as they make corrections.

EXPANDING LEARNERS

- Have students review the steps that Eva and Ethan have taken to complete their report. Then ask students to describe these steps using the following structures: *empezar a, seguir, dejar de, llevar*. For example: *Empezaron a investigar lo que significan las siglas OEA. Siguieron leyendo sobre la OEA. Llevan tiempo estudiando la OEA.* Next, ask students to use these same structures to describe how they have completed a recent school project.

56 Un proyecto para un país ideal

▶ **Escribe.** ¿Cómo sería tu país ideal? Explica tus ideas en estos aspectos.

- El tipo de gobierno.
- Los cargos políticos e instituciones más relevantes.
- Los símbolos nacionales (dibújalos y descríbelos, explicando su significado).

▶ **Habla** con tu compañero(a) y comparen sus países ideales.

Modelo A. *En mi país ideal habría un gobierno democrático. Los ciudadanos elegirían a sus representantes cada dos años.*

B. *En el mío también, pero las elecciones serían cada cinco años porque…*

Final del desafío

ETHAN: ¡Hola, Eva! Perdona, llego un poquito tarde. ¿Llevas mucho tiempo ___1___?

EVA: No, tranquilo. Acabo de ___2___.

ETHAN: He estado pensando, pero no sé por dónde empezar….

EVA: Yo creo que para el reportaje deberíamos empezar explicando qué es la OEA, cuándo se fundó…

ETHAN: Podemos mirar en la página oficial.

EVA: Un momento… aquí está. Uff, cuánta información.

ETHAN: ¿Por qué no pinchas donde dice *Acerca de la OEA*?

EVA: Ah, sí. Aquí están los datos que buscamos. Llevan ___3___ más de sesenta años. Aquí dice que se creó en 1948. Espera, voy a seguir ___4___ ….

ETHAN: Eva, deberíamos empezar a ___5___ sobre los proyectos para decidir de cuáles queremos hablar en el reportaje.

EVA: Eso estará aquí, donde dice *Qué hacemos*.

57 Investiga sobre la OEA

▶ **Completa** el diálogo con estas formas verbales.

| leyendo | esperando | trabajando | llegar | investigar |

▶ **Habla** con tu compañero(a). ¿Creen que Eva y Ethan conseguirán su desafío? ¿Tienen suficiente información para escribir su artículo?

▶ **TU DESAFÍO** Visita la página web. Escucha las preguntas de tu *Minientrevista Desafío 2* y escribe las respuestas.

HERITAGE LANGUAGE LEARNERS

- The OAS offers a highly competitive internship program for university students and young professionals. To qualify, candidates must have a GPA of 3.0 and a command of two of the four official languages of the organization. Ask students to write a letter of application to the OAS stating their qualifications for one of the following internships: Information Technology or Sustainable Development. Students should emphasize their bilingualism in Spanish and English, and their desire to work for an international organization that values democracy, human rights, security, and development.

CRITICAL THINKING

- After students complete activity 56, ask them to work with their partner and another pair and discuss in greater detail how their ideal countries would apply effective problem-solving measures to deal with their problems. Have students brainstorm some problems that affect almost all nations: poverty, unemployment, education, health care, affordable housing, and preserving the environment. Have them follow up with how their countries will work to offer creative solutions. Then encourage a classroom discussion to get feedback from all groups.

56. After comparing their ideal countries, have each pair agree on the best characteristics for an ideal country. Ask pairs to present their ideal country to the class and have the class decide by voting which is the best ideal country and why.

Answer Key

53. 1. Guatemala   3. Uruguay
2. Chile   4. Bolivia
▶ Answers will vary.

54. Answers will vary. Sample answers:
1. ¿Cuándo empezó a interesarse por la política?
2. ¿Cuándo comenzó a estudiar en la universidad? ¿Cuándo lo dejó?
3. ¿Por qué empezó a trabajar tan joven?
4. ¿Siguió estudiando más adelante?
5. ¿Cuándo terminó su maestría?
6. ¿Cuánto tiempo lleva participando en comités y proyectos sociales?

55. Answers will vary. Sample answers:
Perú y los EE. UU.: Repúblicas democráticas con un sistema multipartidario. El presidente de la república es el jefe del Estado y el jefe del Gobierno. El presidente elige a los ministros y al presidente del consejo de ministros.
Perú: Voto obligatorio para los ciudadanos entre los 18 y los 70 años. El presidente es elegido cada cinco años y no puede ser reelegido inmediatamente. El Congreso está formado por una sola cámara de 130 miembros que son elegidos cada cinco años.

56. Answers will vary.
▶ Answers will vary.

57. 1. esperando 3. trabajando 5. investigar
2. llegar   4. leyendo
▶ Answers will vary.

Additional Resources

Fans Online activities
Practice Workbook

419

DESAFÍO 3

Expresar deseos, opinar y valorar

Presentation

■ In *Desafío 3*, Daniel and Michelle need to make a calendar of multicultural events in New York City that will be part of a travel brochure. Students will preview language used to talk about society, and see how the subjunctive mood is used in a variety of contexts.

Activities	Standards	Resources
Texto	1.2, 2.1, 3.2	Vis. Pres.
58.	1.2, 1.3, 3.1	
59.	1.1, 1.3, 2.1, 2.2, 5.1	
60.	1.1, 2.1, 2.2	
61. Comunidades	1.1, 1.2, 2.1, 5.1	

Teaching Suggestions

Warm-Up / Independent Starter

■ Ask students to brainstorm things that they know about New York City and a list of words to describe the city.

Preparation

■ Have students share their Independent Starters. If your students are not from New York City, ask if any of them have visited the city. What were their impressions? How is it similar to or different from where they live?

Texto: Un calendario multicultural

■ Read the introduction to the dialogue. Then have five different pairs of students read the dialogue aloud.

■ As their classmates read, have students take notes on the adjectives that Daniel and Michelle use to describe the city and the events that they mention. Ask students which of the events mentioned they would want to attend, and why.

Activities

59. After students complete this activity, discuss students' answers to question 4 as a class. Have several students suggested similar events? Which events are these?

420

Un calendario multicultural

New York City is world renowned for its multiculturalism. Daniel and Michelle will make a calendar of multicultural events to be published in a travel brochure. Lucas and Asha have invited them to spend a week in New York so that they can attend some of these events.

MICHELLE: Es una suerte que Lucas y Asha nos hayan invitado a Nueva York.

DANIEL: Ya lo creo.

MICHELLE: Yo no conozco la ciudad, pero mis amigas me recomendaron que visitara un montón de lugares famosos.

DANIEL: Bueno, pero aunque vayamos a alguno de esos sitios, recuerda que viajamos allí para resolver nuestro desafío.

MICHELLE: No creo que sea muy difícil. Además, Lucas y Asha nos ayudarán. Daniel, ¿no te parece sorprendente que haya tantos eventos multiculturales en Nueva York?

DANIEL: La verdad es que no porque es una ciudad con una gran herencia cultural. Dudo que haya muchos lugares con tanta diversidad.

MICHELLE: ¿Conoces algún evento cultural que podamos incluir en el calendario?

DANIEL: Sí, el Desfile Puertorriqueño, que se celebra en junio, y el desfile del Año Nuevo chino, que es entre enero y febrero. Y mis amigos me contaron que en enero se celebra el Desfile de los Reyes Magos.

MICHELLE: ¡Qué curioso! Esa es una fiesta de origen hispano, pero no sabía que se celebrara en Nueva York. Bueno, ya tenemos tres eventos. Quizá debamos incluir uno por mes.

DANIEL: Sí, uno por lo menos.

Desfile del Día de Acción de Gracias (Nueva York).

Estación Grand Central (Nueva York).

58 Detective de palabras

▶ **Completa** estas oraciones.

1. Michelle dice que es una suerte que Lucas y Asha los _____ a Nueva York.
2. Sus amigas le recomendaron a Michelle que _____ muchos lugares.
3. Michelle no cree que el desafío _____ muy difícil.
4. A ella le parece sorprendente que _____ tantos eventos multiculturales en Nueva York.
5. Daniel duda que _____ muchos lugares con tanta diversidad.

▶ **Decide.** ¿A qué modo corresponden las formas anteriores: al indicativo o al subjuntivo?

420 cuatrocientos veinte

Differentiated Instruction

DEVELOPING LEARNERS

• Ask pairs of students to take turns reading the dialogue aloud. Monitor their pronunciation and intonation. If they are having difficulties with certain words or phrases, model the pronunciation and have them repeat after you. After students read, ask them to write a narrative that summarizes what has taken place in the dialogue. Invite them to share their narratives with the rest of the class.

EXPANDING LEARNERS

• Ask students to go through the dialogue and make a list of all the verbs that are in the subjunctive mood. Then have students identify the tense of these verbs and explain why they are in the subjunctive. For example, *hayan invitado* is in the present perfect; it follows the expression *es una suerte que* and it refers to an action that happened in the past. *Visitara* is in the imperfect subjunctive because it follows the verb *recomendaron*, which is also in the past (preterite). Have students do this for the rest of the verbs.

59 ¿Comprendes?

▶ **Responde** a estas preguntas.

1. ¿En qué consiste el desafío de Michelle y Daniel?
2. ¿Qué eventos culturales mencionan?
3. ¿Por qué hay tanta diversidad en Nueva York?
4. ¿Conoces otros eventos que podrían incluir en su calendario? ¿Cuáles son y cuándo se celebran?

60 Eventos multiculturales

▶ **Relaciona** estas fotografías con los eventos multiculturales del diálogo. ¿A cuál corresponde cada una?

 ▶ **Habla** con tu compañero(a). ¿Cómo imaginan esos eventos?

 **COMUNIDADES**

EL CORAZÓN DE LA MULTICULTURALIDAD

La ciudad de Nueva York es un lugar único por la mezcla de culturas, etnias y religiones que hay entre sus más de ocho millones de habitantes. Históricamente Nueva York fue el centro de la inmigración europea, pero después se incorporaron emigrantes de todos los continentes. Esta diversidad se refleja en la música, el teatro, la danza, la literatura, la moda y la gastronomía, y ha convertido a la ciudad en referente mundial de la cultura y el arte.

61 **Explica.** En tu opinión, ¿qué ventajas y desventajas tendría vivir en una ciudad tan multicultural como Nueva York?

cuatrocientos veintiuno **421**

Expresar deseos, opinar y valorar

60. Have students describe the photos, the people, and their actions. To expand this activity, have students describe a multicultural event in which they may have participated.

 COMUNIDADES

El corazón de la multiculturalidad

A city of over eight million residents, New York City is truly a center of multiculturalism. There may be as many as 800 languages spoken by its residents, who have migrated there from all over the globe. This diversity is reflected throughout the five boroughs in their museums, restaurants, theaters, and events. Each year, close to fifty million tourists visit the Big Apple to experience its unique culture.

Answer Key

58. 1. hayan invitado 4. haya
2. visitara 5. haya
3. sea
▶ Todas las formas verbales anteriores corresponden al modo subjuntivo.

59. 1. Consiste en crear un calendario de eventos multiculturales para publicarlo en un folleto turístico.
2. Mencionan el Desfile Puertorriqueño, el desfile del Año Nuevo chino y el Desfile de los Reyes Magos.
3. Porque es una ciudad con una gran herencia cultural, pues en ella residen personas de todas las culturas y grupos étnicos del mundo.
4. Answers will vary.

60. 1. Desfile de los Reyes Magos.
2. Año Nuevo chino.
3. Desfile Puertorriqueño.
▶ Answers will vary.

61. Answers will vary.

Additional Resources

Fans Online activities

HERITAGE LANGUAGE LEARNERS

• After students complete activity 59, ask them to choose one of the events they mentioned in their answer to the fourth question and do further research on this celebration. Review students' choices so that there is some variety in their selection of celebrations. After students gather their information, ask them to make an oral presentation to the class. Take a class vote to see which celebration is the one the rest of the students would most likely want to see or participate in.

MULTIPLE INTELLIGENCES:
Intrapersonal Intelligence

• Ask students to imagine that they are from another country and have come to live for a year in a small town in the United States on an academic exchange program. They don't know anyone, and most of the town's residents, including the sponsoring family, have not had much contact with foreigners. Ask students how they think someone in this situation would react. Have them write an entry in their journals that reflects their conflictive feelings: they want to learn from this experience, but everything seems so "foreign."

DESAFÍO 3

Vocabulario – Sociedad

Presentation

■ In this section, students will learn key words to discuss society.

Activities	Standards	Resources
Vocabulario	1.2, 2.1	
62.	1.2	
63.	1.1, 1.2	Audio
64.	1.1, 1.2, 1.3, 4.2, 5.1	
65. Cultura	1.1, 1.2, 2.1, 2.2, 5.1	Video

Teaching Suggestions

Warm-Up / Independent Starter

■ Ask students to list some words that they already know that are related to society and the way people interact in society (e.g., *sociedad*, *comunidad*, *ciudadano*, *cultura*, *diversidad cultural*, *población*).

Preparation

■ Have students read the text silently. When they are finished, read it aloud, emphasizing the pronunciation of the highlighted words. Next, read the words in the *Más vocabulario* feature aloud in order to model correct pronunciation and have students repeat them after you. Some of the terms in this vocabulary presentation are cognates, but might not be words that students use frequently in their daily speech.

■ Ask students to think of other words that are in the same word family as some of the vocabulary words (e.g., *la tolerancia → tolerante, tolerar*). Then have students share their Independent Starters, and review those words as well.

Activities

63. Before students listen to the audio recording, have them look at the questions and think of potential answers to make sure that they understand the vocabulary used. Ask students to state some of the background information they can glean from just reading the instructions and the questions (e.g., *Hablan con una mesera que posiblemente es de otro país.*).

Vocabulario

Sociedad

Es mi primera vez en Nueva York y me ha sorprendido mucho su **diversidad**. Esta es una ciudad verdaderamente **multicultural**.

Históricamente Nueva York es una ciudad de **inmigrantes** de distintas **etnias** procedentes de todas partes del mundo. Muchos de los extranjeros que emigraron a esta ciudad mantienen su **herencia cultural** y sus **valores** como signo de **identidad**.

Algunos ciudadanos participan en **sociedades** culturales **públicas** o **privadas**. Estas sociedades trabajan por los **derechos** y **deberes** de sus miembros y les ofrecen **apoyo** y orientación.

El proceso de **integración** en una nueva cultura es a veces difícil y cuesta trabajo, sobre todo cuando las **normas** son muy distintas. Pero es imprescindible **integrarse**. Yo pienso que la clave está en el **respeto** entre las comunidades. La **convivencia** de tantas culturas en una ciudad como Nueva York es un buen ejemplo de que la **paz** es posible.

Más vocabulario

Vida en comunidad

la igualdad	*equality*	la pluralidad	*plurality*
la justicia	*justice*	la solidaridad	*solidarity*
la libertad (de expresión)	*freedom (of speech)*	la tolerancia	*tolerance*
el mestizaje	*mix of races*		

62 ¿Qué quiere decir?

▶ **Une** las dos columnas.

Ⓐ

1. apoyo
2. norma
3. paz
4. solidaridad
5. inmigrante
6. identidad

Ⓑ

a. Persona que llega a un lugar para establecerse en él.
b. Ayuda, protección.
c. Rasgos propios de un individuo o una comunidad.
d. Regla que hay que seguir.
e. Situación en la que no hay conflictos entre personas.
f. Apoyo a las causas de otros.

422 cuatrocientos veintidós

Differentiated Instruction

DEVELOPING LEARNERS

• Ask students to identify the word that does not belong and explain why.
  1. *mestizaje   tolerancia   solidaridad* (mestizaje)
  2. *identidad   diversidad   pluralidad* (identidad)
  3. *valores   públicas   privadas* (valores)
  4. *diversidad   paz   multicultural* (paz)
  5. *apoyo   etnias   inmigrantes* (apoyo)
  6. *injusticia   justicia   igualdad* (injusticia)
  7. *deberes   derechos   herencia* (herencia)

EXPANDING LEARNERS

• Ask students to complete these analogies:
  1. *públicas : privadas :: ... : censura* (libertad)
  2. *... : variedad :: enorme : inmenso* (diversidad)
  3. *recordar : olvidar :: ... : prejuicio* (tolerancia)
  4. *igual : diferente :: segregación : ...* (integración)
  5. *obligaciones : ... :: apoyo : ayuda* (deberes)
  6. *objetos : cosas :: ... : reglas* (normas)
  7. *famoso : desconocido :: ... : guerra* (paz)
  8. *... : símbolo :: distinto : diferente* (signo)

63 **Conversación en un restaurante**

 ▶ **Escucha** la conversación de los personajes con la mesera de un restaurante y responde a estas preguntas.

1. ¿En qué país nació la mesera?
2. ¿Cuánto tiempo lleva en Nueva York?
3. ¿Cuál es su nacionalidad?
4. ¿Se siente integrada en Nueva York? ¿Por qué?
5. ¿Qué se celebra el próximo jueves?

 64 **Herencias culturales**

 ▶ **Habla** con tu compañero(a) sobre tu herencia cultural. Puedes seguir este guion.

- ¿De dónde es tu familia?
- ¿Cuándo llegaron tus antepasados a los Estados Unidos?
- ¿Con qué cultura te identificas más?
- ¿Qué valores son importantes para tu familia?
- ¿Qué desafíos superaron algunos de tus familiares para integrarse en la cultura estadounidense?

▶ **Presenta** lo que sabes de la herencia cultural de tu compañero(a). Al final, entre todos(as) pueden hacer un gráfico sobre las herencias culturales de la clase.

CULTURA

El Museo del Barrio

En 1969, un grupo de padres, educadores, artistas y otros voluntarios fundaron El Museo del Barrio en un salón de clase público en East Harlem (Nueva York) con la misión de promover y preservar la cultura latina, especialmente la puertorriqueña.

El Museo del Barrio tiene una gran colección de objetos precolombinos y exposiciones temporales de pintura, escultura y fotografía. Además ofrece celebraciones culturales y programas educativos para la comunidad y los visitantes.

Exposición de pintura en el Museo del Barrio (Nueva York).

 65 **Piensa.** Si pudieras fundar un museo en tu comunidad, ¿qué tipo de museo sería? ¿Cuál sería su misión?

cuatrocientos veintitrés 423

---

64. How multicultural is your class? Ask students to compare the graph they created with a similar graph for their state (they can find information on the U.S. Census Bureau website). How does the class compare with the state's population? Is the class more, less, or equally diverse?

 AUDIO SCRIPT
See page 389 J.

 CULTURA

El Museo del Barrio

After noting the lack of Latino representation in museums, Raphael Montañez Ortiz led a group of community individuals to open up *El Museo del Barrio* in New York City. The museum has a permanent collection of over 6,500 pieces and covers 800 years of history. Visitors can see drawings, paintings, sculptures, photography, documentaries, and videos that celebrate and promote Latino culture.

Answer Key

62. 1. b   2. d   3. e   4. f   5. a   6. c

63. 1. Nació en Colombia.
2. Lleva más de diez años en Nueva York.
3. Tiene doble nacionalidad: es colombiana y estadounidense.
4. Sí, se siente totalmente integrada porque hay gente de todas partes del mundo en Nueva York.
5. El próximo jueves se celebra el Día de la Independenciade de Colombia.

64. Answers will vary.
▶ Answers will vary.

65. Answers will vary.

Additional Resources

Fans Online activities
Practice Workbook

423

HERITAGE LANGUAGE LEARNERS

- Ask students to describe their favorite celebration in their family's country of origin. Ask them to name the celebration and to explain when and why it takes place. Encourage students to describe how they prepare for this celebration and how they and their family celebrate it. Ask students to include details that make this celebration unique. Then have them exchange papers with a partner who will proofread their composition. After all corrections have been made, ask students to read their compositions aloud.

CRITICAL THINKING

- Ask students to imagine that they are curators for the *Museo del Barrio*, and they are getting ready for some new exhibits. Ask students to research some of the art, film, and photography collections that have been exhibited at *El Museo*. Have students consider these past exhibits and then have them write a press release that describes the works they are planning to sponsor. Students should consider what would best reflect the diversity of Hispanic cultures, especially to an audience that may not be familiar with them.

DESAFÍO 3

Gramática – Los artículos

Presentation

- In this section, students will learn when the definite and indefinite articles are used.

Activities	Standards	Resources
Gramática	1.2, 3.1	
66.	1.3, 4.1	
67.	1.2, 2.1, 3.1	
68.	1.3	
69.	1.1, 2.2, 5.2	
70. Cultura	1.1, 1.2, 2.1, 2.2, 4.2, 5.1	

Teaching Suggestions

Warm-Up / Independent Starter

- Write the following words on the board and ask students to identify both the definite and indefinite articles that are used with each word: *celebración, inmigrante, popularidad, calendario, problema, agua, derechos, ciudadanía.*

Preparation

- Have students share their Independent Starters. If necessary, review gender and number agreement. Remind students that even though the noun *agua* is feminine, we say *el agua* because the word *agua* begins with a stressed *a.*

- Ask students to read the grammar explanation silently. When they have finished, ask them to identify the examples that differ from the way definite and indefinite articles are used in English.

- Have students write a brief description of themselves, applying definite and indefinite articles as appropriate. Circulate through the room as students are working in order to check their work. Ask volunteers to share what they wrote. Reassure students that the pattern of when to use definite, indefinite, or no articles is something they will learn to "hear" with time.

Activities

67. After completing this activity, ask students to identify the examples that are not equivalent to their English counterparts.

Gramática

Los artículos

El artículo definido

CONTRACCIONES

a + el = al
de + el = del

- The definite article (el, la, los, las) corresponds to *the* in English. It is used when referring to a known person, object, or entity.

Estos son **los** zapatos que me compré ayer.

- Spanish uses a definite article in many places where it is omitted in English:
  – With nouns used in a general sense, or generically, and with abstract nouns.

Los delfines son inteligentes.   Me gusta **el** pan.   Amamos **la** libertad.

  – With body parts and articles of clothing, in place of the possessive.

Ella abrió **los** ojos lentamente.   Carlos se puso **los** zapatos y salió.

  – After jugar a.

Andy juega **al** fútbol muy bien.   No sé jugar **a las** cartas.

El artículo indefinido

- The indefinite article (un, una, unos, unas) is used when referring to an unknown person, object, or entity. The singular forms (un, una) correspond to *a* or *an*. The plural forms (unos, unas) generally correspond to *some* or *a few*.

Vivo en **una** casa cerca de la escuela.   Perdí **unas** monedas de plata.

- In Spanish, indefinite articles are sometimes omitted where they are used in English:
  – After the verb ser and before unmodified nouns referring to occupation, nationality, social status, or religious or political affiliation.

Yo soy doctora.   Tim es estadounidense.   Irene es metodista.

Note that the indefinite article is used if the noun is modified.

Yo soy **una** doctora excelente.   Tim es **un** estadounidense muy simpático.

  – After some verbs like tener and llevar *(to wear)*, when referring to nouns in a general, or generic, sense. In this case, the noun is unmodified.

¿Tienes novio?   Llevo chaqueta porque hace frío.

66 **Compara.** Traduce las siguientes oraciones al español.

a. *She's a Republican.*
b. *My head hurts.*
c. *I'm a good student.*
d. *Put on your shirt.*

67 **El desfile por el barrio**

▶ **Completa** las oraciones con los artículos apropiados cuando sea necesario.

1. ___1___ Día de Reyes es ___2___ fiesta de origen religioso.
2. Hay ___3___ desfile muy largo y van miles de personas.
3. Hay ___4___ camellos desfilando por ___5___ calles de Manhattan.
4. Las personas del desfile llevan ___6___ disfraces.

Differentiated Instruction

DEVELOPING LEARNERS

- Ask students to complete the following sentences with the correct article, or to indicate that no article is needed:
  1. *Marcos estudia en … universidad. (la)*
  2. *… oro cuesta mucho. (El)*
  3. *No me gustan … películas románticas. (las)*
  4. *Todos … sábados voy a la piscina. (los)*
  5. *Como … manzanas todos los días. (X)*
  6. *No tengo … dinero. (X)*
  7. *Vivo en … calle Mayor, 16. (la)*
  8. *Cuando llueve llevo … paraguas. (X)*

EXPANDING LEARNERS

- Introduce students to the following expressions that omit the definite article, even though their English-language equivalents use them. Then ask students to write one sentence with each of these expressions:
  – *a corto/largo plazo* (in the short/long run)
  – *en alta mar* (on the high seas)
  – *en dicho mes* (in the said month)
  – *en manos de* (in the hands of)
  – *en nombre de* (in the name of)

68 Fotos de la ciudad

▶ **Escribe** una descripción de las fotos que sacaron Michelle y Daniel en Nueva York.

Modelo *Esta foto es del puente de Brooklyn. Es un puente muy famoso que une…*

69 Descripciones

▶ **Habla** con tu compañero(a). Describe un lugar famoso del mundo hispano. Él/Ella tiene que adivinar cuál es haciéndote preguntas. Tú solo puedes responder *sí* o *no*.

Modelo A. *Es una de las ciudades más grandes del mundo.*
B. *¿Es la capital de un país?*
A. *Sí.*
B. *¿Es la Ciudad de México?*

CULTURA

El Festival de Comida Internacional

Desde hace más de 38 años, cada mes de mayo se celebra en Nueva York el Festival de Comida Internacional de la Novena Avenida. Más de un millón de personas asisten cada año a esta feria gastronómica para conocer la comida de países hispanos y de todo el mundo. Además de poder degustar los numerosos platos que ofrecen los restaurantes de la zona, hay espectáculos de música y danza en directo. El dinero recaudado se emplea en beneficio de los grupos comunitarios del barrio.

70 **Piensa.** ¿Tu comunidad tiene muchos restaurantes internacionales? ¿Cuáles son los más comunes? ¿Por qué?

cuatrocientos veinticinco 425

Gramática – Los artículos

68. Before beginning this activity, ask students to brainstorm vocabulary that they can use to describe each of the pictures. After students have finished writing their responses, ask them to share a sentence without revealing which picture it relates to. See if the rest of the class can guess which picture it describes.

69. As an alternative to describing places in the Spanish-speaking world, students can describe places in their city or local area.

70. Ask students what their favorite international foods are. If your school allows it, consider planning a multicultural food tasting.

CULTURA

El Festival de Comida Internacional

Since 1973, the Ninth Avenue Association has hosted an annual International Food Festival. The festival helps the association to meet its mission of uniting the business community, helping the neighborhood, and supporting neighborhood causes by providing funding for its projects. Visitors can sample food from around the world, purchase handcrafted items, or speak with representatives from local community groups. There are also children's games and activities.

Answer Key

66. a. Ella es republicana.
b. Me duele la cabeza.
c. Soy un(a) buen(a) estudiante.
d. Ponte la camisa.

67. 1. El   3. un   5. las
2. una 4. X   6. X

68. Answers will vary.

69. Answers will vary.

70. Answers will vary.

Additional Resources

Fans Online activities
Practice Workbook

HERITAGE LANGUAGE LEARNERS

• Students might need reminding that the articles *el* and *un* are used before singular feminine nouns that begin with a stressed *a* or *ha*; however, the adjectives and pronouns that modify these nouns are in the feminine form (e.g., *el agua fría*). Ask students to brainstorm other nouns that fit this pattern. For example: *el/un águila, el/un alba, el/un alma, el/un ancla, el/un área, el/un arma, el/un arpa, el asma, el/un aula, el/un hacha, el/un hada, el/un hambre.*

COOPERATIVE LEARNING

• Ask students to work in small groups and imagine that they are going to organize an international food festival for their neighborhood. Each student in the group will have a different task: some will make a list of the countries whose cuisine will be represented; others will use this list to name the foods that will be available; another might calculate the amounts and prices of these foods; another will take care of the public relations campaign, etc. Once they are finished, ask groups to present their festival plans to the class.

DESAFÍO 3

Gramática – Usos del subjuntivo (repaso)

Presentation

■ In this section, students will review the uses of the subjunctive mood.

Activities	Standards	Resources
Gramática	1.2, 3.1	
71.	4.1	
72.	1.2, 1.3, 3.1	
73.	1.1, 1.2, 1.3, 5.1	
74.	1.1, 5.1	

Teaching Suggestions

Warm-Up / Independent Starter

■ Ask students to write at least five expressions that require the subjunctive mood in the dependent clause.

Preparation

■ Ask students to read the grammar explanation silently, and then ask a volunteer to read it aloud.

■ Have students take their expressions from the Independent Starter and identify the use of the subjunctive to which each expression corresponds. Ask volunteers to share their examples.

■ Ask students to take three of their expressions from the Independent Starter and finish the sentences. Challenge students to write at least one of the statements in the past, applying the imperfect subjunctive. You may want to review the sequence of tenses with students.

Activities

71. If students struggle to identify the subjunctive in English, have them look at the examples in the grammar explanation and ask them to think of the English equivalents. Remind students that the subjunctive is one of the many grammar structures that do not have a direct translation between the two languages. There are, however, some instances in English where the subjunctive is required (e.g., If I *were* you, I would call him).

426

Gramática

Usos del subjuntivo (repaso)

El modo subjuntivo

● In Spanish, the subjunctive mood occurs primarily in the dependent clause when the main clause expresses certain conditions. There is usually a change of subject from the main to the dependent clause. These are some common uses of the subjunctive:

– To express:

wishes and preferences	Deseo que nuestro equipo **gane**.
value judgments	Es bueno que **hagas** ejercicio.
feelings and emotions	Me alegra que **hayas salido** bien en el examen.
opinions in the negative	No pienso que la Física **sea** fácil.
negative expressions	No es verdad que **nieve** en el Caribe.
doubts and uncertainty	Dudo que **ganemos** el partido de baloncesto.
recommendations	La profesora me recomendó que **estudiara**.

– After:

aunque, for unreal or uncertain situations	Aunque **haga** frío, saldré a comer.
para que and a que, to indicate purpose	Te llamo para que me **ayudes**.
donde, for unknown, indefinite, or hypothetical places	Vamos de viaje donde tú **quieras**.
cuando, después de que, and antes de que, for future events	Llámame cuando **llegues**.

– In conditional sentences, to express unlikely, hypothetical, or contrary-to-fact conditions.
   Si **fuera** más alta, jugaría al baloncesto.

– To give a negative command. In this case, use the present tense of the subjunctive.
   No **bebas** tantos refrescos.   No me **digan** las respuestas.

71 **Compara.** ¿Puedes pensar en ejemplos del subjuntivo en inglés? ¿Cómo expresas duda, deseo, emoción e hipótesis en inglés?

72 **Un mundo mejor**

▶ **Une** las dos columnas y escribe las oraciones usando la forma correcta del subjuntivo.

1. Seríamos más felices…
2. Podremos convivir en paz…
3. Quiero vivir en un lugar…
4. Es bueno que todos nosotros…

a. donde _____ ser feliz.
   _{poder}
b. _____ la igualdad.
   _{promover}
c. si no _____ las guerras.
   _{existir}
d. cuando todos _____ más tolerantes.
   _{ser}

Differentiated Instruction

DEVELOPING LEARNERS

● Ask students to complete the following sentences with the correct form of the verb in parentheses:

1. *Quiero que (haber) paz en el mundo. (haya)*
2. *Dudamos que los inmigrantes (integrarse) tan pronto. (se integren)*
3. *No creo que (venir) el profesor. (venga)*
4. *Cuando lo (tú – saber), llámame. (sepas)*
5. *Si (yo – estudiar) más, tendría mejores notas. (estudiara)*
6. *Tengo mucha hambre. Vamos a comer donde (ser). (sea)*
7. *Era imposible que (ellos – respetar) nuestros derechos. (respetaran)*

EXPANDING LEARNERS

● After students complete the activities on these pages, have them take another look at the example sentences in the *Gramática* feature. Ask them to write original sentences applying the uses that are shown: wishes and preferences, value judgments, feelings and emotions, opinions in the negative, etc., and after certain words (*aunque, donde…*), but leaving a space for the verb in the dependent clause. Have them exchange papers with a partner, who will complete each sentence.

73 **Planeando una celebración multicultural**

▶ **Completa** estas notas para un concierto multicultural.

Un concierto multicultural

1. Es necesario que _____ qué tipo de música queremos.
   _{decidir}

2. Es importante que _____ músicos disponibles.
   _{encontrar}

3. Espero que los músicos no _____ mucho dinero.
   _{pedir}

4. Necesitamos a alguien que _____ manejar las luces.
   _{saber}

5. Los profesores nos recomendaron que _____ carteles informativos.
   _{preparar}

6. No creo que _____ difícil encontrar una sala libre para el concierto.
   _{ser}

7. Si el club _____ más miembros, podríamos promocionar mejor el evento.
   _{tener}

8. Aunque nosotros _____ poco tiempo para prepararlo, el concierto será un éxito.
   _{tener}

▶ **Haz** una lista de actividades multiculturales que podrían realizarse en tu escuela.

 ▶ **Habla** con tus compañeros(as). Presenta tus propuestas y escucha las suyas. Al final, hagan una selección de las actividades que más les gusten.

▶ **Escribe** una carta para informar al director de la escuela sobre las actividades multiculturales que quieren organizar.

Modelo

> Estimado Sr. Hall:
>
> Le escribo en nombre del club de Español. Queremos organizar un concierto multicultural para que los estudiantes tengan la oportunidad de conocer y apreciar la música de otras culturas. También...

74 **Las noticias recientes**

 ▶ **Habla** con tu compañero(a) sobre noticias recientes de tu comunidad, de tu estado, de tu país o del mundo. Intercambien sus opiniones sobre esas noticias.

Modelo

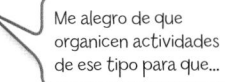 En la biblioteca municipal van a organizar un ciclo de conferencias de escritores latinoamericanos.

Me alegro de que organicen actividades de ese tipo para que...

El escritor peruano Mario Vargas Llosa.

DESAFÍO 3

Gramática – Usos del subjuntivo (repaso)

72. Before beginning this activity, ask students to identify what each sentence starter expresses (e.g., wishes, feelings).

73. For the fourth part of this activity, ask students to include at least five statements that require the subjunctive, including one conditional statement. When students have finished a draft of the letter, have them do a peer review. Ask students to pay special attention to the sentences that have the subjunctive, checking for proper use and correct conjugation.

Answer Key

71. En ciertos casos se usa el infinitivo en inglés (e.g., *I want you to go to the parade*). En otros casos se usa un verbo conjugado, pero no hay una conjugación especial (e.g., *I am happy that you speak many languages*). En las cláusulas condicionales hipotéticas se usa *were* (e.g., *If I were to go to New York, I would visit the museum*). Se expresa duda con expresiones como: *I might be late for work today.*

72.
1. (c) Seríamos más felices si no existieran las guerras.
2. (d) Podremos convivir en paz cuando todos seamos más tolerantes.
3. (a) Quiero vivir en un lugar donde pueda ser feliz.
4. (b) Es bueno que todos nosotros promovamos la igualdad.

73.
1. decidamos
2. encontremos
3. pidan
4. sepa
5. preparáramos
6. sea
7. tuviera
8. tengamos
▶ Answers will vary.
▶ Answers will vary.
▶ Answers will vary.

74. Answers will vary.

Additional Resources

Fans Online activities
Practice Workbook

HERITAGE LANGUAGE LEARNERS

• Students may use the subjunctive correctly, but they may not identify it as subjunctive or know why they are using it. Say or write ten sentences with verbs in both the indicative and the subjunctive; be sure to include different tenses and practice with *cuando, aunque, donde, antes de que,* and *después de que* when these words refer to real events, uncertain situations, or events in the future. Ask students to identify each verb as indicative or subjunctive and explain why each mood was used.

TOTAL PHYSICAL RESPONSE (TPR)

• Have students play a game in which they will practice using the subjunctive. You may want to divide the class into two or four teams. Give players index cards on which they will write an action verb and have them exchange the cards with the opposing team. Then ask players to take turns drawing cards and telling a teammate what to do, using verbs such as *recomendar, querer, decir, sugerir,* etc. For example:
A. *Sugiero que leas este libro.*
B. (Student will pantomime reading a book.)

LECTURA: TEXTO LITERARIO

Presentation

- In this section, students will read a poem by Nicolás Guillen, a Cuban writer, who is well known for his mastery of rhythmic stanzas and his solidarity with the underprivileged—especially the black population of the Antilles.

Activities	Standards	Resources
Lectura: texto literario	1.2, 2.1, 3.1, 3.2	
75.	1.1, 1.2, 2.2, 3.2	
76.	1.2, 1.3	
77.	1.3, 2.1, 3.2	

Teaching Suggestions

Warm-Up / Independent Starter

- Ask students to observe the poem, count the stanzas (estrofas), and note the ones that look alike. Have them note the words that are the same in these stanzas. Can they see a pattern?

Preparation

- Have students work with a partner to read the *Antes de leer* strategies. Then ask pairs to write the answers to the questions posed. Once pairs have finished, discuss their answers to the *Antes de leer* and their Independent Starters as a class.

- Read the poem aloud to model the rhythm and rhyme and have students follow along in their books. Then call on individual students to each read a stanza. Call students' attention to the repetition and the rhyme of certain words. Have them write the words that rhyme on the board (e.g., *muralla – vaya – playa; monte – horizonte; clavel – coronel – laurel; quién es – ciempiés*). Explain that these words have *rima consonante* (i.e., a rhyme where, beginning with the last stressed vowel, the vowels as well as the consonants sound identical).

- Then ask students to find pairs of words in the poem that have related meanings (e.g., *manos negras – manos blancas; playa – monte; rosa – clavel; alacrán – ciempiés; veneno – puñal*). Call students' attention to the fact that these pairs also contribute to the rhythm of the poem.

LECTURA: TEXTO LITERARIO

Antes de leer: estrategias

1. Lee el título. ¿Conoces la palabra *muralla*? Si no la conoces, búscala en el diccionario. Busca también la palabra *pared*. ¿Qué diferencia hay entre las dos?

2. Lee los cuatro primeros versos *(lines)* del poema. Explica cuál crees que será el tema.

3. Lee las dos primeras estrofas *(stanzas)* que empiezan con «¡Tun, tun!». ¿Cuándo se abre y cuándo se cierra la muralla? Escríbelo con tus propias palabras.

La muralla

Para hacer esta muralla,
tráiganme todas las manos:
Los negros, sus manos negras,
los blancos, sus blancas manos.
Ay,
una muralla que vaya
desde la playa hasta el monte[1],
desde el monte hasta la playa, bien,
allá sobre el horizonte.

—¡Tun, tun![2]
—¿Quién es?
—Una rosa y un clavel...
—¡Abre la muralla!

—¡Tun, tun!
—¿Quién es?
—El sable[3] del coronel...
—¡Cierra la muralla!

—¡Tun, tun!
—¿Quién es?
—La paloma y el laurel...
—¡Abre la muralla!

—¡Tun, tun!
—¿Quién es?
—El alacrán[4] y el ciempiés[5]...
—¡Cierra la muralla!

Al corazón del amigo,
abre la muralla;
al veneno[6] y al puñal[7],
cierra la muralla;
al mirto[8] y la yerbabuena[9],
abre la muralla;
al diente de la serpiente,
cierra la muralla;
al ruiseñor[10] en la flor,
abre la muralla...

Alcemos una muralla
juntando todas las manos;
los negros, sus manos negras,
los blancos, sus blancas manos.
Una muralla que vaya
desde la playa hasta el monte,
desde el monte hasta la playa, bien,
allá sobre el horizonte...

NICOLÁS GUILLÉN (Cuba, 1902-1989).

---

1. forest	3. sword	5. centipede	7. dagger	9. peppermint
2. «—Knock, knock!»	4. scorpion	6. poison	8. myrtle	10. nightingale

Differentiated Instruction

DEVELOPING LEARNERS

- Reading and comprehending poetry often presents challenges to students. First, have students scan the poem for unfamiliar words and encourage them to use the footnotes, look for cognates, and use context clues to decode any new words. Then have students practice reading the poem aloud but quietly to themselves before they take turns reading aloud to the group. You may want to have one student read the questions and the exclamations and another, the responses. Monitor students' pronunciation and rhythm as they read the lines.

EXPANDING LEARNERS

- Ask students to try their hand at writing a poem. It does not have to rhyme, but it should be related somehow to the focus of this unit (i.e., *historia, política y sociedad*). Students might use symbolism to describe one of these topics. Encourage students to send a "message" in their poem that is a call to improve society. You may want to consider assigning the poem as homework so students may edit and proofread their work carefully. Call on volunteers to read their poems aloud, and discuss their content with the class.

75 Comprensión

▶ **Responde** a estas preguntas.

1. ¿Quién va a construir esta muralla?
2. ¿Cuál es el propósito de la muralla?
3. ¿Qué tipo de cosas deja fuera la muralla?
4. ¿Qué tipo de cosas deja entrar?

 ▶ **Comenta** estas cuestiones con tu compañero(a).

1. En opinión de ustedes, ¿cómo se relaciona el poema con el tema de esta unidad?
2. ¿Se puede decir que este poema representa un tipo de sociedad ideal? ¿Cómo es esa sociedad? Escriban cuatro o cinco palabras que describan esa sociedad ideal.
3. Una característica de este poema son las repeticiones y los contrastes. Busca ejemplos y expliquen: ¿qué efecto producen en el poema?

 ▶ **Lee** de nuevo el poema. ¿Estás de acuerdo con estas afirmaciones? Coméntalo con tus compañeros(as) y explica tus respuestas.

1. Este poema usa imágenes de la naturaleza para representar las cosas buenas.
2. La sociedad ideal no necesita tener un ejército.
3. La sociedad ideal llegará cuando todos trabajemos con el mismo objetivo.
4. Los valores que trata este poema son la solidaridad, la armonía y la paz.

76 Imágenes

▶ **Completa** una tabla como esta con las imágenes positivas y negativas que hay en el poema. Después, añade otras palabras que te sugieren cosas similares.

	Imágenes positivas	Imágenes negativas
Plantas y flores	rosa	
Animales		

77 Con tus propias palabras

▶ **Escribe** dos estrofas más siguiendo este esquema. No olvides que deben expresar los mismos valores que el poema de Nicolás Guillén.

—¡Tun, tun!
—¿Quién es?
—...
—¡Abre la muralla!

—¡Tun, tun!
—¿Quién es?
—...
—¡Cierra la muralla!

Activities

76. To expand this activity, explain that symbols are words or items that have a significance beyond their obvious meaning. For instance, the word *corazón* means the body organ, but it also means love. Have students explain the symbolic meaning of some of the words in the poem (e.g., *paloma, rosa, laurel, puñal*).

77. Before assigning this activity, have students count the number of syllables that the majority of lines in the poem have. (8; *son versos octosílabos*) Remind students to write two lines that have eight syllables each. The last word of each line or verse should rhyme with the previous or following line in order to preserve the rhythm.

Answer Key

75. 1. Los negros y los blancos van a construir la muralla.
2. Protegerse de lo malo y admitir lo bueno.
3. El odio y la violencia.
4. El amor y la belleza.
▶ Answers will vary.
▶ Answers will vary.

76. Answers will vary. Sample answers:
– Imágenes positivas. Plantas y flores: rosa, clavel, laurel, yerbabuena, flor, mirto. Animales: paloma, ruiseñor.
– Imágenes negativas: Plantas y flores: ninguna. Animales: alacrán, ciempiés.

77. Answers will vary.

Additional Resources

Fans Online activities

HERITAGE LANGUAGE LEARNERS

• Tell students that a few years ago *el Día del Libro* in Spain wanted to pay tribute to words, rather than to literary works or authors. The goal was to find *la palabra más bella del castellano*. More than 41,000 Internet users submitted 7,130 entries. The word *amor* received the most votes, followed by *libertad, paz,* and *vida*. Ask students to conduct their own competition. Have students ask their classmates, friends, family members, or neighbors what is *la palabra más bonita del idioma español*. Tally all students' results to see which word the most people chose.

SPECIAL-NEEDS LEARNERS

• Provide students with information-processing difficulties a quiet area in which to process the directions and the ideas in the poem. Many students with information-processing difficulties can only concentrate for shorter periods of time; therefore, provide additional time for these students and allow them to take several breaks while reading the material or while working on any of these activities.

Unit 8
DESAFÍO 3
Comunicación

Presentation

- In this section, students will integrate the vocabulary and grammar skills from *Desafío 3* to express wishes and opinions about community events.

Activities	Standards	Resources
78.	1.2, 1.3, 2.1	Audio
79.	1.1, 1.2, 2.2, 3.1, 5.1	
80.	1.1, 1.2, 1.3, 2.1, 2.2, 5.1	
81. Final del desafío	1.1, 1.2, 1.3, 2.1, 2.2, 3.1, 5.1	
Tu desafío	1.1, 1.2	

Teaching Suggestions

Warm-Up / Independent Starter

- Have students write a list of multicultural events in their community. Ask them to choose their favorite and write a few sentences about the event.

Preparation

- Ask students to share their Independent Starters. Do students in your class prefer certain types of events or is there a diversity of preferences? Why might this be? Discuss this as a class.

- Have students take their descriptions of their favorite events and rewrite them using the subjunctive. Suggest that they use statements that express emotion or wish. For example: *Me llena de orgullo que celebremos la independencia de nuestra nación. Por eso quiero que mi familia vaya al desfile del Día de la Independencia.*

Activities

78. Ask students to also note other information each speaker provides, such as his or her ethnicity and how he or she describes each event.

79. Before students begin the third part of this activity, ask them what they like about the festival and what they think it lacks. You may also want to review expressions that are used to give suggestions, such as *recomiendo que, sugiero que, aconsejo que.*

430

DESAFÍO 3
Comunicación

78 Mi desfile favorito

 ▶ **Escucha** a varias personas hablando sobre eventos culturales y completa una tabla como esta.

	¿De qué evento habla?	¿Cuándo y dónde se celebra?	¿Por qué le gusta?
Estela			
Manuel Alejandro			
Mariana			

79 SummerStage en la ciudad

▶ **Lee** esta entrada de blog y complétala con los artículos definidos e indefinidos necesarios.

> ### @SUMMERSTAGE: EVENTOS LATINOS EN AGOSTO
> **Lunes, 8 de agosto de 2011. Escrito por ÁLEX GUERRERO**
>
> ¿Quién no se la ha pasado bien en SummerStage? Hace ___1___ año yo estaba cantando y bailando ___2___ ritmo de Los Amigos Invisibles, Natalia Lafourcade y Jovanotti. SummerStage, ___3___ festival gratuito al aire libre más grande de ___4___ ciudad, es parada esencial del verano neoyorquino. ___5___ artistas en cartelera son de primera y muchos de ellos son latinos. Además de Central Park, ___6___ programación de SummerStage abarca otros diecisiete parques de ___7___ ciudad. En ___8___ mes de agosto se presenta ___9___ obra teatral *Sangre*, que es ___10___ adaptación de *Bodas de Sangre*, del escritor español Federico García Lorca. Check it out!
>
> Fuente: http://www.latinoevents.me (texto adaptado)

▶ **Responde** a estas preguntas.

1. ¿Qué es el SummerStage?
2. ¿Dónde tiene lugar?
3. ¿Qué tipo de música piensas que se puede escuchar en los conciertos?
4. Además de los conciertos, ¿qué otras actuaciones hay?

▶ **Escribe** un correo electrónico a los organizadores del SummerStage haciéndoles algunas sugerencias para mejorar el festival.

430 cuatrocientos treinta

Differentiated Instruction

DEVELOPING LEARNERS

- Ask students to complete the following sentences with the correct form of the verb in parentheses:
  1. *Recomiendo que (tú – leer) el poema otra vez. (leas)*
  2. *Termina la tarea antes de que (llegar) tus padres. (lleguen)*
  3. *No pienso que esa palabra (ser) tan bonita. (sea)*
  4. *Quería que tú lo (pasar) bien. (pasaras)*
  5. *Cuando (estar) el director, se lo diré. (esté)*
  6. *Busco alguien que (saber) español. (sepa)*

EXPANDING LEARNERS

- Ask students to work with a partner and write the concluding dialogue for the *Final del desafío*. Students may choose to go into detail about what Michelle and Daniel plan to include, or they might include some problems that the two participants will need to solve before they prepare their multicultural calendar. After they write their dialogues, invite some pairs to come before the class and role-play their conversations.

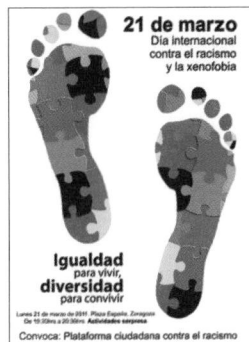

21 de marzo
Día internacional
contra el racismo
y la xenofobia

Igualdad
para vivir,
diversidad
para convivir

Lunes 21 de marzo de 2011 Plaza España, Zaragoza
De 19:30hrs a 20:30hrs **Actividades sorpresa**

Convoca: Plataforma ciudadana contra el racismo

 80 La igualdad y el respeto

▶ **Lee** este cartel. ¿Cuál es el mensaje
que transmite?

▶ **Habla** con tu compañero(a). Compartan su opinión
sobre el cartel.

▶ **Creen** un cartel similar para fomentar la paz,
la solidaridad o la igualdad mundial.

Final del desafío

MICHELLE: ¡Me encanta Nueva York! Ojalá pueda volver
pronto.
DANIEL: A mí también. Me alegro de que nuestra
investigación ___1___ tanto. ¡Tenemos mucho
que contar! Ahora es necesario que ___2___ qué
eventos vamos a incluir en el folleto.
MICHELLE: Yo quiero que ___3___ sobre el Día de Reyes.
Ese festival me parece muy lindo.
DANIEL: ¿Ponemos también el Desfile Puertorriqueño?
MICHELLE: Claro. Y si vamos a incluir la cultura
estadounidense, yo pondría también el desfile del
Día de Brujas. Aunque prefiero hablar de elementos
que ___4___ la pluralidad de la ciudad...
DANIEL: Entonces es mejor que ___5___ un párrafo
sobre la fiesta del Día de la Independencia de
Colombia. El barrio colombiano es muy conocido
aquí y la fiesta dura varios días.
MICHELLE: Muy bien. ¿Y qué más eventos incluimos?

81 Faltan unas palabras

▶ **Completa** el diálogo con las formas correctas de estos verbos.

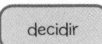 decidir   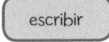 escribir   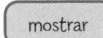 mostrar   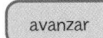 avanzar   hablar

 ▶ **Habla** con tu compañero(a). ¿Qué eventos han seleccionado Daniel y Michelle para el folleto?
¿Qué otros eventos deberían incluir? Busquen información y hagan una lista.

 Visita la página web. Escucha las preguntas de tu *Minientrevista*
Desafío 3 y escribe las respuestas.

cuatrocientos treinta y uno 431

HERITAGE LANGUAGE LEARNERS

• Ask students to bring to class some
brochures, pamphlets, or other forms of
advertisement that promote a cultural or
multicultural event in their family's country
of origin. Students should be prepared to
explain why this event is being celebrated
and when and where it is observed.
Encourage students to give a first-hand
account of their participation, or that of a
family member, in this event. Encourage the
rest of the students to ask questions about
the celebrations described in the material
that was brought to class.

COOPERATIVE LEARNING

• Ask students to imagine that the school
has declared next week as Multicultural
Awareness Week and has asked them to
promote this event. Have students work
in small groups and design an advertising
campaign that includes some flyers, a
poster, and some advertising on local radio
and TV. Each member of the group will work
alone or with a partner on one aspect of the
project. When students finish, have them
gather the promotional materials and display
them in the classroom. Have students vote
for the most effective campaign.

Unit 8
DESAFÍO 3
Comunicación

 AUDIO SCRIPT
See page 389 J.

Answer Key

78. Estela: Habla del Desfile Nacional de
Puerto Rico. Tiene lugar en junio en Nueva
York. Le gusta porque se ven muchas
personas orgullosas de su cultura y de su
identidad nacional.
Manuel Alejandro: Habla del Mes de la
Herencia Dominicana que tiene lugar en
enero en el Museo del Parque, en Queens.
Le gusta porque cree que es importante
que haya iniciativas para que el público
conozca el arte dominicano y su cultura.
Mariana: Habla del Desfile del Día de la
Hispanidad que se celebra el fin de semana
previo al 12 de octubre por la Quinta
Avenida. Le gusta el sentimiento de unidad
que la celebración produce.

79. 1. un   3. el   5. Los   7. la   9. la
2. al   4. la   6. la   8. el   10. una

▶ 1. Es el festival gratuito al aire libre más
grande de Nueva York.
2. En el Central Park y en otros
17 parques de la ciudad.
3. Se puede escuchar música de todo
el mundo.
4. Hay presentaciones de obras
de teatro.

▶ Answers will vary.

80. Answers will vary.
▶ Answers will vary.
▶ Answers will vary.

81. 1. avance   4. muestren
2. decidamos   5. escribamos
3. hablemos
▶ Answers will vary.

Additional Resources

Fans Online activities
Practice Workbook

431

Para terminar

Presentation

- In this section, students will review the unit objectives and put them into practice. They will recognize and talk about events related to history, politics, and society, and they will describe individuals who have had a positive impact on humanity. In addition, students will select one of the following *desafíos* to develop: research one of the indigenous peoples of the Americas and create a map to show where they lived, prepare a presentation about an organization that works for human rights and social justice, or prepare an informational brochure about international celebrations in their community.

Activities	Standards	Resources
82.	1.1, 1.2, 1.3, 2.1, 2.2, 3.1	
83.	1.1, 1.3, 3.1, 5.2	
84. Tu desafío	1.1, 1.2, 1.3, 2.1, 2.2, 3.1, 3.2, 5.1	

Teaching Suggestions

Warm-Up / Independent Starter

- Have students go back and review the vocabulary and grammar for this unit. Ask them to make a list of events that they consider to have had an important impact on the history of the world.

Preparation

- Have students share their Independent Starters with a partner. Then have them select one of the events and describe it in a paragraph. Ask them to include why they consider it to be an important episode. Call on volunteer pairs to come before the class and present their paragraphs.

- Ask students to determine what each of the three pictures shown on this page depict, and brainstorm some words associated with each one. For example: A. *La llegada de los conquistadores españoles al continente americano.* → conquista, explorar, explotar, descubrir, invasión; B. *La llegada de los inmigrantes a Ellis Island.* → inmigración, diversidad, integración, etnias; C. *Machu Picchu* → imperio inca, desaparecer, excavar, reconstruir, arqueólogos, ruinas.

432

Para terminar

Todo junto

HABLAR Y ESCRIBIR

82 **Historia, política y sociedad**

▶ **Relaciona** cada acontecimiento con la(s) foto(s) que le corresponde(n).

1. Este imperio ocupaba gran parte de los Andes.
2. Este hecho histórico ocurrió en 1492.
3. Llegaban de todos los países de Europa.
4. Hablaban español.
5. Construyeron templos impresionantes.
6. Llevaron su religión y su lengua.
7. La Constitución garantizaba la libertad de todos.
8. No conocían el continente.
9. Fueron derrotados por otros pueblos.
10. Llegaron en barcos.
11. Encontraron civilizaciones muy antiguas.
12. Hablaban quechua.

 ▶ **Habla** con tu compañero(a). Comenten todo lo que sepan sobre esos acontecimientos.

▶ **Elige** uno de esos acontecimientos y escribe un párrafo sobre él.

ESCRIBIR

83 **Una persona importante**

▶ **Escribe.** ¿Qué personajes históricos o de la actualidad crees que fueron o son importantes para la Humanidad? Elige uno que te parezca interesante y escribe un párrafo sobre él, sin mencionar su nombre.

Modelo *Fue un músico que cantaba en un grupo muy famoso y se convirtió en un símbolo de la paz mundial.*

▶ **Lee** tu texto a tus compañeros(as). Ellos(as) tienen que adivinar de quién se trata.

432 cuatrocientos treinta y dos

Differentiated Instruction

DEVELOPING LEARNERS

- Ask students to complete these sentences:
  1. *Es importante que los inmigrantes se rechacen / integren en la sociedad.* (integren)
  2. *La alcaldesa / La reina gobierna la ciudad.* (La alcaldesa)
  3. *Los conquistadores invadieron / exploraron el nuevo continente.* (invadieron)
  4. *Los arqueólogos hicieron ruinas / excavaciones.* (excavaciones)
  5. *El dictador llegó al poder mediante una ley / un golpe de estado.* (un golpe de estado)
  6. *La igualdad y la justicia son valores / herencias importantes.* (valores)

EXPANDING LEARNERS

- Ask students to identify the word that does not belong and explain why.
  1. *liberal   cultural   conservador* (cultural)
  2. *reinas   arqueólogos   excavaciones* (reinas)
  3. *imperio   diputado   gobernador* (imperio)
  4. *ministro   mestizaje   parlamento* (mestizaje)
  5. *apoyar   rechazar   aprobar* (rechazar)
  6. *invadir   restaurar   reconstruir* (invadir)
  7. *dirigir   gobernar   descubrir* (descubrir)

Tu desafío

84 **Mapas y eventos**

¿Recuerdas los desafíos de los personajes? ¿Cuál te gusta más? Elige una de estas opciones y resuelve tu desafío.

DESAFÍO Ⓐ

Investiga sobre la historia de uno de los pueblos indígenas de las Américas. Escribe un texto y haz un mapa indicando lo siguiente:

- Quiénes eran y dónde vivían.
- Qué monumentos o sitios arqueológicos se conservan y dónde están.

VACUNACION DE TODOS LOS NIÑOS DEL MUNDO

DESAFÍO Ⓑ

Investiga sobre una organización internacional que trabaje en favor de los derechos humanos, la paz o la igualdad, y prepara una presentación. Incluye esta información:

- Cuándo se fundó.
- Países que forman parte de ella.
- Proyectos a los que se dedica.

DESAFÍO Ⓒ

Investiga sobre las celebraciones internacionales en tu comunidad y haz un folleto incluyendo lo siguiente:

- Fechas y lugares en que se celebran.
- Descripción de esos eventos.

cuatrocientos treinta y tres **433**

Activities

82. Ask students to work with a partner to complete the first part of this activity. Have them read the sentences aloud to practice pronunciation and intonation. Ask them to do the first four sentences and then change pairs to add variety and give students the opportunity to work with different people in the class. After four sentences, have them change pairs once more. Tell students that there may be some statements that apply to more than one picture.

84. Display students' work in the classroom and have the class vote on the best entry in each category.

Answer Key

82. A: 2, 4, 6, 8, 10, 11.
B: 3, 7, 10.
C: 1, 5, 9, 12.
▶ Answers will vary.
▶ Answers will vary. Sample answer: Ellis Island es una pequeña isla situada en el puerto de la ciudad de Nueva York. Entre 1892 y 1954 pasaron por esta isla más de doce millones de inmigrantes, en su mayoría europeos. En la isla se les realizaba un examen médico y se revisaba su documentación, y así se decidía si podían entrar al país. En 1954 se cerró Ellis Island y en 1965 fue declarada Monumento Nacional.

83. Answers will vary.
▶ Answers will vary.

84. Answers will vary.

Additional Resources

Fans Online activities

HERITAGE LANGUAGE LEARNERS

- Explain to students that studying the ruins of ancient cultures gives us insight into how people lived, what their beliefs were, how they constructed their buildings and monuments, and what they contributed to the world. Ask students to make a list of the structures, artifacts, and other materials from our culture that would give archaeologists 1,000 years from now an idea of how we lived, what our values were, and what contributions we made. Then have students work with all members of the group to explain their choices.

CRITICAL THINKING

- Now that students have followed the participants in their *desafíos*, ask them in which challenge they would have liked to have participated in and why. Would they have liked working with one of the participants, or with someone else? With whom? Which *desafío* is more in line with their own interests and abilities? Do students think that they could have done a better job with one of the challenges; if so, which one? Were the pairs a good match, or do students think the participants should have had different partners? Ask students to explain their answers.

MAPA CULTURAL

Una ciudad con historia: Barcelona

Presentation

■ This section presents information about the city of Barcelona (Spain), with a special emphasis on its history. The images serve as a reference point for additional cultural readings and activities that expand on the skills students learned in this unit.

Activities	Standards	Resources
Mapa cultural	1.2, 2.1, 2.2, 3.1	Video
85.	1.1, 1.2, 2.2, 4.2, 5.1	

Cultural Topics

■ **Ciudad de México.** Mexico City, one of the most populous cities in the world and one of the oldest continuously inhabited urban centers in the Western Hemisphere, was founded by the Aztecs in 1325. Tenochtitlan, as it was called then, became the capital of the Aztec empire and it was the largest city in Mesoamerica by the time the Spanish conquered it in 1521. The Spanish made it the capital of the Viceroyalty of New Spain. In 1821, the Mexican army entered Mexico City and liberated it from Spanish rule. Today, Mexico City's history is evident in its architecture—a mix of Aztec ruins, Spanish colonial churches and palaces, nineteenth-century mansions, and modern skyscrapers.

■ **Ciudad de Nueva York.** New York City, the most populous city in the United States and one of the most influential in the world, started as a Dutch settlement in 1626 on land purchased for a pittance from the Native Americans who lived in the area. In 1664, the British took the city and renamed it New York. Trade and international commerce grew and by 1900, it was one of the wealthiest cities in the world. Throughout its history, New York City has attracted a large inflow of immigrants, making it the most ethnically diverse city in America.

Teaching Suggestions

Warm-Up / Independent Starter

■ Ask students to glance at the *Mapa cultural* and jot down some facts they know about Barcelona.

Una ciudad con historia: Barcelona

La historia de una ciudad se manifiesta en su emplazamiento *(location)*, sus barrios y su arquitectura. Por eso, la ciudad cambia, se adapta, crece, se reinventa, y esta evolución va dejando huellas visibles en su fisonomía *(appearance)*.

La antigua Barcino

El origen de la ciudad de Barcelona es muy antiguo: hacia el año 10 a. C. se fundó una colonia romana en una llanura a orillas del Mediterráneo que se llamó Barcino. Como en toda ciudad romana, Barcino tenía una plaza central (el foro), una muralla, templos, acueductos, un sistema de alcantarillado, etc.

Columnas del Templo de Augusto.

La Barcelona medieval

Con el paso del tiempo, Barcelona fue creciendo hasta convertirse en un importante centro comercial a orillas del Mediterráneo. Hoy se puede pasear por las calles estrechas del Barrio Gótico y admirar muchos edificios construidos entre los siglos XIII y XV, como la catedral o el Palacio de la Generalitat.

La Barcelona moderna

La ciudad siguió creciendo y en el siglo XIX se convirtió en una importante ciudad industrial. En esta época se crearon barrios obreros, como el Poblenou, y también se construyó L'Eixample (el Ensanche), un barrio con calles rectas y anchas, y cuadras regulares.
Entre los siglos XIX y XX, la ciudad se embelleció con construcciones de estilo modernista diseñadas por el arquitecto Antonio Gaudí.

Barrio Gótico.

La Pedrera (Antonio Gaudí).

Differentiated Instruction

DEVELOPING LEARNERS

• To help students organize the information presented in this *Mapa cultural*, have them create a four-column chart, with one column for each historical period. Ask students to summarize, in a bulleted list, information about each of these periods. The first bullet should include dates; the second, information about the architectural style and famous buildings of this period; and the third, other miscellaneous information (e.g., neighborhoods that were created during this period, important events that took place).

EXPANDING LEARNERS

• Ask students to relate what they have learned about the history of Barcelona with what they know about a city—other than their city—in the United States. In addition to comparing and contrasting the history of both cities, students should also look at the location, layout, architecture, neighborhoods, and public areas of both cities. Then ask students to list landmarks from the American city that reflect each of the city's historical periods. Invite students to do a class presentation.

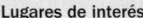

Lugares de interés

Barcelona romana
1. Necrópolis romana
2. Restos de la muralla

Barcelona medieval
3. Catedral
4. Monasterio de Pedralbes
5. Palacio Real Mayor
6. Palacio de la Generalitat

Barcelona moderna
7. Paseo de las Ramblas
8. Basílica de la Merced
9. Plaza de Cataluña
10. Basílica de la Sagrada Familia
11. La Pedrera
12. L'Eixample
13. Parque Güell

Barcelona actual
14. Villa Olímpica
15. Torre Mapfre y hotel Arts
16. Torre Agbar

La Barcelona actual

A finales del siglo XX, la celebración de los Juegos Olímpicos de 1992 dio un nuevo impulso a Barcelona. Se reordenó la ciudad y se construyó la ciudad olímpica, con un puerto deportivo y dos rascacielos *(skyscrapers)* muy característicos: la torre Mapfre y el hotel Arts.
Barcelona es hoy una ciudad moderna en la que se desarrollan nuevas construcciones y áreas como la llamada 22@Barcelona.

85 **Ciudad viva**

▶ **Responde.**

1. ¿Por qué crees que los romanos eligieron el lugar donde está Barcelona?
2. ¿Qué zona de Barcelona te gusta más? ¿Por qué?

▶ **Compara.**

– ¿Cómo es tu localidad: antigua o moderna?
– ¿Cuándo se fundó tu localidad? ¿Quiénes la crearon?
– ¿Hay en tu localidad zonas que pertenecen a distintas épocas? ¿Qué diferencias hay en las casas y en las calles de esas zonas?

Torre Agbar.

Unit 8

MAPA CULTURAL

Una ciudad con historia: Barcelona

Preparation

■ Show students a map of Spain and call on a volunteer to identify Barcelona on the map. Then have students share their Independent Starters. You may want to create a list on the board or on a transparency of the facts and information about Barcelona that students mention. How much do they know about this city?

■ Explain to students that Barcelona is the second-largest city in Spain. The population of the city proper is about 1,630,000, but the metropolitan area has a population of about 5,000,000. Barcelona is located on the Mediterranean coast and is the capital of Cataluña (Catalonia), one of Spain's seventeen autonomous communities. Due to its strategic position on the Mediterranean Sea, Barcelona boasts a large and important port, and is a major commercial and cultural center. Barcelona hosted the Olympic Games in 1992 and it hosts numerous annual conferences, trade fairs, and exhibitions.

Activities

85. For the second part of this activity, you may want to divide the class into small groups and assign each group a different aspect or question to research. The objective is to create a historical account of your city, similar to the one about Barcelona in this *Mapa cultural*. Once the different groups have gathered their information and pictures, ask them to come together as a class to compile and summarize the information to create a *Mapa cultural* of their city.

Answer Key

85. Answers will vary.
   ▶ Answers will vary.

Additional Resources

Fans Online activities
Practice Workbook

HERITAGE LANGUAGE LEARNERS

• Ask students to choose one of the following cities and research the imprints that each of the city's major historical periods (i.e., pre-Hispanic, colonial, and present) left on it.

– *Ciudad de México (México)*
– *Cuzco (Perú)*
– *San Juan (Puerto Rico)*
– *Cartagena (Colombia)*

• Have students organize their information in a visually appealing way and present it to the class. After the presentation, ask the class to compare and contrast the city presented by their classmates with Barcelona.

CRITICAL THINKING

• As a class, discuss the factors that play an important role in the demise or survival of cities. Why might some cities survive and thrive over the millennia, whereas others cease to exist? You may want to have students work in small groups to research the history of several cities; some that have survived (e.g., Cuzco, Peru; Santa Fe, NM; Córdoba, Spain), and others that have disappeared (e.g., Teotihuacan, Mexico; Tikal, Guatemala; Centralia, PA). Ask students to compile a list of factors and try to develop their own theory for the success or demise of a city.

ESCRITURA

Y tú, ¿qué opinas?

Presentation

- In this section, students will practice and extend their writing skills. They will apply the vocabulary and grammar they have learned in this unit in order to write a persuasive essay.

Activities	Standards	Resources
Escritura	1.1, 1.2, 1.3, 3.1	

Teaching Suggestions

Warm-Up / Independent Starter

- Have students read the introduction to the writing task on page 436 silently. Then ask them to think of two issues that are important to them. These topics can range from local to national or international issues—what is important is that students feel strongly about them.

Preparation

- Invite students to share their Independent Starters. Compile a list of topics on the board and briefly discuss as a class the topics that students find most interesting or feel most passionately about. The more they feel about an issue, the more motivated they will be to write about it. Some issues might be somewhat controversial, but emphasize the importance of avoiding extremist points of view, since that will alienate the audience.

- Ask for a volunteer to read the Persuasive Writing box aloud. You may want to bring to class some examples of persuasive writing. Some of these texts may be in English and others in Spanish. Before you or volunteer students read each text aloud, note the purpose of the text and its target audience. As a class, talk about the features of each text and discuss the specific language and techniques that helped the writer persuade his or her audience.

Step-by-Step Instructions

Piensa

- Have students use their Independent Starters and the class discussion of the Preparation activity to help them select a topic for their essay. Once they have their topic, ask students to start listing reasons or arguments in support of their position.

ESCRITURA

Y tú, ¿qué opinas?

Persuasive writing

In persuasive writing, the author uses facts and opinions to convince the reader to agree with his or her point of view. Persuasive writing can be used to motivate people to take a certain action, or simply to change their thinking. Some examples of **persuasive texts** include commercials, op-ed columns in the newspaper, and political speeches.

Los textos de opinión expresan el punto de vista de su autor sobre un tema o una situación. Las opiniones expuestas deben apoyarse en argumentos lógicos, que son los que determinan que el texto sea persuasivo o no. Además, los textos de este tipo siempre deben ir firmados, ya que el autor se hace responsable de las opiniones planteadas.

En esta unidad, vas a escribir un texto de opinión analizando algún tema social o político que consideres interesante y expresando tu opinión sobre él.

Piensa

- Elige un tema político o social y define la tesis o posición que vas a defender.

Modelo *Todas las personas deben ejercer su derecho al voto.*

- Piensa en los argumentos que utilizarás para defender tu tesis y busca información para apoyar tus argumentos.

Modelo *Votar aumenta el compromiso con el futuro del país.*

- Anota tus ideas en un esquema como este:

Introducción Presenta el tema e intenta captar la atención del receptor.	*En los países democráticos los ciudadanos tienen derecho a elegir a sus gobernantes.*
Exposición Explica la información fundamental y expón tu tesis.	*El voto es una forma de ejercer la democracia. Es muy importante que los ciudadanos ejerzan su derecho al voto y participen activamente en los procesos electorales.*
Argumentación Presenta los argumentos con los que vas a defender tu tesis.	– *Votar les permite expresar sus opiniones y preferencias políticas.* – *Votar aumenta el compromiso con el futuro del país.*
Conclusión Resume los aspectos más relevantes de tu argumentación.	*Hay que fomentar la participación para que todos los ciudadanos ejerzan su derecho al voto.*

436 cuatrocientos treinta y seis

Rubric for Evaluation

	Content	Organization	Conventions
1 point	Thesis is not clear. No supporting arguments or they lack substance. No evidence provided. Limited vocabulary.	Focus on issue is not sustained. Details are not in a logical order. Few or no transitions between ideas. Ineffective conclusion.	Many errors in spelling, punctuation, grammar, and usage. Errors obscure meaning.
3 points	Thesis is clear but some supporting arguments are weak. Evidence is accurate. Some inaccurate word choices.	Mostly clear focus. Some effective transitions are present. Conclusion restates thesis, but is not very effective.	Some errors in spelling, punctuation, grammar, and usage. Errors don't interfere with meaning.

Escribe

■ A partir de las ideas que anotaste, escribe el borrador de tu texto. Recuerda que el propósito del texto es expresar tus ideas acerca de un tema determinado y convencer al lector con tus argumentos. Por tanto, tu lenguaje debe ser claro y persuasivo.

■ Para argumentar tus ideas, puedes utilizar ejemplos, citas textuales y preguntas que te ayuden a implicar al lector en tus comentarios.

Modelo *Todos sabemos que ...*

■ Elige un título que capte la atención del lector.

Expresiones útiles

En mi opinión...	*In my opinion ...*
A mi modo de ver...	*The way I see it ...*
Desde mi punto de vista...	*From my point of view ...*
Considero que...	*I think ...*
Estoy de acuerdo con...	*I agree with ...*
No estoy de acuerdo con...	*I disagree with ...*
Por ejemplo...	*For example ...*
Así como...	*As well as ...*
Ya que...	*Since ...*

Votar en las elecciones: un deber social

Desde mi punto de vista, es muy importante que las personas ejerzan su derecho al voto en los procesos electorales.

Todos sabemos que el derecho al voto es una característica fundamental de los gobiernos democráticos. En mi opinión, los ciudadanos deben ejercer su derecho a votar y de este modo expresar sus opiniones y sus preferencias políticas. A mi modo de ver, si las personas no van a votar están perdiendo la oportunidad de expresar sus preferencias políticas. Opino, además, que tener una participación activa a través del voto promueve un mayor compromiso de las personas con su gobierno y su país...

Revisa

■ Intercambia tu trabajo con tu compañero(a) y revisa su texto.

– ¿Las ideas están bien expuestas? ¿La opinión es clara?

– ¿Te convencen los argumentos que da tu compañero(a) para defender su opinión?

– ¿Tiene errores de gramática u ortografía? Señálalos. Si tienes dudas, puedes consultar un diccionario o preguntarle a tu profesor(a).

■ Devuelve el texto a su autor(a) y vuelve a revisar tu trabajo incorporando los cambios que sean necesarios.

Comparte

■ Comparte tu texto con el resto de la clase. ¿Qué opinan tus compañeros(as)? ¿Están de acuerdo con tus ideas?

■ Publica tu trabajo en el blog de la escuela o de tu comunidad.

	Content	Organization	Conventions
5 points	Strong thesis followed by substantive supporting arguments. Evidence is relevant and convincing. Accurate, rich, and purposeful word choices.	Distinct focus and clear structure that enhances the thesis. Effective use of transitions and logical sequencing. Conclusion binds essay together.	Few, if any, errors in spelling, punctuation, grammar, and usage. Excellent command of the Spanish language.

ESCRITURA
Y tú, ¿qué opinas?

■ To help students focus their arguments, have them ask themselves what objections to their position their readers might have. Then, they should focus their arguments on overcoming the readers' objections. Clarify to students that they are not discussing the opposing view; they are just focusing on the validity and benefits of their point of view, but using arguments that address the readers' objections.

Escribe

■ Emphasize to students the importance of backing up their position with evidence (e.g., facts, examples, statistics, quotes from experts, personal experience). Facts are not debatable and can be used to draw the readers in and persuade them to accept the writer's point of view. However, students should take care that the evidence they present is accurate and relevant.

Revisa

■ Ask students to read through their own text before they exchange it with a classmate. Have students try to look at their text from the point of view of someone who objects to the position they have taken in their essay. This will help students discover loopholes in their arguments.

■ As students read their classmates' essays, suggest the following questions: Is the thesis clear? Does it fully address the issue? Do the arguments offer clear support of the thesis? Does the essay follow a clear and logical train of thought? Is the conclusion effective?

Comparte

■ Encourage students to deliver a lively reading of their essay. You may want to hold a class vote to select five or six essays for publication. Students should consider both the relevance of the topic and the effectiveness of the essay when making their selection.

Evaluation

■ Distribute copies of the rubric to students and discuss the evaluation criteria. Ask students to refer to the rubric as they prepare their writing and as they evaluate their classmates' essays.

REPASO

Vocabulario

Presentation

- In this section, students will review all key vocabulary from the unit, organized by themes, to prepare for an assessment. Students will complete practice activities for each of the three *Desafíos*.

Activities	Standards	Resources
1.	1.2, 1.3, 3.1	
2.	1.2, 3.1	
3.	1.1, 2.2, 5.2	

Teaching Suggestions

Warm-Up / Independent Starter

- Ask students to imagine that they have to explain this country's political system to a foreign exchange classmate who knows nothing about it. Have students jot down some facts and descriptions based on what they know. They should mention the Constitution, presidency, House of Representatives, Senate, political parties and elections, and the federal system.

Preparation

- Have students get together in small groups of three and share their notes from the Independent Starter. Then have groups summarize their information in a two-paragraph description of the U.S. political system. They may want to create a graphic organizer to show how the government is organized. Call on volunteer groups to share their explanations and visuals with the class. Then invite students who know or have read about other political systems to compare and contrast those systems to the American system.

- Organize a game to practice the rest of the vocabulary (i.e., *Personajes, acontecimientos, civilizaciones* and *Sociedad*). Divide the class into small groups. Write words from those two vocabulary categories on small index cards, put them in a bag, and have one student from each group pick a card. The student will then write the word vertically on the board, and within a given time limit, write words related to the topic, using each letter of the original word as the initial letter for a word.

438

Personajes, acontecimientos, civilizaciones

la civilización	civilization	**Personas**		**Acciones**	
la estatua	statue	el/la arqueólogo(a)	archaeologist	conquistar	to conquer
la excavación	excavation	el/la conquistador(a)	conqueror	descubrir	to discover
el imperio	empire	el/la explorador(a)	explorer	desaparecer	to disappear
el palacio	palace			excavar	to excavate
las ruinas	ruins	**Hechos históricos**		invadir	to invade
el siglo	century	la batalla	battle	reconstruir	to reconstruct
la época	time, period	la conquista	conquest	restaurar	to restore
		la guerra	war		
		la invasión	invasion		

Política y gobierno

el Congreso	Congress	**Personas, cargos y títulos**	
la Constitución	Constitution	el alcalde/la alcaldesa	mayor
la dictadura	dictatorship	el/la ciudadano(a)	citizen
el golpe de Estado	coup (d'état)	el/la dictador(a)	dictator
la ley	law	el/la diputado(a)	representative
la monarquía constitucional	constitutional monarchy	el/la gobernador(a)	governor
el Parlamento	Parliament	el/la ministro(a)	minister
el poder	power	el/la presidente(a)	president
la república democrática	democratic republic	el príncipe/la princesa	prince/princess
el Senado	Senate	el rey/la reina	king/queen
la votación	vote	el/la senador(a)	senator
		el/la vicepresidente(a)	vice-president

Acciones		**Ideologías**	
apoyar	to support	demócrata	democrat
aprobar	to approve	comunista	communist
dirigir	to direct	conservador(a)	conservative
gobernar	to govern	liberal	liberal
rechazar	to reject	republicano(a)	republican
votar	to vote	socialista	socialist

Sociedad

el apoyo	support	la libertad (de expresión)	freedom (of speech)
la convivencia	coexistence	el mestizaje	mix of races
los deberes	duties	multicultural	multicultural
los derechos	rights	las normas	norms
la diversidad	diversity	la paz	peace
la etnia	ethnicity	la pluralidad	plurality
la herencia cultural	cultural heritage	privado(a)	private
la identidad	identity	público(a)	public
la igualdad	equality	el respeto	respect
el/la inmigrante	immigrant	la sociedad	society
la integración	integration	la solidaridad	solidarity
integrarse	to integrate	la tolerancia	tolerance
la justicia	justice	los valores	values

Differentiated Instruction

DEVELOPING LEARNERS

- Ask students to create a vocabulary booklet with the three categories studied in this unit (i.e., *Personajes, acontecimientos, civilizaciones; Política y gobierno; Sociedad*). The booklet will consist of three spreads (i.e., six pages), one for each vocabulary category. Allow students to organize the vocabulary in each category as they see fit. Encourage them to illustrate their spreads. They may use images from magazines or the Internet. Tell students that they should use this booklet as a study tool. They may also use it to work on the three vocabulary activities from this *Repaso*.

EXPANDING LEARNERS

- Most words in this *Repaso* come from Latin or Greek and are cognates. But there are also some words that mean different things and are used in different contexts in English and Spanish. Ask students to look for these "false cognates" and explain how these words might cause confusion and give examples of usage in both languages. For example, a *diputado* is not a "deputy," but rather a representative or member of Congress. "Deputy" might be translated as *ayudante, suplente,* or *sub-,* depending on the context (e.g., deputy sheriff → *ayudante del sheriff;* deputy director → *subdirector*).

DESAFÍO 1

1 **Dos libros interesantes.** ¿En qué libro puedes leer las siguientes palabras? ¿En el libro de Historia, en el de Arqueología o en los dos? Clasifícalas en dos grupos.

batalla
excavación
ruinas
guerra
siglo
restaurar
invadir
descubrir

DESAFÍO 2

2 **Personas importantes.** ¿A qué persona con título o cargo corresponde cada una de estas definiciones?

① Hijo de un rey y una reina.

② Segunda persona con más poder en el gobierno de un país.

③ Miembro del gobierno de un país que se ocupa de un área en concreto (salud, educación...).

④ Mujer que gobierna en una ciudad o en un pueblo.

DESAFÍO 3

3 **Símbolos.** ¿Qué valores simbolizan estas imágenes? Inventa con tu compañero(a) otros símbolos para estos y otros valores.

①

②

③

Activities

1. To expand this activity, ask students to classify the rest of the vocabulary for *Desafío 1* in a similar manner. Then have students get together with a classmate and compare their classifications.

3. Have students work in small group to come up with other symbols. You may want to assign each group a different value (e.g., *respeto, tolerancia, solidaridad, igualdad, justicia*) so that as many values as possible are represented. Then have each group present and explain their symbol to the class. Post students' symbols around the classroom as a reminder of the importance of these values.

Answer Key

1. Libro de Arqueología: excavación, ruinas, restaurar.
   Libro de Historia: batalla, guerra, invadir.
   Los dos: siglo, descubrir.

2. 1. príncipe
   2. vicepresidente(a)
   3. ministro(a)
   4. alcaldesa

3. Answers will vary. Sample answers:
   1. la justicia
   2. la paz
   3. la libertad

Additional Resources

Fans Online activities
Practice Workbook

HERITAGE LANGUAGE LEARNERS

• Have students research the form of government of their heritage town or city. Ask them to list the following: manner in which the person who heads the town is elected and the frequency of elections, administrative organization of the town's government, services provided by the town, and types of taxes collected by local authorities or ways in which the town finances itself. Ask students to organize their data in a logical and visually attractive manner to do a class presentation. Then have the class compare and contrast this town with their own town or city.

MULTIPLE INTELLIGENCES:
Verbal-Linguistic Intelligence

• Ask students to look for patterns in the *Repaso* vocabulary, list them, and extrapolate a rule for each pattern. Then have students research the topic to find out whether their rule is correct. Students should also address the exceptions to the rule. For example: "Words that end in *-ción* in Spanish have an English equivalent that ends in *-tion.*" This rule is correct in many cases, but not in all (e.g., *canción* → song). Some of these words change in meaning (e.g., *decepción* → disappointment; deception → *engaño*).

REPASO

Gramática

Presentation

- Students will review grammatical structures presented in the unit. Each grammar point is cross-referenced to the corresponding page on which it was introduced. The activities here provide systematic practice by *Desafío*.

Activities	Standards	Resources
4.	1.2, 1.3, 3.1	
5.	1.2	
6.	1.2, 3.1	
7. Cultura	1.1, 2.1, 2.2, 3.1	

Teaching Suggestions

Warm-Up / Independent Starter

- Ask students to think of four historical events that happened at different points in time. One of these events must be recent or still going on.

Preparation

- Draw a timeline on the board and call on volunteers to share their Independent Starters. Write on the timeline some of the events students mention. For example: *El Mayflower llegó a Nueva Inglaterra.* → *EE. UU. se independizó.* → *Armstrong llegó a la Luna.* → *Se creó Internet.* Then ask students to write sentences with the information on the timeline, paying close attention to the use of the different past tenses. For example: *Cuando Armstrong llegó a la Luna, EE. UU. ya se había independizado. Internet ha sido importantísimo en nuestra sociedad.* Invite students to share some of their sentences.

- Go over the rest of the grammar topics from this *Repaso* with the class. If needed, provide additional examples and practice activities for some of the topics.

Activities

4. After students have finished this activity, ask them to explain why sentences 3 and 4 can't be converted into the passive voice. They should explain that sentence 3 has a verb of perception *(escucho)* and sentence 4 has an indirect object *(me: a mí)*.

440

REPASO Gramática

La voz pasiva (pág. 400)

subject (receiver) + verb (ser + past participle) + agent (with por)

Tecnochtitlán fue fundada por los aztecas.

Usos de los tiempos de pasado (pág. 402)

- **Pretérito:** completed actions.
- **Imperfecto:** descriptions, repeated actions, circumstances surrounding an event.
- **Presente perfecto:** actions that began in the past but continue into the present, and recent actions.
- **Pluscuamperfecto:** a past action completed before another.

Hablar de las etapas de una acción (pág. 412)

empezar a + infinitive	dejar de + infinitive
seguir + present participle	acabar de + infinitive
llevar + present participle	

Usos del indicativo (pág. 414)

- To express:
  - Certainty.
  - Opinions in the affirmative.
- To ask about:
  - The purpose of an action.
  - The reason for something.
  - A place or location.
- After:
  - Aunque, for real situations or known outcomes.
  - A lo mejor.
  - Donde, for known, definite, or real places.
  - Cuando and después de que, for habitual or past actions.
- In conditional sentences to express factual or likely conditions.

Los artículos (pág. 424)

EL ARTÍCULO DEFINIDO (EL, LA, LOS, LAS)

Use the definite article when referring to a known person, object, or entity. Spanish uses also the definite article:
- With nouns used in a general sense, or generically, and with abstract nouns.
- With body parts and articles of clothing.
- After jugar a.

EL ARTÍCULO INDEFINIDO (UN, UNA, UNOS, UNAS)

Use the indefinite article when referring to an unknown person, object, or entity. In Spanish, the indefinite article is omitted:
- After the verb ser and before unmodified nouns referring to occupation, nationality, social status, or religious or political affiliation.
- After verbs like tener and llevar, when referring to nouns in a general, or generic, sense.

Usos del subjuntivo (pág. 426)

- To express:
  - Wishes and preferences.
  - Value judgments.
  - Feelings and emotions.
  - Opinions in the negative.
  - Negative expressions.
  - Doubts and uncertainty.
  - Recommendations.
- After:
  - Aunque, for unreal or uncertain situations.
  - Para que and a que, to indicate purpose.
  - Donde, for unknown, indefinite, or hypothetical places.
  - Cuando, después de que, and antes de que, for future events.
- In conditional sentences to express unlikely, hypothetical, or contrary-to-fact conditions.
- To give a negative command.

Differentiated Instruction

DEVELOPING LEARNERS

- Have students complete these sentences:
  1. *Me parece que a veces la Historia se repite / repita. (repite)*
  2. *No creo que existe / exista el gobierno perfecto. (exista)*
  3. *Después de que el alcalde perdió / perdiera la elecciones, se retiró de la política. (perdió)*
  4. *Hace falta respeto para que la convivencia sea / es buena. (sea)*
  5. *Es necesario que rechazamos / rechacemos la violencia. (rechacemos)*
  6. *Cuando votamos / votemos, cumplimos con nuestro deber. (votamos)*

EXPANDING LEARNERS

- Ask students to choose one of the following headlines and write a two-paragraph news report. Have students pay special attention to the use of the different past tenses and the passive voice.
  - *Más de 10 heridos son evacuados en helicóptero.*
  - *El pueblo derribó la estatua del dictador.*
  - *Hallado un manuscrito de más de 2.000 años.*
  - *Los militares derrocaron (overthrew) al gobierno.*
- Have students read their news to the class as if they were newscasters and use appropriate inflection, intonation, and timing.

DESAFÍO 1

4 **En pasiva.** Transforma estas oraciones utilizando la voz pasiva siempre que sea posible.

1. Miles de personas de todo el mundo han leído el último libro del escritor peruano Mario Vargas Llosa.
2. Los estudiantes eligieron al representante de la clase.
3. Yo escucho la radio todas las mañanas mientras desayuno.
4. Mis padres me regalaron unos jeans muy bonitos.
5. Un arquitecto muy famoso diseñará el nuevo centro comercial.

Mario Vargas Llosa.

DESAFÍO 2

5 **Cuestiones de lógica.** Une las dos columnas.

Ⓐ

1. Llegué a la biblioteca a las cinco y son las diez.
2. Mi abuelo no fue a la universidad.
3. Juan se fue hace un minuto.
4. Estoy un poco gordito.
5. ¿Tu hermana dejó el piano?

Ⓑ

a. Tengo que dejar de comer dulces.
b. Llevo estudiando cinco horas.
c. No, sigue estudiando.
d. Empezó a trabajar muy joven.
e. Acaba de salir.

DESAFÍO 3

6 **¿Con qué artículo?** Decide si estas oraciones necesitan artículo y completa las que lo necesiten.

1. Me duele _____ cabeza.
2. Mi amiga Begoña no necesita llevar _____ gafas.
3. Voy a ir al cine con _____ compañero de la escuela.
4. Mi madre es _____ abogada.
5. _____ profesor de Historia es muy simpático.

CULTURA

7 **De ayer a hoy.** Responde a estas preguntas.

1. ¿En qué siglos y en qué regiones se desarrolló la civilización maya?
2. ¿Qué es la OEA?
3. ¿Dónde está el Museo del Barrio? ¿Qué se puede ver allí?

cuatrocientos cuarenta y uno **441**

---

5. To expand this activity, ask students to select one of the sentences and use it as inspiration to write a brief story. Have students use as many structures to talk about the different stages of an action as they can. For example: *Mi abuelo no fue a la universidad. Dejó de estudiar al cumplir los 16 años y empezó a trabajar en una fábrica. Cuando llevaba trabajando 20 años, tuvo un accidente y...*

Answer Key

4. 1. El último libro del escritor peruano Mario Vargas Llosa ha sido leído por miles de personas de todo el mundo.
   2. El representante de la clase fue elegido por los estudiantes.
   3. No se puede transformar.
   4. No se puede transformar.
   5. El nuevo centro comercial será diseñado por un arquitecto muy famoso.

5. 1. b   2. d   3. e   4. a   5. c

6. 1. la
   2. No lleva artículo.
   3. un
   4. No lleva artículo.
   5. El

7. Answers will vary. Sample answers:
   1. La civilización maya se desarrolló entre los siglos III y XV en el sur de México y en zonas de Guatemala, Honduras y El Salvador.
   2. La OEA es la Organización de los Estados Americanos. Realiza proyectos destinados a la protección de los derechos humanos, el desarrollo económico y social y la consolidación de la paz y la democracia.
   3. Está en Nueva York. Tiene una gran colección de objetos precolombinos y exposiciones temporales de pintura, escultura y fotografía.

Additional Resources

Fans Online activities
Practice Workbook

HERITAGE LANGUAGE LEARNERS

• Ask students to imagine that they are the speechwriters of a candidate for the presidency of this country. This candidate is visiting your city and will be briefly addressing the Latino community. Ask students to write this candidate's speech. Have them focus on one or two issues of interest to the Latino community. The speech should be uplifting and encourage listeners to get involved in the political process. Once students have finished, you may want to ask them to choose a classmate who will play the presidential candidate and deliver the speech before the class.

CRITICAL THINKING

• Ask students to analyze these sentences:
   1. *Me puse las manos en la cabeza.* (I placed my hands on my head.)
   2. *Puse mis manos en su cabeza.* (I placed my hands on his head.)

• Why might Spanish use definite articles in the first case and possessive adjectives in the second? Assist students in understanding that possession is marked in the first example with the reflexive pronoun (*me*), so a possessive adjective would be redundant. In the second example, the possessive adjectives are needed to avoid ambiguity because it is not clear whose body is being referred to.

Unit 8

PROYECTO

Un país de Latinoamérica

Presentation

- In this section, students will apply the vocabulary, grammar, and cultural information they have learned in this unit to write a report about an influential period or historical event in a Latin American country.

Activities	Standards	Resources
Paso 1	1.1, 1.2, 2.1, 2.2, 3.1, 5.1	
Paso 2	1.2, 1.3, 2.1, 2.2, 3.1, 5.1	
Paso 3	1.3, 3.1, 5.1	
Paso 4	1.1, 1.2, 1.3, 2.1, 2.2	

Teaching Suggestions

Warm-Up / Independent Starter

- Have students read the introduction to the project silently. Then ask them to list two historical facts about Latin America that they find fascinating. It may be something they have learned in their classes, something they have read or heard in the media, or perhaps something a Spanish-speaking friend or family member told them.

Preparation

- Display a map of Latin America and ask each student to identify a different Spanish-speaking country. Challenge students to mention an interesting fact about the country they identified (e.g., Perú → *en Cuzco estaba la capital del imperio inca*; Paraguay → *hablan guaraní y español*). Then ask students to share their Independent Starters. Encourage students to take notes.

Step-by-Step Instructions

Paso 1

- Ask students to pull out their notes from the previous section and use them to choose a country and an event that piques their interest. Then have students think of research sources they could use. Remind them of the importance of using reliable sources. The Latin American Network Information Center (LANIC) of the University of Texas has a wealth of information on Latin America. To develop research skills, ask students to include a bibliography in their work.

442

PROYECTO

Una presentación sobre

un país de Latinoamérica

The history of Latin America is fascinating and full of great cultures—such as the Aztecs, the Incas, and the Mayas—and of important historical events: the arrival of Spaniards in 1492, the period of colonization, the independence movements of the 19th century, etc. In this project, you are going to write a report about one country, highlighting an influential time period or historical event in its history.

PASO 1 Define el tema de tu presentación

- Elige el país de Latinoamérica que prefieras.
- Busca información sobre ese país. Puedes seguir este esquema:

Historia de...

Culturas indígenas

Período colonial

La independencia

La actualidad

- Elige un período histórico o un hecho de la historia de ese país sobre el que quieras tener más información. Aquí tienes algunos ejemplos:

El reinado de Moctezuma (México)

El grito de Dolores (México)

El hundimiento del Maine (Cuba)

La inauguración del canal de Panamá

El descubrimiento de Machu Picchu (Perú)

La muerte de Eva Perón (Argentina)

El rescate de los mineros de Atacama (Chile)

Doña Marina, traductora de Hernán Cortes, en su conversación con Moctezuma.

442 cuatrocientos cuarenta y dos

Rubric for Evaluation

	Content	Organization	Presentation
1 point	Limited relevance. Information is incomplete or not based on research. Little Spanish is used.	Inefficient use of time. Information is disorganized or unclear. The report is not well designed and organized.	Unclear communication. Delivery is not fluent. Many errors in vocabulary and grammar.
3 points	Relevant and focused information. The information is correct but some of it lacks significance. Spanish is used most of the time.	Time is used well. Information is mostly organized but lacks some clarity. The report is mostly well designed and organized.	Clear communication and fluent delivery. Mostly correct vocabulary and grammar.

PASO 2 Investiga sobre el período o el hecho elegido

- Busca información sobre el período o sobre el hecho que has elegido y toma notas sobre él. Procura dar respuesta a las seis preguntas básicas:

¿Qué?	¿Dónde?
¿Quiénes?	¿Cómo?
¿Cuándo?	¿Por qué?

- Selecciona algunas fotografías o imágenes sobre ese período o ese hecho, y escribe pies de foto.

Hernán Cortés manda prender a Moctezuma. Museo de América (Madrid).

PASO 3 Escribe los textos para tu presentación

- Elige un formato adecuado para tu presentación: un póster, una presentación de PowerPoint, un reportaje, un *collage*...
- Utiliza tus notas para escribir un borrador de tu presentación. Organiza los textos de acuerdo con el formato que has elegido.
- Vuelve a leer el borrador, revísalo, corrígelo y escribe los textos definitivos.

PASO 4 Comparte la información

- Presenta tu tarea a tus compañeros(as) y responde a sus preguntas.
- Escucha las presentaciones de tus compañeros. ¿Qué hecho o qué período te parece más interesante?

Unidad 8

Autoevaluación

¿Qué has aprendido en esta unidad?

Do these activities to evaluate how well you can manage in Spanish.

Evalúa tus habilidades. Para cada punto, di Muy bien, Bien o Necesito practicar más.

a. Can you talk about historical events?

▶ Explain when three famous places were built, discovered, restored, or explored.

▶ Tell five events in history that you think are most significant, using a variety of tenses in the past.

b. Can you describe political events in the past?

▶ Describe the main aspects of your local, state, or national government.

▶ Tell two things you just did, two things you stopped doing, and two things that you continue to do in your free time.

c. Can you express wishes, opinions, and values in relation to a multicultural society?

▶ Describe the diversity present in your city or state. What is your opinion about the effects of this diversity?

▶ Tell three things that you hope for your community's future.

	Content	Organization	Presentation
5 points	Relevant, focused, and interesting information. Many details and significance are highlighted. Spanish is used exclusively.	Time is used wisely. Information is clearly organized visually and logically. The report is very well designed and organized.	Clear and fluent communication. Very motivating, upbeat delivery. Correct and complete vocabulary and grammar.

PROYECTO

Un país de Latinoamérica

Paso 2

- Remind students that history is generally written by the winners. Therefore, historical accounts are not completely impartial. Encourage students to be aware of these biases and to try to write a balanced account.

Paso 3

- Ask students to keep in mind both the purpose of their presentation (i.e., to inform their audience) and their audience's background knowledge. This will help them decide what information to include in their report.

Paso 4

- Ask students to try to anticipate the kind of questions that their classmates might ask and prepare themselves by taking notes that will help them answer these questions.

Evaluation

- Distribute copies of the rubric to students. Discuss the evaluation criteria and explain how this project will be graded. Encourage students to refer to the rubric as they prepare their projects.

Content

- Discuss with students the importance of selecting relevant information and summarizing it in a clear and succinct manner. Students will probably find a lot of information about their chosen historical period or event, but they must keep in mind that they have a limited time for their presentation.

Organization

- Rather than deciding on a pattern of organization (chronological, sequential, cause-effect pattern, etc.) from the beginning, encourage students to try out different patterns and choose the one they think works best.

Presentation

- Ask students to rehearse their presentation and get its length right. Remind students to speak clearly and to pause at the end of each point to give their audience time to process the information. Once they have finished, ask students to thank their audience and invite questions.

RESUMEN DE GRAMÁTICA

Nouns

Nouns are words for people, animals, places, and things. Spanish nouns have gender (masculine or feminine) and number (singular or plural).

Gender of nouns

Most nouns that end in -o are masculine, and most nouns that end in -a are feminine. Nouns that end in -e or in a consonant can be either masculine or feminine.

Masculine form	Feminine form	Examples
Ends in -o.	Changes -o to -a.	el niño → la niña
Ends in a consonant.	Adds -a.	el profesor → la profesora

Casos especiales:

- Masculine nouns that end in -a: día, mapa, planeta
- Feminine nouns that end in -o: foto, moto
- Masculine nouns of Greek origin that end in -ma: clima, drama
- Masculine and feminine nouns with the same ending:
  - ending in -ista: artista, periodista
  - ending in -e: agente, cantante
  - ending in -o: modelo, piloto

Number of nouns

Nouns can be singular (one person or thing) or plural (more than one person or thing).

Singular form	Plural form	Examples
Ends in a vowel.	Adds -s.	el edificio → los edificios
Ends in a consonant.	Adds -es.	el ascensor → los ascensores

Articles

Articles agree in gender and number with the noun they accompany.

Definite articles refer to a specific noun. In English, the definite article has only one form: *the*. In Spanish, there are four forms: el, la, los, and las.

Indefinite articles refer to a nonspecific noun. In Spanish, the indefinite article has four forms: un, una (*a* or *an*) and unos, unas (*some* or *a few*).

DEFINITE ARTICLES

	Masculine	Feminine
Singular	el	la
Plural	los	las

INDEFINITE ARTICLES

	Masculine	Feminine
Singular	un	una
Plural	unos	unas

Unlike in English, Spanish uses a definite article in these cases:

- With nouns used in a general sense and with abstract nouns:
  Los perros son más cariñosos que los gatos.
- With body parts and articles of clothing: Me duele la cabeza.
- After jugar a: Voy a jugar al tenis con Pedro.

Don't use indefinite articles in these cases:

- After the verb ser and before nouns referring to occupation, nationality,
  social status, or religious or political affiliation: Mi padre es médico.
- After some verbs like tener and llevar, when referring to nouns
  in a general, or generic, sense: ¿Tienes coche?

Contractions

The combination of the preposition a and de with the definite article el
results in a contraction.

a + el → al	de + el → del

Adjectives

Adjectives describe nouns and in Spanish usually follow the noun:
el músico **calvo**, la cantante **morena**.

Spanish adjectives can be masculine or feminine, singular or plural.
They must agree with the noun both in gender and in number.

End in -o: 4 forms	el chico simpático	los chicos simpáticos
	la chica simpática	las chicas simpáticas
End in -e: 2 forms	el niño inteligente	los niños inteligentes
	la niña inteligente	las niñas inteligentes
End in a consonant: usually, 2 forms	el señor débil	los señores débiles
	la señora débil	las señoras débiles

Adjectives of Nationality

Adjectives that express nationality also have variation of gender and number.

End in -o or in a consonant: 4 forms	el niño español	los niños españoles
	la niña española	las niñas españolas
End in -e: 2 forms	el señor canadiense	los señores canadienses
	la señora canadiense	las señoras canadienses

Demonstrative adjectives and pronouns

To indicate where something or someone is located in relation
to the person speaking, use demonstratives. Demonstrative adjectives
and pronouns show gender and number.

Demonstrative pronouns can be used to point or to avoid repetition.
They mean *this one/that one* or *these/those*.

Distance from speaker	Singular			Plural	
	Masculine	Feminine	Neutral	Masculine	Feminine
Near	este	esta	esto	estos	estas
At a distance	ese	esa	eso	esos	esas
Far away	aquel	aquella	aquello	aquellos	aquellas

Neutral forms esto, eso, and aquello are always pronouns. They are used
to refer to situations or facts, and to present or to refer to unknown objects.

Possessive adjectives and pronouns

Possessive adjectives and pronouns express ownership. Possessive
adjectives agree with the noun they accompany. They agree with the thing
(or person) possessed, not with the owner. They can be placed before
or after the noun they accompany.

	Before the noun (*mi tío*)				After the noun (*un tío mío*) or pronouns (*el mío*)			
	Singular		Plural		Singular		Plural	
	Masculine	Feminine	Masculine	Feminine	Masculine	Feminine	Masculine	Feminine
my	mi		mis		mío	mía	míos	mías
your (inf.)	tu		tus		tuyo	tuya	tuyos	tuyas
his, her, your	su		sus		suyo	suya	suyos	suyas
our	nuestro	nuestra	nuestros	nuestras	nuestro	nuestra	nuestros	nuestras
your (inf.)	vuestro	vuestra	vuestros	vuestras	vuestro	vuestra	vuestros	vuestras
their, your	su		sus		suyo	suya	suyos	suyas

Indefinites

To indicate existence or quantity in an imprecise way or to indicate absence, use indefinites.

ningún, ninguno(a)	*no, (not) any, none*	alguien	*someone*
algún, alguno(a)(os)(as)	*a few, any, one, some*	algo	*something*
poco(a)(os)(as)	*some, few*	nadie	*nobody*
mucho(a)(os)(as)	*many, a lot of*	nada	*nothing*
demasiado(a)(os)(as)	*too much, too many*	otro(a)(os)(as)	*another*
todo(a)(os)(as)	*all, every, throughout*	cualquier(a)	*whichever*
varios(as)	*several*		

Before a masculine singular noun, use algún or ningún instead of alguno and ninguno.

Alguien and nadie refer to people. Algo and nada refer to things.

Comparatives

To express equality, use:

tan + adjective + como		verb + tanto como	
igual de + adjective / adverb + que	*as ... as*	verb + igual que	*... as much as ...*

To express inequality, use:

más / menos + adjective / adverb / noun + que	*more / less ... than*
verb + más / menos que	*... more / less than*

Superlatives

The superlative is used to express an extreme degree of an adjective. You can also use adverbs like muy before the adjective to express the same idea.

Adjectives ending in a consonant.	Add -ísimo, -ísima, -ísimos, -ísimas. popular + ísimo → popularísimo
Adjectives ending in a vowel.	Drop the vowel and add the superlative ending. triste + ísimo → tristísimo

The relative superlative is used to describe a noun in comparison to a larger group.

el / la / los / las + noun + más / menos + adjective + de... / que...

Pronouns

Subject pronouns

Subject pronouns identify the person who is performing an action.

SUBJECT PRONOUNS

	Singular		Plural
yo	*I*	nosotros nosotras	*we*
tú	*you (informal)*	vosotros vosotras	*you (informal)*
usted él ella	*you (formal)* *he* *she*	ustedes ellos ellas	*you* *they* *they*

Direct object and indirect object pronouns

To avoid repeating words that have already been mentioned, you can replace the direct object or the indirect object with a pronoun.

DIRECT OBJECT PRONOUNS

	Singular		Plural
me	*me*	nos	*us*
te	*you (informal)*	os	*you (informal)*
lo la	*you (formal), him, it* *you (formal), her, it*	los las	*you, them* *you, them*

INDIRECT OBJECT PRONOUNS

	Singular		Plural
me	*to / for me*	nos	*to / for us*
te	*to / for you (informal)*	os	*to / for you (informal)*
le	*to / for you (formal), him, her*	les	*to / for you, them*

Note: The direct object pronoun lo can also refer to situations or facts which are neither masculine nor femenine.

Position of pronouns

Direct and indirect object pronouns are placed before the conjugated verb, or attached to the infinitive, the present participle, or the affirmative command.

Direct and indirect object pronouns may be used in the same sentence. In this case, the indirect object pronoun goes before the direct object pronoun. Le and les become se when placed in front of a direct object pronoun.

The pronoun *se*

To present the information without telling who does the action, use this formula:

> se + verb in the third person

Adverbs

Adverbs of frequency

These adverbs and adverbial phrases express how often something is done.

nunca	*never*	muchas veces	*many times, often*
casi nunca	*almost never*	casi siempre	*usually, normally*
rara vez	*seldom, rarely*	siempre	*always*
a veces	*sometimes*	todos los días	*every day*

Adverbs of quantity

Some verbs can be modified by a word that expresses quantity.

nada	poco	bastante	mucho
not at all	*little, not much*	*quite, enough*	*a lot, much*

Adverbs and phrases about the future

When you express intention or future plans, you can use these adverbs or expressions.

ahora	*now*	mañana	*tomorrow*
luego, después	*later*	pasado mañana	*the day after tomorrow*
en un rato	*in a while*	mañana por la mañana	*tomorrow morning*
en media hora	*in half an hour*	mañana por la tarde	*tomorrow afternoon / evening*
en dos horas	*in two hours*	mañana por la noche	*tomorrow night*
hoy	*today*	el lunes que viene / el próximo lunes	*next Monday*
esta mañana	*this morning*	el mes que viene / el próximo mes	*next month*
esta tarde	*this afternoon*		
esta noche	*tonight*	el año que viene / el próximo año	*next year*

Adverbs and phrases about the past

These adverbs and time expressions refer to the past tense.

antes	*before*	la semana pasada	*last week*
anoche	*last night*	el mes pasado	*last month*
ayer	*yesterday*	el año pasado	*last year*
anteayer	*the day before yesterday*		

Use hace to express the amount of time elapsed since an action was completed.

hace + time expression + que + verb in the preterite tense

verb in the preterite tense + hace + time expression

Use hacía to describe an action or event that began in the past and continued for some time.

hacía + time expression + que + verb in the imperfect tense

verb in the imperfect tense + desde hacía + time expression

Adverbs and phrases of location

Many words and phrases are used to show location.

aquí, acá	*here*	al lado de	*next to*	encima de	*on, on top of*	detrás de	*behind*
ahí	*there*	a la derecha de	*to the right of*	debajo de	*under*	cerca de	*near, close to*
allí, allá	*over there*	a la izquierda de	*to the left of*	delante de	*in front of*	lejos de	*far from*

Adverbs and phrases of possibility or probability

Expressions such as quizá(s), tal vez, and a lo mejor are used to talk about the possibility or probability of an action taking place.

quizá(s) tal vez	+ subjunctive	a lo mejor	+ indicative

Adverbs ending in -*mente*

Many adverbs are formed from adjectives by adding the suffix -mente to the feminine singular form.

Adjectives ending in -o.	Change -o to -a and add -mente.	lento → lentamente
Adjectives ending in -e or in a consonant.	Add -mente.	frecuente → frecuentemente habitual → habitualmente

Prepositions

Prepositions of place

en	*at, in, on, inside* (to express location)	de	*from* (to express origin)
a	*to* (after the verb *ir* indicating destination)	desde... hasta de... a	*from ... to* (to express direction or destination)

The personal *a*

The preposition a works like a marker before certain direct objects:

direct objects referring to a definite or specific person or people
direct objects referring to a definite pet
direct object pronouns referring to people, such as alguien, nadie, alguno, ninguno, or todos

Prepositions *por* and *para*

Por and para can usually be translated as *for* in English.

Uses of por		Uses of para
«in exchange for»	approximate time	deadline
ratio, proportion, «per»	approximate place	purpose
mode of communication	time periods during the day	opinion
mode of transportation	cause or reason	movement toward a place
«on behalf of»	movement within an area	recipient of an action
object of an errand	agent of an action	comparison, «considering»

Interrogatives

Interrogatives are words that are used to ask questions. Normally, interrogatives go at the beginning of a sentence.

¿Qué? *What?*	¿Cuál(es)? *Which?*	¿Quién(es)? *Who?*
¿Cuándo? *When?*	¿Cómo? *How?*	¿Por qué? *Why?*
¿Cuánto(a)? *How much?*	¿Cuántos(as)? *How many?*	¿Para qué? *What for?*
¿Dónde? *Where?*	¿Adónde? *Where to?*	¿De dónde? *Where from?*

Verbs

Verbs are words that express actions, and place these actions in time (past, present, and future). Spanish verbs fall into three conjugations: -ar (*hablar, estudiar…*), -er (*aprender, comer…*), and -ir (*vivir, subir…*).

The infinitive

1st conjugation: -ar	2nd conjugation: -er	3rd conjugation: -ir
comprar, hablar, estudiar…	comer, tener, vender…	abrir, pedir, escribir…

The present participle

The present participle (gerundio) is formed by adding the following endings to the verb stem.

-ando for -ar verbs	lavar → lavando
-iendo for -er, -ir verbs	hacer → haciendo escribir → escribiendo

Irregular present participle forms

e > i		o > u	
decir → diciendo	servir → sirviendo	dormir → durmiendo	
medir → midiendo	vestir → vistiendo	morir → muriendo	
pedir → pidiendo		poder → pudiendo	

The past participle

The past participle (participio) of a verb can be used as an adjective to describe a noun.

Besides, the past participle is used with the verb estar to express the state or condition of a subject as a result of a previous action: Luis hizo las tareas. Las tareas están hechas.

The past participle is formed by adding the following endings to the verb stem.

-ar verbs	Add the ending -ado.	pintar → pintado
-er and -ir verbs	Add the ending -ido.	vestir → vestido

Irregular past participle forms

abrir → abierto	morir → muerto
cubrir → cubierto	poner → puesto
decir → dicho	resolver → resuelto
descubrir → descubierto	romper → roto
escribir → escrito	ver → visto
hacer → hecho	volver → vuelto

The present tense

Use the present tense to speak about the present and to talk about the future when you refer to timetables, pre-arranged events, and when you want to present the information as a fact.

Regular verbs (*-ar, -er, -ir*)

		Comprar *(to buy)*	Vender *(to sell)*	Abrir *(to open)*
Singular	yo	compro	vendo	abro
	tú	compras	vendes	abres
	usted él, ella	compra	vende	abre
Plural	nosotros(as)	compramos	vendemos	abrimos
	vosotros(as)	compráis	vendéis	abrís
	ustedes ellos(as)	compran	venden	abren

Stem-changing verbs

		Cerrar (e > ie) *(to close)*	Poder (o > ue) *(can, to be able)*	Pedir (e > i) *(to ask)*
Singular	yo	cierro	puedo	pido
	tú	cierras	puedes	pides
	usted él, ella	cierra	puede	pide
Plural	nosotros(as)	cerramos	podemos	pedimos
	vosotros(as)	cerráis	podéis	pedís
	ustedes ellos(as)	cierran	pueden	piden

Verbs with irregular yo forms

		Dar (to give)	Conocer[1] (to know)	Hacer (to do)	Poner (to put)	Saber (to know)	Traer[2] (to bring)	Ver (to see)	Salir (to leave)
Singular	yo	doy	conozco	hago	pongo	sé	traigo	veo	salgo
Singular	tú	das	conoces	haces	pones	sabes	traes	ves	sales
Singular	usted él, ella	da	conoce	hace	pone	sabe	trae	ve	sale
Plural	nosotros(as)	damos	conocemos	hacemos	ponemos	sabemos	traemos	vemos	salimos
Plural	vosotros(as)	dais	conocéis	hacéis	ponéis	sabéis	traéis	veis	salís
Plural	ustedes ellos(as)	dan	conocen	hacen	ponen	saben	traen	ven	salen

[1] In general, verbs ending in -ecer, and -ucir add a z in the yo form like conocer (parecer: yo parezco, traducir: yo traduzco).

[2] The verb caer is conjugated as traer (yo caigo).

Verbs ser and estar

Ser (to be)			
Singular		Plural	
yo	soy	nosotros(as)	somos
tú	eres	vosotros(as)	sois
usted él, ella	es	ustedes ellos(as)	son

Estar (to be)			
Singular		Plural	
yo	estoy	nosotros(as)	estamos
tú	estás	vosotros(as)	estáis
usted él, ella	está	ustedes ellos(as)	están

- To identify people, places, and things, and to describe physical characteristics and personality traits, use ser: La señora Flores **es** mi profesora. Ella **es** muy inteligente.

- To express feelings and conditions or when talking about the result of a process, use estar: Ellos **están** tristes porque **están** enfermos. Luis **está** muy guapo con esa camisa.

The verb ir

Ir (to go)			
Singular		Plural	
yo	voy	nosotros(as)	vamos
tú	vas	vosotros(as)	vais
usted él, ella	va	ustedes ellos(as)	van

- To say where someone is going, use ir a + place.
- To express intention or future plans, use ir a + infinitive.

The verb *haber*

To say that someone or something exists or to ask about the existence of something, use the form hay (*there is, there are*).

Hay que and *tener que*, and *deber*

To make recommendations and to express obligation and necessity, use these structures:

hay que + infinitive	tener que + infinitive	deber + infinitive

The verb *gustar*

To express likes or dislikes, use the verb *gustar*.

		Gustar *(to like)*	
Singular	(A mí)	me **gust**a	me **gust**an
	(A ti)	te **gust**a	te **gust**an
	(A usted) (A él/a ella)	le **gust**a	le **gust**an
Plural	(A nosotros/as)	nos **gust**a	nos **gust**an
	(A vosotros/as)	os **gust**a	os **gust**an
	(A ustedes) (A ellos/a ellas)	les **gust**a	les **gust**an

Pronominal verbs

Pronominal verbs are conjugated with a reflexive pronoun: me, te, se, nos, os, se. The pronoun agrees with the subject: Yo me lavo.

Peinarse *(to comb one's hair)*			
Singular		Plural	
yo	me **pein**o	nosotros(as)	nos **pein**amos
tú	te **pein**as	vosotros(as)	os **pein**áis
usted él, ella	se **pein**a	ustedes ellos(as)	se **pein**an

Reflexive verbs are used to express an action that reflects back on the subject: Ana se maquilla.

Reciprocal verbs express reciprocal actions. They are conjugated like reflexive verbs, but always in the plural forms: Ellos se escriben.

Some verbs can be used with or without reflexive pronouns, but with meaning differences: Ayer dormí ocho horas. Me dormí a las diez.

The present progressive

Use the present progressive (presente continuo) to talk about actions that are happening at the moment of speaking. The present progressive is formed with estar + gerundio (present participle).

Lavar *(to wash)*			
Singular		**Plural**	
yo	estoy lavando	nosotros(as)	estamos lavando
tú	estás lavando	vosotros(as)	estáis lavando
usted él, ella	está lavando	ustedes ellos(as)	están lavando

The present perfect

The present perfect (presente perfecto) is equivalent to *have* + past participle. Use the present perfect tense:

- To describe actions that already happened at the time we consider to be the present: He vivido en esta casa toda mi vida.

- To describe actions that have recently ended: He llegado hace un minuto.

Hablar *(to speak)*			
Singular		**Plural**	
yo	he **habl**ado	nosotros(as)	hemos **habl**ado
tú	has **habl**ado	vosotros(as)	habéis **habl**ado
usted él, ella	ha **habl**ado	ustedes ellos(as)	han **habl**ado

The preterite tense

Use the preterite tense to talk about past actions presented as completed, without mentioning the duration.

		Comprar *(to buy)*	Comer *(to eat)*	Escribir *(to write)*
Singular	yo	**compr**é	**com**í	**escrib**í
	tú	**compr**aste	**com**iste	**escrib**iste
	usted él, ella	**compr**ó	**com**ió	**escrib**ió
Plural	nosotros(as)	**compr**amos	**com**imos	**escrib**imos
	vosotros(as)	**compr**asteis	**com**isteis	**escrib**isteis
	ustedes ellos(as)	**compr**aron	**com**ieron	**escrib**ieron

Verbs ending in -car, -gar, and -zar require a spelling change in the yo form: buscar → yo busqué; llegar → yo llegué; empezar → yo empecé.

Irregular verbs: *ser, ir, decir, tener, estar, hacer* and *traer*

		Ser (to be), ir (to go)	Decir (to say)	Tener (to have)	Estar (to be)	Hacer (to make, to do)	Traer (to bring)
Singular	yo	fui	dije	tuve	estuve	hice	traje
	tú	fuiste	dijiste	tuviste	estuviste	hiciste	trajiste
	usted él, ella	fue	dijo	tuvo	estuvo	hizo	trajo
Plural	nosotros(as)	fuimos	dijimos	tuvimos	estuvimos	hicimos	trajimos
	vosotros(as)	fuisteis	dijisteis	tuvisteis	estuvisteis	hicisteis	trajisteis
	ustedes ellos(as)	fueron	dijeron	tuvieron	estuvieron	hicieron	trajeron

Irregular verbs: *pedir* and *dormir*

In Spanish, -ir verbs that are e > i stem-changing in the present tense (pedir > pido) have the same change in the third person of the preterite tense.

The verbs dormir and morir are also irregular in the third person (o > u).

		Pedir (to ask)	Dormir (to sleep)
Singular	yo	pedí	dormí
	tú	pediste	dormiste
	usted él, ella	pidió	durmió
Plural	nosotros(as)	pedimos	dormimos
	vosotros(as)	pedisteis	dormisteis
	ustedes ellos(as)	pidieron	durmieron

Irregular verbs: *dar, poder, poner, querer, saber,* and *venir*

		Dar (to give)	Poder (can, to be able)	Poner (to put)	Querer (to want)	Saber (to know)	Venir (to come)
Singular	yo	di	pude	puse	quise	supe	vine
	tú	diste	pudiste	pusiste	quisiste	supiste	viniste
	usted él, ella	dio	pudo	puso	quiso	supo	vino
Plural	nosotros(as)	dimos	pudimos	pusimos	quisimos	supimos	vinimos
	vosotros(as)	disteis	pudisteis	pusisteis	quisisteis	supisteis	vinisteis
	ustedes ellos(as)	dieron	pudieron	pusieron	quisieron	supieron	vinieron

The imperfect tense

Use the imperfect tense:

- To talk about habitual actions or actions that happened repeatedly in the past.
- To describe characters and setting, and to explain the circumstances surrounding an event.
- To make a polite request.

		Viajar (to travel)	Volver (to return)	Salir (to leave)
Singular	yo	viajaba	volvía	salía
	tú	viajabas	volvías	salías
	usted él, ella	viajaba	volvía	salía
Plural	nosotros(as)	viajábamos	volvíamos	salíamos
	vosotros(as)	viajabais	volvíais	salíais
	ustedes ellos(as)	viajaban	volvían	salían

Irregular verbs

		Ser (to be)	Ir (to go)	Ver (to see)
Singular	yo	era	iba	veía
	tú	eras	ibas	veías
	usted él, ella	era	iba	veía
Plural	nosotros(as)	éramos	íbamos	veíamos
	vosotros(as)	erais	ibais	veíais
	ustedes ellos(as)	eran	iban	veían

The past progressive

Use the past progressive (pasado continuo) to talk about ongoing actions in the past. The past progressive is formed with estar plus the present participle (gerundio).

Cantar (to sing)			
	Singular		Plural
yo	estaba cantando	nosotros(as)	estábamos cantando
tú	estabas cantando	vosotros(as)	estabais cantando
usted él, ella	estaba cantando	ustedes ellos(as)	estaban cantando

The past perfect

Use the past perfect (pluscuamperfecto) to describe an action that was completed before another action in the past: Cuando él llegó, María ya se había ido.

Hablar (to speak)

Singular		Plural	
yo	había **habl**ado	nosotros(as)	habíamos **habl**ado
tú	habías **habl**ado	vosotros(as)	habíais **habl**ado
usted él, ella	había **habl**ado	ustedes ellos(as)	habían **habl**ado

The future

Use the future tense to talk about things that will happen in the future.

The future tense is also sometimes used idiomatically in Spanish to express conjecture or probability in the present.

		Entrar *(to come in)*	**Comer** *(to eat)*	**Seguir** *(to follow)*
Singular	yo	entrar**é**	comer**é**	seguir**é**
	tú	entrar**ás**	comer**ás**	seguir**ás**
	usted él, ella	entrar**á**	comer**á**	seguir**á**
Plural	nosotros(as)	entrar**emos**	comer**emos**	seguir**emos**
	vosotros(as)	entrar**éis**	comer**éis**	seguir**éis**
	ustedes ellos(as)	entrar**án**	comer**án**	seguir**án**

Irregular verbs

poder → podr-	**tener** → tendr-	**decir** → dir-	**saber** → sabr-
poner → pondr-	**venir** → vendr-	**hacer** → har-	**haber** → habr-
salir → saldr-	**valer** → valdr-	**querer** → querr-	**caber** → cabr-

The conditional

The conditional (condicional) is used:

- To express wishes for the present or the future: Me gustaría ir a la fiesta.
- To give advice by putting yourself in the place of the other person: Yo no iría.
- To make polite requests: ¿Podrías prestarme un lápiz?

		Entrar (to come in)	Comer (to eat)	Seguir (to follow)
Singular	yo	entraría	comería	seguiría
	tú	entrarías	comerías	seguirías
	usted él, ella	entraría	comería	seguiría
Plural	nosotros(as)	entraríamos	comeríamos	seguiríamos
	vosotros(as)	entraríais	comeríais	seguiríais
	ustedes ellos(as)	entrarían	comerían	seguirían

Irregular verbs

poder → podr-	tener → tendr-	decir → dir-	saber → sabr-
poner → pondr-	venir → vendr-	hacer → har-	haber → habr-
salir → saldr-	valer → valdr-	querer → querr-	caber → cabr-

The present subjunctive

Use the subjunctive to express wishes, feelings, emotions, or opinions, to express doubt or uncertainty, and to express value judgments.

		Cantar (to sing)	Comer (to eat)	Vivir (to live)
Singular	yo	cante	coma	viva
	tú	cantes	comas	vivas
	usted él, ella	cante	coma	viva
Plural	nosotros(as)	cantemos	comamos	vivamos
	vosotros(as)	cantéis	comáis	viváis
	ustedes ellos(as)	canten	coman	vivan

Verbs ending in -car, -gar, -zar, -ger, -gir, and -guir have spelling changes.

-car → -que: sacar → saque, saques…	-ger, -gir → -ja: dirigir → dirija, dirijas…
-gar → -gue: llegar → llegue, llegues…	-guir → -ga: seguir → siga, sigas…
-zar → -ce: abrazar → abrace, abraces…	

Irregular verbs

Irregular verbs in the **yo** form of the indicative are also irregular in the subjunctive.

yo hago → haga, hagas, haga…	yo tengo → tenga, tengas, tenga…

Stem-changing verbs

		Pensar (to think)	Jugar (to play)	Volver (to return)	Pedir (to ask)	Dormir (to sleep)
Singular	yo	piense	juegue	vuelva	pida	duerma
	tú	pienses	juegues	vuelvas	pidas	duermas
	usted él, ella	piense	juegue	vuelva	pida	duerma
Plural	nosotros(as)	pensemos	juguemos	volvamos	pidamos	durmamos
	vosotros(as)	penséis	juguéis	volváis	pidáis	durmáis
	ustedes ellos(as)	piensen	jueguen	vuelvan	pidan	duerman

Irregular verbs: *dar*, *estar*, *saber*, *ser*, and *ir*

		Dar (to give)	Estar (to be)	Saber (to know)	Ser (to be)	Ir (to go)
Singular	yo	dé	esté	sepa	sea	vaya
	tú	des	estés	sepas	seas	vayas
	usted él, ella	dé	esté	sepa	sea	vaya
Plural	nosotros(as)	demos	estemos	sepamos	seamos	vayamos
	vosotros(as)	deis	estéis	sepáis	seáis	vayáis
	ustedes ellos(as)	den	estén	sepan	sean	vayan

The imperfect subjunctive

Use this tense in the same situations in which you would use the present subjunctive when the verb in the main clause is in the past.

		Cantar (to sing)	Comer (to eat)	Vivir (to live)
Singular	yo	cantara	comiera	viviera
	tú	cantaras	comieras	vivieras
	usted él, ella	cantara	comiera	viviera
Plural	nosotros(as)	cantáramos	comiéramos	viviéramos
	vosotros(as)	cantarais	comierais	vivierais
	ustedes ellos(as)	cantaran	comieran	vivieran

If a verb is irregular in the preterite, it is also irregular in the imperfect subjunctive: No sabía que fueras abogado.

The present perfect subjunctive

Use this tense in the same types of sentences in which you would use the present subjunctive, when the action in the dependent clause is presented as completed: Me alegro de que te hayas casado.

		Cantar (to sing)	Comer (to eat)	Vivir (to live)
Singular	yo	haya cantado	haya comido	haya vivido
	tú	hayas cantado	hayas comido	hayas vivido
	usted él, ella	haya cantado	haya comido	haya vivido
Plural	nosotros(as)	hayamos cantado	hayamos comido	hayamos vivido
	vosotros(as)	hayáis cantado	hayáis comido	hayáis vivido
	ustedes ellos(as)	hayan cantado	hayan comido	hayan vivido

Affirmative commands

To tell one person or more than one person to do something, use an informal or a formal command.

	Caminar (to walk)	Comer (to eat)	Escribir (to write)	
Singular	camina	come	escribe	tú
	camine	coma	escriba	usted
Plural	caminemos	comamos	escribamos	nosotros(as)
	caminad	comed	escribid	vosotros(as)
	caminen	coman	escriban	ustedes

Irregular verbs: *tener, hacer, poner, venir,* and *salir*

	Tener (to have)	Hacer (to do, to make)	Poner (to put)	Venir (to come)	Salir (to leave)	
Singular	ten	haz	pon	ven	sal	tú
	tenga	haga	ponga	venga	salga	usted
Plural	tengamos	hagamos	pongamos	vengamos	salgamos	nosotros(as)
	tened	haced	poned	venid	salid	vosotros(as)
	tengan	hagan	pongan	vengan	salgan	ustedes

Irregular verbs: *ser*, *decir*, *ir*, and *dar*

	Ser (to be)	**Decir** (to say)	**Ir** (to go)	**Dar** (to give)	
Singular	sé	di	ve	da	tú
	sea	diga	vaya	dé	usted
Plural	seamos	digamos	vayamos	demos	nosotros(as)
	sed	decid	id	dad	vosotros(as)
	sean	digan	vayan	den	ustedes

Negative commands

Use negative commands when telling someone what not to do.

	Caminar (to walk)	**Comer** (to eat)	**Escribir** (to write)	
Singular	no camines	no comas	no escribas	tú
	no camine	no coma	no escriba	usted
Plural	no caminemos	no comamos	no escribamos	nosotros(as)
	no caminéis	no comáis	no escribáis	vosotros(as)
	no caminen	no coman	no escriban	ustedes

Irregular verbs: *dar*, *estar*, *ir*, and *ser*

	Dar (to give)	**Estar** (to be)	**Ir** (to go)	**Ser** (to be)	
Singular	no des	no estés	no vayas	no seas	tú
	no dé	no esté	no vaya	no sea	usted
Plural	no demos	no estemos	no vayamos	no seamos	nosotros(as)
	no deis	no estéis	no vayáis	no seáis	vosotros(as)
	no den	no estén	no vayan	no sean	ustedes

The passive voice

Use the passive voice to emphasize the receiver or product of an action rather than the performer: Esta pirámide fue construida por los mayas.

Subject (receiver) + **verb** (ser + past participle) + **agent** (with por)

Do not use passive voice neither with verbs of perception or emotion, nor with an indirect object.

Sentence structures

Expressing certainty and doubt

To express certainty use verbs like saber, or expressions like es verdad or estoy seguro(a) + indicative.

> expression / verb + que + indicative

To express doubt use the verb dudar or expressions like es dudoso or es probable + subjunctive.

> expression / verb + que + subjunctive

To express uncertainty or doubt, use negative expressions like no es verdad or no estoy seguro(a) + subjunctive.

> no + expression / verb + que + subjunctive

Expressing opinion

Use verbs like creer, opinar, parecer, pensar, suponer, or parecer.

verb + que + indicative	When the verb in the main clause states an opinion in the affirmative: Creo que esta foto es bonita.
no + verb + que + subjunctive	When the verb in the main clause states an opinion in the negative: No creo que esta foto sea bonita.

Expressing value statements

Use impersonal expressions like es aconsejable, es importante, es bueno, or the expression me parece followed by a word like bien, mal, or maravilloso.

expression + infinitive	In general statements: Es necesario estudiar todos los días.
expression + que + subjunctive	When referring to one or more people in particular: Es necesario que Ana estudie todos los días.

Expressing wishes, likes and preferences

Use the verbs gustar, encantar, interesar, apetecer, querer, esperar, desear, and preferir.

verb + infinitive	When there is no subject change: Quiero ir a Santo Domingo.
verb + que + subjunctive	When there are two subjects: Quiero que tú vayas a Santo Domingo.

Expressing feelings

Use verbs like alegrar, asustar, divertir, molestar, etc.

verb + infinitive	When the main clause and the dependent clause refer to the same person: Nos encanta jugar.
verb + que + subjunctive	When the main clause and the dependent clause refer to different people: Me molesta que hagas ruido.

Giving advice or making recommendations

Use the verbs aconsejar, recomendar, and sugerir.

verb + infinitive	El médico me aconseja caminar.
verb + que + subjunctive	El médico me aconseja que camine.

Adding details about a noun

Use an adjective clause introduced by que: Tengo un gato que come mucho.

que + indicative	To describe someone or something that exists or is known: Conozco a un chico que habla seis idiomas.
que + subjunctive	To describe someone or something that doesn't exist, is unknown, or whose existence is in question: No hay ningún celular que funcione con energía solar. Necesito una casa que tenga jardín. ¿Hay algo que no entiendas?

Expressing location

Use donde, adonde, de/desde donde, or por donde.

donde adonde de/desde donde por donde	+ indicative	When the main clause refers to a known, definite, or real place: Fuimos de excursión por donde pasa el río.
	+ subjunctive	When the main clause refers to an unknown, indefinite, or hypothetical place: Prefiero comer en restaurantes donde no haya mucha gente.
¿Dónde...? ¿De dónde...? ¿Adónde...? ¿Por dónde...?	+ indicative	To ask about a place: ¿Dónde está el restaurante?

Expressing time

Use the conjunctions cuando, antes de (que), or después de (que).

cuando + indicative	Past or habitual events: Bebo mucha agua cuando hago deporte.
cuando + subjunctive	Future events: Cuando esté de vacaciones, voy a leer muchos libros.

antes de + infinitive después de + infinitive	When there is no subject change: Siempre me peino antes de salir de casa.
antes de que + subjunctive	When there are two subjects: Siempre llego a casa antes de que llegue mi hermano.
después de que + subjunctive después de que + indicative	When there are two subjects: Me acostaré después de que me llames. Me acuesto después de que cenamos.

Expressing difficulty

Use aunque and a pesar de que.

aunque + indicative a pesar de que + indicative	When referring to real situations: Aunque no tengo dinero, soy feliz. Alicia toca muy bien el piano a pesar de que tiene seis años.
aunque + subjunctive a pesar de que + subjunctive	When referring to unreal or uncertain situations, probabilities, or unknown outcomes: Aunque llueva mañana, iré a la playa. Saldré, a pesar de que esté cansado.

Expressing purposes

Use expressions such as para (que) and a (que).

para + infinitive a + infinitive	When there is no subject change: Salí a tomar el sol.
para que + subjunctive a que + subjunctive	When there are two subjects: Traigo fotos para que las veas.
¿Para qué...? + indicative ¿A qué...? + indicative	To ask about the purpose of an action: ¿Para qué llevas esa caja?

Expressing condition

Use conditional sentences with si *(if)* clauses to express what could happen if some condition is met.

si + present indicative, present indicative / future indicative / command	To refer to real or likely conditions in either the present or the future: Si termino pronto las tareas, veré el partido en la televisión.
si + imperfect subjunctive, conditional	To express unlikely, hypothetical, or contrary-to-fact conditions in either the present or the future: Si terminara pronto las tareas, vería el partido en la televisión.

Expressing cause

Use porque and por.

porque + indicative	No saldré porque tengo que estudiar.
por + infinitive	Saldré por acompañarte.

To ask about the reason, use ¿Por qué...? followed by a verb in the indicative mood.

Expressing consequence

Use así (es) que and por eso.

así (es) que + indicative	Llovió mucho, así que se inundó la calle.
por eso + infinitive	Hubo un terremoto, por eso se derrumbaron varios edificios.

Reported speech

To speak in reported speech (estilo indirecto), use a verb like decir, contar, responder... followed by que.

reporting verb + que + indicative	To relay information: El profesor dice que el examen es el viernes.
reporting verb + que + subjunctive	To relay a request or a command: El profesor dice que estudiemos para el examen.

With the verb preguntar, in indirect yes/no questions, use si instead of que: El profesor me pregunta si estudiamos mucho.

In reported speech, it may be necessary to change the verb tense to match the moment of speaking: El profesor me dijo que había pocos errores en mis tareas.

GLOSARIO ESPAÑOL-INGLÉS

A

a   *to* 2
a causa de   *because of* 342
a diario   *every day* 182
a dieta   *on a diet* 182
a fuego lento   *over a low heat* 221
a menudo   *often* 48
A mi modo de ver...   *In my view ...* 437
A mí no.   *Not me.* 286
A mí sí.   *I do.* 286
a orillas del mar   *by the sea* 434
a partir de   *from* 56
a pesar de que   *despite, although* 264
a pie   *on foot* 92
a sus espaldas   *under his belt* 254
a tiempo   *on time* 86
a través de   *through* 23
a veces   *sometimes* 2
A ver...   *Let's see ...* 41
abandonar   *to leave* 403
abarcar   *to cover* 430
el/la **abogado(a)**   *attorney* 187
abrazar   *to hug* 74
el **abrazo**   *hug* 74
abreviar   *to abbreviate* 99
la **abreviatura**   *abbreviation* 99
el **abrigo**   *coat* 125
abrir (irreg.)   *to open* 2
abrirse (irreg.)   *to open* 90
abrocharse   *to fasten* 128
el/la **abuelo(a)**   *grandfather/ grandmother* 32
los **abuelos**   *grandparents* 37
abundante   *abundant* 345
abundantemente   *abundantly* 218
aburrido(a)   *boring* 6 *bored* 22
aburrir   *to bore* 262
acabar de   *to have just* 132 *to finish* 412
académico(a)   *academic* 273
el/la **académico(a)**   *academic* 378
acceder a   *to gain access to (become member)* 244 *to visit (a website)* 338
el **acceso**   *access* 96
el **accesorio**   *accessory* 125
el **accidente**   *accident* 5
la **acción**   *action* 11
el **aceite**   *oil* 179
el **aceite de oliva**   *olive oil* 182
la **aceituna**   *olive* 190
aceptar   *to accept* 52
acerca de   *about* 301
acercarse   *to come closer* 204
acercarse a   *to go to* 104
el **acero**   *steel* 368
el **acompañamiento**   *accompaniment (with food)* 188

acompañar   *to go with* 59 *to serve with* 220
aconsejable   *advisable* 198
aconsejar   *to advise* 210
el **acontecimiento**   *event* 39
acordar (irreg. **ue**)   *to agree* 90
acordarse (de) (irreg. **ue**)   *to remember* 64
acostarse (irreg. **ue**)   *to go to bed* 358
acostumbrarse a   *to get used to* 45
la **actitud**   *attitude* 321
activamente   *actively* 231
la **actividad**   *activity* 3
activo(a)   *active* 281
el **actor**   *actor* 26
la **actriz**   *actress* 29
la **actuación**   *performance* 157
actual   *present* 1 *modern* 30 *current, topical* 382
la **actualidad**   *current situation* 442
la **actualización**   *update* 378
actualmente   *nowadays* 44
actuar   *to perform* 298
acudir   *to go* 289
el **acueducto**   *aqueduct* 434
la **acupuntura**   *acupuncture* 197
la **adaptación**   *adaptation* 163
adaptar   *to adapt* 55
adecuado(a)   *appropriate* 139 *correct* 365
Adelante.   *Go on. (to encourage action)* 1
además   *also* 72
además de   *as well as* 22
adicional   *additional* 173
la **adivinanza**   *riddle* 144
adivinar   *to guess* 33
el **adjetivo**   *adjective* 24
administrativo(a)   *administrative* 165
admirar   *to admire* 157
la **adolescencia**   *adolescence* 44
el/la **adolescente**   *adolescent* 39
adonde   *to where* 318
adónde   *where* 6
la **adopción**   *adoption* 254
adoptar   *to adopt* 403
adoptivo(a)   *adopted* 32
adorar   *to adore* 213
adornar   *to decorate* 155
el **adorno**   *ornament* 140
el/la **adulto(a)**   *adult* 19
aeróbico(a)   *aerobic* 194
el **aeropuerto**   *airport* 233
afectar   *to affect (badly)* 243
Afectuosamente.   *Affectionately,* 275
afeitarse   *to shave* 179
la **afición**   *hobby* 52
el/la **aficionado(a)**   *fan, supporter* 302

la **afirmación**   *statement* 83
afirmar   *to state* 197
afortunadamente   *fortunately* 200
afroamericano(a)   *African-American* 57
afrolatino(a)   *Afro-Latino* 101
afrontar   *to face* 244
las **afueras**   *outskirts* 383
agarrar   *to grab* 320
la **agencia de viajes**   *travel agency* 264
la **agenda**   *diary* 108
el/la **agente**   *agent* 252
el/la **agente de viajes**   *travel agent* 315
agotarse   *to run out* 344
agradable   *pleasant* 249
agregar   *to add* 167
agresivo(a)   *aggressive* 29
agrícola   *agricultural* 143
el/la **agricultor(a)**   *farmer* 233
la **agricultura**   *agriculture* 368
agrio(a)   *sour* 179
el **agua**   *water* 8
el **agua mineral (con/sin gas)**   *(sparkling/flat) mineral water* 182
las **aguas**   *waters* 192
las **aguas termales**   *hot springs* 193
agudo(a)   *high-pitched* 111 *acute* 303
el **águila**   *eagle* 341
la **aguja hipodérmica desechable**   *disposable syringe* 254
el **agujero de la capa de ozono**   *hole in the ozone layer* 344
ahí   *there* 138
el/la **ahijado(a)**   *godson/goddaughter* 32
ahora   *now* 32
ahora mismo   *right now* 3
ahorrar   *to save* 347
el **ahorro**   *conservation* 344
el **aire**   *air* 341
el **ajedrez**   *chess* 71
el **ají**   *chili pepper* 219
el **ajo**   *garlic* 179
ajustado(a)   *tight* 128
al   *to the (followed by noun)* 5
al   *when (followed by infinitive)* 5
al aire libre   *in the open air* 8 *open-air* 94
al extranjero   *abroad* 209
al fin   *finally* 374
Al final...   *Finally ...* 329
al final de   *at the end of* 158
al lado de   *next to* 279
al menos   *at least* 105
Al principio...   *At first ...* 59
al punto   *just right* 182
al respecto   *about it* 135

el **ala** *wing* 252

el **alacrán** *scorpion* 428

alargar *to stretch out* 320

el/la **albañil** *bricklayer, building worker* 152

albergar *to hold (contain)* 380

albino(a) *albino* 401

el **albornoz** *bathrobe* 194

el **álbum** *album* 64

el **alcalde** *mayor (man)* 410

la **alcaldesa** *mayor (woman)* 410

el **alcance** *scope* 417

el **alcantarillado** *sewerage* 434

alcanzar *to reach* 56

alegrar *to make happy* 258

alegrarse *to be glad* 90

la **alegría** *joy* 52

el **alemán** *German (language)* 251

alemán(a) *German* 38

la **alergia** *allergy* 211

la **alfombra** *carpet* 125 *rug* 141

algo *anything* 2 *something* 5

el **algodón** *cotton* 125

alguien *someone* 80

algún, alguno(a), algunos(as) *some* XXVI *any* 24

la **alimentación** *diet* 174 *food* 212

alimentado(a) *well fed* 280

alimentar *to feed* 372

alimentarse *to feed (oneself)* 342

alimenticio(a) *food (adjective)* 191

el **alimento** *food* 179

alistarse en el ejército *to join the army* 254

allá *there* 117

allí *there* 50

el **almacén** *store (shop)* 19

almendrado(a) *almond-shaped* 20

almorzar *(irreg. **ue**) to have lunch* 2

el **almuerzo** *lunch* 352

el **alojamiento** *accommodation* 202

alojarse *to stay (at a hotel, etc.)* 122

la **alpaca** *alpaca* 126

el **alpinismo** *mountaineering* 287

alquilar *to rent* 4

alrededor de *around* 164

los **alrededores** *surrounding area* 383

el **altar** *altar* 374

alterar *to alter* 380

alternativamente *alternately* 320

la **altitud** *altitude* 7

alto(a) *tall* 17 *high* 47

la **altura** *height* 7

el/la **alumno(a)** *student* 166

amable *kind, nice* 20

amado(a) *beloved* 80

el/la **amado(a)** *sweetheart* 47

el/la **amante** *lover* 44

amar *to love* 28

amargo(a) *bitter* 179

amarillo(a) *yellow* 136

el **amarillo limón** *lemon yellow* 140

amazónico(a) *Amazon (adjective)* 260

ambicioso(a) *ambitious* 248

el **ambiente** *environment, atmosphere* 159

el **ámbito** *world (of art, education, etc.)* 417

amenazar *to threaten* 344

americano(a) *American* 57

amerindio(a) *Amerindian* 38

el/la **amigo(a)** *friend* 2

el **aminoácido** *amino acid* 183

la **amistad** *friendship* 74

amistoso(a) *friendly* 20

el **amor** *love* 74

amoroso(a) *loving, affectionate* 320

amplio(a) *loose* 128

ampuloso(a) *exaggerated* 320

el **análisis de sangre** *blood test* 206

analizar *to analyze* 59

la **anatomía** *anatomy* 206

ancho(a) *wide* 128

¡Anda! *Come on!* 311

andaluz(a) *Andalusian* 155

el **andén** *platform* 320

andino(a) *Andean* 131

el **anfibio** *amphibian* 344

el/la **anfitrión(a)** *host/hostess* 86

angelical *angelic* 321

angosto(a) *narrow* 164

el **ángulo** *angle* 303

angustiado(a) *anguished* 104

la **animación** *animation* 288

el **animal** *animal* 212

el **animal de compañía** *pet* 201

animar a hacer algo *to encourage to do something* 389

animar(se) *to cheer up* 232

¡Anímate! *Cheer up!* 232

¡Ánimo! *Cheer up!* 263

el **aniversario** *anniversary* 44

anoche *last night* 7

anotar *to make note of* 59

ante *in the face of* 212 *to* 274 *before (an altar, etc.)* 374

anteayer *the day before yesterday* 48

el **antecedente** *predecessor* 93

el **antepasado** *ancestor* 40

anterior *above* 4 *previous* 33

la **anterioridad** *precedence, previousness* 358

antes *before, in the past* 34

antes de *before* 16

el **antibiótico** *antibiotic* 206

anticipar *to tell in advance* 298

antiguamente *in the past* 31

la **antigüedad** *antiquity, ancient times* 56

las **antigüedades** *antiques* 146

antiguo(a) *old* 28 *ancient* 43

la **antropología** *anthropology* 406

anual *annual* 362

anualmente *annually, yearly* 373

anunciar *to announce* 52

el **anuncio** *announcement, message* 69 *poster* 82 *ad* 100

los **anuncios clasificados** *classified ads* 246

añadir *to add* 17

el **año** *year* 3

los **años mozos** *youth* 254

apagar *to put out (fires)* 236

el **aparato** *machine* 211 *(electrical) appliance* 369

aparecer *(irreg.) to appear* 21

el **apartamento** *apartment* 41

apasionante *fascinating* 1

el **apellido** *surname* 17

aplaudir *to applaud* 290

aportar *to give* 113 *to provide* 180

apoyar a alguien *to support someone* 74

apoyar algo *to support something* 166

el **apoyo** *support* 422

apreciar *to appreciate* 74

aprender *to learn* 1

aprenderse algo *to memorize something* 90

apresar *to capture* 374

aprobar *(irreg. **ue**) to approve* 410

apropiado(a) *suitable, appropriate* 28 *correct* 74

el **aprovechamiento** *use* 378

aprovechar *to use* 352

aproximadamente *approximately* 320

apuesto(a) *handsome* 20

apuntarse a algo *to join something, to sign up for* 317

los **apuntes** *notes* 361

el **apuro** *haste* 113

aquel, aquella *that one* 36 *that* 156

aquello *that* 156

aquellos, aquellas *those* 156

aquí *here* 14

árabe *Arab, Arabic* 151

el **árbol** *tree* 43

el **árbol genealógico** *family tree* 33

el **archipiélago** *archipelago* 344

el **arco** *bow* 92

el **arco iris** *rainbow* 356

el **área** *area* 165

la **arena** *sand* 202

el **arete** *earring* 145

argentino(a) *Argentinean* 15

la **argumentación** *line of argument* 436

argumentar *to argue* 324

el **argumento** *argument* 166 *plot* 328

el **arma** *arm, weapon* 93

el **armario** *wardrobe, closet* 104

la **armonía** *harmony* 429

el **aro** *hoop* 92

la **arqueología** *archeology* 398

arqueológico(a) *archeological* 364

el/la **arqueólogo(a)** *archeologist* 398

el/la **arquitecto(a)** *architect* 233

la **arquitectura** *architecture* 157

arrancar *to pull out (train)* 321

el **arreglar** *to fix* 152

el **arreglo** *repair* 161

arrepentirse (irreg. **ie**) *to regret* 42

arrogante *arrogant* 50

arrojar *to throw out* 383

el **arroz** *rice* 189

el **arroz blanco** *plain rice* 188

arrugarse *to wrinkle* 90

el **Arte** *art (subject)* 2

las **artes marciales** *martial arts* 94

artesanal *handcrafted* 145 *handicrafts (adjective)* 373

la **artesanía** *handicrafts* 118

el/la **artesano(a)** *craftsman/craftswoman* 91

el **artículo** *article* 44

artificial *artificial* 147

el/la **artista** *artist* 15

artístico(a) *artistic* 151

el **asa** *handle* 327

asado(a) *roasted* 179

asar *to roast* 179

ascender (irreg. **ie**) *to be promoted* 248

el **ascensor** *elevator* 125

Asegúrate de... *Make sure you ...* 275

así *this way* 47

Así como... *As well as ...* 437

Así es la vida. *That's life.* 394

así que *so* 63

asiático(a) *Asian* 57

la **asignatura** *subject* 178

asistir (a) *to attend, to go (to)* 5

la **asociación** *association* 44

asociar algo a/con *to associate something with* 112

el **aspecto** *aspect* XXVI *appearance* 25

áspero(a) *rough* 140

la **aspirina** *aspirin* 414

el **astro** *heavenly body* 354

el/la **astronauta** *astronaut* 239

la **astronomía** *astronomy* 362

astronómico(a) *astronomical* 399

el/la **astrónomo(a)** *astronomer* 354

la **astucia** *astuteness* 212

el **asunto** *matter, issue* 274 *affair* 328

asustar *to frighten* 262

asustarse *to be frightened* 375

atacar *to attack* 50

atarse *to tie* 128

la **atención** *attention* 157

la **atención médica** *medical care* 235

la **atención primaria** *primary health care* 197

atender (irreg. **ie**) **a personas mayores** *to attend to the elderly* 260

Atentamente. *Sincerely,* 275

el **Atlántico** *Atlantic Ocean* 57

atlántico(a) *Atlantic* 202

el/la **atleta** *athlete* 302

el **atletismo** *athletics* 302

la **atracción turística** *tourist attraction* 141

atractivo(a) *attractive* 20

atraer (irreg.) *to attract* 119

atreverse a hacer algo *to dare to do something* 90

atribuir (irreg.) *to attribute* 406

el **atún** *tuna* 179

la **audiencia** *audience* 290

la **audioguía** *audio guide, audio tour* 14

el **auditorio** *auditorium* 290

el **aula** *classroom* 273

aumentar *to increase* 182

aumentar de peso *to gain weight* 194

aún más *even more* 56

aunque *although* 87 *even if* 258

austral *Southern* 380

auténtico(a) *genuine* XXVI *real, authentic* 140

la **autobiografía** *autobiography* 38

autobiográfico(a) *autobiographical* 44

el **autobús** *bus* 5

la **autoestima** *self-esteem* 321

el **autógrafo** *autograph* 77

el/la **autor(a)** *creator* 19 *author, writer* 23 *painter* 41 *cartoonist* 55

autoritario(a) *authoritarian* 33

el **autorretrato** *self-portrait* 38

el/la **auxiliar de vuelo** *flight attendant* 233

el **avance** *advance* 398

avanzado(a) *advanced* 56

avanzar *to move forward* 361 *to make progress* 431

el **ave** *bird* 344

la **avenida** *avenue* 28

aventurero(a) *adventurous* 322

averiguar *to find out* 77

el **avión** *airplane* 145

avisar a alguien *to let someone know* 210

¡ay! *oh!* 137

ayer *yesterday* 5

la **ayuda** *help* 19

el/la **ayudante** *assistant* 26

ayudar *to help* XXVI

el **ayuntamiento** *city council* 82 *city hall* 164

el **azahar** *orange/lemon blossom* 156

azteca *Aztec* 56

el **azúcar** *sugar* 83

azul *blue* 38

el **azul oscuro** *dark blue* 140

B

el/la **bailaor(a)** *flamenco dancer* 151

bailar *to dance* XXVI

el/la **bailarín(a)** *dancer* 67

el **baile** *dance* 9

bajar *to come down* 213

bajar de peso *to lose weight* 194

bajar un archivo *to download a file* 248

bajo *in* 374 *under* 399

bajo(a) *short* 17 *low* 355

el **balcón** *balcony* 110

el **ballet** *ballet* 290

el **balneario** *spa* 176

el **balón** *ball* 92

el **baloncesto** *basketball* 302

el **banco** *bank* 112 *bench* 320

la **banda** *sash* 134

la **bandera** *flag* 72

el/la **banquero(a)** *banker* 236

bañarse *to take a bath* 78 *to go for a swim* 301

el **baño** *bath* 192

barato(a) *cheap* 140

la **barba** *beard* 20

el **barco** *ship* 42 *boat* 303

barrer *to sweep* 152

la **barrera** *barrier* 381

el **barrio** *neighborhood* 244

basarse en *to be based on* 197

la **base** *base* 111 *basis* 183

básico(a) *basic* 218

la **basílica** *basilica* 435

bastante *quite* 20 *quite a lot* 204

la **basura** *garbage* 263

la **batalla** *battle* 398

el **bate** *bat* 287

la **batería** *battery* 98

la **batidora** *blender, mixer* 221

batir *to beat* 179

el **bautizo** *baptism* 44

beber *to drink* 90

beberse *to drink up* 90

la **bebida** *drink* 63

la **beca** *scholarship* 416

el **béisbol** *baseball* 88

la **Bella Durmiente** *Sleeping Beauty* 75

bello(a) *beautiful* 113

la **beneficencia** *charity* 205

el **beneficio** *benefit* 343

benéfico(a) *charitable* 259

besar(se) *to kiss* 74

el **beso** *kiss* 74

la **biblioteca** *library* 11

el/la **bibliotecario(a)** *librarian* 49

la **bici** *bicycle* 4

la **bicicleta** *bicycle* 64

bien *fine 5 well 7*

bien situado(a) *well located 314*

bienvenido(a) *welcome 14*

el **bigote** *mustache 20*

bilingüe *bilingual 118*

la **biodiversidad** *biodiversity 381*

la **biografía** *biography 38*

biográfico(a) *biographical 58*

la **Biología** *biology 215*

la **biosfera** *biosphere 343*

el **biotopo** *biotope 347*

la **bisutería** *costume jewelry 373*

blanco(a) *white 40*

blando(a) *soft 140*

el **bloque** *block 317*

la **blusa** *blouse 125*

la **boca** *mouth 321*

el **bocadillo** *speech bubble 29*

el **boceto** *sketch 134*

la **boda** *wedding 32*

el **bolero** *bolero 101*

el **boleto** *ticket 290*

el **bolígrafo** *ballpoint pen 10*

los **bolos** *bowling 308*

la **bolsa** *bag 104*

el **bolsillo** *pocket 128*

la **bomba** *Puerto Rican musical style 57*

el/la **bombero(a)** *firefighter 233*

la **bombilla** *light bulb 376*

bondadoso(a) *kind 20*

bonito(a) *pretty 20*

el **bordado** *embroidery 134*

el **borrador** *draft 275*

borrar *to erase 104*

el **bosque** *woods, forest 4*

el **bosquejo** *sketch 58*

la **bota** *boot 125*

la **botella** *bottle 345*

el **botón** *button 128*

la **boya** *buoy 303*

bravo(a) *angry 193*

el **brazo** *arm 4*

breve *brief 38*

brevemente *briefly 367*

brillante *bright 140*

brillar *to shine 356*

la **broma** *joke 104*

el **bronce** *bronze 368*

la **bruja** *witch 431*

la **brújula** *compass 322*

el **budismo** *Buddhism 44*

budista *Buddhist 186*

buen, bueno(a) *good 8*

Bueno, ... *Well, ... 15 Alright, ... OK, ... 26*

Bueno, depende... *Well, it depends ... 286*

Bueno, según se mire. *Well, depending on how you look at it. 286*

la **bufanda** *scarf 125*

buscar *to look for, to search for 26 to pick up 35*

la **butaca** *seat 290*

el **buzón de voz** *voice mailbox 98*

el **caballero** *knight 23 gentleman 128*

el **caballo** *horse 326*

la **cabaña** *hut, cabin 4*

caber (irreg.) *to fit 102*

la **cabeza** *head 204*

el **cabildo** *city hall 165*

el **cabo** *cape 380*

el **cacique** *chief 47*

el **cactus** *cactus 411*

cada *each 9*

cada cual *each 237*

cada vez más *more and more 75*

cada vez que *every time 74*

la **cadena** *chain 106 TV station 253*

caer(se) (irreg.) *to fall 90*

el **café** *coffee 86 café 387*

la **cafetera** *coffee maker 352*

la **cafetería** *cafeteria 2*

la **caja** *box 130*

el/la **cajero(a)** *cashier 233*

el **calambre** *cramp 194*

el **calcetín** *sock 104*

el **caldo** *stock (for cooking) 190*

el **calendario** *calendar 357*

calentarse (irreg. **ie**) *to warm 90*

la **calidad** *quality 315*

cálido(a) *warm 353*

caliente *warm 164 hot 199*

el **caligrama** *calligram 112*

la **calle** *street, road 11*

calmar *to relieve 195*

el **calor** *heat 157*

la **caloría** *calorie 182*

caluroso(a) *hot 157*

calvo(a) *bald 20*

el **calzado** *shoes, footwear 125*

la **cama** *bed 104*

la **cámara** *chamber 418*

el **camarón** *prawn 179*

el **cambio** *change 59*

el **cambio climático** *climate change 344*

el **camello** *camel 424*

caminar *to walk 50*

el **camino** *way 7 journey 212 road, route 319*

la **camisa** *shirt 125*

la **camiseta** *T-shirt 125*

la **campana** *bell 110*

la **campaña** *campaign 277*

el/la **campeón(a)** *champion 302*

el **campeonato** *championship 302*

el **cámping** *campground 202*

el **campo** *country, countryside 64 field 218*

el **canal** *canal 442*

cancelar una reserva *to cancel a reservation 314*

el **cáncer** *cancer 268*

la **cancha** *court 302*

la **canción** *song 101*

el/la **candidato(a)** *candidate 225*

la **canoa** *canoe 43*

cansado(a) *tired 9*

el **cansancio** *tiredness 212*

el **Cantábrico** *Cantabrian Sea 289*

el/la **cantante** *singer 101*

el/la **cantaor(a)** *flamenco singer 151*

cantar *to sing 71*

el/la **cantautor(a)** *singer-songwriter 298*

la **cantidad** *quantity 142 number 164 amount 220*

la **capacidad** *capacity (room) 28 ability 326*

capaz *capable 55*

la **capital** *capital 50*

captar *to attract 436*

la **cara** *face 136*

el **caracol** *snail 403*

el **carácter** *character (personality) 33 character (nature) 363*

la **característica** *feature 12*

característico(a) *characteristic 218*

caracterizado(a) *characterized 254*

el **carbón** *coal 368*

el **carbono** *carbon 183*

el **cargo** *post, position 228*

caribeño(a) *Caribbean 57*

cariñoso(a) *warm, affectionate 20*

el **carnaval** *carnival 110*

la **carne** *meat 179*

la **carne blanca** *white meat 182*

la **carne roja** *red meat 182*

caro(a) *expensive 129*

el/la **carpintero(a)** *carpenter 152*

la **carrera** *career 237 university course 272 race 302*

la **carretera** *road 387*

la **carretilla** *wheelbarrow 211*

el **carro** *cart 113*

la **carta** *letter 199*

las **cartas** *cards 424*

el **cartel** *poster 54*

la **cartelera** *entertainment guide 290*

la **cartera** *pocketbook 321*

el **cartón** *cardboard 344*

la **cartulina** *piece of card stock (thick paper) 65*

la **casa** *home 22 house 25*

la **casa de campo** *country house 138*

casado(a) *married 32*

casarse *to marry 32*

la **cascada** *waterfall 341*

el **casco** *helmet 111*

casi *almost 43*

el **caso** *case 11*

castaño(a) *chestnut, brown 20*

el **castillo** *castle* 111

catalán(a) *Catalan* 72

las **cataratas del Iguazú** *Iguazu Falls* 43

la **catástrofe ecológica** *ecological catastrophe* 344

la **catedral** *cathedral* 164

la **categoría** *category* 70

el **caucho** *rubber* 92

la **causa** *cause* 258

causar *to cause* 368

la **caverna** *cave* 50

cazar *to hunt* 212

la **cazuela** *casserole dish* 221

la **cebolla** *onion* 179

el **ceibo** *ceibo tree* 347

la **celebración** *celebration* 44 *holding* 118

celebrar *to celebrate* 5

célebre *famous* 273

el **celo** *zeal* 374

celoso(a) *jealous* 74

el **celular** *cell phone* 98

la **cena** *dinner* 34

cenar *to have dinner* 7

central *central* 157

centrarse en *to revolve around* 44

el **centro** *center* 41

el **centro comercial** *shopping mall* 76

centroamericano(a) *Central American* 347

cepillarse los dientes *to brush one's teeth* 179

el **cepillo** *brush* 19 *toothbrush* 179

la **cerámica** *ceramics* 140

cerca de *near, close to* 37 *nearly* 57

cercano(a) *nearby* 73

el **cerdo** *pig* 341

el **cereal** *cereal* 183

el **cerebro** *brain* 206

la **ceremonia** *ceremony* 110

cerrado(a) *closed* 22

cerrar(se) (irreg. **ie**) *to close* 35

cerrar un programa *to close an application* 248

la **certeza** *certainty* 228

el **césped** *lawn* 63

el **champú** *shampoo* 179

el **chango** *monkey* 38

la **chaqueta** *jacket* 104

charlar *to chat* 300

el/la **chico(a)** *boy/girl* 6

chileno(a) *Chilean* 21

la **chimenea** *fireplace* 138

chino(a) *Chinese* 57

chismoso(a) *gossipy* 20

el **chiste** *joke* 33

chocar *to crash* 5

el **chocolate** *chocolate* 72

chorrear *to drip* 374

el **chubasco** *heavy shower* 356

el **chupa-chups** *lollipop* 254

la **cicatriz** *scar* 20

el **ciclismo** *cycling* 302

el/la **ciclista** *cyclist* 302

el **ciclo** *cycle* 45

el **ciclón** *cyclone* 368

el **cielo** *sky* 112

el **ciempiés** *centipede* 428

científico(a) *scientific* 313

el/la **científico(a)** *scientist* 236

cierto(a) *true* 3

la **cifra** *figure* 207

el **cilindro** *cylinder* 327

el **cine** *cinema* 33

el **cinturón** *belt* 128

el **circo** *circus* 290

las **circunstancias** *circumstances* 104

la **cita** *quote* 80 *appointment* 91

citar *to quote* 382

la **ciudad** *city* 5

el/la **ciudadano(a)** *citizen* 260

civil *civil* 164

la **civilización** *civilization* 398

claramente *clearly* 167

la **claridad** *clarity* 65

claro *of course* 14

claro(a) *clear* 59

la **clase** *class* 2

la **clase media** *middle class* 19

clásico(a) *classical* 28

la **cláusula** *clause* 234

la **clausura** *closing ceremony* 308

clavar *to fix (eyes on)* 77

la **clave** *key* 328

el **clavel** *carnation* 428

clicar con el ratón *to click the mouse* 248

el/la **cliente(a)** *customer* 129 *guest* 323

el **clima** *climate* 157

climático(a) *climatic* 345

la **climatología** *climate* 157

climatológico(a) *climatic* 218

el **cobre** *copper* 369

la **cocción** *baking* 352

cocer (irreg. **ue**) *to boil* 179

el **coche** *car* 5

cocido(a) *boiled* 179

la **cocina** *kitchen* 104 *cooking, cookery* 119

cocinar *to cook* 94

el/la **cocinero(a)** *cook* 233

el **códice** *codex* 374

el **código** *code* 99

la **coherencia** *coherence* 167

la **cohesión** *cohesion* 110

la **coincidencia** *coincidence* 72

coincidir *to coincide* 70

la **cola** *tail* 347

la **colaboración** *collaboration* 338

el/la **colaborador(a)** *contributor* 265

colaborar *to collaborate, to work with* 260

la **colección** *collection* 136

coleccionar *to collect* 71

el/la **colega** *colleague* 298

colgar (irreg. **ue**) *to hang* 152 *to upload* 248

colgar el teléfono *to hang up the phone* 98

el **collar** *necklace* 169

colocar *to put, to place* 139

colombiano(a) *Colombian* 30

la **colonia** *colony* 434

colonial *colonial* 56

la **colonización** *colonization* 56

el/la **colono(a)** *colonist* 57

coloquial *colloquial* 210

el **color** *color* 40

colorido(a) *colorful* 95

colosal *colossal* 212

la **columna** *column* 2

columpiarse *to swing (on a swing)* 158

el **columpio** *swing* 158

combatir *to fight* 193

la **combinación** *combination* 137

combinar *to combine* 101

la **comedia** *comedy* 296

el **comedor** *dining room* 125

comentar *to discuss* 25

el **comentario** *comment* 33

comenzar (irreg. **ie**) *to begin* 2

comer *to eat* 3

comercial *commercial* 254 *trade (adjective)* 319

el/la **comerciante** *vendor* 236

comerciar *to trade* 338

el **comercio justo** *fair trade* 338

comerse *to eat up* 73

los **comestibles** *food* 242

cometer *to commit* 26

la **comida** *food* 35

la **comida basura** *junk food* 182

el **comité** *committee* 418

como *as* 21 *since* 77

cómo *how* 7

como el perro y el gato *fighting like cats and dogs* 115

¿Cómo eres? *What are you like?* 12

Como quieras. *As you like, Whatever you like.* 394

¿Cómo te llamas? *What's your name?* 10

cómodo(a) *comfortable* 134

el/la **compañero(a)** *classmate* 3

la **compañía** *company* 201

la **comparación** *comparison* 12

comparar *to compare* 3

la **comparsa** *carnival club* 110

compartir *to share* 49

el/la **compatriota** *compatriot* 298

la **competencia** *competition* 302

el/la **competidor(a)** *competitor* 285

competir (irreg. **i, i**) *to compete* 223

el **complejo** *complex* 193

los **complementos** *accessories* 125
completo(a) *full* 323
complicado(a) *difficult* 81
el **componente** *component* 92
componer (irreg.) *to compose* 113
el **comportamiento** *behavior* 383
la **composición** *composition* 298
el/la **compositor(a)** *composer* 266
la **compra** *purchase, buy (noun)* 140
shopping 171
comprar *to buy* 3
la **comprensión** *understanding*
(comprehension) 51
comprensivo(a) *understanding* 20
comprometido(a) *committed* 260
el **compromiso** *commitment* 417
la **computación** *computing* 249
la **computadora** *computer* 248
común *common* 38 *in common* 75
mutual 408
la **comunicación** *communication* 52
comunicar *to communicate*
(information) 97 *to be busy*
(phone) 98
comunicarse *to communicate*
XXVI
la **comunidad** *community* 75
comunista *communist* 410
comunitario(a) *community*
(adjective) 110
con *with* XXVI *to* 3
con antelación *in advance* 314
con calma *calmly* 320
con destino a *departing for* 314
con detalle *in detail* 162
con el fin de *in order to* 313
con facilidad *easily* 219
con frecuencia *often* 8
con motivo de *on the occasion*
of 82
Con mucho gusto. *With pleasure.*
86
con tranquilidad *calmly* 374
concentrarse *to concentrate* 214
el **concepto** *concept* 285
concienciar *to make aware* 344
el **concierto** *concert* 290
la **conclusión** *conclusion* 107
la **concordancia** *agreement (in*
grammar) 252
concreto(a) *specific* 280
el **concurso** *contest* 68
la **condición** *condition* 218
el **cóndor** *condor* 21
conducir (irreg.) *to drive* 401
conectado(a) *online* 68
conectar *to turn on* 249
el **conector** *connecting phrase* 363
la **conexión** *connection* 72
la **conferencia** *lecture* 85
confesar (irreg. **ie**) *to confess* 317
la **confianza** *trust* 74 *intimacy* 87
confiar en *to trust* 74
la **confirmación** *confirmation* 16

confirmar *to confirm* 104
confirmar una reserva *to confirm a*
reservation 314
el **conflicto** *conflict* 74
conformar *to form* 416
conforme *as* 164
confundido(a) *confused* 104
la **confusión** *confusion* 41
congelado(a) *frozen* 320
el **congelador** *freezer* 352
congregar *to gather* 110
el **congreso** *conference* 378
el **Congreso (de los Diputados)**
Congress 410
la **conjetura** *conjecture* 333
el **conjunto** *outfit* 166
conmemorar *to commemorate* 110
conmigo *with me* 76
conocer (irreg.) *to know* XXVI *to*
meet 38
conocerse (irreg.) *to meet* 52
el **conocimiento** *knowledge* 239
la **conquista** *conquest* 398
el/la **conquistador(a)** *conqueror* 398
conquistar *to conquer* 398
consciente *aware* 417
la **consecuencia** *consequence* 99
conseguir (irreg. **i, i**) *to win* 100 *to*
achieve 103 *to manage* 119 *to*
get, to obtain 123
el/la **consejero(a)** *counselor* 237
el **consejo** *advice* 8 *meeting* 374
el **consejo de ministros** *cabinet* 418
la **conservación** *conservation* 353
conservador(a) *conservative* 410
conservar *to preserve* 56
considerar *to consider* 94
consistir en *to consist of* 99
la **consolidación** *consolidation* 409
constar de *to consist of* 326
la **constelación** *constellation* 356
la **constitución** *constitution* 410
constitucional *constitutional* 410
constituir (irreg.) *to make up* 57
la **construcción** *construction (in*
grammar) 100 *creation* 258
building, construction 280
construir (irreg.) *to construct* 59 *to*
build 143
la **consulta** *query* 185
la **consulta médica** *doctor's office*
visit 206
consultar *to look up* 247
consultar con *to consult with* 314
el **consultorio** *advice column* 185
el/la **consumidor(a)** *consumer* 367
consumir *to consume* 184
el **consumo** *consumption* 182
la **contabilidad** *accounting* 253
contactar con *to contact* 75
el **contacto** *contact* 75
el/la **contador(a)** *accountant* 236
la **contaminación** *pollution* 263
contaminar *to pollute* 371

contar (irreg. **ue**) *to tell* 1
contemplar *to look at* 254
el **contenedor** *recycling bin* 345
contener (irreg.) *to contain* 190
el **contenido** *content* 92 *contents* 183
contento(a) *happy* 11
el **contestador** *answering machine*
104
contestar *to answer* 33
el **contexto** *context* 314
contigo *with you* 293
el **continente** *continent* 56
continuamente *constantly* 110
continuar *to continue* 50
el **contorno** *outline* 112
contra *against* 19
la **contracción** *contraction* 424
contrario(a) *opposing* 305
el **contraste** *contrast* 210
contratar *to hire* 31
el **contrato** *contract* 248
contribuir (irreg.) *to contribute* 258
el **control de pasaportes** *passport*
control 314
controlar *to control* 261
convencer *to convince* 238
conveniente *advisable* 198
el **convento** *convent* 374
la **conversación** *conversation* 11
convertir en (irreg. **ie, i**) *to turn*
into 42
convertirse en (irreg. **ie, i**) *to*
become 186
convincente *convincing* 275
la **convivencia** *coexistence* 260
convivir *coexist* 260
la **convocatoria** *audition* 416
la **cooperación** *cooperation* 260
el/la **cooperante** *aid worker* 260
cooperar *to cooperate* 260
el/la **coordinador(a)** *coordinator* 236
la **copa** *cup* 303
la **copia** *copy* 249
el **copo** *flake* 218
la **coquetería** *vanity* 254
el **coral** *coral* 353
el **corazón** *heart* 206
la **corbata** *tie* 104
el **cordero** *lamb* 73
los **cordones** *shoelaces* 128
la **cordura** *good sense, wisdom* 111
el/la **coronel** *colonel* 428
la **corporación** *corporation* 416
la **corrección** *correction* 59
correctamente *correctly* 383
correcto(a) *correct* 11
corregir (irreg. **i, i**) *to correct* 59
el **correo (electrónico)** *e-mail* 5
correr *to run* 3
corresponder *to correspond* 9
correspondiente *corresponding* 16
la **corriente** *current* 193
cortar *to mow* 63 *to cut* 190

disculparse *to apologize* 74
el **discurso** *speech* 241
la **discusión** *argument* 118
discutir *to argue* 74
el/la **diseñador(a)** *designer* 129
el/la **diseñador(a) gráfico(a)** *graphic designer* 236
diseñar *to design* 65
el **diseño** *design* 128
el **disfraz** *costume* 424
disfrutar *to enjoy* 202
disfrutar de *to enjoy something* 193
disminuir (irreg.) *to reduce* 157
disolverse (irreg.) *to dissolve* 221
disponerse (irreg.) *to get ready* 374
disponible *available* 256
la **disposición** *arrangement* 113
la **distancia** *distance* 87
distante *distant, aloof* 33 *faraway* 374
distinto(a) *different* 147
distintos(as) *various* 56
distraerse (irreg.) *to get distracted* 166
distraído(a) *distracted* 167
distribuir (irreg.) *to distribute* 206
la **diversidad** *diversity* 422
la **diversión** *entertainment, pastime* 54 *entertainment, fun* 327
diversos(as) *various* 21
divertido(a) *enjoyable, fun* 7 *funny* 22
divertirse (irreg. **ie, i**) *to enjoy oneself* 14
dividir *to divide* 43
divorciado(a) *divorced* 32
divorciarse *to divorce* 38
el **divorcio** *divorce* 39
doblar *to turn* 4 *to fold* 152
el/la **doctor(a)** *doctor* 74
la **documentación** *papers, identification* 314
el **documental** *documentary* 44
el **documento** *document* 248
el **dólar** *dollar* 22
doler (irreg. **ue**) *to hurt* 199
el **dolor** *pain* 74
el **dolor de espalda** *backache* 195
el **dolor de estómago** *stomachache* 211
domar *to tame* 326
el **domicilio** *address* 10
dominar *to rule* 398
dominicano(a) *Dominican* 101
el **dominio** *control* 326 *command* 374
don *Mr.* 86
la **donación** *donation* 207
el/la **donante** *donor* 207
donar *to donate* 268
donde *where* 38
dónde *where* 10
doña *Mrs.* 86
dormido(a) *asleep* 23

dormir (irreg. **ue, u**) *to sleep* 3
dormirse (irreg. **ue, u**) *to fall asleep* 90
el **dormitorio** *bedroom* 3
el **dragón** *dragon* 72
el **drama** *drama* 252
la **dramatización** *dramatization* 118
ducharse *to take a shower* 160
la **duda** *doubt* XXVI
dudar *to hesitate* 124 *to doubt* 238
dudoso(a) *doubtful* 238
el/la **dueño(a)** *owner* 149
el **dueto** *duet* 298
dulce *sweet (adjective)* 83
el **dulce** *sweet, treat* 77
la **duna** *dune* 380
la **duración** *duration* 81
durante *during* 2 *for* 31
durar *to last* 355
duro(a) *hard* 140

echar *to put* 179
echar la culpa de algo a *to blame something on* 74
echar un vistazo *to scan* 104
echar una mano a alguien *to give someone a hand* 124
el **eclipse** *eclipse* 357
la **ecología** *ecology* 344
ecológico(a) *ecological* 344 *organic* 371 *environmentally friendly* 376
ecologista *environmental, ecological* 344
la **Economía** *economics* 418
la **economía** *economy* 247
económico(a) *economic* 205 *cheap* 254
el **ecosistema** *ecosystem* 344
ecuatoriano(a) *Ecuadorian* 146
la **edad** *age* 94
la **Edad Media** *the Middle Ages* 272
la **edición** *celebration* 295
la **edificación** *building* 165
el **edificio** *building* 164
la **educación** *education* 241
la **Educación Física** *physical education* 203
educado(a) *polite, well mannered* 27
el/la **educador(a)** *teacher* 423
educar *to educate* 245
educativo(a) *educational* 268
efectivamente *sure enough* 187
efectivo(a) *effective* 19
el **efecto** *effect* 129
el **efecto invernadero** *greenhouse effect* 344
los **efectos especiales** *special effects* 291
eficaz *effective* 242

eficiente *efficient* 248
el **egoísmo** *selfishness* 321
egoísta *selfish* 20
el **ejemplo** *example* 77
ejercer *to practice* 273 *to exercise* 436
el **ejercicio** *exercise* 8
el **ejército** *army* 254
el **ejército del aire** *the Air Force* 254
el *the* XXVI
él *he* 3
el/la cual *which* 91
la **elaboración** *preparation* 220
elaborar *to make* 14 *to prepare* 220 *to draw up* 280
la **elección** *choice* 259
las **elecciones** *elections* 419
electoral *election (adjective)* 436
el/la **electricista** *electrician* 152
eléctrico(a) *electric* 102 *electrical* 369
el **electrodoméstico** *appliance* 103
el **elefante** *elephant* 341
la **elegancia** *elegance* 136
elegante *elegant* 140
elegir (irreg.) *to choose* 10 *to elect* 410
el **elemento** *element* 38
la **élite** *elite* 187
ella *she* 3
ello *it* 408
ellos *they* XXVI
el **e-mail** *e-mail* 171
la **embajada** *embassy* 312
embarazada *pregnant* 52
el **embarazo** *pregnancy* 44
la **embarcación** *boat* 301
embellecer (irreg.) *to freshen up, to beautify* 434
el **emblema** *emblem* 139
la **emigración** *emigration* 56
el/la **emigrante** *emigrant* 235
emigrar *to emigrate* 45
la **emisora (de radio)** *radio station* 96
emitirse *to be broadcast* 310
la **emoción** *emotion* 308
emocionado(a) *excited* 63
emocionante *exciting* XXVI
emocionar *to move, to touch* 262
el **emoticono** *emoticon* 99
emotivo(a) *emotional, moving* 298
la **empanada** *pie, pastry* 180
empanado(a) *breaded* 179
empaparse *to soak up* 254
empatar *to tie* 287
el **empate** *tie* 302
el **emperador** *emperor* 205
empezar (irreg. **ie**) *to begin* 1
el **emplazamiento** *location* 434
el/la **empleado(a)** *employee* 236
emplear *to use* 75
el **empleo** *job* 247
emprendedor(a) *entrepreneurial* 248

la **especialmente** *specially* 87

la **especie** *kind* 134 *species* 347

la **especie en peligro de extinción** *endangered species* 349

la **especie protegida** *protected species* 344

la **especie vegetal** *plant* 347

específico(a) *specific* 147

el **espectáculo** *show* 28 *entertainment* 71

el/la **espectador(a)** *spectator* 28

el **espejo** *mirror* 30

la **espera** *wait* 320

Espera... *Wait ...* 203

la **esperanza** *hope* 374

esperar *to hope* 14 *to wait* 87

las **espinacas** *spinach* 179

el **esplendor** *peak* 399

la **esponja** *sponge* 194

el/la **esposo(a)** *husband/wife* 32

la **espuma de afeitar** *shaving foam* 194

el **esqueleto** *skeleton* 206

el **esquema** *diagram* 275

esquematizar *to outline* 328

el **esquí** *skiing* 287

el **esquí acuático** *water-skiing* 302

el/la **esquiador(a)** *skier* 302

la **esquina** *corner* 4

¿Está...? *May I speak with ...?* 98

establecer (irreg.) *to establish* 133

establecerse (irreg.) *to settle* 56

el **establecimiento** *establishment* 367

la **estación** *station* 287 *season* 338

el **estacionamiento** *parking lot* 5

el **estadio** *stadium* 302

el **estado** *state* 50

el **estado civil** *marital status* 17

el **estado de ánimo** *emotion* 17

estadounidense *American* 21

el **estafador** *con man* 296

el **estampado** *pattern* 136

el **estante** *shelf* 49

la **estantería** *bookcase* 125

el **estaño** *tin* 368

estar (irreg.) *to be* 2

estar de acuerdo *to agree* 22

estatal *state (adjective)* 274

la **estatua** *statue* 398

este, esta *this (one)* XXVI

el **estereotipo** *stereotype* 21

el **estilo** *style* 28

Estimado(a)... *Dear ...* 185

estirar *to stretch* 194 *to reach out* 320

esto *this* 10

el **estómago** *stomach* 206

estornudar *to sneeze* 214

estos(as) *these* 3

la **estrategia** *strategy* 26

estrechar la mano *to shake hands* 87

estrecho(a) *tight* 128 *narrow* 434

la **estrella** *star* 21

la **Estrella Polar** *North Star* 328

estrenar *to open* 290

el **estreno** *premiere, opening night* 293

el **estrés** *stress* 193

estresado(a) *stressed* 194

estresante *stressful* 195

estricto(a) *strict* 58

la **estrofa** *stanza* 113

la **estructura** *structure* 144

estructurar *to structure* 173

el/la **estudiante** *student* 2

estudiar *to study* 2

estudiarse *to learn* 90

el **estudio** *study* 45 *studio* 298

estudioso(a) *studious* 25

estupendo *great* 161

estupendo(a) *great* 187

la **etapa** *stage* 44

eterno(a) *eternal* 42

la **etnia** *ethnicity* 422

étnico(a) *ethnic* 110

evaluar *to evaluate* 65

evaporarse *to evaporate* 190

el **evento** *event* 54

la **evidencia** *evidence* 255

evidente *obvious, evident* 167

evidentemente *obviously, evidently* 393

evitar *to avoid* 182

la **evolución** *development* 434

exactamente *exactly* 285

exacto *exactly* 230

exacto(a) *exact* 180

el **examen** *exam* 16

el **examen físico** *physical exam* 206

examinar *to examine* 207

la **excavación** *excavation* 398

excavar *to excavate* 398

excelente *excellent* 15

la **excepción** *exception* 252

excepcional *exceptional* 146

excepto *except* 223

excesivo(a) *excessive* 261

exclusivamente *exclusively* 204

la **excursión** *excursion* 48

la **excusa** *excuse* 95

la **exhibición** *display* 326

exhibir *to show* 320

exigente *demanding* 248

exigir *to demand* 166

la **existencia** *existence* 142

existente *existing* 164

existir *to exist* 33

el **éxito** *success* 44

exitoso(a) *successful* 26

exótico(a) *exotic* 209

expandir *to expand* 136

la **expedición** *expedition* XXVI

la **experiencia** *experience* 1

experto(a) *expert* 84

la **explicación** *explanation* 81

explicar *to explain* 2

el/la **explorador(a)** *explorer* 398

explorar *to explore* 353

la **explotación agrícola** *farm* 371

exponer (irreg.) *to set out* 166 *to explain* 383

exportar *to export* 345

la **exposición** *exhibition* 71 *presentation* 167

expresar *to express* 1

la **expresión** *expression* 4

extenderse (irreg. **ie**) *to spread* 57

la **extensión** *area* 143

la **extinción** *extinction* 347

extranjero(a) *foreign* 94

el/la **extranjero(a)** *foreigner* 406

extrañar *to seem strange* 262

la **extrañeza** *surprise* 178

extraño(a) *strange* 104

extraordinario(a) *extraordinary* 147

el/la **extraterrestre** *extraterrestrial* 401

el **extremo** *end* 326

extremo(a) *extreme* 300

extrovertido(a) *extroverted* 236

F

la **fábrica** *factory* 233

la **fabricación** *manufacture* 373

fabricar *to manufacture* 126

fabuloso(a) *fabulous* 53

fácil *easy* 80

facilitar *to facilitate* 284

fácilmente *easily* 81

facturar *to check* 287

la **facultad** *faculty* 251

la **falda** *skirt* 125

la **falla** *fault* 199

falso(a) *false* 3

faltar *to fail to turn up, to miss* 136 *to be missing* 253

la **fama** *fame* 24 *reputation* 33

la **familia** *family* 6

la **familia política** *family-in-law* 32

la **familia real** *royal family* 31

familiar *familial* 12

el/la **familiar** *relative* 77

familiarizarse *to familiarize oneself* 14

famoso(a) *famous* XXVI

el/la **fan** *fan* XXVI

fantástico(a) *fantastic* 43

el/la **farmacéutico(a)** *pharmacist* 236

fascinante *fascinating* 14

fascinar *to fascinate* 262

la **fase** *stage* 221

fastidiado(a) *annoyed* 320

el **fastidio** *annoyance* 320

fatal *terrible, awful* 178

la **fauna** *fauna* 343

el **favor** *favor* 122

favorecer (irreg.) *to favor* 371

la **favorito(a)** *favorite* 11
la **fe** *faith* 244
la **fecha** *date* 23
la **fecha de entrada** *check-in date* 314
la **fecha de nacimiento** *birth date* 17
la **fecha de salida** *check-out date* 314
felicidades *congratulations* XXVI
felicitar *to greet* 82
el/la **felino(a)** *feline* 381
feliz *happy* 16
femenino(a) *feminine* 156
la **feminidad** *femininity* 136
fenomenal *great, terrific* 293
el **fenómeno** *phenomenon* 356
la **feria** *fair* 77 *festival* 94
fértil *fertile* 50
el **festival** *festival* 52
la **festividad** *festivity* 357
la **fibra** *fiber* 182
la **ficción** *fiction* 44
la **ficha** *file* 6 *counter* 93
ficticio(a) *fictitious* 23
la **fidelidad** *faithfulness* 74
la **fiebre** *fever* 46
fiel *faithful* 20
la **fiesta** *party* 5 *festivity* 35 *public holiday* 64
la **figura** *shape* 91 *figure (person)* 245 *figure (object)* 301
fijarse en *to pay attention to* 65
fijo(a) *fixed* 270
la **fila** *line* 290
el **filete** *steak* 183
filmar *to film, to shoot* 342
la **filosofía** *philosophy* 245
el **filtro** *filter* 352
el **fin** *end* 406
el **fin de semana** *weekend* 3
final *final (adjective)* 167
el **final** *end* 29
la **final** *final* 303
la **finalidad** *end, purpose* 282
finalizar *to finish* 383
finalmente *finally* 16
la **finca agrícola** *farm* 143
la **firma** *signature* 275
firmado(a) *signed* 436
el/la **firmante** *signatory* 275
firmar *to sign* 19
la **Física** *physics (subject)* 178
físicamente *physically* 27
físico(a) *physical* 9
el/la **físico(a)** *physicist* 273
la **fisonomía** *appearance* 57
el **flamenco** *flamenco* XXVI
el **flan** *flan, crème caramel* 179
la **flecha** *arrow* 92
la **flor** *flower* 63
la **flora** *flora* 343
florecer (irreg.) *to flourish* 374
la **florería** *florist* 155
el **florero** *vase* 142

la **fluidez** *fluidity* 59
folclórico(a) *folkloric* 157
el **folleto** *brochure* 82
fomentar *to promote, to encourage* 344
el **fondo** *back* 157
los **fondos** *funds* 416
forestal *forest (adjective)* 380
la **forma** *form* 8 *shape* 9 *way* 16
la **formación** *formation* 130 *training* 247
formado(a) por *composed of* 30
formal *formal* 137
formar *to form* 43
formar parte de *to be part of* 97
el **formato** *format* 275
la **fórmula** *expression* 282
el **formulario** *form* 10
el **foro** *forum* 253
fortalecer (irreg.) *to strengthen* 406
la **fortificación** *fortification* 165
forzoso(a) *obligatory* 320
la **foto** *photo, picture* 5
la **fotocopiadora** *copier* 248
fotocopiar *to copy* 248
la **fotografía** *photography* 3 *photograph* 9
el **fragmento** *excerpt* 94 *passage* 293
el **francés** *French* 11
la **franja** *stripe* 411
la **frase** *sentence* 59
fray *brother (monk)* 374
frecuente *common* 215
frecuentemente *frequently* 48
fregar (irreg. **ie**) *to scrub* 152
la **fregona** *mop* 254
freír (irreg.) *to fry* 179
el **frente** *front* 265
frente a *in front of* 104
fresco(a) *fresh* 214
el **frijol** *bean* 92
el **frío** *cold* 279
frío(a) *cold* 33
frustrado(a) *frustrated* 17
la **fruta** *fruit* 179
el **fruto** *fruit* 254
los **frutos secos** *dried fruits and nuts* 182
el **fuego** *heat* 190 *fire* 362
los **fuegos artificiales** *fireworks* 362
la **fuente** *fountain* 42 *source* 136
fuerte *strong* 50 *hard* 211 *powerful* 369 *severe* 370
fuertemente *hard* 369
la **fuerza** *strength* 93
la **fuerza de voluntad** *willpower* 197
la **función** *performance* 290
funcionar *to work* 205
el/la **funcionario(a)** *government employee* 236
la **fundación** *foundation* 229
fundamental *essential, fundamental* 84

fundar *to found* 42
funerario(a) *funeral* 362
furioso(a) *furious* 17
la **fusión** *fusion* 101
el **fútbol** *soccer* 88
el **fútbol americano** *football* 287
el **fútbol sala** *indoor soccer* 308
el **futuro** *future* 18
futuro(a) *future* 103

G

las **gafas** *glasses* 125
las **gafas de sol** *sunglasses* 125
la **galaxia** *galaxy* 356
la **galleta** *cookie* 320
la **ganadería** *livestock* 368
ganador(a) *winning* 82
el/la **ganador(a)** *winner* 302
ganar *to win* 49 *to earn* 236
el **garaje** *garage* 125
garantizar *to guarantee* 146
el **garbanzo** *chickpea* 181
la **garganta** *throat* 207
el **gas natural** *natural gas* 368
la **gaseosa** *soda* 320
gastar *to waste* 352
el **gasto** *expense* 416 *spending* 417
la **gastronomía** *gastronomy* 146
gastronómico(a) *gastronomic* 425
el **gato** *cat* 30
el **géiser** *geyser* 199
el **gel** *gel* 179
gemir (irreg. **i**) *to groan* 320
la **generación** *generation* 43
general *general* 59
generalmente *generally* 33
generar *to generate* 352
el **género** *genre* 57 *gender* 156
generoso(a) *generous* 17
el **genio** *genius* 178
la **gente** *people* 50
gentil *kind* 27
genuinamente *genuinely* 255
geográfico(a) *geographic* 308
geométrico(a) *geometric* 136
el **geranio** *geranium* 156
el/la **gerente** *manager* 236
el **gerundio** *gerund* 34
la **gestión** *management* 416
el **gesto** *gesture* 104
gigante *giant (adjective)* 344 *gigantic* 368
la **Gimnasia** *gymnastics* 108
el **gimnasio** *gym* 194
la **gira** *tour* 298
gitano(a) *gypsy* 151
globalmente *globally* 417
el/la **gobernador(a)** *governor* 410
gobernar *to govern* 410
el **gobierno** *government* 164
el **gol** *goal* 303

el **golf** *golf* 287
el **golfo** *gulf* 381
el **golpe** *bump* 206
el **golpe de Estado** *coup (d'état)* 410
    golpear *to hit* 369
    gordito(a) *overweight* 441
    gordo(a) *fat* 17
el **gorro de ducha** *shower cap* 194
la **gota** *drop* 356
    gótico(a) *Gothic* 434
    gozar de *to enjoy* 272
la **grabación** *recording* 417
    grabar *to record* 16
    gracias *thank you* 75
    gracias a *thanks to* 91
    gracioso(a) *funny* 17
el **grado** *degree* 87
la **graduación** *graduation* 44
el/la **graduado(a)** *graduate* 273
    graduarse *to graduate* 44
el **gráfico** *diagram* 17 *chart* 207
    gramatical *grammatical* 167
    gran, grande *big* 20 *great* 44
la **Gran Depresión** *Great Depression* 242
la **grandeza** *size* 164
el **granizo** *hail* 356
la **granja** *farm* 372
el **grano** *grain* 212
la **grasa** *fat* 182
    grasoso(a) *greasy* 182
    gratis *free* 119
    gratuito(a) *free* 430
    grave *serious* 39 *low* 111
el **grifo** *faucet* 171
la **gripe** *flu* 9
    gritar *to scream* 104
el **grito** *scream* 104
    grosero(a) *rude* 320
el **grupo** *group* 40
el **guante** *glove* 125
    guapo *handsome* 20
    guaraní *Guarani* 56
    guardar *to put away* 104 *to keep* 190 *to save* 248
    guatemalteco(a) *Guatemalan* 49
la **guerra** *war* 398
el/la **guerrero(a)** *warrior* 47
la **guía** *guide* 146
    guiar *to guide* 14
el **guion** *outline* 166
el/la **guionista** *scriptwriter* 40
el **guisante** *pea* 179
la **guitarra** *guitar* 150
    gustar *to like* XXVI
el **gusto** *like* 1 *taste* 202

    haber (irreg.) *to have* XXVI
    haber que *to have to* 67
    había *there was/there were* 77

la **habilidad** *skill* 55
la **habitación** *room* 104 *bedroom* 158
el/la **habitante** *inhabitant* 56
    habitar *to inhabit* 56
el **hábitat** *habitat* 338
el **hábito** *habit* 174
los **hábitos alimenticios** *eating habits* 185
    habitual *usual* 35 *regular* 48
    habitualmente *usually* 259
el **habla** *speech* 252
el/la **hablante** *speaker* 264
    hablar *to speak* 2 *to talk* 3
    hablar de *to talk about* 1
    habrá *there will be* 102
    hace... *... ago* 42
    hacer (irreg.) *to do, to make* XXVI
    hacer escala *to stop over* 287
    hacer falta *to be needed* 111
    hacer memoria *to try to remember* 63
    hacer un favor a alguien *to do someone a favor* 124
    hacerse daño *to hurt oneself* 65
    hacia *toward* 50
la **hacienda** *country estate* 122
el **hambre** *hunger* 262
    hambriento(a) *starving* 212
la **hamburguesa** *hamburger* 226
la **hamburguesería** *hamburger bar* 185
la **harina** *flour* 218
    hasta *until* 44 *to* 92
    ¡Hasta la próxima! *See you soon!, See you next time!* 85
    ¡Hasta pronto! *See you soon!* 14
    hay *there is/there are* 22
la **hazaña** *feat* 72
el **hecho** *action* 1 *fact* 43 *event* 329
la **hectárea** *hectare* 268
el **helado** *ice cream* 115
    helar (irreg. **ie**) *to freeze* 356
el **helicóptero** *helicopter* 268
el **hemisferio** *hemisphere* 354
la **herencia** *inheritance* 214
la **herencia cultural** *cultural heritage* 422
la **herida** *injury* 38 *wound* 206
el/la **hermanastro(a)** *step-brother/ step-sister* 32
el/la **hermano(a)** *brother/sister* 17
los **hermanos** *brothers and sisters* 10
    hermoso(a) *beautiful* 146
el **héroe** *hero* 236
la **herradura** *horseshoe* 153
    hervir (irreg. **ie, i**) *to boil* 179
la **hibernación** *hibernation* 350
    hibernar *to hibernate* 343
el **hidrato de carbono** *carbohydrate* 183
el **hielo** *ice* 209
la **hierba** *herb* 193
el **hierro** *iron* 140
el **hígado** *liver* 206
la **higiene** *hygiene* 179

el/la **hijo(a)** *son/daughter* 17
los **hijos** *children (offspring)* 18
el **hilo dental** *dental floss* 194
el **himno** *anthem* 110
    hinchado(a) *swollen* 206
el **hinduismo** *Hinduism* 44
la **hipótesis** *hypothesis* 177
    hispano(a) *Hispanic* XXVI
    hispanohablante *Spanish-speaking* 313
la **Historia** *history* 11
la **historia** *story* 5
    históricamente *historically* 274
    histórico(a) *historical* 101 *historic* 406
la **historieta** *comic strip, cartoon* 21
la **hoguera** *bonfire* 354
la **hoja** *sheet (of paper)* 119
    hojear *to page through* 320
    hola *hello* XXVI
el **hombre** *man* 23
el **hombro** *shoulder* 327
el **homenaje** *tribute* 289
    honesto(a) *honest* 8
el **honor** *honor* 230
    honrar *to honor* 213
la **hora** *hour* 8 *time* 23
el **horario** *timetable* 3 *schedule* 287
el **horario flexible** *flextime* 247
las **horas extraordinarias** *overtime* 256
el **horizonte** *horizon* 428
la **hormiga** *ant* 212
    hornear *to bake* 221
el **horno** *oven* 125
    horrible *horrible* 35
la **hortaliza** *vegetable* 182
el **hospital** *hospital* 45
    hostil *hostile* 380
el **hotel** *hotel* 138
    hoy *today* 7
la **huelga** *strike* 235
la **huella** *trace* 434
el **hueso** *bone* 206
el/la **huésped** *guest* 138
el **huevo** *egg* 343
el **huipil** *huipil (traditional Indian dress)* 134
la **humanidad** *mankind* 151 *humanity* 254
    humanista *humanist* 254
    humano(a) *human* 111
    húmedo(a) *humid* 381
    humilde *humble* 83
el **humo** *smoke* 371
el **humor** *humor* 19
el **hundimiento** *sinking* 442
el **huracán** *hurricane* 368

I

el **icono** *icon* 277
la **idea** *idea* 28
    ideal *ideal* 89

la **ira** *anger, rage* 321
irreal *imaginary* 265
irregular *irregular* 1
irritado(a) *irritated* 320
irse (irreg.) *to leave* 90
la **isla** *island* 44
el **islamismo** *Islam* 44
el/la **italiano(a)** *Italian* 56
la **itálica** *italics* 80
el **itinerario** *itinerary* 325
la **izquierda** *left* 113

el **jabón** *soap* 179
el **jade** *jade* 141
el **jaguar** *jaguar* 381
el **jamón** *ham* 52
japonés(a) *Japanese* 57
el **jarabe** *cough syrup* 207
el **jardín** *yard, garden* 35
el/la **jardinero(a)** *gardener* 152
el/la **jefe(a)** *boss* 236
jerárquico(a) *hierarchical* 403
el **jeroglífico** *hieroglyphic* 399
el/la **jinete** *rider* 326
la **jornada completa** *full-time* 248
la **jornada laboral** *working day* 237
el/la **joven** *young person* 44
la **joya** *jewel* 141
la **jubilación** *retirement* 44
jubilarse *to retire* 45
el **judaísmo** *Judaism* 44
el/la **judío(a)** *Jew* 56
el **juego** *game* 55
el **juego de mesa** *board game* 92
los **juegos competitivos** *competitive games* 92
los **Juegos Olímpicos** *Olympics* 302
el/la **juez(a)** *judge* 236
el/la **jugador(a)** *player* 84
jugar (irreg. **ue**) *to play* 11
el **jugo** *juice* 117
jugoso(a) *juicy* 182
junto(a) *together* 4
junto a *right by* 193
junto con *together with* 219
el **jurado** *jury* 157
jurar el cargo *to be sworn in* 244
la **justicia** *justice* 422
justificar *to justify* 243
justo(a) *fair* 238
juvenil *young* 416
la **juventud** *youth* 44

el **karate** *karate* 308
el **kilo** *kilo* 133
el **kilómetro** *kilometer* 194

la, las *the* XXVI
la **labor** *task* 374
laboral *workers'* 231 *working* 281
lacio(a) *straight* 20
lácteo(a) *dairy* 179
la **ladera** *slope* 381
el/la **ladrón(a)** *thief* 29
el **lago** *lake* 4
la **lágrima** *tear* 112
la **laguna** *lagoon* 373
la **lámpara** *lamp* 125
la **lana** *wool* 125
el **lápiz** *pencil* 294
largo(a) *long* 7
la **lasaña** *lasagna* 180
el **láser** *laser* 401
la **lástima** *pity, shame* 361
la **lata** *can* 344
el **latido** *beat* 211
latino(a) *Latino* 21
latinoamericano(a) *Latin American* 56
el **laurel** *laurel* 428
la **lava** *lava* 380
la **lavadora** *washer* 125
el **lavaplatos** *dishwasher* 125
lavar *to wash* 130
lavar los platos *to wash the dishes* 152
lavarse *to wash up* 78 *to wash* 179
el **lavavajillas** *dishwashing liquid* 152
el **lazo** *tie, bond* 111
le *(to) him/her/you (formal)* 76
la **lección** *lesson* 400
la **leche** *milk* 221
el **lecho** *bed* 374
la **lechuga** *lettuce* 19
el/la **lector(a)** *reader* 59
la **lectura** *reading* 26
leer (irreg.) *to read* XXVI
el **legado** *legacy* 245
la **legibilidad** *legibility* 167
las **legumbres** *legumes, vegetables* 179
lejano(a) *distant* 55
lejos *far* 244
el **lema** *slogan, motto* 111
la **lengua** *language* 46
el **lenguaje** *language* 99
lentamente *slowly* 424
la **lenteja** *lentil* 179
lento *slowly* 401
les *(to) them/you* 76
la **letra** *handwriting* 59 *letter* 99 *lyrics* 101
el **levantamiento** *lifting* 327
levantar *to build (a tower)* 111 *to raise (a hand)* 111 *to lift* 185 *to elicit* 266

levantarse *to get up* 78 *to stand up* 209
la **ley** *law* 410
la **leyenda** *legend* XXVI
el/la **libanés(a)** *Lebanese* 56
liberal *liberal* 410
la **libertad (de expresión)** *freedom (of speech)* 422
libre *free* 71
el **libro** *book* 36
la **licencia de conducir** *driver's license* 6
el/la **líder** *leader* 207
ligero(a) *light* 182
el **limón** *lemon* 298
el **limpiacristales** *window cleaner* 152
limpiar *to clean* 3
limpiar el polvo *to dust* 152
la **limpieza** *cleanliness* 167 *cleaning* 388
limpio(a) *clean* 104
lindo(a) *pretty* 42
la **línea** *line* 39
la **línea aérea** *airline* 314
lineal *linear* 136
el **liquen** *lichen* 380
el **líquido** *liquid* 206
liso(a) *plain* 128
la **lista** *list* 8
listo(a) *ready* 113
literario(a) *literary* 50
la **literatura** *literature* 23
el **litro** *liter* 185
la **llamada** *call* 4
la **llamada perdida** *missed call* 98
llamar *to call* 34
llamarse *to be called* 18
llano(a) *flat* 218
la **llanura** *plain (topographic)* 434
la **llegada** *arrival* 42
llegar *to arrive* 5
llenar *to fill in* 249
llenarse *to fill up* 136
lleno(a) *full* 25
llevar *to have been* 37 *to bring* 109 *to wear* 111 *to take* 145 *to lead* 185 *to have* 188 *to carry* 211
llevarse *to get along* 32
llorar *to cry* 42
llover (irreg. **ue**) *to rain* 155
llover a cántaros *to pour with rain* 356
lloviznar *to drizzle* 356
la **lluvia** *rain* 51
lluvioso(a) *rainy* 356
lo *it* 4 *the* 7
Lo cierto es que... *The truth is that ...* 92
lo fundamental *the most important thing* 84
lo que... *what ...* 3
Lo siento. *I'm sorry.* 86

la **local** *local* 143
la **localidad** *town* 388
la **localización** *location* 392
localizar *to set* 28 *to find* 85
loco(a) *mad* 23
lógicamente *logically* 223
lógico(a) *logical* 2
el **logo** *logo* 376
lograr *to win* 161 *to manage* 212 *to achieve* 241
el **logro** *achievement* 404
el **loro** *parrot* 38
los *the* XXVI
los/las cuales *which* 219
la **lotería** *lottery* 268
la **lucha** *fight* 92
luchar *to fight* 47
luego *then* 8 *later* 77
el **lugar** *place* 7
el **lugar de nacimiento** *birthplace* 17
el **lujo** *luxury* 268
la **luna** *moon* 341
la **luna llena** *full moon* 358
lunar *lunar* 357
el **lunar** *mole (on skin)* 20
la **luz** *light* 104

la **maceta** *flowerpot* 155
la **madera** *wood* 368
la **madrastra** *stepmother* 33
la **madre** *mother* 17
la **madurez** *adulthood* 44
maduro(a) *ripe* 212
la **maestría** *master's degree* 418
el/la **maestro(a)** *teacher* 9
la **magia** *magic* 293
mágico(a) *magic(al)* 328
magnífico(a) *magnificent* 310
el/la **mago(a)** *wizard* 55
el **maíz** *corn* 212
mal *bad* 9 *wrong* 22
maleducado(a) *rude* 295
la **maleta** *suitcase* 322
malo(a) *bad* 24
maltratar *to mistreat* 293
malvado(a) *wicked* 328
la **mamá** *mom* 34
el **mambo** *mambo* 97
el **mamífero** *mammal* 344
el **manantial** *spring (water)* 192
mancharse *to get dirty* 90
mandar *to order* 47 *to send* 63
el/la **mandatario(a)** *head of state* 244
el **mandato** *command* 174
la **mandíbula** *jaw* 212
la **mandioca** *cassava* 219
manejar *to handle* 93 *to drive* 196 *to use* 251 *to operate* 427
la **manera** *way* 1
la **manga** *sleeve* 128

la **manguera** *hose* 156
la **manifestación** *demonstration* 235 *expression* 326
la **manifestación artística** *art form* 151
manifestarse (irreg. **ie**) *to become apparent* 434
la **mano** *hand* 84
manso(a) *gentle* 176
mantener(se) (irreg.) *to keep* 53
el **mantenimiento** *upkeep* 406
la **mantequilla** *butter* 182
manual *manual (adjective)* 197
el **manual** *manual* 254
las **manualidades** *crafts* 118
la **manzana** *apple* 144 *city block* 165
mañana *tomorrow* 22
la **mañana** *morning* 2
el **mapa** *map* 56
mapuche *Mapuche* 57
maquillarse *to make oneself up, to apply makeup* 78
la **máquina** *machine* 211
la **maquinilla de afeitar** *safety razor* 194
el **mar** *sea* 192
el/la **maratón** *marathon* 195
la **maravilla** *wonder* 342
maravilloso(a) *wonderful* 43
la **marca** *target* 92 *brand* 129
el **marcador** *marker* 48 *scoreboard* 302
el **marcapasos** *pacemaker* 211
marcar *to dial* 98 *to mark* 254 *to score* 303
marcharse *to leave* 397
la **marea negra** *oil spill* 344
mareado(a) *dizzy* 206
el **mariachi** *mariachi* 335
el **marido** *husband* 44
la **mariposa** *butterfly* 336
el **marisco** *seafood* 181
marrón *brown* 128
más *more* XXVI
más tarde *later* 98
el **masaje** *massage* 194
la **mascota** *pet* 200 *mascot* 282
masculino(a) *masculine* 156
matar *to kill* 42
matemático(a) *mathematical* 399
la **materia** *subject* 378
la **materia prima** *raw material* 366
material *material (adjective)* 368
el **material** *material* 22 *materials* 352
materno(a) *maternal* 32
el **matorral** *scrubland* 380
el **matrimonio** *marriage* 44
máximo(a) *maximum (adjective)* 119
maya *Mayan* 49
la **mayonesa** *mayonnaise* 179
mayor *older* 24 *bigger* 37 *greatest, highest* 75

el/la **mayor** *eldest* 25
la **mayor parte** *most, largest part* 56
la **mayoría** *majority* 199
la **mayúscula** *capital (letter)* 65
la **mazorca** *corncob* 218
me *(to) me* 76 *myself* 78
Me/Te apetece... *I/you feel like ...* 69
Me da igual. *I don't mind.* 394
Me da lo mismo. *I don't mind.* 394
Me encantaría... *I'd love to ...* 340
Me gustaría... *I'd like to ...* 340
Me parece... *I think ...* 86
Me resulta fácil/difícil... *I find it easy/difficult ...* 232
mecánico(a) *mechanical* 7
el/la **mecánico(a)** *mechanic* 233
el/la **mecenas** *patron* 31
la **medalla** *medal* 308
la **media** *average* 207
la **media jornada** *part-time* 248
mediano(a) *medium-sized* 37 *average* 374
mediante *through, by* 43
el **medicamento** *medicine (drug)* 204
la **medicina** *medicine (science)* 197 *medicine (drug)* 263
medicinal *medicinal* 192
médico(a) *medical* 10
el/la **médico(a)** *doctor* 8
el/la **médico(a) de familia** *family doctor* 204
la **medida** *measure* 199
medieval *medieval* 23
el **medio** *means* 68 *environment* 380
medio(a) *medium* 190 *half* 204
el **medio ambiente** *environment* 133
el **medio de transporte** *means of transport* 315
medioambiental *environmental* 133
los **medios de comunicación** *media* 96
medir (irreg. **i, i**) *to measure* 381
la **meditación** *meditation* 8
mediterráneo(a) *Mediterranean* 354
la **mejilla** *cheek* 87
mejor *better* 8
el/la **mejor** *best* 9
la **mejora** *improvement* 235
mejorar *to improve* 59
el **melón** *melon* 179
el **membrete** *letterhead* 275
memorable *memorable* 147
las **memorias** *memoirs* 45
memorizar *to memorize* 124
mencionar *to mention* 21
la **menina** *noble girl serving at court* 63
menonita *Mennonite* 57
menor *younger* 24 *little* 37 *lower* 254
el/la **menor** *youngest* 25
menos *less* 24 *least* 25

el **mensaje** *message* 109
mentir (irreg. **ie, i**) *to lie* 74
la **mentira** *lie* 55
¡Menudo(a)...! *What a ...!* 108
las **mercaderías** *goods* 319
el **mercadillo** *street market* 140
el **mercado** *market* 35
las **mercancías** *goods* 236
el **merengue** *merengue (dance)* 97
el **mes** *month* 6
la **mesa** *table* 34
el/la **mesero(a)** *waiter/waitress* 7
la **mesita de noche** *nightstand* 104
Mesoamérica *Central America* 85
el **mestizaje** *mix of races* 422
la **meta** *goal* 103
el **metal** *metal* 140
el **meteorito** *meteorite* 356
meteorológico(a) *meteorological* 356
meter *to put in* 51
meterse *to dive* 223
metódicamente *methodically* 104
metodista *Methodist* 424
el **metro** *meter* 7
mexicano(a) *Mexican* 38
la **mezcla** *mixture* 190
mezclar(se) *to mix* 38
mi, mis *my* 2
el **microondas** *microwave* 125
el **miedo** *fear* 50
el **miembro** *member* 40
mientras *while* 34 *meanwhile* 134
la **migración** *migration* 342
migrar *to migrate* 338
migratorio(a) *migratory* 350
miles *thousands* 110
milenario(a) *ancient* 84
militar *military* 164
la **milla** *mile* 196
el **millón** *million* 207
el/la **millonario(a)** *millionaire* 268
la **mina** *mine* 369
el **mineral** *mineral* 368
la **mineralización** *mineralization* 199
la **minería** *mining* 368
el/la **minero(a)** *miner* 442
la **minientrevista** *mini-interview* 29
el/la **ministro(a)** *minister* 410
la **minoría** *minority* 56
el **minuto** *minute* 49
mío, mía *mine* 22 *my* 36
míos, mías *my* 32 *mine* 36
la **mirada** *look* 320
mirar *to look (at)* 5
mirar fijamente (a) *to stare (at)* 320
el **mirto** *myrtle* 428
la **misión** *mission* 183
mismo(a) *same* 34
el **misterio** *mystery* 328
misterioso(a) *mysterious* 23

la **mitad** *half* 118
el **mito** *myth* 49
la **mitología** *mythology* 38
mixteco(a) *Mixtec* 66
la **mochila** *backpack* 22
la **moda** *fashion* 129
el **modelo** *model* 2
modernista *Art Nouveau (adjective)* 434
moderno(a) *modern* 5
la **modificación** *alteration* 143
modificar *to modify* 91 *to change* 167 *to alter* 382
el **modo** *mood* 84 *way* 340
mojado(a) *wet* 333
moler (irreg. **ue**) *to mill* 218
molestar *to bother* 258
el **molino** *mill* 218
el **momento** *moment* 2
la **monarquía** *monarchy* 410
el **monasterio** *monastery* 315
la **moneda** *coin* 71 *currency* 347
el/la **monitor(a)** *sports instructor* 194
el **mono** *monkey* 341
el **monopatín** *skateboard* 37
el **monstruo** *monster* 55
la **montaña** *mountain* 6 *mountains* 34
montañoso(a) *mountainous* 347
montar *to ride* 71 *to put up* 173
el **monte** *forest* 428
(un) montón *a lot* 155
el **monumento** *monument* 363
moreno(a) *tanned* 6 *dark* 17
morir (irreg.) *to die* 38
el **mosquetero** *musketeer* 75
la **mostaza** *mustard* 179
el **mostrador** *counter* 314
mostrar (irreg. **ue**) *to show* 21
motivado(a) *motivated* 281
motivar *to cause* 42 *to motivate* 329
el **motivo** *motive* 26 *reason* 383 *motif* 389
la **moto** *motorbike* 196
la **motocicleta** *motorbike* 252
el **motor** *motor* 206
mover (irreg. **ue**) *to move* 92
el **movimiento** *movement* 388
el/la **muchacho(a)** *boy/girl* 320
mucho *a lot* 3
mucho(a) *a lot of* 8
Mucho gusto. *Pleased to meet you.* 71
muchos(as) *many* XXVI
mudarse *to move* 209
mudo(a) *mute* 99
los **muebles** *furniture* 125
la **muerte** *death* 44
muerto(a) *dead* 26
la **muestra** *proof* 253
la **mujer** *woman* 5
la **multa** *fine (monetary)* 370

multicultural *multicultural* 422
la **multiculturalidad** *multiculturalism* 421
multinacional *multinational* 408
multipartidario(a) *multiparty* 418
multirracial *multiracial* 56
la **multitud** *crowd* 110
mundial *world (adjective)* 18
el **mundo** *world* XXVI
municipal *municipal* 302
la **muñeca** *wrist* 209
el/la **muñeco(a)** *doll* 158
el/la **muralista** *muralist* 38
la **muralla** *wall* 165
el **músculo** *muscle* 206
el **museo** *museum* 35
el **musgo** *moss* 380
la **música** *music* 63
musical *musical (adjective)* 57
el **musical** *musical* 290
la **musicalidad** *musicality* 113
el/la **músico(a)** *musician* 63
mutuo(a) *mutual* 408
muy *very* XXVI
muy hecho(a) *well done* 182
Muy señor(a) mío(a)... *Dear Sir/ Madam ...* 275

nacer (irreg.) *to be born* 44
el **nacimiento** *birth* 44
la **nación** *nation* 25
nacional *national* 28 *domestic* 247
la **nacionalidad** *nationality* 75
nada *nothing* 28
el/la **nadador(a)** *swimmer* 302
nadar *to swim* 7
nadie *nobody* 80
los **naipes** *playing cards* 71
la **narración** *story* 13
narrar *to tell, to narrate* 13
narrativo(a) *narrative* 328
la **natación** *swimming* 302
nativo(a) *native* 139
nato(a) *born* 254
natural *natural* 140
la **naturaleza** *nature* 254
la **navegación a vela** *sailing* 193
el/la **navegante** *sailor* 302
navegar por Internet *to surf the Internet* 248
la **Navidad** *Christmas* 35
necesariamente *necessarily* 192
necesario(a) *necessary* 59
la **necesidad** *necessity* 67 *need* 212
necesitado(a) *needy* 259
necesitar *to need* 11
la **necrópolis** *necropolis* 435
negativamente *negatively* 146
negativo(a) *negative* 19
negociable *negotiable* 247

la **negociación** negotiation 241

el **negocio** business 18

la **negrita** bold 92

negro(a) black 18

neoyorquino(a) New York (adjective) 244

nervioso(a) nervous 17

neutro(a) neutral 170

la **nevada** snowfall 356

nevar (irreg. **ie**) to snow 341

ni nor/or 183 not even, not a single ... 266

el/la **nieto(a)** grandson/daughter 17

la **nieve** snow 47

ningún, ninguno(a) (not) any 138 none 269

la **niñez** childhood 44

el/la **niño(a)** child 18

el **nivel** level 199

el **nivel del mar** sea level 146

no no XXVI not 2

No es de extrañar que... It is not surprising ... 362

No me apetece. I don't feel like it. 86

la **noche** night, evening 7

la **Nochebuena** Christmas Eve 35

nombrar to appoint 31 to mention 188 to name 387

el **nombre** name 17 noun 38

nominado(a) nominated 289

el **nopal** prickly pear cactus 411

la **norma** rule, norm 422

normal normal 7

normalmente normally 48

el **norte** North 192

norteamericano(a) North American 244

nos (to) us 76 ourselves 78

nosotros(as) us XXVI we 2

la **nota** grade 10 note 49

la **noticia** news 19

el **noticiero** news (program) 249

la **novela** novel 23

noveno(a) ninth 425

el/la **novio(a)** boyfriend/girlfriend 32

la **nube** cloud 356

nublado(a) cloudy 341

nublarse to cloud over 356

nuboso(a) cloudy 356

la **nuera** daughter-in-law 32

nuestro(a) our 11

el/la **nuestro(a)** ours 291

nuevo(a) new XXVI

la **numeración** numerals 403

el **número** number 10 shoe size 128

numeroso(a) numerous 56 large 158

nunca never 38

la **nutrición** nutrition 174

el **nutriente** nutrient 218

nutritivo(a) nutritional 182

O

el **objetivo** aim, objective 92

el **objeto** object 37

el **objeto directo** direct object 66

la **obligación** obligation 67

obligar to force 308

obligatorio(a) compulsory 333

la **obra** work 41

la **obra benéfica** charity work 265

la **obra teatral** play 430

el/la **obrero(a)** (blue collar) worker 236

el/la **observador(a)** observer 254

observar to watch 5

el **observatorio** observatory 354

la **obsesión** obsession 38

el **obstáculo** obstacle 265

obtener (irreg.) to obtain 172

obviamente obviously 200

obvio(a) obvious 238

la **ocasión** occasion 68 chance 68

occidental Western 408

el **océano** ocean 193

el **ocelote** ocelot 381

el **ocio** leisure 282

el/la **oculista** ophthalmologist 206

ocupado(a) busy 86

ocupar to occupy 91 to hold 406

ocuparse de (hacer) algo to deal with (doing) something 312

ocurrir to happen 5

odiar to hate 169

odiarse to hate each other 78

el **odio** hate 81

el **oeste** West 193

la **oferta** offer 128 bargain 209 vacancy 246

oficial official 419

la **oficina** office 117

el **oficio** job, profession 152

ofrecer (irreg.) to offer 50 to offer up 73

¡Oh! Oh! 394

el **oído** ear 209

oír (irreg.) to listen 26 to hear 28

ojalá... I hope... 16

el **ojo** eye 20

la **ola** wave 193

el **oleaje** swell 380

olímpico(a) Olympic 305

la **olla a presión** pressure cooker 352

el **olor** smell 383

olvidar(se) to forget 59

el **olvido** oblivion 80

el **ombligo** navel 50

la **ONG** NGO 230

opaco(a) opaque 374

la **opción** option 19

opcional optional 364

la **ópera** opera 290

opinar to think 7

la **opinión** opinion 1

la **oportunidad** opportunity 427

el/la **opresor(a)** oppressor 374

optar a to apply for 271

optimista optimistic 17

la **oración** sentence 2

oral oral 328

el **orden** order (arrangement) 51

la **orden** order (command) 1

la **ordenanza** regulation 164

ordenar to order 4

el **orégano** oregano 190

orgánico(a) organic 372

el **organismo** organization 273

la **organización** organization 260

la **organización no gubernamental** non-governmental organization 230

organizado(a) organized 248

el/la **organizador(a)** organizer 284

organizar to organize 16

el **órgano** organ 206

la **orientación** guidance 422

orientado(a) a aimed at 247

oriental Eastern 381

el **origen** origin 35

original original 83

originalmente originally 181

originario(a) originally 93

originarse to originate 43

el **oro** gold 368

la **orquesta** orchestra 63

la **orquesta sinfónica** symphony orchestra 416

la **orquídea** orchid 347

la **ortografía** spelling 99

ortográfico(a) spelling (adjective) 167

os (to) you (plural, informal) 76 yourselves (informal) 78

oscurecerse (irreg.) to grow dark 374

oscuro(a) dark 112

el **oso** bear 291

ostensible evident 320

el **otoño** fall, autumn 319

otra vez again 21

otro(a) other XXVI another 5

ovalado(a) oval 140

la **oveja** sheep 91

el **oxígeno** oxygen 206

P

paciente patient (adjective) 236

el/la **paciente** patient 206

pacífico(a) peaceful 235

el **padrastro** stepfather 32

el **padre** father 5

los **padres** parents 9

el **padrino** godfather 32

la **paella** paella 196

pagar to pay 145

la **página** page 14

el **país** country XXVI

el **pimentón** *paprika* 190
la **pimienta** *pepper (spice)* 180
el **pimiento** *pepper (vegetable)* 188
pinchar *to click* 419
el **pingüino** *penguin* 380
pintar *to paint* 152
el/la **pintor(a)** *painter* 30 *house painter* 152
la **pintura** *painting* 39
la **piña** *pineapple* 179
la **pirámide** *pyramid* 6
el/la **pirata** *pirate* 393
la **piscina** *swimming pool* 200
el **piso** *floor* 158
la **pista** *clue* 26 *track* 302
el **plan** *plan* 96
la **plancha** *iron* 125
planchar *to iron* 152
planear *to plan* 97
el **planeta** *planet* 18
planificar *to plan* 165
el **plano** *floor plan* 125 *map* 165
plano(a) *low-heeled* 128
la **planta** *plant* 155
la **plantación** *plantation* 345
plantar *to plant* 212
plantear *to pose* 55
plasmar *to reflect* 301
el **plástico** *plastic* 140
la **plastilina** *modeling clay* 158
la **plata** *silver* 368
el **plátano** *banana* 181
el **plato** *plate* 91 *dish* 94
platónico(a) *platonic* 298
la **playa** *beach* 6
la **plaza** *square* 28 *seat* 314
el/la **plomero(a)** *plumber* 152
el **plomo** *lead* 368
la **pluma** *feather* 347
el **plumaje** *plumage* 347
plural *plural* 78
la **pluralidad** *plurality* 422
el **pluscuamperfecto** *past perfect* 121
la **población** *population* 56
el/la **poblador(a)** *inhabitant* 398
poblar (irreg. **ue**) *to populate* 158
Pobrecito(a). *Poor thing.* 342
los **pobres** *the poor* 25
la **pobreza** *poverty* 50
poco *little* 26
poco(a)(os)(as) *some, few* 142
poco a poco *little by little* 53
poco hecho(a) *underdone* 182
poder (irreg. **ue, u**) *to be able* XXVI *to succeed* 46
el **poder** *power* 410
poderoso(a) *powerful* 368
el **poema** *poem* 77
la **poesía** *poetry* 75
el/la **poeta** *poet* 80
la **poetisa** *poet (female)* 113
el/la **policía** *policeman/policewoman* 233

la **policía** *police force* 29
el **poliéster** *polyester* 128
la **polio** *polio* 38
la **política** *politics* 19
político(a) *in-law* 32 *political* 242
el/la **político(a)** *politician* 22
el **pollo** *chicken* 183
poner (irreg.) *to put* 6 *to put on* 153 *to show* 288
poner en marcha *to launch* 277
poner fin a *to put an end to* 398
ponerse (irreg.) *to wear* 9 *to get, to become* 74 *to put on* 128
ponerse al teléfono *to answer the phone* 98
ponerse en contacto con *to get in touch with* 124
popular *popular* 28
popularizar *to popularize* 21
(un) poquito *a little bit* 180
por *in* 2 *for* 5 *around* 6 *because of* 19 *by* 21
por ejemplo *for example* 31
por ello *for that reason* 369
por encima *over* 361
por encima de *rather than* 406
Por eso... *Therefore ...* 383
Por esta razón... *For this reason ...* 167
Por este motivo... *For this reason ...* 383
por favor *please* 72
por fin *finally* 45
por lo general *in general* 35
por lo menos *at least* 9
por qué *why* 10
¿Por qué no? *Why not?* 86
Por supuesto. *Of course.* 1
Por tanto... *So ...* 383
por turnos *in turns* 9
por último *finally* 14
la **porción** *portion* 221
porque *because* 5
el **porqué** *reason* 254
poseer (irreg.) *to have* 82
la **posesión** *possession, ownership* 12
el **posesivo** *possessive* 36
la **posibilidad** *possibility* 236
posible *possible* 95
la **posición** *position* 76
positivo(a) *positive* 8
el **poste** *post* 327
el **póster** *poster* 40
el **postgrado** *postgraduate studies* 272
el **potencial** *potential* 382
la **poza** *pool* 193
la **práctica** *practice* 193
practicar *to practice* 8 *to play* 35
práctico(a) *practical, useful* 140
precalentar (irreg. **ie**) *to pre-heat* 352
precedido(a) *preceded* 200

preciado(a) *highly valued* 212
el **precio** *price* 143
precisamente *in fact* 253 *precisely* 308
preciso(a) *necessary* 198
precocinado(a) *pre-cooked* 185
precolombino(a) *pre-Columbian* 93
predecir (irreg.) *to forecast* 362
la **predicción** *forecast* 364
predominar *to prevail* 92
la **preferencia** *preference* 1
preferible *preferable* 257
preferido(a) *favorite* 107
preferir (irreg. **ie, i**) *to prefer* 34
el **prefijo** *prefix* 92
la **pregunta** *question* 7
preguntar *to ask* 5
preguntarse *to wonder* 254
prehispánico(a) *pre-Hispanic* 85
premiar *to award a prize to* 378
el **premio** *prize* 44
la **prenda (de vestir)** *garment* 125
prender *to arrest* 443
la **prensa** *press* 378
preocupado(a) *worried* 18
preocupar(se) *to worry* 68
la **preparación** *preparation* 179 *training* 301
preparado(a) *ready* 230
preparar *to prepare* 34
prepararse *to get ready* 83 *to train* 300
los **preparativos** *preparations* 313
la **preposición** *preposition* 36
la **presencia** *presence* 57
la **presentación** *presentation* 40 *introduction* 66
el/la **presentador(a)** *presenter* 249
presentar *to present* 11 *to introduce* 20 *to depict* 33
presentarse a *to go in for* 82
el **presente** *present* 1
el **presente continuo** *present progressive* 1
el **presente perfecto** *present perfect* 120
preservar *to preserve* 373
presidencial *presidential* 12
el/la **presidente(a)** *president* 236
la **presión** *pressure* 201
prestar *to pay* 167 *to lend* 242
el **prestigio** *prestige* 272
prestigioso(a) *prestigious* 244
el **pretérito** *preterite, past tense* 1
prevenir (irreg.) *to prevent* 197
previsto(a) *planned* 298
la **primavera** *spring* 136
primer(o)(a) *first* 2
el/la **primo(a)** *cousin* 17
la **princesa** *princess* 410
principal *main* 21

principalmente   *mainly* 91

el   **príncipe**   *prince* 410

el   **principio**   *beginning* 21

la   **prisa**   *haste* 318

la   **prisión**   *prison* 83

privado(a)   *private* 422

la   **probabilidad**   *likelihood* 282

probable   *likely* 234

probablemente   *probably* 147

el   **probador**   *fitting room* 129

probar (irreg. **ue**)   *to try, to taste* 176

probarse (irreg. **ue**)   *to try on* 129

el   **problema**   *problem* 7

la   **procedencia**   *origin* 56

procedente de   *coming from* 57

proceder de   *to come from* 56

el   **proceso**   *process* 221

procurar   *to try* 443

la   **producción**   *production* 219

producir (irreg.)   *to produce* 171

el   **producto**   *product* 141

productor(a)   *producing* 345

el/la   **productor(a)**   *producer* 367

la   **profesión**   *profession* 187

profesional   *professional* 88

el/la   **profesor(a)**   *teacher* 22

profundamente   *deeply* 194

profundizar   *to go into depth* 173

el   **programa**   *program* 25

la   **programación**   *programs* 253 *program* 430

el/la   **programador(a) informático(a)**   *programmer* 236

el   **progreso**   *progress* 361

prohibir   *to forbid* 144

el   **promedio**   *average* 10

prometer   *to promise* 47

prometido(a)   *engaged* 32

la   **promoción**   *promotion* 288

promocionar   *to promote* 68

promover (irreg. **ue**)   *to promote* 96 *to bring about* 353

el   **pronombre**   *pronoun* 36

pronominal   *pronominal* 66

pronto   *soon* 73 *quickly* 84

la   **propiedad**   *property* 183

la   **propina**   *tip* 225

propio(a)   *own* XXVI *himself* 73 *typical* 153

proponer (irreg.)   *to suggest, to propose* 15

la   **proporción**   *proportion* 191

proporcionar   *to provide* 164

el   **propósito**   *purpose* 274

la   **propuesta**   *suggestion, proposal* 86

la   **prórroga**   *overtime* 303

los   **pros y contras**   *the pros and cons* 331

el/la   **protagonista**   *main character* 290

protagonizar   *to star in* 296

la   **protección**   *protection* 280

proteger   *to protect* 260

la   **proteína**   *protein* 182

la   **protesta**   *protest* 242

proveniente de   *coming from* 378

provenir de (irreg.)   *to come from* 189

la   **provincia**   *province* 381

provocar   *to cause* 371

próximo(a)   *next* 94

la   **proyección**   *screening* 118

proyectar   *to screen* 119

el   **proyecto**   *project* XXVI

la   **prueba**   *test* 186

la   **Psicología**   *psychology* 215

el/la   **psicólogo(a)**   *psychologist* 206

públicamente   *publicly* 410

publicar   *to post* 85 *to publish* 215

la   **publicidad**   *advertising* 33 *publicity* 99

publicitario(a)   *advertising (adjective)* 195

el   **público**   *audience* 290

público(a)   *public* 422

el   **pueblo**   *village, town* 21 *people* 56

¿Puedo hablar con...?   *May I speak with ...?* 98

la   **puerta**   *gate* 2 *door* 22

el   **puerto deportivo**   *marina* 435

puertorriqueño(a)   *Puerto Rican* 44

pues   *well* XXVI

el   **puesto**   *stall* 140 *place* 237 *post* 244

el   **pulmón**   *lung* 206

la   **pulsera**   *bracelet* 145

el   **punto**   *point* 58

el   **punto de partida**   *starting point* 328

el   **punto de vista**   *point of view* 159

la   **puntuación**   *punctuation* 65

puntual   *punctual* 117

el   **puñal**   *dagger* 428

la   **pupila**   *pupil* 77

la   **pureza**   *purity* 136

puro(a)   *pure* 349

que   *that* XXVI *than* 18 *who* 19

qué   *what* 2 *how* 6

¡Qué bien!   *Great!* 6

¡Qué le vamos a hacer!   *Never mind!* 394

¡Que se diviertan!   *Enjoy yourselves!* 16

¡Qué suerte!   *How lucky!* 37

¿Qué tal (estás)?   *How are you?* 35

¿Qué tal así?   *What about this?* 95

¿Qué tal se te da...?   *Are you any good at ...?* 178

¡Qué va!   *Not at all!* 286

quechua   *Quechuan* 50

quedar   *to remain* 47 *to arrange to meet* 90 *to be left* 100 *to suit* 126 *to look* 138 *to turn out* 188

quedarse   *to stay* 50 *to go* 186

quedarse sin saldo   *to run out of minutes* 98

quejarse   *to complain* 291

quemar   *to burn* 368

querer (irreg.)   *to want* 6 *to love* 74

querer decir   *to mean* XXVI

quererse (irreg.)   *to love each other* 78

Querido(a)...   *Dear ...* 74

el   **queso**   *cheese* 72

el   **quetzal**   *quetzal* 347

quien   *whom* 109

quién   *who* 6

quieto(a)   *still* 20

la   **Química**   *chemistry* 215

la   **quinceañera**   *celebration of a girl's fifteenth birthday in parts of Latin America* 61

quinto(a)   *fifth* 136

la   **quinua**   *quinoa (grain)* 183

el   **quiosco**   *stand, kiosk* 170

quitar   *to remove* 134

quitarse   *to take off* 128

quizá(s)   *maybe* 137

R

el   **rabillo (del ojo)**   *corner (of the eye)* 320

la   **radio**   *radio* 19

radiofónico(a)   *radio (adjective)* 401

la   **radiografía**   *X-ray* 206

la   **ráfaga**   *burst* 266

la   **raíz**   *root* 212

rallar   *to grate* 221

la   **rambla**   *boulevard* 435

el   **ramo**   *bunch* 83 *bouquet* 333

el   **rancho**   *ranch* 242

rápidamente   *quickly* 4

rápido   *fast* 24 *quickly* 253

rápido(a)   *fast (adjective)* 155

la   **raqueta**   *racket* 287

el   **rascacielos**   *skyscraper* 435

el   **rasgo**   *trait* 12 *feature* 20

el   **ratón**   *mouse* 248

la   **raya**   *stripe* 129 *line* 403

la   **razón**   *reason* 92

razonable   *reasonable* 192

el   **razonamiento**   *reasoning* 254

la   **reacción**   *reaction* 70

reaccionar   *to react* 232

el   **reactor**   *jet plane* 254

real   *real* 43 *royal* 273

la   **realidad**   *reality* 33

realista   *realistic* 328

realizar   *to carry out* 14 *to perform* 72 *to make* 133 *to organize* 308 *to implement* 406

realmente   *really* 191

rebajado(a)   *reduced* 129

rebelarse   *to rebel* 19

recargar *to charge* 99
recaudar *to collect* 261
el/la **recepcionista** *receptionist* 233
el/la **receptor(a)** *recipient* 436
la **receta** *recipe* 118 *prescription* 207
recetar *to prescribe* 206
rechazar *to reject* 410
recibir *to receive* 4 *to have* 193 *to be awarded* 272
reciclable *recyclable* 133
el **reciclaje** *recycling* 133
reciclar *to recycle* 344
recién nacido(a) *newborn* 52
reciente *recent* 120
recíproco(a) *reciprocal* 66
el **recital** *recital* 417
recitar *to recite* 374
la **reclamación** *complaint* 274
el **recogedor** *dustpan* 152
recoger *to pick up* 5 *to gather* 226
recomendable *advisable* 226
la **recomendación** *recommendation* 1
recomendar (irreg. **ie**) *to recommend* 210
reconciliarse *to make up* 74
reconocer (irreg.) *to admit* 254 *to recognize* 362
reconstruir (irreg.) *to reconstruct* 398
la **recopilación** *compilation* 293 *collection* 417
recordar (irreg. **ue**) *to remember* 47 *to remind* 244
recorrer *to travel through* 319
el **recorrido** *route* 303
recortar *to cut out* 159
recrear *to recreate* 347
rectangular *rectangular* 140
recto(a) *straight* 164
el/la **rector(a)** *president* 272
el **recuerdo** *memory* 41 *souvenir* 171 *remembrance* 237
recuperarse *to recover* 38
el **recurso** *means* 113 *resource* 205
los **recursos naturales** *natural resources* 344
la **red** *network* 58 *Internet* 350
la **red social** *social network* 54
la **redacción** *wording* 113
redactar *to write* 59
redondo(a) *round* 140
reducir (irreg.) *to reduce* 182
la **redundancia** *redundancy* 329
reelegir (irreg.) *to re-elect* 418
reescribir (irreg.) *to rewrite* 59
el **referente** *reference* 421
referirse a (irreg. **ie, i**) *to refer to* 228
reflejar *to show* 21 *to reflect* 30
reflexionar *to think* 291
reflexivo(a) *reflexive* 66
reforzar (irreg. **ue**) *to strengthen* 110
el **refresco** *soft drink* 90

el **refrigerador** *refrigerator* 125
el **refugio** *shelter* 353
regalar *to give as a present* 64
el **regalo** *present* 76
la **regata** *boat race* 302
regatear *to bargain* 145
la **región** *region* 97
regional *regional* 120
el **registro** *register* 104
la **regla** *rule* 84
el **regreso** *return* 212
regular *regular* 1 *to control* 211
la **reina** *queen* 410
el **reinado** *reign* 442
reinventarse *to reinvent oneself* 434
reír(se) (irreg. **i**) *to laugh* 20
la **relación** *relationship* 8
la **relación amorosa** *love affair* 52
relacionado(a) *related* 74
relacionar *to link* 16
la **relajación** *relaxation* 8
relajarse *to relax* 194
el **relámpago** *lightning* 341
relativamente *relatively* 164
el **relativo** *relative* 228
relativo(a) a *relating to* 242
el **relato** *story* XXVI
el **relax** *relaxation* 322
relevante *important* 419
la **religión** *religion* 44
religioso(a) *religious* 35
rellenar *to fill in* 247
el **reloj** *watch* 22
el **remedio** *remedy* 197
el **remo** *rowing* 302
remover (irreg. **ue**) *to stir* 221
la **rendija** *crack* 266
rendirse (irreg. **i**) *to give up* 230
reordenar *to restructure* 435
la **reparación** *repair* 253
reparar *to repair, to fix* 152
repartir *to distribute* 227
repasar *to revise* 1
el **repaso** *revision* 60
el **repertorio** *repertoire* 298
la **repetición** *repetition* 429
repetir (irreg. **i, i**) *to repeat* 22
el **repique** *ringing* 111
reponerse (irreg.) *to compose oneself* 104
el **reportaje** *report* 52
la **representación** *performance* 293
el/la **representante** *representative* 410
representativo(a) *representative* 101
el **reproductor** *player* 103
el **reproductor de CD** *CD player* 248
el **reptil** *reptile* 344
la **república** *republic* 410
republicano(a) *republican* 410

requerir (irreg. **ie**) *to require* 185
el **requisito** *requirement* 257
la **res** *beef* 181
rescatar *to rescue* 83
el **rescate** *rescue* 442
reseco(a) *very dry* 321
la **reseña** *profile* 11
la **reserva** *reservation* 314
reservado(a) *shy* 20
reservar *to book* 164
la **residencia** *residence* 164
la **resignación** *resignation* 394
resignado(a) *resigned* 394
la **resistencia** *stamina* 92
resolver (irreg.) *to solve* 55
respecto a *compared to* 417
respetado(a) *respected* 416
respetar *to respect* 74
el **respeto** *respect* 422
respirar *to breathe* 194
respiratorio(a) *respiratory* 376
responder *to answer* 15
la **responsabilidad** *responsibility* 239
responsable *responsible* 248
la **respuesta** *answer* 3
el **restaurante** *restaurant* 7
restaurar *to restore* 398
el **resto** *rest* 50
los **restos** *remnants* 380
el **resultado** *result* 56 *score* 331
el **resumen** *summary* 39
resumir *to summarize* 39
retirarse *to withdraw* 298
retomar *to take up again* 308
retrasado(a) *delayed* 320
el **retraso** *delay* 314
retratar *to portray* 55
el **retrato** *portrait* 29
el **retrato robot** *police sketch* 29
la **reunión** *meeting* 86
reunir *to gather* 172
reunirse *to meet* 35
reutilizable *reusable* 352
reutilizar *to reuse* 347
revelar *to reveal* 254
revisar *to check* 59
la **revisión (médica)** *medical checkup* 206
la **revista** *magazine* 172
revolucionar *to revolutionize* 211
revolucionario(a) *revolutionary* 211
el **rey** *king* 410
los **Reyes Magos** *the three wise men* 158
rico(a) *rich* 25
el **riego** *irrigation* 301
el **riesgo** *risk* 307
la **rima** *rhyme* 77
rimar *to rhyme* 113
el **riñón** *kidney* 207
el **río** *river* 43
la **riqueza** *richness* 406 *wealth* 411

U

V

las **vacaciones** *vacation* 6

el **vagón** *train car* 321

Vale. *OK.* 86

valer (irreg.) *to cost* 102

valer la pena *to be worthwhile* 7

valerse de (irreg.) *to make use of* 374

valiente *brave* 43

valioso(a) *valuable* 220

el **valle** *valley* 51

el **vallenato** *Colombian music style* 119

el **valor** *courage* 111 *value* 422

la **valoración** *value statement* 174

valorar *to make value statements* 70

Vámonos. *Let's go.* 90

el **vapor** *steam* 199

variado(a) *varied* 298

la **variante** *variation* 181

variar *to vary* 127

la **variedad** *variety* 92

varios(as) *several* 27

el/la **vecino(a)** *neighbor* 18 *inhabitant* 164

la **vegetación** *vegetation* 342

vegetal *plant (adjective)* 347

vegetariano(a) *vegetarian* 182

vehemente *vehement* 374

la **vejez** *old age* 44

la **vela** *sailing* 302

la **velocidad** *speed* 308

el/la **vendedor(a)** *sales clerk* 131 *salesperson* 250

el/la **vendedor(a) ambulante** *peddler* 405

vender *to sell* 100

el **veneno** *poison* 428

venerar *to worship* 212

venezolano(a) *Venezuelan* 129

venir (irreg.) *to come* 6

la **venta** *sale* 106

la **ventaja** *advantage* 31

la **ventanilla** *ticket counter* 320

la **ventilación** *ventilation* 164

ver (irreg.) *to watch (television)* 3 *to see* 34

el **verano** *summer* 6

verbal *verbal* 42

el **verbo** *verb* 1

la **verdad** *truth* 46

… **¿verdad?** *… isn't it?/really?/etc.* 16

verdaderamente *truly* 422

verdadero(a) *true* 74

verde *green* 136

verdoso(a) *greenish* 140

la **verdura** *vegetables* 8

verse (irreg.) *to see each other* 78

la **versión** *version* 139

el **verso** *line (of poetry)* 83

vertical *vertical* 411

el **vestíbulo** *hall* 158

el **vestido** *dress* 22

la **vestimenta** *clothes* 127

vestirse (irreg. **i, i**) *to dress* 25 *to get dressed* 78

el/la **veterinario(a)** *veterinarian* 233

la **vez** *time* 5

viajar *to travel* XXVI

el **viaje** *journey* 6 *travel* 42

el **viaje de negocios** *business trip* 314

el **viaje de placer** *personal trip* 314

el **viaje organizado** *package tour* 314

el/la **viajero(a)** *traveler* 146

el/la **vicepresidente(a)** *vice-president* 410

la **victoria** *victory* 302

victorioso(a) *victorious* 47

la **vida** *life* 35

el **video** *video* 40

el **videojuego** *videogame* 55

el **vidrio** *glass* 344

viejo(a) *old* 53

el **viento** *wind* 193

el **viernes** *Friday* 94

la **Villa Olímpica** *Olympic Village* 435

el **vinagre** *vinegar* 179

la **viñeta** *cartoon frame* 29

la **violencia** *violence* 242

la **violeta** *violet* 83

el **virrey** *viceroy* 164

virtual *virtual* 173

la **visa** *visa* 314

el **visado** *visa* 312

visible *visible* 434

la **visita** *visit* 153

el/la **visitante** *visitor* 157

visitar *to visit* 5

la **vista** *view* 193

vistoso(a) *colorful* 135

visual *visual* 134

vital *vital* 61

la **vitamina** *vitamin* 182

el/la **viudo(a)** *widower/widow* 32

la **vivienda** *home* 120

viviente *living* 344

vivir *to live* XXVI

vivo(a) *alive* 166

la **vocal** *vowel* 99

volar (irreg. **ue**) *to fly* 265

el **volcán** *volcano* 47

volcánico(a) *volcanic* 380

el **voleibol** *volleyball* 85

el **volumen** *volume* 104

el **voluntariado** *volunteer work* XXVI

el/la **voluntario(a)** *volunteer* 260

volver (irreg.) *to come back* 23 *to return* 47

volver a hacer algo *to do something again* 2

volverse (irreg.) *to go* 23 *to become* 186

vosotros(as) *you* 76

la **votación** *vote* 410

votar *to vote* 410

el **voto** *vote* 418

la **voz** *voice* 100

el **vuelo** *flight* 314

el **vuelo directo** *direct flight* 314

el **vuelo nacional** *domestic flight* 314

la **vuelta** *return* 314

vuestro(a) *your* 36

el/la **vuestro(a)** *yours* 36

la **wiphala** *Andean indigenous flag* 120

y *and* XXVI

ya *already* XXVI *now* 18

ya no *not any more* 75

ya que *since* 85

el **yacimiento** *site* 402

la **yerbabuena** *peppermint* 428

el **yerno** *son-in-law* 32

yo *I* 2

Yo no. *I don't.* 286

Yo sí. *I do.* 286

el **yoga** *yoga* 194

la **yuca** *cassava* 219

la **zanahoria** *carrot* 181

la **zapatilla** *slipper* 125

el **zapato de tacón** *high-heeled shoe* 128

zaragozano(a) *from Zaragoza (Spain)* 254

el **Zócalo** *main square of Mexico City* 110

la **zona** *zone* 43

GLOSARIO INGLÉS-ESPAÑOL

A

a *un, una* XXVI
a little bit *un poquito* 180
a lot *mucho* 3 *un montón* 155
a lot of *mucho(a)* 8
to **abbreviate** *abreviar* 99
abbreviation *la abreviatura* 99 *las siglas* 393
ability *la capacidad* 326
about *de* 1 *sobre* 1 *acerca de* 301
about it *al respecto* 135
above *anterior* 4
above all *sobre todo* 77
abroad *al extranjero* 209 *en el extranjero* 94 *en el exterior* 315
Absolutely (true). *En absoluto.* 286
abundant *abundante* 345
abundantly *abundantemente* 218
academic *el/la académico(a)* 378
academic *académico(a)* 273
academic year *el curso* 352
to **accept** *aceptar* 52
access *el acceso* 96
accessories *los complementos* 125
accessory *el accesorio* 125
accident *el accidente* 5
accommodation *el alojamiento* 202
accompaniment (with food) *el acompañamiento* 188
according to *según* 29
accountant *el/la contador(a)* 236
accounting *la contabilidad* 253
to **achieve** *conseguir (irreg. i, i)* 103 *lograr* 241
achievement *el logro* 404
acrobat *el/la saltimbanqui* 55
acronym *las siglas* 393
action *el hecho* 1 *la acción* 11
action film *la película de acción* 290
active *activo(a)* 281
actively *activamente* 231
activity *la actividad* 3
actor *el actor* 26
actress *la actriz* 29
acupuncture *la acupuntura* 197
acute *agudo(a)* 303
ad *el anuncio* 100
to **adapt** *adaptar* 55
adaptation *la adaptación* 163
to **add** *añadir* 17 *incorporar* 59 *agregar* 167
additional *adicional* 173
address *el domicilio* 10 *la dirección* 90
to **address** *dirigirse a* 185
addressee *el/la destinatario(a)* 274
adjective *el adjetivo* 24
administrative *administrativo(a)* 165
to **admire** *admirar* 157
to **admit** *reconocer (irreg.)* 254

adolescence *la adolescencia* 44
adolescent *el/la adolescente* 39
to **adopt** *adoptar* 403
adopted *adoptivo(a)* 32
adoption *la adopción* 254
to **adore** *adorar* 213
adult *el/la adulto(a)* 19
adulthood *la madurez* 44
advance *el avance* 398
advanced *avanzado(a)* 56
advantage *la ventaja* 31
adventure film *la película de aventura* 290
adventurous *aventurero(a)* 322
advertising *la publicidad* 33
advertising (adjective) *publicitario(a)* 195
advice *el consejo* 8
advice column *el consultorio* 185
advisable *aconsejable, conveniente* 198 *recomendable* 226
to **advise** *aconsejar* 210
aeronautical engineer *el/la ingeniero(a) aeronáutico(a)* 254
affair *el asunto* 328
to **affect** (badly) *afectar* 243
affectionate *cariñoso(a)* 20 *amoroso(a)* 320
Affectionately, *Afectuosamente,* 275
African-American *afroamericano(a)* 57
Afro-Latino *afrolatino(a)* 101
after *después de* 21
afternoon *la tarde* 5
again *otra vez* 21 *de nuevo* 51
against *contra* 19
age *la edad* 94
agent *el/la agente* 252
aggressive *agresivo(a)* 29
... ago *hace...* 42
to **agree** *estar de acuerdo* 22 *acordar (irreg. ue)* 90
agreement (in grammar) *la concordancia* 252
agricultural *agrícola* 143
agriculture *la agricultura* 368
aid worker *el/la cooperante* 260
aim *el objetivo* 92
aimed at *orientado(a) a* 247 *destinado(a) a* 378
air *el aire* 341
Air Force *el ejército del aire* 254
airline *la línea aérea* 314
airplane *el avión* 145
airport *el aeropuerto* 233
aisle *el pasillo* 290
alarm clock *el despertador* 5
albino *albino(a)* 401
album *el álbum* 64
alive *vivo(a)* 166
all *todo(a), todos(as)* 34
allergy *la alergia* 211
to **allow** *permitir* 86

almond-shaped *almendrado(a)* 20
almost *casi* 43
alone *solo(a)* 200
aloof *distante* 33
alpaca *la alpaca* 126
already *ya* XXVI
alright *bueno* 26
also *también* XXVI *además* 72
altar *el altar* 374
to **alter** *alterar* 380 *modificar* 382
alteration *la modificación* 143
alternately *alternativamente* 320
alternative energy *la energía alternativa* 344
although *aunque* 87 *a pesar de que* 264
altitude *la altitud* 7
always *siempre* 18
amazing *impresionante* 7
Amazon (adjective) *amazónico(a)* 260
ambitious *ambicioso(a)* 248
American *estadounidense* 21 *americano(a)* 57
Amerindian *amerindio(a)* 38
amino acid *el aminoácido* 183
among *entre* 38
amount *la cantidad* 220
amphibian *el anfibio* 344
amusement park *el parque de atracciones* 328
an *un, una* XXVI
to **analyze** *analizar* 59
anatomy *la anatomía* 206
ancestor *el antepasado* 40
ancient *antiguo(a)* 43 *milenario(a)* 84
ancient times *la antigüedad* 56
and *y* XXVI
Andalusian *andaluz(a)* 155
Andean *andino(a)* 131
angelic *angelical* 321
anger *la ira* 321
to **anger** *enojar* 262
angle *el ángulo* 303
angry *enojado(a)* 19 *bravo(a)* 193
anguished *angustiado(a)* 104
animal *el animal* 212
animated film *la película de dibujos animados* 290
animation *la animación* 288
ankle *el tobillo* 211
anniversary *el aniversario* 44
to **announce** *anunciar* 52
announcement *el anuncio* 69
annoyance *el fastidio* 320
annoyed *fastidiado(a)* 320
annual *anual* 362
annually *anualmente* 373
another *otro(a)* 5
answer *la respuesta* 3
to **answer** *responder* 15 *contestar* 33
to **answer the phone** *ponerse al teléfono* 98

answering machine *el contestador* 104

ant *la hormiga* 212

anthem *el himno* 110

anthropology *la antropología* 406

antibiotic *el antibiótico* 206

antiques *las antigüedades* 146

antiquity *la antigüedad* 56

any *algún, alguno(a), algunos(as)* 24 *ningún, ninguno(a)* 138 *cualquier(a)* 247

anything *algo* 2

anyway *en fin* 200

apartment *el apartamento* 41

to **apologize** *disculparse, pedir perdón* 74

to **appear** *aparecer (irreg.)* 21

appearance *el aspecto* 25 *la fisonomía* 57

to **applaud** *aplaudir* 290

apple *la manzana* 144

appliance *el electrodoméstico* 103 *el aparato* 369

application *la solicitud* 94

to **apply for** *solicitar* 256 *optar a* 271

to **apply makeup** *maquillarse* 78

to **appoint** *nombrar* 31

appointment *la cita* 91

to **appreciate** *apreciar* 74

appropriate *apropiado(a)* 28 *adecuado(a)* 139

to **approve** *aprobar (irreg. ue)* 410

approximately *aproximadamente* 320

aqueduct *el acueducto* 434

Arab *árabe* 151

Arabic *árabe* 151

archeological *arqueológico(a)* 364

archeologist *el/la arqueólogo(a)* 398

archeology *la arqueología* 398

archipelago *el archipiélago* 344

architect *el/la arquitecto(a)* 233

architecture *la arquitectura* 157

Are you any good at ...? *¿Qué tal se te da...?* 178

Are you good at ...? *¿Eres bueno(a) en...?* 178

area *la extensión* 143 *el área* 165 *el espacio, la superficie* 380

Argentinean *argentino(a)* 15

to **argue** *discutir* 74 *argumentar* 324

argument *la discusión* 118 *el argumento* 166

to **arise** *surgir* 295

arm *el brazo* 4 *el arma* 93

armchair *el sillón* 125

army *el ejército* 254

around *en* 4 *por* 6 *en torno a* 157 *alrededor de* 164

to **arrange to meet** *quedar* 90

arrangement *la disposición* 113

to **arrest** *detener (irreg.)* 401 *prender* 443

arrival *la llegada* 42

to **arrive** *llegar* 5

arrogant *arrogante* 50

arrow *la flecha* 92

art *el Arte (subject)* 2

art form *la manifestación artística* 151

Art Nouveau (adjective) *modernista* 434

article *el artículo* 44

artificial *artificial* 147

artist *el/la artista* 15

artistic *artístico(a)* 151

as *como* 21 *conforme* 164

As a child ... *De niño(a)...* 59

as ... as *tanto(a)... como* 24

as ... as *tan... como...* 18 *igual de... que...* 24

as much as *tanto como* 24

as well as *además de* 22

As well as ... *Así como...* 437

As you like. *Como quieras.* 394

Asian *asiático(a)* 57

to **ask** *preguntar* 5

to **ask (for)** *pedir (irreg. i, i)* 6

asleep *dormido(a)* 23

aspect *el aspecto* 19

aspirin *la aspirina* 414

assistant *el/la ayudante* 26

to **associate something with** *asociar algo a/con* 112

association *la asociación* 44

assumption *la suposición* 70

astronaut *el/la astronauta* 239

astronomer *el/la astrónomo(a)* 354

astronomical *astronómico(a)* 399

astronomy *la astronomía* 362

astuteness *la astucia* 212

at *en* 2

At first ... *Al principio...* 59

at least *por lo menos* 9 *al menos* 105

at once *enseguida* 77

at the end of *al final de* 158

athlete *el/la atleta* 302

athletics *el atletismo* 302

Atlantic *atlántico(a)* 202

Atlantic Ocean *el Atlántico* 57

atmosphere *el ambiente* 159

to **attack** *atacar* 50

to **attend** *asistir (a)* 5

to **attend the elderly** *atender (irreg. ie) a personas mayores* 260

attention *la atención* 157

attic *el desván* 125

attitude *la actitud* 321

attorney *el/la abogado(a)* 187

to **attract** *atraer (irreg.)* 119 *captar* 436

attractive *atractivo(a)* 20

to **attribute** *atribuir (irreg.)* 406

audience *la audiencia, el público* 290

audio guide *la audioguía* 14

audio tour *la audioguía* 14

audition *la convocatoria* 416

auditorium *el auditorio* 290

aunt *la tía* 17

authentic *auténtico(a)* 140

author *el/la autor(a)* 23

authoritarian *autoritario(a)* 33

autobiographical *autobiográfico(a)* 44

autobiography *la autobiografía* 38

autograph *el autógrafo* 77

autumn *el otoño* 319

available *disponible* 256

avenue *la avenida* 28 *el paseo* 435

average *el promedio* 10 *la media* 207

average (adjective) *mediano(a)* 374

to **avoid** *evitar* 182

to **award a prize to** *premiar* 378

aware *consciente* 417

awful *fatal* 178

Aztec *azteca* 56

back *la espalda* 38 *el fondo* 157

backache *el dolor de espalda* 195

backpack *la mochila* 22

bad *mal* 9 *malo(a)* 24

bag *la bolsa* 104 *el paquete* 320

baggage *el equipaje* 287

to **bake** *hornear* 221

baker *el/la panadero(a)* 72

baking *la cocción* 352

balance *el equilibrio* 4

balanced *equilibrado(a)* 8

balcony *el balcón* 110

bald *calvo(a)* 20

ball *la pelota* 66 *el balón* 92

ballet *el ballet* 290

ballpoint pen *el bolígrafo* 10

banana *el plátano* 181

bank *el banco* 112

banker *el/la banquero(a)* 236

baptism *el bautizo* 44

barefoot *descalzo(a)* 229

bargain *la oferta* 209

to **bargain** *regatear* 145

barrier *la barrera* 381

base *la base* 111

baseball *el béisbol* 88

basement *el sótano* 125

basic *básico(a)* 218

basilica *la basílica* 435

basis *la base* 183

basketball *el baloncesto* 302

bat *el bate* 287

bath *el baño* 192

bathrobe *el albornoz* 194

bathroom *el cuarto de baño* 125

battery *la batería* 98 *la pila* 344

battle *la batalla* 398

to **be** *ser (irreg.), estar (irreg.)* 2 *encontrarse (irreg. ue)* 199

to **be able** *poder (irreg. ue, u)* XXVI

to **be about** *tratar de* 77

to **be awarded** *recibir* 272

to **be based on** *basarse en* 197

to **be born** *nacer (irreg.)* 44

to **be broadcast** *emitirse* 310

to **be busy** (phone) *comunicar* 98

to **be called** *llamarse* 18

to **be careful** *tener cuidado* 370

Be careful! *¡Cuidado!* 131

to **be discouraged** *desanimarse* 185

to **be enriched** *enriquecerse (irreg.)* 56

to **be equivalent to** *equivaler a (irreg.)* 136

to **be flooded** *inundarse* 370

to **be frightened** *asustarse* 375

to **be glad** *alegrarse* 90

to **be hungry** *tener hambre* 209

to **be in a hurry** *tener prisa* 122

to **be in the habit of** *soler (irreg. ue)* 33

to **be inspired by** *inspirarse en* 161

to **be interrupted** *interrumpirse* 104

to **be left** *quedar* 100

to **be left (over)** *sobrar* 352

to **be like** *parecerse a (irreg.)* 32

to **be met** (requirements) *cumplirse* 349

to **be missing** *faltar* 253

to **be needed** *hacer falta* 111

to **be part of** *formar parte de* 97

to **be passed on** *transmitirse* 220

to **be promoted** *ascender (irreg. ie)* 248

to **be right** *tener razón* 74

to **be surprised** *sorprenderse* 321

to **be sworn in** *jurar el cargo* 244

to **be titled** *titularse* 44

to **be useful** *servir (irreg. i, i)* 16

to **be worthwhile** *valer la pena* 7

beach *la playa* 6

bead *la cuenta* 169

bean *el frijol* 92

bear *el oso* 291

beard *la barba* 20

beat *el latido* 211

to **beat** *batir* 179

beautiful *bello(a)* 113 *hermoso(a)* 146

to **beautify** *embellecer (irreg.)* 434

because *porque* 5

because of *por* 19 *a causa de* 342

Because of this … *Debido a esto…* 167

to **become** *ponerse (irreg. u)* 74 *convertirse en (irreg. ie, i), volverse (irreg.)* 186

to **become angry** *enojarse* 43 *enfadarse* 262

to **become apparent** *manifestarse (irreg. ie)* 434

to **become established** *imponerse (irreg.)* 254

to **become independent** *independizarse* 411

bed *la cama* 104 *el lecho* 374

bedroom *el dormitorio* 3 *la habitación* 158

beef *la res* 181

before *antes de* 16 *antes* 34 *ante* 374

to **begin** *empezar (irreg. ie)* 1 *comenzar (irreg. ie)* 2 *iniciar(se)* 308

beginning *el principio* 21

behavior *el comportamiento* 383

behind *detrás* 30 *detrás de* 153

being *el ser* 110

belief *la creencia* 43

to **believe** *creer (irreg.)* 4

bell *la campana* 110 *el timbre* 400

to **belong** *pertenecer (irreg.)* 290

beloved *amado(a)* 80

belt *el cinturón* 128

bench *el banco* 320

benefit *el beneficio* 343

best *el/la mejor* 9

better *mejor* 8

between *entre* 25

to **bewitch** *encantar* 82

bicycle *la bici* 4 *la bicicleta* 64

big *grande* 20 *gran* 50

bigger *mayor* 37

bilingual *bilingüe* 118

biodiversity *la biodiversidad* 381

biographical *biográfico(a)* 58

biography *la biografía* 38

biology *la Biología* (subject) 215

biosphere *la biosfera* 343

biotope *el biotopo* 347

bird *el ave* 344 *el pájaro* 347

birth *el nacimiento* 44

birth date *la fecha de nacimiento* 17

birthday *el cumpleaños* 63

birthplace *el lugar de nacimiento* 17

bitter *amargo(a)* 179

black *negro(a)* 18

to **blame something on** *echar la culpa de algo a* 74

blank space *el espacio en blanco* 113

blender *la batidora* 221

block *el bloque* 317

blond(e) *rubio(a)* 17

blood *la sangre* 73

blood test *el análisis de sangre* 206

blouse *la blusa* 125

to **blow** *soplar* 356

blue *azul* 38

board *el tablero* 92

board game *el juego de mesa* 92

boarding pass *la tarjeta de embarque* 314

boat *la embarcación* 301 *el barco* 303

boat race *la regata* 302

body *el cuerpo* 47 *la entidad* 268

to **boil** *cocer (irreg. ue), hervir (irreg. ie, i)* 179

boiled *cocido(a)* 179

bold *la negrita* 92

bolero *el bolero* 101

bond *el lazo* 111

bone *el hueso* 206

bonfire *la hoguera* 354

book *el libro* 36

to **book** *reservar* 164

bookcase *la estantería* 125

boost *el impulso* 435

boot *la bota* 125

to **bore** *aburrir* 262

bored *aburrido(a)* 22

boring *aburrido(a)* 6

born *nato(a)* 254

boss *el/la jefe(a)* 236

to **bother** *molestar* 258

bottle *la botella* 345

boulevard *la rambla* 435

bouquet *el ramo* 333

bow *el arco* 92

bowling *los bolos* 308

box *el cuadro* 3 *la caja* 130

box office *la taquilla* 290

boy *el chico* 6 *el muchacho* 320

boyfriend *el novio* 32

bracelet *la pulsera* 145

brain *el cerebro* 206

brand *la marca* 129

brave *valiente* 43

bread *el pan* 72

breaded *empanado(a)* 179

to **break** *romper(se) (irreg.)* 4

to **break up** *romper (irreg.)* 74

breakfast *el desayuno* 196

to **breathe** *respirar* 194

bricklayer *el/la albañil* 152

brief *breve* 38

briefly *brevemente* 367

bright *brillante* 140

to **bring** *traer(se) (irreg.)* 6 *llevar* 109

to **bring about** *promover (irreg. ue)* 353

brochure *el folleto* 82

broken *roto(a)* 206

bronze *el bronce* 368

broom *la escoba* 152

brother *el hermano* 17

brother (monk) *fray* 374

brother-in-law *el cuñado* 32

brothers and sisters *los hermanos* 10

brown *castaño(a)* 20 *marrón* 128

brush *el cepillo* 19

drink la bebida 63
to **drink** beber 90
to **drink up** beberse 90
to **drip** chorrear 374
to **drive** manejar 196 conducir (irreg.) 401
driver's license la licencia de conducir 6
to **drizzle** lloviznar 356
drop la gota 356
drought la sequía 341
drum el tambor 110
dry seco(a) 157
to **dry** secar 152
dryer la secadora 130
Due to ... Debido a... 383
duet el dueto 298
dune la duna 380
duration la duración 81
during durante 2 en 6
to **dust** limpiar el polvo 152
dustpan el recogedor 152
duties los deberes 260
dynamic dinámico(a) 284

each cada 9 cada cual 237
eagle el águila 341
ear el oído 209
early temprano 86
to **earn** ganar 236
earring el arete 145
Earth la tierra 341
earthquake el terremoto 368
easily fácilmente 81 con facilidad 219
Eastern oriental 381
easy fácil 80
to **eat** comer 3
to **eat up** comerse 73
eating habits los hábitos alimenticios 185
eclipse el eclipse 357
ecological ecológico(a), ecologista 344
ecological catastrophe la catástrofe ecológica 344
ecology la ecología 344
economic económico(a) 205
economics la Economía 418
economy la economía 247
ecosystem el ecosistema 344
Ecuadorian ecuatoriano(a) 146
to **educate** educar 245
education la educación 241
educational educativo(a) 268
effect el efecto 129
effective efectivo(a) 19 eficaz 242
efficient eficiente 248
effort el esfuerzo 212

egg el huevo 343
eldest el/la mayor 25
to **elect** elegir (irreg.) 410
election (adjective) electoral 436
elections las elecciones 419
electric eléctrico(a) 102
electrical eléctrico(a) 369
electrician el/la electricista 152
elegance la elegancia 136
elegant elegante 140
element el elemento 38
elephant el elefante 341
elevator el ascensor 125
to **elicit** levantar 266
elite la élite 187
e-mail el correo (electrónico) 5 el e-mail 171
to **embarrass** dar vergüenza 232
embassy la embajada 312
emblem el emblema 139
embodiment la encarnación 244
to **embody** encarnar 244
embroidery el bordado 134
to **emerge** surgir 272
emergency (room) las urgencias 210
emigrant el/la emigrante 235
to **emigrate** emigrar 45
emigration la emigración 56
emoticon el emoticono 99
emotion el estado de ánimo 17 la emoción 308
emotional emotivo(a) 298
emperor el emperador 205
empire el imperio 398
employee el/la empleado(a) 236
to **encourage** fomentar 344
to **encourage to do something** animar a hacer algo 389
encyclopedia la enciclopedia 172
end el final 29 la finalidad 282 el extremo 326 el fin 406
to **end up** terminar 4
endangered species la especie en peligro de extinción 349
enemy (adjective) enemigo(a) 165
energy la energía 9
engaged prometido(a) 32
engineer el/la ingeniero(a) 211
engineering la Ingeniería 251
English el inglés 11
enigma el enigma 176
to **enjoy** disfrutar 202
to **enjoy oneself** divertirse (irreg. ie, i) 14
to **enjoy something** disfrutar de 193
Enjoy yourselves! ¡Que se diviertan! 16
enjoyable divertido(a) 7
enough suficiente 173
to **enrich** enriquecer (irreg.) 52
to **enter** entrar 14
entertaining entretenido(a) 311

entertainment la diversión 54 el espectáculo 71 el entretenimiento 383
entertainment guide la cartelera 290
entrance la entrada 50
entrepreneur el/la emprendedor(a) 378
entrepreneurial emprendedor(a) 248
entry la entrada 7
environment el medio ambiente 133 el ambiente 159 el medio 380
environmental ecologista 344
environmentally friendly ecológico(a) 376
equality la igualdad 422
equally igualmente 68
equinox el equinoccio 355
equivalent equivalente 46
era la época 56
to **erase** borrar 104
to **escape** escapar 43
essay el ensayo 166
essential fundamental 85 esencial 218 imprescindible 257
to **establish** establecer (irreg.) 133
establishment el establecimiento 367
eternal eterno(a) 42
ethnic étnico(a) 110
ethnicity la etnia 422
to **evaluate** evaluar 65
to **evaporate** evaporarse 190
even if aunque 258
even more aún más 56
evening la noche 7
event el acontecimiento 39 el evento 54 el suceso 328 el hecho 329
every todos(as) 34
every day todos los días 2 a diario 182
every time cada vez que 74
everyone todos(as) 9 todo el mundo 63
everything todo 25
evidence la evidencia 255
evident patente 57 evidente 167 ostensible 320
evidently evidentemente 393
exact exacto(a) 180
exactly exacto 230 exactamente 285
exaggerated ampuloso(a) 320
exam el examen 16
to **examine** examinar 207
example el ejemplo 77
to **excavate** excavar 398
excavation la excavación 398
excellent excelente 15
except excepto 223
exception la excepción 252
exceptional excepcional 146

excerpt el fragmento 94
excessive excesivo(a) 261
exchange el intercambio 94
to **exchange** intercambiar 59
excited emocionado(a) 63
excited about ilusionado(a) con 263
exciting emocionante XXVI
exclusively exclusivamente 204
excursion la excursión 48
excuse la excusa 95
Excuse me. Perdone. 180
exercise el ejercicio 8
to **exercise** ejercer 436
exhibition la exposición 71
to **exist** existir 33
existence la existencia 142
existing existente 164
exotic exótico(a) 209
to **expand** expandir 136
expedition la expedición XXVI
expense el gasto 416
expensive caro(a) 129
experience la experiencia 1
expert experto(a) 84
to **explain** explicar 2 exponer (irreg.) 383
explanation la explicación 81
to **explore** explorar 353
explorer el/la explorador(a) 398
to **export** exportar 345
to **express** expresar 1
expression la expresión 4 la fórmula 282 la manifestación 326
extinction la extinción 347
extraordinary extraordinario(a) 147
extraterrestrial el/la extraterrestre 401
extreme extremo(a) 300
extroverted extrovertido(a) 236
eye el ojo 20

fabric la tela 129
fabulous fabuloso(a) 53
face la cara 136 el rostro 374
to **face** afrontar 244
to **facilitate** facilitar 284
facilities las instalaciones 143
fact el hecho 43
factory la fábrica 233
faculty la facultad 251
to **fail to turn up** faltar 136
fair la feria 77
fair (adjective) justo(a) 238
fair trade el comercio justo 338
faith la fe 244
faithful fiel 20
faithfulness la fidelidad 74
fall el otoño 319

to **fall** caer(se) (irreg.) 90
to **fall asleep** dormirse (irreg. ue, u) 90
to **fall in love with** enamorarse de 74
false falso(a) 3
fame la fama 24
familial familiar 12
to **familiarize oneself** familiarizarse 14
family la familia 6
family doctor el/la médico(a) de familia 204
family-in-law la familia política 32
family tree el árbol genealógico 33
famous famoso(a) XXVI célebre 273
fan el/la fan XXVI el/la aficionado(a) 302
fang el diente 428
fantastic fantástico(a) 43
far lejos 244
faraway distante 374
farm la finca agrícola 143 la explotación agrícola 371 la granja 372
farmer el/la agricultor(a) 233
to **fascinate** fascinar 262
fascinating apasionante XXVI fascinante 14
fashion la moda 129
fashionable de moda 22
fast rápido 24
fast (adjective) rápido(a) 155
to **fasten** abrocharse 128
fat la grasa 182
fat (adjective) gordo(a) 17
father el padre 5
father-in-law el suegro 32
faucet el grifo 171
fault la falla 199
fauna la fauna 343
favor el favor 122
to **favor** favorecer (irreg.) 371
favorite favorito(a) 11 preferido(a) 107
fear el miedo 50 el temor 374
to **fear** temerse 150
feat la hazaña 72
feather la pluma 347
feature la característica 12 el rasgo 20
fee la tasa 333
to **feed (oneself)** alimentarse 342 alimentar 372
to **feel** sentirse (irreg. ie, i) 64 encontrarse (irreg. ue) 209
feeling el sentimiento 1
feline el/la felino(a) 381
feminine femenino(a) 156
femininity la feminidad 136
fertile fértil 50
festival el festival 52 la feria 94
festivity la fiesta 35 la festividad 357
fever la fiebre 46

few poco(a)(os)(as) 142
fiber la fibra 182
fiction la ficción 44
fictitious ficticio(a) 23
field el campo 218
fifth quinto(a) 136
fight la pelea 50 la lucha 92
to **fight** luchar 47 pelearse 51 combatir 193
fighting like cats and dogs como el perro y el gato 115
figure la cifra 207 la figura 245
figure skating el patinaje (artístico) 308
file la ficha 6
to **fill** (a vacancy) cubrir (irreg.) 253
to **fill in** rellenar 247 llenar 249
to **fill up** llenarse 136
to **film** filmar 342
film director el/la director(a) de cine 44
filming el rodaje 52
filter el filtro 352
final la final 303
final (adjective) final 167
finally por último 14 finalmente 16 por fin 45 definitivamente 149 al fin 374
Finally ... Al final... 329
to **find** encontrar (irreg. ue) 4 localizar 85
to **find it difficult to do something** costar trabajo hacer algo 230
to **find out** saber (irreg.) 46 enterarse 90 averiguar 77
fine (monetary) la multa 370
fine bien 5
to **finish** terminar 2 finalizar 383 acabar de 412
fire el fuego 362 el incendio 368
firefighter el/la bombero(a) 233
fireplace la chimenea 138
fireworks los fuegos artificiales 362
first primer(o)(a) 2
fish el pescado 144 el pez 344
to **fish** pescar 4
fishing la pesca 368
to **fit** caber (irreg.) 102
fitting room el probador 129
to **fix** reparar 152
to **fix** (eyes on) clavar 77
fixed fijo(a) 270
flag la bandera 72
flake el copo 218
flamenco el flamenco XXVI
flamenco dancer el/la bailaor(a) 151
flamenco singer el/la cantaor(a) 151
flan el flan 179
flashing intermitente 104
flat llano(a) 314
flextime el horario flexible 247

to **go with** *acompañar* 59
goal *la meta* 103 *el gol* 303
god(dess) *el/la dios(a)* 47
goddaughter *la ahijada* 32
godfather *el padrino* 32
godson *el ahijado* 32
gold *el oro* 368
golf *el golf* 287
good *buen, bueno(a)* 8
Good luck! *¡Suerte!* 1
good sense *la cordura* 111
goods *las mercancías* 236 *las mercaderías* 319
gossipy *chismoso(a)* 20
Gothic *gótico(a)* 434
to **govern** *gobernar* 410
government *el gobierno* 164
government department *la secretaría* 406
government employee *el/la funcionario(a)* 236
governor *el/la gobernador(a)* 410
to **grab** *agarrar* 320
grade *la nota* 10
graduate *el/la graduado(a)* 273
to **graduate** *graduarse* 44 *titularse* 254
graduation *la graduación* 44
grain *el grano* 212
grammatical *gramatical* 167
granddaughter *la nieta* 17
grandfather/grandmother *el/la abuelo(a)* 32
grandparents *los abuelos* 37
grandson *el nieto* 17
graphic designer *el/la diseñador(a) gráfico(a)* 236
to **grate** *rallar* 221
greasy *grasoso(a)* 182
great *gran, grande* 44 *estupendo* 161 *estupendo(a)* 187 *fenomenal* 293
Great! *¡Qué bien!* 6
Great Depression *la Gran Depresión* 242
greatest *mayor* 75
green *verde* 136
greenhouse effect *el efecto invernadero* 344
greenish *verdoso(a)* 140
to **greet** *felicitar* 82
to **greet one another** *saludarse* 87
grid *la cuadrícula* 164
grief *la pena* 47
to **groan** *gemir (irreg. i)* 320
ground *el suelo* 4 *la tierra* 199
group *el grupo* 40
to **grow** *cultivar* 51 *crecer (irreg.)* 164
to **grow dark** *oscurecerse (irreg.)* 374
growing *creciente* 253
Guarani *guaraní* 56
to **guarantee** *garantizar* 146
Guatemalan *guatemalteco(a)* 49
to **guess** *adivinar* 33

guest *el/la invitado(a)* 86 *el/la huésped* 138 *el/la cliente(a)* 323
guidance *la orientación* 422
guide *la guía* 146
to **guide** *guiar* 14
guilty *culpable* 74
guitar *la guitarra* 150
gulf *el golfo* 381
gulp *el trago* 91
gym *el gimnasio* 194
gymnastics *la Gimnasia* 287
gypsy *gitano(a)* 151

H

habit *el hábito* 174
habitat *el hábitat* 338
hail *el granizo* 356
hair *el pelo* 20
hair dryer *el secador* 179
haircut *el corte de pelo* 225
half *la mitad* 118
half (adjective) *medio(a)* 204
hall *la sala* 150 *el vestíbulo* 158
hallway *el pasillo* 125
ham *el jamón* 52
hamburger *la hamburguesa* 226
hamburger bar *la hamburguesería* 185
hand *la mano* 84
handcrafted *artesanal* 145
handicapped *discapacitado(a)* 280
handicrafts *la artesanía* 118
handicrafts (adjective) *artesanal* 373
handkerchief *el pañuelo* 128
hand-knitted *tejido(a) a mano* 131
handle *el asa* 327
to **handle** *manejar* 93
handsome *guapo* 20
handwriting *la letra* 59
to **hang** *colgar (irreg. ue)* 152
to **hang out** *tender (irreg. ie)* 152
to **hang up the phone** *colgar el teléfono* 98
to **happen** *pasar* 4 *ocurrir* 5 *suceder* 158
happy *contento(a)* 11 *feliz* 16
hard *duro(a)* 140 *fuerte* 211 *fuertemente* 369
hard-working *trabajador(a)* 17
harmony *la armonía* 429
harvest *la cosecha* 357
to **harvest** *cosechar* 212
haste *el apuro* 113 *la prisa* 318
hat *el sombrero* 131
hate *el odio* 81
to **hate** *odiar* 169
to **hate each other** *odiarse* 78
to **have** *haber (irreg.)* XXVI *tener (irreg.)* 6 *poseer (irreg.)* 82 *tomar* 86 *llevar* 188 *recibir* 193 *sufrir* 211

to **have a good time** *pasarlo bien* 14
to **have breakfast** *desayunar* 160
to **have dinner** *cenar* 7
to **have just** *acabar de* 132
to **have lunch** *almorzar (irreg. ue)* 2
to **have to** *haber que* 67
he *él* 3
head *la cabeza* 204
head of state *el/la mandatario(a)* 244
headline *el titular* 268
headquarters *la sede* 390
health *la salud* 174
healthy *sano(a)* 101 *saludable* 174
to **hear** *oír (irreg.)* 28
heart *el corazón* 206
heat *el calor* 157 *el fuego* 190
heavenly body *el astro* 354
heavy *pesado(a)* 327
heavy shower *el chubasco* 356
hectare *la hectárea* 268
heel *el tacón* 128
height *la altura* 7
helicopter *el helicóptero* 268
hello *hola* XXVI
Hello? *¿Diga?* 98
helmet *el casco* 111
help *la ayuda* 19
to **help** *ayudar* 8
hemisphere *el hemisferio* 354
her *su(s)* XXVI
(to) her *le* 76
herb *la hierba* 193
here *aquí* 14
heritage *el patrimonio* 151
hero *el héroe* 236
hers *el/la suyo(a)* 36
herself *se* 78
to **hesitate** *dudar* 124
to **hibernate** *hibernar* 343
hibernation *la hibernación* 350
to **hide** *esconder(se)* 158
hierarchical *jerárquico(a)* 403
hieroglyphic *el jeroglífico* 399
high *alto(a)* 47
high quality *de muy buena calidad* 140
high season *la temporada alta* 314
highest *mayor* 75
high-heeled shoe *el zapato de tacón* 128
to **highlight** *destacar* 77
highly valued *preciado(a)* 212
high-pitched *agudo(a)* 111
hiking *el senderismo* 287
(to) him *le* 76
himself *propio(a)* 73 *se* 78
Hinduism *el hinduismo* 44
to **hire** *contratar* 31
his *su(s)* XXVI *el/la suyo(a)* 36
Hispanic *hispano(a)* XXVI
historic *histórico(a)* 406
historical *histórico(a)* 101

historically *históricamente* 274
history *la Historia* 11
to **hit** *golpear* 369
hobby *la afición* 52
to **hold** *sostener (irreg.)* 320 *albergar* 380 *ocupar* 406
holding *la celebración* 118
hole in the ozone layer *el agujero de la capa de ozono* 344
holiday *el día festivo* 245 *el día feriado* 256
holy *sagrado(a)* 49
holy place *el santuario* 397
home *la casa* 22 *la vivienda* 120
home team *el equipo local* 302
homework *la tarea* 2
honest *honesto(a)* 8
honor *el honor* 230
to **honor** *honrar* 213
hoop *el aro* 92
hope *la esperanza* 374
to **hope** *esperar* 14
horizon *el horizonte* 428
horrible *horrible* 35
horror film *la película de terror* 290
horse *el caballo* 326
horseshoe *la herradura* 153
hose *la manguera* 156
hospital *el hospital* 45
host/hostess *el/la anfitrión(a)* 86
hostile *hostil* 380
hot *picante* 89 *caluroso(a)* 157 *caliente* 199
hot springs *las aguas termales* 193
hotel *el hotel* 138
hour *la hora* 8
house *la casa* 25
house painter *el/la pintor(a)* 152
housework *las tareas domésticas* 121
how *qué* 6 *cómo* 7
How are you? *¿Qué tal (estás)?* 35
How lucky! *¡Qué suerte!* 37
how many *cuántos(as)* 10
how much *cuánto(a)* 7
however *sin embargo* 74
hug *el abrazo* 74
to **hug** *abrazar* 74
huge *enorme* 373
human *humano(a)* 111
human being *el ser humano* 378
human rights *los derechos humanos* 260
humanist *humanista* 254
humanity *la humanidad* 254
humble *humilde* 83
humid *húmedo(a)* 381
humor *el humor* 19
hunger *el hambre* 262
to **hunt** *cazar* 212
hurricane *el huracán* 368
to **hurry** *darse prisa* 84
to **hurt** *doler (irreg. ue)* 199
to **hurt oneself** *hacerse daño* 65

husband *el esposo* 32 *el marido* 44
hut *la cabaña* 4
hygiene *la higiene* 179
hypothesis *la hipótesis* 177

I *yo* 2
I agree. *De acuerdo.* 86
I can ... *Soy capaz de...* 232
I do. *A mí sí./Yo sí.* 286
I don't. *Yo no.* 286
I don't feel like it. *No me apetece.* 86
I don't mind. *Me da igual/Me da lo mismo.* 394
I/you feel like ... *Me/Te apetece...* 69
I find it easy/difficult ... *Me resulta fácil/difícil...* 232
I hope ... *Ojalá...* 16
I think ... *Me parece...* 86
I think you're wrong. *Creo que te equivocas.* 286
I'd like to ... *Me gustaría...* 340
I'd love to ... *Me encantaría...* 340
I'm hopeless at ... *Soy un desastre para...* 178
I'm sorry. *Lo siento.* 86 *Perdona.* 419
ice *el hielo* 209
ice cream *el helado* 115
icon *el icono* 277
idea *la idea* 28
ideal *ideal* 89
idealistic *idealista* 19
ideals *los ideales* 308
identification *la documentación* 314
to **identify** *identificar(se)* 92
identity *la identidad* 422
ideology *la ideología* 410
idol *el ídolo* 50
if *si* 2
ignorance *la ignorancia* 374
ignorant *ignorante* 375
ill *enfermo(a)* 22
illegal *ilegal* 347
illness *la enfermedad* 38
to **illustrate** *ilustrar* 51
illustration *la ilustración* 4
image *la imagen* 429
imaginary *imaginario(a)* 21 *irreal* 265
imagination *la imaginación* 65
imaginative *imaginativo(a)* 53
to **imagine** *imaginar(se)* 23
to **imitate** *imitar* 328
immaterial *inmaterial* 151
immediately *inmediatamente* 418
immigrant *el/la inmigrante* 422
immigration *la inmigración* 56
impact *el impacto* 75
impassive *impasible* 374

impeccable *impecable* 136
imperative *el imperativo* 1
imperfect tense *el imperfecto* 12
impersonal *impersonal* 144
implacable *implacable* 374
to **implement** *realizar* 406
importance *la importancia* 8
important *importante* 26 *relevante* 419
impossible *imposible* 240
impression *la impresión* 70
impressive *impresionante* 7
to **improve** *mejorar* 59
improvement *la mejora* 235
impulse *el impulso* 211
in *en* XXVI *por* 2 *dentro de* 103 *bajo* 374
in a bad mood *de mal humor* 29
in advance *con antelación* 314
in cash *en efectivo* 145
in common *común* 75
in detail *con detalle* 162
in fact *en realidad* 32 *precisamente* 253
in front of *frente a* 104
in general *por lo general* 35 *en general* 322
in its entirety *en su totalidad* 317
in love *enamorado(a)* 74
In my opinion ... *En mi opinión...* 437
In my view ... *A mi modo de ver...* 437
in order to *con el fin de* 313
in particular *en concreto* 439
in shape *en forma* 8
In summary ... *En resumen...* 167
in the face of *ante* 212
In the first place ... *En primer lugar...* 167
in the open air *al aire libre* 8
in the past *antiguamente* 31 *antes* 34
in touch *en contacto* 75
in turns *por turnos* 9
Inca *inca* 50
to **include** *incluir (irreg.)* 23
incomplete *incompleto(a)* 11
to **increase** *aumentar* 182
incredible *increíble* 145
indeed *en efecto* 308
indefinites *los indefinidos* 120
independence *la independencia* 110
independent *independiente* 409
to **indicate** *indicar* 92
indicative *el indicativo* 1
indifference *la indiferencia* 394
indignant *indignado(a)* 320
indirect *indirecto(a)* 66
individual *el individuo* 350
individual (adjective) *individual* 303
individually *individualmente* 92
indoor soccer *el fútbol sala* 308

to **laugh**   reír(se) (irreg. i) 20

to **launch**   poner en marcha 277

laundry detergent   el detergente 152

laurel   el laurel 428

lava   la lava 380

law   la ley 410

Law   el Derecho 251

lawn   el césped 63

lazy   perezoso(a) 17

lead   la entradilla 254

lead   el plomo 368

to **lead**   llevar 185

leader   el/la líder 207

to **lean**   apoyar 166 inclinarse 266

to **learn**   aprender 1 estudiarse 90

least   menos 25

leather   el cuero 128

to **leave**   salir (irreg.) 35 irse (irreg.) 90 dejar 221 marcharse 397 abandonar 403

to **leave a message**   dejar un recado 98

Lebanese   el/la libanés(a) 56

lecture   la conferencia 85

left   la izquierda 113

leftovers   las sobras 181

leg   la pierna 38

legacy   el legado 245

legend   la leyenda XXVI

legibility   la legibilidad 167

legumes   las legumbres 179

leisure   el ocio 282

lemon   el limón 298

lemon blossom   el azahar 156

lemon yellow   el amarillo limón 140

to **lend**   prestar 242

lentil   la lenteja 179

less   menos 24

lesson   la lección 400

to **let**   dejar 177

Let me help you.   Déjame ayudarte./Déjame que te ayude. 124

to **let someone know**   avisar a alguien 210

Let's go!   ¡Vámonos! 90

Let's see …   A ver… 41

letter   la letra 99 la carta 199

letterhead   el membrete 275

lettuce   la lechuga 19

level   el nivel 199

liberal   liberal 410

librarian   el/la bibliotecario(a) 49

library   la biblioteca 11

lichen   el liquen 380

lie   la mentira 55

to **lie**   mentir (irreg. ie, i) 74

life   la vida 35

to **lift**   levantar 185

lifting   el levantamiento 327

light   la luz 104

light (adjective)   ligero(a) 182

to **light**   encender (irreg. ie) 354

light bulb   la bombilla 376

lightning   el relámpago 341

like   el gusto 1

to **like**   gustar XXVI

likelihood   la probabilidad 282

likely   probable 234

liking   la simpatía 321

line   la línea 39 la fila 290 la raya 403

line (of poetry)   el verso 83

line of argument   la argumentación 436

linear   lineal 136

link   el enlace 249

to **link**   relacionar 16 enlazar 383

liquid   el líquido 206

list   la lista 8

to **listen**   escuchar 3 oír (irreg.) 26

liter   el litro 185

literary   literario(a) 50

literature   la literatura 23

little   poco 26 pequeño(a) 35 menor 37

little by little   poco a poco 53

live   en directo 63

to **live**   vivir XXVI

to **live on**   perdurar 244

liver   el hígado 206

livestock   la ganadería 368

living   viviente 344

living room   la sala 125 el salón 158

local   local 143

to **locate**   situar 141

located   ubicado(a) 272

location   la situación 146 la ubicación 307 la localización 392 el emplazamiento 434

locked in   encerrado(a) 328

logical   lógico(a) 2

logically   lógicamente 223

logo   el logo 376

lollipop   el chupa-chups 254

lonely   solitario(a) 274

long   largo(a) 7

look   la mirada 320

to **look**   quedar 138

to **look after**   cuidar 198

to **look at**   mirar 5 contemplar 254

to **look for**   buscar 26

to **look like**   parecerse a (irreg.) 32

to **look up**   consultar 247

loose   amplio(a) 128

to **lose**   perder (irreg. ie) 4

to **lose weight**   bajar de peso 194

loser   el/la perdedor(a) 302

losses   las pérdidas 368

lottery   la lotería 268

love   el amor 74

to **love**   encantar 15 amar 28 querer (irreg.) 74

love affair   la relación amorosa 52

to **love each other**   quererse (irreg.) 78

lover   el/la amante 44 el/la enamorado(a) 47

loving   amoroso(a) 320

low   grave 111 bajo(a) 355

low season   la temporada baja 314

lower   menor 254

low-heeled   plano(a) 128

luck   la suerte 14

lunch   el almuerzo 352

lung   el pulmón 206

luxury   el lujo 268

luxury state hotel   el parador 315

lyrics   la letra 101

machine   el aparato, la máquina 211

mad   loco(a) 23

Madam   Señora 180

magazine   la revista 172

magic   la magia 293

magical   mágico(a) 328

magnificent   magnífico(a) 310

maid   la criada 30

main   principal 21

main character   el/la protagonista 290

mainly   principalmente 91

majority   la mayoría 199

to **make**   hacer (irreg.) XXVI elaborar 14 realizar 133

to **make a clean copy of**   pasar a limpio 167

to **make a mistake**   equivocarse 74

to **make aware**   concienciar 344

to **make happy**   alegrar 258

to **make note of**   anotar 59

to **make one's debut**   debutar 136

to **make oneself up**   maquillarse 78

to **make progress**   avanzar 431

to **make sense**   tener sentido 408

Make sure you …   Asegúrate de… 275

to **make up**   constituir (irreg.) 57

to **make up**   inventar 5 reconciliarse 74

to **make use of**   valerse de (irreg.) 374

to **make value statements**   valorar 70

mambo   el mambo 97

mammal   el mamífero 344

man   el hombre 23 el señor R1

to **manage**   conseguir (irreg. i, i) 119 lograr 212

management   la gestión 416

manager   el/la director(a) 99 el/la gerente 236

mankind   la humanidad 151

manual   el manual 254

manual (adjective)   manual 197

manufacture   la fabricación 373

to **manufacture**   fabricar 126

many   muchos(as) XXVI

map el mapa 56 el plano 165
marathon el/la maratón 195
mariachi el mariachi 335
marina el puerto deportivo 435
marital status el estado civil 17
mark el signo 65
to **mark** señalar 38 marcar 254
marker el marcador 48
market el mercado 35
marriage el matrimonio 44
married casado(a) 32
to **marry** casarse 32
martial arts las artes marciales 94
mascot la mascota 282
masculine masculino(a) 156
massage el masaje 194
master's degree la maestría 418
match el partido 302
material el material 22
material (adjective) material 368
materials el material 352
maternal materno(a) 32
mathematical matemático(a) 399
matter la cuestión 65 el asunto 274
maximum (adjective) máximo(a) 119
May I speak with …? ¿Puedo hablar con…? 98
Mayan maya 49
maybe quizá(s) 137
mayonnaise la mayonesa 179
mayor el alcalde/la alcaldesa 410
(to) me me 76
to **mean** querer decir XXVI significar 15
meaning el significado 46 el sentido 264
means el medio 68 el recurso 113
means of transport el medio de transporte 315
meanwhile mientras 134
measure la medida 199
to **measure** medir (irreg. i, i) 381
meat la carne 179
mechanic el/la mecánico(a) 233
mechanical mecánico(a) 7
medal la medalla 308
media los medios de comunicación 96
medical médico(a) 10
medical care la atención médica 235
medical checkup la revisión (médica) 206
medicinal medicinal 192
medicine (drug) el medicamento 204 la medicina 263
medicine (science) la medicina 197
medieval medieval 23
meditation la meditación 8
Mediterranean mediterráneo(a) 354
medium medio(a) 190

medium-sized mediano(a) 37
to **meet** reunirse 35 conocer (irreg.) 38 conocerse (irreg.) 52 encontrarse (irreg. ue) 205 cumplir con 378
meeting la reunión 86 el consejo 374
melon el melón 179
to **melt** derretir (irreg. i) 221
member el miembro 40
memoirs las memorias 45
memorable memorable 147
to **memorize** aprenderse 90 memorizar 124
memory el recuerdo 41
to **mend the bridges** tender puentes (irreg. ie) 378
Mennonite menonita 57
to **mention** mencionar 21 nombrar 188
merengue (dance) el merengue 97
message el anuncio 69 el mensaje 109
metal el metal 140
meteorite el meteorito 356
meteorological meteorológico(a) 356
meter el metro 7
methodically metódicamente 104
Methodist metodista 424
Mexican mexicano(a) 38
microwave el microondas 125
middle class la clase media 19
middleman el/la intermediario(a) 367
to **migrate** migrar 338
migration la migración 342
migratory migratorio(a) 350
mile la milla 196
military militar 164
milk la leche 221
mill el molino 218
to **mill** moler (irreg. ue) 218
million el millón 207
millionaire el/la millonario(a) 268
mind el pensamiento 374
to **mind** importar 88
mine la mina 369
mine mío(a) 22 míos, mías 36
miner el/la minero(a) 442
mineral el mineral 368
mineral water (sparkling/flat) el agua mineral (con/sin gas) 182
mineralization la mineralización 199
mini-interview la minientrevista 29
mining la minería 368
minister el/la ministro(a) 410
minority la minoría 56
minute el minuto 49
mirror el espejo 30
mischievous travieso(a) 20
to **miss** perder (irreg. ie) 5 faltar 136
missed call la llamada perdida 98

mission la misión 183
mistake el error 41
to **mistreat** maltratar 293
to **mix** mezclar(se) 38
mix of races el mestizaje 422
mixer la batidora 221
mixture la mezcla 190
model el modelo 2
modeling clay la plastilina 158
modern moderno(a) 5 actual 382
to **modify** modificar 91
mole (on skin) el lunar 20
mom la mamá 34
moment el momento 2
monarchy la monarquía 410
monastery el monasterio 315
money el dinero 196
monkey el chango 38 el mono 341
monster el monstruo 55
month el mes 6
monument el monumento 363
mood el modo 84
moon la luna 341
mop el trapeador 152 la fregona 254
more más XXVI
more and more cada vez más 75
morning la mañana 2
moss el musgo 380
most la mayor parte 56
mother la madre 17
mother-in-law la suegra 32
motif el motivo 389
to **motivate** motivar 329
motivated motivado(a) 281
motive el motivo 26
motor el motor 206
motorbike la moto 196 la motocicleta 252
motto el lema 111
mountain la montaña 6
mountaineering el alpinismo 287
mountainous montañoso(a) 347
mountains la montaña 34
mouse el ratón 248
mouth la boca 321
to **move** mover (irreg. ue) 92 mudarse 209 emocionar 262
to **move forward** avanzar 361
movement el movimiento 388
movie la película 11
movie theatre la sala (de cine) 290
moving emotivo(a) 298
to **mow** cortar 63
Mr. señor 86 don 86
Mrs. señora 86 doña 86
multicultural multicultural 422
multiculturalism la multiculturalidad 421
multinational multinacional 408
multiparty multipartidario(a) 418
multiracial multirracial 56
municipal municipal 302

muralist *el/la muralista* 38
muscle *el músculo* 206
museum *el museo* 35
music *la música* 63
musical *el musical* 290
musical (adjective) *musical* 57
musicality *la musicalidad* 113
musician *el/la músico(a)* 63
musketeer *el mosquetero* 75
must *deber* 7
mustache *el bigote* 20
mustard *la mostaza* 179
mutual *común, mutuo(a)* 408
mute *mudo(a)* 99
my *mi, mis* 2 *míos(as)* 32 *mío(a)* 36
myrtle *el mirto* 428
myself *me* 78
mysterious *misterioso(a)* 23
mystery *el misterio* 328
myth *el mito* 49
mythology *la mitología* 38

nail *la uña* 179
nail clippers *el cortaúñas* 194
naïve *inocente* 55
name *el nombre* 17
to **name** *nombrar* 387
to **narrate** *narrar* 13
narrative *narrativo(a)* 328
narrow *angosto(a)* 164 *estrecho(a)* 434
nation *la nación* 25
national *nacional* 28
national team *la selección* 303
nationality *la nacionalidad* 75
native *el/la indígena* 43
native (adjective) *nativo(a)* 139
natural *natural* 140
natural disaster *el desastre natural* 368
natural gas *el gas natural* 368
natural resources *los recursos naturales* 344
nature *la naturaleza* 254
navel *el ombligo* 50
near *cerca de* 37
nearby *cercano(a)* 73
nearly *cerca de* 57
necessarily *necesariamente* 192
necessary *necesario(a)* 59 *preciso(a)* 198
necessity *la necesidad* 67
neck *el cuello* 201
necklace *el collar* 169
necropolis *la necrópolis* 435
need *la necesidad* 212
to **need** *necesitar* 11
needy *necesitado(a)* 259
negative *negativo(a)* 19
negatively *negativamente* 146

negotiable *negociable* 247
negotiation *la negociación* 241
neighbor *el/la vecino(a)* 18
neighborhood *el barrio* 244
neither *tampoco* 33
nephew *el sobrino* 17
nervous *nervioso(a)* 17
network *la red* 58
neutral *neutro(a)* 170
never *nunca* 38
Never mind! *¡Qué le vamos a hacer!* 394
new *nuevo(a)* XXVI
New York (adjective) *neoyorquino(a)* 244
newborn *recién nacido(a)* 52
news *la noticia* 19 *el noticiero* 249
newspaper *el periódico* 11 *el diario* 55
next *próximo(a)* 94
next to *al lado de* 279
NGO *la ONG* 230
nice *simpático(a)* 3 *cortés* 20
Nice to meet you. *Encantado(a).* 71
niece *la sobrina* 17
night *la noche* 7
nightingale *el ruiseñor* 428
nightstand *la mesita de noche* 104
ninth *noveno(a)* 425
no *no* XXVI
no doubt *sin duda* 286
nobody *nadie* 80
noise *el ruido* 266
nominated *nominado(a)* 289
none *ningún, ninguno(a)* 269
non-governmental organization *la organización no gubernamental* 230
non-stop *sin parar* 214
nor *ni* 183
norm *la norma* 422
normal *normal* 7
normally *normalmente* 48
North *el norte* 192
North American *norteamericano(a)* 244
North Star *la Estrella Polar* 328
not *no* 2
not a single ... *ni* 266
not any *ningún, ninguno(a)* 138
not any more *ya no* 75
Not at all! *¡Qué va!* 286
not even ... *ni* 266
Not me. *A mí no.* 286
not to know *desconocer (irreg.)* XXVI
note *la nota* 49
notebook *el cuaderno* 8
notes *los apuntes* 361
nothing *nada* 55
noun *el nombre* 38 *el sustantivo* 252
novel *la novela* 23
now *ya* 18 *ahora* 32
nowadays *actualmente* 44 *en la actualidad* 164

nuclear energy *la energía atómica* 273
number *el número* 10 *la cantidad* 164
numerals *la numeración* 403
numerous *numeroso(a)* 56
nurse *el/la enfermero(a)* 206
nutrient *el nutriente* 218
nutrition *la nutrición* 174
nutritional *nutritivo(a)* 182

object *el objeto* 37
objection *la dificultad* 265
objective *el objetivo* 92
obligation *la obligación* 67
obligatory *forzoso(a)* 320
oblivion *el olvido* 80
observatory *el observatorio* 354
observer *el/la observador(a)* 254
obsession *la obsesión* 38
obstacle *el obstáculo* 265
to **obtain** *conseguir (irreg. i, i)* 123 *obtener (irreg.)* 172
obvious *evidente* 167 *obvio(a)* 238
obviously *obviamente* 200 *evidentemente* 393
occasion *la ocasión* 68
to **occupy** *ocupar* 91
ocean *el océano* 193
ocelot *el ocelote* 381
odd *curioso(a)* 181
of *de* XXVI
of course *por supuesto* 1 *claro* 14
offer *la oferta* 128
to **offer** *ofrecer (irreg.)* 50
to **offer up** *ofrecer (irreg.)* 73
office *la oficina* 117 *el despacho* 234
official *oficial* 419
often *con frecuencia* 8 *a menudo* 48
Oh! *¡ay!* 137 *¡Oh!* 394
oil *el aceite* 179 *el petróleo* 265
oil (adjective) *petrolífero(a)* 265
oil spill *la marea negra* 344
OK. *Vale.* 86
old *antiguo(a)* 28 *viejo(a)* 53
old age *la vejez* 44
older *mayor* 24
olive *la aceituna* 190
olive oil *el aceite de oliva* 182
Olympic *olímpico(a)* 305
Olympic Village *la Villa Olímpica* 435
Olympics *los Juegos Olímpicos* 302
on *en* 3 *sobre* 104
on a diet *a dieta* 182
on foot *a pie* 92
on the occasion of *con motivo de* 82
on the other hand *en cambio* 18

on time   *a tiempo* 86
on top of   *encima de* 134
once   *una vez* 8
Once upon a time ...   *Érase una vez...* 329
one   *uno* 9
One day ...   *Un día...* 329
onion   *la cebolla* 179
on-line   *conectado(a)* 68 *en línea* 69
only   *solo* 18 *único(a)* 416
opaque   *opaco(a)* 374
to **open**   *abrir (irreg.)* 2 *abrirse (irreg.)* 90 *inaugurar* 202 *estrenar* 290
open-air   *al aire libre* 94
opening   *la inauguración* 442
opening night   *el estreno* 293
opera   *la ópera* 290
to **operate**   *manejar* 427
operator   *el/la telefonista* 233
ophthalmologist   *el/la oculista* 206
opinion   *la opinión* 1
opportunity   *la oportunidad* 427
opposing   *contrario(a)* 305
oppressor   *el/la opresor(a)* 374
optimistic   *optimista* 17
option   *la opción* 19
optional   *opcional* 364
or   *u* 67 *ni* 183
oral   *oral* 328
orange blossom   *el azahar* 156
orchestra   *la orquesta* 63
orchid   *la orquídea* 347
order   *la orden (command)* 1 *el orden (arrangement)* 51
to **order**   *ordenar* 4 *mandar* 47
oregano   *el orégano* 190
organ   *el órgano* 206
organic   *ecológico(a)* 371 *orgánico(a)* 372
organization   *la organización* 260 *el organismo* 273
to **organize**   *organizar* 16 *realizar* 308
organized   *organizado(a)* 248
organizer   *el/la organizador(a)* 284
origin   *el origen* 35 *la procedencia* 56
original   *original* 83
originally   *originario(a)* 93 *originalmente* 181
to **originally come from**   *ser originario(a) de* 127
to **originate**   *originarse* 43
to **originate in**   *ser originario(a) de* 93
ornament   *el adorno* 140
other   *otro(a)* XXVI
other people   *los/las demás* 236
otherwise   *en caso contrario* 314
our   *nuestro(a)* 11
ours   *el/la nuestro(a)* 291
ourselves   *nos* 78
outfit   *el conjunto* 166
outline   *el contorno* 112 *el guion* 166
to **outline**   *esquematizar* 328

outskirts   *las afueras* 383
outstanding   *destacado(a)* 273
oval   *ovalado(a)* 140
oven   *el horno* 125
over   *por encima* 361
over a low heat   *a fuego lento* 221
to **overcome**   *superar* 212
overtime   *las horas extraordinarias* 256 *la prórroga* 303
overweight   *gordito(a)* 441
own   *propio(a)* XXVI
owner   *el/la dueño(a)* 149
ownership   *la posesión* 12
oxygen   *el oxígeno* 206

pacemaker   *el marcapasos* 211
package   *el paquete* 196
package tour   *el viaje organizado* 314
paella   *la paella* 196
page   *la página* 14
to **page through**   *hojear* 320
pain   *el dolor* 74
to **paint**   *pintar* 152
painter   *el/la pintor(a)* 30 *el/la autor(a)* 41
painting   *el cuadro* 14 *la pintura* 39
pajamas   *el pijama* 252
palace   *el palacio* 398
Palestinian   *palestino(a)* 56
Pan-American   *panamericano(a)* 282
pantry   *la despensa* 125
paper   *el papel* 344
papers   *la documentación* 314
paprika   *el pimentón* 190
parade   *el desfile* 133
to **parade**   *desfilar* 424
paradise   *el paraíso* 202
paragraph   *el párrafo* 3
parallel   *paralelo(a)* 164
parents   *los padres* 9
park   *el parque* 29
parking lot   *el estacionamiento* 5
Parliament   *el parlamento* 410
parrot   *el loro* 38
part   *la parte* 43
participant   *el/la participante* 111
participation   *la participación* 280
participle   *el participio* 120
particular   *particular* 14
particularly   *particularmente* 374
partner   *la pareja* 32 *el/la socio(a)* 281
part-time   *la media jornada* 248
party   *la fiesta* 5
to **pass**   *pasar* 7
passage   *el fragmento* 293
passenger   *el/la pasajero(a)* 320
passive   *pasivo(a)* 390

passport control   *el control de pasaportes* 314
past   *el pasado* 13
past (adjective)   *pasado(a)* 1
past perfect   *el pluscuamperfecto* 121
past progressive   *el pasado continuo* 12
past tense   *el pretérito* 1
pasta   *la pasta* 180
pastime   *la diversión, el pasatiempo* 54
pastry   *la empanada* 180
to **patent**   *patentar* 254
paternal   *paterno(a)* 32
path   *el curso* 362
patient   *el/la paciente* 206 *el/la enfermo(a)* 211
patient (adjective)   *paciente* 236
patriotic   *patriótico(a)* 415
patron   *el/la mecenas* 31
patron saint   *el patrón* 73
pattern   *el estampado* 136
to **pay**   *pagar* 145 *prestar* 167
to **pay attention to**   *fijarse en* 65
pea   *el guisante* 179
peace   *la paz* 422
peaceful   *pacífico(a)* 235
peacefully   *tranquilamente* 200
peak   *el esplendor* 399
pear   *la pera* 179
peculiar   *curioso(a)* 218
peddler   *el/la vendedor(a) ambulante* 405
pediatrician   *el/la pediatra* 206
to **peel**   *pelar* 179
pencil   *el lápiz* 294
pending   *pendiente* 132
penguin   *el pingüino* 380
peninsula   *la península* 42
people   *la gente* 50 *el pueblo* 56
pepper (spice)   *la pimienta* 180
pepper (vegetable)   *el pimiento* 188
peppermint   *la yerbabuena* 428
perfect   *perfecto(a)* 26
perfection   *la perfección* 136
perfectly   *perfectamente* 253
to **perform**   *realizar* 72 *actuar* 298
performance   *la actuación* 157 *la función* 290 *la representación* 293 *la interpretación* 416
perhaps   *tal vez* 284
period   *la época* 31 *el período* 164
permanent   *permanente* 186
perpendicular   *perpendicular* 164
to **persist**   *perdurar* 244
person   *la persona* XXVI
personal   *personal* 8
personal trip   *el viaje de placer* 314
personality   *la personalidad* 12
perspective   *la perspectiva* 159
persuasive   *persuasivo(a)* 436
Peruvian   *peruano(a)* 7

peso   el peso 140
pessimistic   pesimista 17
pesticide   el pesticida 353
pet   la mascota 200 el animal de compañía 201
petrified   petrificado(a) 50
pharmacist   el/la farmacéutico(a) 236
phenomenon   el fenómeno 356
philosophy   la filosofía 245
phone card   la tarjeta telefónica 98
photo   la foto 5
photograph   la fotografía 9
photography   la fotografía 3
physical   físico(a) 9
physical education   la Educación Física 203
physical exam   el examen físico 206
physically   físicamente 27
physicist   el/la físico(a) 273
physics (subject)   la Física 178
piano   el piano 35
to **pick up**   recoger 5 buscar 35
to **pick up the phone**   descolgar el teléfono 98
picture   la foto 5 la imagen 64
pie   la empanada 180
piece   la pieza 182 el trozo 190
piece of card stock (thick paper)   la cartulina 65
piece of information   el dato 49
pig   el cerdo 341
pigeon   la paloma 112
pilates   el pilates 194
pill   la píldora 206
pillar   el pilar 409
pilot   el/la piloto 252
pineapple   la piña 179
pirate   el/la pirata 393
pity   la pena 300 la lástima 361
place   el lugar 7 el puesto 237 el sitio 307
to **place**   situar 39 colocar 139
plain (topographic)   la llanura 434
plain (adjective)   liso(a) 128
plain rice   el arroz blanco 188
plan   el plan 96 el trazado 164
to **plan**   planear 97 planificar 165
planet   el planeta 18
planned   previsto(a) 298
plant   la planta 155 la especie vegetal 347
plant (adjective)   vegetal 347
to **plant**   plantar 212
plantation   la plantación 345
plastic   el plástico 254
plate   el plato 91
platform   el andén 320
platonic   platónico(a) 298
play   la obra teatral 430
to **play**   tocar 3 jugar (irreg. ue) 11 practicar 35 interpretar 293
player   el/la jugador(a) 84 el reproductor 103

playing cards   los naipes 71
pleasant   agradable 249
please   por favor 72
Pleased to meet you.   Mucho gusto. 71
plot   el argumento 328
plot of land   la parcela 164
plumage   el plumaje 347
plumber   el/la plomero(a) 152
plural   plural 78
plurality   la pluralidad 422
pocket   el bolsillo 128
pocketbook   la cartera 321
poem   el poema 77
poet   el/la poeta 80
poet (female)   la poetisa 113
poetry   la poesía 75
point   el punto 58
point of view   el punto de vista 159
poison   el veneno 428
police force   la policía 29
police sketch   el retrato robot 29
policeman/policewoman   el/la policía 233
polio   la polio 38
polite   educado(a) 27
politely   cortésmente 340
political   político(a) 242
politician   el/la político(a) 22
politics   la política 19
to **pollute**   contaminar 371
pollution   la contaminación 263
polyester   el poliéster 128
pool   la poza 193
Poor thing.   Pobrecito(a). 342
popcorn   las palomitas 145
popular   popular 28
to **popularize**   popularizar 21
to **populate**   poblar (irreg. ue) 158
population   la población 56
portion   la porción 221
portrait   el retrato 29
to **portray**   retratar 55
to **pose**   plantear 55
position   la posición 76 el cargo 228
positive   positivo(a) 8
possession   la posesión 12
possessive   el posesivo 36
possibility   la posibilidad 236
possible   posible 95
post   el puesto 244 el cargo 228 el poste 327
to **post**   publicar 85
poster   el póster 40 el cartel 54 el anuncio 82
postgraduate studies   el postgrado 272
potato   la papa 181
potential   el potencial 382
to **pour with rain**   llover a cántaros 356
poverty   la pobreza 50
power   el poder 410
powerful   poderoso(a) 368 fuerte 369

practical   práctico(a) 140
practice   la práctica 193
to **practice**   practicar 8 ejercer 273
prawn   el camarón 179
preceded   precedido(a) 200
precedence   la anterioridad 358
precious stone   la piedra preciosa 396
precisely   precisamente 308
pre-Columbian   precolombino(a) 93
pre-cooked   precocinado(a) 185
predecessor   el antecedente 93
to **prefer**   preferir (irreg. ie, i) 34
preferable   preferible 257
preference   la preferencia 1
prefix   el prefijo 92
pregnancy   el embarazo 44
pregnant   embarazada 52
to **pre-heat**   precalentar (irreg. ie) 352
pre-Hispanic   prehispánico(a) 85
premiere   el estreno 293
preparation   la preparación 179 la elaboración 220
preparations   los preparativos 313
to **prepare**   preparar 34 elaborar 220
preposition   la preposición 36
to **prescribe**   recetar 206
prescription   la receta 207
presence   la presencia 57
present   el presente 1 el regalo 76
present (adjective)   actual 1
to **present**   presentar 11
present perfect   el presente perfecto 120
present progressive   el presente continuo 1
presentation   la presentación 40 la exposición 167
presenter   el/la presentador(a) 249
to **preserve**   conservar 56 preservar 373
president   el/la presidente(a) 236 el/la rector(a) 272
presidential   presidencial 12
press   la prensa 378
pressure   la presión 201
pressure cooker   la olla a presión 352
prestige   el prestigio 272
prestigious   prestigioso(a) 244
preterite   el pretérito 1
pretty   bonito(a) 20 lindo(a) 42
to **prevail**   predominar 92
to **prevent**   prevenir (irreg.) 197 impedir (irreg. i, i) 254
previous   anterior 33
previousness   la anterioridad 358
price   el precio 143 la tarifa 203
prickly pear cactus   el nopal 411
priest   el sacerdote 401
primary health care   la atención primaria 197

prince *el príncipe* 410

princess *la infanta* 31 *la princesa* 410

principal *el/la director(a)* 82

to **print** *imprimir (irreg.)* 248

printer *la impresora* 248

prison *la prisión* 83

private *privado(a)* 422

prize *el premio* 44

probably *seguramente* 102 *probablemente* 147

problem *el problema* 7 *la dificultad* 45

process *el proceso* 221

procession *el desfile* 110

to **produce** *producir (irreg.)* 171

producer *el/la productor(a)* 367

producing *productor(a)* 345

product *el producto* 141

production *la producción* 219

profession *el oficio* 152 *la profesión* 187

professional *profesional* 88

profile *la reseña* 11 *el perfil* 281

program *el programa* 25 *la programación* 430

programmer *el/la programador(a) informático(a)* 236

programs *la programación* 253

progress *el progreso* 361

project *el proyecto* XXVI

to **promise** *prometer* 47

to **promote** *promocionar* 68 *promover (irreg. ue)* 96 *fomentar* 344

promotion *la promoción* 288

pronominal *pronominal* 66

pronoun *el pronombre* 36

proof *la muestra* 253

property *la propiedad* 183

proportion *la proporción* 191

proposal *la propuesta* 86

to **propose** *proponer (irreg.)* 15

to **protect** *proteger* 260

to **protect against** *prevenir (irreg. i)* 197

protected species *la especie protegida* 344

protection *la defensa* 265 *la protección* 280

protein *la proteína* 182

protest *la protesta* 242

to **provide** *proporcionar* 164 *aportar* 180

province *la provincia* 381

psychologist *el/la psicólogo(a)* 206

psychology *la Psicología* 215

public *público(a)* 422

public holiday *la fiesta* 64

public phone *el teléfono público* 98

publicity *la publicidad* 99

publicly *públicamente* 410

to **publish** *publicar* 215

Puerto Rican *puertorriqueño(a)* 44

to **pull out** (train) *arrancar* 321

punctual *puntual* 117

punctuation *la puntuación* 65

pupil *la pupila* 77

purchase *la compra* 140

pure *puro(a)* 349

purity *la pureza* 136

purpose *el propósito* 274 *la finalidad* 282

to **put** *poner (irreg.)* 6 *colocar* 139 *echar* 179 *depositar* 345

to **put an end** *poner fin a* 398

to **put away** *guardar* 104

to **put in** *meter* 51

to **put on** *ponerse (irreg.)* 128 *poner (irreg.)* 153

to **put out** (fires) *apagar* 236

to **put up** *montar* 173

pyramid *la pirámide* 6

qualification *la cualificación* 247

quality *la cualidad* 20 *la calidad* 315

quantity *la cantidad* 142

Quechuan *quechua* 50

queen *la reina* 410

query *la consulta* 185

question *la pregunta* 7

questionnaire *el cuestionario* 10

quetzal *el quetzal* 347

quick *deprisa* 203

quickly *rápidamente* 4 *pronto* 84 *rápido* 253

quiet *tranquilo(a)* 202

quite *bastante* 20

quite a lot *bastante* 204

quote *la cita* 80

to **quote** *citar* 382

race *la carrera* 302

racket *la raqueta* 287

radio *la radio* 19

radio (adjective) *radiofónico(a)* 401

radio station *la emisora (de radio)* 96

to **raffle off** *sortear* 299

rage *la ira* 321

rain *la lluvia* 51

to **rain** *llover (irreg. ue)* 155

rainbow *el arco iris* 356

raincoat *el impermeable* 125

rainy *lluvioso(a)* 356

to **raise** (a hand) *levantar* 111

to **raise the awareness of** *sensibilizar* 133

ranch *el rancho* 242

rather than *por encima de* 406

raw *crudo(a)* 182

raw material *la materia prima* 366

to **reach** *alcanzar* 56

to **reach** (years of age) *cumplir* 65

to **reach out** *estirar* 320

to **react** *reaccionar* 232

reaction *la reacción* 70

to **read** *leer (irreg.)* XXVI

reader *el/la lector(a)* 59

reading *la lectura* 26

ready *listo(a)* 113 *preparado(a)* 230

real *real* 43 *auténtico(a)* 140

realistic *realista* 328

reality *la realidad* 33

really *realmente* 191

really? *¿verdad?* 16

reason *la razón* 92 *el porqué* 254 *el motivo* 383

reasonable *razonable* 192

reasoning *el razonamiento* 254

to **rebel** *rebelarse* 19

to **receive** *recibir* 4

recent *reciente* 120

receptionist *el/la recepcionista* 233

recipe *la receta* 118

recipient *el/la receptor(a)* 436

reciprocal *recíproco(a)* 66

recital *el recital* 417

to **recite** *recitar* 374

to **recognize** *reconocer (irreg.)* 362

to **recommend** *recomendar (irreg. ie)* 210

recommendation *la recomendación* 1

to **reconstruct** *reconstruir (irreg.)* 398

record *el disco* 36

record (adjective) *discográfico(a)* 298

to **record** *grabar* 16

recording *la grabación* 417

to **recover** *recuperarse* 38

to **recreate** *recrear* 347

rectangular *rectangular* 140

recyclable *reciclable* 133

to **recycle** *reciclar* 133

recycling *el reciclaje* 133

recycling bin *el contenedor* 345

red *rojo(a)* 73

red meat *la carne roja* 182

reddish *rojizo(a)* 140

red-haired *pelirrojo(a)* 21

to **reduce** *disminuir (irreg.)* 157 *reducir (irreg.)* 182

reduced *rebajado(a)* 129

redundancy *la redundancia* 329

to **re-elect** *reelegir (irreg.)* 418

to **refer** *referirse a (irreg. ie, i)* 228

reference *el referente* 421

to **reflect** *reflejar* 30 *plasmar* 301

reflexive *reflexivo(a)* 66

refrigerator *el refrigerador* 125

Regards, *Un cordial saludo.* 275

region *la región* 97

regional *regional* 120

register   el registro 104
registration   la inscripción 10
to regret   arrepentirse (irreg. ie) 42
regular   regular 1 habitual 48
regulation   la ordenanza 164
to rehearse   ensayar 353
reign   el reinado 442
to reinvent oneself   reinventarse 434
to reject   rechazar 410
related   relacionado(a) 74
relating to   relativo(a) a 242
relationship   la relación 8
relative   el/la familiar 77 el relativo 228
relatively   relativamente 164
to relax   relajarse 194
relaxation   la relajación 8 el relax 322
relentless   implacable 374
to relieve   calmar 195
religion   la religión 44
religious   religioso(a) 35
to remain   quedar 47 permanecer (irreg.) 344
remedy   el remedio 197
to remember   recordar (irreg. ue) 47 acordarse (de) (irreg. ue) 64
remembrance   el recuerdo 237
to remind   recordar (irreg. ue) 244
remnants   los restos 380
to remove   suprimir 99 quitar 134
renewable energy   la energía renovable 378
to rent   alquilar 4
repair   el arreglo 161 la reparación 253
to repair   reparar 152
to repeat   repetir (irreg. i, i) 22
repertoire   el repertorio 298
repetition   la repetición 429
to replace   sustituir (irreg.) 112
report   el reportaje 52 el informe 248
to report   denunciar 344
representative   el/la diputado(a), el/la representante 410
representative   representativo(a) 101
reptile   el reptil 344
republic   la república 410
republican   republicano(a) 410
reputation   la fama 33
request   la petición 1
to require   requerir (irreg. ie) 185
requirement   el requisito 257
rescue   el rescate 442
to rescue   rescatar 83
research   la investigación 16
to research   investigar 236
researcher   el/la investigador(a) 378
reservation   la reserva 314
residence   la residencia 164
resignation   la resignación 394

resigned   resignado(a) 394
resource   el recurso 205
respect   el respeto 422
to respect   respetar 74
respected   respetado(a) 416
respiratory   respiratorio(a) 376
responsibility   la responsabilidad 239
responsible   responsable 248
rest   el resto 50
to rest   descansar 194
restaurant   el restaurante 7
to restore   restaurar 398
to restructure   reordenar 435
result   el resultado 56
résumé   el currículum 253
to retire   jubilarse 45
retirement   la jubilación 44
return   el regreso 212 la vuelta 314
to return   volver (irreg.) 47
reusable   reutilizable 352
to reuse   reutilizar 347
to reveal   revelar 254
review   la crítica 44
to revise   repasar 1
revision   el repaso 60
revolutionary   revolucionario(a) 211
to revolutionize   revolucionar 211
to revolve around   centrarse en 44
to rewrite   reescribir (irreg.) 59
rhyme   la rima 77
to rhyme   rimar 113
rhythm   el ritmo 57
rice   el arroz 189
rich   rico(a) 25
riches   las riquezas 212
richness   la riqueza 406
riddle   la adivinanza 144
to ride   montar 71
rider   el/la jinete 326
right by   junto a 193
right in the middle of ...   en pleno(a)... 315
right now   ahora mismo 3
rights   los derechos 422
ringing   el repique 111
ripe   maduro(a) 212
risk   el riesgo 307
rite   el rito 44
ritual   ritual 93
rival   el/la rival 20
river   el río 43
road   la calle 11 el camino 319 la carretera 387
to roast   asar 179
roasted   asado(a) 179
Roman   romano(a) 434
romance   la película romántica 290
romantic   romántico(a) 68
Romanticism   el romanticismo 77
room   el espacio 28 la habitación 104 el cuarto 158

rooming house   la pensión 314
root   la raíz 212
rose   la rosa 72
rough   áspero(a) 140
roughness   la rudeza 321
round   redondo(a) 140
round-trip   de ida y vuelta 314
route   la ruta XXVI el recorrido 303 el camino 319
routine   la rutina 223
rowing   el remo 302
royal   real 273
royal family   la familia real 31
rubber   el caucho 92
rude   maleducado(a) 295 grosero(a) 320
rug   la alfombra 141
to ruin   destrozar 51
ruins   las ruinas 398
rule   la regla 84 la norma 422
to rule   dominar 398
rumba   la rumba 96
to run   correr 3
to run out   agotarse 344
to run out of minutes   quedarse sin saldo 98
rural   rural 127

sacrifice   el sacrificio 241
to sacrifice   sacrificar 43
sad   triste 9
sadness   la tristeza 112
safety razor   la maquinilla de afeitar 194
sailing   la navegación a vela 193 la vela 302
sailor   el/la navegante 302
Saint   san 42 santo(a) 272
salary   el salario 236 el sueldo 248
sale   la venta 106
sales clerk   el/la vendedor(a) 131 el/la dependiente(a) 181
salesperson   el/la vendedor(a) 250
salmon   el salmón 183
salsa   la salsa XXVI
salt   la sal 153
salt flat   el salar 317
salty   salado(a) 179
Salvadoran   salvadoreño(a) 307
salvation   la salvación 376
same   mismo(a) 34 igual 147
sanctuary   el santuario 350
sand   la arena 202
sandal   la sandalia 125
sash   la banda 134
Saturday   el sábado 86
sauce   la salsa 118
sauna   la sauna 193
to save   salvar 236 guardar 248 ahorrar 347

to **stretch out**   *alargar* 320
strict   *estricto(a)* 58
strike   *la huelga* 235
stripe   *la raya* 129 *la franja* 411
strong   *fuerte* 50
structure   *la estructura* 144
to **structure**   *estructurar* 173
student   *el/la estudiante* 2 *el/la alumno(a)* 166
studio   *el estudio* 298
studious   *estudioso(a)* 25
study   *el estudio* 45
to **study**   *estudiar* 2
style   *el estilo* 28
to **subdue**   *someter* 398
subject   *el tema* 26 *la asignatura* 178 *el sujeto* 223 *la materia* 378
subjunctive   *el subjuntivo* 88
to **substitute**   *sustituir (irreg.)* 182
subtitle   *el subtítulo* 119
to **succeed**   *poder (irreg. u, ue)* 46
success   *el éxito* 44
successful   *exitoso(a)* 26
Suddenly ...   *De pronto..., De repente...* 329
to **suffer**   *sufrir* 38
sugar   *el azúcar* 83
to **suggest**   *proponer (irreg.)* 15 *sugerir (irreg. ie, i)* 83
suggestion   *la sugerencia* 59 *la propuesta* 86
suit   *el traje* 125
to **suit**   *quedar* 126
suitable   *apropiado(a)* 28
suitcase   *la maleta* 322
to **summarize**   *resumir* 39
summary   *el resumen* 39
summer   *el verano* 6
sun   *el sol* 85
sunglasses   *las gafas de sol* 125
sunny   *soleado(a)* 356
sunscreen   *la crema solar* 194
super food   *el superalimento* 183
superficially   *superficialmente* 266
superiority   *la superioridad* 24
superlative   *el superlativo* 12
supermarket   *el supermercado* 180
superstition   *la superstición* 153
superstitious   *supersticioso(a)* 153
to **supervise**   *supervisar* 248
supplement   *el suplemento* 55
support   *el apoyo* 422
to **support someone**   *apoyar a alguien* 74
to **support something**   *apoyar algo* 166
supporter   *el/la aficionado(a)* 302
to **suppose**   *suponer (irreg.)* 286
supranational   *supranacional* 408
Supreme Court   *la Corte Suprema* 244
sure enough   *efectivamente* 187
to **surf the Internet**   *navegar por Internet* 248

surface   *la superficie* 199
surfer   *el/la surfista* 302
surfing   *el surf* 193
surname   *el apellido* 17
surprise   *la sorpresa* 143 *la extrañeza* 178
to **surprise**   *sorprender* 262
surprising   *sorprendente* 198
to **surround**   *rodear* 136
surrounding area   *los alrededores* 383
survival   *la supervivencia* 343
to **survive**   *sobrevivir* 343
to **suspect**   *el/la sospechoso(a)* 27
sustainable   *sostenible* 261
sweater   *el suéter* 125
sweatshirt   *la sudadera* 104
to **sweep**   *barrer* 152
sweet   *el dulce* 77 *dulce* 83
sweetheart   *el/la amado(a)* 47
swell   *el oleaje* 380
to **swim**   *nadar* 7
swimmer   *el/la nadador(a)* 302
swimming   *la natación* 302
swimming pool   *la piscina* 200
swing   *el columpio* 158
to **swing** (on a swing)   *columpiarse* 158
swollen   *hinchado(a)* 206
sword   *la espada* 73 *el sable* 428
symbol   *el símbolo* 91
symbolically   *simbólicamente* 163
symbolism   *el simbolismo* 327
to **symbolize**   *simbolizar* 376
symphony orchestra   *la orquesta sinfónica* 416
symptom   *el síntoma* 206
synonym   *el sinónimo* 135
synopsis   *la sinopsis* 297
Syrian   *el/la sirio(a)* 56
system   *el sistema* 91

T

table   *la tabla* 3 *la mesa* 34
tactless   *indiscreto(a)* 33
tail   *la cola* 347
to **take**   *tomar* 3 *sacar* 71 *llevar* 145 *tardar* 320
to **take a bath**   *bañarse* 78
to **take a shower**   *ducharse* 160
to **take care of oneself**   *cuidarse* 194
to **take note**   *tomar nota* 11
to **take off**   *quitarse* 128
to **take one's pulse**   *tomar el pulso* 206
to **take out**   *sacar* 320
to **take part**   *participar* 14 *intervenir (irreg.)* 350
to **take place**   *tener lugar* 308
to **take turns**   *turnarse* 79
to **take up again**   *retomar* 308
talent   *el talento* 39

to **talk**   *hablar* 3
to **talk about**   *hablar de* 1
tall   *alto(a)* 17
to **tame**   *domar* 326
tango   *el tango* 97
tanned   *moreno(a)* 6
tapestry   *el tapiz* 141
target   *la marca* 92
task   *la tarea* 1 *la labor* 374
taste   *el sabor* 94 *el gusto* 202
to **taste**   *probar (irreg. ue)* 176 *degustar* 425
tasteless   *soso(a)* 179
tasty   *sabroso(a)* 182
tea   *el té* 367
to **teach**   *enseñar* 84
teacher   *el/la maestro(a)* 9 *el/la profesor(a)* 22 *el/la educador(a)* 423
team   *el equipo* 89
tear   *la lágrima* 112
teaspoonful   *la cucharadita* 190
technical   *técnico(a)* 247
technician   *el/la técnico(a)* 233
technique   *la técnica* 134
technology   *la tecnología* 89
telephone   *el teléfono* 34
telephone (adjective)   *telefónico(a)* 67
telescope   *el telescopio* 356
television   *la televisión* 3
television set   *el televisor* 104
to **tell**   *contar (irreg. ue)* 1 *narrar* 13
to **tell in advance**   *anticipar* 298
temperature   *la temperatura* 193
temple   *el templo* 212
temporary   *temporal* 186
tennis   *el tenis* 287
tennis shoes   *los tenis* 125
tense   *el tiempo* 54
tent   *la tienda de campaña* 317
term   *el término* 297
terminal   *la terminal* 314
terrace roof   *la terraza* 158
terrible   *terrible* 38 *fatal* 178
terrific   *fenomenal* 293
territory   *el territorio* 91
test   *la prueba* 186 *la suerte* 326
text   *el texto* 244
textual   *textual* 437
texture   *la textura* 140
than   *que* 18
thank you   *gracias* 75
thanks to   *gracias a* 91
Thanksgiving   *el día de Acción de Gracias* 225
that (pronoun)   *eso* XXVI *aquel, aquello(a)* 156
that (conjunction)   *que* XXVI
that (one)   *ese, esa* 7 *aquel, aquella* 36
that is   *es decir* 20
That's life.   *Así es la vida.* 394

the *el, la, los, las* XXVI *lo* 7

the day before yesterday *anteayer* 48

the Middle Ages *la Edad Media* 272

the most important thing *lo fundamental* 84

the poor *los pobres* 25

the pros and cons *los pros y contras* 331

the rest *los/las demás* 165

the same as ... *igual que...* 24

the three wise men *los Reyes Magos* 158

The truth is ... *Lo cierto es que...* 92

theater *el teatro* 26

theft *el robo* 29

their *su(s)* XXVI

theirs *el/la suyo(a)* 36

(to) them *les* 76

themselves *se* 78

then *después* 3 *luego* 8 *entonces* 18

therapeutic *terapéutico(a)* 193

therapy *la terapia* 197

there *allí* 50 *allá* 117 *ahí* 138

there is/there are *hay* 22

there was/there were *había* 77

there will be *habrá* 102

Therefore ... *Por eso...* 383

thermal *termal* 199

thermometer *el termómetro* 207

these *estos(as)* 3

these days *en la actualidad* 164

thesis *la tesis* 166

they *ellos* XXVI

thief *el/la ladrón(a)* 29

thin *delgado(a)* 17

thing *la cosa* XXVI

to **think** *opinar* 7 *pensar (irreg. ie)* 9 *creer (irreg.)* 15 *parecer (irreg.)* 15 *reflexionar* 291

third *tercer(o)(a)* XXVI

this *esto* 10

this (one) *este, esta* XXVI

this way *así* 47

those *aquellos, aquellas* 156

those (ones) *esos, esas* 36

thought(s) *el pensamiento* 8

thousands *miles* 110

to **threaten** *amenazar* 344

thriller *la película de suspenso* 290

throat *la garganta* 207

through *a través de* 23 *mediante* 43

to **throw** *tirar* 95

to **throw out** *arrojar* 383

thunder *el trueno* 356

ticket *el boleto* 290

ticket counter *la ventanilla* 320

tie *la corbata* 104 *el lazo* 111 *el empate* 302

to **tie** *atarse* 128 *empatar* 287

tight *ajustado(a), estrecho(a)* 128

time *la vez* 5 *el tiempo* 7 *la época* 23 *la hora* 23

time (adjective) *temporal* 13

timetable *el horario* 3

tin *el estaño* 368

tip *la propina* 225

tip-toeing *de puntillas* 266

tired *cansado(a)* 9

tiredness *el cansancio* 212

title *el título* 26

to *para* XXVI *a* 2 *hasta* 92 *ante* 274

To begin ... *Para comenzar...* 167

To top it off ... *Para colmo...* 329

to where *adonde* 318

today *hoy* 7

together *junto(a)* 4

together with *junto con* 219

tolerance *la tolerancia* 260

tolerant *tolerante* 264

tomato *el tomate* 117

tomorrow *mañana* 22

tone *el tono* 134

too *demasiado* 137

too many *demasiados(as)* 142

too much *demasiado* 5 *demasiado(a)* 142

toothbrush *el cepillo* 179

toothpaste *la pasta de dientes* 179

top *superior* 158

topic *el tema* 14

topical *actual* 382

topographical *topográfico(a)* 374

topography *la topografía* 375

top-quality *de muy buena calidad* 140

tornado *el tornado* 341

tortilla *la tortilla* 218

total *total* 374

totally *totalmente* 269

touch *el toque* 122

to **touch** *tocar* 85 *emocionar* 262

tour *la gira* 298

tourism *el turismo* 172

tourist *el/la turista* 193

tourist (adjective) *turístico(a)* 7

tourist attraction *la atracción turística* 141

toward *hacia* 50

towel *la toalla* 179

tower *la torre* 111

town *el pueblo* 21 *la localidad* 388

trace *la huella* 434

track *la pista* 302

trade (adjective) *comercial* 319

to **trade** *comerciar* 338

tradition *la tradición* 15

traditional *típico(a)* 7 *tradicional* 14

traditionally *tradicionalmente* 111

traffic *el tráfico* 347

train *el tren* 7

to **train** *entrenar(se)* 194 *prepararse* 300

train car *el vagón* 321

training *la formación* 247 *la preparación* 301 *el entrenamiento* 311 *el perfeccionamiento* 416

trait *el rasgo* 12

to **translate** *traducir (irreg.)* 44

translation *la traducción* 262

translator *el/la traductor(a)* 236

transplant *el trasplante* 207

transportation *el transporte* 103

travel *el viaje* 42

to **travel** *viajar* XXVI *desplazarse* 254

travel agency *la agencia de viajes* 264

travel agent *el/la agente de viajes* 315

to **travel through** *recorrer* 319

traveler *el/la viajero(a)* 146

treasure *el tesoro* 158

treat *el dulce* 77

to **treat** *tratar* 54

treatment *el tratamiento* 192

tree *el árbol* 43

triangle *el triángulo* 303

tribute *el homenaje* 289

tropical *tropical* 368

trousers *los pantalones* 5 *el pantalón* 130

true *cierto(a)* 3 *verdadero(a)* 74

truly *verdaderamente* 422

trust *la confianza* 74

to **trust** *confiar en* 74

truth *la verdad* 46

to **try** *probar (irreg. ue)* 176 *intentar* 209 *procurar* 443

to **try on** *probarse (irreg. ue)* 129

to **try to remember** *hacer memoria* 63

to **try to** *tratar de* 83

T-shirt *la camiseta* 125

tuber *el tubérculo* 219

tulip *el tulipán* 156

tuna *el atún* 179

tundra *la tundra* 380

tunnel *el túnel* 7

Turkish *turco(a)* 44

to **turn** *doblar* 4 *transformar* 47

to **turn into** *convertir en (irreg. ie, i)* 42

to **turn on** *conectar* 249

to **turn out** *salir (irreg.)* 16 *quedar* 188

to **turn up** *subir* 104

turtle *la tortuga* 348

TV station *la cadena* 253

type *el tipo* 10

typical *típico(a)* 3 *propio(a)* 153

umbrella *el paraguas* 128

uncle *el tío* 17

undecided *indeciso(a)* 104

under *debajo de* 199 *bajo* 399
under his belt *a sus espaldas* 254
underdone *poco hecho(a)* 182
underground *subterráneo(a)* 199
to **underline** *subrayar* 59
to **understand** *entender (irreg. ie)* 2
understanding (comprehension) *la comprensión* 51
understanding (adjective) *comprensivo(a)* 20
to **undertake to do something** *encargarse de hacer algo* 206
unexpected *inesperado(a)* 186
unexpectedly *imprevistamente* 320
to **unfasten** *desabrocharse* 128
unforgettable *inolvidable* 54
unfortunately *desgraciadamente* 308
uniform *el uniforme* 166
unique *único(a)* 80
unit *la unidad* 12
united *unido(a)* 25
unity *la unión* 244 *la unidad* 308
universal *universal* 153
universe *el universo* 336
university *la universidad* 44
university course *la carrera* 272
unknown *desconocido(a)* 104
unlikely *improbable* 238
unlimited *ilimitado(a)* 388
to **untie** *desatar(se)* 128
until *hasta* 44
untouched *intacto(a)* 321
untrue *incierto(a)* 265
unwelcome *inoportuno(a)* 153
update *la actualización* 378
upkeep *el mantenimiento* 406
to **upload** *colgar (irreg. ue), subir* 248
urban *urbano(a)* 147
Uruguayan *uruguayo(a)* 192
us *nosotros(as)* XXVI
(to) us *nos* 76
use *el uso* 22 *el aprovechamiento* 378
to **use** *usar* XXVI *emplear* 75 *utilizar* 99 *manejar* 251 *aprovechar* 352
useful *útil* 16 *práctico(a)* 140
user *el/la usuario(a)* 75
usual *habitual* 35
usually *habitualmente* 259

vacancy *la oferta* 246
vacation *las vacaciones* 6
vacation (adjective) *vacacional* 406
valley *el valle* 51
valuable *valioso(a)* 220

value *el valor* 422
value statement *la valoración* 174
vanity *la coquetería* 254
variation *la variante* 181
varied *variado(a)* 298
variety *la variedad* 92
various *diversos(as)* 21 *distintos(as)* 56 *diferentes* 84
to **vary** *variar* 127
vase *el florero* 142
vegetable *la hortaliza* 182
vegetables *la verdura* 8 *las legumbres* 179
vegetarian *vegetariano(a)* 182
vegetation *la vegetación* 342
vehement *vehemente* 374
velvet *el terciopelo* 128
vendor *el/la comerciante* 236
Venezuelan *venezolano(a)* 129
ventilation *la ventilación* 164
verb *el verbo* 1
verbal *verbal* 42
version *la versión* 139
vertical *vertical* 411
very *muy* XXVI
very dry *reseco(a)* 321
very soon *enseguida* 311
veterinarian *el/la veterinario(a)* 233
vice-president *el/la vicepresidente(a)* 410
viceroy *el virrey* 164
victorious *victorioso(a)* 47
victory *la victoria* 302
video *el video* 40
videogame *el videojuego* 55
view *la vista* 193
village *el pueblo* 21
vinegar *el vinagre* 179
violence *la violencia* 242
violet *la violeta* 83
virtual *virtual* 173
visa *el visado* 312 *la visa* 314
visible *visible* 434
visit *la visita* 153
to **visit** *visitar* 5
to **visit** (a website) *acceder a* 338
visiting team *el equipo visitante* 302
visitor *el/la visitante* 157
visual *visual* 134
vital *vital* 61
vitamin *la vitamina* 182
voice *la voz* 100
voice mailbox *el buzón de voz* 98
volcanic *volcánico(a)* 380
volcanic eruption *la erupción volcánica* 368
volcano *el volcán* 47
volleyball *el voleibol* 85
volume *el volumen* 104
volunteer *el/la voluntario(a)* 260

volunteer work *el voluntariado* XXVI
vote *la votación* 410 *el voto* 418
to **vote** *votar* 410
vowel *la vocal* 99

wait *la espera* 320
Wait ... *Espera...* 203
to **wait** *esperar* 87
waiter/waitress *el/la mesero(a)* 7
to **wake up** *despertar(se) (irreg. ie)* 90
walk *el paseo* 71
to **walk** *caminar* 50
wall *la pared* 103 *la muralla* 165
to **want** *querer (irreg.)* 6
war *la guerra* 398
wardrobe *el armario* 104
warm *cariñoso(a)* 20 *caliente* 164 *cálido(a)* 353
to **warm** *calentarse (irreg. ie)* 90
warrior *el/la guerrero(a)* 47
to **wash** *lavar* 130 *lavarse* 179
to **wash up** *lavarse* 78
washer *la lavadora* 125
to **waste** *gastar* 352 *perder (irreg. ie)* 408
watch *el reloj* 22
to **watch** *ver (irreg.)* 3 *observar* 5
water *el agua* 8
water sports *los deportes acuáticos* 193
waterfall *la cascada* 341
watermelon *la sandía* 179
waters *las aguas* 192
water-skiing *el esquí acuático* 302
wave *la ola* 193
way *la manera* 1 *el camino* 7 *la forma* 16 *el modo* 340
we *nosotros(as)* 2
weak *débil* 209
wealth *la riqueza* 411
weapon *el arma* 93
to **wear** *ponerse (irreg. u)* 9 *llevar* 111
weather *el tiempo* 54 *el tiempo meteorológico* 336
website *el sitio web* 74
wedding *la boda* 32
week *la semana* 2
weekend *el fin de semana* 3
weekly *semanal* 248
to **weigh** *pesar* 225
weight *el peso* 194
welcome *bienvenido(a)* 14
well *bien* 7 *bueno* 15
well *pues* XXVI
Well! *¡En fin!* 394
Well, ... *Bueno,...* 15
well done *muy hecho(a)* 182
well fed *alimentado(a)* 280
well located *bien situado(a)* 314

ÍNDICE GRAMATICAL

CRÉDITOS FOTOGRÁFICOS (TEACHER'S EDITION)

Cubierta: J. C. Muñoz; Eitan Simanor, R. Jáuregui/A. G. E. FOTOSTOCK; Tony Anderson/GETTY IMAGES SALES SPAIN; I. PREYSLER/ATREZZO: HELEN CHELTON; **Contracubierta:** J. M.ª Escudero; SERIDEC PHOTOIMAGENES CD; Luis Castañeda/ A. G. E. FOTOSTOCK; Richard Ellis/GETTY IMAGES SALES SPAIN; **T1** I. Preysler/Atrezzo: Helen Chelton; **T4** I. PREYSLER/ ATREZZO: HELEN CHELTON; Museo Nacional de Antropología, México/Jean-Pierre Courau/The Bridgeman Art Library/INDEX **T5** Mauritius/Reinhard Dirscherl/FOTONONSTOP; ARCHIVO SANTILLANA **T7** I. Preysler/Atrezzo: Helen Chelton; Javier Larrea/ A. G. E. FOTOSTOCK; **T8** I. Preysler/Atrezzo: Helen Chelton; SEIS x SEIS; **T9** C. Díez Polanco; FUNDACIÓN SANTILLANA; I. Preysler/Atrezzo: Helen Chelton; ISTOCKPHOTO; **T11** I. Preysler/Atrezzo: Helen Chelton; **T15** I. Preysler/Atrezzo: Helen Chelton; SERIDEC PHOTOIMAGENES CD; The Art Archive/Museo Nacional de Historia Guatemala City/Gianni Dagli Orti/The Picture Desk Limited; **T16** I. Preysler/Atrezzo: Helen Chelton; **T18** Amos Morgan/A. G. E. FOTOSTOCK; **T22** I. Preysler/Atrezzo: Helen Chelton. **T23** I. Preysler/Atrezzo: Helen Chelton; ARCHIVO SANTILLANA

CRÉDITOS FOTOGRÁFICOS (STUDENT BOOK)

Cubierta: J. C. Muñoz; Eitan Simanor, R. Jáuregui/A. G. E. FOTOSTOCK; Tony Anderson/GETTY IMAGES SALES SPAIN; I. PREYSLER/ATREZZO: HELEN CHELTON; **Contracubierta:** J. M.ª Escudero; SERIDEC PHOTOIMAGENES CD; Luis Castañeda/ A. G. E. FOTOSTOCK; Richard Ellis/GETTY IMAGES SALES SPAIN; **I** I. PREYSLER/ATREZZO: HELEN CHELTON **IV** Michael Langford, Travel Ink/GETTY IMAGES SALES SPAIN; I. PREYSLER/ATREZZO: HELEN CHELTON **V** GETTY IMAGES SALES SPAIN; I. PREYSLER/ATREZZO: HELEN CHELTON **VI** REUTERS/CORDON PRESS; Tibor Bognar, Tips/Luis Castaneda/FOTONONSTOP **XI** C. Pérez; J. Montoro; J. V. Resino; , José Fuste Raga/A. G. E. FOTOSTOCK; Alamy Images/ACI AGENCIA DE FOTOGRAFÍA; Santi Palacios/EFE; I. PREYSLER/ATREZZO: HELEN CHELTON **XIII** C. Pérez; J. Montoro; J. V. Resino; M. Barcenilla; S. Enríquez; Alamy Images/ACI AGENCIA DE FOTOGRAFÍA; Santi Palacios/EFE; I. PREYSLER/ATREZZO: HELEN CHELTON **XV** C. Pérez; I. Sabater; J. Montoro; J. V. Resino; S. Enríquez; Alamy Images/ACI AGENCIA DE FOTOGRAFÍA; Santi Palacios/EFE; I. PREYSLER/ATREZZO: HELEN CHELTON **XVII** C. Pérez; J. Montoro; J. V. Resino; Halfdark/A. G. E. FOTOSTOCK; Alamy Images/ACI AGENCIA DE FOTOGRAFÍA; Santi Palacios/EFE; I. PREYSLER/ATREZZO: HELEN CHELTON **XIX** C. Pérez; J. Montoro; J. V. Resino; Zoonar/R. Laschon, a collectionRF/A. G. E. FOTOSTOCK; Alamy Images/ACI AGENCIA DE FOTOGRAFÍA; Santi Palacios/EFE; I. PREYSLER/ATREZZO: HELEN CHELTON **XXI** C. Pérez; J. Montoro; J. V. Resino; SERIDEC PHOTOIMAGENES CD; M&M Valledor/A. G. E. FOTOSTOCK; Alamy Images/ACI AGENCIA DE FOTOGRAFÍA; Santi Palacios/EFE; I. PREYSLER/ATREZZO: HELEN CHELTON **XXIII** C. Pérez; J. Montoro; J. V. Resino; Gunnar, Zoonar/Paul Mayall/A. G. E. FOTOSTOCK; Alamy Images/ACI AGENCIA DE FOTOGRAFÍA; Santi Palacios/EFE; I. PREYSLER/ATREZZO: HELEN CHELTON **XXV** C. Pérez; J. Montoro; J. V. Resino; OEA/Juan Manuel Herrera; Tomás Abad/A. G. E. FOTOSTOCK; Alamy Images/ACI AGENCIA DE FOTOGRAFÍA; Santi Palacios/EFE; I. PREYSLER/ATREZZO: HELEN CHELTON; **000** I. PREYSLER/ATREZZO: HELEN CHELTON **001** I. PREYSLER/ ATREZZO: HELEN CHELTON **002** I. PREYSLER/ATREZZO: HELEN CHELTON **003** J. Jaime; Prats i Camps; Hill Street Studios/ A. G. E. FOTOSTOCK; COMSTOCK **004** Prats i Camps **005** Prats i Camps; Photos.com Plus/GETTY IMAGES SALES SPAIN; AbleStock.com/HIGHRES PRESS STOCK **006** Thinkstock/GETTY IMAGES SALES SPAIN; I. PREYSLER/ATREZZO: HELEN CHELTON; ISTOCKPHOTO **007** S. Padura; Alamy Images/ACI AGENCIA DE FOTOGRAFÍA **008** Prats i Camps **009** Prats i Camps; S. Enríquez; ISTOCKPHOTO **010** I. PREYSLER/ATREZZO: HELEN CHELTON **011** A. G. E. FOTOSTOCK **012** Algar/THE MUSEUM OF MODERN ART, NEW YORK; PROCINES/ALBUM **013** J. Montoro; Private Collection/DACS/The Stapleton Collection/The Bridgeman Art Library/INDEX **014** I. PREYSLER/ATREZZO: HELEN CHELTON **015** Prats i Camps/I. PREYSLER/ATREZZO: HELEN CHELTON **016** Prats i Camps; Juan Martín/EFE; I. PREYSLER/ATREZZO: HELEN CHELTON; ISTOCKPHOTO **017** Photos.com Plus/GETTY IMAGES SALES SPAIN **019** Mario Guzmán/EFE **020** I. PREYSLER/ATREZZO: HELEN CHELTON **021** ALBUM; AFP/ Martín Bernetti/GETTY IMAGES SALES SPAIN **023** CORBIS/A. G. E. FOTOSTOCK; Photos.com Plus, Rubberball/Mike Kemp/ GETTY IMAGES SALES SPAIN; AbleStock.com/HIGHRES PRESS STOCK; The Bridgeman Art Library/MUSEUM ICONOGRAFÍA **025** Photos.com Plus/GETTY IMAGES SALES SPAIN **026** STOCK PHOTOS **028** Alamy Images/ACI AGENCIA DE FOTOGRAFÍA **030** Algar/THE MUSEUM OF MODERN ART, NEW YORK; J. Martin/MUSEO NACIONAL DEL PRADO/MUSEUM ICONOGRAFÍA **031** INTERFOTO/A. G. E. FOTOSTOCK; REUTERS/CORDON PRESS; J. Martin/MUSEUM ICONOGRAFÍA **032** Prats i Camps **033** WALT DISNEY PRODUCTIONS/ALBUM **035** Prats i Camps; Ariel Skelley/GETTY IMAGES SALES SPAIN **036** Photos.com Plus/GETTY IMAGES SALES SPAIN **037** J. Jaime; UNIVERSAL TV/20TH CENTURY FOX TV/KLASKY-SCUPO/ALBUM; ISTOCKPHOTO **038** SIPA-PRESS/SOTHEBY'S/EFE **039** GARCÍA-PELAYO/Juancho; **040** GARCÍA-PELAYO/Juancho; ISTOCKPHOTO **041** J. V. Resino; S. Enríquez; I. PREYSLER/ATREZZO: HELEN CHELTON **042** Bettmann/CORBIS/CORDON PRESS; Private Collection/DACS/The Stapleton Collection/The Bridgeman Art Library/INDEX **043** Prats i Camps **044** Paco Torrente/EFE **047** SuperStock/GETTY IMAGES SALES SPAIN **049** Algar/CASA MUSEO DE DIEGO RIVERA, GUANAJUATO, MÉXICO; I. PREYSLER/ ATREZZO: HELEN CHELTON **050** E. Ferro; Richard Price/GETTY IMAGES SALES SPAIN **051** Rick Nederstigt/EFE; Reynaldo Álvarez/GETTY IMAGES SALES SPAIN **052** AFP/Dominique Faget/GETTY IMAGES SALES SPAIN **053** GARCÍA-PELAYO/Juancho; S. Enríquez; COMSTOCK; Dorgie Productions, Stockbyte/GETTY IMAGES SALES SPAIN; I. PREYSLER/ATREZZO: HELEN CHELTON **054** Image Source, Patryce Bak/GETTY IMAGES SALES SPAIN; AbleStock.com/HIGHRES PRESS STOCK; ISTOCKPHOTO **055** BIBLIOTECA NACIONAL DE ESPAÑA/Laboratorio Biblioteca Nacional; Oronoz/ALBUM; SIPA-PRESS/SOTHEBY'S/EFE **056** DEA/G. Dagli Orti/ALBUM **057** Sherrie Nickol/A. G. E. FOTOSTOCK; Oronoz, akg-images/ALBUM; Laurence Monneret/ GETTY IMAGES SALES SPAIN **058** Photos.com Plus/GETTY IMAGES SALES SPAIN **061** ISTOCKPHOTO **063** ORONOZ/REAL ACADEMIA ESPAÑOLA DE LA LENGUA, MADRID; Photos.com Plus/GETTY IMAGES SALES SPAIN **064** GARCÍA-PELAYO/Juancho; Dennis Curran, Stuart Pearce/A. G. E. FOTOSTOCK; GETTY IMAGES SALES SPAIN; AbleStock.com/HIGHRES PRESS STOCK **065** Prats i Camps; I. PREYSLER/ATREZZO: HELEN CHELTON **066** Pelota Mixteca Arellanes; Julián Martín/EFE **067** Carlos Durán Araújo/EFE; I. PREYSLER/ATREZZO: HELEN CHELTON **068** I. PREYSLER/ATREZZO: HELEN CHELTON **069** Jesús Prats i Pino; S. Enríquez; I. PREYSLER/ATREZZO: HELEN CHELTON **070** Prats i Camps; I. PREYSLER/ATREZZO: HELEN CHELTON; ISTOCKPHOTO **071** J. Lucas; Prats i Camps; Fotosearch/A. G. E. FOTOSTOCK; Photos.com Plus/GETTY IMAGES SALES SPAIN; AbleStock.com/HIGHRES PRESS STOCK **072** Julián Martín/EFE; ISTOCKPHOTO **073** MUSEO DE MALLORCA; Prats i Camps **074** I. PREYSLER/ATREZZO: HELEN CHELTON **075** Prats i Camps; Orban/SYGMA/CONTIFOTO **076** GARCÍA-PELAYO/Juancho; ISTOCKPHOTO **077** MATTON-BILD; Photos.com Plus/GETTY IMAGES SALES SPAIN **080** Getty Images Sales Spain/Thinkstock; I. PREYSLER/ATREZZO: HELEN CHELTON **081** Prats i Camps; Lane Oatey/Blue Jean Images/ GETTY IMAGES SALES SPAIN; ISTOCKPHOTO **083** AbleStock.com/HIGHRES PRESS STOCK; I. PREYSLER/ATREZZO: HELEN CHELTON **084** Pelota Mixteca Arellanes; Thinkstock; Getty Images Sales Spain; I. PREYSLER/ATREZZO: HELEN CHELTON **085** Pelota Mixteca Arellanes; Alex Cruz/EFE **086** Prats i Camps; Keith Brofsky/Thinkstock/GETTY IMAGES SALES SPAIN